D1746922

THE AUSTRALIAN COOK BOOK

THE AUSTRALIAN COOK BOOK

PR BOOKS

Compiled by Anne Thorpe

The publishers would like to thank the following people for lending props and equipment to assist in photography:

**Accoutrement Cook Shops
Kosta-Boda Australia Pty Ltd
National Panasonic (Aust) Pty Ltd
Villeroy & Boch (Aust) Pty Ltd**

Photographer: Norman Nicholls
Food Artist: Di Kirby
Cover Photographer: Per Ericson
Cover Food Artist: Sheridan Rogers
Additional photography supplied by the contributors.

This edition published by PR Books,
5 Skyline Place, Frenchs Forest, NSW,
Australia, 2086
First published in 1986 by
Child & Associates Publishing Pty Ltd
Reprinted 1987
Second edition published by
PR Books 1989
Reprinted 1990

© Australian Dairy Corporation 1986, 1989
© Australian Meat and Livestock Corporation 1986, 1989
© National Broiler Council 1986, 1989
© Bread Research Institute of Australia Ltd 1986, 1989
© Department of Sea Fisheries, Tasmania 1986, 1989
© Department of TAFE, Meadowbank, New South Wales 1986, 1989
© New South Wales Egg Corporation 1986, 1989
© Pork Promotion Centre 1986, 1989
© Primary Products Promotion Unit, Department of Agriculture 1986, 1989
© Queensland Fish Management Authority 1986, 1989
© Ricegrowers' Co-operative Mills Ltd 1986, 1989
© San Remo Macaroni Co. Pty Ltd 1986, 1989
© Anne Thorpe 1986, 1989

Typeset by Deblaere Typesetting Pty Ltd
Printed in Singapore by Kyodo-Shing Loong Printing Industries Pte Ltd

**National Library of Australia
Cataloguing-in-Publication Data**

The Australian cook book.

Includes index.
ISBN 1 875113 03 7

1. Cookery, Australian, I. Thorpe, Anne.

641.5994

All rights reserved. No part of this publication may be reproduced, stored in a retrieval system, or transmitted in any form or by any means, electronic, mechanical, photocopying, recording, or otherwise, without the prior permission in writing of the Publisher.

CONTENTS

Introduction	7
Pantry List	8
Weights and Measures	9
Equipment	12
First Course	15
Soups	16
Appetisers	27
Sauces	37
Stocks	40
Eggs	41
Egg Drinks	52
Beef	55
Lamb	105
Veal	147
Pork	159
Ham	189
Chicken	193
Other Poultry	262
Seafood	263
Pasta and Rice	291
Spaghetti	292
Noodles	294
Rice	307
Vegetables	369
Salads	381
Desserts	393
Baking	439
Glossary	460
Index	461

Apricot Egg Flip (page 54).

INTRODUCTION

The revolution in Australian cooking over the last few years has led to new sophistication in the way we prepare and present food. More and more publications have a gourmet image which looks, and often is, very difficult to attain. Perhaps we have lost sight of the real values in food preparation and this is the reason for this book.

The Australian Cook Book is a compilation of the very best ways to prepare food in Australia. The recipes have been carefully prepared by the leading food authorities and corporations which specialise in particular food groups.

Australia has probably the greatest array of fresh food available anywhere in the world and because of this, Australians have always had a consuming interest in what they eat. Only the best quality will do – after all why should we accept second best? We produce the best so it should be ours for the choosing. Also, because our country began with one industry – farming, we still think of it as a leading primary producer. We do still produce an abundance of primary products but we also excel in food processing – a fact not always recognised. The recipes here are a superb cross-section of all the best ways to use these resources in simple and up-to-date text.

The task of compiling a book of the magnitude of the *The Australian Cook Book* has been awesome and without the overwhelming co-operation of the people involved in Australian food, it would have been impossible. Each person I have contacted has reacted with the utmost encouragement and has worked unceasingly to provide copy on time. Being the representatives of the bodies set up to promote these individual products, they have become expert in the methods of preparation and as such we must heed their advice.

All the ingredients show imperial equivalents so anyone world-wide knows how much to buy and what temperature to cook all the food and where possible I have shown the alternative names for ingredients, such as zucchini (courgette). This also assists in the use of the book in other places. The methods are concise and use equipment available in almost every kitchen and where possible the photographs are placed opposite the recipe.

The whole idea of including recipes from a variety of sources naturally leads to overlapping. The decision on which to choose has been entirely mine. The choice is by no means definitive – other people may have other choices but I feel the final result gives a fair representation of Australian food style. Even though our country is now so very multicultural I still believe there is room for Australian cooking as such and I hope this volume establishes how very special our food is in preserving our culture and our heritage.

The actual production of the book involved many headaches, each one being more than compensated for by the marvellous moments and laughs from a great team of people. Invariably after completing a chapter, my typists vowed never to eat the products again but soon began recalling favourite recipes that they would try at home. Particular thanks to Velda, Jan and Marilyn and especially to Rona Veldhuis and Dawn Hope for helping to establish style, assistance in editing and proof reading.

I hope we have put together a usable volume that will last through the years and be the first book opened when looking for your favourite dish.

This is not a complete book – no cookbook ever is, it is simply the best.

Anne Thorpe.

PANTRY LIST

allspice
arrowroot
basil
bay leaf
bicarbonate of soda
   (baking soda)
bouquet garni
breadcrumbs
caraway seeds
cardamom
chilli powder
cinnamon –
   ground
   stick
cloves –
   ground
   whole
cocoa
coconut –
   desiccated
   shredded
coffee –
   ground
   instant
cornflour
   (cornstarch)
cream of tartar
cumin
curry powder
custard powder

dried fruit –
   apricots
   currants
   dates
   figs
   raisins
   sultanas
flour –
   plain (all-purpose)
   self-raising (self rising)
   wholemeal (wholewheat)
food colourings
garam masala
gelatine
glacé fruits –
   cherries
   pineapple
ginger –
   ground
golden syrup
hoi sin sauce
honey
mace
milk –
   condensed
   evaporated
   powdered
mint flakes
mixed herbs
mixed spice

mustard –
   powder
   seeds
nutmeg
nuts –
   almonds
   hazelnuts
   peanuts
   walnuts
oil –
   olive
   peanut
   safflower
   vegetable
onions – dried flakes
oregano
parsley flakes
pasta –
   egg noodles
   spaghetti
peel – mixed
pepper –
   black
   cayenne
   white
pine nuts
rice –
   basmati
   brown
   white

rosemary
saffron
sage
salt
stock cubes –
   beef
   chicken
   fish
   onion
soy sauce
sugar –
   caster (powdered)
   icing (confectioners')
   raw (demerara)
   soft brown
   white (crystalline)
Tabasco
tarragon
tea
thyme
turmeric
vanilla essence
vinegar –
   brown
   cider
   tarragon
   white
Worcestershire sauce

[M] - Indicates that the recipe is suitable for cooking in a microwave or convection/microwave oven.

Unless otherwise stated all flour used is plain (all-purpose).

WEIGHTS & MEASURES

MASS

METRIC g	AVOIRDUPOIS oz
15	½
30	1
60	2
125	4 (¼ lb)
155	5
185	6
220	7
250 (0.25 kg)	8 (½ lb)
285	9
315	10
345	11
375	12 (¾ lb)
410	13
440	14
470	15
500 (0.5 kg)	16 (1 lb)
750	24 (1½ lb)
1000 (1 kg)	32 (2 lb)
1500 (1.5 kg)	48 (3 lb)
2000 (2 kg)	64 (4 lb)

TEMPERATURE

Description	C°	F°	Gas Mark
Very Cool	110	225	¼
	120	250	½
Cool	140	275	1
	150	300	2
Moderate	160	325	3
	180	350	4
Moderately Hot	190	375	5
	200	400	6
Hot	220	425	7
	230	450	8
Very Hot	240	475	9
	260	500	10

LIQUID

METRIC cups		IMPERIAL fl oz
1 tablespoon + 2 teaspoons (30 ml)		1
¼		2
⅓		2½
5 tablespoons	(100 ml)	3
½		4
⅔	(150 ml)	5 (¼ pint)
¾		6
1	(0.25 litre or 250 ml)	8
1¼		10 (½ pint)
1½		12
1¾		14
2	(0.5 litre or 500 ml)	16
2½		1 pint
41 litres		32
51.25 litres		1 quart
184.5 litres		1 gallon

1 (20 ml) tablespoon = 4 (5 ml) teaspoons

COMMON EQUIVALENTS

barbecue	grill
beef – fillet	boneless tenderloin
– mince	ground beef
– rump	boneless sirloin
bicarbonate of soda	baking soda
butter – unsalted	sweet
chicory	endive
cornflour	cornstarch
crayfish	lobster
cream	single or light cream for pouring
	double or heavy cream for whipping
eggplant	aubergine
essence	extract
flour – plain	all-purpose
– self-raising	self-rising
– wholemeal	wholewheat
golden syrup	corn syrup
grill	broil
jam	jelly
kiwifruit	Chinese gooseberry
peppers red and/or green	capsicum/bell pepper
pumpkin	squash
spring onion	scallion
scone	biscuit
sugar – caster	powdered
– icing	confectioners'
– raw	demerara
zucchini	courgette

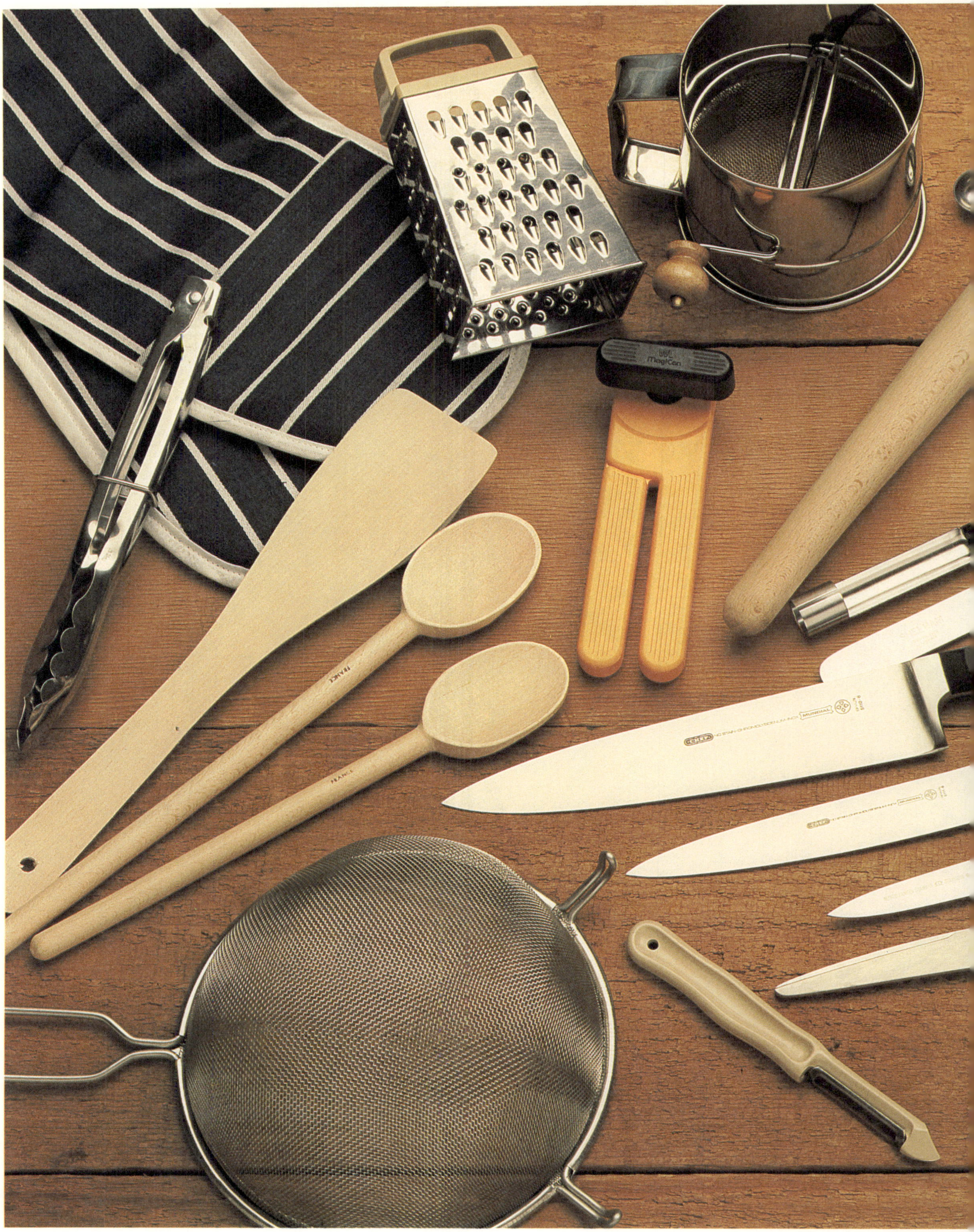
MagiCan

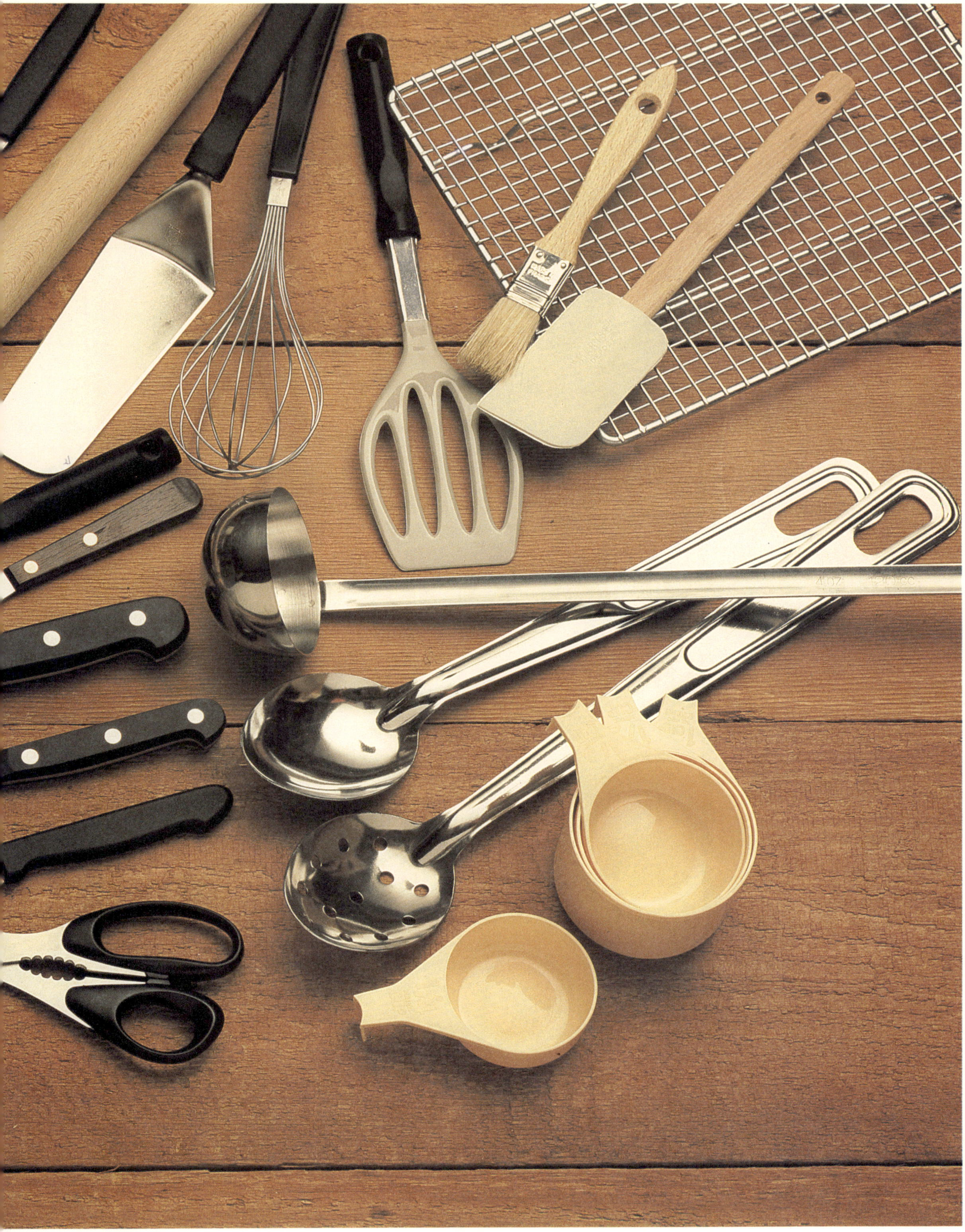

EQUIPMENT

There are an unlimited number of appliances available for use in our kitchens today. Most are made with a specific task in mind but many overlap in their usefulness. The choice of a particular appliance must be left with the person undertaking the major responsibility for food preparation. Listed below are the main appliances available. Perhaps this brief description will guide you in the right choice.

Small Appliances

Food Processor
A food processor is a compact, powerful appliance that performs an amazing number of kitchen tasks in a few seconds. It is unequalled in the performance of repetitive chores. It will grate, chop, purée, blend, slice, shred, and knead the best pastry dough you have ever made. It is the ideal appliance for the blending of royales or quenelles which require speed to keep the mixture cool. However, a food processor will not liquefy nor will it aerate egg whites to make meringue, or whip cream.

Electric Mixer or Beater
One of the first electric appliances made for the home kitchen, a mixer is still one of the most useful tools you can own. Creaming butter and sugar for cake batter or whipping cream can best be achieved in an electric mixer. Although purists will say only a copper bowl and an egg whisk will do the job, it is still easier and quicker to whisk egg whites with an electric beater. Mixers are available hand-held or mounted on a detachable stand and are usually supplied with bowls in two sizes. They are also available in rechargeable models.

Blender
Nothing quite surpasses a blender for liquefying. It produces delicious creamed soups and is perfect for puréeing livers for a pâté. Because it requires liquid to move the mixture about in the container it is not suitable for creamed vegetables or other immovable food. It is a very useful appliance but unless you have a great demand for drinks, soups and other liquid food products it should not be the first appliance purchased.

Mini-blender or Hand-held Mixer
This small appliance has become almost essential in every kitchen. Because of its portability and ease of operation it will probably be the first appliance you use. It is capable of mixing very small quantities even in a glass or similar fragile container. It will be invaluable in cocktail mixing and produces the best creamed vegetables you have tasted. Usually supplied with a small selection of fittings, it can be wall mounted for ease of storage.

Previous page: *Although there are hundreds of small utensils available for use in the kitchen, we have shown here those essential to any home. With these available, any basic kitchen task can be performed.*

Slow Cooker
A slow cooker is great for dishes which improve with slow gentle cooking. Curries and pot roasts just melt in your mouth after a few hours in the slow cooker. Casseroles are perfect too but because the cooking is so slow the gravy and juices tend not to thicken as much as using a conventional cooking method. With time being as important as it is today, these appliances are losing their appeal but must be considered according to your life style.

Electric Frypan
An electric frypan is a thermostatically controlled frying pan usually supplied with a high domed lid. It can be used for simple frying as well as baking with the lid on. It is a useful appliance for the small family and there is a great power saving when used for smaller meals.

Deep-fryer
A deep-fryer is a very versatile appliance for those who love the taste of crisp, crunchy food. It is thermostatically controlled, which is a safety feature and helps to reduce the possibility of fire which is always a problem when heating oil or fat on a conventional heat source.

Electric Skillet
Similar to an electric frypan this can be used for the smaller family or for preparing a quick breakfast. Ideal for sautéeing or frying small quantities of vegetables or meats, it can also be used on the table for flaming desserts.

Toast and Griller Combination
This is perfect for single persons or those preparing tiny meals. Almost four appliances in one, it will toast bread, grill (broil), top-brown and bake, usually with a thermostat control.

Sandwich Maker
Golden fried sandwiches or jaffles are mouth-watering on a cold winter's day. This small appliance makes the job simple and is the ideal method of using leftover food. The jaffles can be made sweet or savoury and are easy and simple to prepare.

Juicer
Fresh fruit or vegetable juice is made in seconds with this appliance. Great for those interested in health drinks, for those with young children and those with a large supply of fruit and vegetables on hand.

Electric Knife
Although nothing can replace the feel of carving with a perfectly balanced steel carving knife, an electric knife is quicker and, what is more important, is always sharp. Be sure that the knife you purchase has blades that are easily removed and that the motor can be serviced readily. The blades are liable to jam in some circumstances.

Major Appliances

Fan-forced or Conventional Oven (Gas or Electric)
Many homes today have only a microwave or microwave/convection oven installed in the kitchen. Although this seems sensible because of its speed, it is still essential to have a conventional oven. Firstly, it will invariably be larger, a fact which is important in day-to-day living. Nothing is worse than trying to co-ordinate a meal by moving dishes in and out of small appliances with a hungry family waiting.

Hotplates (Gas or Electric)
These are essential to every home and are installed in every kitchen. Electricity will give steady cooking and cleanliness while gas will give you speed and the ability to regulate temperature quickly. If you tend to cook Asian food you will find gas the better choice because of the heat control. Also most ranges come equipped with a wok stand. These ranges can also be supplied with a built-in grill (broiler) with a vacuum-type exhaust fan to eliminate fumes. This is the ideal way to cook the perfect steak indoors but is only for those with plenty of bench space.

Microwave Oven
All kitchens designed today have a microwave oven built-in. It has filled the gap in our busy life style because of its speed and ease of operation. Microwaves are high frequency, non-ionizing, electromagnetic waves, similar to radio waves, which are confined within the walls of the oven and activate the particles in food molecules. This activation causes friction which produces heat in the food. All ovens manufactured today are perfectly safe from leakage but if you are unsure a special gauge can be purchased to measure any problems.

Microwave ovens with a turntable are the most efficient as they distribute the energy more evenly and thus cook the food more efficiently. Use the microwave for melting chocolate and butter or for heating that one cup of coffee. It will make the fluffiest scrambled eggs and reheat almost any food without any deterioration in taste or moisture. A microwave is an appliance to be used every day in a thousand different ways. The more you use it the more ways you will find it useful. A conventional microwave oven will not brown any food without the use of a browning dish made especially for use in microwave ovens.

Microwave/Convection Oven
This type of oven has been on the market for the last few years and is taking over from the conventional microwave oven because of its multi-purpose functions. It can perform all of the tasks of the microwave oven as well as a conventional fan-forced oven. It can cook food using only microwave energy and then switch to convection for finishing and browning, it can switch on and off from one energy source to the other during the entire cooking time or it can use any or all of the combinations to produce the desired result.

The microwave/convection oven produces the golden appearance and crunchy texture desirable in much of our food.

Food Preparation

The first step in any meal is the purchase of the food. If using a recipe then the choice of ingredients is listed for you but the selection available for any particular food is immense and therefore careful consideration must be given before any purchase is made. The end result will rest on how discriminating you are. Wilted vegetables will not lead a cook to great inspiration while crisp vegetables with bright greens and yellows will enliven the spirits to bring out that extra flavour. Always choose the freshest ingredients even if it means a little extra time and travel; food is too expensive to waste on second best.

Preparation of the ingredients is the secret of success in any dish. All food is judged by its appearance before taste and the way you prepare the food behind-the-scenes will lead to praise later on. Preparation is time consuming and sometimes laborious. Cutting masses of vegetables for a soup or preparing days in advance for an important meal is not glamourous but the end result will always show this care of good food.

All hotels employ a finishing chef whose sole responsibility is to place the food on the plates and garnish it so as to give that gourmet look. This seemingly simple task is the most important step in presentation. Those dishes you see in leading food magazines are not difficult to prepare nor overly time-consuming – they are just placed on the plate in the right way.

Make sure that any sauce for the dish does not completely coat the food. (The exception to this is of course dishes such as Blanquette de Veau where the coating is the dish.) Usually a sauce looks better around the food with perhaps a tiny dribble on one corner.

Think of the colours of the food when placing it on the plate. One colour dishes do not tempt the taste-buds. If the dish has tones of only one colour, garnish with a contrast to attract the eye.

Do not serve heavy courses one after the other. If the main course is rich, serve a light first course and finish with a fruit dessert rather than a heavy chocolate cream pie.

Always garnish with a delicate hand. Two tiny leaves of parsley are better than 5 cm of stalk covered in leaves. Always garnish with something edible; it is not always pleasant to spend an entire meal dodging a foreign item on your plate.

Lastly, remember food is just that – it is meant to be eaten. Do not spoil your enjoyment or your guests' by giving the feeling that the first person to touch the buffet is ruining your life's work. Relax and enjoy.

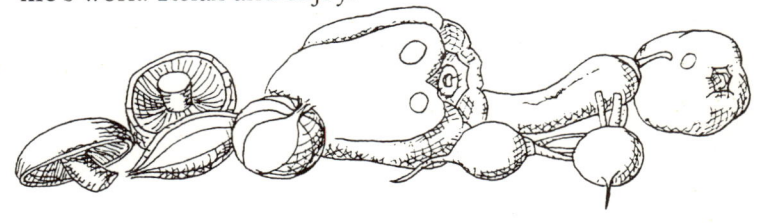

Clockwise from top: *Drunken Prawns* (page 28); *Cheese Pillows* (page 29); *Hot Mozzarella Avocados* (page 30).

FIRST COURSE

The first course of any meal can be chosen from a wide variety of dishes including very light soups or fruit to the more substantial fare such as quiche or pâté. Because of our need for lighter meals and less kilojoules the trend now is to serve quite light and fresh ingredients to begin a meal. Sometimes a simple salad is sufficient when followed by a rich main course and a succulent dessert. This first dish should leave diners hungry and eager for what is to follow. However don't leave your guests for too long before serving this course, they will fill up on nuts and drink your wine and won't notice the time and care you have put into the remainder of the meal.

This chapter contains recipes for stocks and sauces which form the basis of many recipes included in the book.

The recipes in this chapter have been supplied by many of the contributors whose credits appear later in the book, but in particular the **Australian Dairy Corporation**.

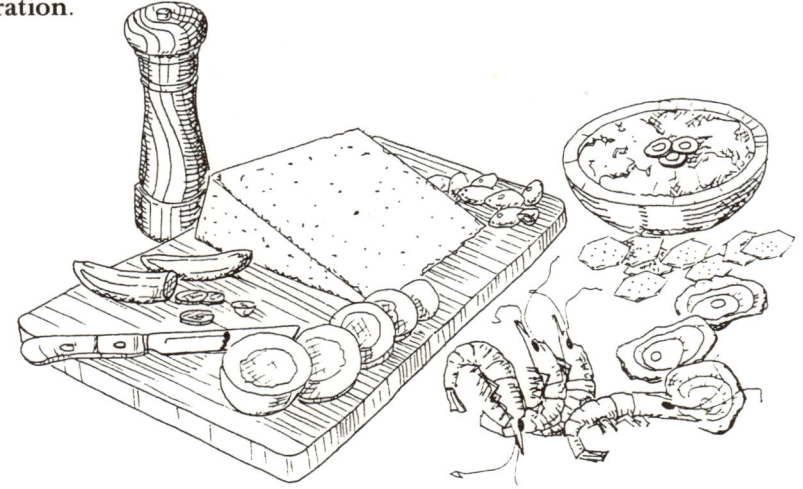

The **Australian Dairy Corporation** is a Commonwealth Statutory Authority funded by Australian dairy farmers. The overall objective of the Corporation is to enhance the profitable production and marketing of Australian dairy produce. Its functions are to improve the marketability and consumption of Australian dairy produce and to assist in the marketing on both the national and international markets.

The Dairy Foods Advisory Bureau is an integral part of the National Marketing Division and as such is involved in the preparation and production of recipe leaflets, food photography, T.V. commercials and educational materials related to the dairy industry. From time to time the Bureau is called upon to test new dairy products produced by Australian dairy manufacturers and to assist in the development of recipes for these products.

The Bureau is staffed by three home economists and a dietitian and is based in the head office of the Corporation in Melbourne. The recipes here have been devised, developed and tested in the Bureau's test kitchen and include a wide variety of Australian dairy products.

First Course

Soups

Cream of Chicken Soup
Serves 4

3 tablespoons (1 ½ oz) rice
½ cup diced celery
½ cup finely chopped onion
3 cups (24 fl oz) chicken stock
2 cups (16 fl oz) milk
salt and pepper
1 ½ cups chopped cooked chicken, optional
chopped fresh parsley

Cook the rice, celery and onion in the stock until quite soft, then push through a sieve or whirl in a blender. Heat the milk and add the rice-vegetable mixture. Season and heat, stirring, until just boiling. Add the cooked chicken, if using, and serve sprinkled with parsley.

Cream of Vegetable Soup
Serves 4

¼ cup (2 oz) rice
4 cups (1 litre) boiling water
2 teaspoons salt
2 cups chopped vegetables (carrots, celery, onion, turnips, tomatoes, peas, beans)
2 cups (16 fl oz) milk
pepper

Boil the rice in the water until almost tender about 10 minutes. Add the salt and vegetables and simmer, covered, until the vegetables are tender. Add the milk, check seasoning and reheat.

Chicken Curry Soup
Serves 6

30 g (1 oz) butter
3 rashers bacon, chopped
2 chicken breasts, finely chopped
1 onion, chopped
1 garlic clove, crushed
2 teaspoons curry powder
2 teaspoons flour
5 cups (1.25 litres) chicken stock
1 large carrot, grated
1 x 440 g (14 oz) can cream-style corn
¾ cup (5 oz) rice
pinch of dried herbs
salt and pepper
chopped fresh parsley

Heat the butter in a large pan and sauté the bacon, chicken, onion, garlic and curry powder for 3 minutes. Stir in the flour and the remaining ingredients except the parsley. Bring to the boil and simmer gently for 40 minutes. Serve piping hot sprinkled with parsley.

Mulligatawny (Curried) Soup with Rice
Serves 4

4 cups (1 litre) chicken stock, preferably made from the carcase of a roast chicken or a small boiling fowl, or from cans of chicken consommé
60 g (2 oz) margarine or 1 tablespoon cooking oil
1 large onion, sliced
1 level teaspoon curry powder, or curry paste
vinegar
1 tablespoon flour
salt
1 cup hot boiled rice
lemon wedges

Heat the chicken stock. Meanwhile, melt the margarine in a pan and sauté the onion until it is transparent. In a cup, mix the curry powder with a little vinegar and, with a wooden spoon, stir into the onion and cook over a low heat for 5 minutes. Sprinkle with flour and mix well, and cook for a further 2 to 3 minutes. Pour in the strained stock, a little at a time, stirring so that the curry mixture blends thoroughly with the stock. Cook for several minutes until it is bubbling, taste and add salt if needed. Strain again and serve into soup bowls. On the table, provide a bowl of hot boiled rice and a bowl of lemon wedges. Each person usually adds about 2 tablespoons of rice and some lemon juice to their soup.

If you prefer, the curry powder may be replaced by the same quantity (or more or less depending on your preference) of a mixture of 1 teaspoon ground ginger, ½ teaspoon chilli powder, ½ teaspoon pepper and a pinch of powdered cloves.

Summer Day Soup
Serves 6

3 cups peas, fresh or frozen
5 cups (1.25 litres) chicken stock, made with stock cubes
1 onion, chopped
½ cup cooked rice
½ cup (4 fl oz) cream or milk
salt and pepper
sour cream and chopped chives

Combine the peas, chicken stock, onion and rice, place over moderate heat and simmer for about 20 minutes or until peas are tender. Purée in a blender or push through a coarse sieve. Add cream to the pea purée and season with salt and pepper. Chill in the refrigerator before serving garnished with sour cream and chives.

Old Style Chicken Broth

Serves 6

1 kg (2 lb) chicken pieces, breasts and thighs
8 cups (2 litres) water
a few lemon slices
1 teaspoon salt
freshly ground pepper
1 bay leaf
¼ cup (2 oz) rice
2 carrots, thinly sliced
1 stalk celery, sliced
2 leeks, washed thoroughly and sliced, or
2 white onions, thinly sliced
2 tablespoons chopped fresh parsley

Where possible remove the skin from the chicken pieces. Cover them with water, add the lemon slices and allow to soak for half an hour. Bring to the boil, season and add the bay leaf, then simmer for 30 minutes. Add the rice and continue to cook for another 40 minutes. When the chicken is quite tender remove from broth. While the chicken is cooling add the carrots, celery and leeks to the broth and simmer until tender. Remove any remaining skin from the chicken pieces and chop them into small dice. Replace in the broth and check seasoning. Allow the broth to cool and then skim off the fat. When serving reheat and sprinkle with parsley.

Hearty Cabbage Soup

Serves 6

45 g (1 ½ oz) butter
1 onion, chopped
2 carrots, sliced
1 small cabbage, shredded
6 cups (1.5 litres) beef stock
½ cup (3 oz) rice
1 teaspoon salt
freshly ground pepper
½ teaspoon paprika or ¼ teaspoon nutmeg
2 tablespoons chopped fresh parsley
½ cup (4 fl oz) sour cream or yoghurt or ½ cup (2 oz) grated cheese

Heat the butter and sauté the onion, carrots and cabbage until well coated with butter. Add the beef stock and simmer for 15 minutes. Add the rice and season with salt, pepper and paprika. Simmer for another 25 minutes. Serve sprinkled with parsley and topped with sour cream.

Note: To make this soup a complete meal, add sliced frankfurt to the soup and simmer for 5 minutes.

Hearty Cabbage Soup

First Course

Minestrone Soup

Serves 6

- 125 g (4 oz) haricot beans, soaked overnight
- 125 g (4 oz) bacon or salt pork, chopped
- 2 garlic cloves, chopped
- 3 sprigs fresh parsley, chopped
- 2 onions, thinly sliced
- 4 potatoes, peeled and diced
- 3 carrots, peeled and diced
- 3 stalks celery, chopped
- 3 zucchini (courgettes), chopped
- 3 tomatoes, peeled and chopped or 2 tablespoons tomato paste
- 12 cups (3 litres) water
- salt
- freshly ground pepper
- ½ cabbage (Savoy is preferable), shredded
- 1 cup frozen peas
- 1 cup sliced beans
- 1 cup (6 oz) rice
- 125 g (4 oz) cubed ham, cooked chicken or salami
- 1 tablespoon chopped fresh parsley or basil
- freshly grated Parmesan cheese

Cook the haricot beans in boiling water until almost tender, about 1 hour. Do not add salt to the water as it will toughen the beans at this stage. Heat the bacon, garlic and parsley in a heavy based saucepan until the bacon fat melts. Add the onions and cook for a few minutes. Add the haricot beans and all the remaining vegetables except the cabbage, peas and beans. Cover with water and season well with salt and pepper. Cover with a lid and simmer for about 1½ hours. This slow simmering is important to develop the flavour. Add the cabbage, peas and beans, cook for about 10 minutes and then add the rice. Continue simmering until the rice is tender, about 15 minutes. Add the ham and serve sprinkled with parsley and plenty of Parmesan cheese.

Note: If you wish, you may add extra ham to this recipe to make a more sustaining soup. Chicken or beef stock cubes may be added to the water and cubed cooked chicken can be added during the last 5 minutes of cooking.

Tomato Chicken Bouillon

Serves 6

- 2 cups (16 fl oz) chicken stock, made with stock cubes
- 4 cups (1 litre) tomato juice
- ¼ cup diced celery
- 1 teaspoon chopped onion or chives
- 2 cloves, optional
- small garlic clove, crushed
- salt
- 2 teaspoons brown sugar
- 1 teaspoon Worcestershire sauce
- 1 teaspoon vinegar or lemon juice
- 1 cup cooked rice

Combine all the ingredients except the rice, bring to the boil then simmer for 25 minutes. Add the rice and cook for another 5 minutes. Add more stock if soup is too thick.

Rice Florentine Soup

Serves 6

- 2 tablespoons olive oil
- 1 small leek, white part chopped
- 2 small onions, chopped
- 1 garlic clove, crushed
- 2½ cups chopped fresh spinach
- 5 cups (1.25 litres) chicken stock
- ⅓ cup (2 oz) rice
- 1 tablespoon grated Parmesan cheese
- salt and pepper
- nutmeg

Heat the oil in a large saucepan and add the leek, onions and garlic. Cook until softened, but not browned. Add the spinach and cook for 5 minutes. Add the stock and rice. Bring to the boil, reduce heat and simmer for about 15 to 20 minutes. Stir the cheese into the soup and season to taste with salt, pepper and nutmeg.

Greek Lemon Soup

Serves 6

- 6 cups (1.5 litres) rich chicken stock
- ¼ cup (2 oz) rice
- 2 eggs
- juice of 2 lemons
- grated rind of 1 lemon
- salt and pepper
- chopped parsley and thin lemon slices, to garnish

Bring the chicken stock to the boil, add the rice, and then simmer over moderate heat until the rice is cooked, about 20 minutes. Beat the eggs, lemon juice and rind until well blended. Very gradually add about 1 cup (8 fl oz) boiling stock to the egg mixture, stirring all the time. Pour the egg mixture into the stock, season and stir well. Gently heat the soup but do not boil. Serve garnished with parsley and lemon slices.

Note: Finely chopped chicken may be added to the soup.

Brown Rice Broth

Serves 6

- 2 cups chopped carrot
- 1 onion, chopped
- 1 cup chopped celery
- 1 cup chopped parsnip or turnip
- 10 cups (2.5 litres) lamb or beef stock
- 3 whole fresh parsley stalks
- 1 bay leaf
- 1 tablespoon tomato paste
- ½ cup (3 oz) brown rice
- salt
- freshly ground pepper
- chopped fresh parsley

Place the prepared vegetables, stock, parsley, bay leaf, tomato paste and rice in a saucepan, season with salt and pepper and cover. Simmer for 1½ hours. Remove parsley stalks, check seasoning and serve sprinkled with chopped parsley.

Note: This soup develops a better flavour if allowed to stand overnight.

Highland Fish Soup

Serves 4

15 g (½ oz) butter
1 onion, sliced or
   4 spring onions
   (scallions), sliced
1 tablespoon flour
2 cups (16 fl oz) chicken
   stock
1 x 425 g (13 ½ oz) can
   tomatoes
2 cups flaked cooked
   haddock, salmon or tuna
1 cup cooked rice
salt and pepper
chopped fresh parsley

Heat the butter and fry the onion until golden. Blend in the flour, and gradually add the chicken stock, stirring until smooth. Add the tomatoes, haddock and rice and season to taste. Simmer for about 10 minutes. Sprinkle with chopped parsley before serving.

Hurry Curry Soup

Serves 6

2 teaspoons butter
1 onion, grated
4 rashers bacon, chopped
1 tablespoon curry powder
3 tablespoons flour
4 cups (1 litre) chicken stock
1 ½ cups (12 fl oz) milk
1 carrot, grated
1 parsnip, grated
1 stalk celery, finely
   chopped
1 cup peas
juice of 1 lemon
1 ½ cups cooked rice, kept
   warm
chopped fresh parsley

Melt the butter and very gently sauté the onion, bacon and curry powder for 3 minutes. Remove from the heat and blend in the flour, stock and milk. Add the remaining ingredients, except the rice and parsley. Bring to the boil and simmer very gently for 20 minutes. Spoon rice into each soup bowl and top with piping hot soup. Sprinkle with parsley before serving.

Cream of Carrot Soup

Serves 6

45 g (1 ½ oz) butter
750 g (1 ½ lb) carrots,
   thinly sliced
1 onion, finely chopped
6 cups (1.5 litres) chicken
   stock, made with stock
   cubes
2 tablespoons rice
¼ teaspoon dried basil or
   dried mint
salt and pepper
sour cream, to garnish
chopped fresh mint or fresh
   chives, to garnish

Melt the butter, add the carrots and onion, and cook gently, covered, for about 10 minutes. Add the stock, rice and basil. Cover and simmer over low heat for about 20 to 25 minutes. Push through a sieve or whisk in an electric blender until smooth. Check the seasoning. Serve with a dob of sour cream and sprinkled with chopped mint or chives.

Corn and Rice Chowder with Prawns

Serves 6

250 g (8 oz) pickled pork,
   cubed
2 onions, chopped
½ cup chopped celery with
   tops
3 tablespoons chopped
   green pepper (capsicum)
3 tablespoons finely
   chopped carrot
½ bay leaf, crumbled
3 tablespoons flour
4 cups (1 litre) water
2 x 450 g (14 ½ oz) cans corn
   kernels
1 x 425 g (13 ½ oz) can
   evaporated milk
500 g (1 lb) cooked prawns
   (shrimp), cleaned
salt and pepper
3 cups cooked rice
chopped fresh parsley, to
   garnish

Cook the pickled pork in a large saucepan until browned and crisp. Remove the pork and pour off all but 3 tablespoons of fat. Add the next 5 ingredients and cook for 5 minutes. Stir in the flour, then add the water, stirring until blended and boiling. Reduce the heat and simmer for 15 minutes, stirring occasionally. Add the corn, evaporated milk and prawns; heat well but do not boil. Season to taste. Add the pork pieces and the rice and heat again without boiling. Serve garnished with chopped parsley.

Salmon Tomato Chowder

Serves 4

1 cup (6 oz) rice
3 cups (24 fl oz) chicken
   stock made with stock
   cubes
1 cup canned tomatoes
1 onion, thinly sliced
1 bay leaf
1 x 250 g (8 oz) can salmon,
   drained and flaked
45 g (1 ½ oz) butter
2 tablespoons flour
3 cups (24 fl oz) milk
1 teaspoon seasoned salt
freshly ground black pepper
½ teaspoon grated lemon
   rind
chopped fresh parsley, to
   garnish

Combine the rice, stock, tomatoes, onion and bay leaf and simmer until the rice is just tender, about 20 minutes. Fork the salmon into the rice.

   In another saucepan, melt the butter, blend in the flour and cook for 1 minute, then remove from the heat. Gradually blend in the milk until smooth. Replace over the heat, stir constantly until it boils and thickens and then add the salt, pepper and lemon rind. Pour the milk mixture onto the rice and salmon and stir gently until well blended. Check the seasoning and add a little extra stock if required. Serve hot and sprinkle each bowl with a little parsley.

First Course

Mexican Chilli Soup

Serves 4

1 tablespoon oil
500 g (1 lb) good quality topside mince (ground beef)
1 small onion, chopped
1 garlic clove, crushed
1 x 125 g (4 oz) can tomato paste
1 tablespoon chilli seasoning mix
4 cups (1 litre) water
¾ cup (5 oz) rice
1 x 315 g (10 oz) can kidney beans
¾ cup (3 oz) grated cheese

Heat the oil in a large saucepan or Dutch oven. Add the meat, onion and garlic and cook until the meat is browned and crumbly. Add the tomato paste and chilli seasoning mix. Mix well and add the water. Bring to the boil and simmer for 30 minutes.

Add the rice, cover and simmer for 25 minutes. Add the undrained kidney beans and heat through. Ladle the soup into 6 serving bowls and top each serving with some of the grated cheese. Serve with corn chips if desired.

Pumpkin Zucchini Soup

Serves 4

250 g (8 oz) pumpkin, peeled and roughly chopped
2 medium-sized zucchini (courgettes), roughly chopped
2 cups (16 fl oz) water
seasonings to taste
thyme
½ cup (1 ½ oz) skim milk powder

Place the pumpkin, zucchini and water in a saucepan. Bring to the boil. Add the seasonings. Simmer gently for 15 minutes or until the vegetables are tender. Strain and reserve the liquid. Purée the vegetables in a blender. Stir the skim milk powder into the vegetable liquid, add this to the vegetable purée and blend until smooth. Return to the saucepan and heat through. Serve with toasted croûtons.

Avocado and Prawn Soup

Serves 6 – 8

½ onion
2 medium-sized avocados
juice of 1 lemon
salt and freshly ground black pepper
dash of Tabasco sauce
1 garlic clove, crushed
500 g (1 lb) prawns (shrimp), peeled
2 ½ cups (20 fl oz) fish or chicken stock
2 ½ cups (20 fl oz) milk or ½ milk and ½ cream

Purée the onion and avocados and add the lemon juice, salt and pepper, Tabasco, crushed garlic and half the prawns. Blend until smooth. Heat the stock and milk and add the avocado mixture and the remaining prawns, roughly chopped. Heat through without boiling and serve piping hot, garnished with cayenne pepper.

Oyster and Dill Soup

Serves 4

60 g (2 oz) butter
2 spring onions (scallions), finely chopped
½ cup (2 oz) flour
1 ½ cups (12 fl oz) fish stock and oyster liquor
1 ¼ cups (10 fl oz) milk
1 tablespoon fresh dill, finely chopped
salt and pepper
juice of 1 lemon
20-24 oysters

Melt the butter in a large saucepan and add the spring onions. Cook for 1 minute. Add the flour and stir to make a paste. Stir in the stock and milk and simmer whilst stirring until a smooth sauce results.

Add the dill and season to taste with salt, pepper and lemon juice. Add the oysters and simmer for 2 minutes. Serve in warm soup bowls and garnish with a sprig of dill.

Cheese and Corn Soup

Serves 6

90 g (3 oz) butter
1 large onion, chopped
3 rashers bacon, diced
¼ cup (1 oz) flour
2 cups (16 fl oz) water
2 chicken stock cubes, crumbled
1 medium-sized carrot, diced
1 x 440 g (14 oz) can corn kernels, drained
2 cups (16 fl oz) milk
2 cups grated Australian cheese
1 tablespoon chopped fresh parsley

Melt the butter and fry the onion and bacon for 5 minutes. Stir in the flour and cook for 3 minutes. Add the water and stir until smooth. Add the stock cubes, carrot and corn and simmer for 30 minutes. Stir in the remaining ingredients and reheat without boiling. Serve with crusty buttered bread.

Apple Chicken Soup

Serves 4

500 g (1 lb) cooking apples, peeled, cored and roughly chopped
1 large onion, roughly chopped
2 cups (16 fl oz) chicken stock
1 cup (8 fl oz) condensed cream of chicken soup
seasonings
½ cup (4 fl oz) natural yoghurt

Place the chopped apples, onion and chicken stock in a saucepan. Bring to the boil. Cover and simmer until the apples are tender, approximately 10 minutes. Blend or purée until smooth. Return to the saucepan and add the undiluted chicken soup. Season to taste. Reheat or serve chilled, garnished with a spoonful of yoghurt.

Creole Beef Soup

Serves 6

1 tablespoon oil
3 rashers bacon, chopped
250 g (8 oz) minced (ground) meat (pork or veal if possible)
1 onion, chopped
1 garlic clove, crushed
1 red or green pepper (capsicum), chopped
pinch of chilli powder or cayenne pepper
¼ teaspoon Tabasco sauce or 1 teaspoon Worcestershire sauce
6 cups (1.5 litres) beef stock
1 x 440 g (14 oz) can tomatoes
1 tablespoon (½ oz) brown sugar
1 bay leaf
salt and pepper
3 cups cooked rice

Heat the oil and fry the bacon and the minced meat until the meat changes colour. Remove the meat and bacon and drain off all but 1 tablespoon of oil. Add the onion, garlic and chopped pepper and cook for a few minutes. Add the chilli powder, Tabasco sauce, beef stock, tomatoes, sugar, bay leaf, salt and pepper. Replace the meat and bacon and simmer the soup over a low heat for 35 minutes. Check the seasoning. Spoon ½ cup hot rice into each soup bowl and spoon over the soup.

Mock Rice Bouillabaisse

Serves 6

1 medium-sized carrot
500 g (1 lb) smoked cod or haddock
500 g (1 lb) flake or bream
125 g (4 oz) butter
2 medium-sized onions, sliced
1 large garlic clove, crushed
½ cup (3 oz) rice
1 bay leaf
1 x 450 g (14 ½ oz) can tomato purée
3 cups (24 fl oz) water
juice of 2 lemons
2 teaspoons salt
¼ cup (2 fl oz) dry sherry
freshly ground black pepper
grated Parmesan cheese

Peel the carrot, cut through the centre lengthwise and slice thinly into half rings. Cut the fish into 5 cm (2 inch) pieces. Melt the butter and sauté the onions, garlic and rice until lightly golden. Add the fish and sauté a few minutes, tossing frequently. Add the bay leaf, tomato purée, water, lemon juice and salt and bring to the boil. Cover and simmer for about 15 to 20 minutes, until the rice is cooked. Add the sherry and season with pepper. Accompany with Parmesan cheese.

Creole Beef Soup

First Course

Chinese Watercress Soup

Serves 6 - 8

250 g (8 oz) minced (ground) chicken meat
1 x 440 g (14 oz) can water chestnuts, drained and finely chopped
2 teaspoons grated fresh ginger
3 teaspoons soy sauce
1 egg
10 cups (2.5 litres) chicken stock
⅛ teaspoon pepper
1 teaspoon sesame oil
3 cups watercress, torn into 8 cm (3 inch) lengths
30 g (1 oz) cellophane noodles

Combine the chicken with the water chestnuts, half the ginger and soy sauce and the egg. Form into tiny balls to float in the soup. Bring 4 cups (1 litre) of the chicken stock to the boil. Add the chicken balls and allow to cook gently for 3 minutes. Remove and set aside.

Bring the remaining stock to the boil and flavour with pepper, the remaining ginger and soy sauce and the sesame oil. Add the watercress and cellophane noodles. Cook for 3 minutes.

Place the chicken balls in a serving bowl. Pour the boiling soup into the bowl. Serve immediately.

Pumpkin and Apple Soup

Serves 8

1 large onion, chopped
45 g (1 ½ oz) butter
1.5 kg (3 lb) pumpkin, peeled and chopped
1 large Granny Smith apple, peeled and chopped
2 tablespoons tomato paste
½ teaspoon nutmeg
6 cups (1.5 litres) chicken stock
½ cup (4 fl oz) sour cream
½ cup (2 oz) chopped pecans

Sauté the onion in the butter until golden. Add the pumpkin, apple, tomato paste, nutmeg and 4 cups (1 litre) of the stock. Simmer for 30 minutes. Purée in a blender or food processor. Add the remaining stock and reheat before serving.

Serve with a dollop of sour cream and chopped pecans.

Iced Tomato Soup

Serves 2

4 large ripe tomatoes, peeled
2 tablespoons lemon juice
2 tablespoons olive oil
1 teaspoon chopped chives
1 teaspoon chopped fresh mint or 1 teaspoon chopped fresh basil

Place all the ingredients in a blender or food processor and purée until smooth. Serve over ice cubes.

Parsnip and Orange Soup

Serves 4

500 g (1 lb) parsnips
60 g (2 oz) butter
1 white onion, finely chopped
½ teaspoon curry powder
3 cups (24 fl oz) chicken stock
grated rind of 1 orange
3 tablespoons orange juice
salt and pepper

Peel the parsnips, remove any hard or woody parts and slice into rings. Melt the butter. Add the parsnips and onion and gently fry until they are glazed and slightly softened.

Stir in the curry powder and fry for 1 minute. Add the stock and orange rind, cover, and cook gently until the parsnips are quite soft. Add the orange juice, salt and pepper and heat through.

French Onion Soup

Serves 6 - 8

500 g (1 lb) brown onions
90 g (3 oz) butter or margarine
¼ cup (1 oz) flour
8 cups (2 litres) beef or vegetable stock
salt and pepper
1 bay leaf
1 French loaf
1 garlic clove, crushed
olive oil or melted butter
125 g (4 oz) Gruyère cheese, finely grated

Peel the onions and slice thinly. Heat the butter in a large pan, add the onions and gently fry until golden brown. (It is important to fry the onions slowly in order to caramelise their natural sugar content.)

Sprinkle the flour over the onions and stir over the heat for 1 to 2 minutes. Add the boiling stock and bring to the boil. Season to taste with salt and pepper. Add the bay leaf and simmer for 30 minutes.

Cut the French loaf into 12 or 16 slices. Place on a baking tray and bake at 150°C (300°F/Gas 2) for 15 minutes. Mix the crushed garlic with a little olive oil, brush on the bread and continue baking until golden.

Place the bread in the bottom of a large casserole. Ladle the soup on top and sprinkle the cheese over. Bake the soup, uncovered, in a 190°C (375°F/Gas 5) oven until the cheese has melted and is golden. Serve hot.

Minted Cucumber Soup

Serves 6 - 8

2 cucumbers, peeled, seeded and sliced
2 cups (16 fl oz) chicken stock
2 tablespoons chopped fresh mint
1 cup (8 fl oz) natural yoghurt

Cook the cucumbers in the stock until tender. Chill. Add the finely chopped mint and purée in a blender. Stir in the yoghurt just before serving.

Fresh Corn Chowder

Serves 4 - 6

4 cobs corn
45 g (1 ½ oz) butter
2 onions, chopped
1 stalk celery, sliced
2 potatoes, peeled and cut into 2 cm (¾ inch) cubes
salt and freshly ground pepper to taste
1 ½ cups (12 fl oz) chicken stock
1 tablespoon chopped fresh basil
1 tablespoon chopped fresh thyme
2 cups (16 fl oz) milk
1 cup (8 fl oz) cream

Remove the corn kernels from the cobs. In a large heavy pan melt the butter and sauté the onions and celery until tender. Add the potatoes, corn, salt, pepper, stock and herbs. Cover and simmer for 15 minutes or until the potatoes and corn are tender.

Add the milk and cream and heat through. Serve hot with cracker biscuits.

Chilled Cherry Soup

Serves 8

2 kg (4 lb) cherries, stewed
1 ¼ cups (10 fl oz) milk
2 tablespoons honey
4 cups (1 litre) water
freshly grated nutmeg
whipped cream for serving, optional

Drain the cherries and reserve the syrup. Halve the cherries and remove the stones. Place in a bowl with the reserved syrup, milk and honey. Cover and leave overnight in the refrigerator.

Next day, combine the cherry mixture with the water in a pan. Bring to the boil, remove from the heat and cool. Add the nutmeg to taste and chill thoroughly.

If liked, top each bowl of chilled soup with a spoonful of cream.

Fruit Soup

Serves 6

3 cups (24 fl oz) orange juice
1 banana
1 Granny Smith apple, peeled and chopped
juice of 1 lemon
¼ rockmelon, peeled and chopped
1 cup (8 fl oz) buttermilk
yoghurt for serving

Combine all the ingredients in a blender until smooth. Chill before serving. Top each serving with a spoonful yoghurt.

Cressy Soup

Serves 6 - 8

4 large carrots
1 large onion
1 stalk celery
1 rasher bacon
30 g (1 oz) butter or margarine
5 cups (1.25 litres) chicken or vegetable stock
2 tablespoons cornflour (cornstarch)
⅔ cup (5 fl oz) cream
pinch of sugar
salt and pepper
chopped fresh parsley for garnish

Scrape or peel the carrots and dice finely. Peel the onion and chop finely. Wash the celery, remove the coarse pieces and slice thinly. Remove the rind and bones from the bacon and chop. Heat the butter in a large, heavy based pan. Add the vegetables, bacon and bacon rind. Cover and sauté for 5 minutes, shaking the pan occasionally, until the vegetables have absorbed nearly all the fat. Remove the rind.

Add the stock, cover and bring to the boil, then simmer for 30 minutes. Cool, then mix to a purée in a blender or food processor and return to the pan.

Blend the cornflour smoothly with the cream. Add to the soup and bring to the boil, stirring continuously. Add the sugar and salt and pepper to taste, and simmer for 3 minutes before serving. Serve hot, garnished with chopped parsley.

Celery and Chicken Soup

Serves 4

30 g (1 oz) butter
½ bunch celery, finely chopped
1 cup chopped cooked chicken meat
3 cups (24 fl oz) chicken stock
¼ cup chopped fresh parsley
60 g (2 oz) cream cheese
2 spring onions (scallions), thinly sliced
freshly ground black pepper

Melt the butter in a large heavy pan, add celery and chicken and sauté, covered, for 5 minutes. Add the stock, bring to the boil and simmer for 15 minutes. Add the parsley, cream cheese, spring onions and pepper. Stir until the cheese is melted.

For a creamier soup, purée in a blender until smooth. Serve hot with hot wholemeal toast.

First Course

Prawn and Pumpkin Soup
Serves 4

600 g (1 ¼ lb) pumpkin
1 onion, chopped
1 garlic clove, crushed
4 cups (1 litre) fish or chicken stock
⅛ teaspoon nutmeg
freshly ground pepper
200 g (6 ½ oz) prawn (shrimp) meat, roughly chopped
juice of 1 lemon
chopped fresh parsley

Bring the pumpkin, onion, garlic and stock to the boil in a large saucepan. Simmer until the pumpkin is tender.

In a blender place all the cooked ingredients, nutmeg, pepper and half the prawns and blend until smooth. Return to the saucepan and add the remaining prawns. Cook for a further 2 to 3 minutes and add the lemon juice. Check the consistency and if too thick add a little milk or stock. Garnish with chopped parsley or a teaspoon of sour cream or yoghurt.

Fish Soup
Serves 4

600 g (1 ¼ lb) head and backbone of snapper or red emperor
8 cups (2 litres) water
30 g (1 oz) butter
1 garlic clove, crushed
¼ cup (1 oz) flour
1 carrot, peeled and grated
1 onion, peeled and grated
1 large potato, peeled and grated
⅔ cup (5 fl oz) white wine
salt and pepper to taste
¼ cup (2 fl oz) lemon juice
1 tablespoon chopped fresh parsley
¾ cup (6 fl oz) cream
freshly grated nutmeg

Rinse the bones under cold running water and drain. Place in a large saucepan and cover with the water. Bring to the boil and simmer until the flesh comes away from the bones (approximately 45 minutes). Allow to cool. Remove the flesh from the bones and head, particularly around the cheeks, and set aside. Strain the liquid and reserve. Discard the bones.

Melt the butter and sauté the garlic for 1 minute before stirring in the flour. Add the fish stock, grated vegetables, white wine, pepper and reserved fish flesh. Simmer for 30 minutes until the vegetables have disintegrated. Add the lemon juice, salt and pepper to taste. Stir in the parsley and cream and heat but do not boil. Serve garnished with freshly grated nutmeg.

Broccoli and Scallop Soup
Serves 6

500 g (1 lb) broccoli
1 onion, chopped
4 cups (1 litre) fish or chicken stock
200 g (6 ½ oz) scallops
¼ teaspoon nutmeg
¼ teaspoon coriander
freshly ground pepper
30 g (1 oz) butter
¼ cup (1 oz) flour
juice of 1 lemon

Cook the broccoli and onion in the fish or chicken stock until tender but still deep green in colour. Remove the vegetables from the liquid and purée in a blender until smooth. Cook the scallops for 2 minutes in the vegetable liquid. Blend the scallops, reserving some for garnish, and liquid into the broccoli purée and season with nutmeg, coriander and pepper.

Melt the butter, stir in the flour and cook for 3 minutes. Pour in the broccoli mixture and stir until thickened and smooth. Add the lemon juice and check the flavour. Salt may need to be added. Serve in warm bowls garnished with slices of cooked scallop.

Prawn Bisque
Serves 4

200 g (6 ½ oz) butter
400 g (12 ½ oz) prawn (shrimp) meat (bug or crab meat can be substituted), some reserved for garnish
400 g (12 ½ oz) combined onion, carrot, leek and celery, roughly chopped
3 tablespoons tomato paste
½ cup (3 oz) rice, cooked
⅓ cup (2 ½ fl oz) white wine
¼ cup (2 fl oz) brandy
bouquet garni
4 cups (1 litre) fish stock (chicken stock may be substituted)

Melt the butter and fry the prawns, onion, carrot, leek and celery for 3 to 5 minutes until soft. Add the tomato paste and cooked rice, wine, brandy and bouquet garni. Season and moisten with some of the stock. Simmer until partially reduced, about 20 minutes.

Purée the soup and correct the consistency with the remaining stock. Check the seasonings and serve garnished with diced prawn flesh.

Chicken Soup Indienne
Serves 4 – 5

60 g (2 oz) butter
1 medium-sized onion, chopped
1 garlic clove, crushed
1 medium-sized apple, peeled and chopped
125 g (4 oz) mushrooms, chopped
2 stalks celery, chopped
¼ cup (1 oz) flour
2 teaspoons curry powder
1 tablespoon tomato paste
¼ teaspoon dried thyme
white pepper, to taste
½ teaspoon salt
2 ½ cups (20 fl oz) chicken stock
1 cup (8 fl oz) water
1 cup cooked rice
½ cup (4 fl oz) cream

Melt the butter in a large saucepan. Add the onion, garlic, and apple and cook gently for about 5 to 6 minutes. Add the mushrooms and celery and cook for a further 4 minutes. Add the flour and curry powder and cook for 2 minutes. Add the tomato paste, thyme, pepper, salt and stock mixed with water. Bring to the boil, stirring occasionally. Cover and simmer for 30 minutes. Purée the soup in a blender or food processor in 2 or 3 lots until smooth. Adjust seasoning. Stir in the rice and cream. Heat through but do not boil.

Beef 'n' Rice Potage
Serves 6

500 g (1 lb) gravy beef, cut into 2.5 cm (1 inch) strips
30 g (1 oz) butter
4 cups shredded cabbage
2 stalks celery, cut into 1.25 cm (½ inch) pieces
2 small carrots, cut into 1.25 cm (½ inch) pieces
1-2 teaspoons salt
12 peppercorns, tied in cheesecloth
2 beef stock cubes, crumbled
1 x 440 g (14 oz) can whole peeled potatoes
1 leek or onion, sliced
7 cups (1.75 litres) water
¾ cup (5 oz) rice
1 tablespoon paprika
¼ teaspoon ground cloves
1 x 310 g (10 oz) can corn kernels
¾ cup (3 oz) grated Parmesan cheese

Sauté the beef for 15 minutes in the butter. Add the remaining ingredients, except the corn and cheese, and simmer for 1¼ hours. Add the corn, adjust the seasoning and remove peppercorns. Serve the cheese separately or sprinkled on the soup.

Beef 'n' Rice Potage

First Course

Pumpkin Soup

Serves 6

2 kg (4 lb) pumpkin
250 g (8 oz) potatoes
2½ cups (20 fl oz) milk
salt and freshly ground
   black pepper
⅓ cup (2½ fl oz) sour
   cream mixed with
   2 beaten eggs
extra sour cream
chopped chives or parsley

Peel and slice the pumpkin and potatoes. Place in a large pan and add the milk. Season lightly. Slowly bring to the boil, lower the heat and continue to cook over low to moderate heat until very soft. Stir until the vegetables have completely dissolved. Taste for seasoning.

Blend or process the soup and return to the saucepan. The soup should be a little thicker than you would normally eat. If too thick, add a little more milk. Reheat the soup and when it reaches boiling point, remove from the heat. Beat the cream and eggs together and add to the soup. DO NOT return the soup to the heat once the cream and eggs have been added. Serve with a teaspoon of sour cream in the soup and garnish with chopped chives or parsley.

Note: This soup can be served hot or cold. If serving cold, cut the top from a pumpkin and carefully remove the flesh. Serve soup in the pumpkin shell.

Tomato and Egg Soup

Serves 6

375 g (12 oz) ripe tomatoes
5 cups (1.25 litres) chicken
   stock
1½ tablespoons cornflour
   (cornstarch)
3 teaspoons sesame oil
1 egg
1 teaspoon vegetable oil
1 tablespoon sherry
1 tablespoon soy sauce
2 spring onions (scallions),
   finely chopped

Peel and halve the tomatoes and cut into chunks. Combine ¼ cup (2 fl oz) stock, the cornflour and sesame oil until blended.

In a separate bowl, whisk together the egg and vegetable oil. Heat the remaining stock, sherry and soy sauce until boiling. Add the tomatoes. Gradually stir in the cornflour mixture and return to the boil, stirring until thickened. Remove from the heat and while stirring in a circular motion add the egg mixture in a thin stream. The egg should cook in thin shreds. Garnish with spring onions and serve immediately.

Borsch

Serves 6

1 x 750 g (1½ lb) can sliced
   beetroot
1 x 410 g (13 oz) can
   tomatoes
1 small garlic clove
1 cup (8 fl oz) consommé or
   stock
1 teaspoon salt
1 teaspoon sugar
1½ tablespoons lemon juice
freshly ground pepper
1 cup (8 fl oz) sour cream
2 eggs, beaten
finely chopped spring
   onions (scallions)

Blend the first three ingredients until puréed. Add the remaining ingredients except the sour cream, eggs and spring onions. Strain the soup and chill. Before serving combine the sour cream and eggs and fold through the soup. Serve garnished with the spring onions.

Note: This soup is a marvellous first course as the colour is superb. Some sieved hard-boiled egg yolk can be scattered next to the spring onions for greater colour presentation. If too thick, add more consommé.

Egg and Lemon Soup

Serves 6

3 eggs
juice of 1 lemon
5 cups (1.25 litres) chicken
   stock
freshly ground black pepper
2 teaspoons chopped
   fresh parsley

Beat the eggs and lemon juice together and strain. Heat the chicken stock. Remove 1 cup (8 fl oz) of hot stock and blend into the egg mixture. Return to the remaining stock, season with pepper, heat and serve immediately, sprinkled with parsley.

Royal Soup

Serves 6

3 hard-boiled eggs
125 g (4 oz) cooked ham,
   chopped
250 g (8 oz) finely chopped
   cooked chicken
4 cups (1 litre) chicken stock
2 tablespoons sherry
salt and black pepper
2 tablespoons chopped
   fresh parsley

Finely chop the hard-boiled eggs. Combine with the ham and chicken. Heat the stock and sherry and bring to the boil. Add the eggs, chicken and ham and simmer for 1 minute. Season and garnish with chopped parsley. Serve immediately.

Appetisers

Souffléed Beer Pots

Serves 4

- 125 g (4 oz) Australian cream cheese, at room temperature
- 1 cup (4 oz) Australian grated cheese
- ½ cup (4 fl oz) beer
- 2 teaspoons gelatine
- 2 tablespoons hot water
- ¼ cup chopped spring onions (scallions)
- freshly ground black pepper to taste
- 2 egg whites
- extra chopped spring onions (scallions)

Blend the softened cream cheese, grated cheese and beer together until smooth. Sprinkle the gelatine over the water and stir briskly until dissolved to a clear golden liquid. Stir into the cheese mixture. Add the spring onions and pepper. Whisk the egg whites until stiff peaks form and gently fold into the cheese mixture. Divide the mixture between 4 individual pots and sprinkle with the extra spring onions. Refrigerate until set. Serve as a first course with crisp celery sticks, carrot slices and rye bread fingers.

Crabmeat Ramekins

Serves 4

- 1 x 200 g (6 ½ oz) can crabmeat, drained (or shrimp)
- ½ cup (4 fl oz) white wine
- pinch of nutmeg
- ¼ teaspoon cayenne pepper
- 15 g (½ oz) butter
- 2 tablespoons flour
- ½ cup (4 fl oz) milk
- ½ cup (4 fl oz) cream
- 125 g (4 oz) Australian Swiss cheese, cut into thin strips
- 4 sprigs parsley

Simmer the crabmeat in the white wine, nutmeg and cayenne pepper for 5 minutes. Strain and reserve the liquid. Divide the crabmeat into 4 ramekins. Melt the butter, add the flour and cook for a few minutes. Gradually add the milk and bring to the boil. Stir in the cream and reserved liquid. Heat, but do not boil. Pour over the crabmeat and sprinkle the top with cheese. Place under a hot griller (broiler) until the cheese is melted and golden brown. Garnish with sprigs of parsley. Accompany with lightly toasted triangles of bread.

Creamy Blue Cheese Celery Sticks

Serves 6

- 250 g (8 oz) blue castello (a mild blue cheese)
- 100 g (3 ½ oz) softened cream cheese
- 2 teaspoons tarragon vinegar
- 4 spring onions (scallions), finely chopped
- ½ cup (2 oz) coarsely chopped pecans
- 6 stalks celery, cut into 5 cm (2 inch) lengths
- 2 tablespoons chopped fresh parsley

Mix the cheeses and vinegar in a food processor and blend until creamy. Transfer to a bowl. Stir in the spring onions and nuts.

Spread the mixture into the celery sticks. Sprinkle with chopped parsley. Refrigerate before serving. Serve as a savoury or party appetiser.

Mediterranean Dip

Makes 2 - 3 cups

- 1 large eggplant (aubergine)
- 2 tablespoons chopped fresh parsley
- 1 tablespoon onion, chopped
- 1 garlic clove
- juice of 2 lemons
- 1 cup (8 fl oz) olive oil
- ¾ cup (1 ½ oz) fresh breadcrumbs
- 1 tomato, peeled and chopped
- ½ cup (4 fl oz) yoghurt

Leave the skin on the eggplant and bake in a moderate oven, 180°C (350°F/Gas 4), for 30 minutes. Peel and chop. Place the parsley, onion and garlic in a blender or food processor. Add the eggplant and lemon juice and process until smooth.

Gradually add the olive oil, breadcrumbs, tomato and yoghurt and blend until smooth. Pour into a bowl and chill. The mixture will thicken slightly on standing. Serve with vegetable crudités for dipping and black olives.

First Course

Drunken Prawns

Serves 4

30 g (1 oz) butter
750 g (1 ½ lb) shelled green prawns (shrimp), deveined
2 tablespoons Scotch whisky
4 spring onions (scallions), cut diagonally into 2.5 cm (1 inch) lengths
¼ cup (2 fl oz) cream
1 tablespoon cornflour (cornstarch), blended with 1 tablespoon water
seasonings to taste
¼ cup (1 oz) toasted flaked almonds

Melt the butter in a pan. Add the prawns and gently sauté for a few minutes. Add the whisky and spring onions and continue cooking for a further 2 minutes. Stir in the cream, then the blended cornflour. Bring to simmering point. Season to taste. Garnish with almonds. Serve with crusty French bread.

Crab and Asparagus Pâté

Makes 1 small dish

155 g (5 oz) crabmeat (meat from 1 large sand crab)
50 g (1 ½ oz) asparagus
dash of Tabasco sauce
1 tablespoon tomato sauce
squeeze of lemon juice
salt and freshly ground pepper
⅓ cup (2 ½ fl oz) sour cream
155 g (5 oz) cream cheese, softened

Add all the ingredients to the cream cheese and blend thoroughly. Check the seasonings and refrigerate in small individual ramekin dishes or one small soufflé dish for 2 hours before serving with fresh French bread or water crackers. Garnish with parsley sprigs.

Note: Instead of asparagus, 200 g (6 ½ oz) of crab and prawn (shrimp) meat may be used.

Prawn Pâté

Serves 4

2 eggs
250 g (8 oz) peeled prawns (shrimp)
60 g (2 oz) butter
1 tablespoon cream
1 tablespoon brandy
salt
small pinch of cayenne pepper
¼ teaspoon mace

Separate the eggs and gently beat the yolks. Devein the prawns and chop finely. Melt the butter in a large heavy frying pan. Add the prawns, cream and egg yolks and stir over a low heat until thickened. Do not boil. Remove from the heat and add the brandy, salt, cayenne and mace. Grease 4 ramekins and fill with the prawn mixture, chill and serve with Melba Toast (*page 32*).

Mozzarella Stacks

Serves 4

3 eggs
1 cup (4 oz) self-raising flour, sifted
2 teaspoons soft brown sugar
90 g (3 oz) butter, melted
½–¾ cup (4-6 fl oz) buttermilk
4 slices ham, grilled (broiled)
125 g (4 oz) Australian mozzarella cheese, sliced

Beat the eggs for 2 minutes until light and fluffy. Add the flour and sugar and beat until smooth. Melt one third of the butter and add sufficient buttermilk to make a batter of pouring consistency. Melt a little extra butter in a frying pan and pour in approximately ¼ cup (2 fl oz) batter and make a pancake 10 cm (4 inch) in diameter. When bubbles appear, turn and brown the second side. Remove and keep warm. Repeat this process to make 8 pancakes. Spread 4 pancakes with the remaining butter and top with a second pancake. Place a slice of ham on each stack and cover with cheese. Grill (broil) for 2 to 3 minutes until the cheese melts. Serve with Tomato Toppa (*see below*) poured over the top as a breakfast, brunch or light meal.

Tomato Toppa

Serves 4

60 g (2 oz) butter
1 large onion, chopped
1 garlic clove, crushed
3 tomatoes, diced
2 tablespoons tomato paste
½ teaspoon dried oregano leaves
½ teaspoon dried basil leaves
1 teaspoon lemon juice
seasonings to taste

Melt the butter in a saucepan and fry the onion and garlic for 4 to 5 minutes until transparent. Add remaining ingredients and simmer for 5 minutes.

Camembert Hot Bread

Serves 4–6

1 French bread stick
125 g (4 oz) Australian Camembert cheese, finely chopped
60 g (2 oz) butter
salt and freshly ground pepper
chopped fresh parsley
poppy or sesame seeds

Cut the bread stick into 2 cm (¾ inch) wide slices almost through to the base. Combine the cheese and butter, salt, pepper and chopped parsley. Beat well. Spread the cheese mixture onto each slice of bread. Sprinkle with poppy or sesame seeds. Wrap in foil and bake in a hot oven, 200°C (400°F/Gas 6), for 15 minutes.

Mini Edam Quiches

Dipaway Meatballs

Serves 8 – 10

500 g (1 lb) lean minced (ground) steak
1 medium-sized onion, finely chopped
2 tablespoons chopped dill cucumber
1 tablespoon chopped fresh parsley
soft brown sugar

Combine the meat, onion, dill cucumber and parsley together. Roll into 30 bite-sized balls. Place on a baking tray. Sprinkle lightly with sugar. Bake at 200°C (400°F/Gas 6) for 15 minutes. Arrange in a serving bowl. Serve as a toothpick savoury with Mustardy Yoghurt Dip *(see below)*.

Mini Edam Quiches

Makes 24

1 x 375 g (12 oz) packet puff pastry
1 cup (4 oz) Australian Edam cheese
125 g (4 oz) sliced ham, finely diced
3 tablespoons cream
1 tablespoon French mustard
1 egg
1 tablespoon chopped fresh parsley
freshly ground black pepper

Roll out the pastry 3 mm (⅛ inch) thick. Using a 6 cm (2½ inch) pastry cutter, cut 24 circles and press into patty tins. Combine the remaining ingredients thoroughly. Spoon the mixture into patty cases and bake in a hot oven 200°C (400°F/Gas 6), for 20 minutes, or until puffed and brown. Serve as a party snack.

Cheese Pillows

Makes 18

1 cup (4 oz) grated Australian cheese
¼ cup finely chopped mortadella sausage
2 tablespoons cream
6 sheets filo pastry
melted butter
egg glaze

Combine the cheese, mortadella and cream. Brush one sheet of pastry with butter, place second sheet on top and brush again with butter. Using a sharp knife, cut the pastry into 6 rectangles. Place a small spoonful of cheese mixture in the centre of each pastry portion. Fold into a parcel, tucking ends well under. Continue in this way with remaining pastry and filling to make 18 savouries. Place on a buttered tray, brush with a little egg glaze and bake at 200°C (400°F/Gas 6) for 15 minutes. Serve hot.

Mustardy Yoghurt Dip

Makes 1 cup

1 cup (8 fl oz) natural yoghurt
½-1 teaspoon dry mustard
1 teaspoon Worcestershire sauce
seasonings to taste

Combine all the ingredients and pour into a serving bowl. Refrigerate for several hours to allow flavour to develop.

First Course

Mushroom Roulade with Cheesy Sauce

Serves 8

75 g (2 ½ oz) butter
 plus extra 30 g (1 oz)
½ cup (2 oz) flour
2 cups (16 fl oz) milk
4 eggs, separated
250 g (8 oz) mushrooms,
 sliced

1 cup (4 oz) grated
 Australian cheese
1 quantity Cheesy Sauce
 (see below)

Cheesy Sauce
60 g (2 oz) butter
2 tablespoons flour
1 cup (8 fl oz) milk

½ cup (2 oz) grated
 Australian cheese
pepper to taste

Preheat the oven to 190°C (375°F/Gas 5). Grease, line, then flour a Swiss roll tin. Melt the 75 g (2 ½ oz) butter in a saucepan and stir in the flour. Cook for 1 to 2 minutes without colouring. Stir in the milk gradually and heat until the mixture thickens. Beat the egg whites until stiff. Add the egg yolks to the mixture then fold in the egg whites. Pour into the prepared tin and bake for 25 to 30 minutes or until the mixture springs back when touched. Turn out onto a tea towel and peel off the lining. Melt the extra butter and fry the mushrooms until soft. Spoon over the cooked roulade then sprinkle with half the cheese. Roll up as for a Swiss roll and place on a serving plate with the join underneath. Pour Cheesy Sauce over the roulade and sprinkle with the remaining cheese. Serve immediately.

Cheesy Sauce: Melt the butter and stir in the flour. Cook for 1 to 2 minutes. Gradually add the milk and cook until the sauce thickens. Add the cheese and pepper.

Egg Mousse

Serves 4

6 hard-boiled eggs
¾ cup (6 fl oz) mayonnaise
2 teaspoons gelatine
¾ cup (6 fl oz) chicken
 stock
½ cup (4 fl oz) thickened
 cream

1 tablespoon anchovy sauce
3 drops Tabasco sauce
1 small lettuce
1 tomato
4 black olives

Shell and roughly chop the eggs and combine with the mayonnaise. Add the gelatine to the stock and stir over low heat until dissolved. Cool slightly. Add the gelatine mixture to the eggs and mix well. Fold in the softly beaten cream, anchovy sauce and Tabasco. Pour mixture into a lightly oiled 20 cm (8 inch) sandwich tin. Refrigerate until set. Garnish with lettuce, sliced tomato and olives.

Hot Mozzarella Avocados

Serves 4

2 medium-sized firm
 avocados
seasonings to taste
½ cup finely chopped
 bacon

1 ½ cups (6 oz) grated
 Australian mozzarella
 cheese

Halve the avocados lengthwise and remove the stones. Lightly season. Combine the bacon and cheese. Spoon over the entire top surface of the avocados. Bake at 200°C (400°F/Gas 6) for 15 minutes. Serve immediately.

Pickled Eggs

Makes 12

5 cups (1.25 litres) vinegar
½ cup (4 oz) sugar
8 cloves
2 teaspoons cinnamon
½ level teaspoon
 horseradish powder
2 small garlic cloves
½ teaspoon mustard seed
 or dry mustard

½ level teaspoon mace
1 level teaspoon salt
2 teaspoons cornflour
 (cornstarch)
2 teaspoons dry mustard
1 level teaspoon sugar
½ level teaspoon salt
yellow food colouring
12 hard-boiled eggs

Place the vinegar, sugar, cloves, cinnamon, horseradish, garlic, mustard seed, mace and salt in a saucepan. Bring slowly to the boil and simmer for 25 minutes. Cool. Blend the cornflour with a little water and stir in the dry mustard. Add to the vinegar mixture with 1 teaspoon sugar and ½ teaspoon salt. Stir in about 2 teaspoons of yellow food colouring. Bring to the boil and simmer for 3 minutes. Shell the eggs, place in a large sterilised jar and pour over the hot vinegar mixture. Seal airtight and store in a cool dark place.

Note: The longer they are pickled, the more flavour they will have.

Baby Quiche

Makes approximately 36

5 sheets ready-rolled
 shortcrust pastry
2 cups (8 oz) grated cheese
 or 1 cup (4 oz) grated
 Gruyère and 1 cup (4 oz)
 grated Emmenthal

½ cup finely chopped ham
1 onion, finely chopped
4 eggs, beaten
1 cup (8 fl oz) cream
salt and pepper
¼ teaspoon nutmeg

Lightly grease patty tins and line with the pastry. Mix the remaining ingredients and pour into each pastry case. Bake at 190°C (375°F/Gas 5) for 25 minutes until golden. Serve warm.

Egg 'n' Crunchy Peanut Butter Dip

Makes 2 cups

3 hard-boiled eggs
2-3 slices ham or cooked bacon, finely chopped
2 tablespoons crunchy peanut butter
2 tablespoons gherkin relish
250 g (8 oz) cream cheese
salt and pepper

Chop the eggs and combine with the other ingredients. Serve as a dip or spread. Season with freshly ground pepper.

Egg and Salmon Dip

Makes 2 cups

3 hard-boiled eggs
1 x 125 g (4 oz) can pink salmon, drained and flaked
1 cup chopped celery
125 g (4 oz) cream cheese

Chop the eggs and combine with the remaining ingredients. Refrigerate and serve as a dip or spread. Garnish with slices of lemon or lemon pepper.

Egg 'n' Apple Dip

Makes 2 cups

3 hard-boiled eggs
3 spring onions (scallions)
1 red apple, cored and chopped
250 g (8 oz) cream cheese
2 slices ham, finely chopped
salt and pepper
green grapes, halved

Chop the eggs and combine with the other ingredients. Serve as a dip or spread. Garnish with halves of green grapes.

Egg 'n' Onion Dip

Makes 1 cup

3 hard-boiled eggs
1 tablespoon finely chopped onion or ½ packet onion soup
½ teaspoon paprika
½ cup (4 fl oz) sour cream
salt and pepper
chopped fresh parsley

Chop the eggs and combine with the other ingredients. Serve as a dip or spread. Garnish with freshly chopped parsley.

Egg 'n' Corn Relish Dip

Makes 1 cup

3 hard-boiled eggs
3 tablespoons corn relish
½ cup (4 fl oz) sour cream
3 spring onions (scallions), finely chopped
salt and pepper

Chop the eggs and combine with the other ingredients. Serve as a dip or spread. Season with freshly ground black pepper.

Egg 'n' Cheese Dip

Makes 2 cups

3 hard-boiled eggs
2 tablespoons gherkin relish
1 cup (4 oz) grated cheese
1 tablespoon mayonnaise
salt and pepper
chives, finely chopped

Chop the eggs and combine with the other ingredients. Serve as a dip or spread. Garnish with finely chopped chives.

Egg 'n' Celery Dip

Makes 1 cup

3 hard-boiled eggs
¼ cup finely chopped celery
¼ cup finely chopped red pepper (capsicum)
½ cup (4 fl oz) sour cream
salt and pepper

Chop the eggs and combine with the other ingredients. Serve as a dip or spread. Sprinkle with freshly ground black pepper.

Egg 'n' Chicken and Almond Spread

Makes 1 cup

3 hard-boiled eggs
½ packet cream of chicken soup
½ tablespoon crushed nuts
½ cup (4 fl oz) sour cream
gherkins, cut into strips

Chop the eggs and combine with the other ingredients. Serve as a dip or spread. Garnish with strips of gherkin.

First Course

Dip à la Ritz

Makes 2 cups

6 hard-boiled eggs
1 tablespoon olive oil
½ small onion
2 flat anchovy fillets
1 stalk celery
½ red or green pepper (capsicum)
¼ cup (2 fl oz) mayonnaise
1 teaspoon tarragon vinegar
4 drops Tabasco sauce
salt and freshly ground black pepper
half slices of lemon

Place the eggs in a food processor and chop them very finely. Add the oil, onion, anchovies, celery and red pepper and blend until chopped very finely. Add the mayonnaise, vinegar, Tabasco, a little salt and pepper and blend until smooth. Spoon into a serving bowl and garnish with half slices of lemon.

Salmon Salad Dip

Makes 2 cups

1 x 200 g (6½ oz) can salmon, drained and flaked
3 eggs, hard boiled and chopped
¼ cup chopped spring onions (scallions)
½ cup chopped celery
1 cup (8 fl oz) mayonnaise
1 teaspoon lemon juice
½ teaspoon chilli powder
salt and pepper
1 teaspoon chopped fresh parsley

Combine all the ingredients and mix well. Chill before serving. Use as a dip or spread.

Egg 'n' Pine Dip

Makes 2 cups

3 hard-boiled eggs
185 g (6 oz) crushed drained pineapple
250 g (8 oz) cream cheese
½-1 teaspoon mint jelly
2 stalks celery, finely sliced
salt and pepper
chopped fresh mint

Chop the eggs and combine with the other ingredients. Serve as a dip or spread. Garnish with chopped mint.

Melba Toast

Trim away all crusts from a square loaf of white unsliced bread. Use an electric knife or extremely sharp knife to cut slices as thinly as possible. Cut each slice into triangles. Place the triangles on ungreased flat oven trays, bake at 180°C (350°F/Gas 4) for about 20 minutes, or until the bread is golden brown, curled and crisp. It must be completely dried out, or it will develop mould during storage. Cool before storing in an airtight container.

Savoury Egg Rolls

Makes approximately 10

⅓ cup (2½ fl oz) water
2 tablespoons cornflour (cornstarch)
6 large eggs
½ cup (4 fl oz) milk
30 g (1 oz) butter
1 small onion, very finely chopped
2 teaspoons tomato paste
2 tablespoons finely sliced spring onions (scallions)
salt and pepper
1 packet frozen flaky or puff pastry sheets, thawed
beaten egg for glazing
Parmesan cheese

Combine the water and cornflour. Beat together the eggs, milk and cornflour mixture. Melt the butter in a pan, add the egg mixture and cook as for scrambled eggs. Add the onion, tomato paste, spring onions, salt and pepper and cool. Pipe onto strips of flaky or puff pastry approximately 10 x 30 cm (4 x 12 inch) and roll to form a casing. Cut into desired lengths and prick the top of each using a fork. Glaze with beaten egg and sprinkle with the Parmesan cheese. Bake at 220°C (425°F/Gas 7) for 10 to 15 minutes or until golden.

Scots Eggs

Makes 4

4 hard-boiled eggs
flour
125 g (4 oz) sausage mince
125 g (4 oz) lean mince (ground beef)
1 small onion, finely chopped
1 teaspoon dried basil
1 garlic clove, crushed
1 egg, beaten
dry white breadcrumbs
oil for deep frying

Peel the eggs and roll in the flour. Combine the next five ingredients, then wrap the mince around each egg to enclose completely. Brush each with beaten egg before rolling in breadcrumbs. Deep fry in hot oil for approximately 7 minutes. Drain well on kitchen paper and serve hot or cold.

Stuffed Cottage Eggs

Makes 8

4 hard-boiled eggs
2 teaspoons vinegar
1 tablespoon chutney
250 g (8 oz) cottage cheese
¼ teaspoon salt
1 teaspoon chives
pinch of cayenne pepper
parsley to garnish

Cut the eggs in half lengthwise and remove the yolks. Mash with the remaining ingredients. Pipe or spoon the mixture back into the whites and garnish with parsley.

Egg Nibblers

Makes 20

2 rashers bacon
4 hard-boiled eggs, chopped
1 small onion, very finely grated
pinch of nutmeg
pinch of dry mustard
¼ teaspoon salt
1 teaspoon mayonnaise
1 cup (4 oz) finely grated cheese
5 teaspoons chopped fresh parsley
toasted sesame seeds

Chop the bacon very finely. Sauté for about 5 minutes until crisp and golden. Combine the eggs, onion, nutmeg, mustard and salt with the bacon. Mix in enough mayonnaise to bind the ingredients together. Chill for at least 2 hours. Mix together the cheese, parsley and sesame seeds. Shape the mixture into tiny balls and roll in the mixture. Chill again before serving on lettuce leaves.

Peppered Eggs

Serves 4

2 green or red peppers (capsicums)
250 g (8 oz) mushrooms
1 tablespoon tomato paste
dried oregano
4 eggs
salt
freshly ground black pepper
½ cup (2 oz) grated cheese

Cut the peppers in half lengthwise and remove the cores and seeds. Blanch the shells in boiling water for 2 minutes and drain on absorbent paper. Place in a buttered ovenproof dish. Slice the mushrooms finely and divide between each of the pepper shells. Put 1 teaspoon tomato paste into each shell, sprinkle with a little oregano and break an egg into each. Season with salt and pepper then cover with cheese. Place in 190°C (375°F/Gas 5) oven for about 15 minutes, or until the eggs are set and the cheese is melted and golden.

Savoury Bites

Makes 30

6 hard-boiled eggs
1 teaspoon finely chopped fresh parsley
250 g (8 oz) minced (ground) cooked chicken or ham
¼ cup (2 fl oz) mayonnaise, approximately
salt and pepper
¾ cup finely crushed potato crisps

Shell the eggs and mash with parsley and chicken. Mix in mayonnaise gradually to bind the mixture then season. Chill the mixture for 1 hour. Shape into small balls and coat with finely crushed potato crisps. Serve on lettuce leaves.

Egg Nibblers

Egg and Apple Croquettes

Makes 20

4 hard-boiled eggs, chopped
1 tablespoon chopped celery
1 tablespoon chopped fresh parsley
1 tablespoon lemon juice
¼ teaspoon nutmeg
1 Granny Smith apple, peeled, cored and finely chopped
3 tablespoons finely chopped spring onion (scallion)
2 cups (4 oz) fresh breadcrumbs
1 egg, beaten
dry white breadcrumbs
oil for deep frying

White Sauce
60 g (2 oz) butter
3 tablespoons flour
¾ cup (6 fl oz) milk

Combine all the ingredients except the beaten egg, dry breadcrumbs and oil, and add the white sauce to bind. Refrigerate for 1 hour before rolling into bite-sized balls. Coat with beaten egg and roll in the dry breadcrumbs. Deep fry in hot oil until golden brown.

White Sauce: Melt the butter and add the flour, then cook for 1 minute. Remove from the heat and add the milk gradually, stirring after each addition. Return to the heat and stir continuously until thickened, then put aside to cool.

First Course

Scotch Egg Roll

Serves 6

250 g (8 oz) sausage mince
1 teaspoon dried basil
1 garlic clove, crushed
2 teaspoons chopped fresh parsley
1 small onion, finely chopped
4 hard-boiled eggs, shelled
flour
1 x 375 g (12 oz) packet ready-rolled puff pastry
egg for glazing
grated Parmesan cheese

Combine the mince with the basil, garlic, parsley and onion. Cut eggs in half lengthwise and roll in the flour. Flatten out the mince into a rectangular shape. Lay the egg halves down the centre, flat side down. Mould the mince around the eggs to enclose completely. Roll out puff pastry 6 mm (¼ inch) thick. Roll the egg roll in the pastry, moistening the edges with milk to seal. Press the ends closed firmly. Using a fork, make holes in the top to allow steam to escape. Glaze with egg and sprinkle with Parmesan cheese. Bake in a pre-heated oven at 220°C (425°F/Gas 7) for 20 minutes or until the pastry is golden brown.

Egg and Tuna Aspic

Makes 4

2 teaspoons gelatine
3 tablespoons cold water
4 hard-boiled eggs, chopped
1 x 185 g (6 oz) can tuna
1 cup (8 fl oz) water
pinch each of sugar and salt
2 tablespoons lemon juice
a few drops of Worcestershire sauce
1 small onion, chopped
chopped fresh parsley

Soak the gelatine in 3 tablespoons water for 10 minutes. Arrange the egg and tuna in layers in 4 moulds.
 Combine the water, sugar, salt, lemon juice, Worcestershire sauce and onion in a saucepan. Bring to the boil, remove, and stir in the gelatine. Strain the liquid and pour into the moulds over the egg and tuna. Sprinkle with parsley and refrigerate. Turn out of the moulds and serve with salad.

Ham and Melon Wraps

Serves 6 - 8

1 rockmelon, cubed

10 slices prosciutto ham

Marinade
½ teaspoon grated fresh ginger
black pepper
1 tablespoon honey
2 tablespoons water

Combine all marinade ingredients. Add the marinade to the melon cubes. Slice the ham into strips 4 cm (1 ½ inch) wide. Roll the melon cubes in the ham and secure with toothpicks. Serve on lettuce leaves.

Calypso Eggs

Makes 12

6 hard-boiled eggs
90 g (3 oz) prawns (shrimp) or crabmeat
1 teaspoon curry paste
4 drops Tabasco sauce
a few drops Worcestershire sauce
ground basil
squeeze of lemon juice
1 ¼ cups (10 fl oz) mayonnaise
salt
freshly ground black pepper
1 small lettuce
½ small cucumber

Cut the eggs in half lengthwise. Remove the yolks and press them through a sieve. Mix the prawns, curry paste, Tabasco, Worcestershire sauce and basil, and squeeze a little lemon juice over the top. Stir in sufficient mayonnaise to make the mixture stiff and creamy. Season with salt and pepper. Pipe back into the egg whites. Serve on lettuce leaves and decorate with cucumber twists.

Vegetable Terrine

Serves 10 - 12

The secret of this recipe is to season the batter very well with salt and cayenne pepper. If under seasoned it will be too bland.

410 g (13 oz) mushrooms, sliced and sautéed in butter
315 g (10 oz) baby carrots, peeled and cut into 8 cm (3 inch) lengths and blanched
500 g (1 lb) asparagus, blanched or green beans, topped, tailed and blanched
mayonnaise, flavoured with mustard or curry powder

Batter
¾ cup (3 oz) flour
1 ½ cups (12 fl oz) chicken stock
7 eggs
salt and cayenne pepper

Pour enough batter into a well-buttered 5 cup (1.25 litre) terrine to cover the base. Place a layer of mushrooms in the terrine, packing them closely together over the base. Cover with batter. Repeat the layers with the remaining vegetables and batter, finishing with batter. Cover with buttered foil or baking paper and place in a small baking dish. Pour boiling water into the dish to come three quarters of the way up the side of the terrine. Bake at 180°C (350°F/Gas 4) for 1 ½ hours or until set. Allow to cool in the terrine for at least 2 hours to set. Unmould, cut into slices and serve with mustard- or curry-flavoured mayonnaise.

Batter: Sift the flour into a bowl. Make a well in the centre, pour in the chicken stock and whisk until smooth. Whisk in the eggs and seasonings. Strain the batter to remove any lumps.

Irish Eggs

Serves 4 - 6

3 large potatoes, boiled and mashed
3 eggs, beaten
2 spring onions (scallions), finely chopped
1 Granny Smith apple, unpeeled, cored and finely chopped
½ teaspoon dried thyme leaves
½ cup (2 oz) breadcrumbs
oil for deep frying

Mix together the mashed potatoes, eggs, spring onions, apple and thyme. Flour your hands, then take 2 tablespoons of the mixture and form into cylinders. Roll in breadcrumbs and deep fry in hot oil until golden brown, about 2 minutes. Drain on absorbent kitchen paper and serve.

Stuffed Mushrooms

Serves 4

4 large mushrooms, wiped clean
15 g (½ oz) butter
1 rasher bacon, rind removed and chopped
½ cup (1 oz) fresh breadcrumbs
2 teaspoons chopped fresh parsley
1 hard-boiled egg, finely chopped
grated rind of ½ lemon
1 tablespoon lemon juice
salt and pepper
½ cup (2 oz) finely grated cheese

Remove the stalks from the mushrooms and chop finely. Heat the butter and fry the mushroom stalks and bacon for a few minutes. Remove from the heat and stir in the breadcrumbs, parsley, egg, lemon rind and juice. Season well.

Place the mushroom caps on a greased baking tray. Divide the filling between each, top with grated cheese and bake at 180°C (350°F/Gas 4) for 10 to 15 minutes. Serve hot as a first course, or as an accompaniment to pork or lamb.

Curry Nibblers

Makes 24

2 cups cooked rice
1 x 185 g (6 oz) can red salmon
2 eggs
⅔ cup (2½ oz) self-raising flour
2 tablespoons chopped fresh parsley
3 teaspoons curry powder
2 tablespoons lemon juice
1 garlic clove, chopped
dry breadcrumbs
vegetable oil

Combine all the ingredients, except the breadcrumbs and vegetable oil. Cover and chill for 1 hour. Roll into bite-sized balls, coat with breadcrumbs and deep fry in the hot oil until golden in colour. Drain well and serve.

Egg and Anchovy Pâté

Serves 8 - 10

2 x 60 g (2 oz) cans anchovy fillets in oil
6-8 stuffed olives, halved
30 g (1 oz) butter
1 onion, chopped
1-2 garlic cloves, crushed
¼ cup (1 oz) flour
⅔ cup (5 fl oz) fish or chicken stock
3 eggs, beaten
1½ cups (3 oz) fresh brown or white breadcrumbs
2 tablespoons capers
3 hard-boiled eggs, chopped
pepper

Grease a loaf tin and line the base with greaseproof paper. Arrange 8 anchovy fillets and the olives on the base. Chop the remaining anchovies and reserve, with the oil.

Melt the butter in a pan, and gently fry the onion and garlic for 5 minutes. Stir in the flour and cook for 1 minute, then add the stock a little at a time, stirring after each addition until smooth. Bring to the boil, stirring until thickened. Remove from the heat and stir in the anchovies and oil. Cool slightly then add the remaining ingredients, with pepper to taste. Leave for 15 minutes, then spoon into the tin. Bake at 180°C (350°F/Gas 4) for 1 hour or until set. Leave until completely cold. Turn out and serve with salad.

Tarragon Chicken Mousse

Serves 4 - 6

3 eggs, separated
1½ tablespoons cornflour (cornstarch)
⅔ cup (5 fl oz) chicken stock
⅔ cup (5 fl oz) sour cream
1 tablespoon tarragon vinegar
1 tablespoon chopped fresh or 2 teaspoons dried tarragon
2 tablespoons gelatine dissolved in 2 tablespoons boiling water
375 g (12 oz) minced (ground) cooked chicken
salt and pepper
lemon slices
tarragon

Whisk the egg yolks, cornflour and stock in a pan. Place over moderate heat and whisk continuously until thickened. DO NOT BOIL. Remove from the heat and cool slightly. Stir in the sour cream, vinegar, tarragon, dissolved gelatine and chicken. Season, then leave until just beginning to set, stirring occasionally.

Whisk the egg whites until stiff and fold into the mixture carefully but thoroughly. Turn into a 5 cup (1.25 litre) soufflé dish or mould and refrigerate for about 2 hours or until set. Turn out onto a serving dish and garnish with lemon slices and tarragon.

First Course

Camembert Puffs

Makes 24

1 cup (8 fl oz) water
60 g (2 oz) butter or margarine
½ teaspoon salt
½ teaspoon dried mixed herbs
⅛ teaspoon pepper
1 cup (4 oz) flour
4 eggs
125 g (4 oz) Camembert cheese, cut into tiny cubes
¼ cup (1 oz) chopped toasted almonds
3 tablespoons chopped fresh parsley

Combine the water, butter, salt, herbs and pepper. Heat until boiling. Add all the flour at once. Stir vigorously over low heat until the mixture forms a ball. Cool for 5 minutes.

Add the eggs, one at a time, beating well after each addition. Stir in the remaining ingredients. Drop one tablespoon at a time onto a lightly greased tray. Bake at 200°C (400°F/Gas 6) for 15 to 20 minutes or until puffed and golden. Cool.

Note: Puffs can be stored overnight at room temperature, in an airtight container, or wrapped and frozen for up to 1 week. Reheat briefly in a moderately hot oven before serving.

Shrimp Pâté

Serves 4 – 6

½ onion
2 x 200 g (6 ½ oz) cans cocktail prawns (shrimp), drained
125 g (4 oz) butter, softened
1 tablespoon lemon juice
2 tablespoons mayonnaise
1 teaspoon tomato paste
Tabasco sauce
3 teaspoons chopped fresh parsley

Chop the onion in a blender until very fine. Add the prawns and purée. Add remaining ingredients and blend until smooth. Spoon into a pâté pot and refrigerate. Serve with toast triangles.

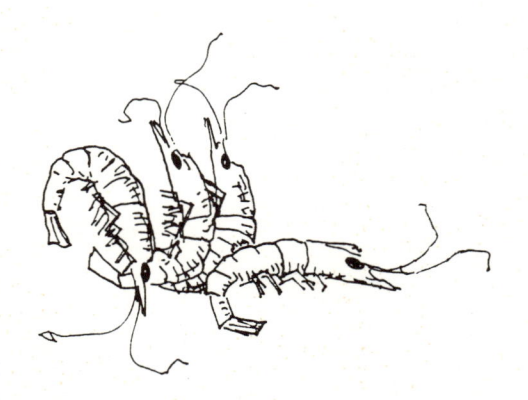

Herb and Blue Cheese Pinwheels

Makes approximately 40

Crêpes
⅓ cup (1 ½ oz) flour
2 eggs
¾ cup (6 fl oz) milk
1 tablespoon oil
½ cup chopped fresh parsley
2 tablespoons chopped chives
¼ teaspoon dried basil leaves

Filling
250 g (8 oz) cream cheese
125 g (4 oz) blue vein cheese
125 g (4 oz) unsalted butter
1 tablespoon brandy
1 teaspoon French mustard

Crêpes: Place all the ingredients in a blender or processor and blend until smooth. Pour the mixture into a jug and allow to stand for 30 minutes. Heat a crêpe pan, grease with butter and pour about ¼ cup (2 fl oz) of the batter into the pan. Cook until lightly browned, turn and cook the other side for 15 seconds. Repeat until the batter is used.

Fill the crêpes with filling, fold up firmly like a Swiss roll and refrigerate for 15 minutes. Cut into 2.5 cm (1 inch) slices.

Filling: Blend or process all the ingredients until smooth.

Vol au Vent Provençale

Serves 4

250 g (8 oz) puff pastry
1 egg, beaten
2 hard-boiled eggs
60 g (2 oz) mushrooms
15 g (½ oz) butter
½ cup (4 fl oz) velouté sauce (*page 38*)
75 g (2 ½ oz) bacon, finely chopped
1 teaspoon Madeira
salt
freshly ground black pepper

Roll out the pastry about 3 mm (⅛ inch) thick. Cut out four circles measuring 10 cm (4 inch) across, and a circle of 5 cm (2 inch) diameter from the centre of each. Cut out another four 10 cm (4 inch) circles. Place these last circles on a buttered baking tray. Brush the edges with the lightly beaten egg, and place the large rings on top of them, making a border. Brush with beaten egg. Place the smaller circles, which will be caps, on the tray and brush with beaten egg. Bake at 230°C (450°F/Gas 8) for 10 minutes or until golden brown.

Chop the hard-boiled eggs. Slice the mushrooms and lightly fry in the butter. Mix together the sauce, chopped eggs, mushrooms, bacon, Madeira, salt and pepper. Fill the pastry cases, place the caps on top and serve hot.

Condiments and Sauces

Chinese Mixed Pickles

Makes 2 jars

- 1 x 5 cm (2 inch) piece fresh ginger, peeled and julienned
- 2 large carrots, peeled and julienned
- 1 large Chinese white radish, peeled and julienned
- ½ red pepper (capsicum), julienned
- ½ green pepper (capsicum), julienned
- 4 stalks celery, julienned
- 2 small Spanish onions, julienned
- 1 large cucumber, julienned
- 1 cup (8 oz) sugar
- 2 cups (16 fl oz) white wine or lemon vinegar
- ½ teaspoon salt
- 1 ¼ cups (10 fl oz) water

Blanch the vegetables separately, depending on their texture, until tender-crisp. Drain and refresh. Dry on kitchen paper. Arrange in preserving jars.

Mix the remaining ingredients in a saucepan, stirring constantly to dissolve the sugar. Bring to the boil, then cool. Pour the liquid over the vegetables and seal well.

Note: Serve as an accompaniment to Chinese meals or use in sauces in place of commercial mixed pickles.

Plum and Ginger Chutney

- 1 kg (2 lb) plums
- 4 cups (2 lb) soft brown sugar
- 3 cups (24 fl oz) vinegar
- 3 onions, chopped
- 2 garlic cloves, crushed
- 1 ½ cups (8 oz) sultanas
- 1 teaspoon salt
- 1 tablespoon mixed spice
- 1 tablespoon ground ginger
- 1 tablespoon mustard seed
- 60 g (2 oz) fresh or preserved root ginger, chopped

Place the plums, sugar, vinegar, onions, garlic and sultanas in a stainless steel or ceramic-lined pan. Bring to the boil, stirring continuously until the sugar has dissolved, then simmer for 30 minutes. Skim the stones and any coarse plum skins from the surface with a slotted spoon.

Add the remaining ingredients and simmer for 15 minutes. Pour the chutney into warm, dry pots. Cover, seal and label. Store in a cool dry cupboard. Serve with cold meats and salad or with curry.

Chinese Mixed Pickles

First Course

Avocado Sauce

Makes about 1 ½ cups

1 ripe avocado
¼ onion
1 cup (8 fl oz) milk or stock, either chicken or fish
¼ teaspoon curry powder or chilli powder
¼ teaspoon salt
freshly ground pepper
1 tablespoon lemon juice

Combine all the ingredients in a blender and purée. Gently heat without bringing to the boil.

Lemon and Orange Sauce

Makes about 1 ½ cups

½ cup (4 fl oz) mayonnaise
¾ cup (6 fl oz) sour cream
3 teaspoons lemon juice
¼ cup (2 fl oz) orange juice
1 teaspoon each finely grated orange and lemon rind
1 teaspoon prepared horseradish

Blend all the ingredients. Serve with shellfish, such as prawns (shrimp) and crab.

Peppercorn Sauce

Makes 2 cups

1 tablespoon spring onions (scallions), finely chopped
15 g (½ oz) butter
½ teaspoon green peppercorns
⅓ cup (2 ½ fl oz) dry sherry
½ teaspoon cornflour
½ cup (4 fl oz) evaporated skim milk
½ teaspoon chopped fresh parsley

Fry the spring onions lightly in the butter. Add the peppercorns and mash with a fork. Add the dry sherry and allow to reduce by half. Mix the cornflour into the evaporated skim milk. Add to the peppercorn mixture and stir until thickened. Add the parsley. Do not allow the sauce to boil.

Velouté Sauce

Makes 2½ cups (20 fl oz)

125 g (4 oz) butter
½ cup (2 oz) flour
2½ cups (20 fl oz) stock (veal, chicken or fish)
2 egg yolks
salt
freshly ground black pepper

Melt two thirds of the butter in a saucepan. Remove from the heat and stir in the flour. When the flour and butter are well mixed, slowly pour in the stock, a little at a time, stirring continuously to prevent the sauce going lumpy. Return to the heat and bring to the boil, stirring continuously. Remove from the heat and let cool a little. Whisk in the remaining butter and the egg yolks with salt and pepper.

Tomato Sauce

Makes 2½ cups

1 onion, finely chopped
1 garlic clove, crushed
3 tablespoons oil
2 ripe tomatoes, chopped
freshly ground pepper
1 tablespoon dried dill
½ cup (4 fl oz) dry white wine
½ teaspoon chilli powder
salt and sugar to taste

Lightly fry the onion and garlic in the oil. Add the tomatoes and simmer until soft. Add the remaining ingredients and simmer for 10 minutes. Check the seasoning and adjust to your taste. If it is too sharp add ¼ teaspoon sugar.

Sweet and Sour Sauce

Makes 1 ½ cups (12 fl oz)

1 cup (8 fl oz) water
½ cup (4 fl oz) white vinegar
½ cup (4 oz) sugar
2 tablespoons cornflour (cornstarch) mixed with a little water
red food colouring

Place the water, vinegar and sugar in a small saucepan. Stir over gentle heat until the sugar is dissolved. Blend in the cornflour mixture and stir over medium heat until the sauce is slightly thick. Stir in red food colouring, a few drops at a time, until the sauce has the desired colour.

Tartare Sauce

Makes 2 cups

2 cups (16 fl oz) mayonnaise
2 teaspoons white vinegar
6 gherkins, finely diced or chopped
2 teaspoons capers, chopped
1 tablespoon chopped fresh tarragon
1 tablespoon chopped fresh chives or chervil
salt and pepper

Mix the mayonnaise and vinegar. Add the gherkins, capers, herbs and seasoning. Mix well and refrigerate.

Basil Sauce (Pesto)

Makes 1 cup

1 large bunch of fresh basil
2 garlic cloves, crushed
1 cup (8 fl oz) olive oil
salt and pepper

Crush the basil leaves and garlic, or process in a food processor. With the motor running, slowly pour in the oil or beat with an electric mixer. Season well. Serve over veal or with pasta.

Béarnaise Sauce

Makes 1 cup

½ cup (4 fl oz) white wine vinegar
2 spring onions (scallions), finely chopped
1 sprig tarragon, finely chopped
salt and pepper
3 egg yolks, at room temperature
185 g (6 oz) butter

Place the vinegar in a saucepan and add the spring onions, tarragon and salt and pepper. Bring to the boil and reduce to 1 tablespoon. Strain well and place the liquid in a double saucepan. Discard the herbs.

Place the egg yolks in the double saucepan with the vinegar. Whisk over low heat until creamy. Add the butter in tiny pieces at a time, whisking continuously. Add the next piece only after the first is thoroughly incorporated. Continue until all the butter is used. Serve immediately.

Note: Clarified butter or ghee is the best for this sauce but the result is still satisfactory with unclarified. The sauce may be made in a food processor, adding melted butter in a slow stream.

Mayonnaise

Makes 2 cups

2 egg yolks, at room temperature
1 tablespoon prepared mustard
2 cups (16 fl oz) peanut oil
2 tablespoons lemon juice
salt and pepper

Place the egg yolks and mustard in food processor. With the motor running, very slowly dribble in the oil. Continue until all the oil is added. Add the lemon juice and salt and pepper.

Note: If the mayonnaise curdles, add another beaten egg yolk very slowly with the motor running.

Yoghurt

Makes 2 cups

2 cups (16 fl oz) milk
1 tablespoon natural yoghurt

Bring the milk to the boil and cool to lukewarm. Mix the yoghurt through the milk. Pour into a warm clean ovenproof container with a lid. Cover and place in a very cool oven 43°C (110°F/Gas ¼) for 8-12 hours. Refrigerate.

Hollandaise Sauce

Makes 1 cup

2 egg yolks
1 tablespoon water
2 tablespoons lemon juice
125 g (4 oz) butter
pinch of salt

Place the egg yolks, water and half the lemon juice in the top of a double saucepan. Whisk over gentle heat until thick and lemon-coloured. Whisk in the butter, small pieces at a time, until the sauce is thick and creamy. Add the salt and remaining lemon juice to taste.

Tarragon Vinegar

Makes 4 cups

3-4 sprigs fresh tarragon
4 cups (1 litre) white wine vinegar

Wash the tarragon and remove any bruised leaves. Trim the stalks. Pour the vinegar into a clean airtight bottle, and put in the sprigs. Seal the bottle and leave in a dark place to steep for approximately 1 month before using.

Strawberry Wine Vinegar

Makes 2 cups

2 punnets strawberries
2 cups (16 fl oz) white wine vinegar
1 tablespoon sugar

Wash and hull the strawberries. Place in a bowl, crush with a fork and add the vinegar. Cover and refrigerate for three days.

Place a fine clean cloth inside a strainer. Strain the mixture, pressing with a wooden spoon to extract as much liquid as possible. Discard the pulp. Combine the liquid and sugar in a saucepan. Stir over heat until the sugar is dissolved. Bring to the boil, reduce the heat and simmer gently for 5 minutes. Skim the surface as the mixture simmers. Pour into hot sterilized bottles, seal when cold. Use in French dressing and in game sauces.

First Course

Stocks

Chicken Stock

Makes 4 cups (1 litre)

This is a traditional recipe and takes some time to prepare. However the result is worth the effort and cannot be compared with stock cubes. Freeze the stock in ice cube trays for use in sauces, soups, etc.

1 onion, roughly chopped
2 stalks celery, roughly chopped
30 g (1 oz) butter
chopped parsley
salt and pepper
1 boiling fowl or bones and carcase from a roasting fowl
4 cups (1 litre) water

Sweat the vegetables in the butter for a few minutes then add the boiling fowl or carcase. Add a good quantity of chopped parsley. Season well. Cover with water and simmer very gently for at least 2 hours. The addition of crushed egg shells will keep the stock clean. Skim the surface occasionally. Strain the stock, cool and freeze in ice cube trays when cold.

Beef Stock

Fish Stock

head and bones of a medium-sized fish
1 small onion, studded with 2 whole cloves
1 bay leaf
6 peppercorns
1 small carrot
celery tips, if available

Place the fish head and bones in a large saucepan together with the remaining ingredients. Cover with cold water and bring to the boil. Simmer for 20 minutes. Strain and use as needed.

To freeze: Place in small containers, cover and freeze.

Demi Glace

Makes 4 cups (1 litre)

500 g (1 lb) beef bones (preferably shanks or bones with marrow)
1 carrot, roughly chopped
1 onion, roughly chopped
4 cups (1 litre) water
bouquet garni
salt and pepper

Place the bones, carrot and onion in a roasting pan and bake at 200°C (400°F/Gas 6) for about 1 ½ hours or until dark brown.
 Place the pan contents in a large pot. Rinse the brown bits from the pan and add to the bones. Cover with the water. Add the bouquet garni and season well. Simmer for 2 hours, uncovered. Strain well and freeze in ice cube trays when cool.

Beef Stock

Makes 4 cups (1 litre)

500 g (1 lb) beef bones
1 carrot, thickly sliced
1 onion, thickly sliced
2 sprigs parsley
salt and freshly ground black pepper
4 cups (1 litre) water

Place all the ingredients in a large saucepan and bring to the boil. Simmer for 2 hours. Strain and freeze in ice cube trays.

EGGS

Because of their inclusion in most recipes, we tend to neglect eggs as a main course or a meal on their own. Eggs are economical and quick to prepare and are ideal for everyday use. You may choose to perfect a soufflé, try a delicious egg combo using left-over ingredients or brighten up a simple meal by drawing a face on the shell of that boiled egg cooked for someone special.

The colour of egg shell and yolk is determined by the hen's diet and in no way affects the nutritional value. Eggs should be stored in the refrigerator but are best brought to room temperature before use.

The recipes in this chapter have been supplied by the **New South Wales Egg Corporation**.

The **New South Wales Egg Corporation** is a statutory authority which was established by the Egg Industry Act, 1983. The Corporation is under the direction and control of the Minister for Agriculture and Fisheries and reports through him to the New South Wales Parliament. The Act specifies that it is the duty of the Corporation to ensure that eggs and egg products comply with the prescribed standards of quality and grade when sold by wholesale or retail and to ensure the efficient marketing and distribution of a continuous supply of high quality eggs and egg products. The Corporation is also required to devise and implement suitable policies to ensure egg products are sold at the lowest possible price to the consumer, whilst providing a reasonable return to efficient producers.

Research and development is undertaken by the Corporation to introduce new egg products onto the market. The recipes here and through the book have been supplied by Hilary Wright.

Eggs

Boiling [M]

Use eggs at room temperature, or if cold, run them under the hot tap for a few seconds. Pierce the large end of the egg with a pin to prevent cracking. Eggs that are very fresh are difficult to peel when they are hard-boiled.

Method 1: Boil enough water to cover the egg. Reduce the heat to a simmer then lower the egg gently into the water. Cook for 4 minutes for a soft egg and 10 minutes for hard. Lift out the egg and lightly tap the top to allow the steam to escape, otherwise the egg will continue cooking.

Method 2: Put the egg into cold water. Bring the water to the boil then reduce the heat to a simmer. Cook for 2½ minutes for a soft egg and 6½ minutes for hard from the time the water boiled.

Note: Hard-boiled eggs should be immediately cooled in cold water to prevent a grey ring forming around the yolk

Poaching
Serves 1 [M]

½ cup (4 fl oz) water
¼ teaspoon salt
1 egg

Conventional method: Boil about 3 cm (1¼ inch) of water in a frying pan. Add the salt. Reduce the heat until the water is barely simmering.

Crack the egg into a cup and gently slip the egg into the water. Cook for about 3 minutes. Lift out with a perforated spoon.

Microwave method (650 watt oven): Place the water in a small dish. Microwave on high until the water boils.

Break the egg onto a plate and gently slide into the water. Gently prick the yolk and white several times with a toothpick or skewer. Microwave on high for 30 seconds or until the white is opaque.

Frying
Serves 1 [M]

15 g (½ oz) butter
1 egg

Conventional method: Gently heat the butter in the base of a pan.

Break the egg into the pan and cook gently, basting continuously, or turn over the egg halfway through the cooking time (about 3 minutes).

Microwave method (650 watt oven): Place the butter in a custard cup, small soufflé dish or plate. Microwave on high for 30 seconds or until the butter has melted.

Break the egg onto a dish. Prick the egg yolk and white with a skewer or toothpick. Microwave on high for 30 seconds.

Scrambled Eggs
Serves 1 [M]

2 eggs
2 tablespoons milk
salt and pepper
30 g (1 oz) butter or margarine

Conventional method: Beat the eggs and the milk with a fork, adding a little salt and pepper. Melt the butter over low heat in a heavy based saucepan. Pour in the eggs. (Too much heat will make the eggs leathery).

Stir slowly and continuously with a wooden spoon until thick and creamy. Remove from the heat just before the eggs are thoroughly cooked. Serve immediately.

Microwave method (650 watt oven): Beat the eggs, butter, milk and seasonings together in small bowl or jug. Cover with plastic wrap.

Microwave on high for 1 minute. Stir. Microwave on high for 30 seconds. Stir and serve.

Note: Gentle heat and gentle mixing are what make really creamy scrambled eggs.

Flat Omelette
Serves 1

2 eggs
2 tablespoons water
15 g (½ oz) butter
¼ cup (1 oz) grated cheese
filling of your choice (*see below*)

Lightly beat the eggs and water together. Preheat a pan until very hot. Place the butter in the pan. Pour in the egg mixture.

Using a spatula draw the cooked egg mixture into the centre of the pan allowing the uncooked egg to flow underneath. Continue until the mixture no longer flows.

Fill one side of the omelette with any of the suggestions below. Fold and turn out onto a serving plate.

Fillings:

1. 1 rasher bacon, lightly sautéed
   30 g (1 oz) mushrooms, lightly sautéed

2. 2 tablespoons cream
   ¼ cup (1 oz) grated Gruyère cheese
   1 teaspoon chopped chives

3. 1 tomato, sliced
   ¼ cup (1 oz) grated cheese
   pinch of basil

4. 1 x 220 g (7 oz) can salmon or tuna
   ¼ cup chopped celery
   pinch of nutmeg
   ¼ cup (1 oz) grated cheese, optional

Note: Fillings for omelettes are limited only by your imagination. They should be at room temperature and precooked if necessary.

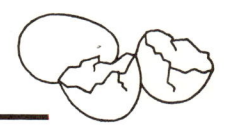

Fluffy Omelette

Serves 1

2 eggs, separated
30 g (1 oz) butter
filling of your choice (see below)

Whisk the egg whites until stiff, then fold in the beaten yolks and the filling.

Melt the butter in an omelette pan and pour in the egg mixture. Cook the omelette until the base is set, then place the pan under a griller (broiler) until the top is set.

Fillings:
1. ½ cup (2 oz) grated cheese
   1 tablespoon chives
   1 tablespoon tarragon
   1 tablespoon finely chopped fresh parsley
2. ¼ cup chopped ham
   ¼ cup chopped tomato
   ¼ cup (2 oz) grated cheese
   pinch of dried basil
   freshly ground black pepper

Note: Fillings for omelettes are limited only by your imagination. They should be at room temperature and precooked if required.

Basic Hot Soufflé

Serves 2

125 g (4 oz) butter
½ cup (2 oz) flour
1¼ cups (10 fl oz) milk
½ cup (2 oz) grated Parmesan cheese
salt and freshly ground pepper
4 eggs, separated

Preheat the oven to 200°C (400°F/Gas 6). Lightly grease a soufflé dish. Melt the butter in a saucepan, remove from the heat and stir in the flour. Gradually pour in the milk, stirring after each addition, until smooth. Return the saucepan to the heat and continue stirring until the sauce is smooth and thick. Remove from the heat and add the cheese, salt and pepper to taste. Beat the egg yolks into the mixture.

Whisk the whites until soft peaks are formed and then gently fold them through the mixture. Pour into the greased dish. Using a sharp knife, cut a circle into the mixture approximately 1 cm (½ inch) in from the rim (this helps the soufflé to rise). Bake the soufflé for 40 to 45 minutes.

Variation:

Fish Soufflé
1 x 315 g (10 oz) can smoked fish fillets, flaked
1 tablespoon grapefruit juice
1 tablespoon chopped fresh parsley

Add the fish, grapefuit juice and parsley to the basic mixture at the same time as the egg yolks. Omit the cheese.

Cheese and Tomato Soufflé
15 g (½ oz) butter
1 small onion, chopped
1 garlic clove, crushed
375 g (12 oz) tomatoes, chopped
2 rashers bacon, chopped
2 tablespoons dried oregano
salt and freshly ground pepper
½ cup (2 oz) grated Gruyère cheese

Melt the butter in a pan and fry the onion, garlic, tomatoes and bacon for 3 to 4 minutes. Add the oregano and season with the salt and pepper to taste. Allow to cool, then spread in the base of the soufflé dish.

Cover with the basic soufflé mixture to which the extra cheese has been added and cook as for a basic hot soufflé (above).

Chocolate Soufflé
1 tablespoon cocoa
125 g (4 oz) grated dark chocolate
omit the Parmesan cheese, salt and pepper

Sift the cocoa with the flour. Prepare and cook as for a basic hot soufflé mixture (above), replacing the cheese with the grated dark chocolate.

Strawberry Soufflé
1 punnet strawberries, washed, hulled and mashed
omit the cheese, salt and pepper

Add the strawberries to the hot sauce before adding the egg yolks. Prepare and cook as for a basic hot soufflé (above).

Eggs

Egg Combos

(Egg combinations suitable for all occasions and all ages.)

Serves 3 - 4

30 g (1 oz) butter or margarine	1 quantity egg combo mixture (*see below*)
1 quantity egg combo filling (*see below*)	

Heat a frypan to 120°-150°C (260°-300°F). Melt the butter in the pan. Stir fry or sauté the ingredients (*see below*) from the egg combo filling until the desired consistency.

Pour the egg combo mixture evenly over the cooked ingredients. As the egg sets around the edges, lift evenly with a spatula and allow the uncooked egg to flow underneath. Tilt the pan if necessary. When the egg mixture is almost cooked, add the remaining ingredients from the filling. Place the lid on the pan for 3 to 8 minutes or until heated through.

Cut into squares and serve hot, straight from the pan.

Savoury Basic Combo Mixture

6 eggs, lightly beaten together with	salt and pepper to taste
¼ cup (2 fl oz) water	1-2 tablespoons melted butter or oil

Sweet Basic Combo Mixture

6 eggs, lightly beaten together with	¼ cup (2 oz) raw (demerara) sugar
¼ cup (2 fl oz) milk or cream and	1-2 tablespoons oil

Savoury Combo Fillings

Tomato Combo Filling

2 tomatoes, roughly chopped and stir fried	1 cup cooked mixed vegetables, stir fried
1 medium-sized onion, sliced and stir fried	1 tomato, sliced
2 rashers bacon or ham, chopped and stir fried	½ cup (2 oz) grated cheese chopped fresh parsley

Brunch Combo Filling

1 medium-sized onion, sliced and stir fried	1 tablespoon tomato sauce
1 cup cooked seafood (fish, tuna, calamari, salmon, prawns (shrimp) or any combination of these)	1 tablespoon Worcestershire sauce
	1 tomato, peeled and sliced
	2 tablespoons chopped fresh parsley

Mushroom Combo Filling

½ cup (2 oz) finely grated cheese	¼ cup chopped ham, stir fried
1 tablespoon chopped fresh parsley	1 garlic clove or ¼ teaspoon dried garlic, stir fried
4 large mushrooms, sliced and stir fried	¼ teaspoon dried thyme, stir fried
1 large onion, chopped and stir fried	extra chopped fresh parsley
1 rasher bacon, chopped and stir fried	

Add the grated cheese and 1 tablespoon parsley to the beaten egg mixture and proceed as above.

Seafood Combo Filling

1 large onion, sliced and stir fried	squeeze of lemon juice
1 x 440 g (14 oz) can peeled tomatoes, drained	chopped fresh parsley
1 x 220 g (7 oz) can salmon, drained and flaked	asparagus spears or prawns (shrimp), optional

Add the tomatoes to the stir fried onion and proceed as above.

Sweet Combo Filling

Sweet combos can be topped with maple syrup, and either brandy orange, whisky caramel, or rum chocolate sauces.

Apple and Cream Combo Filling

1 cup lightly cooked apple, sautéed	1 tablespoon honey
45 g (1½ oz) butter	1½ teaspoons cinnamon
	½ cup (3 oz) mixed fruit

Sauté the apple in the butter. Sprinkle the honey and cinnamon over the apple and proceed as above. Serve with cream, ice cream or sour cream.

Fruit Combo Treat Filling

3 bananas, peeled and sliced	chopped glacé cherries
45 g (1½ oz) butter	icing (confectioners') sugar and/or crushed nuts
¼ cup (1½ oz) dried mixed fruit, sautéed	

Melt the butter in pan. Add the sliced bananas and the dried mixed fruit and sauté gently. Proceed as above. Serve with whipped cream, ice cream or sour cream.

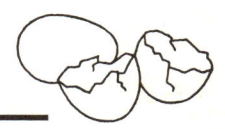

Special Occasion Combo Filling

Substitute ¼ cup (2 oz) caster (powdered) sugar with ¼ cup (1½ oz) soft brown sugar.

1 ½ cups (6 oz) chopped dried apricots	¼ teaspoon nutmeg
brandy, rum, marsala or orange juice	45 g (1½ oz) butter
	1-2 apples, peeled and thinly sliced
½ teaspoon cinnamon	extra cinnamon
1-1½ teaspoons mixed spice	crushed nuts

Soak the dried apricots overnight or as long as possible in brandy. Add the spices to the egg mixture and mix well. Reserve ½ cup of the marinated fruit for the topping. Melt the butter and gently fry the apples until lightly cooked. Sprinkle with the extra cinnamon. Add the remaining marinated fruit and heat gently. Pour the egg mixture evenly over the apples and fruit. Proceed as above. Serve with whipped cream, ice cream or sour cream, and crushed nuts.

Crêpes

Makes 6 - 8

2 eggs	pinch of salt
1 cup (8 fl oz) milk	2 tablespoons melted butter
1 cup (4 oz) flour	

Beat together the eggs and milk. Sift the flour and salt together, then add to the eggs. Beat until smooth and stir in the melted butter. Cover and refrigerate for approximately 30 minutes.

Heat a 15 cm (6 inch) crêpe pan or heavy frying pan, then grease lightly with butter.

Pour approximately 2 tablespoons of the mixture into the pan. Quickly rotate the pan to spread the mixture evenly across the base. Lightly colour the underside and flip over.

Brunch Egg Combo

Eggs

Basic Roulade

60 g (2 oz) butter
1/3 cup (1 1/2 oz) flour
1 cup (8 fl oz) milk
4 eggs, separated
grated Parmesan cheese
chopped fresh parsley

Melt the butter and add the flour. Cook for 1 minute. Gradually add the milk, stirring continuously until sauce thickens. Stir in the egg yolks and place the mixture in a bowl. In a separate bowl beat the egg whites until soft peaks form, then fold through the mixture.

Pour into a greased and lined Swiss roll tin. Bake at 200°C (400°F/Gas 6) for 10 to 16 minutes or until golden brown. Remove from the oven and turn onto a tea towel or greaseproof paper sprinkled with the Parmesan cheese and chopped parsley. Remove the lining paper, spread with the desired filling and roll gently as you would a Swiss roll.

Variation

Add any of the following to the sauce mixture:

grated cheese
cooked spinach
chopped fresh parsley and spring onions (scallions)
tomato paste
different herbs

Filling 1: Mushroom

30 g (1 oz) butter
1 onion, chopped
185 g (6 oz) sliced
    mushrooms
1 tablespoon flour
pinch of nutmeg
2/3 cup (5 fl oz) milk

Heat butter and fry onion, add mushrooms and cook for 2 to 3 minutes. Stir in the flour and nutmeg. Gradually add the milk and stir until thickened.

Filling 2: Tomato and Zucchini (Courgettes)

30 g (1 oz) butter
1 onion, chopped
1 garlic clove, crushed
3 tomatoes, chopped
2-3 small zucchini
    (courgettes), sliced
1/2 teaspoon dried oregano
1/4 teaspoon dried basil
1 teaspoon dried mixed
    herbs
1 tablespoon cornflour
    (cornstarch)

Melt the butter and sauté the onion and garlic lightly. Add the tomatoes, zucchini and herbs and simmer for 5 minutes. Combine the cornflour with a little water, add to the mixture and stir until thickened.

Filling 3: Salmon

2 x 200 g (6 1/2 oz) cans
    red salmon
4 spring onions (scallions),
    chopped
1/2 cup (4 fl oz) sour cream
2 teaspoons lemon juice
1 tablespoon chopped
    fresh dill

Drain and flake the salmon. Combine all the ingredients until mixed well.

Spinach Roulade
Serves 4

500 g (1 lb) spinach
4 eggs, separated
salt and pepper
nutmeg

Filling
2 tablespoons oil
1 onion, chopped
185 g (6 oz) mushrooms,
    sliced
1 tablespoon wholemeal
    flour
2/3 cup (5 fl oz) milk
salt and pepper
1 tablespoon grated
    Parmesan cheese

Wash the spinach and cook in a large pan with just the water clinging to the leaves. Cook for 6 minutes, drain thoroughly and chop finely. Place in a bowl with the egg yolks, salt, pepper and nutmeg to taste, and mix well. Whisk the egg whites until stiff and fold into the mixture. Spread the mixture evenly in a lined and greased 30 x 20 cm (12 x 8 inch) Swiss roll tin. Cook in a preheated oven at 200°C (400°F/Gas 6) for 10 to 15 minutes until risen and firm.

Filling: Heat the oil in a pan, add the onion and fry until soft. Add the mushrooms and fry for 2 to 3 minutes. Stir in the flour, then gradually stir in the milk. Add salt and pepper to taste and simmer for 2 to 3 minutes. Sprinkle the cheese over a sheet of greaseproof paper. Turn the roulade out onto the paper and peel off the lining paper. Spread with the filling and roll up like a Swiss roll. Serve immediately.

Zucchini Slice
Serves 6 - 8

375 g (12 oz) zucchini
    (courgettes)
1 large onion
3 rashers bacon
1 cup (4 oz) grated cheese
1 cup (4 oz) self-raising
    flour, sifted
1/2 cup (4 fl oz) oil
5 eggs
salt and pepper

Wash and coarsely grate the unpeeled zucchini. Finely chop the onion and bacon. Combine all the ingredients well. Pour into a greased 15 x 25 cm (6 x 10 inch) lamington tin. Bake at 180°C (350°F/Gas 4) for 35 to 45 minutes or until browned.

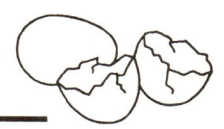

Savoury Egg Pillow

Serves 4

1 x 375 g (12 oz) packet frozen puff pastry, thawed
4 hard-boiled eggs, chopped
1 x 125 g (4 oz) can sardines, drained
1-2 teaspoons curry powder
1 tablespoon chopped parsley
4 tablespoons mayonnaise
salt and pepper
beaten egg to glaze

Roll the pastry into a 30 cm (12 inch) square, then cut in half. Place one piece on a baking tray. Mix together the remaining ingredients, adding salt and pepper to taste. Spread the filling over the pastry on the baking tray, leaving a 1 cm (½ inch) border. Brush the edges with water and place the remaining pastry on top. Seal the edges, brush with beaten egg and decorate with shapes cut from the trimmings. Bake on the top shelf of a preheated hot oven at 220°C (425°F/Gas 7) for 15 minutes. Serve hot.

Herby Tomato Quiche

Serves 6

Pastry
1 cup (4 oz) flour
90 g (3 oz) butter
1 egg yolk
1 tablespoon lemon juice

Filling
30 g (1 oz) butter
1 cup chopped spring onions (scallions)
3 small ripe tomatoes, sliced
3 eggs and 1 egg white from Pastry
1 cup (8 fl oz) cream
1 cup (4 oz) grated cheese
¾ cup chopped fresh basil
½ cup chopped fresh parsley
1 tablespoon grated Parmesan cheese
salt and pepper

Pastry: Sift the flour into a bowl and rub in the butter. Add the egg yolk and lemon juice to make a firm dough. Cover and refrigerate for 15 to 30 minutes. Roll out to line a 23 cm (9 inch) flan tin. Bake blind at 200°C (400°F/Gas 6) for 10 minutes.

Filling: Melt the butter and lightly sauté the spring onions. Arrange two of the sliced tomatoes in the pastry case. Combine the eggs, cream, grated cheese, spring onions, basil and parsley and pour into the pastry case. Arrange the remaining sliced tomato on top and sprinkle with Parmesan cheese, salt and pepper. Bake at 180°C (350°F/Gas 4) for 30 minutes.

Quizza

Serves 6

15 g (½ oz) compressed yeast
½ cup (4 fl oz) lukewarm water
½ teaspoon sugar
1½ cups (6 oz) flour
salt
2 tablespoons oil

Filling
1 x 50 g (1¾ oz) can tomato paste
3 eggs
½ teaspoon garlic salt
2 teaspoons mixed herbs
¼ teaspoon black pepper
½ teaspoon dried oregano
¼ teaspoon dried basil
125 g (4 oz) mushrooms, cooked and sliced
1-2 slices ham, chopped
1 x 45 g (1½ oz) can anchovies, optional
1 cup (4 oz) grated mozzarella cheese
2 tablespoons grated Parmesan cheese

Pastry: Crumble the yeast into the lukewarm water and add the sugar. Stir gently until dissolved and let stand for 10 minutes or until bubbles appear on the surface.

Sift the flour and salt into a bowl, make a well in the centre and add the oil and the yeast mixture. Mix to a firm dough by hand. Turn the dough onto a floured surface and knead for 10 minutes or until soft and elastic. Place in a lightly oiled bowl, cover and let stand for 30 minutes or until doubled in size.

Knock the dough down and knead into a smooth ball. Flatten dough into a circle about 2.5 cm (1 inch) thick and roll from the centre to fit a 25 cm (10 inch) pizza pan.

Filling: Spread the dough with the tomato paste. Beat the eggs and seasonings together and then pour over the dough. Arrange the mushrooms, ham and anchovies on top. Sprinkle with the mozzarella and Parmesan cheeses. Bake at 200°C (400°F/Gas 6) for 15 to 20 minutes or until set and the crust is golden brown.

Seasoned Egg Ramekins

Serves 4

½ onion, chopped
1 green or red pepper (capsicum), chopped
pinch of basil
4 eggs
½ cup (2 oz) grated cheese
salt and freshly ground black pepper
30 g (1 oz) butter

Lightly grease 4 ramekins. Sprinkle the onion, green pepper and basil into each. Break 1 egg into each dish, top with the cheese, sprinkle with salt and pepper, and put a knob of butter on the top. Bake at 220°C (425°F/Gas 7) for 8 minutes or until the eggs are cooked, and serve immediately.

Eggs

Egg Lasagne

Egg Lasagne

Serves 4

1 bunch spinach
1 x 250 g (8 oz) packet instant lasagne noodles
10 hard-boiled eggs, sliced

250 g (8 oz) mozzarella cheese, grated
grated Parmesan cheese

Sauce
2 tablespoons oil
1 onion, chopped
1 green or red pepper (capsicum), chopped
2 x 140 g (4 ½ oz) cans tomato paste

2 x 410 g (13 oz) cans peeled tomatoes
2 teaspoons basil
½ teaspoon thyme

Wash and cook the spinach. Drain well to remove the excess moisture. Place a little of the sauce in the bottom of a lasagne dish, then arrange in layers the noodles, sauce, sliced eggs, spinach and mozzarella cheese. Repeat the layers, sprinkle with Parmesan cheese and bake at 180°C (350°F/Gas 4) for 30 to 35 minutes.

Sauce: Place the oil in a frying pan, heat and then lightly sauté the onion and green pepper. Add the tomato paste, peeled tomatoes and herbs and mix well. Simmer gently for 20 minutes.

Egg Stroganoff

Serves 4

30 g (1 oz) butter
3 medium-sized onions, sliced
1 large red or green pepper (capsicum), sliced
250 g (8 oz) button mushrooms
½ cup (4 fl oz) water
2 beef stock cubes

2 tablespoons tomato paste,
1 cup (8 fl oz) sour cream, combined with
1 teaspoon cornflour (cornstarch)
6 hard-boiled eggs, shelled and halved
salt and pepper
chopped fresh parsley

Heat the butter in a large deep frying pan. Lightly fry the onions. Cut the pepper in half and discard the membrane and seeds. Slice the pepper and add to the pan with the mushrooms. Gently fry for 2 to 3 minutes. Add the water, crumbled stock cubes and tomato paste and stir until combined.

Lower the heat and add the sour cream and cornflour mixture. Add the eggs to the vegetables and sour cream. Season to taste. Serve on a bed of hot boiled rice, or hot cooked noodles. Decorate with chopped parsley.

Egg Curry

Serves 4

2 tablespoons oil
2 onions, chopped
2 garlic cloves, chopped
½ teaspoon ground ginger or 2.5 cm (1 inch) piece fresh ginger, chopped
½ teaspoon cinnamon
1 teaspoon paprika
1 teaspoon salt
1 tablespoon mild curry powder

2 tablespoons desiccated coconut
½ cup (4 fl oz) pineapple juice
1 ¼ cups (10 fl oz) chicken stock
1 cup (8 fl oz) yoghurt
10 hard-boiled eggs, shelled
1 tablespoon garam masala

Heat the oil in a large frying pan. Add the onions, garlic and ginger and fry for 3 minutes. Add the cinnamon, paprika, salt and curry powder. Cook gently for approximately 10 minutes, stirring occasionally.

Add the coconut, pineapple juice, stock and yoghurt to the curry mixture. Add the whole eggs. Heat slowly until simmering then simmer for 20 minutes. Stir in the garam masala and simmer for another 2 minutes. Serve hot with boiled rice.

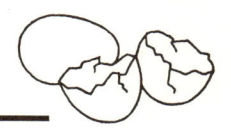

Quiche Lorraine

Serves 4

1 small onion, cut into fine rings
15 g (½ oz) butter
185 g (6 oz) shortcrust pastry
60 g (2 oz) sliced Gruyère cheese
4 eggs
1 cup (8 fl oz) cream
125 g (4 oz) bacon, chopped
1 teaspoon finely chopped fresh parsley
freshly ground black pepper
salt

Lightly fry the onion rings in the butter. Line a flan tin with shortcrust pastry and lay the Gruyère slices over the bottom. Beat the eggs and cream together, add the bacon pieces, onion and parsley and season with pepper. Pour the egg mixture onto the cheese and bake at 200°C (400°F/Gas 6) for 30 minutes. Sprinkle with a little salt. Allow to cool, then remove from the flan tin. Serve with a fresh salad.

Pizza Omelette

Serves 2

6 eggs
30 g (1 oz) butter
1 x 185 g (6 oz) can tuna, well drained
185 g (6 oz) tomatoes, sliced
60 g (2 oz) mushrooms, chopped and lightly sautéed
1 tablespoon capers, drained
1 teaspoon basil
1 teaspoon oregano
1 garlic clove, crushed
freshly ground black pepper
¾ cup (3 oz) grated cheese

Separate the eggs and whisk the whites until fluffy and peaks form. Lightly beat the egg yolks and fold through the whites. Melt the butter in a frying pan and cook the omelette until the base is set. Arrange the remaining ingredients on the top and place under the griller (broiler) for a few minutes until the omelette is set and the cheese has melted and is golden brown.

Egg Fondue

Serves 4

4 egg yolks
1 cup (4 oz) grated Gruyère cheese
salt
pepper
nutmeg
90 g (3 oz) butter
6 teaspoons milk
2 teaspoons sherry

Mix together the yolks, cheese, salt, pepper and nutmeg. Heat gently, stirring constantly. Add the butter a little at a time, then add the milk and sherry. Stir until blended. Do not boil. Serve with cubes of bread, fresh or fried in butter.

Note: This dish may be cooked at the table in a fondue dish.

Spinach Pie (Spanakopita)

Serves 6

If you can't get spinach, substitute silverbeet, or even lettuce if you like, but try to get the spinach.

1 kg (2 lb) spinach
1 cup chopped spring onions (scallions)
15 g (½ oz) butter
125 g (4 oz) feta cheese, crumbled
3 tablespoons Parmesan cheese
1 teaspoon chopped fresh dill or 1 teaspoon chopped dried basil
4 eggs, lightly beaten
2 tablespoons chopped fresh parsley
½ teaspoon nutmeg
freshly ground black pepper
3 rashers bacon, diced
puff pastry or 10 sheets filo pastry
beaten egg
poppy seeds

Wash and coarsely shred the spinach. Cover and steam for 8 minutes in a colander over boiling water, then squeeze out all the moisture and leave to cool. Gently fry the spring onions in the butter. Add to the spinach and stir in the cheeses, herbs, eggs, parsley, nutmeg, pepper and bacon. Lightly grease an ovenproof dish. Pour in the spinach mixture and spread evenly over the bottom. Cover with a layer of puff or filo pastry (see Note) about 3 mm (⅛ inch) thick, allowing the pastry to hang over the edges of the dish about 2.5 cm (1 inch) all round. Tuck this overhang under the lip of the dish, or just let it hang down. Brush the pastry with beaten egg, sprinkle with poppy seeds and bake at 230°C (450°F/Gas 8) for 25 minutes or until the pastry is golden brown. Let stand for 5 minutes before serving.

Note: If you use filo pastry, line the ovenproof dish with 5 sheets of filo, brushing each sheet with melted butter. Put in the filling, brush and moisten the edges of the pastry with beaten egg, and place the remaining filo pastry on top, brushing each sheet and the top with melted butter. Tuck the pastry into the side of the dish, sprinkle it with poppy seeds and cook as directed above. This mixture works well as a filling for small pies or turnovers.

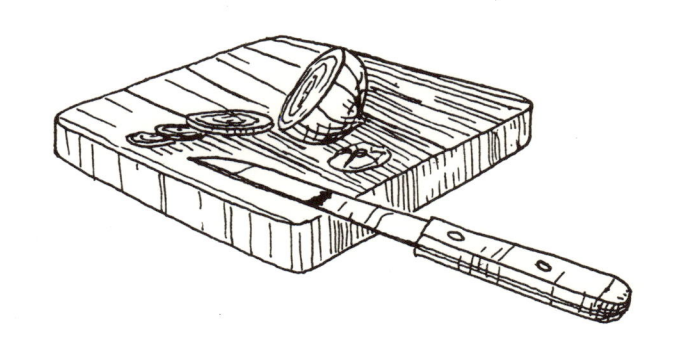

Eggs

Pumpkin Flan

Serves 6

Pastry
1 cup (4 oz) wholemeal flour
125 g (4 oz) butter or margarine
1 egg yolk
¼ cup (2 fl oz) water

Filling
3 spring onions (scallions)
15 g (½ oz) butter
500 g (1 lb) pumpkin, boiled or steamed
250 g (8 oz) feta cheese
3 eggs and 1 egg white from Pastry
⅔ cup (5 fl oz) cream
2 tablespoons drained chopped glacé ginger
3 tablespoons chopped fresh parsley
salt and pepper

Pastry: Sift the flour and return the husks to the bowl. Rub in the butter and add the egg yolk and just enough water to make a firm dough. Cover and refrigerate for 15 to 30 minutes. Roll out the pastry to line a 23 cm (9 inch) flan tin and bake blind at 190°C (375°F/Gas 5) for 10 minutes.

Filling: Lightly sauté the spring onions in the butter. Sieve the pumpkin and feta cheese. Add the beaten eggs, cream, spring onions, ginger, parsley, salt and pepper and mix well. Pour into the pastry case and bake at 180°C (350°F/Gas 4) for 25 to 30 minutes.

Pumpkin Flan

Farmland Treat

Serves 10

10 slices square sandwich ham
2 onions, finely chopped
30 g (1 oz) butter
2 cups (8 oz) finely grated cheese
10 eggs
2 cups (16 fl oz) natural yoghurt
2 tablespoons chopped fresh parsley

Line 10 x 1 cup (8 fl oz)-capacity ovenproof dishes with the ham. Lightly sauté the onions in the butter and divide evenly between the ham-lined dishes. Sprinkle evenly with half the cheese. Beat together the eggs and yoghurt and pour into dishes. Sprinkle with the remaining cheese and the parsley. Place on an oven tray and bake at 180°C (350°F/Gas 4) for 30 minutes. Turn out immediately and serve.

Tomato Nests

Serves 6

6 tomatoes
6 hard-boiled eggs
½ cup (4 fl oz) mayonnaise
lemon juice
salt
freshly ground black pepper
chopped fresh basil
1 small lettuce

Cut the tomatoes in half and remove the seeds. Invert the tomatoes and let drain.
   Cut the eggs in half and remove the yolks, being careful not to break them. Finely chop the whites and combine with the mayonnaise, lemon juice, salt and pepper. Fill the tomato halves with the egg white mixture. Place half an egg yolk in each tomato, flat side down. Garnish with the basil. Serve on a bed of washed lettuce.

No-Name Eggs

Serves 4

8 hard-boiled eggs
1 large onion
15 g (½ oz) butter
4 tomatoes
125 g (4 oz) mushrooms, sliced
pinch of dried oregano
salt and freshly ground black pepper
5 rashers bacon

Slice 4 eggs and place them in the base of a greased heatproof dish. Finely chop the onion. Melt the butter in a heavy frying pan and gently fry the onion until soft. Chop the tomatoes and place them in the pan together with the mushrooms, oregano, salt and pepper. Stir and cook gently for about 5 minutes. Pour the mixture over the eggs. Add another layer of sliced eggs and lay the bacon rashers on top. Place the dish under the griller (broiler) until the bacon is crisp and golden.

Stuffed Peppers

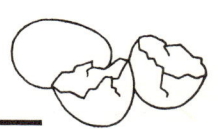

Eggs au Gratin

Serves 4

4 hard-boiled eggs
½ cup chopped spring onions (scallions), sautéed
60 g (2 oz) butter
3 tablespoons flour
pinch of nutmeg
¼ teaspoon mixed dried herbs
1 cup (8 fl oz) milk
1 cup (4 oz) grated cheese
1 tablespoon chopped fresh parsley
salt and pepper
extra parsley

Cut the eggs in half and place in a casserole dish. Sprinkle with the spring onions. Melt the butter and add the flour, nutmeg and mixed herbs. Mix well to combine. Gradually add the milk a little at a time, stirring continuously to prevent lumps forming. Continue stirring until thickened, then fold through half the cheese and the parsley. Season and pour over the eggs and sprinkle with the remaining cheese. Place under griller (broiler) until cheese has browned. Garnish with parsley.

Note: Extras may include sautéed bacon and/or additional cheese for a real cheesy sauce.

Stuffed Peppers

Serves 6

3 red or green peppers (capsicums)
2 cups (4 oz) fresh breadcrumbs
8 green olives, pitted and sliced
1 small garlic clove, crushed
4 anchovy fillets, chopped
2 tablespoons chopped fresh parsley
1 teaspoon dried oregano
squeeze of lemon juice
2 eggs

Cut the peppers in half lengthwise, core and remove the seeds. Place on a lightly greased baking tray. Combine all the remaining ingredients except the eggs and mix well. Add the lightly beaten eggs last and mix through. Divide the filling between each pepper and bake for 10 to 15 minutes at 180°C (350°F/Gas 4).

Note: This filling is also ideal to stuff mushrooms, tomatoes or eggplants (aubergines). Just include the mushroom stalks or tomato and eggplant flesh in with the filling.

Egg Drinks

Edinburgh Egg Nog

Makes 1 cup

1 egg, separated
1 teaspoon honey
½ cup (4 fl oz) milk
pinch of cinnamon
2 teaspoons rum or brandy
pinch of ground ginger

Beat the egg white until stiff. Beat together the yolk and remaining ingredients then pour onto beaten white. Mix lightly and chill.

The Snowie

Makes 1 cup

1 egg, separated
1 teaspoon sugar
50 ml (1 ½ oz) Bacardi light rum
1 teaspoon powdered malt honey
½ cup (4 fl oz) hot milk

Beat egg white until stiff. Add the sugar and beat quickly until peaks are formed. Mix together the Bacardi, egg yolk, malt and honey. Add the hot milk and top with the meringue mix.

Old Style Egg Nog

Makes 10 cups

60 ml (2 fl oz) Bacardi light rum
1 ½ cups (12 fl oz) milk
3 eggs
1 teaspoon vanilla essence
3 tablespoons powdered malt
nutmeg or cinnamon

Mix all ingredients in the blender until well combined. For a cold egg nog, use icy cold milk and some crushed ice. For a winter warmer, use warmed milk.

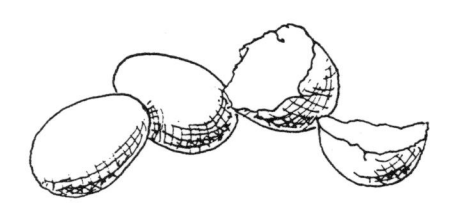

Brandy Egg Nog

Makes 1 cup

1 egg
1 egg
1 ¼ cups (10 fl oz) chilled milk
1 teaspoon honey
nip of brandy or orange juice
cinnamon

Combine the egg, milk, honey and brandy in a blender. If you don't like brandy, use a nip of orange juice. Blend and pour into a glass. Sprinkle with cinnamon.

Apple Nog

Makes 1 cup

1 egg
¾ cup (6 fl oz) apple juice
¼ cup (2 fl oz) milk
1 teaspoon honey
¼ teaspoon cinnamon

Combine all the ingredients in a blender until well blended. Pour into a tall glass.

Peachy Keen Nog

Makes 2 cups

1 ½ cups vanilla or peach ice cream
2 fresh or canned peaches, peeled
2 eggs

Combine all the ingredients in a blender. Blend at medium speed until smooth, about 15 seconds. Serve immediately.

Egg Nog

Makes 1 cup

1 egg
1 teaspoon sugar
vanilla essence
½ cup (4 fl oz) milk, chilled or warmed
nutmeg

Beat together the egg, sugar and vanilla essence. Add the milk and beat again. Pour into a glass if chilled or mug if warmed. Sprinkle a little nutmeg on top before serving.

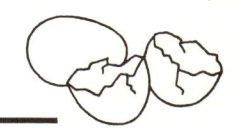

Norwegian Egg Cream

Makes 10 cups

10 egg yolks
½ cup (4 oz) sugar
1 cup (8 fl oz) brandy
cinnamon

Blend the egg yolks and sugar together until thick and creamy. It could take about 5 minutes. Slowly add the brandy and beat until well blended. Pour into individual cups and sprinkle with cinnamon.

Tomato Cocktail

Makes 3 cups

3 eggs
3 teaspoons Worcestershire sauce
salt and pepper
2 cups (16 fl oz) tomato juice
a few slices of cucumber

Whisk eggs with the sauce and season. Whisk in the juice. Chill and pour into glasses. Top with cucumber slices.

Butterfly Flip

Makes 1 cup

60 ml (2 fl oz) brandy
30 ml (1 fl oz) Crème de Cacao
4 egg yolks
2 tablespoons cream
2 teaspoons sugar
1 cup crushed ice
nutmeg

Beat or blend all ingredients together. Serve sprinkled with nutmeg.

Party Punch

Makes 12 cups

¼ cup (2 oz) sugar
½ teaspoon cinnamon
¼ teaspoon ground ginger
6 eggs
4 cups (1 litre) chilled orange juice
4 cups (1 litre) chilled pineapple juice
2 cups (16 fl oz) chilled ginger ale
orange sherbet, optional

Mix the sugar and spices. Add the eggs and beat well. Stir in the chilled juices and ginger ale, blending well. Add scoops of sherbet if desired.

Hot Coffee Brandy Cream

Makes 8 cups

6 eggs
½ cup (4 oz) caster sugar
4 tablespoons brandy
2 ½ cups (20 fl oz) milk
2 ½ cups (20 fl oz) strong black coffee
½ cup (4 fl oz) cream
2 tablespoons grated chocolate

Whisk the eggs, sugar and brandy together. Heat the milk and coffee until at boiling point then gradually whisk into the egg mixture. Whip the cream lightly and top each drink with cream. Sprinkle with grated chocolate.

Sunrise Cocktail

Makes 1 - 2 cups

1 egg
60 ml (2 fl oz) lemon juice
60 ml (2 fl oz) orange juice
60 ml (2 fl oz) pineapple juice
dash of grenadine
30 ml (1 fl oz) vodka

Blend or shake all ingredients together and pour into long glasses over crushed ice.

Malted Mallow

Makes 3 cups

2 tablespoons malt powder
4 tablespoons boiling water
2 ½ cups (20 fl oz) milk
3 eggs
6 marshmallows

Mix the malt powder with the boiling water. Heat the milk and stir into the mixture. Whisk the eggs well and gradually whisk in the milk. Pour into glasses and serve topped with 2 marshmallows in each glass.

Prairie Oyster

Makes 1 cup

1 egg
Worcestershire sauce
lemon juice
salt and pepper

Break the egg into a glass. Add a few drops of Worcestershire sauce and a little lemon juice. Season. Swallow in one gulp.

Eggs

Grapefruit Bubbly

Makes 8 cups

2 oranges
¼ cup (2 oz) caster (powdered) sugar
4 cups (1 litre) canned grapefruit juice
6 eggs
1 cup (8 fl oz) ginger ale
2 or 3 ice cubes
mint leaves

Squeeze the juice from the oranges and pour into a saucepan. Add the sugar and 4 strips of orange rind without pith. Heat gently to dissolve the sugar, then cool.

Whisk together the grapefruit juice, eggs, strained orange juice and pour into a serving jug. Add the ginger ale and ice cubes just before serving. Top with mint leaves.

Advocaat

Makes 4 cups

6 egg yolks
½ cup (4 oz) caster (powdered) sugar
2 cups (16 fl oz) milk
½ cup (4 fl oz) dark rum
2 cups (16 fl oz) cream, whipped
nutmeg

Beat the egg yolks until thick and creamy. Add the sugar and continue beating. Stir in the milk and rum and chill for 2 to 3 hours. Fold in the whipped cream and chill for another hour. Sprinkle with nutmeg to serve.

Egg Flip

Makes 1 cup

1 egg
1 cup (8 fl oz) cold milk
dribble of honey
grated nutmeg

Whisk the egg, milk and honey. Pour into glass. Sprinkle with nutmeg. Serve chilled, garnished with a cherry.

Apricot Egg Flip

Makes 1 cup

1 egg
1 cup (8 fl oz) apricot juice
crushed ice

Whisk the egg and juice together. Serve with crushed ice. For a richer drink, add 2-4 teaspoons of fresh cream and garnish with a strawberry.

Muscle Tucker

Makes 1 cup

½ cup (4 fl oz) chilled orange juice
½ cup (4 fl oz) cold milk
2 eggs
dribble of honey
nutmeg or cinnamon

Blend the orange juice, milk, eggs and honey together. Pour into a cold glass and sprinkle with nutmeg or cinnamon.

Egg 'n' Malt Flip

Makes 1 cup

1 egg
1 cup (8 fl oz) cold milk
3 drops vanilla essence
4 teaspoons powdered malt

Mix milk, egg, vanilla and malt. Pour into a glass and serve chilled, garnished with an orange segment.

Banana Bender

Makes 1 cup

1 banana
squeeze of lemon juice
1 egg
dribble of honey
1 scoop ice cream
½ cup (4 fl oz) cold milk
cinnamon

Mash or blend the banana with the lemon juice. Add the egg, honey, ice cream and milk and beat until frothy. Pour into a tall glass and sprinkle with cinnamon.

Egg Whisk

Makes 1 cup

1 egg
1 tablespoon strawberry jam
¼ cup (2 fl oz) milk
¼ teaspoon vanilla essence
cinnamon

Beat the egg with the jam. Add the milk and vanilla essence and beat well. Serve cold, sprinkled with cinnamon.

For a fluffy Egg Whisk, separate the egg, whisk egg white until stiff then fold into egg yolk mixture. Serve hot or cold.

Tropics

Makes 1 cup

1 egg
30 ml (1 fl oz) Bacardi gold
60 ml (2 fl oz) orange juice
60 ml (2 fl oz) lemon juice
60 ml (2 fl oz) pineapple juice

Shake or blend all ingredients and pour over crushed ice.

BEEF

Beef has been eaten world-wide since time began. It has always been a traditional source of protein and still remains the major source today. Although we now consume less meat, Australia still has one of the highest intakes of beef per capita in the world.

Australian beef is inexpensive and beautifully fresh. It is available in almost any cut desired and the family butcher can still make or break a meal. Ask his advice and he will look after you. Beef should always be bright red and have a layer of firm creamy white fat. The more expensive cuts have a smooth texture compared to the coarse appearance of the stewing cuts.

The new short cut recipes have opened up a wide range of dishes to the busy household and reduced preparation and cooking times to a minimum. The recipes here offer a wide range of traditional and international fare.

The majority of the recipes in this chapter have been supplied by the **Australian Meat and Livestock Corporation** while others have been provided by contributors whose credits appear elsewhere in the book.

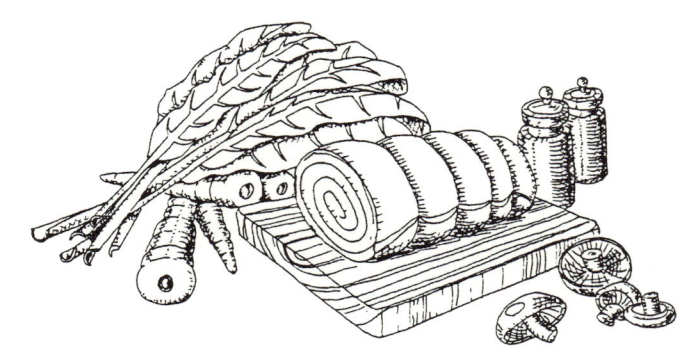

The **Australian Meat and Livestock Corporation** is the marketing arm of the Australian red meat industry. It is responsible for the marketing of beef, lamb, veal, goat and buffalo overseas, as well as within Australia.

The AMLC respresents the Australian Meat Industry in negotiating access arrangements with the EEC, Japan and the USA, and it is always on the lookout for new markets for Australian red meat overseas.

On the domestic front, it advertises meat, bearing in mind consumer tastes and trends. Campaigns are planned after extensive research into consumer needs.

The Corporation promotes red meat by supplying merchandising material to retailers, to inform the public of the very positive factors of meat in diet. It is constantly liaising with the catering and hospitality industry and investigating new products that will enhance the produce as well as open new avenues for the marketing of meat.

The Corporation is also very active in the field of recipe development, and like any modern marketing corporation, it fully utilizes modern methods of market research to best carry out its job.

The recipes here have been supplied by Tess Mallos.

Beef

CARVING

Rib of Beef

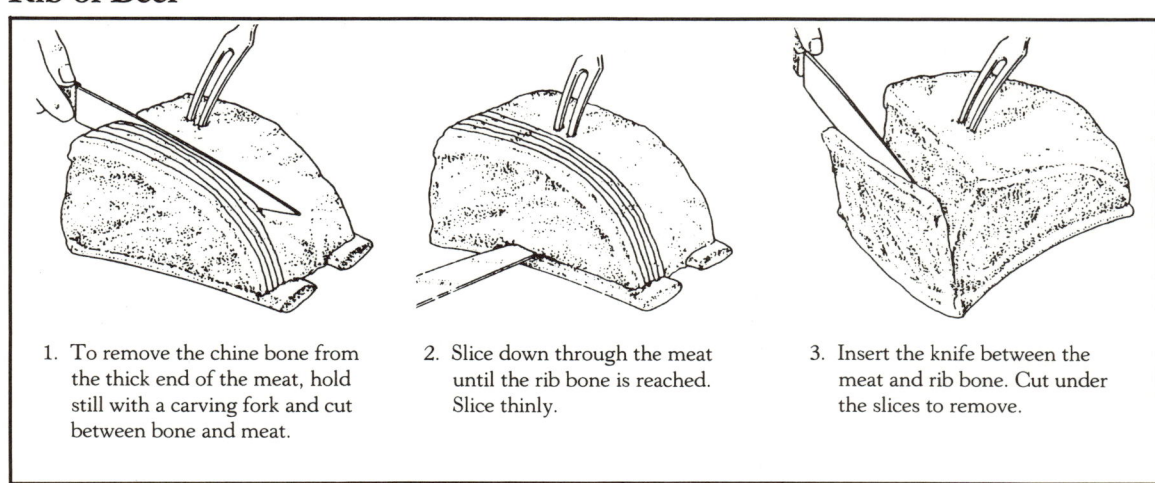

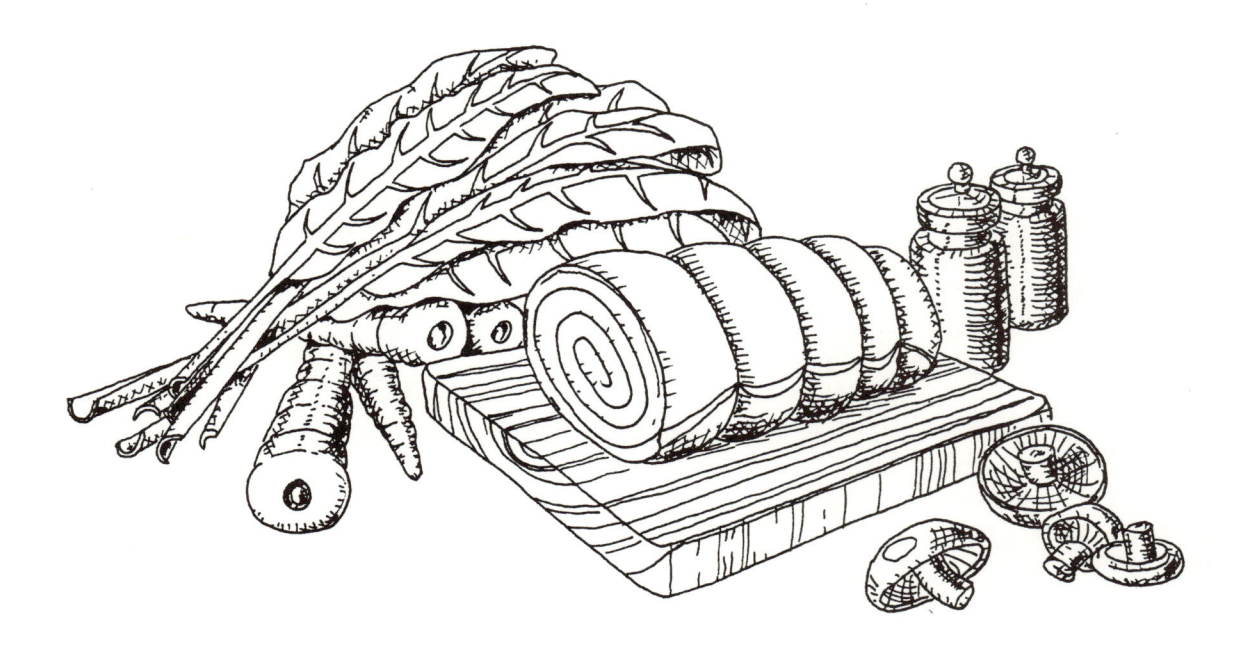

1. To remove the chine bone from the thick end of the meat, hold still with a carving fork and cut between bone and meat.

2. Slice down through the meat until the rib bone is reached. Slice thinly.

3. Insert the knife between the meat and rib bone. Cut under the slices to remove.

Meat Ring

Serves 6 [M]

750 g (1 ½ lb) finely minced (ground) beef
1 small onion, grated
1 small carrot, grated
½ cup (2 oz) quick cooking rolled oats
2 tablespoons chopped parsley
1 tablespoon tomato sauce
2 teaspoons barbecue or thick Worcestershire sauce
2 eggs, lightly beaten
salt and pepper
1 tablespoon dry breadcrumbs

Place the mince in a bowl and break up with a fork. Add the remaining ingredients except the breadcrumbs, mix lightly and leave for 5 minutes, then mix lightly and thoroughly until combined. Grease a glass or plastic ring mould with butter and dust with the breadcrumbs. Pack the mince mixture evenly into the mould. Cook on medium high for 15 minutes, giving the mould a half turn after 7 minutes. Stand for 10 minutes, unmould onto a serving dish and brush with a mixture of extra tomato and barbecue sauce. Cut in slices to serve.

Variation – Meat Loaf: Pack the above mixture into a greased and crumbed microwave meat loaf dish. Wrap a 3 cm (1 ¼ inch) wide strip of foil around the top rim and fold in over the edge of the loaf. Cook on medium high for 30 minutes, giving the dish a quarter turn each 10 minutes. Remove the foil for the last 10 minutes of cooking. Stand for 10 minutes before turning out and serving.

Rib Eye Roast

Serves 6 - 8

1 beef rib eye, about 1.5 kg (3 lb)
freshly ground pepper
15 g (½ oz) butter
1 cup (8 fl oz) stock
2 tablespoons port or Madeira

Season the meat liberally with pepper and place on a rack in a roasting dish. Spread the butter on top and cook in a hot oven at 220°C (425°F/Gas 7) for 1 hour for rare beef or 1 ½ hours for medium. Check with a meat thermometer. Turn twice during cooking and baste with pan drippings occasionally. Remove to a platter when cooked, cover with foil and leave in a warm place for 10 minutes.

Drain the fat from the dish and add the stock. Stir well to lift the browned juices. Strain into a small pan and add the port. Bring to the boil and thicken lightly with a cornflour (cornstarch) and water paste if desired. Adjust the seasoning. Serve the sliced beef with the sauce, boiled or sautéed potato balls and other vegetables of your choice.

Pineapple Meat Loaf

Serves 6

250 g (8 oz) finely minced (ground) beef
250 g (8 oz) veal and pork or sausage mince
2 tablespoons finely chopped bacon
1 cup cooked rice
1 small onion, finely chopped
¼ cup (2 fl oz) liquid from canned pineapple
1 tablespoon tomato sauce
1 egg
1 teaspoon curry powder
salt and pepper
butter or oil
4 slices canned pineapple

Glaze
¼ cup (2 fl oz) liquid from canned pineapple
1 tablespoon soft brown sugar
½ teaspoon ground ginger

Combine the minced meats with the bacon, rice, onion, pineapple liquid, tomato sauce, egg, curry powder and about 1 teaspoon salt and pepper to taste. Mix lightly and thoroughly. Grease a loaf pan with butter or oil. Halve the pineapple slices and overlap these along the base of the pan. Carefully pack the meat mixture into the pan, pressing it in firmly. Grease a lamington dish and invert the loaf pan on this; do not unmould as the loaf will release itself during cooking.

Bake at 180°C (350°F/Gas 4) for 30 minutes, then remove the loaf pan. Mix the glaze ingredients and pour over the loaf. Return to the oven for 15 minutes, basting occasionally with glaze. Serve sliced with fruit chutney and vegetables of your choice.

Beef

Barbecued Rib Eye

Serves 8 - 10

1 whole rib eye (Scotch fillet) roast, about 1.5 kg (3 lb)
¾ cup (6 fl oz) port
freshly ground pepper
oil or melted butter

Carefully trim the visible membrane on the outside of the roast to prevent the meat losing its shape. Do not trim off the fat. Tie at intervals with butcher's twine (more heat resistant than string). Prick the beef all over with a fine metal skewer, place in a sturdy plastic bag and put in a dish. Pour the port over the roast and seal the bag with an elastic band. Leave to marinate in the refrigerator for several hours or overnight, turning the bag occasionally.

When ready to cook, remove the meat and pat dry. Most of the port should be absorbed. Rub with pepper and place on a barbecue over medium heat. Brush well with oil or melted butter and cook for 45 minutes to 1 hour, depending upon the thickness of the roast. Turn often to brown evenly, and brush with oil frequently. If using a barbecue with a cover, place the drip pan in the centre of the coals as directed by the manufacturer, close the cover and cook.

When meat is cooked, remove to a carving platter, cover with foil and leave for 10 minutes before carving into thick slices. Serve with foil-wrapped potatoes, halved butternut pumpkin brushed with butter and sprinkled with nutmeg, and corn cobs all cooked on the barbecue with the beef. Supply a selection of mustards.

Barbecued Rib Eye

Sausage Rolls

Makes 40

1 kg (2 lb) sausage mince (ground beef)
1 cup (2 oz) soft breadcrumbs
1 onion, grated
1 tablespoon finely chopped parsley
2 tablespoons tomato sauce
4 sheets ready-rolled puff pastry
1 egg, beaten

Mix the sausage mince with the crumbs, onion, parsley and sauce until combined. Divide into 8 even portions and shape each into a roll the length of a pastry sheet. Dust the work surface and your hands with flour to shape the mince.

Cut the pastry sheets in halves. Place a roll of sausage mince along one edge of one strip, moistening the opposite edge with water. Turn the pastry over the filling and tuck the moistened edge underneath, pressing lightly to seal the join. Cut the roll into 5 even portions and place on a lightly greased baking sheet. Shape the remaining rolls. Glaze the tops with beaten egg and cut 2 to 3 small diagonal slits on top of each roll. Bake in a preheated very hot oven, 230°C (450°F/Gas 8), for 15 minutes. Reduce the heat to 180°C (350°F/Gas 4) and cook for a further 10 to 15 minutes.

Note: Sausage rolls may be prepared and frozen. Place on oiled baking sheets, do not glaze. Cover with foil and freeze until firm, lift off and pack into foil containers, separating layers with plastic film. Seal, label and return to freezer. Store for up to 2 months. When required, place frozen rolls on baking sheets, thaw and complete as above.

Peppered Rump Steak

Serves 4   [M]

1 slice middle cut rump steak 4 cm (1 ¾ inch) thick, about 750 g (1 ½ lb)
2 tablespoons crushed peppercorns
1 tablespoon oil or clarified butter

Trim the fat on the steak and coat each side with crushed peppercorns. Heat a large browning grill on high for 8 minutes. Add the oil and the steak. Cook for 3 minutes on high, turn with tongs and cook for a further 4 minutes on medium for rare, 5 minutes for medium done. Remove the steak to a serving platter and leave for 2 minutes. Carve in thick slices with the knife held at a 45° angle. While well-done steak is not recommended because of the risk of toughening, slices can be microwaved on medium for a few seconds for those who prefer steak that way.

Note: Use black or white peppercorns; if available a mixture of black, white and freeze-dried pink and green peppercorns may be used.

Roast Beef with Yorkshire Pudding

Serves 12

1 bone-in rib or sirloin roast, about 2.5 kg (5 lb)
salt and freshly ground pepper
oil
potatoes, pumpkin, onions, etc, peeled and cut into pieces

Yorkshire Pudding
1 cup (4 oz) flour
½ teaspoon salt
3 eggs
½ cup (4 fl oz) milk
approximately ½ cup (4 fl oz) water

The roast should be prepared by the butcher, that is with chine bone (backbone) sawn through just above the rib bones so that carving will be easier. The chine bone can be removed if desired. If using a rib roast, the thick cartilage (paddywack) should also be removed. Have the roast tied securely between the rib bones if the chine is taken off.

Bring the beef to room temperature (about 2 hours). Rub the meat surfaces with pepper and the fat with salt and pepper. Brush all over with oil. Place in roasting dish, fat side up, with the rib bones forming a natural rack. Cook in a moderate oven, 180°C (350°F/Gas 4) for 1½ hours for rare, 2 hours for medium. Place the vegetables around roast 1 hour before the end of cooking, or cook them in oil in a separate dish.

Remove the roast when cooked, place on a platter and cover with foil. Leave in a warm place to rest for 30 minutes. Carve the roast and serve with the vegetables, a green vegetable and the Yorskshire Pudding. Provide mustard and horseradish. A prime beef roast does not need gravy, however directions follow for gravy fans.

Yorkshire Pudding: Make the batter when the vegetables go into the oven. Sift the flour and salt and add the eggs and milk. Beat with a whisk until smooth, gradually adding water to make a thin batter. Beat for 5 minutes, then cover and leave for at least 20 minutes. Put a teaspoon of fat from the roast into each of 12-14 large muffin pans and place in the oven. Increase the oven to 190°C (375°F/Gas 5). When the fat is smoking, half fill each with batter. Place on the upper shelf and cook for 25 minutes or until puffed and golden.

Beef Gravy: Cook vegetables in a separate dish so that juices will not be lost. Drain fat from roasting dish, placing 1 tablespoon fat in a small saucepan. Leave any juices in the dish and add 1½ cups (12 fl oz) light stock or water. Place over the heat and stir to dissolve the sediment. Place the saucepan with the fat on the heat and stir in 1 tablespoon flour. Cook until lightly coloured and stir in the dissolved juices. Stir constantly until bubbling. Simmer for 5 minutes and adjust the seasoning. Strain into a gravy boat. Beef gravy should be thin.

Roast Beef with Yorkshire Pudding

Beef

Roast Beef with Vegetables Provençale

Serves 5 - 6

1 piece rib eye or eye fillet (beef tenderloin), about 1 kg (2 lb)

Vegetables Provençale
2 small onions
1 green pepper (capsicum)
1 red pepper (capsicum)
4 zucchini (courgettes)
2 large ripe tomatoes, peeled
freshly ground pepper
1 tablespoon melted butter or oil

1 tablespoon olive oil
1 garlic clove, crushed
salt and pepper
white wine, optional
chopped fresh herbs to garnish

Wipe the beef with paper towels and tie at intervals with white string. Rub the meat with pepper and brush all over with the butter. Place on a rack set in a roasting dish and cook in a preheated hot oven, 220°C (425°F/Gas 7), for 30 minutes for eye fillet, 40 minutes for rib eye. These times give medium-rare beef; if medium beef is required, increase the time by 5 to 7 minutes. Remove to a platter, cover with foil and rest in a warm place for 10 minutes before carving. Remove the string and serve carved in thick slices with Vegetables Provençale.

Vegetables Provençale: Halve the onions and cut into slender wedges. Remove the stems and seeds from the peppers and cut into thick strips. Cut the zucchini diagonally into thick slices and dice the tomatoes. Heat the oil in a pan and add the onions and garlic. Cook on low heat, stirring often, for 5 minutes. Add the remaining vegetables, season with salt and pepper and a pinch of sugar, if desired. Cover the pan and cook the vegetables gently for 15 minutes or until just tender. A little dry white wine may be added if additional moisture is required during cooking. Sprinkle with chopped fresh herbs before serving.

Note: Cooked beef and vegetables can be served cold. Wrap cooled beef in foil and refrigerate; chill cooked vegetables in a covered bowl, or leave to cool to room temperature and serve.

Chateaubriand

Serves 4

1 piece eye fillet (tenderloin), about 750 g (1 ½ lb)
freshly ground black pepper
30 g (1 oz) butter
¾ cup (6 fl oz) veal stock
¼ cup (2 fl oz) port
2 teaspoons cornflour (cornstarch)
salt

Trim eye fillet if necessary so that no silver skin remains. Tie the fillet at intervals with white string so that it keeps its shape during cooking. Rub with pepper. Heat the butter in a frying pan until foaming subsides. Add the fillet and brown on all sides over medium high heat. Remove the fillet to a roasting dish and retain the pan with juices. Cook fillet in a preheated hot oven, 220°C (425°F/Gas 7), for 30 minutes, turning occasionally during cooking. Remove to a warm dish, cover and keep warm.

Deglaze the roasting dish with the stock. Heat the frying pan, pour in the stock from the dish and add the port. Stir well and bring to the boil. Mix the cornflour with a little cold water and gradually pour into the pan, stirring constantly. Simmer gently for 2 minutes, adjust the seasoning and strain onto a hot serving platter to coat the base. Slice the fillet thickly and overlap the slices down the centre of the dish.

Note: Demi glace should be used for the sauce, so if you have some on hand, use in place of the veal stock and omit the cornflour thickening. Then again if you have no veal stock, use ½ teaspoon each of beef and vegetable bouillon powder with ¾ cup (6 fl oz) water. Remember the browned meat juices are full of flavour.

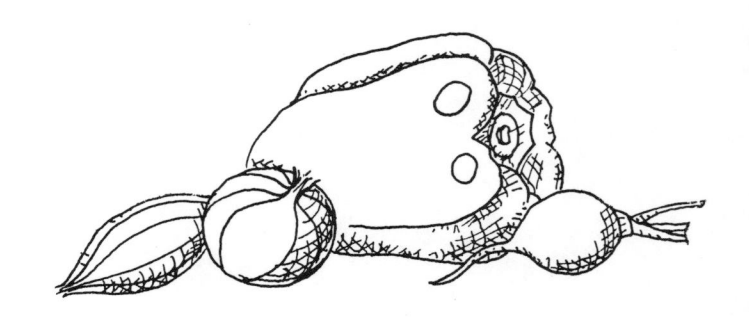

Beef Rolls with Spinach and Pine Nuts

Serves 5 - 6

2 thick flank skirt steaks, each about 500 g (1 lb)
freshly ground pepper
2 tablespoons oil
1 tablespoon flour
½ cup (4 fl oz) beef stock
½ cup (4 fl oz) red wine

Spinach and Pine Nut Stuffing
1 cup cooked spinach leaves
4 spring onions (scallions), chopped
15 g (½ oz) butter
2 tablespoons pine nuts
¼ cup (½ oz) soft breadcrumbs
salt and pepper
a little freshly grated nutmeg
beaten egg

Trim the skirt steaks if necessary. Using a sharp knife, score the smooth side of each steak in diamonds. Turn the steaks scored side down on a board. Spread the stuffing onto the steaks. Roll up from one long side into neat rolls and secure with toothpicks or fine metal skewers. Season with pepper and place in an oiled roasting dish. Brush the rolls with oil and cook in a moderately hot oven, 190°C (375°F/Gas 5), for 45 minutes, turning occasionally to brown evenly. Remove to a warm platter, cover and keep warm.

Place the roasting dish over the heat and sprinkle in the flour. Stir well and cook for 1 minute. Pour in the stock and wine, stirring constantly. When thickened and bubbling, simmer gently for 2 minutes. Strain into a sauceboat.

Remove the toothpicks from the rolls and carve into thick slices. Serve with the sauce.

Spinach and Pine Nut Stuffing: Drain the spinach thoroughly, squeezing out any excess moisture. Chop roughly and place in a bowl. Cook the spring onions in the butter until soft and add to the spinach with the pine nuts, crumbs, salt and pepper to taste and the nutmeg. Add enough beaten egg to bind lightly.

Fillet with Béarnaise Sauce

Serves 5 - 6 [M]

1 piece beef fillet (tenderloin), about 750 g (1½ lb)
freshly ground pepper
1 tablespoon clarified butter or oil

Béarnaise Sauce
¼ cup (2 fl oz) white wine
1 tablespoon white vinegar
1 ¼ teaspoons dried tarragon
2 chopped spring onions (scallions)
6 peppercorns
125 g (4 oz) butter
pepper
3 egg yolks

Trim the fillet and carefully trim off the fat and silver skin, taking care not to separate the muscles if using butt fillet. If using eye fillet, this only has a single muscle. Tie the fillet at intervals with white string then weigh. Calculate cooking time per 500 g (1 lb) at 7 minutes for rare, 8 minutes for medium or 10 minutes for well done. Season with pepper. Heat a browning grill on high for 6 minutes for small grill, 8 minutes for large. Add the butter or oil and the fillet. Cook on high for 3 minutes, turning the fillet across the grill surface during this time to brown it evenly. Reduce to medium and cook for the remaining cooking time. When cooked, cover loosely with foil, shiny side down, and leave for 10 minutes. Serve cut in thick slices with Béarnaise Sauce and vegetables of your choice.

Béarnaise Sauce: Place the wine, vinegar, 1 teaspoon of the tarragon, the spring onions and peppercorns in a 2-cup glass measure and heat on medium high for 4 minutes until the liquid is reduced by half. Strain liquid into a jug or bowl, pressing the flavourings with a spoon to extract the moisture. Add the butter, the remaining tarragon and a grinding of pepper. Heat on high for 1 minute until the butter is melted. Beat the egg yolks and stir into the bowl with a balloon whisk. Heat on medium for 40 to 45 seconds, whisking at 15-second intervals until thickened. Do not let the sauce boil or it will curdle. If the sauce does curdle, remove from the oven and whisk briskly until smooth. The sauce can be served warm but do not attempt to reheat it.

Beef

Beef Stroganoff

Serves 4 - 5 [M]

- 500 g (1 lb) lean round, topside or blade steak
- 1 cup (8 fl oz) strong beef stock
- 2 teaspoons Worcestershire sauce
- ¼ teaspoon ground nutmeg
- 1 tablespoon tomato paste
- 1 tablespoon cornflour (cornstarch)
- 1 teaspoon seasoned meat tenderiser
- 1 large onion, halved and sliced in slender wedges
- 15 g (½ oz) butter
- 250 g (8 oz) mushrooms, sliced
- ¼ cup (2 fl oz) sour cream

Cut the meat into 6 mm (¼ inch) wide strips and place in a bowl. Mix the beef stock with the Worcestershire sauce, nutmeg, tomato paste and cornflour. Mix the meat tenderiser into the meat. Place the onion in a large casserole dish with the butter and cook on high for 4 minutes. Add the mushrooms and cook on high for 1 minute. Stir the liquid mixture and pour into the dish. Cover and cook on high for 5 to 7 minutes, stirring occasionally, until thickened and bubbling. Remove the cover and stir in the meat. Cook uncovered on high for 5 to 7 minutes, stirring occasionally, until the meat changes colour and is cooked through. Cover and cook for a further 3 to 4 minutes on high. Stir in the sour cream and cook for 30 seconds. Stand for 5 minutes before serving with boiled rice or noodles.

Tripe and Onions

Country Beef Casserole

Serves 6

- 1 kg (2 lb) chuck steak
- 30 g (1 oz) butter
- 1 medium-sized onion, chopped
- 1 garlic clove, crushed
- 2 tablespoons flour
- 3 tablespoons tomato paste
- 1 cup (8 fl oz) light stock
- ½ teaspoon sugar
- salt and pepper to taste
- 2 medium-sized carrots, cut into chunks
- bouquet garni
- 8-10 small whole onions
- 1 turnip, sliced
- 12 small whole potatoes, peeled
- 1 cup shelled green peas
- chopped parsley

Trim the beef and cut into 3 cm (1 ¼ inch) cubes. Heat the butter in a large frying pan, add the meat cubes and brown on each side. Transfer to a casserole dish. Add the chopped onion and cook gently on low until transparent. Add the garlic and cook a few seconds. Sprinkle in the flour, stir well and cook for 1 minute, then stir in the tomato paste mixed with the stock. Stir constantly until thick and bubbling. Add the sugar, salt and pepper and pour over the meat. Add the carrots and place the bouquet garni in the centre.

Cook in a moderately slow oven, 160°C (325°F/Gas 3), for 1 hour. Add the onions, turnip, potatoes and peas. Cover and return to the oven for a further hour or until the meat and vegetables are tender. Skim any fat from the surface and remove the bouquet garni and discard. Sprinkle with chopped parsley.

Tripe and Onions

Serves 4

- 500 g (1 lb) tripe
- cold water
- 2 white onions, peeled
- 2 teaspoons salt
- 30 g (1 oz) butter
- 3 tablespoons flour
- 1 ½ cups (12 fl oz) liquid from tripe
- 1 ½ cups (12 fl oz) milk
- 1 tablespoon chopped parsley
- white pepper, optional

Wash the tripe and blanch by placing in a pan of cold water. Bring to the boil and pour off the water.

Cut the blanched tripe into 2 cm (¾ inch) squares. Return to the cleaned saucepan, cover with cold water and add the onions and salt. Bring to the boil, reduce heat and simmer, covered, for 1 ½ to 2 hours until the tripe is tender. To test if cooked, remove a piece and when cool enough to handle, pull with both hands. It should break apart easily.

When cooked, drain off the liquid, reserving 1 ½ cups. Remove the tripe and onions to a dish. Cut the onions into small pieces. Clean the saucepan and return to heat. Melt the butter, stir in the flour and cook on medium heat for 1 to 2 minutes without allowing the flour to colour. Pour in the tripe liquid and milk, stirring constantly. Keep stirring until thickened and bubbling. Stir in the tripe, onions, parsley and pepper if used, heat through gently and serve garnished with grilled bacon rolls and toast triangles.

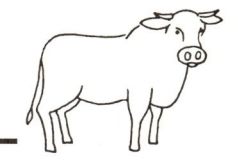

Corned Beef Dinner

Serves 6

1 piece corned brisket, about 2 kg (4 lb)
1 onion, quartered
1 teaspoon whole peppercorns
1 carrot, quartered
1 stalk celery, cut into pieces
1 bay leaf
6 small whole carrots
6 small whole onions
6-8 medium-sized potatoes
6-8 cabbage wedges

Parsley Sauce
30 g (1 oz) butter
2 tablespoons flour
1 ¼ cups (10 fl oz) milk
salt and pepper
2 tablespoons finely chopped parsley

Rinse the beef in cold water and place in a large saucepan with the onion, peppercorns, carrot, celery and bay leaf. Cover with warm water. Bring slowly to the boil, skimming when necessary. Cover and simmer for 1 ½ hours.

Add the whole carrots and onions, with root end of onions cross-cut to prevent the centres popping. Cover and simmer for 45 minutes, add potatoes and cook for 30 minutes.

Prepare the cabbage so that each wedge has some core attached. Place on top of pan contents, cover and cook 10 minutes longer or until the vegetables are tender. Remove the vegetables to a platter and keep hot. Leave the beef in water for 10 minutes before carving. Serve the beef and vegetables with the Parsley Sauce.

Parsley Sauce: Melt the butter in a heavy saucepan and stir in the flour. Cook for 2 minutes without browning, remove from heat and stir in the milk. Return to heat and stir constantly until the sauce thickens and bubbles. If lumps form, stir them out with a balloon whisk. Season to taste and stir in the parsley. Simmer for 1 minute, then pour into a sauceboat.

Corned Beef Dinner

Beef

Buderim Beef Salad

Serves 6

500 g (1 lb) cold cooked roast beef
185 g (6 oz) snow peas (mange-tout)
1 x 220 g (7 oz) can water chestnuts

Orange Vinaigrette
grated rind of 1 orange
⅓ cup (2 ½ fl oz) orange juice
1 teaspoon grated fresh ginger
¼ cup (2 fl oz) good salad oil

julienne shreds of fresh ginger
orange to garnish

3 teaspoons French mustard
3 teaspoons sugar
1 tablespoon wine vinegar

Slice the roast beef thinly and cut the slices in half if large. Top and tail the snow peas if desired and boil for 2 minutes. Drain and refresh under cold water. Drain well. Drain the water chestnuts and slice thinly.

Arrange the beef and other salad ingredients attractively on a large platter and spoon half the Orange Vinaigrette on top. Cover with plastic film and refrigerate for 30 minutes for the flavours to mingle. Leave at room temperature for 10 minutes before serving. Serve garnished with orange and with the remainder of the dressing served separately. A tossed salad of mixed greens can accompany the beef salad if desired.

Orange Vinaigrette: Place the ingredients in a blender and blend until thick, or whisk in a bowl until thickened. The dressing may have to be beaten again just before use. This stores for up to 4 days in a sealed jar in the refrigerator.

Beef with Blackberries

Serves 6

1 butt fillet (tenderloin) of beef or small rib eye, about 1 kg (2 lb)
freshly ground pepper
15 g (1 oz) butter
1 cup (8 fl oz) water
½ cup (4 fl oz) port

1 teaspoon beef bouillon powder
2 teaspoons cornflour (cornstarch)
1 cup fresh or frozen blackberries
sugar and salt

Trim the fat and silver skin from the fillet, taking care not to separate the muscles. If using rib eye, trim if necessary. Tie the beef at intervals with white string and sprinkle with pepper. Heat the butter in a frying pan and brown the beef on all sides. Transfer the beef to a rack set in a roasting dish and keep the frying pan aside. Cook the beef in a hot oven, 200°C (400°F/Gas 6), for 35 minutes for medium rare, 40 minutes for medium; for rib eye, allow an extra 5 minutes on these times. Brush occasionally with a little butter during cooking. When the beef is cooked, remove to a warm platter, cover with foil and leave in a warm place for 10 minutes. Drain any fat from the roasting dish, add the water and stir well to dissolve the crusty bits in the pan. Pour into the frying pan in which the beef was browned.

Add the port and bouillon powder to the liquid in the frying pan and heat, stirring often to lift the sediment. Mix the cornflour with a little cold water and stir into the liquid. Heat, stirring constantly until thickened and bubbling. Boil to reduce a little, then add the blackberries (thaw first if frozen) and adjust the flavour with sugar and salt. Bring to the boil and serve with the sliced beef. As accompaniments, serve a lightly cooked green vegetable such as asparagus or snow peas (mange-tout), and puréed sweet potatoes mixed with coconut.

Note: If fresh or frozen blackberries are not available, use a 425 g (13 ½ oz) can of blackberries. Drain, reserving the syrup, and add some of this to the sauce if necessary. Do not add sugar.

Opposite: *Beef with Blackberries*

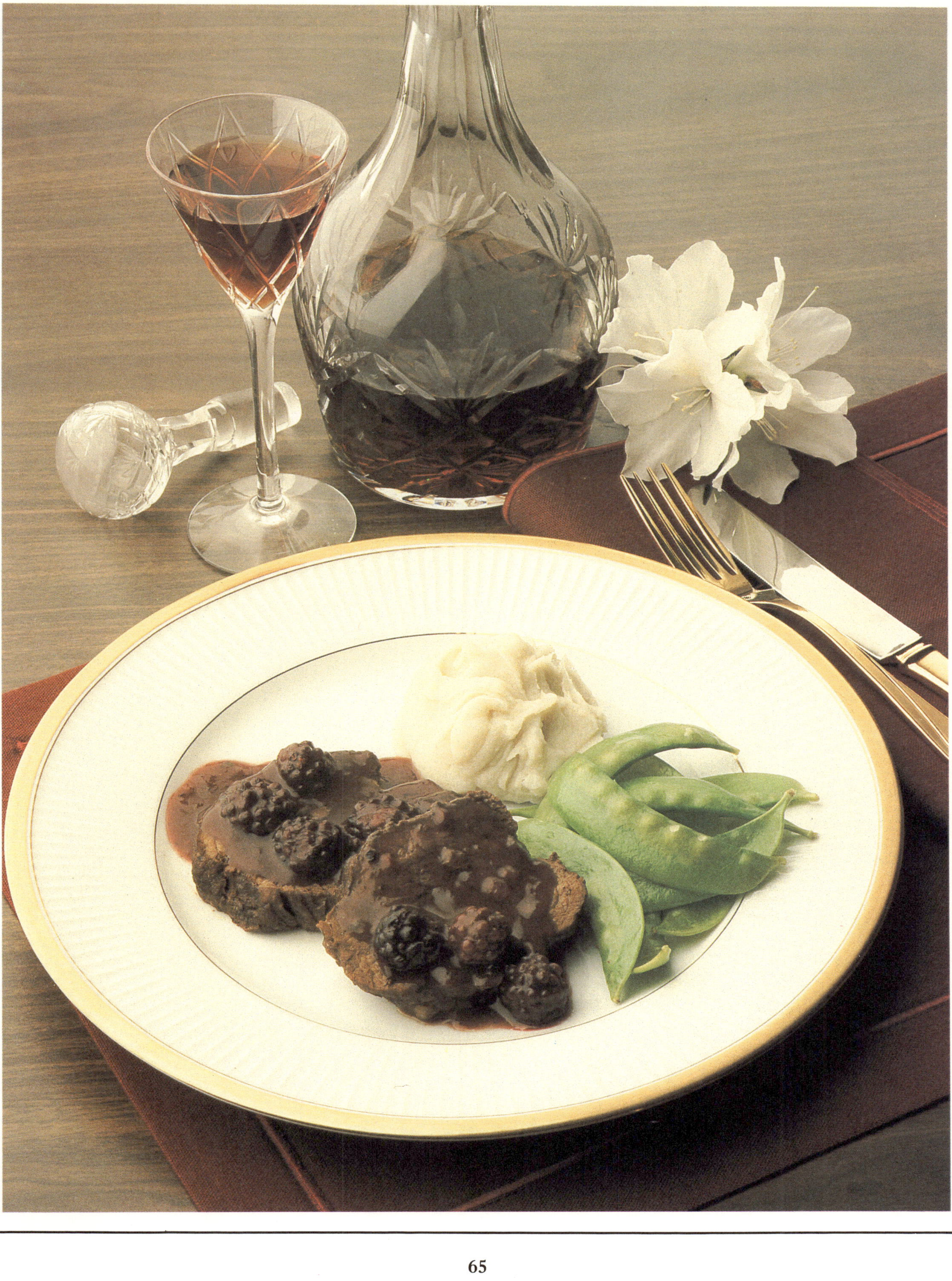

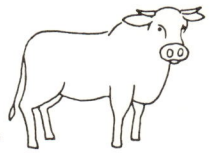

Beef

Roast Stuffed Topside
Serves 5 - 6

1 topside roast, about 1.5 kg (3 lb)
salt and pepper
oil
1 cup (8 fl oz) stock or water

Herb Stuffing
1 small onion, finely chopped
15 g (½ oz) butter
1 cup (2 oz) soft breadcrumbs
1 tablespoon chopped parsley
½ teaspoon dried thyme leaves
½ teaspoon dried marjoram
salt and pepper
beaten egg to bind

Have the butcher cut a pocket in the topside, or cut one yourself in the following way. Cut a thin slice at the narrow meaty end of the topside, but do not cut all the way through – the slice must be attached at the base. Then cut a deep pocket into the meat. The partly cut slice is used later to hold in the stuffing.

Insert the stuffing into the pocket. Lift the flap over the opening and fasten the end to the top of the roast with a poultry skewer. Season with salt and pepper and brush with a little oil. Place on a rack in a roasting dish and cook in a moderate oven, 180°C (350°C/Gas 4), for 1½ hours for medium beef. Remove to a carving platter, cover with foil and leave in a warm place for 15 minutes. Drain the fat from the dish and dissolve the crusty bits in the pan with the stock. Boil, thicken if desired, and serve with the sliced beef. Baked vegetables and a green vegetable are traditional accompaniments.

Herb Stuffing: Cook the onion in the butter until soft. Add to the crumbs with the herbs, and season to taste with salt and pepper. Add enough beaten egg to bind the stuffing, mixing it in lightly.

Capricornia Beef and Rice Salad
Serves 6

315 g (10 oz) sliced cold roast beef
1 cup (8 fl oz) natural yoghurt
1 ½ teaspoons curry powder
¼ cup (3 oz) mango chutney
¼ cup (¾ oz) coconut
¼ cup (1 ½ oz) sultanas
1 ½ cups canned pineapple pieces, drained
1 large green apple, diced
3 cups cold boiled rice
crisp lettuce leaves
¼ cup (1 ½ oz) cashew nuts or peanuts
1 red apple, optional

Trim the fat from the beef if necessary and cut into strips or small squares. Place the yoghurt in a large bowl and stir in the curry powder, chutney, coconut and sultanas. Drain the pineapple, core the apple and dice with the skin on. Mix the fruit into the yoghurt mixture with the rice and beef pieces. Cover and chill until required.

To serve, pile into a large salad bowl lined with crisp lettuce leaves and sprinkle the nuts on top. Salad may be further garnished with slender wedges of red apple (skin on) tossed with a little lemon juice to prevent discolouring.

Easy-as-Pie
Serves 6

⅓ cup (1 ½ oz) dry breadcrumbs
½ cup (4 fl oz) evaporated milk
½ packet French onion soup mix
2 tablespoons chopped parsley
pinch of dried thyme
½ teaspoon salt
freshly ground pepper
pinch of ground nutmeg
1 tablespoon tomato sauce
1 teaspoon Worcestershire sauce
500 g (1 lb) finely minced (ground) lean beef
2 sheets ready-rolled shortcrust pastry
egg or milk to glaze

Put the crumbs in a bowl with the evaporated milk, soup mix, parsley, thyme, salt, pepper, nutmeg and sauces. Mix well, leave for 5 minutes, then mix in the mince lightly and thoroughly.

Place a sheet of pastry in the centre of a greased baking sheet. Spread the meat mixture evenly on top, leaving a 4 cm (1 ½ inch) border of pastry. Moisten the pastry edge with water and place a second sheet of pastry on top. Press pastry closely over the meat, press the edges together and trim with a sharp knife. Seal by pressing with a fork. Glaze the pastry with a little beaten egg and prick the top in several places.

Bake the pie in a preheated hot oven, 200°C (400°F/Gas 6), for 40 minutes until golden. Serve hot, cut into squares. For cold service, cool on a tray and refrigerate in a sealed container until needed. Serve cold with tomato chutney and salad.

Steak Canton

Serves 4

500 g (1 lb) rump or boneless blade steak
3-4 cups prepared vegetables
1 tablespoon oil
2-3 tablespoons bottled stir fry sauce

Trim the steak and cut into thin strips. Prepare a selection of vegetables – spring onions (scallions), snow peas (mangetout), broccoli, red pepper (capsicum), baby corn, mushrooms, green beans. Slice or break into pieces as necessary. Heat the oil in a wok or deep frying pan. Add the vegetables and stir fry for 3 to 4 minutes, sprinkling in a little water to create steam. Remove to a bowl. Increase the heat, add the beef strips to the wok with a little more oil if needed and stir fry until the colour changes. Do not overcook. Return the vegetables to the wok and add stir fry sauce to taste. Toss over heat until the meat and vegetables are hot and serve with boiled noodles.

Beef and Tomato Flan

Serves 4 - 5

2 tablespoons finely chopped bacon pieces
1 medium-sized onion, chopped
1 tablespoon oil
500 g (1 lb) finely minced (ground) beef
2 tablespoons tomato paste
1 teaspoon Worcestershire sauce
½ teaspoon sugar
1 teaspoon garlic salt
freshly ground pepper
1 sheet ready-rolled shortcrust pastry
2 eggs
4 tablespoons sour cream
2 small tomatoes, sliced
oil
sugar
salt and pepper
1 tablespoon snipped chives

Put the bacon in a heated pan and cook until the fat runs and the bacon browns a little. Add the onion with the oil and cook gently until soft. Add the beef and stir over high heat to break up the lumps. Cook until the colour changes and the juices run. Stir in the tomato paste, Worcestershire sauce, sugar, garlic salt and pepper. Cook gently for 2 minutes, remove from the heat and cool.

Line a greased 20 cm (8 inch) flan dish with the pastry and trim the edge. Spread the meat over the pastry. Beat the eggs with the sour cream and pour evenly over the meat. Top with the sliced tomatoes, brush with oil and season lightly with sugar, salt and pepper.

Bake in a preheated moderately hot oven, 200°C (400°F/Gas 6), for 40 minutes, until set in the centre. Sprinkle with chives and serve hot or cold cut in wedges.

Regal Roast Beef

Serves 12

1 beef rib roast on the bone, 5-6 ribs
30 g (1 oz) butter
1 onion, finely chopped
1 ½ cups chopped mushrooms
½ cup (3 oz) chopped walnuts or pecans
155 g (5 oz) pâté de foie oil
½ teaspoon each salt, dry mustard and paprika
freshly ground pepper
½ cup (4 fl oz) red wine
½ cup (4 fl oz) stock

Stand the roast on a board. With a sharp pointed knife cut deep pockets into the meat from the top of the roast, just in front of each rib bone. Melt the butter in a pan, add the onion and mushrooms and cook gently until soft. Cool and combine with the nuts and pâté. Spoon the mixture into each pocket, pressing it down with the back of a teaspoon. Rub a little oil over the outside of the roast and sprinkle with a mixture of salt, spices and pepper.

Place the roast fat side up in a roasting dish with the ribs forming a natural rack. Cook in a moderate oven, 180°C (350°F/Gas 4), for 2½ hours for rare, 3 hours for medium, 3½ hours for well done. Check with a meat thermometer. When cooked remove to a platter, cover with foil and leave in a warm place for 20 minutes before carving. Drain the fat from the dish, dissolve the juices with red wine and stock and bring to the boil. Strain into a jug.

To carve, remove 2 rib bones by cutting around them with the point of a knife and slice across the grain of the meat. Remove other rib bones as required. Serve with boiled jacket potatoes, glazed carrots and a green vegetable.

Carpetbag Steaks

Serves 4 - 6

4-6 fillet (tenderloin) or rib eye steaks, cut 3 cm (1 ¼ inch) thick
12-18 oysters
lemon juice
freshly ground pepper
about 1 tablespoon firm butter
melted butter or oil

Cut a pocket into the side of each steak, making it as large as possible within the steak while keeping the opening small. Drain the oysters, sprinkle with lemon juice and pepper and place 3 oysters in each pocket with a small knob of butter. Secure the openings with toothpicks or fine metal skewers. Season with pepper.

Place the steaks on a grill (broiler) tray or barbecue grid and brush with melted butter. Grill (broil) or barbecue on high heat for 2 to 3 minutes on each side until sealed. Reduce the heat and cook for a further 3 to 5 minutes each side for rare or medium-rare steaks, a little longer for medium. Serve immediately.

Beef

Peppered Beef in Filo
Serves 8

8 fillet steaks (tenderloin), cut 3 cm (1¼ inch) thick
freshly ground pepper
1 tablespoon oil
15 g (½ oz) butter
2 tablespoons brandy
salt
16 sheets filo pastry
melted butter

Peppercorn Sauce
1½ tablespoons flour
¾ cup (6 fl oz) beef stock
⅓ cup (2 ½ fl oz) dry sherry
pinch of sugar
1 tablespoon drained green peppercorns
½ cup (4 fl oz) cream

Season the steaks with pepper. Heat the oil and butter in a large frying pan, add the steaks and cook on high heat for 1 minute each side to brown and seal. Pour the brandy over the steaks and ignite immediately. Shake the pan until the flames die down. Remove the steaks to a plate and leave until cool. Keep the pan juices aside.

When the steaks are cold, season lightly with salt if desired. Brush a sheet of filo pastry lightly with melted butter, top with another sheet and brush with butter. Fold in half to give almost a square of pastry. Brush with butter and place a steak in the centre. Bring up the 2 sides over the steak, double-fold across the top, fold in the corners and tuck the ends under. Place on a greased baking sheet and brush the top and sides with butter. Make the remaining packages in the same way. Bake in a preheated hot oven, 220°C (425°F/Gas 7), for 10 minutes for rare steak, 12 minutes for medium, 15 minutes for well done.

Peppercorn Sauce: Heat the pan in which the steaks were cooked until any moisture evaporates, leaving the fat. Add a little butter if necessary, and stir in the flour. Cook 1 minute, then stir in the stock, sherry and sugar, scraping up any brown sediment. Add the peppercorns and squash lightly with a fork. Stir in the cream and simmer for 1 minute. Spread the sauce in the centre of hot dinner plates and place a beef package on top. Serve with steamed asparagus or snow peas (mange-tout) and pumpkin balls.

Note: This recipe can be prepared ahead of time. Prepare the packages ready for baking, cover with foil and refrigerate. Make the sauce to the stage before adding the peppercorns, transfer to a bowl, cover and refrigerate. To finish, bring the packages to room temperature 1 hour before cooking; put the sauce into a saucepan, add the peppercorns and complete just before serving.

Beef Fillet with Avocado Béarnaise
Serves 6

1 eye fillet of beef (tenderloin), about 750 g (1 ¾ lb)
30 g (1 oz) butter
watercress

Avocado Béarnaise
½ cup (4 fl oz) dry white wine
2 tablespoons white vinegar
1 teaspoon dried tarragon
2 chopped spring onions (scallions)
2 cracked peppercorns
3 egg yolks
250 g (8 oz) soft butter, divided into 8 portions
1 tablespoon lemon juice
1 large ripe avocado

Trim the silver membrane from the fillet and tie at intervals with white string. Heat the butter in a large frying pan and lightly brown on all sides. Transfer to a rack set in a roasting dish and cook in a preheated hot oven, 200°C (400°F/Gas 6), for 30 minutes. Remove and leave to cool. Take off the string, wrap in foil and refrigerate until required. Fillet may be served within 2 hours, or stored for up to 2 days.

To serve, cut in 1 cm (½ inch) slices and arrange on a platter. Garnish with watercress sprigs and serve with the Avocado Béarnaise and salads.

Avocado Béarnaise: Put the wine, vinegar, tarragon, spring onions and peppercorns in a small pan and boil until reduced by half. Strain the liquid into a heatproof bowl and cool. Add the egg yolks and beat with a balloon whisk until light and fluffy. Stand the bowl in a wide pan of barely simmering (not boiling) water and beat with a whisk until light and fluffy. Whisk in a portion of the butter at a time, adding each lot as the previous amount is incorporated. The mixture will become thick and creamy. Remove the bowl from the water bath and whisk in the last piece of butter. Beat in the lemon juice and leave until cold. Purée the avocado flesh and mix into the sauce. Cover the sauce and leave at room temperature until required. The sauce should be made not more than 4 hours before serving.

Note: Eye fillet is the centre section cut from a full fillet and will have to be ordered ahead. If you order a full fillet, cut off tapered tip and cut off the butt (thick) end where the main eye muscle begins to taper into the other two muscles.

Toad-in-the-Hole

Serves 4

8 thick beef sausages
1 tablespoon beef dripping

Yorkshire Pudding Batter
1 cup (4 oz) flour
½ teaspoon salt
3 eggs
½ cup (4 fl oz) milk
about ½ cup (4 fl oz) water

Place oven shelf just above centre and preheat to 220°C (425°F/Gas 7). Separate the sausages and place in a baking dish with the dripping and heat in the oven until the dripping is very hot. Quickly pour in the prepared Yorkshire Pudding batter, return to the oven and cook on shelf just above centre for 25 to 35 minutes until batter is well risen, crisp and nicely browned. Time depends on size of dish and thickness of batter. Serve hot with rich brown gravy (a commercial gravy mix is fine) or tomato sauce and a green vegetable.

Yorkshire Pudding Batter: Make this at least 20 minutes before required. Sift the flour and salt into a bowl and add the eggs and milk. Beat with a balloon whisk until smooth, gradually adding some water to make a thin batter. Beat for 5 minutes, cover and leave for 20 minutes or so. Use as directed.

Blue Vein Cheese Roast

Serves 6 – 8

1½-2 kg (3-4 lb) piece Scotch fillet
seasonings to taste
1 x 250 g (8 oz) packet frozen spinach, thawed
2 medium-sized onions, finely chopped
125 g (4 oz) Australian blue vein cheese, cut into 1 cm (½ inch) sticks
30 g (1 oz) butter, melted

Trim the meat if necessary and make a lengthwise cut along the side to form a deep pocket. (Cut to within 2 cm (¾ inch) of the other side and the ends.) Sprinkle the inside with the seasonings. Squeeze the excess moisture from the spinach, loosen the leaves a little and spread into the pocket. Add the onions and blue vein cheese. Close the pocket and tie with white string at intervals of about 4 cm (1½ inch). Brush the meat all over with the melted butter, sprinkle with seasonings and place on a rack in a roasting pan. Bake for 20 minutes at 200°C (400°F/Gas 6), then reduce temperature to 180°C (350°F/Gas 4) and bake a further 1½ hours or until the meat is cooked as desired. As the meat is cooking, baste occasionally with pan juices. Serve with baked vegetables and beans.

Blue Vein Cheese Roast

Beef

Barbecue Beef Spare Ribs
Serves 6 - 8

2.5-3 kg (5-6 lb) beef spare ribs

Barbecue Sauce
1 large onion, grated
2 tablespoons oil
1 garlic clove, crushed
1 cup (8 fl oz) tomato sauce
2 tablespoons Worcestershire sauce
2 tablespoons brown vinegar
1 tablespoon soft brown sugar
½ cup (4 fl oz) apple cider

Trim some of the fat from the spare ribs and score the remaining fat with deep diagonal slashes. Place fat side up in a baking dish and cook in a hot oven, 200°C (400°F/Gas 6), for 40 minutes until lightly browned, turning after 20 minutes. Drain off any fat. Cover the dish with foil, shiny side down, and continue to cook in a moderate oven, 180°C (350°F/Gas 4), for a further hour until meat is fork tender. Remove the ribs from the dish, and if not required immediately, store in a covered container and refrigerate.

To finish the spare ribs, place on a barbecue grid over glowing coals and brush well with the sauce. Cook until well glazed and crisp, basting frequently with the sauce. Turn often with tongs. Heat the sauce in a pan at the side of the barbecue and serve any remaining sauce with the spare ribs. Serve with hot boiled rice or a rice salad and a platter of prepared salad vegetables.

Barbecue Sauce: Place the onion and oil in a saucepan and cook for 5 minutes. Add the garlic, cook a few seconds, then add the remaining ingredients. Cover and simmer for 15 minutes until thick. Cool and store in a sealed jar in the refrigerator until required.

Sausage Breakfast for One
[M]

2 thin sausages
1 small tomato, halved
1 egg

Prick the sausages well. Heat a small browning dish for 4 minutes on high. Add the sausages and tomato. Cook on high for 1 minute. Turn the sausages and tomato and break an egg into the dish. Prick the egg yolk twice with a skewer. Cook on high for 1 ½ minutes. Serve immediately.

Hamburgers
Serves 6

1 egg
1 medium-sized onion, grated
½ cup (2 oz) dry breadcrumbs
½ teaspoon salt
pepper to taste
1 tablespoon chopped parsley
500 g (1 lb) hamburger mince (ground beef) or finely minced (ground) beef

Beat the egg in a large bowl and stir in the onion, crumbs, seasoning and parsley. Stand for 5 minutes, then add the mince and mix lightly and thoroughly. Divide into 6 even portions and shape into thick patties 8 cm (3 inch) in diameter. Pan grill in a greased pan or cook under a hot grill (broiler) or on a barbecue until cooked to taste. A light brush of oil will assist browning if the mince is lean.

Serving suggestions
1. Serve cooked hamburgers in toasted, buttered buns with onion slices, lettuce, sliced tomato and beetroot, and sauce or pickles of your choice.
2. Split 3 buns, toast and butter them. Spread with tomato sauce and top each half with a hamburger. Add a slice of tomato and cheddar cheese. Grill (broil) until the cheese melts and serve with salad.
3. As for 2, topping hamburgers with sliced, canned pineapple instead of tomato, top with cheese and grill (broil). Garnish with pickled gherkins.
4. As for 2, topping hamburger with creamy mashed potato instead of tomato and cheese. Sprinkle with crumbled, crisply cooked bacon and grated cheese. Grill (broil) until the cheese melts.

Blue Cheese Steaks
Serves 6 - 8

6-8 rib eye steaks or 6-8 portions rump steak
200 g (6 ½ oz) blue vein cheese
2 tablespoons port
freshly ground pepper
melted butter

Ask for steaks from the rib end, not the neck end, so that the main eye muscle is as large as possible. Cut a deep pocket through the side of each steak, keeping the opening as small as possible. Mash the blue vein cheese and mix in the port. Insert into pockets and close with toothpicks. Season the steaks with pepper and brush with melted butter. Cook on a barbecue for about 3 minutes on each side or until cooked to taste. Serve with hot potato salad and a tossed mixed salad.

High Fibre Rissoles

Serves 4

½ cup (2 oz) quick-cooking rolled oats
1 onion, grated
1 medium-sized carrot, grated
2 tablespoons water
1 tablespoon skim milk powder
1 egg
grated rind of ½ lemon
1 tablespoon lemon juice
1 tablespoon chopped parsley
pinch of dried mixed herbs
½ teaspoon salt
freshly ground pepper
500 g (1 lb) finely minced (ground) lean beef
2 tablespoons wholemeal flour
2 tablespoons oil for frying

Place the oats in a mixing bowl with the remaining ingredients except the mince, flour and oil. Mix lightly and leave for 10 minutes, then add the beef and mix lightly and thoroughly to combine. Cover and stand for 15 minutes. Mix lightly and with moistened hands shape into 8 thick patties. Coat lightly with the flour.

Heat the oil in a large frying pan and cook the rissoles over medium heat 3 to 4 minutes on each side until cooked through. If desired the pan may be deglazed with ½ cup (4 fl oz) dry red wine and thickened with 1 teaspoon cornflour (cornstarch) mixed with a little cold water. Pour this sauce over the rissoles. Serve hot with vegetables of your choice.

Microgrill and Vegetables

Serves 1 [M]

2 lamb loin or chump chops or 1 portion rump steak
pepper to taste
1 small potato, halved
2 small pieces pumpkin
6-8 green beans, sliced
knob of butter

Trim the chops or steak and season with pepper. Place the vegetables with the butter in a medium-sized plastic freezer bag and place in the microwave oven, tucking the end of the bag loosely underneath the vegetables. Place the browning grill next to vegetables. Heat the grill and vegetables on high for 6 minutes. Remove the vegetables, leave in the bag and place on a plate, covering with foil. Heat the browning grill on high for a further 2 minutes. Add the meat and cook for 2 minutes on high, turning after 1 minute. Remove to a plate, turn the vegetables out of the bag and serve immediately.

Pizza Burgers

Serves 6

1 medium-sized onion, grated
½ cup (2 oz) dry breadcrumbs
1 egg
1 tablespoon tomato sauce
½ teaspoon dried oregano
1 tablespoon chopped parsley
½ teaspoon salt
freshly ground pepper
500 g (1 lb) finely minced (ground) beef
oil or butter
3 tomatoes, sliced
1 onion, sliced
1 green pepper (capsicum), seeded and sliced
6 hamburger buns
6 slices mozzarella cheese

Put the onion in a bowl with the crumbs, egg, sauce, herbs, salt and pepper. Mix well and leave for 10 minutes. Add the beef and mix lightly and thoroughly. Leave for 10 minutes then shape into 12 thin patties. Place on a tray, cover and chill until required.

Assemble the other ingredients, splitting the hamburger buns. Grease a heated barbecue hotplate with oil or butter and place patties on to cook. Place the tomato, onion and pepper slices onto the hotplate around the patties and put the buns, cut side down, around the edge to toast. Turn the patties and vegetables to complete cooking. Turn the buns right side up and place a cooked patty on each. Top with vegetable slices and cover each with a slice of cheese. Leave the buns around the side of the barbecue for a minute or so until the cheese begins to melt. If vegetables and patties are hot, there should be sufficient heat to melt the cheese. Serve with a tossed salad.

Salisbury Steaks

Serves 5 - 6

1 kg (2 lb) finely minced (ground) beef
1 packet French onion soup
2 tablespoons soy sauce
2 eggs
½ teaspoon garlic salt
dash of cayenne pepper
2 tablespoons snipped chives
oil or butter for cooking

Break up the mince in a bowl and add the dry soup mix with the remaining ingredients except the oil or butter. Mix lightly, leave for 10 minutes, then mix again lightly until thoroughly combined. Divide into 8 equal portions and shape each portion into a thick patty. Keep the hands moist to make shaping easier. Grease a barbecue hotplate with a little butter or oil, add the patties and cook for 5 to 6 minutes on each side. They should be slightly pink in the centre for maximum enjoyment. Serve with potato salad and a tossed mixed salad.

Beef

Barbecued Herbed Steaks

Serves 6 - 8

1-1.5 kg (2-3 lb) rib, oyster or bone-in blade steaks

Herb-wine Marinade
¾ cup (6 fl oz) red wine
3 spring onions (scallions), chopped
1-2 garlic cloves, crushed
1 tablespoon oil
2 tablespoons white vinegar
½ teaspoon dried rosemary
½ teaspoon dried thyme
1 tablespoon chopped parsley
freshly ground pepper
1 teaspoon soft brown sugar

If bone-in blade steaks are used, cut into serving portions if large. Mix the marinade ingredients in a large plastic container with a lid. Add the steaks, turn to coat, seal and refrigerate overnight or for up to 2 days. Shake the container occasionally to distribute the marinade.

To cook, drain the marinade into a small pan. Cook the steaks on a barbecue grid, brushing occasionally with the marinade. Turn with blunt-ended tongs so that the sealed surface is not pierced.

The remaining marinade may be thickened with a little cornflour (cornstarch) mixed with cold water and served as a sauce with the steaks.

Summer Loafers

Serves 4 - 6

1 slice middle-cut rump steak 3 cm (1 ¼ inch) thick
freshly ground pepper
French bread sticks or other bread accompaniments (*see below*)

Trim the steak and season with pepper. Cook under a heated grill (broiler) or on a barbecue for 12 to 16 minutes, turning with tongs. Remove to a carving board and carve at an angle in thin slices. Arrange on halved and lightly buttered bread sticks or thick slices of crusty bread with desired accompaniments.

Accompaniments: Select a combination from the following: crisp lettuce, sprouts, cucumber, tomato, mustards, horseradish, cress, herbs, onion, cottage or ricotta cheese, pickles, chutney, sliced orange, kiwifruit, apple, pear.

Open Steak Sandwiches

Serves 6 - 8

2 slices middle-cut rump steak
barbecue seasoning or steak spice
60 g (2 oz) butter
2 onions, sliced
6-8 medium-sized tomatoes, halved
250 g (8 oz) mushroom caps
2 tablespoons chopped chives
crisp lettuce leaves
sliced buttered rye or wholemeal bread

Slash the fat on the steak in 3 or 4 places. Sprinkle with barbecue seasoning or steak spice (available from spice section of supermarket) and place on the barbecue. Cook until done to taste, turning with tongs. While the steak is cooking, melt the butter in a large frying pan set on the barbecue and add the onions. Cook until transparent and push the rings to one side. Add the tomatoes, cut side down first, cook for 2 minutes then turn and push aside. Add the mushrooms and cook for 2 to 3 minutes. Sprinkle with chives and leave at the side of the barbecue until the steak is ready.

When steak is cooked, sprinkle again with seasoning if desired and lift onto carving board. Place lettuce leaves on the bread. Slice the steak into strips with the knife held at an angle and arrange on top of the lettuce. Garnish with some onion rings and serve with remaining onion rings, tomatoes and mushrooms. Provide a selection of mustards and barbecue sauces to be added to individual tastes.

Pepper Steaks

Serves 4 - 6

4-6 fillet (tenderloin) or rib eye steaks
1-1½ tablespoons cracked black peppercorns
30 g (1 oz) butter
2 tablespoons brandy
squeeze of lemon juice
⅓ cup (2 ½ fl oz) cream

Trim the steaks if necessary and coat lightly with the crushed peppercorns, pressing them in lightly with the heel of the hand. Leave for 10 minutes. Heat the butter in a frying pan until foaming subsides, add the steaks and cook on medium high for 3 to 5 minutes on each side until cooked to taste. Warm the brandy in a small pan, ignite and pour over the steaks. Shake the pan until the flames subside. Remove to a warm dish, sprinkle with lemon juice and keep warm.

Swirl the cream into the pan juices, adjust the seasoning and heat well. Pour over the steaks, and serve with boiled jacket potatoes, glazed carrots and steamed broccoli or asparagus.

Opposite: *Pepper Steaks*

73

Beef

Chinese Beef

Serves 4 [M]

500 g (1 lb) round, topside or blade steak
½ teaspoon bicarbonate of soda (baking soda)
1 tablespoon dry sherry
1 tablespoon cornflour (cornstarch)
½ cup (4 fl oz) strong beef stock
3 tablespoons bottled stir fry sauce
1 teaspoon sugar, optional
375 g (12 oz) prepared vegetables; snow peas (mange-tout), broccoli sprigs, red or green pepper (capsicum) pieces, onion leaves or spring onion (scallion) pieces, green beans, sliced mushrooms, baby corn
1 teaspoon grated fresh ginger
1 garlic clove, crushed
1 tablespoon oil

Cut the beef into very thin strips and place in a bowl. Mix in the soda, sherry and half the cornflour. Leave for 30 minutes. Mix the stock with the sauce, sugar if the sauce is not sweet, and the remaining cornflour. Prepare the vegetables or use a packet of frozen Chinese vegetables.

Place the ginger and garlic with the oil in a large casserole dish. Cook on high for 4 minutes, stirring once. Stir the liquid mixture and pour into the dish. Stir, cover and cook on high for 4 minutes, stirring occasionally, until thickened and boiling. Remove the cover and add vegetables. Stir, cover and cook on high for 6 minutes, stirring once. If using frozen vegetables, cook for only 3 minutes. Add the meat, stir well and cook uncovered for 6 minutes, stirring 3 or 4 times. Check that meat is cooked. Stand 3 minutes and serve with boiled or fried rice.

Steak Teriyaki

Serves 4 - 6

4-6 portions fillet (tenderloin) or boneless sirloin steak
1 garlic clove, crushed
½ cup (4 fl oz) teriyaki sauce
½ cup (4 fl oz) dry sherry
¼ cup (4 fl oz) light stock
1 teaspoon cornflour (cornstarch)
1 tablespoon oil

Trim the steaks. Mix the garlic with the sauce and sherry. Add the steaks, turn in the marinade and leave for 30 minutes. Drain the steaks. Mix the marinade in a small pan with the stock and cornflour and stir over heat until thickened. Leave to simmer gently. Heat the oil in a large frying pan or griddle. Add the steaks and cook on medium high until done to taste. Spoon some sauce over the steaks and serve immediately with the remaining sauce, boiled rice, and onion rings which can be cooked alongside the steaks.

Steaks Rosemary

Serves 4

4 fillet (tenderloin) or rib eye steaks
freshly ground pepper
ground rosemary
1 garlic clove, halved
30 g (1 oz) butter
¼ cup (2 fl oz) Madeira
1 tablespoon fresh rosemary leaves
2 teaspoons flour
¾ cup (6 fl oz) beef stock
squeeze of lemon juice
Potato Cakes (see below)

Sprinkle the steaks on both sides with pepper and a little ground rosemary. Leave aside for 15 minutes.

Rub a frying pan with the cut surfaces of the garlic. Add the butter and heat until the foaming subsides. Add the steaks and cook on medium high for 2 to 3 minutes on each side for rare, 4 minutes for medium, a little longer for well done. Add the Madeira to the pan and ignite immediately. Shake the pan until the flames die down. Remove the steaks to a warm dish.

Add the fresh rosemary to the pan and press well into the juices with a fork to extract the flavour. Stir in the flour, cook a few seconds, then add the stock and lemon juice and stir until bubbling. Place each steak on a hot Potato Cake, pour on the sauce and serve immediately with lightly cooked carrot and zucchini (courgette) strips.

Potato Cakes

Serves 4

2 large old potatoes, peeled
salt and pepper
30 g (1 oz) butter
2 tablespoons oil

Grate the potatoes coarsely and place in a sieve. Rinse under cold water and press out the moisture. Turn into a bowl and mix in salt and pepper to taste. Heat the butter and oil in a large frying pan and add potato in 4 mounds. Flatten with a spatula and cook 3 to 4 minutes on each side until brown and crisp. Drain on paper towels.

Brochettes Tropicana
Serves 6

750 g (1 ½ lb) rump
 or boneless blade steak
1 small pineapple
½ pawpaw (papaya)
2 firm bananas
3 kiwifruit

Tropical Fruit Baste
30 g (1 oz) butter
1 teaspoon curry powder
grated rind of 1 orange
1 tablespoon lime or lemon
 juice
⅓ cup (2 ½ fl oz) pineapple
 juice
⅓ cup (2 ½ fl oz) orange
 juice
1 tablespoon soft brown
 sugar

Trim the steak and cut into 2 cm (¾ inch) cubes. Peel the fruit and cut into chunky pieces. Thread the meat onto 6 skewers and the fruit onto another 6 skewers. Brush the meat with the baste and cook under a heated grill (broiler) or on a barbecue for 7 to 8 minutes, basting frequently. During the last 3 minutes of cooking, place the fruit skewers alongside the meat. Baste and cook until just heated through. Serve with rice pilaf tossed with coconut, sultanas and grated orange rind.
Tropical Fruit Baste: Melt the butter in a small pan, add the remaining ingredients and heat gently. Do not boil. Remove from heat.

Beefy Fried Rice
Serves 4 - 5

2 eggs
2 tablespoons cold water
salt
2 tablespoons oil
1 teaspoon grated fresh
 ginger
1 garlic clove, crushed
¼ cup chopped smoked
 beef or bacon
375 g (12 oz) finely minced
 (ground) beef
1 cup chopped spring
 onions (scallions)
½ cup chopped red pepper
 (capsicum)
4 cups cold boiled rice
1 ½ cups cooked green peas
2 tablespoons soy sauce
1 tablespoon dry sherry
bottled spicy plum and
 chilli sauces for serving

Beat the eggs lightly with the water and a pinch of salt. Heat half the oil in a large frying pan, add the eggs and cook until set. Remove to a plate, cut into small squares and keep aside.
 Add the remaining oil with the ginger, garlic and smoked beef and cook for 5 minutes. Add the minced beef and cook until the colour changes, stirring often to break up the lumps. When the liquid evaporates add the spring onions and red pepper. Cook for 2 to 3 minutes, then add the rice and peas. Cook, stirring often, until thoroughly heated. An egg lifter or Chinese stirrer is ideal for lifting and stirring the ingredients.
 Mix in the egg pieces and sprinkle in the soy sauce and sherry. Stir well and serve immediately in bowls. Serve the sauces separately.

Scotch Eggs
Serves 6

6 hard-boiled eggs,
 shelled
2 tablespoons seasoned
 flour
500 g (1 lb) sausage mince
1 tablespoon grated onion
1 tablespoon finely chopped
 parsley
1 tablespoon tomato sauce
2 tablespoons soft
 breadcrumbs
 (rub through a sieve)
1 egg, beaten with
 1 tablespoon milk
dry breadcrumbs to coat
oil for deep frying

Coat the eggs with seasoned flour. Combine the sausage mince with the onion, parsley, tomato sauce and soft breadcrumbs. Mix thoroughly and divide into 6 even portions. Shape a portion around each egg, enclosing it completely. Coat again with seasoned flour, brush with egg beaten with milk, and coat with dry breadcrumbs. Chill for 15 minutes.
 Deep fry the eggs in hot oil for 5 to 7 minutes. Do not fry too quickly, as the sausage mince must cook through without the coating browning too much. Serve hot or cold, sliced in halves, as a snack, picnic food or a meal with vegetables or salad.

Ginger Beef Skewers
Serves 4 - 5

2 thin slices topside steak,
 about 750 g (1 ½ lb)
⅓ cup (2 ½ fl oz) light
 soy sauce
1 tablespoon oil
1 tablespoon soft brown
 sugar
1 tablespoon dry sherry
1 teaspoon grated fresh
 ginger
1 garlic clove, crushed

Ask for second and third slice from the topside as these are more tender with little muscle separation. Cut into strips about 3 cm (1 ¼ inch) wide. Mix the remaining ingredients in a square plastic container. Add the meat strips and turn to coat. Seal and store in the refrigerator for several hours, shaking the container occasionally to distribute the marinade.
 Weave the strips onto flat metal skewers and place on a barbecue. Pour the marinade into a small pan. Barbecue the skewers for a minute or so on each side, basting with the marinade. Do not overcook or the meat will toughen. Serve immediately with boiled Chinese noodles, drained and tossed in a pan on the barbecue with some oil, marinade from meat, and sliced vegetables such as mushrooms, spring onions (scallions), celery and red peppers (capsicums).

Beef

Barbecued Sausages

Serves 6

1-1.5 kg (2-3 lb) thick beef sausages
water
plum or other fruity barbecue sauce

Place the sausages in a large saucepan, cover with cold water and place on low heat. Bring slowly to simmering point. Do not boil. Remove from the heat when the sausages are firm. Leave to cool in water, drain and refrigerate in a sealed container.

To cook, place on a barbecue and cook on medium heat until browned. Baste with sauce towards the end of cooking. Serve as they are or in the following ways:

Carpetbag Sausages: Slit the sausages down the centre and place 2 or 3 oysters in each slit. Pass around with napkins as finger food.

Mushroom Sausages: Cook sliced mushrooms in butter with a squeeze of lemon juice. Slit the sausages and fill with mushrooms. Serve on plates with other barbecued meats and vegetable accompaniments.

Sausage Rolls: Slit the sausages and fill with fruit chutney, barbecue or tomato sauce. Place in long buttered bread rolls with fried onion rings and salad ingredients, if desired.

Crunchy Sausage Sticks: Blunt the ends of butchers' skewers by rubbing points on a rough surface. Push a sausage onto the end of each skewer. Barbecue, basting towards the end of cooking with fruit sauce. When cooked, brush again with sauce and roll in crushed potato crisps to coat. Excellent food-in-the-hand for children.

Sausage and Pineapple Skewers: Peel and slice fresh pineapple and cut the slices in half, or use canned pineapple slices, halved. Thread a sausage crosswise onto 2 long metal skewers, passing them through each end. Pass the skewers crosswise through a halved slice of pineapple. Repeat until skewers are filled and prepare another 2 in the same way. The filled skewers will resemble a ladder. Place on a barbecue and baste with a mixture of ½ cup (4 fl oz) lemon or lime juice, ¼ cup (3 oz) honey, pinch of ground ginger and 1 tablespoon each of oil and light soy sauce. Turn and baste frequently while cooking.

Pasta with Summer Sauce

Serves 4 - 5

250 g (8 oz) sliced cold roast beef
250 g (8 oz) wholemeal pasta
1 ½ cups chopped, peeled tomatoes
¾ cup chopped pepper (capsicum)
½ cup chopped spring onions (scallions)
¼ cup (1 ½ oz) chopped black olives
2 tablespoons chopped fresh basil, optional
salt and pepper
2-3 tablespoons olive oil
chopped parsley
2-3 tablespoons grated Parmesan cheese

Trim any fat from the beef and cut the meat into thin strips. Cook the pasta in boiling water until just tender to the bite. While the pasta is cooking, heat the chopped tomatoes well in a saucepan. Stir in the chopped pepper, spring onions, olives, beef strips, basil, if used, and season to taste with salt and pepper. Remove from the heat.

Drain the pasta in a colander and return to the saucepan. Add the tomato-beef mixture, olive oil to taste, and about one tablespoon each of the parsley and Parmesan cheese. Toss well. The heat of the pasta warms the other ingredients. Serve immediately, sprinkled with additional parsley and cheese.

Sherried Beef Stew

Serves 4

750 g (1 ½ lb) boneless blade or round steak
15 g (½ oz) butter or oil
1 onion, chopped
2 tablespoons dry sherry
1 cup (8 fl oz) beef stock or vegetable water
1 carrot, sliced
1 small parsnip, cubed
2 tablespoons chopped parsley
salt
freshly ground pepper
6 small new potatoes, scrubbed and halved
4 zucchini (courgettes), sliced
chopped parsley

Trim the beef and cut into 2 cm (¾ inch) cubes. Heat the butter in a deep pan and brown the meat cubes quickly. Remove to a plate and keep aside. Reduce the heat, add the onion to the pan and cook on low heat until soft. Add the sherry and stock and stir well to lift the browned sediment. Return the beef to the pan with the carrot, parsnip and parsley and season to taste. Cover and simmer gently for 1 hour. Add the potatoes, cover and cook for 15 minutes, then add the zucchini and cook until the beef and vegetables are tender. Serve sprinkled with additional chopped parsley.

Fillet Steak with Four Peppers

Serves 6

6 fillet steaks (tenderloin), about 3 cm (1 ¼ inch) thick
1 tablespoon white peppercorns
1 tablespoon black peppercorns
1 tablespoon oil
30 g (1 oz) butter
2 tablespoons brandy
3 teaspoons flour
¾ cup (6 fl oz) beef stock
squeeze of lemon juice
about ½ cup (4 fl oz) cream
1 teaspoon drained green peppercorns
1 teaspoon drained pink peppercorns
salt, optional

Trim the fillet steaks, removing any visible silver skin and fat. Mix the white and black peppercorns and crush coarsely. Coat the steaks lightly on each side with the peppercorns and press into meat. Heat the oil and butter in a large frying pan and sauté the steaks on medium high heat for 3 to 5 minutes on each side until cooked to taste. Pour the brandy over and ignite. Shake the pan until the flames die down, then remove the steaks to a warm dish.

Pour off the excess fat and sprinkle the flour into the pan. Stir well with a fork and add the stock, stirring constantly until lightly thickened and bubbling. Stir in the lemon juice and cream and boil gently for a few minutes to reduce. Add the green and pink peppercorns and mash lightly with a fork, add salt to taste if desired and serve the sauce with the steaks.

Note: To prevent the pepper flavour overpowering the meat and sauce, do not pepper the steaks ahead of time, and add green and pink peppercorns just before serving the sauce.

Chinese Sizzling Steak

Serves 4

2 thin slices round steak, about 500 g (1 lb)
½ teaspoon bicarbonate of soda (baking soda)
2 teaspoons water
4 small onions
2 tablespoons oil
1 garlic clove, crushed
1 teaspoon grated fresh ginger
⅓ cup (2 ½ fl oz) plum sauce
1 tablespoon Worcestershire sauce
1 tablespoon soy sauce
1 tablespoon dry sherry

Trim the fat from the steak and cut the meat into pieces about 3 cm (1 ¼ inch) square (some will be triangular in shape). Flatten the steak pieces between 2 sheets of plastic wrap and place in a bowl. Mix the soda with the water, pour over the steak and mix thoroughly. Leave for 30 minutes.

Peel the onions, cut out the roots, then cut into quarters and separate the segments. Put a cast iron sizzle plate onto a hotplate or burner to heat gently. Heat half the oil in a frying pan and add the steak pieces. Brown quickly on each side and transfer to a plate. Add the onions and remaining oil to the pan and stir fry quickly until the edges brown (the onions should remain crisp). Remove to another plate, leaving the oil in the pan.

Add the garlic and ginger to the pan. Cook for a few seconds, then stir in the sauces. When boiling, return the meat to the pan and toss over the heat until the slices are glazed. Place the onions on hot sizzle plate. Remove the plate from the heat, and place into the wooden holder. Top with the meat, pour the sherry over to sizzle and serve immediately with boiled rice and lightly cooked Chinese-style vegetables.

Pasta with Summer Sauce

Beef

Samosa with Meat Filling
Makes about 48

1 large onion, finely chopped
15 g (1 oz) butter or oil
2 garlic cloves, crushed
2 teaspoons grated fresh ginger
¼-½ teaspoon chilli powder
1 teaspoon ground coriander
½ teaspoon ground turmeric
500 g (1 lb) finely minced (ground) beef
½ cup (4 fl oz) water
salt and pepper
2 tablespoons chopped fresh coriander leaves or mint
1 teaspoon garam masala
1 tablespoon lemon juice
8 sheets filo pastry or 12 large spring roll wrappers
oil for deep frying

Cook the onion gently in the butter until transparent. Add the garlic, ginger, chilli powder to taste, coriander and turmeric and cook for a further minute. Increase the heat, add the meat and cook over high heat, stirring to break up the lumps. When the colour changes reduce the heat, add the water and salt and pepper to taste. Cover and simmer gently for 15 minutes. Add the coriander and garam masala and cook, uncovered, until most of the liquid evaporates. Stir in the lemon juice and leave until cool.

Cut the filo sheets into strips about 6 cm (2 ½ inch) wide, stack and cover. Place a generous spoonful of filling at the base of each strip and bring the bottom of the pastry across the filling to line up with one side. Make a straight fold up, then fold across to the other side of the strip. Continue folding the triangle to the end of the strip. Lightly brush the end of the strip with water and complete the fold. Place fold side down onto a cloth and cover while shaping remaining triangles.

Heat the oil and fry **5-6** samosa at a time, turning to brown evenly. Remove with a draining spoon and drain on paper towels. Cooked samosa may be kept warm in a slow oven. Serve hot with chutney for dipping.

Crockpot Apricot Beef
Serves 6

1 kg (2 lb) boneless shin (gravy) beef
2 tablespoons seasoned flour
1 onion, grated
1 ¼ cups (10 fl oz) apricot nectar
¼ cup (1 oz) dried apricots
2 teaspoons soft brown sugar
2 tablespoons tomato sauce
2 teaspoons Worcestershire sauce
1 tablespoon brown vinegar
¼ teaspoon ground cinnamon
2 teaspoons curry powder

Cut the beef into 2 cm (1 ¾ inch) cubes and toss in seasoned flour to coat. Place in a crockpot or slow cooker with the remaining ingredients. Cover and cook on low for 7 to 8 hours, or high for 4 to 5 hours until the meat is very tender. Serve with boiled brown rice and a green vegetable or salad.

To cook in oven: Place the flour-coated beef in a casserole dish with the remaining ingredients, cover and cook in a moderately slow oven, 160°C (325°F/Gas 3), for 2 to 2 ½ hours until tender.

Steak Diane
Serves 2

2 fillet steaks (tenderloin) about 3 cm (1 ¼ inch) thick
freshly ground pepper
30 g (1 oz) butter
2 teaspoons Worcestershire sauce
2 garlic cloves, finely chopped
2 tablespoons chopped parsley

Flatten each steak between 2 pieces of plastic wrap until very thin. Season with pepper. Have the remaining ingredients prepared and on hand.

Heat the butter in a large frying pan and when the foam subsides add the Worcestershire sauce. Add the steaks. Cook on high heat for 1 minute, sprinkle garlic and parsley over the steaks, then turn and cook for another minute. Remove to two warm plates and pour the butter and garlic mixture from the pan over the steaks. Serve immediately with steamed asparagus or zucchini (courgettes), glazed carrot straws and boiled new potatoes tossed with chives.

Note: If more than 2 serves are required, the first 2 steaks can be kept warm in a low oven for a short while, or use a second frying pan. Double or triple the ingredients as necessary.

Frypan Moussaka

Serves 5 - 6

1 large onion, chopped
1 tablespoon oil
1 garlic clove, crushed
750 g (1 ½ lb) finely minced (ground) lean beef
⅓ cup (2 ½ fl oz) red wine
3 tablespoons tomato paste
¼ teaspoon ground cinnamon
1 teaspoon sugar
2 tablespoons chopped parsley
salt and pepper to taste
3 medium-sized potatoes, peeled
4-5 zucchini (courgettes)
5 slices processed cheddar cheese
1 tablespoon grated Parmesan cheese

Cook the onion in oil until soft in a 23-25 cm (8-10 inch) frying pan with a lid. Add the garlic, increase the heat and add the mince. Stir over high heat to break up the mince and cook until the colour changes. Reduce the heat to medium low and add the wine, tomato paste, cinnamon, sugar, parsley and season to taste. Cover and simmer for 15 minutes.

Cut the potatoes into 6 mm (¼ inch) slices. Trim the zucchini and cut lengthwise into slices. When meat is cooked, remove to a bowl. In the same pan, place a layer of potato slices on the base, top with half the mince and spread the zucchini over this. Spread the remaining mince on top and cover with the remaining potatoes. Cover and cook on low heat for 20 minutes until the potato is tender. Place the cheese slices on top and sprinkle with Parmesan. Cover and cook for 2 to 3 minutes until the cheese melts. Stand for 5 minutes then cut into wedges and serve with a tossed salad.

Bolognese Sauce

Serves 5 - 6

500 g (1 lb) coarsely minced (ground) beef
1 large onion, chopped
1 carrot, grated
½ cup chopped red pepper (capsicum)
1 garlic clove, crushed
1 cup chopped mushrooms
1 x 425 g (13 ½ oz) can tomatoes, chopped
¼ cup (2 fl oz) red wine
⅓ cup (2 ½ fl oz) tomato paste
½ teaspoon dried basil
1 tablespoon chopped parsley
1 teaspoon sugar
seasoning to taste

Heat a heavy pan and add the mince. Stir over high heat to break up the lumps. Cook until the juices evaporate and the meat begins to brown. Drain off the fat. Add the onion, carrot and red pepper, reduce the heat and cook, stirring occasionally, for 10 minutes. Add the garlic and mushrooms and cook for 5 minutes. Add the remaining ingredients. Cover and simmer on low heat for 30 minutes. Serve with boiled spaghetti and grated Parmesan cheese.

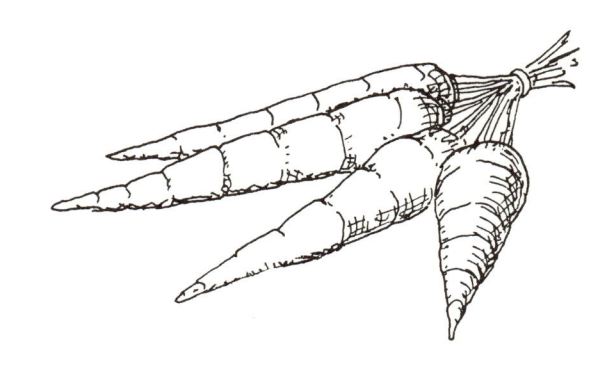

Cranberry Corned Beef

Serves 5 - 6 for 2 meals

1 piece corned silverside, about 2 kg (4 lb)
1 teaspoon whole allspice
2 tablespoons soft brown sugar
2 tablespoons brown vinegar
3 cloves
½ orange

Cranberry Glaze

¾ cup (6 fl oz) fresh orange juice
⅓ cup (4 oz) cranberry jelly or sieved cranberry sauce
2 tablespoons julienne shreds of orange rind

Rinse the corned beef in cold water and place in a large saucepan. Cover with warm water and add the allspice, sugar and vinegar. Insert the cloves into the orange half and add to the pan. Cover, bring to a slow simmer and cook for 2 hours, timing from simmering point. Remove the pan from the heat and leave for 15 minutes.

Remove the joint and place in a roasting dish, fat side up. Pour the orange juice over the beef and spread the cranberry jelly or sieved sauce over the fat. Cook in a moderate oven, 180°C (350°F/Gas 4), for 30 minutes, basting occasionally with juice. Take care not to displace the topping. While the beef cooks, blanch the orange shreds in boiling water to cover for 5 minutes, drain and reserve.

To serve, place the corned beef on a platter and top with shreds of orange rind. Slice and serve hot with mustard and vegetables of your choice.

Note: Cold corned beef can be sliced thinly and rolled up with a filling of ricotta cheese with fruit chutney to taste and white seedless grapes. Serve the rolls with salad or as a packed lunch.

Beef

Baked Dinner for Two
Serves 2 with meat left over [M]

1 thick skirt (flank) steak, about 500 g (1 lb)
1 rasher bacon, chopped
2 spring onions (scallions), chopped
2 teaspoons chopped parsley
¼ teaspoon mixed dried herbs
lemon pepper
2 slices wholemeal bread, crusts removed
butter or margarine
pepper
oil
6 vegetable pieces (potato, sweet potato, pumpkin)
stock

Lightly score one side of the steak into diamonds and turn upside down on a board. Place the bacon in a bowl and cook on high for 1 minute. Mix in the spring onions and herbs. Season the steak with lemon pepper and sprinkle on half the bacon and spring onions. Lightly spread each side of the bread slices with butter and place side by side along the steak. Sprinkle the remaining bacon and spring onions on top and roll up lengthwise. Secure with wooden toothpicks or white string. Season the roll with pepper and brush with oil. Brush oil on the vegetable pieces. Heat a browning grill on high for 6 minutes. Add the beef and vegetable pieces and cook for 4 minutes on high. Turn the roll during this time to brown it evenly, and turn the vegetable pieces once. Reduce to medium and cook for 12 minutes, turning the meat and vegetables once during cooking. For well-done beef, cook for 14 minutes. Remove to a plate, cover with foil and stand for 5 minutes. Dissolve the browned juices on the grill with the stock, pour into a bowl and make gravy. Remove the string or picks and cut the meat into thick slices to serve.

Mini Meat Loaves
Serves 5 - 6

1 packet French onion soup or brown onion sauce mix
⅓ cup (1 ½ oz) dry breadcrumbs
⅔ cup (5 fl oz) evaporated milk
1 tablespoon chopped parsley
500 g (1 lb) finely minced (ground) beef

Place the dry soup or sauce mix in a bowl with the crumbs, evaporated milk and parsley. Mix well and leave for 5 minutes. Add the mince and mix lightly and thoroughly until combined. Grease 12 deep muffin or patty pans with oil and lightly pack the meat mixture into them, mounding it over the tops of the pans. Brush the tops with oil and bake at 180°C (350°F/Gas 4) for 25 minutes.

Beef Pizza
Serves 4 - 6

½ pack (1 loaf) frozen bread dough or 2 Lebanese pita bread
2 tablespoons oil
500 g (1 lb) finely minced (ground) beef
1 ¼ cups (10 fl oz) bottled tomato spaghetti sauce
1 cup chopped green pepper (capsicum)
1 cup sliced mushrooms
1 onion, sliced and separated into rings
2 tablespoons (1 oz) sliced, stuffed olives
2 cups (8 oz) shredded mozzarella cheese

Thaw the frozen bread dough or have ready 2 large cooked pita bread. Heat 1 tablespoon of the oil in a frying pan. Add the beef and cook on high heat, stirring to break up the lumps. When the meat begins to brown, drain off the fat and keep the meat aside.

Divide the thawed bread dough into two and shape into balls. Roll out to fit 2 greased 30 cm (12 inch) pizza pans. If using pita bread, place these on a lightly greased baking sheet. Spread the tomato spaghetti sauce on the dough or bread and sprinkle the minced beef on top. Toss the green pepper, mushrooms, onion rings and olives with the remaining oil and scatter over the mince. Top with the shredded cheese. Bake in a preheated hot oven, 220°C (425°F/Gas 7), for 12 to 15 minutes until the top is bubbly and the crust is golden (if bread dough is used as the base). Serve in wedges.

Mini Meat Loaves

Beef Wellington

Serves 4 - 5

1 butt fillet (tenderloin), about 750 g (1¾ lb)
freshly ground pepper
15 g (½ oz) butter
1 tablespoon oil
2 tablespoons brandy
¼ cup chopped spring onions (scallions)
1 cup sliced mushrooms
1 x 375 g (12 oz) packet puff pastry
60 g (2 oz) pâté de fois
beaten egg

Trim the visible silver skin and fat from the fillet without separating the muscles. Tie at intervals with white string to keep in shape and season with pepper. Heat the butter and oil in a frying pan and brown the fillet quickly on all sides. Warm the brandy in a small pan, ignite and pour over the fillet. Spoon the juices over the fillet until the flames die down and remove meat to a rack set in a dish. Leave until cold. Add the spring onions to the pan and cook for 1 minute. Add the mushrooms and cook until the juices evaporate. Set aside.

Roll out the pastry to 3 mm (⅛ inch) thick. Trim to a rectangle and reserve the trimmings. Remove the strings from the fillet and place towards one side of the pastry. Spread the top of the meat with the pâté and press the spring onion and mushroom mixture on top. Fold the pastry over the fillet, tucking the ends under. Moisten the pastry edges to seal. Place on a greased baking sheet and decorate with a rose and leaves cut from the pastry trimmings. Secure in place with a little water. Glaze with the beaten egg and cook in a preheated hot oven at 220°C (425°F/Gas 7) for 30 minutes or until golden brown. This time gives rare beef; for medium beef, cook for a further 5 minutes. Carve in thick slices and serve with steamed asparagus and sautéed mushrooms.

Steak Rolls Teriyaki

Serves 4 - 5

2 thick skirt (flank) steaks, each about 500 g (1 lb)
1 garlic clove, crushed
1 teaspoon grated fresh ginger
¼ cup (2 fl oz) dry sherry
2 tablespoons soy sauce
3 teaspoons sugar
pepper to taste
1 tablespoon oil
1 large carrot
12 green beans
4 spring onions (scallions)
1 packet frozen spinach, thawed
¾ cup (6 fl oz) hot beef stock
2 teaspoons cornflour (cornstarch)

Ask for flank skirt steaks, the ones almost oval in shape. Lightly score one side of each steak into diamonds. Mix the garlic, ginger, sherry, soy sauce, sugar, pepper and oil in a flat dish. Add the steaks and turn to coat. Marinate for 1 hour. Scrape the carrot and cut into strips; top and tail the beans; trim the spring onions to the same length as the beans and slit in halves. Parboil the carrot and beans for 4 minutes and drain. Drain the thawed spinach.

Drain the steaks and place scored side down on a board. Retain the marinade. Spread the spinach over the meat and arrange the other vegetables on top lengthwise with the grain of the steak. Roll each up lengthwise. Secure with poultry skewers or tie with string. Place the rolls in a greased baking dish and brush with marinade. Cook in a moderate oven at 180°C (350°F/Gas 4) for 45 minutes for medium beef, or 55 minutes for well done. Turn occasionally to brown evenly.

Remove the rolls to a platter, cover with foil and keep warm. Add the reserved marinade to a pan with the hot stock. Stir over heat to dissolve the juices. Boil and thicken with the cornflour mixed with a little cold water. Remove the skewers or ties from the rolls, slice and serve with the sauce, boiled rice and some lightly steamed snow peas (mange-tout) or broccoli.

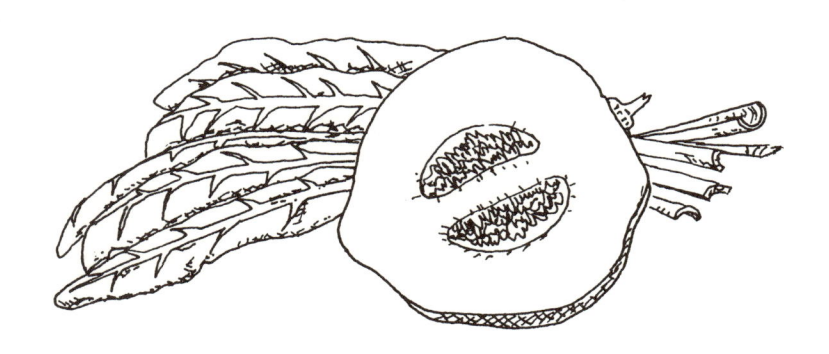

Beef

Satays with Peanut Sauce

Serves 6 - 8

1 kg (2 lb) boneless blade or round steak (first cuts)
2 tablespoons soy sauce
1 garlic clove, crushed
1 teaspoon ground coriander
½ teaspoon ground cumin
1 tablespoon soft brown sugar
grated rind of 1 lemon
2 teaspoons lemon juice
2 tablespoons canned coconut milk
⅛ teaspoon chilli powder
1 teaspoon sesame seeds, optional

Peanut Sauce

1 onion, finely chopped
1 chilli, seeded and chopped
2 teaspoons oil
1 garlic clove, crushed
½ cup (4 oz) crunchy peanut butter
2 teaspoons soy sauce
2 teaspoons sugar
½ cup (4 fl oz) coconut milk

Cut the beef into 2 cm (¾ inch) cubes. Mix the remaining ingredients in a glass bowl, add the beef and stir well. Cover and leave to marinate at room temperature for 1 hour, or in the refrigerator for 2 hours or overnight. Stir occasionally. Soak bamboo skewers in cold water for 1 hour at least.

Thread 6–8 meat cubes onto the ends of the skewers and cook under a hot grill (broiler) or on a barbecue, turning often and basting with any remaining marinade. Serve with Peanut Sauce, boiled rice and salad.

Peanut Sauce: Place the onion and chilli in a pan with the oil and cook until softened. Add the garlic, cook a few seconds and stir in the peanut butter, soy sauce, sugar and coconut milk. Remove from the heat and thin down with more coconut milk and water if necessary to make thick or thin Peanut Sauce as desired. Serve hot or cold.

Smoked Beef Carbonara

Serves 4 - 5

375 g (12 oz) pasta
250 g (8 oz) sliced smoked beef
30 g (1 oz) butter
2 garlic cloves, crushed
⅓ cup (2 ½ fl oz) cream
½ teaspoon paprika
chilli pepper, optional
2 eggs
¼ cup chopped parsley
⅓ cup (1 ½ oz) grated Parmesan cheese
pepper to taste

Choose tagliatelle, fettucine noodles or spaghetti and cook in boiling, salted water until al dente, that is, firm to the bite. While the pasta is cooking, prepare the other ingredients as speed is essential in the final assembly of the dish.

Cut the smoked beef into strips. Heat the butter in a frying pan, add garlic and beef strips and cook on medium low for 2 to 3 minutes. Stir in the cream, paprika and a light sprinkling of chilli pepper, if used. Bring to the boil and remove from the heat.

Break the eggs into a bowl and beat with a fork. Beat in the parsley, cheese and pepper to taste. Keep aside.

When the pasta is cooked, drain in a colander and return to the saucepan. Bring the smoked beef mixture back to the boil and pour over the hot pasta with the egg and cheese mixture. Toss well and serve immediately with additional grated Parmesan cheese. The heat of the pasta sets the egg lightly. Carbonara should not be reheated.

Note: When purchasing smoked beef, ask for medium thick slices.

Peppered Steak and Peaches

Serves 6

1 x 1 kg (2 lb) whole beef fillet
1 x 425 g (13 ½ oz) can sliced peaches, drained, juice reserved
15 g (½ oz) butter
1 tablespoon green peppercorns
2 tablespoons flour
½ cup (4 fl oz) light sour cream

Make a slit in the beef and fill with the peaches. Bake at 180°C (350°F/Gas 4) for 50 to 60 minutes. Remove the meat to a serving tray and keep warm. Melt the butter with the meat juices and cook the peppercorns for 2 minutes. Add the flour and cook for 1 minute. Add the peach juice and stir until smooth and thickened. Add a little water if too thick. Stir in the sour cream and heat without boiling. Cut the beef into 6 steaks and serve with the sauce poured over. Accompany with potatoes, parsley, pumpkin and broccoli.

Beer Casserole

Serves 4

3 kg (1 ½ lb)) round steak
125 g (4 oz) butter or margarine
2 medium-sized onions, sliced
2 tablespoons brown malt vinegar
3 tablespoons flour
1 ¼ cups (10 fl oz) water
1 beef stock cube
1 x 375 ml (12 fl oz) can or bottle beer
2 teaspoons sugar
1 bay leaf
2 tablespoons chopped parsley
½ teaspoon dried thyme
salt and pepper

Remove any excess fat from the steak and cut into large serving-sized pieces. Pound with a meat mallet until thin.

Heat the butter in a pan and fry the steak until well browned on both sides. Sprinkle with pepper and remove the steak from the pan. Add the onions to the remaining butter in the pan. Cook, stirring, until the onions are brown. Remove from the pan. Add the flour to the pan with the vinegar, water, crumbled stock cube, and beer. Continue stirring until the gravy is smooth and thickened. Add the sugar, bay leaf, parsley, thyme, and salt and pepper to taste.

Return the steak and onions to the pan. Cover and simmer gently until the steak is tender. Remove the bay leaf before serving.

Steak Rolls in Curry Sauce

Serves 4

3 kg (1 ½ lb) topside steak, thinly sliced
375 g (12 oz) sausage mince
⅓ cup (1 ½ oz) seasoned flour
90 g (3 oz) butter
2 large onions, sliced
2 beef stock cubes
3 cups (24 fl oz) boiling water
2 teaspoons curry powder
½ cup (4 fl oz) milk
salt and pepper

Pound the steaks until very thin. Cut into oblong pieces and place approximately 1½ tablespoons of sausage mince on each piece. Roll up and secure with toothpicks. Coat in seasoned flour.

Melt the butter and fry the steak rolls and onions until lightly browned. Drain off the excess fat. Dissolve the beef cubes in boiling water. Add the curry powder and milk. Pour over the steak rolls and stir well. Bring to the boil, cover and reduce the heat. Simmer for 1 hour or until tender, stirring occasionally. Season to taste. Serve with hot rice.

Smoked Beef Carbonara

Beef

Corned Beef Orana

Serves 10 - 12

2 kg (4 lb) piece corned silverside	small pinch of ground cloves
warm water to cover	¼ cup (2 fl oz) dry red wine
2 tablespoons soft brown sugar	¾ cup (6 fl oz) water
2 tablespoons malt vinegar	2-3 tablespoons sugar
2 cups (12 oz) pitted fresh cherries	thin strip of lemon rind
	1 teaspoon lemon juice
	1 tablespoon arrowroot

Rinse the corned beef, place in a boiler or slow cooker and cover with warm water. Add the brown sugar and vinegar. Cover, bring to a slow simmer, and simmer gently for 2 hours. If using a slow cooker, cook on low for 7 to 8 hours, on high for 4 to 6 hours (check manual for cooking times as appliances vary). When cooked, cool completely in the liquid, drain and store in a sealed container in the refrigerator until required for serving.

Place the cherries in a stainless steel or enamel saucepan with the cloves, wine, water, 2 tablespoons of the sugar and the lemon rind. Bring slowly to the boil then cover and simmer gently for 15 minutes or until the cherries are just tender. Remove the lemon rind. Mix the lemon juice with the arrowroot and a little cold water and stir into the simmering cherries until thickened and bubbling. Adjust the flavour with a little more sugar if necessary. (The flavour should be pleasantly sweet-sour.) Pour into a bowl and cool, stirring occasionally.

When ready to serve, trim the fat from the beef until a thin layer remains and place on a serving platter. Spoon some of the cooled cherry sauce on top and garnish with watercress sprigs, little bunches of cherries and lemon slices. Serve the remaining cherry sauce separately.

Note: When fresh cherries are not available, heat the contents of a 425 g (13 ½ oz) can of pitted cherries with the wine, ground cloves and lemon rind. When boiling remove the lemon rind and thicken with arrowroot, adding a little lemon juice to the sauce.

Reuben Sandwich

sliced rye bread, buttered	caraway seeds, optional
thinly sliced pastrami or corned silverside	sliced or shredded Emmenthal cheese
sauerkraut	dill pickles for serving

Top the buttered rye bread with thin slices of pastrami or corned beef. Rinse and drain the sauerkraut well if desired, and mix in a few caraway seeds if used. Pile onto the meat and top with sliced or shredded cheese. Place under a hot grill (broiler) for a few seconds to melt the cheese and top with another slice of buttered rye. Serve with dill pickles.

Ox Tongue with Cumberland Sauce

Serves 6 - 8

1 corned ox tongue	½ teaspoon whole peppercorns
½ cup (4 fl oz) white wine	
1 orange, sliced	
1 tablespoon soft brown sugar	

Cumberland Sauce

2 tablespoons julienne shreds of orange rind	½ cup (4 fl oz) orange juice
1 tablespoon julienne shreds of lemon rind	¼ cup (2 fl oz) port
½ cup (5 oz) redcurrant jelly	1 teaspoon dry mustard
	3 teaspoons arrowroot
	2 tablespoons lemon juice

Rinse the tongue in cold water and place in a large pan with the wine and warm water to cover, the sliced orange, sugar and peppercorns. Cover, bring to a slow simmer and continue to simmer gently for 3 to 4 hours until tender. Remove the tongue to a bowl of cold water just long enough to cool the outside, then tear off the outer skin and remove the gristle and small bones from the root end. Return the tongue to the cooking liquid to cool completely, then drain and refrigerate in a sealed container. Serve thinly sliced with Cumberland Sauce and salads.

Cumberland Sauce: Put the orange and lemon shreds in a small pan, cover with cold water and bring to the boil. Boil for 3 minutes and drain off water. Add the jelly, orange juice, port and mustard. Stir over moderate heat until the jelly melts. Mix the arrowroot with the lemon juice and stir into the pan. Stir constantly until thickened and bubbling. Cool, stirring occasionally, and serve at room temperature. This sauce goes with any corned meat.

Beef Olives

Serves 4

750 g (1 ½ lb) minute steaks (topside or silverside)
freshly ground pepper
15 g (½ oz) butter or oil
1 onion, chopped
1 carrot, diced
½ cup sliced celery
¼ cup (2 fl oz) dry red wine
½ cup (4 fl oz) light stock
bouquet garni

Herb Stuffing:
¼ cup chopped spring onions (scallions)
1 ½ cups (3 oz) soft breadcrumbs
1 tablespoon chopped parsley
1 teaspoon chopped fresh thyme
grated rind and juice of ½ lemon
salt and pepper
1 small egg, beaten

Cut the steaks in half if large. Spread a tablespoon of Herb Stuffing on each piece. Roll up and secure with toothpicks or white string. Season with pepper. Heat the butter in a pan, brown the rolls on all sides and remove to a plate. Reduce the heat, add the vegetables to the pan, cover and cook gently until softened. Return the rolls to the pan and add the wine, stock and bouquet garni. Cover and simmer gently for 1 hour until tender.

Transfer the rolls to a dish, remove the toothpicks or string, cover and keep warm. Discard the bouquet garni and purée the vegetables with the juices. Return to the pan to heat thoroughly and season to taste. Pour over the rolls and serve with mashed potatoes and a green vegetable.

Herb Stuffing: Mix the stuffing ingredients lightly, adding the lemon juice and seasoning to taste and enough beaten egg to bind.

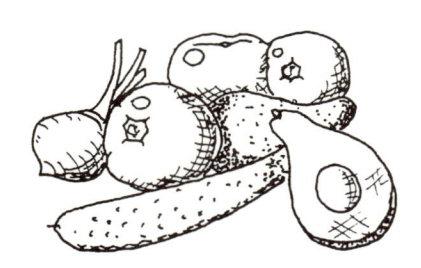

Economical Beef Stroganoff

Serves 4 - 5

750 g (1 ½ lb) round, topside or boneless blade steak
30 g (1 oz) butter
1 onion, chopped
185 g (6 oz) mushrooms, sliced
1 cup (8 fl oz) beef stock
2 teaspoons Worcestershire sauce
pinch of ground nutmeg
salt
freshly ground pepper
3 teaspoons cornflour (cornstarch)
½ cup (4 fl oz) sour cream

Trim the meat and cut into thin strips. Heat half the butter in a frying pan, add the meat and brown quickly on high heat. Remove to a plate. Reduce the heat and add remaining butter to the pan with the onion. Cook on low heat until soft, add the mushrooms and cook until their moisture runs out. Stir in the stock and return the beef to the pan. Add the sauce, nutmeg and salt and pepper to taste. Cover and simmer gently for 1 hour or until meat is tender. Mix the cornflour to a paste with a little cold water and pour gradually into the simmering stew, stirring constantly. When thickened and bubbling, stir in the sour cream and heat gently. Serve with boiled rice or noodles and a tossed salad.

Chilli Beef and Beans

Serves 4 - 5

600 g (1 ¼ lb) boneless blade or skirt steak
1 tablespoon oil
1 large onion, chopped
2 garlic cloves, crushed
1 cup chopped peeled tomatoes
2 tablespoons tomato paste
1 cup (8 fl oz) beef stock
2 teaspoons Mexican style chilli powder
1 teaspoon soft brown sugar
1 x 440 g (14 oz) can white (cannellini style) beans
½ cup chopped red pepper (capsicum)

Trim the meat and cut into 2 cm (¾ inch) cubes. Heat the oil in a saucepan, add the beef and brown on all sides. Remove to a plate, leaving the oil in the pan. Add the onion with the garlic and cook gently until soft. Stir in the tomatoes, tomato paste, stock, chilli powder and sugar. Return the beef to the pan, cover and simmer gently for 1 ¼ hours. Add the beans and some of their liquid if necessary, and the red pepper. Cover and simmer for 15 to 20 minutes until the beef is tender. Serve with crusty bread and a side salad.

Note: Take care that the chilli powder is the blended chilli powder used for Chilli con Carne, not the pure hot chilli powder. If the hot one is the only one available, use ¼ to ½ teaspoon and add ½ teaspoon each dried oregano, cumin and coriander.

Beef

Steak and Kidney Pie
Serves 6

1 kg (2 lb) chuck steak
4 lamb kidneys or 250 g (8 oz) veal or beef kidney
¼ cup (1 oz) flour
salt and freshly ground pepper
30 g (1 oz) butter or 1 tablespoon oil
1 large onion, chopped
¾ cup (6 fl oz) beef stock
¼ cup (2 fl oz) red wine
2 teaspoons Worcestershire sauce
2 tablespoons chopped parsley
1 x 375 g (12 oz) packet puff pastry

Trim the steak and cut into 2 cm (¾ inch) cubes. Halve the kidneys and remove the fatty core with kitchen scissors. Cut into cubes. Mix the flour with salt and plenty of pepper and coat the steak and kidney with the mixture. Heat the butter or oil in a heavy based saucepan and brown the meats, adding a single layer to the pan at a time. Transfer to a dish when browned. Add the onion to the pan and cook gently on low heat until transparent. Return the meat to the pan and add the stock, wine, sauce and chopped parsley. Cover and simmer gently for 1 ½ hours or until the meat is tender. Mix any remaining flour from coating the meat with a little cold water and gradually stir into the bubbling stew to thicken it further. Simmer gently for 2 minutes and remove from heat. Cool.

Preheat the oven on 230°C (450°F/Gas 8). Roll out the pastry on a floured board and using a deep pie dish as a guide, cut the pastry 1.25 cm (½ inch) larger than the top of the dish. Keep this aside, and cut a 3 cm (1 ¼ inch) wide strip from the remaining pastry. Cut the leaves and make a pastry rose from the trimmings. The pastry should be allowed to rest for 30 minutes after the initial rolling, and another 15 minutes after cutting.

Turn the cooled steak and kidney mixture into the pie dish and place a pie funnel in the centre. Moisten the rim of the dish with water and place the strip of pastry on the rim. Brush this with water and place the pastry top in position. Press gently to seal. Trim around the edge with a very sharp knife. Cut a vent in the centre and place the leaves and pastry rose in position, holding them in place with a little water. Knock up the edge of the pie with the back of a knife blade. Glaze the top and decorations with beaten egg or milk, but take care not to brush the cut edge as the pastry will not puff evenly.

Bake the pie in a very hot oven, 240°C (475°F/Gas 9), for 15 minutes. Reduce to moderate, 180°C (350°F/Gas 4), and cook for a further 20 to 25 minutes until puffed and golden.

An easy way to serve the pie: Roll out the pastry and cut 6 rounds a little larger than the top of individual soufflé dishes. The point of a very sharp knife gives better results than a pastry cutter. Turn upside down onto a lightly greased baking sheet and glaze. (Rest the pastry after rolling and cutting.) Bake in a preheated hot oven, 220°C (425°F/Gas 7), for 8 to 10 minutes until puffed and golden. Pile the hot steak and kidney mixture into warmed soufflé dishes, sprinkle with chopped parsley and perch a round of pastry on top.

Carbonnade for a Crowd
Serves 18 - 20

4 kg (8 lb) round or boneless blade steak
2 packets French onion soup mix
3 tablespoons flour
2 tablespoons soft brown sugar
3 teaspoons dry mustard
¼ teaspoon ground nutmeg
2 bouquets garnis
1 ½ cups (12 fl oz) stout
2 medium-sized onions, sliced
30 g (1 oz) butter

Trim the beef and cut into 2 cm (¾ inch) cubes. Combine the onion soup mix with the flour, brown sugar, mustard and nutmeg. Place a quarter of this mixture in a plastic bag, add a quarter of the meat cubes and shake to coat. Tip into a large greased casserole dish and coat the remaining meat in the same way.

Place the bouquets garnis amongst the meat cubes and sprinkle any remaining coating mixture on top. Pour in the stout and cover. Cook in a moderately slow oven, 160°C (325°F/Gas 3), for 1 hour. Stir well then continue to cook for a further hour until the meat is almost tender. Remove the bouquets garnis and cool the carbonnade. Cover and store in the refrigerator for up to 4 days.

To serve, bring to room temperature, then heat in a moderate oven 180°C (350°F/Gas 4), for 1 ½ hours. Stir occasionally. Fry the onion slices in the butter until golden and sprinkle on top of the carbonnade just before serving.

Note: Carbonnade can be cooked in a large boiler. If handles or knob are bakelite, cover with foil.

Chilli con Carne
Serves 5 - 6 **M**

500 g (1 lb) finely minced (ground) beef
1 tablespoon oil
1 large onion, chopped
1 garlic clove, crushed
1 red pepper (capsicum), chopped
3 teaspoons Mexican style chilli powder
1 x 440 g (14 oz) can tomato soup
1 beef stock cube
1 x 440 g (14 oz) can red kidney beans, drained

Press the mince into a flat cake, or use flat-packed mince straight from the freezer. Place the oil, onion, garlic, red pepper and chilli powder in a large casserole dish and cook on high for 5 minutes, stirring twice. Add the mince to the dish, cover and cook on high for 8 minutes. Break up the mince into chunks with a fork and stir in the tomato soup, stock cube and beans. Cover and cook on medium-high for 10 minutes. Serve with crusty bread and a salad.

Note: See Chilli Beef and Beans (*page 85*).

Opposite: *Carbonnade for a Crowd*

87

Beef

Corned Silverside
Serves 8 - 10 [M]

1 piece corned silverside, about 1.5 kg (3 lb)
1 tablespoon soft brown sugar
1 tablespoon malt vinegar
2 teaspoons pickling spice
4 cups (1 litre) hot tap water

Weigh the corned silverside and calculate the cooking time at 25 minutes per 500 g (1 lb). For 1.5 kg (3 lb), 75 minutes. Rinse the meat well in cold water and place in a casserole dish just large enough to contain it. Add the remaining ingredients, cover and cook on high for 10 minutes. Turn the meat, re-cover and cook on medium for the remainder of the cooking time, turning once more halfway through cooking. Leave to stand, covered, for 15 minutes before carving if serving hot, or until cool if required cold. Store the drained corned beef in a sealed container in the refrigerator.

Oven Bag Method: (Suitable for corned beef which is known not to be salty; e.g. freshly pumped beef is usually not salty.)

Weigh and calculate the cooking time at 24 minutes per 500 g (1 lb) and rinse as above. Shake 1 tablespoon flour in an oven bag and arrange in an oven dish. Place the corned silverside in the bag and add the sugar, vinegar and spices. Carefully pour in 1 ½ cups (12 fl oz) hot tap water and tie the bag loosely with string. Cook for 10 minutes on high, turn the bag and beef and cook for remaining time on medium, turning again halfway through cooking time. Stand as above before carving or storing.

Burgundian Beef and Beans
Serves 4

500 g (1 lb) boneless blade or chuck steak
1 tablespoon oil
1 onion, chopped
1 garlic clove, crushed
1 rasher bacon, chopped
1 carrot, diced
½ cup chopped celery
1 cup (8 fl oz) dry red wine
1 tablespoon tomato paste
bouquet garni
salt
freshly ground pepper
1 x 440 g (14 oz) can white beans

Trim the beef and cut into 2 cm (¾ inch) cubes. Heat half the oil in a heavy saucepan and brown the meat quickly. Remove to a plate. Add the remaining oil with the onion, garlic and bacon and cook gently until the onion is soft. Add the carrot, celery, wine and tomato paste. Return the beef to the pan and place the bouquet garni in the pan. Season with a little salt and pepper to taste, cover and cook for 1 ¼ hours or until the meat is just tender. Drain the beans and add to the pan. Cover and simmer for 20 minutes. Serve with a tossed salad and wholemeal bread to mop up juices.

Drover's Dream
Serves 6

1 kg (2 lb) chuck steak
2 tablespoons dripping or oil
1 large onion, chopped
1 large carrot, sliced
½ cup chopped celery
3 tablespoons flour
1 ½ cups (12 fl oz) beef stock
2 teaspoons Worcestershire sauce
½ teaspoon dried thyme
salt and pepper

Scone Topping (optional)
2 cups (8 oz) self-raising flour
pinch of salt
¾ cup (6 oz) milk
4 tablespoons melted butter
2 tablespoons finely chopped parsley
1 tablespoon grated Parmesan cheese
onion salt

Trim and cube the steak. Heat 1 tablespoon of dripping or oil in a frying pan and brown the meat quickly. Transfer to a casserole dish. Reduce the heat, add the remaining dripping with the vegetables and cook gently until the onion is soft. Sprinkle in the flour, stir and cook for 2 minutes. Stir in the stock and keep stirring until thickened and bubbling. Pour over the meat, add the sauce, thyme and season to taste. Cover and cook in a moderately slow oven, 160°C (325°F/Gas 3), for 2 hours until the meat is tender. Serve with mashed potatoes and a green vegetable, or finish as follows.

Increase the oven to 230°C (450°F/Gas 8), leaving the casserole in the oven. Make the scone topping as directed below and cut into rounds. Place on top of the hot casserole, overlapping the slices a little. Brush with milk and return to the oven, uncovered, for 15 to 20 minutes until the topping is golden brown and cooked through. Serve with a green vegetable.

Scone Topping: Sift the flour and salt into a bowl and make a well in the centre. Pour in the milk and 2 tablespoons melted butter. Mix lightly with a round bladed knife and turn onto a floured board. Dust with flour and knead lightly, about 10 turns. Roll out to a rectangle 1 cm (½ inch) thick. Brush with the remaining butter and sprinkle evenly with parsley, cheese and a little onion salt. Roll up firmly from the longer edge and cut into 1 cm (½ inch) slices with a floured knife.

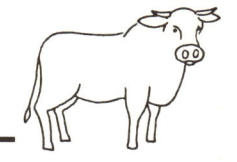

Keema Curry

Serves 6

30 g (1 oz) butter or
  1 tablespoon oil
2 medium-sized onions,
  chopped
1 teaspoon grated fresh
  ginger
1 garlic clove, crushed
3-4 teaspoons curry powder
750 g (1 ½ lb) finely
  minced (ground) beef or
  lamb
¾ cup chopped, peeled
  tomatoes
salt
¾ cup (6 fl oz) water
1 ½ cups fresh or frozen
  peas
1 teaspoon sugar
1 tablespoon lemon juice
1 teaspoon garam masala or
  ground allspice
2 tablespoons chopped fresh
  mint or coriander leaves

Heat the butter in a heavy pan and add the onions. Fry gently until transparent. Add the ginger, garlic and curry powder to taste. Cook gently for a further 5 minutes. Increase the heat and add the mince. Cook, stirring often, until the meat changes colour and the lumps are broken up. Reduce the heat, add the tomatoes, about 1 teaspoon salt and the water. Cover and simmer gently for 25 minutes. Add the peas and sugar. Cover and cook gently for a further 10 minutes or until the peas are tender. Stir in the lemon juice, garam masala and mint. If desired, thicken with a cornflour and water paste. Served on boiled rice with traditional curry accompaniments.

Curried Sausages

Serves 4 - 6

750 g (1 ½ lb) beef sausages
1 tablespoon oil
1 large onion, chopped
1 garlic clove, crushed
1 tablespoon curry powder
1 tablespoon flour
½ cup sliced celery
1 carrot, chopped
1 large ripe tomato, peeled
  and chopped
1 cup frozen green peas
1 ½ cups (12 fl oz) beef
  stock
salt and pepper

Par-boil the sausages by placing them in a saucepan with cold water to cover. Bring slowly to simmering point. Do not boil. Remove from heat, cover and leave for 10 minutes until the sausages are firm. Drain and cut into thick slices.
  Heat the oil in a deep pan and brown the slices on all sides. Lift out and keep aside. Add the onion and garlic and cook gently for 10 minutes. Sprinkle in the curry powder and flour, stir well and cook for a further 3 to 4 minutes. Add the remaining vegetables, stock, salt and pepper to taste, stirring well when the stock is added. Bring slowly to simmering point, cover and simmer gently for 15 minutes. Add the sausage slices and simmer, covered, for a further 15 to 20 minutes. Serve with boiled rice and fruit chutney.

Corned Beef Richmond

Serves 10 - 12

2 kg (4 lb) piece corned
  silverside
warm water to cover
2 tablespoons soft brown
  sugar
2 tablespoons malt vinegar
½ orange
3 cloves
⅓ cup (4 oz) lime
  marmalade
2 limes or lemons

Rinse the corned silverside under cold water and place in a boiler with warm water. Add the sugar, vinegar and the half orange studded with cloves. Cover and bring to a slow simmer. Simmer gently for 2 hours, remove from the heat and leave to cool in the liquid. When cool, drain the beef and store in a sealed container in the refrigerator until required.
  Place the marmalade in a small pan and heat gently until melted, stirring occasionally. Trim the fat from the beef leaving a thin layer. Brush the top and sides with half the marmalade. Slice the limes thinly and overlap slices on the top. Cover with the remaining marmalade. Chill for 30 minutes; for longer storage, place in a sealed container. Slice thinly to serve, and accompany with a salad of honeydew, rockmelon and pawpaw (papaya) balls or cubes mixed with watercress, tossed with a dressing of ⅓ cup (2½ fl oz) French dressing beaten with the grated rind and juice of 1 orange and ¼ teaspoon mustard.

Note: A piece of cooked corned silverside can be purchased from the delicatessen and presented in this way; about 1.5 kg (3 lb) would be sufficient. For cooking corned beef in other ways, pressure cook for 45 minutes; in a slow cooker on low setting for 7 to 8 hours, on high setting for 4 to 6 hours. Check manuals for cooking times as appliances can vary.

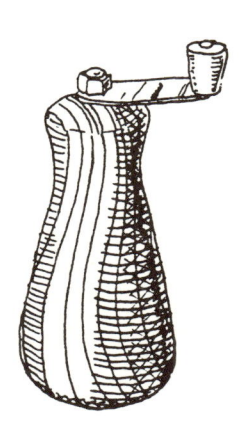

Beef

Family-Size Meat Pie
Serves 6 - 8

1 ½ cups (6 oz) flour
½ teaspoon salt

½ cup (4 fl oz) water
45 g (1 ½ oz) beef dripping

Filling
500 g (1 lb) minced (ground) steak
2 onions, chopped
½ teaspoon salt
¼ teaspoon pepper
pinch of nutmeg
2½ cups (20 fl oz) water

1 beef stock cube
¼ cup (1 oz) flour
2 teaspoons Worcestershire sauce
2 teaspoons parisian essence
185 g (6 oz) puff pastry

Base: Sift the flour and salt. Place the water and dripping in a saucepan. Heat gently to melt the dripping. Pour hot liquid into a well in the centre of the flour. Mix with knife to begin with and when cool enough use the hands. Knead on a lightly floured board until free of cracks. Roll out and line a 23 cm (9 inch) pie plate.

Filling: Fry the meat and onions in a saucepan until well browned. Drain off any surplus fat. Add the salt, pepper, nutmeg, 2 cups water and crumbled stock cube. Bring to the boil, reduce the heat, and simmer, covered, for 20 minutes. Blend the flour with the remaining water and add to the meat mixture, stirring continuously until the mixture boils and thickens. Add the Worcestershire sauce and parisian essence. Allow mixture to cool. Place the meat mixture into the pastry case. Glaze the pastry edge with the milk. Roll the puff pastry to cover the top of the pie. Press the edges together. Glaze the pie with milk and slit the top in 2 or 3 places. Bake in a hot oven, 200°C (400°F/Gas 6), for 20 minutes then reduce the temperature to 180°C (350°F/Gas 4) for 20 to 25 minutes or until the pastry is golden brown.

Meatballs in Beer Sauce
Serves 4 - 5

500 g (1 lb) finely minced (ground) beef
1 small onion, grated
⅓ cup (1 oz) quick-cooking rolled oats
1 egg

¼ teaspoon ground allspice
½ teaspoon salt
pepper to taste
1 tablespoon oil

Beer Sauce
1 packet French onion soup
1 ½ cups (12 fl oz) beer
1 tablespoon soft brown sugar

pinch of ground nutmeg
2 tablespoons sour cream

Place the meatball ingredients, except the oil, in a bowl and mix lightly and thoroughly. With moistened hands, shape into balls the size of a walnut. Heat the oil in a pan and brown the meatballs on all sides. Drain off any fat.

Beer Sauce: Sprinkle the soup mix into a pan and stir in the beer, sugar and nutmeg. Bring to the boil, stirring carefully. Cover the pan, reduce the heat to low and simmer for 25 minutes, stirring occasionally. Stir in sour cream and serve with boiled noodles and vegetables or salad.

Steak Satay
Serves 4 – 6

½ cup (4 fl oz) oil
¼ cup (2 fl oz) soy sauce
¾ cup grated onion
1 garlic clove

2 teaspoons lemon juice
1 teaspoon cumin
4 kg (2 lb) rump steak
1 tablespoon sesame seeds

Combine the oil, soy sauce, onion, crushed garlic, lemon juice, and cumin. Cut the steak into 2.5 cm (1 inch) cubes and add to the marinade. Stir well and marinate approximately 1 hour.

Using a rolling pin, crush the sesame seeds to a pulp. Add to the meat and marinade and leave to stand a further 1 hour. Thread the meat on skewers and grill (broil) lightly, turning occasionally.

Opposite: *Meatballs in Beer Sauce*

91

Beef

Coconut Beef Curry
Serves 6

1.25 kg (2 ½ lb) chuck steak
1 large onion, chopped
1 garlic clove, chopped
1 teaspoon chopped fresh ginger
¼ cup (½ oz) toasted coconut
5 cm (2 inch) strip of lemon rind
30 g (1 oz) ghee or butter
2 tablespoons curry paste
1 cup (8 fl oz) canned coconut milk
salt and pepper
2 tablespoons chopped fresh coriander
1 tablespoon lemon juice

Trim the steak and cut into 2 cm (¾ inch) cubes. Place the onion in a food processor fitted with a steel blade. Add the garlic, ginger, coconut and lemon rind. Process to a paste, adding a little of the coconut milk if necessary.

Heat the ghee in a heavy saucepan and add the onion mixture with the curry paste. Cook gently for 10 minutes, stirring often, then increase the heat and add the beef cubes. Cook on high, stirring often, until the meat changes colour. Reduce the heat, add the coconut milk and season to taste. Cover and simmer gently for 1 ½ to 2 hours or until the meat is tender and the sauce is thick. Stir in the coriander and the lemon juice. Serve with boiled rice and traditional curry accompaniments.

Note: Curry is the perfect dish for cooking ahead as the flavour improves on standing. If preparing beforehand, cook until the meat is just tender, and do not add the coriander and lemon juice. Transfer to a bowl, cover and refrigerate for up to 3 days. Complete the cooking when reheating, adding coriander and lemon juice just before serving.

Beef Goulash
Serves 5 - 6

1 kg (2 lb) chuck steak
2 tablespoons oil
1 large onion, chopped
1 tablespoon tomato paste
1 tablespoon paprika
1 cup chopped, peeled tomatoes
¾ cup (6 fl oz) beef stock
1 teaspoon sugar
salt and pepper
1 cup diced green and red peppers (capsicum)
3 tablespoons sour cream

Trim the beef and cut into cubes. Heat the oil in a saucepan and brown the beef, adding a single layer at a time. Remove to a plate as the cubes brown. Reduce the heat and add the onion. Cook gently until soft, stir in the tomato paste and paprika and cook gently for 3 to 4 minutes, stirring often. Return the meat to the pan with the tomatoes, stock, sugar and salt and pepper to taste. Cover and simmer gently for 1 ½ hours. Add the peppers and cook for a further 15 minutes or until the beef is tender. Stir in the sour cream, heat gently and serve with boiled noodles tossed with butter and caraway or poppy seeds.

Pastrami and Spinach Salad
Serves 6

15 spinach leaves or 6 silverbeet leaves
250 g (8 oz) thinly sliced pastrami
4 hard-boiled eggs
2 tablespoons chopped pecan nuts

Tomato-Onion Dressing
⅓ cup (2 ½ fl oz) tomato sauce
¼ cup (2 fl oz) cider vinegar
¾ cup (6 fl oz) salad oil
1 garlic clove, crushed
1 teaspoon sugar
½ teaspoon celery salt
freshly ground pepper
1 teaspoon dry mustard
1 teaspoon Worcestershire sauce
3 spring onions (scallions), chopped

Remove the stems from the spinach or silverbeet and wash the leaves well. Shake dry, roll loosely in a tea towel and place in a plastic bag. Refrigerate for 2 to 3 hours to crisp. Break the leaves into large pieces and place in 6 individual salad bowls or plates. Curl the pastrami slices on top. Shell the eggs and cut into quarters. Place 3 egg quarters on each salad and sprinkle the pecan nuts over. Place all the dressing ingredients except the spring onions in a bowl and beat well with a rotary or electric beater. Stir in the spring onions. Spoon a little dressing over each salad and serve the remaining dressing separately. Serve with an assortment of breads and curls of butter.

Note: The salad can be assembled in a large bowl as part of a buffet spread, adding crisp leaves of mignonette lettuce to increase quantity. Pastrami can be cut into strips instead of leaving it in slices.

Cornucopias
Makes about 40

½ cup (2 oz) dried apricots
½ cup (4 fl oz) cream sherry
375g (12 oz) thinly sliced smoked veal or corned silverside
500 g (1 lb) ricotta cheese
½ cup (1 ½ oz) chopped pecan nuts

Place the apricots in a bowl with the sherry and leave for several hours or overnight. Cut the smoked veal into pieces about 5 cm (2 inch) square. Drain the apricots and add the cheese and pecans. Mix lightly.

Place a heaped teaspoon of cheese mixture diagonally along the centre of the meat and roll into a cone shape, fastening with a toothpick. Shape the remaining ingredients in the same way. When all are shaped, put a little more filling in the top of each cone. Arrange on a serving platter, cover with plastic wrap and refrigerate until required for serving.

Aberdeen Sausage

Serves 6 - 8

500 g (1 lb) finely minced (ground) beef	freshly ground pepper
185 g (6 oz) bacon	pinch of ground nutmeg
¾ cup quick-cooking rolled oats	grated rind of ½ lemon
1 tablespoon tomato sauce	2 tablespoons chopped parsley
2 teaspoons Worcestershire sauce	1 egg
1 teaspoon salt	dry breadcrumbs for coating

Place the mince in a large mixing bowl. Trim the bacon and chop very finely. Add to the beef with the remaining ingredients except the breadcrumbs and mix lightly and thoroughly. Lightly dampen a board and turn the mixture onto it. Shape into a roll with wet hands, making the roll the same diameter and length as a nut roll tin. Grease a nut roll tin with butter and gently push in the meat roll. Put a piece of greased foil over each end and push top and base of the tin into place.

Bring 4 cups (1 litre) of water to the boil in a pressure cooker with a trivet in the base. Put in the tin on its side, cover and bring to high pressure and cook for 40 minutes. Reduce the pressure and remove the tin. Cool for 20 minutes, remove the roll from the tin and coat completely with dry breadcrumbs. Wrap in foil and chill. Serve sliced with salad and relishes or in sandwiches.

Note: Shaping the roll before packing into the tin gives a more even shape when cooked. If you do not have a pressure cooker, the roll (in the nut loaf tin) can be boiled in a saucepan of water for 2 hours, using a trivet in the base.

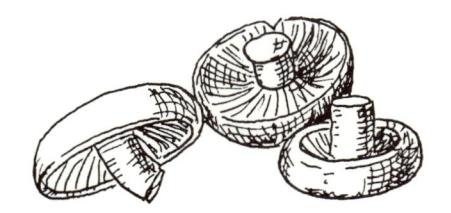

Corned Beef Hash

Serves 4

2 cups diced, cooked corned beef	salt and pepper
3 cups diced, boiled potatoes	2 eggs
60 g (2 oz) butter	¼ cup (2 fl oz) cream
1 medium-sized onion, chopped	pinch of ground nutmeg

Put the diced beef and potatoes into a bowl. Heat a little of the butter in a large frying pan and cook the onion gently until transparent. Add to the beef and potatoes with salt if necessary and pepper to taste. Beat the eggs with the cream and nutmeg and add to the bowl. Stir thoroughly.

Heat a little more butter in a frying pan and add the corned beef mixture. Press evenly to cover the base of the pan. Cook on medium low heat until a brown crust forms on the bottom – about 20 minutes. Loosen with a spatula, then place a dinner plate on top of the pan and invert hash onto the plate. Add the remaining butter, heat well and slide the hash back into the pan. Cook for a further 15 to 20 minutes until browned on the second side. Serve cut in wedges with a spicy or chilli sauce. Fried eggs are traditionally served with hash.

Riverina Beef Casserole

Serves 5 - 6

750 g (1 ½ lb) round or boneless blade steak	1 teaspoon Worcestershire sauce
30 g (1 oz) butter	1 tablespoon vinegar
1 onion, chopped	1 ½ tablespoons soft brown sugar
1 teaspoon curry powder	¼ cup (2 fl oz) water
½ teaspoon ground ginger	salt to taste
¼ teaspoon ground allspice	2 tablespoons chopped bacon pieces
1 cup (8 fl oz) apricot nectar	12 prunes, pitted
¼ cup (2 fl oz) tomato sauce	grated rind of 1 lemon

Cut the steak into thick strips. Heat the butter in a frying pan and brown the strips, adding a single layer at a time. Transfer to a casserole dish. Add the onion with more butter if necessary and cook gently until soft. Stir in the curry powder and cook for 2 minutes. Add the spices, apricot nectar, sauces, vinegar, brown sugar and water. Stir well to lift the browned juices, add salt and pour over the beef.

Cover and cook in a moderately slow oven, 160°C (325°F/Gas 3), for 1½ hours. Fry the bacon in a heated pan until crisp, drain on absorbent paper and add to the casserole with the prunes and lemon rind. Cover and cook for a further 30 minutes. Serve with boiled rice and a tossed salad.

Beef

Kofta Curry
Serves 4

1 medium-sized onion, grated
2 teaspoons grated fresh ginger
¼ cup (1 oz) dry breadcrumbs
1 teaspoon garam masala
salt
freshly ground pepper
1 egg
2 teaspoons finely chopped fresh mint
500 g (1 lb) finely minced (ground) beef
15 g (½ oz) ghee or oil
1 large onion, chopped
1 garlic clove, crushed
3 teaspoons curry powder
1 cup chopped, peeled tomatoes
½ cup (4 fl oz) beef stock
1 tablespoon chopped fresh mint or coriander leaves

Place the onion and 1 teaspoon of the ginger in a mixing bowl and stir in the breadcrumbs, ½ teaspoon garam masala, ½ teaspoon salt, pepper, the egg and mint. Leave for 5 minutes, then add the beef and mix thoroughly. Stand for 15 minutes and mix again, then shape into balls the size of a walnut.

Heat the ghee in a saucepan and brown the meatballs on all sides. Remove to a plate, leaving the oil in the pan. Reduce the heat, add the onion and cook gently until soft. Add the garlic, the remaining ginger and curry powder, stir well and cook for 5 minutes. Stir in the tomatoes and stock, return the meatballs, cover and simmer for 30 minutes until the meatballs are tender and the sauce is thick. Stir in the remaining garam masala and fresh mint. Simmer for 2 to 3 minutes and adjust the seasoning. Serve with boiled rice, yoghurt mixed with chopped mint, crushed garlic and sliced cucumber, and sliced tomatoes mixed with chopped spring onions (scallions) and a little vinegar.

Beef Bourguignonne

Beef Bourguignonne
Serves 5 - 6

1 kg (2 lb) chuck or boneless blade steak
2 rashers bacon, chopped
30 g (1 oz) butter
1 onion, chopped
1 garlic clove, crushed
1 ½ tablespoons flour
1 cup (8 fl oz) burgundy or other red wine
1 tablespoon tomato paste
1 teaspoon sugar
salt
freshly ground pepper
bouquet garni
8 small whole onions
125 g (4 oz) small mushrooms
chopped parsley for serving

Trim the beef and cut into 3 cm (1 ¼ inch) cubes. Heat a frying pan on medium heat and add the bacon. Cook until lightly browned and remove to a casserole dish, leaving the fat in the pan. Add half the butter, increase the heat and add the meat cubes. Brown quickly on each side, transferring to the casserole when browned. Add the remaining butter with the onion and garlic and cook on low heat until the onion is soft. Sprinkle in the flour, stir well, then add the wine. Keep stirring until thickened and bubbling, and stir in the tomato paste, sugar, and salt and pepper to taste.

Pour the sauce over the meat in the casserole dish and place the bouquet garni in the centre of the contents. Cover and cook in a moderately slow oven, 160°C (325°F/Gas 3), for 30 minutes. Add the peeled whole onions and trimmed mushrooms, stir gently, then cover and cook for a further 1 to 1 ½ hours until the meat is tender. Skim any fat from the surface or mop up with a paper towel. Remove the bouquet garni and serve sprinkled with chopped parsley.

Swiss Steak
Serves 5 - 6

1 thick slice round steak, about 1 kg (2 lb)
2 tablespoons seasoned flour
30 g (1 oz) butter
2 onions, sliced
425 g (13 ½ oz) can peeled tomatoes, chopped
1 tablespoon tomato sauce
2 teaspoons Worcestershire sauce
salt and pepper

Trim the fat from the steak and lightly nick the edges to prevent curling during cooking. Sprinkle the seasoned flour over the steak and pound it in lightly with a meat mallet. Heat the butter in a frying pan with lid to fit, and when foaming subsides add the steak and brown on each side on high heat. Reduce heat and add the onion slices around the steak. Stir and cook gently until they soften. Move some onion onto the top of the steak and add the tomatoes and their liquid, sauces and seasoning to taste. Cover and simmer gently for 1 to 1 ½ hours until the meat is tender.

Lift the steak onto a platter, cover with foil and leave for 5 minutes. Keep the sauce hot in pan. Cut the steak at an angle in thin slices and serve with the sauce, creamy mashed potatoes and a green vegetable.

Dinner Loaf

Serves 4

1 cottage loaf, wholemeal or white
15 g (½ oz) butter
1 onion, chopped
2 garlic cloves, crushed
500 g (1 lb) finely minced (ground) beef
1 tablespoon flour
¾ cup (6 fl oz) beef stock
2 zucchini (courgettes), sliced
2 teaspoons Worcestershire sauce
salt
freshly ground black pepper
¾ cup (1 ½ oz) soft breadcrumbs, made from the cottage loaf
2 tablespoons chopped parsley
additional 1 tablespoon melted butter

Cut around base of the cottage loaf, 3 cm (1 ¼ inch) in from the sides. Remove the bottom crust and keep aside. Hollow out the centre of the loaf and make into crumbs.

Heat the butter in a saucepan and add the onion and garlic. Cook gently until the onion is soft. Add the mince and increase the heat. Cook on high heat, stirring to break up the mince, and when browned and the juices have evaporated, sprinkle in the flour and stir well. Cook for 1 minute, then add the stock and stir constantly until thick and bubbling. Stir in the zucchini, Worcestershire sauce and salt and pepper to taste. Cover and simmer on low heat for 15 minutes, stirring occasionally. Remove from the heat and fold in breadcrumbs and parsley.

Spoon the mixture into the hollowed loaf and replace the bottom crust to act as a stopper. Brush the top of the loaf with the melted butter and wrap in foil. Bake in a moderate oven, 180°C (350°F/Gas 4), for 25 minutes. Open the foil and cook for a further 5 minutes. Serve hot cut in wedges with a side salad.

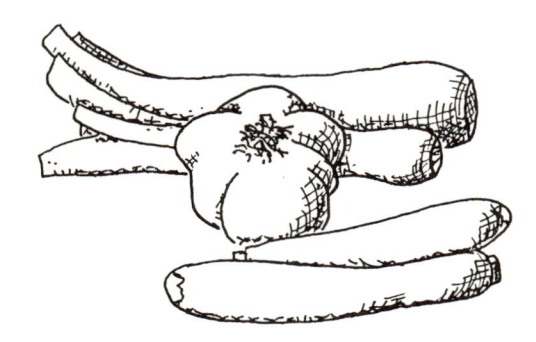

Irish Pot Roast

Serves 6 - 8

1 rolled chuck or boneless blade pot roast, about 2 kg (4 lb)
¼ cup (1 oz) flour
salt and pepper
1 teaspoon dry mustard
30 g (1 oz) butter
1 tablespoon oil
1 bay leaf
2 large onions, sliced
1 carrot, chopped (optional)
1 cup (6 oz) pitted prunes
1 cup (8 fl oz) stout

Wipe the meat with paper towels. If using blade pot roast, tie into a neat shape with white string. Mix the flour with salt and pepper to taste and mustard and use to coat the meat. Reserve the remaining flour.

Heat the butter and oil in a Dutch oven or heavy saucepan with the bay leaf. Add the beef and brown on all sides. Remove the beef to a plate and add the onions to the pan with the carrot, if used. Cook gently on low heat, stirring often, until the onion is transparent. Return the meat to the pan, add the prunes and stout. Cover and simmer gently for 2 ½ hours until the beef is tender. Turn the meat occasionally.

Remove the beef to a platter. Cover and keep warm. Skim the fat from the pan liquid and bring to the boil over high heat. Boil rapidly to reduce by half. Thicken if necessary with the remaining flour mixture mixed with cold water. Boil for 2 minutes. Slice the pot roast and coat the slices with prune and onion sauce.

Florentine Beef Cakes

Makes 12

6 silverbeet leaves, blanched and halved
250 g (8 oz) finely minced (ground) beef
250 g (8 oz) finely minced (ground) veal
1 cup cooked brown rice
1 small onion, grated
1 zucchini (courgette), grated
1 carrot, grated
½ cup (4 fl oz) beef stock
⅓ cup (2 ½ fl oz) tomato purée
1 egg, beaten
1 tablespoon curry powder
3 tablespoons wheatgerm

Line greased deep patty tins with silverbeet leaves. Combine the remaining ingredients thoroughly. Spoon the meat mixture into the tins. Pack down firmly and fold the silverbeet leaves over to cover.

Bake in a moderate oven at 180°C (350°F/Gas 4) for 20 to 30 minutes. Allow to stand for 5 minutes before turning out. Serve with a crisp salad.

Beef

Poached Fillet with Tapenade

Serves 6 - 8

1 butt fillet (tenderloin) of beef, about 1 kg (2 lb)
1 x 500 g (1 lb) can beef consommé

Tapenade
1 x 45 g (1 ½ oz) can anchovy fillets
12 black olives, pitted
1 garlic clove
1 tablespoon drained capers
water
freshly ground pepper
capers, chives and black olives to garnish

1 teaspoon French mustard
1 tablespoon brandy
1 tablespoon lemon juice
¼ cup (2 fl oz) olive oil

Trim the silver skin and fat from the beef taking care not to separate the muscles. Tie at intervals with white string. Put the consommé in a saucepan just large enough to take the fillet and add an equal quantity of water and pepper to taste. Bring to the boil, add the fillet and boil for 3 minutes. Reduce the heat so the liquid barely simmers. Cover and simmer very gently for 30 minutes. Remove from the heat, stand for 5 minutes and remove the fillet from the liquid. Wrap in foil and leave until cool. The consommé can be strained and stored in a jar in the refrigerator. Use as beef stock in other recipes.

Slice the beef thinly and arrange the slices on a platter. Spoon the Tapenade over the beef and garnish with capers, chives and olives. Cover with plastic wrap and store in the refrigerator if necessary, but bring to room temperature for serving. Serve with crusty bread and a platter of crisp salad vegetables.

Tapenade: Drain the oil from the anchovies then place them in a blender or food processor with the remaining ingredients except the olive oil. Blend until smooth and gradually pour in the oil. Blend for a few seconds.

Green Lasagne

Serves 6 - 8

1 tablespoon oil
1 onion, chopped
1 garlic clove, crushed
750 g (1 ½ lb) finely minced (ground) beef
440 g (14 oz) can peeled tomatoes
¼ cup (2 fl oz) tomato paste
¼ cup (2 fl oz) red wine
½ teaspoon each dried oregano and basil

2 tablespoons chopped parsley
1 teaspoon sugar
salt and pepper
375 g (12 oz) green lasagne noodles
500 g (1 lb) ricotta cheese
⅓ cup (1 ½ oz) grated Parmesan cheese

White Sauce
30 g (1 oz) butter
3 tablespoons flour
1 ½ cups (12 fl oz) milk
salt and pepper
pinch of ground nutmeg

Heat the oil in a deep pan. Add the onion and cook gently until soft. Add the garlic then increase heat. Add the mince and stir over high heat to break up the lumps. When the colour changes reduce the heat and add the chopped tomatoes and their liquid, tomato paste, wine, herbs, sugar, salt and pepper. Cover and simmer for 30 minutes, removing lid for last 10 minutes to evaporate some of the moisture. Cook the lasagne noodles according to the directions on the packet.

Grease a 30 x 23 cm (12 x 9 inch) oven dish with butter and place a layer of lasagne noodles in the base. Spread a third of the meat sauce on top and cover with a third of the softened ricotta. Sprinkle with 1 tablespoon Parmesan cheese. Repeat the layers, then finish with a layer of lasagne noodles. Spread white sauce on top and sprinkle on the remaining Parmesan.

Bake the lasagne in a moderate oven, 180°C (350°F/Gas 4), for 30 to 35 minutes until golden brown. Stand for 10 minutes before cutting into squares. Serve with a salad of mixed greens, tomato, capsicum (green or red pepper), olives and anchovies tossed with salad dressing.

White Sauce: Melt the butter in a saucepan and stir in the flour. Cook for 2 minutes without browning and stir in the milk. Stir constantly until thickened and bubbling and season to taste with salt, pepper and a pinch of nutmeg.

Freezer Beef Stew

Serves 6 for 3 meals

3 kg (6 lb) blade, chuck or round steak
4 tablespoons oil
2 large onions, chopped
about 2 cups (16 fl oz) water
2 beef stock cubes
salt and pepper
1 carrot, cut into chunks

Trim the meat and cut into 3 cm (1 ¼ inch) cubes. Heat 1 tablespoon of the oil in a large heavy saucepan until very hot and add enough beef cubes to cover the base. Brown quickly on all sides and transfer to a large bowl. Add more oil and beef cubes in batches until all the meat is browned.

Reduce the heat and add 1 tablespoon oil and the onions. Cook gently until soft. Stir in 1 cup (8 fl oz) of water and the crumbled stock cubes. Return the meat to the pan, add salt and pepper to taste, and the carrot. Cover and simmer for 30 minutes, stirring occasionally. After this time, check liquid level. Add more water only if the meat is not covered by liquid. Simmer for a further 30 minutes. The meat should still be fairly firm. Skim any fat from the surface.

Place the saucepan in a sinkful of cold water and cool, stirring occasionally. Ladle into containers; divide into 3 portions if 6 are to be served from each portion, or 4 portions if serving 4. Place the carrot chunks in one of the portions, leaving the other portions without carrots. Seal, label and store in freezer for up to 2 months.

Remove a portion of frozen stew from the freezer to the refrigerator to thaw, about 24 hours before required. Alternatively, defrost in a microwave oven, or unmould into a saucepan and thaw over gentle heat, with a lid on the pan.

To reheat and serve
Beef and Vegetable Casserole: Use the portion containing the carrots. Place the thawed stew in a casserole dish. Add ¼ cup (2 fl oz) red wine, ½ cup sliced celery, 1 small sliced turnip, 4-6 small whole peeled onions, 3-4 medium-sized potatoes, peeled and quartered, 1 cup green peas or sliced green beans, a bouquet garni, 2 tablespoons tomato paste and 1 teaspoon sugar. Cover and cook in a moderate oven, 180°C (350°F/Gas 4), for 1 ¼ hours or until the meat and vegetables are tender. Remove the bouquet garni. Sprinkle with chopped parsley and serve.

Beef Stroganoff: In a saucepan heat 15 g (½ oz) butter and add 1 ½ cups sliced mushrooms with a squeeze of lemon juice. Cook with a lid on the pan until the mushrooms are limp. Add the stew, a good pinch of nutmeg, 2 teaspoons Worcestershire sauce, ½ teaspoon sugar and 1 tablespoon tomato paste. Cover and simmer gently for 45 minutes until the meat is tender. Thicken with 3 teaspoons cornflour (cornstarch) mixed with cold water. Boil for 1 minute, then stir in 2–3 tablespoons sour cream. Serve with boiled noodles tossed with butter, and a green vegetable.

Freezer Beef Stew

Beef Goulash: Heat 15 g (½ oz) butter in a saucepan and add 1 large chopped onion. Cook gently until soft, add 1 crushed garlic clove, 2 tablespoons tomato paste, 1 ½ tablespoons paprika and ½ teaspoon sugar. Cook gently, stirring often, for 5 minutes. Add the stew, stir well, cover and simmer for 45 minutes or until the meat is tender and the sauce is thick. Stir in 2–3 tablespoons sour cream and serve with boiled noodles.

Steak and Kidney Pie: Cook 1 chopped onion in 15 g (½ oz) butter until soft. Remove the core from 250 g (8 oz) beef kidney or from 3 lamb kidneys and cut the kidney into small cubes. Add to the onion and stir over medium heat until the kidney changes colour. Add the stew, 2 tablespoons chopped parsley and 1 tablespoon Worcestershire sauce. Cover and simmer for 45 minutes until meat is tender. Thicken with 2 tablespoons flour shaken in a screw-topped jar with ¼ cup (2 fl oz) water. Boil for 2 minutes, remove from the heat and cool. Place in a deep pie dish and moisten the rim with water. Place a sheet of ready-rolled puff or short crust pastry on top and trim edge. Decorate with pastry trimmings, glaze with beaten egg or cream and bake in a preheated hot oven, 220°C (425°F/Gas 7), for 30 minutes or until pastry is golden brown.

Beef

Party Chilli con Carne

Serves 20 - 24

This recipe is designed for those catering for a party, allowing for previous preparation.

2 large onions, chopped
2 tablespoons oil
3 garlic cloves, crushed
2 green peppers (capsicums), grated
2.5 kg (5 lb) coarsely minced (ground) beef
2 x 440 g (14 oz) cans peeled tomatoes, chopped
1/3 cup (2 1/2 fl oz) tomato paste
2 teaspoons ground coriander
1 teaspoon ground cumin
2 teaspoons dried oregano leaves
1/2-1 teaspoon hot chilli powder
2 teaspoons sugar
salt and pepper
2 x 675 g (1 lb 14 oz) cans red kidney beans
1/4 cup chopped fresh coriander

Corn Bread
3 cups (12 oz) flour
2 tablespoons baking powder
1 1/2 tablespoons caster (powdered) sugar
1 teaspoon salt
3 cups yellow cornmeal (polenta)
4 eggs
2 1/2 cups (20 fl oz) milk
185 g (6 oz) butter, melted

Cook the onions in the oil until soft in a large, heavy saucepan. Add the garlic and peppers and cook for a further minute. Increase the heat and add the beef. Cook, stirring often to break up the lumps, until the meat changes colour. It is easier if mince is added in 3 lots, adding the second lot only after the first has changed colour.

Reduce the heat and add the tomatoes with their liquid, tomato paste, ground coriander, cumin, oregano, chilli powder to taste, sugar, salt and pepper. Cover and simmer gently for 30 minutes. The mince may be cooled quickly and stored in refrigerator at this stage for up to 3 days, or in a freezer in 3 lots for longer storage. If frozen, thaw in refrigerator for 24 hours when needed.

If the mince has been stored, bring to the boil in a large boiler and add the drained kidney beans and a little of their liquid if the mixture looks dry. Taste and add more chilli powder if not hot enough. Cover and simmer gently for 30 minutes, stir in the coriander and serve with boiled rice, hot corn bread and a tossed salad.

Corn Bread: Sift the flour with the baking powder into a bowl. Mix in the sugar, salt and cornmeal. Beat the eggs and add to the dry ingredients with the milk and melted cooled butter. Stir well to combine. Grease 2 lamington pans with butter and spread the batter evenly in the pans. Bake in a hot oven, 200°C (400°F/Gas 6), for 30 minutes. Serve hot cut into squares. Corn bread may be baked the day before required and heated in a moderate oven for 15 minutes.

Spiced Beef Pâté

Serves 6 - 8

1 kg (2 lb) shin beef with bone
1/2 cup (4 fl oz) red wine
1 cup (8 fl oz) water
1 teaspoon ground allspice
1/4 teaspoon ground nutmeg
1 teaspoon salt
freshly ground pepper
2 teaspoons soft brown sugar
1 bay leaf
90 g (3 oz) ham pieces
2 tablespoons butter
1 tablespoon brandy

Aspic
1/3 cup (2 1/2 fl oz) water
1 teaspoon gelatine
1/3 cup (2 1/2 fl oz) canned beef consommé
fresh herb sprigs

Have the beef shin cut in slices on the bone. Rinse the beef well and place in a deep pan with the wine and water. Bring to a slow simmer, skimming off the froth when necessary. Add the spices, salt, pepper to taste, sugar and bay leaf. Cover and simmer gently for 2 1/2 to 3 hours until the meat is very tender and falling off the bones. Lift the beef from the liquid. Remove the bones, fat and any hard gristle and place the meat in a bowl. Strain the hot cooking liquid over the meat, cool and refrigerate until the fat is set on top.

Remove the set fat and place the meat and jellied liquid in a food processor fitted with a steel blade. Process to a paste. Add the ham, butter and brandy and process until smooth. Pack into 1 large or 2 small crocks or bowls and smooth the top.

Spoon a thin layer of aspic on top of the pâté and arrange the herb sprigs on top. Chill until set, then spoon more aspic on top to cover the herbs completely. Return to refrigerator, and when set, cover with plastic wrap and keep chilled until required. Serve with crackers, crusty bread or Melba toast, and a selection of crisp salad vegetables.

Aspic: Place the water in a small pan. Add the gelatine and stir well. Heat gently until the gelatine is dissolved. Stir in the consommé and cool.

Note: Pâté keeps for about 1 week in the refrigerator; it is also very good as a sandwich filling.

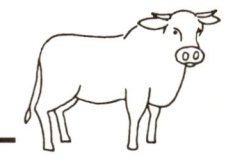

Chilli Bitter Melon Beef

Serves 4

- 250 g (½ lb) fillet steak (tenderloin), trimmed and thinly sliced
- 2 tablespoons soy sauce
- 1 tablespoon sesame oil
- 1 teaspoon chilli sauce
- 2 small bitter melons
- 1 teaspoon caster (powdered) sugar
- 2 garlic cloves, crushed
- 1 teaspoon grated fresh ginger
- 1 small red chilli, very finely chopped
- 1 tablespoon oil
- ½ cup (4 fl oz) stock
- 1 tablespoon cornflour (cornstarch) with 2 tablespoons water
- 4 spring onions (scallions), thinly sliced

Marinate the steak in the soy sauce, sesame oil and chilli sauce for 2 hours. Halve the bitter melons and remove and discard the seeds. Slice very finely and parboil for 3 minutes. Drain and sprinkle with the sugar. Set aside.

Stir fry the garlic, ginger and chilli in the heated oil. Add half the beef and stir fry until well browned. Remove and repeat with the remaining beef.

Stir fry the bitter melon, adding extra oil if required. Drizzle with stock, cover and cook until tender-crisp. Return the beef to the wok with blended cornflour and spring onions. Stir fry until a glossy sauce is formed. Serve immediately.

Note: Bitter melon has a bitter flavour which can be an acquired taste. Snake beans or Chinese cabbage may be substituted if preferred.

Spiced Beef Loaf

Serves 6 - 8

Ingredients are much the same as for Spiced Beef Pâté (see page 98). Increase the shin beef to 1.5 kg (3 lb) and omit the ham, butter and brandy. Cook with the same quantity of other ingredients and for the same length of time. When cooking is completed, lift the meat from the liquid and remove the bone, hard gristle and fat. Shred the meat finely with two forks. Place in a bowl and press plastic wrap closely over the meat to prevent it drying.

Strain the hot liquid into a bowl, cool a little then refrigerate until the surface fat is set. Remove this fat and heat the liquid if necessary to melt it. Stir in the shredded beef.

Make aspic as directed and pour into the base of a loaf tin previously rinsed with cold water. Refrigerate until the aspic begins to thicken and arrange the herb sprigs decoratively in the aspic. Chill until set, then pour the beef and its liquid into the tin. Cover and chill until set. When required for serving, run a knife blade around the edge of the loaf and immerse in hot water for a few seconds. Invert onto a serving platter to unmould. Garnish with watercress and radishes and serve sliced with salad and a selection of pickles, chutney and relishes.

Pastrami

Serves 6 - 8

- 2 kg (4 lb) piece rolled corned brisket
- 3 large garlic cloves, crushed
- 2 teaspoons pickling spice
- 2 teaspoons paprika
- ¼ teaspoon chilli powder
- ½ teaspoon ground allspice
- ½ teaspoon saltpetre
- 2 tablespoons soft brown sugar
- warm water
- 1 onion, sliced
- 2 sprigs parsley
- 1 tablespoon malt vinegar

Remove the strings from the brisket and open out. Rinse and dry with paper towels. Mix the garlic with spices, saltpetre and sugar and rub all over the meat. Wrap closely in plastic wrap and place in a glass or ceramic dish. Cover the dish with plastic wrap to prevent strong flavours escaping. Refrigerate for 1 week, turning the meat each day while still in its wrapping.

Remove the meat from the wrapping and drain well. Cold smoke in a smoker for 30 minutes. Place in a pan with warm water to cover. Add the onion, parsley and vinegar. Bring to a slow simmer and simmer gently for 2 hours until tender. Cool for 15 minutes in liquid. Carve in very thin slices to serve.

Note: Saltpetre may be obtained from a gunsmith.

Beer-Sauced Garlic Steak

Serves 4

- 2 teaspoons garlic salt
- 4 x 200 g (6 ½ oz) porterhouse steaks
- 1 x 370 ml can beer

Sprinkle ¼ teaspoon of the garlic salt onto either side of each steak. Press into the meat with the back of a wooden spoon. Arrange the steaks in a large shallow dish. Pour over the beer, making sure all the meat surfaces are covered. Cover and marinate for at least 2 hours. Remove the steaks from the beer. Reserve the liquid for the sauce. Cook the steaks as desired under a hot grill (broiler). Serve masked with Cheese Sauce (see below) and accompanied by a crisp tossed salad and baked potatoes.

Cheese Sauce

Serves 4

- 1 cup (8 fl oz) reserved marinade (see above)
- 1 cup (4 oz) grated Australian cheese
- 1 tablespoon cornflour (cornstarch)

Heat the marinade to simmering point in a heavy based pan. Toss the grated cheese and cornflour together. Add a little at a time to the simmering liquid, stirring well until combined to a smooth, thickened sauce.

Beef

Short Cut Recipes

Mustard Glazed Steaks

Serves 4

Preparation time: 15 minutes
Cooking time: 15 minutes

12 small new potatoes
2 tablespoons French mustard
4 garlic cloves, crushed
2 teaspoons Worcestershire sauce
1 carrot, cut into strips
125 g (4 oz) green beans
6-8 button squash
4 rib eye or boneless sirloin steaks

Put the potatoes on to boil. Heat the grill (broiler) to high. Combine the mustard, garlic and sauce. Put the other vegetables with the potatoes to boil.

Place the steaks under the grill (broiler) and cook for 4 to 6 minutes. Turn the steaks and spread the uncooked side with the mustard mixture and grill (broil) for a further 4 to 6 minutes. Drain the vegetables and serve on 4 warm plates with the steaks.

French Onion Steak

Serves 4

Preparation time: 15 minutes
Cooking time: 20 minutes

600 g (1 ¼ lb) lean rump or topside steak
2 large onions
12 small new potatoes
30 g (1 oz) butter
broccoli sprigs
1 tablespoon Worcestershire sauce
2 tablespoons cream
pepper
paprika

Cut the steak into strips. Halve the onions and slice each half thinly. Put the potatoes on to boil. Put another pan of water on to boil. Melt two-thirds of the butter in a frying pan. Add the onions and stir well to coat with the butter. Cook on medium low heat for 10 minutes, stirring occasionally, until they are soft and lightly coloured. Remove from the pan. Prepare the broccoli and add to the boiling water. Cook for 6 to 8 minutes until just tender.

Increase the heat to high and add the steak strips with the remaining butter. Cook for 4 to 5 minutes, stirring often to brown the strips well. Do not let the meat boil in its juices. Return the onions to the pan, stir in the Worcestershire sauce and cream and season to taste. Dish out the steak and onions onto plates, dust with paprika and serve with the potatoes and broccoli.

Beef Satays

Serves 4

Preparation time: 20 minutes
Cooking time: 15 minutes

1 cup (6 oz) rice
600 g (1 ¼ lb) lean rump or boneless blade steak
½ cup (4 fl oz) white wine
1 tablespoon soft brown sugar
1 tablespoon sesame oil
2 teaspoons grated fresh ginger
1 garlic clove, crushed
¼ teaspoon five spice powder
¼ teaspoon chilli powder, optional
1 medium-sized cucumber
½ cup roughly chopped red pepper (capsicum)
½ cup (4 fl oz) yoghurt
juice of ½ lemon
2 tablespoons chopped fresh coriander or parsley
bottled satay sauce

Put the rice on to boil. Cut the steak into 2.5 cm (1 inch) cubes and thread 4–5 pieces onto the ends of 16–20 small bamboo skewers so that the skewers are half filled. Mix the wine with the sugar, sesame oil, ginger, garlic and five spice powder, adding chilli powder if liked. Add the satays, turn to coat in marinade and leave aside.

Wash the cucumber, halve lengthwise and slice into semicircles. Mix with the red pepper and toss with the yoghurt, lemon juice and coriander. Drain the cooked rice, return to the pan and keep hot on the side of the barbecue. Barbecue the satays for 5 to 6 minutes, basting with the marinade. Serve on rice with the cucumber salad and satay sauce.

Steak with Tangy Apricots

Serves 4

Preparation time: 10 minutes
Cooking time: 16 minutes

250 g (8 oz) noodles
salad greens
4 rib eye steaks
pepper
2 teaspoons oil
1 small onion, chopped
1 x 425 g (13 ½ oz) can unsweetened apricots
2 teaspoons tomato paste
2 tablespoons mango chutney
finely chopped fresh herbs
French dressing

Bring a pan of water to the boil. Add the noodles and boil until tender. While they boil, prepare a tossed green salad. Season the steaks with pepper. Heat the oil in a large pan on medium high heat. Add the steaks and quickly brown on each side to seal. Reduce the heat to medium and cook for 4 minutes on each side or until the meat feels springy to the touch. Remove and keep warm.

Add the onion and cook for 2 minutes. Drain the apricots, reserving ¼ cup (2 fl oz) juice. Add the apricots to the pan with the reserved juice, tomato paste and mango chutney. Stir and heat until bubbling. Drain the noodles and toss with the herbs. Toss the salad with a splash of French dressing. Place the steaks onto plates, spoon on the sauce and serve with the noodles and salad.

Steak with Tangy Apricots

Beef

Honey Beef Kebabs
Serves 4

Preparation time: 15 minutes
Cooking time: 10 minutes

500 g (1 lb) lean rump steak
125 g (4 oz) button mushrooms
8 small onions, peeled
red or green pepper (capsicum) pieces
1 orange or 1 small can mandarin segments
3 cups finely shredded cabbage
fresh orange juice
2 tablespoons warmed honey
3 teaspoons cooking oil
a few drops sesame oil
1 ½ tablespoons lemon juice
4 small wholemeal pita bread

Cut the steak into 2 cm (¾ inch) cubes. Thread onto 8 metal skewers alternating with mushrooms, onions and pepper pieces. Prepare the segments from the orange or drain the can of mandarin segments and toss with the cabbage and orange juice to taste.

Combine the honey with the cooking oil, sesame oil and lemon juice. Brush over the kebabs. Grill (broil) or barbecue the kebabs under medium heat for 8 to 10 minutes, turning and brushing frequently with the honey mixture. Serve on pita bread with the orange-cabbage salad.

Town and Country Hot Pot
Serves 4

Preparation time: 12 minutes
Cooking time: 20 minutes

600 g (1 ¼ lb) lean round topside steak
2 teaspoons oil
1 x 440 g (14 oz) can mushroom soup
½ cup frozen broad beans
½ cup frozen peas
4 spring onions (scallions), sliced
1 tablespoon tomato paste
2 tablespoons chopped parsley
1 ½ cups (9 oz) rice
butter
additional chopped parsley and spring onions (scallions)

Put a pan of water on to boil for the rice. Slice the steak into fine strips. Heat the oil in a frying pan. Add the beef and cook over high heat, stirring often, until the meat changes colour and is lightly browned. Don't let the meat boil in its juices. Add the mushroom soup, beans and peas, spring onions, tomato paste and parsley. Stir well, cover and simmer gently on low heat for 15 minutes. Add the rice to the boiling water and cook until tender.

Drain the rice and toss with a little butter and chopped parsley and divide between 4 warm plates. Top with the beef mixture and garnish with chopped spring onions.

Pronto Beef Parmigiana
Serves 4

Preparation time: 7 minutes
Cooking time: 20 minutes

4-6 lean oyster blade steaks
pepper
green vegetables; broccoli, zucchini (courgettes) and snow peas (mange-tout)
250 g (8 oz) wholemeal macaroni
2 teaspoons oil
1 onion, sliced
1 x 425 g (13 ½ oz) can tomatoes
pinch of dried basil
2 tablespoons white wine
¼ cup (1 ¼ oz) black olives
4 slices mozzarella cheese

Put 2 pans of water on to boil. Season the steaks with pepper and prepare the green vegetables. Stir the macaroni into one pan of boiling water and cook for 15 minutes until tender.

Heat the oil in a large frying pan over medium high heat. Add the steaks and seal quickly on each side. Reduce the heat to medium and cook for 4 minutes on each side. Remove and set aside. Add the onion to the pan. Cook for 1 minute then add the tomatoes with their liquid, the basil and wine. Boil rapidly, uncovered, for 8 minutes, and while the sauce cooks, add the vegetables to the boiling water.

Reduce the heat under the sauce to low. Return the steaks to the pan, turn in the sauce and top with olives and cheese slices. Cover and simmer on very low heat until cheese melts – about 2 minutes. Serve with drained macaroni tossed with herbs, and the green vegetables.

Mexican Sausages with Chilli Beans
Serves 4

Preparation time: 15 minutes
Cooking time: 10-12 minutes

155 g (5 oz) cream cheese
chilli sauce
8-10 snow peas (mange-tout)
2 small carrots
salad greens
1 x 440 g (14 oz) can red kidney beans
1 teaspoon ground cumin
1 tomato, chopped
pinch of chilli powder
8-10 thick beef sausages
French dressing

Mix the cream cheese with the chilli sauce to taste. String the snow peas and slice the carrots thinly lengthwise. Prepare a green salad. Drain the kidney beans, put in a saucepan on the barbecue with the cumin, tomato and chilli powder and heat gently.

Prick the sausages and barbecue 10 to 12 minutes until cooked. Slice them lengthwise, but don't cut right through. Fill with the cream cheese mixture and put a snow pea and carrot slice in each. Toss the salad with the French dressing and serve with the sausages and beans.

Beef and Salad Pillows

Serves 4

Preparation time: 15 minutes
Cooking Time: 10-12 minutes

2 rump or boneless blade steaks, each about 350 g (11 oz)
¼ cup (2 fl oz) olive oil
1 tablespoon wine vinegar
2 tablespoons chopped parsley or basil
1 garlic clove, crushed
½ teaspoon mustard
freshly ground pepper
1 cup sliced red pepper (capsicum)
½ cup sliced celery
1 small onion, sliced
1 ½ cups alfalfa sprouts
4-5 small wholemeal pita bread
cherry tomatoes and mignonette lettuce

Place the steaks under a hot grill (broiler) and cook for 5 to 6 minutes each side. Combine the oil, vinegar, herbs, garlic and mustard. Beat well with a fork and season to taste. Remove the steaks from the grill. With a sharp knife trim off the fat if necessary and cut the steaks in thin slices. Add to the dressing and toss to coat. Prepare a salad with the red pepper, celery, onion and sprouts. Warm the pita bread in a moderate oven. Halve the warmed bread, fill the pockets with salad and top with the sliced meat. Drizzle over any remaining dressing and serve garnished with cherry tomatoes and lettuce leaves.

Stuffed Rib Eye Steak with Hot Potato Salad

Serves 4

Preparation time: 20 minutes
Cooking time: 8-12 minutes

10-12 small new potatoes
sliced tomatoes
sliced green pepper (capsicum)
salad dressing
4 rib eye or boneless sirloin steaks
bread-and-butter cucumbers
sliced Swiss cheese
chutney
½ cup chopped spring onions (scallions)
¼ cup chopped parsley
seasoning to taste

Wash the potatoes, halve them, leaving the skin on, and put on to boil. Make a side salad of the tomatoes and green pepper and moisten with salad dressing. Cut a pocket in each steak taking care not to cut right through. Insert 3–4 slices of bread-and-butter cucumbers, a small slice of Swiss cheese and some chutney. Close the pocket with a skewer.

Barbecue the steaks on an oiled grid for 8 to 12 minutes until cooked to taste, turning once. Drain the potatoes and toss with the spring onions, parsley and salad dressing and season to taste. Remove the skewers from the steaks and serve with the two salads.

Teriyaki Meatballs

Serves 4

Preparation time: 20 minutes
Cooking time: 15 minutes

3 spring onions (scallions), chopped
1 garlic clove, crushed
1 teaspoon grated fresh ginger
¼ cup (2 fl oz) soy sauce
1 tablespoon sugar
500 g (1 lb) finely minced (ground) lean beef
1 cup (6 oz) rice
2 medium-sized carrots, thinly sliced
155 g (5 oz) snow peas (mange-tout)
1 tablespoon oil
⅓ cup (2 ½ fl oz) water
1 teaspoon cornflour (cornstarch)

Put a pan of water on to boil. Mix the spring onions with the garlic, ginger, soy sauce and sugar. Put the beef into another bowl and pour in half the soy mixture. Mix well to combine and shape into 20 meatballs. Add the rice to the boiling water and put another pan of water on to boil. Prepare the carrots and top and tail the snow peas.

Heat the oil in a large frying pan and fry the meatballs, turning often until they are browned and cooked through, about 10 minutes. Add the carrot to the boiling water, cook 5 minutes, then add the snow peas and cook for a further 3 minutes. Mix the water and cornflour into the remaining soy mixture and add to the meatballs, stirring constantly until the sauce thickens and bubbles. Boil for a minute or so, then serve the meatballs and sauce with the drained rice and vegetables.

Fruity Barbecued Blade

Serves 4

Preparation time: 10 minutes
Cooking time: 10-12 minutes

4 blade steaks
freshly ground pepper
1 tablespoon plum sauce
1 tablespoon vinegar
1 tablespoon tomato paste
½ cup (4 fl oz) juice from canned pears
4 canned pear halves
250 g (8 oz) Polish salami
alfalfa sprouts
crusty bread rolls, buttered

Sprinkle the steaks with pepper and place on a plate. Mix the plum sauce with the vinegar, tomato paste and pear juice in a bowl. Cut the pear halves into quarters. Remove the skin from the salami and cut into chunks. Thread the salami and pear chunks alternately onto 4 skewers. Rinse and drain the alfalfa sprouts.

Brush the steaks with the sauce and barbecue for 10 to 12 minutes, turning occasionally and basting with more sauce if necessary. Place the skewers next to the steaks, brush with the sauce and barbecue for 4 minutes, turning once. Place some alfalfa sprouts onto 4 plates and top with the filled skewers. Add the steaks and serve with the bread rolls.

Beef

Skewered Beef Waldorf

Skewered Beef Waldorf

Serves 4

Preparation time: 16 minutes
Cooking time: 6-7 minutes

600 g (1 ¼ lb) lean boneless blade or round steak
¼ cup (4 fl oz) apple cider or whisky
2 tablespoons cider vinegar
1 tablespoon soft brown sugar
1 tablespoon oil
1 garlic clove, crushed
3 cups shredded savoy cabbage
2 sliced or diced apples
½ cup (3 oz) pecan nuts
¼ cup (2 fl oz) coleslaw dressing
2 slices fresh pineapple with skin
2 small onions, peeled

Slice the steak into 6 mm (¼ inch) strips and marinate in a mixture of apple cider, cider vinegar, brown sugar, oil and garlic. Toss the cabbage with the apples (prepared with skin on), pecan nuts and coleslaw dressing.

Cut the pineapple into wedges and quarter the onions. Thread a piece of pineapple and onion onto each of 8 skewers then weave on the drained meat strips, retaining the marinade. Barbecue the skewers, turning frequently and basting with the marinade, and cook for 6 to 7 minutes. Serve with the Waldorf cabbage.

Sang Cho Bau

Serves 4

Preparation time: 18 minutes
Cooking time: 6 minutes

2 cups (16 fl oz) water
1 cup (6 oz) rice
8 lettuce leaves
sliced red or green pepper (capsicum)
1 cucumber
1 tomato
1 tablespoon cooking oil
a few drops of sesame oil
1 teaspoon grated fresh ginger
1 garlic clove, crushed
500 g (1 lb) finely minced (ground) lean beef
1 tablespoon dry sherry
1 tablespoon soy sauce
½ cup sliced canned water chestnuts, optional
freshly ground pepper
1 tablespoon cornflour (cornstarch), mixed with 2 tablespoons cold water
½ cup chopped spring onions (scallions)
additional soy sauce

Boil the water and add the rice. Stir, return to the boil, reduce the heat to low and cover the pan. Cook on low heat for 15 minutes. While the rice is cooking, place the lettuce leaves in a bowl of iced water to keep crisp. Prepare a salad of red or green pepper, cucumber and tomato.

Heat the cooking and sesame oils in a wok or frying pan. Add the ginger, garlic and beef. Stir fry on high heat for 3 minutes until the meat changes colour and is broken up. Remove the pan from the heat and add the sherry, soy sauce, water chestnuts, if used, and pepper to taste. Mix the cornflour and cold water and add to the meat. Return to the heat and stir fry for 2 minutes. Remove from the heat and stir in the spring onions.

Drain the lettuce leaves and place 2 leaves on each plate. Scoop spoonfuls of rice into the leaves and top with the beef mixture. Serve with additional soy sauce and the salad.

LAMB

Australian lamb is succulent and inexpensive. It is meat from a sheep less than one year old while mutton is obtained from older sheep.

Almost the whole of a lamb is easily prepared and cooked and can be used in a variety of recipes. Lamb has a higher fat content than beef but because of this it is more tender.

Lamb is now being presented in many new cuts which enable the preparation of many dishes inherited from our multi-cultural society. Try these new tastes, but do not forget that very special roast leg of lamb with baked vegetables.

The majority of the recipes in this chapter have been supplied by the **Australian Meat and Livestock Corporation** while others have been provided by contributors whose credits appear elsewhere in the book.

Lamb

CARVING

Leg of Lamb

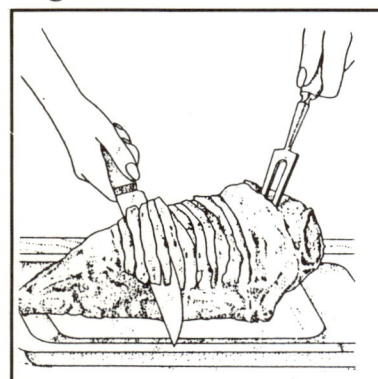

1. Place, fat side up, on the board. Cut vertically down through the meat to the bone. Slip the knife under the slices and cut away from the bone.

2. From the side of the leg, cut thick slices parallel to the bone. Repeat on the other side.

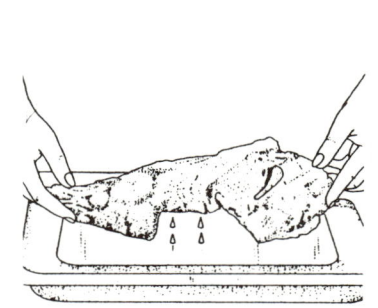

3. Turn the leg over and cut a wedge-shaped piece from the centre.

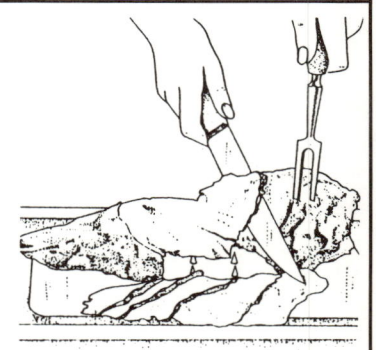

4. Holding the knife at an angle, carve thick slices from either side of the wedge, down towards the bone.

Shoulder of Lamb

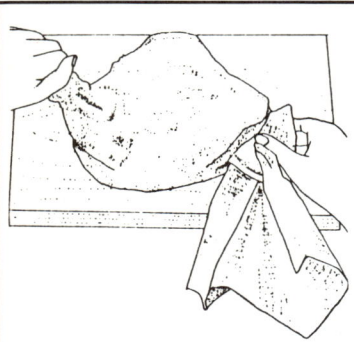

1. Hold the joint firmly and use a cloth to draw out the loosened blade bone after cooking.

2. Hold the shank bone and slice thickly through the meat where the bone has been removed. Continue until the shank bone has been reached.

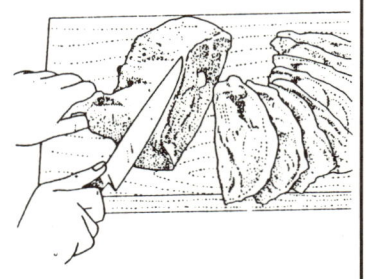

3. Position the shoulder with the shank pointing away and slice through the meat until the bone is reached again. Carve until the bone is clean.

Loin of Lamb

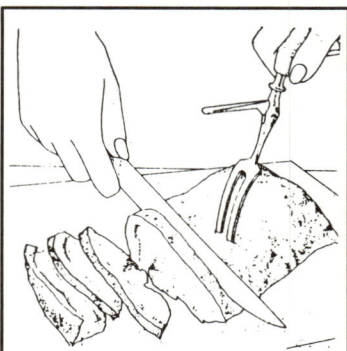

1. Place on the board, fat side up. Cut thick slices down through the meat.

Baked Lamb Dinner

Serves 5 – 6

1 leg lamb, about
   1.5 kg (3 lb)
salt and pepper
potatoes, pumpkin,
   carrots, parsnips for
   baking
green peas, beans or
   Brussels sprouts
1 ½ tablespoons flour
1 cup (8 fl oz) hot stock
mint sauce or jelly for
   serving

Wipe the lamb with paper towels and season with salt and pepper. Place on a small rack in a large roasting dish and cook in a moderate oven, 180°C (350°F/Gas 4), for 1 hour. Prepare two or three of the vegetables for baking, cutting them in even-sized pieces. Place around the lamb, season to taste, and pour a little melted dripping or oil over them if there is insufficient fat in the dish. Return to the oven and cook for a further hour, turning the lamb and vegetables to brown evenly during cooking.

When the lamb and vegetables are tender, remove the lamb to a platter, cover with foil and leave in a warm place (not the oven) for 15 minutes. Place the vegetables in an ovenproof dish and return to a slow oven to keep hot. Put the green vegetable on to cook.

Drain off the excess fat in the dish, leaving about 1 tablespoon. Place over the heat and sprinkle in the flour. Stir the flour into the pan drippings and cook gently 2 to 3 minutes to lightly brown the flour. Remove the dish from the heat and stir in the hot stock. Return to the heat and keep stirring until the gravy thickens and bubbles. Simmer gently for 2 minutes and strain into a gravy boat. Carve the lamb and serve on hot plates with the vegetables, gravy and mint sauce.

Note: Other lamb roasting joints may be cooked in the same way; rolled shoulder or forequarter with stuffing, or the same cuts bone in. Allow 1 ½ hours total cooking time for shoulder, 2 ½ for forequarter and add the vegetables 1 hour before the end of cooking.

Benalla Lamb and Apricot Terrine

Serves 10 – 12 as a first course, 6 as a main course

8 rashers bacon
1 large onion, chopped
1¾ cups (7 oz) dried
   apricots, chopped
1 kg (2 lb) finely minced
   (ground) lamb
1 teaspoon dried thyme
   leaves
1 teaspoon dried marjoram
   leaves
salt and pepper to taste

Trim the rind from the bacon and line a terrine tin or loaf pan with the bacon. Combine the remaining ingredients, mixing well. Pack the mixture evenly in the bacon-lined tin. Place the tin in a dish with water to come halfway up the side of the tin. Cover the dish of water and the terrine with a lid or a sheet of foil, shiny side down. Cook in a moderate oven, 180°C (350°F/Gas 4), for 1¼ to 1½ hours or until the terrine is firm. Pour off the excess liquid and leave to cool.

Unmould onto a serving platter, cover with plastic wrap and chill well. Serve thinly sliced with dry toast triangles and salad garnish as a first course, or with tossed salad for a summer lunch.

Lamb Boulangère

Serves 6 – 8

1 leg lamb, about
   2 kg (4 lb)
2 garlic cloves
freshly ground pepper
1 tablespoon oil
1 tablespoon fresh rosemary
   leaves
30 g (1 oz) butter
5 medium-sized onions,
   sliced
1.25 kg (2 ½ lb)
   potatoes
2 bay leaves
1 cup (8 fl oz) light
   stock

Wipe the leg with paper towels. Insert 1 garlic clove in the shank end of the lamb close to the bone. Season the leg with pepper, rub with oil and place in a roasting dish. Sprinkle on half the rosemary and cook in a moderate oven, 180°C (350°F/Gas 4), for 1 hour.

Heat the butter in a frying pan, crush the remaining garlic and add to the pan with the onions. Cook gently until the onions are transparent. Peel the potatoes, slice thinly and soak in cold water for 30 minutes. Drain well.

After lamb has cooked for 1 hour, remove from the oven and take the lamb from the dish. Drain the fat from the dish and add the potatoes. Top with the onions, the remaining rosemary and the bay leaves. Place the lamb in the centre, upside down, and pour in the stock. Return to the oven and cook for a further 1½ hours, turning the lamb once. As the vegetables slow down the cooking of the lamb, it should be pink and juicy after this time. Remove the lamb to a platter, cover and leave in a warm place for 20 minutes, keeping the vegetables hot in a low oven. Carve the lamb and serve on hot plates with the vegetables, dish juices and a tossed salad.

Lamb

Lamb Cutlets in Pastry

Serves 4

16 dried apricot halves
¼ cup (2 fl oz) orange juice
¼ cup (1 oz) slivered almonds
8 lamb cutlets
pepper to taste
8 sheets filo pastry
3 tablespoons melted butter

Put the apricots in a small pan with the orange juice and bring to the boil. Remove from the heat and leave aside. Toast the almonds on a baking sheet while the oven is heating. Trim the cutlets and sprinkle with pepper.

Fold a sheet of filo pastry in half, brush lightly with melted butter and fold across to give a rectangle. Brush with butter and place a cutlet towards the shorter edge with the bone protruding. Top with 2 teaspoons almonds and 2 apricot halves. Fold the pastry over the meaty end of the cutlet, then bring the flap of pastry over the top and tuck underneath. Twist the pastry around the bone, using a dab of water to make it stick. Wrap the remaining cutlets.

Place the wrapped cutlets on a greased baking sheet and brush the tops lightly with butter. Bake in a preheated hot oven, 200°C (400°F/Gas 6), for 18 minutes. Serve with boiled sweet potato cubes tossed with a little orange juice and ground ginger, and a steamed green vegetable.

Lamb Loin with Mustard Sauce

Serves 6

2 lamb mid loins, boned
freshly ground black pepper
3 tablespoons grainy mustard
½ cup (4 fl oz) dry white wine
½ cup (4 fl oz) light stock
2 teaspoons cornflour (cornstarch)
cream, optional

Have the butcher bone out 2 lamb mid loins. Remove the fine skin covering the loins and trim off the excess fat. Place the loins fat side down on a board, leave the fillet in the centre and sprinkle the meat with the pepper. Spread about 2 teaspoons mustard on each loin and roll them up separately. Tie with string. Rub the rolls with more pepper and place in a roasting dish. Cook in a moderate oven, 180°C (350°F/Gas 4), for 45 minutes, turning to brown evenly.

Remove the lamb to a platter, cover with foil and leave in a warm place. Drain the fat from the dish and stir in the wine and stock to dissolve the dish juices. Pour into a small saucepan and add the remaining mustard. Bring to the boil, adjust seasoning and thicken with the cornflour mixed with a little cold water. A little cream may be added if desired. Slice the lamb and serve with the mustard sauce, puréed parsnips mixed with a dash of grated nutmeg, boiled pumpkin cubes and steamed green beans.

Crown Roast with Cherries

Serves 5 – 6

1 crown roast of lamb, about 16 ribs
freshly ground pepper
½ cup (4 fl oz) light stock
¾ cup (6 fl oz) liquid from cherries (see below)
3 teaspoons cornflour (cornstarch)
¼ cup (2 fl oz) port
pinch of cinnamon
1 teaspoon sugar

Cherry Stuffing
1 onion, finely chopped
15 g (½ oz) butter
2 cups (4 oz) soft wholemeal breadcrumbs
grated rind of 1 lemon
1 cup bottled morello cherries, drained and pitted
¼ teaspoon cinnamon
1 small egg, beaten

When ordering the crown roast, ask the butcher to remove some of the fat before assembling it. Rub the crown roast with pepper and place in a greased roasting dish. Spoon the stuffing into centre of roast and cover the rib bones with foil. Cook in a moderately hot oven, 190°C (375°F/Gas 5), for 1¼ hours. Remove the roast to a platter, cover with foil and leave in a warm place for 10 minutes.

Pour off any fat from the roasting dish, add the stock and stir to dissolve the browned juices. Strain into a small pan, add the cherry liquid and bring to the boil. Mix the cornflour with the port and stir into the simmering liquid. Add the cinnamon and sugar, adjust the seasoning and strain into a sauceboat. Serve the crown roast with the sauce and vegetables of your choice.

Cherry Stuffing: Gently cook the onion in the butter until soft. Turn into a bowl. Add the remaining ingredients, lightly mixing in enough egg to bind. The mixture will be fairly moist.

Roast Lamb Sesame

Serves 6

grated rind of 1 orange and 1 lemon
1 teaspoon dry mustard
freshly ground pepper to taste
1 leg lamb, about 1.5 kg (3 lb)
¾ cup (6 fl oz) orange juice
1 tablespoon honey
¼ teaspoon ground ginger
1 tablespoon sesame seeds
¾ cup (6 fl oz) light stock
2 teaspoons cornflour (cornstarch)

Mix the orange and lemon rind with the mustard and pepper. Rub the mixture all over the lamb and leave for 30 minutes. Place upside down in a roasting dish and cook in a moderate oven, 180°C (350°F/Gas 4), for 30 minutes. Turn the leg right side up. Mix the orange juice with the honey and ginger and pour over the lamb, then sprinkle with the sesame seeds. Return to the oven and cook for a further 1½ to 2 hours, basting often. Remove to a platter, cover with foil and keep warm. Skim the fat from the dish and add the stock. Heat and stir well to dissolve the juices. Strain into a saucepan and stir in the cornflour mixed with a little cold water. Bring to the boil, stirring constantly until thickened, and adjust the seasoning. Serve the lamb with the sauce, baked or boiled jacket potatoes, carrots cooked in orange juice and a green vegetable.

Honeyed Barbecue Lamb

Serves 8 – 10

1 large leg lamb, about 2.5 kg (5 lb)
2 garlic cloves, cut in slivers
½ lemon
2 teaspoons fresh rosemary leaves
salt and pepper
about ¼ cup (3 oz) honey

Make incisions over the lamb leg with the point of a knife and insert the garlic slivers. Rub well with the cut lemon. Place the rosemary in a bowl and press well with the back of a spoon to bruise the leaves. Rub onto the lamb with the salt and pepper. Place in a dish, cover and refrigerate for 2 to 3 hours or overnight.

Push the leg onto a barbecue spit. Secure with the spit forks and check the balance, repositioning if necessary. Cook over glowing coals for about 2 hours. If the lamb is lean, brush with oil occasionally. Five minutes before removing from the barbecue, drizzle the honey over the leg. Remove to a large platter and brush with more honey. Leave for 15 minutes before carving.

If barbecue has a cover, place the leg on the grid with a drip pan in the centre of the coals, close the cover and cook for 1½ to 2 hours. Brush with honey towards the end of cooking. Serve with roast potatoes cooked in a dish on the barbecue and vegetables or salad.

Roast Lamb Sesame

Lamb

Roast Lamb with Fruity Stuffing

Forequarter serves 6 – 8; shoulder serves 4 – 5

1 lamb forequarter or shoulder, boned
salt and pepper

Fruity Stuffing
¼ cup (1 oz) chopped dried apricots
2 tablespoons sultanas
1 small onion, chopped
15 g (½ oz) butter
2 cups (4 oz) soft breadcrumbs
2 teaspoons chopped parsley
grated rind of ½ lemon
1 tablespoon lemon juice
1 small egg, beaten
salt

Open out the lamb and trim off the excess fat. Spread the stuffing over the inside surface of the lamb. Roll up, skewer into shape, then tie with white string. Rub the lamb with salt and pepper and place on a rack in a roasting dish. Roast in a moderate oven, 180°C (350°F/Gas 4), for 2 to 2 ½ hours for forequarter, 1 ¼ hours for shoulder. Turn twice during cooking to brown evenly. Remove to a platter, cover with foil and keep warm. Make the gravy from the dish juices. Serve with baked vegetables and a green vegetable.

Fruity Stuffing: Soak the apricots and sultanas in hot water for 15 minutes. Cook the onion gently in the butter until soft and tip into a bowl. Add the drained fruit and remaining stuffing ingredients, adding enough egg to bind. Mix lightly and add salt to taste.

Note: Other cuts suitable for the above recipe are boned lamb leg or 2 boned mid loins, each filled with stuffing and rolled separately. Cook the leg for 2 hours; mid loins for 45 to 60 minutes. Leg or loins serve 6-8.

Chutneyed Chops Banana

Serves 4

30 g (1 oz) butter
8 middle loin chops, excess fat removed
1 large onion, peeled and cut into rings
1 tablespoon curry powder
1 tablespoon flour
½ cup (4 fl oz) water
2 tablespoons fruit chutney
1 banana, peeled and sliced
½ cup (4 fl oz) sour cream

Melt the butter in a large heavy based pan. Lightly brown the chops on both sides. Add the onion rings, cover and cook for 2 to 3 minutes or until the onion is tender. Place the chops on one side of the pan. Stir in the curry powder and flour. Gradually blend in the water and chutney. Stir over the heat until the sauce thickens. Mask the chops with the sauce. Cover and simmer for 10 to 15 minutes or until the chops are tender. Stir in the banana and sour cream. Reheat. Serve with buttered parsley rice and a cucumber salad.

Lamb Smithton

Serves 8

2 whole mid loins lamb, boned
2 tablespoons pine nuts or slivered almonds
15 g (½ oz) butter
½ cup chopped spring onions (scallions)
1 ½ cups blackberries
2 tablespoons honey
1 ½ cups (3 oz) wholemeal breadcrumbs
grated rind of ½ lemon
1 teaspoon chopped fresh thyme or ½ teaspoon dried thyme
salt and pepper to taste
1 small egg, beaten
1 cup (8 fl oz) light stock
3 teaspoons cornflour (cornstarch)

Remove the fine outer skin from the loins and trim off the excess fat if necessary. Place the lamb fat side down on a board. Place the pine nuts in a small frying pan with the butter and stir over medium heat until golden. Add the spring onions, cook for 1 minute, then add half the blackberries and 1 tablespoon honey. Cook gently for 4 to 5 minutes, stirring occasionally. Turn into a bowl and add the breadcrumbs, lemon rind and thyme. Mix lightly to combine, season to taste and lightly mix in the egg, adding enough to bind.

Spread the stuffing along the centre of the lamb loins, roll up and tie at intervals with white string. Season with salt and pepper and place in a roasting dish. Cook in a moderately hot oven, 190°C (375°F/Gas 5), for 50 minutes, turning occasionally to brown evenly. Add a little water to the dish if the juices begin to scorch.

Remove the lamb to a warm dish and keep warm. Drain the fat from the dish and dissolve the dish juices with the stock. Pour into a small pan and add the remaining honey and blackberries. Heat and simmer gently for 3 to 4 minutes. Thicken with the cornflour mixed with a little cold water. Adjust the flavour and seasoning with honey, salt and pepper and boil for 1 minute. Remove the strings from the loins and carve in thick slices. Serve with the sauce, scalloped potatoes, glazed carrots and a green vegetable.

Note: The stuffing may be used to fill a crown roast of lamb. Have the butcher trim off some of the fat before shaping the roast. Prepare the stuffing as directed. Place the crown roast in the base of the roasting dish and fill the centre with the stuffing. Cover the ends of the rib bones with foil and cook as for loins. Finish as directed.

Rack of Lamb with Herb and Pine Nut Crust

Serves 6

6 racks of lamb, each with 3-4 ribs
¾ cup (6 fl oz) dry vermouth
1 tablespoon oil
1 sprig each rosemary, thyme and parsley

2 garlic cloves, chopped
freshly ground pepper
2 teaspoons cornflour (cornstarch)
Madeira, optional

Herb and Pine Nut Crust

2 cups (4 oz) soft white breadcrumbs
2 tablespoons melted butter
¼ cup pine nuts
½ cup chopped fresh herbs (parsley, thyme, rosemary, chives)
grated rind of 1 lemon
salt and pepper to taste
beaten egg to bind

If lamb racks are small, ask for 4-rib racks, otherwise 3-rib racks should be sufficient for each serving. Trim the fat, leaving a thin layer of fat on each. Mix the vermouth, oil, herb sprigs, garlic and pepper to taste in a plastic container with a good seal. Add the racks, seal and shake well to distribute the marinade. Leave at room temperature for 1 hour, shaking occasionally; if marinating for longer, store in the refrigerator.

Place the crumbs in a bowl and add all the crust ingredients except the egg. Mix lightly, then add enough beaten egg to bind.

Drain the lamb racks, reserving the marinade, and place fat side up on a roasting rack set in an oven dish. Add a little water to the dish. Cook in a hot oven, 200°C (400°F/Gas 6), for 20 minutes. Remove from the oven and press the crust mixture evenly on top of the racks. Return to the oven and cook for a further 20 to 25 minutes.

Remove the racks to a warm plate and keep warm. Drain the fat from the oven dish and add the marinade. Stir well to dissolve the baked-on juices and strain into a small pan. Heat until boiling, and thicken with the cornflour mixed to a paste with a little cold water. If too tart for your taste, add a little Madeira to soften the flavour. Adjust the seasoning, spoon some sauce onto hot plates and place the lamb racks upright in the centre of the sauce.

Herbed Roast Lamb

Serves 8

1 leg lamb, about 2 kg (4 lb)
⅓ cup finely chopped fresh parsley
2 tablespoons chopped fresh herbs (thyme, marjoram, chervil etc)
½ teaspoon dried tarragon
2 garlic cloves, crushed
1 tablespoon finely chopped spring onions (scallions)

grated rind of ½ lemon
15 g (½ oz) soft butter
freshly ground pepper
salt
oil
½ cup (4 fl oz) dry white wine or vermouth
¾ cup (6 fl oz) light stock
3 teaspoons cornflour (cornstarch)

Choose a leg which has the outer covering intact. Have the shank bone sawn. Remove this and keep aside for use in another recipe. Ask for the pelvic bone to be removed, or do this yourself with a sharp boning knife.

Beginning at the top end of the leg, carefully pull back the fine skin covering the meat. Ease it away gently with the aid of a small knife. Pull it down so that the top of the leg is exposed. Don't worry if the skin tears a little. Trim off the excess fat from the inside of the skin and from the meat.

Mix the herbs with the garlic, spring onions, lemon rind and butter. Add pepper to taste and ½ teaspoon salt and spread over the exposed meat. Carefully pull the skin over the herb paste.

Using a large needle and doubled thread, sew the skin onto the meat around the sides and top. Sprinkle with salt and pepper, brush with oil and place in roasting dish with the shank. Roast in a moderate oven, 180°C (350°F/Gas 4), for 1 hour. Add the wine and stock and cook for a further hour or until cooked to taste, basting occasionally.

When cooked remove the lamb to a platter, cover with foil and leave in a warm place for 15 minutes. Remove the stitches from the lamb. Skim the fat from the dish juices, add a little water and dissolve the sediment. Pour into a small pan and heat, then thicken with cornflour mixed with a little cold water. Strain into a sauceboat and serve with the lamb.

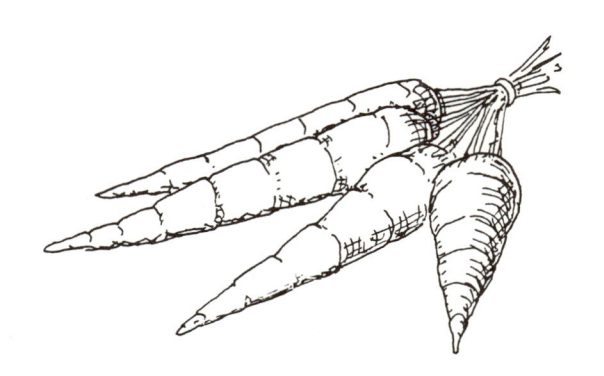

Lamb

Navarin of Lamb

Serves 6

- 1 kg (2 lb) boneless lamb from leg or shoulder
- 30 g (1 oz) butter
- 1 medium-sized onion, chopped
- 1 garlic clove, crushed
- 2 tablespoons flour
- 3 tablespoons tomato paste
- 1 cup (8 fl oz) light stock
- ½ teaspoon sugar
- salt and freshly ground pepper to taste
- 2 medium-sized carrots, cut into chunks
- bouquet garni
- 8-10 small, whole onions
- 1 turnip, sliced
- 12 small whole potatoes, peeled
- 1 cup shelled green peas
- chopped fresh parsley

Trim the lamb and cut into 2 cm (¾ inch) cubes. Heat the butter in a large frying pan, add the lamb and brown on each side. Transfer to a casserole dish. Add the chopped onion to the pan and cook gently on low heat until transparent. Add the garlic and cook for a few seconds. Sprinkle in the flour, stir well and cook for 1 minute, then stir in the tomato paste mixed with the stock. Stir constantly until thickened and bubbling. Add the sugar, salt and pepper and pour over the lamb. Add the carrots and place the bouquet garni in the centre of the casserole contents.

Cook in a moderately slow oven, 160°C (325°F/Gas 3), for 1 hour. Add the onions, turnip, potatoes and peas, cover and return to the oven for a further hour or until the meat and vegetables are tender. Skim any fat from the surface and remove the bouquet garni and discard. Clean around the edge of the casserole dish and sprinkle with chopped parsley. Serve at the table from the dish, and accompany with crusty bread.

Navarin of Lamb

Fruity Lamb Pot Roast

Shoulder serves 4; forequarter serves 6 – 8

- 1 boned lamb shoulder or forequarter
- salt and pepper
- 15 g (½ oz) butter
- 1 onion, chopped
- 1 cooking apple, peeled and chopped
- 1 cup (8 fl oz) apple cider
- ½ teaspoon ground allspice
- ⅓ cup (2 oz) dried prunes
- ⅓ cup (1½ oz) dried apricots
- 1 large sweet potato, peeled and sliced
- 3 teaspoons cornflour (cornstarch)

Trim the lamb, roll up firmly and tie with white string or have the butcher do this for you. Season with salt and pepper. Heat the butter in a heavy pan or Dutch oven and brown the lamb on all sides. Reduce the heat and add the onion and apple to the pan around the lamb. Cook gently until soft and add the cider and allspice. Cover and simmer for 45 minutes for shoulder, 1½ hours for forequarter, turning occasionally.

Add the prunes, apricots and sweet potato to the pan around the lamb, cover and cook for a further 45 minutes or until the meat is tender. Remove the lamb to a warm platter and take off the string. Surround with apricots, prunes and sweet potato. Cover with foil and leave in a warm place. Skim the fat from the liquid in the pan and bring to the boil. Boil rapidly to reduce a little and thicken with cornflour mixed with a little cold water. Pour into a sauceboat and serve with the sliced lamb.

Apricot-Nut Rack of Lamb

Serves 4 – 6

- 2 x 8-rib racks of lamb, trimmed and cut into cutlets
- ½ teaspoon turmeric
- ½ teaspoon ground cumin
- ½ cup (2 oz) pie-pack apricots
- 1 cup (8 fl oz) natural yoghurt
- 1 cup (3 oz) desiccated coconut
- 2 tablespoons self-raising flour
- seasonings to taste

Reshape the cutlets to resemble racks again. Run a long skewer through each to hold in place. Rub the turmeric and cumin over the top surface of the lamb racks. Spread the apricots evenly on top. Combine the remaining ingredients and spoon carefully over the apricots. Smooth the surface with a knife or spatula. Place the racks on a baking tray. Cook at 180°C (350°F/Gas 4) for approximately 1 hour until the surface is golden brown and the lamb is cooked. Place on a serving dish and gently remove the skewers. Serve either hot or cold accompanied with slices of fresh pineapple and a rice pilaf. Alternately, use 16 separate cutlets and place flat on a baking tray. Place the topping over the eye of each cutlet and bake for 15 to 20 minutes.

Lamb Balls with Egg and Lemon Sauce

Serves 6

- 750 g (1½ lb) finely minced (ground) lamb
- 1 small onion, finely chopped
- 1 egg, beaten
- ⅓ cup (2½ oz) short grain rice
- 2 tablespoons finely chopped parsley
- 1 teaspoon finely chopped fresh mint
- 1 teaspoon salt
- freshly ground black pepper
- flour for coating
- 3 cups (24 fl oz) light stock
- 15 g (½ oz) butter
- 3 teaspoons cornflour (cornstarch)
- 2 eggs, separated
- 3 tablespoons lemon juice

Put the lamb in a bowl and add the onion, beaten egg, rice, herbs and seasoning. Mix lightly until combined. Shape into balls the size of a large walnut and coat the balls lightly with flour.

Bring the stock to the boil in a large saucepan, add butter and lamb balls and return to the boil. Cover and simmer on low heat for 45 minutes.

Strain the stock from the meatballs into a small saucepan; keep the lamb balls hot on a low heat. Heat the stock and thicken with cornflour mixed with a little cold water. Beat the egg whites until stiff then beat in the egg yolks and lemon juice. Gradually pour the hot stock onto the eggs, beating constantly, return to the saucepan and stir over low heat for 2 to 3 minutes. Serve the lamb balls with the sauce poured on top. Sprinkle with chopped parsley and serve with creamy mashed potatoes and a green vegetable.

Note: Make light stock from some lamb bones with carrot, celery and onion added, or use 2-3 chicken stock cubes with hot water.

Lamb

Roast Lamb with Pears
Serves 8–10

1 leg lamb, about 2 kg (4 lb)
salt and pepper
8-10 poached or canned pear halves
1 tablespoon flour
¾ cup (6 fl oz) light stock
¼ cup (2 fl oz) pear syrup
1 tablespoon lemon juice
mint jelly

Rub the lamb with salt and pepper and place on a rack in a roasting dish. Roast in a moderate oven, 180°C (350°F/Gas 4), for 1½ to 2 hours until cooked to taste. Fifteen minutes before the end of cooking, place the pear halves on the rack around the lamb to heat, or place in a covered casserole dish and heat in the oven.

When the lamb is cooked, remove the lamb and pears to a warm platter, cover and leave in a warm place for 15 minutes. Drain the fat from the dish, leaving about 1 tablespoon of fat in the dish. Stir in the flour and heat for 2 minutes. Stir in the stock, pear syrup and lemon juice until thickened and bubbling. Adjust the seasoning and strain into a gravy boat. Arrange the lamb on a platter with the pear halves and fill the hollows of the pears with mint jelly. Serve with oven-baked vegetables and a green vegetable.

Lamb Montmorency
Serves 6–8

1 leg lamb, about 2 kg (4 lb)
salt and pepper
1 teaspoon juniper berries, crushed
1 cup (8 fl oz) water or light stock
1 tablespoon port
1 cup sour cherries with liquid
3 teaspoons cornflour (cornstarch)
additional ¼ cup (2 fl oz) port
3 teaspoons soft brown sugar

Dry the leg with paper towels. Rub with the salt, pepper and juniper berries. Place in a roasting dish without a rack and add the water to the dish with the 1 tablespoon port. Cook in a moderate oven, 180°C (350°F/Gas 4), for 2 to 2½ hours or until cooked to taste. Baste occasionally with the liquid in the dish, adding a little water if the dish juices begin to scorch. Turn the leg to brown evenly. When cooked remove to a platter, cover with foil and leave in a warm place for 15 minutes before carving. Skim the fat from the dish juices and dissolve with about ½ cup (4 fl oz) water.

Pour the juices into a small pan and add the cherries and their liquid. Mix the cornflour into the port with the sugar and stir into the cherries. Bring to the boil, stirring constantly, then simmer gently for 3 minutes. Pour into a sauceboat and serve with the sliced lamb.

Honey-Glazed Lamb Racks
Serves 6

3 lamb racks, each with 6-8 ribs
¼ cup (3 oz) honey
¼ cup (2 fl oz) lemon juice
¾ cup (6 fl oz) dry white wine
freshly ground pepper
ground rosemary
½ cup (4 fl oz) light stock
cornflour (cornstarch), optional

Trim the fat from the racks leaving a thin covering. Cut each rack in half to give individual racks of 3 or 4 ribs, depending on the amount required for serving. Score the fat into diamonds. Mix the honey with the lemon juice and ¼ cup (2 fl oz) of the wine in a plastic container. Add the racks, seal the container and shake well to coat. Refrigerate for at least 2 hours or overnight, shaking the container occasionally.

Remove the racks from the marinade, place fat side up on a roasting rack set in a dish and season with pepper and rosemary. Pour the remaining wine and the stock into the dish and cook in a moderately hot oven, 190°C (375°F/Gas 5), for 50 minutes, brushing occasionally with marinade. Remove to a warm platter, cover and keep warm.

Skim the fat from the dish juices and add the marinade. Place over heat and stir well to lift the browned sediment. Bring to the boil and thicken if desired with a cornflour and water paste. Adjust the seasoning and strain into a sauceboat. Serve the racks with the sauce, lightly cooked cherry tomatoes and steamed button squash.

Apricot Lamb
Serves 4–5

1 kg (2 lb) lamb forequarter chops
1 packet French onion soup mix
1 teaspoon curry powder
1 x 425 g (13 ½ oz) can apricot nectar
1 tablespoon tomato sauce
¼ cup (1 oz) dried apricots

Trim the chops and cut the edges in 2 or 3 places. Combine the dry soup mix with the curry powder and coat the chops. Place in a single layer in a roasting dish. Sprinkle any remaining soup mix on top.

Mix the remaining ingredients and pour over the lamb. Cover with foil, shiny side down, and cook in a moderate oven, 180°C (350°F/Gas 4), for 1¼ hours, turning halfway through cooking. When cooked, tilt the dish and skim off any fat. Serve on warm plates with rice pilaf and lightly cooked beans or broccoli.

Opposite: *Honey-Glazed Lamb Racks*

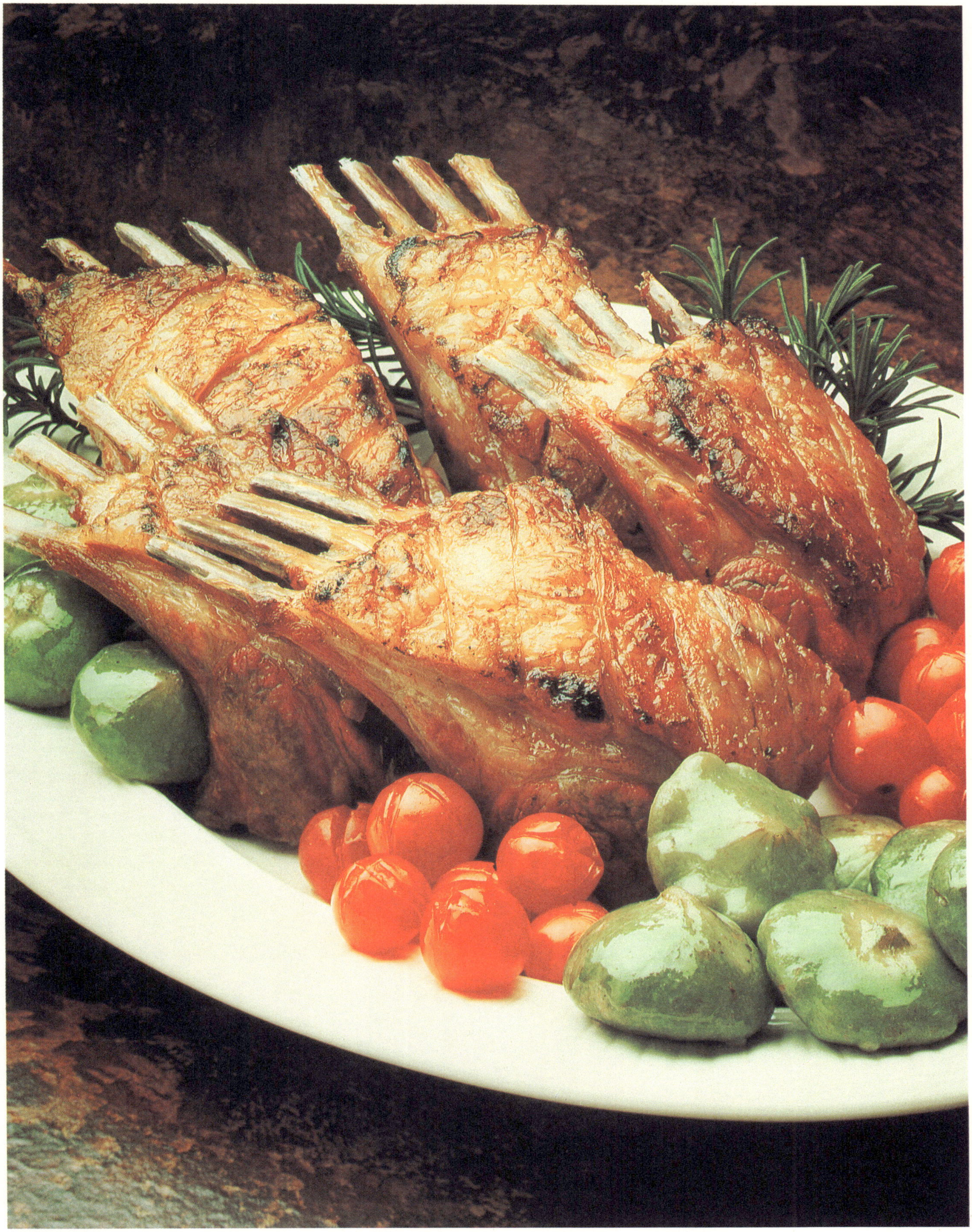

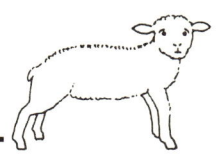

Lamb

Ladies' Fingers
Makes 36 rolls

30 g (1 oz) ghee or butter
½ cup pine nuts
1 large onion, finely chopped
500 g (1 lb) lean minced (ground) lamb or beef
¼ teaspoon cinnamon
salt
freshly ground black pepper
¼ cup chopped fresh parsley
1 tablespoon chopped fresh mint
2 teaspoons lemon juice
18 sheets filo pastry
melted butter

Heat the ghee in a frying pan, add the pine nuts and fry until golden, stirring often. Remove to a plate with a draining spoon.

Add the onion to the pan and cook on gentle heat until transparent. Increase the heat, add the meat and cook, stirring often to break up the lumps. When the meat changes colour, reduce the heat, add the cinnamon, about ½ teaspoon salt and plenty of pepper. Cover and let simmer for 15 minutes. Remove the lid and evaporate most of the juices. Stir in the parsley, mint, lemon juice and browned pine nuts. Leave until cool.

Cut the filo sheets in half, stack and cover with a piece of plastic wrap. Brush a sheet of filo lightly with melted butter and fold in half to give a strip of pastry about 10-12 cm (4-4½ inch) wide. Brush the strip with butter and place a scant tablespoon of filling along the folded edge. Turn the pastry over the filling, fold in the sides and roll up into a neat roll. Place flap side down on a greased baking sheet. Make the remaining rolls in the same way.

Brush the completed rolls lightly with melted butter. At this stage they may be covered with plastic wrap, placed in the freezer until frozen, then removed and packed into a rigid container with freezer film between the layers. Label and store in freezer. Cook the rolls in a moderately hot oven, 190°C (375°F/Gas 5), for 12 to 15 minutes until golden brown. If cooked directly from the freezer, cook about 3 minutes longer. Serve hot with a bowl of natural yoghurt for dipping.

Guard of Honour
Serves 6

2 lamb racks, each with 6-8 ribs
1 cup (8 fl oz) apricot nectar

Fruit Stuffing
½ cup (2 oz) chopped dried apricots
½ cup (3 oz) chopped pitted prunes
1 small onion, finely chopped
30 g (1 oz) butter
salt and pepper to taste
½ teaspoon ground ginger
water or stock

2 cups (4 oz) soft white breadcrumbs
grated rind of 1 lemon
1 tablespoon lemon juice
salt and pepper
1 small egg, beaten

Ask for racks from the opposite sides of the carcase, and have them prepared with the blade bone cartilage removed without disturbing the outside fat cover. (Butchers often remove this cartilage by cutting off the fat covering this section.)

Remove the fine skin covering the fat on the racks and score the fat into diamonds. Mix the apricot nectar with the salt, pepper and ginger, add the racks and turn to coat with the marinade. Cover and leave for 1 to 2 hours, turning occasionally.

Drain the racks and place on a board. Interlock the rib bones so that an arch is formed. Tie each end with string, passing it between the rib bones at each end and around the racks to hold them together. Place the racks in a roasting dish. Fill the arch with the stuffing. Pour the apricot marinade into the dish and cover the rib bones with foil.

Cook in a moderately hot oven, 190°C (375°F/Gas 5), for 1¼ hours, basting occasionally. When cooked remove to a platter, cover with foil and keep warm. Skim the fat from the dish juices and stir in a little water or stock. Place over heat and stir well until boiling. Strain into a sauceboat. Replace the foil on the bones with cutlet frills and serve the Guard of Honour with the sauce, pumpkin balls, boiled new potatoes and broccoli.

Fruit Stuffing: Put the chopped apricots and prunes in a bowl and cover with boiling water. Leave for 20 minutes then drain. Cook the onion in the butter until soft and add to the fruit with the crumbs, lemon rind and juice, and salt and pepper to taste. Add enough egg to bind the mixture, mixing it lightly.

Lamb Lima

Serves 4

500 g (1 lb) boneless lamb from leg or shoulder	½ cup (4 fl oz) dry white wine
1 tablespoon oil	bouquet garni
1 large onion, chopped	freshly ground pepper
2 garlic cloves, crushed	½ teaspoon sugar
1 cup chopped, peeled tomatoes	2 x 300 g (9 ½ oz) cans lima beans
1 tablespoon tomato paste	chopped fresh parsley for serving
½ cup (4 fl oz) water	

Trim the lamb and cut into 2 cm (¾ inch) cubes. Heat half the oil in a heavy saucepan and brown the lamb cubes quickly. Remove to a plate. Add the onion and garlic with the remaining oil and cook gently until the onion is soft. Add the tomatoes, tomato paste and liquids and stir well. Return the lamb to the pan and add the bouquet garni, pepper and sugar. Cover and simmer gently for 1 hour. Drain the lima beans, add to the pan and cover and cook for a further 20 minutes or until the meat is tender. If the sauce is preferred thickened, remove about ¼ cup of the beans, mash well with a fork and stir into the pan contents. Sprinkle with parsley. Serve with a tossed salad and crusty bread.

Middle Eastern Kebabs

Serves 6

750 g (1 ½ lb) boneless lamb from leg	1 tablespoon finely chopped parsley
½ cup (4 fl oz) lemon juice	2 crumbled bay leaves
1 teaspoon dried rigani* or marjoram	1 chopped onion
	¼ cup (2 fl oz) olive oil
	freshly ground pepper

To Serve

cos lettuce leaves	natural yoghurt mixed with mint and garlic, optional
tabouleh	
pita bread	

Trim the lamb and cut into 2 cm (¾ inch) cubes. Place in a bowl with the lemon juice, herbs, onion, oil and pepper to taste. Stir well, cover and marinate in the refrigerator for 2 hours at least or overnight, stirring occasionally.

Thread the lamb onto 6 skewers and grill (broil) or barbecue, basting frequently with marinade. Cook to the pink stage. Do not overcook or the lamb will toughen. Place the lettuce and tabouleh onto warmed pita bread and top with the lamb cubes. Add some yoghurt mixed with mint and garlic if desired, and roll up for eating.

* Rigani is a dried Greek herb available from Greek delicatessens and food stores. While it is a wild marjoram, and oregano is often given as a substitute, oregano is not the same. Dried marjoram with a pinch of dried sage added approximates the flavour of rigani.

Hasty Tasty Lamb Casserole

Serves 4

1 kg (2 lb) lamb forequarter chops	1 cup frozen peas
1 packet spring vegetable soup mix	½ cup (4 fl oz) tomato purée
1 tablespoon flour	¾ cup (6 fl oz) light stock
1 carrot, sliced	¼ cup (2 fl oz) red wine
3 potatoes, peeled and quartered	

Trim the chops and cut the edges in 2 or 3 places. Empty the soup mix into a casserole dish and mix in the flour. Turn the chops in this mixture to coat and leave them in the dish. Add the remaining ingredients and cover. Cook in a moderate oven, 180°C (350°F/Gas 4), for 1¼ hours or until the lamb is tender. Serve with crusty wholemeal bread.

Plum Lamb Chops for Two

Serves 2 [M]

4 lamb shoulder chops or 2-3 forequarter chops	¼ cup sliced celery
1 tablespoon seasoned flour	½ cup (4 fl oz) stock
2 teaspoons oil	2 tablespoons plum jam
1 small onion, sliced	1 tablespoon tomato sauce
1 small carrot, thinly sliced	1 teaspoon Worcestershire sauce

The times given are for 500 g (1 lb) trimmed meat, so purchase the number of chops accordingly. Trim the fat from the chops and coat with the seasoned flour. Place the oil in a small casserole dish with the onion, carrot and celery. Cook on high for 3 minutes. Mix the stock with the jam and sauces. Place the chops in a dish and pour on the liquid. Cover and cook on medium for 10 minutes, turning the chops after 5 minutes. Reduce to defrost and cook for 25 minutes. Stand for 5 minutes and serve with jacket potatoes and a green vegetable.

Lamb

Corned Lamb with Cranberry Glaze

Serves 8

- 1 corned lamb leg
- 1 tablespoon vinegar
- 2 tablespoons soft brown sugar
- ½ teaspoon whole allspice
- ½ teaspoon whole peppercorns
- ½ cup (4 fl oz) cranberry sauce

Ask the butcher to crack the shank so that the leg can fit into the pan. Rinse the leg and place in a large boiler with warm water to cover. Add the vinegar, sugar, allspice and peppercorns, cover and bring to a slow simmer. Simmer gently for 2½ hours (60 minutes per kg), timing from simmering point. Leave to cool in the liquid, remove and refrigerate in a sealed container. Chill for 2 to 3 hours or overnight.

About 2 hours before serving, prepare the glaze. Press the cranberry sauce through a fine sieve and place in a small pan. Heat just long enough to thin it down. Brush the glaze over the cold leg, refrigerate for 30 minutes, then brush again with glaze to give a good coating. Chill until required for serving. Extra cranberry sauce (unsieved) and a couple of salads should be served with the lamb.

Note: While the leg can be cooked in a slow cooker, you may have difficulty in fitting it in. Have the butcher saw the shank almost at the joint of the shank. Cook for 7 to 8 hours on low, or 4 to 6 hours on high; check manual.

Lamb with Prunes

Serves 6

- 1 kg (2 lb) boneless lamb from leg or shoulder
- 30 g (1 oz) butter
- 1 onion, chopped
- ½ cup (4 fl oz) dry red wine
- ¼ cup (2 fl oz) light stock
- salt and freshly ground pepper
- thin strip of lemon rind
- ½ teaspoon cinnamon
- ¼ teaspoon ground ginger
- 18 pitted prunes
- 1 tablespoon toasted pine nuts or slivered almonds

Trim the lamb and cut into 3 cm (1 ¼ inch) cubes. Heat half the butter in a heavy pan. Add the lamb cubes and brown quickly on each side. Remove to a plate. Reduce the heat and add the onion with the remaining butter. Cook gently until the onion is soft. Stir in the wine and stock and return the lamb to the pan. Add the salt and pepper to taste, then the lemon rind, cinnamon and ginger. Cover and simmer gently for 45 minutes, add the prunes and cook for a further 45 minutes or until the lamb is tender.

Remove the lemon rind and transfer the stew to a serving dish. Sprinkle with pine nuts. Serve with a rice pilaf and a green vegetable or tossed salad.

Note: If desired, the stew can be thickened with 2 teaspoons cornflour (cornstarch) mixed to a paste with a little cold water.

Corned Lamb with Cranberry Glaze

Moroccan Lamb and Chick Pea Stew

Serves 4

1 cup dried chick peas	1 garlic clove, crushed
4 cups (1 litre) water	1 teaspoon turmeric
600 g (1¼ lb) boneless lamb from leg or shoulder	½ teaspoon cumin
	⅛ teaspoon cayenne pepper
1 tablespoon oil	2-3 tablespoons lemon juice
1 large onion, chopped	

Pick over the chick peas to remove small stones. Wash well in cold water and place in a saucepan with the water. Bring to the boil, boil for 2 minutes, cover and remove from heat. Leave aside for 1 hour until plump, then return to the boil and cook gently for 1 hour.

Trim the lamb and cut into 2 cm (¾ inch) cubes. Heat the oil in a deep, heavy pan and brown the lamb on each side. Remove to a plate. Reduce the heat and add the onion and garlic with a little more oil if necessary. Cook gently until the onion is soft. Stir in the turmeric, cumin and cayenne and cook for 2 to 3 minutes. Return the lamb to the pan and add the partly cooked chick peas with their cooking liquid. Cover and cook on low heat for 1½ hours or until the lamb and chick peas are tender. Add the lemon juice to taste and serve with a tossed salad.

Mediterranean Lamb Stew

Serves 4 – 5

750 g (1½ lb) boneless lamb from leg	1 small onion studded with 3 cloves
2 tablespoons oil	1 bay leaf
1 onion, chopped	2 tablespoons chopped fresh parsley
1 garlic clove, crushed	1 teaspoon sugar
½ cup sliced celery	salt
1 carrot, sliced	freshly ground pepper
1 x 425 g (13½ oz) can peeled tomatoes, chopped	3 medium-sized potatoes
	4 zucchini (courgettes), sliced
1 tablespoon tomato paste	250 g (4 oz) prepared green beans
¼ cup (2 fl oz) dry red wine	
1 cup (8 fl oz) water	

Trim the lamb and cut into 3 cm (1¼ inch) cubes. Heat the oil in a heavy saucepan and brown the lamb on each side. Remove to a plate. Reduce the heat and add the onion, garlic and celery to the pan. Cover and cook gently until soft. Return the meat to the pan and add the carrot, tomatoes, including their liquid, tomato paste, wine, water, onion, herbs, sugar, and salt and pepper to taste. Cover and simmer gently for 30 minutes. Peel and quarter the potatoes, add to the stew and cook for a further 30 minutes. Place the zucchini and beans on top of the meat and potatoes, cover and continue to cook for a further 30 minutes or until the meat and vegetables are tender. Remove the onion and bay leaf and discard. Serve with crusty bread.

Plum Lamb Casserole

Serves 5 - 6

1 kg (2 lb) lamb stewing chops (forequarter, shoulder, best neck)	1 carrot, sliced
	½ cup sliced celery
	¼ cup (3 oz) plum jam
2 tablespoons seasoned flour	½ cup (4 fl oz) light stock
	2 tablespoons tomato sauce
1 onion, sliced	2 teaspoons Worcestershire sauce
15 g (½ oz) butter	

Trim the chops and coat with seasoned flour. Cook the onion in the butter until soft. Layer the chops in a casserole with the cooked onion, carrot and celery. Mix the remaining ingredients, pour over the lamb, cover and cook in a moderate oven, 180°C (350°F/Gas 4), for 1½ hours or until the lamb is tender. Serve from the casserole with jacket backed potatoes, boiled pumpkin cubes and a green vegetable.

Mediterranean Lamb Stew

Lamb

Rich Scotch Broth

Serves 6

6 lamb shanks
8 cups (2 litres) water
¼ cup pearl barley
1 large onion, chopped
1 large carrot, diced
1 leek, chopped
1 small turnip, diced
1 small parsnip, diced
2 tablespoons tomato paste
salt to taste
freshly ground pepper
chopped fresh parsley for serving

Have the lamb shanks sawn into 2 or 3 pieces. Rinse in cold water and place in a large saucepan with the water. Bring to a slow simmer, skimming when necessary. When well skimmed and boiling gently, add the rinsed barley and remaining ingredients except the parsley. Cover and simmer gently for 2 hours until the meat is very tender.

Remove the shanks to a dish, using a slotted spoon. Trim the meat from the bones and cut into small pieces. Return the meat to the soup and return to the boil. Ladle into bowls, sprinkle with chopped parsley and serve with crusty wholemeal bread.

Persian Lamb with Sour Cherries

Serves 6

1 kg (2 lb) boneless lamb from leg or shoulder
15 g (½ oz) ghee or butter
1 large onion, finely chopped
1 teaspoon turmeric
3 cm (1¼ inch) piece cinnamon bark
¾ cup (6 fl oz) water
salt
freshly ground pepper
1½ cups bottled Morello cherries
½ cup (4 fl oz) liquid from cherries
lime or lemon juice to taste
soft brown sugar to taste

Trim the lamb and cut into cubes. Heat half the ghee in a heavy pan and brown the lamb cubes on each side. Remove to a plate. Reduce the heat, add the remaining ghee with the onion and cook gently until transparent. Stir in the turmeric and cook for 2 minutes.

Return the lamb to the pan and add the cinnamon, water, and season to taste with salt and pepper. Cover and simmer gently for 1¼ hours. Add the cherries and their liquid, and adjust the flavour with lime juice and brown sugar to give a pleasant sweet-sour flavour. Cover and simmer for a further 10 minutes. While this dish is not traditionally thickened, you can thicken it if preferred. Mix 2 teaspoons cornflour (cornstarch) with a little cold water and gently stir into the pan contents until thickened and bubbling. Serve with boiled long grain rice cooked by the absorption method *(page 307)*, with a knob of butter tossed through the grains.

Corned Lamb with Mustard Sauce

Serves 6 [M]

1 corned lamb leg, about 2 kg (4 lb)
1 large oven bag
2 cups (16 fl oz) warm water

Mustard Sauce
15 g (½ oz) butter
1½ tablespoons flour
1 tablespoon dry mustard
1 teaspoon salt
1 tablespoon soft brown sugar
¾ cup (6 fl oz) milk
¼ cup (2 fl oz) malt
1 egg
vinegar

Rinse the lamb and dry with paper towels. Weigh and calculate the cooking time at 20 minutes per 500 g (1 lb). Flour an oven bag and arrange in a large oven dish. Place the lamb in the bag and shield the shank end with a piece of foil. Carefully pour in the water. Tie the bag loosely with string. Cook on high for 20 minutes, turning the bag and the lamb over after 10 minutes. Reduce to medium and cook for half the remaining time.

Carefully pour the water from the bag, turn the lamb over and add another 2 cups (16 fl oz) fresh warm water. Retie the bag loosely and return to the oven on medium for the remaining time. Leave the lamb in the bag and cover with foil. Stand for 20 minutes if served hot; if served cold, leave until cool then remove to a container, seal and refrigerate. Serve hot with vegetables or cold with salad accompaniments and hot or cold Mustard Sauce.

Mustard Sauce: Melt the butter in a medium-sized bowl on high for 30 seconds. Stir in the flour, mustard, salt and sugar and cook on high for 30 seconds. Stir in the milk and cook on high for 3 minutes, stirring each minute, until thickened and bubbling. Beat the egg well with the vinegar and stir into the sauce. Heat on high for 2 to 3 minutes, stirring occasionally, until bubbling. Serve immediately if served hot. If served cold, stir in an additional ¼ cup (2 fl oz) milk at the end of cooking, and cool, stirring occasionally to prevent a skin forming.

Sweet Lamb Curry
Serves 4 – 5 [M]

750 g (1½ lb) lamb chump, shoulder or forequarter chops
1½ tablespoons seasoned flour
1 large onion, chopped
2 green apples, peeled and chopped
15 g (½ oz) butter
3 teaspoons curry powder
2 tablespoons sultanas
1 cup (8 fl oz) beef stock
1 tablespoon soft brown sugar
1 tablespoon soy sauce

Trim the lamb and coat with seasoned flour. Place the onion, apples and butter in a large casserole dish and cook on high for 4 minutes, stirring once. Add the curry powder and cook on high for 2 minutes. Add the chops to the dish with the sultanas. Mix the stock with the brown sugar and soy sauce, and pour over the chops. Cover and microwave on medium for 10 minutes, rearranging the chops after the first 5 minutes. Reduce to defrost and cook for 40 minutes.

Let the curry stand, covered, for 5 minutes and serve with boiled rice and traditional curry accompaniments or with vegetables.

Mango Lamb
Serves 4 [M]

8 lamb chump or shoulder chops
2 tablespoons flour
grated rind of 1 orange
1 teaspoon dry mustard
2 teaspoons soft brown sugar
pepper to taste
1 tablespoon oil
¼ cup (2 fl oz) water
½ cup (4 fl oz) orange juice
¼ cup (2 fl oz) port
1 chicken stock cube
2 teaspoons cornflour (cornstarch)
salt to taste
1 x 425 g (13½ oz) can mangoes, or 1 large ripe mango, sliced

Trim the chops. Mix the flour with the orange rind, mustard, brown sugar and pepper and coat the chops with the mixture. Heat a browning casserole on high for 6 minutes, add the oil and chops and cook on high for 2 minutes. Turn and rearrange the chops. Cook on high for a further 1 minute. Alternatively the chops may be browned in a frying pan on the stove, then transferred to the casserole dish.

Mix any remaining flour mixture with the water (shake in a jar to mix smoothly), and mix in the orange juice, port, crumbled stock cube and cornflour. Add salt to taste. Pour over the chops, cover and cook on defrost for 40 minutes, turning and rearranging the chops halfway through cooking. When the chops are cooked, add the drained mango slices. Cover and cook on defrost for a further 5 minutes. Stand for 5 minutes and serve with boiled turmeric rice mixed with fine shreds of orange rind, and a tossed salad.

Farmhouse Casserole
Serves 5 – 6

1 kg (2 lb) lamb forequarter chops
2 tablespoons oil
1 large onion, sliced
2 garlic cloves, crushed
½ cup sliced celery
1 x 425 g (13½ oz) can tomatoes, chopped, and their liquid
2 tablespoons tomato paste
½ cup (4 fl oz) red wine
1 bay leaf
1 tablespoon chopped fresh parsley
½ teaspoon dried thyme
1 teaspoon sugar
salt and pepper to taste
1 green pepper (capsicum), sliced
1 red pepper (capsicum), sliced
4-5 zucchini (courgettes), sliced thickly

Trim the lamb. Heat the oil in a frying pan, brown the chops and remove to a casserole dish. Add the onion, garlic and celery to the pan and cook gently until soft. Stir in the tomatoes and their liquid, tomato paste, wine, herbs, sugar, salt and pepper. Pour over the lamb, cover and cook in a moderately slow oven, 160°C (325°F/Gas 3), for 1 hour. Add the peppers and zucchini, cover and cook for a further 45 minutes until tender. Skim any fat from the surface.

Stew Method: Brown the lamb in a deep, heavy saucepan and remove to a plate. Cook the onion etc, add the other ingredients and return the lamb to the pan. Add the peppers and zucchini after 45 minutes.

Lamb Hot Pot
Serves 4 – 6

1 kg (2 lb) lamb best neck chops
2 lamb kidneys
2 tablespoons seasoned flour
1 large onion, sliced
1 carrot, sliced
½ cup chopped celery
1 cup (8 fl oz) hot beef stock
500 g (1 lb) potatoes, sliced
melted butter
salt and pepper
finely chopped fresh parsley

Trim the chops if necessary. Remove the skin from the kidneys, halve and cut out the fatty cores. Slice each half. Coat the chops and kidneys with seasoned flour. Place a layer of onion in the base of a casserole dish, top with half the meat and kidneys. Add the carrot slices and celery, spreading evenly over the meat, then add the remaining meat and top with the remaining onion. Pour the hot stock carefully over the casserole contents, cover and cook in a moderate oven, 180°C (350°F/Gas 4), for 1 hour.

Remove the lid and place the potato slices on top of the meat. Brush the potatoes with butter and season with salt and pepper. Cover and return to the oven for a further 30 minutes. Remove the lid and leave in the oven for 15 to 20 minutes until the potatoes brown. Sprinkle with chopped parsley and serve from the casserole.

Lamb

Orange Lamb Kebabs

Serves 4

750 g (1 ½ lb) boneless shoulder lamb
orange segments
fresh pineapple
banana
red-skinned apple

Orange Butter

125 g (4 oz) butter, melted
2 teaspoons grated orange rind
2 teaspoons curry powder
a few drops of Worcestershire sauce
seasonings to taste

Cut the meat into 5 cm (2 inch) cubes and threat onto 4 x 20 cm (8 inch) skewers. On another 4 skewers, alternately thread pieces of fresh fruit. Brush all the kebabs with orange butter. Place the lamb kebabs under a hot grill (broiler) or on a barbecue and cook to desired taste, turning often and brushing with orange butter each time the skewers are turned. Add the fruit kebabs 5 minutes before the lamb is ready, brushing with butter also.

Orange Butter: Combine all ingredients thoroughly.

Oven Chops and Vegetables

Serves 5 – 6

1 kg (2 lb) lamb shoulder or forequarter chops
salt and pepper
½ teaspoon dried marjoram
2 tablespoons oil
2 onions, sliced
1 carrot, sliced
1 cup shelled green peas
1 teaspoon sugar
3 ripe tomatoes, peeled and sliced
4 potatoes, peeled and sliced
2 tablespoons chopped fresh parsley

Trim the chops and place in an oiled baking dish in a single layer. Sprinkle with salt, pepper, marjoram and a little oil. Cover with sliced onions and carrot and pour on the remaining oil. Cook, uncovered, in a moderately hot oven, 190°C (375°F/Gas 5), for 45 minutes.

Turn the chops, then add the peas with the sugar, tomato and potato slices. Season lightly and cover with foil, shiny side down. Return to the oven and cook for a further 45 minutes until the meat and vegetables are tender. Remove the foil for the last 10 minutes of cooking to brown lightly. Serve sprinkled with chopped parsley.

Jumbuck Stew

Serves 5 – 6

1 kg (2 lb) lamb shoulder or forequarter chops
2 tablespoons seasoned flour
1 teaspoon curry powder
¼ teaspoon ground ginger
15 g (½ oz) butter
1 large onion, sliced
1 tablespoon brown vinegar
2 tablespoons tomato sauce
2 tablespoons Worcestershire sauce
1 tablespoon soft brown sugar
½ cup (4 fl oz) stock
500 g (1 lb) pumpkin, cut into large pieces

Trim the chops. Mix the seasoned flour with the curry powder and ginger and coat the chops with the mixture. Heat half the butter in a heavy saucepan and brown the lamb on each side. Remove to a plate. Add the remaining butter to the pan with the onion and cook gently until soft. Return the lamb to the pan. Mix the vinegar, sauces, sugar and stock and pour over the lamb. Cover, bring to a simmer, reduce the heat to low and simmer gently for 1 hour. Skim any fat from the surface and add the pumpkin pieces. Cover and cook for a further 30 minutes or until the lamb and pumpkin are tender. Serve with hot herbed damper.

Casserole Method: Use one of the lamb cuts given above. Trim the meat and coat with flour mixture. Cook the onion gently until soft in 30 g (1 oz) butter. Layer the lamb and onion in the casserole and pour the liquid over. Cover and cook in a moderately slow oven, 180°C (350°F/Gas 4), for 1 hour. Skim off the fat, add the pumpkin and cook for a further 30 to 45 minutes until lamb and vegetables are tender.

Lamb Shank Curry Casserole

Serves 4 – 6

6-8 lamb shanks, cracked
3 tablespoons flour
1 tablespoon curry powder
salt and pepper
2 tablespoons plum jam
2 tablespoons tomato paste
1 cup (8 fl oz) light stock
1 large onion, sliced
2 carrots, sliced
1 parsnip, sliced
½ cup sliced celery

Separate the cracked shanks into chunky pieces. Mix the flour with the curry powder, about 1 teaspoon salt, and pepper to taste. Coat the lamb pieces and place in a casserole dish. Mix any remaining flour into the plum jam with the tomato paste and gradually mix in the stock. Add the vegetables to the dish and pour the mixed liquids over the contents. Cover and cook in a moderate oven, 180°C (350°F/Gas 4), for 1½ hours or until the meat is tender. Skim the fat from the surface and serve with boiled rice and a green vegetable.

Opposite: *Jumbuck Stew*

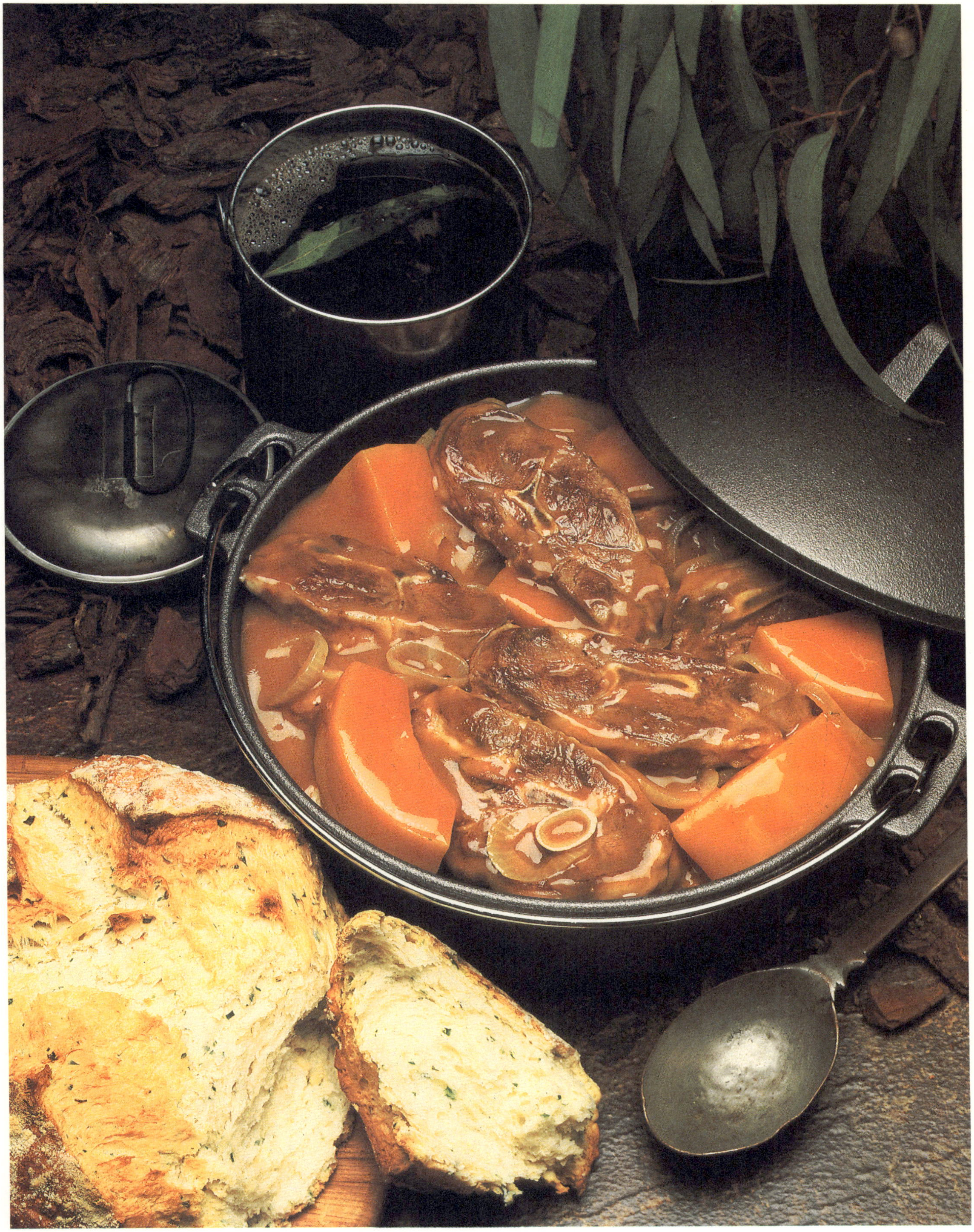

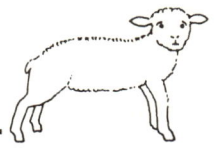

Lamb

Lamb Cassoulet

Serves 6 – 8

1½ cups dried haricot or cannellini beans
5 cups (1.25 litres) water
1 lamb shoulder, boned
½ cup bacon pieces
1 tablespoon oil
1 large onion, chopped
2 garlic cloves, crushed
1 x 500 g (1 lb) can peeled tomatoes, chopped
2 tablespoons tomato paste
1 teaspoon sugar
salt and pepper to taste
2 chicken stock cubes
bouquet garni
chopped fresh parsley to garnish

Wash the beans well, place in a large pan with the water, bring to the boil and boil for 2 minutes. Cover and remove from the heat. Stand for 1 hour or until the beans are plump. Return to the boil and boil gently for 1 hour or until the beans are barely tender.

Trim the lamb and cut into cubes. Put the bacon in a heated pan and fry until browned. Remove to a casserole dish, leaving the fat in the pan. Add the oil to the pan and brown the lamb quickly. Transfer to a casserole dish. Add the onion and garlic and cook gently until soft. Add the tomatoes and their liquid, tomato paste, sugar, salt and pepper. Stir well and add to the lamb.

Drain the beans, reserving the liquid. Mix the stock cubes with 2 cups (16 fl oz) liquid and add with the beans to the casserole. Place the bouquet garni in the centre of the contents, cover the dish and cook in a moderately slow oven, 160°C (325°F/Gas 3), for 2½ hours. Stir occasionally during cooking, adding more bean liquid if needed. Remove the bouquet garni and discard. Skim off the fat if necessary and sprinkle the chopped parsley over the cassoulet. Serve from the casserole with crusty bread and a tossed green salad.

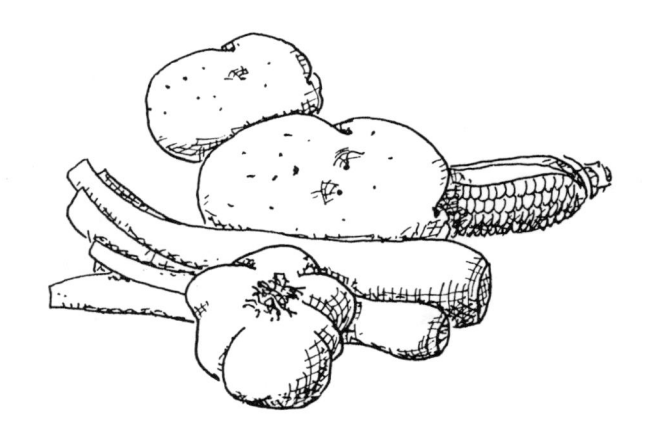

Middle Eastern Keftes

Serves 4 – 5

1 onion, grated
½ cup (2 oz) dry breadcrumbs
2 tablespoons chopped parsley
½ teaspoon dried mint
1 tablespoon lemon juice
1 egg
½ teaspoon salt
freshly ground pepper to taste
750 g (1 ½ lb) finely minced (ground) lamb
flour for coating
oil for shallow frying

To Serve
salad ingredients such as cos lettuce, cucumber and tomato
pita bread

Place the onion, crumbs, herbs, lemon juice and egg into a bowl and mix well. Add salt and pepper and leave for 10 minutes. Lightly mix in the lamb, leave for another 10 minutes, then mix again. With moistened hands, shape into thick patties. Coat lightly with flour and shallow fry in hot oil for about 3 minutes on each side until cooked through. Drain on paper towels and serve 2-3 hot keftes in pita bread with salad vegetables. If desired, a mixture of natural yoghurt, crushed garlic, mint and grated, well-drained cucumber can be served as a sauce, spooned over the keftes.

Lamb and Coconut Curry

Serves 6

1 kg (2 lb) boneless lamb leg or shoulder
2 large onions, chopped
2 teaspoons chopped fresh ginger
1 chilli, seeded
2 garlic cloves
2 tablespoons fresh coriander
2 tablespoons toasted coconut
15 g (½ oz) ghee or oil
1 tablespoon curry powder
1 ripe tomato, peeled and chopped
1 cup (8 fl oz) canned coconut milk
1 teaspoon soft brown sugar
salt
2 teaspoons garam masala

Trim the meat and cut into 2 cm (¾ inch) cubes. Put half the chopped onion in a food processor and add the ginger, chilli, garlic, coriander and toasted coconut. Purée, adding a little water if necessary.

Heat the ghee in a heavy pan and add the remaining chopped onion. Cook gently until transparent, add puréed ingredients and curry powder and cook, stirring occasionally, for 10 minutes.

Increase the heat and add the lamb cubes. Stir often until the meat changes colour. Add the tomato, coconut milk, sugar and salt, reduce heat and cover pan. Simmer gently for 1½ hours until the lamb is tender. Stir in garam masala, cook a further 5 minutes, and serve with boiled rice and traditional curry accompaniments.

Lamb Pot Roast

Shoulder serves 4 – 5; forequarter serves 6 – 8

1 tablespoon oil
1 lamb shoulder or forequarter, boned, rolled and tied
1 medium-sized onion, chopped
½ cup sliced celery
½ cup diced carrot
½ cup (4 fl oz) light stock
¼ cup (3 oz) plum jam
1 bay leaf
½ teaspoon dried thyme
salt and pepper
2-3 medium-sized carrots
6-8 small, whole onions
1 tablespoon flour
¼ cup (2 fl oz) water

Heat the oil in a heavy saucepan or Dutch oven and brown the lamb on all sides. Reduce the heat and add the onion, celery and carrot around the lamb. Cook gently for 10 minutes, then add the stock, jam, bay leaf, thyme, and salt and pepper to taste. Cover and simmer gently for 1 hour for shoulder, 1½ hours for forequarter.

Cut the carrots into thick chunks, and cut a cross in the trimmed root end of each onion to prevent the centres popping. Place around the lamb, cover and continue to cook until the lamb and vegetables are tender, about 1 hour. Remove the lamb and larger vegetable pieces to a serving platter and keep warm.

Skim the fat from the liquid in the pan and remove the bay leaf. Reduce the liquid over high heat if necessary, then purée the flavouring vegetables with the liquid. Return to the pan. Mix the flour with the water until smooth and stir into the sauce. Stir constantly until thickened and boiling. Serve the sauce over the sliced lamb.

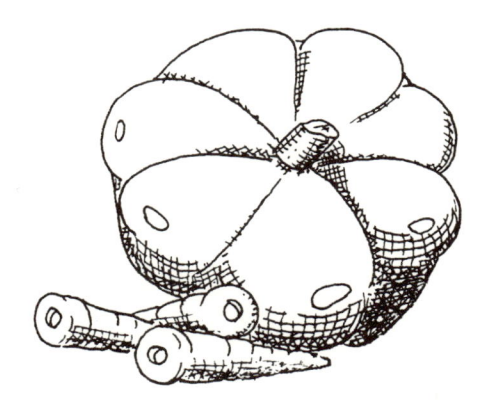

Orange Lamb Chops

Serves 6

1 kg (2 lb) lamb shoulder or forequarter chops
15 g (½ oz) butter
grated rind of 1 orange
½ cup (4 fl oz) orange juice
2 tablespoons honey
1 teaspoon dry mustard
1 teaspoon chopped fresh mint
salt and pepper
2 teaspoons cornflour (cornstarch)
orange slices and blanched strips of orange rind to garnish

Trim the chops and nick the edges to prevent curling. Heat the butter in a frying pan and brown the chops on each side on high heat. Reduce the heat to low.

Mix the orange rind and juice with the honey, mustard and mint. Pour over the chops, add salt and pepper to taste. Cover and simmer gently for 1½ hours or until the chops are tender. Juices from the lamb will add to the liquid content. If the liquid is low after 30 minutes, add a little water or orange juice.

When cooked, tilt the pan and skim off the fat. Thicken the sauce with cornflour mixed with a little cold water. Arrange the chops on a serving platter, spoon on the sauce and garnish with orange slices and strips of rind. Serve with a brown rice pilaf and lightly cooked snow peas (mange-tout) and carrots.

Smoked Lamb Leg with Marmalade Glaze

Serves 6 – 8

1 smoked lamb leg
½ cup (4 fl oz) orange juice
¼ cup (2 fl oz) port
2 teaspoons prepared English mustard
½ cup (5 oz) shredded orange marmalade

Have the shank sawn so that it will fit into a boiler. Soak the leg in cold water for 1 hour, drain and place in a boiler with warm water to cover. Bring to a slow simmer, cover and simmer gently for 2 hours. Leave to cool in the liquid, drain and store in a sealed container in the refrigerator if not required immediately.

To serve, place the leg in a roasting dish and make shallow slashes diagonally across the top. Mix the orange juice with the port and mustard and pour over the lamb. Cook in a moderate oven, 180°C (350°F/Gas 4), for 20 minutes, basting occasionally with the liquid in the dish, adding water if the liquid begins to scorch.

Spread the marmalade on top of the lamb and cook for a further 25 minutes. Let the lamb stand in a warm place for 15 minutes before carving. Serve hot with boiled new potatoes tossed with sour cream and chives, and salads.

Lamb

Devilled Chops and Kidneys

Serves 4 – 6

6-8 lamb chump or mid loin chops	1 tablespoon fruit chutney, chopped
2-3 lamb kidneys	1 teaspoon prepared English mustard
2 tablespoons tomato sauce	1 tablespoon lemon juice
1 tablespoon Worcestershire sauce	dash of cayenne pepper

Trim the chops and if using mid loin, secure the tails with toothpicks. Halve the kidneys and cut out the fatty cores. Thread the kidneys onto 2 fine skewers with the skewers about 2.5 cm (1 inch) apart through each kidney half (this prevents them curling during cooking). Mix the remaining ingredients in a bowl.

Place the chops on a grill (broiler) tray and brush with the sauce mixture. Grill (broil) under high heat for 2 minutes on each side, brushing the second side with the mixture. Reduce the heat or lower the tray. Brush the kidneys with the mixture and place next to the chops. Continue to cook for a further 6 to 8 minutes, turning occasionally and brushing with the mixture. Kidneys should not be overcooked or they will toughen.

Slide the kidneys off the skewers and serve 1-2 chops and half a kidney for each serving. Grilled (broiled) tomato halves and mushrooms can accompany the lamb and kidneys.

Noisettes with Mushroom Sauce

Serves 4 – 6

30 g (1 oz) butter	¼ cup (2 fl oz) Madeira
6-8 lamb noisettes*	½ cup (4 fl oz) light stock
1 cup sliced small mushrooms	salt
½ cup chopped spring onions (scallions)	freshly ground pepper
3 teaspoons flour	2 tablespoons cream

Heat a large frying pan on medium high heat. Add a third of the butter and when foaming, add the noisettes. Fry for 4 to 5 minutes on each side for pink lamb. Remove to a warm platter and keep warm. Drain the fat from the pan and add the remaining butter with the mushrooms and spring onions. Cook on medium heat until the mushrooms are limp. Sprinkle in the flour and stir well. Deglaze the pan with Madeira and stock, stirring well with a fork to lift the browned juices. Boil to reduce a little, season to taste with salt and pepper and stir in the cream. Remove string from noisettes, pour sauce over and serve immediately.

*Noisettes are thick, boneless, lamb mid loin chops tied into neat rounds with string. They should be about 3 cm (1¼ inch) thick.

Chilli-Plum Glazed Cutlets

Serves 6

2 lamb racks, each with 8 ribs	1 tablespoon light soy sauce
salt and pepper	½ teaspoon Chinese chilli sauce
1 teaspoon finely grated fresh ginger	¼ cup (2 fl oz) dry sherry
1 garlic clove, crushed	2 cm (¾ inch) piece fresh ginger, bruised
¾ cup (6 fl oz) bottled spicy plum sauce	2 tablespoons toasted sesame seeds
2 tablespoons plum jam	

Trim the fat from the lamb racks, leaving a very thin layer. Season with salt and pepper. Mix the grated ginger and garlic with 1 tablespoon plum sauce and brush over the racks. Place fat side up in a roasting dish and cook in a moderately hot oven, 190°C (375°F/Gas 5), for 45 minutes. Leave until cool.

Mix the remaining plum sauce with the jam, soy and chilli sauces, sherry and bruised ginger. Heat until the ingredients combine and begin to boil. Remove from the heat.

Cut the lamb racks into cutlets and brush each with glaze. Place in a single layer on a tray. Spread the remaining glaze on top. Do not glaze the rib bones. Sprinkle with toasted sesame seeds and serve within 1 hour, or cover carefully with plastic wrap and refrigerate overnight.

To serve, arrange the cutlets on a platter, placing cutlet frills on the bones if desired. Garnish with watercress sprigs and serve with a salad of watercress, bean sprouts and lettuce dressed with vinaigrette.

Curry Crumbed Cutlets

Serves 4 – 5

8-10 lamb cutlets	2 tablespoons milk
2 tablespoons flour	dry breadcrumbs
salt	oil for shallow frying
2 teaspoons curry powder	lemon wedges and fruit chutney for serving
grated rind of 1 lemon	
1 egg	

Trim the cutlets and flatten if necessary. Mix the flour with salt to taste, the curry powder and lemon rind. Beat the egg with the milk in a shallow dish. Coat the cutlets with seasoned flour mixture, dip into beaten egg, then coat with crumbs, pressing them on firmly. Place on a tray and chill for about 15 minutes.

Heat about ¼ cup (2 fl oz) oil in a large frying pan and shallow fry the cutlets for 3 minutes each side until golden brown and crisp. Drain on absorbent paper. Serve garnished with lemon wedges and provide a bowl of fruit chutney.

Opposite: *Noisettes with Mushroom Sauce*

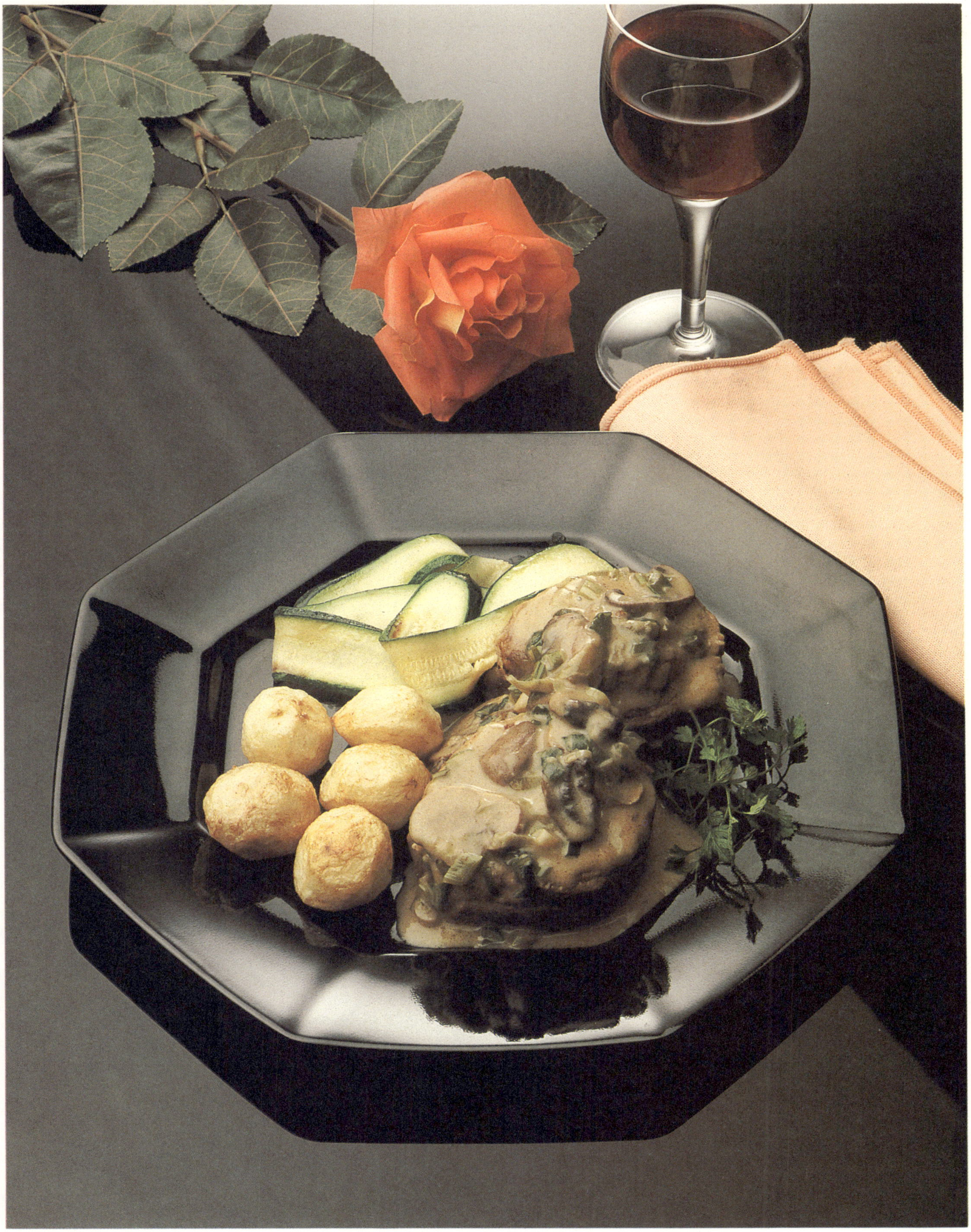

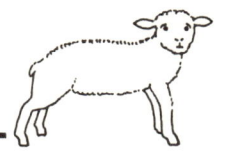

Lamb

Orange Ginger Lamb Chops

Serves 5–6

10-12 lamb mid loin chops
grated rind of 1 orange
¾ cup (6 fl oz) fresh orange juice
2 tablespoons cider vinegar
1 tablespoon honey
1 tablespoon soft brown sugar
1 tablespoon soy sauce
1 teaspoon grated fresh ginger
freshly ground pepper
1 large orange

Trim the chops and secure the tails with toothpicks. Rub the orange rind into the meat and place in a glass or ceramic dish. Mix the remaining ingredients except the whole orange and pour over the chops. Marinate for 1 hour or more, turning occasionally. Peel the orange, removing the pith with the peel. Cut into 5-6 thick slices and remove the pips.

Lift the chops from the marinade and pour the marinade into a small saucepan. Bring to the boil and leave on low heat. Grill the chops for 10 to 12 minutes under a preheated grill (broiler), basting occasionally with marinade. Towards the end of cooking, place orange slices around the lamb, brush with marinade.

Thicken the remaining marinade if desired with a little cornflour mixed with cold water. Serve the chops with the sauce and the orange slices, and accompany with boiled pumpkin cubes and broccoli.

Lamb Steaks Wangaratta

Serves 4

4 thick lamb chump chops, boned
2 tablespoons finely chopped walnuts
8 dried apricot halves, finely chopped
1 large orange
knob of butter
¾ cup (6 fl oz) chicken stock

Trim the chops and slit each slice almost through the centre from the side opposite the fat selvedge, opening out flat. Sprinkle the walnuts on one side of each slice, pressing them in with the back of a spoon. Put the apricots on top, fold the meat over to enclose and secure with toothpicks.

Remove the rind from the orange with a zester, or use a vegetable peeler to remove some strips, then cut these into fine shreds. Juice the orange and set the juice aside with the rind.

Heat the butter in a frying pan. Quickly cook the lamb for 3 minutes on each side and transfer to a warm dish. Deglaze the pan with the stock and add the orange juice. Boil until the sauce thickens slightly. Pour over the meat and garnish with the orange rind. Serve with boiled new potatoes, glazed carrots and a green vegetable.

Lamb Sweet and Sour

Serves 4–5

500 g (1 lb) lamb leg steaks
2 tablespoons oil
2 onions, quartered and segmented
1 green pepper (capsicum), cut into strips
1 medium-sized carrot, thinly sliced
½ teaspoon ground ginger
1 x 425 g (13 ½ oz) can pineapple pieces
1 tablespoon cornflour (cornstarch)
¼ cup (2 fl oz) white vinegar
2 tablespoons dry sherry
1 tablespoon soy sauce
2 teaspoons sugar
salt

Trim the lamb and cut into thin strips. Heat 1 tablespoon of the oil in a wok or large frying pan and stir fry the lamb strips over high heat until lightly browned and just cooked through. Remove with a slotted spoon and keep aside.

Add the remaining oil to the wok with the onions, green pepper and carrot and stir fry over medium heat for 3 to 4 minutes, sprinkling in a little water to create steam to soften the vegetables. Remove the wok from the heat and stir in the ginger.

Drain the pineapple and measure the liquid and make it up to 1 cup (8 fl oz) with water. Add the pineapple and liquid to the wok. Mix the cornflour with the vinegar, sherry and soy sauce. Return the wok to the heat and stir in the cornflour mixture, sugar and salt to taste. Stir constantly until the sauce thickens and bubbles. Boil gently for 2 minutes, then return the lamb to the wok and heat gently for 2 to 3 minutes without boiling. Serve with boiled rice.

Lemon Mint Chops

Serves 4

6-8 lamb grilling (broiling) chops (forequarter, mid loin or chump)
grated rind and juice of 1 lemon
2 tablespoons olive oil
1 tablespoon chopped fresh mint or 1 teaspoon dried mint
1 garlic clove, crushed
freshly ground pepper
salt

Trim the chops. If using mid loin, secure the tails with toothpicks. Mix the remaining ingredients except the salt in a glass dish. Add the chops and turn to coat. Marinate for at least 30 minutes. Drain and cook under a preheated grill (broiler), basting often with marinade. Season with salt after cooking.

Mango Lamb Sauté

Serves 4

- 500 g (1 lb) lamb fillets (tenderloin)
- 2 tablespoons flour
- grated rind of 1 orange
- 1 teaspoon soft brown sugar
- 1 teaspoon dry mustard
- salt and pepper
- 2 teaspoons oil
- 15 g (1 oz) butter
- ¼ cup (2 fl oz) water
- ¼ cup (2 fl oz) port
- juice of 1 orange (about ⅓ cup; 2 ½ fl oz)
- 1 x 425 g (13 ½ oz) can mango slices or 1 large ripe mango, sliced
- 2 tablespoons cream

Trim the fat and silver membrane from the fillets and cut in half if large. Mix the flour with the orange rind, sugar, mustard, salt and pepper to taste. Coat the lamb with the mixture.

Heat the oil and butter in a frying pan until foaming. Add the fillets and sauté on medium heat until lightly browned on all sides and pink in the centre. Thin pieces cook in 8 to 10 minutes, thick pieces 12 minutes. Remove to a plate as pieces cook and keep warm.

Add the remaining flour coating mix to the pan and stir over heat for 1 minute. Stir in the water, port and orange juice and stir well to lift the browned sediment. Add the mango slices and season to taste with salt and pepper. Simmer gently for 2 minutes and stir in the cream. Return the fillets to the pan, spoon the sauce over, cover and leave on very low heat for 2 to 3 minutes. Do not boil. Serve with rice pilaf and tossed green salad.

Lamb Diane

Serves 4

- 4 lamb leg chops or 8 chump chops
- 30 g (1 oz) butter
- 1 tablespoon Worcestershire sauce
- 2-3 garlic cloves, finely chopped
- 3 tablespoons chopped parsley

Trim the chops and flatten lightly with a meat mallet. Heat the butter in a large frying pan until foaming. Add the Worcestershire sauce, then the lamb and cook for 3 minutes on medium high heat. Sprinkle the garlic into the pan, turn the chops and cook for a further 3 minutes or until done to taste. Add the parsley, turn the chops and cook for a further minute. Serve with garlic and parsley mixture poured on top.

Smoked Lamb with Blueberry Sauce

Serves 4

- 2 lamb loins, boned
- 2 teaspoons oil
- 15 g (½ oz) butter
- ½ cup (4 fl oz) veal stock
- 1 tablespoon red wine vinegar
- 1 tablespoon redcurrant jelly
- freshly ground black pepper
- 1 x 425 g (13 ½ oz) can blueberries, drained
- a little syrup from the blueberries

Remove the eye muscle and the fillet from each of the loins. Keep the fillets for another use. Trim the silvery membrane covering the eyes of the loins and cold smoke the two meat pieces for about 3 hours if this is possible, otherwise use the lamb as it is.

Heat the oil and butter in a frying pan. Add the lamb and brown quickly on all sides. Reduce the heat and continue to cook for a further 8 to 10 minutes, turning often, until the lamb feels slightly springy when pressed. Adjust the heat while cooking so that the lamb fries gently and does not boil in its juices. Remove to a warm dish.

Deglaze the pan with the veal stock (or use a mixture of chicken and beef stock) and stir in the wine vinegar and redcurrant jelly. Simmer until the jelly melts and the sauce thickens slightly. Add the pepper to taste, the blueberries and a little of their syrup. Simmer again until the sauce thickens slightly. Spoon the sauce onto 4 warm plates, cut the lamb into thick slices and fan 3-4 slices on top of the sauce. Serve with snow peas, glazed carrots and jacket boiled potatoes.

Note: While this calls for smoked lamb, it is just as delicious if lamb is not smoked.

Spicy Barbecued Chops

Serves 6

- 1 kg (2 lb) lamb forequarter (barbecue) chops
- ¼ cup (2 fl oz) tomato sauce
- 2 tablespoons barbecue sauce
- 2 teaspoons Worcestershire sauce
- 1 tablespoon brown vinegar
- 1 teaspoon prepared English mustard
- 2 teaspoons soft brown sugar

Trim the chops if necessary. Mix the remaining ingredients in a small pan and place at the side of the barbecue. Sear the chops on each side, brush with glaze and continue to cook for 4 to 5 minutes on each side, brushing often with glaze. Serve with coleslaw and potato salad.

Lamb

Pineapple Lamb Riblets

Serves 8 – 10

4-5 lamb breasts with bone in
salt and pepper
1 large onion, grated
1 garlic clove, crushed
2 teaspoons curry powder
1 cup (8 fl oz) pineapple juice
2 tablespoons soft brown sugar

Ask the butcher to cut the lamb breasts from the carcase a little wider than normal if possible, then have them cut into strips between the bones. Discard the fatty ends. Season the riblets with salt and pepper and place in a greased frying pan on a barbecue grid or on a hotplate. Brown the riblets, turning often, then cover the pan and move to the side of the barbecue so that they can cook more slowly. If cooking on a hotplate, push to the side of the hotplate and invert a metal baking dish over the riblets so that they can cook slowly in their own steam. Cook for 45 minutes, turning occasionally. Drain off the fat if using a pan.

Mix the remaining ingredients in a small saucepan and bring to the boil on the barbecue. Brush the pineapple glaze over the lamb. Continue to cook on medium heat, basting often with glaze, until well glazed and tender. Serve as finger food.

Note: Initial cooking can be carried out in the kitchen either in a frying pan on the stove, or in a baking dish in the oven. Cover the dish after the lamb is browned. Drain, store in a sealed container in the refrigerator, and finish on the barbecue with the pineapple mixture.

Pineapple Lamb Riblets

Skewered Lamb and Mushrooms

Serves 4

600 g (1 ¼ lb) boneless lamb leg
½ cup (4 fl oz) dry white wine
1 tablespoon lemon juice
2 teaspoons oil
2 garlic cloves, crushed
1 tablespoon chopped fresh herbs (rosemary, parsley, thyme)
2 spring onions (scallions), chopped
freshly ground pepper
200 g (6 ½ oz) small mushroom caps

Trim the lamb and cut into 3 cm (1 ¼ inch) cubes. Mix the wine in a glass or ceramic dish with the remaining ingredients except the mushrooms. Add the lamb and turn the meat to coat. Cover and marinate at room temperature for 1 hour or for several hours in the refrigerator. Turn the meat occasionally.

Lift the lamb from the marinade and thread the cubes onto 4 skewers alternately with the mushrooms. Cook for 10 to 12 minutes under a preheated grill (broiler) or on the barbecue, turning often and brushing with marinade. Serve with brown rice pilaf and a tossed salad.

Note: The remaining marinade may be boiled with ½ cup (4 fl oz) stock and thickened with 2 teaspoons cornflour (cornstarch) mixed with a little cold water. Strain into a sauceboat and serve with the lamb skewers.

Lamb's Fry and Bacon Sauté

Serves 4 – 6

1 lamb's fry
2 rashers bacon, rind removed
15 g (½ oz) butter or 15 ml (½ fl oz) oil
2 onions, sliced
3 tablespoons seasoned flour
1 tablespoon cider vinegar
chopped parsley

Soak the lamb's fry in cold water for 1 hour. Drain and remove the skin and larger tubes. Slice thinly, halving the slices if large. Chop the bacon.

Heat a large frying pan, add the bacon and cook, stirring often, until the fat renders and the bacon begins to brown. Add the butter or oil with the onions and cook gently until transparent. Coat liver with seasoned flour.

Increase the heat and add the liver slices. Fry quickly, stirring to brown the pieces evenly. When liver is just cooked through, and lightly pink in the centre, sprinkle on the vinegar, stir and serve immediately sprinkled with the chopped parsley. Serve with mashed potatoes and a green vegetable.

Lamb Venetian Style

Lamb Chops with Marmalade Sauce

Serves 4

4 lamb leg chops
   or 8 chump chops
2 garlic cloves, crushed
2 tablespoons lemon juice
1 teaspoon rosemary leaves
1-2 eggplants (aubergines)
2 tablespoons olive oil
1 large onion, finely
   chopped
1 cup chopped, peeled
   tomatoes
½ teaspoon sugar
freshly ground pepper
4-8 slices mozzarella
   cheese

Trim the lamb chops and marinate for 1 hour in a mixture of the garlic, lemon juice and rosemary, turning often. Cut thin slices from the outside of the eggplants to give 4-8 oval pieces of skin with 6 mm (¼ inch) flesh on them. Score the skin lightly with 3 diagonal slashes. Heat the oil in a frying pan and sauté the slices until browned. Drain on paper towels. Add the onion to the pan, cook gently until soft, and add the tomatoes, sugar and season to taste. Simmer until thick.

Drain the chops and grill (broil) for 5 to 7 minutes on each side until cooked to taste. Spoon a little tomato sauce on each and top with cheese. Return to the grill until the cheese melts, then top each with a slice of eggplant, skin side up. Heat for 1 minute and serve with the remaining tomato sauce, boiled pasta and a tossed salad.

Lamb Chops with Marmalade Sauce

Serves 4

8 lamb mid loin chops
freshly ground black pepper
15 g (½ oz) butter
1 onion, finely chopped
1 garlic clove, crushed
¼ cup (2 fl oz) orange
   juice
1 tablespoon lemon juice
¼ cup (3 oz) marmalade
2 teaspoons chopped fresh
   mint

Trim the chops if necessary and season with pepper. Heat a large frying pan and grease with a little butter. Add the chops and cook on medium heat for about 8 to 10 minutes, turning often. When cooked to taste, remove to a dish and keep warm.

Drain the fat from the pan and return to the heat. Add the butter, onion and garlic, and cook gently until the onion has softened. Add the juices, marmalade and mint. Stir well to lift the browned sediment and bring to the boil. Simmer for a minute or so to reduce to a syrup.

Return the chops to the pan and turn in the sauce to glaze. Serve with boiled chokoes (summer squash) tossed with low fat yoghurt and chopped mint, and boiled rice with sultanas and toasted almonds added after cooking.

Lamb

Lamb with Skewered Fruits

Serves 6 – 8

6-8 lamb mid loin chops cut 3 cm (1 ¼ inch) thick

1 small pineapple
½ pawpaw (papaya)
3 kiwifruit

Butter-fruit Baste
60 g (2 oz) butter
grated rind of 1 orange
1 teaspoon curry powder
¼ cup (2 fl oz) pineapple juice
¼ cup (2 fl oz) orange juice
1 tablespoon soft brown sugar

Trim the chops and secure the tails with toothpicks. Peel the fruit, cut into chunky pieces and thread onto flat metal skewers, stainless steel for preference. Melt the butter in a small pan and mix in the remaining baste ingredients. Place the pan at the side of the barbecue.

Brush the lamb chops with the basting mixture and barbecue over medium heat so that they cook through without charring. Turn with tongs and baste frequently. Towards the end of cooking, place the fruit skewers beside the lamb. Baste well and cook for 2 to 3 minutes, turning often. The fruit should just warm through, but remain firm. Serve the lamb with the fruit, and drizzle any remaining baste over the lamb.

Accompaniments: Make a rice pilaf and toss through toasted slivered almonds, some sultanas and a little grated orange rind. Tossed green salad can also be served.

Herbed Lamb Chops

Serves 4

8 lamb mid loin chops
lemon juice
freshly ground pepper
30 g (1 oz) butter
1 tablespoon chopped parsley
2 teaspoons chopped fresh thyme or marjoram
1 teaspoon chopped fresh rosemary leaves
1 tablespoon chopped chives or spring onions (scallions)

Trim the chops if necessary. Place on a plate and sprinkle lemon juice and pepper on each side. Leave for 15 minutes. Heat half the butter in a large frying pan. Add the chops and cook on medium high heat until browned on each side and just cooked through. Do not overcook. Remove to a hot dish and keep warm. Drain off all the fat from the pan and add the remaining butter with the chopped herbs. Cook a few seconds, add 1 tablespoon lemon juice and pour immediately over the chops. Garnish with fresh herbs and lemon slices and serve immediately. If desired some stock and white wine can be stirred into the herbs and boiled for a minute or so.

Lebanese Lamburgers

Serves 6

1 boned lamb shoulder
½ teaspoon salt
freshly ground pepper
½ teaspoon ground allspice
½ teaspoon ground cumin
⅛ teaspoon chilli powder
juice of ½ lemon
3 large pita bread
1 cup (8 fl oz) natural yoghurt
1 teaspoon finely chopped fresh mint
1 garlic clove, crushed
shredded lettuce
sliced tomato, cucumber and onion

Place the lamb on a board. Mix the salt with pepper to taste and the spices. Rub the lamb all over with the lemon juice, then rub in the spice mixture. Place in a dish, cover and refrigerate for 2 hours or overnight. Bring to room temperature and push 2 long metal skewers crosswise through the lamb so that it will remain flat during cooking.

Place the lamb on a barbecue grid and brown on each side. Move to the side of the barbecue and continue to cook more slowly for 45 minutes, turning frequently.

Cut the pita bread in half. Mix the yoghurt with the mint and garlic and season to taste with salt and pepper.

When lamb is cooked, remove to a carving board, cover with foil and leave for 10 minutes. Remove the skewers and carve the lamb into thin slices. Place the lettuce, tomato and cucumber into the pockets in the bread. Top with lamb and onion slices and spoon on some yoghurt sauce. Tabouleh may also be added if desired.

Lamb Cutlets Parmigiana

Serves 4

8 lamb cutlets
freshly ground black pepper
1 egg, beaten
2 tablespoons milk
¾ cup (3 oz) dry breadcrumbs
3 tablespoons grated Parmesan cheese
2 tablespoons oil
⅓ cup (2 ½ fl oz) tomato spaghetti sauce
shredded or sliced mozzarella cheese

Trim the cutlets and season with pepper. Mix the egg with the milk in a shallow dish. Mix the crumbs with 2 tablespoons of the Parmesan cheese on kitchen paper. Dip the cutlets in the egg mixture and coat with crumbs.

Heat the oil in a large frying pan. Add the cutlets and cook on medium heat for 2 to 3 minutes on each side until golden. Drain on kitchen paper and place on a grill (broiler) rack lined with foil. Spoon some of the spaghetti sauce onto each cutlet and top with shredded or sliced mozzarella. Sprinkle with the remaining Parmesan and place under the heat for 2 minutes until the cheese melts. Serve onto warm plates and accompany with ribbon noodles tossed with chopped parsley and lightly cooked zucchini (courgettes) or tossed salad.

Lamb Teppanyaki

Serves 4

500 g (1 lb) boneless lean lamb from leg, chump or loin
pepper
8 dried Chinese mushrooms
60 g (2 oz) small mild green chillies or 1 green pepper (capsicum)
oil for cooking
1 onion, sliced
½ cup shredded white radish

Sauce 1
½ cup (4 fl oz) light soy sauce
1 tablespoon lemon juice
2 tablespoons Japanese chilli paste

Sauce 2
¼ cup (2 fl oz) sesame paste
1 teaspoon finely chopped fresh ginger
1 garlic clove, crushed
2 tablespoons light soy sauce
2 tablespoons mirin or sweet sherry

Have the lamb in one piece, either part of the leg, or a whole chump or mid loin with the bone removed. Trim off all the fat and cut into very thin slices. Cut the slices in half if necessary to give pieces approximately 4 cm (1 ½ inch) square. Season lightly with pepper.

Rinse the mushrooms and soak in hot water for 30 minutes. Drain, squeeze out the moisture and remove the stems. Leave the mild chillies whole or, if using green pepper, seed and cut into strips. Prepare either or both of the sauces and mix the ingredients in small bowls.

Heat a griddle on the stove, or a barbecue hotplate. Pour on a little oil and add the lamb pieces, onion slices, chillies and mushrooms, keeping each ingredient separate. Cooking, particularly for the meat, should be very brief. If the hot plate or griddle is not very large, only small amounts of each ingredient should be cooked at a time. Serve out onto plates, with the shredded radish and sauce (or sauces) to be added to individual taste. Boiled rice can also be served.

Sherried Lamb Kidneys

Serves 4 – 6

8-12 lamb kidneys
1 large onion, chopped
1 tablespoon oil
15 g (½ oz) butter
3 tablespoons flour
salt to taste
freshly ground black pepper
½ cup (4 fl oz) beef stock
½ cup (4 fl oz) dry sherry
2 teaspoons cornflour (cornstarch)
1 tablespoon water
chopped parsley

Remove the skin from the kidneys, halve and cut out the fatty cores. Gently cook the onion in the oil and butter in a frying pan until soft and golden. Remove with a slotted spoon, leaving the fat in the pan. Increase the heat and when the pan is hot, add the kidneys and brown quickly on each side, doing this in two lots if necessary. Sprinkle the flour over the kidneys and stir and toss the kidneys over the heat for a minute or so. Reduce the heat, return the onion to the pan, add the seasoning, stock and sherry, stirring constantly until the liquid thickens and bubbles gently. If necessary, the liquid may be thickened with the cornflour mixed with the water. Leave on a very low heat for a minute or two, taking care that kidneys do not overcook and toughen – they are best when pink in the centre. Sprinkle with chopped parsley and serve immediately with toast triangles or creamy mashed potatoes.

Lamburgers Pizza-Style

Serves 4

750 g (1 ½ lb) finely minced (ground) lamb
1 small onion, finely chopped
2 tablespoons chopped parsley
½ teaspoon salt
pepper to taste
1 tablespoon oil
1 large onion, sliced
1 garlic clove, crushed
1 green pepper (capsicum), chopped
1 x 440 g (14 oz) can tomatoes, chopped
½ teaspoon dried basil
8 slices mozzarella cheese

Mix the lamb with the onion, parsley, salt and pepper. Divide into 12 equal portions and shape each into a thick patty.

Put the oil into a large frying pan and heat well. Add the lamburgers and cook on medium high heat until browned on each side. Reduce the heat and add the onion, garlic and green pepper around the burgers. Cook for 3 to 4 minutes, then add the remaining ingredients except cheese. Simmer uncovered for 15 minutes.

Top each burger with a slice of cheese, cover the pan and simmer for 2 to 3 minutes until the cheese melts, or place under a heated griller (broiler) for 2 to 3 minutes. Serve with the sauce on toasted split muffins or hamburger buns. Add a salad tossed with a little Italian dressing.

Lamb

Roast Lamb with Peppercorn Soufflé Crust

Serves 6

- 1 leg lamb, about 2 kg (4 lb)
- juice of ½ lemon
- salt
- freshly ground pepper
- 1 tablespoon oil
- 1 tablespoon drained green peppercorns
- 2 tablespoons chopped fresh parsley
- 1 tablespoon prepared French mustard
- 2 egg whites
- ¼ cup (½ oz) fine soft breadcrumbs
- ½ cup (4 fl oz) light stock
- ½ cup (4 fl oz) dry white wine
- 2 teaspoons cornflour (cornstarch)

Wipe the lamb with paper towels and trim off any excess fat. Rub all over with lemon juice, salt and pepper. Place in a baking dish and brush with oil. Cook in a moderate oven, 180°C (350°F/Gas 4), for 2 hours or until cooked to taste, turning occasionally to brown evenly. When cooked, remove to an ovenproof platter, cover with foil and leave in a warm place for 15 minutes. Increase the temperature to 220°C (425°F/Gas 7).

Mash the green peppercorns lightly with a fork and mix with the parsley and mustard. Beat the egg whites in a clean bowl until stiff. Fold in the peppercorn mixture and breadcrumbs and spread over the top and sides of the lamb. Return to the hot oven and cook for 6 to 8 minutes until puffed and lightly browned.

Drain any fat from the baking dish and add the stock and wine. Stir well to dissolve the browned juices and strain into a small saucepan. Heat and thicken with the cornflour mixed to a paste with a little water or wine. Carve the lamb from the shank end, making a 'V' cut and carving slices down towards the bone so that each slice has some of the crust on it. Serve with the sauce and vegetables of your choice.

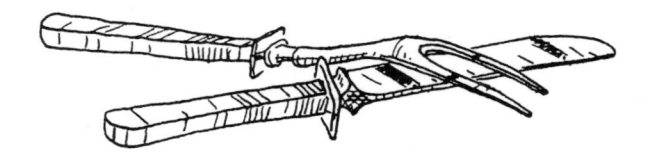

Crown Roast with Fruit Stuffing

Serves 5 – 6 [M]

- 1 crown roast of lamb with 14-16 ribs
- 1 garlic clove, crushed
- 1 tablespoon lemon juice
- 1 tablespoon oil
- ½ cup (4 fl oz) light stock
- 1 cup (4 fl oz) apricot nectar
- 1 tablespoon cornflour (cornstarch)
- salt and pepper

Fruit Stuffing
- 1 small onion, finely chopped
- 30 g (1 oz) butter
- ⅓ cup (1 ½ oz) chopped dried apricots
- 1 tablespoon currants
- 1 tablespoon sherry
- 2 tablespoons apricot nectar
- 2 cups (4 oz) soft wholemeal breadcrumbs
- 1 teaspoon grated lemon rind
- 1 tablespoon chopped fresh parsley
- salt and pepper
- 1 small egg, beaten

Ask the butcher to trim most of the fat from the lamb racks before assembling into a crown roast. Weigh the roast and calculate the total cooking time at 10 to 12 minutes per 500 g (1 lb), depending on taste. Mix the garlic with the lemon juice and oil and brush on the inside and outside of the roast. Place the stuffing in the centre of the roast, packing it in loosely.

Heat a browning grill on high for 8 minutes. Place the crown roast on hot grill, lifting it on with an egg lifter to prevent the stuffing from dislodging. Cook on high for 2 minutes, then on medium for the remainder of the cooking time. Covering with paper is not necessary, but it may be necessary to remove the juices from the gutter during cooking with a bulb baster. Keep these aside.

When cooked, remove to a plate, cover loosely with foil and leave for 10 minutes. Deglaze the browning grill with the stock and apricot nectar and pour into a bowl with the previously removed juices. Skim well. Mix the cornflour with a little cold water and stir into the liquid. Heat on high for 4 to 5 minutes, stirring occasionally until thickened and boiling. Adjust the seasoning with salt and pepper and strain into a sauceboat. Brush a little of the sauce over the crown roast and garnish as desired.

Fruit Stuffing: Place the onion and butter in a bowl, then microwave on high for 2 minutes. Add the apricots, currants and sherry and microwave on high for 1 minute. Cool and lightly mix in the remaining stuffing ingredients, adding enough beaten egg to bind. It should be rather moist, but still hold its shape.

Apple Lamb Loin

Apple Lamb Loin

Serves 4

1 lamb mid loin, boned
15 g (½ oz) butter
2 cooking apples, peeled and grated
2 tablespoons raisins
2 tablespoons pecans or walnuts
pinch of ground cinnamon
grated rind of ½ lemon
salt and pepper
1 cup (8 fl oz) apple cider
2 tablespoons port
2 teaspoons cornflour (cornstarch)

Open out the loin, remove the fine skin covering the fat and trim fat if necessary. Melt the butter in a small pan, add the apples and stir over the heat for a few minutes until soft. Remove from the heat and stir in the raisins, nuts, cinnamon and lemon rind.

Place the lamb fat side down on a board and season the inside lightly with salt and pepper. Spread the stuffing along the centre, roll up and secure with skewers. Tie at intervals with white string and remove the skewers. Rub the outside of the roll with salt and pepper.

Place the loin in a baking dish and cook in a hot oven, 200°C (400°F/Gas 6), for 15 minutes. Add the cider to the dish and cook for a further 20 to 25 minutes, basting often with cider. The lamb will be pink at this stage; cook a little longer for well done.

Remove the lamb to a warm dish, cover with foil and leave for 10 minutes. Skim the fat from the dish juices, add the port and place the dish over the heat. Stir to lift the browned juices, adding a little water if necessary. Thicken with the cornflour mixed with cold water, adjust seasoning and serve with the sliced loin.

Peachy Lamb

Serves 6 [M]

1 leg lamb, about 2 kg (4 lb)
½ cup (4 fl oz) puréed canned peaches
¼ cup (3 oz) honey
2 tablespoons lemon juice
1 tablespoon soy sauce
1 small onion, grated
1 garlic clove, crushed
¼ teaspoon ground ginger
¼ teaspoon ground allspice
salt and pepper to taste
6 peach halves
1 tablespoon cornflour (cornstarch)

Weigh the lamb and calculate the total cooking time at 18 minutes per 500 g (1 lb). Mix the peach purée with the honey, lemon juice, soy sauce, onion, garlic, spices and salt and pepper. Flour an oven bag with 1 tablespoon flour and arrange in an oven dish. Place the leg in the bag upside down and pour the peach mixture over it. Tie the bag loosely with string. Microwave for 5 minutes on high, reduce to medium and cook for the remainder of the calculated cooking time, turning the bag and the lamb carefully halfway through cooking. Remove the lamb to a plate, cover with foil and leave to stand for 15 minutes. Drain the liquid from the bag into a bowl and skim off the fat.

Place the peach halves on a flat dish and brush with a little of the bag liquid. Microwave on high for 2 minutes. Keep aside. Mix the cornflour with a little cold water and stir into the liquid. Microwave on high for 3 to 4 minutes, stirring occasionally, until boiling and thickened. Place the lamb on a serving platter with the peach halves. Brush a little of the sauce over the lamb and serve the remainder separately.

Roasting Dish Method: Calculate the cooking time at 12 minutes per 500 g (1 lb) for pink lamb, 15 minutes for well done. Brush lamb well with the peach mixture. Place upside down on a microwave-safe rack in an oven dish. Microwave for 5 minutes on high, then medium for the remainder of the cooking time, covering the leg with a piece of greaseproof paper if spattering occurs. Brush occasionally with the peach mixture, and turn halfway through cooking. Stand the leg, covered with foil, for 15 minutes. Skim the fat from the dish juices and pour into the remaining peach mixture. Thicken the sauce and heat the peaches as above.

Lamb

Minced Lamb Kebabs

Serves 6

1 kg (2 lb) finely minced (ground) lamb
½ cup coarsely chopped parsley
1 large onion, chopped
1 ½ teaspoons salt
½ teaspoon ground allspice
⅛ teaspoon chilli powder
½ teaspoon ground cumin
½ teaspoon ground coriander
½ teaspoon paprika
oil for cooking

To Serve
pita bread
cos lettuce, sliced tomatoes and cucumber, chopped onion
Yoghurt Sauce (see below)

Place the meat in a bowl and lightly mix in the parsley, onion, salt and spices. Pass through a meat mincer twice using the fine screen, or process in 4 batches in a food processor. Knead to a smooth paste by hand to blend the flavours evenly.

Moisten hands with water, take generous tablespoons of the paste and mould it around flat, sword-like skewers in finger shapes about 10 cm (4 inch) long. Place two shapes on long skewers, one if skewers are short. As the skewers are prepared, set them across a baking dish with the ends resting on each side. Cover and chill if time permits.

Remove the grid from the barbecue if possible and place skewers so that the ends rest on the sides of the barbecue. An Hibachi barbecue is ideal for cooking these. Otherwise place the skewers on a grid so that the meat lies between the grid bars. Brush the kebabs lightly with the oil and barbecue for 2 to 3 minutes, turning skewers frequently.

To serve, slide kebabs off the skewers and serve in split pita bread with lettuce, sliced tomatoes and cucumber and chopped onion. Spoon on some Yoghurt Sauce if desired.

Yoghurt Sauce: Mix a crushed clove of garlic into 1 cup (8 fl oz) thick natural yoghurt with 1 teaspoon dried mint flakes and salt to taste. Chill until required for serving.

Mongolian Lamb

Serves 6 [M]

750 g (1 ½ lb) boneless lamb leg
2 tablespoons soy sauce
3 teaspoons sugar
½ teaspoon bicarbonate of soda (baking soda)
3 teaspoons cornflour (cornstarch)
2 tablespoons oil
1 garlic clove, crushed
1 teaspoon grated fresh ginger
1 onion, thinly sliced
¼ teaspoon five-spice powder
2 teaspoons hoi sin sauce
1 tablespoon dry sherry

Trim the lamb and cut into 2 cm (¾ inch) cubes. Mix the soy sauce with the sugar, soda and cornflour and add the lamb. Stir well and leave for 20 to 30 minutes, stirring occasionally.

Heat a browning casserole dish on high for 6 minutes. Add the lamb, oil, garlic and ginger and cook on high for 10 minutes, stirring occasionally. Add the remaining ingredients, stir well and cook on high, uncovered, for 4 to 5 minutes, stirring twice. Stand, covered, for 5 minutes, and serve with boiled rice and microwave-cooked snow peas (mange-tout) or Chinese cabbage.

Note: If the dish has to be reheated, then use medium power, stirring occasionally to distribute heat evenly. Do not reheat for too long as the meat may toughen.

Noisettes with Citrus Sauce

Serves 4

30 g (1 oz) butter
8 lamb noisettes (thick boneless loin chops tied into rounds)
freshly ground pepper
½ cup (4 fl oz) dry red wine
¼ cup (2 fl oz) water
1 tablespoon lime marmalade
½ tablespoon orange marmalade
½ teaspoon prepared English mustard
2 teaspoons cornflour (cornstarch)

Grease a heavy frying pan with a little of the butter. Heat the pan and add the noisettes and sprinkle with the pepper. Cook on medium heat, turning often, for 12 to 14 minutes for pink lamb. Remove to a dish and keep warm.

Drain the fat from the pan and deglaze with the wine and water. Stir over heat to lift the browned sediment and stir in the remaining butter and the marmalades and mustard. Heat gently until the marmalade has melted into the liquid, then thicken with the cornflour mixed with a little cold water. Adjust the seasoning and simmer for a minute or so. Serve the noisettes with sauce, boiled sweet potato cubes tossed with a little ground ginger and a lightly cooked green vegetable.

Herbed Lamb Skewers

Serves 5–6

750 g (1 ½ lb) boneless
    lamb from leg

Herbed Marinade

¾ cup (6 fl oz) white
    wine or dry vermouth
2 tablespoons lemon juice
2 tablespoons olive oil
freshly ground pepper
1 teaspoon sugar
1 garlic clove, crushed
1 small onion, sliced
1 crumbled bay leaf
2–3 tablespoons chopped
    fresh herbs (rosemary,
    thyme, parsley, oregano
    etc.)

Trim the lamb and cut into cubes. Mix the marinade ingredients in a glass or ceramic bowl, add the lamb and stir well. Cover and marinate for at least 2 hours, or for several hours in refrigerator, stirring occasionally. When required, remove the lamb from the marinade and thread onto skewers. Vegetable pieces, or herbs such as bay leaves or rosemary, can be placed between lamb cubes. Cook under a preheated grill (broiler) or on a barbecue, basting occasionally with marinade. Rice pilaf and a tossed salad can be served as accompaniments.

Herb substitutes: When fresh herbs are not available, use 2 teaspoons in total of dried thyme, rosemary, oregano and tarragon with 1 tablespoon chopped fresh parsley.

Lamb Satsuma

Serves 4–6

8-12 lamb cutlets or
    mid loin chops
freshly ground pepper
15 g (½ oz) butter or oil
⅔ cup (5 fl oz) puréed
    canned satsuma plums
salt to taste
⅓ cup (2½ fl oz)
    syrup from plums
⅛ teaspoon ground
    cinnamon
2 teaspoons Worcestershire
    sauce

Trim the cutlets neatly. If using chops, trim and secure the tails with toothpicks. Season the lamb with pepper. Heat the butter or oil in a large frying pan and cook the lamb on medium heat until browned on each side and cooked to taste. Remove to a hot dish. Drain the fat from the pan and return to the heat. Add the remaining ingredients and stir well to lift the browned sediment. Bring to the boil and simmer for 1 minute. Serve the plum sauce with the chops, and garnish with plum pieces if desired. Suitable accompaniments are rice pilaf or boiled new potatoes, mashed pumpkin and green beans or broccoli.

Lamb Pommery with Parsnip Purée

Serves 6

600 g (1 ¼ lb) parsnips
salt
½ teaspoon sugar
freshly grated nutmeg
freshly ground pepper
3 lamb mid loins, boned
15 g (½ oz) butter
½ cup (4 fl oz) dry
    white wine
½ cup (4 fl oz) light
    stock
2 tablespoons Pommery or
    other grainy mustard
¼ cup (2 fl oz) cream

Scrape the parsnips, trim and slice into a saucepan. Add salt to taste, then the sugar and water to cover. Bring to the boil, partly cover and cook on low heat until tender and most of the liquid has evaporated. Mash well or purée. Mix in the nutmeg and pepper to taste, cover and keep warm.

Remove the main eye muscle from each of the lamb loins. Reserve the fillets for another use. Trim the gristle from the eyes of the loins, leaving 3 longish, thick pieces of pure lamb meat. Season with pepper. Heat the butter in a frying pan and brown the lamb on all sides. Reduce the heat and cook for a further 10 minutes, turning frequently. The lamb is pink and juicy after this time. Cook for a further 2 to 3 minutes for well done. Remove to a dish and keep warm.

Deglaze the pan with the wine and stock and stir in the mustard. Bring to the boil and simmer to reduce and thicken slightly, then stir in the cream. Leave the sauce to simmer gently.

Cut the lamb into thick slices with the knife at an angle. Pile the parsnip purée into mounds on 6 dinner plates, spoon some sauce on the purée and overlap slices of lamb on top. Serve with vegetables of your choice.

Lamb Mildura

Serves 4

8 lamb mid loin or
    chump chops
pepper
½ cup (4 fl oz) water or
    light stock
¼ cup (3 oz) fruit
    chutney
lemon juice
canned apricot halves or
    peach slices, drained

Trim lamb if necessary. Season with pepper to taste. Heat a frying pan, add the lamb and cook on medium heat, turning occasionally. Drain off the fat as it accumulates. When cooked to taste, remove to a hot dish and keep warm.

Drain any fat from the pan and add the water or stock. Heat, stirring well to lift the browned sediment. Stir in the chutney and lemon juice to taste and boil until slightly thickened. Add the drained fruit, allowing 2–3 apricot halves per serve or 4-5 peach slices. Heat gently, adjust the flavour with lemon juice and spoon over the chops.

Lamb

Lamb and Mint Sausages

Makes approximately 20 sausages

- 1.5 kg (3 lb) boneless lamb from leg or forequarter
- ½ teaspoon freshly ground pepper
- ½ teaspoon calcium ascorbate*
- 2 ½ teaspoons salt
- ¼ cup (2 fl oz) iced water
- 1 cup chopped white onion
- ⅓ cup firmly packed chopped fresh mint leaves
- 1 cup ice
- 1 ¼ cups (5 oz) wholemeal flour
- thick sausage casings from the butcher

For 1.5 kg (3 lb) boneless lamb you will need a leg over 2 kg (4 lb) in weight. If the leg is small, purchase an additional 2 or 3 chump chops and remove the bones. A boned forequarter should provide sufficient meat. Trim the fine skin and any thick gristle from the lamb, but leave a good proportion of fat. Cut into 2 cm (¾ inch) cubes and check the weight to ensure you have the right amount. Place in a large dish and sprinkle the pepper and calcium ascorbate evenly over the lamb. Stir the salt into the iced water and add to the lamb. Mix well.

Divide the meat roughly into 6 portions and process each portion separately in a food processor with steel blade until finely minced (ground). Remove each batch to a large dish. Place the onion and mint in the processor and process to a coarse purée. Add the ice and process until the ice is crushed. Add the flour and process until combined. Do not overmix. Pour this mixture over the meat, mix thoroughly and process again in 4 batches in the food processor. Turn into a dish.

Rinse the salt from the sausage casings and soak in warm water for 30 minutes. Run cold water through each length of casing to check there are no holes. Fit about a metre (yard) of casing onto the nozzle of a sausage filler attachment. Pass the lamb mixture through the sausage filler. When meat appears at the end of the nozzle, switch off the filler and pull the casing over the end of the nozzle. Tie the casing, then continue with the filling. Let the sausage curl into a dish. When the casing is filled, leave the end unfilled and untied, and fill more casings as necessary.

Beginning at the tied end of each long sausage, twist the sausage into links, twisting first in one direction, then in the opposite direction. Tie off the other end close to the filling and snip off any excess casing at each end.

Store loosely covered in the refrigerator for 1 day before cooking for flavours to develop. Cook within 3 days, otherwise store properly wrapped in a freezer.

To cook, separate the sausages and prick with a fork. Cook in a little butter in a frying pan on medium low heat, turning frequently to brown evenly. Do not overcook. Serve with mint jelly or redcurrant jelly.

Note: Sausage fillers are available as attachments for food processors and mincers.

* Calcium ascorbate is a more stable form of ascorbic acid or vitamin C powder, available at pharmacies and health food stores. Ascorbic acid is a meat preservative, but it loses potency once the jar contents are exposed to air. Purchase unflavoured calcium ascorbate or ascorbic acid.

Lamb Steaks with Port Sauce

Lamb Steaks with Port Sauce

Serves 5 – 6

- 750 g (1 ½ lb) lamb leg steaks
- freshly ground pepper
- 30 g (1 oz) butter
- ¼ cup (2 fl oz) port
- ½ cup (4 fl oz) light stock
- 1 teaspoon cornflour (cornstarch)
- 2 tablespoons cold water
- 1 tablespoon chopped chives

Trim the steaks and season with pepper. Heat the butter in a large frying pan until the foaming subsides. Add the lamb and cook on medium heat about 2 minutes on each side for pink lamb, a little longer for well done. Remove to a warm dish.

Deglaze the pan with the port and stock and stir over heat to lift the browned sediment. Mix the cornflour with the water until smooth and stir into the pan liquid to thicken. Add the chives, adjust the seasoning and simmer 1 minute. Pour over the steaks and serve with vegetables of your choice.

Lamb Rosemary

Serves 4 – 6

4-6 lamb leg steaks or chops
freshly ground pepper
15 g (½ oz) butter
1 garlic clove, crushed
1 tablespoon fresh or dried rosemary leaves
⅓ cup (2½ fl oz) red or white wine
½ teaspoon sugar
2 teaspoons cornflour (cornstarch)
½ cup (4 fl oz) light stock
2 tablespoons cream, optional

Trim the lamb. If using chops, the bones can be removed to give lamb steaks. Season with pepper. Heat the butter until foaming in a frying pan and add the lamb. Cook on medium high heat for 3 to 4 minutes on each side for pink lamb. Remove to a hot dish, cover and keep warm. Reduce the heat and add the garlic and rosemary to the pan. Cook a few seconds, then deglaze the pan with the wine. Stir well and press the rosemary leaves with a fork to release the flavour. Mix the sugar and cornflour into the stock and pour into the pan, stirring constantly until thickened and bubbling. Stir in the cream, if used, then pour over the lamb steaks and serve with carrot straws, lightly cooked spinach and boiled new potatoes or ribbon noodles tossed with a little butter and chopped chives.

Apple Isle Lamb

Serves 4

8 lamb chump chops
freshly ground black pepper
15 g (½ oz) butter
1 tablespoon brandy
1 onion, thinly sliced
2 green apples, cored and sliced
1 tablespoon flour
¾ cup (6 fl oz) apple cider
1 teaspoon prepared mustard
2 tablespoons cream

Trim the chops if necessary and season with pepper. Melt the butter in a large frying pan until foaming. Add the chops and cook on medium heat for 8 to 10 minutes, turning occasionally. Pour on the brandy, ignite immediately, and shake the pan until the flames die down. Remove the chops to a dish and keep warm.

Add the onion and apple slices and cook on medium low heat, stirring occasionally, until softened. Sprinkle in the flour, stir well, then pour in the cider and stir to lift the browned sediment. When thickened and bubbling, stir in the mustard, adjust the seasoning and add the cream. Return the chops and reheat gently for 1 to 2 minutes. Do not let them boil in the sauce. Serve the chops on warm plates, top with apple mixture and accompany with glazed carrots and boiled new potatoes tossed with chopped chives.

Apple Isle Lamb

Lamb

Lamb Shogayaki

Serves 4

500 g (1 lb) lean lamb (see Lamb Teppanyaki; page 133)
1 teaspoon grated fresh ginger
1 dried chilli, soaked and chopped
½ cup (4 fl oz) light soy sauce
3 tablespoons saki or dry sherry
1 teaspoon Japanese mustard (kalashi)
1 medium-sized carrot, cut into fine strips
2 spring onions (scallions), cut into fine strips
1 green pepper (capsicum), cut into fine strips
1 stalk celery, cut into fine strips
chopped parsley or chives
oil for cooking

Trim the lamb of all visible fat and cut into thin slices, halving the slices if large. Mix the ginger with the chilli, soy sauce, saki and mustard. Add the lamb and mix well. Leave to marinate for 1 hour or more, stirring occasionally. Prepare the vegetables and toss together; keep the parsley separate.

Heat a griddle or barbecue hotplate. Add a little oil and the lamb. Cook the lamb on high heat, tossing it often, until just cooked through and lightly browned. Serve on plates, sprinkle with the parsley, and add some of the vegetable strips to each plate.

Note: Japanese mustard is mildly hot and available from Japanese food stores. If unavailable, use French mustard mixed with a little English mustard for heat.

Oregano Lamb with Quick Ratatouille

Serves 4

8 lamb chump chops
juice of 1 lemon
1 teaspoon dried oregano
pepper to taste
2 teaspoons olive oil

Quick Ratatouille
1 cup (8 fl oz) tomato spaghetti sauce
½ cup (4 fl oz) white wine or water
1 cup sliced green beans
1 cup sliced zucchini (courgettes)
1 green pepper (capsicum), sliced
1 eggplant (aubergine), cubed

Trim the chops if necessary. Mix the lemon juice with the oregano, pepper and oil in a shallow dish. Add the chops and turn to coat. Leave aside for a few minutes.

Heat the griller (broiler), drain the chops and place under medium heat. Grill (broil) for 8 to 10 minutes, turning and brushing occasionally with marinade.

Serve on hot plates with the ratatouille and accompany with crusty bread and a tossed green salad.

Quick Ratatouille: Place the spaghetti sauce in a saucepan. Add the wine with the vegetables and bring to the boil, stirring occasionally. Cover and simmer gently for 20 minutes until the vegetables are tender.

Curried Lamb Fingers

Serves 4

500 g (1 lb) finely minced (ground) lamb
¾ cup cooked rice
2 teaspoons curry powder
1 small onion, finely chopped
1 egg
½ teaspoon salt
pepper to taste
½ cup (3 oz) chopped raisins
flour for coating
1 tablespoon oil
fruit chutney for serving

Combine the lamb with the rice, curry powder, onion, egg, salt, pepper and raisins. Mix lightly and thoroughly and divide into 12 portions. With moistened hands form into little finger shapes about 1 cm (½ inch) thick. Coat with flour.

Heat the oil in a pan and cook the lamb fingers on medium high heat until golden brown on each side and cooked through. Drain on paper towels and serve topped with fruit chutney. Serve with mashed potatoes, glazed carrots and a green vegetable. Also good with salad.

Lamb and Pawpaw Curry

Serves 6

¼ cup (2 fl oz) oil
1.5 kg (3 lb) lean lamb, cubed
2 medium-sized onions, chopped
1 garlic clove, crushed
2 teaspoons grated fresh ginger
1 tablespoon coriander
1 teaspoon cumin
½ teaspoon chilli
1 cup (8 fl oz) beef stock
1 pawpaw (papaya)
½ cup (4 fl oz) natural yoghurt
½ cup (2 oz) flaked almonds, toasted

Heat the oil, add the lamb, brown well and remove. Add the onions, garlic and ginger and sauté for 2 minutes. Add the spices and cook a further 1 minute. Return the meat, add the stock, cover and simmer for 30 to 40 minutes or until tender. Halve the pawpaw and prepare balls with a melon baller. Add the pawpaw and yoghurt to the meat. Heat gently and serve immediately topped with flaked almonds.

Note: Brown rice and sambals make an ideal accompaniment.

Apricot Cider Lamb

Serves 6 - 8

- 1 x 1.5 kg (3 lb) boned leg of lamb
- 8 apricots, stoned and sliced
- 1 onion, chopped
- finely grated rind and juice of 1 lemon
- 1 tablespoon fresh dill, chopped
- 1 cup breadcrumbs
- freshly ground black pepper
- ½ cup (5 oz) honey
- 2 cups (16 fl oz) apple cider

Lay the lamb skin side down on a board. Using a sharp knife, cut the meat in several places to open out the leg, making it suitable for stuffing and rolling.

Place the apricots and onion in a pan. Cover and heat gently for 5 minutes or until tender, stirring occasionally. Mix the lemon rind, dill, breadcrumbs and pepper and spread over the lamb. Roll the lamb to enclose the stuffing and secure with skewers or string. Place in a roasting tin and brush with the honey and apple cider and bake in a moderate oven at 180°C (350°F/Gas 4) for approximately 1 hour. Baste occasionally and if over browning cover with foil. Add extra cider if the pan juices are very thick.

Remove the foil, add the lemon juice and return to the oven for a further 30 minutes or until cooked. Rest the meat for 20 minutes before carving.

Heat the remaining pan juices until slightly reduced and serve as a sauce with the lamb. Add extra cider to the sauce if too thick. Serve with green peas and new potatoes.

Lamb in the Pink

Serves 4

- 1 medium-sized onion, finely chopped
- 2 rashers bacon, chopped
- 1 cup cooked brown rice
- 2 tamarillos, peeled and chopped
- 1 teaspoon rosemary
- freshly ground black pepper
- ½ cup pine nuts, toasted
- 2 boned loins of lamb

Sauce
- 1 cup (8 fl oz) stock
- 2 tablespoons red wine
- 2 tamarillos, peeled and puréed
- 1 tablespoon cream

Sauté the onion and the bacon until the onion is transparent. Combine with the rice, tamarillos, rosemary, pepper and pine nuts. Stuff the boned lamb with the seasoning and tie securely with white string. Place the remaining seasoning in an ovenproof dish. Bake the lamb and seasoning in a moderate oven at 180°C (350°F/Gas 4) for 45 minutes, or until cooked. Remove and drain. Carve the lamb and serve with the sauce and seasoning, the sliced tamarillos and vegetables in season.

Sauce: Combine the pan juices with the stock, wine and tamarillos. Simmer until reduced and thickened. Swirl in the cream.

Lamb Chops with Mandarin Sauce

Serves 4 - 6

- 6 shortloin lamb chops
- pepper

Mandarin Sauce
- 3 tablespoons blackcurrant jelly
- ⅓ cup (2 ½ fl oz) orange juice
- ½ cup (4 fl oz) port
- 2 tablespoons lemon juice
- 1 teaspoon dry mustard
- ½ teaspoon ground ginger
- ½ teaspoon cornflour (cornstarch)
- 1 tablespoon cold water
- 6 mandarins, segmented, with pith removed

Season the lamb chops with pepper and grill (broil) for approximately 5 minutes on each side or until cooked. Spoon the mandarin sauce over the chops and serve.

Sauce: Blend the jelly, juice, port, lemon juice, mustard and ginger together in a pan and heat, stirring, until well combined. Remove from the heat. Blend the cornflour with the water to make a paste and stir into the hot sauce. Return to the heat and cook, stirring continually, until thickened. Add the mandarins.

Peppercorn Lamb

Serves 4

- 8 thick lamb mid loin or chump chops
- lemon juice
- freshly ground pepper
- 15 g (½ oz) butter
- 3 teaspoons flour
- 2 teaspoons drained green peppercorns
- ½ cup (4 fl oz) light stock
- ¼ cup (2 fl oz) white wine
- salt
- 3 tablespoons cream

Trim the chops. If using mid loin chops, remove the bone if desired and shape into rounds, securing with toothpicks. Rub the lamb with lemon juice and season generously with pepper. Heat the butter in a large frying pan, add the lamb and cook on medium heat until browned and cooked to taste. Remove to a hot dish. Drain off all but 1 tablespoon fat from the pan and stir in the flour. Cook for 1 minute, add the peppercorns and mash lightly with a fork. Add the stock and wine and stir constantly until bubbling. Add salt to taste and a little lemon juice. Stir in the cream and serve with the lamb.

Note: If green peppercorns are not available, 1 tablespoon chopped chives can be stirred into the sauce with the cream.

Lamb

Short Cut Recipes

Glazed Lamb Cutlets

Serves 4

Preparation time: 10 minutes
Cooking time: 5 minutes

2 large potatoes
2 tablespoons oil
1 packet frozen broccoli
8-10 lean lamb cutlets
freshly ground pepper
15 g (½ oz) butter
2 teaspoons French mustard
1 tablespoon redcurrant jelly

Peel the potatoes and cut into tiny cubes. Heat the oil in a frying pan, add potatoes and cook on medium heat, tossing occasionally. Put a pan of water on to boil, when boiling add the broccoli and cook until tender.

Season the cutlets with pepper. Melt the butter in a large frying pan, add the cutlets and cook for 2 to 3 minutes on each side. Drain off the fat. Mix the mustard with the redcurrant jelly and add to the pan. It will start to bubble immediately. Turn the cutlets over so that both sides are coated with glaze. Drain the potatoes and broccoli and serve immediately with the glazed cutlets.

Lamb Roast Seville

Serves 4

Preparation time: 5 minutes
Cooking time: 38 minutes

2 boneless lamb chump roasts, each about 500 g (1 lb)
grated rind of 1 orange
pepper to taste
a little oil
½ cup (4 fl oz) orange juice
1 teaspoon dry mustard
1 tablespoon honey
2 tablespoons mint sauce
cubed pumpkin
asparagus spears
2 teaspoons cornflour (cornstarch)

Trim the fat from the lamb chumps if necessary and rub with grated orange rind and pepper. Heat a large frying pan and grease with oil. Add the lamb and brown on each side on medium-high heat. When browned, reduce the heat to medium-low, cover and cook for 20 minutes, turning once.

Mix the orange juice with the mustard, honey and mint sauce. Pour over the lamb in the pan. Cover and cook for a further 15 minutes, turning the lamb occasionally. Put pumpkin cubes on to boil and put a second pan of water on to boil for the asparagus. Add the asparagus when boiling.

Remove the lamb to a platter and cover with foil. Skim the pan juices if necessary and thicken with the cornflour mixed with a little cold water. Boil gently for 1 minute and adjust the seasoning. Slice the lamb onto hot plates, spoon on the sauce and serve with the drained pumpkin and asparagus.

Minted Lamb Chops

Serves 4

Preparation time: 12 minutes
Cooking time: 10 – 12 minutes

8 lamb mid loin chops
1 tablespoon French mustard
2 teaspoons Worcestershire sauce
2 tablespoons chopped fresh mint
lettuce
avocado
red pepper (capsicum)
cucumber
black olives
4 corn cobs
1 teaspoon sugar
salad dressing

Secure the tails of the chops with toothpicks. Mix the mustard with the Worcestershire sauce and mint and spread half the mixture on the chops. Put a pan of water on to boil for the corn and heat the grill (broiler). Prepare a salad with the lettuce, avocado, red pepper, cucumber and black olives. Put the corn in boiling water with the sugar and cook for 8 to 10 minutes.

Cook the chops under the grill (broiler) for 4 to 6 minutes. Turn and spread with the remaining mustard mixture and cook a further 4 to 6 minutes. Drain the corn, toss the salad with the dressing and serve with the chops.

Honey-Soy Lamb Chops

Serves 4

Preparation time: 8 minutes
Cooking time: 10 minutes

8 lamb mid loin chops
2 tablespoons soy sauce
1 tablespoon honey
1 tablespoon lemon juice
1 garlic clove, crushed
½ teaspoon ground ginger
1 teaspoon oil
1 packet frozen Chinese stir fry vegetables
1 tablespoon toasted sesame seeds

Trim the chops if necessary. Put the griller (broiler) on to heat. Mix the soy sauce with honey, lemon juice, garlic and ginger. Place the chops on the grill (broiler) rack and brush with honey-soy mixture. Grill (broil) for about 5 minutes on each side, brushing the second side with the mixture.

While the chops are cooking, heat the oil in a wok or frying pan. Add the Chinese vegetables and stir fry 4 to 5 minutes or until cooked, adding any remaining soy mixture from the chops.

Sprinkle the chops with toasted sesame seeds and serve with the vegetables.

Opposite: *Lamb Roast Seville*

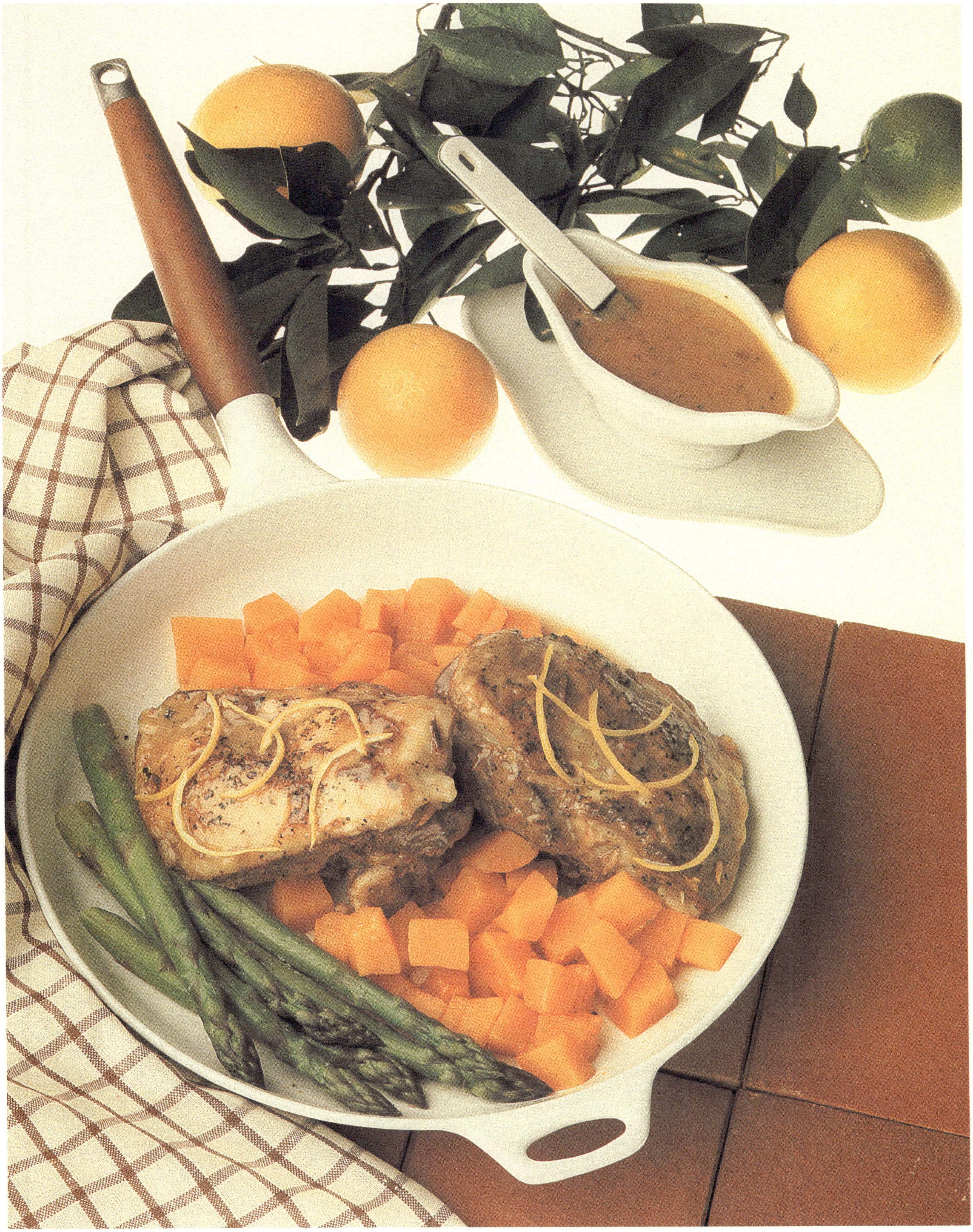

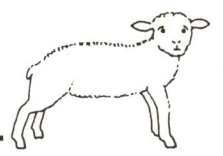

Lamb

Quick Microroast Lamb Dinner

Serves 4 [M]

Preparation time: 7 minutes
Cooking time: 37-40 minutes

1 kg (2 lb) lamb shoulder roast with fruity stuffing (*page 110*)
freshly ground pepper
2 tablespoons oil
1 ½ tablespoons light gravy powder
4 potatoes
4 pieces pumpkin
1 ½ cups frozen peas
water
sugar
¾ cup (6 fl oz) warm stock

Rub the roast with pepper, 2 teaspoons of the oil and ½ tablespoon gravy powder. Place fat side down on an upturned saucer or rack in a microwave dish and microwave on high for 5 minutes. Reduce to medium-high and cook for a further 6 minutes. Turn the roast over and cook for 11 minutes. Peel and halve the potatoes and prepare the pumpkin. Heat the remaining oil in a frying pan, add the vegetables and brown on all sides on medium heat. Put the peas in a bowl with a little water and sugar, cover and leave aside.

Remove the roast from the dish and wrap in foil. Stand for 15 minutes. Drain the meat juices into a bowl, remove the rack and place the vegetables in the dish. Microwave on high 8 to 10 minutes. Remove and cover. Microwave the peas on high for 4 to 5 minutes. Skim the fat from the juices and add the stock. Stir in the remaining gravy powder. After the vegetables are cooked, microwave the gravy on high for 3 minutes, stirring 3 times, until thickened. Carve the lamb and serve with the vegetables and gravy.

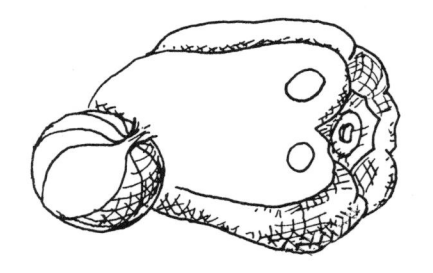

Lamb Chops with Plum Sauce

Serves 4

Preparation time: 10 minutes
Cooking time: 12 minutes

4-6 lamb forequarter chops
250 g (8 oz) sliced small mushrooms
½ red pepper (capsicum), thinly sliced
½ cup chopped parsley
4 chopped spring onions (scallions)
salad dressing
¼ cup (3 oz) plum jam
¼ cup (2 fl oz) orange juice
2 garlic cloves, crushed
1 teaspoon ground cumin
foil-wrapped garlic bread

Trim the chops if necessary and leave aside. Put the mushrooms in a bowl and add the red pepper, parsley and spring onions and toss with salad dressing. Make a basting sauce with the plum jam and orange juice mixed in a small pan with the garlic and cumin. Place the pan on a barbecue to heat gently with the garlic bread.

Place the chops on the barbecue and cook for about 6 minutes each side, basting frequently with the warm plum sauce. Serve the chops with any remaining sauce, the mushroom salad and garlic bread.

Lamb Cutlets and Vegetables in Pastry

Serves 4

Preparation time: 27 minutes
Cooking time: 18 minutes

8 lamb cutlets
freshly ground black pepper
15 g (½ oz) butter
1 small onion, finely chopped
1 medium-sized carrot, finely chopped
2 cups chopped mushrooms
1 cup frozen green peas
4 sheets frozen puff pastry, thawed
1 small egg, beaten
green salad of lettuce, watercress, avocado

Season the cutlets with pepper. Heat a large frying pan, grease with a little of the butter and brown the cutlets on each side. Do not cook through. Remove and set aside. Add the remaining butter with the onion and carrot and cook on medium low heat until slightly softened. Add the mushrooms and peas and cook for a further 5 minutes. Remove and cool if time allows. Set oven to 220°C (425°F/Gas 7).

Cut the pastry sheets in half. On each half place a tablespoon of vegetable mixture, top with a cutlet and put another tablespoon of vegetables on top of cutlet. Fold the pastry over to enclose, sealing the edges with beaten egg. Place on a greased baking sheet and glaze with beaten egg. Bake for 15 to 18 minutes until golden. Prepare the salad while they cook. Serve the cutlets with the salad.

Honey Lamb Chops

Serves 4

Preparation time: 25 minutes
Cooking time: 12 minutes

4-6 lamb chump chops	1 x 850 g (1 ¾ lb) can
juice of 1 orange and 1 lemon	baby beetroot
1 tablespoon soy sauce	canned or fresh orange segments
1 tablespoon warmed honey	1 tablespoon finely shredded orange rind
2 teaspoons dried rosemary leaves	lettuce cups
1 garlic clove, crushed	foil-wrapped garlic bread

Make small cuts in the edges of the chops to prevent them curling during cooking. Combine the fruit juices with the soy sauce, honey, rosemary and garlic. Add the chops and turn to coat. Drain the beetroot and place in a bowl with the orange segments and rind. Prepare the lettuce cups and fill with the beetroot mixture.

Place the garlic bread on a barbecue to heat. Drain the chops well and pour the marinade into a small pan and place on the barbecue to heat. Barbecue the chops for 8 to 10 minutes, turning and brushing frequently with marinade. Place the filled lettuce cups on 4 plates and spoon a little of the hot marinade on top. Add the steaks and serve with slices of garlic bread.

Greek Kebabs and Salad

Serves 4

Preparation time: 15 minutes
Cooking time: 10 minutes

500 g (1 lb) cubed lamb leg	freshly ground black pepper
¼ cup (2 fl oz) olive oil	dash of Tabasco sauce
¼ cup (2 fl oz) lemon juice	2 tomatoes
	4 small pita bread
1 small onion, finely chopped	cubed feta cheese
2 tablespoons finely chopped parsley	onion rings
	black olives
	shredded lettuce

Thread the lamb cubes onto 4 bamboo skewers. Combine the oil, lemon juice, onion, parsley, pepper and Tabasco. Add the lamb skewers and turn to coat. Cut the tomatoes into wedges. Drain the lamb skewers, place them under a heated grill (broiler) and cook for 10 minutes, turning often and basting with the marinade.

While the lamb cooks, warm the pita bread in a moderate oven. Toss the feta cheese with the onion rings and black olives. Place the bread on warm plates with the lettuce, tomato wedges and feta mixture. Using a fork, push the lamb cubes from each skewer onto the bread and serve.

Barbecued Lemon Chops

Serves 4

Preparation time: 15 minutes
Cooking time: 18 minutes

4-6 lamb chump chops	2 tomatoes, sliced
¼ cup (2 fl oz) dry sherry	3-4 radishes, sliced
¼ cup (2 fl oz) lemon juice	salad dressing
1 tablespoon oil	1 tablespoon chopped fresh mint
1 teaspoon dried rosemary leaves	⅓ cup (2 oz) black olives
2 garlic cloves, crushed	4 corn cobs
2 cups sliced celery	butter

Trim the chops if necessary and place in a marinade made with the sherry, lemon juice, oil, rosemary leaves and garlic. Place the celery in a bowl with the tomato and radish slices. Toss with salad dressing and scatter the top with mint and olives.

Strip the husks and silk from the corn. Place on a large piece of foil, top with a little butter and a sprinkle of water. Wrap and seal with double folds. Put the package on a barbecue grid and cook for 15 to 18 minutes, turning the package occasionally. After corn has been cooking for 5 minutes or so, drain the chops and barbecue 5 to 6 minutes on each side, brushing occasionally with marinade. Serve chops with the salad and corn.

Little Lamb Sausages

Serves 4

Preparation time: 15 minutes
Cooking time: 15 minutes

500 g (1 lb) finely minced (ground) lamb	onion wedges
	red pepper (capsicum) pieces
1 small onion, finely chopped	mushrooms
1 garlic clove, crushed	cherry tomatoes
1 tablespoon chopped fresh mint	oil
	bean sprouts
seasoning to taste	

Mix the lamb with the chopped onion, garlic and mint, adding seasoning to taste. Shape into small balls and form these into sausage shapes on skewers; about 3 to a skewer. Thread the onion wedges, red pepper, mushrooms and cherry tomatoes onto other skewers and brush with oil.

Grill (broil) or barbecue the sausages and vegetables using medium heat, turning to brown evenly. The sausages should be pink in the centre – if overcooked they will become dry. Serve the sausage and vegetable skewers on a bed of bean sprouts.

Lamb

Roman-Style Lamb

Serves 4

Preparation time: 10 minutes
Cooking time: 14 minutes

1 small red chilli, optional
2 garlic cloves
4 boneless lamb leg steaks
2 teaspoons oil
1 teaspoon dried rosemary leaves
½ cup (4 fl oz) white wine
1 teaspoon cider vinegar
3 medium-sized tomatoes, sliced
1 medium-sized onion, sliced
chopped parsley
salad dressing
185 g (6 oz) snow peas (mange-tout)

If using the chilli, seed and chop finely with the garlic. Nick the edges of the steaks with a sharp knife. Heat the oil in a large frying pan on high heat. Add the steaks and cook for 2 to 3 minutes on each side until browned. Remove the steaks to a plate and remove the pan from the heat. Put chilli and garlic into a hot pan and stir in the rosemary, wine and vinegar. Return to the heat and bring to the boil. Reduce the heat, return the steaks and simmer very gently for 5 to 6 minutes, turning the steaks often.

Meanwhile put a saucepan of water on to boil for the snow peas. Arrange the tomatoes and onion in overlapping circles on a plate, sprinkle the top with parsley and splash on a little salad dressing. Add the peas to the boiling water, cook 3 to 4 minutes, drain. Serve the steaks with the sauce, snow peas and the tomato salad.

Lamb and Pea Stroganoff

Serves 4

Preparation time: 5 minutes
Cooking time: 15 minutes

1 boneless lamb chump, about 500 g (1 lb)
15 g (½ oz) butter
1 ½ cups frozen green peas
½ cup (4 fl oz) cream
salt and pepper
4 slices bread
wedges of tamarillo or tomato

Slice the chump and cut slices into strips. Heat a frying pan on high heat, add the butter and when foaming, add the lamb strips. Brown quickly, tossing the strips frequently. Add the peas, cream and season to taste. Reduce the heat to low and cover the pan. Cook gently for 10 to 12 minutes until the peas are tender.

Meanwhile toast the bread and place on warm plates with wedges of tamarillo. Serve the stroganoff on a warm serving dish.

Note: 4 large chump chops or 500 g (1 lb) lamb leg steaks may be used in place of the boneless chump; trim off fat and bone, then slice into strips.

Satay Lamb

Serves 4

Preparation time: 6 minutes
Cooking time: 8 minutes

1 cup (6 oz) rice
3 small onions
shredded cabbage
lemon juice
2 teaspoons oil
500 g (1 lb) cubed boneless lamb leg
1 garlic clove, crushed
1 teaspoon grated fresh ginger
3-4 tablespoons bottled satay sauce
1 tablespoon soy sauce
sliced spring onion (scallion) tops

Put the rice on to boil. Quarter the onions, cut out the roots and segment. Prepare the shredded cabbage and toss with lemon juice.

Heat a wok or large frying pan and add the oil. When very hot add the lamb cubes, garlic and ginger and stir fry on high heat until the cubes are browned and almost cooked through. Add the onion leaves and continue to stir fry for 2 to 3 minutes to lightly cook the onion. Add the satay sauce to taste and the soy sauce and toss over heat for 1 minute. Put the satay lamb onto plates, sprinkle with spring onion tops and serve with the boiled rice and cabbage salad.

Note: Boneless lamb may be prepared from chump chops if desired; you will need about 6 chops.

Lebanese Lamb Pockets

Serves 4

Preparation time: 15 minutes
Cooking time: 10 minutes

1 onion, sliced
1 tablespoon oil
¼ cup pine nuts
500 g (1 lb) lean minced (ground) lamb
2 garlic cloves, crushed
1 teaspoon ground cumin
¼ teaspoon chilli powder, optional
⅓ cup (2 oz) sultanas (seedless raisins)
¼ cup (2 fl oz) apple cider or white wine
4-6 wholemeal pita bread
½ cucumber
2 tomatoes
fresh mint
8 black olives
1 lemon

Sauté the onion in the oil for 2 minutes. Add the pine nuts, cook for 1 minute, add the mince and increase the heat. Cook on high heat for 3 minutes, stirring often to break up the mince. Reduce the heat to low, add the garlic, spices, sultanas and cider. Season to taste and simmer gently for 10 minutes.

Meanwhile warm the pita bread. Halve the cucumber lengthwise, scrape out seeds and cut into half-moon slices. Cut the tomatoes into wedges and chop the mint. Cut the bread in half and place some cucumber, tomato and mint into the pockets with the lamb mince and serve garnished with olives and lemon wedges.

VEAL

Veal is a low cholesterol meat from a calf. It is pale in colour and tender. Because of its very low fat content it must be cooked with care and not for long periods. Milk-fed veal is also available but is a little more expensive. Veal bones are very soft and can be cut easily. Veal is very easily digested and is suitable for invalids and children.

Veal cuts are usually very similar to lamb but are best cooked with a sauce or stuffing to enhance the delicate flavour. Almost everyone has tasted Vienna Schnitzel but there are many more exciting recipes that will give you a new insight into this often neglected meat.

These recipes have been specially chosen to make the most of this delicate meat and will lead the adventurous cook to experiment with new taste sensations.

The majority of the recipes in this chapter have been supplied by the **Australian Meat and Livestock Corporation** while others have been provided by contributors whose credits appear elsewhere in the book.

Veal

Prune and Nut Veal

Serves 4 [M]

1 veal loin, boned
freshly ground pepper
oil
1 cup (8 fl oz) chicken stock
3 teaspoons cornflour (cornstarch)
2 tablespoons Madeira or port
3 teaspoons soft brown sugar
2 teaspoons lemon juice

Prune and Nut Stuffing
1 small onion, chopped
15 g (½ oz) butter
½ cup (3 oz) chopped, pitted prunes
½ cup (3 oz) finely chopped pecan nuts
grated rind of 1 lemon
½ teaspoon ground ginger

Ask the butcher to leave a fairly long flap on the loin so that stuffing can be contained. Weigh and calculate the cooking time at 18 minutes per 500 g (1 lb). Spread the stuffing on the inside of the loin. Roll up and tie securely with white string, tying along the length of the loin as well as around. Season with pepper and brush with oil.

Heat a browning grill on high for 6 minutes. Add the veal and cook on high for 5 minutes, turning to brown evenly. Reduce to medium and cook for the remainder of the cooking time, turning once. Remove to a plate, cover with foil and stand for 10 minutes.

Deglaze the browning grill with the stock and pour into a bowl. Mix the cornflour with Madeira and stir into the liquid with the sugar and lemon juice. Cook on high, stirring occasionally, for 4 minutes until thickened and bubbling. Strain and serve with the sliced veal. Pumpkin or sweet potato and a green vegetable can be served as accompaniments.

Prune and Nut Stuffing: Place the onion and butter in a bowl and cook on high for 2 minutes. Mix in the remaining ingredients, adding pepper to taste.

Citrus Rack of Veal

Serves 5 – 6

1 rack of veal with 5-6 ribs
freshly ground black pepper
1 tablespoon melted butter
grated rind of 1 orange
juice of 2 oranges
juice of 1 lemon
¼ cup (3 oz) honey
1 cup (8 fl oz) light stock
2 teaspoons cornflour (cornstarch)

Tie the veal rack between the rib bones with white string and season with pepper. Place upright in a baking dish and brush with melted butter. Cook in a moderate oven, 180°C (350°F/Gas 4), for 20 minutes. Mix the orange rind and fruit juices with honey and pour over the veal. Cook, basting occasionally with juices, for a further hour or until the juices run clear when veal is pierced. Remove to a platter, cover with foil and keep warm.

Add the stock to the dish and stir to dissolve the brown bits in the pan. Bring to the boil and thicken with cornflour mixed with a little cold water. Adjust seasoning and strain into a sauceboat. Carve the veal into chops and serve with the sauce.

Mustard Cream Rack of Veal

Serves 6

1 rack of veal with 8-9 ribs, about 2 kg (4 lb)
freshly ground pepper
2 tablespoons melted butter
½ cup (4 fl oz) white wine
½ cup (4 fl oz) light stock
2 tablespoons Dijon mustard
grated rind of 1 orange
1 cup (8 fl oz) cream

Tie the rack between each second rib bone to keep the flap in place. Season with pepper and place upright in a roasting dish. Brush with butter and cook in a moderate oven, 180°C (350°F/Gas 4), for 30 minutes. Pour the wine and stock over the veal and cook for a further 30 minutes. Remove from the oven and remove the strings.

Place the veal in a dish so that it rests on rib bones, meat side up. Mix the mustard with the orange rind and spread on top. Pour the cream over the veal and return to the oven for a further 30 to 45 minutes, basting often with dish juices.

Remove the rack to a platter, cover with foil and leaves in a warm place for 15 minutes. Scrape the browned bits from the sides of the dish into the sauce and thin down with a little wine or stock. Place over heat and stir well until boiling. Strain into a sauceboat. Carve the rack between the rib bones and serve with the sauce.

Veal Marsala

Serves 4

500 g (1 lb) thin veal steaks
2 tablespoons seasoned flour
1 tablespoon oil
15 g (½ oz) butter
½ cup (4 fl oz) chicken stock
¼ cup (2 fl oz) marsala
squeeze of lemon juice

Flatten the veal steaks if necessary and coat lightly with seasoned flour, keeping the remaining flour aside. Heat the oil and butter in a large frying pan on high and when foaming subsides, add the veal and brown quickly for about 1 minute on each side until just cooked through. Remove to a dish and keep aside.

Reduce the heat and sprinkle the remaining flour in the pan. Stir well with a fork and cook for a minute or so, then pour in the stock and marsala, stirring constantly. Keep stirring until thickened and bubbling. Boil until reduced by half and syrupy, then add the lemon juice and return the veal to the pan. Keep the heat low and turn the veal in the sauce to glaze the slices. Serve immediately with sautéed potatoes and lightly cooked zucchini (courgettes).

Vienna Schnitzels

Serves 4

500 g (1 lb) thin veal steaks
2 tablespoons seasoned flour
1 egg
1 tablespoon milk
dry breadcrumbs
oil for shallow frying
1 hard-boiled egg, sliced
anchovy fillets
lemon wedges

Flatten the veal steaks if necessary and coat them lightly with seasoned flour. Beat the egg in a flat dish with the milk. Dip the veal in the egg mixture then coat with breadcrumbs. Place on a tray and chill for 15 minutes. Put oil in a frying pan to a depth of 6 mm (¼ inch) and heat well. Add the veal and fry for about 2 minutes on each side until golden brown and just cooked through. Drain. Place on a hot serving dish with a slice of egg and a rolled anchovy fillet on each. Garnish with lemon wedges.

Avocado Veal in Filo

Serves 6

6 thick veal leg steaks
freshly ground pepper
60 g (2 oz) butter
½ cup chopped spring onions (scallions)
1 ½ cups sliced small mushrooms
½ teaspoon dried tarragon
lemon juice
1 large ripe avocado
12 sheets filo pastry
melted butter
4 tablespoons soft breadcrumbs
salt

Sherry Cream Sauce
15 g (½ oz) butter
1 tablespoon flour
⅓ cup (2 ½ fl oz) dry sherry
¾ cup (6 fl oz) light stock
¼ teaspoon dried tarragon
salt and pepper
1 tablespoon snipped chives
¼ cup (2 fl oz) cream
lemon juice

Steaks should be cut 1.5 cm (½ inch) thick. Nick any membrane on the sides of the veal and season with pepper. Heat half the butter in a large frying pan and add the spring onions, mushrooms, tarragon and a squeeze of lemon juice. Cook gently until soft, drain and remove to a plate.

Add the remaining butter and when foaming, add the veal and fry on high heat to brown each side. Do not cook through. Remove to a plate and leave until cold. Keep the pan aside for the sauce. Peel the avocado, slice into slender wedges and sprinkle with lemon juice.

Butter 2 sheets filo pastry and lay one on the other. Brush the top with butter and fold in half lengthwise. Sprinkle a scant tablespoon of crumbs in the centre and place a veal steak on top. Season lightly with salt, top with 2 – 3 slices avocado and some of the mushroom mixture. Bring up the sides of the pastry over the top, double fold and fold in sides. Tuck the sides under. Place on a greased baking sheet and brush lightly with butter. Make the remaining parcels in the same way. These may be covered and refrigerated at this stage.

Cook in a preheated hot oven, 200°C (400°F/Gas 6), for 15 minutes until puffed and golden. Serve immediately with the sherry cream sauce passed separately.

Sherry Cream Sauce: Melt the butter in the pan in which the veal was browned and stir in the flour. Cook for 1 minute and pour in the sherry and stock, stirring constantly. When bubbling, add the tarragon and simmer until thickened. Adjust the seasoning, add the chives, cream and a little lemon juice and heat gently. Pour into a sauceboat.

Veal

Veal with Mango

Serves 4

500 g (1 lb) thin veal steaks
2 tablespoons flour
salt
freshly ground pepper
1 tablespoon oil
15 g (½ oz) butter
2 tablespoons brandy or Grand Marnier
½ cup (4 fl oz) veal or other light stock
½ cup (4 fl oz) white wine
1 teaspoon French mustard
grated rind of ½ orange, optional
2 mangoes, peeled and sliced
2 tablespoons cream

Nick any membrane on the edges of the steaks to prevent them curling. Flatten the steaks if necessary. Coat with flour seasoned with salt and pepper. Heat the oil and butter in a large frying pan until foaming. Add the veal and fry quickly on high heat for 2 minutes each side. Add the brandy and ignite immediately. Shake the pan until the flames are extinguished. Remove the veal to a hot dish and keep warm.

Return the pan to the heat and leave until the moisture evaporates and only the fat remains. Stir in the remaining flour from coating the veal and cook for 1 minute. Pour in the stock and wine, stirring constantly, and continue to stir until thickened and bubbling. Add the mustard and stir well to lift the brown sediment. Stir in the orange rind if brandy was used to flame the veal. Add mango slices to sauce. Heat gently, adjust seasoning, and swirl cream into sauce. Serve sauce and mango slices with the veal, and accompany with lightly cooked snow peas (mange-tout).

Veal with Mango

Veal Steaks with Blueberry Sauce

Serves 4

500 g (1 lb) thin veal leg steaks
2 tablespoons seasoned flour
60 g (2 oz) butter
additional 2 teaspoons flour
½ cup (4 fl oz) light stock
⅓ cup (2 ½ fl oz) marsala
¾ cup fresh blueberries
1 teaspoon lemon juice
1 teaspoon sugar
salt and pepper

Coat the veal with seasoned flour. Heat half the butter in a large frying pan, and when foaming subsides, add 2–3 steaks. Sauté over medium high heat until browned and just cooked through. Remove to a warm dish and keep warm. Cook the remaining steaks, adding butter as required. When the steaks are cooked, stir the extra flour into the pan drippings and cook for 1 minute. Stir in the stock and marsala and heat until boiling. Add the blueberries, simmer gently for 3 to 4 minutes. Add the lemon juice, sugar and adjust the seasoning with salt and pepper. Pour over the steaks and serve immediately with rice boiled in chicken stock with butter added, and grated orange rind and toasted, slivered almonds tossed through just before serving. Accompany with a green salad.

Tarragon Veal Cutlets

Serves 5–6

1 kg (2 lb) veal cutlets
½ cup (4 fl oz) white wine
1 tablespoon lemon juice
1 tablespoon oil
1 tablespoon finely chopped spring onions (scallions)
½ teaspoon dried tarragon
freshly ground pepper
1 egg
1 tablespoon milk
½ teaspoon salt
breadcrumbs
oil for shallow frying
1 chicken stock cube, crumbled
2 teaspoons cornflour (cornstarch)
2 tablespoons water
¼ cup (2 fl oz) cream

Place the veal cutlets in a glass dish in a single layer. Mix the wine with the lemon juice, oil, spring onions, tarragon and pepper. Pour over the cutlets and marinate 1 to 2 hours, turning occasionally. Drain and reserve the marinade.

Beat the egg with the milk and salt. Dip the cutlets into the egg, then coat with breadcrumbs. Chill for 15 minutes, then shallow fry in hot oil until lightly browned on each side. Reduce the heat and continue to fry until cooked through. Drain on absorbent paper and keep warm.

Drain the oil, add the marinade and stock cube and bring to the boil. Mix the cornflour with the water and add to the pan, stirring constantly until thickened and bubbling. Boil for 1 minute, adjust seasoning and stir in the cream. Heat through, pour over cutlets and serve with jacket boiled potatoes and broccoli.

Opposite: *Veal Steaks with Blueberry Sauce*

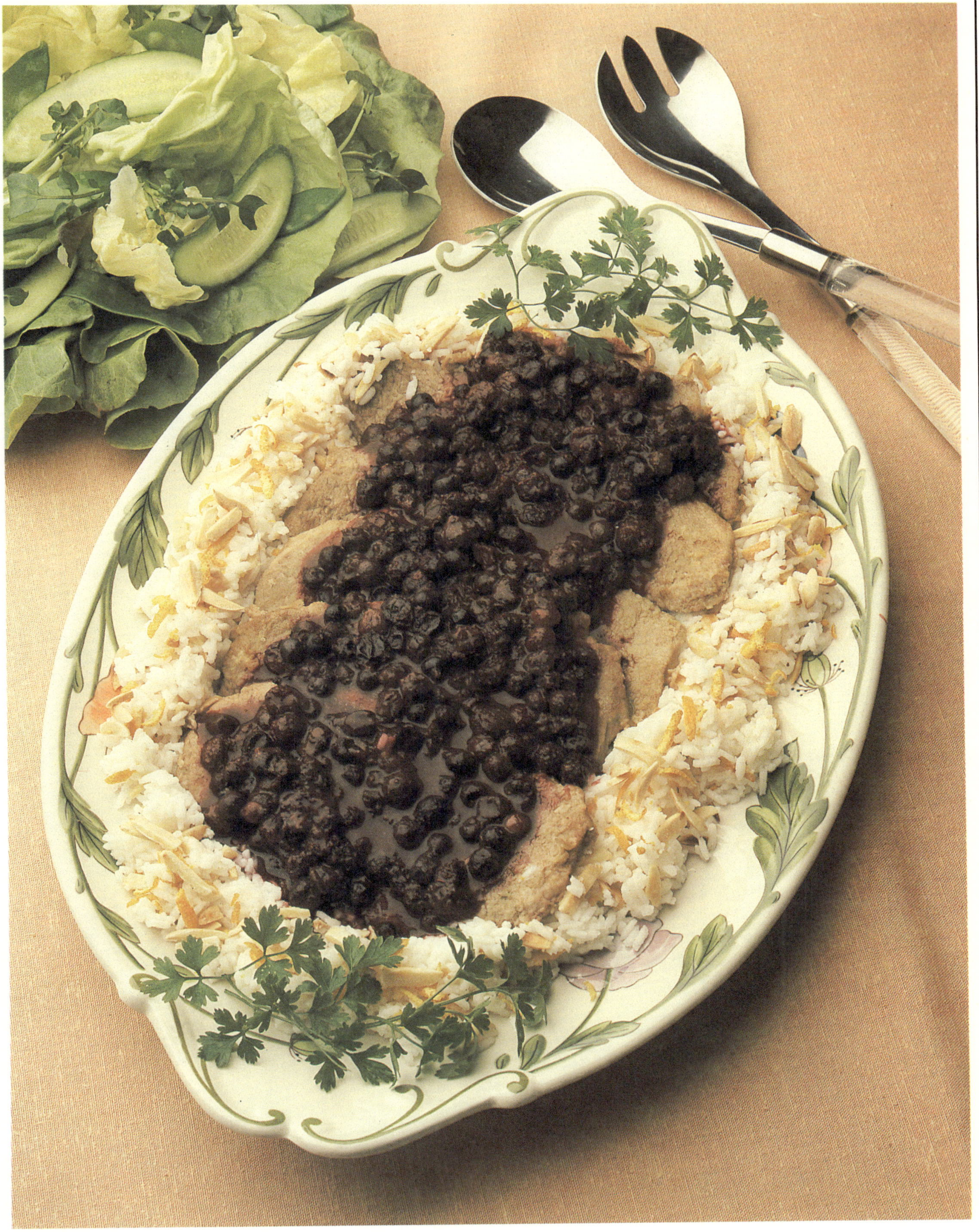

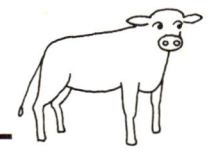

Veal

Veal with Peppercorn Sauce

Serves 6

1 tablespoon oil
15 g (½ oz) butter
12 thin veal steaks
3 teaspoons flour
½ cup (4 fl oz) dry white wine or vermouth
pinch of salt
¼ teaspoon sugar
1-2 teaspoons green peppercorns
1 teaspoon pink peppercorns, optional
squeeze of lemon juice
½ cup (4 fl oz) cream

Heat a frying pan on medium high heat and add the oil and butter. Place the veal slices in a pan and fry for about 2 minutes each side until just cooked through. Remove to a warm dish and keep warm.

Spinkle flour into the pan and stir well with a fork. Pour in the wine to deglaze and stir until thickened, adding a little water if necessary. Add the salt, sugar and drained peppercorns, using 2 teaspoons green peppercorns if pink peppercorns are not available. Mash lightly with a fork and stir in a little lemon juice. Add the cream, stir well and simmer briefly. Pour over veal and serve immediately with vegetables in season.

Veal Goulash for Two

Serves 2   [M]

500 g (1 lb) cubed veal
1 tablespoon seasoned flour
1 medium-sized onion, chopped
1 garlic clove, crushed
2 teaspoons oil
2 tablespoons tomato paste
1 tablespoon paprika
½ cup chopped red pepper (capsicum)
½ teaspoon sugar
¾ cup (6 fl oz) stock
1 tablespoon sour cream

Coat the veal with seasoned flour. Place the onion, garlic and oil in a small casserole dish and cook on high for 3 minutes, stirring once. Add the tomato paste and paprika and cook on high for 2 minutes. Add the veal, chopped pepper, sugar and stock, stir, cover and cook on medium for 5 minutes. Continue cooking on defrost for 30 minutes, stirring once. Stir in the sour cream, stand 5 minutes and serve with boiled noodles and a green vegetable or salad.

Blanquette of Veal

Serves 6

60 g (2 oz) butter
1 kg (2 lb) cubed veal
1 onion studded with 3 cloves
2 medium-sized carrots, sliced
1 ½ cups (12 fl oz) veal stock
1 teaspoon salt
white pepper to taste
bouquet garni
2 tablespoons flour
12 small onions, parboiled
125 g (4 oz) button mushrooms
additional knob of butter
squeeze of lemon juice
2 egg yolks
¼ cup (2 fl oz) cream
¼ teaspoon ground nutmeg

Heat one third of the butter in a heavy saucepan. Add the veal and cook on high heat, stirring often, until the colour changes. Do not brown. Reduce the heat, add the clove-studded onion, the carrots, stock, salt, pepper and bouquet garni. Cover and bring to a slow boil, skimming if necessary, then boil gently for 45 minutes. Remove the veal pieces and carrot slices with a slotted spoon and keep aside. Strain the stock through a muslin lined sieve and reserve. Clean the saucepan and return to the heat with the remaining butter. Stir in the flour and cook for 2 minutes. Add the stock, stirring constantly until thickened and bubbling. Reduce the heat and add the veal and carrots with the parboiled onions. Cover and simmer gently for 20 to 30 minutes until the veal is tender.

Trim the mushrooms and sauté in the extra butter with a squeeze of lemon juice. When the veal is tender, add the mushrooms and remove from the heat.

Beat the egg yolks in a bowl with the cream and nutmeg. Beat in a little of the hot sauce from the veal, then pour the egg mixture into the veal, stirring it in gently. Reheat gently for 2 to 3 minutes without allowing it to boil. Serve with boiled rice or noodles and a green vegetable.

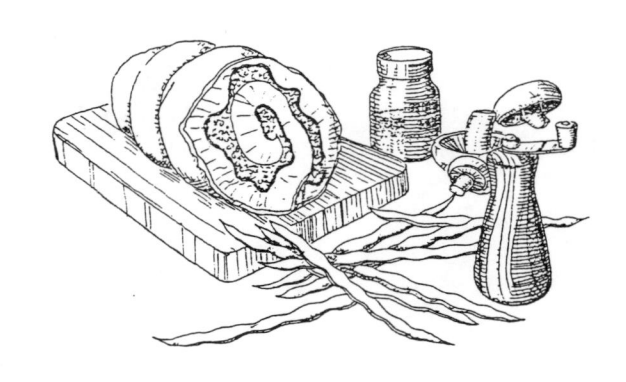

Osso Buco

Serves 4 - 6

1.5-2 kg (3-4 lb) veal knuckles cut in 5 cm (2 inch) pieces
flour
salt and pepper
2 tablespoons olive oil
30 g (1 oz) butter
1 large onion, finely chopped
2 garlic cloves, crushed
1 x 440 g (14 oz) can Italian tomatoes
2 tablespoons tomato paste
½ cup (4 fl oz) dry white wine
1 teaspoon sugar
thinly peeled strip of lemon rind
1 teaspoon dried marjoram
3 tablespoons chopped fresh parsley
stock
grated rind of ½ lemon and ½ orange

Tie the knuckle pieces with white string if desired. This keeps them intact. Coat with the flour seasoned with salt and pepper. Heat the oil and butter in a large, heavy pan and brown the veal on all sides. Remove to a plate. Reduce the heat and add the onion. Cook gently until soft, then add the garlic and cook for a few seconds.

Chop the tomatoes and add to the pan with their liquid. Stir in the tomato paste, wine and sugar. Add the lemon rind, marjoram and half the parsley. Return the veal with the pieces upright so that the marrow stays in the bones. Cover and simmer gently for 1 ½ hours or until the meat is tender. Add a little stock after 1 hour if needed.

When cooked, transfer the veal pieces to a serving dish and remove the strings. Adjust the seasoning of the sauce and pour over the veal. Mix the remaining parsley with the grated rinds and sprinkle on top. Serve with saffron rice and a tossed salad.

Note: The marrow is the highlight of this dish. While there is a special tool for removing it, a fondue fork does just as well. Provide one for each diner.

Paupiettes of Veal

Serves 6

750 g (1 ½ lb) thin veal steaks
2 tablespoons flour
salt
freshly ground pepper
30 g (1 oz) butter

Herb Stuffing
¼ cup chopped spring onions (scallions)
30 g (1 oz) butter
1 ½ cups (3 oz) soft breadcrumbs
1 tablespoon chopped fresh parsley
1 onion, chopped
½ cup chopped celery
¼ cup (2 fl oz) dry red wine
½ cup (4 fl oz) light stock
bouquet garni

1 tablespoon chopped fresh herbs (thyme, marjoram)
grated rind of 1 lemon
1 small egg, beaten
salt and pepper

Cut the veal steaks in half if large. Spread about 1 tablespoon of the Herb Stuffing on each piece of veal. Roll up and secure with fine skewers or tie with white string. Season the flour with salt and pepper and coat the rolls lightly.

Heat the butter in a frying pan with lid to fit and brown the rolls on all sides. Remove to a plate. Reduce the heat and add the vegetables. Cook gently for 10 minutes, stirring often. Add the wine, stock and bouquet garni. Stir well to lift the sediment and place the rolls on top of the vegetables. Season to taste, cover and simmer gently for 45 minutes or until tender. Transfer the rolls to a warm dish and remove the skewers or string.

Remove the bouquet garni from the pan and discard. Strain the contents through a sieve into a clean pan and rub the vegetables through a sieve. Bring to the boil, thicken if necessary with a cornflour (cornstarch) and water paste and pour over the rolls. Alternatively thicken the liquid in the pan with the vegetables and serve with the veal.

Herb Stuffing: Gently cook the spring onions in the butter until soft and add to the crumbs with the remaining ingredients, adding enough beaten egg to bind. Mix lightly and season to taste.

Veal

Cold Veal Pie

Serves 6 – 8

1.25 kg (2 ½ lb) cubed veal
500 g (1 lb) veal bones, sawn into pieces
3 cups (24 fl oz) water
½ cup (4 fl oz) dry white wine
1 carrot, quartered
1 onion, quartered
bouquet garni
salt
½ teaspoon whole peppercorns
½ teaspoon whole allspice
3 eggs
½ teaspoon ground mace
½ teaspoon ground allspice
¼ teaspoon each ground thyme, sage and marjoram
2 tablespoons finely chopped parsley
grated rind of 1 lemon
375 g (12 oz) shortcrust pastry
beaten egg for glazing

Rinse the veal and bones in cold water and place in a large pan with the water, wine, carrot and onion. Bring slowly to the boil, skimming when necessary. Add the bouquet garni, about 2 teaspoons salt, the peppercorns and whole allspice. Cover and simmer gently for 1 hour until the veal is tender. Cool, then remove the veal to a bowl with a slotted spoon. Return the pan to the heat and simmer, uncovered, until reduced by half.

Hard boil the eggs, cool under running water, and shell immediately to prevent the yolks darkening. Add the ground spices and herbs, the parsley and lemon rind to the veal. Moisten with 2 tablespoons of the veal stock and toss thoroughly.

Grease a 23 x 12 cm (9 x 5 inch) loaf pan and line with strips of strong baking paper, cut to width of sides, with sufficient length to line the pan and overlap the rim by 5 cm (2 inch). Roll out three quarters of the pastry and line the pan, cutting the corners so that they fit evenly. Press all joins to seal. Roll out the remaining pastry for the top.

Spread half the veal in the base and place the eggs along the centre. Fill with the remaining veal. Do not pack too tightly. Moisten the pastry edge with water and put the top in position. Press the edges to seal and trim. Crimp the edges, roll out the trimmings and cut out leaves and stem – gum leaf shapes give an Australian touch. Roll the small pieces into gum nuts.

Brush the top of the pie with beaten egg and arrange the decoration on top. Shape another gum nut and place on a greased section of a baking sheet and place the pie on the sheet. Cut a vent in the centre of the pie.

Bake in a preheated hot oven, 220°C (425°F/Gas 7), for 15 minutes. Reduce to moderate and remove the pie from the oven. Glaze the top with beaten egg and return to the oven to cook for a further 35 to 40 minutes until golden brown. Cool for 1 hour.

Strain the reduced stock through a muslin lined sieve and leave until cool but still liquid. Place a funnel in the vent and slowly pour in the stock. Check the level in the pie occasionally so that the stock does not overflow. Place the extra gum nut over the vent. Chill in the refrigerator for 4 hours.

Lift the pie out of the pan with the aid of the paper liner. If it does not yield, place the pan briefly on a warm hotplate as a little jelly may have seeped out. Store in a sealed container if not required immediately. Serve in thick slices with salad accompaniments.

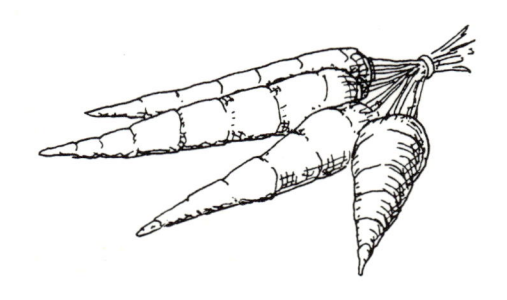

Cold Veal Pie

Veal and Spinach Pie

Serves 4

- 2 teaspoons oil
- 500 g (1 lb) finely minced (ground) veal
- ¾ cup chopped spring onions (scallions)
- 1 chicken stock cube, crumbled
- 1 cup chopped, peeled tomatoes
- 1 cup chopped, cooked spinach
- ½ cup (2 oz) ricotta cheese
- 1 tablespoon chopped fresh parsley
- ½ teaspoon ground rosemary
- salt
- freshly ground pepper
- 1 egg
- 8 sheets filo pastry
- melted butter

Heat the oil in a pan, add the mince. Cook over high heat, stirring often, until the meat has browned and the juices evaporate. Turn into a bowl and mix in the spring onions, stock cube, tomatoes and well drained spinach. Mash the cheese with a fork and add to the meat mixture with the parsley, rosemary and seasoning to taste. Beat the egg lightly and stir into the mixture.

Lightly grease a lamington tin or oven dish of a similar size. Line with 4 sheets filo pastry, brushing each sheet lightly with melted buter. Spread the filling in the dish and top with 4 sheets pastry, brushing each with melted butter. Trim the edges and brush the top lightly with butter. Bake in a moderately hot oven, 190°C (375°F/Gas 5), for 30 to 35 minutes or until puffed and golden. Cut into squares and serve hot for a lunch or light meal.

Veal and Spinach Pie

Veal

Vitello Tonnato
Serves 8

- 1.5 kg (3 lb) nut of veal or rolled shoulder
- 4 bay leaves
- 15 g (½ oz) butter
- 1 tablespoon oil
- 1 onion, chopped
- 1 carrot, sliced
- 1 stalk celery, sliced
- 2 sprigs fresh parsley
- 1 cup (8 fl oz) dry white wine
- 3 cups (24 fl oz) water
- ½ teaspoon whole peppercorns
- salt

Tuna Sauce
- 1 x 185 g (6 oz) can tuna in oil, drained
- 6 anchovy fillets
- 2 egg yolks
- ½ teaspoon dry mustard
- 3 teaspoons drained capers
- 2 tablespoons lemon juice
- ¾ cup (6 fl oz) olive oil
- cold strained stock from veal
- salt and pepper

If using nut of veal, 2 may be necessary depending on size. Tie the veal nut into a neat roll with white string. If using a shoulder, ask the butcher to roll and tie it. Push the bay leaves under the strings on the veal. Heat the butter and oil in a deep pan and sear the veal lightly on all sides. Do not brown. Add the chopped and sliced vegetables, parsley, wine, water, peppercorns and about 1 teaspoon salt and bring to a slow simmer. Cover and simmer gently for 1½ to 2 hours until the veal is tender. Cool in the stock, remove and wrap in foil. Refrigerate overnight or for up to 2 days. Strain the stock through a muslin lined sieve and store in a separate container in the refrigerator.

A few hours before serving, remove the strings from the veal and slice the meat thinly. Arrange the slices slightly overlapping on a platter. Spread half the sauce over the veal. Cover with plastic wrap and refrigerate for several hours.

Just before serving, remove the plastic and spread on a little more sauce. Sprinkle with the remaining capers and garnish with sprigs of watercress. Serve with remaining sauce separately. A selection of salads should accompany the dish.

Tuna Sauce: Place the tuna, anchovy fillets, egg yolks, mustard, 1 teaspoon capers and half the lemon juice in a blender or food processor with a steel blade fitted. Process until smooth and gradually pour in the oil while processing. Pour the sauce into a bowl and stir in a little veal stock to give a thin cream consistency. Add more lemon juice if necessary and adjust seasoning with salt and pepper. The remaining capers are used for garnishing.

Note: The remaining veal stock may be frozen and used the next time you prepare the dish, or freeze it in small quantities and use when veal or light stock is required.

Veal and Pepper Casserole
Serves 6

- 750 g (1 ½ lb) veal steak
- 30 g (1 oz) butter
- 2 onions, thinly sliced
- 1 garlic clove, crushed
- 1 tablespoon paprika
- 1 tablespoon flour
- 1 ½ cups (12 fl oz) stock
- 3 tablespoons tomato paste
- salt and pepper
- 3 medium-sized tomatoes, quartered
- 1 medium-sized green pepper (capsicum), chopped
- ½ cup (4 fl oz) sour cream

Cut the meat into 2.5 cm (1 inch) cubes. Melt the butter in a saucepan and fry the meat until sealed. Remove the meat and fry the onions and garlic lightly. Stir in the paprika and flour, blend in the stock and stir until boiling. Return the meat, add the tomato paste, season to taste and simmer gently for 1½ hours. Add the tomatoes and green pepper. Simmer a further 5 to 10 minutes. Just before serving stir in the sour cream. Serve with buttered noodles.

Veal Marengo
Serves 4

- 2 tablespoons oil
- 750 g (1 ½ lb) cubed stewing veal
- 2 tablespoons oil
- 2 onions, finely chopped
- 1 garlic clove, crushed
- 1 x 425 g (13 ½ oz) can peeled tomatoes, chopped
- 1 tablespoon tomato paste
- ½ cup (4 fl oz) light stock
- ¼ cup (2 fl oz) dry white wine
- 1 bay leaf
- ¼ teaspoon dried thyme
- 1 tablespoon chopped fresh parsley
- 1 teaspoon sugar
- salt
- freshly ground pepper
- 125 g (4 oz) small mushrooms
- chopped parsley to garnish

Heat half the oil in a heavy saucepan, add the veal and brown quickly. Remove to a plate. Add the onion with the remaining oil and cook gently until soft. Add the garlic, cook a few seconds, then stir in the tomatoes with their liquid, tomato paste, stock and wine. Return the veal to the pan and add the bay leaf, herbs, sugar and salt and pepper to taste. Cover and simmer gently for 1 hour. Add the trimmed mushrooms, cover and cook for a further 30 minutes until veal is tender. Serve sprinkled with additional chopped parsley, with boiled rice or noodles and a tossed salad as accompaniments.

Fruity Veal 'n' Pork Rolls

Serves 4 – 6

500 g (1 lb) minced (ground) veal and pork
1 medium-sized onion, finely chopped
¼ cup (1 oz) flour
1 cup (8 fl oz) soda water
1 beaten egg
seasonings to taste
155 g (5 oz) Australian cheese, cut into eight 6 x 1 x 1 cm (2 ½ x ½ x ½ inch) sticks
60 g (2 oz) butter

Combine all the ingredients except the cheese and butter and cover the mixture with plastic wrap. Refrigerate for 1 hour. Divide the meat into 8 portions. Mould each around a stick of cheese, ensuring the cheese is completely covered. Melt the butter in a heavy based frying pan. Sauté the patties slowly for 10 to 12 minutes on each side or until golden brown. Serve with Fruit Sauce (see below).

Fruit Sauce

Makes 1 cup

½ cup (2 oz) chopped dried apples
¼ cup (1 oz) chopped dried apricots
¼ cup (1 oz) chopped sultanas
1 cup (8 fl oz) hot water
1 tablespoon lemon juice or to taste

Place the fruit in a small saucepan. Pour over the hot water. Stand at least 30 minutes then bring to the boil. Reduce the heat and simmer gently until the remaining liquid is reduced by half. Beat with a fork to combine the ingredients. Stir in the lemon juice.

Italian Veal Roll

Serves 6

2-3 kg (1-1½ lb) veal or yearling steak in 1 piece
salt and pepper
1 large rasher bacon
2-3 hard-boiled eggs
1 tablespoon oil
dried sage
½ cup (4 oz) white wine

Flatten out the meat and season. Lay the bacon rasher, with the rind removed, on top of the meat, then the whole hard-boiled eggs, end to end. Roll up the meat securely around the eggs and tie firmly with string. Heat the oil in a frying pan and brown the meat well on all sides.

Transfer to a casserole, season well with salt, pepper and sage, and pour the wine over. Cover and cook in a moderate oven, 180°C (350°F/Gas 4), for about 2 hours.

Casserole Veal Chops

Serves 6

2 medium-sized onions
125 g (4 oz) mushrooms
1 small eggplant (aubergine), sliced
6 veal chops
salt and pepper
4 tablespoons oil
1 cup (4 oz) dry breadcrumbs
¼ teaspoon dried basil
¼ cup (2 fl oz) wine
1 cup (8 fl oz) stock

Slice the onions and mushrooms. Peel and slice the eggplant. Season the chops with salt and pepper. Heat the oil in the pan and brown the chops on both sides. Remove the chops and keep warm.

Sauté the eggplant in the hot oil until just coloured on both sides, then remove and keep warm. Quickly sauté the onions and mushrooms, then place in the bottom of a casserole. Place the chops on top, then the eggplant. Sprinkle with the breadcrumbs, basil, salt and pepper. Pour over the wine and stock. Cover and bake in moderately hot oven at 190°C (375°F/Gas 5) for 1 hour. Remove the cover for last 15 minutes.

Veal with Mushrooms and Paprika

Serves 6

1 kg (2 lb) veal steak
½ cup (2 oz) flour
salt and pepper
90 g (3 oz) butter or margarine
1 onion, chopped
125 g (4 oz) mushrooms, sliced
3 teaspoons paprika
1 cup (8 fl oz) water
1 chicken stock cube
1¼ cups (10 fl oz) sour cream

Flatten the veal and cut into serving pieces. Coat with the flour seasoned with salt and pepper. Heat the butter in a frying pan and fry the veal until cooked and browned on both sides. Remove from the pan. In the same pan sauté the onion and mushrooms for 5 minutes. Add the paprika and salt and pepper. Mix well. Reduce the heat to low. Stir in the water, crumbled stock cube and sour cream. Mix thoroughly. Bring the sauce slowly to the boil; add the veal and heat through gently.

Serve with hot boiled noodles tossed with a little butter and chopped parsley.

Veal

Veal Louisa
Serves 6

1 garlic clove
1 onion
1 kg (2 lb) lean stewing veal
1 teaspoon paprika
1 teaspoon salt
3 tablespoons flour
4 tablespoons oil
2 teaspoons Worcestershire sauce
1 cup (8 fl oz) chicken stock
½ cup (4 fl oz) dry white wine
½-1 cup (4-8 fl oz) sour cream
pepper

Crush the garlic and chop the onion. Cut the meat into 5 cm (2 inch) pieces and toss in a combination of paprika, salt and flour. Heat the oil in a large pan and brown the meat well on all sides. Add the garlic, onion, Worcestershire sauce, stock and wine. Bring to the boil, reduce the heat and cover. Simmer for 1 to 1½ hours or until the meat is tender.

Just before serving, stir in the sour cream to taste and season with salt and pepper. Reheat gently. Serve with hot noodles, sprinkled with parsley.

Paprika Veal Chops
Serves 4

2 tablespoons oil
750 g (1 ½ lb) veal chops or pork chops
3 tablespoons minced onion
1 teaspoon minced garlic
1 tablespoon flour
1 tablespoon paprika
1 x 425 g (13 ½ oz) can peeled tomatoes, liquid reserved
1 teaspoon salt
¼ teaspoon ground black pepper
½ cup (4 fl oz) sour cream
1 tablespoon vinegar
6 cups cooked rice
45 g (1 ½ oz) butter
parsley flakes

Heat the oil and brown the chops on both sides. Remove the chops and add a little extra oil if needed. Add the onion and garlic and cook for a few minutes. Replace the chops in the pan, sprinkle with the flour and blend. Add the paprika and cook for 1 minute, stirring. Add the tomatoes with liquid, season with salt and pepper. If the chops are not covered with tomato liquid add a little water. Cover and simmer over low heat until tender, about half an hour. Add the sour cream mixed with the vinegar and heat but do not boil. Serve with hot rice tossed in butter. Garnish with parsley flakes.

Veal Zarina and Lemon Rice
Serves 4

60 g (2 oz) margarine
½ cup chopped spring onions (scallions)
½ cup canned or fresh green pepper (capsicum)
small garlic clove, crushed
250 g (8 oz) fresh mushrooms, sliced
2 teaspoons flour, seasoned
1 ¼ cups (10 fl oz) thick sour cream
¼ cup chopped cucumber or dill pickle
salt and pepper
750 g (1 ½ lb) veal steaks
2 firm red tomatoes, sliced
extra 30 g (1 oz) margarine
4 cups cooked rice
1 tablespoon lemon juice
½ teaspoon grated lemon rind
1 tablespoon chopped fresh parsley
extra chopped cucumber or black olives, to garnish

Heat half the margarine in a pan and sauté the spring onions, green pepper and garlic for 1 minute. Add the mushrooms and sauté until just tender. Sprinkle the flour over the mushrooms, stir and cook for 1 minute. Gradually add the sour cream and stir, then add the cucumber and season to taste. Remove from the pan and keep warm.

Wipe out the frypan and add the remaining margarine. Trim the veal, cut into serving sized pieces, toss in a little seasoned flour and sauté in the frypan until brown on both sides, about 10 to 15 minutes. Push the veal to one side and lightly sauté the tomato slices. Remove the veal and tomatoes and keep warm.

Add the extra 2 tablespoons of margarine to the frypan, add the rice, lemon juice and rind and toss continuously with the fork until the rice has heated. Add the parsley. Lay the veal down the centre of the rice, spoon over the mushroom sauce and garnish with chopped cucumber or black olives on reserved tomato slices.

PORK

Roast pork is always a favourite but today pork has been 'new-fashioned' to give the cook a huge variety of recipes from which to choose.

Pork fat should be white and firm and the flesh pale pink and the old saying 'you cannot overcook pork' is now untrue; pork should be cooked with as much care as any meat. Pork is available in the form of chops as well as roasts and spare ribs and a side of pork is always a good buy. Bacon is taken from specially-bred pigs, usually the leaner ones, while ham is taken from pigs with a high fat content.

Pork is a rich meat and is best cooked in simple dishes rather than with heavy sauces and stuffings. It is excellent served with piquant fruit sauces. Make sure the crackling on your roast leg is crisp and serve it separately so it doesn't get covered in gravy.

The majority of the recipes in this chapter have been supplied by the **Pork Promotion Centre**, while others have been provided by contributors whose credits appear elsewhere in the book.

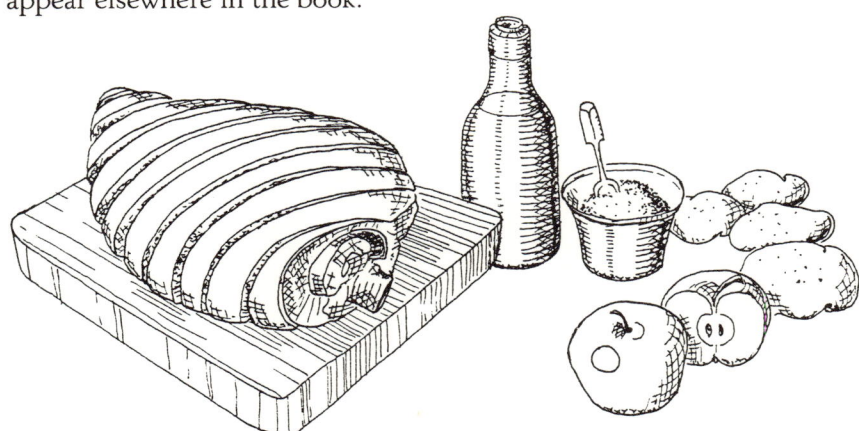

The Pork Promotion Committee is a statutory body established in 1975 by the Department of Primary Industry under the Pork Promotion act. The Pork Promotion Committee's principal objectives are to educate consumers and other public groups about pigmeat and its processed products, and to increase the consumption of pork in Australia.

The **Pork Promotion Centre** is the vehicle through which the Committee works. The activities of the Centre cover television commercials, recipe leaflets in butcher shops and supermarkets, recipe booklets in women's magazines, radio and newspaper advertising, cutting demonstrations, educational material and promotional activities related to broadening the use of all pork products including hams and bacon.

The **Pork Promotion Centre** also developed and promoted a new range of cuts of pork, known as New-Fashioned Pork. These are fat-trimmed and mainly bone-free and were developed in answer to growing consumer demand for a more nutritious meat.

The recipes here have been supplied by Julie Kerim.

Pork

CARVING

Leg of Pork

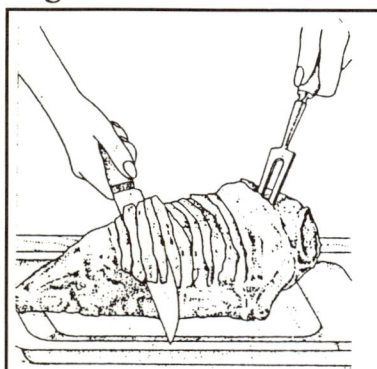

1. Place the leg, fat side up, on a board. Cut vertically down through the meat to the bone. Slip the knife under the slices and cut away from the bone.

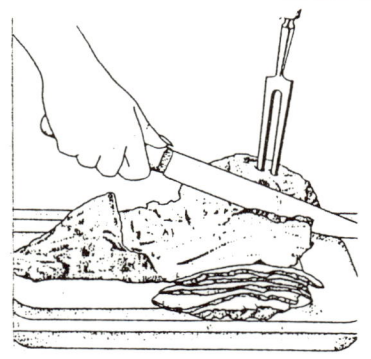

2. Cut thick slices parallel to the bone from the side of the leg. Repeat on the other side.

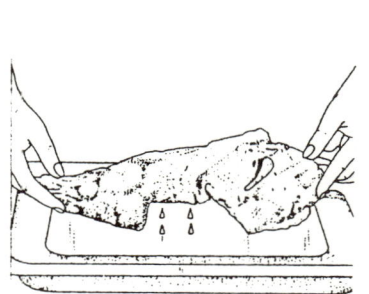

3. Turn the leg over and cut a wedge-shaped piece from the centre.

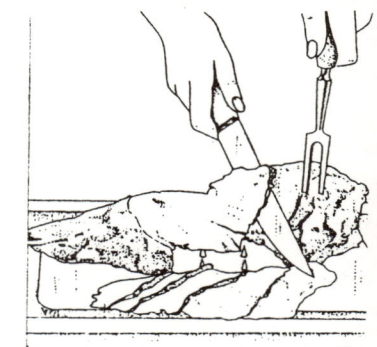

4. Holding the knife at an angle, carve thick slices from either side of the wedge, down towards the bone.

Loin of Pork

1. Place the thickest part of the loin down on the plate. Cut into thick slices between the rib bones.

Pork in Lemon Sauce

Serves 4

750 g (1 ½ lb) diced pork from the shoulder
1 tablespoon lard
1 onion, finely chopped
1 garlic clove, crushed
2 stalks celery, chopped
1 cup (8 fl oz) chicken stock
½ teaspoon salt
3 peppercorns
sprig of fresh dill or fennel
½ cup (4 fl oz) lemon juice
1 tablespoon flour
2 egg yolks
1 tablespoon brandy

Fry the pork in the lard with the onion and garlic until browned. Add the celery, stock, seasonings and dill, then cover and simmer slowly for 40 minutes. Blend the lemon juice into the flour and thicken the pork mixture, stirring until the mixture boils and thickens. Simmer for 3 minutes, then remove from the heat and whisk in the egg yolks and brandy. Cover and stand for 3 minutes. Serve with hot rice.

Pork and Quince Casserole

Serves 6

1 kg (2 lb) diced pork from the shoulder
2 tablespoons lard or oil
1 onion, chopped
½ cup (4 fl oz) tomato purée
½ cup (4 fl oz) red wine
½ teaspoon salt
½ teaspoon cinnamon
1 tablespoon honey
1 garlic clove, crushed
1 large quince

Brown the pork in the hot lard in small batches until golden. Place in a casserole. Fry the onion and add the liquids to the pan with the salt, cinnamon, honey and garlic. Bring to the boil and pour over the pork. Peel the quince, cut into quarters and remove the core, and add to the pork. Cover and bake at 160°C (325°F/Gas 3) for 1 hour. Thicken the casserole if desired with 1 tablespoon cornflour blended with extra wine. Adjust the seasonings and cook a further 10 minutes.

Mild Pork Curry

Serves 6

1 ½ tablespoons oil
750 g (1 ½ lb) lean diced pork
1 ½ cups chopped spring onions (scallions)
1 tablespoon curry powder
2 large ripe tomatoes, chopped
1 tablespoon chopped fresh coriander or parsley
¼ teaspoon cardamom
1 tablespoon roasted unsalted peanuts, chopped

Heat the oil in a saucepan and sauté the pork and spring onions for 3 minutes. Add the curry powder and continue to cook just long enough to seal the pork. Add the tomatoes, coriander and cardamom, then cover and simmer slowly for 30 minutes. Stir in the peanuts and cook for a further 10 minutes. Serve with steamed rice and vegetables.

Pork Chop Suey

Serves 4

3 cups sliced mixed fresh vegetables
3 tablespoons oil
100 g (3 ½ oz) peeled green prawns (shrimp)
500 g (1 lb) diced pork
1 large onion, sliced
2 garlic cloves, chopped
1 cm (4 inch) piece fresh ginger, finely chopped
1 cup (8 fl oz) chicken stock
1 teaspoon soy sauce
3 teaspoons cornflour (cornstarch)
1 tablespoon sweet sherry or wine
sliced spring onions (scallions)

Plunge the vegetables into boiling water for 2 minutes to blanch. Drain and cool under cold water; drain. Heat the oil and cook the prawns over medium heat until just pink. Remove. Add the pork and sauté with the onion, garlic and ginger until the pork is cooked, about 5 minutes. Add a little extra oil if necessary. Add the blanched vegetables and toss. Add all the remaining ingredients except the spring onions and stir until thickened. Simmer for 1 minute with the prawns to reheat. Top with spring onions.

Pork

Pork Curry
Serves 4 - 6

30 g (1 oz) butter
1 ½ cups chopped spring onions (scallions)
750 g (1 ½ lb) diced pork
1 tablespoon mild curry paste
1 teaspoon fish paste or sauce
1 cup (8 fl oz) unsweetened coconut milk
½ teaspoon chopped fresh basil or dried herbs
1 tablespoon chopped fresh coriander or parsley
red chilli or pepper (capsicum) rings

Melt the butter in a saucepan and sauté the spring onions until just soft. Add the pork with the curry paste and stir fry for about 3 minutes to seal the pork. Add remaining ingredients except the chilli, then cover and simmer slowly for 50 to 60 minutes. Stir in the chilli and cook uncovered for a further 15 minutes. Serve hot.

Fruity Pork Braise

Fruity Pork Braise
Serves 4

2 tablespoons oil
1 large onion, diced
500 g (1 lb) diced pork from the shoulder
1 teaspoon ground fennel
1 cup (8 fl oz) apple juice or chicken stock
10 seedless prunes
1 teaspoon mild chilli sauce
pinch of salt
8 dried apricots
155 g (5 oz) fine ham strips
1 tablespoon chives, chopped

Heat the oil and sauté the onion and pork with the fennel. Stir often. Purée the apple juice, 6 prunes, the sauce and salt in a blender and add to the pork. Cover and cook for 15 minutes. Stir often and garnish with the remaining prunes, the apricots, ham strips and chives.

Pork and Ham in Pineapple Sauce
Serves 4 [M]

2 tablespoons oil
375 g (12 oz) diced pork
1 x 220 g (7 oz) can pineapple pieces
1 tablespoon soy sauce
1 tablespoon cornflour (cornstarch)
2 tablespoons tomato sauce
1 tablespoon soft brown sugar
375 g (12 oz) ham steaks, diced

Conventional Method: Heat the oil in a large frying pan and add the pork. Cook quickly and stir until brown on all sides. Drain off the excess fat. Drain the pineapple and add the pineapple juice with the soy sauce to the pork. Cover and simmer gently for about 40 minutes or until the meat is tender. Blend the cornflour with the tomato sauce and brown sugar. Add to the pan and stir until boiling. Add the pineapple pieces and ham and simmer for 10 minutes.

Microwave Method: Heat the oil in a casserole on high for 1 minute. Toss the pork in the oil and cook a further 2 minutes. Add the pineapple juice and soy sauce. Cover and cook on medium high for 20 minutes. Add the pineapple pieces and ham. Blend the cornflour with the tomato sauce and brown sugar. Stir into the meat and season to taste. Microwave on medium for 10 minutes, stirring twice.

Pork with Chickpeas Creole

Serves 4

750 g (1 ½ lb) diced pork
2 tablespoons oil
1 tablespoon curry paste or 2 tablespoons curry powder
2 onions, sliced
5 cups diced mixed firm vegetables
2 cups (16 fl oz) chicken stock
1 x 250 g (8 oz) can chickpeas
boiled rice
toasted shredded coconut

Sauté the pork in the oil with the curry paste for about 2 minutes. Add the onions and cook a further 2 minutes. Add the vegetables with the stock, then cover and simmer for 10 minutes. Add the chickpeas and cook the creole a further 5 minutes. The diced pork requires a total of 45 minutes. Serve with boiled rice sprinkled with toasted coconut.

Note: Use any canned beans available. Alternatively, dried chickpeas must be soaked overnight in the refrigerator, drained and cooked for 45 minutes with the pork.

Pork and Mushrooms in a Rice Ring

Serves 2

1 cup mushrooms
30 g (1 oz) margarine
2 tablespoons flour
1 ½ cups (12 fl oz) skim milk
250 g (8 oz) cooked diced pork
1 tablespoon lemon juice
salt and pepper
1 cup hot boiled rice
parsley sprigs and lemon slices for garnish

Wipe the mushrooms with a damp cloth and cut into slices. Melt the margarine in a heated pan. Add the mushrooms and sauté for 3 minutes. Add the flour and stir until well blended with the mushroom mixture. Remove from the heat and add the skim milk, stirring until smooth. Add the pork, lemon juice and seasonings, return to the heat and stir until the mixture boils and thickens.

Mould the rice into a ring shape and pour the pork with the sauce into the centre. Garnish with parsley and lemon slices.

Pork with Chickpeas Creole

Pork

Pork Satay

Serves 2

½ teaspoon seasoned pepper
½ teaspoon ground coriander
2 tablespoons light soy sauce
2 teaspoons white wine
1 teaspoon soft brown sugar
¼ cup (2 fl oz) lime or lemon juice
2 teaspoons peanut oil
375 g (12 oz) leg or fillet of pork, diced
1 cup hot boiled rice
8 tomato wedges

Combine the pepper, coriander, soy sauce, wine, sugar, lime juice and peanut oil in a flat dish. Add the pork and toss until well coated. Cover and set aside for 2 hours. Arrange an equal number of pork cubes on 4 small or 2 large metal skewers. Place on a rack and grill (broil) for 10 minutes, turning frequently. Brush with any remaining marinade during cooking. Place ½ cup rice on each of 2 warm plates and set the pork satays on top. Garnish with 4 tomato wedges on each plate.

Pork and Vegetable Creole

Serves 4

½ cup (3 oz) red lentils
2 onions, coarsely chopped
1 ½ tablespoons oil
3 teaspoons curry paste
750 g (1 ½ lb) diced pork
¾ cup (6 fl oz) tomato purée
⅓ cup (2 ½ fl oz) stock
1 teaspoon salt
2 cups sliced carrots
1 ½ cups cauliflower florets

Soak the lentils in water for 1 hour, rinse clean and drain. Sauté the onions in the oil, add the curry paste and pork and stir fry together for about 5 minutes. Add the lentils, tomato purée and stock and simmer slowly for 30 minutes, covered. Season, add the carrots and mix through, then arrange the cauliflower florets on top. Cover and cook a further 30 minutes.

Pork and Noodle Toss

Serves 4

2 x 85 g (2 ½ oz) packets 3-minute noodles
3 tablespoons oil
500 g (1 lb) diced pork from the shoulder
1 teaspoon curry powder
2 onions, finely chopped
1 tablespoon chilli sauce
1 cup sliced green beans
½ cup sliced celery
salt and pepper

Prepare the noodles according to the directions on the packet and drain. Heat the oil and sauté the pork with the curry powder and onions for about 4 minutes. Stir often until browned. Add the sauce, cover and simmer slowly for 7 minutes. Add the beans and celery and stir together until tender. Adjust the seasoning, add the noodles and toss together.

Pork Minute Steak

Serves 2

6 thin pork schnitzels
60 g (2 oz) garlic butter (*page 277*)
2 tablespoons tomato sauce
2 tablespoons Worcestershire sauce
3 tablespoons sherry
chopped fresh parsley

Flatten the pork into small thin steaks. Preheat a heavy frying pan, then add the butter and quickly fry the pork for 1 minute on each side. Combine the sauces with the sherry, then add to the pan with the steaks and simmer a further 1 minute to coat the pork. Add the parsley and serve.

Pork Rarebit

Serves 4

4 pork loin medallion steaks	1 tablespoon Worcestershire sauce
¼ teaspoon garlic salt	1 teaspoon dry mustard
⅓ cup (2 ½ fl oz) tomato sauce	½ cup (2 oz) grated cheese

Season the pork medallions with the garlic salt, then secure into a round shape with toothpicks. Place under a medium hot griller (broiler) and cook 5 to 7 minutes each side depending on thickness. Mix all the remaining ingredients and spoon on top of each medallion during the final 2 minutes of cooking.

Note: Pork can be cooked on a browning tray in a microwave oven. Top with the mixture and cook just a few seconds. For a crispy finish pop under a hot griller (broiler) for a few minutes longer.

Saucy Tomato Pork

Serves 4

4-6 pork medallions from the loin	1 teaspoon chilli sauce
flour	3 tablespoons sour cream
1 teaspoon dry mustard	1 teaspoon horseradish relish
1 large onion, sliced	1 tablespoon chopped chives
15 g (½ oz) butter	
1 cup (8 fl oz) tomato soup	

Coat the pork with flour and mustard. Sauté the onion in the butter until soft, then remove. Brown the pork on both sides over low heat. Add the tomato soup, chilli sauce and onion and cook together for about 15 to 30 minutes. Combine the sour cream with the horseradish and spoon into the centre of a serving dish. Garnish with chopped chives and surround with the pork.

Pork in Pepper Sauce

Serves 2 - 4

4 x 150 g (5 oz) pork loin medallion steaks	2 tablespoons sherry or wine
15 g (½ oz) butter	1 tablespoon cream
1 packet pepper steak sauce mix	
½ cup (4 fl oz) water	

Secure the pork medallions with skewers into neat round shapes. Melt the butter in a deep frying pan and lightly brown the pork on both sides. Remove any excess fat from the pan. Blend the sauce mix with the water and sherry and add to the pork, stirring until smooth. Cover and simmer gently for about 30 minutes. Remove the pork and keep warm. Add the cream to the pan and quickly boil the sauce for 1 minute.

Tarragon Pork Medallions

Serves 4 - 6

4-6 pork medallions from the loin	1 teaspoon dried tarragon
⅓ cup (2 ½ fl oz) white wine	1 tablespoon oil
¼ teaspoon salt	1 teaspoon chopped fresh parsley
⅛ teaspoon pepper	1 tablespoon sour cream

Marinate the pork in a mixture of the wine and seasonings for several hours. Turn often. Remove the pork and wipe dry. Sauté the pork in a heavy pan with the oil. Cook about 7 minutes on each side or until just cooked and brown. Mix the parsley and sour cream into the remaining marinade and pour over the pork in the pan. Heat and turn the pork to coat with the mixture.

Pork in Ginger Wine

Serves 4

4 pork loin medallion steaks	⅔ cup (5 fl oz) green ginger wine
dash of ground cinnamon	3 teaspoons soy sauce
30 g (1 oz) butter	4 tablespoons cream
2 small apples, sliced	
1 onion, sliced into rings	

Season the pork with a little cinnamon and stand aside. Melt half the butter and sauté the apples without browning. Remove, then fry the onion until soft. Remove. Add the remaining butter to the pan and cook the pork steaks about 7 minutes on each side, turning often to keep moist and golden. Remove and keep warm. Add the ginger wine, soy sauce and cream and stir until boiling. Reduce for about 3 minutes. Return the onion, pork and apples and heat to coat with the sauce.

Swiss Style Schnitzels

Serves 4 - 6

6-8 pork schnitzels from the leg	1 egg, beaten with a little water
6-8 slices Swiss or Cheddar cheese	1 ½ cups (6 oz) dry breadcrumbs
6-8 slices ham	oil
seasoned flour	

Flatten the pork out into larger shapes. Place a slice each of cheese and ham over half the pork and fold over to make a sandwich. Secure with toothpicks. Dust the pork with seasoned flour, then dip into the beaten egg. Coat with the crumbs and press on firmly. Chill for 30 minutes. Shallow fry in hot oil for about 3 minutes on each side depending on thickness.

Pork

Sauté Médaillon Suzette

Serves 4 - 6

- 4-6 pork medallions from the loin
- 2 tablespoons seasoned flour
- 2 oranges, juiced to yield 1 cup (8 fl oz) juice
- 30 g (1 oz) butter
- 1 tablespoon brandy
- 1 tablespoon sugar
- ½ teaspoon chilli sauce
- chopped fresh parsley
- red pepper (capsicum) slices

Secure the pork medallions into a round shape with a skewer. Toss in the seasoned flour. Peel the oranges, remove the pith and cut the rind into fine strips. Juice the oranges. Melt the butter and fry the pork on both sides until golden and almost cooked. Remove and place under a grill (broiler) or in the oven to keep warm.

Pour off the excess pan drippings, add the juice, brandy, sugar and chilli sauce and stir until boiling. Add the orange shreds and simmer for 4 minutes. Add the pork medallions and reheat in the sauce. Garnish with parsley and red pepper slices.

Sauté Médaillon Suzette

Plum Pork Medallions

Serves 4 [M]

- 4 x 125 g (4 oz) pork loin medallion steaks
- 15 g (½ oz) butter or margarine
- 1 x 454 g (14 ½ oz) can plums in syrup
- 2 teaspoons cider vinegar
- pinch of cinnamon
- ground pepper
- 2 teaspoons cornflour (cornstarch)

Conventional Method: Secure the pork medallions with a wooden toothpick to make a neat round shape. Heat the butter in a frying pan and brown the medallions for 2 minutes on each side. Combine ⅓ cup (2½ fl oz) of the plum syrup with the vinegar, cinnamon and pepper. Pour over the medallions. Cover and cook gently for 15 minutes or until tender. Remove the medallions. Blend the cornflour with 1 tablespoon extra syrup and stir into the frying pan with the plums. Cook for 2 minutes. Pour the sauce and plums over the medallions.

Microwave Method: Prepare the medallions and brown as above. Transfer to a casserole. Pour the syrup mixture over, cover and microwave on medium high for 5 minutes. Remove the pork, add the blended cornflour and plum syrup. Microwave on high for 1 minute. Add the plums and microwave for 1 minute. Pour the sauce and plums over the medallions.

Cranberry Pork Steaks

Serves 4 [M]

- 4 pork steaks
- 1 cup (8 fl oz) wine
- 1 onion, sliced
- 1 bay leaf
- 2 cm (¾ inch) piece cinnamon stick

Sauce
- ½ cup (4 fl oz) wine marinade from the pork
- 4 tablespoons bottled cranberry sauce
- 1 teaspoon each chilli and garlic sauces
- 1 teaspoon cornflour (cornstarch)

Conventional Method: Place the pork in an ovenproof casserole. Add the wine, onion, bay leaf and cinnamon. Cover and stand several hours. Place in a moderate oven, 180°C (350°F/Gas 4), and cook for 40 minutes. Drain the pork into a serving dish and keep warm.

Sauce: Boil the wine marinade and when reduced, strain and measure off ½ cup (4 fl oz). Add the other sauce ingredients and stir until thickened. Spoon over the pork steaks and bake for 7 minutes.

Microwave Method: Marinate the pork as above, then microwave on medium for 15 minutes. Make the sauce as above, pour over the drained pork steaks and microwave on high for 2 minutes.

Cranberry Pork Steaks

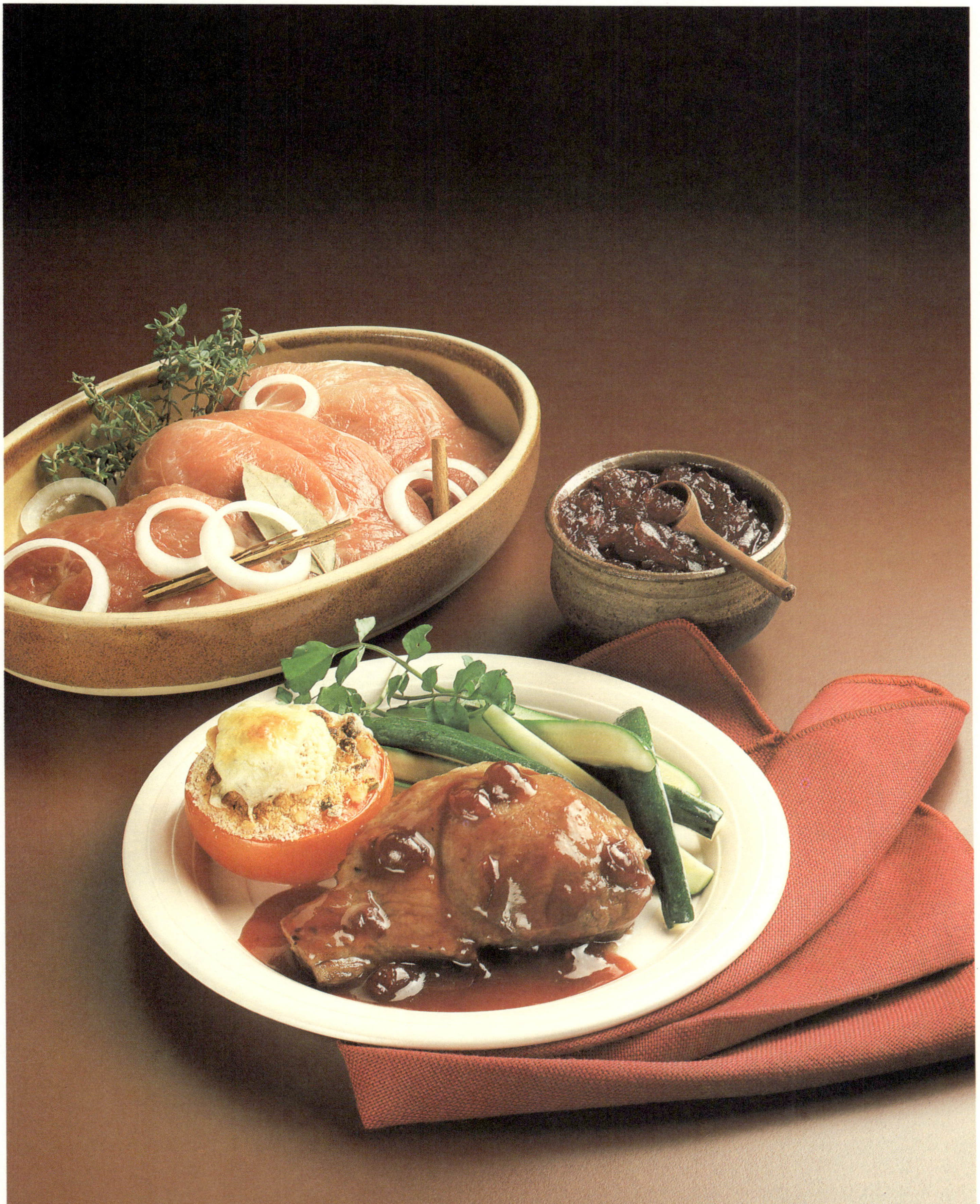

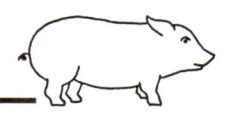

Pork

Pot Luck Pork Casserole

Serves 4 - 6

4-6 pork loin medallion steaks	1 small red pepper (capsicum), sliced
salt and pepper	1 cup chopped, peeled tomatoes
1 garlic clove, crushed	½ cup (2 ½ oz) stuffed olives
60 g (2 oz) butter	
3 lamb kidneys, sliced	
125 g (4 oz) sliced leek	

Season the pork with salt and pepper. Sauté the pork medallions in the garlic and butter until just brown on both sides. Remove to a casserole. Add the sliced kidneys to the pan and sauté over low heat. Spoon over the pork.

Top with sliced leek, red pepper, tomatoes and olives. Cover and bake in a moderate oven, 180°C (350°F/Gas 4), for about 1 hour.

Pancake Pork Schnitzels

Serves 2

4 large thin pork leg schnitzels	2 tablespoons grated Parmesan cheese
2 tablespoons flour	3 tablespoons chopped parsley or chives
oil	
3 large eggs	

Flatten the pork until really thin. Lightly dust with the flour. Preheat an electric frypan or heavy based grill-type frying pan, then add the oil to grease the base just prior to cooking. Beat the eggs, add the cheese and parsley. Quickly coat the pork in the egg, then immediately cook in the greased pan for about 1 ½ minutes on each side. Turn with an egg slice.

Parma Pork Schnitzels

Serves 4

4 pork schnitzels	4 tablespoons grated Parmesan cheese
2 tablespoons seasoned flour	cooking oil
1 egg, beaten, or milk	1 lemon, sliced
1 cup (4 oz) fine dry breadcrumbs	capers, optional

Flatten the pork schnitzels between plastic wrap until thin. Toss in the seasoned flour, then dip in the beaten egg. Coat in a mixture of breadcrumbs and cheese, pressing evenly and firmly, then refrigerate for 30 minutes before cooking. Shallow fry in medium hot oil for 3 minutes each side, depending on thickness. Remove, drain and serve with slices of lemon and capers.

Peasant Style Pork

Serves 4

4 x 125 g (4 oz) pork loin medallions	1 x 400 g (13 oz) can borlotti beans
1 tablespoon oil	2 teaspoons chopped fresh basil
1 garlic clove, crushed	zucchini (courgettes) or green beens
1 brown (Spanish) onion, sliced	
2 large tomatoes, diced	

Slash the edges of the pork medallions with a sharp knife and secure into a round shape with toothpicks. Season if desired. Heat the oil in a pan and sauté the garlic and onion until soft. Add the tomatoes and cook for 3 minutes. Drain and rinse the borlotti beans, then add to the tomato mixture with the basil. Cook for 2 minutes. Grill (broil) or pan fry pork medallions for approximately 3 ½ minutes on each side on a medium heat according to thickness. Serve with zucchini julienne or green beans.

Zippy Pork in Sauce

Serves 2 - 4

4 x 150 g (5 oz) pork loin medallion steaks	1 red pepper (capsicum), sliced
ground white pepper	1 x 220 g (7 oz) can tomato soup
15 g (½ oz) butter	¼ cup (2 fl oz) water
1 onion, sliced	

Lightly season the pork with the pepper but no salt. Heat the butter in a deep pan and lightly fry the pork on both sides with the onion and red pepper. Add the soup with the water and stir well. Cover and simmer gently for 30 minutes. Remove the lid. Reduce the sauce over high heat for 7 minutes then serve.

Pork in Taco Sauce

Serves 4

2 tablespoons flour	½ cup (4 fl oz) tomato purée or juice
2 tablespoons taco seasoning mix	½ cup (4 fl oz) stock or wine
4-6 thin pork steaks from the shoulder	chopped spring onions (scallions)
60 g (2 oz) butter	
2 small onions, sliced	

Combine the flour with the taco seasoning and lightly coat the pork. Melt the butter in a pan and sauté the onions until just soft. Remove. Pan fry the steaks on both sides, then remove. Add a little extra butter and the remaining spiced flour and stir in the liquids to make a smooth sauce. Return the pork and onions and simmer, covered, for 20 minutes. Serve with spring onions.

Pork Parmigiana

Serves 4

500 g (1 lb) pork leg schnitzels
1 egg, beaten
½ cup (2 oz) dry breadcrumbs
4 tablespoons oil
1 cup Italian style tomato sauce
125 g (4 oz) mozzarella cheese, sliced
1 tablespoon grated Parmesan cheese

Conventional Method: If necessary flatten the pork until very thin. Dip in the beaten egg and coat with breadcrumbs. Fry in hot oil until golden brown on both sides. Drain and place in an ovenproof baking dish and pour over the Italian tomato sauce. Top with mozzarella and Parmesan cheese and bake in a preheated oven 200°C (400°F/Gas 6) for 20 minutes or until the top is golden.

Microwave Method: Prepare the pork and fry in the oil as above. Drain. Transfer to a microwave-safe casserole dish. Pour the sauce over the pork. Cover and cook on high for 5 minutes. Top with the cheeses and cook uncovered a further 2 minutes. The cheese may be browned under a hot grill (broiler) if preferred.

Pork with Blackbean Sauce

Serves 4

1 large carrot
1 large white radish
2 spring onions (scallions)
2 tablespoons oil
1 large onion, sliced
6 large pork leg schnitzels or steaks
¾ cup (6 fl oz) bottled blackbean sauce
⅓ cup (2 ½ fl oz) chicken stock
1 teaspoon each chilli and garlic sauces
2 packets 3-minute noodles

Peel the carrot and radish and trim the spring onions. Fill a bowl with ice cold water. Using the point of a small sharp knife score the vegetables lengthwise with deep long cuts. Use a vegetable peeler to make wafer-thin long slices to give fine shredded vegetables. Place in cold water. Finely slice the spring onions into julienne strips and mix with the vegetables to crisp.

Heat the oil over a medium heat and sauté the onion. Remove when soft, do not overcook. Flatten out the pork if necessary and cut into smaller 'scaloppine' shapes. Sauté in oil for 2 minutes on each side. Combine the blackbean sauce with the stock, chilli and garlic sauces and pour over the pork. Sauté a further 2 minutes, turning to coat evenly in mixture. Add the onion. Cook and drain the noodles and drain the crisp salad shreds. Serve with the pork.

Spicy Plum Pork

Serves 4

6 pork medallions
1 tablespoon teriyaki sauce
2 tablespoons plum sauce or jam
2 tablespoons tomato sauce
2 teaspoons Worcestershire sauce
finely chopped spring onions (scallions) or herbs

Conventional Method: Slash the edges of the pork medallions with a sharp knife, then secure into a round shape with toothpicks. Brush over the teriyaki sauce and cook under a medium hot griller (broiler) for 5 minutes each side. Combine the other sauces and spread over each side of the pork during the last minute of grilling. Serve topped with spring onions.

Microwave Method: Prepare the pork medallions as above. Preheat a browning dish. Brush over a little oil or butter and add the medallions brushed with the sauce. Spoon on some topping and cook on high for 5 minutes. Turn the pork. Spread with more topping and cook a further 4 minutes. Stand 1 minute before serving.

Pork Schnitzel Kiev

Serves 4

500 g (1 lb) thin pork leg steaks
60 g (2 oz) smoked or tasty cheese
1 small zucchini (courgette)
1 teaspoon prepared mild mustard
2 tablespoons seasoned flour
1 egg, beaten
¾ cup (3 oz) fine dry breadcrumbs
1 teaspoon each sesame seeds and dried herbs
3 rashers bacon
oil for shallow frying

Flatten the pork schnitzels until thin. Cut the cheese and zucchini into strips. Lightly spread the pork with the mustard and divide the cheese and vegetables on top. Roll firmly, then coat in the seasoned flour. Dip in the egg, then roll in the breadcrumbs mixed with the sesame seeds and herbs. Remove the rind from the bacon and cut the rashers into strips. Fold round the centre of each pork roll and secure with toothpicks. Chill for 30 minutes. Shallow fry in medium hot oil for about 7 minutes without over-browning. Drain and serve. Alternatively these may be baked in a moderately hot oven, 180°C (350°F/Gas 4), for 45 minutes.

Note: The strips of bacon rind can also be used to tie the pork rolls.

Pork

Pork Medallions in Tomato Sauce

Serves 4 - 6

- 6 x 150 g (5 oz) pork medallions from the loin
- 2 tablespoons seasoned flour
- 4 tablespoons oil
- 1 onion, sliced
- 1 red pepper (capsicum), sliced
- 1 x 440 g (14 oz) can peeled tomatoes
- 1 teaspoon each salt and sugar
- 1 teaspoon chilli sauce
- ⅓ cup (2 oz) sliced stuffed olives

Cut the edge of the pork to prevent curling. Secure with small skewers into a round shape. Lightly coat with seasoned flour, then sauté in half the oil for about 5 minutes on each side or until golden. Using a separate pan, fry the onion and red pepper in the oil until soft without browning. Add the tomatoes and simmer together for 10 minutes to reduce the excess liquid. Season with salt, sugar, chilli sauce and olives.

Italian Style Schnitzels

Serves 4 - 6

- 6-8 pork schnitzels from the leg
- ⅓ cup (1 ½ oz) flour
- ½ teaspoon each dried oregano, marjoram and basil
- ¼ teaspoon garlic salt
- 1 egg, beaten with a little water
- 1 cup (4 oz) fine dry breadcrumbs
- ⅓ cup (1 ½ oz) grated Parmesan cheese
- oil for frying
- 100 g (3 ½ oz) ham slices, chopped
- 60 g (2 oz) mozzarella cheese slices

Flatten the pork thinly if desired. Mix the flour with the herbs and garlic salt and coat the pork. Dip in the beaten egg, then coat in a mixture of breadcrumbs and Parmesan cheese. Chill for at least 30 minutes. Shallow fry in hot oil for about 3 minutes, turning to cook evenly. Drain and place on a griller (broiler). Top with ham and mozzarella cheese and heat until just bubbling.

Italian Style Schnitzels

Oven Fried Pork Schnitzel

Pork and Mushroom Rolls

Serves 4

8 small pork schnitzels
250 g (8 oz) pork mince (ground pork)
⅓ cup chopped cooked ham
1 ½ tablespoons finely chopped spring onions (scallions)
½ teaspoon each chilli and garlic sauce
salt and pepper
2 small eggs, beaten
2 cups (8 oz) fine dry breadcrumbs
4 tablespoons melted butter or oil
1 garlic clove, crushed

Trim the pork schnitzels into round shapes. Finely chop any off cuts and add to the mince. Combine the pork mince, ham, spring onions, chilli and garlic sauces, salt and pepper. Mould the mixture in the centre of each pork schnitzel. Brush the beaten egg completely over the schnitzel and topping, then toss in the breadcrumbs. Chill for 30 minutes.

Heat the butter and garlic in an oven tray. Add the pork schnitzels and spoon a little butter on top. Bake in a moderately hot oven, 180°C (350°F/Gas 4), for 30 minutes.

Pork and Mushroom Rolls

Serves 4 - 5

8 pork schnitzels from the leg
salt and pepper
60 g (2 oz) butter
100 g (3 ½ oz) mushrooms
⅓ cup chopped spring onions (scallions)
½ cup cooked rice
¼ cup chopped water chestnuts
1 tablespoon lard
¾ cup (6 fl oz) chicken stock
2 tablespoons cream
1 tablespoon chopped fresh parsley

Flatten the pork schnitzels if necessary and season with salt and pepper. Melt half the butter and sauté the sliced mushrooms with the spring onions until soft. Season and mix with the rice and water chestnuts. Spread over the pork, roll up and secure with string. Brown in a pan with the lard and remaining butter, turning to cook evenly. Add the stock, then cover and simmer for 30 minutes. Remove the lid, add the cream and simmer a further 3 minutes. Add the parsley.

Pork

Hot and Spicy Pork Strips
Serves 4

- 500 g (1 lb) pork schnitzels from the leg
- 3 tablespoons cornflour (cornstarch)
- ⅛ teaspoon chilli powder
- ¼ teaspoon five spice powder
- ½ teaspoon salt
- 2 tablespoons oil
- 1 garlic clove, crushed
- ½ cup diced red pepper (capsicum)
- ½ cup chopped spring onions (scallions)
- 1 ¾ cups (14 fl oz) stock
- 2 teaspoons soy sauce
- 1 tablespoon vinegar

Cut the pork into strips and coat in a mixture of 2 ½ tablespoons cornflour and the spices. Fry in hot oil until crisp, about 5 minutes. Remove and keep warm. Sauté the garlic, red pepper and spring onions for 1 minute. Remove. Place the remaining ingredients including the cornflour in a saucepan and stir until thickened. Simmer for 2 minutes, then add the pork and vegetables and reheat.

'Stir-Fried' Pork
Serves 2

- 3 teaspoons oil
- ½ cup chopped onion
- 2 small garlic cloves, minced
- 1 cup diagonally sliced celery
- ½ cup snow peas (mange-tout)
- 1 cup bean sprouts
- ½ cup sliced champignons
- ¼ cup bamboo shoots
- 250 g (½ lb) cooked pork, thinly sliced
- 1 tablespoon light soy sauce
- 1 chicken stock cube mixed with ¼ cup (2 fl oz) water

Heat the oil in a wok or pan. Add the onion, garlic and celery. Stir fry for 2 minutes. Add the next 5 ingredients, stir and toss until well combined and heated through. Add the soy sauce and chicken stock, and toss until well mixed.

Pork Ragout
Serves 4

- 1 kg (2 lb) pork forequarter steaks
- 1 bouquet garni
- 1 cup (8 fl oz) tomato purée
- 1 tablespoon oil
- 1 large onion, sliced
- 1 cup sliced mushrooms
- sour cream and chopped chives

Place the pork steaks in a crockpot. Add the bouquet garni with the purée and add to the pot. Heat the oil and sauté the onion and mushrooms and stir into the pork. Cover and cook on high for at least 5 hours, then add the cream and chopped chives.

Casanova Pork Rolls
Serves 4 - 6

- 6 large pork leg steaks
- 2 tablespoons seasoned flour
- 2 tablespoons oil
- 60 g (2 oz) butter
- 1 cup (8 fl oz) wine or stock
- chopped fresh herbs

Omelette Filling
- 3 eggs, beaten
- 1 teaspoon chopped fresh herbs
- 15 g (½ oz) butter
- ¾ cup finely chopped ham
- ¼ cup chopped spring onions (scallions)
- ¼ cup chopped red pepper (capsicum)
- salt and pepper

Place the steaks on a board. Top each with a piece of omelette, then roll from the wide end and secure with a toothpick. Dust the pork rolls in the seasoned flour and chill for 10 minutes. Sauté in the pan with the oil and butter until sealed and golden. Add the wine, then cover and cook for 20 minutes. Remove the rolls and thicken the sauce if desired. Strain pan juices over the rolls and serve with chopped herbs on top.

Filling: Combine the eggs in a bowl with the herbs. Melt the butter and sauté the ham, spring onions and red pepper until soft. Add to the eggs and season with salt and pepper. Heat a frying pan with a little extra butter, add the egg mixture and make an omelette. Allow to cook, then invert onto a plate and cut into 6 triangles.

Crunchy Pork Butterflies with Mushroom Sauce
Serves 4   [M]

- 1 packet Chasseur (mushroom) Sauce Mix
- ½ cup (2 oz) dry breadcrumbs
- 4 x 125 g (4 oz) midloin butterfly steaks
- 1 egg, beaten
- 4 tablespoons oil
- ½ cup (4 fl oz) water
- 125 g (4 oz) mushrooms, sliced
- 2 tablespoons white wine

Conventional Method: Combine ½ packet of the Chasseur Sauce Mix with the breadcrumbs. Dip the steaks in beaten egg and coat with the breadcrumb mixture. Press on firmly. Heat half the oil and fry the steaks for 5 minutes on each side until golden and tender. Blend the remaining sauce mix with the water and cook as directed on the packet. Sauté the mushrooms in the remaining hot oil and add to the sauce mix with the wine. Pour the sauce over the steaks.

Microwave Method: Prepare the butterfly steaks and cook in a frying pan as above. Blend the remaining sauce and mix in a basin with the water. Cook in a microwave on medium high for 3 minutes. Stand for 5 minutes, add the sautéed mushrooms and wine and return to the microwave for 2 minutes.

Fruity Pork Parcels

Serves 6 - 9 [M]

- 8 pork leg steaks
- 2/3 cup (7 oz) fruit chutney
- 1/3 cup (1 1/2 oz) dry breadcrumbs
- 1 spring onion (scallion), finely chopped
- 1 mango, peach or banana, peeled
- 1 tablespoon oil
- 30 g (1 oz) butter
- 1 1/2 cups (12 fl oz) chicken stock
- 1 tablespoon tomato paste
- 3 teaspoons soy sauce
- 1 tablespoon cornflour (cornstarch)

Conventional Method: Flatten the pork until very thin. Mix together the chutney, crumbs and spring onion and spread over the pork. Place a thick slice of peeled fruit at one end and roll firmly. Tie with cotton like a parcel. Heat the oil and butter in a deep pan and brown the pork parcels over a medium heat for 7 minutes, turning often. Blend remaining ingredients, then pour into the pan and stir until thickened. Cover and simmer very slowly for 35 minutes until the pork is tender, turning often. Remove the cotton and serve.

Microwave Method: Prepare the pork parcels as above and sauté until golden. Remove to a microwave dish. Place the stock, paste, sauce and cornflour in a deep bowl and cook on high for 3 minutes. Stir during cooking. Pour the sauce over the pork, cover and microwave on medium for about 15 minutes.

Grand Pork Chops

Serves 4 - 6

- 6 pork medallions from the loin
- salt and freshly ground pepper
- 1 tablespoon Grand Marnier liqueur
- 30 g (1 oz) butter
- 1/3 cup (1 1/2 oz) flaked almonds
- 2 teaspoons soft brown sugar
- 3 teaspoons flour
- grated rind of 1 orange
- 3/4 cup (6 fl oz) orange juice

Season the pork with the salt and pepper, then spoon over half the liqueur and stand for 30 minutes. Melt half the butter and brown the almonds until golden. Remove. Add the remaining butter to the pan and slowly brown the chops for about 7 minutes on each side, turning to cook evenly. Remove and keep warm. Add the sugar to the pan drippings and stir to melt. Mix in the flour and cook a further 3 minutes. Add the rind and juice and stir until the sauce boils and thickens. Add the remaining liqueur and return the pork to heat and coat with saucy glaze. Garnish with the almonds.

Pork and Ham Rolls

Serves 4

- 4-6 pork leg schnitzels or steaks
- 1 1/2 teaspoons French mustard
- 4-6 slices leg ham
- 4-6 drained asparagus spears
- 1 tablespoon oil
- 30 g (1 oz) butter
- 1 garlic clove, crushed
- 2 tablespoons cream
- 2 teaspoons chopped chives

Flatten the pork until very thin. Lightly spread with mustard and top with a slice of ham and an asparagus spear. Roll firmly and secure with a toothpick. Heat the oil, add the butter and garlic and sauté the pork rolls over a medium heat for 10 minutes, turning often. Add the cream and chives and stir in all the pan residue to form a glaze to pour over the pork rolls.

Pork Niçoise

Serves 4 [M]

- 4-6 midloin butterfly steaks
- black olives and fresh herbs

Marinade
- 1/3 cup (2 1/2 fl oz) white wine or stock
- 1 teaspoon grated lemon rind
- 1/4 teaspoon seasoned pepper
- 1 garlic clove, crushed

Sauce
- 15 g (1/2 oz) butter
- 1 large onion, sliced
- 3/4 cup sliced red pepper (capsicum)
- 2 teaspoons light gravy powder mix
- 1 cup (8 fl oz) white wine or stock
- 2 large tomatoes, peeled and diced
- 1/2 teaspoon dried basil or thyme

Conventional Method: Slash or cut the edges of the steaks to prevent curling during cooking. Cook under a medium hot griller (broiler) for 5 minutes each side, depending on thickness. Brush with marinade to keep moist. Serve the pork chops with the sauce and garnish with olives and herbs.

Marinade: Place marinade ingredients in a shallow dish. Add the pork and turn to coat both sides then stand at least 30 minutes.

Sauce: Melt the butter and lightly fry the onion and red pepper without browning. Remove, then blend in the gravy powder and wine and stir. Simmer the mixture. Add the tomatoes, onion, red pepper and herbs and simmer for 7 minutes.

Microwave Method: First prepare the sauce in a basin in a microwave oven. Thicken and reheat after the pork chops are cooked on a browning tray.

Pork

Pork Steaks with Dates

Serves 4 [M]

2/3 cup (3 oz) chopped pitted dates	4 pork butterfly steaks
1 tablespoon chopped glacé ginger	salt and pepper
	15 g (½ oz) butter
2 teaspoons honey	2 tablespoons cream
	½ teaspoon cinnamon

Conventional Method: Mix the dates, ginger and honey together and spread on each butterfly steak. Fold over and secure with a toothpick. Season the pork with salt and pepper. Melt the butter and pan fry the steaks for about 5 minutes each side over a medium heat. Remove when cooked and keep warm. Add the cream and cinnamon to the pan residue and stir until simmering. Spoon over each steak.

Microwave Method: Prepare the steaks as above. Preheat the browning plate for 7 minutes. Brush with butter, add the pork steaks and cook on high for 4 minutes each side. Pour any pan juices into a separate little dish with the cream and cinnamon and heat on low for 1 minute. Spoon over the pork.

Deep Pork Pie

Pork in Peanut Sauce

Serves 4

2 teaspoons soy sauce	1 small garlic clove, crushed
1 teaspoon finely chopped fresh ginger	4 x 180 g (6 oz) pork loin steaks
Peanut Sauce	
2 tablespoons crunchy peanut butter	¼ teaspoon Sambal Oelek or chilli paste
¼ cup finely chopped onion	2 teaspoons lemon juice
	½ cup (4 fl oz) water

Combine the soy sauce, ginger and garlic. Spread evenly over each pork steak. Set aside for 30 minutes. Place the pork steaks on a rack and grill (broil) under medium heat for 10 to 12 minutes until cooked. Keep warm. Serve with Peanut Sauce.

Peanut Sauce: Place all the ingredients in a small saucepan and simmer gently until thickened.

Note: Sauce may be cooked in a microwave on high for 4 minutes, stirring to combine after 2 minutes.

Deep Pork Pie

Serves 4

750 g (1 ½ lb) pork shoulder steaks	2 small apples, cored and thickly sliced
3 tablespoons seasoned flour	1 teaspoon chopped lemon thyme
3 tablespoons oil	3 pickled walnuts or prunes
2 rashers bacon, chopped	250 g (8 oz) shortcrust pastry
2 onions, sliced	
1 cup (8 fl oz) apple juice	beaten egg or cream
salt and pepper	

Cut the pork steaks into large cubes and toss in the seasoned flour. Sauté in 3 batches in the oil until lightly browned. Place in a deep casserole dish. Lightly fry the bacon and onions and spoon into the casserole. Add the excess flour to the pan drippings and blend in the apple juice. Stir until thickened, adjust the seasonings and strain into the casserole. Add the sliced apples, thyme, halved walnuts or chopped pitted prunes.

Cut the pastry into wide strips and cover the mixture in a basket weave pattern. Glaze with egg or cream and bake in a moderately hot oven, 180°C (350°F/Gas 4), for 15 minutes. Lower the heat and cook a further 1 hour.

Pork Steaks with Dates

175

Pork

Spinach-Stuffed Pork

Serves 4

4 butterfly pork steaks from the mid loin
salt and pepper
15 g (½ oz) butter
1 small onion, chopped
2 spinach leaves, shredded
2 tablespoons cottage cheese
¼ teaspoon nutmeg
2 tablespoons lemon juice
1 tablespoon oil

Season the pork with the salt and pepper. Melt the butter and fry the onion until soft. Add the spinach and stir until tender without browning. Strain this mixture, pressing out any excess moisture with the back of a spoon. Chop finely. Combine the spinach with the cheese, nutmeg and a dash of the lemon juice. Divide over the pork. Fold over the steaks and secure with toothpicks. Pan fry in the oil for 10 minutes on each side according to thickness. Remove the pork, deglaze the pan with lemon juice, stir and pour over the steaks.

Pork au Blanc

Serves 4

1 ½ tablespoons flour
1 ½ tablespoons soft brown sugar
1 teaspoon cocoa
¼ teaspoon ground nutmeg
4 thick pork steaks from the shoulder
15 g (½ oz) butter
1 garlic clove, crushed
¾ cup (6 fl oz) evaporated milk
1 cup chopped spring onions (scallions)
1 tablespoon chopped fresh dill, thyme or parsley
¼ cup (2 fl oz) stock or wine

Combine the flour, sugar, cocoa and nutmeg and dust the pork. Heat the butter and sauté the pork over a low heat to seal, about 1 minute on each side. Add the garlic and milk and simmer, uncovered, for 20 minutes. Turn the pork steaks, add the spring onions and dill and simmer for a further 7 minutes. Remove the pork to a serving dish and keep warm. Add the stock to the residue in the pan. Pour over the steaks.

Oven-Fried Pork Steaks

Serves 4

15 g (½ oz) butter
2 garlic cloves, crushed
pinch each of dried basil, oregano and marjoram
4 pork midloin butterfly steaks

Topping
1 medium-sized eggplant (aubergine)
salt
2 small tomatoes, sliced
8 small slices mozarella cheese

Place the butter and seasonings in an ovenproof dish and melt in a moderate oven at 180°C (350°F/Gas 4) for a few minutes. Coat the pork steaks in this butter and bake in a moderately hot oven, 190°C (375°F/Gas 5), for 15 minutes on each side. Wipe and slice the eggplant. Sprinkle with salt and stand for 20 minutes. Turn in the salt to sweat the eggplant, then drain and dry. Drain the pork butter drippings into a saucepan. Add the eggplant and simmer for 5 minutes. Arrange alternate slices of eggplant, tomatoes and cheese on top of the pork and bake a further 7 minutes.

Note: Oven-fried pork steaks can be topped with any mixture of sliced vegetables and cheese of your choice.

Old English Casserole

Serves 4

4-6 pork forequarter steaks or chops
1 ½ tablespoons seasoned flour
salt and pepper
15 g (1 oz) butter
2 onions, sliced
2 large potatoes, peeled and sliced
½ cup (4 fl oz) chicken stock
½ teaspoon each salt and dried thyme
2 rashers bacon, chopped
2 tablespoons grated cheese
½ teaspoon ground paprika

Season the pork with the flour, salt and pepper. Lightly fry in the butter, then place in a casserole. Fry the onions in the pan drippings until soft and spoon over the pork. Arrange the potatoes down and around the side of the casserole and some on top. Combine the chicken stock with the salt and thyme and place in the casserole. Cover and bake at 160°C (325°F/Gas 3) for 1 hour. Remove the lid and top with the bacon, cheese and paprika. Bake uncovered a further 10 minutes.

Butterfly Pork Steaks Supreme

Serves 4 - 6

4-6 butterfly pork steaks	2 small apples
salt and pepper	6-8 prunes
1 teaspoon oil	

Sauce

15 g (½ oz) butter	½ cup (4 fl oz) wine or water
1 onion, finely chopped	
2 tablespoons light gravy powder	2 teaspoons mixed herb mustard
1 cup (8 fl oz) chicken stock	2 tablespoons cream

Season the pork with salt and pepper. Grease a heavy pan with the oil. Add the pork to the pan and cook over a medium heat for 7 minutes on each side, depending on thickness. Slice the apples and fry on both sides. Stir in the prunes. Serve with the pork.

Sauce: Sauté the onion in the butter until soft. Add the gravy powder and blend in the stock. Add the wine and mustard. Stir the sauce until the mixture boils and thickens. Cook for 3 minutes, then add the cream.

Butterfly Steak Royale

Serves 4

4 pork midloin butterfly steaks	1 cup (8 fl oz) water or part cherry syrup
15 g (½ oz) garlic butter (page 277)	1 cup drained pitted dark cherries
1 packet red wine sauce	4 slices firm pâté

Slit the edges of the pork steaks to prevent curling and cook under a medium hot griller (broiler) for 7 minutes on each side. Spread with a little garlic butter while cooking. Prepare the packet sauce with the water as directed and stir until thickened. Add the cherries. Place a slice of pâté on top of each steak during the final cooking, then serve immediately with the sauce.

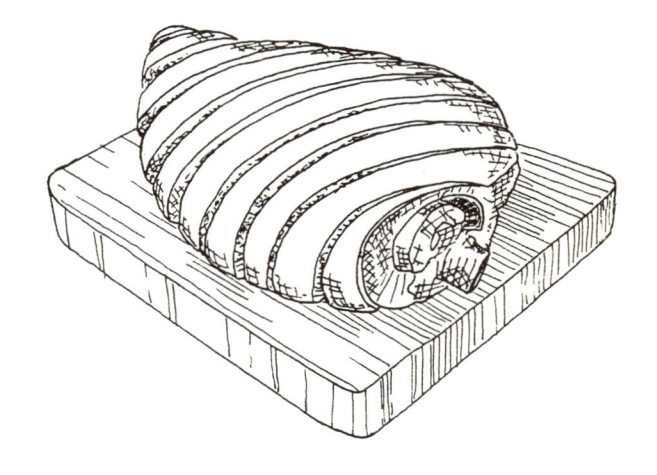

Pork Supreme Casserole

Serves 3 - 4

1 kg (2 lb) pork forequarter chops	1 packet salt-reduced chicken soup
2 tablespoons oil	1 cup (8 fl oz) water
2 onions, sliced	1 x 310 g (10 oz) can corn kernels
1 cup sliced celery	
100 g (3 ½ oz) smoked bacon bones	

Cut the chops into large pieces and if necessary discard excess fat. Heat the oil and lightly brown the pork on both sides with the sliced onions. Place in a casserole with the celery and bacon bones. Blend the soup mix with the water and add to the pan drippings with the undrained corn. Stir until thickened and pour over the pork. Cover and bake at 180°C (350°F/Gas 4) for 1 hour.

Pork

Stuffed Pork with Herbs

Serves 4

- 4 butterfly pork steaks from the mid loin
- salt and pepper
- ½ cup (1 oz) soft white breadcrumbs
- ½ cup finely choppped spring onions (scallions)
- 1 tablespoon finely chopped fresh parsley
- ½ teaspoon dried marjoram
- ½ teaspoon dried tarragon
- 2 tablespoons melted butter
- ½ cup (4 fl oz) chicken stock
- ½ cup (4 fl oz) tomato purée
- ¼ teaspoon chopped fresh basil

Season the pork with salt and pepper. Combine the breadcrumbs with the spring onions and herbs. Mix with the melted butter and divide between the pork steaks. Fold and secure with toothpicks, then place on a greased ovenproof tray. Mix the stock, tomato purée and basil with salt and pepper to taste and spoon over the pork. Bake in the centre of a moderately hot oven, 180°C (350°F/Gas 4), for 30 minutes, basting with juices during cooking.

Apricot Pork Roast

Serves 5 - 6

- 1 x 1 kg (2 lb) piece pork, bone and rind removed
- 3 teaspoons seasoned flour
- 30 g (1 oz) butter
- 12 dried apricots or pitted prunes
- 2 teaspoons cornflour (cornstarch)
- ¼ cup (2 fl oz) pan juices or stock
- ⅔ cup (5 fl oz) apricot nectar

Coat the pork in seasoned flour. Melt the butter and brown the pork on all sides. Remove to a rack over a baking tray containing water to make a stock while cooking. Make about 6 deep incisions down into the pork and press an apricot or piece of prune well down into the meat. Bake at 190°C (375°F/Gas 5) for 1 ¼ hours. Cover and stand in a warm place for 10 minutes prior to carving.

Chop the remaining apricots, place in a small saucepan with the cornflour and blend in the pan juices and nectar. Stir until boiling and thickened. Serve with the pork.

Rosy Pork Roast

Serves 8 - 10

- 2.5 kg (5 lb) pork roast from the leg
- 1 teaspoon tandoori spice mixture
- ½ teaspoon salt
- 3 rashers bacon, cut into strips
- 8 dried apricots
- 4 pickled walnuts or prunes
- 1 ½ tablespoons oil
- 3 garlic cloves, crushed
- 2 tablespoons chopped chives
- 2 tablespoons chopped fresh parsley
- 1 teaspoon paprika

Score the pork rind in a diamond pattern. Remove the bone if necessary to make a pocket in the meat and season with the spice and salt. Add the strips of bacon with the apricots and whole pickled walnuts. Secure the filling with skewers or sew with string. Place the pork on a rack in a roasting pan. Combine the remaining ingredients and brush or spoon into the scored pork rind. Bake at 180°C (350°F/Gas 4) for 1 ½ hours. Increase the heat to 220°C (425°F/Gas 7) during the final 10 minutes of cooking to puff the crackling. Stand the pork in a warm place for 15 minutes prior to carving.

Roast Pork with Mango

Serves 6 - 8

- 1.5 kg (3 lb) pork roast from the shoulder
- grated rind of 1 orange
- 1 teaspoon curry powder
- 1 teaspoon honey
- 1 garlic clove, crushed
- ½ teaspoon salt
- 1 x 410 g (13 oz) can mango pieces in nectar
- ½ cup (4 fl oz) orange juice
- 1 tablespoon cornflour (cornstarch)
- 2 teaspoons white rum or vodka

Score the pork rind finely. Blend the orange rind, curry powder, honey, garlic and salt and press into the slits between the rind. Place pork on a rack in a baking dish and pour over the drained mango nectar. Bake in the centre of a moderately hot oven, 190°C (375°F/Gas 5), for 30 minutes. Reduce the heat and continue to roast in a barely moderate oven, 160°C (325°F/Gas 3), for a further 1 ¼ hours. Baste the meat during cooking. Drain off the pan drippings and quickly freeze to remove fat from the surface. Combine this stock with the orange juice blended with the cornflour and stir until the sauce boils and thickens. Add the mango pieces and flavour with rum or vodka. Serve with the pork.

Pork Wellington

Serves 6

1 kg (2 lb) pork shoulder roast
salt and pepper
1 tablespoon oil
15 g (½ oz) butter
2 cups chopped mushrooms
2 tablespoons chopped spring onions (scallions)
1 cup (2 oz) soft breadcrumbs
1 tablespoon chopped fresh dill or parsley
1 x 375 g (12 oz) packet puff pastry
beaten egg

Trim the roast into a neat shape. Season with a little salt and pepper. Brown evenly in the oil, turning often. Remove and cool. Add the butter to the pan and sauté the mushrooms with the spring onions. Mix in the breadcrumbs, dill, salt and pepper. Mound the mixture on top of the pork. Roll the pastry thinly into an oblong shape and wrap around the pork, sealing the pastry underneath. Place on a roasting rack on a baking tray. Glaze with beaten egg and decorate as desired. Bake at 220°C (425°F/Gas 7) for 15 minutes. Reduce the temperature to 180°C (350°F/Gas 4) for a further 1 hour. Stand for 10 minutes prior to carving.

Pork Pot Roast

Serves 8

2 tablespoons tomato paste
1 x 2 kg (4 lb) piece pork shoulder roast, boned
2 medium-sized carrots, sliced
1 onion, sliced
8 green beans, left whole
½ cup chopped fennel tops
salt and pepper
oil
1 cup (8 fl oz) chicken stock
1 cup (8 fl oz) white wine
2 medium-sized fennel bulbs, cut into sections
1 tablespoon light gravy powder blended with a little water

Spread tomato paste over the inside of the pork. Arrange the carrot, onion, beans and fennel tops on top and season with salt and pepper. Roll up into a neat shape and secure with skewers and string. Insert a meat thermometer. Heat an electric frypan or heavy saucepan with a little oil and brown the pork on the outside. Add the stock and wine, and season. Cook, covered, on medium heat for 15 minutes, then reduce the heat. Add the fennel bulbs, then cover and simmer slowly a further 1½ hours. The internal temperature should read 76°C (170°F). Remove the roast and thicken the pan residue with the blended gravy powder. Simmer for 3 minutes. Serve the gravy with the sliced pork and fennel.

Polish Pork Roast

Serves 6 - 8

1.5 kg (3 lb) pork forequarter roast, boned and scored
salt and pepper
1 tablespoon prepared mustard
250 g (8 oz) kransky sausage or salami
100 g (3 ½ oz) sliced sweet and sour gherkins

Season the pork with salt and pepper and spread with mustard. Remove the outside casing of the sausage and place on the pork with slices of gherkin, then roll up and tie with string and secure with skewers if necessary. Place the pork on a rack in an oven tray and insert a meat thermometer. Bake at 190°C (375°F/Gas 5) for 30 minutes. Reduce the heat to 160°C (325°F/Gas 3) and bake a further 1 ¼ hours or until the internal temperature is 76°C (170°F). Stand for 10 minutes prior to carving.

Barbecued Roast Pork

Serves 8 - 10

1.5 kg (3 lb) pork forequarter roast, boned
oil
salt
3 tablespoons Chinese barbecue sauce (hoi sin)

Remove the rind and score with a sharp knife. Rub in oil and sprinkle over salt ready to bake in a hot oven or under a griller (broiler) until puffed and crisp for serving as a separate side dish. Spread the barbecue sauce over the pork and stand for 30 minutes. Place on a roasting rack over a pan containing some water to prevent burning and insert a meat thermometer. Bake at 220°C (425°F/Gas 7) for 1½ hours or until the internal temperature reaches 76°C (170°F). Slice hot or cold and serve with rice, the crackling and stir fried vegetables.

Fast Pork Burgers

Serves 3 - 4

500 g (1 lb) pork mince (ground pork)
1 onion, finely chopped
1 small carrot, grated
½ cup chopped mushrooms
½ teaspoon mixed dried herbs
salt and pepper
oil
hot meat gravy

Combine all ingredients except the oil and gravy. Place in a food processor and chop finely, adding the pork mince last to mix evenly. Shape with lightly floured hands into 8 flat burgers. Shallow fry in medium hot oil for 5 minutes on each side. Serve hot with gravy.

Pork

Roast Pork Calvados
Serves 6 - 8

1 x 1.5 kg (3 lb) piece pork foreloin steak, boned
1 garlic clove, cut into slivers
2 tablespoons Calvados liqueur
1 teaspoon finely chopped fresh sage or thyme
salt and pepper
2 cups diced apple
60 g (2 oz) butter

Sauce
1 tablespoon sugar
1 tablespoon lemon juice or vinegar
½ cup (4 fl oz) chicken stock
2 tablespoons Calvados liqueur
1 cup (8 fl oz) cream
1 ½ teaspoons tomato paste
15 g (½ oz) soft butter
1 tablespoon flour
1 tablespoon preserved pink peppercorns
salt and pepper

Trim the pork and insert a few slices of garlic. Brush over the Calvados and sprinkle on the herbs. Season with salt, pepper and insert a meat thermometer. Place on a rack on a baking tray and roast for 1 ¼ hours at 180°C (350°F/Gas 4). Internal temperature should be 76°C (170°F). Stand for 7 minutes prior to carving. In a frying pan, sauté the diced apple in the butter in a frying pan then transfer to the oven and bake 15 minutes. Serve with the sliced pork and peppercorn sauce.

Sauce: Heat a heavy frying pan. Sprinkle in the sugar and allow to caramelise. Add the juice and allow to evaporate over gentle heat. Combine the stock with the Calvados, cream and tomato paste and add to the pan. Stir and allow to simmer for 15 minutes until half the volume. Cream the butter and flour together, gradually mix into the sauce and cook for a further 7 minutes. Add the roasting pan juices, then strain the sauce into a small saucepan. Add the peppercorns and adjust seasonings with salt and pepper.

Pork Tacos
Serves 4

3 teaspoons oil
1 onion, finely chopped
500 g (1 lb) pork mince, (ground pork)
1 x 30 g (1 oz) packet taco seasoning mix
⅔ cup (5 fl oz) tomato purée or juice
8 taco shells
shredded lettuce
grated cheese
diced tomatoes

Heat the oil in a saucepan and fry the onion, without browning, until soft. Add the pork and stir until it changes colour. Blend in the seasoning mix with the purée and simmer together for 30 minutes, stirring often. Serve the mixture spooned into warm taco shells and topped with lettuce, cheese and tomato.

Yankee Noodle Pork Roast
Serves 6

1 x 1.5 kg (3 lb) pork forequarter roast, boned
oil and salt
1 packet 2-minute noodles, curry flavour
2 cups (16 fl oz) water
1 small banana, mashed
2 tablespoons spicy chutney
1 tablespoon fruit chutney, optional

Score the pork rind and rub in a little oil and salt into the skin before cooking. Cook the noodles in 2 cups (16 fl oz) water for 2 minutes, then drain well and mix in the spice sachet. Mash the banana with the chutney and spread into the boned pocket of the roast, then fill with cooled noodles and secure with skewers and string into a good shape. Place the pork on a rack over a baking dish of water and roast at 180°C (350°F/Gas 4) for 1¼ hours. Increase the temperature for 10 minutes to crisp the rind. Stand for 10 minutes before carving. Use the pan drippings to make a gravy, discarding any excess fat. Add a little fruit chutney if desired.

Note: Stuffing can also be made with cooked rice, stale breadcrumbs or minced meats. Flavour with your favourite chutney or chopped dried fruits

Pork and Bacon Loaf
Serves 5 - 6

¾ cup burghul
2 large onions, finely chopped
2 garlic cloves, crushed
1 tablespoon oil
750 g (1 ½ lb) pork mince (ground pork) from the shoulder
1 teaspoon salt
2 teaspoons chilli sauce
1 tablepoon light soy sauce
1 red pepper (capsicum), sliced
100 g (3 ½ oz) green beans, left whole
4 rashers bacon
1 ½ tablespoons sesame seeds

Soak the burghul in warm water for 30 minutes. Drain. Place the onions and garlic with the oil in a pan and stir over low heat to just soften. Place in a basin with the pork, salt, chilli sauce, soy sauce and drained burghul. Mix well to combine. Blanch the red pepper and green beans, then drain and cool under cold water. Remove the rind from the bacon. Press the pork mixture over a sheet of foil approximately 35 x 20 cm (14 x 8 inch). Arrange the bacon on top with alternate rows of red pepper and beans. Roll up as for a Swiss roll, remove foil, then roll the loaf in sesame seeds. Place the loaf on a greased tray and bake at 180°C (350°F/Gas 4) for 1¼ hours. Serve in slices.

Pork Balls and Bean Soup

Serves 6

The choice of dried beans will influence the colour of the soup; light coloured beans give a colourful appearance while dark or red beans give a rich hearty colour with only slight differences in flavour.

- ½ cup dried cannellini or red kidney beans
- 4 cups finely diced fresh mixed vegetables, including onions
- 6 cups (1.5 litres) stock or water
- 1 large tomato, peeled and diced
- 1 tablespoon chopped fresh herbs
- 100 g (3 ½ oz) smoked ham or rib bones
- 250 g (8 oz) pork mince (ground pork)
- 1 garlic clove, crushed
- 1 teaspoon chopped fresh herbs
- freshly ground black pepper
- 1 small egg

Soak the beans in water overnight, or in the refrigerator for at least 6 hours. Drain. Place the vegetables in a large soup saucepan with the stock, tomato and herbs. Add the drained beans and smoked ham bones. Simmer for 1 hour. Place the pork and remaining ingredients in a food processor and process until fine and smooth. Shape into 18-20 small balls, cover and chill. Check the bean soup for flavour and ensure the beans are tender. Add the pork balls and simmer slowly without boiling for 15 minutes. Remove the bones. Serve with hot crusty bread.

Note: Cooked canned beans may be substituted; use 2 x 300 g (9 ½ oz) cans, drained and rinsed.

Speedy Pork Pies

Serves 6

- 2 rashers bacon, chopped
- 500 g (1 lb) pork mince (ground pork)
- 1 apple, cored and diced
- 2 tablespoons sultanas
- 1 cup (8 fl oz) stock
- 2 tablespoons cornflour (cornstarch)
- ½ teaspoon caraway seeds
- pinch of salt, pepper, cumin
- 3 x 125 g (4 oz) ready-rolled puff pastry sheets
- beaten egg for glazing

Fry the bacon until almost crisp. Add the remaining ingredients except the pastry and stir until the pork filling thickens. Simmer for 5 minutes, then spread out on a tray to quickly cool. Cut each pastry sheet into 4 squares. Divide the pork filling over 6 pastry bases arranged on a lightly greased oven tray. Moisten the edges and cover with the remaining puff pastry squares. Press to seal the edges. Glaze the tops and make centre slits as vents then bake at 200°C (400°F/Gas 6) for 15 minutes. Lower the heat and bake a further 10 minutes.

Pork Pâté Loaf

Serves 10

- 500 g (1 lb) minced (ground) pork from the shoulder
- 60 g (2 oz) pâté de foi gras
- ¼ cup (2 fl oz) brandy
- ½ cup (4 fl oz) white wine
- ½ cup chopped spring onions (scallions)
- 2 garlic cloves, crushed
- 1 teaspoon salt
- ½ teaspoon white pepper
- 500 g (1 lb) shortcrust pastry (page 458)
- 4 whole pickled walnuts
- 6 chicken livers
- egg glaze

Combine the pork mince, foi gras, brandy, wine, spring onions, garlic, salt and pepper in a food processor and mix well. Roll out two thirds of the pastry to line a deep oval pâté or loaf tin and half fill with the pork mixture. Arrange the whole walnuts with the chicken livers down the centre, then cover with the remaining pork. Roll out the remaining pastry and cover. Glaze and crimp the edges, make a centre vent, glaze and decorate the top. Bake at 190°C (375°F/Gas 5) for 30 minutes. Reduce the heat and bake a further 1 hour. Cool until barely warm and if desired fill pie with 1 cup (8 fl oz) flavoured stock combined with 1 tablespoon gelatine. Chill and allow the flavours to develop for 2 days before slicing and serving.

Canadian Pork Pie

Serves 4 - 6

- 750 g (1 ½ lb) minced (ground) pork from the shoulder
- 1 rasher bacon, chopped
- 2 hard-boiled eggs, chopped
- 2 garlic cloves, crushed
- 1 large onion, finely chopped
- 1 carrot, grated
- 1 tablespoon tomato paste
- 1 teaspoon salt
- ½ teaspoon white pepper
- ½ teaspoon each sage and thyme
- 1 tablespoon chopped fresh parsley
- 350 g (11 oz) prepared puff pastry
- beaten egg for glazing

Thoroughly combine the mince with the bacon, eggs and all ingredients except the pastry and beaten egg. Divide the pastry into two portions. Roll the base into a 20 cm (8 inch) circle and mould the pork filling over the base in a dome shape, within 1 cm (½ inch) from the edge. Roll the second portion of pastry into a slightly larger circle, about 25 cm (10 inch), and place over the meat. Glaze the edges and crimp or press together, make a centre vent and glaze the top. Decorate with the edge of a sharp knife and make pastry leaves. Chill for 30 minutes before baking at 200°C (400°F/Gas 6) for 15 minutes, then reduce the heat and continue to bake at 180°C (350°F/Gas 4) for 50 to 60 minutes.

Pork

Pork Cabbage Rolls
Serves 6

24 cabbage leaves
500 g (1 lb) minced (ground) pork from the shoulder
1 potato, grated
2 onions, finely chopped
1 cup (2 oz) soft white breadcrumbs
1 tablespoon chopped fresh parsley
1 teaspoon salt
pepper
1 small egg, beaten
1 onion, sliced
15 g (½ oz) butter
1 x 440 g (14 oz) can peeled tomatoes
½ cup (4 fl oz) yoghurt, optional

Blanch the cabbage in boiling water, drain and refresh under cold water, drain again and pat dry. Combine the pork, potato, onions, breadcrumbs, parsley, salt, pepper and egg and mix well. Divide over two overlapping cabbage leaves to make 12 rolls and roll up firmly. Squeeze each roll to seal the edges, then arrange in a shallow greased casserole. Cover with foil and bake at 160°C (325°F/Gas 3) for 45 minutes. Sauté the onion in butter. Add the tomatoes and season with salt and pepper. Simmer to evaporate the excess juices. Drain off the juices from the cabbage rolls, cover with tomato mixture and top with yoghurt if desired. Reheat in the oven for a further 10 to 15 minutes.

Pork Sukiyaki
Serves 4

750 g (1 ½ lb) pork mince (ground pork)
2 teaspoons curry powder
1 tablespoon soy sauce
1 tablespoon vinegar
3 cups (24 fl oz) water
1 chicken stock cube
2 teaspoons sugar
¼ cup (2 oz) rice
60 g (2 oz) noodles
1 cup thinly sliced green beans
2 tablespoons sultanas
2 cups shredded cabbage

Place the pork mince in a saucepan, cover with water and bring to the boil. Cook for 15 minutes. Remove the pork from the liquid. Heat a pan, add the curry powder. Stir in the combined soy sauce, vinegar and water. Add the crumbled stock cube, sugar, reserved pork mince, rice and noodles. Mix well. Allow to cook steadily for 20 minutes, or until the rice and noodles are just cooked. Add the remaining ingredients and cook gently a further 10 minutes.

Pork and Tomato Sauce (for pasta)
Serves 2

100 g (3 ½ oz) bacon pieces
2 tablespoons oil
1 large onion, finely chopped
250 g (8 oz) fine pork mince (ground pork)
1 x 445 g (14 ½ oz) can Italian style tomato sauce
sprig of fresh rosemary and basil, optional
cooked pasta and grated cheese

Chop the bacon finely, and place in a saucepan with the oil and onion and fry for 1 minute. Add the pork and stir until sealed. Add the contents of the can and the herbs, then stir until just simmering. Cover and cook slowly for 20 minutes. Serve with cooked pasta and grated cheese.

Stuffed Pork Chops with Mushrooms
Serves 4

4 x 250 g (8 oz) thick pork loin chops
30 g (1 oz) butter
1 cup (2 oz) soft stale breadcrumbs
½ cup finely chopped mushrooms
¼ cup finely chopped spring onions (scallions)
1 tablespoon cream
1 teaspoon chopped fresh mint
salt and pepper
3 tablespoons tomato sauce

Cut a deep pocket into the side of each chop. Melt half the butter and fry the breadcrumbs until toasted, then remove. Melt the remaining butter and fry the mushrooms and spring onions over a brisk heat to evaporate the moisture. Spoon into a dish. Bind with a little cream and season with mint, salt and pepper. When cool, fill the chops and place in an ovenware dish. Spread with the tomato sauce and season. Bake at 200°C (400°F/Gas 6) for 30 minutes or according to thickness.

Pork Rockets

Serves 2 - 4

750 g (1 ½ lb) pork mince (ground pork)
2 rashers bacon, chopped
1 cup (2 oz) soft stale breadcrumbs
½ teaspoon salt and pepper
1 teaspoon chopped fresh herbs
1 large onion, finely chopped
2 garlic cloves, crushed
½ cup finely chopped red pepper (capsicum)
8 x 1 cm (½ inch) pieces cabanossi
redcurrant jelly, warmed

Place the pork mince in a basin with the other ingredients, except the cabanossi and jelly, and mix well. Place a piece of cabanossi on the end of small satay sticks then mould the mince around into a rocket shape. Place on an oven tray and bake at 180°C (350°F/Gas 4) for 50 minutes. Glaze with warm redcurrant jelly.

Stuffed Pork Chops

Serves 4

4 thick pork chops from the loin
2 teaspoons grated orange rind
4 tablespoons orange juice
1 garlic clove, crushed
1 teaspoon teriyaki sauce

Stuffing
1 medium-sized banana
1 tablespoon crunchy peanut butter
2 tablespoons chopped dates
½ teaspoon mild chilli sauce

Make a pocket in the side of each chop. Place in a shallow dish with half the rind, the juice, garlic and sauce, and marinate for at least 30 minutes. Turn the meat often. Combine the stuffing ingredients and fill each chop, then secure with a skewer. Cook under a medium hot griller (broiler) for 7 minutes on each side, according to thickness. Brush with marinade while cooking. Garnish with the remaining rind.

Portuguese Pork

Serves 4   [M]

1 kg (2 lb) pork forequarter chops
1 tablespoon oil
½ cup (4 fl oz) dry white wine
½ teaspoon ground cumin
1 small garlic clove, crushed
pinch of salt
pepper to taste
1 teaspoon coriander
thin lemon slices to garnish

Conventional Method: Cut the forequarter chops into bite-sized cubes. Cut off the rind if necessary. Heat the oil in a large pan and brown the pork quickly on all sides. Drain the excess liquid, add the wine, cumin, garlic, salt and pepper. Cover and cook gently for 40 minutes or until the pork is tender. Stir in the coriander, adjust the seasoning and top with lemon slices.

Microwave Method: Prepare the pork as above and brown in a frypan. Transfer the meat to a glass casserole, add the wine, cumin, garlic, salt and pepper. Cover and cook in a microwave on medium for 20 minutes, stirring once. Adjust the seasoning, add the coriander and lemon slices and reheat for 1 minute. Stand for 5 minutes before serving.

Marinated Pork Chops

Serves 6

6 lean pork chops or steaks

Marinade
2 tablespoons lemon juice
1 teaspoon mixed French mustard with herbs
1 teaspoon each chopped fresh lemon thyme and parsley
1 teaspoon sesame or salad oil
1 garlic clove, crushed

Slash the edges of the chops. Place the marinade ingredients in a shallow dish and coat each side of the pork. Stand covered for 1 hour or in the refrigerator overnight. Cook under a medium hot griller (broiler) or barbecue for about 5 minutes on each side. Brush with the marinade during cooking. Serve with savoury pasta and steamed, mixed green vegetables.

Variation:
Apricot Marinade
½ cup (4 fl oz) apricot or mango nectar
1 teaspooon ground cinnamon
1 tablespoon finely chopped onion
1 teaspoon each chilli and garlic sauces

Pork

Smoked Pork and Cucumber Sauce

Serves 6

15 g (½ oz) butter
4 slices smoked pork loin chops
1 onion, sliced

Sauce
1 small cucumber
1 cup (8 fl oz) chicken stock
30 g (1 oz) butter
1 ½ tablespoons flour
1 tablespoon dry vermouth
2 tablespoons cream
2 teaspoons chopped fresh dill or chives

Heat a heavy frying pan. Add the butter and sauté the smoked pork on both sides. Add the onion and cover the pan. Simmer for 5 minutes. Serve the smoked pork topped with onion rings and cucumber sauce.

Sauce: Peel the cucumber, cut off the ends and remove the centre seeds with a spoon. Cut into rounds, place in a saucepan with the chicken stock and cook for 5 minutes. Melt the butter, add the flour and cook over a low heat until golden. Strain and measure 1 cup (8 fl oz) stock from the cucumber, add the vermouth and stir until the sauce boils and thickens. Simmer for 7 minutes. Add the cream, chopped dill and drained cucumber and keep warm.

Pork Pantry Casserole

Serves 4 - 5

6 pork forequarter steaks or chops
2 tablespoons seasoned flour
345 g (11 oz) sweet potato
1 ½ tablespoons oil
1 large onion, sliced
2 carrots, cut into straws
2 tablespoons golden syrup
4 tablespoons tomato sauce
½ teaspoon ground nutmeg
½ teaspoon instant garlic granules
salt and pepper

Coat the pork steaks in seasoned flour. Peel the sweet potato and cut into thick slices. Lightly fry in the oil with the onion until just soft. Spoon into a casserole dish. Add a layer of carrot straws, then place the pork on top.

Heat the remaining ingredients in a saucepan and when boiling pour over the pork. Cover and bake at 180°C (350°F/Gas 4) for about 1 ¼ hours. Stand for 5 minutes before serving.

Note: This style of casserole can be made with plain potato or pumpkin, parsnips etc, seasoned to your own taste.

Herb Pork Casserole

Serves 4 - 6 [M]

6 pork forequarter chops or steaks
salt and pepper
2 tablespoons oil
2 garlic cloves, chopped
2 onions, sliced
1 x 425 g (13 ½ oz) can peeled tomatoes
sprig each of fresh rosemary, basil, and marjoram or ½ teaspoon each dried rosemary, basil and marjoram
3 teaspoons cornflour (cornstarch)
1 cup sliced mushrooms

Conventional Method: Trim the pork and cut into large serving size pieces. Season with a little salt and pepper. Heat the oil in a frying pan and seal the pork on both sides. Remove to a crockpot. Sauté the garlic and onions until soft, then add the tomatoes, reserving the juice, and the herbs. Break up with a spoon and stir until simmering. Pour over the pork and cook on high in the crockpot for 1 ½ hours (or in a barely moderate oven). Ladle out the excess juice and place in a saucepan with the reserved tomato juice and thicken with the cornflour. Return the sauce to the crockpot with the mushrooms. Cover and cook on low for 30 minutes.

Microwave Method: Sauté the pork, garlic and onions in the oil. Transfer to a covered microwave dish. Add the drained tomatoes, the herbs and mushrooms and cook on high for 20 minutes. Pour off the excess juices from the casserole into a basin. Add the reserved tomato juice and the cornflour and cook on high for 2 minutes. Pour over the pork and reheat a further 3 minutes.

Pork Chops with Pernod

Serves 4

4 thick superporker chops or medallions from the loin
salt and pepper
1 large apple, cored and sliced
60 g (2 oz) butter
16 stoned prunes
½ cup (4 fl oz) white wine
1 tablespoon Pernod
⅓ cup (2 ½ fl oz) cream

Season the pork with salt and pepper. Sauté the apple in part of the butter. Plump the prunes in the wine over low heat without overcooking. Fry the chops in the remaining butter over medium heat for 15 minutes until golden, then remove. Add the Pernod, ignite to flame and return to the heat with the liquid from the prunes. Add the cream and stir to make a sauce. Serve with slices of apple and prunes on top.

Crunchy Pork Grill

Serves 4

4 pork loin chops
freshly ground black pepper
3 tablespoons crunchy peanut butter
½ teaspoon ground coriander
¼ teaspoon chilli powder
1 teaspoon sesame seeds
1 teaspoon curry powder
1 garlic clove, crushed

Season the pork with pepper and cook under a medium hot griller (broiler) for 5 to 7 minutes on each side, depending on thickness. Combine the remaining ingredients and spread lightly over each side of the pork during the final cooking stages.

Pork Chops with Cheese

Serves 4 - 6

4-6 pork loin chops, skin and excess fat removed
salt and pepper
½ cup (2 oz) grated cheese
2 tablespoons sour cream
½-1 teaspoon prepared mustard
dash of paprika

Grill (broil) the pork chops, seasoned with salt and pepper, under a medium hot griller (broiler) for about 4 minutes on each side, according to thickness. Mix together the cheese, cream and mustard, then spread over each chop. Sprinkle on some paprika and grill a further 1 to 2 minutes until melted and golden.

Dry-Spiced Spareribs

Serves 4

750 g (1 ½ lb) pork spareribs or slices
1 cup (8 fl oz) stock or water
1 tablespoon each chilli and garlic sauces
3 teaspoons caster (powdered) sugar
1 teaspoon Chinese five spice powder or cinnamon
1 tablespoon tandoori spice mix or paprika

Cut each sparerib into approximately 5 pieces. Place in a saucepan with the stock and chilli and garlic sauces. Cover and simmer slowly for 30 minutes, then drain. Combine the sugar, five spice powder and tandoori spices and toss the pork pieces in this mixture. Place on a lightly greased oven tray and bake at 200°C (400°F/Gas 6) for 30 minutes. Alternately, the spareribs may be grilled (broiled) under a moderate heat, turning often to prevent burning.

Braised Chinese Spareribs

Serves 4

250 g (8 oz) broccoli
1 x 420 g (13 ½ oz) can baby corn cob pieces
3 tablespoons oil
1 small onion, sliced
1 cup sliced spring onions (scallions)
750 g (1 ½ lb) pork spareribs or slices
1 tablespoon light soy sauce
1 teaspoon sugar
2 teaspoons chilli sauce
½ cup (4 fl oz) stock
3 teaspoons cornflour (cornstarch)
¼ cup (2 fl oz) sherry

Trim the broccoli and blanch in boiling salted water for 1 minute. Drain and refresh under cold water, then drain well. Drain the corn pieces. Heat half the oil, then sauté the broccoli. Remove the broccoli and sauté the onion, then the spring onions. Remove from the pan.

Cut the pork into small pieces and fry in the remaining oil until almost cooked, about 10 minutes. Add the soy sauce and sugar and fry a further 2 minutes. Add chilli sauce and stock, allow to simmer. Thicken with the cornflour blended with the sherry and stir until cooked, about 2 minutes. Quickly toss through the broccoli, onion, corn and spring onions and reheat. Serve topped with the spring onions.

Spareribs with Sauerkraut

Serves 4

1 x 440 g (14 oz) can sauerkraut
2 smoked frankfurts
1 cup shredded green cabbage
2 tablespoons oil
750 g (1 ½ lb) pork spareribs or slices
1 onion, sliced
½ cup (4 fl oz) apple cider
¼ teaspoon caraway seeds
½ teaspoon salt
¼ teaspoon pepper
sliced apple rings
15 g (½ oz) butter

Drain the sauerkraut and rinse under running water. Drain again. Slice the frankfurts into chunky pieces. Sauté the cabbage in the oil until soft then remove. Sauté spareribs over a medium heat for about 10 minutes, turning often to brown evenly. Drain off the excess fat from the pan, add the onion and cider and cover with the sauerkraut, caraway seeds, salt and pepper. Cover and simmer for 30 minutes, then remove the lid. Add the cabbage and the frankfurt slices and stir into the mixture. Simmer a further 10 minutes, adding extra apple cider if desired. Fry the apple slices in the butter until just tender and serve with the pork and sauerkraut.

Pork

Eastern Spareribs

Serves 4

- 1 kg (2 lb) pork spareribs or slices
- 2 tablespoons oil
- 1 cup (8 fl oz) water
- 2 teaspoons soy sauce
- 2 teaspoons each chilli and garlic sauces
- ½ cup (3 oz) soft brown sugar
- boiled rice
- bottled Chinese vegetables in ginger sauce

Cut the spareribs into small pieces about 5 cm (2 inch) long. Remove any large bones. Heat the oil in a wok or deep pan. Add the pork pieces and stir fry until crisp and brown, about 7 to 10 minutes. Drain off the excess fat. Add the water and cook rapidly until the liquid is foamy and nearly evaporated. Add the sauces and stir fry to evenly coat. Sprinkle over the brown sugar and continue stirring and cooking for a further 7 to 10 minutes. Take care not to allow the pork and sugar to burn. Serve immediately with rice and Chinese vegetables in ginger sauce.

Lemon-Spiced Spareribs

Serves 4

- 2 tablespoons lemon juice
- 1 garlic clove, crushed
- 1 tablespoon honey
- 1 tablespoon soy sauce
- 750 g (1 ½ lb) pork spareribs
- 1 tablespoon lard
- ½ cup prepared lemon sauce or jam
- boiled rice

Combine the lemon juice, garlic, honey and soy sauce in a flat dish. Cut each sparerib into 3 pieces and toss in the marinade. Stand at least 1 hour, turning often. Melt the lard in a frying pan or wok and brown the spareribs. Lower the heat and stir fry until almost cooked. Mix in the lemon sauce and remaining marinade, and allow to boil and coat the spareribs. Serve hot with boiled rice and a green vegetable.

Note: Lemon sauce or lemon jam is obtainable at leading Chinese food stores.

Redcurrant-Glazed Pork Spareribs

Serves 4 [M]

- 750 g (1 ½ lb) pork spareribs
- ⅓ cup (4 oz) redcurrant jelly
- 2 teaspoons grated lemon rind
- 3 tablespoons lemon juice
- 1 tablespoon cornflour (cornstarch)
- 1 garlic clove, crushed

Conventional Method: Place the spareribs on a rack in a baking dish. Pour water in the bottom of the baking dish. Place the remaining ingredients in a saucepan and blend with a wooden spoon. Stir until boiling and simmer for 2 minutes. Brush the spareribs with the glaze and bake at 190°C (375°F/Gas 5) for 40 minutes or until tender. Turn the spareribs and brush frequently with the glaze during cooking.

Microwave Method: Place the ingredients for the glaze in a basin. Blend together and cook on high for 2 minutes. Stir well. Place the spareribs on a rack and brush with the glaze. Cook on medium for 20 minutes, turning and brushing with the glaze several times. Stand for 10 minutes before serving.

Honey Pork with Pineapple

Serves 4

- 750 g (1 ½ lb) pork spareribs
- 2½ tablespoons cornflour (cornstarch)
- ¼ teaspoon Chinese five spice powder
- pinch of chilli powder
- 4 tablespoons oil
- ½ red pepper (capsicum), cut into strips
- 1 cm (½ inch) piece fresh ginger, sliced
- 1 onion, sliced
- 1 zucchini (courgette), sliced
- 1 garlic glove, crushed
- 1 cup of unsweetened pineapple pieces with 1 cup (8 fl oz) syrup
- 2 teaspoons soy sauce
- 3 teaspoons honey

Remove the rind and bones from the spareribs and cut into pieces. Dust with half the cornflour seasoned with the five spice and chilli powders. Heat the oil and stir fry the prepared vegetables and the garlic for 2 minutes. Remove and drain, then add the pork and cook for about 7 to 10 minutes until crisp. Drain. Place the pineapple, pineapple syrup, soy sauce and honey in the pan and stir until the mixture boils and thickens. Simmer for 2 minutes, then add the pork with the vegetables and reheat.

Hungarian Casserole

Serves 4

- 750 g (1½ lb) pork spareribs or slices
- 1½ tablespoons flour
- 3 teaspoons paprika
- ½ teaspoon salt
- ¼ teaspoon pepper
- 3 tablespoons oil
- 1 large onion, sliced
- 1 eggplant (aubergine), sliced
- 2 small peppers (capsicums), sliced
- 1 garlic clove
- 1 cup (8 fl oz) tomato purée
- ½ cup (4 fl oz) wine or stock
- 2 bay leaves

Cut the spareribs in half. Toss in the flour seasoned with paprika, salt and pepper. Sauté the pork in the oil until evenly browned. Remove to a casserole dish. Sauté the onion, eggplant and peppers until just soft, without browning, and add to the pork with the garlic, tomato purée, wine and bay leaves. Cover and cook at 160°C (325°F/Gas 3), for approximately 1¼ hours. Thicken if desired.

Barbecued Pork Spareribs

Serves 4

- 2 tablespoons soy sauce
- 2 tablespoons honey
- 2 tablespoons sherry
- 4 garlic cloves, crushed
- ½ teaspoon grated fresh ginger
- ½ teaspoon Chinese five spice powder
- 1 teaspoon salt
- 1 kg (2 lb) pork spareribs or slices

Blend the soy sauce, honey and sherry. Mix in the garlic, ginger, five spice powder and salt. Add pork spareribs and coat well. Cover and marinate in the refrigerator overnight or for several hours. Cook over a medium hot barbecue or under the griller (broiler) for about 30 minutes, turning often to cook evenly.

Alternately, roast on a rack over a tray of water at 160°C (325°F/Gas 3) for about 45 minutes. Turn the spareribs during baking.

Mexicano Spareribs

Serves 4

- 1 kg (2 lb) pork spareribs or slices
- 1 cup (8 fl oz) stock
- 1 packet taco seasoning mix
- ⅔ cup (5 fl oz) tomato sauce
- 2 teaspoons soft brown sugar

Place the spareribs in a shallow frying pan. Pour over the stock and sprinkle in 2 teaspoons of taco seasoning mix then cover and simmer for 20 minutes. Mix the remaining taco seasoning into the tomato sauce and brown sugar and stand aside for 10 minutes while the spareribs cook. Drain the spareribs and place on a grill (broiler) rack. Spread with the taco sauce mix and cook under a medium heat for 7 to 10 minutes, depending on the thickness. Turn the spareribs, spread over the taco sauce and cook until tender, about 7 minutes.

Mandarin Style Spareribs

Serves 4

- 1 kg (2 lb) pork spareribs
- ½ cup (4 fl oz) vegetable oil
- 1 x 315 g (10 oz) can mandarin segments, liquid reserved
- 1 x 425 g (13½ oz) can baby corn cob pieces, liquid reserved
- 1 chicken stock cube
- 1 garlic clove, crushed
- 1 cm (½ inch) piece fresh ginger, chopped
- 1½ cups (12 fl oz) sweet and sour sauce (*page 38*)
- rice
- spring onions (scallions)
- soy sauce

Cut the spareribs in half. Heat the oil in a deep wok or frying pan and when medium hot add the spareribs. Fry gently for 7 minutes, turning the pieces to cook evenly. Remove and drain the spareribs and place in a clean saucepan with the reserved mandarin and corn liquids measured to make 1 cup (8 fl oz). Add the stock cube, garlic and ginger. Simmer briskly until all the liquid has evaporated, then add the sweet and sour sauce and the drained corn cob pieces. Stir fry until hot and coated. Add the drained mandarins. Serve immediately with rice and garnish with spring onions and a little soy sauce if desired.

Pork

Pork with Snake Beans

Serves 4

2 tablespoons peanut oil
250 g (8 oz) pork shoulder, finely diced
1 teaspoon finely chopped garlic
2 tablespoons light soy sauce
pinch of pepper
500 g (1 lb) snake beans, cut into 5 cm (2 inch) lengths
1 red pepper (capsicum), cut into 1.25 cm (½ inch) squares
5 spring onions (scallions), finely chopped
½ teaspoon sesame oil
3 tablespoons toasted sesame seeds

Heat a wok, add the oil and when hot, fry the pork and garlic until the pork changes colour. Season with the soy sauce and pepper. Add the beans and red pepper and cook, covered, until the pork is tender. Add the spring onions and sesame oil and serve hot, sprinkled with the sesame seeds and accompanied by boiled white rice.

Apricot and Pork Kebabs

Serves 4

500 g (1 lb) pork shoulder, cut into 2.5 cm (1 inch) cubes
500 g (1 lb) apricots, halved and stoned
1 garlic clove, crushed
2 tablespoons soy sauce
1 teaspoon soft brown sugar
½ teaspoon Chinese five spice powder
1 teaspoon ground coriander

Mix all the ingredients together well. Marinate in the refrigerator for at least 1 hour. Stir occasionally.

Thread the pork cubes alternately with the apricots on bamboo skewers. Grill (broil), turning, until the pork is cooked and the apricots are glazed, about 10 minutes. Brush occasionally with the remaining marinade. Serve hot with savoury rice.

Pork and Pineapple Boats

Serves 4

1 kg (2 lb) pork fillet (tenderloin)
¼ cup (1 oz) seasoned flour
1 pineapple
2 tablespoons sherry
2 tablespoons oil
1 garlic clove, crushed
1 teaspoon curry powder
1 teaspoon dried oregano
freshly ground black pepper
1 large onion, diced
2 stalks celery, sliced
125 g (4 oz) button mushrooms
1 cup (8 fl oz) chicken stock
fresh dill sprigs

Cut the pork into 2.5 cm (1 inch) cubes. Toss in seasoned flour. Cut the pineapple in half lengthwise and scoop out the flesh from each pineapple shell. Cut into cubes. Reserve the shells for serving. Place the pineapple flesh in a bowl, pour over the sherry and set aside.

Heat the oil in a large pan. Add the garlic, curry powder, oregano and pepper. Stir until combined. Add the onion, celery and mushrooms. Sauté for a few minutes without browning. Remove from the pan. Add the pork to the pan and brown well on all sides. Cover with stock and simmer until the meat is tender, about 30 minutes.

Add the sautéed onion, celery, mushrooms and the pineapple to the pan. Cook for a further 5 to 10 minutes and season to taste with pepper.

Spoon back into the pineapple shells. Garnish with sprigs of dill. Serve with noodles and poppy seeds.

Honey Taro Root Pork

Serves 4

1 garlic clove, crushed
1 teaspoon grated fresh ginger
2 tablespoons oil
250 g (8 oz) pork fillet, cut into thin strips
1 cup julienned and parboiled taro root
1 red pepper (capsicum), julienned
pepper
½ cup (4 fl oz) chicken stock
2 tablespoons soy sauce
1 ½ tablespoons honey
½ teaspoon sesame oil
3 tablespoons sesame seeds
1 ½ tablespoons cornflour (cornstarch), blended with 3 tablespoons water
½ cup chopped garlic cloves

Stir fry the garlic and ginger in the heated oil. Add the pork and stir fry until well browned. Remove and drain. Add the taro root and red pepper. Stir fry until tender-crisp.

Return the pork with the remaining ingredients and stir fry until a glossy sauce is formed. Serve immediately.

Ham

Ham in Peppercorn Sauce
Serves 4

4 ham steaks
cinnamon, optional
30 g (1 oz) garlic butter (*page 277*)
1 tablespoon green peppercorns in brine
1 tablespoon brandy
½ cup (4 fl oz) cream

Season the ham steaks with a little cinnamon, if desired, then fry in a preheated pan with the garlic butter for 2 minutes on each side. Remove and keep warm. Add the peppercorns to the pan and crush slightly with a spoon. Add the brandy and cream and stir until boiling. Evaporate slightly to thicken, then return the ham steaks to reheat in this mixture.

Juicy Ham Steaks with Curried Fruits
Serves 4

2 teaspoons soft brown sugar
4 thick ham steaks

Sauce

1 ½ cups (12 fl oz) orange and mango juice
2 tablespoons cornflour (cornstarch)
1 teaspoon curry paste or powder
1 tablespoon oil
15 g (½ oz) butter
¼ cup (2 fl oz) wine or stock
1 ½ cups sliced fresh fruit in season

Sprinkle the sugar over the ham and set aside. Preheat a heavy pan, and lightly grease with the oil and butter. Quickly brown the ham steaks, turning to cook both sides, about 3 minutes. Serve with the curried fruit on top.

Sauce: Heat the fruit juice, then add the cornflour and curry paste blended together with the wine. Stir to thicken the juice, then simmer for 3 minutes. Wash the fruit and slice if necessary, then add to the sauce and cook a further 1 minute.

Ham Puff Pie
Serves 3 - 4

375 g (12 oz) shoulder ham, roughly chopped
1 onion, chopped
375 g (12 oz) chicken livers or chicken breast
30 g (1 oz) garlic butter (*page 277*)
1 packet Sauce Provençale or red wine sauce
¾ cup (6 fl oz) water
1 x 125 g (4 oz) sheet ready-rolled puff pastry

Place the ham in a small pie dish. In a frying pan sauté the onion and chicken livers in the garlic butter to seal and lightly brown. Remove to the pie dish. Blend the sauce mix with the water in the frying pan and stir until thickened. Spoon into the pie dish and mix well. Moisten the edges and cover with the rolled pastry. Trim and decorate the edges and make a vent in the centre. Bake at 200°C (400°F/Gas 6) for 25 minutes and serve immediately.

Ham and Parsley Flapjacks
Makes 1 - 2

15 g (½ oz) butter
1 ½ tablespoons flour
½ cup (4 fl oz) milk
⅓ cup (2 ½ fl oz) cream
2 eggs, separated
⅔ cup chopped ham
pinch each of nutmeg, garlic salt and dry mustard
2 tablespoons chopped fresh parsley
extra butter

Melt the butter, stir in the flour and cook until golden. Stir in the milk and cream and cook until the batter thickens, stirring often. Cook for 2 minutes, then add the egg yolks, ham and seasonings. Beat the egg whites until foamy and thick then fold into the sauce with the parsley. Heat a large pan with extra butter, and when bubbling add the batter and cook gently until golden on each side. Serve immediately.

Pork

Ham Paella

Serves 3 - 4

Always a favourite casual meal, this versatile recipe uses leftover ham and other ingredients to make a dish fit for a king!

1 onion, sliced
1 red pepper (capsicum), sliced
2 tablespoons oil
1 cup diced cooked chicken or meat
150 g (5 oz) smoked leg ham, chopped
2 ½ cups cooked saffron rice (page 314)
¾ cup peeled prawns (shrimp) or seafood
extra prawns (shrimp), olives, chopped fresh parsley for garnish

Sauté the onion and red pepper in the oil. Add the chicken and ham and toss, then spoon in the cooked rice. Add the prawns and the garnish, then cover with foil or a lid and heat over a low heat for 15 to 20 minutes.

Crusty Ham Grill

Serves 4

4 thick ham steaks
2 tablespoons chutney
8 slices banana or pineapple
15 g (½ oz) garlic butter
1 cup (2 oz) soft brown breadcrumbs
⅓ cup (1 ½ oz) grated cheese
dash of cayenne pepper or paprika

Cut the ham steaks in half and make a side pocket in each. Spread with some of the chutney and fill with banana or pineapple. Melt the garlic butter and fry the breadcrumbs until toasted, then remove to a dish. Cool, then mix in the cheese with a little cayenne. Grill (broil) the ham steaks for about 2 minutes on each side. Spread with the remaining chutney and spoon on the breadcrumb topping. Grill (broil) under a low heat for a further 1 minute without burning.

Ham Pizza Steak

Serves 4

4 round ham steaks
3 tablespoons tomato paste
2 tomatoes, sliced
dried basil
salt and pepper
seasonings of choice
4 slices tasty or mozzarella cheese

Place the ham steaks under a medium hot griller (broiler) and turn to cook each side. Spread over some tomato paste, top with sliced tomato and grill a further 1 minute. Season with basil, salt and pepper. Sprinkle over any other seasoning of your choice, then top with cheese and cook until golden and bubbling.

Ham Pasta

Serves 4

350 g (11 oz) shoulder ham, cut into strips
2 garlic cloves, crushed
60 g (2 oz) butter
¾ cup (6 fl oz) white wine
1 ¼ cups (10 fl oz) cream
¾ cup (3 oz) grated Parmesan cheese
¼ teaspoon each salt and white pepper
250 g (8 oz) each white and green pasta, cooked
chopped chives or herbs

Sauté the ham and garlic in the butter for 3 minutes. Remove some ham for the garnish. Add the wine and cream and simmer for 10 minutes. Mix in the cheese and allow to melt. Season with salt and pepper. Serve over the cooked noodles, garnished with the remaining ham and the chives.

Pantry Ham Steak

Serves 4

4 ham steaks
2 teaspoons soft brown sugar
2 teaspoons prepared mustard, optional
30 g (1 oz) butter
24 baby button mushrooms
1 bunch fresh asparagus spears, cooked
¾ cup (3 oz) grated cheese

Wipe the ham steaks and arrange on a grill (broiler) rack and sprinkle with some of the sugar. Cook under a medium hot griller (broiler) until glazed. Turn, add more sugar and continue to cook. Spread with mustard if desired.
Melt the butter and sauté the mushrooms until just soft. Spoon onto the ham. Add the asparagus spears and cheese and cook until hot and bubbly.

Bonjour Croissants

Serves 2 - 4

A good morning cup of coffee with a delicate croissant filled with ham and cheese makes the best start to any busy day!

4 baked plain croissants
8 small slices Swiss style cheese
8 thin slices leg ham
½ cup alfalfa sprouts or shredded lettuce

Preheat the oven to 160°C (325°F/Gas 3). Slice the croissants across in half and place on an oven tray. On the base of each croissant arrange a slice of cheese, ham, then more cheese on top and bake for about 10 minutes until crisp and melted. Sprinkle with alfalfa or fine shredded lettuce and top with the other half of the croissant. Serve immediately with steaming coffee or tea.

Yummy Ham Loaf

Serves 5 - 6

slices of pineapple or peaches
500 g (1 lb) shoulder ham
500 g (1 lb) sausage mince (ground beef)
2 cups (4 oz) brown breadcrumbs
1 egg, beaten
½ cup finely chopped spring onions (scallions)
2 tablespoons finely chopped red pepper (capsicum) or nuts
tomato sauce or gravy

Grease a loaf tin and arrange the fruit in a pattern on the base. Cut the ham into fine small cubes and combine thoroughly with remaining ingredients except the sauce. Pack firmly into the tin. Bake in a preheated oven, 200°C (400°F/Gas 6), for 45 minutes. Remove and stand for 5 minutes before slicing and serving with tomato sauce or gravy.

Ham Potato Boats

Serves 2 - 4

2 large roasting potatoes
15 g (½ oz) garlic butter (page 277)
½ cup finely chopped ham
¼ cup chopped spring onions (scallions)
2 tablespoons cream or milk
dash of pepper, nutmeg or herbs
4 slices cheese
pinch of cayenne pepper or paprika

Scrub the potatoes and place in a moderate oven, 180°C (350°F/Gas 4), for about 1 hour. Meanwhile, sauté in garlic butter the ham and spring onions, then add the cream with the seasoning. Cut the potatoes across in half and scoop out the cooked potato. Add to the ham and mash well until creamy. Return the filling to the potato shells and top with a slice of cheese and a pinch of cayenne pepper. Bake for a further 10 minutes.

Pasta Ham Salad

Serves 4 - 6

2 cups leg ham strips
2 cups cooked pasta shapes
1 cup shredded or grated raw zucchini (courgettes)
¾ cup sliced celery
1 small red apple
1 tablespoon lemon juice
1 cup (8 fl oz) Italian style dressing or mayonnaise
walnut pieces and chopped chives

Place the ham in a basin with the pasta, zucchini and celery. Core the apple, slice with the skin and toss in the lemon juice. Add to the salad and toss with the dressing. Cover and chill before serving, then mix again. Add extra dressing if desired and scatter over the walnut pieces and chives.

French Ham Bake

Serves 4 - 6

375 g (12 oz) double-smoked ham
6 thick slices brown or rye bread
1 ½ cups (6 oz) shredded Edam cheese
3 small eggs, beaten
⅓ cup (2 ½ fl oz) cream or beer
1 teaspoon dry mustard
salt and pepper
extra ham

Slice the ham very thinly. Lightly toast the bread and arrange on an oven tray. Place the cheese, beaten eggs, cream and mustard in a bowl and season with a little salt and pepper. Allow the mixture to stand 15 minutes. Spoon half the mixture over the toast, arrange the sliced ham on top, then the remaining cheese mixture. Bake at 200°C (400°F/Gas 6) for 15 minutes until golden and puffed. Serve at once with extra ham and a side salad.

Ham Milano Bake

Serves 2

1 x 200 g (6 ½ oz) eggplant (aubergine)
salt
1 cup cooked pasta or sliced cooked potato
1 tablespoon chopped fresh herbs
1 x 425 g (13 ½ oz) can Italian style tomato sauce
½ cup (4 fl oz) oil
250 g (8 oz) sliced leg ham
60 g (2 oz) sliced mozzarella cheese

Wipe and slice the eggplant, sprinkle with salt on both sides and stand for 15 minutes. Place the cooked pasta in the base of a shallow ovenproof dish. Mix the herbs into the tomato sauce. Wipe the eggplant with kitchen paper, then shallow fry in hot oil until golden. Drain. Spoon half the sauce over the pasta and arrange alternate slices of ham and eggplant on top. Spoon the remaining sauce over and dot with pieces of sliced cheese. Bake at 200°C (400°F/Gas 6) for 30 minutes.

Ham and Noodles in a Pot

Serves 3 - 4

15 g (½ oz) butter
1 small onion, chopped
1 cup sliced mushrooms
1 ½ cups chopped ham
1 cup peeled, diced tomatoes
1 ½ cups (12 fl oz) chicken stock
½ cup peeled and cooked prawns (shrimp)
1 tablespoon chopped fresh herbs
1 packet instant noodles

Melt the butter in a saucepan and sauté the onion and mushrooms until soft. Add the remaining ingredients except the noodles and simmer for 7 minutes. Add the noodles and cook a further 3 minutes.

Pork

Ham Steaks with Pineapple Sauce

Serves 4

15 g (½ oz) butter
4 ham steaks

4 slices pineapple

Sauce

15 g (½ oz) butter
2 tablespoons cornflour (cornstarch)
¾ cup (6 fl oz) pineapple juice
⅓ cup finely sliced spring onions (scallions)
1 tablespoon red pepper (capsicum) strips
1 tablespoon maple syrup or honey
soy sauce, optional

Melt the butter in a pan and add the ham steaks to seal and brown. Remove and keep warm while quickly pan frying the pineapple. Serve the ham topped with the pineapple and sauce.

Sauce: Melt the butter. Add the cornflour and blend in the juice. Stir until the sauce boils and thickens. Add the spring onions, red pepper and syrup, and simmer for 3 minutes. Adjust the flavour taste and colour with a little soy sauce if desired and keep warm.

Delicate Ham Puffs

Serves 6

1 tablespoon chopped red pepper (capsicum)
1 small onion, chopped
15 g (½ oz) butter
2 cups chopped shoulder ham
⅛ teaspoon white pepper
1 tablespoon chopped chives

Sauce

30 g (1 oz) butter
3 tablespoons flour
1 cup (8 fl oz) milk, warmed
3 egg yolks
5 egg whites

Grease 6 large soufflé or ramekin dishes. Preheat the oven to 190°C (375°F/Gas 5). Sauté the red pepper and onion in the butter until soft, then place in a food processor with the ham and mix until smooth. Season with pepper but no salt. Add the chives. Make the sauce and add the ham mixture as directed, then spoon into soufflé dishes. Bake in the centre of the oven for about 20 minutes. Serve immediately.

Sauce: Melt the butter, add the flour and stir until golden. Gradually add the warm milk and stir until the sauce boils and thickens. Simmer for 2 minutes, then remove and add the egg yolks and the ham mixture. Mix until evenly combined. Whisk the egg whites until firm peaks form. Beat one third of the whites into the ham, then lightly fold in the remaining whites.

Ham and Chicken with Spaghetti

Serves 4

60 g (2 oz) butter
1 tablespoon oil
4 chicken drumsticks
2 garlic cloves, crushed
1 onion, sliced
1 cup diced, peeled tomatoes
1 cup button mushrooms
½ teaspoon ground cardamom
1 cup (8 fl oz) chicken stock
4 thick slices leg ham
2 tablespoons cornflour (cornstarch) mixed with a little water
250 g (8 oz) spaghetti

Garnish

1 red apple, cored
15 g (½ oz) butter
1 tablespoon lemon juice
1 tablespoon caster (powdered) sugar

Heat the butter and oil and sauté the chicken legs with the garlic and onion until golden. Add the tomatoes, mushrooms and cardamom. Pour in the stock, add the ham and simmer gently for about 10 minutes. Thicken with the blended cornflour. Cook for a further 3 minutes. Meanwhile, cook the spaghetti in 8 cups (2 litres) boiling salted water for 13 minutes, drain and keep warm. Serve the hot spaghetti, topped with chicken and ham, with the apple garnish.

Garnish: Cut the apple into wedges and cook separately in the butter until golden on each side. Add the lemon juice and sugar and cook for a further 3 minutes.

Stand-by Ham au Gratin

Serves 4 - 6

12 slices leg ham
1 ½ tablespoons herb mustard
1 x 400 g (12 ½ oz) can artichokes or asparagus
1 x 190 g (6 oz) can whole button mushrooms
½ cup (2 oz) grated Gruyère cheese
1 cup (8 fl oz) white sauce, warmed (*page 33*)
1 egg, beaten
15 g (½ oz) butter
1 garlic clove, crushed
1 slice bread, diced
extra grated Gruyère
pinch of paprika
fresh herbs in season

Grease a shallow ovenproof dish and line the base with 3 slices of ham. Spread the mustard over the remaining ham slices and add the drained sliced artichokes and the mushrooms. Fold the ham and pack into the dish. Add the cheese to the warm white sauce, then the beaten egg. Pour over the ham.

Melt the butter with the garlic, add the diced bread and toss. Spoon over the sauce and top with extra grated cheese, if desired, and the paprika. Bake at 180°C (350°F/Gas 4) for 30 minutes. Increase the heat for a crisp golden topping and bake for a further 5 minutes. sprinkle with fresh herbs.

CHICKEN

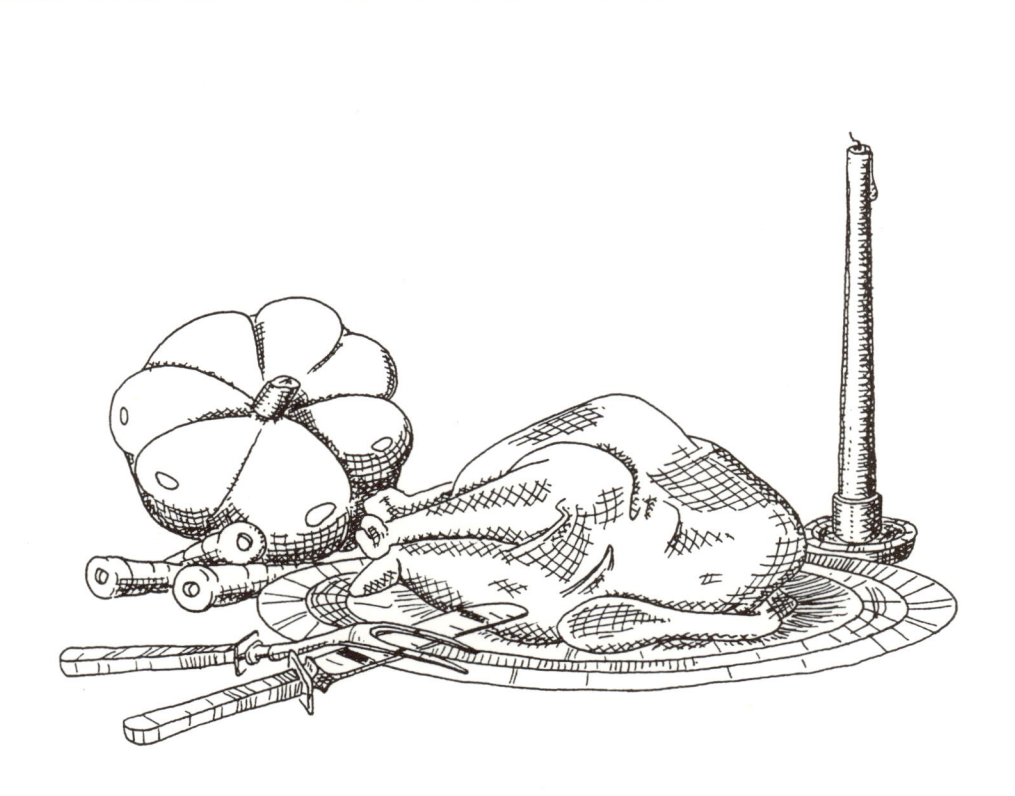

Chicken is now eaten as frequently as red meat, mainly because of its availability and price. Chicken is very versatile and is always at its best combined with other flavours that enhance the delicate flavour of the flesh. With the influx of speciality chicken shops we are able to purchase chicken meat in forms previously unheard of. Boneless, minced and cubes of chicken meat are all popular. Boneless meat should be watched very carefully as it takes only a few minutes to cook through and becomes very dry if overcooked. Experiment with the new cuts and discover new delights of this family favourite.

The majority of the recipes in this chapter have been provided by the **Australian Poultry Federation**, in particular Dr Ian Fairbrother, from booklets published as a result of the National Chicken Cooking Contest run annually. Other recipes have been provided by contributors whose credits appear elsewhere in the book.

Chicken

Carving

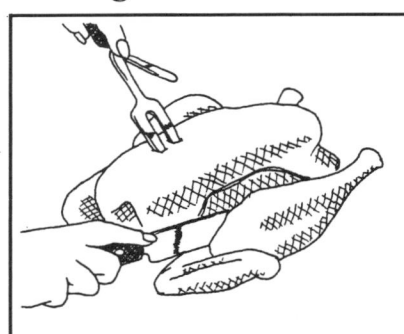

1. Cut through the joint where leg is attached to the body. Remove the legs and divide at the joint into thigh and drumstick.

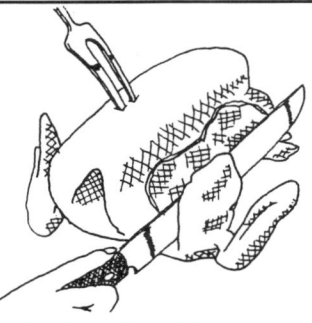

2. Cut down through front corner of breast through wing joint and remove wing with a portion of the breast. Repeat on the other side.

3. Turn chicken sideways. Slip knife behind the wishbone and cut through to remove it with a portion of breast.

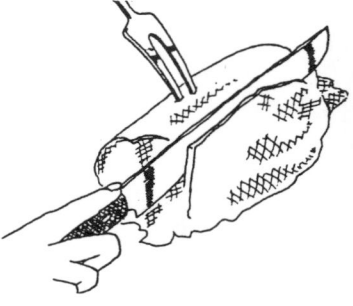

4. Turn dish so wishbone end is nearest you. Cut thin, even slices from the breast. Repeat on the other side.

Trussing

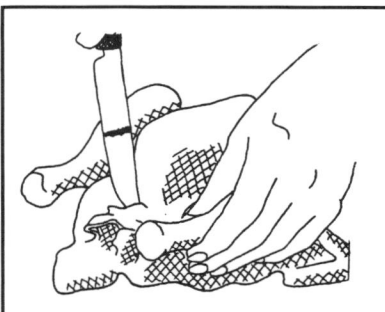

1. Turn the chicken on its back and cut a small hole and push the tail through. This should close the vent.

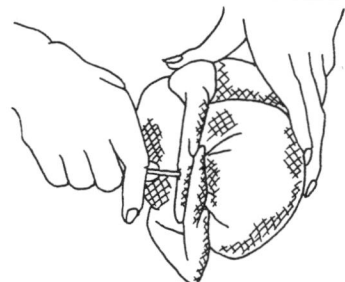

2. Pull the skin over the neck and fold the wing tips back over the skin. Run a skewer through the wings.

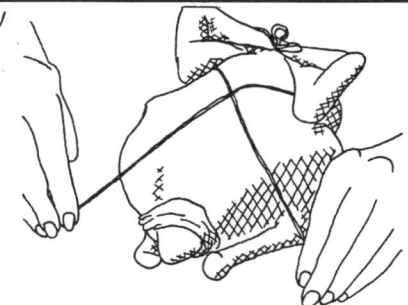

3. Run a piece of string around the skewer and cross it over the back.

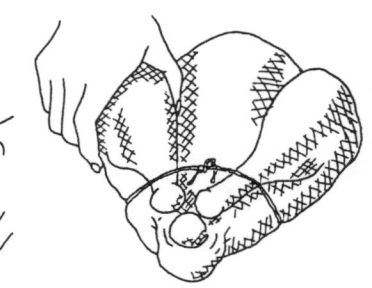

4. Turn the chicken over and tie the legs together, keeping them close to the body.

Jointing

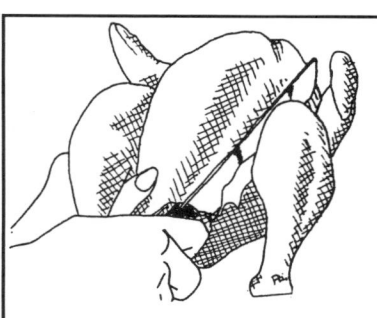

1. Place the chicken, breast side up, on the cutting board. Cut the skin between the thighs and body.

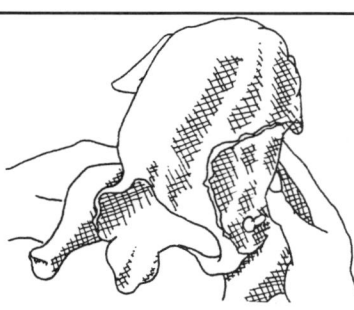

2. Grasping the leg, lift and bend back until the bones break at the hip joint. Repeat on the other side.

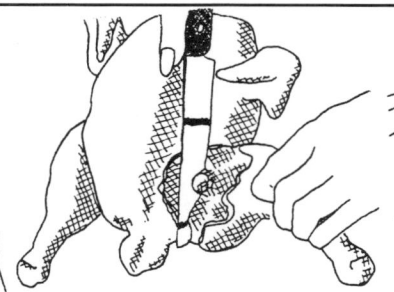

3. Remove the leg and thigh from the body by cutting from the tail towards the shoulder, between the joints. Repeat on the other side.

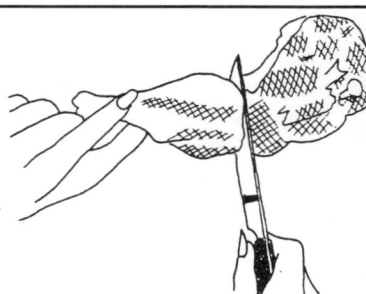

4. To separate the thigh and drumstick, locate the knee joint by bending thigh and leg together. With skin side down, cut through the joints to each leg.

5. With the chicken on its back, remove the wings by cutting the inside of the wing just over the joint. Pull from the body and cut from the top down, through the joint.

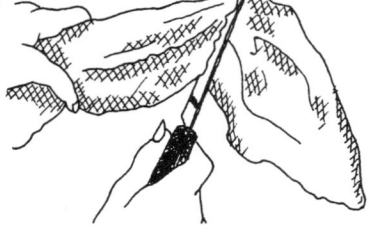

6. Separate the breast and back by placing the chicken on the neck end or back and cutting towards the board, through the joint along each side of the rib cage.

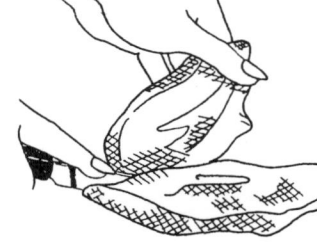

7. The breast may be left whole or halved. Place, skin side down, on the board and cut the wishbone into two at the joint of the bone.

Roast Chicken

Serves 4

1 teaspoon salt	1 x 1.5 kg (3 lb) chicken
¼ teaspoon pepper	

Mix together the salt and pepper and sprinkle over the outside of the chicken and inside the cavity. If desired, fill the cavity with stuffing. Hook the wing tips under the back. Place the chicken, breast side up, in a shallow baking pan. Bake at 180°C (350°F/Gas 4) for about 1 hour or until a fork can be inserted in the chicken with ease and the leg moves freely when lifted or twisted. (If stuffed, add 30 minutes to the cooking time.) Allow to stand 10 minutes for easier carving.

Oven-Fried Chicken

Serves 4

60 g (2 oz) margarine	½ cup (2 oz) breadcrumbs
1 teaspoon salt	1 x 1.5 kg (3 lb) chicken,
¼ teaspoon pepper	cut into serving pieces

Melt the margarine in a small pan over medium heat. Remove from the heat and stir in the salt and pepper. Place the breadcrumbs in a shallow dish. Dip the chicken, one piece at a time, first in the margarine, then in the breadcrumbs, turning to coat on all sides. Place the chicken in a single layer on a lightly greased baking sheet. Bake at 190°C (375°F/Gas 5) for about 40 minutes, or until brown and crisp and a fork can be inserted in the chicken with ease.

Poached Chicken

Serves 4

1 x 1.5 kg (3 lb) chicken	1 teaspoon salt
2 cups (16 fl oz) water	¼ teaspoon pepper

Place the chicken in a deep saucepan. Add the water, salt and pepper. Cover and simmer for about 45 minutes or until a fork can be inserted in the chicken with ease. Remove the chicken from the pan and cool. Reserve the broth for later use, if desired. Separate the meat from the bones. Discard the bones and skin. Cut the chicken into bite-sized pieces. A 1.5 kg (3 lb) chicken yields about 3 cups of diced cooked chicken and 2 to 2½ cups (16 to 20 fl oz) of broth.

Variation: For extra flavour, 1 small onion, sliced, and the leaves from 3 stalks of celery may be added to the water when cooking chicken.

Note: Chicken broth is tasty and nutritious. Keep covered in the refrigerator for up to three days or freeze for later use in ice trays and store the cubes in a plastic freezer bag. Add one or two cubes to water when cooking vegetables, stew, soup or other dishes which are enhanced by the flavour of chicken.

Chicken on the Grill

Tips for grilling (broiling) chicken:

1. The process should never be hurried. Keep a close eye on the chicken to avoid burning.
2. Adjust rack 15 to 20 cm (6 to 8 inch) from heat.
3. Place the chicken skin side up.
4. Apply any sauce or marinade during the last 30 minutes of cooking, turning the chicken often and applying liberally after each turning.
5. Chicken is ready to serve if a fork can be inserted with ease.

Fried Chicken

Serves 4

½ cup (2 oz) flour	1 x 1.5 kg (3 lb) chicken,
1 teaspoon salt	cut into serving pieces
¼ teaspoon pepper	½ cup (4 fl oz) cooking oil

Mix together the flour, salt and pepper in a paper or plastic bag. Add the chicken, a few pieces at a time, and shake to coat thoroughly. Place the oil in a large pan and heat to high. Add the chicken, skin side down, and cook for about 10 minutes, turning to brown on all sides. Reduce the heat to medium low, cover and cook for about 20 minutes longer or until a fork can be inserted in the chicken with ease.

Oven-Barbecued Chicken

Serves 4

1 x 1.5 kg (3 lb) chicken, cut into serving pieces	1 cup (8 fl oz) vinegar
1 teaspoon salt	¼ cup (2 fl oz) tomato sauce
3 tablespoons flour	¾ teaspoon red (cayenne) pepper
90 g (3 oz) margarine	
1 cup (8 fl oz) water	¼ teaspoon paprika

Place the chicken in a single layer in a baking pan. Coat with the salt and flour. Melt the margarine, add remaining ingredients and heat thoroughly. Pour the sauce over the chicken and bake at 180°C (350°F/Gas 4) for about 1½ hours.

Chicken

Chicken Southern Style

Serves 4

1 x 1.5 kg (3 lb) chicken
1 ¼ cups (5 oz) flour, seasoned
250 g (8 oz) butter or margarine
1 tablespoon paprika
2 cups diced celery
2 cups diced carrots
2 cups diced onions
1.25 litres (5 cups) chicken broth
pinch of red (cayenne) pepper
¼ cup (2 fl oz) sherry

Quarter the chicken and dredge in the seasoned flour. Melt the butter in a roasting pan and put in the chicken, skin side up. Sprinkle with the paprika, add the vegetables, and brown lightly. Add the broth, pepper and sherry. Cook, uncovered, in the oven at 180°C (350°F/Gas 4) for 1 to 1½ hours.

Chicken Florentine

Serves 4

1 x 1.5 kg (3 lb) chicken, cut into serving pieces
2 teaspoons salt
¼ teaspoon pepper
2 tablespoons cooking oil
1 x 500 g (1 lb) can peeled tomatoes
½ cup (4 fl oz) dry red wine
1 cup (6 oz) rice
3 tablespoons sliced olives
1½ cups (12 fl oz) boiling water
2 x 315 g (10 oz) packets frozen chopped spinach, thawed
1 cup (4 oz) ricotta cheese
1 egg
¼ teaspoon dried marjoram
¼ teaspoon ground nutmeg
¼ cup (1 oz) grated Parmesan cheese

Sprinkle the chicken with 1 teaspoon of the salt and the pepper. Place the cooking oil in a pan and heat gently. Add the chicken and cook for about 10 minutes, turning, until brown on all sides.

In a medium-sized bowl, mix together the tomatoes and the wine. Lightly grease a large baking pan and mix in 1 cup of the tomato mixture, the rice, olives, ½ teaspoon of the salt and the boiling water. Place the chicken on top. Cover tightly with foil and bake at 180°C (350°F/Gas 4) for 45 minutes.

Press the spinach until very dry and mix with the ricotta cheese, egg, marjoram, nutmeg and remaining salt. Spoon the spinach mixture around the edges of the baking pan and pour the remaining tomato sauce mixture over the centre. Sprinkle with the Parmesan cheese. Continue baking, uncovered, for a further 10 minutes or until a fork can be inserted in the chicken with ease.

Chicken Corn Pudding

Chicken Corn Pudding

Serves 6

1 x 1.5 kg (3 lb) chicken, cut into serving pieces
1½ teaspoons salt
¼ teaspoon pepper
½ cup (4 fl oz) cooking oil
1 cup (8 fl oz) milk
2 eggs
1 cup (4 oz) flour, unsifted
¼ teaspoon dried sage
1 tablespoon finely chopped onion
1 tablespoon finely chopped fresh parsley
1 x 500 g (1 lb) can corn kernels, drained
15 g (½ oz) butter
1 teaspoon paprika

Sprinkle the chicken with 1 teaspoon of the salt and the pepper. Place the oil in a pan over medium heat. Add the chicken and cook for about 15 minutes, turning, until brown on all sides. Cover, reduce heat to low and simmer a further 25 minutes.

Place the milk, eggs, flour, remaining salt, sage, onion and parsley in a large bowl. Mix with a whisk or beater until just smooth. Add the corn, stirring to blend. Place the chicken in a warm, greased casserole dish. Add the butter to the pan and melt over medium heat. Pour the pan drippings over the chicken. Pour the corn mixture over the chicken and sprinkle with paprika. Bake, uncovered, at 220°C (425°F/Gas 7) for about 30 minutes or until a fork can be inserted in the chicken with ease and the pudding is puffed and golden.

Orange-Ginger Chicken

Serves 4

- 1 x 1.5 kg (3 lb), chicken, cut into serving pieces
- 1 teaspoon salt
- 1 teaspoon paprika
- 90 g (3 oz) butter or margarine
- 3 tablespoons flour
- 2 tablespoons soft brown sugar
- 1 cup (8 fl oz) water
- 1½ cups (12 fl oz) orange juice
- ½ teaspoon ground ginger
- a few drops of Tabasco sauce
- 1 orange, unpeeled and thinly sliced
- 250 g (8 oz) sweet potatoes, peeled and cubed

Sprinkle the chicken with the salt and paprika. In a deep flameproof casserole, place half the butter and heat gently. Add the chicken and cook, turning, for about 10 minutes or until brown on all sides. Remove the chicken and set aside. Add the remaining butter, melt and stir in the flour and sugar. Slowly stir in the water and orange juice, scraping the brown bits from the bottom of the pan. Cook, stirring, for about 5 minutes or until the sauce is smooth and thickened. Add the ginger and Tabasco sauce. Return the chicken to the sauce.

Cover and bake at 180°C (350°F/Gas 4) for 15 minutes. Add the orange slices and sweet potatoes and bake for a further 20 minutes or until a fork can be inserted in the chicken with ease.

Lime Chicken

Serves 4

- ¼ cup (2 fl oz) lime juice
- ¼ cup (2 fl oz) cooking oil
- ½ teaspoon salt
- ⅛ teaspoon pepper
- 1 tablespoon chopped parsley
- 1 tablespoon capers
- 1 x 1.5 kg (3 lb) chicken
- 2 carrots, cooked and cut into lengthwise strips
- 3 boiled potatoes, peeled and cut into wedges
- 2 leeks, cut lengthwise
- 250 g (8 oz) mushrooms, halved

Mix together the lime juice, cooking oil, salt, pepper, parsley and capers. Place the chicken in a roasting pan. Pour the lime juice mixture over the chicken and inside the cavity. Allow to marinate for 1 hour, turning often. Bake at 200°C (400°F/Gas 6) for 20 minutes. Turn and baste, then bake a further 20 minutes. Turn and baste again, then add the carrots, potatoes, leeks and mushrooms. Bake another 20 minutes or until a fork can be inserted in the chicken with ease. Carve the chicken and serve with the vegetables, spooning the juices over. Garnish with lime slices.

Orange-Ginger Chicken

Chicken

Chicken Skillet Supreme

Serves 4

1 tablespoon freshly squeezed lemon juice
½ teaspoon crushed garlic
¼ cup (2 fl oz) water
1 x 185 g (6 oz) can marinated artichoke hearts, marinade reserved
1 x 1.5 kg (3 lb) chicken, cut into serving pieces
½ cup (4 fl oz) dry white wine
1 chicken stock cube, crumbled
4 small potatoes, halved
12 small mushrooms, halved
1 tablespoon chopped fresh parsley

In a small bowl, mix together the lemon juice, garlic and water. Set aside. In a large pan, place the reserved artichoke marinade and heat gently. Add the chicken and cook, turning, for about 10 minutes or until brown on all sides. Skim off the fat and with the chicken skin side up, add the wine, lemon-garlic mixture, stock cube and potatoes. Bring to the boil, cover; reduce heat to low and cook for about 15 minutes or until potatoes are tender and a fork can be inserted in the chicken with ease. Stir in the mushrooms and artichoke hearts and sprinkle with parsley. Cover and cook a further 5 minutes.

Remove the chicken and vegetables to a heated serving plate. Continue cooking to reduce the liquid until slightly thickened. Pour over the chicken.

Chicken Basil

Serves 4

¼ cup (2 fl oz) olive oil
1 x 1.5 kg (3 lb) chicken, cut into serving pieces and skinned
1 large onion, chopped
2 green peppers (capsicums), chopped
1 garlic clove, crushed
½ cup basil leaves, well packed
½ cup finely chopped parsley
½ teaspoon sugar
1 cup (5 oz) pitted olives, drained
500 g (1 lb) whole fresh mushrooms
1 cup (8 fl oz) spaghetti sauce
1 teaspoon salt
1 teaspoon ground rosemary

Place the oil in a pan and heat gently. Add the chicken and cook, turning, for about 10 minutes or until brown on all sides. Remove the chicken and set aside. Add the onion, green peppers, garlic and basil and sauté for about 3 minutes or until the onion is transparent. Add the parsley, sugar, olives, mushrooms and spaghetti sauce and sauté for about 10 minutes.

Arrange the chicken on the vegetable sauce in the pan and sprinkle with the salt and rosemary. Cover tightly and cook over low heat for about 30 minutes or until a fork can be inserted in the chicken with ease. Serve over spaghetti or fettucine.

Chicken Paprika

Serves 4

1 x 1.5 kg (3 lb) chicken, cut into serving pieces
1 ¼ teaspoons salt
2 teaspoons paprika
butter or margarine
¾ cup (6 fl oz) water
60 g (2 oz) onions, finely chopped
⅔ cup (5 fl oz) yoghurt
2 teaspoons chopped fresh parsley

Sprinkle the chicken with 1 teaspoon of salt and 1 teaspoon of paprika. Brown the chicken in the butter, then put the pieces in a pan and add the water and onion. Cover and simmer for 40 minutes, then remove the chicken.

Add the remaining salt and paprika and the yoghurt to the mixture in the pan and heat, stirring constantly, but do not boil. Pour this sauce over the chicken and sprinkle with the parsley.

Ginger Lemon Chicken

Serves 6

1 x 1.5 kg (3 lb) chicken
2 teaspoons salt
4 tablespoons peanut oil
3 slices fresh ginger
1 spring onion (scallion), cut into 4 cm (1 ½ inch) pieces
2 tablespoons soy sauce
2 tablespoons Worcestershire sauce
1 large lemon, thinly sliced and seeds removed
½ cup (4 fl oz) dry white wine
4 tablespoons sugar
12 mushroom caps
1 tablespoon cornflour (cornstarch)
½ cup (4 fl oz) water

Rub the chicken inside and out with the salt. Place the peanut oil in a Dutch oven, and heat over a high temperature for 1 minute. Add the ginger and spring onion and stir fry 1 minute. Remove the ginger and spring onion and reserve. Add the chicken to the Dutch oven and brown on all sides. Reduce heat to low. Add the soy sauce, Worcestershire sauce, lemon, wine, sugar, mushrooms, reserved ginger and spring onion. Simmer, covered, for 20 minutes. Turn the chicken and simmer for a further 25 minutes or until a fork can be inserted with ease.

Remove the chicken to a carving board and slice. Arrange on a serving dish, keeping the mushroom mixture warm. Remove the mushroom caps and lemon slices from the Dutch oven and arrange on the chicken slices. Increase the temperature to medium. Remove and discard the ginger. Mix together the cornflour and water and stir into the pan juices. Cook, stirring, until thickened. Spoon some of the sauce over the chicken and serve the remainder separately.

Baked Mustard Chicken

Serves 4

1 x 1.5 kg (3 lb) chicken, cut into serving pieces
125 g (4 oz) butter
½ cup (4 fl oz) Dijon mustard
¼ teaspoon crushed dried tarragon leaves
1 cup (2 oz) fresh breadcrumbs
¼ cup (1 oz) grated Parmesan cheese
3 tablespoons chopped parsley
pinch of red (cayenne) pepper

Place the chicken in a shallow baking pan. In a small saucepan, mix together the butter, mustard and tarragon. Cook over low heat until the butter is melted. Spoon evenly over the chicken, turning to coat all sides. Set aside. In a small bowl, mix together the breadcrumbs, Parmesan cheese, parsley and pepper. Dredge the chicken, one piece at a time, in the breadcrumb mixture, patting with hands to coat.

Arrange the chicken in a single layer in the same baking pan. Bake, uncovered, at 180°C (350°F/Gas 4) for 30 minutes. Turn the chicken over and bake a further 15 minutes or until the chicken is crisp and a fork can be inserted with ease. Arrange on a serving dish.

Baked Chicken Remoulade

Serves 4

1 x 1.5 kg (3 lb) chicken, cut into serving pieces
1 teaspoon salt
½ cup (4 fl oz) mayonnaise
¼ cup (2 fl oz) prepared mustard
2 teaspoons horseradish
1 teaspoon paprika
½ cup chopped onion
2 medium-sized tomatoes, diced
½ cup (2 ½ oz) sliced black olives

Parsley Rice
½ cup finely chopped parsley
2 cups cooked rice

Place the chicken, skin side up in a baking pan and sprinkle with salt. In a small bowl, mix together the mayonnaise, mustard, horseradish and paprika and spread over the chicken. Bake, uncovered, at 180°C (350°F/Gas 4) for 30 minutes. Drain well. Add the onion, tomatoes and black olives to the chicken. Cover and bake for a further 30 minutes or until a fork can be inserted in the chicken with ease. Serve over Parsley Rice.

Parsley Rice: Mix together the parsley and the rice.

Lemon-Coconut Chicken

Serves 4

30 g (1 oz) butter
125 g (4 oz) flaked coconut
¾ cup finely crushed wheat crackers
1 teaspoon grated lemon peel
½ teaspoon salt
½ teaspoon ginger
2 eggs
1 x 1.5 kg (3 lb) chicken, cut into serving pieces

Place the butter in a shallow baking pan and melt in 190°C (375°F/Gas 5) oven. Remove pan from oven. In a shallow bowl, mix together the coconut, cracker crumbs, lemon peel, salt and ginger. Place the eggs in another shallow bowl and beat with a fork. Dip the chicken, one piece at a time, first in the egg, then in the cracker crumb mixture, dredging to coat.

Arrange chicken in a single layer in the baking pan. Bake for about 1 hour, turning occasionally, until a fork can be inserted in the chicken with ease.

Chicken Andouille

Serves 6

185 g (6 oz) Andouille sausage, diced or pork sausages
1 green pepper (capsicum), diced
1 onion, diced
2 stalks celery, diced
2 tablespoons chicken stock
60 g (2 oz) cornmeal (polenta)
1 day old French bread stick, cubed
3 drops Tabasco sauce
½ teaspoon Worcestershire sauce
1 teaspoon salt
¼ teaspoon pepper
1 teaspoon chopped parsley
½ teaspoon dried oregano
¼ teaspoon dried thyme
60 g (2 oz) margarine
2 eggs, beaten
1 x 1.8 kg (3 ½ lb) chicken, boned or 6 whole chicken breasts, boned

Make the stuffing by placing the sausage, green pepper, onion and celery in a large pan. Sauté lightly. Add the chicken stock and cook, stirring, for about 5 minutes. Remove pan from heat. Mix together cornmeal, bread cubes, Tabasco sauce, Worcestershire sauce, salt, pepper, parsley, oregano, thyme and margarine. Add the sausage-vegetable mixture, then the eggs and mix well. Place the chicken on a flat surface and pound gently with a mallet to form one rectangular piece. If breasts are used, overlap slightly to make one flat piece.

Place the stuffing on top of the chicken and wrap the chicken around to form a loaf. Carefully lift and place the chicken on a sheet of greased aluminium foil. Seal the ends tightly. Bake at 190°C (375°F/Gas 5) for about 40 minutes. Remove from the oven and cool before unwrapping. Brown lightly under the griller (broiler). Slice to serve.

Chicken

Chicken Sweet 'n' Sour

Serves 4

- 60 g (2 oz) butter or margarine
- 2 tablespoons oil
- 1 large onion, chopped
- 1 large carrot, grated
- 1 large green pepper (capsicum), seeded and sliced
- 2 tablespoons soft brown sugar
- 2 tablespoons soy sauce
- 4 tablespoons vinegar
- 1 x 425 g (15 oz) can pineapple pieces, chopped and juice reserved
- 2 tablespoons tomato purée
- 1 kg (2 lb) cooked chicken, diced
- 250 g (8 oz) bean sprouts
- 60 g (2 oz) almonds, toasted

Heat the butter and oil in an ovenproof pan for 2 minutes, add the onion, carrot and green pepper and cook in the oven at 180°C (350°F/Gas 4) for 8 minutes. Stir in the remaining ingredients except the bean sprouts and almonds and cook for a further 10 minutes.

Heat the bean sprouts in a pan for 3 minutes, drain and serve with the chicken, sprinkled with the toasted almonds.

Roasted Plum Chicken

Serves 4

- 1 ¼ cups herb stuffing (*page 262*)
- 1 apple, finely chopped
- ⅓ cup finely chopped celery
- ¾ cup (6 fl oz) hot water
- 60 g (2 oz) margarine, melted
- 2 tablespoons chopped walnuts
- 1 tablespoon finely chopped onion
- 1 x 1.5 kg (3 lb) chicken
- ½ cup (4 fl oz) dry white wine
- ½ cup (5 oz) plum jam
- ¼ cup (2 fl oz) lemon juice
- 1 ½ teaspoons ground ginger
- ½ teaspoon salt
- 2 tablespoons flour

Mix together the stuffing, apple, celery, 5 tablespoons of the water, margarine, walnuts, and onion. Spoon into the cavity of the chicken. Hook the wing tips under the back and tie the legs together. Place the chicken in a large shallow baking pan. Make the plum sauce by mixing together the wine, jam, lemon juice, ginger and salt. Pour the sauce over the chicken, carefully brushing to coat. Bake, uncovered, at 160°C (325°F/Gas 3), basting occasionally, for about 1¾ hours or until the leg moves freely when lifted or twisted. Remove the chicken to a serving dish. Skim the fat from the juices in the pan. Mix the flour and remaining water. Stir until smooth. Add the flour mixture to the contents of the baking pan. Cook, stirring, over medium heat for about 5 minutes or until thick. Serve with chicken.

Hawaiian Chicken Salad

Serves 6

- 4 chicken half-breasts (suprêmes)
- 2 cups (16 fl oz) water
- ½ teaspoon salt
- 3 celery tops
- 250 g (8 oz) medium-sized pasta shells, cooked
- 1 x 250 g (8 oz) can pineapple pieces, drained and juice reserved
- 1 orange, peeled and cut into pieces
- 1 cup julienne carrots
- ½ medium-sized green pepper (capsicum), seeded and thinly sliced
- ⅓ cup diced cheese
- shredded lettuce
- ¼ cup (1 oz) chopped macadamia nuts

Dressing

- ½ cup (4 fl oz) reserved pineapple juice
- salt and pepper
- ¼ cup (2 fl oz) oil

Place the chicken, water, salt and celery tops in a saucepan. Cover and simmer for about 30 minutes or until a fork can be inserted in the chicken with ease. Cool, then separate the meat from the bones. Discard the bones and skin. Cut the chicken into bite-sized pieces and place in a large bowl. Add the drained, cooked pasta, pineapple, orange, carrots, green pepper and cheese. Pour the dressing over and toss gently to mix. Arrange the salad on a bed of lettuce and sprinkle with the macadamia nuts.

Dressing: Mix together all the ingredients and stir until well blended.

Sweet and Spicy Chicken

Serves 4

- ½ teaspoon white pepper
- ½ teaspoon ground ginger
- ½ teaspoon ground cinnamon
- ¼ teaspoon ground cloves
- 1 x 1.5 kg (3 lb) chicken
- ¼ cup (2 fl oz) soy sauce
- 2 tablespoons honey
- ½ cup (5 oz) plum jam
- 2 teaspoons sugar
- 2 teaspoons vinegar
- ¼ cup (3 oz) chutney

Mix together the white pepper, ginger, cinnamon and cloves. Rub the inside of the chicken with half the spice mixture. To the remaining spice mixture, stir in 1 tablespoon of the soy sauce and rub on the outside of the chicken. Refrigerate for 1 hour. Remove the chicken from the refrigerator and place, breast side up, on a rack in a wok, over 5 cm (2 inch) of boiling water. Cover and steam for 1 hour. Remove the chicken to a shallow baking pan. Bake at 180°C (350°F/Gas 4) for about 15 minutes, or until a leg moves freely when lifted or twisted.

Mix the remaining soy sauce and the honey and brush on the chicken. Mix together the jam, sugar, vinegar and chutney and rub on the chicken. Return the chicken to the oven and bake at 230°C (450°F/Gas 8) for about 10 minutes, or until the chicken is brown and a fork can be inserted in the chicken with ease.

Opposite: *Hawaiian Chicken Salad*

201

Chicken

Chicken Divan
Serves 4

1 x 1.5 kg (3 lb) chicken
1 bunch broccoli
4 tablespoons sherry
1 cup (4 oz) grated Parmesan cheese
2 cups (16 fl oz) milk
90 g (3 oz) butter
3 tablespoons flour
¼ teaspoon ground nutmeg
½ cup (4 fl oz) cream
¾ cup (6 fl oz) Hollandaise sauce, warmed (page 39)
½ teaspoon paprika

Steam or roast the chicken. When cool, remove and discard the skin and bones. Slice the chicken into long pieces, as large as possible. Cook the broccoli only until tender-crisp, retaining the bright green colour. Drain and arrange in the bottom of a warm baking dish. Sprinkle with 1 tablespoon of the sherry and ¼ cup (1 oz) of the Parmesan cheese. Place the chicken on the broccoli, first the dark meat and then the white. Sprinkle with 1 tablespoon of the sherry and ¼ cup (1 oz) of the Parmesan cheese. Set aside, keeping the ingredients in the baking dish warm while making the sauce.

Heat the milk to boiling point and keep hot. Make the white sauce by melting the butter over medium heat. Stir in the flour and blend until smooth, about 1 minute. Slowly add the hot milk, stirring until the sauce is thick and smooth, about 2 minutes. Add the nutmeg, set aside and keep warm. Whip the cream and add to the white sauce, stirring gently. Gently stir in the warm Hollandaise sauce. Add the remaining sherry. Pour over the chicken and broccoli and sprinkle with the remaining Parmesan cheese and paprika. Grill (broil) until lightly browned and bubbly, about 2 minutes.

Merry Berry Chicken
Serves 6

½ cup (2 oz) flour
1 teaspoon salt
½ teaspoon garlic salt
1 teaspoon curry powder
6 chicken half-breasts (suprêmes)
90 g (3 oz) butter
¼ cup (2 fl oz) white wine
¼ cup (2 fl oz) lemon juice
1 x 500 g (1 lb) can whole cranberry sauce
1 teaspoon grated lemon peel
3 tablespoons honey

In a plastic bag, mix together the flour, salt, garlic salt and curry powder. Add the chicken breasts one at a time, and shake well to coat. Place the butter in a large pan and melt. Add the chicken and cook for about 10 minutes, turning often, until brown on all sides. Sprinkle the wine and lemon juice over chicken, reduce the heat to low, cover and simmer for about 15 minutes.

Spoon the cranberry sauce over the chicken, then sprinkle with the lemon peel and honey. Cover and simmer a further 15 minutes or until a fork can be inserted in the chicken with ease. Serve over hot rice and pour the pan drippings over.

Sunshine Chicken Pie
Serves 4

1 x 1.5 kg (3 lb) chicken
2 cups (16 fl oz) water (approximately)
3 celery tops
1 tablespoon salt
1 bay leaf
1 cup (8 fl oz) cream
1 cup (4 oz) flour
½ teaspoon Worcestershire sauce
⅛ teaspoon pepper
⅛ teaspoon mace
125 g (4 oz) butter
12 small onions, cooked
1 x 315 g (10 oz) packet frozen peas, cooked, seasoned and buttered

Carrot Scones
1 quantity dry scone dough, without the liquid added (page 458)
½ cup grated carrot
cream

Place the chicken in a deep saucepan. Add the water, celery, salt and bay leaf. Cover and simmer for about 45 minutes or until a fork can be inserted in the chicken with ease. Cool. Strain and reserve the broth. Add water, if needed, to measure 2 cups (16 fl oz) liquid. Separate the meat from the bones. Discard the bones and skin. Cut the chicken into bite-sized pieces and place in a large baking pan or casserole. Mix together the cream, flour, Worcestershire sauce, pepper and mace. Melt the butter over medium heat. Gradually add the reserved flour mixture and reserved 2 cups of chicken broth. Cook, stirring, for about 7 minutes or until the mixture is thick and bubbly. Pour the sauce over the chicken. Top with the onions, then the scones. Bake, uncovered, at 220°C (425°F/Gas 7) for about 20 minutes or until the scones are golden. To serve, place a spoonful of peas in the centre of each scone.

Carrot Scones: Place 2 cups of dry scone dough in a large bowl. Add the grated carrot. Mix well. Add the milk or water (from the scone recipe) and mix until a soft dough forms. Roll out dough to 1.25 cm (½ inch) thickness and cut out with a doughnut cutter dipped in flour. Brush the tops with cream.

Rosemary Chicken Supreme

Serves 6

- 3 tablespoons lemon juice
- 1 teaspoon lemon pepper
- ¼ cup (2 fl oz) plus 2 tablespoons Worcestershire sauce
- 6 chicken half-breasts (suprêmes), skinned
- 1 x 500 g (1 lb) can peeled tomatoes
- 1 x 470 g (15 oz) can chickpeas, drained
- 1 cup thinly sliced carrots
- 1 cup diced onion
- 1 cup diced celery
- 1 cup sliced mushrooms
- 1 teaspoon garlic salt
- 1 teaspoon dried rosemary
- 1 cup (4 oz) flour
- brown rice, cooked

Mix together the lemon juice, lemon pepper and 2 tablespoons of the Worcestershire sauce. Add the chicken, turning to coat, then set aside in the marinade. In a medium bowl, mix together the tomatoes, chickpeas, carrots, onion, celery, mushrooms, garlic salt and remaining Worcestershire sauce. Mix well and sprinkle with the rosemary. Place the flour in an oven cooking bag. Add the vegetable mixture and knead to mix the juice with the flour, holding the bag securely closed. Place the marinated chicken on top of the vegetable mixture in the bag, and secure the opening. Place in a baking pan and cut 6 slits in the bag. Bake at 180°C (350°F/Gas 4) for about 1 hour or until a fork can be inserted in the chicken with ease. Serve over brown rice.

Orange-Avocado Chicken

Serves 8

- 60 g (2 oz) margarine
- 8 chicken half-breasts (suprêmes)
- 1 teaspoon grated orange peel
- 1 cup (8 fl oz) orange juice
- ½ cup chopped onion
- 1 teaspoon salt
- 1 teaspoon paprika
- ½ teaspoon ground ginger
- ½ teaspoon dried tarragon leaves, crushed
- 2 tablespoons cornflour (cornstarch)
- 2 oranges, peeled and sliced crosswise
- 1 avocado, peeled and sliced

Place the margarine in a large pan and melt over medium heat. Add the chicken and cook for about 10 minutes, turning, until brown on all sides. Pour off all but 1 tablespoon of the margarine. Add the orange peel, ½ cup (4 fl oz) of the orange juice, onion, salt, paprika, ginger and tarragon. Reduce heat to low, cover and simmer for about 30 minutes or until a fork can be inserted in the chicken with ease. Remove the chicken to a serving dish and keep warm.

In a small bowl, mix the remaining orange juice and cornflour, stirring until smooth. Add to the pan drippings and cook over a low heat until thickened. Arrange the orange and avocado slices around the chicken. Pour the sauce over.

Chicken St. Basil

Serves 8

- 8 whole chicken breasts, boned and skinned
- 3 tablespoons white wine
- 1 cup (8 oz) cottage cheese
- 8 whole basil leaves
- 2 teaspoons prepared horseradish sauce
- ½ teaspoon dry mustard
- 3 eggs
- 2 tablespoons water
- 2½ cups (5 oz) wholewheat breadcrumbs
- 2 tablespoons finely chopped parsley
- ⅛ teaspoon garlic salt
- ⅛ teaspoon white pepper

Place the chicken in a large shallow dish. Add the wine, cover and set aside. Whip the cottage cheese until smooth. Add the basil, horseradish sauce and dry mustard and continue whipping until smooth and creamy. Set aside. In a shallow bowl, beat the eggs and add the water. In a separate shallow bowl, mix together the breadcrumbs, parsley, garlic salt and pepper. Set aside. Place each chicken breast between 2 pieces of plastic wrap on a hard surface. Using a meat mallet or similar, gently pound the chicken to 20 cm (8 inch) diameter.

Place a heaped tablespoon of basil mixture on each chicken breast. Roll and tuck the chicken to enclose the filling. Secure with toothpicks. Dip each chicken roll, first in the egg mixture, then in the breadcrumb mixture, coating well. Place the chicken in a large non-stick baking pan and bake at 190°C (375°F/Gas 5) for about 20 minutes or until a fork can be inserted in the chicken with ease.

Note: Each chicken roll may be sliced into quarters to make 32 hot hors d'oeuvres.

Pollo Verde Chicken

Serves 4

- ⅓ cup (1½ oz) flour
- ½ teaspoon salt
- ¼ teaspoon pepper
- 4 chicken half-breasts (suprêmes)
- 45 g (1½ oz) butter
- 2 tablespoons cooking oil
- 125 g (4 oz) green chillies, cut into strips
- 125 g (4 oz) cheddar cheese, cut into strips
- 1 x 60 g (2 oz) jar pimientos, drained and cut into strips

Place the flour, salt and pepper in a shallow bowl. Add the chicken, one piece at a time, dredging to coat. Heat the butter and oil over a medium heat until bubbling. Add the chicken, skin side down, and cook for about 10 minutes, turning, until brown on all sides. Remove the chicken from the pan and drain on paper towels. Place the chicken in a shallow baking pan and top with strips of chillies, cheese and pimiento. Bake at 180°C (350°F/Gas 4) for 10 minutes or until a fork can be inserted in the chicken with ease and the cheese is melted.

Chicken

Little Legs Tempura

Makes 20

10 chicken wings
½ cup (4 fl oz) ginger ale
½ cup (2 oz) flour
1 egg, well beaten
1 teaspoon soy sauce
1 teaspoon salt
1 cup (8 fl oz) cooking oil

Remove the tips from each chicken wing. Cut the remainder of the wing into two parts. Mix together the ginger ale, flour, egg, soy sauce and salt very quickly and with as few strokes as possible. Dip each chicken piece in the batter. Place the oil in a large pan and heat to 180°C (350°F). Add the chicken and cook 8 to 10 minutes, turning to brown evenly. Serve hot with sweet and sour sauce or chutney.

Basil-Garlic Chicken Pastries

Serves 4

4 chicken half-breasts, (suprêmes), skinned
220 g (7 oz) butter
1 carrot, cut into 8 cm (3 inch) strips
1 stalk celery, cut into 8 cm (3 inch) strips
1 small onion, cut into 8 wedges
½ teaspoon lemon pepper
½ teaspoon dried basil
¼ teaspoon ground ginger
¾ teaspoon garlic salt
4 filo pastry sheets
parsley sprigs

Basil-Garlic Cream Sauce
60 g (2 oz) butter
½ teaspoon dried basil
1 teaspoon garlic salt
2 tablespoons flour
½ cup (4 fl oz) chicken stock
1 cup (8 fl oz) milk
salt and pepper

On one half of each chicken breast portion, place 1½ teaspoons butter, 1 strip each of the carrot and celery, and 1 onion wedge. Mix together the lemon pepper, basil, ginger and ¼ teaspoon of the garlic salt. Sprinkle evenly over the chicken. Fold the other half of the chicken over the vegetables. Melt the remaining butter and brush on the filo sheets. Place the chicken in the centre at one end of each sheet. Roll and fold each breast in the pastry. Trim any excess and seal the edges. Place, seam side down, in a buttered baking dish and brush with extra melted butter. Bake at 180°C (350°F/Gas 4) for 1 hour or until golden brown. Decorate with parsley sprigs and serve with Basil-Garlic Cream Sauce.

Basil-Garlic Cream Sauce: Melt the butter and add the basil and salt. Blend in the flour to a smooth paste. Add the stock and milk and stir over medium heat until smooth and thickened. Season well.

Little Legs Tempura

Teen's Easy Cheesy Chicken

Serves 4

¼ cup (1 oz) flour
¼ teaspoon salt
¼ teaspoon freshly ground pepper
½ teaspoon dried thyme
½ teaspoon red (cayenne) pepper
4 chicken half-breasts (suprêmes)
2 tablespoons cooking oil
8 thin slices tomato
1 egg, beaten
½ cup (4 fl oz) mayonnaise
1 cup (4 oz) grated cheese
¼ cup chopped onion
½ teaspoon Worcestershire sauce
parsley
tomato wedges

In a plastic bag, mix together the flour, salt, pepper, thyme and red pepper. Add the chicken, one piece at a time, shaking to coat. Place the oil in a 20 cm (8 inch) square baking pan. Arrange the chicken, skin side down, in a single layer. Bake, uncovered, for 30 minutes at 200°C (400°F/Gas 6). Turn the chicken and bake for a further 10 minutes. Place 2 tomato slices on each chicken breast.

In a small bowl, mix together the egg, mayonnaise, cheese, onion and Worcestershire sauce and pour over the chicken. Bake a further 10 minutes or until a fork can be inserted in the chicken with ease and the cheese is bubbly. Garnish with parsley and tomato wedges.

Chicken Rolls

Serves 4

4 chicken half-breasts (suprêmes), skinned
1 x 125 g (2 oz) packet cream cheese
1 teaspoon lemon juice
knob of butter
2 tablespoons chopped onion
1 x 125 g (4 oz) can prawns (shrimp)

2 tablespoons flour
1 cup (4 oz) seasoned breadcrumbs
1 egg
1 tablespoon white wine
½ cup (4 fl oz) cooking oil
lemon slices
parsley

East Coast Sauce
1 egg
¼ teaspoon salt
¼ teaspoon grated lemon peel

½ teaspoon chopped onion
1 cup (8 fl oz) cooking oil
2 tablespoons cream
2 tablespoons cocktail sauce

Pound the chicken to 6 mm (¼ inch) thickness and cut lengthwise to form 8 pieces. In a small bowl, mix together the cream cheese, lemon juice and butter. Stir in the onion. Divide the mixture into 8 portions and spread on the chicken to within 6 mm (¼ inch) of the edges. Chop the prawns into 1.25 cm (½ inch) slices and place on the cream cheese mixture. Roll up the chicken and secure with toothpicks. Place the flour and breadcrumbs on two separate pieces of greaseproof paper. In a shallow bowl, mix together the egg and wine. Dredge the chicken in flour, one piece at a time. Dip the chicken in the egg mixture, then roll in breadcrumbs, coating well.

Heat the oil to medium temperature. Add the chicken and cook about 10 minutes, turning, until brown on all sides. Remove the chicken to a baking pan and bake uncovered at 180°C (350°F/Gas 4) for 20 minutes or until a fork can be inserted in the chicken with ease. Remove the toothpicks. Garnish with the lemon slices and parsley. Serve with East Coast Sauce.

East Coast Sauce: In a blender, place the egg, salt, lemon peel and onion. Blend. Slowly pour in the oil and process until the mixture begins to thicken. Stir in the cream and sauce. Chill.

Chicken Rolls

Chicken

Chicken in Brandy
Serves 6

60 g (2 oz) butter
6 chicken half-breasts (suprêmes)
½ teaspoon salt
½ teaspoon garlic salt
¼ teaspoon onion salt
⅛ teaspoon ground nutmeg
500 g (1 lb) small mushrooms
1 ½ cups sliced zucchini (courgettes)
1 ½ tablespoons lemon juice
1 cup (8 fl oz) cream
2 tablespoons brandy
2 tablespoons sherry

Place half the butter in a large non-stick pan and melt over medium heat. Add the chicken and cook, turning, for about 10 minutes or until brown on all sides. Sprinkle the chicken with the salt, garlic salt, onion salt and nutmeg. Cover and cook for about 10 minutes or until a fork can be inserted in the chicken with ease.

In another large pan place the remaining butter and melt over medium heat. Add the mushrooms, zucchini and lemon juice and sauté for about 10 minutes. Set aside.

Remove the chicken from the pan and keep warm. Pour the cream into the pan drippings and bring to the boil. Add the brandy and sherry and simmer for 2 minutes. Add the mushroom-zucchini mixture to the sauce. Heat and serve over the chicken.

Chicken Lemon Fillet
Serves 4   [M]

4 chicken half-breasts (suprêmes), skinned
1 teaspoon light sesame oil
1 tablespoon dried parsley flakes
½ teaspoon minced garlic
⅛ teaspoon freshly ground fennel seed
1 teaspoon lemon pepper
2 tablespoons chopped onion
¼ teaspoon freshly ground pepper
⅛ teaspoon salt
½ teaspoon fresh lemon juice
1 teaspoon honey
pinch of paprika
lemon wedges
parsley sprigs

Place the chicken in a large shallow microwave dish lined with double-folded plastic wrap. Drizzle the sesame oil over the chicken and sprinkle evenly with the parsley flakes, garlic, fennel, lemon pepper, onion and pepper. Cover loosely with double-folded plastic wrap and microwave on high for 5 minutes. Allow to stand for 4 minutes. If a fork cannot be inserted in the chicken with ease, then return to the oven for additional cooking.

Place the chicken on a large platter. Pour the cooking juice over and sprinkle with salt. Mix together the lemon juice and honey and drizzle over the chicken. Sprinkle with paprika and garnish with lemon wedges and parsley.

Chicken Kiev
Serves 8

125 g (4 oz) butter
2 teaspoons chopped chives
2 teaspoons lemon juice
4 whole chicken breasts, boned
salt and pepper
3 eggs, beaten
¼ cup (2 fl oz) water
1 ½ cups (6 oz) fine dry breadcrumbs
deep-frying oil

Blend together the butter, chives and lemon juice, and chill. Halve the breasts, remove the skin, then cut through the thickest part of each half-breast to form a pocket. Sprinkle with salt and pepper. Place 2 teaspoons of the firm chive-butter into each pocket.

Combine the eggs and water and dip the stuffed chicken breasts into this egg mixture, then roll in breadcrumbs and repeat. Chill for 1 hour. Deep fry in the hot oil at 180°C (350°F) for 10 minutes. Serve immediately.

Carrot-Topped Chicken
Serves 4

4 chicken half-breasts (suprêmes)
¾ teaspoon salt
½ teaspoon pepper
1 ½ cups grated carrot
1 apple, peeled and chopped
¼ teaspoon ground nutmeg
1 tablespoon mayonnaise
1 ½ cups (3 oz) fresh breadcrumbs
15 g (½ oz) margarine, melted
2 tablespoons grated Parmesan cheese
¼ teaspoon paprika
fresh apple rings
carrot strips
chopped parsley

Sprinkle the chicken with ½ teaspoon of the salt and the pepper. Place in a buttered square baking pan. In a medium-sized bowl, mix together the carrots, apple, remaining salt and the nutmeg. Add the mayonnaise and toss well. Spread the carrot mixture over the chicken. Cover with foil and bake at 190°C (375°F/Gas 5) for 25 minutes. Remove from the oven and uncover.

In a small bowl, toss the breadcrumbs with the margarine and spread over the chicken and carrots. Sprinkle with the Parmesan cheese and paprika. Bake uncovered for a further 20 minutes or until a fork can be inserted in the chicken with ease. Garnish with fresh apple rings, carrot strips and chopped parsley.

Nutty Oven-Fried Chicken

Serves 6

½ cup (4 fl oz) buttermilk
2 tablespoons fresh lime juice, rind reserved
1 tablespoon Worcestershire sauce
1 tablespoon soy sauce
1½ teaspoons paprika
½ teaspoon salt
½ teaspoon pepper
¼ teaspoon garlic salt
3 chicken half-breasts (suprêmes), skinned
3 slices whole wheat bread, broken into pieces
45 g (1½ oz) margarine
¾ cup (3 oz) cashews
½ cup (2½ oz) sesame seeds
lime slices

Make the marinade by mixing together the buttermilk, lime juice, Worcestershire sauce, soy sauce, 1 teaspoon of the paprika, salt, pepper and garlic salt. Add the chicken, turning to coat. Set aside.

In a blender, place the bread, margarine and the remaining paprika. Blend, then remove to a shallow dish. In the blender, place the rind from one quarter of the lime, cut into strips, and the cashews. Blend, then add to the bread mixture and stir in the sesame seeds.

Remove the chicken from the marinade, drain and place in the bread mixture, one piece at a time, dredging to coat. Arrange the chicken in a lightly greased shallow baking pan and bake uncovered at 180°C (350°F/Gas 4) for about 30 minutes or until a fork can be inserted in the chicken with ease. Garnish with the lime slices.

Chicken Picante

Serves 6

½ cup (4 fl oz) bottled taco sauce
¼ cup (2 fl oz) Dijon mustard
2 tablespoons fresh lime juice
6 chicken half-breasts (suprêmes)
45 g (1½ oz) butter
½ cup (4 fl oz) yoghurt
1 lime, peeled and sliced into 6 segments, membranes removed

Make the marinade by mixing the taco sauce, mustard and lime juice. Add the chicken, turning to coat. Marinate for at least 30 minutes. Place the butter in a large pan and melt over medium heat until foamy. Remove the chicken from the marinade and place in a pan. Cook for about 10 minutes, turning, until brown on all sides. Add the marinade and cook a further 5 minutes or until a fork can be inserted in the chicken with ease and the marinade is slightly reduced and beginning to glaze.

Remove the chicken to a warmed serving dish. Raise the heat to high and boil the marinade for 1 minute. Pour over the chicken. Place 1 tablespoon of the yoghurt on each piece and top each with a lime segment.

Chicken with Olive Scones

Serves 6

2 tablespoons flour
½ teaspoon salt
⅛ teaspoon pepper
2 whole chicken breasts, skinned, boned and cut into pieces
1 tablespoon cooking oil
¼ cup finely chopped onion
½ cup (4 fl oz) white wine
½ cup (4 fl oz) chicken stock
1 teaspoon crushed dried rosemary
6 large mushrooms, chopped
1 cup (8 fl oz) sour cream

Olive Scones

90 g (3 oz) butter or margarine, melted
¼ cup (1 oz) breadcrumbs
1 teaspoon poppy seeds
2 tablespoons finely chopped green olives
1 cup (4 oz) flour
1 tablespoon sugar
2 teaspoons baking powder
¼ teaspoon salt
⅓ cup (2½ fl oz) milk

Prepare the scone dough as instructed. In a small bowl, mix together the flour, salt and pepper. Sprinkle over the chicken and toss to coat. Heat the oil, then add the chicken and the onion. Cook for about 10 minutes, turning, until the chicken is brown on all sides. Add the wine, chicken stock, rosemary and mushrooms. Cover and simmer for 20 minutes, then remove from the heat and add the sour cream. Pour into a square baking pan, cover with foil and keep warm.

Cut the scone dough into 12 slices. Arrange the scones on top of the chicken and bake, uncovered, at 200°C (400°F/Gas 6) for about 20 minutes or until the scones are brown.

Olive Scones: In a small bowl, mix together one third of the butter, the breadcrumbs, poppy seeds and olives. Set aside. In a medium-sized bowl, mix together the flour, sugar, baking powder and the salt. Add the remaining butter and mix until crumbly. Stir in the milk. Turn onto a lightly floured board and knead until the dough holds together. Roll into a 30 x 40 cm (12 x 16 inch) rectangle. Spread the breadcrumb mixture over the dough and roll up, starting with the long edge. Wrap in greaseproof paper and chill.

Chicken

Vegetable Chicken

Serves 4   M

- 2 cups thinly-sliced fresh vegetables in any combination
- 4 chicken half-breasts (suprêmes)
- 3 tablespoons French mustard
- 3 tablespoons melted butter

Arrange the vegetables in a shallow microwave dish. Cover with plastic wrap and microwave on high for 3 minutes. Dry the chicken with a paper towel. Mix together the mustard and butter and brush on the chicken, covering all sides. Place the chicken on the vegetables with the bony parts towards the centre and the meaty parts towards the outside of the dish. Cover with greaseproof paper and microwave on high for 18 minutes, rotating the dish one half-turn halfway through cooking. Let stand, covered, for 5 minutes. If a fork cannot be inserted in the chicken with ease, return to the microwave, covered, for brief additional cooking.

Chicken Chablis

Serves 4

- 8 chicken half-breasts (suprêmes), skinned
- 1½ teaspoons salt
- ⅛ teaspoon pepper
- ¼ cup (2 fl oz) milk
- 1 egg, beaten
- ½ cup (2 oz) flour
- 2 tablespoons cooking oil
- 15 g (½ oz) butter
- 1 teaspoon garlic salt
- 250 g (8 oz) mushrooms, sliced
- 1 green pepper (capsicum), chopped
- 1 small onion, diced
- ¾ cup (6 fl oz) chicken stock
- 1 cup (8 fl oz) chablis

Place the chicken on a hard surface. Using a meat mallet or similar, gently pound the chicken to 6 mm (¼ inch) thickness. Sprinkle with the salt and pepper. In a small bowl, mix together the milk and egg. Place the flour in a shallow bowl. Dip the chicken, one piece at a time, first in the egg mixture, then in the flour. Repeat to coat well. Place the chicken in a shallow pan and refrigerate for 30 minutes.

Place the oil and butter in a pan and melt over medium heat. Add the chicken and cook for about 10 minutes, turning, until brown on all sides and a fork can be inserted with ease. Remove the chicken from the pan and set aside.

To the pan, add the garlic salt, mushrooms, green pepper and onion. Sauté for about 5 minutes or until tender. Remove and set aside. To the same pan, add the stock and wine and boil for about 10 minutes. Return the chicken to the pan. Spoon the wine mixture over the chicken and top with the vegetable mixture. Heat thoroughly over low heat and serve on buttered noodles.

Opposite: *Vegetable Chicken*

90-Second Chicken

Serves 4

- 2 tablespoons cooking oil
- 3 garlic cloves, peeled and thinly sliced
- 8 thin slices ginger
- 2 teaspoons whole peppercorns
- 4 chicken half-breasts (suprêmes), sliced into 1.25 cm (½ inch) strips
- 250 g (8 oz) sweet potatoes, peeled, thinly sliced and cut into 1.25 cm (½ inch) squares
- ¼ cup frozen baby lima beans
- 2 tablespoons Worcestershire sauce
- 4 tablespoons red wine
- 1 teaspoon cornflour (cornstarch)
- a few drops of Tabasco sauce
- ⅛ teaspoon salt
- ⅛ teaspoon pepper
- ⅓ cup (2 oz) unsalted peanuts
- 6 spring onions (scallions), chopped

Place the cooking oil in a wok or large pan and heat to low. Add the garlic, ginger and peppercorns and stir fry for 90 seconds. Remove these ingredients and discard. Increase the heat to high, add the chicken and stir fry for 90 seconds. Add the sweet potatoes and stir fry a further 90 seconds. Add the lima beans and stir fry another 90 seconds. Add the Worcestershire sauce, red wine, cornflour, Tabasco sauce, salt and pepper, and stir fry for 90 seconds. Add the remaining ingredients, stir to mix and serve.

Chicken Breasts Provençale

Serves 6

- 60 g (2 oz) butter
- 2 tablespoons olive oil
- 6 chicken half-breasts (suprêmes)
- 1 medium-sized onion, finely chopped
- 4 tablespoons flour
- 1½ cups (12 fl oz) chicken stock
- ½ cup (4 fl oz) tomato juice
- ½ cup diced tomatoes
- 1 teaspoon salt
- ¼ teaspoon pepper
- ¼ cup (2 fl oz) sherry
- 2 tablespoons chopped parsley

Place the butter and olive oil in a large pan and heat to medium high. Add the chicken and cook for 10 minutes, turning to brown on both sides. Remove the chicken from the pan, add the onion and stir fry for about 1 minute to brown lightly. Stir in the flour and slowly add the chicken stock. Continue stirring and add the tomato juice and diced tomatoes. Bring to the boil and sprinkle with salt and pepper. Return the chicken to the pan. Add the sherry and parsley, cover and simmer about 30 minutes or until a fork can be inserted with ease.

Chicken

Mustard Chicken

Serves 4

- 8 chicken half-breasts (suprêmes)
- 1 teaspoon seasoned salt
- 30 g (1 oz) butter
- 1 rounded tablespoon dry mustard
- 1/8 teaspoon dried rosemary
- 3/4 cup (4 oz) sliced pitted black olives
- 3/4 cup sliced mushrooms
- 4 shallots, grated
- 2 cups (16 fl oz) white wine

Sprinkle the chicken with the seasoned salt. Place the chicken, butter, mustard, rosemary, olives, mushrooms, shallots and wine in a large pan. Cover and place over a medium high heat. Cook for about 30 minutes. Remove the lid and cook a further 15 minutes or until a fork can be inserted in the chicken with ease and the liquid is reduced.

Chicken Chow Mein

Serves 4

- 500 g (1 lb) Chinese egg noodles
- 5 tablespoons cooking oil
- 1/2 teaspoon salt
- 2 kg (1 lb) chicken half-breasts (suprêmes), cut into 6 x 40 mm (1/4 x 1 1/2 inch) pieces
- 1 teaspoon sherry
- 2 cups sliced mushrooms
- 1 cup sliced bamboo shoots
- 1 cup diagonally sliced Chinese cabbage
- 1 cup sliced water chestnuts
- 1 medium-sized onion, sliced
- 2 stalks celery, diagonally sliced
- 1 green pepper (capsicum), cut into wedges
- 1 cup bean sprouts
- 4 tablespoons cornflour (cornstarch)
- 1 teaspoon ground ginger
- 4 tablespoons soy sauce
- 1/8 teaspoon pepper
- 1 teaspoon sesame oil
- 1 teaspoon oyster sauce
- 1 cup (8 fl oz) chicken stock, warmed

Place the noodles in plenty of boiling salted water. Cook for about 8 minutes, then drain. Place 2 tablespoons of the oil in a wok and heat to medium high. Spread half the noodles in the wok and cook, without stirring, until light brown. Turn the pancake-like noodles and cook the other side until brown, about 3 minutes. Remove and keep warm.

Add 1 tablespoon of the oil to the wok and repeat with the remaining noodles. Add the remaining oil and sprinkle with the salt, add the chicken and sherry, and stir fry. Push the chicken to one side, add the mushrooms, bamboo shoots, Chinese cabbage, water chestnuts, onion, celery and green pepper. Stir fry about 3 minutes. Add the bean sprouts and stir. Mix the cornflour and ginger, stir in the soy sauce and set aside. Sprinkle the chicken with the pepper, sesame oil and oyster sauce. Stir in the chicken stock and bring to the boil. Add the cornflour mixture, stirring. Serve over the noodles.

Cold Lemon Chicken

Serves 6

- 90 g (3 oz) butter
- 6 chicken half-breasts (suprêmes)
- 1/2 cup (4 fl oz) white wine
- 1/3 cup (2 1/2 fl oz) lemon juice
- 1 teaspoon salt
- 1/4 teaspoon pepper
- 1 1/2 cups (12 fl oz) mayonnaise
- 1/4 cup (2 fl oz) lemon juice

Melt the butter in a large pan over medium high heat. Add the chicken and sauté about 10 minutes, turning, until brown on all sides. Add the white wine and cook to reduce the liquid to 1/3 cup (2 1/2 fl oz). Add 1/3 cup lemon juice, the salt and pepper. Remove the chicken to an ovenproof dish and pour over the liquid from the pan. Cover and bake at 180°C (350°F/Gas 4), basting several times, for about 30 minutes or until a fork can be inserted in the chicken with ease. Remove the chicken and reduce the sauce by one half. Pour the sauce over the chicken. Cover and refrigerate overnight.

When ready to serve, mix the mayonnaise and lemon juice and pour over the chicken before serving at cool room temperature.

Pecan Chicken with Dijon Sauce

Serves 4

- 4 chicken half-breasts (suprêmes)
- 125 g (4 oz) butter
- 4 tablespoons Dijon mustard
- 185 g (6 oz) pecans, finely ground
- 2 tablespoons safflower oil
- 2/3 cup (5 fl oz) sour cream
- 1 teaspoon salt
- freshly ground pepper

Place the chicken between two pieces of greaseproof paper. Using a meat mallet or similar, gently pound the chicken to 6 mm (1/4 inch) thickness. Melt 90 g (3 oz) of the butter over medium heat. With a wire whisk, beat in 3 tablespoons of the mustard until well blended. Place the pecans in a shallow dish. Dip the chicken, one piece at a time, first in the butter-mustard mixture, then in the pecans, dredging to coat. Place the remaining butter in a large pan. Add the oil and heat to medium. Add the chicken and sauté for about 3 minutes on each side, or until brown. Remove to a baking pan and bake at 150°C (300°F/Gas 2) for about 15 minutes, or until a fork can be inserted in the chicken with ease. Drain the pan and deglaze with the sour cream. Using a wire whisk, add the remaining mustard, salt and pepper. For each serving, place the chicken over a small portion of the sauce.

Baked Chicken Reuben

Serves 4

- 8 chicken half-breasts (suprêmes)
- ¼ teaspoon salt
- ⅛ teaspoon pepper
- 1 x 500 g (1 lb) can sauerkraut, drained (press out excess liquid)
- 4 slices Swiss cheese, each about 10 x 15 cm (4 x 6 inch)
- 1 ¼ cups (10 fl oz) Thousand Island salad dressing
- 1 tablespoon chopped parsley

Place the chicken in a greased baking pan. Sprinkle with salt and pepper. Place the sauerkraut over the chicken. Top with the Swiss cheese. Pour the dressing evenly over the cheese. Cover with foil and bake at 160°C (325°F/Gas 3) for about 1 ½ hours or until a fork can be inserted in the chicken with ease. Sprinkle with the chopped parsley to serve.

Chicken with Lime Butter

Serves 6

- 6 chicken half-breasts (suprêmes)
- ½ teaspoon salt
- ½ teaspoon pepper
- ⅓ cup (2 ½ fl oz) cooking oil
- juice of 1 lime
- 125 g (4 oz) butter
- ½ teaspoon snipped chives
- ½ teaspoon finely chopped dill weed

Sprinkle the chicken on both sides with the salt and pepper. Place the oil in a large pan and heat to medium. Add the chicken and sauté about 4 minutes or until lightly browned. Turn the chicken, cover and reduce the heat to low. Cook for 10 minutes, or until a fork can be inserted in the chicken with ease. Remove the chicken and keep warm. Drain off the oil and discard.

In the same pan, add the lime juice and cook over low heat until the juice begins to bubble. Add the butter, stirring, until the butter becomes opaque. Stir in the chives and dill. Spoon the sauce over the chicken.

Chicken Ratatouille

Serves 4

- ¼ cup (2 fl oz) corn oil
- 4 chicken half-breasts (suprêmes), cut into 2.5 cm (1 inch) pieces
- 2 small zucchini (courgettes), thinly sliced
- 1 small eggplant (aubergine), peeled and cut into 2.5 cm (1 inch) cubes
- 1 large onion, thinly sliced
- 1 medium-sized green pepper (capsicum), seeded and cut into 2.5 cm (1 inch) pieces
- 250 g (8 oz) mushrooms, sliced
- 1 x 500 g (1 lb) can tomatoes
- 2 teaspoons garlic salt
- 1 teaspoon dried basil, crushed
- 1 teaspoon dried parsley
- ½ teaspoon black pepper

Heat the oil to medium in a large pan. Add the chicken and sauté, stirring, for about 2 minutes. Add the zucchini, eggplant, onion, green pepper and mushrooms. Cook, stirring occasionally, for about 15 minutes or until tender but not soft. Add the tomatoes, stirring carefully. Add the garlic salt, basil, parsley and pepper. Simmer, uncovered, for about 5 minutes or until a fork can be inserted in the chicken with ease. Serve the chicken on a large serving dish with a mound of rice in the centre.

Curried Chicken Rolls

Serves 4

- 4 chicken half-breasts (suprêmes)
- ½ teaspoon salt
- ⅛ teaspoon pepper
- 30 g (1 oz) margarine
- ½ onion, finely chopped
- ¾ cup cooked rice
- ¼ cup (1 oz) raisins
- 1 tablespoon chopped parsley
- 1 teaspoon curry powder
- 1 teaspoon soft brown sugar
- pinch of garlic salt
- 1 tablespoon cooking oil
- ½ cup (4 fl oz) white wine
- 1 chicken stock cube

Using a meat mallet or similar, gently pound the chicken on a hard surface to 1 cm (⅜ inch) thickness. Sprinkle the salt and pepper on the chicken. Melt the margarine in a pan over medium heat. Add the onion and sauté for 3 minutes or until soft. Add the rice, raisins, parsley, curry powder, sugar and garlic salt. Stir until well mixed. Divide the stuffing into 4 portions and place one portion on each piece of chicken. Roll and fasten with toothpicks.

In another pan, heat the oil to medium. Add the chicken rolls and cook for about 15 minutes, turning, until brown on all sides. Add the wine and stock cube. Cover and simmer for 30 minutes or until a fork can be inserted in the chicken with ease.

Chicken

Nugget Chicken

Serves 4

2 cups (16 fl oz) corn oil
1 egg, beaten
⅓ cup (2 ½ fl oz) water
⅓ cup (1 ½ oz) flour
2 teaspoons sesame seeds

Nippy Pineapple Sauce
1 x 375 g (12 oz) jar pineapple jam
¼ cup (2 fl oz) prepared mustard

Dill Sauce
½ cup (4 fl oz) sour cream
½ cup (4 fl oz) mayonnaise
1 teaspoon dried dill

Royalty Sauce
1 cup (8 fl oz) tomato sauce
½ teaspoon dry mustard
1 tablespoon soft brown sugar

1 ½ teaspoons salt
4 chicken half-breasts (suprêmes), cut into 2.5 x 1.25 cm (1 x ½ inch) pieces

¼ cup (2 fl oz) prepared horseradish sauce

2 tablespoons finely chopped dill pickle

2 tablespoons vinegar
125 g (4 oz) margarine

Place the oil in a deep fryer, filling to no more than one third. Heat to medium. Place the egg and water in a large bowl and mix well. Add the flour, sesame seeds and salt, stirring until a smooth batter is formed. Dip the chicken in the batter, draining off the excess. Add the chicken to the hot oil, a few pieces at a time. Fry for about 4 minutes or until golden brown. Drain on paper towels. Serve with the three sauces.

Nippy Pineapple Sauce: Mix together the pineapple jam, mustard and horseradish sauce. Cook over low heat, stirring, for about 5 minutes.

Dill Sauce: Mix together the sour cream, mayonnaise, dill and dill pickle. Let stand at room temperature for about 1 hour, allowing the flavours to blend.

Royalty Sauce: Mix together the tomato sauce, mustard, sugar, vinegar and margarine. Cook over low heat for 5 minutes, stirring constantly.

Chicken Extraordinaire

Serves 6

½ cup (2 oz) flour
6 chicken half-breasts (suprême)
¼ cup (2 fl oz) corn oil
30 g (1 oz) butter
250 g (8 oz) mushrooms, sliced

⅔ cup (5 fl oz) white wine
1 teaspoon salt
¼ teaspoon pepper
6 thick slices French bread stick
6 slices Swiss cheese

Place the flour in a shallow dish. Add the chicken, one piece at a time, dredging to coat. Place the oil in a pan and heat to medium. Add the chicken and cook for about 10 minutes, turning, until brown on all sides. Reduce the heat, cover and simmer about 10 minutes or until a fork can be inserted in the chicken with ease. Remove the chicken and keep warm.

Add the butter to the pan, then the mushrooms and sauté over low heat for about 3 minutes. Push the mushrooms to the side, pour in the wine and stir to loosen any browned bits. Add the salt and pepper. Return the chicken to the pan and simmer, uncovered, for about 10 minutes or until the sauce is slightly thickened. Arrange the slices of bread in a single layer on a baking sheet. Top each with a slice of cheese. Place in a 200°C (400°F/Gas 6) oven until the cheese is melted. Remove to a serving dish and place a chicken piece on top of each slice of bread. Spoon the mushrooms and sauce over the chicken.

Chicken Cordon Bleu

Serves 4

8 chicken half-breasts (suprêmes)
½ teaspoon salt
⅛ teaspoon pepper
8 thin slices Gruyère cheese
8 thin slices prosciutto ham
½ cup (2 oz) flour

½ cup (2 oz) fine breadcrumbs
½ cup (2 oz) grated Parmesan cheese
1 egg, beaten
250 g (8 oz) butter
lemon wedges

Using a meat mallet or similar, gently pound each chicken half-breast to 6 mm (¼ inch) thickness. Sprinkle with the salt and pepper. On each half-breast, place 1 slice of Gruyère cheese and 1 slice of prosciutto ham. Roll the chicken, tucking in the sides to secure the cheese and ham. Tie at three intervals with cotton thread or string (toothpicks may be used but are not as effective).

Mix together the flour, breadcrumbs and Parmesan cheese. Dip each chicken roll, one at a time, first in the egg, then in the flour mixture, dredging to coat on all sides. Place the butter in a large pan and melt over medium heat. Add the chicken and cook, turning, for about 20 minutes or until a fork can be inserted in the chicken with ease. Serve hot with lemon wedges.

Chicken Scaloppine

Serves 4

½ cup (4 fl oz) cooking oil
60 g (2 oz) margarine
500 g (1 lb) mushrooms, sliced
4 spring onions (scallions), sliced
1 garlic clove, crushed
4 tablespoons grated Parmesan cheese
4 tablespoons flour
2 whole chicken breasts, halved, boned and quartered
1 x 250 g (8 oz) can peeled tomatoes
⅛ teaspoon chilli powder
3 tablespoons chopped parsley
1 teaspoon salt
¼ teaspoon pepper
⅛ teaspoon dried thyme
1 cup (8 fl oz) white wine

Place the oil and margarine in a large pan and heat to medium. Add the mushrooms, spring onions and garlic and cook, stirring occasionally, for about 5 minutes. Remove from the pan and reserve. Mix together the Parmesan cheese and flour. Add the chicken, dredging to coat. In the same pan place the chicken and cook for about 5 minutes or until opaque. Remove the chicken and set aside.

Drain the oil and drippings from the pan and discard. Return the mushroom mixture to the pan and add the tomatoes, chilli powder, parsley, salt, pepper and thyme. Stir well. Simmer over medium heat for 5 minutes. Add the chicken and simmer a further 10 minutes or until a fork can be inserted in the chicken with ease. Add the wine during the last few minutes of cooking and stir well. Serve with hot buttered noodles sprinkled with Parmesan cheese and chopped fresh parsley.

Chicken Breasts in Tarragon Cream

Serves 6

12 chicken half-breasts (suprêmes)
water
¼ cup (2 fl oz) white wine
2 tablespoons chopped tarragon
salt and pepper
1 cup (8 fl oz) mayonnaise
¼ cup (2 fl oz) cream, lightly whipped
sliced cucumber
lemon half slices

Put the chicken breasts into a baking dish and cover with water. Add the wine, 1 tablespoon tarragon and salt and pepper. Cover with foil and bake at 180°C (350°F/Gas 4) for 30 minutes until cooked and tender. Cool.

Mix together the mayonnaise, cream and remaining tarragon and season. Arrange the chicken breasts on a serving dish. Coat with tarragon cream and garnish with half slices of cucumber and lemon. Serve chilled.

Chicken Portuguese

Serves 4

2 tablespoons olive oil
1 x 1.5 kg (3 lb) chicken, cut into serving pieces
2½ cups (20 fl oz) water
1 cup (6 oz) rice
1 teaspoon salt
¾ teaspoon pepper
4 tomatoes, quartered
2 green peppers (capsicums), cut into 2.5 cm (1 inch) squares
1 large onion, chopped
1 cup sliced mushrooms
½ cup (2 ½ oz) pitted, chopped green olives
1 garlic clove, crushed
¾ cup (6 fl oz) dry white wine
¾ cup (6 fl oz) buttermilk

Place the oil in an ovenproof pan and heat to medium. Add the chicken and cook for about 10 minutes, turning, until brown on all sides. Remove the chicken and drain the oil. In the same pan place the water and rice and stir. Arrange the browned chicken over the rice. Cover and bake at 190°C (375°F/Gas 5) for about 45 minutes or until the liquid is absorbed. Remove the chicken and set aside. Stir in the salt and pepper.

Arrange the tomatoes, green peppers, onion, mushrooms, olives and garlic over the rice. Place the chicken over the vegetables. Bake, uncovered, at 200°C (400°F/Gas 6) for 10 minutes, or until a fork can be inserted in the chicken with ease. Remove the chicken again and add the wine and buttermilk. Mix lightly. Place the chicken on top of the rice and vegetables.

Country Club Chicken

Serves 4

60 g (2 oz) margarine
4 chicken half-breasts (suprêmes)
¼ teaspoon salt
¼ teaspoon pepper
1 sheet frozen puff pastry, thawed
4 slices mozzarella cheese
1 x 315 g (10 oz) packet frozen chopped spinach, cooked and well drained
1 teaspoon onion salt
½ teaspoon lemon pepper
1 x 125 g (4 oz) can sliced mushrooms, drained
½ teaspoon paprika

Place the margarine in a pan and melt over medium heat. Add the chicken and cook for about 10 minutes, turning, until brown on all sides. Sprinkle with the salt and pepper. On a floured board gently unfold the pastry and roll out to approximately 30 x 37 cm (12 x 15 inch). Divide into quarters.

Place a slice of cheese on each pastry quarter, then place a chicken breast on the diagonal. Top the chicken with one quarter of the spinach, then with the onion salt, lemon pepper and mushrooms. Roll the pastry around the assembled ingredients to form a neat parcel. Pinch to seal the edges. Sprinkle with the paprika. Bake at 180°C (350°F/Gas 4) for about 25 minutes or until a fork can be inserted in the chicken with ease.

Chicken

Chicken Zucchini Parmesan

Serves 4

- 6 tablespoons olive oil
- 1 medium-sized onion, diced
- 2 garlic cloves, crushed
- 2 x 315 g (10 oz) cans peeled tomatoes
- 1 ¼ teaspoons salt
- ¼ teaspoon pepper
- ⅛ teaspoon dried oregano
- 1 egg, beaten
- ¼ cup (1 oz) dry breadcrumbs
- ½ cup (2 oz) grated Parmesan cheese
- 4 chicken half-breasts (suprêmes)
- 250 g (8 oz) sliced mozzarella cheese
- 500 g (1 lb) zucchini (courgettes), sliced

Heat 3 tablespoons of the olive oil to medium. Add the onion and garlic and cook about 5 minutes or until the onion is transparent. Add the peeled tomatoes, salt, pepper and oregano. Stir. Cover and simmer over low heat, stirring occasionally, for 30 minutes. Place the egg in a shallow dish. Mix together the breadcrumbs and half the Parmesan cheese. Dip the chicken in the egg, then in the breadcrumb mixture, one piece at a time, turning to coat. Place the remaining oil in a large pan and heat to medium. Add the chicken and cook for about 8 minutes, turning, until brown on both sides.

Place the chicken in a large shallow baking pan. Spread with half the tomato sauce, then with half the mozzarella cheese. Arrange the zucchini over. Spread with the remaining tomato sauce, then the remaining mozzarella cheese. Sprinkle with the remaining Parmesan cheese. Bake, uncovered, at 190°C (375°F/Gas 5) for 30 minutes.

Chicken Maçedoine

Serves 4

- 60 g (2 oz) butter
- 1 medium-sized onion, chopped
- 1 x 1.5 kg (3 lb) chicken, cut into serving pieces
- 1 medium-sized green pepper (capsicum)
- 3 carrots, chopped
- 2 fresh tomatoes, peeled and diced
- 1 ½ cups (12 fl oz) chicken stock
- ½ teaspoon paprika
- ½ teaspoon pepper
- 1 tablespoon flour
- ¼ cup (2 fl oz) sour cream

Melt the butter in a large pan over medium heat. Add the onion and sauté until tender. Set aside. Add the chicken to the pan and cook for about 10 minutes, turning, until brown on all sides. Return the onion to the pan and add the green pepper, carrots, tomatoes, chicken stock, paprika and pepper. Bring to the boil. Cover and simmer for about 25 minutes or until a fork can be inserted in the chicken with ease.

Mix together the flour and sour cream and stir into the chicken mixture. Serve over rice.

Tahitian Chicken

Serves 4 - 6

- 1 egg, well beaten
- ½ cup (2 oz) cornflour (cornstarch)
- 4 chicken half-breasts (suprêmes), cut into bite-sized pieces
- 3 tablespoons cooking oil
- 1 x 440 g (14 oz) can pineapple pieces, drained and syrup reserved
- ⅓ cup (3 oz) sugar
- ⅓ cup (2 ½ fl oz) cider vinegar
- 2 tablespoons soy sauce
- ¼ teaspoon ground ginger
- ¾ cup thinly sliced carrots
- 1 medium-sized green pepper (capsicum), cut into 2.5 cm (1 inch) squares
- 2 tablespoons cold water
- ½ cup (2 oz) slivered almonds, toasted
- 4 cups hot cooked rice
- 1 tablespoon chopped parsley

Place the egg in a small bowl. Place half the cornflour in another small bowl. Coat the chicken, a few pieces at a time, first in the egg and then in the cornflour. Place the oil in a pan and heat to medium. Add the chicken and cook for about 7 minutes, turning, until brown. Remove the chicken and drain on paper towels. Reserve the pan drippings. Add water to the reserved pineapple syrup to make 1 cup (8 fl oz) of liquid and add to the reserved drippings in the pan. Stir in the sugar, vinegar, soy sauce and ginger. Bring to the boil and cook, stirring, until the sugar is dissolved. Add the carrots and green pepper, cover and simmer for about 5 minutes or until the carrots are tender-crisp.

Stir the remaining cornflour into the water until smooth and add to the pan. Cook, stirring constantly, until the mixture boils and becomes thick; continue for 1 minute. Add the chicken, pineapple pieces and almonds and cook, stirring, until hot.

Mix together the rice and parsley. Pack into an oiled mould. Immediately invert onto a warm serving dish. Spoon the chicken around the rice.

Baked Chilli Chicken

Serves 4

- 4 chicken half-breasts (suprêmes)
- 1 ½ cups (12 fl oz) condensed tomato soup
- 250 g (4 oz) mild green chillies, diced
- 60 g (2 oz) cream cheese, whipped
- 2 drops of Tabasco sauce

Place the chicken, skin side up, in a single layer in a shallow baking pan. Mix together the soup, chillies, cream cheese and Tabasco sauce. Spread evenly over the chicken. Bake, uncovered, at 190°C (375°F/Gas 5) for about 1 hour or until a fork can be inserted in the chicken with ease.

Puffed Ricotta Chicken

Serves 4

- 4 chicken half-breasts (suprêmes)
- ½ teaspoon salt
- ¼ teaspoon white pepper
- 60 g (2 oz) butter
- ½ cup (4 oz) ricotta cheese
- ¼ cup (2 fl oz) orange juice
- 2 teaspoons grated orange rind
- ½ teaspoon dried rosemary
- 1 sheet frozen puff pastry, thawed
- 1 egg, beaten

Sprinkle the chicken with the salt and pepper. Place the butter in a pan and melt over medium heat. Add the chicken and cook for about 3 minutes on each side or until a fork can be inserted in the chicken with ease. Mix together the ricotta cheese, orange juice, orange peel and rosemary.

On a lightly floured board unfold the pastry sheet. Cut into 4 equal squares. Roll out each square large enough to enclose the chicken half-breast. Place a piece of chicken on each pastry square and spread each with one quarter of the cheese mixture. Carefully wrap the pastry around the chicken. Pinch the edges to seal. Place on an ungreased baking sheet and brush with the egg. Bake at 180°C (350°F/Gas 4) for about 20 minutes or until golden brown.

Chicken Tamale

Serves 4

- ⅓ cup (2 ½ fl oz) cooking oil
- 4 chicken half-breasts (suprêmes), cut into 2.5 cm (1 inch) cubes
- 1 medium-sized onion, diced
- 1 x 500 g (1 lb) can peeled tomatoes
- 1 cup (4 oz) yellow cornmeal (polenta)
- 1 x 250 g (8 oz) can corn kernels, undrained
- 1 small green pepper (capsicum), chopped
- ½ cup chopped celery
- 2 eggs
- 1 ½ teaspoons salt
- 1 teaspoon chilli powder
- ½ cup (2 oz) grated cheese
- ½ cup (2 ½ oz) pitted ripe olives

Place the oil in a large pan and heat to medium. Add the chicken and cook for about 8 minutes or until brown. Push the chicken to one side. Add the onion and sauté for about 3 minutes or until clear. Add the tomatoes and heat. Gradually add the cornmeal and cook, stirring, for about 10 minutes. Remove from the heat.

Add the corn, green pepper, celery, eggs, salt and chilli powder. Mix well. Pour into a greased loaf pan. Sprinkle with the cheese. Arrange the olives evenly over the top. Bake, uncovered, at 180°C (350°F/Gas 4) for about 50 minutes.

Chicken Deluxe

Serves 4

- 2 tablespoons cooking oil
- 1 tablespoon lemon juice
- 6 chicken half-breasts (suprêmes)
- 2 tablespoons teriyaki sauce
- 2 tablespoons soy sauce
- 2 teaspoons lemon pepper
- 1 teaspoon freshly ground pepper
- ¼ teaspoon garlic salt
- ½ cup (5 oz) honey
- 3 medium-sized onions, cut into 6 mm (¼ inch) wedges
- 1 x 500 g (16 oz) packet whole frozen okra
- ¾ cup (6 fl oz) condensed mushroom soup
- 4 medium-sized tomatoes, cut into 6 mm (¼ inch) wedges
- 3 medium-sized green peppers (capsicums), cut into 2 cm (¾ inch) squares

Place 1 tablespoon of the cooking oil and the lemon juice in a pan with a lid. Add the chicken, turning to coat. Heat to medium, then cover and simmer for 20 minutes. Add the teriyaki sauce, soy sauce, lemon pepper, ground pepper and garlic salt. Stir well. Cover and cook, stirring occasionally, a further 10 minutes or until a fork can be inserted in the chicken with ease. Remove the pan from the heat and stir in the honey.

Place the remaining cooking oil in a separate pan and heat to medium. Add the onions and sauté for 5 minutes. Add the okra and mushroom soup, stirring, and simmer for 10 minutes. Add to the chicken. Stir in the tomatoes and green peppers. Bring to the boil over medium heat. Cook for a further 2 minutes or until the mixture is hot. Serve with hot cooked rice.

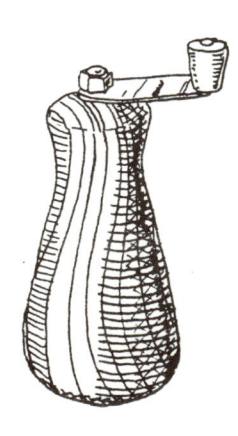

Chicken

Chicken Escalope

Serves 4

4 chicken half-breasts (suprêmes)
2 tablespoons plus 1 teaspoon lemon juice
½ teaspoon salt
pinch of white pepper
125 g (4 oz) butter
125 g (4 oz) mushrooms, sliced
2 small shallots, minced
2 tablespoons flour
1 cup (8 fl oz) dry white wine
1 cup (8 fl oz) chicken stock
1 teaspoon dried tarragon
1 teaspoon dried thyme
1 cup (8 fl oz) cream

Place the chicken on a hard surface and, using a meat mallet or similar, gently pound to 6 mm (¼ inch) thickness. Rub with 1 teaspoon of the lemon juice and sprinkle with the salt and pepper. Place one third of the butter in a pan and melt over medium heat. Add the chicken and cook for about 3 minutes or until firm and opaque and a fork can be inserted in the chicken with ease. Remove to a heated serving dish, cover, and keep warm.

In the same pan add another one third of the butter to the drippings and melt. Add the mushrooms, shallots and remaining lemon juice. Cook for about 2 minutes or until tender. Spoon the mushrooms and shallots over the chicken.

Make the sauce in the same pan by adding the remaining butter. Melt over medium heat. Add the flour, stirring, until absorbed. Stir in the wine, chicken stock, tarragon and thyme and cook, stirring, until the mixture boils and becomes thick. Simmer, uncovered, over low heat for about 9 minutes. Gradually stir in the cream and cook until the sauce reduces to about 1 ½ cups (12 fl oz). Pour the sauce over the chicken and serve.

Indian Chicken Savouries

Makes 36

1 tablespoon Dijon mustard
2 tablespoons cream sherry
½ cup (2 oz) cornflour (cornstarch)
4 egg whites, slightly beaten
4 chicken half-breasts (suprêmes), cut into 2.5 cm (1 inch) cubes
2 cups (8 oz) finely chopped dry-roasted peanuts
3 cups (24 fl oz) corn oil
2 cups (16 fl oz) yoghurt
2 tablespoons lemon juice
2 tablespoons curry powder

Mix the mustard, sherry, cornflour and egg whites. Coat the chicken cubes with the batter and roll in the chopped peanuts. Heat the corn oil in a deep fryer or heavy saucepan to 190°C (375°F). Add the chicken in small amounts and cook for 2 to 3 minutes or until golden brown and a fork can be inserted with ease. Drain on a paper towel. Mix together the yoghurt, lemon juice and curry powder to make a smooth dip.

Savoury Chicken and Squash

Serves 4

2 tablespoons cornflour (cornstarch)
1 teaspoon salt
¼ teaspoon lemon pepper
4 chicken half-breasts (suprêmes), cut into 2.5 cm (1 inch) pieces
60 g (2 oz) butter
2 small zucchini (courgettes), cut into 5 cm (2 inch) pieces
2 small yellow squash, cut into 5 cm (2 inch) pieces
1 cup (8 oz) ricotta cheese
1 cup (8 fl oz) condensed chicken soup
¼ cup (2 fl oz) sherry

Onion, Cheddar, Poppy Seed Crumbs

60 g (2 oz) butter
3 tablespoons dried onion flakes
1 cup crushed cheese biscuits
¼ teaspoon paprika
¼ teaspoon poppy seeds

Mix together the cornflour, salt and lemon pepper. Add the chicken, a few pieces at a time, dredging to coat. Place the butter in a large pan and melt over medium heat. Add the chicken, zucchini and yellow squash and cook for about 10 minutes or until a fork can be inserted in the chicken with ease. Place the ricotta cheese, soup and sherry in a blender and purée. Add to the pan. Cook, stirring constantly, over low heat for about 10 minutes or until thick. Sprinkle with the crumbs.

Onion, Cheddar, Poppy Seed Crumbs: Place the butter in a small pan and melt over medium heat. Add the onion flakes and cheese biscuit crumbs. Sauté for 5 minutes. Stir in the paprika and poppy seeds.

Brown Baked Chicken

Serves 2

3 tablespoons chilli sauce
2 tablespoons soy sauce
1 tablespoon olive oil
½ teaspoon spicy brown mustard
4 chicken pieces

Mix together the chilli sauce, soy sauce, olive oil and spicy brown mustard. Place the chicken in the mixture, one piece at a time, turning to coat on all sides. Arrange the chicken in a single layer in a shallow baking pan. Bake at 180°C (350°F/Gas 4) for about 45 minutes or until a fork can be inserted in the chicken with ease.

Spiced Chicken Microwave

Serves 4 [M]

- 4 chicken half-breasts (suprêmes), cut into bite-sized pieces
- ¼ cup (2 fl oz) cooking oil
- 1 teaspoon microwave browning sauce
- ¼ cup (1 oz) flour
- 1 cup (8 fl oz) water
- ¼ cup diced onion
- 2 teaspoons dried parsley
- 1 teaspoon salt
- 1 teaspoon cinnamon
- ½ teaspoon minced garlic
- ¼ teaspoon ground cloves
- ⅛ teaspoon freshly ground pepper

Mix together the chicken, oil and browning sauce in a large, shallow glass baking dish, taking care the chicken is well coated. Cover with greaseproof paper. Microwave on high for 1½ minutes. Stir and continue to microwave a further 2½ minutes. Set aside, covered. Place the flour in a small bowl. Gradually add the water, stirring until smooth. Add the onion, parsley, salt, cinnamon, garlic, cloves and pepper. Stir to mix well. Pour over the chicken and mix. Microwave, stirring every 2 minutes, for 6 minutes. Remove from oven and let stand, covered, for about 5 minutes. Return to the oven for additional cooking if a fork cannot be inserted in the chicken with ease. Serve on hot fluffy rice.

If available, use a microwave browning dish. Preheat the dish, without the lid, in the microwave oven on high for 6 minutes. Mix together the chicken, oil, browning sauce and place in the heated dish without removing it from the oven. Proceed as above.

Chicken Marengo

Serves 4

- 4 tablespoons olive oil
- 1 x 1.5 kg (3 lb) chicken, cut into serving pieces
- 1 cup finely chopped onions
- 1 garlic clove, quartered
- ½ cup (4 fl oz) white wine
- 1 teaspoon salt
- ¼ teaspoon pepper
- 1 x 440 g (14 oz) can tomatoes
- 1 cup sliced mushrooms
- 2 tablespoons chopped parsley
- 1 bay leaf
- ⅛ teaspoon dried thyme

Place the oil in a deep pan or Dutch oven, and heat to medium high. Add the chicken and cook until brown, about 20 minutes. Move the chicken to one side of the pan. Add the onion and garlic and stir fry until golden brown, about 5 minutes. Add the wine and cook, stirring, for about 5 minutes. Sprinkle the chicken with the salt and pepper. Add the tomatoes, mushrooms, parsley, bay leaf and thyme. Reduce the heat to low, cover and cook for about 20 minutes. Remove the lid and cook a further 10 minutes or until the sauce is thickened and a fork can be inserted in the chicken with ease.

Chicken Pizza

Serves 4

- 1 sheet ready-rolled frozen pastry, thawed
- ¼ cup (2 fl oz) cooking oil
- 4 chicken half-breasts (suprêmes), cut into 2.5 cm (1 inch) pieces
- 1 large onion, sliced into thin rings
- 1 large green pepper (capsicum), seeded and sliced into thin rings
- 250 g (8 oz) mushrooms, sliced
- ½ cup (2 ½ oz) sliced pitted ripe olives
- 1 x 250 g (8 oz) can tomato paste
- ½ cup (2 oz) grated cheese
- 1 teaspoon garlic salt
- 1 teaspoon dried oregano
- ¼ cup (1 oz) grated Parmesan cheese
- 2 cups (8 oz) grated mozzarella cheese

Press the pastry into a lightly oiled 30 cm (12 inch) pizza pan. Place the oil in a pan and heat to medium. Add the chicken, onion, green pepper, mushrooms and olives and cook, stirring, for about 5 minutes or until a fork can be inserted in the chicken with ease.

Spread the tomato paste and cheese over the crust. Spoon the chicken mixture evenly over the sauce. Sprinkle the garlic salt, oregano and Parmesan cheese over. Top with the mozzarella cheese. Bake, uncovered, at 220°C (425°F/Gas 7) for 20 minutes or until the crust is done. Cut into wedges to serve.

Chicken Licken Rice

Serves 4

- 30 g (1 oz) margarine
- 1 small onion, chopped or 4 spring onions (scallion), chopped
- 2 stalks celery, chopped
- 1 x 315 g (10 oz) can cream of celery soup
- 1 cup (8 fl oz) milk
- 3 cups cooked rice
- 2 cups cooked diced chicken
- 4 hard-boiled eggs, sliced
- salt and pepper
- 1 tablespoon chopped fresh parsley
- ¼ cup (1 oz) dried breadcrumbs
- ½ cup (2 oz) grated cheese
- extra 30 g (1 oz) margarine

Heat the margarine and sauté the onion and celery until tender. Add the celery soup, milk, rice, chicken, eggs, salt, pepper and parsley. Spoon the rice mixture into a greased ovenproof dish. Combine the breadcrumbs and cheese, sprinkle over the rice, top with knobs of margarine and bake in a 180°C (350°F/Gas 4) oven for about 25 minutes.

Chicken

Chicken-Topped Eggplant Boats
Serves 6

3 small eggplants (aubergines)
250 g (8 oz) butter
1 medium-sized green pepper (capsicum), diced
12 spring onions (scallions), finely chopped
½ cup chopped parsley
3 garlic cloves, crushed
½ teaspoon dried thyme
2 bay leaves
2 cups cooked rice
1 teaspoon salt
½ teaspoon pepper
½ teaspoon Tabasco sauce
250 g (8 oz) fetta cheese, drained and crumbled
3 eggs, beaten
1 ½ cups (6 oz) breadcrumbs
½ teaspoon red (cayenne) pepper
1 teaspoon garlic salt
6 chicken thighs, skinned, boned and flattened

Place the eggplants in a large saucepan and boil for 15 minutes. Drain, cool and cut in half lengthwise. Scoop out the centres and reserve, leaving 1.25 cm (½ inch) shells. Drain the inverted shells on paper towels. Dice the reserved eggplant centres and drain. Place half the butter in a Dutch oven and melt over medium heat. Add the green pepper, spring onions, parsley, garlic, thyme and bay leaves. Sauté until tender, about 5 minutes. Remove the bay leaves, add the rice and cook a further 10 minutes. Remove from the heat, then add the salt, pepper, Tabasco sauce, fetta cheese and diced eggplant. Add the eggs and stir to mix. Fill the eggplant shells with the vegetable mixture, piling higher in the centre.

In a shallow dish, mix together the breadcrumbs, red pepper and garlic salt. Melt the remaining butter and dip the chicken thighs first in the butter, then in the breadcrumb mixture. Place 1 thigh on top of each eggplant half and sprinkle with any remaining breadcrumbs. Bake at 180°C (350°F/Gas 4) for about 45 minutes or until a fork can be inserted in the chicken with ease.

Tasty Chicken Thighs
Serves 4

½ cup (4 fl oz) Italian salad dressing
8 chicken thighs
2 cups (2 oz) crushed cornflakes
2 tablespoons grated Parmesan cheese
½ teaspoon salt
⅛ teaspoon pepper

Pour the Italian salad dressing over the chicken and marinate, turning frequently, for about 1 hour at room temperature. Mix together the cornflake crumbs, Parmesan cheese, salt and pepper. Place the chicken, one piece at a time, in the crumb mixture and turn to coat evenly. Place the chicken in a lightly oiled shallow baking pan. Bake, uncovered, at 200°C (400°F/Gas 6) for about 1 hour or until a fork can be inserted in the chicken with ease.

Chicken Asparagus Casserole
Serves 4

⅛ teaspoon pepper
4 chicken half-breasts (suprêmes), cut into 2 x 10 cm (¾ x 4 inch) strips
¼ cup (2 fl oz) corn oil
1 x 315 g (10 oz) packet frozen asparagus
1 ¼ cups (10 fl oz) condensed cream of chicken soup
⅓ cup (2 ½ fl oz) mayonnaise
1 teaspoon lemon juice
½ teaspoon curry powder
¼ cup (1 oz) grated cheese

Sprinkle the pepper on the chicken. Place the oil in a pan and heat to medium. Add the chicken and cook for about 5 minutes, turning, until the chicken is brown. Partially cook the asparagus for about 4 minutes, following the directions on the packet. Drain. Mix together the soup, mayonnaise, lemon juice and curry powder.

Place the asparagus in a single layer in a large shallow baking pan. Place the chicken over the asparagus. Spoon the soup mixture over and sprinkle the cheese on top. Cover with foil and bake at 190°C (375°F/Gas 5) for about 30 minutes or until a fork can be inserted in the chicken with ease and the sauce is bubbly.

South-of-the-Border Baked Chicken
Serves 4

4 eggs
¾ cup (6 fl oz) bottled taco sauce
3 cups (12 oz) fine breadcrumbs
1 garlic clove, crushed
¼ teaspoon salt
2 teaspoons chilli powder
1 teaspoon ground cumin
½ teaspoon dried oregano
1 cup (4 oz) flour
4 chicken drumsticks
4 chicken thighs
125 g (4 oz) margarine
½ head of lettuce, shredded
12 cherry tomatoes
12 large black olives

In a shallow bowl, mix together the eggs and taco sauce. Set aside. In a separate bowl, mix together the breadcrumbs, garlic, salt, chilli powder, cumin and oregano. Set aside. Place the flour in another bowl. Dip the chicken, one piece at a time, first in the flour, then in the egg mixture and then in the breadcrumbs, dredging to coat. Dip each piece again, first in the egg mixture, then in the breadcrumbs.

Place the margarine in a shallow baking pan and melt. Add the chicken and turn to coat in the margarine. Place the chicken in the oven and bake at 190°C (375°F/Gas 5) for 45 minutes or until a fork can be inserted in the chicken with ease. Place the chicken on a heated platter and surround with the shredded lettuce, cherry tomatoes and black olives.

Yummy Chicken Balls

Serves 5

¾ cup (5 oz) rice
60 g (2 oz) butter
6 spring onions (scallions), sliced
1 red pepper (capsicum), diced
1 garlic clove, crushed
2 tablespoons flour
½ cup (4 fl oz) wine
½ cup (4 fl oz) milk

2 chicken stock cubes, crumbled
1 cup (4 oz) grated Australian cheese
1 cooked chicken, flesh finely diced
2 tablespoons dried tarragon leaves
2 tablespoons chopped parsley

Coating

½ cup (2 oz) seasoned flour
2 eggs beaten with ¼ cup (2 fl oz) milk

1 cup (4 oz) dry breadcrumbs
ghee for frying

Cook the rice in boiling salted water then drain well. Melt the butter in a saucepan and fry the spring onions, red pepper and garlic for 3 minutes. Stir in the flour and cook for 1 minute. Add the wine gradually, then the milk, stock cubes, cheese, chicken, rice, tarragon and parsley. Chill until firm enough to handle. Roll into balls 5 cm (2 inch) in diameter.

Coating: Coat the balls in the flour, egg-milk mixture, then the breadcrumbs. Press the crumbs on firmly and refrigerate, preferably overnight. Melt the ghee and deep fry 3 or 4 chicken balls at a time until golden brown. Remove, drain and place in oven at 180°C (350°F/Gas 4) for 10 minutes. Serve with carrots, broccoli and potato.

Chicken and Brussels Sprouts Casserole

Serves 6

1 kg (2 lb) chicken pieces
½ teaspoon salt
½ teaspoon pepper
1½ teaspoons paprika
125 g (4 oz) butter
250 g (8 oz) mushrooms, halved

2 tablespoons flour
⅔ cup (5 fl oz) chicken stock
3 tablespoons sherry
500 g (1 lb) Brussels sprouts, blanched

Sprinkle the chicken with salt, pepper and paprika. Place half the butter in a pan and melt over medium heat. Add the chicken and cook for about 10 minutes, turning, until brown on all sides. Remove the chicken and place in a large shallow baking pan. Place the remaining butter in the pan, add the mushrooms and sauté for about 5 minutes. Sprinkle with the flour, stir in the chicken broth and sherry. Cook a further 5 minutes or until thickened.
Arrange the Brussels sprouts among the chicken pieces. Pour the mushroom mixture over. Cover and bake at 190°C (375°F/Gas 5) for about 50 minutes or until a fork can be inserted in the chicken with ease.

Chicken Salad Drumsticks

Serves 4

½ cup (2 oz) flour
2 teaspoons salt
½ teaspoon pepper
1 tablespoon onion salt
8 chicken drumsticks
250 g (8 oz) vegetable shortening

8 frozen uncooked dinner rolls
2 cups coleslaw
2 tablespoons melted butter
2 tablespoons sesame seeds

In a plastic bag, mix together the flour, salt, pepper and onion salt. Add the chicken, two pieces at a time, shaking to coat. Place the shortening in a pan and melt over medium heat. Add the chicken and cook, uncovered, turning occasionally, for about 35 minutes or until a fork can be inserted with ease. Remove from the heat and drain on paper towels.
Separate the roll dough into 8 triangles. Place 2 tablespoons of coleslaw on each. Place the meaty portion of each drumstick in the centre of the slaw, wrap the dough around and seal firmly. Place the wrapped chicken in an ungreased shallow baking pan. Brush the tops with butter and sprinkle with the sesame seeds. Bake at 190°C (375°F/Gas 5) for about 15 minutes or until golden brown. Cool slightly, then chill in the refrigerator and serve cold.

Chicken with Turnips

Serves 4

90 g (3 oz) butter
1 x 1.5 kg (3 lb) chicken, quartered
500 g (1 lb) small turnips, peeled
500 g (1 lb) small onions
1 bay leaf
½ teaspoon dried thyme
½ teaspoon dried parsley

½ teaspoon salt
¼ teaspoon freshly ground pepper
1 tablespoon sugar
1 tablespoon hot water
1 tablespoon chopped chives
juice of ¼ lemon

Melt half the butter over medium heat. Add the chicken and cook for about 10 minutes, turning, until brown on all sides. Remove the chicken to a Dutch oven and cover. Drain the pan, leaving 2 tablespoons of the drippings. Add the remaining butter and melt over low heat. Plunge the turnips and onions into boiling water, then remove and dry on paper towels. Sauté for about 5 minutes. Add the turnips, onions, bay leaf, thyme, parsley, salt and pepper. Cover and simmer for about 35 minutes or until a fork can be inserted in the chicken with ease and the vegetables are tender. Arrange the chicken on a serving dish and surround with the vegetables.
Add the sugar to the drippings and stir until caramelized. Stir in the hot water and pour over the vegetables and chicken. Sprinkle with the chives and lemon juice.

Chicken

Hazelnut Chicken

Serves 4

¾ cup seasoned crumb coating mix	2 egg whites
½ cup (2 oz) ground hazelnuts	5 tablespoons Dijon mustard
½ teaspoon paprika	1 x 1.5 kg (3 lb) chicken, cut into serving pieces
½ teaspoon salt	hazelnuts
½ teaspoon pepper	parsley sprigs

In a plastic bag, place the coating mix, ground hazelnuts, paprika, salt and pepper. Shake well to mix. Beat the egg whites until frothy. Beat in the mustard. Dip the chicken, one piece at a time, in the egg mixture and place on a rack. Then place the chicken in the plastic bag, one piece at a time, and shake to coat.

Arrange the chicken in a lightly oiled baking pan. Bake at 190°C (375°F/Gas 5) for 40 minutes or until a fork can be inserted in the chicken with ease. If the chicken browns too quickly, cover with foil and remove for the last 10 minutes. When the chicken is done, remove from the oven and cover with foil for 5 minutes before placing on a warm serving dish. Garnish with whole hazelnuts and parsley sprigs.

Fiesta Chicken with Chilli Sauce

Serves 4

30 g (1 oz) butter	½ teaspoon salt
1 medium-sized green pepper (capsicum), chopped	½ teaspoon pepper
	4 chicken thighs
	4 chicken drumsticks
1 medium-sized onion, chopped	¼ cup (2 fl oz) corn oil
	1 cup (8 fl oz) chicken stock
2 tablespoons chopped green chillies	1 cup (4 oz) grated cheese
	¼ cup chopped pimiento-stuffed olives
1 garlic clove, crushed	
¼ cup (1 oz) yellow cornmeal (polenta)	

Place the butter in a small pan and melt over medium heat. Add the green pepper, onion, chillies and garlic. Sauté for about 3 minutes or until soft. Set aside. Mix together the polenta and the salt and pepper. Dip the chicken, one piece at a time, dredging to coat. Heat the oil to medium in a deep pan. Add the chicken, skin side down, and cook for about 6 minutes or until brown. Turn and cook a further 5 minutes. Drain the oil and discard.

Mix together the chicken stock and green pepper mixture. Pour over the chicken. Cover and simmer for 30 minutes or until a fork can be inserted in the chicken with ease. Place the chicken on a warm dish, pour 1 cup (8 fl oz) of the sauce from the pan over the chicken and sprinkle with the cheese and olives. Serve the remaining sauce separately.

Cheesy Chicken and Cabbage Bake

Serves 6

1 x 1.8 kg (3½ lb) chicken, cut into serving pieces	grated rind of 1 lemon
	2 teaspoons caraway seeds
1 teaspoon salt	1 teaspoon sugar
¼ teaspoon pepper	¼ cup (2 fl oz) water
1 small head of cabbage, cut into 1.25 cm (½ inch) wedges	2 cups (8 oz) grated Swiss cheese
	¼ cup (1 oz) chopped walnuts
3 large apples, unpeeled and cut into 1.25 cm (½ inch) wedges	1 teaspoon paprika
	chopped parsley
1 medium-sized onion, thinly sliced	

Place the chicken in a large shallow baking pan. Sprinkle with salt and pepper. Bake at 180°C (350°F/Gas 4) for 1 hour or until a fork can be inserted in the chicken with ease. Place the cabbage, apples and onion in a shallow baking dish. Sprinkle with the lemon rind, caraway seeds and sugar. Pour the water over the cabbage mixture. Cover and place in the oven with the chicken during the last 30 minutes of cooking.

Remove the chicken and cabbage from the oven. Sprinkle half the Swiss cheese over the cabbage mixture and arrange the chicken on top. Add the pan drippings from the chicken and sprinkle the remaining cheese, walnuts and paprika over the chicken. Return to the oven and bake a further 5 minutes or until the cheese begins to melt. Garnish with the chopped parsley.

Spicy Grilled Chicken

Serves 4

1 teaspoon poultry seasoning	2 garlic cloves, crushed
	⅛ teaspoon chilli powder
½ teaspoon dried mint	1 x 1.5 kg (3 lb) chicken, cut into serving pieces
¼ cup (2 fl oz) cider vinegar	1 cup (8 fl oz) chicken stock
¼ cup (2 fl oz) soy sauce	2 tablespoons tomato sauce
2 tablespoons cooking oil	¼ cup (2 fl oz) yoghurt

Make the marinade by mixing together the poultry seasoning, mint, vinegar, soy sauce, cooking oil, garlic and chilli powder. Add the chicken, turning to coat, and marinate for at least 30 minutes. Place the chicken on the griller (broiler), skin side down, and grill (broil) about 12 cm (5 inch) from the heat for about 15 minutes. Turn the chicken, brush with marinade and cook a further 15 minutes or until a fork can be inserted in the chicken with ease. Remove to a warm dish.

Place the chicken stock, tomato sauce and any remaining marinade over medium heat and reduce by one third. Add the yoghurt and bring to the boil. Serve with the chicken.

Spanish Chicken

Serves 4

1 cup (4 oz) flour
2 teaspoons salt
½ teaspoon pepper
1 x 1.5 kg (3 lb) chicken, cut into serving pieces
¼ cup (2 fl oz) cooking oil
1 cup chopped onion
2 garlic cloves, crushed
½ cup chopped green pepper (capsicum)
⅓ cup canned pimiento, cut into strips
1 cup (5 oz) long grain rice
2½ cups (20 fl oz) chicken stock
1½ teaspoons turmeric
⅛ teaspoon chilli powder

Mix together the flour, 1 teaspoon of the salt and ¼ teaspoon of the pepper. Dip the chicken, one piece at a time, dredging to coat. Place the oil in a large pan and heat gently. Add the chicken and cook for about 10 minutes, turning, until brown on all sides. Remove the chicken and set aside. Add the onion, garlic and green pepper. Sauté about 5 minutes or until the onion is golden. Reduce the heat to low, then add the pimiento and rice, stirring for about 2 minutes. Add half the stock, the turmeric, chilli powder and the remaining salt and pepper. Bring to the boil.

Pour the rice mixture into a casserole and arrange the chicken on top. Bake at 180°C (350°F/Gas 4) for about 1½ hours or until a fork can be inserted in the chicken with ease. Add the remaining ½ to ¾ cup (4 to 6 fl oz) stock as needed.

Chicken Scampi

Serves 4

250 g (8 oz) broccoli, cut into bite-sized pieces
500 g (1 lb) fettuccine noodles
60 g (2 oz) butter
⅓ cup (2½ fl oz) olive oil
1 large onion, sliced
1 large green pepper (capsicum), cut into bite-sized pieces
3 whole chicken breasts, boned, skinned and cut into bite-sized pieces
juice of ½ lemon
1 teaspoon salt
½ teaspoon pepper
¼ cup (1 oz) grated Parmesan cheese

Steam the broccoli in salted water for 4 minutes or until crisp. Meanwhile boil the noodles in salted water for 9 minutes and drain. Place the butter and olive oil in a large pan over medium heat. Add the onion and green pepper and sauté for 5 minutes. Remove from the pan and reserve. Add the chicken and continue to cook, stirring, for about 5 minutes. Return the onion and green pepper to the pan, add the cooked broccoli and sauté a further 5 minutes. Sprinkle with the lemon juice, salt and pepper. Place the noodles in a serving dish, top with the chicken-vegetable mixture and sprinkle with Parmesan cheese.

North Carolina Grilled Chicken

Serves 8

90 g (3 oz) margarine
⅓ cup (2½ fl oz) vinegar
1 cup (8 fl oz) tomato sauce
¼ cup (2 oz) sugar
1½ teaspoons lemon juice
1 tablespoon Worcestershire sauce
¼ teaspoon Tabasco sauce
2 x 1.5 kg (3 lb) chickens, quartered

Place the margarine, vinegar, tomato sauce, sugar, lemon juice, Worcestershire sauce and Tabasco sauce in a small saucepan. Bring to the boil. Reduce temperature to low and simmer for 10 minutes. Place the chicken under the griller (broiler), skin side down. Grill (broil) for about 10 minutes or until browned. Turn the chicken and cook a further 10 minutes. Brush the chicken liberally with sauce and continue to grill (broil), turning and adding more sauce, for a further 20 minutes or until a fork can be inserted with ease.

Apricot Chicken

Serves 4

¼ cup (2 fl oz) cooking oil
1 x 1.5 kg (3 lb) chicken, cut into serving pieces
½ cup (2 oz) plus 1 tablespoon flour
2 tablespoons chopped onion
¼ cup chopped celery
1 cup (8 fl oz) chicken stock
1 teaspoon salt
¼ teaspoon white pepper
½ teaspoon ground ginger
¼ teaspoon nutmeg
⅛ teaspoon ground cloves
1 large egg, beaten
2 tablespoons fresh lemon juice
1 teaspoon grated lemon rind
¼ cup (2 fl oz) apricot nectar
1 x 780 g (1½ lb) can apricot halves
½ cup (2 oz) slivered almonds, toasted
parsley sprigs

Place the oil in a pan and heat to medium. Dredge the chicken in ½ cup (2 oz) of the flour and cook for about 10 minutes, turning, until brown on all sides. Remove from the pan and set aside. Add the onion and celery and sauté for about 3 minutes. Sprinkle the remaining flour over the onion-celery mixture, stirring. Gradually stir in the chicken stock and heat thoroughly. Return the chicken to the pan. Mix together the salt, pepper, ginger, nutmeg and cloves. Sprinkle over the chicken. Cover and simmer for about 30 minutes or until a fork can be inserted in the chicken with ease. Remove the chicken from the pan and keep warm. Mix together the egg, lemon juice, lemon rind and apricot nectar and add to the pan. Cook, stirring, until thickened. Return the chicken to the pan. Top with 1 cup of the apricot halves and the almonds. Heat thoroughly. Place the chicken on a warm serving dish. Cover with apricot sauce. Garnish with parsley and the remaining apricot halves.

Chicken

Oyster-Stuffed Chicken
Serves 6

1 bottle oysters
90 g (3 oz) butter
3 tablespoons chopped green pepper (capsicum)
2 tablespoons chopped celery
3 tablespoons chopped fresh parsley
2 tablespoons chopped onion
1 garlic clove, crushed
1 ½ cups (3 oz) soft breadcrumbs
1 teaspoon salt
¼ teaspoon red (cayenne) pepper
¼ teaspoon freshly ground pepper
3 x 1.5 kg (3 lb) chickens, halved
½ cup (4 fl oz) water

Drain and chop the oysters, reserving the liquid. Place half the butter in a large pan. Add the oysters, green pepper, celery, parsley, onion and garlic. Sauté for 10 minutes. Add 1 cup (2 oz) of the breadcrumbs, the salt, red pepper, pepper and ½ cup (4 fl oz) of the reserved oyster liquid. Stir to mix well. Place the chicken halves, skin side up, in a shallow baking pan. Dot with half the remaining butter. Add the water to the pan. Bake at 190°C (375°F/Gas 5) for 30 minutes or until brown. Remove the chicken from the oven, turn skin side down and fill each cavity with oyster stuffing. Melt the remaining butter, add the remaining breadcrumbs and sprinkle over the stuffing. Return the chicken to the oven and bake a further 20 minutes or until the crumbs are golden brown and a fork can be inserted in the chicken with ease.

Carolina Chicken
Serves 10

2 x 1.8 kg (3½ lb) chickens, cut into serving pieces
5 cups (1.25 litres) water
250 g (8 oz) bacon
1 onion, chopped
1 green pepper (capsicum), chopped
6 cups (1.5 litres) chicken broth
1 teaspoon salt
pepper to taste
4 cups (1 ½ lb) rice
60 g (2 oz) butter
6 hard-boiled eggs, chopped

Place the chicken and water in a heavy Dutch oven. Cover and cook about 45 minutes or until a fork can be inserted in the chicken with ease. Remove the chicken and reserve the broth. When cool enough to handle, remove the chicken meat from the bones. Discard the bones and skin. Cook the bacon in a pan until crisp. Drain on paper towels, crumble coarsely and set aside. Drain all but 3 tablespoons of the bacon drippings and add the onion and green pepper. Stir fry for about 5 minutes or until the onion is transparent. Place reserved chicken broth, salt and pepper in the Dutch oven. Add the onion and green pepper and bring to the boil over medium heat. Add the chicken, rice and butter. Stir to mix well. Reduce the heat to low and cook approximately 1 hour, stirring twice during cooking. Add the bacon and eggs and mix well.

Chutney Chicken
Serves 6

1 x 1.5 kg (3 lb) chicken, cut into serving pieces and skinned
5 medium-sized red apples, unpeeled and thickly sliced
1 medium-sized mild white onion, thinly sliced
1 ½ cups (12 fl oz) apple cider
3 tablespoons lemon juice
1 teaspoon white pepper
2 tablespoons chopped crystallized ginger
4 tablespoons soft brown sugar
½ cup (3 oz) peanuts
½ cup (3 oz) raisins
30 g (1 oz) butter
3 cinnamon sticks
parsley sprigs

Apple Cinnamon Rice
1 cup (6 oz) rice
1 cup (8 fl oz) apple cider
1 cup (8 fl oz) water
1 cinnamon stick
½ cup (3 oz) raisins

Place the chicken in a single layer in a large casserole. Top with the apple slices, reserving at least 6 for garnish. Place the onion on the apple slices and pour the apple cider and lemon juice over. Sprinkle with the pepper, chopped ginger and brown sugar. Add the peanuts, raisins and butter. Baste the chicken several times with the juices in the casserole. Cover and bake at 180°C (350°F/Gas 4) for 1 hour or until a fork can be inserted in the chicken with ease.

Mound the Apple Cinnamon Rice in the centre of a serving dish. Arrange the chicken around and spoon the pan juices over the chicken. Place the cinnamon sticks vertically in the rice. Garnish with the apple slices and parsley sprigs.

Apple Cinnamon Rice: Cook the rice in the apple cider and water with the cinnamon stick. Add the raisins when the rice is done.

Tomato-Chilli Chicken
Serves 2

1 x 315 g (10 oz) can peeled tomatoes
2 small green chillies, finely chopped
½ cup finely chopped celery
1 tablespoon steak sauce
2 chicken quarters
½ teaspoon garlic salt
2 cups hot cooked rice

Make the sauce by mixing together the tomatoes, chillies, celery and steak sauce. Place the chicken in a square baking pan. Pour the sauce over the chicken and sprinkle with the garlic salt. Bake at 180°C (350°F/Gas 4) for about 30 minutes. Remove from the oven.

Place the pan under the griller (broiler) 15 cm (6 inch) from the heat. Continue to cook the chicken until brown and a fork can be inserted with ease, about 5 minutes. Remove the chicken from the pan and add the hot cooked rice to the sauce. Stir until well mixed. Serve the rice with the chicken.

Chicken and Pears

Serves 4

- 1 x 500 g (1 lb) can pear halves in light syrup, reserved
- 1½ teaspoons salt
- ½ teaspoon pepper
- 1 x 1.5 kg (3 lb) chicken, cut into serving pieces
- 3 tablespoons cooking oil
- 1 medium-sized onion, sliced
- 3 tablespoons flour
- ½ teaspoon dried basil
- ¾ cup (6 fl oz) water
- ⅓ cup (2½ fl oz) dry white wine
- 250 g (8 oz) cherry tomatoes

Drain and quarter the pears. Sprinkle 1 teaspoon of the salt and ¼ teaspoon of the pepper over the chicken. Place the cooking oil in a large pan over medium heat. Add the chicken and cook for about 10 minutes, turning, until brown on all sides. Remove the chicken to a large baking dish with a lid. Add the onion to the pan and sauté until transparent, about 3 minutes. Blend in the flour and basil, stirring well. Add the water gradually and stir for about 5 minutes or until thick and bubbly. Add the white wine and ⅓ cup (2½ fl oz) of the reserved pear syrup. Add the tomatoes and pears and cook about 3 minutes. Add the remaining salt and pepper. Pour the pear sauce over the chicken, cover and bake at 180°C (350°F/Gas 4) for 45 minutes or until a fork can be inserted in the chicken with ease. Remove the lid for the last 5 minutes of cooking. Serve with parsley rice.

Capital Chicken Casserole

Serves 4

- 90 g (3 oz) butter
- 1 tablespoon cooking oil
- 1 x 1.5 kg (3 lb) chicken, cut into serving pieces
- 250 g (8 oz) mushrooms, sliced
- 1 tablespoon flour
- 1 x 315 g (10 oz) can cream of chicken soup
- 1 cup (8 fl oz) dry white wine
- 1 cup (8 fl oz) water
- ½ cup (4 fl oz) cream
- 1 teaspoon salt
- ¼ teaspoon dried tarragon
- ¼ teaspoon pepper
- 1 x 470 g (15 oz) can artichoke hearts, drained
- 6 spring onions (scallions), chopped
- 2 tablespoons chopped parsley

Place the butter and oil in a large pan and heat to medium until the butter melts. Add the chicken and cook for about 10 minutes, turning, until brown on all sides. Remove the chicken and place in a baking pan or casserole. In the same pan, sauté the mushrooms for about 5 minutes or until tender. Stir in the flour. Add the soup, wine and water and simmer, stirring, for about 10 minutes or until the sauce thickens. Stir in the cream, salt, tarragon and pepper and pour over the chicken.

Bake, uncovered, at 180°C (350°F/Gas 4) for 1 hour. Mix in the artichoke hearts, spring onions and parsley. Bake a further 5 minutes or until a fork can be inserted in the chicken with ease.

Latin American Chicken

Serves 8

- 60 g (2 oz) butter
- 2 x 1.5 kg (3 lb) chickens, quartered
- ½ cup chopped onion
- 1 garlic clove, crushed
- ½ cup (4 fl oz) dry white wine
- 1 x 500 g (1 lb) can tomatoes
- 1 chicken stock cube
- 1 bay leaf
- 1 tablespoon Worcestershire sauce
- 1 teaspoon dried thyme
- 1 teaspoon salt
- 1 cup (6 oz) pitted dried prunes
- 1 cup mashed ripe bananas
- 3 green-tipped bananas, peeled and cut into 2.5 cm (1 inch) pieces

Melt the butter in a large pan over medium heat. Add the chicken, four pieces at a time, and cook for about 10 minutes, turning, until brown on all sides. Remove the chicken and keep warm. To the same pan, add the onion and garlic and sauté for 1 minute. Add the wine, the tomatoes with their liquid, the stock cube, bay leaf, Worcestershire sauce, thyme, salt and prunes. Bring to the boil and return the chicken to the pan. Cover, reduce the heat to low and simmer about 30 minutes or until a fork can be inserted in the chicken with ease. Remove the chicken to a serving dish. Remove the bay leaf from the sauce and discard then add the mashed bananas and banana pieces to the pan. Cook, stirring frequently, for about 2 minutes. Spoon the sauce over the chicken.

Hot Chinese Chicken Salad

Serves 4

- ¼ cup (1 oz) cornflour (cornstarch)
- 8 chicken thighs, skinned, boned and cut into bite-sized pieces
- ¼ cup (2 fl oz) corn oil
- 1 large ripe tomato, roughly chopped
- 1 x 125 g (4 oz) can water chestnuts, drained and sliced
- 125 g (4 oz) mushrooms, sliced
- 1 cup coarsely chopped spring onions (scallions)
- 1 cup diagonally sliced celery
- ⅛ teaspoon garlic salt
- ¼ cup (2 fl oz) soy sauce
- 2 cups finely shredded lettuce

Place the cornflour in a shallow dish. Add the chicken, one piece at a time, dredging to coat. Place the oil in a wok and heat to medium. Add the chicken and cook for about 3 minutes or until brown. Add the tomato, water chestnuts, mushrooms, spring onion, celery, garlic salt and soy sauce. Stir gently. Cover and simmer for about 5 minutes or until a fork can be inserted with ease. Place the lettuce in a large bowl. Add the chicken and vegetable mixture and toss lightly. Serve hot with rice.

Chicken

Chicken Andaluza

Serves 6

- ¼ cup (2 fl oz) dry sherry
- 2 tablespoons raisins
- 2 tablespoons orange juice
- 1 ½ teaspoons chopped parsley
- 1 garlic clove, crushed
- 6 chicken half-breasts (suprêmes)
- ½ cup (2 oz) flour
- 1 teaspoon salt
- ½ teaspoon freshly ground pepper
- ½ cup (4 fl oz) olive oil
- 60 g (2 oz) butter
- 2 tablespoons sliced almonds
- 1 x 90 g (3 oz) jar Spanish olives, drained

Place the sherry and raisins in a small bowl and set aside to soak. Rub the orange juice, parsley and garlic on the chicken breasts. Mix together the flour, salt and pepper. Add the chicken, two pieces at a time, shaking to coat. Place the oil in a pan and heat to medium. Add the chicken and cook for about 10 minutes, turning, until brown on both sides. Remove the chicken and drain the oil from the pan.

Remove the raisins from the sherry. Place the butter and sherry in the same pan and simmer over medium heat for about 15 minutes or until reduced to a glaze. Add the raisins, almonds and olives. Stir to mix. Return the chicken to the pan. Simmer, uncovered, over low heat for about 15 minutes or until a fork can be inserted in the chicken with ease. Spoon the sauce over the chicken and serve.

Golden Chicken

Serves 6

- 6 chicken thighs
- 6 chicken drumsticks
- 1 teaspoon salt
- 1 teaspoon dried basil
- ¼ teaspoon freshly ground pepper
- ½ cup (4 fl oz) soy sauce
- ½ cup (4 fl oz) tomato sauce
- ¼ cup (3 oz) honey
- ¼ cup (2 fl oz) corn oil
- 2 garlic cloves, crushed

Poached Oranges

- ¾ cup (6 fl oz) water
- 1 ½ cups (12 oz) sugar
- 3 tablespoons slivered orange rind
- segments of 3 oranges
- 2 tablespoons orange-flavoured liqueur

Sprinkle the chicken with the salt, basil and pepper. Mix together the soy sauce, tomato sauce, honey, corn oil and garlic. Place the chicken in a large shallow baking pan, skin side up, in a single layer. Pour about half the soy sauce mixture over the chicken. Bake at 180°C (350°F/Gas 4), basting frequently, for about 1 hour or until a fork can be inserted in the chicken with ease. Pour the remaining soy sauce mixture, the Poached Oranges and their sauce over the chicken.

Poached Oranges: Mix together the water, sugar and orange rind. Cook until slightly thickened. Add the orange segments and cook a further 3 minutes. Add the liqueur, mixing thoroughly.

Coq au Vin

Serves 4

- 2 ½ cups (20 fl oz) water
- 1 x 1.5 kg (3 lb) chicken, cut into serving pieces (giblets included)
- 1 small onion, quartered
- 1 stalk celery, quartered
- 1 teaspoon rock salt
- freshly ground pepper
- 2 tablespoons finely diced bacon
- 30 g (1 oz) butter
- 4 tablespoons flour
- 1 teaspoon sugar
- 1 ½ cups (12 fl oz) dry red wine
- 12 very small onions
- 1 bay leaf
- ¼ teaspoon dried marjoram
- ¼ teaspoon dried thyme
- 2 tablespoons chopped parsley

Place the water, chicken giblets, neck and back, onion, celery, ½ teaspoon of the rock salt, and some pepper in a saucepan. Bring to the boil, reduce the heat, cover and simmer about 25 minutes. Drain and reserve the broth (about 1 ½ cups (12 fl oz) should remain). Finely chop the giblets and reserve. Discard the neck and bones. In a large heavy saucepan or Dutch oven, place the diced bacon and cook over medium heat until crisp. Remove from the pan and set aside to drain. Add the butter to the pan drippings and melt. Add the chicken pieces and cook for about 15 minutes, turning, until brown on all sides. Remove the chicken from the pan, set aside and keep warm.

Remove all but 4 tablespoons of the butter drippings from the pan. Add the flour and sugar, stirring until dark brown. Stir in the reserved broth from the giblets, then add the red wine. Stir and bring to the boil. Return the chicken to the pan, add the giblets, bacon, onions, bay leaf, marjoram, thyme, the remaining rock salt and pepper. Cover and simmer for about 45 minutes or until a fork can be inserted in the chicken with ease. Sprinkle with parsley and serve on rice.

Coriander Chicken

Serves 4

- 4 tablespoons soy sauce
- 2 teaspoons ground coriander
- 1 teaspoon soft brown sugar
- 8 peppercorns, crushed
- 2 garlic cloves, crushed
- 8 chicken thighs

Mix together the soy sauce, coriander, brown sugar, peppercorns and garlic. Stir. Add the chicken, turning to coat. Cover and marinate at room temperature for 30 minutes, basting occasionally. Reserve the marinade. Place the chicken under the griller (broiler). Cook gently on one side for 10 minutes. Turn the chicken, basting with the reserved marinade and cook a further 20 minutes or until a fork can be inserted in the chicken with ease.

Opposite: *Chicken Andaluza*

225

Chicken

Chicken Country Captain
Serves 4

- 4 rashers bacon
- 1 x 1.5 kg (3 lb) chicken, cut into serving pieces
- 1 teaspoon salt
- ½ teaspoon pepper
- 2 stalks celery, chopped
- 1 onion, finely chopped
- 1 green pepper (capsicum), chopped
- 2 garlic cloves, crushed
- 1 x 440 g (14 oz) can tomatoes
- 2 teaspoons curry powder
- ½ teaspoon dried thyme
- 1 cup (8 fl oz) chicken stock, heated
- ½ cup (2 ½ oz) currants
- 1 tablespoon chopped parsley
- ½ cup (3 oz) toasted almonds

Place the bacon over medium heat in a Dutch oven or deep pan, and cook until crisp, about 5 minutes. Remove the bacon, drain on a paper towel, crumble and reserve. Add the chicken to the pan and cook for about 15 minutes, turning, until brown on all sides. Sprinkle with half the salt and the pepper. Remove the chicken and keep warm. To the drippings in the pan, add the celery, onion, green pepper and garlic. Stir fry for about 5 minutes or until the onion is clear and lightly browned. Add the tomatoes, curry powder, thyme and remaining salt. Bring to the boil, reduce the heat to low, cover and simmer about 10 minutes. Pour the chicken stock over the currants and let stand for 30 minutes until the currants are plump. Return the chicken to the pan, cover and cook for about 20 minutes. Add the currants and broth and continue cooking, covered, for a further 10 minutes or until a fork can be inserted in the chicken with ease. Sprinkle with the parsley, crumbled bacon and toasted almonds. Serve on rice with chutney as an accompaniment.

Country-Style Chicken
Serves 4

- 3 whole chicken breasts, skinned and boned or 8 chicken thighs, skinned and boned
- 1 teaspoon salt
- ¼ teaspoon pepper
- ½ cup (2 oz) flour
- ½ cup (4 fl oz) cooking oil
- 1 ¼ cups (10 fl oz) chicken stock
- 1 cup (8 fl oz) hot water
- 2 tablespoons white wine
- ⅛ teaspoon dried marjoram

Cut the chicken into narrow 2.5 cm (1 inch) strips. Sprinkle the chicken with salt and pepper. Place the flour in a shallow dish, add the chicken strips, a few at a time, and dredge to coat on all sides.

Place the oil in a pan over medium high heat. Add the chicken and cook about 10 minutes, turning to brown on all sides. Pour off the excess oil. Add the stock and hot water to the contents of the pan. Reduce the heat to low, cover and simmer for 15 minutes. Stir in the wine and marjoram, cover and cook a further 5 minutes. Serve the chicken with gravy over rice.

Chicken and Dumplings
Serves 4

- 60 g (2 oz) butter
- 1 x 1.5 kg (3 lb) chicken, cut into serving pieces
- 1 ½ teaspoons salt
- freshly ground pepper
- ⅔ cup finely chopped celery
- ⅔ cup finely chopped onion
- juice of 1 lemon
- 1 tablespoon chopped parsley
- 3 cups (24 fl oz) water
- 1 ¾ cups (7 oz) flour
- 2 teaspoons baking powder
- 1 ¾ cups (14 fl oz) milk

Place half the butter in a large Dutch oven or heavy saucepan, and melt. Add the chicken and cook, turning, until brown on all sides, about 15 minutes. Sprinkle the chicken with 1 teaspoon of the salt and the pepper. Sprinkle the celery and onion over the chicken and add the lemon juice, parsley and water. Bring to the boil, cover, reduce heat to low and simmer for about 45 minutes. Sift together three times 1 ½ cups (6 oz) of the flour, the baking powder and remaining salt. Blend in the remaining butter, then add ¾ cup (6 fl oz) of the milk and stir only until mixed. With a tablespoon, drop the dough on top of the simmering chicken, allowing the dough to rest on the chicken. Cover and cook for 20 minutes (do NOT uncover while cooking) or until a skewer comes out clean when inserted in the dumplings. Remove the chicken with the dumplings on top to a large serving bowl or tureen, leaving the broth in the pan.

To the remaining flour, slowly add the remaining milk, stirring to make a smooth paste. Add milk-flour mixture slowly to the broth in the pan, stirring to avoid lumps. Continue to stir and cook until the gravy boils and thickens, about 2 minutes. Pour over the chicken and dumplings and serve immediately.

Chicken and Noodles
Serves 2

- 1 x 315 g (10 oz) cook-in-pouch frozen Chinese-style vegetables
- 2 tablespoons cooking oil
- 4 chicken thighs, skinned and cut into bite-sized pieces
- ¼ teaspoon salt
- 1 cup (8 fl oz) water
- 1 x 90 g (3 oz) packet Oriental flavour noodles
- 1 teaspoon soy sauce

Place the pouch of vegetables in a saucepan of boiling water and cook for about 5 minutes. Place the oil in a wok and heat to high. Sprinkle the chicken with salt. Add the chicken and stir fry until it loses its pink colour, about 4 minutes. While the chicken is cooking, place the water in a saucepan and bring to the boil over high heat. Add the Oriental noodles with their flavour sachet. Cook 3 minutes, stirring occasionally. Add the cooked vegetables, noodles and soy sauce to the chicken. Stir until well mixed and thoroughly heated, about 1 minute.

Lemon Honey Chicken

Serves 4

½ cup (4 fl oz) lemon juice
1 tablespoon honey
¼ teaspoon dried marjoram
¼ teaspoon dried tarragon
1 x 1.5 kg (3 lb) chicken, cut into serving pieces
1 teaspoon salt
½ teaspoon pepper
¾ cup (3 oz) flour
2 cups (16 fl oz) cooking oil
2 cups (16 fl oz) hot water

Mix together the lemon juice, honey, marjoram and tarragon. Place the chicken in this mixture, one piece at a time, turning to coat. Reserve the excess mixture. Sprinkle the chicken with the salt and pepper. Place ½ cup (2 oz) of the flour in another shallow dish and add the chicken, one piece at a time, dredging to coat.

Place the oil in a large pan over high heat. Add the chicken and cook for about 5 minutes, turning to brown on all sides. Reduce the heat to medium high and continue cooking a further 15 minutes or until a fork can be inserted in the chicken with ease. Remove the chicken from the pan, set aside and keep warm. Drain all but 2 tablespoons of the oil and pan drippings. Add the remaining flour and stir to brown, about 1 minute. Slowly stir in the hot water and 2 tablespoons of the reserved lemon juice mixture. Cook about 3 minutes, stirring, or until thickened. Serve the hot gravy with the chicken.

Chicken Noodle Soup

Serves 6

1 x 1.5 kg (3 lb) chicken, cut into serving pieces
6 cups (1.5 litres) water
1 cup finely chopped onion
¾ cup finely chopped celery
2 teaspoons salt
2 teaspoons chopped parsley
½ teaspoon pepper
2 cups egg noodles
slices of hard-boiled egg

Place the chicken in a large saucepan or Dutch oven. Add the water, onion, celery, salt, parsley and pepper. Cover and simmer over low heat for about 1 hour or until a fork can be inserted in the chicken with ease. Remove the chicken from the broth. When cool enough to handle, remove the chicken from the bones, discarding the skin and bones. Cut the chicken into bite-sized pieces.

Break the noodles into small pieces and cook according to the directions on the packet. Drain. Skim the fat from the broth and discard. Bring the broth to the boil. Add the chicken and cooked noodles to the broth and simmer for about 5 minutes. Garnish with slices of hard-boiled egg.

Stir-Fried Chicken and Broccoli

Serves 6

8 chicken thighs, skinned and boned
¼ teaspoon ground ginger
¼ teaspoon pepper
3 tablespoons peanut oil
1 bunch broccoli, cut into small pieces
1 cup sliced spring onions (scallions)
¾ cup (6 fl oz) chicken stock
1 teaspoon salt
½ teaspoon sugar
1 tablespoon cornflour (cornstarch)
2 tablespoons water
¼ cup (1 oz) grated Parmesan cheese

Whole Wheat Croûtons
4 slices whole wheat bread
2 tablespoons melted butter
1 tablespoon chopped parsley
½ teaspoon garlic salt

Cut the chicken into bite-sized pieces. Sprinkle with the ginger and pepper. Pour the oil into a large pan or wok, and heat to high. Add the chicken and stir fry for 3 minutes or until brown. Push the chicken to one side. Add the broccoli and spring onion. Stir fry a further 3 minutes. Mix together the stock, salt and sugar and stir into the pan. Reduce the heat to medium high, cover and cook for 2 minutes. Add the cornflour to the water and stir until smooth. Stir into the pan and cook for 1 minute. Remove from heat. Stir in the cheese and sprinkle with Whole Wheat Croûtons.

Whole Wheat Croûtons: Cut the bread into 2.5 cm (1 inch) cubes. Mix together the bread cubes, melted butter, parsley and garlic salt. Spread in a single layer and toast in the oven at 150°C (300°F/Gas 2) for about 20 minutes or until crisp.

Curried Chicken

Serves 2

1 tablespoon cooking oil
60 g (2 oz) butter or margarine
1 garlic clove, crushed
salt and pepper
2 tablespoons apricot jam (jelly)
3 tablespoons vinegar
1 teaspoon curry powder
½ cup (4 fl oz) water
4 chicken pieces
1 large onion, sliced into rings

Place the oil and butter in a small pan and heat to medium. Add the chicken and cook for about 10 minutes, turning, until brown on all sides. Add the onion rings and garlic and sauté until the onion is clear, about 3 minutes. Pour off the excess oil. Sprinkle the chicken with the salt and pepper. Mix together the apricot jam, vinegar and curry powder. Stir in the water. Pour the mixture over the chicken and bring to the boil. Reduce the heat to low, cover and simmer about 20 minutes or until a fork can be inserted in the chicken with ease. Remove the lid and continue to cook 5 minutes to reduce the liquid. Serve over rice.

Chicken

Quick Pepper Chicken

Serves 4

- ¼ cup (2 fl oz) cooking oil
- 1 x 1.5 kg (3 lb) chicken, cut into serving pieces
- 1 teaspoon celery salt
- 1 teaspoon chilli powder
- 2 large green peppers (capsicum), sliced into strips
- 1 large red pepper (capsicum), sliced into strips
- 2 large onions, sliced into rings

Place the oil in a large heavy Dutch oven and heat to medium high. Add the chicken and sprinkle with ½ teaspoon of the celery salt and ½ teaspoon of the chilli powder. Cook until the chicken is brown on one side, about 5 minutes. Turn the chicken and sprinkle the other side with the remaining celery salt and chilli powder. Cook a further 5 minutes or until the chicken is brown. Reduce the heat to medium low. Cover and continue cooking for about 15 minutes or until a fork can be inserted in the chicken with ease. Drain off any accumulated fat and adjust temperature to medium high. Add the peppers and onions and cook for about 5 minutes, stirring, until the onion is clear. Sprinkle lightly with chilli powder to garnish.

Crispy Lemon Chicken

Crispy Lemon Chicken

Serves 4

- 2 eggs
- 2 teaspoons dry sherry
- 1 cup (4 oz) plus 1 teaspoon cornflour (cornstarch)
- 1 teaspoon soy sauce
- ½ teaspoon salt
- ¼ teaspoon sugar
- ⅛ teaspoon white pepper
- ⅓ cup (2 ½ fl oz) peanut oil
- 4 chicken half-breasts (suprêmes), quartered
- 3 tablespoons iced water (approximately)

Lemon Sauce
- 1 cup (8 fl oz) water
- ⅓ cup (3 oz) sugar
- ⅓ cup (2 ½ fl oz) cider vinegar
- 1 lemon, thinly sliced
- lettuce and parsley
- 2 tablespoons cornflour (cornstarch), mixed with 3 tablespoons water

Separate 1 egg and reserve the egg yolk. Place the egg white in a large bowl and beat lightly. Add the sherry, 1 teaspoon of the cornflour, the soy sauce, half the salt, the sugar, pepper and ¼ teaspoon of the peanut oil. Mix well. Add the chicken, turning to coat. Marinate at room temperature for 30 minutes. Beat the remaining egg and the reserved egg yolk. Add the remaining cornflour, the water and 1 teaspoon of the oil. Mix well. Add additional iced water if needed to attain a good batter consistency.

Dip the chicken, one piece at a time, to coat. Place the remaining oil in a large pan and heat to fairly hot. Add the chicken and cook for about 7 minutes, turning once, until light brown and a fork can be inserted in the chicken with ease. Drain well. Sprinkle with the remaining salt. Serve on a bed of lettuce and parsley. Spoon the Lemon Sauce over the chicken.

Lemon Sauce: Mix together the water, sugar, vinegar and lemon. Place over medium heat and bring to the boil. Simmer, stirring occasionally, for 10 minutes. Remove from the heat. Slowly pour in the cornflour mixture while stirring. Return to medium heat and cook, stirring constantly, for about 5 minutes or until the sauce is thick.

Sweet Surprise Chicken

Serves 6

- 3 whole chicken breasts, halved
- 1 x 500 g (1 lb) can jellied cranberry sauce
- 1 cup (8 fl oz) creamy French dressing
- 1 packet dried onion soup mix

Place the chicken in a shallow greased baking pan, skin side up, in a single layer. Mix together the cranberry sauce, French dressing and onion soup mix. Pour over the chicken. Bake, uncovered, at 120°C (250°F/Gas ½) for about 2 hours or until a fork can be inserted in the chicken with ease.

Chicken-Chilli Sandwich

Serves 4

- 4 chicken half-breasts (suprêmes)
- 2 cups (16 fl oz) water
- ¼ cup chopped celery
- ¼ cup chopped onion
- ¼ cup chopped green pepper (capsicum)
- 3 tablespoons chopped green chillies
- 2 tablespoons mayonnaise
- ¼ teaspoon chilli powder
- 8 slices firm white bread
- 4 slices cheese
- 2 eggs
- ¼ cup (2 fl oz) milk
- 30 g (1 oz) butter

Place the chicken in a deep saucepan and add the water. Cover and simmer for about 15 minutes or until a fork can be inserted in the chicken with ease. Cool. Separate the meat from the bones, if any. Dice the chicken. Discard the bones and skin. Mix together the celery, onion, green pepper, chillies, mayonnaise and chilli powder. Add the chicken and mix well. Spread the chicken mixture on 4 slices of bread. Top each with a slice of cheese, then the remaining bread slice, pressing lightly.

Beat the eggs and milk together. Dip the sandwiches into the egg mixture, turning to coat both sides. Drain briefly. Place the butter in a large pan and melt over medium heat. Place the sandwiches in the pan, cover and cook about 2½ minutes or until golden brown. Turn and cook a further 2½ minutes, until golden brown.

Chicken-Chilli Sandwich

Chicken

Chicken and Pineapple
Serves 4

- 2 tablespoons cornflour (cornstarch)
- 1 teaspoon ground ginger
- 4 tablespoons soy sauce
- 1 tablespoon olive oil
- ¼ cup (2 fl oz) pineapple juice
- 1 tablespoon finely chopped chives
- 4 chicken drumsticks
- 4 chicken thighs
- 1 teaspoon garlic salt
- 8 pineapple slices

Mix together the cornflour and ginger. Add the soy sauce and olive oil, stirring until smooth. Add the pineapple juice and chives. Brush the chicken with the mixture and arrange on an ovenproof dish, skin side up. Sprinkle the chicken with ½ teaspoon of the garlic salt. Place the pan on the grill so the chicken is about 20 cm (8 inch) from the heat. Grill (broil) until brown on one side, about 15 minutes. Turn the chicken and sprinkle with the remaining garlic salt. Grill (broil) a further 10 minutes.

Brush the pineapple slices with the remaining sauce and place in the pan with the chicken. Continue to cook a further 5 minutes or until a fork can be inserted in the chicken with ease. Serve over rice or soft noodles.

Chicken Jambalaya
Serves 4

- ⅔ cup (2½ oz) flour
- 2 tablespoons mild chilli powder
- 1 tablespoon plus ½ teaspoon salt
- 1 x 1.5 kg (3 lb) chicken, cut into serving pieces
- ⅓ cup (2½ fl oz) olive oil
- 1 large onion, chopped
- ⅔ cup (4 oz) rice
- 1 garlic clove, crushed
- 1 x 875 g (1 lb 12 oz) can peeled tomatoes, undrained
- ¼ cup (2 fl oz) water
- ⅛ teaspoon ground red (cayenne) pepper

Mix together the flour, chilli powder and 1 tablespoon of the salt. Add the chicken, one piece at a time, dredging to coat. Place the oil in a Dutch oven and heat to medium. Add the chicken and cook for about 10 minutes, turning, until brown on all sides. Remove the chicken and drain. Remove all but 1 tablespoon of the oil, then add the onion, rice and garlic.

Stir fry for about 4 minutes or until the rice is golden brown. Add the tomatoes, water, red pepper and the remaining salt. Mix well. Heat gently until the mixture boils. Return the chicken to the Dutch oven, making sure the hot mixture covers the chicken. Cover and bake at 180°C (350°F/Gas 4) for 1 hour or until a fork can be inserted in the chicken with ease.

Chicken Cannelloni
Serves 4

- 1 x 1.5 kg (3 lb) chicken, cut into serving pieces
- 2 cups (16 fl oz) water (approximately)
- 60 g (3 oz) butter
- 2½ tablespoons flour
- 2 cups (16 fl oz) hot milk
- ⅔ cup (2½ oz) grated Parmesan cheese
- 1 teaspoon salt
- ½ teaspoon pepper
- 4 eggs, beaten
- 1 tablespoon dried parsley flakes
- 1 teaspoon Italian seasoning
- 2½ cups (20 fl oz) spaghetti sauce
- 1 x 250 g (8 oz) packet cannelloni noodles, cooked and drained
- 1 cup (4 oz) grated mozzarella cheese

Place the chicken in a deep saucepan. Add the water, cover and simmer for about 45 minutes or until a fork can be inserted in the chicken with ease. Cool. Separate the meat from the bones. Discard the bones and skin. Cut the chicken into bite-sized pieces and reserve. Make a white sauce by placing 45 g (1½ oz) of the butter in a pan and melting over medium heat. Stir in the flour. Gradually add the hot milk, stirring, and cook for about 5 minutes or until thick and bubbly. Add half the Parmesan cheese, half the salt, and half the pepper. Set aside.

Place the remaining butter in a large pan and melt over low heat. Add the eggs, the remaining Parmesan cheese, the parsley flakes, Italian seasoning, and the remaining salt and pepper. Cook, stirring, until thick. Add the reserved chicken and mix well. Remove from the heat. Spread 1½ cups (12 fl oz) of the spaghetti sauce in a large shallow baking pan. Fill the cannelloni with the chicken mixture and place in a single layer, close together, over the spaghetti sauce. Spoon the remaining spaghetti sauce over the filled noodles, then top with the white sauce. Sprinkle with the mozzarella cheese. Bake, uncovered, at 180°C (350°F/Gas 4) for about 25 minutes.

Chicken Burgoo
Serves 4

- 10 chicken wings
- 4 cups (1 litre) water
- 2 cups grated cabbage
- 1 x 500 g (1 lb) can peeled tomatoes
- 1 packet dry onion soup mix
- 30 g (1 oz) margarine
- ½ teaspoon salt
- 1¼ cups (10 fl oz) condensed vegetable soup
- ½ cup (1 oz) instant mashed potato flakes

Place the chicken in a Dutch oven. Add the water, cabbage, tomatoes, soup mix, margarine and salt. Cover and bring to the boil. Reduce the heat and simmer for 1 hour. Remove the chicken wings from the Dutch oven. Cool. Separate the meat from the bones. Discard the bones and skin. Cut the chicken into bite-sized pieces and return to the Dutch oven. Add the vegetable soup and potato flakes. Stir to mix. Bring to the boil over medium heat and cook for 2 minutes.

Chicken with Artichokes

Serves 4

60 g (2 oz) butter
1 x 1.5 kg (3 lb) chicken, cut into serving pieces
4 small white onions, quartered
1 x 500 g (1 lb) can artichoke hearts, drained and halved
1 tablespoon chopped parsley
2 tablespoons water
1 teaspoon Italian seasoning
⅛ teaspoon garlic salt
1 tomato, chopped
¼ cup (2 fl oz) chablis

Place the butter in a large pan and heat to medium. Add the chicken and cook for about 10 minutes, turning, until brown on all sides. Remove the chicken to a medium baking pan or casserole. In the same pan place the onions, artichokes, parsley, water, Italian seasoning and garlic salt. Cook, stirring occasionally, over medium heat for about 5 minutes or until the onion is tender and the brown bits in the pan have dissolved. Stir in the tomato and wine. Pour over the chicken.

Cover and bake at 180°C (350°F/Gas 4) for about 50 minutes or until a fork can be inserted in the chicken with ease. Remove the cover, sprinkle with cheese, and return to the oven for 5 minutes or until the cheese melts.

Confetti Chicken Quiche

Serves 4 - 6

1 x 1.5 kg (3 lb) chicken, cut into serving pieces
2 cups (16 fl oz) water
1 cup (5 oz) grated cheese
1½ cups (6 oz) flour
½ cup diced onion
60 g (2 oz) butter or margarine
2 cups (16 fl oz) milk
4 eggs
⅔ cup cooked rice
1½ cups whole kernel corn
2 tablespoons chopped spring onion (scallion) tops
2 tablespoons chopped canned pimientos
½ teaspoon pepper
¼ teaspoon salt

Place the chicken in a deep saucepan. Add the water. Cover and simmer for about 45 minutes or until a fork can be inserted in the chicken with ease. Cool. Separate the meat from the bones. Discard the bones and skin. Cut the chicken into small pieces about 6 mm (¼ inch) square. Mix the cheese into the flour then add the onion. Mix well. Cut the butter through the mixture and add water, if necessary, to make a firm dough. Roll out to cover the base and sides of a 25 cm (10 inch) quiche dish or deep pie pan. Line the dish and set aside.

Place the milk, eggs and rice in an electric mixer and mix well. Add the corn, spring onion tops, pimiento, pepper, salt and the chicken. Stir to blend. Pour into the prepared crust. Bake, uncovered, at 180°C (350°F/Gas 4) for about 55 minutes or until a knife inserted near the centre comes out clean.

Chicken à la Brandy Wine

Serves 4

¼ teaspoon salt
¼ teaspoon paprika
1 x 1.5 kg (3 lb) chicken, cut into quarters, skinned and boned
100 g (3 ½ oz) butter
4 slices pineapple
125 g (4 oz) diced salt-cured ham
¼ cup chopped spring onions (scallions)
1 tablespoon brandy, warmed
½ cup (4 fl oz) white wine
1 tablespoon plus 1 teaspoon flour
½ cup (4 fl oz) cream
¼ cup (1 oz) slivered almonds

Sprinkle the salt and paprika on the chicken. Clarify the butter by melting half over low heat. Remove from the heat and let stand a few minutes, allowing the white milk solids to settle to the bottom. Skim the top for clarified butter. Place 2 tablespoons of the clarified butter in a large pan over very low heat. Add the chicken, top with pineapple slices, ham and spring onions. Cover and simmer for about 45 minutes or until a fork can be inserted in the chicken with ease, but avoid browning the chicken. Pour the warmed brandy over the chicken, then light a match to flambé.

Transfer the contents of the pan, as undisturbed as possible, to a warm serving dish. In the same pan make the sauce by pouring in the wine and cooking over high heat for about 2 minutes. Stir the flour into the cream and mix until smooth. Add the cream mixture to the wine in the pan, stirring well, and simmer about 1 minute or until thick. Add half the remaining butter to the sauce and stir until melted.

To serve, spoon part of the sauce over the chicken. Melt the remaining clarified butter over medium heat. Add almonds and cook, turning, until light brown. Sprinkle over chicken. Serve the remaining sauce separately.

Bravo Chicken

Serves 4

30 g (1 oz) butter
4 large potatoes, roughly chopped
6 carrots, roughly chopped
250 g (8 oz) Italian sausage, cut into 2.5 cm (1 inch) pieces
1 x 1.5 kg (3 lb) chicken, cut into serving pieces
1 tablespoon dried rosemary
¼ teaspoon salt
⅛ teaspoon pepper

Place the butter in a large shallow baking pan and melt over low heat. Add the potatoes and carrots. Toss to coat with butter. Add the sausage. Place the chicken on top of the vegetables and sausage. Sprinkle with the rosemary, salt and pepper. Cover and bake at 180°C (350°F/Gas 4) for 1 ½ hours. Uncover and bake a further 30 minutes or until a fork can be inserted in the chicken with ease.

Chicken

Olive-Rosemary Honey Chicken

Olive-Rosemary Honey Chicken

Serves 4

1 x 1.5 kg (3 lb) chicken, cut into serving pieces
60 g (2 oz) butter
¼ cup (2 fl oz) lime juice
1 tablespoon dried rosemary, crushed
1 teaspoon paprika
1 lime, thinly sliced
¼ cup (1 ½ oz) sliced olives
1 cup (12 oz) honey
1 teaspoon dried mint, crushed
1 teaspoon salt
¼ teaspoon pepper
¼ cup finely chopped parsley

Arrange the chicken, skin side up, in a large greased baking pan. Melt the butter over a medium heat. Add the lime juice, rosemary and paprika. Pour this mixture over the chicken and bake at 200°C (400°F/Gas 6) for 30 minutes, basting occasionally. Remove the chicken from the oven and top with the lime and olive slices. In a small bowl, mix together the honey, mint, salt and pepper. Pour slowly over the chicken. Return to the oven and bake a further 15 minutes or until a fork can be inserted in the chicken with ease. Garnish with the parsley.

Chicken in a Pot

Serves 4

1 apple, quartered
1 x 1.5 kg (3 lb) chicken
2 tablespoons lemon juice
2 teaspoons onion salt
½ teaspoon dried rosemary
⅛ teaspoon crushed garlic

Place the apple in the cavity of the chicken. Fold the wings across the back. Place the chicken, breast side up, in a casserole. Brush with the lemon juice and sprinkle with the onion salt, rosemary and garlic. Cover and roast at 190°C (375°F/Gas 5) for about 1 ½ hours or until a leg moves freely when lifted or twisted.

Chicken Tetrazzini

Serves 2

1 tablespoon cooking oil
4 chicken pieces
185 g (6 oz) mushrooms, thinly sliced
½ teaspoon salt
½ teaspoon paprika
⅛ teaspoon pepper
1 ½ tablespoons flour
¾ cup (6 fl oz) chicken stock
¼ cup (2 fl oz) sherry
1 teaspoon chopped parsley
2 cups hot, cooked vermicelli noodles

Place the oil in a small pan and heat to medium. Add the chicken and cook for about 10 minutes, turning, until brown on all sides. Move the chicken to one side of the pan and add the mushrooms. Sprinkle with the salt, paprika and pepper. Reduce the heat to low and cook, uncovered, for about 20 minutes or until a fork can be inserted in the chicken with ease. Transfer the chicken to a warm dish. Drain off all but 1 tablespoon of the oil. Leave the mushrooms and drippings in the pan. Sprinkle the flour in the pan and brown, stirring, over medium heat, for about 1 minute. Stir in the stock and sherry, add the parsley and stir. Cook a further 2 minutes or until smooth and thickened. Stir the hot, cooked noodles into the sauce and pour the mixture into a serving bowl.

Chicken in Curry Cream Sauce

Serves 4

1 x 1.5 kg (3 lb) chicken, cut into serving pieces
seasoned flour
oil and butter or margarine
1 onion, chopped
2 teaspoons curry powder
1 ¼ cups (10 fl oz) white sauce (*page 33*)
2 tablespoons cream

Roll the chicken pieces in the seasoned flour. Heat a mixture of oil and butter in a sauté pan and add the chicken pieces, the onion and the curry powder. Sauté for approximately 15 minutes, then remove the chicken pieces and keep warm. Mix the white sauce into the onion and curry mixture and stir well. Return the chicken to the pan and continue cooking gently until the chicken is tender. Add the cream just before serving.

Opposite: *Chicken in a Pot*

233

Chicken

Herby Chicken Pie
Serves 8

- 3 ¾ cups (30 fl oz) chicken stock (*page 40*)
- 1 cup (7 oz) pearl barley
- 3 leeks
- 90 g (3 oz) butter or margarine
- salt and pepper
- 750 g (1 ½ lb) cooked chicken, diced
- 2 teaspoons chopped parsley
- ½ teaspoon dried thyme
- 1 ½ cups (6 oz) grated cheese
- 3 large tomatoes, sliced

Boil the chicken stock and add the barley. Simmer for 40 to 45 minutes or until just cooked. Coarsely shred the leeks and sweat them in the butter without colouring, then season and sprinkle them in a suitable shallow dish.

Combine the chicken meat, cooked barley, half the chopped parsley, the thyme, salt and pepper, and evenly cover the leeks with this mixture. Sprinkle with the grated cheese, arrange slices of tomato on top and bake in the oven at 190°C (375°F/Gas 5) for 25 minutes until the cheese is coloured. Sprinkle with the remaining chopped parsley and serve.

Lazy Day Chinese Chicken
Serves 4

- 1 tablespoon cooking oil
- 1 x 1.5 kg (3 lb) chicken
- ¼ cup (2 fl oz) sherry
- ¾ cup (6 fl oz) soy sauce
- ¼ cup (2 fl oz) water
- ¼ cup chopped spring onions (scallions)
- 3 garlic cloves, crushed
- 1 tablespoon sugar
- 1 teaspoon finely chopped fresh ginger

Place the oil in a Dutch oven or casserole and heat to high. Add the chicken and cook on all sides until brown. Pour the sherry over the chicken. Mix together the soy sauce, water, spring onion, garlic, sugar and ginger. Add this mixture to the chicken. Cover and simmer for 25 minutes. Turn the chicken and simmer a further 10 minutes or until the leg moves freely when lifted or twisted. Serve whole, sliced, or chopped, with the juices.

Chicken au Poivre
Serves 4

- ⅓ cup (1 ½ oz) flour
- 1 teaspoon salt
- ½ teaspoon pepper
- 1 x 1.5 kg (3 lb) chicken, cut into serving pieces
- 60 g (2 oz) butter, melted
- ½ cup (4 fl oz) hamburger dressing
- ¼ cup (1 oz) raisins
- ¼ cup chopped onion
- 1 teaspoon vinegar
- ¼ teaspoon ground ginger
- ¼ cup (2 fl oz) water
- ½ teaspoon cornflour (cornstarch)
- 4 pears, halved and cored

Mix together the flour, salt and pepper. Add the chicken, one piece at a time, dredging to coat. Place the butter in a large shallow baking pan. Arrange the chicken, skin side up, in a single layer in the butter. Bake, uncovered, at 220°C (425°F/Gas 7), basting once, for 35 minutes. Mix together the hamburger dressing, raisins, onion, vinegar and ginger and stir. Simmer over medium heat for 10 minutes. Remove from heat.

Mix the water and cornflour, stirring until smooth. Gradually add to the sauce. Cook, stirring constantly, for about 4 minutes or until slightly thick. Arrange the pears among the chicken pieces in the baking pan. Spoon the sauce over the chicken and pears. Bake, uncovered, at 180°C (350°F/Gas 4) for 30 minutes or until a fork can be inserted in the chicken with ease.

Creamy Lemon Chicken
Serves 6

- ½ cup (2 oz) flour
- ½ teaspoon paprika
- ½ teaspoon salt
- ½ teaspoon pepper
- 1 egg, beaten
- 1 ½ cups (6 oz) seasoned breadcrumbs
- 3 whole chicken breasts, halved
- 125 g (4 oz) butter
- ¼ cup (2 fl oz) chicken consommé
- ½ cup (2 oz) slivered almonds
- 3 tablespoons chopped chives
- ¾ cup (6 fl oz) cream, whipped
- 1 lemon, thinly sliced

Mix together the flour, paprika, salt and pepper. Place the egg in a shallow dish and in another dish place the crumbs. Add the chicken, one piece at a time, to the flour mixture, dredging to coat. Then dip the chicken in the egg and roll in the crumbs. Place the butter in a heavy pan and melt over medium heat. Add the chicken and cook for about 10 minutes, turning, until brown on all sides. Add the consommé and almonds. Cover and simmer for about 25 minutes or until a fork can be inserted in the chicken with ease. Fold the chives into the whipped cream and chill until time to serve. When the chicken is done, remove to a warm serving dish and place a lemon slice on each piece of chicken and then top with a spoonful of cream.

Zippy Fruit Chicken

Serves 4

1 x 1.5 kg (3 lb) chicken, cut into serving pieces
½ cup (2 fl oz) crushed cracker crumbs
1½ teaspoons salt
¼ teaspoon pepper
¼ cup (2 fl oz) cooking oil
1 x 500 g (1 lb) can pear halves, drained and syrup reserved
1 tablespoon lemon juice
1 tablespoon soy sauce
2 teaspoons cornflour (cornstarch)
1½ teaspoons dry mustard
¾ teaspoon grated lemon rind

Roll the chicken in the crumbs, one piece at a time, to coat, then sprinkle with the salt and pepper. Place the oil in a large pan and heat to medium. Add the chicken and cook for about 10 minutes, turning, until brown on all sides. Mix together the reserved pear syrup, lemon juice, soy sauce, cornflour, mustard and lemon rind. Pour this sauce over the chicken, stirring occasionally and simmer about 5 minutes or until the sauce becomes thick.

Place the chicken, skin side up, in a single layer in a large shallow baking pan. Pour the sauce over the chicken. Bake, uncovered, at 180°C (350°F/Gas 4), basting occasionally, for 45 minutes or until a fork can be inserted in the chicken with ease. Arrange the pear halves among the chicken pieces and baste with the sauce. Bake a further 10 minutes or until the pears are heated through. Baste again before serving.

Riverboat Chicken Wheel

Serves 6

12 chicken drumsticks
2 teaspoons salt
1 teaspoon pepper
½ cup (4 fl oz) cooking oil
1 tablespoon garlic salt
½ cup (4 fl oz) Italian salad dressing
½ cup (4 fl oz) soy sauce
1 tablespoon soft brown sugar
½ teaspoon curry powder
3 cups (24 fl oz) water
3 cups (1 ¼ lb) quick cooking rice
1 tablespoon chopped parsley flakes

Sprinkle the chicken with the salt and pepper. Place the oil in a large pan and heat to high. Add the chicken and cook for about 5 minutes, turning, until brown on all sides. Sprinkle with garlic salt and cook a further 1 minute. Add the Italian salad dressing and soy sauce. Sprinkle the brown sugar and curry powder on the chicken. Cover and cook over high heat for about 12 minutes or until a fork can be inserted in the chicken with ease. Remove the chicken from the pan and keep hot. Add the water to the pan drippings, stirring to loosen brown bits, and bring to the boil. Add the rice and stir. Cover and simmer for 10 minutes or until the rice is cooked. Place the rice on a large round serving dish and sprinkle with parsley. Arrange the chicken over the rice in a wheel pattern.

Spicy Chicken with Rice

Serves 4

1 x 1.5 kg (3 lb) chicken, quartered
2 cups (16 fl oz) water (approximately)
1 tablespoon cooking oil
500 g (1 lb) mushrooms, sliced
1 green pepper (capsicum), chopped
1 onion, chopped
1 cup (6 oz) brown rice
2 cups canned tomatoes
1 cup (8 fl oz) dry sherry
1 x 90 g (3 oz) jar sliced stuffed olives, juice reserved
3 garlic cloves, crushed
3 bay leaves
½ teaspoon dried basil
½ teaspoon dried marjoram
½ teaspoon dried oregano
½ teaspoon dried thyme
½ teaspoon Tabasco sauce
500 g (1 lb) frozen green peas
1 x 500 g (1 lb) can artichoke hearts with juice

Place the chicken in a deep saucepan. Add the water. Cover and simmer for about 45 minutes or until a fork can be inserted in the chicken with ease. Cool. Make the broth up to 2 cups (16 fl oz) with water if necessary and reserve. Separate the meat from the bones. Discard the bones and skin. Cut the chicken into bite-sized pieces and reserve.

Place the oil in a large pan and heat to medium. Add the mushrooms, green pepper, onion and brown rice and stir. Cover and cook for 10 minutes. Add the tomatoes, sherry, olives with their juice, garlic, bay leaves, basil, marjoram, oregano, thyme and Tabasco sauce. Stir to mix well. Cover and simmer for 15 minutes. Add the reserved chicken and broth and simmer for 30 minutes. Stir in the peas and artichokes and simmer a further 10 minutes or until the peas and rice are tender.

Chicken Vermouth

Serves 4

1 x 1.5 kg (3 lb) chicken, cut into serving pieces
2½ teaspoons salt
½ teaspoon pepper
3 medium-sized carrots, sliced
2 stalks celery, thinly sliced
1 medium-sized onion, thinly sliced
6 garlic cloves, peeled
2 tablespoons chopped parsley
⅓ cup (2½ fl oz) dry white vermouth
¼ cup (2 fl oz) sour cream

Sprinkle the chicken with the salt and pepper. Place the chicken, skin side up, in a single layer in a large covered casserole. Add the carrots, celery, onion, garlic, parsley and vermouth. Cover tightly and bake at 190°C (375°F/Gas 5) for about 1½ hours or until a fork can be inserted in the chicken with ease. Add the sour cream to the liquid in the baking pan. Stir to warm through. Serve over hot rice.

Chicken

Cherry Chicken

Cherry Chicken

Serves 4

1 x 1.5 kg (3 lb) chicken, cut into serving pieces
1¼ teaspoons salt
¼ teaspoon pepper
¼ teaspoon paprika
60 g (2 oz) butter
1 tablespoon flour
1 teaspoon sugar
⅛ teaspoon ground allspice
⅛ teaspoon ground cinnamon
1 x 500 g (1 lb) can pitted red sour cherries, drained and juice reserved
1 x 250 g (8 oz) can crushed pineapple
1 chicken stock cube, crushed
a few drops of red food colouring

Sprinkle the chicken with 1 teaspoon of the salt, the pepper and paprika. Place the butter in a large pan and melt over medium heat. Add the chicken and cook for about 10 minutes, turning, until brown on all sides. Remove the chicken from the pan and set aside.

In the same pan place the flour, sugar, remaining salt, allspice and cinnamon. Stir to mix with the pan drippings. Gradually pour in the reserved cherry juice. Stir to mix. Add the pineapple, stock cube and food colouring and mix until blended. Return the chicken to the pan. Cover and simmer for 40 minutes or until a fork can be inserted in the chicken with ease. Add the cherries during the last 5 minutes of the cooking time. Place the chicken on a serving dish and pour over the sauce.

Ginger Wine Chicken

Serves 4

8 chicken thighs
½ cup (4 fl oz) sherry
30 g (1 oz) margarine
2 tablespoons vinegar
2 tablespoons tomato sauce
2 tablespoons honey
1 tablespoon cornflour (cornstarch)
½ teaspoon salt
¼ teaspoon garlic salt
¼ teaspoon ground ginger
⅛ teaspoon coarsely ground pepper

Place the chicken, skin side up, in a single layer in a shallow baking pan. Mix together the sherry, margarine, vinegar, tomato sauce, honey, cornflour, salt, garlic salt, ginger and pepper. Place over medium heat and bring to the boil. Cook, stirring occasionally, for about 5 minutes or until thick and clear. Baste the chicken with one third of the sauce. Bake, uncovered, at 190°C (375°F/Gas 5) for 20 minutes. Baste with more sauce and return to the oven for 10 minutes. Baste again and continue to bake a further 30 minutes or until a fork can be inserted in the chicken with ease.

Skillet Chicken

Serves 4

¼ cup (2 fl oz) olive oil
1 x 1.5 kg (3 lb) chicken, cut into serving pieces
1 large onion, chopped
2 small zucchini (courgettes), sliced into 1.25 cm (½ inch) pieces
1 large green pepper (capsicum), chopped
2 tablespoons flour
1 teaspoon paprika
1 teaspoon salt
¼ teaspoon pepper
½ cup tomato pulp
1¼ cups (10 fl oz) yoghurt

Place the oil in a large pan and heat to medium. Add the chicken and onion and cook for about 10 minutes or until the onion is golden. Cover the pan and simmer for about 30 minutes, stirring occasionally, until nearly tender. Add the zucchini and green pepper.

Stir fry for about 5 minutes, or until the zucchini is transparent. Mix together the flour, paprika, salt and pepper and add to the chicken slowly, stirring to prevent lumps. Add the tomato pulp and cook over high heat for about 5 minutes or until a fork can be inserted in the chicken with ease. Turn the heat to low and blend in the yoghurt.

Chicken with Avocado

Chicken with Avocado

Serves 4

- 125 g (4 oz) butter
- 1 x 1.5 kg (3lb) chicken, cut into serving pieces
- 1 medium-sized onion, chopped
- 1 chicken stock cube, crumbled
- ¾ teaspoon salt
- ¼ teaspoon pepper
- ½ teaspoon chilli powder
- pinch of cinnamon
- 3 tablespoons flour
- ½ cup (4 fl oz) orange juice
- ½ cup (4 fl oz) dry white wine
- 1 large avocado, peeled and sliced
- 2 tablespoons grated orange rind

Place half the butter in a pan and melt over medium heat. Add the chicken and cook for about 10 minutes, turning, until brown on all sides. Remove the chicken to a large casserole. Add the onion to the pan and sauté for about 2 minutes. Stir in the stock cube, ½ teaspoon of the salt, the pepper, chilli powder and cinnamon. Spread the onion mixture over the chicken. Cover and bake at 180°C (350°F/Gas 4) for 20 minutes. Drain any excess oil from the pan. Add the remaining butter and melt. Stir in the flour. Cook over medium heat for about 3 minutes until smooth. Add the orange juice and wine and cook a further 3 minutes or until thickened. Pour over the chicken in the casserole. Cover and bake a further 25 minutes or until a fork can be inserted in the chicken with ease. Top with the avocado slices and sprinkle with the remaining salt. Bake a further 10 minutes, uncovered. Sprinkle with orange rind.

Saucy Chicken

Serves 4

- ¼ cup (1 oz) flour
- 1 x 1.5 kg (3 lb) chicken, cut into serving pieces
- 125 g (4 oz) margarine
- 1 large onion, diced
- 1¼ cups sliced mushrooms
- 1½ cups (10 fl oz) cream of mushroom soup
- ⅔ cup (5 fl oz) evaporated milk
- ½ cup (2 oz) grated cheese
- ½ cup (2 oz) grated Swiss cheese
- ½ teaspoon salt
- ¼ teaspoon dried dill
- ⅛ teaspoon pepper

Place the flour in a shallow dish. Add the chicken, one piece at a time, dredging to coat. Place half the margarine in a shallow baking pan. Melt the margarine. Place the chicken, skin side down, in a single layer in the margarine. Bake, uncovered, at 220°C (425°F/Gas 7) for 30 minutes. Turn the chicken and continue baking a further 15 minutes or until brown. Remove the chicken and turn the oven to 160°C (325°F/Gas 3). Drain the excess drippings from the pan. Melt the remaining margarine over medium heat. Add the onion and sauté for about 5 minutes or until golden. Stir in the mushrooms and continue cooking a further 3 minutes. Add the mushroom soup, milk, both the cheeses, salt, dill and pepper. Stir well and pour over the chicken. Cover and bake for about 15 minutes or until the sauce bubbles and a fork can be inserted in the chicken with ease.

Chicken

Green Pepper Chicken

Serves 4

- 1 x 1.5 kg (3 lb) chicken, cut into serving pieces
- ½ teaspoon garlic salt
- ¼ teaspoon ground ginger
- 2 tablespoons cooking oil
- 125 g (4 oz) mushrooms
- 1 medium-sized green pepper (capsicum), sliced into rings
- ¼ cup (2 fl oz) dry sherry
- ¼ cup (2 fl oz) soy sauce
- 1 tablespoon sugar
- 1 tablespoon cornflour (cornstarch)

Sprinkle the chicken with the garlic salt and ginger. Place the oil in a large pan and heat to medium. Add the chicken and cook for about 10 minutes, turning, until brown on all sides. Reduce the heat to low. Cover and simmer for 30 minutes. Add the mushrooms and green pepper. Cover and cook for about 3 minutes or until the pepper is tender-crisp. Place the sherry, soy sauce, sugar and cornflour in a jar. Cover and shake to mix, then gradually pour over the chicken, stirring. Simmer for about 2 minutes or until clear and thick and a fork can be inserted in the chicken with ease. Serve with hot fluffy rice.

Chicken-Endive au Gratin

Serves 6

- 500 g (1 lb) endive (chicory)
- 2½ cups (20 fl oz) chicken stock
- juice of ½ lemon
- 60 g (2 oz) butter
- ¼ cup (1 oz) flour
- 1 cup (8 fl oz) cream
- 2 tablespoons dry cooking sherry
- 1½ teaspoons salt
- 1¼ teaspoons pepper
- 1 teaspoon dried thyme
- 3 cups cooked chicken, diced
- 2 tablespoons grated Parmesan cheese
- 2 teaspoons paprika
- 2 tablespoons chopped parsley

Trim and discard the tough outer stalks and darker ends of the endive. Split each endive shoot in half and cut crosswise into 2.5 cm (1 inch) lengths. Place the endive pieces in a saucepan and add 1 cup (8 fl oz) of the chicken stock and the lemon juice. Cover and simmer on low heat for 10 minutes or until barely limp. Melt the butter over medium heat, then add the flour, stirring with a wire whisk. Add the remaining stock, stirring well to blend. Add the cream, sherry, salt, pepper and thyme. Blend with a whisk and heat to make a smooth white sauce.

With a slotted spoon, remove the endive from the saucepan and place in a greased shallow baking pan. Add the diced chicken and cover with the white sauce. Sprinkle with the Parmesan cheese and paprika. Bake at 190°C (375°F/Gas 5) for about 20 minutes or until bubbly. Sprinkle with the chopped parsley.

Stuffed Chicken Legs

Serves 5

- 30 g (1 oz) butter
- 2 garlic cloves, crushed
- 1 x 315 g (10 oz) packet frozen chopped broccoli, cooked and drained
- 250 g (4 oz) mushrooms, sliced
- 1 egg, beaten
- 2 eggs, hard-boiled and coarsely chopped
- ¼ cup (1 oz) breadcrumbs
- 2 tablespoons grated Parmesan cheese
- ½ teaspoon salt
- ¼ teaspoon pepper
- 5 chicken maryland pieces
- ⅛ teaspoon paprika

Tomato Sauce
- 1 cup stewed or canned tomatoes
- ½ cup (4 fl oz) chicken stock
- ⅓ cup (2½ fl oz) white wine
- 1 rounded tablespoon cornflour (cornstarch)
- 1 tablespoon chopped parsley
- 1½ teaspoons sugar
- ¼ teaspoon salt
- ¼ teaspoon dried oregano

Melt the butter over medium heat. Add the garlic and sauté for 2 minutes. Add the broccoli, mushrooms, beaten egg, hard-boiled eggs, breadcrumbs, cheese, ⅛ teaspoon of the salt and ⅛ teaspoon of the pepper. Toss lightly to mix and set aside. Place the chicken, skin side down, on a hard surface. Cut the meat down to the bone the length of thigh and drumstick. Pull or scrape the meat away from the bone, keeping the meat in one piece. Flatten slightly with a meat mallet. Sprinkle with ¼ teaspoon of the salt and the remaining pepper. Divide the stuffing into 5 equal portions and place one portion on each piece of chicken. Shape the chicken to form a ball, fasten with toothpicks and place, open end down, on a greased baking sheet. Sprinkle with the remaining salt and paprika. Bake, uncovered, at 180°C (350°F/Gas 4) for 45 minutes. Spoon some Tomato Sauce over the chicken. Bake a further 30 minutes or until a fork can be inserted in the chicken with ease. Serve the remaining sauce with the chicken.

Tomato Sauce: Mix together the tomatoes, chicken stock, white wine, cornflour, parsley, sugar, salt and oregano. Cook, stirring, over medium heat until the mixture boils. Reduce the heat and simmer for 2 minutes.

Chicken Mini-Drumsticks

Makes 36 hors d'oeuvres

- 1 cup (8 fl oz) pineapple juice
- 1 cup (8 fl oz) beer
- ½ cup (4 fl oz) soy sauce
- ¼ cup (1½ oz) soft brown sugar
- 2 tablespoons finely chopped onion
- 1 teaspoon ground ginger
- 1 garlic clove, crushed
- 36 chicken wings, tips removed
- 60 g (2 oz) butter

Mix together the pineapple juice, beer, soy sauce, brown sugar, onion, ginger and garlic and stir until the sugar is dissolved. Add the chicken, stirring to coat. Cover and marinate at room temperature for about 1 hour. Drain the chicken and reserve the marinade. Place the butter in a large pan and melt over medium heat. Add the chicken and cook for about 10 minutes, turning, until brown on all sides. Add ¼ cup (2 fl oz) of the reserved marinade to the chicken. Cover and simmer, stirring occasionally, over low heat for about 15 minutes or until a fork can be inserted in the chicken with ease. Keep the chicken moist by adding additional marinade if needed.

Texas Chicken

Serves 4

- ¼ cup (2 fl oz) cooking oil
- 2 large tomatoes, sliced
- 2 large onions, sliced
- 8 chicken thighs
- ½ cup (4 fl oz) evaporated milk
- 4 garlic cloves, crushed
- 1½ tablespoons soft brown sugar
- 1½ tablespoons lemon juice
- 2 teaspoons crushed peppercorns
- 1½ teaspoons salt
- ¼ teaspoon ground mace
- 2 bay leaves

Place the oil in a large pan and heat to medium. Add the tomatoes and onion and cook about 5 minutes. Add the chicken, stirring several times. Add milk, garlic, brown sugar, lemon juice, peppercorns, salt, mace and bay leaves and bring to the boil. Cover and simmer for 50 minutes, stirring frequently. Remove the cover and cook a further 10 minutes over high heat, reducing most of the liquid and until a fork can be inserted in the chicken with ease. Discard the bay leaves before serving.

Spicy Chicken and Peaches

Serves 4

- 1½ cups sliced canned peaches, drained
- 1 cup (8 fl oz) orange juice
- 2 tablespoons soft brown sugar
- 2 tablespoons vinegar
- 1 teaspoon dried basil
- 1 teaspoon ground nutmeg
- 1 garlic clove, crushed
- ½ cup (2 oz) flour
- 1 teaspoon salt
- ⅛ teaspoon pepper
- 8 chicken thighs
- ¼ cup (2 fl oz) cooking oil

Mix together the peaches, orange juice, brown sugar, vinegar, basil, nutmeg and garlic. Simmer over low heat for 10 minutes and reserve. Mix together the flour, salt and pepper. Add the chicken, one piece at a time, dredging to coat. Place the oil in a pan and heat to medium. Add the chicken and cook for about 10 minutes, turning, until brown on all sides. Drain the oil from the pan. Pour the reserved peach mixture over the chicken. Cover and simmer for 20 minutes or until a fork can be inserted in the chicken with ease. Spoon some sauce over the chicken and serve the remainder separately.

Chicken Vino

Serves 4

- ¾ cup (6 fl oz) chicken stock
- ¼ cup (2 fl oz) tomato paste
- 1 cup (8 fl oz) dry white wine
- ½ teaspoon garlic salt
- ½ teaspoon dried oregano
- ¼ teaspoon salt
- ¼ teaspoon dried basil
- 1 x 1.5 kg (3 lb) chicken, cut into serving pieces
- 4 medium-sized potatoes, roughly chopped
- 3 carrots, sliced 6 mm (¼ inch) thick
- 1 medium-sized zucchini (courgette), sliced 6 mm (¼ inch) thick
- 1 medium-sized onion, sliced
- 3 stalks celery, sliced 6 mm (¼ inch) thick
- 250 g (8 oz) small whole mushrooms

Warm the chicken stock over medium heat. Stir in the tomato paste until smooth. Add the wine, garlic salt, oregano, salt and basil. Stir. Heat until warm. Place the chicken in a large clay pot or Dutch oven. Add the potatoes, carrots, zucchini, onion, celery and mushrooms. Pour in the sauce. Cover and place in a preheated oven and bake at 200°C (400°F/Gas 6) for 1 ¾ hours or until a fork can be inserted in the chicken with ease.

Chicken

Chicken Cacciatore

Serves 4

- 1 x 1.5 kg (3 lb) chicken, cut into serving pieces
- 1 teaspoon salt
- ½ teaspoon pepper
- ½ cup (2 oz) flour
- 5 tablespoons olive oil
- 2 onions, sliced
- 1 large green pepper (capsicum), cut into strips
- 1 garlic clove, crushed
- 2 cups sliced mushrooms
- 1 x 440 g (14 oz) can peeled tomatoes, crushed
- 1 teaspoon chopped fresh basil
- 1 bay leaf
- ½ cup (4 fl oz) dry white wine
- cooked vermicelli

Sprinkle the chicken with half the salt and half the pepper. Place the flour in a shallow dish and add the chicken, one piece at a time, dredging to coat. Place the olive oil in a large pan and heat to medium high. Add the chicken and cook for about 10 minutes, turning, until brown on all sides. Remove the chicken and keep warm. To the oil in the pan, add the onions, green pepper and garlic. Sauté over medium heat for about 5 minutes. Add the mushrooms and cook, stirring, for about 3 minutes. Add the crushed tomatoes, the remaining salt and pepper, the basil and bay leaf. Simmer, uncovered, on low heat for 5 minutes. Return the chicken to the pan, spooning the sauce and vegetables over. Cover and cook on low heat for 30 minutes. Add the wine, cover and cook a further 15 minutes. Serve over cooked vermicelli.

Chicken Cacciatore

Chicken-au-Feu

Serves 4

- ¼ cup (2 fl oz) corn oil
- 1 x 1.5 kg (3 lb) chicken, cut into serving pieces
- 5 cups (1.25 litres) plus 1 tablespoon water
- 1 onion, halved
- 2 carrots, sliced
- 2 stalks celery, sliced
- 2 chicken stock cubes
- 3 sprigs parsley
- 1½ teaspoons salt
- 1 small head of cabbage, cut into eighths
- 315 g (10 oz) frozen peas
- 1 tablespoon cornflour (cornstarch)
- 1 tablespoon water

Place the oil in a Dutch oven or casserole and heat to medium. Add the chicken and cook for about 10 minutes, turning, until brown on all sides. Add the 5 cups (1.25 litres) water, the onion, carrots, celery, stock cubes, parsley and salt. Cover and simmer for about 30 minutes or until a fork can be inserted in the chicken with ease. Remove the parsley. Add the cabbage and peas. Cover and simmer for about 15 minutes or until the vegetables are tender. Remove the chicken and vegetables and keep warm.

Place the cornflour in a bowl and stir in 1 tablespoon of water. Add the juices in the pot and boil for 1 minute, stirring constantly. Return the chicken and vegetables to the pot and heat through.

Opposite: *Chicken-au-Feu*

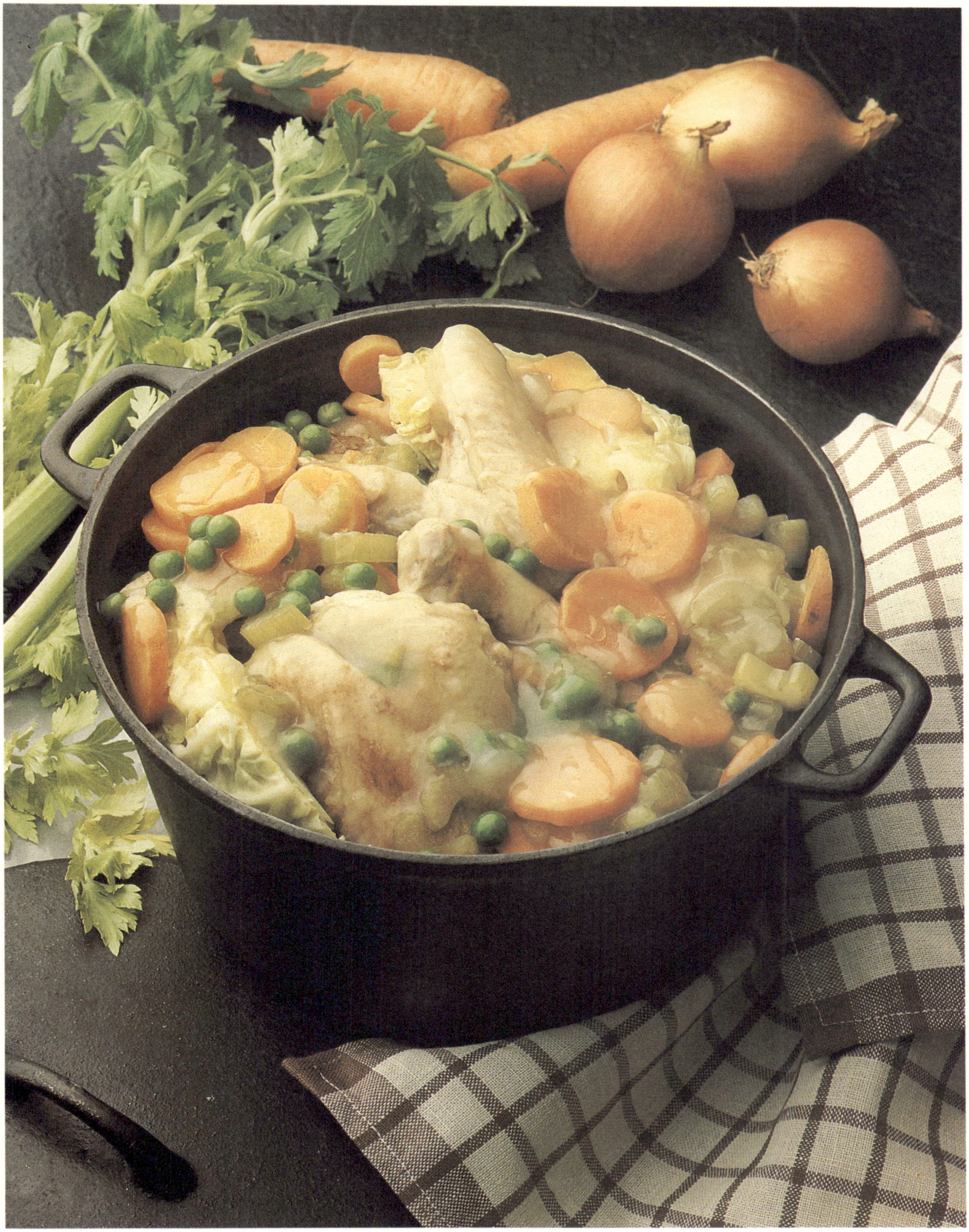

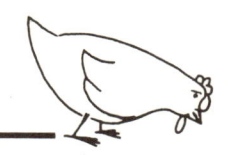

Chicken

Gingered Pear Chicken

Serves 4

60 g (2 oz) margarine	¼ cup (1½ oz) soft brown sugar
4 chicken half-breasts, (suprêmes)	3 tablespoons soy sauce
¼ teaspoon salt	2 teaspoons cornflour (cornstarch)
1 x 500 g (1 lb) can pear halves, drained, each half cut into 2 wedges, and juice reserved	¼ cup (2 fl oz) water
	¼ teaspoon ground ginger
¾ cup (6 fl oz) ginger ale	¼ cup (1 oz) walnuts, coarsely chopped

Place the margarine in a pan and melt over medium heat. Add the chicken and cook for about 10 minutes, turning, until brown on both sides. Sprinkle with the salt. Place the pear juice in a measuring cup and add water, if necessary, to make ¾ cup (6 fl oz) liquid. Mix together the pear juice, ginger ale, brown sugar and soy sauce. Pour over the chicken. Cover and cook over medium heat, turning occasionally, for about 25 minutes or until a fork can be inserted in the chicken with ease.

Remove the chicken from the pan and place in a single layer in a large shallow baking pan. Place the pear wedges around the chicken. Mix the cornflour with the water, stirring until smooth. Add the ginger and stir. Pour the cornflour mixture into the pan juices and cook for about 5 minutes, stirring until thick. Pour the thickened mixture over the chicken and pears. Sprinkle the walnuts over. Bake, uncovered, at 180°C (350°F/Gas 4) for about 10 minutes.

Italian Chicken Liver Pâté

60 g (2 oz) butter	¼ teaspoon dried basil
⅔ cup finely chopped onion	¼ teaspoon dried oregano
⅓ cup finely chopped celery	250 g (8 oz) chicken livers
	2 tablespoons tomato sauce
1 teaspoon garlic salt	1 cup (4 oz) grated mozzarella cheese
¼ teaspoon pepper	thinly sliced mushrooms

Melt the butter in a heavy pan. Sauté the onion and celery for 3 minutes. Stir in the garlic salt, pepper, basil and oregano. Add the chicken livers and sauté 3 to 4 minutes on each side. Pour all the ingredients except the cheese into a blender or food processor and add the tomato sauce. Blend very lightly; the texture should be coarse, not puréed.

Refrigerate the liver mixture and when chilled pour into a small mixing bowl. Add the grated cheese and beat until completely mixed. Pack into a 2 cup (16 fl oz) mould and refrigerate for at least 2 hours. At serving time unmould and garnish with thinly sliced mushrooms. Sprinkle with freshly chopped parsley and serve with thin wheat wafers.

Yoghurt-Lemon Chicken

Serves 4

1 cup (8 fl oz) yoghurt	½ teaspoon freshly ground pepper
¼ cup (2 fl oz) wine vinegar	½ teaspoon ground ginger
1 tablespoon lemon juice	⅛ teaspoon ground cloves
1 garlic clove, crushed	5 drops of Tabasco sauce
1 teaspoon ground coriander	1 x 1.5 kg (3 lb) chicken, cut into serving pieces
1 teaspoon dry mustard	

Mix together the yoghurt, vinegar, lemon juice, garlic, coriander, mustard, pepper, ginger, cloves and Tabasco sauce. Add the chicken, turning to coat, and marinate in the refrigerator for about 1½ hours. Reserve the marinade. Place the chicken, skin side up, on the griller (broiler). Cook gently, turning and basting with the reserved marinade, until a fork can be inserted in the chicken with ease.

Sesame Chicken

Serves 4

2 teaspoons curry powder	1 x 1.5 kg (3 lb) chicken, quartered
½ teaspoon dried mint	
½ teaspoon ground sage	3 tablespoons cooking oil
¼ teaspoon salt	1 cup (8 fl oz) water
1 teaspoon lemon juice	3 tablespoons sesame seeds

Make a paste by mixing together the curry powder, mint, sage, salt and lemon juice. Spread the paste evenly over the chicken pieces. Place the oil in a large pan and heat to medium. Add the chicken and cook for about 10 minutes, turning, until brown on all sides. Add the water. Cover and simmer for 20 minutes. Turn the chicken and continue cooking a further 25 minutes or until a fork can be inserted in the chicken with ease. Sprinkle the sesame seeds over the chicken.

Rosemary's Chicken

Serves 4

2 whole chicken breasts, halved	⅛ teaspoon pepper
	½ cup (4 fl oz) white wine
1 teaspoon finely chopped lemon rind	60 g (2 oz) butter
	½ teaspoon dried rosemary
½ teaspoon salt	

Place the chicken, skin side up, in a single layer in a shallow baking pan. Sprinkle with the lemon rind, salt and pepper. Heat the wine and butter. Do not boil. Add the rosemary and pour over the chicken. Cover and bake at 180°C (350°F/Gas 4) for about 30 minutes or until a fork can be inserted in the chicken with ease.

Buttered Honey Chicken Bites

Makes 36 - 48

6 chicken thighs, boned
60 g (2 oz) butter
4 tablespoons honey
1 teaspoon teriyaki sauce
1 teaspoon seasoned salt
½ teaspoon garlic salt
¼ teaspoon pepper
½ cup sesame seeds, toasted

Cut each chicken thigh into 6 or 8 pieces. Pat dry and chill overnight. Melt the butter and honey over low heat. Add the teriyaki sauce. Sprinkle the chicken with seasoned salt, garlic salt and pepper. Dip each piece into the honey-butter sauce and roll in sesame seeds. Place the chicken pieces on a baking sheet. Bake at 180°C (350°F/Gas 4) for about 30 minutes, turning once to brown evenly. Reheat the remaining honey-butter sauce to serve with the cooked chicken pieces.

Chicken and Macaroni

Serves 4

½ cup (2 oz) flour
2 teaspoons seasoned salt
1 x 1.5 kg (3 lb) chicken, cut into serving pieces
½ cup (4 fl oz) cooking oil
5 spring onions (scallions), chopped
1 cup chopped green pepper (capsicum)
500 g (1 lb) mushrooms, sliced
1 x 750 g (1¾ lb) can tomatoes, drained and coarsely chopped, liquid reserved
¼ cup (2 fl oz) sherry
3 teaspoons salt
1 teaspoon freshly ground black pepper
2 tablespoons grated horse-radish
1½ teaspoons dry mustard
½ teaspoon dried tarragon
2 chicken stock cubes
1 cup (8 fl oz) water (approximately)
2 cups macaroni

Mix the flour and the seasoned salt. Add the chicken, a few pieces at a time, and shake to coat. Heat the oil to medium in a pan and add the chicken. Cook for about 15 minutes, turning, until brown on all sides. Remove the chicken and set aside.

In the same pan place the spring onions and green pepper. Sauté for about 5 minutes or until soft. Add the mushrooms and sauté for 2 minutes. Add the tomatoes, sherry, salt, pepper, horseradish, mustard and tarragon. Stir and remove from the heat. Place the stock cubes in the water and stir until dissolved. Add to the tomato mixture. Add water, if necessary, to the reserved tomato juice to make 2 cups (16 fl oz). Add to the tomato mixture.

Spread the macaroni in a large shallow baking pan. Arrange the chicken, skin side up, in a single layer on the macaroni. Pour the tomato mixture over the top. Cover and bake at 180°C (350°F/Gas 4) for about 40 minutes or until a fork can be inserted into the chicken easily.

Chicken Mushroom Dinner

Serves 4

1 teaspoon salt
1 x 1.5 kg (3 lb) chicken
4 rashers bacon
60 g (2 oz) margarine
250 g (8 oz) mushrooms, sliced
¼ teaspoon white pepper
2 tablespoons finely chopped parsley
3 tablespoons flour
1 teaspoon paprika
1 teaspoon dried oregano
1 teaspoon caraway seeds
2 medium-sized potatoes, cut into thick slices
½ cup (4 fl oz) white wine
1 cup (8 fl oz) chicken stock

Rub the salt on the chicken and set aside. Grill the bacon until crisp, drain and crumble. Melt the margarine over medium heat. Add the mushrooms and pepper. Cook, stirring, for 5 minutes. Add the parsley and remove from the heat and cool. Add 2 tablespoons of the flour and the bacon. Stir well. Stuff the chicken with the mushroom mixture and place in an ovenproof pan. Sprinkle the paprika, oregano and caraway seeds over and arrange the potatoes around the chicken. Add the wine and ½ cup (4 fl oz) of the stock. Roast, uncovered, at 180°C (350°F/Gas 4), basting occasionally, for 1 hour or until the leg moves freely when twisted. Mix the remaining flour and stock. Add to the chicken and potatoes and cook a further 5 minutes.

Creole Chicken

Serves 4

¼ cup (1 oz) flour
1 teaspoon salt
½ teaspoon dried thyme
¼ teaspoon paprika
4 chicken half-breasts (suprêmes)
⅓ cup (2½ fl oz) oil
1 medium-sized onion, chopped
1 medium-sized green pepper (capsicum), chopped
1 x 750 g (1½ lb) can tomatoes
¼ teaspoon Tabasco sauce
1 bay leaf, crumbled
¼ cup chopped parsley

Mix the flour, salt, thyme and paprika. Add the chicken, one piece at a time, dredging to coat. Heat the oil to medium. Add the chicken and cook for about 10 minutes, turning, until browned. Move the chicken to one side of the pan. Add the onion and green pepper and sauté for about 3 minutes or until the onion is soft. Add the tomatoes, Tabasco sauce and bay leaf, stirring to break up the tomatoes slightly. Cover and simmer for 30 minutes. Add the parsley. Cover and simmer for a further 30 minutes or until a fork can be inserted in the chicken with ease. Serve over rice.

Chicken

Limacado Chicken

Serves 4

- 4 chicken half-breasts (suprêmes), schnitzels or escalopes
- 30 g (1 oz) butter
- 2 tablespoons oil
- 1 large avocado, peeled and mashed
- ½ teaspoon finely chopped lime rind
- 1 tablespoon lime juice
- 1 teaspoon grain seed mustard
- freshly ground black pepper
- 2 tablespoons cream

Sauté the chicken in the heated butter and oil in a heavy based pan until well browned and cooked through. Remove, drain and keep warm. Combine the avocado with the lime rind and juice, mustard, pepper and cream.

Heat very gently in the pan until warm. Coat the hot chicken with the lime avocado sauce and serve with a sauté of fresh vegetables.

Limacado Chicken

Colonial Chicken

Serves 4

- 1 x 1.5 kg (3 lb) chicken
- 1 teaspoon salt
- ½ lemon
- 2 small apples, cored and quartered
- 8 chipolata sausages
- 60 g (2 oz) butter
- ¼ cup (3 oz) honey

Rub the cavity of the chicken with salt. Rub the outer surface of the chicken with lemon. Stuff the cavity with the apples and sausages and tie the legs and wings. Mix the butter and honey and baste the chicken thoroughly. Place the chicken on a foil-lined baking pan and cover the chicken loosely with foil. Bake at 160°C (325°F/Gas 3) for about 1 hour or until the leg moves freely when lifted or twisted. Remove the foil for the last few minutes to brown the chicken and baste again with the butter-honey mixture. Serve the apple and sausage with the chicken.

Spiced Custard Apple Chicken

Serves 4

- 30 g (1 oz) butter
- 4 chicken half-breasts (suprêmes), cubed
- 2 onions, chopped
- 2 garlic cloves, crushed
- 1 tablespoon grated fresh ginger
- 1 teaspoon ground cumin
- 1 teaspoon coriander
- 2 teaspoons chilli powder
- 1 teaspoon garam masala
- ½ teaspoon ground turmeric
- freshly ground black pepper
- 1 cup (8 fl oz) chicken stock
- ⅓ cup (2 ½ fl oz) lemon juice
- 1 custard apple, peeled, seeded, flesh flaked
- ½ cup (2 oz) coarsely ground almonds
- 2 tablespoons toasted flaked almonds

Melt the butter in a large pan. Sauté the chicken until golden. Add the onion, garlic and ginger and cook a further 2 minutes. Add the spices and sauté for 1 to 2 minutes.

Add the chicken stock and lemon juice and simmer for 15 to 20 minutes or until cooked. Stir in the custard apple flesh and ground almonds and heat through gently. Serve on a bed of brown rice garnished with flaked almonds, accompanied by curry sambals.

Sambals: Mango chutney; sliced tomatoes, spring onions (scallions) and mint; chopped cucumber and mint with yoghurt; sliced banana tossed in lemon juice and shredded coconut.

Slimmers Chicken and Choko Salad

Serves 4

4 boneless chicken breasts
¼ cup (2 fl oz) white wine
2 teaspoons chopped fresh tarragon or ½ teaspoon dried tarragon
1 tablespoon lemon juice
1 teaspoon French mustard
1 choko (summer squash), peeled, cored and sliced
2 teaspoons shredded lemon rind

Place the chicken, wine, tarragon, lemon juice and mustard in a pan. Arrange the sliced choko over the chicken and sprinkle with lemon rind. Cover and simmer for 15 minutes or until the chicken is tender. Accompany with tomato salad.

Pepino Chicken Salad

Serves 6

2 cups cooked chicken
1 cup chopped celery
1 pepino, peeled, seeded and cubed
½ cup (2 oz) pecan nuts
½ cup (4 fl oz) sour cream
½ cup (4 fl oz) mayonnaise
1 teaspoon lemon rind
2 tablespoons lemon juice
3 teaspoons grated fresh ginger
1 teaspoon honey
¼ cup chopped fresh parsley

Combine the chicken, celery, pepino and pecans. Shake together the remaining ingredients in a screw-top jar and toss with the chicken mixture. Serve well chilled in mignonette lettuce cups.

Chicken and Melon Salad with Ginger Mayonnaise

Serves 6

6 chicken fillets
1 cup (8 fl oz) white wine vinegar
1 cup (8 fl oz) water
1 teaspoon black peppercorns
celery tops
2 stalks celery, finely chopped
1 tablespoon chopped fresh parsley
¼ large melon

Ginger Mayonnaise

½ cup (4 fl oz) mayonnaise
½ cup (4 fl oz) sour cream
1 teaspoon grated lemon rind
2 tablespoons lemon juice
1 teaspoon honey
3 teaspoons peeled and grated fresh ginger
freshly ground black pepper

Gently poach the chicken in a stock made with the wine vinegar and water. Flavour with the peppercorns and celery tops. When cooked, remove the chicken from the stock and cut diagonally into bite-sized cubes.

Place the chicken in a bowl with the celery, parsley and melon which has been peeled and cut into pieces. Fold the Ginger Mayonnaise into the chicken salad and serve salad in honeydew melon shells.

Ginger Mayonnaise: Mix the mayonnaise with the sour cream, lemon rind, lemon juice and honey. Add the ginger. (More or less can be added depending on personal preference.) Season with pepper.

Chicken and Melon Salad with Ginger Mayonnaise

Chicken

Cherry Chicken Salad

Serves 6 – 8

- 2 cups diced cooked chicken or turkey
- 1 cup diced celery
- 2 tablespoons finely chopped pimiento
- ½ cup (2 oz) coarsely chopped walnuts
- 1 cup cherries, pitted and halved
- ½ cup pineapple pieces
- 1 tablespoon lemon juice
- 2 tablespoons French dressing
- ½ cup (4 fl oz) mayonnaise

Toss all ingredients together. Serve on a bed of lettuce leaves, accompanied with a green salad and hot French bread.

Sautéed Chicken Breasts with Blueberry Sauce

Serves 4

- 4 boneless chicken breasts
- seasoned flour for coating
- 60 g (2 oz) butter or margarine
- 2 onions, thinly sliced
- 125 g (4 oz) blueberries
- ¾ cup (6 fl oz) dry white wine
- ¼ cup (2 fl oz) cream
- salt and pepper

Remove the skin, tissues and any fat from the chicken breasts. Wash in cold water, pat dry with paper towels and coat with seasoned flour. Heat the butter in a heavy pan and gently fry the onions until soft and transparent. Add the chicken breasts and fry until browned, then turn and fry for 2 to 3 minutes.

Add the blueberries and wine and bring to the boil, stirring to loosen the pan sediment. Simmer for 5 minutes or until the chicken is tender. Stir in the cream and heat through gently. Season to taste with salt and pepper. Serve hot with sautéed potatoes or boiled rice and a green vegetable.

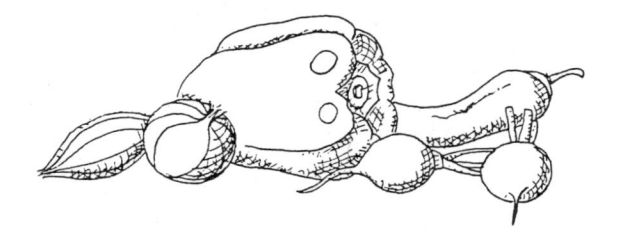

Gingered Lychees with Chicken

Serves 4

- 3 kg (6 lb) chicken breasts
- 6 spring onions (scallions)
- 2 small pieces preserved ginger and 2 tablespoons syrup
- 1 red pepper (capsicum)
- cornflour (cornstarch)
- 3 tablespoons oil
- 500 g (1 lb) fresh lychees, shelled and stones removed
- ½ cup (4 fl oz) hot water
- 2 chicken stock cubes
- salt and pepper
- 2 teaspoons sugar
- 2 tablespoons tomato sauce
- 1 teaspoon cornflour (cornstarch), mixed to a smooth paste with 2 teaspoons water

Remove the chicken from the bone and cut into 6 pieces. Cut each in half lengthwise. Cut each half into 3 pieces.

Chop the spring onions into 5 cm (2 inch) lengths. Slice the ginger. Remove the seeds from the pepper and cut into large pieces.

Coat the chicken pieces in cornflour. Heat the oil in a wok or pan, add the chicken pieces and cook until light golden brown. Add the 2 tablespoons ginger syrup and the remaining ingredients except the cornflour paste. Mix well.

Cover and simmer until the chicken is tender, about 3 to 5 minutes. Add the cornflour and water paste to the mixture. Stir until boiling and serve immediately.

Hungarian Chicken Paprika

Serves 4

- ¼ cup (2 fl oz) cooking oil
- 1 onion, chopped
- 1½ tablespoons paprika
- 1 tablespoon caraway seeds
- 8 chicken thighs
- 2 tomatoes, quartered and seeded
- 2 green peppers (capsicums), sliced
- 1½ cups (12 fl oz) water
- 1 teaspoon salt
- 1 cup (8 fl oz) sour cream
- 2 tablespoons flour

Place the oil in a pan and heat to medium. Add the onion and sauté for about 5 minutes or until soft and golden. Stir in the paprika and caraway seeds. Add the chicken, turning to coat. Add the tomatoes, green peppers, water and salt. Stir to mix. Simmer, uncovered, over low heat for about 1 hour or until a fork can be inserted in the chicken with ease. Remove the chicken and set aside.

Mix the sour cream and flour, stirring until smooth. Add to the contents of the pan. Cook, stirring, over medium heat for about 3 minutes or until thick. Do not boil. Return the chicken to the pan and cook for about 3 minutes or until hot. Serve with noodles.

Cucumber-Stuffed Chicken Breasts

Serves 4

- 2 whole chicken breasts, halved and skinned
- ½ teaspoon salt
- 60 g (2 oz) butter
- ¾ cup (1 oz) cornflake crumbs
- 2 tablespoons diced onion
- ¾ cup (3 oz) breadcrumbs
- 2 teaspoons dill seeds
- ¼ teaspoon dried basil
- ¾ cup (6 fl oz) chicken stock
- 1½ cups chopped cucumber
- 12 cucumber slices

Cut each chicken breast down the centre lengthwise to the bone, leaving about 1.25 cm (½ inch) uncut at the top and bottom. Then lift the breast meat off the bones about 2.5 cm (1 inch) on each side of the cut and push the meat back and up to form a ridge around the cavity thus formed. Sprinkle the chicken with half the salt. Melt the butter over medium heat. Brush the chicken pieces lightly with part of the butter and sprinkle with 1½ tablespoons of the cornflake crumbs. Set aside.

Sauté the onion in the remaining melted butter for about 5 minutes or until transparent. Make the stuffing by mixing together the breadcrumbs, remaining cornflake crumbs, the dill seeds, basil and remaining salt. Add the sautéed onion, chicken stock and the chopped cucumber. Toss gently to mix. Mound the stuffing into the cavity of each chicken breast.

Place the chicken, stuffing side up, in a single layer in a large shallow baking pan. Cover and bake at 200°C (400°F/Gas 6) for 25 minutes. Uncover and place 3 cucumber slices on top of each chicken breast. Bake a further 10 minutes or until a fork can be inserted in the chicken with ease.

Italian Chicken

Serves 6 [M]

- 2 large onions, chopped
- 1 large green pepper (capsicum), seeded and sliced
- 2 tablespoons oil
- salt and pepper
- 750 g (1½ lb) cooked chicken, chopped
- 12 large baps, cut in half
- 6 tomatoes, sliced
- 1½ cups (6 oz) grated cheese
- 2 x 50 g (1 ¾ oz) cans anchovy fillets
- stuffed green olives, sliced

Place the onions, green pepper, oil and seasoning in a bowl and cook in the microwave oven on high for 5 minutes. Cool and add the chicken. Cover two halves of bap with the cooked mixture, top with the sliced tomatoes, cheese and a lattice of anchovy strips.

Cook in the microwave on high for about 2 minutes or until hot and bubbling, rotating once during cooking. Serve garnished with olive slices.

Touch o' Mint Chicken

Serves 4

- 1 large lime
- 1 x 1.5 kg (3 lb) chicken, cut into serving pieces
- ½ cup (2 oz) flour
- 1½ teaspoons salt
- ½ teaspoon paprika
- ¼ cup (2 fl oz) cooking oil
- 2 tablespoons soft brown sugar
- ½ cup (4 fl oz) chicken stock
- ½ cup (4 fl oz) dry white wine
- ½ teaspoon dried mint

Grate the lime rind and set aside. Cut the lime in half and squeeze the juice over the chicken. Mix together the flour, salt and paprika. Add the chicken, a few pieces at a time, and shake to coat each piece evenly. Place the oil in a pan and heat to medium. Add the chicken and cook for about 10 minutes, turning, to brown on all sides.

Remove the chicken from the pan and place in a shallow baking dish. Add the brown sugar to the lime rind and sprinkle over the chicken. Pour the stock and wine over the chicken and sprinkle the mint on top. Cover and bake at 190°C (375°F/Gas 5) for about 45 minutes or until a fork can be inserted in the chicken with ease.

Curried Chicken Salad

Serves 4

- 6 chicken thighs
- 1 teaspoon salt
- 1 stalk celery
- 1 onion, sliced
- 2 cups (16 fl oz) water
- ¼ cup chopped green pepper (capsicum)
- ½ cup chopped onion
- ¼ cup chopped celery
- ½ teaspoon garlic salt
- 2 teaspoons curry powder
- ½ cup (4 fl oz) yoghurt
- 2 tablespoons mayonnaise
- 1 tablespoon lemon juice
- lettuce
- sliced tomatoes
- ½ cup (2 oz) chopped salted peanuts

Place the chicken, salt, celery stalk, sliced onion and water in a deep saucepan. Cover and simmer for about 40 minutes or until a fork can be inserted in the chicken with ease. Cool. Separate the meat from the bones. Discard the bones and skin. Cut the chicken into bite-sized pieces and place in a large bowl. Add the green pepper, the chopped onion and celery, and the garlic salt. Mix together the curry powder, yoghurt, mayonnaise and lemon juice. Stir into the chicken mixture and chill.

At serving time, place the chicken on a bed of lettuce. Garnish with sliced tomatoes and sprinkle the peanuts over the top.

Chicken

Mushroom-Stuffed Chicken

Mushroom-Stuffed Chicken

Serves 4

- 2 x 1 kg (2 lb) chickens, halved
- 1 lemon
- 2 teaspoons salt
- ⅛ teaspoon pepper
- ½ teaspoon paprika
- 125 g (4 oz) butter, melted
- ¼ cup (2 fl oz) sherry

Mushroom Stuffing
- 60 g (2 oz) butter
- 250 g (8 oz) mushrooms, sliced
- 1 tablespoon flour
- 1 tablespoon chopped parsley
- ½ cup (4 fl oz) cream
- ½ teaspoon salt
- ⅛ teaspoon pepper

Place the chicken halves on the griller (broiler). Cut the lemon in half and rub the entire surface of the chicken, squeezing so there is plenty of juice. Mix together the salt, pepper and paprika and sprinkle over the chicken. Grill (broil), skin side down, for about 15 minutes, basting occasionally with the butter and sherry mixed together. Turn the chicken and continue to cook for a further 15 minutes, basting occasionally. Place the chicken halves in a baking dish, skin side down. Fill the cavities with Mushroom Stuffing and bake at 190°C (375°F/Gas 5) for about 15 minutes or until a fork can be inserted in the chicken with ease.

Mushroom Stuffing: Melt the butter and add the mushrooms. Cook for about 4 minutes or until the mushrooms are soft but not brown. Stir in the flour and parsley. Add the cream, stirring constantly until the mixture is smooth. Add the salt and pepper.

Apple Butter Chicken

Serves 4

- 1 medium-sized onion, finely chopped
- 250 g (8 oz) butter
- ½ cup (4 fl oz) apple cider vinegar
- 2 tablespoons soft brown sugar
- 30 g (1 oz) margarine
- 3 tablespoons prepared mustard
- 1 teaspoon celery seeds
- 1 x 1.5 kg (3 lb) chicken, quartered
- 1 teaspoon salt
- ⅛ teaspoon pepper

Mix together the onion, butter, vinegar, brown sugar, margarine, mustard and celery seeds. Bring to the boil (it will be rather thick). Place the chicken quarters in a large bowl and add the sauce. Marinate in the refrigerator for at least 1 hour. At cooking time brush off the excess sauce.

Place the chicken on a covered barbecue (if no top on the barbecue, make a tent of foil), skin side up, about 20 cm (8 inch) from the heat. Cook, turning, every 15 minutes, for about 1¼ hours or until a fork can be inserted in the chicken with ease. Brush generously with the sauce during the last 15 minutes of grilling (broiling). Sprinkle with salt and pepper.

Peanut Butter Chicken

Serves 4

- 60 g (2 oz) butter
- 1 tablespoon peanut butter
- 1 cup (8 fl oz) tomato purée
- juice of 1 lemon
- 2 tablespoons white wine
- 1 teaspoon chilli powder
- 1 teaspoon salt
- 1 teaspoon freshly ground black pepper
- 1 x 1.5 kg (3 lb) chicken, quartered

Melt the butter and peanut butter over medium heat. Stir in the tomato purée, lemon juice, wine, chilli powder, salt and pepper. Place the chicken pieces on the barbecue, skin side up, about 20 cm (8 inch) from the heat. Baste the chicken with the sauce about every 15 minutes, turning the chicken after basting. Cook the chicken for about 1 hour or until a fork can be inserted in the chicken with ease.

Peanut Butter Chicken

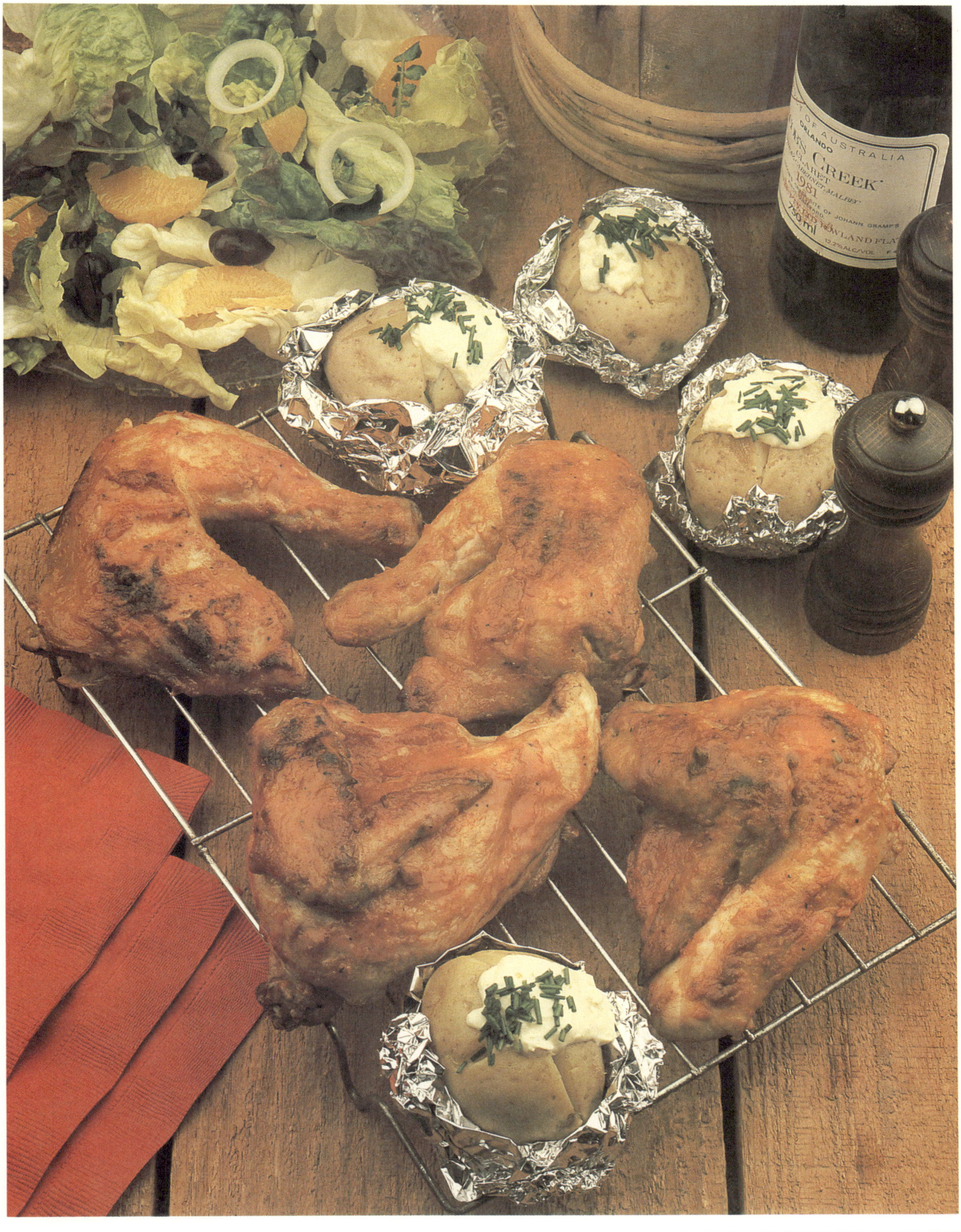

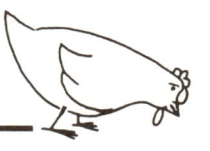

Chicken

Chicken with Fresh Vegetables

Serves 4

60 g (2 oz) butter
4 chicken breast quarters
3 large zucchini (courgettes)
3 large tomatoes
1 cup chopped spring onions (scallions)
1 teaspoon lemon juice
1 teaspoon salt
½ teaspoon pepper

Place the butter in a large pan and melt over medium-high heat. Add the chicken and brown on all sides for about 30 minutes. Slice the zucchini lengthwise and cut into 2.5 cm (1 inch) pieces. Cut the tomatoes into 2.5 cm (1 inch) chunks. Stir in the spring onions, zucchini and tomatoes. Reduce the heat to low, add the lemon juice, salt and pepper. Cook, uncovered, for about 20 minutes or until a fork can be inserted in the chicken with ease.

Chicken Stew

Serves 4 - 6

6 rashers bacon
1 x 1.5 kg (3 lb) chicken, cut into serving pieces
1 cup chopped onion
1 cup chopped celery
2 cups chopped cabbage
1 x 500 g (16 oz) can tomatoes, cut into quarters
1 teaspoon salt
⅛ teaspoon pepper

Place the bacon in a large pan and cook on medium heat for about 8 minutes or until crisp. Remove the bacon and turn the heat to high. Add the chicken and cook for about 10 minutes, turning, to brown on all sides. Push the chicken to one side of the pan, add the onion and celery and stir fry for 5 minutes. Add the cabbage and cook a further 5 minutes. Remove any excess fat, add the tomatoes, salt and pepper and bring to the boil. Cover and simmer over low heat for about 20 minutes or until a fork can be inserted in the chicken with ease. Crumble the bacon on top and serve over rice if desired.

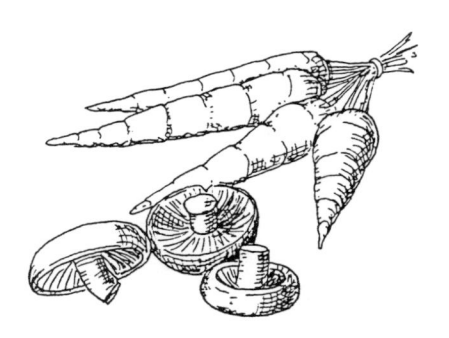

Chicken Chilli

Serves 6

¼ cup (2 fl oz) corn oil
9 chicken thighs, skinned, boned and cut into 2.5 cm (1 inch) cubes
2 large onions, chopped
3 small green peppers (capsicums), chopped
2 garlic cloves, crushed
1 tablespoon mild chilli powder
1½ teaspoons ground cumin
1½ teaspoons dried oregano
½ teaspoon salt
⅛ teaspoon pepper
1 x 750 g (1½ lb) can peeled tomatoes, with liquid
¼ cup (1 oz) grated extra-sharp cheddar cheese

Place the oil in a pan and heat to medium. Add the chicken and cook for about 10 minutes, turning, until brown on all sides. Add the onions, green peppers, garlic, chilli powder, cumin, oregano, salt and pepper. Stir to blend the ingredients, then add the tomatoes. Cover and simmer on low heat for about 45 minutes or until a fork can be inserted in the chicken with ease. Uncover and simmer until most of the liquid has evaporated and the mixture is thick. Spoon into a serving dish and top with the grated cheese. Serve in bowls over hot cooked red beans or rice, or both.

Chicken and Corn Stew

Serves 4

6 rashers bacon
1 x 1.5 kg (3 lb) chicken, cut into serving pieces
6 spring onions (scallions), chopped
2½ cups (20 fl oz) water
1 cup (8 fl oz) tomato sauce
1½ teaspoons salt
4 drops of Tabasco sauce
1 x 315 g (10 oz) packet frozen whole kernel corn

Place the bacon in a Dutch oven and cook over medium heat for about 8 minutes or until crisp. Remove the bacon, drain, crumble and set aside. Add the chicken to the Dutch oven and cook slowly, turning, for 15 minutes. Add the spring onions and continue cooking a further 15 minutes or until the chicken is brown. Drain off the excess fat. Add the water, tomato sauce, salt and Tabasco sauce. Bring to the boil. Add the frozen corn and separate with a fork. Reduce the heat to medium low, cover and cook for an additional 20 minutes. Just before serving, sprinkle with the crumbled bacon.

Barbecued Chicken Suprême

Serves 4

1 x 1.5 kg (3 lb) chicken, quartered
1 cup (8 fl oz) chicken stock
¼ cup (2 fl oz) tomato sauce
2 tablespoons vinegar
2 tablespoons Worcestershire sauce
2 tablespoons grated onion
1 teaspoon garlic salt
1 teaspoon dry mustard
½ teaspoon celery salt
¼ teaspoon pepper

Place the chicken in a shallow dish. Mix together the stock, tomato sauce, vinegar and Worcestershire sauce. Add the onion, garlic salt, mustard, celery salt and pepper. Stir. Place the saucepan over high heat and bring the sauce to the boil. Pour sauce over the chicken and marinate at room temperature for at least 30 minutes. When ready to cook, drain chicken and place on the barbecue, skin side up, about 20 cm (8 inch) from the heat. Cook, turning frequently, for 30 minutes. Baste the chicken with the remaining sauce and continue to cook, turning and basting, for about 35 minutes or until a fork can be inserted in the chicken with ease.

Taco Chicken Grill

Serves 4

1 small onion, grated
1 x 250 g (8 oz) can tomato purée
1 x 125 g (4 oz) can taco sauce
¼ cup (3 oz) molasses
2 tablespoons vinegar
1 tablespoon cooking oil
1 teaspoon salt
½ teaspoon dried oregano
⅛ teaspoon pepper
1 x 1.5 kg (3 lb) chicken, cut into serving pieces
½ cup (2 oz) grated cheese

Mix together the onion, tomato purée, taco sauce, molasses, vinegar, oil, salt, oregano and pepper. Bring to the boil. Place the chicken in a large bowl and add the sauce. Marinate for several hours in the refrigerator. When ready to cook, drain the excess sauce and reserve.

Place the chicken on the barbecue, skin side up, about 20 cm (8 inch) from the heat and cook for about 50 minutes or until a fork can be inserted in the chicken with ease. Turn every 10 minutes to brown evenly and brush with the reserved sauce during the last 15 minutes of cooking time. When the chicken is cooked, place on a serving dish, top with the remaining sauce and sprinkle with the cheese.

Chicken with Broccoli

Serves 4 [M]

2 x 315 g (10 oz) packets frozen broccoli
60 g (2 oz) butter
4 tablespoons flour
1 ½ cups (12 fl oz) milk or cream
½ cup (2 oz) grated Parmesan cheese
1 teaspoon salt
½ teaspoon dry mustard
½ teaspoon pepper
2½ cups cooked chicken, chopped or sliced
½ cup (2 oz) breadcrumbs, toasted
1 teaspoon paprika

Pierce the broccoli packets several times with a fork. Place in the microwave oven and microwave on high 6 to 8 minutes. Cool slightly and drain well. Microwave the butter on high for 1 minute to melt. Stir in the flour, microwave on high for 1 to 1½ minutes to cook. Gradually stir in the milk, using a wire whisk to blend well.

Microwave on high 2 to 4 minutes to thicken, stirring once during cooking. Add the Parmesan cheese, salt, mustard and pepper. Stir until the cheese melts. Arrange the broccoli in an even layer in a shallow casserole. Top with the chicken. Spread the sauce over the chicken and sprinkle with the breadcrumbs and paprika. Cover with greaseproof paper. Microwave on medium high 8 to 10 minutes. Let stand, covered, for 5 minutes before serving.

Hot Tomato Chicken

Serves 4 - 6

2 tablespoons cooking oil
½ cup finely chopped onion
1 garlic clove, crushed
1 chicken stock cube
½ cup (4 fl oz) hot water
1 cup (8 fl oz) bottled taco sauce or tomato purée
1 teaspoon salt
¼ teaspoon dried oregano
2 tablespoons vinegar
1 tablespoon prepared mustard
4-5 large chicken pieces
1 tablespoon mild chilli powder

Place the oil in a small pan and heat to medium. Add the onion and garlic, stir and cook for about 3 minutes or until clear and soft. Dissolve the stock cube in the hot water and add to the pan, along with the sauce, salt, oregano, vinegar and mustard. Dip the chicken into the sauce mixture, then lightly sprinkle the chilli powder on all sides of the chicken. Add any remaining chilli powder to the sauce, bring to the boil and remove from the heat. Just before cooking, dip each piece into the sauce again. Cook over a charcoal grill for 45 to 60 minutes or until the chicken can easily be pierced with a fork (the white meat will be cooked before the dark). Turn every 10 minutes during cooking, basting with the sauce during the last half of cooking time.

Note: The chicken may also be cooked in the oven, at 180°C (350°F/Gas 4), for 50 to 60 minutes. Turn and baste every 15 minutes. Spoon any excess sauce over before serving.

Chicken

Drumsticks Italian Style

Serves 4 [M]

- 8 chicken drumsticks
- 1 cup (8 fl oz) tomato purée
- 1 garlic clove, crushed
- ½ teaspoon fresh basil
- 1 tablespoon finely chopped parsley
- 1 tablespoon finely chopped onion
- 1 x 125 g (4 oz) can sliced mushrooms, drained
- ½ cup (2 oz) grated Parmesan cheese
- 8 slices mozzarella cheese

Arrange the drumsticks in a 30 cm (12 inch) round or 30 x 20 cm (12 x 8 inch) shallow microwave casserole. Place the meaty parts to the outside. Mix together the tomato purée, garlic, basil, parsley, onion and mushrooms. Spoon the sauce over the chicken and cover with greaseproof paper. Microwave on high for 6 to 7 minutes. Rotate the dish half a turn. Microwave on a high a further 6 to 7 minutes.

Remove from the oven and let stand, covered, for 3 minutes before testing if cooked. Return to the oven for additional cooking if a fork cannot be inserted in the chicken with ease. Sprinkle with the Parmesan cheese. Cover each drumstick with a mozzarella slice. Microwave on high 1 to 2 minutes or until the cheese is melted. Cover with greaseproof paper and let stand 3 minutes before serving.

Drumsticks Italian Style

Stuffed Chicken Thighs

Serves 4 - 6

- 12 chicken thighs, boned
- 90 g (3 oz) butter
- ¼ cup finely chopped celery
- ¼ cup finely chopped spring onions (scallions)
- ¼ cup finely chopped green pepper (capsicum)
- 2 cups (8 oz) dry breadcrumbs
- 1 teaspoon salt
- ½ teaspoon pepper
- ½ cup (4 fl oz) chicken stock, warmed
- 2 tablespoons dry white wine

Flatten the chicken thighs to a rectangular shape. Place half the butter in a small pan and melt over medium heat. Add the celery, spring onion and green pepper. Sauté for 5 minutes or until soft. Stir in the breadcrumbs, ½ teaspoon of the salt and ¼ teaspoon of the pepper. Cook for about 5 minutes or until slightly brown. Add the chicken stock and stir until the mixture has the consistency of stuffing. Spoon 1½ to 2 tablespoons of the mixture onto each flattened thigh. Roll up and fasten with toothpicks or skewers. Place the remaining butter in a pan and melt over medium heat. Remove from the heat and stir in the wine. Dip the stuffed thighs in the mixture and carefully place on the barbecue, skin side down. Cook about 15 minutes or until brown on one side, turn and continue cooking for 15 minutes or until brown. The chicken is done when it can easily be pierced with a fork, about 30 to 40 minutes.

Note: To hasten the cooking time, the chicken may be precooked in a microwave oven, covered loosely with greaseproof paper. Cook on medium for about 8 minutes, rotate half a turn, increase heat to high and cook a further 8 minutes. Then dip in the butter-wine mixture and cook 3 to 5 minutes on each side. Add the remaining butter-wine sauce to the drippings in the microwave pan. Heat and pour over the chicken before serving. To cook the rolled thighs in a conventional oven, bake at 180°C (350°F/Gas 4), covered, for 15 to 20 minutes. Remove the cover and cook a further 15 minutes or until the chicken can easily be pierced with a fork.

Mustard Vegetable Chicken

Serves 4 [M]

- 2 cups thinly sliced fresh vegetables (*see note*)
- 1 x 1.5 kg (3 lb) chicken, cut into serving pieces
- 3 tablespoons French mustard
- 30 g (1 oz) butter, melted

Arrange the sliced vegetables evenly over the bottom of a shallow microwave casserole. Place the chicken on top of the vegetables, with the meaty parts towards the outside of the dish. Mix the mustard and butter and brush on the chicken. Cover with greaseproof paper and microwave on high for 18 to 22 minutes. Halfway through cooking, rotate the dish half a turn. Remove from the oven and let stand, covered, for 5 minutes before testing if cooked. Return to the oven for additional cooking if a fork cannot be inserted in the chicken with ease.

Note: Any combination of celery, carrots, zucchini (courgettes), squash and tomatoes may be used.

Tangy Sweet Chicken

Serves 4 [M]

- 1 x 1.5 kg (3 lb) chicken, cut into serving pieces
- 1/3 cup (2 oz) soft brown sugar
- 2 tablespoons prepared mustard
- 1/2 cup (4 fl oz) sweet pickle juice
- 1/2 teaspoon salt
- 1/4 teaspoon pepper

Dry the chicken pieces thoroughly with a paper towel. Mix together the brown sugar and mustard. Brush each chicken piece on all sides with the sugar-mustard mixture and arrange in a large shallow baking dish. Place the meaty parts to the outside. Pour the pickle juice in the bottom of the dish, not directly on the chicken. Cover with greaseproof paper. Microwave on high for 9 to 11 minutes. Rotate the dish half a turn. Microwave, still covered, on high a further 9 to 11 minutes. Sprinkle with the salt and pepper. Return to the oven for additional cooking if a fork cannot be inserted in the chicken with ease. Spoon the sauce over the chicken to serve.

Tangy Sweet Chicken

Chicken

Chicken Breasts Rockefeller

Serves 4 [M]

- ½ teaspoon seasoned salt
- ½ teaspoon paprika
- 4 chicken half-breasts (suprêmes), flattened
- 1 x 315 g (10 oz) packet frozen chopped spinach, thawed and well drained
- ½ cup finely chopped spring onions (scallions)
- 4 chicken half-breasts, (suprêmes)
- 1 cup (4 oz) grated sharp cheese
- 1¼ cups (10 fl oz) cream of chicken soup
- 2 tablespoons cream
- 1 tablespoon Worcestershire sauce
- 2 tablespoons toasted buttered breadcrumbs

Sprinkle the seasoned salt and half the paprika on the chicken. Mix the spinach and spring onions. Place 1 tablespoon of the spinach mixture on each chicken half-breast. Place 1 tablespoon of the cheese on top of the spinach mixture. Roll the chicken and fasten with toothpicks. Mix together the soup, cream, Worcestershire sauce, any remaining cheese and the remaining spinach mixture. Microwave on high for 2 minutes. Stir, then microwave a further 2 minutes or until the cheese is melted.

Place the soup mixture in a glass dish and add to the chicken rolls in a glass dish. Spoon the soup mixture over the chicken and top with the breadcrumbs. Sprinkle the remaining paprika on top of the crumbs. Cover with greaseproof paper. Microwave, turning the dish every 5 minutes, for about 20 minutes or until a fork can be inserted in the chicken with ease. Let stand, covered, for 5 minutes.

Note: For conventional oven, mix the sauce ingredients and cook, stirring, over medium heat for about 5 minutes or until the cheese is melted. Follow the procedures with the chicken as described above. Bake, uncovered, at 180°C (350°F/Gas 4) for about 50 minutes or until a fork can be inserted in the chicken with ease.

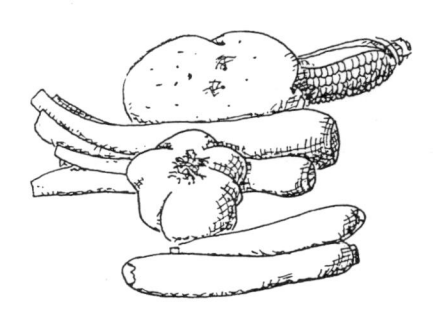

Chicken-Broccoli Dinner

Serves 2 [M]

- 15 g (½ oz) margarine
- ½ cup (4 fl oz) white wine
- 1 teaspoon microwave browning sauce
- ½ teaspoon paprika
- 2 chicken breast quarters
- 1 x 315 g (10 oz) packet frozen broccoli
- ½ teaspoon salt
- ⅛ teaspoon pepper
- 1 cup cooked rice
- 1 teaspoon chopped parsley

Mix together the margarine, wine, browning sauce and paprika. Place in the microwave oven and cook on high for 1 minute. Arrange the chicken in a small baking dish and baste with the sauce. Cover and microwave on high for 6 minutes. Rotate the chicken, baste again and add the broccoli, salt and pepper. Cover and microwave a further 6 minutes on high. Add the rice and parsley, stirring into the pan juices. Cover and microwave an additional 3 minutes on high or until a fork can be inserted in the chicken with ease. Let stand 5 minutes, covered, before serving.

Spaghetti Chicken

Serves 6

- 60 g (2 oz) butter
- 375 g (12 oz) mushrooms, sliced
- 1 green pepper (capsicum), chopped
- 1 garlic clove, crushed
- 3 tablespoons flour
- 3 teaspoons salt
- ¼ teaspoon pepper
- 5 cups (1.25 litres) chicken stock, warmed
- 1 cup (8 fl oz) cream, warmed
- ¼ cup (2 fl oz) dry white wine
- 2 egg yolks, slightly beaten
- 1 x 1.8 kg (3½ lb) chicken, cooked, skinned, boned and cut into serving pieces
- 250 g (8 oz) thin spaghetti
- 1 bay leaf
- ⅔ cup (2½ oz) grated Parmesan cheese

Place the butter in a large pan and melt over medium heat. Add the mushrooms, green pepper and garlic and sauté for about 5 minutes. Stir in the flour, 1 teaspoon of the salt and the pepper. Slowly add 1½ cups (12 fl oz) of the warm chicken stock and cream, stirring until thickened, about 3 minutes. Reduce the heat to low and add the wine. To the beaten egg yolks, add several tablespoons of the hot wine sauce, then add the egg mixture to the pan, continuing to stir. Add the chicken pieces, stirring until thoroughly heated, about 3 minutes.

While making the sauce, cook the spaghetti in the remaining stock with enough water to make 15 cups (3.75 litres) liquid. Add the remaining salt and bay leaf to the stock-water. When done (*al dente*), drain the spaghetti and arrange in a shallow greased baking dish. Spoon the sauce evenly over the spaghetti and sprinkle with the Parmesan cheese. Bake at 150°C (300°F/Gas 2) for about 30 minutes or until bubbly. Garnish with black olives if desired.

Roasted Chicken

Serves 4   M

1 x 1.5 kg (3 lb) chicken
60 g (2 oz) butter, melted
1 tablespoon seasoned salt

Dry the chicken thoroughly with paper towels. Place the chicken, breast side down, on a roasting rack in a shallow dish. Brush the entire surface of the chicken with butter. Cover with greaseproof paper and microwave on medium for 15 minutes. Turn the chicken breast side up. Cover with greaseproof paper.

Microwave on medium a further 15 to 20 minutes, rotating dish half a turn midway through cooking. Sprinkle the salt on the chicken and let stand, covered, for 5 to 10 minutes before checking if cooked. Return to the oven for additional cooking if a leg does not move freely when lifted or twisted. Serve hot as roasted chicken, or cool in the refrigerator and use for casseroles, salads or other recipes calling for cooked chicken.

Quick Chicken Cassolette

Serves 4

1 medium-sized chicken, jointed into 8-10 pieces
1 x 440 g (14 oz) can cream of asparagus soup
½ cup (4 fl oz) milk
freshly ground black pepper to taste
1 cup (4 oz) grated Australian cheese
1 cup (2 oz) fresh breadcrumbs
2 tablespoons chopped fresh parsley

Place the chicken pieces in a shallow casserole dish. Mix together the soup, milk and pepper and pour over chicken. Combine the cheese, breadcrumbs and parsley and sprinkle on top. Bake at 180°C (350°F/Gas 4) for 1 hour. Serve with butter-tossed rice or noodles.

Pan Whiskied Chicken

Serves 4

4 large or 8 small chicken half-breasts (suprêmes), skin removed
seasoned flour for coating
30 g (1 oz) butter
salt and pepper
1 garlic clove, crushed
½ cup (4 fl oz) whisky
½ cup (4 fl oz) cream

Dip the chicken into the flour and shake off the excess. Melt the butter in a large pan. Add the chicken and sauté gently for approximately 15 minutes, turning frequently until golden brown. Season to taste. Add the garlic and whisky. Simmer and reduce liquid to ½ cup (4 fl oz). Stir in the cream until the sauce returns to the boil. Serve immediately and accompany with lemon-buttered fresh asparagus.

Chicken Calypso

Serves 4

4 chicken half-breasts (suprêmes), skin removed
30 g (1 oz) butter
⅓ cup (1 oz) desiccated coconut
1 x 425 g (13 ½ oz) can peaches, drained and chopped
1 teaspoon ground ginger
salt and pepper

Ginger Butter

60 g (2 oz) butter
1 teaspoon ground ginger

Lightly flatten out the chicken half-breasts. Melt the butter, add the coconut and stir constantly over low heat until golden brown. Combine the peaches and ginger and season to taste. Place some peach filling down the centre of each chicken piece. Roll up, encasing the filling, and secure with toothpicks. Place on a baking tray and brush well with Ginger Butter. Bake at 180°C (350°F/Gas 4) for 30 minutes, occasionally basting with butter. Serve with fried rice and a crisp lettuce and orange salad.

Ginger Butter: Melt the butter and stir through the ginger.

Chicken Provençale

Serves 4

6 large tomatoes
1 x 1.5 kg (3 lb) chicken
60 g (2 oz) butter or margarine
4 garlic cloves, unpeeled
1 wineglass sherry or brandy
1 teaspoon tomato purée
salt and pepper
1 tablespoon chopped mixed herbs

Scald and skin the tomatoes, remove the seeds and chop the flesh very finely. Joint the chicken. Melt the butter in a frying pan, add the garlic cloves and the chicken joints, skin side down, and cook slowly for 15 minutes or until the joints are half-cooked. Turn the chicken over, remove the garlic and pour in the sherry. Set this alight and when the alcohol has burnt out, simmer until the liquid has evaporated. Add the tomato flesh, tomato purée and seasoning, and cook until the chicken is tender, about 15 minutes. Remove the chicken and arrange on a serving dish. Boil the tomato mixture to reduce further, then pour over the chicken. Sprinkle with the chopped herbs.

Chicken

Puffed Chilli Chicken

Serves 8

8 chicken half-breasts (suprêmes), skinned
¾ teaspoon salt
¼ teaspoon pepper
¼ cup (1 oz) flour
1 tablespoon yellow cornmeal (polenta)
8 cheese slices
125 g (4 oz) green chillies, cut lengthwise into 8 slices, seeds removed
60 g (2 oz) butter
2 eggs, separated
1 tablespoon grated Parmesan cheese
1 cup (8 fl oz) bottled taco sauce

Place the chicken on a hard surface. Using a meat mallet or similar, gently pound the chicken to 6 mm (¼ inch) thickness. Sprinkle with ½ teaspoon of the salt and the pepper. In a shallow bowl, mix the flour and cornmeal. Wrap one piece of cheese around each chilli slice, place on each chicken breast and roll, tucking in the sides. Fasten with toothpicks. Place each chicken roll in the flour mixture, dredging to coat. Melt the butter in a heavy ovenproof pan. Add the chicken, seam side down, and cook for about 10 minutes, turning, until brown on all sides. Baste the chicken and place the pan in a 180°C (350°F/Gas 4) oven for 25 minutes.

Place the egg whites in a small bowl and beat until stiff. Fold in the slightly beaten egg yolks and gently mix. Add the remaining salt and the Parmesan cheese. Remove the toothpicks from the chicken and increase the temperature to 190°C (375°F/Gas 5). Spoon a mound of egg mixture over each chicken breast, covering completely. Bake a further 12 minutes or until a fork can be inserted in the chicken with ease and the chicken is golden brown. Remove the chicken to a warm serving dish. To the pan drippings, add the taco sauce. Heat, stirring to loosen the brown bits in the pan. Serve over the chicken.

Opposite: *Chicken Pie*

Chicken Pie

Serves 4

1 x 1.5 kg (3 lb) chicken
1 carrot, peeled
1 onion, peeled
bouquet garni
1 wineglass white wine
3 ¾ cups (30 fl oz) water
250 g (8 oz) mushrooms
30 g (1 oz) butter or margarine
salt and pepper
pinch of ground mace
pinch of cayenne pepper
2-3 drops anchovy essence
handful of parsley
5 tablespoons cream
1 quantity shortcrust pastry (*page 458*)
beaten egg

Velouté Sauce
45 g (1 ½ oz) butter or margarine
2 rounded tablespoons flour
1 ¼ cups (14 fl oz) chicken stock
salt and pepper

Cook the chicken in a covered saucepan with the vegetables, bouquet garni, wine and water until tender, approximately 1 hour. Sauté the mushrooms whole in the butter, season, add the spices and anchovy essence and then set aside. Skin and bone the chicken and cut the meat into bite-sized pieces. Make a parsley purée by boiling the parsley for 10 minutes in a little water, then drain and pass through a fine strainer. Add the purée and cream to the sauce. Season, then arrange the chicken in layers in a 25 cm (10 inch) pie dish with the mushrooms, moistening well with the sauce. Leave the chicken mixture until cold then cover with the pastry. Brush with beaten egg and bake until well browned at 220°C (425°F/Gas 7) for 25 to 30 minutes.

Velouté Sauce: Melt the butter, add the flour and cook for 5 seconds. Take off the heat and cool slightly, then blend in the stock. Stir over the heat until thickened, then season. Bring to the boil and cook for several minutes until syrupy.

Mango Chicken

Serves 4

1 x 1.25-1.5 kg (2 ½-3 lb) roasting chicken
1 tablespoon seasoned flour
30-60 g (1-2 oz) butter or margarine
2 onions, finely sliced
1 mango, sliced
⅔-1 ¼ cups (5-10 fl oz) jellied chicken stock
salt and pepper
⅔ cup (5 fl oz) cream

Joint the chicken and roll in the seasoned flour. Heat a sauté pan, put in the butter and then add the chicken, skin side down, and brown slowly on all sides. Remove and keep warm. Put the onions into the pan and cook slowly until they are turning colour, then add the mango and continue cooking until golden brown.

Replace the chicken in the pan, pour on the stock and season. Cover the pan and simmer for 35 to 40 minutes. Stir in the cream and serve.

Chicken

Curried Chicken Pancakes

Serves 6 M

1 quantity crêpe batter (page 45)
frying oil

Filling
60 g (2 oz) butter
2 tablespoons oil
1 large onion, chopped
375 g (12 oz) mushrooms, sliced
⅓ cup (1½ oz) flour
1 tablespoon concentrated curry sauce
apple slices dipped in lemon juice
3 tablespoons orange juice
1¼ cups (10 fl oz) chicken stock
1 kg (2 lb) cooked chicken, sliced

Make the crêpes as directed. Interleave with greaseproof paper and keep stacked, wrapped in foil, in the refrigerator until required.

Fill the pancakes and reheat two per portion in the microwave oven for about 5 minutes. Serve garnished with the apple slices.

Filling: Heat the butter and oil in a bowl in the microwave oven on high for 2 minutes. Stir in the onion and mushrooms and cook for a further 5 minutes. Stir in the remaining ingredients and cook another 10 minutes, stirring frequently. Cool.

Chicken Chinoise

Chicken à la King

500 g (1 lb) cold diced, chicken meat
250 g (½ lb) mushrooms, peeled and sliced
60 g (2 oz) butter
lemon juice

Sauce
60 g (2 oz) butter
2 green or red peppers (capsicums), finely sliced
¼ cup (1 oz) flour
½ teaspoon paprika
salt and pepper
1 ¾ cups (14 fl oz) chicken stock

Bring the sauce to the boil, add the chicken and simmer gently. Cook the mushrooms in the butter and a little lemon juice for just a few minutes. Fold the mushrooms into the chicken mixture and leave a few to garnish. Serve on rice or toast fingers.

Sauce: Melt the butter and soften the peppers for a few minutes. Add the flour, paprika and salt and pepper. Cook for a few minutes then gradually add the stock. Stir until smooth.

Chicken Chinoise

Serves 6

2½ cups (20 fl oz) water
½ cup (4 fl oz) soy sauce
¼ teaspoon garlic salt
¾ teaspoon ground ginger
6 chicken half-breasts (suprêmes)
2 tablespoons cooking oil
250 g (8 oz) snow peas (mange-tout)
6 spring onions (scallions)
2 cups sliced fresh mushrooms
4 garlic cloves, crushed
125 g (4 oz) green chillies, diced
1 cup (8 fl oz) chicken stock
½ teaspoon pepper
1 tablespoon honey
1 tablespoon cornflour (cornstarch)
1 cup (6 oz) rice, boiled
½ cup (2 oz) sliced almonds

In a large saucepan, place 2 cups (16 fl oz) of the water, ¼ cup (2 fl oz) of the soy sauce, the garlic salt and ¼ teaspoon of the ginger. Bring to the boil. Add the chicken and poach for about 20 minutes or until a fork can be inserted with ease. Cool. Cut the chicken into bite-sized pieces and set aside.

Place the oil in a pan or wok, and heat gently. Add the snow peas, spring onions, mushrooms, garlic cloves and chillies. Sauté for about 3 minutes. Add the stock, the remaining soy sauce, ginger and pepper and bring to the boil. Cover, reduce the heat and simmer for about 5 minutes or until the vegetables are tender. In a small bowl, mix together the remaining water, the honey and cornflour and set aside. Add the chicken, rice and almonds to the vegetable mixture. Add the cornflour mixture and simmer for about 5 minutes or until thickened.

Apple-Glazed Chicken Thighs

Serves 4

- 3 tablespoons cooking oil
- ½ cup (2 oz) flour
- 8 chicken thighs, skinned
- ½ cup (5 oz) apple or pineapple marmalade
- ½ cup (4 fl oz) white wine
- 2 teaspoons lemon juice
- 1 tablespoon dried onion flakes
- 1 garlic clove, crushed
- 8 whole cloves
- ½ teaspoon curry powder
- 1 teaspoon salt
- ¼ teaspoon pepper
- cherry tomatoes
- spring onion (scallion) tops
- parsley

Place the oil in a large pan and heat gently. Place the flour in a shallow bowl and add the chicken, one piece at a time, dredging to coat. Place the chicken in the pan and cook for about 10 minutes, turning, until brown on all sides. Remove the excess oil from the pan. In a small saucepan, mix together the apple marmalade, wine, lemon juice, onion flakes, garlic, cloves, curry powder, salt and pepper. Heat until the marmalade melts. Pour this sauce over the chicken, cover and simmer, basting occasionally, for about 15 minutes.

Remove the cover and simmer a further 5 minutes or until a fork can be inserted in the chicken with ease and the chicken is glazed. Place the chicken on a serving platter and garnish with cherry tomatoes, spring onion tops and parsley.

Chicken Mountains

Serves 6 [M]

- 12 potatoes, each about 185 g (6 oz)

Filling
- 6 rashers streaky bacon, rind removed and chopped
- 6 tomatoes, chopped
- 250 g (8 oz) chicken livers, chopped
- 1 level teaspoon dried thyme
- 500 g (1 lb) cooked chicken, chopped
- salt and pepper

Wash and prick the skins of the potatoes and place as far apart as possible on absorbent paper in the microwave. Cook for about 20 minutes depending on the potatoes, moving them several times. When cooked, halve them and break up the centres with a fork, being careful not to damage the skins.

Filling: In a bowl, heat the bacon for 2 minutes on high, then add the tomatoes, chicken livers and thyme and cook for a further 3 minutes, stirring twice. Add the chicken and season. Pile on top of the potatoes and reheat each portion for 2 minutes on high before serving.

Chicken Mountains

Chicken

Arroz con Pollo

Serves 4

1 x 1.5 kg (3 lb) chicken	1 teaspoon salt
¼ cup (2 fl oz) olive oil	¼ cup (2 fl oz) rice
1 onion, chopped	pinch of saffron
2 garlic cloves, crushed	2 green peppers (capsicums), sliced
3 tomatoes	60 g (2 oz) peas
5 cups (1.25 litres) water	pimientos
1 bay leaf	

Cut the chicken into quarters and fry in the oil with the onion and the garlic. When the chicken is lightly browned, add the tomatoes and water and boil for 5 minutes. Add the bay leaf, salt, rice, saffron and green pepper. Stir thoroughly and bake at 190°C (375°F/Gas 5) for 20 minutes. Garnish with the peas and pimientos.

Curried Chicken Amandine

Serves 4

- 1 cup (8 fl oz) mayonnaise
- 1-2 teaspoons concentrated curry sauce
- 1 tablespoon mango chutney
- 1 kg (2 lb) cooked chicken, sliced into finger length pieces
- 1 head of celery, chopped
- 1 bunch spring onions (scallions), sliced
- 1 cup (4 oz) flaked almonds, toasted
- lettuce leaves
- raisins
- toasted desiccated coconut

Mix together the mayonnaise, curry sauce and mango chutney. Stir in the chicken, celery, spring onions and almonds. Pile onto a serving dish, garnish with lettuce and top with raisins and coconut.

Chicken Veronique

Serves 6

- 12 chicken breasts, skinned
- salt and pepper
- 1 ¼ cups (10 fl oz) dry white wine
- 125 g (4 oz) butter
- 1 ½ cups (6 oz) flour
- 6 cups (1.5 litres) milk
- 1 ¼ cups (10 fl oz) cream
- 185 g (6 oz) seedless green grapes

Put the chicken breasts in ovenproof dish. Season and pour over the white wine. Cover and cook at 190°C (375°F/Gas 5) for 25 to 30 minutes until tender and cooked. Drain off the liquid and reserve. Melt the butter and stir in the flour to make a paste. Stir in the milk and the reserved liquid and season to taste. Add the cream and pour over the chicken breasts. Garnish with the grapes. Serve hot.

Chicken Cobbler

Serves 6

- 60 g (2 oz) butter
- 4 tablespoons oil
- 2 large onions, chopped
- 2 green peppers (capsicums), chopped
- 2 level tablespoons flour
- 1 x 275 g (10 oz) can condensed tomato soup
- 2 ½ cups (20 fl oz) chicken stock
- 250 g (8 oz) mushrooms, sliced
- 1 kg (2 lb) cooked chicken, cubed
- seasoning
- 8 cups (2 lb) and 2 level tablespoons flour
- 3 level teaspoons baking powder
- 250 g (8 oz) margarine
- 1 level tablespoon mixed herbs
- 1 level teaspoon salt
- 2 ½ cups (20 fl oz) milk

Melt the butter and oil and fry the onions until softened. Add the peppers and flour and stir in. Cook for 5 minutes. Add the soup and stock and stir until thickened. Add the mushrooms and chicken and season. Put into individual ovenproof dishes. Sift together the flour and baking powder and rub in the margarine. Add the herbs and salt and mix with the milk to a soft dough. Roll out, cut into rounds 4 cm (1 ½ inch) in diameter and place around the dishes. Brush the tops with milk and bake at 200°C (400°F/Gas 6) for 25 to 30 minutes until golden and risen.

Suprêmes de Volaille Amandine

Serves 6

- 3 whole chicken breasts, boned
- salt and pepper
- 125 g (4 oz) butter or margarine
- 2 teaspoons finely chopped onion
- ⅓ cup (1 ½ oz) slivered almonds
- 1 teaspoon tomato paste
- 2 teaspoons flour
- 1 ¼ cups (10 fl oz) chicken broth
- pinch of dried tarragon

Halve the breasts, remove the skin, then sprinkle with the salt and pepper. Melt three quarters of the butter in a pan. Add the chicken breasts and brown, turning occasionally, for approximately 25 minutes. Remove the chicken. Add the remaining butter, the onion and almonds. Cook over a low heat until the almonds are brown. Blend in the tomato paste and the flour. Gradually add the chicken broth and cook stirring constantly, until the mixture thickens and comes to the boil. Add the cooked chicken breasts and the tarragon, then cover and simmer for 20 minutes.

Chicken Wellington

Serves 8

2 x 1.5 kg (3 ½ lb) chickens, boned
750 g (1 ½ lb) puff pastry
2 eggs, beaten

Stuffing

350 g (12 oz) cooked ham, minced (ground)
2 cups (4 oz) fresh breadcrumbs
2 chicken livers, finely chopped
1 small onion, grated
grated rind of 1 lemon

Fill the centre of each chicken with the stuffing. Form into a roll, wrap in foil and bake at 200°C (400°F/Gas 6) for about 1 hour or until cooked. Cool. Roll out the pastry and cut the rectangles to completely enclose the chicken. Wrap and seal with beaten egg. Use the trimmings for decoration. Brush with egg and bake at 220°C (425°F/Gas 7) for about 25 minutes, until risen and golden. Served sliced, hot or cold.

Stuffing: Mix all the ingredients together.

Chicken in Red Wine

Serves 4

125 g (2 oz) butter or margarine
1 small garlic clove, crushed
1 white onion, sliced
1 teaspoon salt
1 x 1.5 kg (3 lb) chicken
dash of pepper
2 rashers bacon, chopped
1 ¼ cups (10 fl oz) burgundy wine
1 ¼ cups (10 fl oz) dry white wine
1 teaspoon flour
2 egg yolks
1 ¼ cups (10 fl oz) cream

Melt the butter in a pan and add the garlic, onion and salt. Brown the dry chicken pieces quickly on all sides, then season. Add the bacon and pour the burgundy and white wine over the chicken. Cover and simmer until the chicken is tender, about 45 to 60 minutes.

Remove the chicken and keep warm. Blend the flour, egg yolks and cream until smooth. Stir into the wine mixture over a low heat until blended, then bring to the boil, stirring constantly. Strain the sauce and pour over the chicken. Serve immediately.

Chicken Maryland

Serves 4

1.5-2 kg (3-4 lb) chicken, cut into serving pieces
2 tablespoons seasoned flour
2 tablespoons oil
2 eggs, beaten
2 bananas, sliced lengthwise
4 slices pineapple
2 cups (4 oz) fresh white breadcrumbs
125 g (4 oz) clarified butter
8 rashers streaky bacon, fried and chopped

Roll the chicken pieces in the seasoned flour. Add the oil to the beaten eggs, then brush the chicken, bananas and pineapple with this egg mixture, and roll in the breadcrumbs. Press on firmly. Heat the clarified butter in a large frying pan. Put in the chicken, bananas and pineapple, and fry gently, turning occasionally so that they are well browned on all sides. Garnish with the fried bacon.

Chicken Tandoori

Serves 4

2 x 1.5 (3 lb) chickens, halved
2 large onions, coarsely chopped
2 green peppers (capsicums), diced
2 tomatoes, coarsely chopped
2 teaspoons curry powder
2 teaspoons coriander
2 teaspoons ground cumin
1 teaspoon turmeric
½ teaspoon cinnamon
½ teaspoon garlic powder
2 teaspoons salt
1 teaspoon black pepper
125 g (4 oz) butter or margarine, melted
2 ½ cups (20 fl oz) water

Place the chicken in a shallow baking pan. Sprinkle over the onion, green pepper, tomato and spices, then pour in the melted butter. Turn the chicken to mix with all the ingredients. Cover and marinate in the refrigerator for several hours, or overnight.

Stir in the water and bake in a moderate oven, 190°C (375°F/Gas 5), for 50 minutes. Garnish with tomato slices, green pepper rings and celery stalks. Serve with hot cooked rice.

Chicken

Other Poultry

Roast Turkey

Serves 10 - 16

Choose either stuffing for your roast turkey.

1 x 5-6 kg (10-12 lb)
  turkey, thawed

Stuffing
125 g (4 oz) bacon, finely chopped
1 small onion, chopped
250 g (8 oz) sausage mince
¼ teaspoon dried sage
1 cup (2 oz) fresh breadcrumbs
1 egg, beaten
salt and pepper

Herb Stuffing
1 small onion, chopped
30 g (1 oz) butter
2 cups (4 oz) fresh breadcrumbs
½ teaspoon dried sage
½ teaspoon dried thyme
½ teaspoon dried tarragon
2 tablespoons chopped parsley
2 eggs, beaten

Place some of the stuffing in the neck cavity of the turkey. Pack it in well but leave enough room for slight expansion during cooking. Close the neck flap over and secure with poultry skewers. Place the remaining stuffing in the main cavity of the turkey after removing the giblets. Tie with string or use special poultry skewers to secure the opening. Place in a roasting pan and bake at 180°C (350°F/Gas 4) for 3 hours. Pierce the skin in several places and return to the oven at 200°C (400°F/Gas 6) for 20 to 30 minutes or until golden brown. Test if cooked and, if not, return to the oven on the lower temperature. If parts of the bird begin to brown too quickly during the cooking time, cover them with foil.

Remove from the oven, place on a carving tray and set aside for 15 minutes before carving. Serve with roast vegetables and gravy. Cranberry sauce is traditionally served with roast turkey. It is available in most supermarkets.

Stuffing: Place the bacon and onion in a pan and cook until the fat begins to run. Add the mince and cook over medium heat until the mince is cooked through. Remove from the heat and stir in the breadcrumbs and the egg. Stir until combined. Season well.

Herb Stuffing: Cook the onion in the butter until soft. Remove from the heat and stir in the breadcrumbs and herbs. Add the beaten eggs to bind the stuffing.

Roast Duck with Cherry Sauce

Serves 4

1 x 2 kg (4 lb) duck, cut into serving pieces
salt and pepper
1 small onion, peeled

Cherry Sauce
juices from the roasting pan
1 x 500 g (1 lb) can pitted dark cherries
grated rind of 1 lemon
1 tablespoon lemon juice

Sprinkle the duck pieces with salt and pepper and place in a roasting pan, preferably on a rack. Place the onion in the pan around the duck. Bake at 190°C (375°F/Gas 5) for 1 ¼ hours or until the pieces are cooked and golden brown. Remove from the pan and place on a warm serving dish. Serve with Cherry Sauce.

Cherry Sauce: Skim the fat from the pan reserving 2 tablespoons. Pour the juice from the cherry can into the pan and reduce over high heat for 5 minutes. Stir in the lemon juice and grated rind. Add the cherries and heat well.

Roast Duck with Orange Sauce

Serves 4

1 x 2 kg (4 lb) duck
salt and pepper
1 small onion, peeled
1 small apple, peeled and chopped
orange slices

Orange Sauce
juices from the roasting pan
juice and finely grated rind of 2 oranges
1 tablespoon sugar
salt and pepper
brandy, optional

Sprinkle the duck inside and out with salt and pepper. Place the onion and apple inside the duck. Place the duck in a roasting pan, preferably on a rack. Prick the skin to reduce the fat during cooking. Bake at 190°C (375°F/Gas 5) for 1 ¾ hours or until the juice runs clear when pricked with a skewer in the fleshy part of the thigh.

Place on a warmed carving tray, garnish with orange slices and serve with Orange Sauce.

Orange Sauce: Skim the fat from the juices in the pan, reserving 2 tablespoons. Add the orange juice, sugar, salt, pepper, and brandy to taste, if desired. Stir over low heat until well combined. Stir in the orange rind.

SEAFOOD

Being a country surrounded by sea, Australia is blessed with the very finest selection of seafood. Whether it be barramundi, freshwater crayfish, coral perch, snapper or the superb scallops and crustaceans from Tasmania, it may be found in our shops.

Fish has a very tender flesh and should only be cooked for a few minutes. It is best quickly deep fried in batter, steamed in foil or grilled (broiled) in a little butter. Cook only until the flesh near the backbone has just turned opaque. When eating a whole fish, don't dive into the middle scattering bones through the remainder of the flesh. All fish have a small row of bones along the top and bottom. Lift off small sections of the flesh and remove the bones in rows. This will make the whole dish more appetising as you will not be removing bones from every bite.

Crabs, crayfish, bugs, prawns, squid, octopus and oysters all have their own special cooking methods so take note of the recipes and watch the cooking times. These seafoods dry out quickly too.

The recipes in this chapter have been supplied by the **Queensland Fish Promotion Advisory Committee** and the **Tasmanian Department of Sea Fisheries**.

In November 1983 the Queensland Government appointed eight fishing industry representatives to the **Queensland Fish Promotion Advisory Committee**. The Committee members represent all sectors of the industry, including catching, wholesaling, retailing, administration and restaurants. The charter of the Committee is to improve the image of the fishing industry and create a greater awareness of seafood for consumption.

The natural gifts from the sea provide an excellent high quality protein and nutrient rich food that is easy to prepare. The recipes here have been developed and tested by Judith Ham to represent Queensland seafoods at their best.

Tasmania is unique in having relatively cold waters – a recognised factor for quality fish. Its unique geographic situation, with many crystal clear bays and inlets, also lends itself to aquaculture or sea farming. Some of the varieties of fish and seafood that are now becoming readily available include blueye (deep sea trevally), a superb eating fish, and the Dory family (including the John Dory). Others which are well known throughout Australia include flounder, flathead, blue grenadier, orange roughy, gemfish, warehou and squid. Tasmanian oysters now find their way into many of Melbourne's top restaurants, and the cultured blue mussel is increasingly sought after. But probably even more exciting is the farming of Atlantic salmon – the king of fish – enabling Australians to enjoy this magnificent fish.

The **Department of Sea Fisheries** in Hobart is responsible for the development and control of fishing and sea farming in Tasmania. The recipes here have been supplied by Barbra Blomberg.

Seafood

Mullet Rollmops

Makes 4 - 6

- 500 g (1 lb) small mullet fillets
- 1 red pepper (capsicum), cut into strips
- 1 large onion, cut lengthwise and then sliced
- 1 cm (½ inch) piece fresh ginger, cut into thin slices
- ½ cup (4 oz) sugar
- 2 cups (16 fl oz) wine vinegar
- 1 tablespoon pickling spices
- grated rind of 1 lemon

Remove any bones from the fillets, and skin if preferred. Wash and pat dry. Beginning at the thickest part of the fillet, roll each mullet fillet around two strips of red pepper and onion. Secure with a toothpick.

Arrange the rolled fillets and ginger slices in layers in a clean 4 cup (1 litre) jar. Slowly bring the remaining ingredients to the boil. Pour over the fish and seal. Gently shake the jar to circulate the liquid and release any air bubbles. Allow to cool, then refrigerate.

Note: These keep well for 2 to 3 weeks. Serve in salads, with drinks, or as an appetiser garnished with lemon wedges, sour cream and tomato slices.

Diver Whiting and Fennel

Makes 1 jar

- 600 g (1¼ lb) diver whiting or other small fish
- 1 small bunch fennel
- 2 cups (16 fl oz) cider vinegar
- ½ cup (4 oz) sugar
- 1 garlic clove, finely sliced
- ¼ teaspoon mustard seeds
- 6 peppercorns
- 1 bay leaf

Head, scale and gut the fish, wash and pat dry. Remove the strings from the fennel and cut it into strips, leaving the green strings intact. Lay a 4 cup (1 litre) jar on its side and layer the whole fish and the fennel in the jar until the jar can be placed upright with the fish in place vertically. Place them top to tail. Bring the remaining ingredients to the boil and pour over the fish and seal. Shake the jar to release any air bubbles. Allow to cool, then refrigerate. Serve with sour cream and slices of cucumber, or with kiwifruit and orange segments as an appetiser.

Warehou in Parsley Wine Sauce

Serves 6

- 1 kg (2 lb) warehou fillets
- 2 tablespoons oil
- 1 large onion, finely chopped
- 1 cup chopped parsley
- 2 garlic cloves, crushed
- ½ cup (4 fl oz) white wine
- salt and pepper

Cut the fish into strips about 2.5 cm (1 inch) wide and place in a shallow ovenproof dish. Heat the oil and sauté the onion until soft but not coloured.

Add the parsley, garlic and wine and bring to the boil. Season with salt and pepper. Pour over the fish. Bake at 180°C (350°F/Gas 4) for 20 minutes.

Seafood Collation

Makes 3 jars

- 500 g (1 lb) fresh mixed seafood (mackerel, squid, snapper, green prawns (shrimp), and scallops)
- 300 g (9½ oz) mixed vegetables, cut into bite-sized pieces (carrots, celery, red or green pepper (capsicum), and cauliflower)
- grated rind of 1 lemon
- 2 cm (¾ inch) piece fresh ginger cut into thin strips
- 3 cups (24 fl oz) vinegar
- ¾ cup (6 oz) sugar
- 8 peppercorns
- 1 bay leaf
- 1 sprig parsley
- 1 sprig dill
- 1 teaspoon pickling spices

Thoroughly wash the seafood and cut the fish into large bite-sized pieces. Peel and devein the prawns. Cut the squid tubes into rings and wash the tentacles thoroughly. Remove the beaks. Arrange the seafood, vegetables, lemon rind and ginger in layers in two 3 cup (24 fl oz) airtight jars. Do not pack down.

Slowly bring the remaining ingredients to the boil and strain into the jars. Fill to cover the seafood and vegetables. Seal and gently shake to release any air bubbles. Allow to cool, and refrigerate for up to 3 weeks.

Serve with a dipping sauce of sour cream and horseradish cream, or add to a green salad of lettuce and cucumber as a first or main course.

Scallops Kebabs with Curry Mayonnaise

Serves 6

500 g (1 lb) scallops
⅓ cup (2½ fl oz) orange juice
1 teaspoon curry powder
1 cm (½ inch) piece fresh ginger, finely chopped or grated
freshly ground pepper
seasoned flour
1 egg, beaten
½ cup (2 oz) breadcrumbs
1 cup (1½ oz) shredded coconut
oil for frying

Curry Mayonnaise
¾ cup (6 fl oz) mayonnaise
½ teaspoon spicy curry powder
¼ cup (2 fl oz) cream
1 tablespoon chopped fresh parsley

Marinate the scallops in the orange juice, curry powder, ginger and pepper for 20 to 30 minutes, then drain. Thread the scallops onto skewers.

Roll in the flour, then the egg and the combined breadcrumbs and coconut. Roll again in the egg and breadcrumbs-coconut. Deep fry in oil for 3 to 4 minutes until golden brown. Serve on a bed of rice (savoury or saffron), accompanied by Curry Mayonnaise.

Curry Mayonnaise: Combine all the ingredients.

Kiwi Fish Fillets

Serves 2

2 fish fillets
¼ cup (1 oz) seasoned flour
45 g (1½ oz) butter, melted
1 spring onion (scallion), finely sliced
2 kiwifruit, peeled and diced
½ cup (4 fl oz) dry white wine
¼ cup (2 fl oz) cream
salt and black pepper to taste
dash of chilli sauce
extra kiwifruit, peeled and sliced

Coat the fish with the seasoned flour. Gently fry in the melted butter until golden and cooked. Remove from the pan and keep warm.

Gently fry the spring onion for 30 seconds, add the kiwifruit and wine and simmer until reduced by half. Remove from the heat. Stir in the cream when the bubbles have subsided. Season to taste and add the chilli sauce.

Serve the fish fillets with sauce spooned over, and garnished with sliced kiwifruit.

Fish Soup with Potatoes and Saffron

Serves 4

8 medium-sized potatoes, peeled and cut into pieces
4 cups (1 litre) fish stock
1 onion, chopped
1 stalk celery, chopped
15 g (½ oz) butter
1 teaspoon saffron strands
½ teaspoon salt
500 g (1 lb) barracouta, cut into 2 cm (¾ inch) pieces
lemon juice
½ cup finely chopped parsley

Place the potatoes in a large saucepan with the stock. Bring to the boil, add the onion and celery and simmer for 20 minutes. Put through a blender or food processor and purée until smooth.

Melt the butter in another saucepan. Add the saffron which has been crushed in the salt and stir for a few minutes until a good yellow colour has appeared. If saffron is not available use ½-1 teaspoon turmeric instead. Add the fish and simmer for approximately 3 minutes. Flavour with lemon juice to taste. Just before serving add the parsley.

Coral Trout Oskar

Serves 4

650 g (1¼ lb) coral trout, cut into fillets
lemon juice
freshly ground pepper
oil
melted butter
1 crayfish (lobster) tail, cooked (prawns (shrimp) or bug meat may be used)
1 cup (8 fl oz) Hollandaise sauce (*page 39*)
lemon wedges
fresh parsley sprigs

Marinate the fillets in lemon juice and pepper for 30 minutes to 1 hour. Preheat the griller (broiler), brush the rack with oil and cover the base of the tray with water. Place the fillets skin side up, brush with butter and season with pepper. Cook, allowing 5 minutes per cm (½ inch) thickness, turning once. Season the other side after turning.

Slice the crayfish meat into medallions and arrange on top of each portion of coral trout. Mask the crayfish with Hollandaise sauce. Grill (broil) until the Hollandaise is browned and the crayfish meat is hot. Serve garnished with wedges of lemon and sprigs of parsley.

Seafood

Reef Seafood Terrine with Yoghurt and Dill Sauce

Serves 4

500 g (1 lb) reef fish fillets (barra or threadfin may be used)
2 tablespoons finely chopped spring onions (scallions)
1 teaspoon chopped fresh dill
¼ teaspoon salt
freshly ground pepper
155 g (5 oz) prawn (shrimp) meat
10 oysters
100 g (3 ½ oz) scallops
⅓ cup (2 ½ fl oz) lemon juice
2 eggs, separated
⅓ cup (2 ½ fl oz) cream
lemon slices
dill sprigs

Yoghurt and Dill Sauce
¾ cup (6 fl oz) natural yoghurt
1 tablespoon finely chopped fresh dill or ½ tablespoon dried dill
juice of ½ lemon

Remove all the bones and skin the fish. Put the fish fillets (cut into chunks), spring onions, dill, salt and pepper in a food processor fitted with steel blade and process for 30 seconds until the fish is roughly chopped.

Combine the fish mixture, prawn meat, oysters, scallops, lemon juice and egg yolks. Add the cream and mix well. Beat the egg whites until stiff and stir into the mixture. Spoon into a greased loaf tin or individual ramekins. Place in a dish half filled with water and bake at 180°C (350°F/Gas 4) for 30 minutes or until set. Allow to cool slightly before turning out of the loaf tin. Garnish with lemon slices and sprigs of dill. Serve warm with Yoghurt and Dill Sauce or cold with homemade mayonnaise.

Yoghurt and Dill Sauce: Combine all the ingredients and mix well.

Barbecued Prawns

Serves 4

1 kg (2 lb) green king prawns (shrimp)
½ cup (4 fl oz) tomato sauce
3 garlic cloves, crushed
½ teaspoon chilli powder
pinch of salt
¼ cup (2 fl oz) lemon juice
2 tablespoons soy sauce
1 teaspoon honey
oil

Peel and devein the prawns and wash thoroughly. Combine the remaining ingredients and mix well.

Marinate the prawns in the sauce for 30 minutes. Stir fry the prawns for approximately 4 to 6 minutes in a pan or cook on the barbecue.

Blue Grenadier Chowder

Serves 4 – 6

500 g (1 lb) grenadier fillets, finely chopped
1 ¼ cups (10 fl oz) yoghurt
½ small cucumber, peeled, seeded and finely chopped
1 cup corn kernels
2 tablespoons lemon juice
2 tablespoons cornflour (cornstarch)
salt and pepper

Combine the fish, yoghurt and cucumber. Bring to the boil and simmer for 5 minutes. Add the corn and lemon juice. Thicken with the cornflour dissolved in a small amount of cold water and stir until creamy. Season with salt and pepper to taste.

Tomato Fish Casserole

Serves 4

600 g (1 ¼ lb) red cod fillets
15 g (½ oz) butter
3 onions, chopped
1 x 425 g (13 ½ oz) can tomatoes
1 teaspoon dried basil
salt and pepper
4 potatoes, cut into small squares and parboiled for 5 minutes
1 cup (4 oz) grated cheese

Cut the fish into serving pieces and place in the centre of a lightly greased ovenproof dish. Melt the butter and sauté the onions until soft but not coloured. Add the tomatoes, basil and salt and pepper to taste. Cook rapidly for 10 minutes. Place the potatoes on both sides of the fish and sprinkle with grated cheese. Pour the tomato mixture over the fish and bake at 200°C (400°F/Gas 6) for 25 minutes.

Fried Fillets with Lemon Caper Sauce

Serves 6

1 kg (2 lb) mirror dory fillets
flour
salt and freshly ground pepper
60 g (2 oz) butter
2 tablespoons capers, chopped
1 tablespoon chopped fresh parsley
4 tablespoons lemon juice

Coat the fish lightly in the flour, salt and pepper. Heat two thirds of the butter in a large shallow frying pan. Add the fish and cook quickly on both sides until golden brown. Set aside on a warm serving dish. Add the remaining butter to the pan and heat. Add the capers, parsley and lemon juice and heat through. Pour over the fish and serve immediately.

Mullet and Mushroom in Filo

Serves 4

500 g (1 lb) mullet fillets
lemon juice
freshly ground pepper
8 sheets filo pastry
155 g (5 oz) butter, melted
155 g (5 oz) mushrooms, sliced
paprika
1 onion, finely chopped
1 tablespoon oil
tomato sauce
3 large ripe tomatoes
1 garlic clove, crushed
¼ teaspoon basil
½ cup (4 fl oz) red wine
salt and sugar to taste

Skin and bone the fillets and cut into strips 2 cm (¾ inch) wide. Marinate in lemon juice and pepper. Brush a sheet of filo pastry with the butter and place another on top. Cut in half. Continue with the remaining sheets. Place the fish at one end of each layered filo pastry and top with mushrooms. Fold in the ends, brush with butter and roll up to make a parcel. Repeat with the other sheets. Place on a greased tray, brush with butter and sprinkle paprika lightly over the top. Bake at 200°C (400°F/Gas 6) for 10 minutes or until golden.

Fry the onion in oil and add the remaining ingredients. Simmer until the tomatoes are a pulp and the wine is reduced by half. Serve over the pastries.

Seafood Soufflé

Serves 4 [M]

60 g (2 oz) butter
2 tablespoons flour
½ teaspoon cayenne pepper
1 cup (8 fl oz) milk
4 eggs, separated
100 g (3½ oz) cooked fish fillets, flaked
155 g (5 oz) prawns (shrimp), cooked, peeled and finely chopped
salt
freshly ground pepper
1 extra egg white
parsley sprigs
lemon wedges

Melt the butter in a saucepan and stir in the flour and cayenne pepper. Gradually stir in the milk until thick. Beat in the egg yolks one at a time, and add the fish and prawns, blending well. Check the seasonings. Allow to cool slightly while whisking the egg whites to form soft peaks. Fold half the egg whites lightly through the seafood sauce, then add the second half until just blended. Pour into a large well greased soufflé dish or 4 small soufflé dishes.

Bake in a preheated oven at 190°C (375°F/Gas 5) for 30 minutes or until well risen and golden brown. Serve garnished with parsley sprigs and wedges of lemon.

Note: This bakes beautifully in a convection/microwave on low for 20 minutes.

Reef Seafood Terrine with Yoghurt and Dill Sauce

Seafood

Green Peppers with Seafood Filling

Serves 4 [M]

- 4 large firm green peppers (capsicums)
- 1 onion, finely chopped
- 1 teaspoon grated fresh ginger
- 2 tablespoons olive oil
- 1 cup cooked prawns (shrimp)
- 1 cup flaked cooked fish
- 1½ cups cooked rice
- 2 tablespoons lemon juice
- ¼ cup (2 fl oz) coconut milk
- freshly ground pepper
- ¼ cup (¼ oz) shredded coconut
- 4 whole prawns (shrimp) for garnish

Conventional Method: Slice the tops off the peppers and chop the tops finely. Remove the seeds and membrane from inside the peppers. Drop the peppers into boiling water and simmer for 5 minutes. Drain well.

Sauté the onion, chopped pepper and ginger in the oil until lightly coloured. Add the remaining ingredients, except the coconut, and mix well.

Stuff each pepper with the seafood filling and sprinkle the coconut on top. Place upright in a greased baking dish and bake at 180°C (350°F/Gas 4) for 20 to 35 minutes. Garnish with whole prawns and serve.

Microwave Method: Combine the seafood filling ingredients until well mixed and fill each unblanched pepper. Top with coconut and place in a greased glass dish. Cover loosely with plastic wrap and microwave on high for 10 to 15 minutes until the peppers are tender.

Troppo Fish Fillets

Serves 6

- 1 kg (2 lb) fish fillets
- seasoned flour
- 2 eggs, beaten
- 1½ cups (4½ oz) desiccated coconut
- butter or oil for frying

Wash and pat dry the fillets and coat lightly with seasoned flour. Dip the fillets in beaten egg and then into coconut. Press the coconut firmly into the flesh. For a good coating repeat the egg and coconut step. Refrigerate for 1 hour. Fry until golden brown in the butter in a pan on medium heat. This should take approximately 6 minutes, turning once.

Note: For best results, cook the flesh side of the fillet first.

Baked Stuffed Mullet with Oyster Sauce

Serves 4

- 4 medium-sized mullet
- 3 cups (6 oz) soft breadcrumbs
- 1 onion, finely chopped
- 1 garlic clove, crushed
- 1 small green pepper (capsicum), finely diced
- 1 tablespoon chopped fresh parsley
- 1 tablespoon chopped fresh mint
- grated rind and juice of 1 lemon
- dash of Tabasco sauce
- 2 tomatoes, finely diced
- 2 stalks celery, finely diced
- freshly ground pepper
- ½ teaspoon salt

Oyster Sauce

- 30 g (1 oz) butter
- ¼ cup (1 oz) flour
- 2½ cups (20 fl oz) fish stock
- ⅓ cup (2½ fl oz) white wine
- 30 oysters (1 large bottle)
- 4 spring onions (scallions)
- 1 tablespoon chopped fresh parsley
- 3 tablespoons cream

Enlarge opening in the mullet, rinse and pat dry. Scale fish and remove as many bones as possible. Combine remaining ingredients for the stuffing and fill the fish. Tie securely, use small skewers or sew up the sides of the fish where necessary. Place the fish on an oiled tray and bake at 200°C (400°F/Gas 6). Reduce the heat to 180°C (350°F/Gas 4) and cook slowly for 35 minutes according to the size of the fish. Test to check if cooked through. Remove the skewers before serving with Oyster Sauce.

Oyster Sauce: Melt the butter and add the flour. Stir to combine and cook for 2 minutes. Add the fish stock and white wine and stir until thick and smooth. Stir in the remaining ingredients until well combined and piping hot – do not allow to boil. Serve at once.

Steamed Mud Crab

Serves 4

- 1 kg (2 lb) live mud crab
- 3 sprigs fresh dill

Kill the mud crab by placing it in the refrigerator for 2 to 3 hours. Bring a large pan of water to the boil and add the dill. Place the crab over the boiling water in a steamer and steam for 18 minutes. Remove from the steamer, break apart and serve.

Whole Baked Fish

Serves 4 – 6 [M]

1 x 2 kg (4 lb) snapper or other reef fish
stuffing of your choice (see below)
½ cup (4 fl oz) oil
½ cup (4 fl oz) white wine

Conventional Method: Wash and pat dry the fish. Make 3 incisions on each side of the fish through to the backbone. Stuff the cavity and secure with a skewer or toothpick. Place in a baking dish and pour over the oil and wine. Bake for 30 to 35 minutes at 180°C (350°F/Gas 4), basting regularly.

Microwave Method: Place in a large shallow dish. Shield the head and the last one third of the tail with foil. Cook for 6 minutes on high. Remove the foil and continue cooking for a further 8 minutes or until the flesh flakes away from the bone.

Oyster Stuffing

1 cup (2 oz) white breadcrumbs
3 spring onions (scallions), chopped
2 rashers bacon, finely chopped and fried
1 bottle oysters (about 12)
½ stalk celery, chopped
2 tablespoons chopped fresh parsley
½ cup (4 fl oz) lemon juice
seasonings

Combine all the ingredients.

Wild Rice Stuffing

1 cup cooked brown rice
½ cup pine nuts
½ cup chopped red pepper (capsicum)
½ teaspoon caraway seeds
½ cup (4 fl oz) white wine
seasonings

Combine all the ingredients.

Note: These stuffings can also be used for squid tubes.

Sesame Sorcery

Serves 6

1 kg (2 lb) flathead fillets (any firm fresh fillets may be used)
salt and freshly ground pepper
2 cups (4 oz) soft white breadcrumbs
¼ cup toasted sesame seeds
60 g (2 oz) butter, melted

Place the fish in a shallow greased baking dish. Sprinkle with salt and pepper. Combine the breadcrumbs, sesame seeds and butter and spoon over the fish. Bake at 180°C (350°F/Gas 4) for 20 minutes.

Mud Crab in Black Bean Sauce

Serves 4 – 6 [M]

3 tablespoons black beans
2 garlic cloves, crushed
½ cup (4 fl oz) water
¼ cup (2 fl oz) oil
4 cm (1 ½ inch) piece fresh ginger, sliced
6 medium-sized mud crabs (for best results use green crabs)
½ bunch spring onions (scallions), cut diagonally into 4 cm (1 ½ inch) pieces
1 egg, beaten

Live Shellfish

When buying live shellfish, ask your seafood retailer to kill and break it up for you. To do it yourself, refrigerate for 2 to 3 hours. This will put the crab or crayfish (lobster) into a permanent sleep. Wash well to remove any dirt. Lift the flap under the crab and pull off the hard round back. With a small, sharp knife, cut away any grey fibrous tissue and rinse again to clean the inside. Chop off any claws or big nippers and crack these with a meat mallet or the back of a cleaver. Chop down the centre to separate the body into 2 halves.

Conventional Method: Place the black beans in a bowl of cold water and stand for 10 to 20 minutes, then drain and rinse in clean water. Mash the black beans and garlic well with a fork. Add the water. Heat the oil in a wok or large pan and add the ginger. Cook over a medium heat for 1 minute and remove the ginger. Add the mud crabs to the wok and cook for 3 to 4 minutes until the crabs turn red. Remove the crabs and add the black bean mixture. Reduce the heat to a low simmer and cook for 1 minute.

Return the crabs to the wok and toss until well coated with the sauce. Cook for a further 4 minutes on a low heat. Add the spring onions and toss again. Pour over the beaten egg, cook for a further minute and serve immediately.

Note: If using cooked crab, break up as directed and eliminate the first cooking step. Finely chop the ginger and add it to the black beans when mashing.

Microwave Method: Place the crabs in a large casserole dish, cover and cook on high for 1 minute. Remove the crabs and add the black bean mixture with the oil to the dish. Microwave on high for 2 minutes. Toss the crabs and finely chopped ginger in the sauce and microwave for 2 minutes. Add the spring onions and beaten egg and microwave for a further 1 minute. Serve.

Seafood

Whole Baked Mullet

Serves 4 [M]

- 2 large or 4 small mullet
- 1 onion, sliced
- ½ teaspoon caraway seeds
- ½ teaspoon dried oregano
- 1 cup (8 fl oz) tomato juice or V8 juice
- 1 cup (8 fl oz) white wine
- 1 tablespoon Worcestershire sauce
- ½ teaspoon grated lemon rind
- lemon slices
- chopped fresh parsley

Conventional Method: Clean and scale the fish, making sure all the black cavity lining is removed. Wash thoroughly and pat dry. Make 3 to 4 incisions through the flesh to the backbone on both sides of each fish. Stuff the onion slices in the cavity of each fish and place in a shallow baking dish. Combine the other ingredients except the lemon slices and parsley and pour over the fish.

Bake at 180°C (350°F/Gas 4) for 35 to 40 minutes, basting regularly with the sauce. Garnish with lemon slices and chopped parsley before serving.

Microwave Method: Cook on high, covered with plastic wrap, for 15 to 20 minutes.

Bouillabaisse

Serves 6

- 3 kg (6 lb) mixed fish (whole green prawns (shrimp), mussels, crabs, scallops, oysters and bugs)
- 2 tablespoons olive oil
- 1 onion, roughly chopped
- 2 garlic cloves, crushed
- 8 cups (2 litres) fish stock
- 2 cups (16 fl oz) white wine
- 1 cup (8 fl oz) water
- 400 g (12½ oz) tomatoes, chopped
- 1 teaspoon dried dill
- salt
- freshly ground pepper
- ¼ teaspoon saffron
- 2 tablespoons chopped fresh parsley

Cut the fish into large chunks. Scrub the crabs, bugs and mussels. Split the bug tails in half lengthwise and clean. Break each crab into 6 portions. Heat the oil and sauté the onion and garlic until soft. Add the stock, wine, water, tomatoes, dill, salt and pepper and bring to the boil. Add the seafood, saffron and parsley and boil rapidly for 15 minutes. Serve with crusty French bread.

Note: The seafood can be lifted out of the soup and served separately on a platter to be eaten first, followed by the soup.

Seafood Pie

Serves 6

- 500 g (1 lb) flathead fillets, boned and skinned (jewfish, flake or reef fish may be used)
- 300 g (9½ oz) of green prawns (shrimp), scallops, squid or crab meat

Butter Sauce
- 60 g (2 oz) butter
- 1 tablespoon flour
- 1 cup (8 fl oz) milk
- 1 cup (8 fl oz) stock (strained from the cooking of the seafood)
- salt
- 10 oysters
- 2 sheets filo pastry or 2 cups seasoned mashed potato
- 1 tablespoon melted butter
- ½ cup (2 oz) grated cheese
- paprika
- freshly ground pepper
- pinch each of dried dill, dried basil and nutmeg
- bay leaf
- ¼ cup (2 fl oz) lemon juice

Cook the fish fillets in a court bouillon (*page 460*) for 5 minutes. Add the prawns and scallops and cook for a further 2 minutes. Remove the seafood and strain the liquid for use in the sauce. Flake the fish and place in layers in a 20 cm (8 inch) pie dish. Poach the oysters in 1 cup (8 fl oz) of water and the juice from the oyster bottle for 2 minutes. Drain, place on top of the fish and then top with the prawns. Pour the Butter Sauce over the seafood filling.

Brush the filo pastry sheets with some of the butter. Layer together and sprinkle with half the cheese. Fold in half, place over the pie dish and trim.

Brush the top with the remaining butter and sprinkle with cheese and paprika. The pie may also be topped with mashed potato, cheese and butter. Cook at 240°C (475°F/Gas 9) for 15 to 20 minutes or until golden.

Butter Sauce: Melt the butter in a saucepan and add the flour, stirring until blended. Add the milk and stock and stir until smooth. Add the seasonings, herbs, nutmeg and bay leaf. Simmer for 5 minutes, add the lemon juice and check the seasonings. Remove the bay leaf.

Opposite: *Seafood Pie*

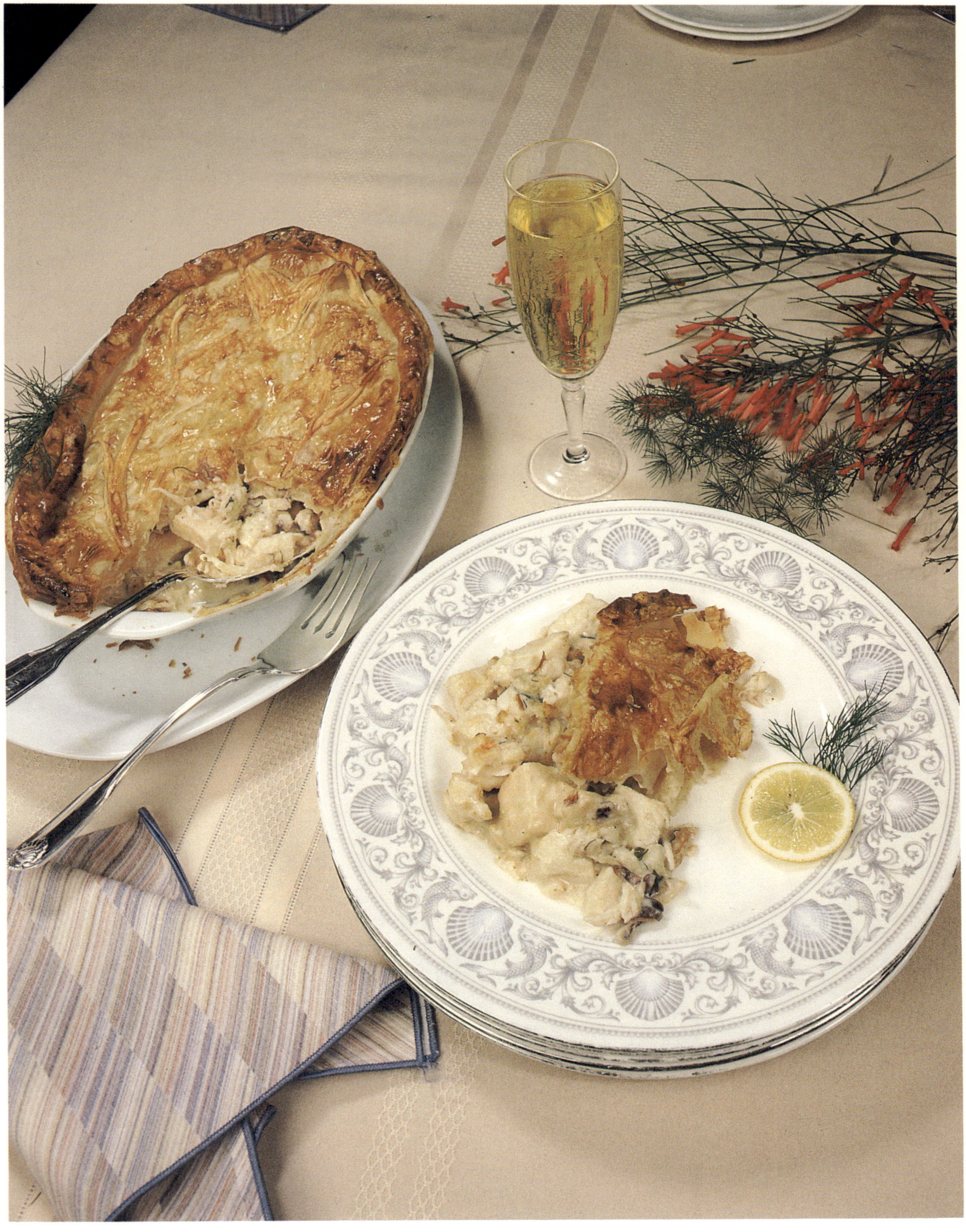

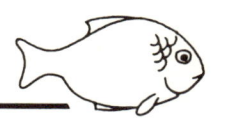

Seafood

Stir Fry Seafood

Serves 4 – 6

½ cup (4 fl oz) oil
1 cm (½ inch) piece fresh ginger, finely chopped
1 garlic clove, crushed
1 red pepper (capsicum), cut into strips
100 g (3½ oz) snow peas (mange-tout)
2 stalks celery, sliced diagonally
200 g (6½ oz) squid, cut in rings or criss-cross pattern
200 g (6½ oz) green prawn (shrimp) meat
200 g (6½ oz) scallops
2 tablespoons soy sauce
2 tablespoons dry vermouth
4 spring onions (scallions), cut into thin diagonal slices

Heat oil in a wok or large saucepan. Add the ginger and garlic and cook for 1 minute. Add the vegetables and toss while cooking for 3 to 4 minutes. Add the seafood, toss and cook for 3 minutes. Add the soy sauce and dry vermouth, cook for 1 minute. Serve garnished with spring onions.

Chinese Style Squid and Peppers

Serves 4 – 6

1 kg (2 lb) squid, cleaned
½ cup (4 fl oz) oil (preferably sesame oil)
2 onions, cut into quarters
2 teaspoons grated fresh ginger
2 red peppers (capsicums), cut into strips
2 green peppers (capsicums), cut into 1 cm (½ inch) squares
2 stalks celery, cut diagonally
½ cup (4 fl oz) chicken or fish stock
3 tablespoons oyster sauce
1 tablespoon soy sauce
½ teaspoon sugar
½ teaspoon salt, optional
1 egg, beaten
4 spring onions (scallions), cut diagonally

Score the squid in a criss-cross pattern and cut into 5 cm (2 inch) squares. Heat the oil in a pan or wok. Add the squid and cook until it curls, remove from the pan and drain on paper towels. Add the onions, ginger, peppers and celery and sauté for 2 to 4 minutes.

Add the remaining ingredients except the egg and spring onions and mix well. Stir until the sauce boils. Add the squid and egg and stir for 1 minute. Place in a serving dish and top with spring onions.

Fish au Gratin

Serves 4

600 g (1 ¼ lb) Blue Grenadier fillets
1 cup (8 fl oz) water
½ cup (4 fl oz) white wine
salt
fresh dill (if available)
500 g (1 lb) broccoli
30 g (1 oz) butter
3 tablespoons flour
2 egg yolks
½ cup (4 fl oz) cream
2 tablespoons lemon juice
½ teaspoon dried tarragon leaves
salt and freshly ground pepper

Cut the fish into serving pieces. Bring the water, wine, salt and dill to the boil, add the fish and poach gently for 3 to 5 minutes, depending on the thickness of the fish fillets. Remove with a slotted spoon and place in a lightly greased ovenproof dish. Strain and reserve the stock.

Parboil the broccoli in salted boiling water for 5 minutes. Drain and place around the fish. Melt the butter, add the flour and stir well. Cook for 1 minute. Gradually add the fish stock and bring to the boil. Simmer for 2 minutes. Remove from the heat, mix the egg yolks and cream and add to the sauce together with the lemon juice and tarragon. Season with salt and pepper to taste. Return to the heat and stir until thickened, but do not boil. Pour over the fish and broccoli. Place in a preheated oven at 200°C (400°F/Gas 6) for 20 minutes. Serve with rice and salad.

Baked Fish with Zucchini

Serves 4

600 g (1 ¼ lb) fish fillets (bream, morwong, flathead)
1 tablespoon lemon juice
2 tablespoons oil
345 g (11 oz) zucchini (courgettes), sliced
1 x 400 g (12 ½ oz) can tomatoes, drained
sprig of fresh rosemary or ½ teaspoon dried rosemary
½ teaspoon dried basil
salt and freshly ground pepper
1 tablespoon dry breadcrumbs
butter or margarine

Remove the skin and bones from the fish, then place in an ovenproof dish. Sprinkle with lemon juice. Heat the oil in a frypan and sauté the zucchini for a couple of minutes without browning.

Add the tomatoes, chopped, or put through a blender, together with the rosemary and basil. Season with salt and pepper and cook for 3 minutes. Pour over the fish. Sprinkle with breadcrumbs and dot with butter. Bake at 180°C (350°F/Gas 4) for 20 to 25 minutes.

Lettuce Roll-Ups

Serves 6

500 g (1 lb) barracouta fillets
2 bacon rashers, chopped and fried
200 g (6 ½ oz) cottage cheese
1 ½ cups (3 oz) fresh breadcrumbs
salt and freshly ground pepper
12 lettuce leaves
½ cup (2 oz) grated cheese

Chop the fish finely. Mix with the bacon, cottage cheese and 1 cup (2 oz) of the crumbs. Season to taste. Blanch the lettuce leaves in boiling water for 10 to 15 seconds, plunge into cold water and drain well. Divide the filling between the leaves and roll up like a parcel. Place in a lightly greased dish, sprinkle with the remaining breadcrumbs and the cheese. Bake at 180°C (350°F/Gas 4) for 20 minutes.

Dory Fillets in Anchovy Sauce

Serves 4

8 fillets king dory
salt
1 medium-sized onion, finely chopped
1 ¼ cups (10 fl oz) cream
beurre manié
 (1 tablespoon flour and 1 tablespoon butter kneaded together)
1 can flat anchovies
2 tablespoons chopped fresh parsley
salt and freshly ground pepper

Rinse the fillets quickly and sprinkle lightly with salt. Place close together in a steamer or saucepan (if a saucepan is used, sprinkle with 3 tablespoons water). Steam for 10 to 12 minutes, depending on thickness. Place the onion in a small saucepan with the cream and bring to the boil. Simmer for 5 minutes. Thicken with a small amount of beurre manié. Chop the anchovies (reserve 4 for decoration) and add to the sauce together with the parsley. Season with salt and pepper to taste.

Remove the fish from the saucepan and place on a heated serving platter. Mask with the sauce and decorate with the reserved anchovies.

Flounder Parmesan

Serves 4

8 flounder fillets
1 tablespoon seasoned flour
1 egg, beaten
4 tablespoons dry breadcrumbs
2 tablespoons grated Parmesan cheese
125 g (4 oz) butter
2 bananas
2 tablespoons lemon juice
8 almonds, blanched and shredded

Cut the flounder fillets into 2 or 3 pieces, depending on size and dry them well on absorbent paper. Coat with the flour and dip in the egg, then breadcrumbs and cheese mixed together, pressing the crumbs onto the fish well. Heat three quarters of the butter in a frypan. Fry the fish until golden brown, drain and place on a serving platter. Wipe out the frypan and heat again. Cut the bananas on a slant and fry quickly in the remaining butter. Add the lemon juice and almonds and fry for a couple of minutes, taking care not to break up the fruit. Arrange around the flounder fillets and serve at once.

Baked Flathead Fillets

Serves 4 [M]

4-8 flathead fillets
2 tablespoons melted butter
½ cup (4 fl oz) white wine
1 garlic clove, crushed

Filling

1 medium-sized onion, finely chopped
½ cup (1 oz) soft breadcrumbs
2 tablespoons melted butter
2 tablespoons sour cream
1 teaspoon chopped fresh thyme
1 teaspoon chopped fresh tarragon

Conventional Method: Put a quarter of the filling on the end of each fillet, fold over and press down to secure. Place in a casserole dish. Mix the butter, wine and garlic and pour over the fish. Cover and bake below the centre of the oven at 180°C (350°F/Gas 4) for 20 to 25 minutes, or until the fish flakes easily.

Filling: Combine all the ingredients and mix well.

Microwave Method: Proceed as above and cook on high for 10 to 12 minutes.

Seafood

Dutch Fish

Fish Fillets in Ginger Sauce

Serves 6

3 tablespoons flour
1 tablespoon ground ginger
salt and freshly ground pepper
800 g (1 ¾ lb) fish fillets (gemfish or morwong)
seasoned flour for coating
60 g (2 oz) butter
2 tablespoons oil
2 tablespoons seasoned flour
½ cup (4 fl oz) cream
1 ½ cups (12 fl oz) fish or chicken stock
1 tablespoon finely chopped fresh ginger

Mix the flour, ground ginger, salt and pepper together. Cut the fish into serving pieces and dust with seasoned flour. Heat the butter and oil in a frying pan and quickly cook the fish fillets, do not overcook. Remove and keep warm.

Pour off all but 3 tablespoons of fat from the pan and sprinkle in the 2 tablespoons seasoned flour. Cook for 1 minute. Gradually add the cream and stock, mixing well until the sauce is smooth. Add the ginger and check the seasoning. Simmer until thickened, do not boil. Place the fish fillets on a serving plate and pour the sauce over each fillet.

Dutch Fish

Serves 6

2 large onions, sliced
60 g (2 oz) butter
2 tablespoons flour
2 cups (16 fl oz) fish stock
salt and freshly ground pepper
juice of 1 lemon
1 teaspoon prepared mustard
1 kg (2 lb) fish fillets, steamed or poached
1 kg (2 lb) potatoes, cooked and mashed with butter

Gently fry the onions in half the butter until golden brown. Melt the remaining butter in a saucepan. Add the flour and cook for 1 minute without browning. Gradually add the fish stock and cook until thickened. Simmer for 2 minutes. Season with salt, pepper, lemon juice and mustard. Arrange layers of fish, potato, onion and sauce in a deep ovenproof dish, finishing with a layer of potato. Bake at 200°C (400°F/Gas 6) for 15 minutes until golden brown on top.

Oven-Baked Morwong with Yoghurt Sauce

Serves 4–6 [M]

- 1 kg (2 lb) morwong fillets
- 2 cups (16 fl oz) non-fat plain yoghurt
- 2 tablespoons light mayonnaise
- 1 cup finely chopped celery
- 1-2 tablespoons lemon juice
- salt and freshly ground pepper
- 2 tablespoons toasted sesame seeds

Conventional Method: Cut the morwong fillets into serving pieces and place in a lightly greased ovenproof dish. Combine the yoghurt, mayonnaise, celery and lemon juice and season with salt and pepper to taste. Spread the mixture over the fish and sprinkle with sesame seeds. Bake at 180°C (350°F/Gas 4) for 20 minutes.

Microwave Method: Prepare as above and cook in a microwave oven on high for 6 minutes. Leave to stand for 1 to 2 minutes.

Braised Ling in Vegetables

Serves 4–6

- 15 g (½ oz) butter
- 1 leek, sliced
- 2 carrots, cut into julienne strips
- 2 stalks celery, cut into julienne strips
- 1 red pepper (capsicum), seeded and cut into rings
- 750 g (1 ½ lb) ling fillets, cut into 5 cm (2 inch) pieces
- ¾ cup (6 fl oz) white wine
- ½ cup (4 fl oz) cream
- ⅓ cup chopped fresh dill or parsley
- salt and freshly ground pepper

Melt the butter in a frypan or wide saucepan, add the leek and soften for a few minutes. Add the carrots, celery and red pepper and place the fillets on top. Pour the wine and cream over, bring to simmering point and simmer for 7 to 10 minutes, depending on thickness.

Add the dill and season with salt and pepper.

Braised Ling in Vegetables

Seafood

Crispy Trout

Serves 2

- 2 rashers bacon, chopped
- 2 trout
- salt
- 2 spring onions (scallions), finely chopped
- 1 tablespoon chopped fresh parsley
- 1 tablespoon lemon juice
- freshly ground pepper
- 1 tablespoon melted butter
- ½ cup (2 oz) finely crushed *jatz* biscuits
- lemon wedges

Fry the bacon pieces until crisp. Remove and reserve the fat. Rinse and wipe the trout. Bone the trout by carefully extending the stomach opening. Snip the backbone just behind the head then at the tail end, but do not cut through the skin. With a sharp knife run the blade between the rib cage and the flesh until you come to the backbone, repeat on the other side, then carefully lift out the complete skeleton. Sprinkle inside with salt.

Mix the spring onions, parsley, lemon juice and pepper to taste. Spread this mixture inside the trout and top with bacon. Brush lightly with the melted butter and coat well with the biscuit crumbs. Reheat the bacon fat and fry the trout until lightly brown on each side, about 4 to 5 minutes on each side. Place on a serving platter and decorate with lemon wedges.

Parsley Fillets

Serves 4 – 6

- 800 g (1 ¾ lb) gemfish fillets
- 2 tablespoons lemon juice
- salt and freshly ground pepper
- 75 g (2 ½ oz) butter
- 1 garlic clove, crushed
- 1 cup (2 oz) fresh breadcrumbs
- 1 cup chopped fresh parsley
- ¾ cup (3 oz) grated cheese
- 4 tomatoes

Cut the fish into serving pieces. Place on a greased ovenproof dish, sprinkle with lemon juice and salt and pepper to taste. Cover with foil and cook at 200°C (400°F/Gas 6) for 15 minutes. Melt the butter in a small saucepan, add the garlic, crumbs, parsley and ½ cup (2 oz) of the cheese. Mix well. Remove the fish from the oven and spread the parsley mixture evenly on top of the fillets.

Cut the tomatoes in half and place on each side of the fish. Sprinkle the remaining cheese over the tomatoes, together with salt and pepper. Return to the oven and continue to bake for 15 minutes.

Quick and Easy Fish Casserole

Serves 4

- 600 g (1 ¼ lb) flake fillets
- salt
- 1 can mushroom soup
- 4 thin slices lemon
- ¼ cup (2 fl oz) cream
- ½ cup chopped fresh parsley and dill
- ¼ teaspoon paprika

Cut the fish into serving pieces and sprinkle with salt. Place the remaining ingredients in a saucepan, mix well and bring to the boil. Add the fish and simmer for 5 to 7 minutes until cooked.

Serve with rice or potatoes and tomato salad.

Morwong Ambrosia

Serves 6

- 6 morwong fillets (other firm white fish may be substituted)
- salt and freshly ground pepper
- ¼ cup (2 fl oz) sherry
- ½ cup (2 oz) dry breadcrumbs
- ¾ cup (3 oz) grated cheese
- 30 g (1 oz) butter

Place the fillets in a greased baking dish. Sprinkle with salt and pepper, add the sherry. Combine the breadcrumbs and cheese and sprinkle evenly over the fillets. Dot with butter and bake at 180°C (350°F/Gas 4) for 20 to 25 minutes until golden brown.

Apple Baked Ling

Serves 4

- 600 g (1 ¼ lb) ling fillets, cut into small pieces
- 1 tablespoon melted butter
- 2 apples, cored and chopped
- 1 teaspoon grated fresh ginger
- salt and freshly ground pepper
- ½ cup (4 fl oz) apple or tomato juice
- ½ cup (4 fl oz) white wine or apple cider

Place the fish in an ovenproof dish and drizzle with melted butter. Sprinkle the apples and ginger over the fish. Season with salt and pepper. Pour the juice and wine over and bake at 180°C (350°F/Gas 4) for 20 to 25 minutes.

Fish with Zucchini and Tomatoes

Serves 6

2 tablespoons oil
1 medium-sized onion, finely chopped
1 garlic clove, crushed
500 g (1 lb) tomatoes, chopped
salt and freshly ground pepper
1 kg (2 lb) trumpeter fillets or steaks
juice of 1 lemon
¼ cup (2 fl oz) white wine
500 g (1 lb) zucchini (courgettes), sliced
1 green pepper (capsicum), seeded and sliced

Heat the oil in a pan and add the onion, garlic, tomatoes and salt and pepper and stir fry for 2 minutes. Add the fish, and sprinkle with lemon juice and wine. Lower the heat, cover with a tightly fitting lid and simmer gently until the fish is almost cooked, about 5 minutes. Add the zucchini and green pepper, replace the lid and simmer gently for 5 minutes.

Fish Kiev

Serves 4

4 thin round fish fillets e.g. sea perch or butterfish
garlic butter (see below)
1 egg
¼ cup (2 fl oz) milk
flour
breadcrumbs
ghee
lemon twists

Trim the fillets and place a piece of garlic butter in the middle of each piece. Roll up the fish so the butter is encased. Secure with toothpicks. Whisk together the egg and milk. Roll fish in flour, dip in the egg and milk, then roll in breadcrumbs. Refrigerate for 15 to 30 minutes. Fry in ghee until golden brown, remove the toothpicks and serve garnished with lemon twists.

Garlic Butter

125 g (4 oz) butter
2-3 garlic cloves, crushed
2 teaspoons lemon juice
1 tablespoon chopped fresh parsley

Beat the butter until smooth. Add the remaining ingredients and mix well. Roll in greaseproof paper or foil to form a thin cylinder shape. Refrigerate until hard. Cut into 4.

Orange Roughy with Mushrooms

Serves 4

600 g (1 ¼ lb) orange roughy fillets
salt and freshly ground pepper
½ cup (4 fl oz) white wine
1 onion, chopped
15 g (½ oz) butter
1 x 440 g (14 oz) can champignons, stems and pieces, drained
1 garlic clove, crushed
½ teaspoon paprika
½ cup chopped fresh parsley

Cut the fillets into serving pieces and place in a dish. Sprinkle with salt and pepper, pour the wine over and leave for 10 to 15 minutes. Sauté the onion in the butter for a few minutes without browning. Add the champignons and garlic and cook for 2 minutes. Place the fish and wine on top of the vegetables and sprinkle with paprika. Simmer for 5 to 7 minutes. Serve sprinkled with parsley.

Spiced Trumpeter

Serves 4

15 g (½ oz) butter
1 medium-sized onion, chopped
1 garlic clove, crushed
1 teaspoon curry powder
60 g (2 oz) mushrooms, sliced
2 teaspoons Worcestershire sauce
1 teaspoon soy sauce
1 x 410 g (13 oz) can tomatoes, chopped
600 g (1 ¼ lb) trumpeter fillets, cut into 2 cm (¾ inch) pieces
salt and freshly ground pepper
chopped fresh parsley

Melt the butter in a large saucepan, add the onion, garlic and curry powder. Stir fry for 2 to 3 minutes. Add the mushrooms and cook for a few minutes. Add the sauces and tomatoes, bring to the boil and simmer for 10 minutes, uncovered, so that some of the liquid will evaporate. Add the fish and simmer for 2 minutes. Season with salt and pepper. Serve sprinkled with parsley.

Seafood

Crispy Baked Orange Roughy

Serves 4

600 g (1 ¼ lb) orange roughy fillets
salt and freshly ground pepper
100 g (3 ½ oz) mushrooms, finely chopped
2 tablespoons chopped fresh parsley
½ cup (1 oz) fresh breadcrumbs
½ cup (2 oz) grated cheese

Place the fillets in an ovenproof dish and season with salt and pepper. Mix the mushrooms and parsley and sprinkle over the fish. Combine the breadcrumbs and cheese and sprinkle over the top. Bake at 200°C (400°F/Gas 6) for 15 to 20 minutes.

Fish with Mango and Kiwifruit

Serves 4 [M]

4 trevally fillets
30 g (1 oz) butter
2 kiwifruit
1 mango
salt and freshly ground pepper

Conventional Method: Place the fish under the griller (broiler). Melt half the butter. Brush the fish with the melted butter and grill (broil) for 3 to 5 minutes on each side, depending on thickness. Peel and slice the kiwifruit and mango and sauté lightly in the remaining butter. Do not brown. Serve on top of the fish.

Microwave Method: Use a browning dish and cook the fish for 2 to 3 minutes on each side. Place the kiwifruit and mango on a plate and heat for 2 minutes. Serve with the fish.

Dory Fillets with Avocado Hazelnut Cream

Serves 4

1 ripe avocado, peeled and seeded
60 g (2 oz) roasted hazelnuts
125 g (4 oz) cream cheese
2 teaspoons lemon juice
pinch of salt
30 g (1 oz) butter
750 g (1 ½ lb) John or mirror dory fillets

Place the avocado, hazelnuts, cream cheese, lemon juice and salt in a food processor or blender and process to form a smooth purée.

Heat the butter in a frying pan, add the fish fillets in a single layer. Add the avocado cream and poach gently for 10 minutes. Serve hot with new potatoes and beans.

Tahitian Fish Kiwi

Serves 4

500 g (1 lb) fresh tuna steaks or snapper fillets
1 onion, chopped
1 chilli, seeded and chopped
1 teaspoon grated fresh ginger
½ cup (4 fl oz) lemon juice
½ cup (4 fl oz) coconut milk
2 firm ripe tomatoes, chopped
freshly ground black pepper
3 kiwifruit, peeled and chopped
lettuce leaves for serving

Cut the fish into bite-sized pieces and place in a bowl. Mix together the onion, chilli, ginger, lemon juice and coconut milk. Pour over the fish and marinate in the refrigerator for about 4 hours or until the fish turns white and has a cooked appearance. Stir occasionally.

Add the tomatoes, pepper and kiwifruit and serve on lettuce leaves.

Ginger Bream

Serves 4 [M]

4 whole bream, cleaned and scaled (450-600 g/ ¾-1 ¼ lb each)
2 spring onions (scallions), cut into thin strips
2 cm (¾ inch) piece fresh ginger, cut in thin matchstick strips
1 tablespoon soy sauce
1 tablespoon lemon juice
½ cup (4 fl oz) wine
sprig of parsley

Score each fish 3 times on each side. Combine the remaining ingredients except the wine and parsley and spoon over each fish and into the cavity.

Place in a steamer with the wine and parsley in the water. Cook over simmering water for 8 to 10 minutes or until the flesh comes away from the bone.

Note: This can also be cooked in foil on the barbecue or in the oven. To microwave, place in a shallow baking dish, cover with a lid or plastic wrap and cook for 5 to 7 minutes.

Opposite: *Ginger Bream*

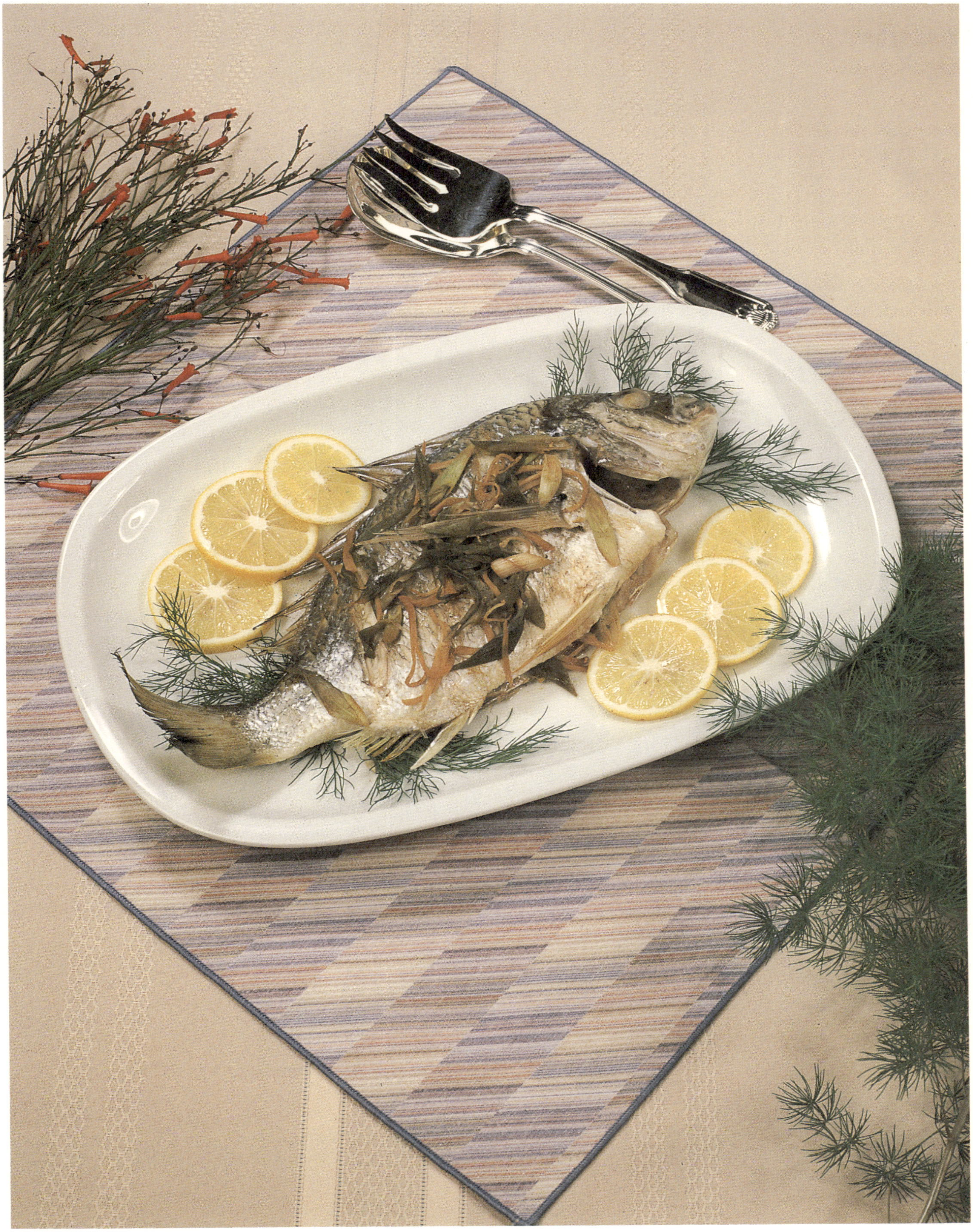

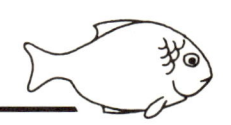

Seafood

Prawns with Snow Peas

Serves 4

- 2 garlic cloves, crushed
- 2 teaspoons grated fresh ginger
- 2 tablespoons peanut oil
- 500 g (1 lb) green prawns (shrimp), peeled and deveined
- 200 g (6 ½ oz) snow peas (mange-tout), topped and tailed
- 4 spring onions (scallions), diagonally sliced
- 1 tablespoon soy sauce
- 1 tablespoon dry sherry
- ½ medium-sized lemon, thinly sliced
- cooked egg noodles

Stir fry the garlic and ginger in 1 tablespoon of the heated oil in a wok for 1 minute. Add the prawns and stir fry until pink, approximately 4 minutes. Remove from the wok.

Heat the remaining oil in the wok and stir fry the snow peas and spring onions for 1 minute. Return the prawns with the remaining ingredients and combine well. Serve immediately with egg noodles.

Oyster Mushroom Prawns

Serves 4

- 2 garlic cloves, crushed
- 2 teaspoons grated fresh ginger
- 2 tablespoons peanut oil
- 500 g (1 lb) green prawns (shrimp), peeled and deveined
- 300 g (9 ½ oz) oyster mushrooms, sliced
- 4 spring onions (scallions), diagonally sliced
- 1 tablespoon soy sauce
- 1 tablespoon dry sherry
- ½ medium-sized lemon, thinly sliced
- cooked egg noodles

Stir fry the garlic and ginger in 1 tablespoon of the heated oil in a wok for 1 minute. Add the prawns and stir fry until pink, approximately 2 minutes. Remove from the wok.

Heat the remaining oil and stir fry the mushrooms and spring onions for 1 minute. Return the prawns with the remaining ingredients and heat through. Serve immediately with egg noodles.

Scallops with Snow Peas

Serves 2 - 3

- 250 g (8 oz) scallops
- 2 leeks
- 125 g (4 oz) snow peas (mange-tout)
- 2 tablespoons peanut oil
- ½ teaspoon finely chopped fresh ginger
- 1 garlic clove, crushed
- 2 teaspoons cornflour (cornstarch)
- ¼ cup (2 fl oz) water
- 1 teaspoon soy sauce
- 1 teaspoon oyster sauce

Remove the dark vein and any marks from the scallops. Leave the orange roe intact. Wash the leeks thoroughly and cut the white part into thin diagonal slices. Remove the strings from the snow peas.

Heat the oil in a wok and stir fry the ginger, garlic and leeks for 1 minute. Add the scallops, cook on high heat for 1 minute, then add the snow peas and toss for a further minute. Push to the side of the wok and add the cornflour blended with the water, the soy and oyster sauces. Stir until thickened, about 1 minute. Stir in the scallops and vegetables. Heat through and serve immediately with boiled rice.

Passionfruit Perch

Serves 4

- ⅓ cup (2 ½ fl oz) vermouth
- ½ cup (4 fl oz) fresh lime juice
- 750 g (1 ½ lb) perch fillets
- pulp of 6 passionfruit
- ¼ cup (2 fl oz) cream
- freshly ground black pepper

Bring the vermouth and lime juice to the boil in a shallow pan. Add the perch fillets and cook covered until the flesh flakes, about 8 to 10 minutes. Remove the fish and keep warm. Add the passionfruit pulp to the poaching liquid. Simmer, uncovered, until reduced and thickened. Swirl in the cream and season with pepper. Mask the fish fillets with creamy passionfruit sauce and garnish with dill. Serve with sautéed potatoes and fresh asparagus.

Fish Curry

Serves 4 – 6 [M]

1 kg (2 lb) warehou fillets
1 tablespoon oil
1 tablespoon curry powder
2 teaspoons grated lemon rind
4 onions, chopped
1 ½ cups (12 fl oz) tomato juice
1 cup (8 fl oz) water
salt and pepper

Conventional Method: Cut the fish fillets into serving pieces and place in a casserole dish. Heat the oil in a saucepan, add the curry powder and rind, stir for 1 minute. Add the onions and cook for a few minutes without browning. Add the tomato juice and water, bring to the boil and season with salt and pepper to taste. Pour over the fish. Place below the centre of the oven at 180°C (350°F/Gas 4) for 20 minutes.

Microwave Method: Heat the oil in a casserole dish, add the curry powder, rind and onions and cook on high for 2 minutes. Add the juice, water and seasoning and bring to the boil. Place the fish in the boiling liquid and microwave on high for 6 to 8 minutes. Leave to stand for 2 minutes.

Baked Whole Fish with Macadamia Stuffing

Serves 8 – 10

3 kg (6 lb) fish, cleaned, scaled and trimmed
4 rashers bacon, rind removed
lemon juice
freshly ground black pepper
125 g (4 oz) butter
1 ½ cups chopped celery
½ cup minced onion
1 garlic clove, crushed
⅔ cup macadamia nuts, coarsely chopped
2 cups (4 oz) fresh breadcrumbs
1 teaspoon salt
½ teaspoon marjoram
½ teaspoon cayenne pepper
milk

With a very sharp knife, cut two lengthwise slits along each side of the fish. Press the bacon into the slits. Place the fish on a double thickness of buttered aluminium foil. Rub all over with lemon juice and black pepper. Melt the butter and sauté the celery, onion and garlic until the celery is slightly soft and the onion transparent. Add the nuts and toss thoroughly. Combine with the breadcrumbs and seasonings. Add milk, if necessary, to moisten the stuffing to desired consistency.

Stuff mixture firmly into the cavity of the fish and fasten with poultry skewers. Enclose the fish completely in foil, crimping the edges to seal. Bake at 190°C (375°F/Gas 5), allowing 20 minutes per kg (2 lb), or until done. To serve, unwrap and cut away foil. Remove the bacon strips.

Crispy Fish Slices with Sweet and Sour Sauce

Serves 4

500 g (1 lb) fish fillets (any firm white fish)
½ teaspoon salt
oil for deep frying
extra 1 tablespoon oil
2 tablespoons chopped fresh ginger
2 garlic cloves, chopped
2 teaspoons cornflour (cornstarch)
¼ cup (2 oz) sugar
¼ cup (2 fl oz) brown vinegar
½ cup (4 fl oz) water
1 tablespoon soy sauce
1 tablespoon white wine
½ teaspoon salt
1 teaspoon sesame oil

Batter
1 cup (4 oz) flour
½ cup (2 oz) cornflour (cornstarch)
½ teaspoon salt
1 egg, beaten
¾ cup (6 fl oz) cold water, approximately

Cut the fish into bite-sized thin slices. Place in a bowl with the salt and allow to stand. Heat the oil in a deep fryer to 180°C (350°F). Dip the fish into the batter and deep fry for 2 minutes until golden brown. Remove and drain. Heat the tablespoon of oil in a large saucepan. Add the ginger and garlic and sauté for 1 minute. Combine the remaining ingredients and stir until thickened. Reheat the fish for a further minute, drain and place on a serving dish, add the sauce. Serve immediately.

Batter: Mix the flour, cornflour and salt with the beaten egg and water to make a batter just thick enough to coat a spoon.

Baked Whole Trevally

Serves 6

1 x 2-2 ½ kg (4-5 lb) trevally
salt and pepper
1 onion, finely chopped
30 g (1 oz) butter
1 large green apple, peeled, cored and chopped
2 cups (4 oz) fresh breadcrumbs
1 egg or ⅓ cup (2 ½ fl oz) milk
½ cup (4 fl oz) apple juice or lemon juice

Rinse and dry the fish well. Sprinkle lightly with salt and pepper. Sauté the onion in half the butter until soft but not coloured. Add the apple and breadcrumbs and bind with the egg. Season. Grease a large piece of strong aluminium foil with the remaining butter. Put the stuffing loosely into the fish and carefully lift onto the foil. Fold up the edges and pour the juice over. Fold the foil over to secure. Bake below the centre of the oven at 200°C (400°F/Gas 6) for 40 to 50 minutes. Approximately 10 minutes for each 500 g (1 lb).

Seafood

Special Fish Pie
Serves 8

60 g (2 oz) butter
⅓ cup (1 ½ oz) flour
¾ cup (6 fl oz) fish stock
¾ cup (6 fl oz) white wine

2 egg yolks
½ cup (4 fl oz) cream
salt and pepper

Filling
500 g (1 lb) flounder fillets, cut into bite-sized pieces
200 g (6 ½ oz) prawns (shrimp), halved
200 g (6 ½ oz) scallops, halved
200 g (6 ½ oz) mushrooms, sliced

Pastry
200 g (6 ½ oz) shortcrust pastry (*page 458*)
beaten egg

Melt the butter, add flour and cook for 1 minute. Gradually add the stock and wine and cook for a few minutes. Beat the yolks and cream together and add to the sauce. Stir until thickened, do not boil. Season with salt and pepper.

Layer a greased ovenproof dish with the fish, prawns, scallops and mushrooms. Cover with sauce and repeat until the filling and sauce are used up.

Roll out the pastry. Place it on top of the dish and wet the edges with beaten egg. Trim the edges. Decorate the pie with the pastry trimmings. Brush with beaten egg. Bake at 200°C (400°F/Gas 6) for 30 to 45 minutes.

Orange and Onion Pickled Scallops

Gravlax
Serves 8

This is a Scandinavian dish. The raw fish is marinated then served in paper thin slices with a mustard dressing.

1 kg (2 lb) fresh salmon fillets
2 tablespoons salt
2 tablespoons sugar

1 teaspoon crushed peppercorns
⅓ cup chopped dill
dill sprigs

Sauce
1 tablespoon prepared mild mustard
3 teaspoons French mustard
1 ½ tablespoons sugar
1 egg yolk

⅓ cup (2 ½ fl oz) oil
2 teaspoons vinegar
salt and pepper
½ cup finely chopped dill

Place half the salmon fillets skin side down in a glass dish. Mix together the salt, sugar, pepper and dill and sprinkle half over the salmon. Cover with the remaining fillets, thick part over thin part. Sprinkle with the remaining mixture. Cover well with plastic wrap. Leave to marinate for 36 to 48 hours, turning the fillets every 8 hours. Drain well. The salmon will keep for up to a week well covered in the refrigerator.

Carefully scrape off the dill and peppercorns and with a very sharp knife (a ham knife is ideal) cut paper thin slices on the slant. Place on a serving dish and decorate with sprigs of dill and the sauce beside.

Sauce: Place the mustards, sugar and egg yolk in a small bowl. Beat well and add the oil drop by drop. When the mixture thickens, gradually add the remaining oil. Season with vinegar and salt and pepper to taste. Stir in the dill and leave in the refrigerator for at least 1 hour. If the sauce separates add 1–2 teaspoons cold water.

Orange and Onion Pickled Scallops
Makes 1 jar

600 g (1 ¼ lb) scallops
2 oranges
1 onion, thinly sliced
¼ cup (2 oz) sugar

1 cup (8 fl oz) wine vinegar
8 black peppercorns
1 bay leaf
½ stick cinnamon

Wash and drain the scallops. Finely grate the rind of the oranges or cut into thin strips. Peel and segment the oranges. Arrange the scallops, orange segments and onion rings in a 3 cup (24 fl oz) airtight jar. Combine the orange rind and the remaining ingredients in a saucepan and bring to the boil. Pour over the scallops, seal and allow to cool.

Baked Fish Loaf

Serves 4 [M]

- 400 g (12 ½ oz) fish fillets
- 3 eggs
- 1 ¼ cups (10 fl oz) sour cream
- salt and pepper
- oil
- breadcrumbs
- ½ cup chopped dill or 1 packet frozen spinach, thawed and well drained

Conventional Method: Place one third of the fish in a food processor with 1 egg and one third of the cream. Process until smooth. Continue with the remaining fish, egg and cream in third lots. Season with salt and pepper.

Brush a loaf tin with a small amount of oil and sprinkle lightly with breadcrumbs. Pour half the fish mixture into the tin. Top with dill or spinach then carefully add the remaining fish. Place the tin in a baking dish half filled with water and cook below the centre of the oven at 200°C (400°F/Gas 6) for 40 to 50 minutes. Serve hot or cold.

Microwave Method: Proceed as above and place the mixture in a microwave dish. Cook on high for 8 minutes, turning the dish a few times during cooking, even if using a turntable.

Microwave Mackerel Bake

Serves 4 [M]

- 2 tomatoes, sliced
- 1 onion, sliced into rings
- 2 medium-sized zucchini (courgettes), cut into fingers
- freshly ground pepper
- 750-850 g (1 ½-1 ¾ lb) mackerel fillets or cutlets
- ⅔ cup (5 fl oz) tomato juice or V8 juice
- ⅔ cup (5 fl oz) dry white wine
- chopped fresh parsley

Layer half the tomatoes, onion and zucchini in a shallow microwave dish and season with pepper. Arrange the fillets over the vegetables and season. Top with the remaining vegetables and season. Pour over the juice and white wine. Cover with plastic wrap or a lid. Microwave on high for 8 to 10 minutes. Garnish with chopped parsley.

Note: To oven bake, follow the method as above but omit the covering and bake in a moderate 180°C (350°F/Gas 4) oven for 20 minutes.

To barbecue, envelope individual portions of fish and vegetables in foil and cook on the barbecue for 8 to 10 minutes.

Microwave Mackerel Bake

Seafood

Marinated Fish Salad

Serves 6

500 g (1 lb) trevally fillets (any firm fresh fish may be substituted)
¾ cup (6 fl oz) lemon juice
1 small onion, sliced
2 spring onions (scallions), finely sliced
½ cup finely diced cucumber
½ cup grated carrot
½ cup finely sliced celery
1 tablespoon mayonnaise
1 tablespoon yoghurt
salt and freshly ground black pepper

Cut fish into 2.5 cm (1 inch) cubes. Place in a glass dish. Add the lemon juice and onion rings. Leave to marinate until the inside of the fish becomes white, approximately 20 to 24 hours, stirring occasionally. Drain well.

Combine the spring onions, cucumber, carrot, celery, mayonnaise, yoghurt and season to taste. Add the fish and mix well. Place in serving dishes and serve really cold with hot bread rolls.

Tangy Baked Fish

Serves 4 – 6

1 x 2-3 kg (4-6 lb) fish
salt and pepper
1 large grapefruit
butter
1 tomato
1 onion
½ cup (4 fl oz) dry sherry

Rinse and dry the fish well and sprinkle lightly with salt and pepper. Cut 4 thin slices off the grapefruit, then cut the remaining fruit into thin wedges. Place the wedges inside the fish cavity. Grease a large double piece of foil with butter and place the fish on the foil.

Thinly slice the tomato and onion and place on top of the fish together with the grapefruit slices. Dot with butter, fold up the sides of the foil and pour the sherry around the fish. Secure the foil. Bake below the centre of the oven at 200°C (400°F/Gas 6) for 45 to 60 minutes. Approximately 10 minutes per 500 kg (1 lb).

Queensland Threadfin Salmon Parcels

Serves 4

600 g (1½ lb) threadfin salmon fillets
1 tablespoon crystallized ginger, finely chopped
4 spring onions (scallions), finely chopped
freshly ground black pepper
seafood seasoning
½ cup (4 fl oz) lemon juice or white wine

Place individual portions of threadfin salmon on sheets of lightly oiled aluminium foil. Top each with the ginger, spring onions, pepper and seafood seasoning. Pour over a tablespoon of lemon juice. Fold over the foil and crimp the edges to make a parcel. Cook for 5 to 10 minutes on the barbecue.

Fish Patties

Serves 4

500 g (1 lb) Jack mackerel fillets
1 onion
1 potato, boiled
½ teaspoon paprika
1 egg
½ cup chopped parsley or dill
salt and pepper
½ cup (2 oz) dry breadcrumbs
30 g (1 oz) butter
2 tablespoons oil
1 lemon, sliced

Chop the fish, onion and potato finely, or put into a food processor or blender and process until fine. Place in a bowl and mix with paprika, egg, parsley or dill. Season with salt and pepper. Form into patties and coat with breadcrumbs.

Heat the butter and oil. Add the patties and fry on medium heat for 3 to 4 minutes on each side. Drain and place a thin lemon slice on each patty.

Deep-Fried Scallops

Serves 4

12 large or 24 small scallops
juice of 1 lemon
4 tablespoons olive oil
1 teaspoon chopped parsley
1 cup (4 oz) flour, sifted
salt
¾ cup (6 fl oz) tepid soda water or water
2 egg whites, stiffly beaten
oil for deep frying
parsley sprigs
lemon wedges
tartare sauce

Cut large scallops in half and place in a bowl. Mix the juice with 2 tablespoons of the oil and the parsley and pour over the scallops. Toss carefully and leave to marinate for 30 minutes. Drain. Put the flour into a bowl. Add the salt and soda water and fold carefully together to prevent elasticity. Leave for 30 minutes. Fold in the beaten egg whites.

Dip each scallop in the batter and deep fry in hot oil at 190°C (375°F) for a couple of minutes. Drain and place on a serving dish. Deep fry the parsley sprigs in the hot oil for 10 to 15 seconds. Drain and serve with the scallops together with lemon wedges and tartare sauce.

Ginger Honey Scallops

Serves 4

¼ cup sesame seeds
3 tablespoons lemon juice
2 tablespoons oil
1 tablespoon honey
1 tablespoon soy sauce
2 teaspoons finely chopped fresh ginger
1 small garlic clove, crushed
500 g (1 lb) scallops

Heat a frying pan and toast the sesame seeds until golden brown. Set aside on greaseproof paper. Combine the lemon juice, oil, honey, soy sauce, ginger and garlic. Add the scallops and mix until well coated in the marinade. Cover and chill for at least 3 hours, stirring occasionally.

Remove the scallops from the marinade, reserving the liquid. Thread the scallops onto skewers. Place under a pre-heated griller (broiler), for approximately 3 minutes, turning frequently and basting with marinade. Remove the scallops from the skewers, sprinkle with sesame seeds and serve at once.

Squid

How to Clean and Prepare Squid

1. Detach the head and internal organs from inside the hood.
2. Slide the stiff, clear membrane from the hood.
3. Cut the head and beak from the tentacles.
4. Remove the skin from the tentacles and cut as required.
5. Remove the skin from the hood. Use a paper towel for ease of removal. The hood can be used whole, cut into rings or sliced open and cut into strips.
6. Remove the fins carefully, if required.

Stuffed Squid or Calamarie Farcie

Serves 6

6 large squid
2 large onions, chopped
2 rashers bacon, finely chopped
3 garlic cloves, crushed
2 tablespoons oil
1½ cups (3 oz) white breadcrumbs
white wine
½ cup chopped fresh parsley
salt and freshly ground pepper
extra chopped parsley

Sauce

500 g (1 lb) tomatoes
1 tablespoon tomato paste
½ cup (4 fl oz) red wine
salt, pepper and sugar
paprika
Tabasco sauce

Remove the body, backbone and skin of each squid. Finely chop the tentacles. Fry the tentacles with the onions, bacon and garlic in the oil until lightly coloured. Add a little white wine to the breadcrumbs. They should be moist but not wet. Pour off any excess liquid. Add the fried ingredients and the parsley. Season.

Fill each squid two thirds full, allowing room for the stuffing to swell without splitting the tube. Secure the open end with a toothpick. Lay them in a single layer in a pan and pour over the Tomato Sauce. Bake at 180°C (350°F/Gas 4) for 30 minutes. Garnish with chopped parsley and serve.

Sauce: Chop the tomatoes roughly. Combine the tomato paste, tomatoes and red wine in a saucepan and simmer for 25 minutes until the tomatoes become a pulp. Pick out any pieces of skin and season with the salt, pepper, sugar, paprika and Tabasco sauce to taste. Set aside.

Seafood

Deep-Fried Squid

Serves 4

4 medium-sized squid
seasoned flour
beaten egg and milk
dry breadcrumbs
oil for deep frying
lemon wedges

Clean and prepare the squid (*page 285*). Cut the hoods crosswise into 6 mm (¼ inch) slices, forming rings. The tentacles may be cooked whole or sliced across. Coat first in the flour, then the egg and milk, then breadcrumbs. Allow to set for 15 minutes, preferably in the refrigerator.

Heat oil to fairly hot and quickly deep fry for about 1 minute until lightly browned. Squid becomes tough if overcooked. Drain on paper. Serve with lemon wedges.

Note: Batter may be substituted for egg and breadcrumbs.

Apricot Squid

Serves 6

½ cup (2 oz) finely
  chopped apricots
4 tablespoons brandy
2 cups cooked brown rice or
  2 cups (4 oz) fresh brown
  breadcrumbs
1 teaspoon oregano
1 garlic clove, crushed
salt and pepper
6 medium-sized squid
  hoods
15 g (½ oz) butter
1 cup (8 fl oz) white wine

Soak the apricots in the brandy for at least 1 hour. Mix with the rice or breadcrumbs, oregano and garlic. Season with salt and pepper. Fill the hoods with the stuffing and secure the opening with skewers or toothpicks.

Sauté the hoods in the butter and place in a casserole dish. Pour the wine over, cover and bake below the centre of the oven at 180°C (350°F/Gas 4) for 50 to 60 minutes or until tender.

Sweet and Sour Squid

Serves 4

2 medium-sized squid
2 tablespoons oil
2 garlic cloves, crushed
2 teaspoons finely chopped
  fresh ginger
1 onion, thinly sliced
125 g (4 oz) mushrooms,
  sliced
2 stalks celery, thinly
  sliced
1 green pepper (capsicum),
  thinly sliced

Sauce

3 teaspoons cornflour
  (cornstarch)
2 teaspoons soy sauce
1 teaspoon sugar
1 teaspoon vinegar
½ cup (4 fl oz) fish or
  chicken stock

Clean and skin the squid. Slit the hoods in half lengthwise, then cut crosswise into 1 cm (½ inch) wide strips. Cut tentacles into 2 or 3 pieces. Heat the oil in a pan or wok. Add the garlic, ginger and onion and stir fry for 1 minute. Add the mushrooms, celery and green pepper and continue to stir fry for 2 minutes. Add the squid and stir fry for 1 to 2 minutes. Add the sauce mixture and stir until thickened. Serve at once.

Sauce: Blend all the ingredients for sauce together.

Stuffed Squid and Mushrooms

Serves 4

4 medium-sized squid
2 tablespoons oil
2 onions, 1 chopped and
  1 sliced
¾ cup (4 oz) rice
fish stock or water
2 tomatoes, peeled and
  chopped
1 teaspoon salt
30 g (1 oz) butter
1 cup sliced mushrooms

Clean the squid and finely chop the tentacles. Heat the oil and fry the tentacles and chopped onion for 1 minute. Add the rice and stir until the grains are coated in oil. Add the stock or water and the tomatoes so that the liquid barely covers the rice. Season to taste and simmer for 10 minutes. Stuff the hood with this mixture and secure the ends. Fry in the butter for 5 minutes. Place in an ovenproof dish.

Toss the mushrooms and sliced onion in the remaining juice in the pan. Season to taste and pour over the squid. Cover with foil and bake at 180°C (350°F/Gas 4) for 30 minutes. Remove the foil and cook a further 15 minutes.

Opposite: *Stuffed Squid and Mushrooms*

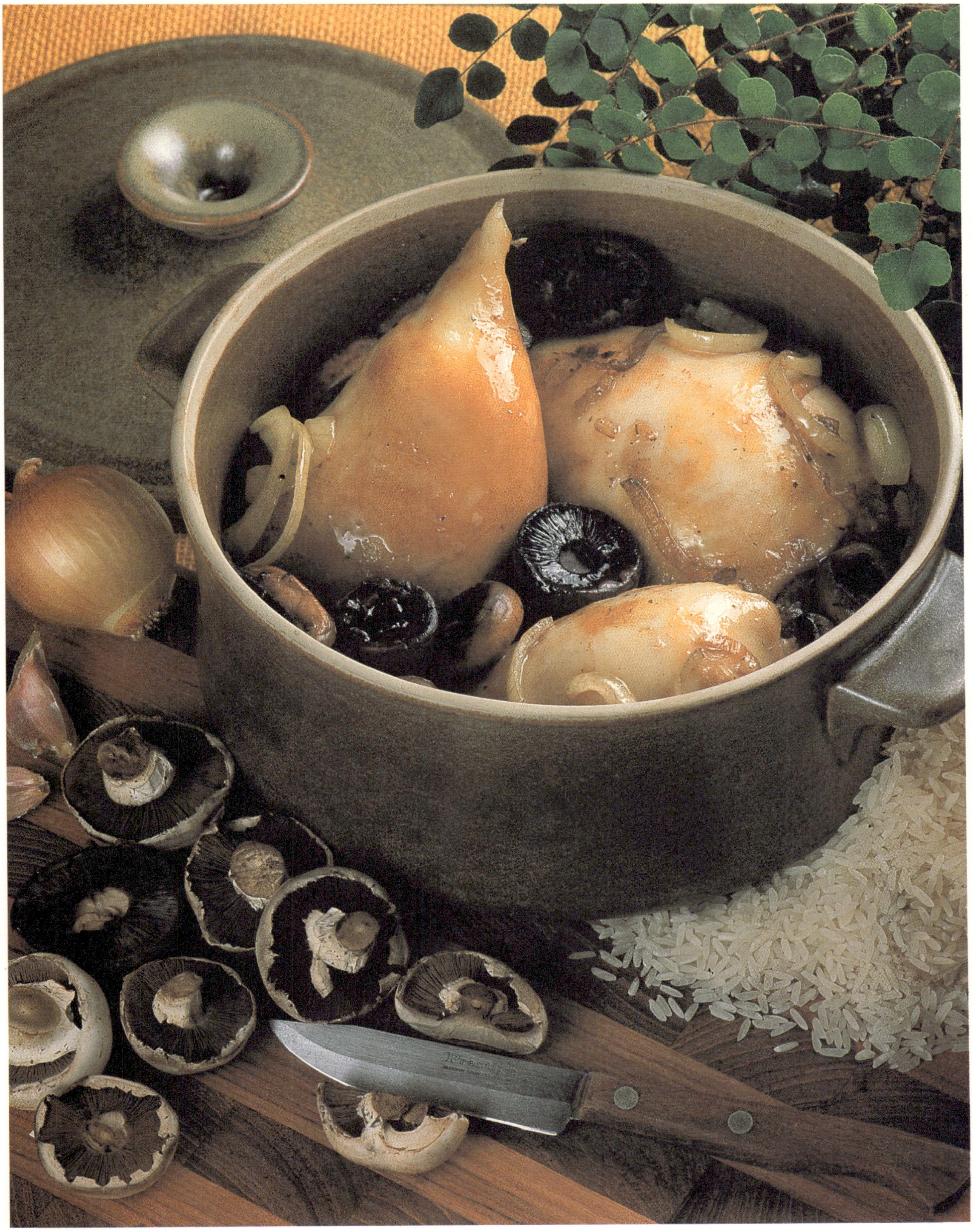

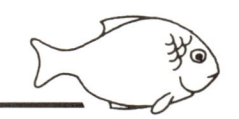

Seafood

Octopus

How to Clean and Tenderise Octopus

1. Cut off the tentacles in one piece. Remove the beak and eyes and discard.
2. Turn the hood inside out and remove the internal organs. Rinse well under running water.
3. Place the octopus in a large saucepan with no liquid (it will produce its own juices) and cook over a moderate heat for about 1 to 1 ½ hours depending on size. This can also be done in a casserole dish in the oven. A pressure cooker may also be used which will reduce the tenderizing time to 20 to 25 minutes.
4. Remove from the saucepan and remove the skin and suckers under running water. They will come off very easily. In some Mediterranean dishes the skin is left on as it is considered to give extra flavour to the dish.
5. Chop the octopus into pieces according to the dish in which it will be used.

Marinated Octopus Greek Style

Serves 8

1 kg (2 lb) octopus, prepared as above and cut into bite-sized pieces
1 cup (8 fl oz) wine vinegar
1 teaspoon dried oregano or sprigs of fresh oregano
⅓-½ cup (3-4 oz) sugar

1 teaspoon salt
½ cup (4 fl oz) olive oil
1 large lemon, chopped
lettuce leaves
black olives
cucumber slices
tomato wedges

Dressing
2 tablespoons olive oil mixed with 2 tablespoons lemon juice

Place the octopus in a large glass jar. Bring the vinegar, oregano, sugar and salt to the boil. Simmer for a few minutes. Pour over the octopus together with the oil and chopped lemon. Mix well and marinate for 24 hours.

Drain and toss in the oil and lemon dressing. Place in lettuce leaves and decorate with black olives, cucumber slices and tomato wedges.

Octopus Casserole

Serves 6

⅓ cup (2 ½ fl oz) oil
3 medium-sized onions, thinly sliced
3 garlic cloves, crushed
3 tomatoes, skinned, seeded and chopped

1 kg (2 lb) octopus, cleaned, tenderized and cut into bite-sized pieces
2 cups (16 fl oz) red wine
salt and pepper

Heat the oil in a deep saucepan. Sauté the onions and garlic for a few minutes without colouring. Add the tomatoes, octopus and wine and season with salt and pepper. Bring to the boil and simmer for 2 hours.

Abalone Amandine

Serves 4 – 6

4 abalone
100 g (3 ½ oz) butter
½ cup (2 oz) slivered almonds

½ cup (4 oz) flour
salt and pepper
1 tablespoon lemon juice

Remove the abalone flesh from the shells with a sharp knife, leaving the small gut section in the shell. Scrub the black frill as clean as possible. Cut off the rough section at the bottom of the foot and discard. Cut remainder horizontally into thin slices, about ½ cm (¼ inch) thick. Gently pound the slices with the flat side of a meat mallet to tenderize the abalone, taking care not to break the slices.

Heat half the butter and quickly fry the almonds. Remove with a slotted spoon and set aside. Dip the abalone steaks in the flour mixed with salt and pepper. Shake off the excess flour. Fry quickly in hot butter, no more than 30 seconds on each side. Long cooking will toughen the abalone. Place on a warm serving dish. Wipe out the pan, add the remaining butter and heat. Add the lemon juice and almonds and pour over the abalone. Serve at once.

Grilled Abalone Steaks

Serves 4

3 tomatoes, peeled, seeded and chopped
1 garlic clove, crushed
½ teaspoon dried basil leaves
2 tablespoons red wine
½ cup (1 oz) green olives, pitted and sliced
4 abalone
2 eggs
salt and pepper
¾ cup (3 oz) dry breadcrumbs
½ cup (2 oz) grated Parmesan cheese
4 tablespoons oil
100 g (3 ½ oz) grated mozzarella cheese

Place the tomatoes and garlic in a saucepan and sauté for a few minutes. Add the basil and wine and simmer until thickened. Add the olives and mix well. Prepare the abalone as in the previous recipe. Beat the eggs lightly with the salt and pepper and dip each abalone slice in egg then coat with breadcrumbs and Parmesan mixed together.

Heat the oil and quickly fry the abalone steaks for 30 seconds on each side. Place on a foil-covered grill (broiler) tray. Spoon the tomato mixture evenly over each slice. Top with the mozzarella and place under a preheated griller (broiler) until the cheese melts. Serve at once.

Garlic Mussels

Serves 2

4-8 large mussels
fresh breadcrumbs
100 g (3 ½ oz) butter mixed with 2 garlic cloves, crushed

Plunge the mussels into boiling salted water for 20 to 30 seconds. Do not overcook. Remove the top shell from the mussels. Cool, then sprinkle with breadcrumbs.

Place a dot of garlic butter over each mussel and arrange on an ovenproof serving dish. Place under a hot grill (broiler) or in a microwave oven until the butter melts and sizzles.

Herbed Mussels

Serves 4

4-8 large mussels
100 g (3 ½ oz) butter, softened
2 tablespoons finely chopped parsley
2 tablespoons finely chopped chives or spring onions (scallions)
1 tablespoon lemon juice
fresh breadcrumbs

Prepare the mussels as in the recipe above. Combine the butter with the parsley, chives and lemon juice. Mix well.

Sprinkle with breadcrumbs and place a dot of herb butter on each mussel. Put under a hot griller (broiler) or in a microwave oven until the butter melts and sizzles.

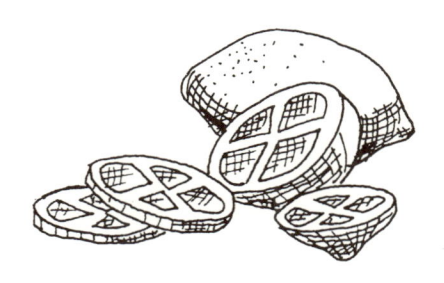

Mornay Mussels

Serves 4

24 mussels in half shells
30 g (1 oz) butter
2 tablespoons flour
1 ½ cups (12 fl oz) milk
¾ cup (3 oz) grated cheese
salt and pepper
1 rasher bacon, cut into very fine strips

Place the mussels on an ovenproof tray. Melt the butter, add the flour and cook for 1 minute. Gradually add the milk and bring to the boil. Remove from the heat and add ½ cup (2 oz) of the grated cheese. Stir until melted. Season with salt and pepper.

Cover mussels with 1-2 teaspoons of the mornay sauce, top with a small amount of grated cheese and a strip of bacon. Place under a very hot griller (broiler) and cook until the cheese melts.

Mussels - the Italian Way

Serves 4

2 onions, finely chopped
4 garlic cloves, crushed
¼ cup (2 fl oz) oil
2 stalks celery, chopped
1 teaspoon chopped dried basil
1 x 440 g (14 oz) can tomatoes, chopped
¾ cup (6 fl oz) red wine
1-2 tablespoons tomato paste
cooked spaghetti for 4
40 mussels removed from the shell
chopped parsley

Cook the onions and garlic in oil until translucent. Add the celery, basil, tomatoes, wine and paste and cook gently for 15 minutes.

Arrange the hot spaghetti on a plate. Add the mussels to the sauce and pour over the spaghetti. Sprinkle with parsley.

Seafood

Crispy Oysters

Serves 4

24 oysters
salt and pepper
pinch of nutmeg
2 rashers bacon, chopped and fried
½ cup (2 oz) grated Swiss cheese
½ cup (4 fl oz) cream
½ cup (2 oz) crushed cracker biscuits
15 g (½ oz) butter

Grease 4 shallow ovenproof dishes and arrange the oysters evenly in them. Sprinkle salt, pepper and nutmeg over the oysters. Top with bacon pieces and cheese. Pour the cream evenly all over, then cover with the biscuit crumbs and dot with butter. Bake above the centre of the oven at 200°C (400°F/Gas 6) for about 10 minutes.

Oyster Casino

Serves 4 – 6

48 oysters in half shells
4 thin rashers bacon, chopped
15 g (½ oz) butter
1 medium-sized onion, very finely chopped
½ cup red pepper (capsicum), very finely chopped
½ cup green pepper (capsicum), very finely chopped
freshly ground pepper
2 tablespoons sherry
oyster juice
1 teaspoon Worcestershire sauce
1 teaspoon lemon juice

Drain the juice from the oysters and reserve. Place the oysters on a foil-covered griller (broiler) tray. Fry the bacon until crisp, remove and drain well.

Melt the butter in a saucepan. Sauté the onion until soft but not coloured. Add the red and green pepper and simmer for a few minutes until soft. Season with pepper. Remove from heat. Add the bacon, sherry, oyster juice, Worcestershire sauce and lemon juice. Mix well. Top each oyster with the mixture. Just before serving place under preheated griller (broiler), for about 3 minutes.

Oyster Cocktail

Serves 4

24 oysters in half shells
2 tablespoons oil
2 tablespoons lemon juice
2 tablespoons tomato paste
Tabasco sauce
lettuce leaves
lemon wedges
toasted bread triangles

Place the oysters on a flat dish. Beat together the oil, lemon juice, tomato paste and a few drops of Tabasco sauce. Spoon over the oysters and leave in the refrigerator for ½ to 1 hour.

Place the lettuce leaves on four plates and place 6 oysters on each plate. Decorate with lemon wedges and serve with toasted bread triangles.

Baked Crayfish with Mustard Butter

Serves 4

2 x 600 g (1 ¼ lb) crayfish (lobster)
60 g (2 oz) butter
2 teaspoons prepared mustard
1 cup (2 oz) fresh brown breadcrumbs
1 tablespoon chopped parsley
1 tablespoon oil

Cook the crayfish in salted water for 10 minutes. Drain and split lengthwise while still hot or use ready-cooked crayfish. Remove the digestive systems and intestinal tracts. Mix the butter and mustard together. Spread this over the crayfish. Sprinkle with the breadcrumbs and parsley mixed together. Drizzle with a small amount of oil. Bake at 180°C (350°F/Gas 4) for 10 minutes. Decorate with lemon wedges.

PASTA AND RICE

Pasta and rice have become substitutes for the staples such as potatoes. Pasta is made from flour or semolina and water and is extruded from a special machine to give the desired shape. Egg noodles are exactly that; flour and water, with the addition of eggs. Strictly speaking, any pasta shape can be used for any dish, but traditionally there are certain shapes for certain dishes. Pasta should always be cooked 'al dente' which means firm to the bite, not mushy and soggy. Pasta is available dried or fresh and it is now possible to purchase machines to extrude your own.

Rice has been a staple food in Eastern countries for centuries. It is the seed of an annual grass and is the most versatile of foods. With the increase of Asian food in our diet, the intake of rice in the Western world has increased rapidly in the last few years. The very best rice is wild rice but this is very hard to obtain and is extremely expensive. Basmati, which is only grown in India, has a superb perfume when cooked and is almost impossible to overcook. Australia produces most of its own rice and it is available as white, short and long grain and brown, short and long grain. White rice is much quicker to cook as the husk has been removed in processing. Brown rice is chewy and takes almost twice as long to cook. Their uses are almost interchangeable.

The majority of the recipes for pasta and rice have been supplied by **San Remo Macaroni Company** and the **Ricegrowers' Co-operative Mills Limited**. Other recipes have been supplied by contributors whose credits appear elsewhere in the book.

The Australian rice industry was launched commercially in 1924 after considerable work to lay out and construct the Murrumbidgee Irrigation Area in south-western New South Wales. In the 1930s the Murray River's power was harnessed through a similar storage and channel system to create the irrigated lands which now extend east and west. In the early 1960s work was completed on a third irrigation area south of the Murrumbidgee Irrigation Area. In 1950 leading members of the Ricegrowers' Association of Australia decided that they would build their own mill and run it as a co-operative from which all farmer members would get a fair return for their produce. The growers called their enterprise **Ricegrowers' Co-operative Mills Limited**. The co-operative went from strength to strength as more and more farmers saw the benefit of their rice being milled and marketed by their own organisation.

Over the years the rice farmers of New South Wales have increased their productivity dramatically. The tonneage of paddy rice harvested each year depends a lot on the water which is available, but a record was set in 1985 when the growers of three irrigation areas harvested more than 850 000 tonnes. The growers are among the top producers, per hectare, in the world.

More than 90 per cent of this rice is exported, making the rice industry one of the major export earners for the State. At the same time, New South Wales rice satisfies the needs of more and more Australian families. The popular Sunwhite, Sunlong, Sungold and Sunbrown range of rices are on sale throughout Australia.

The recipes here have been supplied by Marcia Murphy and Trevor Wiles.

Pasta and Rice

Spaghetti

Cooking Instructions: For every 375 g (12 oz) packet of spaghetti use 12 cups (3 litres) of boiling water and 1 heaped tablespoon of salt. Bring the salted water to the boil. Add the spaghetti and continue boiling until cooked (12 to 19 minutes according to your taste), stirring occasionally. Drain immediately. Serve with your favourite sauce, or by itself with plenty of butter and grated cheese.

Wholemeal Spaghetti with Eggplant and Tomatoes

Serves 4

1 large eggplant (aubergine)
salt
2 garlic cloves, crushed
5 tablespoons olive oil
freshly ground pepper
6 medium-sized ripe tomatoes, peeled and chopped
1 x 375 g (12 oz) packet wholemeal spaghetti
butter
1-2 tablespoons finely chopped fresh parsley

Dice the eggplant into 2.5 cm (1 inch) cubes. (If the skin seems tough peel it as well.) Sprinkle with salt and leave in a colander for 2 hours so the bitter juice is drained. Heat the garlic in the olive oil in a large frying pan. Add the drained eggplant. Stir well and season with salt and pepper. Fry over moderate heat until the eggplant is tender, stirring occasionally. Add the tomatoes. Simmer for 15 to 20 minutes or until the sauce is thick. Cook the spaghetti, drain and mix in a serving bowl with some dots of butter and the parsley. Serve on individual hot plates with the sauce spooned on top.

Spaghettini alla Marinara

4 tablespoons olive oil
20 black pitted olives
1 tablespoon capers, finely chopped, optional
1 garlic clove, crushed
5 or 6 large ripe peeled tomatoes, finely chopped
3 or 4 basil leaves or 2 bay leaves, finely chopped
salt and freshly ground black pepper
1 x 375 g (12 oz) packet thin spaghetti

Place the oil, olives, capers, garlic, tomatoes and basil in a saucepan and leave to marinate for 30 minutes. When ready to prepare the meal, place the pan with this marinated sugo over a moderate heat and cook until thick and creamy, about 25 to 35 minutes. Season to taste. Cook the pasta, drain immediately and mix with the sauce in a deep serving bowl. Grated cheese is not served with this dish.

Wholemeal Spaghetti with Tomato and Basil

Serves 4

6 large ripe tomatoes, peeled
2 tablespoons olive oil
1 clove garlic, crushed
4 or 5 basil leaves, chopped
salt and freshly ground black pepper
1 x 375 g (12 oz) packet wholemeal spaghetti or macaroni
½ cup (2 oz) grated pecorino or Parmesan cheese

Cut the tomatoes into small pieces and take care not to lose the juice. Heat the oil, add the garlic, tomatoes, basil, salt and pepper. Cook over a moderate heat for about 30 minutes or until the sauce is thick. Stir occasionally so that it does not burn. Cook the spaghetti, drain and mix with the sauce. Serve the grated cheese separately.

Wholemeal Spaghetti and Chicken

Serves 4 – 6

½ cup (4 fl oz) olive oil
1 onion, finely chopped
1 x 1.5 kg (3 lb) chicken, cut into serving pieces
1 tablespoon flour
½ cup (4 fl oz) dry white wine
3 whole ripe tomatoes, peeled and chopped
salt and freshly ground pepper
1 x 375 g (12 oz) packet wholemeal spaghetti or macaroni, cooked
grated cheese
finely chopped parsley

Heat the oil, add the onion and chicken pieces and sauté until golden brown all over. Sprinkle with the flour, add the wine and cook until it evaporates. Add the tomatoes and cook for about 5 minutes, stirring frequently. Season with salt and pepper, and cook slowly until the chicken is tender and the sauce thick. Remove the chicken pieces. Pour the sauce over the pasta, add some grated cheese and mix well. Place on a large flat serving dish surrounded by the chicken pieces and garnished with parsley.

Wholemeal Spaghetti with Butter and Vegetables

Serves 4

- 1 x 375 g (12 oz) packet wholemeal spaghetti, cooked
- butter
- ½ cup (2 oz) grated mozzarella cheese
- ¼ cup (1 oz) grated Parmesan cheese
- 500 g (1 lb) peas, beans, spinach or broccoli, cooked
- 3 large potatoes, cooked and sliced
- salt and freshly ground pepper

Mix plenty of butter which has been cut into pieces (do not melt) into the hot prepared pasta. Add the mozzarella cheese and the Parmesan cheese. To this add the cooked vegetables and potatoes. Season with salt and pepper and serve piping hot.

Spaghetti al Sugo

Serves 4

- 4 tablespoons oil
- 1 onion, finely chopped
- 1 garlic clove, crushed
- 500 g (1 lb) diced lean beef
- ½ teaspoon dried oregano
- 6 tablespoons dry wine
- 4-5 ripe peeled tomatoes, finely chopped
- salt and freshly ground black pepper
- 1 x 375 g (12 oz) packet spaghetti, cooked
- ½ cup (2 oz) grated cheese
- butter

Heat the oil and lightly brown the onion and garlic. Add the meat and brown. Season with oregano. Increase the heat, add the wine and cook until it evaporates. Add the tomatoes. Season to taste. Cook over a moderate heat until the sauce is thick. Drain the pasta, stir in the grated cheese, a little butter and the meat sauce.

Spaghetti alla Carbonara

Serves 4

- 1 cup diced bacon
- 30 g (1 oz) butter
- 2 tablespoons oil
- 4 egg yolks
- 3 tablespoons cream
- 2 tablespoons grated Parmesan cheese
- freshly ground black pepper
- 1 x 375 g (12 oz) packet spaghetti, cooked
- extra grated Parmesan cheese

Brown the bacon in the butter and oil. Remove from the heat. Beat the egg yolks and add the cream, cheese and pepper. Add the hot, just cooked, drained spaghetti to the bacon in the pan. Return to the heat for 2 minutes. Mix well. Remove from the heat and pour in the egg mixture, stirring well. Serve piping hot with more grated cheese.

Spaghetti con Salsa di Pomodoro

Serves 4

- 6 ripe peeled tomatoes
- 2 bay leaves
- 4 tablespoons olive oil
- salt and freshly ground black pepper
- 1 x 375 g (12 oz) packet spaghetti, cooked
- grated cheese

Thinly slice 3 tomatoes and cook gently with the bay leaves for about 20 minutes or until the sauce is thick. Remove the bay leaves. Add 2 tablespoons of the olive oil and simmer for 7 minutes. Add another 3 tomatoes, coarsely chopped, the remaining oil and salt and pepper to taste. Simmer for 5 minutes, then mix with the cooked, drained spaghetti and grated cheese.

Note: Vary this recipe by adding any one of the following cooked vegetables: peas, beans, spinach, broccoli, asparagus or cauliflower.

Spaghetti Aglio e Olio

Serves 4

- 4 garlic cloves crushed
- 1 small hot chilli pepper, roughly chopped, optional
- 2 tablespoons chopped fresh parsley
- 5 tablespoons olive oil
- 1 x 375 g (12 oz) packet spaghetti
- freshly ground black pepper
- extra chopped fresh parsley

Sauté the garlic, chilli pepper, if used, and parsley in the olive oil for 1 or 2 minutes over a low heat or until the garlic is golden. Do not let it brown. Remove the garlic and chilli pepper and discard. Cook the spaghetti according to the directions on the packet. Drain and immediately mix with the hot oil in a heated serving bowl. Season with pepper, mix well and serve piping hot with a sprinkle of parsley.

Pasta and Rice

Noodles

Cooking Instructions: For 375 g (12 oz) of egg noodles, use 12 cups (3 litres) of boiling water and 1 heaped tablespoon of salt. Bring the salted water to the boil, add the noodles and continue boiling until cooked, approximately 10 minutes, stirring occasionally. Drain immediately. Serve with your favourite sauce or by itself with plenty of butter and grated cheese.

Note: If cooking more or less noodles, adjust the water and salt. To separate cold cooked noodles, run under cold water.

Soyaroni alla Beppina
Serves 6

- 500 g (1 lb) shelled green peas or broad beans
- 2 tomatoes, peeled and diced
- 3 spring onions (scallions), finely chopped
- 4 tablespoons olive oil
- 1 teaspoon sugar
- salt and freshly ground black pepper
- 1 x 250 g (8 oz) packet *soyaroni*, cooked
- grated or diced mozzarella cheese

Place the peas, tomatoes, spring onions, olive oil, sugar, salt and pepper in a saucepan. If the tomatoes are not very juicy add a little water. Cover and cook gently until the peas have changed colour and are cooked. Add the *soyaroni* to the peas and stir over a moderate heat for 1 or 2 minutes. Serve piping hot with grated or diced mozzarella cheese.

Soyaroni with Tuna and Béchamel Sauce

Soyaroni alla Marinara
Serves 6

- 2 tablespoons oil
- 30 g (1 oz) butter
- 1 garlic clove, crushed
- 1 onion, finely chopped
- 500 g (1 lb) fish fillets, chopped into small pieces
- ½ cup (4 fl oz) dry white wine
- 500 g (1 lb) cooked peeled prawns (shrimp)
- 2 tablespoons chopped fresh parsley
- 1 tablespoon fresh or dried basil
- salt and freshly ground black pepper
- 2 x 250 g (8 oz) packets *soyaroni*, cooked
- butter

Heat the oil, butter and garlic in a large, heavy pan and gently fry the onion until soft. Add the fish pieces and sauté until the fish is cooked, stirring often. Still stirring, add the wine and cook until it has evaporated. Add the prawns, parsley and basil and season with salt and plenty of pepper. Stir gently for 2 to 3 minutes. Place the hot drained *soyaroni* in a deep serving dish and dot with butter. Add the fish sauce and serve immediately.

Soyaroni with Tuna and Béchamel Sauce
Serves 4

- 60 g (2 oz) butter
- 1 onion, finely chopped
- 1 large red or green pepper (capsicum), diced
- 1 tablespoon flour
- 1 x 200 g (6 ½ oz) can tuna in oil
- 2 cups (16 fl oz) milk
- nutmeg
- salt and freshly ground black pepper
- 1 x 250 g (8 oz) packet *soyaroni*, cooked
- breadcrumbs
- grated cheese
- butter
- chopped fresh parsley

Heat the butter, add the onion and red pepper and sauté over a low heat until the onion has changed colour and the pepper is tender. Add the flour and stir constantly until it is a golden brown. Add the tuna and its oil (and a squeeze of lemon juice if you like). Remove from the heat and slowly add the milk, stirring continuously. Return to the heat and continue stirring until thick. Add a pinch of nutmeg, salt and pepper to taste. Pour this sauce into a baking dish with the cooked drained *soyaroni* and mix well. Sprinkle with breadcrumbs, grated cheese and dot with butter and bake at 200°C (400°F/Gas 6) for about 10 minutes or until the top is brown and crusty. Sprinkle with parsley and serve.

Opposite: *Soyaroni alla Marinara*

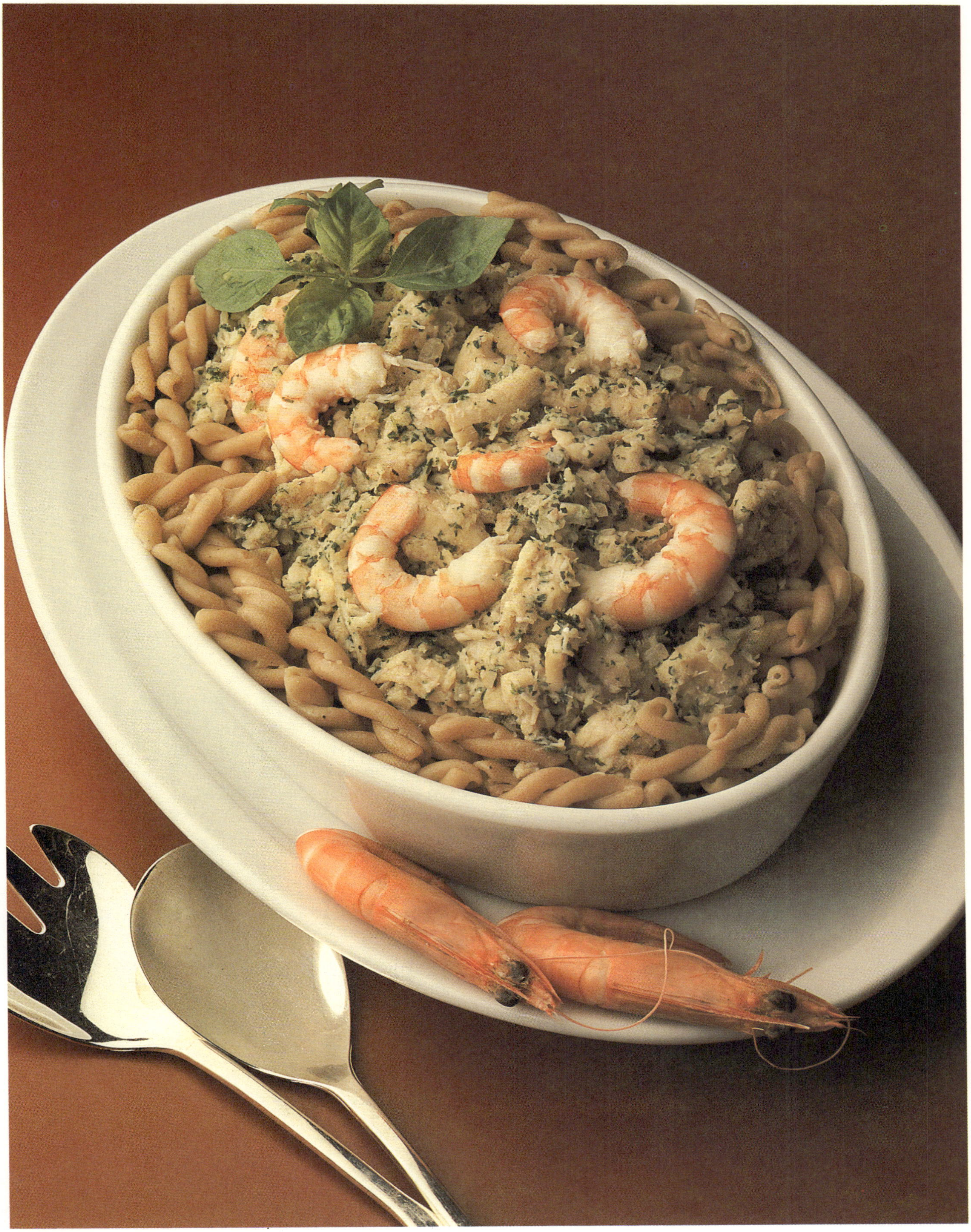

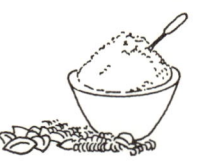

Pasta and Rice

Soyaroni with Peas

Serves 6

60 g (2 oz) lean bacon, finely chopped
1 small onion, finely chopped
1 small garlic clove, crushed
1 stalk celery, finely chopped
chopped fresh parsley

60 g (2 oz) butter
250 g (8 oz) shelled green peas
salt and pepper
1 x 250 g (8 oz) packet *soyaroni*, cooked
grated cheese
butter curls

Toss the bacon, onion, garlic, celery and parsley in a casserole with the butter over medium heat. When the ingredients are coloured add the peas. Season with salt and pepper. Add the noodles to the casserole. Mix well and serve sprinkled with cheese and butter curls.

Soyaroni con Tonno

Serves 6

45 g (1 ½ oz) butter
1 x 155 g (5 oz) can tuna in oil
2 tablespoons finely chopped fresh parsley
1 cup (8 fl oz) cream

salt and freshly ground black pepper
1 x 250 g (8 oz) packet *soyaroni*, cooked
fresh parsley sprigs

Melt the butter and add the flaked tuna with its oil and the parsley. Cook gently on a low heat, uncovered, for 5 minutes. Stir in the cream in a slow stream, add the salt and pepper and simmer, covered, for another 4 to 5 minutes. Do not boil. Mix the drained *soyaroni* with the tuna and serve garnished with parsley sprigs.

Soyaroni with Mushrooms

Lightly fry mushroom slices in butter. Cook *soyaroni* according to instructions, drain and mix in curls of butter. Add the mushrooms. Sprinkle with freshly ground pepper.

Soyaroni and Butter

Cook a sliced onion in butter. When golden add the cooked and drained *soyaroni* and mix. Add grated cheese and serve very hot.

Nidi con Pesto di Formaggio

Serves 4

½ cup finely chopped fresh basil
3 garlic cloves
salt
½ cup (2 oz) grated pecorino cheese

½ cup (2 oz) grated Parmesan cheese
1 cup (8 fl oz) olive oil
1 x 375 g (12 oz) packet noodles
freshly ground black pepper

Mash the basil, garlic and salt in a mortar, or a blender, adding the cheeses a little at a time. Beat in the oil very slowly until well blended. Cook the noodles in plenty of boiling water to which 1 heaped tablespoon of salt has been added. Cooking time will depend on the type of noodle used. Drain noodles and place in a serving dish with the pesto sauce. Season with pepper and serve.

Nidi Verdi con Aglio

Serves 6

1 x 375 g (12 oz) packet Nidi green ribbon noodles
125-185 g (4-6 oz) butter
1-3 garlic cloves, crushed (depending on taste)

8 tablespoons grated Parmesan cheese
salt and freshly ground black pepper

Cook the noodles according to the directions on the packet. Heat the butter in a frying pan and sauté the garlic over a very low heat. Do not brown. When noodles are *al dente*, drain and pour into a hot serving dish along with the hot garlic butter, the cheese, salt and pepper to taste. Mix well and serve immediately on hot plates.

Nidi al Mascarpone

Serves 4

1 x 375 g (12 oz) packet noodles
30 g (1 oz) butter, melted
⅔ cup (2 ½ oz) grated Parmesan cheese

½ cup cream cheese or non fat cream cheese
½ cup lean ham, finely chopped

Cook the noodles, drain and put in a deep serving dish. Pour the melted butter over the noodles and mix together with the grated cheese. Dot with pieces of cream cheese, sprinkle with the ham and serve.

Nidi with Whiting

Serves 6

250 g (8 oz) whiting fillets
4 tablespoons olive oil
1 small onion, finely chopped
salt and freshly ground black pepper
5 large ripe peeled tomatoes
2 tablespoons finely chopped fresh parsley
1 x 375 g (12 oz) packet Nidi wide or medium ribbon noodles

Chop the whiting fillets into small pieces. Heat the oil and brown the onion and whiting pieces over moderate heat with some salt and pepper. Blend, sieve, or very finely chop the tomatoes and add to the fish.

Simmer gently until fairly thick, about 20 to 30 minutes, then add the parsley. Cook the noodles until *al dente*, then drain. Place in a deep serving dish with the whiting sauce.

Nidi alla Romagnola

Serves 6

4 or 5 large tomatoes, peeled
4 tablespoons olive oil
2 tablespoons chopped fresh parsley
1 garlic clove, crushed
salt and freshly ground black pepper
1 x 375 g (12 oz) packet Nidi ribbon noodles
extra olive oil

Blend, pulp or sieve the tomatoes. Put the oil in a pan and cook the parsley, garlic and tomatoes over medium heat until the sauce is thick, about 20 to 35 minutes. Season with salt and pepper. Cook the noodles, drain, toss in a heated serving dish with a little extra oil to make them more slippery and light, and then mix with the tomato sauce. Grated cheese is not usually served with this dish.

Nidi with Spinach

Serves 6

500 g (1 lb) spinach
60 g (2 oz) butter
2 tablespoons olive oil
1 garlic clove, crushed
salt and freshly ground black pepper
½ cup (2 oz) grated Parmesan cheese
1 x 375 g (12 oz) packet Nidi noodles, cooked

Wash the spinach well and steam for a few minutes in an airtight saucepan in which ¼ cup (2 fl oz) of water has been brought to the boil. Drain well and chop. Heat the butter and oil, and brown the garlic in a frying pan, then remove the garlic. Add the spinach, season with salt and pepper and cook for a few minutes, then stir in the grated cheese. Place the cooked, drained noodles in a heated serving dish, cover with the spinach and serve.

Nidi Smalzade

Serves 6

Wide ribbon noodles with wine and cream. The robust flavour of tender veal makes this a superb late night supper, luncheon or even main course. The aroma alone is a treat.

500 g (1 lb) lean veal, cubed
flour
60 g (2 oz) butter
1 medium-sized onion, quartered
½ cup (4 fl oz) white wine
2 tablespoons stock
salt and freshly ground black pepper
½ cup (4 fl oz) cream
1 x 375 (12 oz) packet Nidi wide ribbon noodles
2-3 tablespoons grated Parmesan cheese

Roll the veal pieces in the flour. Melt the butter in a large pan and brown the veal on all sides with the onion. Add the wine and cook rapidly until it has evaporated, then add the stock. When the veal is tender, reduce the heat. Season with salt and pepper and stir in the cream. Cook the noodles, drain and mix with the veal, sauce and grated cheese.

Noodles with Lamb

Serves 6

125 g (4 oz) butter
2 tablespoons olive oil
1 sprig rosemary
1 kg (2 lb) boned lean lamb (leg or shoulder)
3 tablespoons dry white wine
salt and freshly ground black pepper
1 x 375 g (12 oz) packet Nidi wide, medium or thin noodles
2 tablespoons grated Parmesan cheese

Heat the butter and oil in a pan with the rosemary. Chop the lamb into small pieces and brown in the pan over a low heat. Increase the heat to high and add the wine, allowing it to boil for a few minutes until almost evaporated. Stir well and season with salt and pepper. Reduce the heat to low, cover and continue to cook gently until the meat is tender. Add a tablespoon or so of water whenever needed. Cook the noodles as directed on the packet. Drain and place in a deep serving bowl with the sauce, lamb and Parmesan cheese.

Pasta and Rice

Noodles alla Carbonara
Serves 4 – 6

375 g (12 oz) thin ribbon egg noodles
1 cup x 3 cm (1 ¼ inch) bacon strips
30 g (1 oz) butter
1 tablespoon oil
4 egg yolks
3 tablespoons cream
2 tablespoons grated Parmesan cheese
freshly ground black pepper to taste
extra grated Parmesan cheese

Cook and drain the noodles and keep hot. Fry the bacon in butter and oil and remove from the heat. Beat together the egg yolks, cream, cheese and pepper. Add the bacon to the hot noodles and reheat for 2 minutes. Mix well. Remove from the heat and pour in the egg mixture, stirring until well coated. Serve hot with extra Parmesan cheese.

Mexican Noodles
Serves 4 – 6

150 g (5 oz) medium ribbon egg noodles
2 large onions, sliced
15 g (½ oz) butter
1 x 440 g (14 oz) can tomato soup
½ cup (4 fl oz) mayonnaise
½ teaspoon chilli powder
½ teaspoon salt
freshly ground black pepper
¼ cup (1 oz) grated cheese
3 hard-boiled eggs, sliced

Cook and drain the noodles. Lightly fry the onions in the butter until soft and golden. Drain. Combine the tomato soup, mayonnaise and seasonings, and heat slowly. Add the onions and cheese and stir until the cheese melts. Add the cooked noodles and the eggs. Coat gently with sauce and reheat. Do not boil.

Eggs in Noodle Nests

Eggs in Noodle Nests
Serves 4 – 6

375 g (12 oz) thin ribbon egg noodles
1 large onion, chopped
1-2 rashers bacon, chopped
1 cup (4 oz) finely grated cheese
¾ cup (6 fl oz) tomato sauce
salt and freshly ground black pepper to taste
4-6 poached eggs

Cook and drain the noodles and keep hot. Fry the onion and bacon until soft. Add to the hot noodles with the cheese and sauce. Stir well over low heat until the cheese has melted. Season with salt and pepper. Shape each serving of noodles into a nest and place a poached egg on top. Serve immediately.

Custard-Topped Noodle Casserole
Serves 4 – 6

200 g (6 ½ oz) wide ribbon egg noodles
1 large onion, chopped
1 green pepper (capsicum), sliced
15 g (½ oz) butter
500 g (1 lb) minced (ground) steak
2 beef stock cubes dissolved in ½ cup (4 fl oz) hot water
2 heaped tablespoons tomato paste
1 teaspoon Worcestershire sauce
salt and pepper to taste
2 medium-sized tomatoes, sliced

Custard
1 ¼ cups (10 fl oz) milk
3 eggs, beaten
½ cup (2 oz) grated cheese

Cook the noodles and drain. Fry the onion and green pepper in the butter. Add the meat and fry until brown. Add the beef stock, tomato paste, Worcestershire sauce and seasonings and cook for 5 minutes. Check for flavour, adding more paste and Worcestershire sauce if desired. Combine the meat mixture and noodles. Place in an ovenproof dish and arrange the tomato slices on top. Lightly season with salt and pepper. Pour over the tomatoes and sprinkle with cheese. Bake at 190°C (375°F/Gas 5) for 15 to 20 minutes. Lightly brown under the grill (broiler) for 2 minutes.

Custard: Heat the milk until hot and whisk in the beaten eggs. Cook over low heat until the custard thickens.

Curried Eggs and Noodles

Curried Noodle Bake

Serves 6 – 8

- 175 g (5 ½ oz) medium ribbon egg noodles
- 2 large onions, cut into rings
- 15 g (½ oz) butter
- 2 cups (8 oz) grated cheese
- 1 tablespoon chopped fresh parsley
- ¼ teaspoon pepper
- ½ teaspoon salt
- 1 packet chicken noodle soup
- 1 ½ cups (12 fl oz) hot water
- 1 ½ cups (12 fl oz) milk
- 1 tablespoon curry powder
- 4 eggs

Cook and drain the noodles and keep hot. Fry the onion rings in butter until soft. Remove from the pan, and add to the hot noodles together with 1 cup (4 oz) of the cheese, the parsley and seasonings. Place in a large casserole dish. Dissolve the soup in hot water, cool slightly and add the milk. Mix the curry to a paste with 1 beaten egg, then beat in the remaining eggs. Add the egg mixture to the soup and mix well. Pour over the noodles and sprinkle with the remaining cheese. Bake at 180°C (350°F/Gas 4) for 30 minutes.

Curried Eggs And Noodles

Serves 4 – 6

- 375 g (12 oz) thin or medium ribbon egg noodles
- 1 onion, chopped
- 1 small green pepper (capsicum), chopped
- 30 g (1 oz) butter
- 2 tablespoons flour
- 1 tablespoon curry powder
- 1 garlic stock cube
- 1 x 450 g (14 ½ oz) can chicken soup
- 1 soup can of milk
- 6-8 hard-boiled eggs, sliced
- salt and freshly ground black pepper
- melted butter
- 2 teaspoons chopped fresh parsley

Cook and drain the noodles and keep hot. Fry the onion and green pepper in butter until soft. Stir in the flour, curry powder and crumbled garlic cube and cook for 1 to 2 minutes. Add the soup and the milk, and stir until thickened. Add the sliced eggs. Season to taste, then reheat but do not boil. Serve with hot noodles, tossed in melted butter. Garnish with chopped parsley.

Pasta and Rice

Cannelloni Stuffed with Lamb
Serves 3 - 4

30 g (1 oz) butter
½ cup mushrooms, finely chopped
1 cup cooked minced (ground) lamb
3 level tablespoons grated Parmesan cheese
salt and freshly ground black pepper
nutmeg
stock
1 x 250 g (8 oz) packet cannelloni
1 tablespoon grated cheese
1 quantity Béchamel sauce (*page 306*)
extra 30 g (1 oz) butter
extra grated Parmesan cheese

Melt the butter in a heavy pan, add the mushrooms and fry gently for 2 to 3 minutes. Stir in the lamb, Parmesan cheese, seasoning, nutmeg to taste and enough stock to make a fairly soft mixture. Cook the cannelloni according to the directions on the packet. Allow to cool, then, using a teaspoon, fill with the cooked mixture. Arrange in a single layer in a greased ovenproof dish.

Add the grated cheese to the Béchamel sauce and pour over the cannelloni. Dot with the extra butter, sprinkle thickly with extra Parmesan cheese and cook at 200°C (400°F/Gas 6) until lightly browned, about 15 to 20 minutes.

Cannelloni alla Napolitana
Serves 4 - 6

8 cannelloni tubes
6-8 tablespoons olive oil
2 kg (4 lb) ripe tomatoes, peeled and chopped
salt
1 tablespoon chopped fresh basil
6 anchovy fillets, chopped
375 g (12 oz) mozzarella cheese, diced
4-5 tablespoons grated Parmesan cheese

Cook the cannelloni according to the directions on the packet. Drain and set aside to cool.

Heat the olive oil in a heavy pan, add the tomatoes, season lightly with salt and cook over a high heat for 20 minutes. Rub half the tomatoes through a sieve or purée in a blender. Flavour with the basil and set aside. Mix the remaining unsieved tomatoes with the anchovies, mozzarella and 3 tablespoons of the Parmesan cheese. Fill the cannelloni with this mixture. Arrange the cannelloni in a single layer in a shallow greased baking dish. Cover with the puréed tomatoes and the remaining Parmesan cheese. Bake at 180°C (350°F/Gas 4) for about 20 minutes.

Stuffed Cannelloni with Mushrooms
Serves 6

1 x 250 g (8 oz) packet cannelloni tubes

Filling
½ onion, finely chopped
½ carrot, finely chopped
½ stalk celery, finely chopped
60 g (2 oz) butter
250 g (8 oz) lean minced (ground) veal or beef
250 g (8 oz) lean minced (ground) pork
2 rashers bacon, diced
125 g (4 oz) mushrooms, finely chopped

Sauce
1 onion, finely chopped
30 g (1 oz) butter
1 tablespoon olive oil
2 ½ cups tomato purée
5 fresh basil leaves or 2 bay leaves

grated Parmesan cheese
butter

1 small lamb's brain, boiled and skinned, optional
⅔ cup (5 fl oz) white wine
1 tablespoon flour
1 cup chopped peeled tomatoes
salt and freshly ground black pepper
pinch of nutmeg

salt and freshly ground black pepper
3 tablespoons cream

Cook cannelloni as directed, drain and allow to cool. Gently fill the cooked cannelloni tubes with the filling. Spoon a thin layer of the sauce into a greased, shallow baking dish. Arrange the cannelloni in a single layer on top of the sauce. Cover with the remaining sauce, sprinkle with Parmesan cheese and dot with a generous amount of butter. Bake at 200°C (400°F/Gas 6) for 30 minutes, or if preparing in advance, wrap well in foil or plastic wrap and refrigerate until ready to bake.

Filling: Simmer the chopped vegetables in the butter in a pan. Add the veal, pork, bacon, mushrooms and chopped brain and sauté over medium heat until the meat is brown. Add the wine and allow to evaporate; then add the flour and tomatoes. Cook, stirring occasionally until the liquid is thick, about 30 minutes. Season to taste with salt, pepper and nutmeg and allow to cool.

Sauce: Sauté the onion in the butter and oil until soft and changed in colour. Add the purée, basil, salt and pepper. Cook over moderate heat until thick, about 20 to 25 minutes. Remove the basil, stir in the cream and remove from the heat.

Cannelloni 'à la King'

Serves 6

Fill cooked cannelloni with chopped crayfish (lobster). Arrange in a baking dish and stud with small pieces of butter. Cover with a Béchamel sauce (*page 306*) and top with grated cheese, or with a tomato sauce (*page 38*), topped with grated cheese. Bake at 200°C (400°F/Gas 6) for 15 to 20 minutes.

Vegeroni al Burro

Serves 4

- 1 x 375 g (12 oz) packet vegeroni
- ⅓ cup diced mozzarella cheese
- 2 tablespoons grated Parmesan cheese
- freshly ground black pepper
- 2-3 tablespoons butter
- finely chopped fresh parsley

Cook the pasta, drain, then add the mozzarella cheese, Parmesan cheese and pepper. Mix well, then gradually add the butter, cut into small pieces. Sprinkle with parsley or serve plain as a side dish.

Vegeroni with Cottage Cheese

Serves 4

- 3 large ripe peeled tomatoes
- 30 g (1 oz) butter
- salt and freshly ground black pepper
- ¾ cup cottage cheese
- 1 x 250 g (8 oz) packet vegeroni

Put the tomatoes through a sieve or purée in a blender and then cook with the butter over a good heat until thick and creamy. Season with salt and pepper and remove from heat. Mash the cottage cheese with a fork and mix with the tomato purée. Cook the vegeroni in plenty of salted boiling water for about 15 minutes and while still *al dente*, drain and place in a serving bowl with the tomato and cheese sauce. Mix well, add more pepper to taste, and serve hot with your favourite vegetable on the side.

Vegeroni with Cheese and Onions

Serves 4

- 30 g (1 oz) butter
- 1 onion, finely sliced
- 1 level tablespoon flour
- 2 ½ cups (20 fl oz) milk
- 1 cup (4 oz) grated cheese
- 1 x 250 g (8 oz) packet vegeroni, cooked
- paprika

Melt the butter and cook the onion until just golden and tender. Remove from the heat and stir in the flour. Gradually add the milk. Return to heat and stir until boiling. Add the cheese and stir well. Combine with the cooked vegeroni and sprinkle with paprika before serving.

Vegeroni with Ham and Mushroom Sauce

Serves 4

- 1 medium-sized onion, finely diced
- 30 g (1 oz) butter
- 1 x 500 g (1 lb) can mushrooms
- 1 cup chopped ham
- ½ cup (2 oz) grated Parmesan cheese
- 1 x 250 g (8 oz) packet vegeroni, cooked

Sauté the onion in the butter. Add the mushrooms and ham. Heat slowly to simmering point. Simmer for 3 minutes, sprinkle with cheese and serve over hot cooked vegeroni.

Vegeroni Tuna Tomato

Serves 4

- 2 bay leaves
- 1 small garlic clove, crushed
- ⅓ cup (2 ½ fl oz) cooking oil (preferably olive oil)
- 1 x 470 g (15 oz) can peeled tomatoes
- salt and freshly ground black pepper
- 1 x 200 g (6 ½ oz) can tuna, drained and flaked
- 1 x 250 g (8 oz) packet vegeroni

Cook the bay leaves and garlic in the oil for 2 to 3 minutes. Add the tomatoes and their juice, and salt and pepper to taste. Cook over moderate heat for 15 minutes. Add the tuna and cook for a further 5 minutes. Cook the vegeroni according to the directions on the packet. Serve topped with the sauce.

Pasta and Rice

Vegeroni con Tonno
Serves 4

45 g (1 ½ oz) butter
1 x 200 g (6 ½ oz) can tuna in oil
2 tablespoons finely chopped fresh parsley
1 cup (8 fl oz) cream
salt and freshly ground black pepper
1 x 250 g (8 oz) packet vegeroni

Heat the butter in a saucepan until melted. Add the flaked tuna and its oil and the parsley. Leave uncovered and cook gently on low heat for 5 minutes. Stir in the cream slowly, then add the salt and pepper. Cover and simmer a further 4 minutes. Do not allow to boil. Cook the vegeroni according to the directions on the packet and drain thoroughly. Mix with the sauce until well blended and serve piping hot.

Vegeroni al Mascarpone
Serves 4

1 x 375 g (12 oz) packet vegeroni
30 g (1 oz) butter, melted
¼ cup (1 oz) grated Parmesan cheese
⅓ cup fresh mascarpone cheese
⅓ cup lean ham, finely chopped

Cook the vegeroni, drain and put in a deep serving dish. Pour the melted butter over the pasta and mix together with the grated cheese. Dot with pieces of mascarpone cheese and sprinkle with the ham.

Chicken Casserole Vegeroni

Chicken Casserole Vegeroni
Serves 6

30 g (1 oz) butter or 1 tablespoon oil
1 x 1.8 kg (3 ½ lb) chicken
1 small onion, finely chopped
4 teaspoons tomato purée
1 ¼ cups (10 fl oz) stock
salt and freshly ground black pepper
1 teaspoon cornflour (cornstarch)
1 x 185 g (6 oz) can mushrooms
60 g (2 oz) ham, chopped
1 x 250 g (8 oz) packet vegeroni, cooked

Heat the butter in a large casserole dish and slowly brown the chicken all over. Add the onion and cook until golden brown. Blend in the purée and stock, season, and bring to the boil. Cover the casserole and cook slowly for about 1 hour or until the bird is tender. Remove the chicken. Stir in the cornflour and boil, stirring continuously. Add the mushrooms and ham. Cut the chicken into serving pieces, return to the casserole and garnish. Serve with cooked hot vegeroni.

Vegeroni Tuna Salad
Serves 6

1 x 250 g (8 oz) packet vegeroni, cooked
1 x 200 g (6 ½ oz) can tuna
1 onion, diced
1 teaspoon chopped fresh parsley
juice of 1 lemon
¼ cup (2 fl oz) mayonnaise or 2 tablespoons salad oil

In a large bowl combine the cooked vegeroni with the tuna, onion, parsley, lemon juice and mayonnaise. Cover and chill in refrigerator for a short time to allow the flavours to blend.

Vegeroni and Tuna Italian Style
Serves 4

½ cup (4 fl oz) olive oil
1 x 200 g (6 ½ oz) can tuna, flaked
2 teaspoons tomato paste, diluted with ⅓ cup (2½ fl oz) water
salt and freshly ground black pepper
1 x 250 g (8 oz) packet vegeroni, cooked

Heat the oil in a frying pan and add the tuna. Add the tomato paste and salt and pepper to taste. Cook for 15 minutes. Mix the sauce through the cooked vegeroni and serve piping hot.

Vegeroni Niçoise

Vegeroni Niçoise
Serves 8

500 g (1 lb) vegeroni, cooked
1 x 200 g (6 ½ oz) can tuna, broken into small pieces
1 small onion, finely chopped
1 stalk celery, chopped
1 large red or green (capsicum), sliced
1 spring onion (scallion), finely chopped
½ cup cooked green beans
2 carrots, sliced and boiled
2 tablespoons chopped fresh parsley
2 firm tomatoes, cut into wedges
juice of 1 lemon
2 tablespoons mayonnaise diluted with 1 tablespoon olive oil
salt and freshly ground black pepper
1 large head of lettuce
1 cucumber, chopped
6 black olives, pitted

Combine the cooked vegeroni with the tuna, onion, celery, red pepper, spring onion, beans and carrots, parsley, tomatoes, lemon juice and mayonnaise. Season with salt and pepper. Cover and chill in the refrigerator for a short time to allow the flavours to blend. When ready to serve place on chilled crisp lettuce leaves and add the cucumber and olives.

Vegeroni con la Balsamella
Serves 4

60 g (2 oz) butter
2 tablespoons flour
1 ¼ cups (10 fl oz) hot milk
salt and white pepper
1 x 250 g (8 oz) packet vegeroni, cooked
butter
⅔ cup (2 ½ oz) grated Parmesan cheese

Heat two thirds of the butter and when foaming stir in the flour. Let it brown a little, then gradually stir in the hot milk. Season with salt and pepper and bring to the boil, stirring constantly. Cook over a low heat for about 15 minutes. Place the cooked and drained vegeroni in a serving dish, dot with butter and add grated cheese. Add the sauce, mix quickly and serve with green vegetables.

Variation: Add flaked red salmon or tuna, 1 tablespoon lemon juice and toasted chopped almonds to the cooked vegeroni and sauce. Sprinkle with breadcrumbs and dot with butter and grated cheese. Bake at 200°C (400°F/Gas 6) for 10 to 15 minutes or until the crust is golden.

Pasta and Rice

Wholemeal Pasta with Capers and Anchovies

Serves 4

1 tablespoon capers
1 anchovy fillet or salt-cured anchovy
5 tablespoons olive oil
1 garlic clove, crushed
5 large ripe tomatoes
1 red or green pepper (capsicum), thinly sliced
salt and freshly ground black pepper
3 basil leaves, finely chopped
1 x 375 g (12 oz) packet wholemeal long or short pasta
grated cheese

Rinse and finely chop the capers. Coarsely chop the anchovy. Heat the oil and garlic in a pan. Chop the tomatoes into pieces and add to the oil. Simmer, uncovered, for about 10 minutes, then add the anchovy, capers, and red pepper. Season with salt, pepper and basil and cook over a moderate heat until the sauce is fairly thick. Cook the spaghetti, drain, and place in a hot serving dish with the anchovy sauce and grated cheese. Mix well and serve immediately.

Pasta alla Bolognese

Serves 6

1 medium-sized onion
1 small stalk celery
1 medium-sized carrot
125 g (4 oz) bacon, unsmoked
60 g (2 oz) butter
250 g (8 oz) minced (ground) lean veal
1 teaspoon flour
1 cup (8 fl oz) beef stock
salt and freshly ground black pepper
a little nutmeg
1 chicken liver, chopped
½ cup (4 fl oz) cream
375 g (12 oz) pasta of your choice
grated Parmesan cheese

Chop the onion, celery, carrot and bacon. Melt the butter in a large, heavy frying pan and gently brown the chopped vegetables, bacon and veal, stirring gently. Stir in the flour, then the stock. Season with salt, pepper and nutmeg. Cook over low heat, stirring occasionally, for about 30 to 40 minutes. Add the chicken liver and cook for a further 1 or 2 minutes. Just before removing the pan from the heat, stir in the cream. Cook the pasta as directed, and mix in a serving dish with the sauce. Serve the grated cheese separately.

Red, White and Green Pasta

Serves 4

30 g (1 oz) butter
½ cup finely chopped ham
¾ cup (6 fl oz) cream
salt
1 x 250 g (8 oz) packet vegeroni, cooked
grated cheese

Melt the butter and lightly brown the ham, then stir in the cream. Season with salt and simmer for 2 minutes. Drain the vegeroni, place in the pan and stir gently over low heat for 1 to 2 minutes. Serve sprinkled with plenty of grated cheese.

Short Pasta Salad

Serves 6

375 g (12 oz) short pasta
4 tablespoons olive oil
1 x 125 g (4 oz) can tuna, flaked
12 black olives, pitted
1 large red or green pepper (capsicum), diced
1 onion, finely chopped
2 stalks celery, chopped
1 ½ tablespoons cider vinegar
salt and freshly ground black pepper
1 large firm tomato, quartered
2 hard-boiled eggs, quartered

Cook the pasta and allow to cool. Place the pasta, olive oil, tuna, olives, red pepper, onion and celery in a serving bowl. Mix well, then add the vinegar, salt and pepper to taste. Decorate with tomato and egg quarters.

Chicken Macaroni

Serves 6

1 x 1.5 kg (3 lb) chicken
4 tablespoons olive oil
1 medium-sized onion, finely chopped
2 sprigs parsley, finely chopped
flour
½ cup (4 fl oz) dry white wine
4 large ripe peeled tomatoes
salt and freshly ground black pepper
375 g (12 oz) short pasta
grated Parmesan cheese

Cut the chicken into small serving pieces. Heat the oil and cook the onion and parsley over moderate heat until the onion is transparent. Roll the chicken pieces in flour, add to the pan and brown on all sides. Raise the heat, add the wine and cook until it evaporates. Blend or purée the tomatoes, add to the pan and cook for about 5 minutes, stirring frequently. Season. Reduce the heat, cover the pan and simmer until the chicken is tender and the sauce thick. Stir occasionally to prevent burning. Cook the pasta as directed, then pour over some of the sauce, sprinkle with cheese and mix well. Add more sauce and pieces of chicken to each helping, and serve extra Parmesan cheese separately.

Lasagna with Butter and Grated Cheese

Serves 6

Grease a deep dish and cover with a layer of grated cheese, a layer of cooked lasagna, and a generous amount of butter which has been cut into small pieces. Repeat this until all the lasagna has been used. Cover with a layer of breadcrumbs mixed with grated cheese and dot with butter. Brown under a griller (broiler) for 15 to 20 minutes.

Baked Lasagna with Tomato and Meat Sauce

Serves 6

60 g (2 oz) butter
1 small onion, finely chopped
1 small stalk celery, finely chopped
1 small carrot, finely chopped
125 g (4 oz) unsmoked bacon, chopped
300 g (9 ½ oz) lean minced (ground) veal or beef
185 g (6 oz) lean minced (ground) pork
½ cup (4 fl oz) dry white wine
1 kg (2 lb) tomatoes, peeled
salt and freshly ground black pepper
1 teaspoon dried oregano (or pinch of mixed herbs)
pinch of nutmeg
4 tablespoons cream, optional
1 x 375 g (12 oz) packet thick lasagna sheets, cooked
1 quantity Béchamel sauce (page 306)
1 cup (4 oz) grated Parmesan cheese
finely sliced mozzarella cheese
butter

Heat the butter in a pan. Add the chopped vegetables and bacon and cook over a low heat for several minutes until the vegetables are transparent. Add the veal and pork, increase the heat to medium and cook the meat, stirring often, until brown on all sides. Raise the heat to high and add the wine, allowing it to evaporate. Blend, sieve or finely chop the tomatoes and add to the meat. Stir well. Lower the heat; season with salt, pepper, oregano and nutmeg. Cover and simmer until the sauce is thick, about 1 hour. If the sauce seems too dry, add a little stock or water. If you wish to use cream for a rich flavour, add it just before you take the pan from the heat.

While the sauce is cooking, prepare the lasagna and the Béchamel sauce. Grease an ovenproof dish. Line the base with a layer of lasagna, cover with meat sauce, then a thin layer of Béchamel and finally a sprinkling of grated cheese. Repeat the layers until the dish is full (usually 4 or 5 layers are enough). The final layer should be meat sauce and Béchamel sauce, and then a complete covering of sliced mozzarella cheese. Dot with butter. Bake at 200°C (400°F/Gas 6) for 25 to 30 minutes.

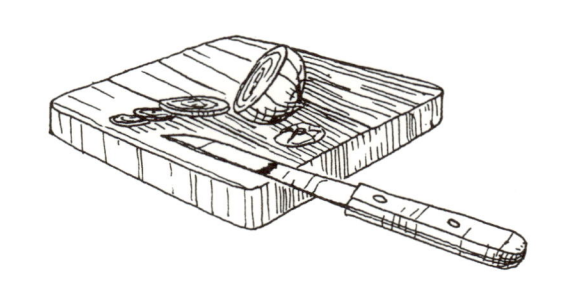

Pasta and Rice

Baked Lasagna with Eggplant

Serves 6

1 large eggplant (aubergine)
salt
flour
4 tablespoons olive oil
1 quantity Béchamel sauce (see below)
1 x 375 g (12 oz) packet lasagna noodles, cooked

440 g (14 oz) mozzarella cheese, cut into thin slices
¾ cup (3 oz) grated Parmesan cheese
butter

Tomato Sugo
5 ripe tomatoes, peeled
4 tablespoons olive oil
1 garlic clove, halved
3 fresh basil leaves, finely chopped
salt and freshly ground black pepper

Thinly slice the eggplant and salt each slice. Place in a colander to drain. Let stand, preferably for a few hours. When the eggplant has drained, dry the pieces with a clean cloth. Flour the pieces on both sides and fry them in the hot olive oil until golden brown on both sides. Drain on greaseproof paper. Repeat this process until all the slices are cooked. Eggplant done in this way absorbs the oil quite quickly, so you will need to keep adding more olive oil as needed.

Prepare the Béchamel sauce and lasagna as directed. Line a greased ovenproof dish with a layer of lasagna. Top with a layer of Tomato Sugo and eggplant, then some Béchamel, a few slices of mozzarella cheese and a sprinkling of Parmesan cheese. Repeat this 3 or 4 times, ending with a layer of Tomato Sugo and Béchamel. Cover completely with slices of mozzarella. Dot with butter and cook at 200°C (400°F/Gas 6) for 25 to 30 minutes.

Tomato Sugo: Blend, sieve or finely chop the tomatoes. Heat the oil and fry the garlic, basil, tomatoes, salt and pepper and cook over a moderate heat until thick and creamy. Remove the garlic. Add the cooked eggplant slices, 2 tablespoons grated Parmesan cheese, stir well for 1 minute and remove from the heat.

Green Lasagna with Meat Sauce

Serves 6

75 g (2 ½ oz) butter
1 small carrot, finely chopped
1 small onion, finely chopped
1 stalk celery, finely chopped
250 g (8 oz) minced (ground) veal or beef
salt and freshly ground pepper

a little wine, stock or water
250 g (8 oz) prosciutto, chopped
1 x 500 g (1 lb) packet green lasagna, cooked
1 quantity Béchamel sauce (see below)
1 ⅓ cups (5 oz) grated Parmesan cheese
butter

Heat the butter in a pan and cook the chopped vegetables for a few minutes, then add the veal. Season with salt, pepper and cook slowly, adding a little stock, water or better still, wine, if the mixture seems too dry. When it is quite thick, add the prosciutto. Remove from the heat when the meat is cooked. Grease an ovenproof dish and cover with a layer of lasagna, then a layer of meat sauce, a layer of Béchamel sauce and some grated cheese. Repeat these layers (3 or 4 layers of lasagna is usually sufficient), ending with a layer of lasagna, then Béchamel. Sprinkle with Parmesan cheese and dot with butter.

Place the lasagna in a moderate to hot oven, 180°-200°C (350°-400°F/Gas 4-6), and bake for 25 to 30 minutes. The top should be golden brown. If not place under the grill (broiler) for 2 or 3 minutes.

Béchamel Sauce

Makes 3 cups (24 fl oz)

60 g (2 oz) butter
3 tablespoons flour
3 cups (24 fl oz) hot milk

salt and white pepper
nutmeg

Heat the butter and when it starts to foam, add the flour. Mix the flour with the butter and cook, stirring constantly, until the mixture is a golden brown. Slowly pour in the hot (not boiling) milk a little at a time, stirring constantly. Remove from the heat when the sauce is smooth and thick. Season with salt and pepper and a little nutmeg. If the sauce is too thin, return to the heat with a small piece of butter kneaded with some flour and stir well until smooth. Set aside until needed.

Rice

How to Cook White Rice

Rapid boil method

Pour 8 cups (2 litres) water into a large saucepan. Use a large saucepan, because when you bring the water to the boil, you're setting up the maximum saucepan area for the rice grains to expand. Add 2 teaspoons salt to the boiling water, then slowly add 1 cup (6 oz) rice. Stir several times with a fork and boil rapidly, uncovered, for 12 to 15 minutes. Remember, 1 cup of rice becomes 3 cups of cooked rice. Tip the expanded cooked rice into a colander, drain well, then fluff up the rice with a fork.

Absorption Method

Bring 2 cups (16 fl oz) water or stock to the boil, then slowly add 1 cup (6 oz) rice and some salt to taste. Return to the boil and stir once. Cover tightly with saucepan lid, then turn heat as low as possible. Simmer gently for 25 minutes or until the rice is tender and all liquid is absorbed.

Fried Rice

Refrigerated or even frozen boiled rice can be used to make Chinese Fried Rice.

Finely chop ½ cup spring onions (scallions), ½ cup mushrooms, ½ cup green pepper (capsicum) and add 1 chopped fried egg. Heat ¼ cup (2 fl oz) oil in a wok or electric frying pan and stir in the vegetables. Toss for 3 to 4 minutes. Add 3 cups refrigerated rice and keep tossing. Add salt and soy sauce to taste, and for the final touch, 1 tablespoon sherry.

Storing Rice

Store rice in an airtight container in the fridge. It will keep as long as fresh milk. For longer storage, keep the container in the freezer.

Reheating Rice

Place rice in a colander over simmering water and allow to heat through. Or reheat in a microwave oven – follow the instructions in your microwave cookbook.

How to Cook Brown Rice

Absorption method

Bring 2 cups (16 fl oz) water or stock to the boil, then slowly add 1 cup (6 oz) brown rice with salt to taste. Return to the boil, stir once, cover and turn heat as low as possible. Simmer gently for 1 hour or until all liquid is absorbed.

Rapid boil method

Bring 8 cups (2 litres) water or stock to the boil in a large saucepan then add 2 teaspoons salt. Slowly add 1 cup (6 oz) brown rice and stir several times with a fork. Boil rapidly, uncovered, for 35 to 40 minutes. Tip into a colander and drain well. Fluff up with a fork.

Variations

Stock made from soup cubes is ideal for this method, or use a combination of tomato and vegetable juices. For chicken or seafood dishes, use half chicken broth and half oyster liquid. If preparing rice for desserts, substitute fruit juices. For further savoury variations, fry lightly in butter any of the following: onion, crushed garlic, spring onions (scallions), celery, green pepper (capsicum), mushrooms, etc. Add raw rice, toss for a few minutes over moderate heat, then add 2 cups (16 fl oz) boiling liquid and continue cooking as above.

Apple Rice

Cook 1 cup (6 oz) rice in 1 cup (8 fl oz) apple juice, 1 cup (8 fl oz) stock and salt to taste. Garnish with chopped apple, and serve with roast pork or pork chops.

Orange Rice

Cook 1 cup (6 oz) rice with 1 cup (8 fl oz) orange juice, 1 cup (8 fl oz) stock and salt to taste. Add nuts and sultanas if you like and serve with chicken.

Onion Rice

Cook 1 cup (6 oz) rice, ½ packet onion soup mix and 2 cups (16 fl oz) water, with salt to taste. Garnish with fried onion rings.

Lemon Rice

Cook 1 cup (6 oz) rice using 1 ¾ cups (14 fl oz) water, ¼ cup (2 fl oz) lemon juice, 1 teaspoon grated lemon rind, ¼ teaspoon turmeric and salt to taste. Serve with fish.

Pasta and Rice

Mushroom Rice

Cook 1 cup (6 oz) rice, 2 cups (16 fl oz) water, 2-3 mushroom stock cubes, 1 beef stock cube and salt to taste. Garnish with sliced sautéed mushrooms.

Tomato Rice

Cook 1 cup (6 oz) rice in 1 cup (8 fl oz) tomato juice and 1 cup (8 fl oz) beef stock, with salt to taste. Garnish with sliced green onions (scallions).

Yellow Rice

Cook 2 cups (12 oz) rice by rapid boil method (*page 307*), adding 1 teaspoon turmeric to the water. When cooked, drain well, and toss 1 teaspoon grated lemon rind through rice.

Chinese-Style Steamed Rice

2 cups (12 oz) rice
water
½ teaspoon salt

Place rice in a sieve or colander and run cold water over until water is quite clear. Drain and allow rice to dry. Place in a heavy based saucepan, and add enough cold water to reach 2.5 cm (1 inch) above rice. (This measurement applies to any quantity of rice.) Add salt, then bring to the boil, boiling rapidly until steam holes appear in the rice. Turn heat down as low as possible and cover with a lid, sealing with foil if not a good fit. Allow rice to simmer gently for 15 to 20 minutes until tender. Remove from heat, uncover and allow to stand 5 minutes before serving.

Rice Ravenna
Serves 6

2 tablespoons oil
2 bacon rashers, chopped
1 onion, chopped
1 garlic clove, crushed, optional
4 cups cooked rice
125 g (4 oz) sausage, salami or devon, cut into thin strips
½ cup (2 oz) grated cheese
salt and pepper
3 eggs, beaten
chopped fresh parsley
a few olives, to garnish

Heat the oil, brown the bacon, then drain and reserve. Add the onion and garlic and cook for 2 minutes. Add the rice, sausage, grated cheese, salt and pepper, and toss well to heat evenly, then add the beaten eggs and toss quickly until rice is just coated. Remove from the heat and garnish with the reserved bacon, parsley and a few sliced olives.

Lemon Butter Rice

500 g (1 lb) rice
juice and rind of ½ lemon
30 g (1 oz) butter
salt and pepper

Cook rice by rapid boil method (*page 307*). Drain well, then add lemon rind and juice, and butter. Toss to blend, and season with salt and pepper to taste.

Bacon Brown Rice
Serves 4

15 g (½ oz) butter
4 rashers bacon, chopped
2 onions, thinly sliced
3 bananas, sliced
2 tomatoes, chopped
4 cups cooked brown rice
½ cup (2 oz) grated cheese
salt and pepper

Heat the butter, fry the bacon and onion until golden, then add the bananas and tomatoes and fry for a few minutes. Add the rice and toss continuously over moderate heat. Add the cheese and allow to melt. Season to taste.

Ham and Rice Bake
Serves 4

3 cups cooked rice
1 onion, grated
1 cup (4 oz) grated cheese
2 eggs, beaten
1¼ cups (10 fl oz) milk
2 tablespoons chopped celery
1 teaspoon paprika
dash of Worcestershire sauce
8 slices ham
1 x 310 g (10 oz) can corn kernels, drained
2 tablespoons chopped red pepper (capsicum)
2 tablespoons melted butter
2 tablespoons (1 oz) brown sugar
1 teaspoon mixed mustard

Boil the rice, drain well, and while still hot add the onion and the cheese. Toss with a fork until the cheese has melted. Add the eggs, milk, celery, paprika and Worcestershire sauce, blending with a fork. Spoon the mixture into a well-greased ovenproof dish and bake in a 180°C (350°F/Gas 4) oven until mixture sets, about 40 minutes. Remove from the oven and overlap the ham slices on the top. Combine the corn and the red pepper and spoon this mixture into the centre of the dish. Combine the butter, brown sugar and mustard, brush over ham. Place dish back in oven and bake for another 15 minutes. A little grated cheese may be sprinkled over the corn and red pepper mixture. Asparagus spears or pineapple slices may be substituted for corn.

Brown Rice and Cheese Casserole

Serves 6

30 g (1 oz) butter
2 tablespoons oil
1 large onion, finely chopped
500 g (1 lb) brown rice
5 cups (1.25 litres) hot water
3 onion stock cubes
1 teaspoon salt
½ teaspoon black pepper
1 ½ cups diced cooked vegetables
2 cups (8 oz) grated cheese
½ cup finely chopped fresh parsley

Heat the butter and oil in a heavy based saucepan and fry the onion over medium heat, stirring frequently, until it is soft and golden. Add the rice and continue frying, stirring constantly, for 5 minutes. Add the hot water, stock cubes, salt and pepper. Bring to the boil, stirring to dissolve the stock cubes. Lower heat, cover tightly and cook for 40 minutes without stirring or lifting the lid. Lightly mix in the vegetables, half the cheese and the parsley. Turn the rice mixture into a buttered ovenproof dish, smooth the top and sprinkle with the remaining cheese. Bake at 180°C (350°F/Gas 4) for 10 minutes or until top is golden.

Curried Eggs

Serves 2

45 g (1 ½ oz) butter
1 onion, finely chopped
1 apple, peeled and chopped
⅔ teaspoon curry powder, or to taste
2 tablespoons flour
2 ½ cups (20 fl oz) milk
1 chicken stock cube
salt and pepper
juice of ½ lemon
3 cups hot cooked rice
extra 15 g (½ oz) butter
1 tablespoon chopped fresh parsley
4 hard-boiled eggs, halved

Heat the butter and fry the onion and apple until tender. Add the curry powder and flour, blend well and cook, stirring constantly, for a few minutes. Add the milk gradually with the crumbled stock cube and stir until the sauce boils. Season with salt and pepper and add the lemon juice. Cover the sauce and simmer for about 15 minutes.

Toss the rice with the extra butter and the parsley and place in a serving dish. Arrange the eggs on the rice, pour the curry sauce over and garnish with a little extra parsley and lemon slices.

Baked Luncheon Rice

Serves 4

15 g (½ oz) butter
1 onion, finely chopped
1 green or red pepper (capsicum), chopped
1 ½ cups cooked rice
1 ½ cups (3 oz) fresh breadcrumbs
1 cup corn kernels, drained
1 x 425 g (13 ½ oz) can tomatoes, drained and chopped
1 tablespoon chopped fresh parsley
1 egg, beaten
salt and pepper
1 x 315 g (10 oz) can tomato soup
1 tablespoon brown sugar
¼ teaspoon dried oregano, optional
1 cup (4 oz) grated cheese

Heat the butter and fry the onion and green pepper until tender. Add the rice, breadcrumbs, corn, tomatoes and parsley. Remove from the heat and add the egg, salt and pepper. Spoon into a greased ovenproof dish. Blend the soup with the brown sugar and oregano. Spoon one third of the soup over the rice mixture and sprinkle with the cheese. Bake at 180°C (350°F/Gas 4), for about 20 to 25 minutes. Heat the remaining soup with a little water added, and serve with the rice as a sauce.

Rice Savoury Supper

Serves 4

2 beef stock cubes
2 cups (16 fl oz) boiling water
1 cup (6 oz) rice
2 onions, thinly sliced
1 tablespoon margarine
2 rashers bacon, diced
2 tomatoes, chopped
½ cup (2 oz) grated cheese
salt and pepper
4 eggs

Dissolve the stock cubes in the boiling water then add the rice, cover and cook over moderate heat for 20 minutes or until the rice is tender. While the rice is cooking sauté the onions in the margarine until tender, then sauté the bacon until crisp. Add the onions, bacon and tomatoes to the cooked rice with half the cheese. Season to taste with salt and pepper.

Spread the rice mixture into an ovenproof dish and make 4 hollows in the rice. Break the eggs into a cup and slide an egg into each hollow. Sprinkle with the remaining cheese and bake at 200°C (400°F/Gas 6) for about 10 minutes or until the eggs are set.

Pasta and Rice

Broccoli Rice Bake

Broccoli Rice Bake

Serves 6

15 g (½ oz) butter
2 rashers bacon, chopped
1 onion, chopped
6 cups cooked brown rice
1 cup (4 oz) grated cheese
salt and pepper
2 cups hot broccoli or any other cooked vegetable such as peas, beans, carrots or cauliflower
2 tomatoes, sliced

Heat the butter and sauté the bacon and onion for 2 minutes. Add the rice and toss well over moderate heat for 2 minutes. Add half the cheese and season with salt and pepper. Place the rice in an ovenproof serving dish and surround the rice with a ring of broccoli. Add a ring of sliced tomatoes, sprinkled with the remaining cheese. Place in the oven or under the griller (broiler) until the tomatoes heat and the cheese melts.

Note: This is an interesting way to serve rice and goes particularly well with grills and casseroles.

Cheese Fried Rice

Serves 6

500 g (1 lb) brown rice
45 g (1 ½ oz) butter
1 cup (4 oz) grated cheese
1 medium-sized carrot, grated

Cook the rice (*page 307*) and drain well in a colander for 30 minutes. Alternatively, prepare in advance and store in refrigerator until required. Heat the butter in a pan and add the rice, tossing continuously with a fork while heating. When hot add the cheese and carrot, toss again lightly and serve with meatballs.

Brown Rice Mushroom Medley

Serves 4

45 g (1 ½ oz) butter
2 rashers bacon, chopped
1 garlic clove, crushed
2 onions, thinly sliced
250 g (½ lb) open flat mushrooms, sliced
2 teaspoons dried oregano or basil
4 cups cooked brown rice
salt and pepper
1 cup cooked peas or beans or 1 tomato, chopped
2 cups shredded lettuce (outside leaves)
grated cheese, optional

Heat the butter, add the bacon, garlic and onions and fry until the onion is just tender. Add the mushrooms and toss over moderate heat for 1 minute, then add the oregano, rice, seasoning and peas. Toss continuously to heat. During the last few minutes add the lettuce. A little grated cheese may be added for extra flavour.

Brown Rice Pie

Serves 4

45 g (1 ½ oz) butter
4 cups cooked brown rice
1 cup (4 oz) chopped peanuts
½ cup chopped celery
1 tomato, diced
1 onion, chopped
1 tablespoon chopped fresh parsley
2 eggs, beaten
1 teaspoon salt
pepper
½ teaspoon ground ginger, nutmeg or dried sage
½ cup (2 oz) grated cheese
tomato wedges
parsley

Combine the first 11 ingredients and blend well. Press into a buttered 23 cm (9 inch) pie plate and sprinkle with grated cheese. Bake at 180°C (350°F/Gas 4) for 25 minutes. Garnish with tomato and parsley.

Spanish Paella

Serves 6 – 8

½ cup (4 fl oz) olive or peanut oil
1 kg (2 lb) chicken pieces, cut into serving sized portions
3 rashers bacon, chopped
2 onions, chopped
2 garlic cloves, crushed
1 green pepper (capsicum), cut into thin strips
2½ cups (1 lb) rice
1 x 450 g (14½ oz) can tomatoes, drained
¼ teaspoon saffron threads, soaked in boiling water for 20 minutes
1 teaspoon paprika
5 cups (1.25 litres) chicken stock
1 cup frozen peas
salt and pepper
250 g (8 oz) peeled prawns (shrimp)
250 g (8 oz) scallops, poached 2 to 3 minutes
12 mussels, bottled or fresh in shell (scrub well and steam until open, about 5 minutes)
1 small crayfish (lobster), chopped in shell, optional
6-8 whole prawns (shrimp), to garnish
lemon wedges, to garnish

Heat the oil in a paella pan or use a large shallow frypan. Fry the chicken, turning frequently until golden. Remove the chicken and set aside. Add the bacon, onions, garlic and pepper strips (reserve a few for garnish) and fry until just tender. Add the rice to the pan and toss over moderate heat for about 3 minutes. Add the tomatoes, saffron liquid, paprika, chicken stock and peas. Check the seasoning, then add salt and pepper to taste. Stir until the mixture comes to the boil. Then replace the chicken and reduce the heat to very low to simmer for about 15 minutes or until most of the liquid has been absorbed. Add all the seafood and garnish the centre of the paella with the whole prawns and the reserved pepper strips. Cook without stirring until the chicken and rice are tender – about another 10 to 15 minutes. Add a little extra boiling stock if required. Remove the pan from the heat and cover with a tea towel or some foil for about 5 to 8 minutes to enhance the flavour. Serve with lemon wedges.

Note: Ingredients may be varied. Replace the bacon with slices of chorizo or some spicy sausage. Anchovy strips may be used to garnish the dish. Canned artichoke hearts make an attractive addition. Some of the chicken stock used may be replaced with ½ cup (4 fl oz) of dry white wine.

Spanish Paella

Pasta and Rice

Brown Rice Medley

Serves 4

60 g (2 oz) butter
1 garlic clove, crushed
1 onion, finely chopped
3 stalks celery, chopped
125 g (4 oz) mushrooms, sliced
4 cups cooked brown rice
¼ teaspoon dried oregano
½ cup (4 fl oz) milk or sour cream
salt and freshly ground pepper
1 cup (4 oz) grated cheese
chopped fresh parsley

Heat the butter and sauté the garlic, onion and celery until just tender. Add the mushrooms and toss for a few minutes. Add the rice, oregano, milk and seasoning and toss continuously until heated. Add the cheese and sprinkle with the parsley.

Brown Rice Scramble

Serves 4

45 g (1 ½ oz) butter
1 cup sliced mushrooms
1 cup finely chopped celery or green pepper (capsicum)
3 cups cooked brown rice
½ cup (4 fl oz) mayonnaise or sour cream
2 tablespoons onion soup mix or 1 onion, finely chopped
3 sliced hard-boiled eggs, or 1 cup of any of the following: drained, canned salmon or tuna, cold cooked diced lamb, beef, chicken or ham
1 cup diced cheese
2 tomatoes, sliced
chopped fresh parsley

Heat the butter and fry the mushrooms and celery for a few minutes before adding the rice. Combine the mayonnaise and soup mix. Add to the rice mixture and toss with a fork to blend. Add the hard-boiled eggs and cheese and continue to toss with the fork until heated. Serve garnished with fried tomato slices. Sprinkle with the parsley.

Fried Brown Rice

Serves 4 - 6

1 cup brown rice
3 tablespoons oil
1 onion, finely chopped
4 spring onions (scallions), thinly sliced
2 carrots, diced
3 cabbage leaves, shredded
2 tomatoes, chopped
4 mushrooms, sliced
6 large prawns (shrimp), deveined and chopped
salt and pepper

Boil the rice in 8 cups (2 litres) boiling, salted water for 35 to 40 minutes or until tender. Drain, rinse under running hot water and leave to cool in a colander or strainer. Heat the oil in a large, heavy based frying pan or wok and gently fry the onion, spring onions, carrots and cabbage for 5 minutes, stirring frequently with a wooden spoon. Add the tomatoes, mushrooms and prawns and fry a further 5 minutes, stirring frequently. Add the rice and stir until hot, about 5 minutes. Season to taste and serve immediately as a main course accompanied by chickpea dip and pumpernickel bread.

Tropical Curry

Serves 4

1 tablespoon peanut oil
6 spring onions (scallions), cut into thin strips or 2 onions, sliced
½ teaspoon chopped fresh ginger or ground ginger
1 garlic clove, crushed
1 red or green pepper (capsicum), cut into thin strips
3 teaspoons curry powder, or to taste
1 cup sliced water chestnuts or canned bean sprouts
1 ½ cups (12 fl oz) chicken stock, made with stock cubes
the grated rind and juice of ½ lemon
1 x 450 g (14 ½ oz) can pineapple pieces, drained and ½ cup (4 fl oz) liquid reserved
arrowroot or cornflour (cornstarch), to thicken
500 g (1 lb) fresh or canned prawns (shrimp)
4 cups hot cooked rice

Heat oil and fry the spring onions, ginger, garlic and pepper over moderate heat for 1 minute. Add curry powder, stir to blend and cook for another minute. Add the water chestnuts, chicken stock, lemon rind and juice and reserved pineapple liquid. Bring to the boil and thicken with arrowroot dissolved in a little water. Add the prawns and pineapple pieces and heat thoroughly. Spoon the curry over a mound of hot rice.

Note: 250 g (8 oz) of cooked chicken or a 500 g (1 lb) can of tuna may replace the prawns.

Summer Rice Pilaf

Serves 4

- 1 cup (6 oz) rice
- 45 g (1 ½ oz) butter
- ½ teaspoon finely chopped fresh ginger
- ½ cup (2 oz) pecan, macadamia or cashew nuts
- 6 spring onions (scallions), sliced diagonally
- salt and pepper
- 1 small pawpaw (papaya) or rock melon (cantaloup)
- 1 x 450 g (14 ½ oz) can sliced pineapple, or use fresh pineapple
- 2 teaspoons caster (powdered) sugar
- chopped fresh mint

Cook the rice by the rapid boil method (*page 307*). Drain, rinse with hot water and keep hot. Heat the butter, add the ginger and nuts and fry until the nuts are pale golden. Add the spring onions and cook for 1 minute. Discard the ginger and spoon the nuts and spring onions onto the rice, tossing lightly with a fork to mix through. Season to taste with salt and pepper. Peel the pawpaw, remove seeds and cut into thin wedges. Cut pineapple slices in half. Add extra butter to pan if needed and lightly fry pawpaw and pineapple, sprinkled with sugar, until golden. Place the rice in the centre of a serving dish and surround with pawpaw and pineapple slices. Sprinkle with chopped mint.

Bacon Rice Bake

Serves 4

- 1 tablespoon melted butter
- salt and pepper
- 2 eggs, beaten
- 1 cup (4 oz) grated cheese
- 4 cups cooked rice
- 1 cup corn kernels
- 2 rashers bacon, chopped
- 2 hard-boiled eggs, chopped
- ½ cup (1 oz) breadcrumbs
- extra ¼ cup (1 oz) grated cheese
- extra 45 g (1 ½ oz) butter, cut into small pieces

Blend the melted butter, the salt and pepper, the beaten eggs and ½ cup (2 oz) of the cheese with the rice, then add the corn. Spoon half the rice mixture into a greased ovenproof dish. Heat half the remaining butter, and fry the bacon until golden. Add the hard-boiled eggs and remaining ½ cup (2 oz) of grated cheese. Spoon over the rice base and top with the remaining rice mixture. Sprinkle with the breadcrumbs and the extra grated cheese and dot with pieces of butter. Bake at 180°C (350°F/Gas 4) for about 25 minutes or until the rice is firm to the touch.

Citrus Curried Rice with Orange Steaks

Serves 4

- 15 g (½ oz) butter
- 4 spring onions (scallions), chopped
- 2 teaspoons curry powder
- ¼ teaspoon cinnamon or ground ginger
- 1 cup (6 oz) rice
- 1 ½ cups (12 fl oz) chicken stock
- ½ cup (4 fl oz) orange juice
- salt and pepper

Orange Steaks

- 4 lamb steaks or short loin chops
- 1 tablespoon oil
- 2 medium-sized oranges, sliced
- grated rind of 1 orange
- juice of 2 oranges, about 1 cup (8 fl oz)
- 2 teaspoons soy sauce
- 3 teaspoons honey
- 2 teaspoons sherry
- a few mint sprigs

Heat the butter and sauté spring onions a few minutes, blend in curry powder and cinnamon, stir over moderate heat. Add rice and stir until coated with curry mixture. Combine stock and orange juice, add to rice and cook by absorption method (*page 307*) for about 25 minutes.

Orange Steaks: While rice is cooking, trim steaks, snip edges slightly to prevent curling. Heat the oil and brown the steaks, then reduce heat and cook to taste. Remove and keep warm. Heat the orange slices in the pan and reserve with steaks. Combine orange rind and juice with soy sauce, honey and sherry. Cook over moderate heat for a few minutes and check seasoning. When rice is cooked, spoon onto serving dish, top with steaks, place orange slices on steaks, spooning over orange glaze. Garnish with mint sprigs.

Curried Puffs

Serves 4

- 2 ½ cups cooked rice
- 2 eggs
- 3 teaspoons curry powder
- ½ cup (2 oz) self-raising flour
- ¼ cup (2 fl oz) milk
- 2 tablespoons chopped fresh parsley
- 1 x 310 g (10 oz) can tuna or salmon, drained and flaked
- juice of 1 lemon
- dry breadcrumbs
- oil for frying
- lemon wedges

Thoroughly combine all the ingredients except the breadcrumbs and oil. Shape the mixture into balls and toss in breadcrumbs. Deep or shallow fry in hot oil until golden. Drain and serve with lemon wedges.

Pasta and Rice

Red Mexican Rice

Serves 4

45 g (1 ½ oz) butter
1 onion, finely chopped
3 rashers bacon, chopped
1 garlic clove, crushed
2 cups (12 oz) rice
3 cups (24 fl oz) chicken stock, made with stock cubes
1 cup (8 fl oz) tomato juice
1 x 440 g (14 oz) can kidney beans, drained
pinch of cayenne pepper or dash of Tabasco sauce
salt and pepper
4 corn cobs, cooked

Heat the butter and fry the onion, bacon and garlic, reserving a little bacon for garnish. Add the rice to the bacon mixture and toss over moderate heat for a few minutes. Add the stock and tomato juice. Bring to the boil, cover, lower the heat to simmer and cook for 20 to 25 minutes or until the rice is tender. Add the drained kidney beans, toss with a fork to blend, heat then season with the cayenne, salt and pepper. Sprinkle the rice with the reserved bacon and serve with the corn cobs.

Red Mexican Rice

Saffron Rice

Serves 6

45 g (1 ½ oz) ghee or butter
2 onions, thinly sliced
¼ teaspoon saffron threads or ½ teaspoon turmeric
6 peppercorns
4 whole cloves
4 cardamom pods, cracked
1 x 8 cm (3 in) cinnamon stick
2 cups (12 oz) rice
4 cups (1 litre) stock, made with stock cubes
salt and pepper
½ cup (3 oz) sultanas
½ cup (3 oz) toasted almonds
4 slices hard-boiled egg
1 cup cooked peas

Heat the ghee and fry the onions until golden. Remove half the onions and reserve. Add all the spices to the pan and cook over moderate heat for 1 minute to develop the flavour. Add the rice and toss for 2 minutes to coat with the spice mixture. Add the stock, salt and pepper. Bring to the boil, cover, lower heat and simmer gently for about 20 to 25 minutes. Add the sultanas during the last 10 minutes of cooking but do not stir the rice. Keep covered until ready to serve, then remove the lid and allow the steam to escape for a few minutes. Serve sprinkled with the almonds and reserved onions, egg slices and peas.

Tangy Rice

Serves 4

½ cup finely chopped celery
3 tablespoons chopped onion
60 g (2 oz) butter
1 ½ cups (12 fl oz) water
1 cup (8 fl oz) fresh orange juice
1 tablespoon grated orange rind
pepper
1 cup (5 oz) long grain rice
chopped fresh parsley

Sauté the celery and onion in the butter until soft but not brown. Stir in the water, orange juice, orange rind and pepper. Bring to the boil and add the rice.

Cover and cook on low heat for 20 minutes or until tender. Fluff with a fork and add the chopped parsley. Serve hot with roast pork or veal.

Biriyani Rice

Serves 6

1 ½ cups (10 oz) rice
60 g (2 oz) ghee or butter
⅓ cup (2 oz) almonds, blanched
3 hard-boiled eggs
pinch of salt
pinch of turmeric
1 large onion, finely sliced
3 chicken stock cubes
¾ teaspoon salt
2 cloves
5 peppercorns
2.5 cm (1 inch) piece of cinnamon stick
pinch of saffron
2 ½ cups (20 fl oz) water
¼ teaspoon garam masala
12 cardamom seeds
⅓ cup (2 oz) sultanas
extra 1 ½ cups (12 fl oz) water

Wash the rice thoroughly, drain in colander and allow to dry for 1 hour. Heat ghee in frypan and lightly fry the almonds. Set aside. Rub the hard-boiled eggs with a pinch of salt and the turmeric and fry, whole, until golden brown. Set aside. Add the sliced onion to the pan and fry until golden. Add the rice and fry for 5 minutes, stirring occasionally. Crush the chicken stock cubes and add to the rice, mix thoroughly and fry for a further 2 minutes. Stir in ¾ teaspoon salt, the cloves, peppercorns, cinnamon stick, saffron and water. Reduce the heat, place lid on pan and simmer for 15 minutes. Stir in garam masala, cardamom seeds, sultanas and extra water. Cook with lid on for a further 10 minutes until all the water is absorbed. Serve the rice garnished with the almonds and eggs cut in half.

South Pacific Rice Salad

Serves 4

3 cups cooked rice
1 cup diced cooked chicken or prawns (shrimp)
½ cup chopped spring onions (scallions)
½ cup each chopped red and green pepper (capsicum)
½ cup thinly sliced water chestnuts or radishes
1 x 450 g (14 ½ oz) can pineapple pieces, drained
⅔ cup (5 fl oz) French dressing
¼ teaspoon ground ginger
¼ teaspoon garlic salt
½ teaspoon curry powder
1 teaspoon soy sauce
1 teaspoon toasted sesame seeds
salt and pepper

Combine the rice with the chicken, spring onions, peppers, water chestnuts and pineapple pieces. Blend the French dressing with the next 5 ingredients, pour over the rice mixture and toss well. Season to taste with salt and pepper.

Tomato Rice Salad

Serves 6

6 large firm ripe tomatoes
2 cups cooked rice
½ red pepper (capsicum), finely diced
½ green pepper (capsicum), finely diced
½ cup chopped black olives
3 tablespoons oil
juice of 1 lemon
salt or garlic salt
pepper
¼ teaspoon paprika or curry powder

Cut the tops off the tomatoes and reserve. Spoon out some of the pulp. Turn the tomatoes upside down to drain and chill in the refrigerator for about 1 hour. Combine the rice with the red and green peppers and olives. Mix together the oil, lemon juice, salt, pepper and paprika. Pour over the rice mixture, tossing to blend well. Fill the tomato shells with the rice mixture and replace tops. Heat gently and serve warm.

Pasta and Rice

Formosa Fried Rice

Serves 4, with other dishes

- 6 dried Chinese mushrooms, fresh may be used
- 1/3 cup (2 1/2 fl oz) peanut oil
- 1 garlic clove, crushed
- 2.5 cm (1 inch) piece fresh ginger, chopped
- 125 g (4 oz) peeled prawns (shrimp)
- 125 g (4 oz) chopped ham or bacon
- 1 cup chopped spring onions (scallions)
- 1/4 cup (1 oz) almonds
- 6 cups cooked rice, refrigerated overnight
- 1 tablespoon soy sauce
- 1 tablespoon sherry
- salt
- 1 cup drained crushed pineapple or fresh pineapple, finely chopped

Soak the Chinese mushrooms in hot water for about 15 minutes until tender. Chop in small dice. Heat the oil, add the garlic, ginger, prawns, ham, 1/2 cup spring onions, the mushrooms and almonds. Fry for a few minutes. Add the rice and toss with a fork continuously until well heated.

Season with soy sauce, sherry and salt if required, add pineapple and toss well to heat. Garnish with remaining spring onions.

Chinese Fried Rice

Serves 6

- 2 1/2 cups (1 lb) rice
- 2 1/2-3 cups (20-24 fl oz) water
- 8 dried Chinese mushrooms
- 4 tablespoons peanut oil
- 2 garlic cloves, finely chopped
- 1 teaspoon finely grated fresh ginger
- 2 stalks celery, finely sliced diagonally
- 1 carrot, coarsely grated
- 125 g (4 oz) green beans, finely sliced
- 125 g (4 oz) fresh bean sprouts or diced bamboo shoots
- 1/3 cup (2 1/2 fl oz) light soy sauce
- 1/2 cup finely chopped spring onions (scallions)
- salt

Cook the rice in the water by the absorption method (*page 307*) a day before or at least some hours ahead. Refrigerate overnight.

Soak the Chinese mushrooms in hot water for 20 minutes, then cut off and discard stems and slice the mushrooms finely. Heat the oil in a large frypan and stir fry the garlic and ginger for a few seconds. Add the mushrooms and vegetables and stir fry over high heat for 3 minutes. Add the rice, toss and fry with the vegetables until heated through. Sprinkle with the soy sauce, continue stirring and frying, then add the spring onions and fry for a minute longer. Taste and add salt if desired. Serve hot.

Citrus Curried Rice

Serves 4

- 15 g (1/2 oz) butter
- 4 spring onions (scallions), chopped
- 2 teaspoons curry powder
- 1/4 teaspoon ground cinnamon or ginger
- 1 cup (6 oz) rice
- 1 1/2 cups (12 fl oz) chicken stock
- 1/2 cup (4 fl oz) orange juice
- salt and pepper

Heat butter and sauté spring onions for a few minutes, then blend in the curry powder and cinnamon and stir over moderate heat. Add the rice and stir until coated with the curry mixture. Combine the stock and orange juice, add to the rice and cook by absorption method (*page 307*), covered, over low heat, until rice has absorbed liquid and is tender, about 25 minutes. Season to taste.

Spiced Indian Pilau

Serves 4 – 6

- 45 g (1 1/2 oz) butter
- 2 onions, thinly sliced into rings
- 2 cups (12 oz) rice
- salt and pepper
- 1 teaspoon ground turmeric
- 3 cloves
- 8 peppercorns
- 4 cardamom pods, crushed
- 1 cinnamon stick
- 4 cups (1 litre) hot chicken stock, made with stock cubes
- 1 cup cooked peas
- 1/2 cup (3 oz) sultanas

Heat the butter in a heavy based saucepan and fry half the onions until golden, reserve. Add the rice, salt, pepper and spices and fry, stirring, for about 2 minutes. Add the hot stock, stir, cover, and cook on low heat for 20 to 25 minutes. Remove from heat, allow steam to escape, then fluff up the rice with a fork. Serve garnished with the peas, reserved onion rings and sultanas.

Nut Rice

Serves 4

- 45 g (1 1/2 oz) butter
- 6 cups cooked rice
- 1/2 cup (2 oz) pecans or chopped almonds
- salt and pepper

Melt the butter in a pan and, with a fork, toss the rice and nuts over moderate heat until warmed through. Season with salt and pepper and serve.

Rice Rissoles, Chinese Style

Serves 4

Chinese Sauce
- 1 x 425 g (13½ oz) can crushed pineapple
- ¼ cup (2 oz) sugar
- 1 tablespoon vinegar
- 2 tablespoons tomato sauce
- 3 teaspoons soy sauce
- 1 carrot, grated
- 2 tablespoons finely chopped red or green pepper (capsicum)
- 2 teaspoons cornflour (cornstarch), dissolved in a little water

Rissoles
- 2 cups cooked rice
- 1½ cups finely chopped cooked chicken, beef, or pork
- 4 spring onions (scallions) finely chopped or 1 small onion, grated
- 1 egg, beaten
- salt and pepper
- 3 teaspoons soy sauce
- 1 tablespoon tomato sauce
- flour
- oil for frying
- 4 cups hot cooked rice
- spring onions (scallions) or parsley, to garnish

Chinese Sauce: Combine the first 7 sauce ingredients, add the cornflour and stir until the sauce boils and thickens. Keep warm.

Rissoles: Combine the first 7 ingredients, blend well and check seasoning. Divide evenly into 8 portions. Toss each portion generously in flour, and shape into 8 rissoles. Chill in the refrigerator for at least 30 minutes. Fry the rissoles in hot oil until crisp and golden. Serve on a bed of rice, spoon over the Chinese Sauce. Garnish with spring onions or parsley.

Sweet Yellow Rice

Serves 4

- pinch of saffron threads
- 3 cups (24 fl oz) milk
- 3 cups cooked rice
- 2 cardamom pods, cracked
- 2.5 cm (1 inch) piece cinnamon stick
- 15 g (½ oz) butter
- ⅓ cup (3 oz) sugar
- ½ cup (3 oz) sultanas or currants
- ¼ cup (1 oz) toasted almond slivers
- cream
- ground cinnamon

Soak the saffron threads in ¼ cup (2 fl oz) of milk. Place the rice, remaining milk, spices and butter in a saucepan and stir over moderate heat for about 15 minutes until the rice has absorbed the milk. Add the saffron milk and the sugar and cook for another 2 minutes, stirring continuously. Top with the sultanas and almond slivers.

Serve with cream sprinkled with cinnamon.

Oriental Fried Rice

Serves 6

- 6 dried Chinese mushrooms, optional
- 4 tablespoons peanut oil
- 1 small garlic clove, crushed
- ½ teaspoon fresh ginger, chopped
- 2 eggs, beaten with a little soy sauce
- ½ cup cooked diced chicken or barbecued pork
- ½ cup peeled prawns (shrimp)
- 6 spring onions (scallions), chopped
- 6 cups cooked rice, refrigerated overnight
- salt
- 1 tablespoon soy sauce
- 1 tablespoon Chinese rice wine or dry sherry
- spring onions (scallions), to garnish

Soak the mushrooms in hot water for 20 minutes or until tender. Cut into small dice. Heat half the oil with the garlic and ginger, and fry the eggs without stirring until set and golden. Remove, cut in small dice and reserve. Heat the remaining oil and fry the mushrooms, chicken, prawns and spring onions. Add the rice and toss continuously with a fork until heated. Season with salt. Add the reserved egg. Combine the soy sauce and wine, sprinkle over rice and toss again. Serve garnished with spring onion curls.

Vegetable Pilau

Serves 4 – 6

- 2 tablespoons vegetable oil
- 45 g (1 ½ oz) ghee or butter
- 1 cup sliced onion
- 2½ cups (1 lb) rice
- 4 cups (1 litre) hot water
- 2½ teaspoons salt
- 4 whole cloves
- 1 small cinnamon stick
- 4 cardamom pods
- 125 g (4 oz) beans, thinly sliced
- ½ cup carrots cut in matchstick strips
- ½ cup diced potato
- ½ cup fresh or frozen peas
- freshly ground black pepper

Heat the oil and ghee in a heavy based saucepan and fry the onion, stirring occasionally, until it is golden. Add the rice and fry, stirring, for about 3 minutes or until all the grains are coated with the oil. Add the hot water, 2 teaspoons of salt and the whole spices. Bring to the boil, then lower the heat to simmer. Cover the pan tightly, cook for 10 minutes then arrange the vegetables on top of the rice but do not stir. Sprinkle with remaining salt and the pepper. Replace the saucepan lid and cook on low heat for a further 10 minutes. The vegetables should be tender but not overcooked. Serve hot.

Note: This dish may be accompanied by yoghurt seasoned with salt and ground cumin, or mixed with finely sliced cucumbers. Vegetable Pilau can be a main dish or an accompaniment to curries.

Pasta and Rice

Pilau Rice

Serves 4 – 6

- 45 g (1 ½ oz) ghee or butter
- 2 small onions, thinly sliced into rings
- pinch of saffron threads or ½ teaspoon ground turmeric
- 6 peppercorns
- 4 whole cloves
- 4 cardamom pods, cracked
- 1 x 7.5 cm (3 inch) piece cinnamon stick
- 2 cups (12 oz) rice
- 4 cups (1 litre) chicken stock, made with stock cubes
- salt and pepper
- ½ cup (3 oz) sultanas

Garnish

- 1 cup cooked peas
- ½ cup (3 oz) toasted almonds
- 4 hard-boiled eggs, quartered

Heat the ghee in a pan and fry the onions until golden brown. Remove and reserve. Add the saffron, peppercorns, cloves, cardamom pods and cinnamon stick and fry over moderate heat, stirring for 1 minute. Add the rice and stir to coat well with butter spice mixture. Cook for 1 minute. Add the chicken stock, salt and pepper, then bring to the boil, cover, lower heat and simmer for about 20 to 25 minutes. Add the sultanas after 15 minutes but do not stir the rice.

Keep covered until ready to serve. Allow the steam to escape for a few minutes just before serving. Place on a serving platter, garnish with the peas, reserved onion rings and the almonds and surround with the hard-boiled eggs.

Rice Bolognese

Serves 4

- 1 tablespoon oil
- 500 g (1 lb) minced steak (ground beef)
- 1 garlic clove, crushed
- 1 onion, chopped
- 1 carrot, grated
- 1 x 450 g (14½ oz) can tomatoes
- 2 tablespoons tomato paste
- 1 bay leaf
- ¼ teaspoon ground oregano
- 2 teaspoons brown sugar
- salt and pepper
- 4 cups cooked rice
- grated cheese (Parmesan if possible)

Heat the oil and brown the meat, garlic, onion and carrot. Stir frequently to prevent the mince forming lumps. Add the tomatoes, tomato paste and seasonings. Cover and cook over low heat for at least an hour. This slow cooking develops the best flavour. Serve the sauce spooned over hot rice and dust generously with the cheese.

Note: This sauce freezes well.

Nasi Goreng

Serves 6

- 4 tablespoons oil
- 2 eggs, beaten with a pinch of salt
- 2 garlic cloves, crushed
- 2 onions, thinly sliced
- 1 red or green pepper (capsicum), chopped
- 2 chillies, chopped, or a pinch of chilli powder or a dash of Tabasco sauce
- 250 g (8 oz) chicken breast, diced
- 250 g (8 oz) pork fillet (tenderloin), diced
- 1 cup fresh or canned bean sprouts
- 6 cups cooked rice, refrigerated overnight
- 250 g (8 oz) peeled prawns (shrimp)
- 1 tablespoon soy sauce

Meatballs

- 250 g (8 oz) minced (ground) beef
- 1 onion, finely chopped
- pinch of chilli powder or dash of Tabasco sauce
- salt
- 1 teaspoon curry powder
- 1 egg white, beaten
- oil

Heat 1 tablespoon of the oil in a pan and cook the eggs, without stirring, until set and golden. Remove the eggs, dice half and cut the remainder into long thin strips, reserve. Add the rest of the oil to the pan and stir fry the garlic, onions, red or green pepper and chillies. Add the chicken breast and pork fillet and cook for 10 minutes. Then add bean sprouts, rice and prawns and toss continuously until heated. Season to taste with the soy sauce. If not using chillies add a pinch of chilli powder or Tabasco sauce. Add the reserved chopped egg to the rice and spoon the rice mixture onto a serving platter. Top with the reserved egg strips in a lattice pattern. Arrange meatballs around the dish.

Meatballs: Blend all the ingredients thoroughly then shape, with wet hands, into small meatballs. Brown in hot oil then thread onto short bamboo skewers.

Additional Garnishes: Fried pineapple, bananas, cucumber and tomato slices, chutney, fried prawn crisps, dry fried onion rings.

Opposite: *Nasi Goreng*

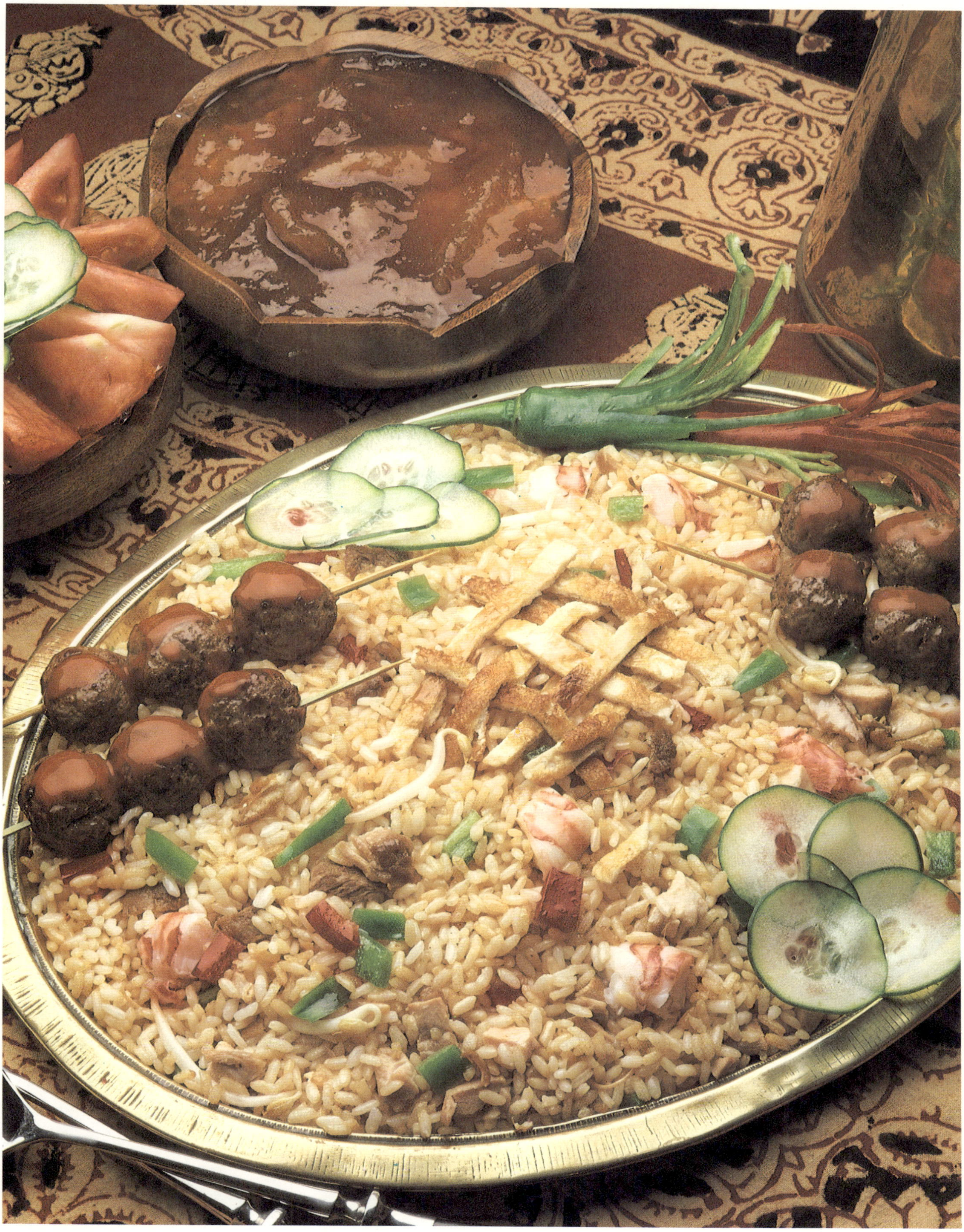

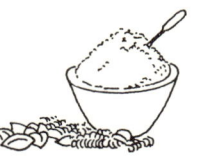

Pasta and Rice

Dolmades

Serves 6

- ½ cup (3 oz) rice, cooked in boiling salted water for just 10 minutes
- 1 onion, finely chopped
- 500 g (1 lb) minced meat (ground beef)
- 1 egg, beaten
- 1 tablespoon (½ oz) currants, optional
- 1 tablespoon chopped fresh parsley
- 1 teaspoon chopped fresh mint
- 1 tablespoon oil
- grated rind of ½ a lemon
- ¼ cup (2 fl oz) water
- salt and pepper
- canned vine leaves
- 1½ cups (12 fl oz) canned beef consommé
- 1½ cups (12 fl oz) water or beef stock, made with stock cubes
- 1 tablespoon lemon juice
- 1 teaspoon tomato paste

Drain the rice well. Blend the onion, meat, egg, currants, parsley and mint and add to the rice along with the oil, lemon rind, water, and salt and pepper. Rinse the vine leaves in hot water. Place the leaves shiny side down and spoon a little filling into the centre of the leaves. Roll up carefully, and seal in the filling.

Arrange seamside down in a large saucepan, making more than 1 layer if needed. Add the beef consommé, water, lemon juice and tomato paste. Cover and simmer on gentle heat for about 40 to 45 minutes. Transfer to a serving plate. Serve on a bed of hot rice, spoon over the sauce. Dolmades may also be eaten cold as an entrée.

Stuffed Eggplant

Serves 4

- 2 medium eggplants (aubergines), halved
- 2 tablespoons oil
- 4 spring onions (scallions), chopped
- 1 garlic clove, crushed
- 1 tomato, cubed
- 2 cups cooked rice
- ½ teaspoon dried oregano
- salt and pepper
- 1 cup (8 fl oz) tomato juice
- 1 tablespoon chopped fresh parsley

Scoop out some of the inside of each eggplant leaving a 2.5 cm (1 inch) shell. Sprinkle salt over the shells and allow to stand for 30 minutes. Meanwhile, chop the eggplant flesh (removed from shells) into small dice. Heat 1 tablespoon of the oil in a pan and fry the eggplant flesh, spring onions, garlic and tomato until the eggplant is just tender. Add the rice, oregano, salt and pepper.

Drain any liquid from the eggplant shells. Pat dry with a paper towel. Spoon the rice mixture evenly into the shells and place them in a shallow ovenproof dish. Spoon over the tomato juice. Place in a 180°C (350°F/Gas 4) oven and bake for 35 to 40 minutes or until the eggplant is tender. Serve sprinkled with parsley.

Baked Tomatoes

Serves 6

- 6 large firm tomatoes
- 45 g (1½ oz) butter
- ¼ teaspoon minced garlic
- 125 g (4 oz) mushrooms, finely chopped
- ¼ teaspoon paprika
- 2 tablespoons chopped spring onions (scallions)
- 2 cups cooked rice
- 2 teaspoons lemon juice
- salt and pepper
- sugar
- ½ cup (2 oz) grated cheese

Cut the tops off the tomatoes, and carefully scoop out the flesh. (Use the flesh to flavour soups or casseroles.) Invert the tomato shells and allow to drain. Heat the butter in a pan and fry the garlic and mushrooms for a few minutes. Add the paprika, spring onions and rice and season with the lemon juice, salt and pepper. Sprinkle each tomato case with a pinch of sugar. Then fill each tomato with the rice/mushroom mixture. Place the stuffed tomatoes in a shallow ovenproof dish. Sprinkle each one with grated cheese and bake at 180°C (350°F/Gas 4) for about 15 to 20 minutes.

Baked Savoury Mushrooms

Serves 6

- 12 large cup-shaped mushrooms
- 45 g (1½ oz) butter
- 1 onion, finely chopped
- 1 bacon rasher, finely chopped
- ½ cup cooked rice
- 1 tablespoon chopped fresh parsley
- melted butter
- salt and pepper
- 125 g (4 oz) cheese, cut into small cubes
- extra chopped fresh parsley

Remove the mushroom stalks and chop them finely. Heat the butter and fry the stalks, onion and bacon for about 2 minutes. Add the rice and parsley and toss to mix well. Brush the mushroom caps on both sides with melted butter. Arrange them in a greased, shallow ovenproof dish with hollow side upwards. Season the rice mixture with salt and pepper. Divide the mixture evenly between the mushroom caps. Top each mushroom with the cheese cubes, then spoon a little extra melted butter over the mushrooms. Bake at 180°C (350°F/Gas 4) for about 15 minutes or until the cheese is melted. Add extra butter if the mushrooms appear dry. Sprinkle with extra chopped parsley.

Cabbage Rolls

Serves 6

30 g (1 oz) butter
1 onion, chopped
1 garlic clove, crushed
500 g (1 lb) minced meat, (ground beef)
1 tablespoon curry powder
salt and pepper
2½ cups (20 fl oz) stock
2 tomatoes, peeled and chopped
¾ cup (5 oz) rice
12 large cabbage leaves, blanched
2 cups (16 fl oz) tomato juice
1 tablespoon Worcestershire sauce

Melt the butter in a pan and sauté onion, garlic, meat and curry powder until the meat is crumbly. Add the salt, pepper, stock, tomatoes and rice. Bring to the boil, cover and simmer for 20 minutes, stirring occasionally. Cool slightly and spoon a portion into each cabbage leaf. Roll up and place seamside down in a greased, shallow casserole dish. Mix the tomato juice and Worcestershire sauce and pour over the cabbage rolls. Bake at 180°C (350°F/Gas 4) for 25 minutes. Serve hot.

Rice and Sardine Ramekins

Serves 4

1 onion, finely chopped
1 cup celery, chopped
1 tablespoon margarine
1 cup (6 oz) rice
2 cups (16 fl oz) chicken stock, made with stock cubes
½ teaspoon grated lemon rind
2 x 105 g (3½ oz) cans sardines
salt and pepper
lemon juice
1 cup (4 oz) dry breadcrumbs tossed in 1 tablespoon melted margarine
½ cup (2 oz) grated cheese
½ cup (4 fl oz) mayonnaise, optional
fresh parsley
sliced stuffed olives, to garnish

Sauté the onion and celery in margarine until just tender then add the rice and toss for 2 minutes. Combine the chicken stock and lemon rind, add to the rice, cover and bring to the boil. Reduce heat to simmer, and cook for 20 minutes until the rice is tender. Remove the lid and allow to stand for 5 minutes. Open the sardines, chop one can, leave the second can whole. Lightly fork the chopped sardines through the rice. Season with salt, pepper and lemon juice. Spoon the rice mixture into ramekins or small ovenproof serving dishes. Top each dish with breadcrumbs, cheese and whole sardines and grill (broil) or bake until the cheese has melted.

To serve, top the sardines with just a dob of mayonnaise, sprinkle with parsley and garnish with olive slices.

Note: This recipe may be prepared with 1 x 220 g (7 oz) can pink salmon.

Mushroom-Rice Piroshki

Makes 48

Sour Cream Pastry
2¼ cups (9 oz) flour
½ teaspoon salt
185 g (6 oz) butter
2 tablespoons sour cream
1 egg, beaten

Filling
30 g (1 oz) butter
1 small onion, finely chopped
250 g (8 oz) mushrooms, finely chopped
¾ teaspoon salt
pepper to taste
pinch of nutmeg
2 hard-boiled eggs, finely chopped
1 teaspoon dried dill
1 cup cooked rice
1½ tablespoons sour cream
beaten egg, to glaze

Sour Cream Pastry: Place the flour and salt in a mixing bowl, then rub in the butter until the mixture resembles breadcrumbs. Add the sour cream and the egg and mix to form a soft dough. Wrap in greaseproof paper and chill for at least 1 hour.

Filling: Melt the butter in a frying pan. Add the onion and cook gently until softened. Add the mushrooms and cook over high heat until all the liquid has evaporated. Add the salt, pepper and nutmeg. Set aside to cool. Combine the eggs with the cooled mushroom mixture, dill, rice and sour cream.

Divide the pastry into 4 pieces. Roll each piece out thinly and cut into 5 cm (2 inch) rounds with a pastry cutter. Put a teaspoonful of the filling onto each round, moisten the edges with a little beaten egg and fold the pastry over to form a crescent shape. Use a fork to press down the edges firmly to seal. Brush the piroshki with beaten egg to glaze and arrange on lightly greased baking sheets. Bake at 200°C (400°F/Gas 6) for about 10 to 15 minutes or until golden brown.

Rice Savoury Fingers

½ cup cooked rice
1 onion, finely chopped
1 tomato, finely chopped
2 slices ham or bacon, finely chopped
1 teaspoon curry powder
salt and pepper

Combine all ingredients and simmer gently for 10 minutes. Thicken with a little dissolved cornflour (cornstarch) if the sauce becomes very liquid. Serve hot on fried bread croûtons or toast fingers.

Pasta and Rice

Golden Risotto

Serves 3

45 g (1 ½ oz) butter
2 rashers bacon, chopped
1 small onion, chopped
2 cups diced pumpkin, butternut is ideal
1 cup (6 oz) rice
1 ½ cups (12 fl oz) stock, chicken or beef
grated Parmesan cheese
fresh parsley, to garnish

Heat butter and fry the bacon, onion and pumpkin for 2 minutes. Add the rice and toss for 1 minute. Add the stock, stir to blend, then bring to the boil. Cover, lower the heat and simmer for about 20 to 25 minutes. Remove the lid and allow to steam for 5 minutes. Toss with a fork, sprinkle with Parmesan cheese and parsley and serve.

Golden Rissotto

Rice Sardine Pizza

Serves 4

3 cups cooked rice
1 onion, grated
1 tablespoon margarine, melted
1 tomato, diced
1 tablespoon tomato paste
1 tablespoon chopped fresh parsley
2 x 105 g (3 ½ oz) cans sardines
lemon juice, to taste
salt and pepper
2 eggs, beaten
1 cup (8 fl oz) chicken stock, made with stock cubes

Garnish
1 cup (4 oz) grated cheese
1 tomato, sliced
½ green pepper (capsicum), cut in thin strips

Combine the rice, onion, margarine, tomato, tomato paste and parsley. Open the sardines, chop one can and add to the rice with the oil from the can. Reserve the second can whole. Add the lemon juice, salt and pepper to the rice. Blend the eggs with the chicken stock, add to the rice and mix thoroughly. Spoon the rice into a well greased 23 cm (9 inch) pie plate. Top with grated cheese. Bake at 180°C (350°F/Gas 4) for 25 minutes or until the mixture is firm. Lay the whole sardines in a wheel spoke design on the pie, alternating with the tomato slices and pepper strips. Sprinkle the sardines with oil from the can and bake for an extra 10 minutes.

Sunbrown Risotto

Serves 4

60 g (2 oz) butter or margarine
250 g (8 oz) sliced fresh mushrooms
6 spring onions (scallions) or 2 onions, chopped
¼ teaspoon dried oregano, basil or mixed herbs
2 tomatoes, chopped
salt and freshly ground pepper
3 cups cooked brown rice
1 cup (4 oz) grated cheese

Heat the butter and fry the mushrooms until just tender, reserving some for garnish. Add the spring onions, oregano, tomatoes, salt and pepper. Add the rice to the pan and toss with a large fork until heated. Lastly add the cheese and garnish with the reserved mushrooms. Serve with green salad.

Rice Athena

Rice Athena

Serves 6

- 1 cup (4 oz) dried apricots, chopped
- 1 cup (6 oz) sultanas
- 60 g (2 oz) butter or margarine
- 2 onions, thinly sliced
- 1 garlic clove, crushed
- 3 cups cooked chicken, cut into bite-sized pieces
- 2 tomatoes, peeled and chopped
- 6 cups cooked rice, rinsed and well drained
- salt and pepper
- 2 cups (16 fl oz) hot chicken stock, made with stock cubes
- grated rind of 1 lemon
- 1/4 teaspoon saffron threads or turmeric
- 1/4 cup (1 oz) slivered toasted almonds, to garnish

Soak the apricots and sultanas in boiling water for about half an hour. Preheat the frypan, add half the butter and fry the onions and garlic for a few minutes. Drain the fruit, pat dry, add to the pan and cook over moderate heat for 1 minute, then add the chicken and tomatoes and toss to heat. Remove the chicken/fruit mixture from the pan.

Add the remaining butter to the pan and spoon in half the cooked rice. Spoon half the chicken mixture over the rice and season with salt and pepper. Add the lemon rind and saffron to the chicken stock. Pour 1 cup (8 fl oz) of stock over the rice mixture and repeat layers with remaining ingredients. Reduce heat to low, cover and cook for about 4 to 5 minutes. Serve sprinkled with almonds.

Stuffed Tomatoes

Serves 4

- 4 large firm tomatoes
- 1/2 cup (2 oz) cheese
- 3/4 cup (1 1/2 oz) fresh breadcrumbs
- 15 g (1/2 oz) melted butter
- 1 green pepper (capsicum)
- 30 g (1 oz) butter
- 1 cup cooked rice
- 1/2 teaspoon Worcestershire sauce
- salt and pepper

Cut a 6 mm (1/4 inch) slice from the top of the tomatoes. Scoop out the pulp and discard. Place the tomatoes upside down on absorbent paper and leave for 30 minutes to drain. Combine one third of the cheese with the breadcrumbs and melted butter and set aside. Remove the seeds and membrane from the pepper and cut into 1.25 cm (1/2 inch) dice. Melt 30 g butter in a small saucepan, add the green pepper, cook gently for about 2 to 3 minutes. Place the rice in a mixing bowl, add the green pepper, remaining cheese, Worcestershire sauce, salt and pepper and mix lightly to combine. Lightly fill the tomatoes with the rice mixture, heaping slightly. Top with the reserved breadcrumb mixture. Place in a buttered baking dish and cover with lightly buttered greaseproof paper. Bake in a 180°C (350°F/Gas 4) oven for 10 minutes. Remove the paper and bake for a further 10 minutes.

Pasta and Rice

Irish Fried Rice

Serves 4

45 g (1 ½ oz) butter or margarine
4 spring onions (scallions), chopped
1 garlic clove, crushed
2 zucchini (courgettes), thinly sliced
2 stalks celery, chopped
1 green pepper (capsicum), chopped
3 cups cooked rice, refrigerated overnight
1 tablespoon chopped fresh parsley
salt and pepper
grated cheese, optional

Heat the butter and fry the spring onions, garlic and zucchini. Cook until the zucchini are almost tender, then add the celery and green pepper and toss for about 2 minutes. The vegetables should still be just crisp. Add the rice and parsley and toss well with a fork until heated thoroughly. Season to taste, add grated cheese if desired.

Gourmet Rice and Mushrooms

Serves 4

60 g (2 oz) butter
1 onion, finely chopped
250 g (8 oz) fresh button mushrooms, thinly sliced
1 cup (6 oz) rice
2 cups (16 fl oz) beef consommé or beef stock
1 tablespoon dry sherry
salt and pepper
chopped fresh chives or parsley

Heat the butter and fry the onion and mushrooms for 2 minutes. Add the rice and toss well with butter/mushroom mixture. Add the beef consommé, sherry and salt and pepper to taste. Cover and cook over low heat for about 20 to 25 minutes, until the rice is tender, adding a little extra hot liquid if needed. Serve sprinkled with chives.

Rice Royale

Serves 4

45 g (1 ½ oz) butter
1 cup sliced fresh mushrooms or 1 x 125 g can mushrooms
1 small onion, chopped or 4 spring onions (scallions), chopped
3 cups cooked rice
salt and pepper
1 teaspoon soy or Worcestershire sauce
chopped fresh chives, to garnish

Heat the butter and fry the onion and mushrooms for 2 minutes. Add the rice and toss well with butter/mushroom mixture. Add the beef consommé, sherry and salt and pepper to taste. Cover and cook over low heat for about 20 to 25 minutes, until the rice is tender, adding a little extra hot liquid if needed. Serve sprinkled with chives.

Cabbage Rolls in Tomato Cream Sauce

Serves 4

8 large cabbage leaves
4 tablespoons oil
3 large onions, finely chopped
2 teaspoons finely chopped garlic
500 g (1 lb) minced steak (ground beef)
1 cup (6 oz) rice
1 ½ teaspoons salt
¼ teaspoon black pepper
1 x 440 g (14 oz) can peeled tomatoes
1 tablespoon flour
15 g (½ oz) soft butter
315 ml (10 fl oz) sour cream

Soften the cabbage leaves by pouring boiling water over them in a large bowl, or steam them for a few minutes until slightly soft. Lay the leaves on a board and slice off some of the thick central leaf rib, without tearing the leaf.

Heat the oil, then fry the onions and garlic over low heat, stirring occasionally until soft and starting to turn golden. Remove from heat. Add one third of the onion mixture to the meat and rice. Add 1 teaspoon of salt and the pepper and mix well. Divide into 8 equal portions and form each into a compact roll. Wrap the meat mixture neatly in the cabbage leaves, turning the sides in and enclosing the meat completely.

Place the rolls in a saucepan and pour in water to almost cover the rolls. Simmer for 30 minutes. Carefully transfer to a greased ovenproof dish.

Add the tomatoes and remaining salt to the rest of the onion. Cover and simmer until the tomatoes are soft. Mix the flour and butter together and add to the sauce a little at a time, stirring constantly until it boils and thickens. Pour the tomato sauce over the rolls and bake, uncovered, at 180°C (350°F/Gas 4) for 10 minutes. Spoon the sour cream over the top and bake for about 15 minutes longer, until the top is bubbly. Serve hot.

Rice Pilaf with Spinach

Serves 4

½ cup (4 fl oz) oil
½ cup finely chopped onion
1 kg (2 lb) fresh spinach, washed and cut into small pieces or equivalent amount of frozen spinach
2 cups (16 fl oz) water
salt and pepper
1 cup (6 oz) rice, well washed

Heat the oil and fry the onion until transparent. Add the well-dried spinach and sauté until it softens. Pour in the water, season with the salt and pepper and simmer until the spinach is cooked. Add the rice, stir it in well with the spinach and onion and cook, covered, for about 15 to 20 minutes, until the water is absorbed and the rice cooked. Ten minutes before the rice is due to be served, take off the lid, put a thick cloth over the pan, replace the lid and fold the ends of the cloth above it, then finish cooking over very low heat. This will make the rice more fluffy. Serve hot as a vegetable dish.

Venetian Rice Ring

Serves 4

45 g (1½ oz) butter
2 rashers bacon, chopped
1 onion, chopped
1 cup fresh or frozen peas
2½ cups (20 fl oz) chicken stock
1 cup (6 oz) rice
2 tablespoons (1½ oz) grated Parmesan cheese

Heat the butter and sauté the bacon and onion for a few minutes. Add the peas and ½ cup (4 fl oz) of the stock and simmer for 10 minutes. Add the remaining stock, bring to the boil, then add the rice and stir. Cover and simmer on low heat until the rice is tender, about 25 minutes. Spoon the rice into a greased ring tin, press down firmly, then turn out onto a serving plate. Sprinkle with cheese. Ideal served with fish, chicken or veal.

Spiced Rice and Lentils

Serves 4

¼ teaspoon cumin
¼ teaspoon ground ginger
1 teaspoon turmeric
½ teaspoon cinnamon
salt and pepper
6 cardamom seeds
1 tablespoon margarine or oil
1 medium onion, finely chopped
1 cup small red lentils, washed well and soaked for 30 minutes in cold water
1 cup (6 oz) rice, washed well and drained
1 teaspoon salt
1 tablespoon mango chutney
4 cups (1 litre) hot water
2 bananas, sliced and sprinkled with lemon juice, to garnish

Mix the first 6 ingredients together to make the spice mixture. Melt the margarine in a deep, heavy based saucepan. Fry the onion until transparent, add the spice mixture and stir well, cooking over a low heat for 5 minutes. Drain the lentils and rice and add them separately to the mixture in the pan, stirring well so that every grain is well covered with the spice mixture and coated with oil. Add the salt and chutney and stir them into the mixture.

Pour in the water. There should be enough to cover the ingredients by about 2.5 cm (1 inch). Increase the heat until the water boils. Then lower the temperature and simmer for 15 to 20 minutes, stirring occasionally, until the water is absorbed. Test to see that the lentils and rice are both cooked. If necessary add a little more boiling water. When the rice and lentils are cooked (but the mixture is not sloppy), serve in bowls and garnish with the bananas.

Note: The traditional name for this is Khichri. It may be eaten with a meat or chicken curry. It may also be served with sliced cucumber in yoghurt, and with chutney. As in all Anglo-Indian recipes, the amount and proportion of spices may be changed to suit your taste.

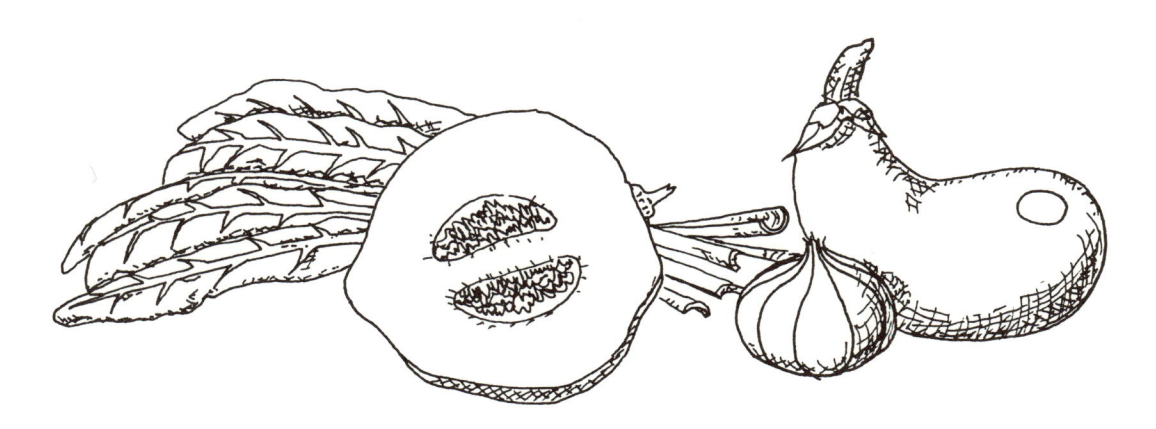

Pasta and Rice

Brown Rice Country Casserole

Serves 4

45 g (1 ½ oz) butter
1 cup chopped ham or bacon
1 cup chopped frozen or fresh spinach or cooked peas
1 green pepper (capsicum) chopped
1 onion, chopped
1 garlic clove, crushed
2 cups cooked brown rice
salt and pepper
½ teaspoon paprika
¼ teaspoon nutmeg
3 beaten eggs
1 cup (4 oz) grated cheese

Heat the butter, fry the ham for a few minutes, then add the spinach, green pepper, onion and garlic. Toss and cook for 2 minutes. Add the rice and seasonings, and cook for another few minutes. Place in a greased ovenproof dish and fold in the beaten eggs and half of the cheese. Top with the remaining cheese and bake at 180°C (350°F/Gas 4) until set, about 35 minutes.

Note: This dish is ideal served with grilled (broiled) chops or sausages. Tuna may be substituted for ham, simply add with the rice.

Creole Stuffed Tomatoes

Serves 6

6 large firm tomatoes
45 g (1 ½ oz) butter
1 small onion, chopped
1 garlic clove, crushed
125 g (4 oz) mushrooms, finely chopped
⅓ cup ham paste, optional
1 cup cooked rice
1 teaspoon Worcestershire sauce
salt and pepper
a little sugar
½ cup (2 oz) grated cheese

Cut the tops off the tomatoes, scoop out the flesh and drain the tomato shells on absorbent paper. Drain the pulp through a sieve, and reserve.

Heat the butter in a pan, add the onion, garlic and mushrooms and cook for a few minutes before adding the ham paste, rice and Worcestershire sauce. Remove from the heat, add the reserved tomato pulp, and salt and pepper.

Sprinkle a little sugar in the base of each tomato. Fill each tomato shell with the rice mixture and sprinkle with the cheese. Place the tomatoes in a well-greased ovenproof dish and bake at 180°C (350°F/Gas 4) for 15 to 20 minutes.

Italian Mushroom Risotto

Serves 6

60 g (2 oz) butter
1 onion, finely chopped
1 garlic clove, crushed
250 g (8 oz) mushrooms, sliced
2 cups (12 oz) rice
½ cup (4 fl oz) dry white wine or extra stock
1 tablespoon tomato paste
5 cups (1.25 litres) hot beef or chicken stock
extra 30 g (1 oz) butter
2 tablespoons (1 ½ oz) grated Parmesan cheese

Melt the butter in a frypan, and cook the onion and garlic until golden. Add the mushrooms and cook over low heat for 2 minutes. Add the rice, toss and cook for a few minutes. Add the wine, tomato paste and half the stock. Stir until it reaches boiling point. Allow to simmer over low heat, about 5 minutes, then add the remaining stock. Continue simmering until the rice is tender, about 20 to 25 minutes. Remove from heat and add the extra butter and the cheese and toss with a fork to blend.

Cheese and Rice Puffs

Makes about 15

1 cup cooked rice
15 g (½ oz) butter
1 tablespoon flour
¼ teaspoon salt
⅓ cup (2 ½ fl oz) milk
¾ cup (3 oz) grated cheese
¼ cup (2 fl oz) Worcestershire sauce
¼ teaspoon dry mustard
4 dashes of Tabasco sauce
1 egg
1 tablespoon milk
fine dry breadcrumbs
oil for deep frying

Place the rice in a medium-sized mixing bowl. Melt the butter in a small saucepan, add the flour and cook for 1 minute. Stir in the salt and milk and cook, stirring constantly, until very thick. Add the grated cheese to the sauce and simmer very gently until the cheese melts. Stir in the Worcestershire sauce, mustard and Tabasco sauce. Add the sauce to the rice and mix well. Chill until the rice mixture is firm and completely cold.

Lightly beat the egg with the milk. Shape the rice mixture into small balls about the size of a walnut. Dip into the egg mixture and then into the breadcrumbs. Deep fry the rice balls in hot oil until golden brown. Do not overcrowd the pan. Drain on absorbent paper. Serve with a spicy dipping sauce.

Note: If possible chill the rice balls for at least 1 hour after coating with breadcrumbs.

Opposite: *Italian Mushroom Risotto*

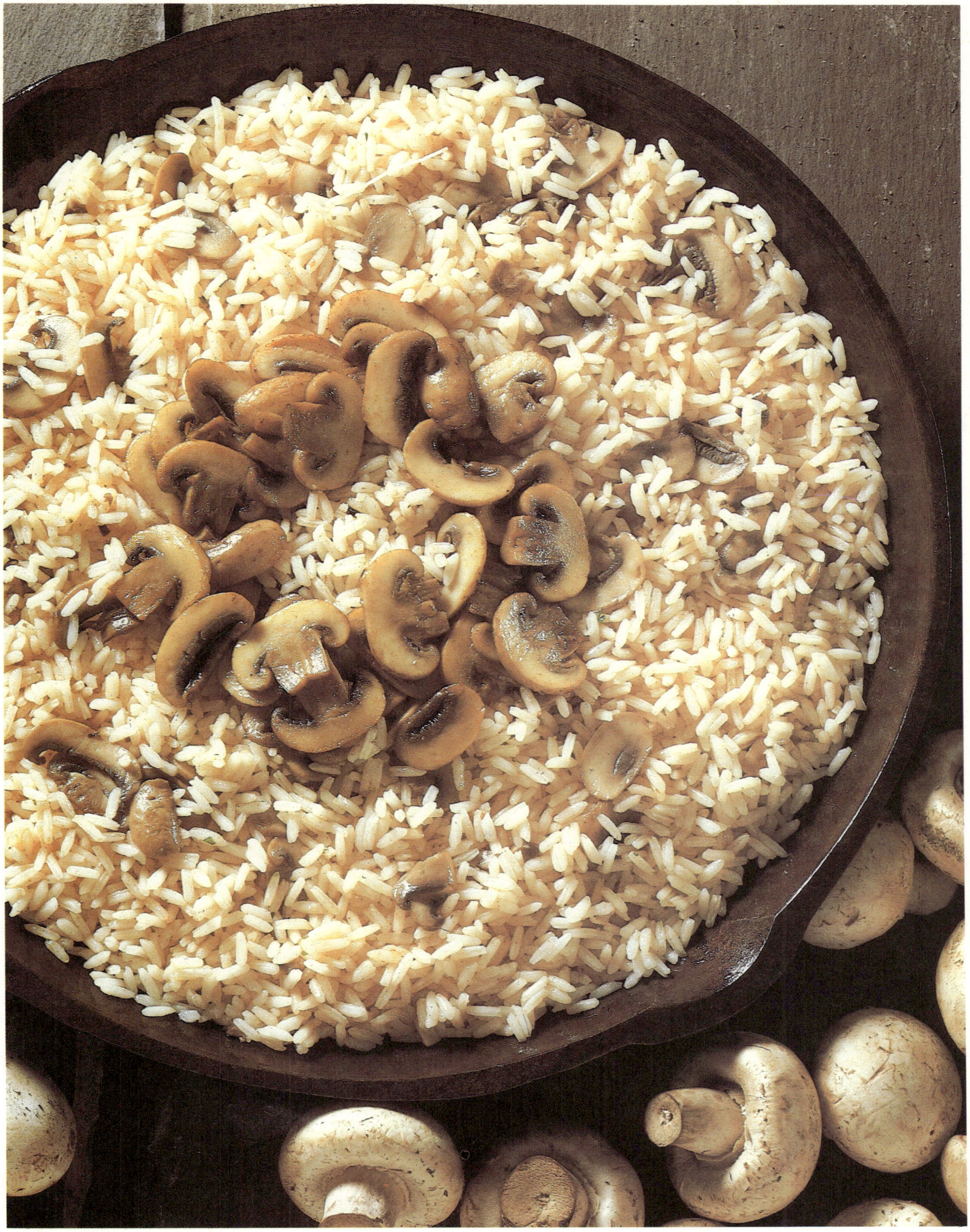

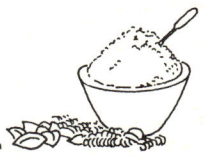

Pasta and Rice

Brown Rice O'Reilly

Serves 4

1 green pepper (capsicum), chopped
4 spring onions (scallions), chopped or
1 onion, chopped
45 g (1½ oz) butter
3 cups cooked brown rice
1 tablespoon chopped gherkins
1 tablespoon chopped stuffed olives or
1 tablespoon chopped fresh parsley
salt and pepper

Fry the green pepper and spring onions in butter until tender. Add the remaining ingredients and heat through thoroughly, tossing with a fork.

Fruity Rice Stuffing for Duck

30 g (1 oz) butter
1 garlic clove, crushed
1 medium onion, chopped
1 small green pepper (capsicum), chopped
1½ cups (9 oz) rice
⅓ cup (1½ oz) chopped dried apricots
⅓ cup (2 oz) chopped dates
⅓ cup (1½ oz) chopped walnuts
¼ cup (2 fl oz) dry white wine
a generous pinch each of salt, paprika and cinnamon

Melt the butter in a frying pan, add the garlic, onion and green pepper and cook until the onion has softened. Stir in the rice, dried fruits, nuts and wine and simmer for about 5 to 8 minutes. Season to taste with the salt, paprika and cinnamon. Allow to cool slightly. Fill the cavity of a large duck with the stuffing. Roast duck as usual.

Cuban Beans and Rice

Serves 4 – 6

30 g (1 oz) butter
1 medium onion, finely chopped
1 garlic clove, crushed
2 medium-sized tomatoes, peeled, seeded and chopped
1 green pepper (capsicum), seeded and diced
salt and pepper
1¼ cups (8 oz) rice
2 cups (16 fl oz) water
1 x 300 g (9½ oz) can kidney beans, drained

Melt the butter in a large saucepan and cook the onion and garlic until softened. Add the tomatoes and green pepper and cook until the mixture is quite thick and well blended. Season to taste with salt and pepper. Stir in the rice and water then cover and cook over a low heat for 20 minutes. Add the beans and heat through for 5 minutes.

Mexican Fried Rice

Serves 6

2 tablespoons oil
1 onion, chopped
3 rashers bacon, chopped
¼ teaspoon dried oregano
½ cup chopped red pepper (capsicum)
½ cup chopped green pepper (capsicum)
1 cup diced ham or salami sausage
1 cup corn kernels, drained
1 cup 3-bean-mix, drained
3 cups cooked rice, refrigerated overnight
1 cup (4 oz) diced cheese
dash of Tabasco sauce or chilli powder
salt and pepper

Heat the oil and fry the onion, bacon, oregano, chopped peppers, ham, corn and 3-bean-mix. Add the rice to the pan and toss with a fork until heated. Add the cheese, Tabasco, salt and pepper and toss lightly through the rice.

Egg and Bacon Rice

Serves 4

250 g (8 oz) bacon, chopped
2 tablespoons oil
4 cups cooked rice
60 g (2 oz) butter
4 eggs, beaten
1 cup chopped spring onions (scallions)
salt and pepper

Fry the chopped bacon in a wok or large frying pan until the fat is transparent. Remove the bacon from the pan. Heat the oil, add the rice and fry, tossing constantly, until very hot. Remove the rice from the pan. Heat the butter and fry the eggs, mixed with the spring onions and well seasoned with salt and pepper. Stir constantly until the eggs are cooked and set. Return the bacon and rice to the pan and mix all ingredients together, stirring and tossing until thoroughly combined. Taste and add more salt and pepper if necessary.

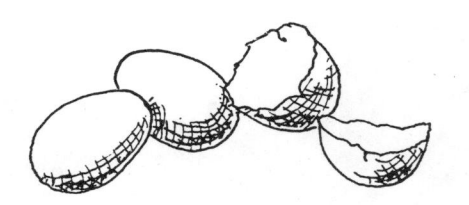

Rio Grande Fried Rice

Serves 6

- 3 tablespoons oil
- 3 rashers bacon, chopped
- 1 onion, chopped
- 1 garlic clove, crushed
- 1 green pepper (capsicum), chopped
- 2 teaspoons tomato paste
- dash of Tabasco sauce or chilli powder
- 6 cups cooked rice, refrigerated overnight
- 1 cup corn kernels, drained
- ½ cup (2 oz) diced cheese, to garnish
- 1 tomato, cut in wedges, to garnish

Heat the oil in a frypan, and sauté the bacon, onion, garlic and green pepper. Blend in the tomato paste and Tabasco sauce. Add the rice and toss to mix with a fork. Then add the corn and continue tossing until the rice is heated. Garnish with the cheese and tomato. Ideal with grilled (broiled) chops or sausages.

Egg Curry with Raisin Brown Rice

Serves 4

- 1 ½ cups (10 oz) brown rice
- ⅓ cup (2 oz) raisins
- 2 tablespoons oil
- 1 onion, thinly sliced
- 1 cup (4 oz) blanched almonds, slivered
- 3 teaspoons curry paste or curry powder
- 1 ¼ cups (10 fl oz) chicken stock
- 1 tablespoon cornflour (cornstarch)
- 1 tablespoon mango chutney
- ½ cup cooked peas
- ½ cup cooked sliced carrots
- 4 hard-boiled eggs

Cook rice by the absorption method (*page 307*). Add the raisins and toss mixture with a fork. Heat the oil in a frying pan and cook the onion and almonds until the onion is golden. Mix the onion and almonds into the rice and keep warm.

Blend the curry paste with a little of the stock then blend in the cornflour, chutney and remaining stock. Cook until the sauce thickens, then add the peas and carrots and simmer for 5 minutes. Peel and quarter the eggs, arrange on the rice and top with sauce.

Creole Casserole and Rice Puffs

Serves 4

- 2 tablespoons margarine
- 1 onion, chopped
- ½ green pepper (capsicum), chopped
- 1 cup chopped celery
- 1 x 410 g (13 oz) can tomatoes, retain liquid
- 2 beef stock cubes
- ½ cup (4 fl oz) water
- 1 tablespoon tomato sauce
- 2 teaspoons Worcestershire sauce
- ½ teaspoon dry mustard, chilli powder or paprika
- 2 cups any cooked meat or poultry, cubed
- salt and pepper
- 3 teaspoons cornflour (cornstarch), dissolved in a little water

Rice Puffs
- 1 stock cube
- ½ teaspoon garlic, onion or celery salt
- 1 egg, beaten
- 1 tablespoon milk
- 2 cups cooked rice
- ½ cup (2 oz) grated cheese

Heat the margarine and sauté the onion, green pepper and celery until tender. Add the tomatoes with liquid, beef stock cubes and water. Then add the tomato and Worcestershire sauces, mustard, meat, salt and pepper. Cover and simmer for 10 minutes. Add the blended cornflour and stir until the mixture boils and thickens.

Rice Puffs: Crumble the stock cube and add with the garlic salt to the beaten egg and milk. Add the egg mixture to the cooked rice with half the cheese. Stir with a fork until well blended.

To Assemble: Spoon the meat mixture into a shallow ovenproof dish. With wet hands, roll the Rice Puff mixture into small balls.

Drop the Rice Puffs onto the meat mixture and sprinkle with the remaining cheese. Bake at 180°C (350°F/Gas 4) for 15 minutes or until the cheese is golden.

Note: Rice Puff mixture may be spooned into the centre of the casserole if preferred.

Pasta and Rice

Fruity Fried Rice

Serves 4

1 tablespoon vegetable oil
3 rashers bacon, chopped
2 onions, finely chopped
½ cup (3 oz) chopped prunes or dried apricots
½ cup red or green pepper (capsicum), chopped
3 cups cooked brown rice
2 tomatoes, chopped, or 1 cup drained, chopped canned tomatoes
salt and pepper
1 cup diced cheese
a little chopped fresh parsley

Heat the oil and fry the bacon and onions until the onion is tender. Add the prunes and the red pepper, cook a few minutes then add the rice. Toss with a large fork until heated, then add the tomatoes and seasoning. Lastly add the cheese and parsley.

Tropical Touch Fried Rice

Serves 8

2 tablespoons peanut oil
6 spring onions (scallions) or 1 onion, chopped
1 cup chopped celery
6 cups cooked rice, refrigerated overnight
1 x 450 g (14 ½ oz) can crushed pineapple, well drained
2 cups diced cooked chicken
salt and pepper
¼ cup (1 oz) chopped peanuts or macadamia nuts

Heat the oil and fry the spring onions and celery for about 2 minutes. Add the rice and toss with a large fork. Add the pineapple and chicken and continue tossing until thoroughly heated. Season with salt and pepper and sprinkle with nuts.

Fried Mushroom Rice

Serves 6

60 g (2 oz) butter or margarine
1 cup chopped celery
3 rashers bacon, chopped
¼ teaspoon dried oregano or basil
1 onion or 4 spring onions (scallions), chopped
1 cup sliced mushrooms
3 cups cooked brown rice, drained for 30 minutes
1 x 310 g (10 oz) can corn kernels, drained
salt and pepper
1 cup diced Cheddar cheese

Heat the butter and sauté the celery, bacon, the oregano, onion and mushrooms until just tender. Add the rice, corn kernels, salt and pepper to taste. Toss until well heated. Add the cheese and serve immediately.

Siamese Fried Rice

Serves 6

3 tablespoons oil
1 garlic clove, crushed
2 teaspoons finely chopped fresh ginger or ground, to taste
125 g (4 oz) pork loin, thinly sliced, or chicken breast
125 g (4 oz) peeled fresh or canned prawns (shrimp)
6 cups cooked rice, refrigerated overnight
1 cup spring onions (scallions), chopped
1 tablespoon soy sauce
dash of Tabasco sauce or chilli powder, optional
2 eggs, lightly beaten

Garnish
2 tomatoes, sliced
½ cucumber, thinly sliced
4 spring onions (scallions), cut in thin strips

Preheat frypan, add the oil, garlic and ginger and cook for 1 minute. Add the pork and stir fry over high heat for about 2 to 3 minutes or until pork is well done. Less time is required if using chicken. Add half the prawns to the pan, reserve others for garnish. Add the rice, lower heat and continue to toss with a fork until the rice is heated. Add spring onions, soy sauce and Tabasco sauce. Gradually add the eggs to the rice and stir fry continuously until eggs are set. Place the reserved prawns in the centre of the frypan, surround with slices of tomato and cucumber and spring onion strips. Serve the rice straight from the frypan or arrange on a serving platter.

Rice Vegetable Loaf

Serves 6

2 rashers bacon, chopped
45 g (1 ½ oz) butter
3 cups cooked brown rice
4 spring onions (scallions) or 1 onion, chopped
½ cup chopped celery
½ cup corn kernels
1 cup grated carrot
¼ cup (1 oz) chopped nuts, peanuts or pecans
1 cup (4 oz) grated cheese
3 eggs, beaten
½ teaspoon paprika
salt and pepper

Brown the bacon in the butter. Pour bacon and drippings onto the rice, then add the next 5 ingredients. Add ½ cup (2 oz) of the cheese with the beaten eggs, paprika, salt and pepper and blend the mixture thoroughly. Spoon into a well greased medium-sized loaf tin and sprinkle remaining cheese on top. Bake at 180°C (350°F/Gas 4) for about 45 minutes or until firm. Allow to stand for 10 minutes, then turn out carefully. Serve with a tossed salad, or as an accompaniment for casseroles.

Opposite: *Siamese Fried Rice*

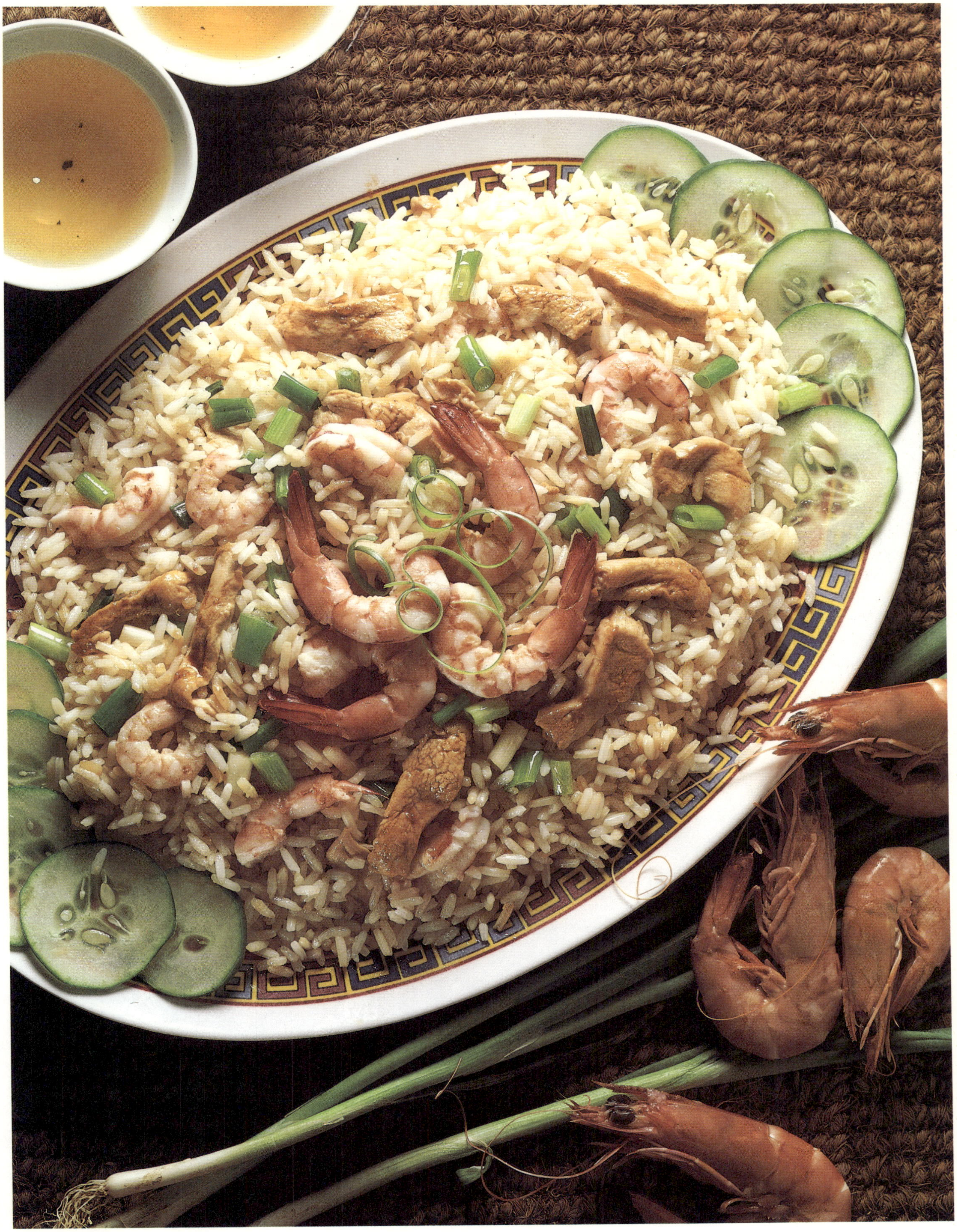

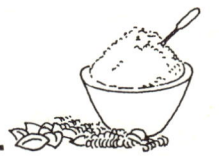

Pasta and Rice

Meatballs with Curry Fruit Sauce

Serves 4

750 g (1½ lb) minced steak (ground beef)
1 egg, beaten
½ cup cooked rice

Curry Sauce
1 tablespoon peanut oil
1 onion, finely chopped
1 garlic clove, crushed
3 teaspoons curry powder, or to taste
1 x 410 g (13 oz) can tomatoes
1 beef stock cube

1 teaspoon curry powder
salt and pepper
oil for frying

1 tablespoon (½ oz) brown sugar
1 tablespoon vinegar
1 tablespoon (1 oz) apricot jam
1 apple, peeled and diced
½ cup (3 oz) sultanas

Banana Rice
1 tablespoon margarine
2 bananas, thinly sliced
3 cups hot, cooked rice

1 tablespoon (½ oz) peanuts

Meatballs: Mix together the mince, egg, rice, curry powder and salt and pepper. Blend thoroughly and shape into small meatballs. Heat the oil in a frying pan and sauté the meatballs until they are brown on all sides. Remove meatballs and reserve.

Curry Sauce: Add more oil to the pan and sauté the onion and garlic for 2 minutes then add the curry powder and cook for 1 minute, stirring to develop the flavour. Add the remaining Curry Sauce ingredients. Replace the meatballs in the Curry Sauce, cover and simmer for about 25 minutes. Serve over Banana Rice.

Banana Rice: Sauté the banana slices in the margarine and toss through the rice. Garnish with peanuts.

Note: For special occasions, place the meatballs on small skewers and grill (broil). Simmer the sauce for 25 minutes. Place skewered meatballs on the rice and spoon over the Curry Sauce.

Beef Apricot Rolls

Serves 4

500 g (1 lb) thinly sliced topside or round steak
2 rashers bacon
2 spring onions (scallions) or 1 small onion, chopped
salt and pepper
flour

45 g (1½ oz) butter
1 x 470 g (15 oz) can apricot nectar
1 packet French onion soup mix
2 teaspoons Worcestershire sauce
chopped fresh parsley

Pound the steak with a meat mallet to flatten, then cut into 8 even-sized pieces about 10 cm (4 inch) square. Finely chop the bacon and sauté in a hot pan with the spring onions. Season the meat with salt and pepper, then spoon a little bacon and spring onion onto each piece. Roll up and secure with toothpicks or string. Roll in the flour and sauté in hot butter until golden brown. Place the beef rolls in a greased ovenproof dish. Combine the apricot nectar, onion soup mix and Worcestershire sauce and pour over the rolls. Cover and bake at 190°C (375°F/Gas 5) for about 1 hour or until tender. Serve on brown rice.

Minute Beef 'n' Walnuts

Serves 4

1 packet French onion soup
1½ cups (12 fl oz) water
1 tablespoon Worcestershire sauce
2 tablespoons tomato paste
¼ teaspoon sugar
60 g (2 oz) butter
2 large green peppers (capsicum), cut into strips

½ cup (1½ oz) halved walnuts
750 g (1½ lb) topside steak, trimmed and cut into fine strips

Noodle Rice
125 g (4 oz) butter
1 cup fine uncooked vermicelli noodles

4 cups cooked rice
1 tablespoon salt
freshly ground pepper

Place the soup, water, Worcestershire sauce, tomato paste and sugar in a saucepan, bring to the boil, and then reduce the heat and simmer for 5 minutes. Melt the butter in a large, heavy based pan and sauté the peppers and walnuts quickly until crisply cooked. Remove. Add the beef and hot sauce and stir over high heat until the meat is cooked, about 5 minutes. Return the peppers and walnuts to the pan and serve immediately with Noodle Rice.

Kofta Curry (Meatballs)

Serves 4

Meatballs
- 500 g (1 lb) minced meat (ground beef)
- 1 onion, finely chopped
- ½ teaspoon minced fresh ginger
- 1 teaspoon garam masala, optional
- 2 garlic cloves, crushed
- ½ cup finely chopped green pepper (capsicum)
- 1 teaspoon salt
- freshly ground pepper
- 1 tablespoon finely chopped fresh mint
- oil for frying

Sauce
- 45 g (1 ½ oz) ghee or butter
- 2 onions, finely chopped
- 2 garlic cloves, crushed
- 1 teaspoon minced fresh ginger
- 2 tomatoes, peeled and chopped
- 1 cup (8 fl oz) beef stock, made with stock cubes
- ¼ teaspoon chilli powder or paprika
- 1 teaspoon garam masala, optional
- ½ teaspoon turmeric
- ½ cup (4 fl oz) yoghurt
- salt and pepper
- a little extra chopped fresh mint

Combine all the meatball ingredients. Blend well and shape with wet hands into small balls about the size of walnuts. Heat the oil and fry the meatballs until brown.

Remove and drain away the oil. Heat the ghee in the same pan, add the onions, garlic, ginger, tomatoes, stock, chilli powder, garam masala and turmeric. Cover the sauce with a lid and simmer for about 25 minutes. Replace the meatballs and simmer for another 15 minutes. Lastly stir in the yoghurt and season. Serve Kofta on hot rice and sprinkle with chopped mint.

Chinese Beef Strips

Seraves 4

- 500 g (1 lb) good quality beef, fillet, rump or round
- 1 tablespoon cornflour (cornstarch)
- 1 teaspoon salt
- 1 egg white
- 4 tablespoons peanut oil
- 2 onions, cut in very thin strips
- 1 tablespoon dry sherry
- 1 tablespoon (¼ oz) sugar
- 1 tablespoon soy sauce

Pound the beef with the back of a large knife to flatten. Cut into thin strips, 5 cm (2 inch) long by 6 mm (¼ inch) wide. Toss the beef strips in the cornflour, salt and egg white and allow to stand for 5 minutes. Heat the oil and fry the onions until just soft. Remove, add the beef and deep fry for 30 seconds. Drain away most of the oil, leaving 1 tablespoon. Replace the onions, add the sherry, sugar and soy sauce and heat well.

Serve over steamed rice.

Beef Curry (Mild)

Serves 4

- 1 kg (2 lb) chuck or blade steak
- 2 tablespoons oil
- 2 onions, finely chopped
- 1 garlic clove, crushed
- 1 tablespoon curry powder, or to taste
- 1 tablespoon (1 oz) brown sugar
- 1 tablespoon vinegar or lemon juice
- 1 cup (8 fl oz) stock, made with beef cubes
- salt
- ½ cup (4 fl oz) coconut milk or extra stock

Cut the meat into 5 cm (2 inch) cubes. Heat the oil, add the onions and garlic and fry for 2 minutes. Add the curry powder and cook over gentle heat, stirring until a strong aroma arises. Add the sugar and vinegar, then add the meat and toss until well coated with the curry mixture. Add the beef stock and salt to taste. Reduce heat, cover and simmer until the meat is quite tender. Add the coconut milk and simmer until heated through.

Serve with Yellow Rice (*page 308*).

Beef with Broccoli

Serves 4

- 500 g (1 lb) good quality beef, rump or round
- 1 tablespoon cornflour (cornstarch)
- 1 teaspoon salt
- 1 egg white
- 4 tablespoons peanut oil
- 2 onions, cut in wedges
- 1 red pepper (capsicum), cut into squares
- 250 g (8 oz) broccoli, broken into florets and finely sliced
- 1 tablespoon dry sherry
- 1 tablespoon hoi sin sauce
- 1 cup (8 fl oz) water
- 2 beef stock cubes
- extra 3 teaspoons cornflour (cornstarch), dissolved in a little water

Pound the beef with the back of a large knife to flatten out and cut the meat into thin strips. Combine the cornflour, salt and egg white with 1 tablespoon of the oil. Add to the beef in the bowl, toss to blend well, and allow to stand for about 30 minutes.

Heat the remaining oil in a pan and stir fry the onions, pepper, and broccoli until just crisp, not soft. Remove the vegetables and stir fry the beef for about 1 minute.

Drain off all but 1 tablespoon of the oil and replace the vegetables and all the remaining ingredients. Stir until it boils and thickens. Serve spooned over steamed rice.

Pasta and Rice

Rice Lasagne

Serves 8 – 10

3 cups cooked rice

Italian Sauce
1 medium-sized eggplant (aubergine) or
1 kg (2 lb) minced steak (ground beef)
4 tablespoons oil
1 cup chopped onions
2 garlic cloves, crushed
½ teaspoon ground basil or ground oregano
1 x 815 g (1 lb 10 oz) can peeled tomatoes
2 tablespoons (1 oz) brown sugar
½ cup (4 fl oz) red wine or beef stock made with stock cubes
3 tablespoons tomato paste
1 teaspoon salt
freshly ground pepper
250 g (8 oz) sliced cooked mushrooms or canned mushrooms

Cheese Filling
2 eggs, beaten
2 tablespoons chopped fresh parsley
½ cup (4 fl oz) sour cream or evaporated milk
1 ½ teaspoons salt
freshly ground pepper
500 g (1 lb) cottage or ricotta cheese
½ cup (2 oz) grated Parmesan cheese
250 g (8 oz) mozarella cheese, sliced
red and green pepper (capsicum) strips, to garnish
stuffed olives, to garnish

Italian Sauce: Cut the eggplant into small cubes, sprinkle with salt, cover and stand for 30 minutes. Drain away the liquid and pat dry. Heat the oil and fry the eggplant until just golden. Drain and set aside. (If using minced steak, add extra oil if needed and cook the mince, breaking up with a fork, over moderate heat.) Add the remaining sauce ingredients and simmer, uncovered, for about 35 to 40 minutes, stirring occasionally.

Cheese Filling: Thoroughly blend all cheese filling ingredients except for the mozarella slices and grated Parmesan.

Assembly: Grease an extra large, shallow ovenproof dish. Spread half the Italian Sauce on the base, spoon over half the rice, then half the cheese filling and the cheese slices. Repeat the layers. Sprinkle the surface with Parmesan cheese. Bake at 180°C (350°F/Gas 4) for 35 to 40 minutes. During the last 5 minutes of baking garnish with red and green pepper strips and stuffed olives. Allow to stand for 10 to 15 minutes after baking and then cut into squares.

Rice Shepherds Pie

Serves 4

1 tablespoon peanut oil
500 g (1 lb) minced steak (ground beef)
1 onion, chopped,
1 beef stock cube
1 tablespoon tomato sauce
1 teaspoon soy sauce
1 x 125 g (4 oz) can mushrooms
salt and pepper
1 egg, beaten with ⅓ cup (2½ fl oz) milk
3 cups cooked rice
2 tomatoes, sliced
½ cup (2 oz) grated cheese

Heat the oil and sauté the meat and onion, breaking up mince with a fork. Crumble the stock cube into the mince, then add the tomato sauce, soy sauce, mushrooms and salt and pepper to taste. Cook over low heat until the mince is tender. Add the beaten egg and milk to the rice and spoon half of the rice into an ovenproof dish. Cover with the meat mixture and lay half of the tomato slices on the meat. Top with the remaining rice. Garnish with the remaining tomato slices and sprinkle with the cheese. Bake at 180°C (350°F/Gas 4) for 25 minutes until heated and cheese is golden.

Note: Finely chopped cooked meat (roast lamb or beef) may replace the mince. Add ½ cup (4 fl oz) water to the meat with the onion and simmer for 5 minutes to blend the flavour.

Barbecue Spare Ribs

Serves 4

750 g (1½ lb) spare ribs
1 x 375 g (12 oz) can sweet and sour sauce
2 teaspoons chilli sauce
1 tablespoon Worcestershire sauce
1 tablespoon tomato paste
1 tablespoon soy sauce
1 x 450 g (14½ oz) can crushed pineapple, drained

Lemon Rice
2 cups (12 oz) rice
grated rind of 1 lemon
15 g (½ oz) butter

Trim excess fat from the spare ribs and place them in a shallow dish. Mix the next 5 ingredients and pour them over the spare ribs. Allow to marinate in the refrigerator for at least 1 hour or overnight if possible.

Lift the spare ribs out of the marinade and barbecue or grill (broil), using extra marinade as a baste. Cook until golden brown. Add the crushed pineapple to the remaining marinade, heat and serve spooned over the spare ribs on a bed of Lemon Rice.

Lemon Rice: Rapid boil the rice (*page 307*). Drain well then toss the lemon rind and butter through the rice.

Mexicani Mince

Serves 4

1 tablespoon peanut oil
500 g (1 lb) minced steak (ground beef)
½ packet dry onion soup mix
¾ cup (6 fl oz) water
2 teaspoons brown sugar

1 tablespoon tomato paste
1 cup corn kernels
¼ teaspoon chilli powder or paprika, to taste
salt and pepper
tomato wedges, to garnish
onion rings, to garnish

Pronto Rice

15 g (½ oz) butter
3 cups cooked rice
½ cup chopped green pepper (capsicum)
4 stuffed olives, sliced

Heat the oil in a frypan and brown the meat, using a fork to break up the lumps. Sprinkle the soup mix over the meat then add the water, sugar, tomato paste, corn and chilli powder. Check the seasoning and simmer for 10 to 15 minutes or until the meat is tender. Melt the butter and toss the rice, green pepper and olives until heated. Spoon the rice onto a serving plate, top with the meat and garnish with the tomato wedges and thinly sliced onion rings.

Note: Orange segments may be used instead of onion rings.

Mini Meat Loaves with Rice

Serves 4

¾ cup cooked rice
1 onion, finely chopped
2 teaspoons curry powder or 1 teaspoon paprika
1 egg, beaten
2 teaspoons soy sauce
500 g (1 lb) minced meat (ground beef)

1 teaspoon salt
freshly ground pepper
grated rind of 1 lemon
¼ cup (1 ½ oz) sultanas
1 tablespoon melted butter
a little sweet fruit chutney or tomato sauce

Lightly combine the rice, onion, curry powder, egg and soy sauce. Add this mixture to the meat with the salt, pepper, lemon rind and sultanas. Pat into a round loaf and cut into quarters. Shape into 4 small meat loaves, round, oval or square. Brush the tops with the melted butter, place in a greased baking dish and bake at 180°C (350°F/Gas 4) for 35 minutes. When cooked, top each with about 1 tablespoon of chutney and return to the oven for 5 minutes to glaze. Serve on a bed of rice.

Mexicani Rice

Pasta and Rice

Saturday Supper Rice Pie
Serves 4

45 g (1½ oz) butter
3 cups cooked rice
1 cup (4 oz) chopped peanuts
½ cup chopped celery
1 cup cooked chopped chicken, beef, lamb or tuna
1 cup corn kernels, drained
3 eggs, beaten
1 onion, chopped
1 tablespoon chopped fresh parsley
½ teaspoon dried oregano or sage
salt and pepper
1 cup (4 oz) grated cheese
tomato slices or egg slices, to garnish
sprigs of parsley, to garnish

Combine all the ingredients except the cheese and the tomato slices. Press into a well-greased 20 cm (8 inch) pie plate and sprinkle the surface with the grated cheese. Bake at 180°C (350°F/Gas 4) for about 25 minutes. Garnish with the tomato slices and parsley sprigs. Cut in wedges and serve with tossed salad.

Rice and Pepper Pinwheel
Serves 4

1 cup (8 fl oz) water
½ teaspoon salt
1 beef stock cube
2 green peppers (capsicums), quartered, seeds removed
250 g (8 oz) minced steak (ground beef)
1 tablespoon peanut oil
1 onion, chopped
1 tablespoon tomato sauce
½ cup corn kernels or cooked peas
pinch of dried oregano or paprika or garlic salt
salt and pepper
3 cups cooked rice
½ cup (2 oz) grated cheese

Combine the water, salt and stock cube in a saucepan, add the green pepper quarters, bring to the boil and boil for 5 minutes. Drain and reserve the liquid. Place the green pepper quarters in a well-greased shallow baking dish.

Brown the minced steak in hot oil, breaking it up with a fork, then add the onion, tomato sauce, corn, oregano, salt and pepper. Simmer the mince for 10 minutes. Then combine the meat mixture with the rice, add the green pepper liquid and toss with a fork until well blended.

Preheat the oven to 180°C (350°F/Gas 4) for at least 2 minutes. Spoon the rice mixture onto the peppers, mounding towards the centre so the edges of the peppers are visible. Sprinkle with the cheese, place the dish on an oven tray and bake for 25 minutes until the cheese is golden. Remove the dish from the oven immediately.

Note: Four thickly sliced tomatoes may be used instead of the green peppers.

Cheesy Rice Franks
Serves 4

8 large frankfurts
15 g (½ oz) butter
1 onion, chopped
1 red pepper (capsicum), seeded and chopped
1 green pepper (capsicum), seeded and chopped
salt and pepper
2 cups cooked rice
1 large tomato, chopped
1 tablespoon chopped fresh parsley
1 cup (4 oz) finely grated cheese

Place the frankfurts in boiling water and cook for 5 minutes. Drain them, then slit each lengthwise without cutting right through to the base, open out and place on a serving dish. Set aside.

Melt the butter, and sauté the onion and chopped peppers for a few minutes. Season with salt and pepper, then add the rice, tomato and parsley and stir until well combined. Top each frankfurt with a spoonful of the rice mixture and sprinkle with the cheese. Place in a 180°C (350°F/Gas 4) oven and heat until the cheese begins to melt. Serve with a tossed salad and a crusty French loaf.

Riverina Rice Meat Loaf
Serves 4

4½ cups cooked rice
750 g (1½ lb) minced steak (ground beef)
2 beef stock cubes
¼ cup (2 fl oz) boiling water
1 tablespoon soy sauce
1 tablespoon tomato sauce
1 apple, peeled and grated
½ cup (3 oz) sultanas
½ cup cottage cheese
1 egg, beaten
salt and pepper
15 g (½ oz) butter
extra 1 tablespoon sultanas
1 red-skinned apple, chopped

Glaze
2 tablespoons tomato sauce
1 tablespoon brown sugar
2 tablespoons vinegar
1 teaspoon sweet fruit chutney

Mix 1½ cups of the rice with the minced steak. Blend the stock cubes, boiling water, soy sauce and tomato sauce and add to the meat with the next 5 ingredients. Mix well and spoon into a greased loaf pan. Combine the glaze ingredients and spoon 1 tablespoon over the meat. Bake at 180°C (350°F/Gas 4) for about 1 hour. Stand for 5 minutes, then turn out onto a serving plate.

Heat the remaining 3 cups rice in the butter with 1 tablespoon sultanas and the apple. Surround the meat loaf with rice. Heat the glaze and spoon over the meat loaf before serving.

Rice with Red Beans

Serves 6

250 g (8 oz) dried red kidney beans
10 cups (2.5 litres) cold water
1 cup finely chopped onion
2 teaspoons salt
¼ teaspoon freshly ground black pepper
1 garlic clove, finely chopped
1 small cinnamon stick
3 tablespoons vegetable oil or 60 g (2 oz) butter
2 ½ cups (1 lb) rice
salt

Wash the beans well, then cover with cold water and leave to soak overnight. When ready to cook, drain, cover with the fresh cold water and bring to the boil. Add the onion, salt, pepper, garlic and cinnamon, cover and simmer until tender but not mushy, about 30 to 40 minutes. Drain the beans, reserving the liquid. If necessary add water to make up to 4 cups (1 litre) liquid.

In another saucepan, heat 2 tablespoons of the oil and fry the rice for 4 or 5 minutes, stirring all the time. Add the reserved bean liquid, the extra salt, stir well and bring to the boil. Cover with a well fitting lid, turn heat as low as possible and cook for 20 minutes without stirring. The rice should absorb all the liquid. Uncover and fluff gently with a fork.

Heat the remaining tablespoon of oil and fry the beans, stirring gently with a metal spoon to avoid crushing them. When they are heated through serve either tossed with the rice or on top of the rice.

Family Favourite Meatballs

Serves 4

750 (1 ½ lb) minced steak (ground beef)
1 cup cooked rice
1 small onion, grated
1 egg, beaten

2 tablespoons tomato sauce
1 tablespoon soy or Worcestershire sauce
1 teaspoon salt
pepper

Sauce
1 cup (8 fl oz) tomato purée
½ cup beef stock, made with stock cubes
1 tablespoon brown sugar
¼ teaspoon dried basil, oregano or mixed herbs
1 tablespoon chopped fresh parsley
1 x 190 g (6 oz) can whole champignons, optional

Combine all the meatball ingredients and blend well. With wet hands shape into small meatballs. Combine the first 4 ingredients for the sauce. Stir, bring to the boil, then simmer for 5 minutes. Add the meatballs to the sauce and simmer, covered, for about 45 to 50 minutes or until tender. Sprinkle the meatballs with parsley and serve with Cheese Fried Rice (*page 310*). Canned whole champignons may be added to the sauce.

Creole Jambalaya

Serves 6

45 g (1 ½ oz) butter
2 cups (12 oz) rice
1 green pepper (capsicum), chopped
2 onions, thinly sliced
1 garlic clove, crushed
1 cup cooked diced chicken
1 cup peeled prawns (shrimp)
1 cup cubed ham
1 cup canned peeled tomatoes
3 cups (24 fl oz) chicken stock
2 teaspoons Worcestershire sauce
pinch of cayenne pepper or dash of Tabasco sauce
4 teaspoons tomato paste
salt and pepper
chopped fresh parsley

Melt the butter and fry the rice, green pepper, onions and garlic for 2 minutes, tossing well to coat the rice with butter. Add the remaining ingredients and stir well to blend. Cover and cook over low heat for about 20 to 25 minutes. Remove the lid, and allow to stand for 5 minutes. If required, place in a 180°C (350°F/Gas 4) oven to dry out for about 5 minutes.

Spicy Beef and Rice Casserole

Serves 4

1 tablespoon oil
1 medium-sized onion, chopped
1 green pepper (capsicum), chopped
500 g (1 lb) minced (ground beef)
500 g (1 lb) ripe tomatoes, peeled, seeded and chopped
1 garlic clove, crushed
1 teaspoon salt
pepper
1 teaspoon mild chilli powder, or to taste
1 cup (6 oz) rice
1 x 310 g (10 oz) can corn kernels, drained
½ cup (2 oz) grated cheese
paprika

Heat the oil in a heavy based frying pan and add the onion and green pepper. Cook until softened, then stir in the minced beef. Cook until the meat is browned and crumbly. Add the tomatoes, garlic, salt, pepper and chilli powder. Bring to the boil and simmer, uncovered, for 15 minutes. Meanwhile, cook the rice, then add to the meat mixture together with the corn. Spoon into a 2 litre (8 cup) casserole dish and sprinkle with the cheese. Bake, uncovered, at 180°C (350°F/Gas 4) for 30 minutes. Sprinkle with paprika just before serving.

Pasta and Rice

Cowra Lamb Casserole
Serves 6

- 15 g (½ oz) butter
- 6 lamb chops, excess fat removed
- 2 onions, sliced
- 1 cup (6 oz) rice
- 1 x 425 g (13½ oz) can tomatoes
- chicken or beef stock made with stock cubes
- 1 bay leaf
- salt and pepper
- 1 tablespoon (½ oz) brown sugar
- 2 slices bread, cut in small dice
- ½ cup (2 oz) grated cheese
- extra butter

Heat butter in pan, brown the chops on both sides and put aside. Fry the onions until just tender, remove and reserve. Place rice in greased ovenproof dish. Drain tomatoes, and add sufficient chicken stock to tomato liquid to make up 2 cups (16 fl oz). Bring the stock to boiling point, add bay leaf, salt and pepper and pour over the rice. Place the chops on the rice, top with onion slices, top with roughly chopped tomatoes and brown sugar. Cover and cook in 180°C (350°F/Gas 4) oven for about 35 minutes or until the rice and chops are tender. Combine the bread and cheese and sprinkle over the chops. Dot with butter and bake until the cheese melts.

Lemon Lamb Casserole
Serves 6

- 750 g (1½ lb) best end neck chops
- flour
- 2 tablespoons peanut oil
- 2 onions, sliced
- 1 cup (8 fl oz) chicken stock, made with stock cubes
- 1 teaspoon salt
- freshly ground pepper
- 1 bay leaf
- ½ lemon, thinly sliced
- 1 carrot, sliced
- 2 zucchini (courgettes), sliced
- lemon slices
- parsley sprigs

Buttered Rice Border

- 2 cups cooked rice
- 1 tablespoon melted butter
- 1 egg, beaten
- 1 tablespoon chopped fresh parsley
- salt and pepper

Dust the chops evenly with flour, and brown both sides in hot oil. Place in casserole, add the onions, chicken stock, salt and pepper, bay leaf and lemon slices. Cover and simmer gently for about 1½ hours until tender. Add the carrot and cook for another 15 minutes. Then add the zucchini and cook for an extra 10 minutes. Place in a deep oval or round ovenproof dish.

Combine the rice, melted butter, egg, parsley and seasoning. Spoon rice mixture around border of casserole. Bake uncovered at 190°C (375°F/Gas 5) for 15 minutes. Serve garnished with lemon slices and parsley sprigs.

This casserole may be prepared in advance and the rice border added after reheating.

Lamb Kebabs with Fruity Rice
Serves 4

- 750 g (1½ lb) boneless lamb, from leg or shoulder
- 1 onion, grated
- 1½ cups (12 fl oz) apricot nectar
- 1 tablespoon lemon juice
- 1 tablespoon (½ oz) brown sugar
- 2 tablespoons tomato sauce
- 2 tablespoons oil
- 1 teaspoon curry powder
- salt and pepper
- ¼ cup (1½ oz) sultanas
- ¼ cup (2 fl oz) orange juice
- 1½ cups (8 oz) rice
- ½ teaspoon grated orange rind
- 15 g (½ oz) butter

Cut the lamb into cubes. Combine the next 8 ingredients and put 1½ cups (12 fl oz) of this mixture in a pan and simmer until thick. Reserve this sauce to serve with the kebabs. Add the lamb to the remainder of the mixture and marinate for at least 30 minutes. Soak the sultanas in the orange juice. Cook the rice by absorption method (*page 307*) and 10 minutes before the end of cooking top with the soaked sultanas, rind and butter.

Thread the lamb onto skewers and grill (broil) or barbecue for about 12 to 15 minutes, basting with marinade and turning often. Mix the sultanas through the rice and pile on a platter. Top with the kebabs and reserved sauce.

Spicy Lamb Pilaf
Serves 4

- 750 g (1½ lb) lamb forequarter chops
- 2 tablespoons oil
- 2 onions, sliced
- 1 garlic clove, crushed
- 3 cardamom pods
- 1 teaspoon ground cinnamon
- ½ teaspoon ground turmeric
- 1 cup (6 oz) rice
- 15 g (½ oz) butter
- 1 cup (8 fl oz) stock
- salt
- freshly ground black pepper
- 1 cup (6 oz) sultanas
- grated rind of ½ lemon
- 2 teaspoons honey
- juice of ½ lemon
- lemon slices, to garnish
- toasted almonds or pine nuts, to garnish

Remove fat and bone from the chops and cut into small cubes. Heat oil in pan and cook meat, onions, garlic and spices over moderate heat for about 5 minutes, tossing all the time. Add the stock, salt and pepper, sultanas and lemon rind. Cover and simmer over moderate heat until the rice and meat are tender. Lastly add the honey and lemon juice and toss through with a fork. Steam for 5 minutes before serving. Garnish with the lemon slices, almonds or pine nuts.

Spring Rice and Lamb

Serves 4

2 cups (12 oz) rice
4 cups (1 litre) chicken stock, made with stock cubes
½ teaspoon ground turmeric
salt and pepper
45 g (1½ oz)) butter
3 onions, thinly sliced
1 garlic clove, crushed
2 cups diced, cooked spring lamb
grated rind of 1 lemon
½ cup (3 oz) currants or sultanas
2 tomatoes, peeled and chopped
½ cup (4 fl oz) yoghurt or sour cream
¼ cup (1 oz) chopped toasted almonds or pine nuts

Combine the rice, chicken stock and turmeric. Bring to the boil, cover and simmer over low heat for about 20 to 25 minutes or until just tender. Uncover and allow to steam for 5 minutes. Season to taste with salt and pepper.

While the rice is cooking, prepare the other ingredients. Heat the butter and cook the onions and garlic until tender. Add the lamb to the pan with the lemon rind, currants and tomatoes. Toss until ingredients are heated. Add the rice to the pan and toss with a fork to blend thoroughly. Add extra butter if needed. Top with yoghurt and sprinkle with nuts.

Lamb Rice Salad

Serves 6

4 cups cooked rice
2 cups cooked lamb, cut into thin strips
½ cup (3 oz) sultanas
½ cup (3 oz) peanuts
salt and pepper
2 red-skinned apples, thinly sliced
juice of ½ lemon
½ cup (4 fl oz) mayonnaise or salad dressing
½ teaspoon curry powder, or to taste

Combine the rice, lamb, sultanas and peanuts. Season with salt and pepper. Toss the apple slices in the lemon juice and add to the rice, reserving a few for garnish. Blend the mayonnaise and curry powder, add to the rice and toss well. Garnish with the reserved apple slices.

Rice with Lamb and Chickpeas

Serves 6

½ cup (3 oz) dried chickpeas, soaked overnight
2½ cups (1 lb) rice
90 g (3 oz) ghee or butter
500 g (1 lb) lean lamb, cubed
2 large onions, finely chopped
3 teaspoons salt
½ teaspoon ground black pepper
1 teaspoon ground cumin
½ teaspoon ground cinnamon
5 cups (1.25 litres) hot water

Rinse the chickpeas, put into a saucepan with water to cover, bring to the boil and boil for 2 minutes. Remove from heat and leave to soak overnight.

Wash the rice and drain well. Heat the ghee in a large, heavy saucepan and brown the lamb over high heat. Add the onions and keep frying and stirring until the onions are golden. Add the chickpeas, salt and spices and hot water. Bring to the boil, then turn heat low, cover and simmer until the lamb and chickpeas are soft, about 1½ hours.

Measure liquid left in the pan and make up to 4 cups (1 litre) with more hot water. Add the rice to the pan together with measured liquid and bring to the boil over high heat. Then cover tightly, turn the heat to low and cook for 25 minutes by which time the rice will be cooked and the liquid all absorbed. Turn off heat, uncover and let the steam escape for a few minutes before serving.

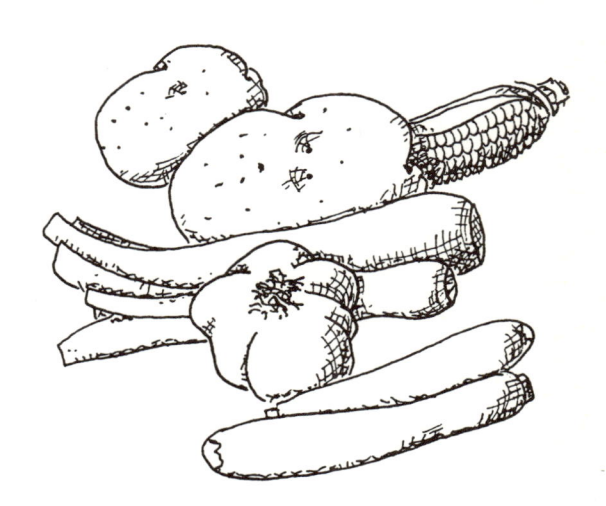

Pasta and Rice

Lamb Biriyani

Serves 4

- 1 kg (2 lb) lamb
- 3 tablespoons oil or ghee
- 2 large onions, finely chopped
- 2 teaspoons finely grated fresh ginger, optional
- 2 garlic cloves, crushed
- ½ teaspoon ground cinnamon
- ½ teaspoon ground cardamom
- 2 teaspoons salt
- 2 teaspoons ground coriander
- 2 teaspoons ground cumin
- 1 teaspoon ground turmeric
- 1 teaspoon chilli powder
- 2 ripe tomatoes, peeled and chopped
- Pilau Rice (page 318)
- extra 1 tablespoon oil or ghee

Trim the fat from the lamb and cut into cubes. Heat the oil or ghee in a large, heavy saucepan and fry the onions until soft. Add the garlic and ginger and continue frying, stirring frequently, until golden brown. Add the ground spices and salt and fry for a minute longer, then add the lamb and continue to stir fry until the meat has lost its pink colour and is covered with the spice mixture. Add the tomatoes, cover and cook over a very low heat for about 1 hour, stirring occasionally. Turn off the heat when lamb is tender and gravy very thick and almost dry. Put aside while preparing Pilau Rice.

Allow Pilau Rice to cool slightly. Heat extra oil in a large ovenproof casserole and pack in one third of the rice, then half the spiced lamb mixture. Repeat layers, finishing with rice. Cover the casserole and cook at 160°C (325°F/Gas 3) for about 20 to 30 minutes. Serve in the casserole.

Lamb and Ricotta Casserole

Serves 4

Casserole
- 60 g (2 oz) clarified butter
- 750 g (1½ lb) leg of lamb, boned and cut into 2.5 cm (1 inch) cubes
- 1 cup sliced onion
- 1 tablespoon flour
- 1 beef stock cube dissolved in 1 cup (8 fl oz) water
- 1 teaspoon lemon rind
- ½ teaspoon sweet dried basil
- salt and pepper

Topping
- 1 x 250 g (8 oz) eggplant (aubergine)
- salt
- 250 g (8 oz) ricotta cheese
- ¼ cup (2 fl oz) sour cream
- 2 eggs
- ½ cup cooked rice
- 2 cups roughly chopped tomatoes
- 1 cup (4 oz) freshly grated Parmesan cheese

Casserole; Melt the butter in a heavy based frying pan and brown the lamb a third at a time. Place in a large saucepan, add the onion, sauté until lightly browned, then sprinkle over the flour. Add the stock and stir until boiling, scraping in the meat juices from the pan base. Sprinkle remaining ingredients over lamb. Cover the saucepan tightly and simmer for 1½ hours.

Topping: Cut the eggplant into thin slices, sprinkle with salt and stand for 30 minutes. Dry well on absorbent paper. Beat the ricotta, sour cream and eggs together thoroughly. Stir in the rice. Place the lamb in an 8 cup (2 litre) ovenproof casserole and cover completely with the cheese topping. Arrange the eggplant and tomatoes on top, and sprinkle with Parmesan cheese. Bake in a 180°C (350°F/Gas 4) oven for 45 minutes.

Spicy Lamb Kebabs

Serves 8

1 kg (2 lb) boned leg of lamb
2 onions
2 red or green peppers (capsicums)

Marinade
½ cup (4 fl oz) oil
¼ cup (2 fl oz) lemon juice
2 bay leaves
½ teaspoon minced garlic
1 teaspoon onion flakes
¼ teaspoon ground thyme
¼ teaspoon dried rosemary leaves
1 teaspoon parsley flakes
¼ teaspoon lemon pepper
1 teaspoon seasoned salt

Buttered Rice
2½ cups (1 lb) rice
45 g (1½ oz) butter
1 teaspoon parsley flakes

Trim any excess fat from the lamb and cut into 4 cm (1½ inch) cubes. Cut the onions into wedges and the pepper into the same sized cubes as the lamb. Mix all marinade ingredients in a glass or ceramic bowl, add the lamb cubes, cover and refrigerate for 4 to 6 hours. Turn occasionally. Thread the lamb onto skewers alternately with the onion and the peppers.

Preheat the griller (broiler) to hot and grill (broil) the kebabs for 15 to 20 minutes, brushing with the marinade during cooking. Serve the kebabs on a mound of Buttered Rice.

Buttered Rice: Cook the rice by the rapid boil method (*page 307*). Drain well, add the butter and parsley flakes, and toss with a fork.

Lamb Ragôut with Celery Rice

Serves 6

Lamb Ragôut
1.5 kg (3 lb) shoulder of lamb, boned
45 g (1½ oz) butter
2 tablespoons oil
1 large onion, quartered
2 tablespoons (¾ oz) flour
1 garlic clove, crushed
1 ¼ cups (10 fl oz) beef stock
1 tablespoon tomato paste
bouquet garni
salt and pepper
6 pickling onions
3 rashers bacon, diced
½ cup peas
finely chopped fresh parsley

Celery Rice
60 g (2 oz) butter
1 cup (6 oz) rice
½ teaspoon salt
2 stalks celery, sliced
1½ cups (12 fl oz) boiling stock

Trim the lamb of excess fat and cut into 2.5 cm (1 inch) cubes. Heat the butter and oil in a large saucepan and brown the lamb and onion. Drain off the butter and reserve. Sprinkle the meat with flour and cook for 1 minute. Add the garlic, stock and tomato paste and cook until the liquid thickens and comes to the boil. Add the bouquet garni and salt and pepper to taste. Cover and simmer for 1 hour. Cook the pickling onions and bacon in the reserved butter until golden, drain, then add to the saucepan. Cover and simmer for a further 40 minutes. Add the peas 7 minutes before the end of the cooking time.

Serve with Celery Rice and sprinkle with chopped parsley.

Celery Rice: Melt the butter in a heavy saucepan. Add the rice and cook for 4 to 5 minutes, stirring until each grain of rice is coated with the butter. Add the salt, celery and boiling stock. Bring to the boil, cover and simmer for 15 minutes until the stock is absorbed.

Pasta and Rice

Swiss Veal with Rice Ring

Serves 6

90 g (3 oz) butter
1 onion, finely chopped
500 g (1 lb) veal steaks
½ cup (4 fl oz) dry white wine
¼ cup (2 fl oz) chicken stock
250 g (8 oz) button mushrooms, sliced
¾ cup (6 fl oz) milk
½ cup (4 fl oz) cream
1 teaspoon salt
freshly ground pepper
3 teaspoons cornflour (cornstarch), dissolved in a little water
4 cups hot cooked rice
15 g (½ oz) butter
1 tablespoon chopped fresh parsley

Heat half the butter and sauté onion until just tender. Cut the veal into thin strips, add to the pan and sauté over high heat until golden. Add the wine and the stock and simmer the veal for about 15 to 20 minutes or until tender. Heat the remaining butter in another pan and sauté the mushrooms until tender. Add the mushrooms to the veal with the milk and cream, stir to blend and simmer over low heat. Season to taste. Add the blended cornflour and stir until the sauce thickens. Toss the 15 g (½ oz) butter through the hot rice and season with salt and pepper.

Invert the rice onto a serving plate. Spoon the Swiss veal into the rice ring and garnish with chopped parsley.

Chinese Fried Rice with Mixed Meats

Serves 6

2½ cups (1 lb) rice
8 dried Chinese mushrooms
2 pairs dried Chinese sausages
peanut oil for frying
250 g (8 oz) beef, finely shredded
3 tablespoons soy sauce
250 g (8 oz) barbecued pork, thinly sliced
12 spring onions (scallions), finely chopped
salt and pepper

Cook the rice by the absorption method (*page 307*) using 3 cups (24 fl oz) of water. If possible, cook rice the day before.

Soak the Chinese mushrooms in very hot water for 20 minutes. Discard the stems and cut the mushroom caps into thin slices. Steam the sausages over boiling water for about 6 to 8 minutes, then slice finely. Heat 2 tablespoons of peanut oil and stir fry the beef over high heat for 2 minutes or just until the colour changes. Remove to a plate, sprinkle with 1 tablespoon of the soy sauce. Heat 4 tablespoons of peanut oil in a wok and toss the barbecued pork and the sliced sausages for 1 minute. Add the cold cooked rice and keep tossing on high heat until the rice is heated through. Add the beef and spring onions and toss to combine, then sprinkle with the remainder of the soy sauce and mix well. Remove from heat. Taste and add salt and pepper if necessary. Serve hot.

Veal Bacon Rolls with Mushroom Rice

Serves 6

6 even-sized veal steaks
salt and pepper
6 rashers bacon
60 g (2 oz) butter
1 onion, finely chopped
1 tablespoon flour
1 teaspoon paprika
1½ cups (12 fl oz) chicken stock
1 tablespoon tomato paste
salt and pepper

Mushroom Rice
4 cups (1 litre) chicken stock
2 cups (12 oz) rice
125 g (4 oz) mushrooms, sliced
45 g (1½ oz) butter

Pound veal between sheets of greaseproof paper until thin. Season steak with salt and pepper. Roll each steak up evenly until quite tight. Wrap 1 bacon rasher around each roll, tie with string or cotton. Heat the butter in a pan and sauté the onion until tender. Add the veal and cook until golden brown, about 10 minutes. Reduce the heat, remove the rolls and blend the flour and paprika into the pan drippings. Add a little extra butter if required and blend until smooth. Then gradually add the stock, stirring well. Add the paste and seasonings, replace the rolls, cover and simmer until the veal is tender, about 1 hour. Serve over Mushroom Rice.

Mushroom Rice: Bring stock to the boil and gradually add the rice. Return to the boil, stir once, cover and simmer over low heat for about 20 to 25 minutes or until the rice is tender. Meanwhile sauté the mushrooms in butter until tender. Uncover the rice and stand for 5 minutes to allow the steam to escape. Spoon the rice onto a serving dish, mix with the mushrooms and season to taste.

Easy Pork Biriyani

Serves 4

- 90 g (3 oz) ghee or butter
- 24 almonds
- 3 tablespoons onion flakes or 1 onion, chopped
- 1 garlic clove, crushed
- ½ teaspoon fresh ginger, finely chopped
- 8 whole cloves
- 4 cardamom pods
- 1 teaspoon ground cinnamon
- ½ teaspoon ground turmeric
- ¼ cup (2 fl oz) yoghurt
- 1 cup (6 oz) rice
- 1 kg (2 lb) cooked pork, diced, or beef, lamb or veal
- 3 ½ cups (28 fl oz) beef stock, made with stock cubes
- 2 teaspoons salt
- ½ cup (3 oz) raisins

Heat the ghee and fry the almonds until pale golden. Drain on paper and reserve. Fry the onion with the garlic, ginger, cloves, cardamom and cinnamon for a few minutes. Lower heat, add the turmeric and yoghurt. Blend well then add the rice and pork. Pour on the beef stock, season and cover. Simmer for about 20 minutes until all liquid is absorbed and the rice is tender. Serve on a platter, garnished with the almonds and raisins.

Pineapple Pork Packets

Serves 6

- 6 pork chops
- 1 teaspoon salt
- freshly ground pepper
- 6 spring onions (scallions), chopped
- 1 garlic clove, crushed
- 15 g (½ oz) butter
- ½ cup (2 oz) chopped dried apricots
- ½ cup (3 oz) raisins
- ½ teaspoon ground ginger
- 1 cup (6 oz) rice
- 1 cup (8 fl oz) chicken stock made with stock cubes
- ¼ cup (2 fl oz) reserved pineapple liquid
- ½ cup (4 fl oz) dry white wine
- ¼ cup (2 fl oz) water
- 1 x 450 g (14 ½ oz) can pineapple pieces, drained

Trim excess fat from the chops and brown them in a pan over high heat. Do not cook completely. Place each chop on a 20 x 25 cm (8 x 10 inch) sheet of foil and season with salt and pepper. Fry the spring onions and garlic in the butter for a few minutes, then add the apricots, raisins and ginger. Add the rice with some extra butter if needed and fry the rice for 2 minutes. Add the stock, pineapple liquid, wine and water, cover and cook over low heat for 5 minutes. Spoon some rice and pineapple pieces on top of each chop. Close packages securely, leaving room inside for the rice to expand. Place in a baking dish and cook in a 180°C (350°F/Gas 4) oven for 45 minutes.

Chinese Spiced Pork

Serves 4

- 375 g (12 oz) pork fillet
- 3 tablespoons oil
- 1 red pepper (capsicum), cut in large pieces
- 2 stalks celery, sliced diagonally
- 6 spring onions (scallions), sliced diagonally
- 1 x 220 g (7 oz) can whole baby corn, drained
- 2 teaspoons cornflour (cornstarch)
- 1 chicken stock cube dissolved in ½ cup (4 fl oz) water
- 2 teaspoons soy sauce

Marinade
- 2 tablespoons soy sauce
- ½ teaspoon finely chopped fresh ginger
- 1 garlic clove, crushed
- 1 tablespoon sherry
- 1 teaspoon brown sugar
- ¼ teaspoon Chinese five spice powder

Lemon Butter Rice
- 30 g (1 oz) butter
- 4 cups cooked rice
- 1 tablespoon lemon juice
- grated rind of 1 lemon
- 1 tablespoon chopped fresh parsley

Remove any fat or skin from the pork and cut the meat into paper thin slices. Blend the 6 marinade ingredients. Place the blended marinade ingredients in a bowl, add the pork, stir, and allow to stand for at least 30 minutes, stirring occasionally. Heat 2 tablespoons of the oil and stir fry the pork slices for about 5 minutes or until the pork is tender. Remove and drain on absorbent paper. Add enough oil to make up 2 tablespoons, heat, add the red pepper and celery and fry for 1 minute. Add the spring onion and corn and replace the pork. Stir fry for 1 minute to heat and then blend the cornflour in the chicken stock, pour into the pan and stir until the mixture thickens. Add soy sauce to taste. Serve the pork with Lemon Butter Rice.

Lemon Butter Rice: Heat the butter, add the rice, lemon juice and rind and parsley. Toss until heated.

Pasta and Rice

Pork Chops on Cider Rice
Serves 4 – 6

4-6 short loin pork chops, medium-sized
flour
salt and pepper
1 teaspoon ground ginger
45 g (1 ½ oz) butter
1 onion, sliced
½ cup chopped celery
1 red-skinned apple, chopped
1 cup (6 oz) rice
2 cups (16 fl oz) apple cider
pinch of cloves
ground cinnamon
ground nutmeg
salt and pepper
2 apples, sliced
1 tablespoon flour mixed with 2 teaspoons sugar
¼ cup (1 ½ oz) glacé ginger, thinly sliced

Trim the excess fat from the chops. Combine the flour, salt, pepper and ginger. Toss the chops in this mixture, then brown them in the butter over high heat. Remove from the pan.

Add the onion, celery, apple and rice to the pan and toss over moderate heat for about 2 minutes. Then add the apple cider and spices with salt and pepper to taste. Stir to blend the rice. Spoon the rice into a greased ovenproof dish. Replace the chops on the rice and cover with a lid or alfoil. Bake in a 180°C (350°F/Gas 4) oven for about 35 to 40 minutes, or until the chops and the rice are tender.

Meanwhile, sprinkle the apple slices with flour and sugar mixture and fry in extra butter until golden. Serve the apple on the chops and sprinkle the rice with the glacé ginger.

Chicken Rice and Noodles
Serves 3

90 g (3 oz) butter
1 chicken breast, cubed
1 medium-sized red pepper (capsicum), cut in strips
1 tablespoon oil
125 g (4 oz) vermicelli noodles
1 cup (6 oz) rice
2 ½ cups (20 fl oz) boiling chicken stock
salt and pepper

Heat half the butter in a pan and cook chicken and red pepper for 2 minutes until the chicken is golden. Remove the chicken and pepper, and reserve. Heat the remaining butter and oil in the pan, crush the vermicelli straight into the pan and toss rapidly over moderate heat, until noodles are golden. Add the rice to the pan and toss until coated with butter. Replace the chicken and red pepper, add boiling stock. Cover and simmer over low heat for about 30 to 35 minutes until the rice is tender. Add a little extra stock if required. Season with salt and pepper and serve.

Baked Ham, Spiced Apple Ring
Serves 4

Ham
1 x 1 kg (2 lb) can ham
whole cloves
½ cup (3 oz) brown sugar
½ cup (4 fl oz) apple cider
2 teaspoons vinegar
2 teaspoons mustard
¼ teaspoon ground cinnamon

Spiced Rice
45 g (1 ½ oz) butter
1 onion, finely chopped
1 cup chopped celery
1 apple, chopped
1 cup (6 oz) rice
extra 2 cups (16 fl oz) apple cider
pinch of ground cinnamon and cloves
1 tablespoon brandy, optional
2 tablespoons chopped fresh parsley

Garnish
1 apple, cored and sliced
flour
brown sugar
butter
2 tablespoons (½ oz) walnuts

Ham: Remove the jelly from the ham. Place the ham in a baking dish, and with a sharp knife mark the top surface in a diamond pattern. Insert a clove in each diamond. Combine the next 5 ingredients and spoon this mixture evenly over the ham. Bake the ham, uncovered, in a 180°C (350°F/Gas 4) oven for 35 minutes. Baste frequently. Cook the rice while the ham is baking.

Spiced Rice: Sauté the onion, celery and apple for a few minutes in the butter, then add the rice and the extra apple cider and cook by the absorption method (*page 307*). Add the spices, brandy and parsley and toss with a fork to mix thoroughly. Serve the ham on the spiced rice and garnish with fried apple slices and walnuts.

Garnish: Dust the apple slices with flour and brown sugar and fry in butter until golden, then arrange around the base of the ham with the walnuts in the centre of the slices.

Kashmiri Chicken Curry

Serves 4

1.5 kg (3 lb) chicken pieces
1 tablespoon oil
45 g (1 ½ oz) butter
2 onions, chopped
1 garlic clove, crushed
1 teaspoon chopped fresh ginger or ground ginger
1 tablespoon curry powder, or to taste
½ cup (4 fl oz) tomato purée or tomato juice
2 teaspoons brown sugar
1 tablespoon lemon juice
2 cups (16 fl oz) chicken stock, made with stock cubes
salt and freshly ground pepper
2 tablespoons yoghurt or sour cream, optional
chopped fresh mint, to garnish

Yellow Rice

1 ¼ cups (8 oz) rice
1 teaspoon ground turmeric
sultanas and toasted slivered almonds, to garnish

Cut the chicken pieces into serving sized portions. Separate the legs from the thighs and cut each whole breast into 4 pieces. Pat the chicken quite dry, and fry in oil and butter until just golden, remove and reserve. In the same pan fry the onion, garlic, ginger and curry powder over moderate heat for 2 minutes to develop the flavour. Add the tomato purée, brown sugar, lemon juice, stock, salt and pepper. Simmer, covered, over low heat for 10 minutes. Place the chicken in the sauce and cook over low heat for 35 minutes or until the chicken is tender. Thicken with a little cornflour (cornstarch) if needed, add the yoghurt just before serving and sprinkle with chopped mint. Serve with Yellow Rice.

Yellow Rice: Boil rice, adding turmeric to water to colour the rice yellow. Drain well and garnish with toasted, slivered almonds and a few sultanas.

Chicken Fillets on Orange Rice

Serves 6

6 chicken fillets
1 tablespoon oil
15 g (½ oz) butter
3 oranges, sliced
grated rind of 1 orange
½ cup (4 fl oz) orange juice concentrate
½ cup (4 fl oz) coconut milk
2 teaspoons soy sauce
3 teaspoons honey
½ teaspoon ground ginger
mint sprigs
toasted slivered almonds

Orange Rice

Serves 6

15 g (1 ½ oz) butter
4 spring onions (scallions) or 1 onion, chopped
pinch of saffron or ½ teaspoon turmeric
1 cup (6 oz) rice
1 ¼ cups (10 fl oz) chicken stock made with stock cubes
½ cup (4 fl oz) orange juice
grated rind of 1 orange
salt and pepper

Pat the chicken fillets quite dry and carefully sauté in the oil and butter until cooked and golden, about 10 to 15 minutes. Sauté the orange slices. Remove the slices and reserve with the chicken. Combine the orange rind, juice, coconut milk, soy sauce, honey and ginger. Cook over moderate heat until well blended then check seasoning.

Serve chicken on a bed of Orange Rice (*see below*), pour over the orange glaze. Top with the fried orange slices and garnish with mint sprigs and almonds.

Orange Rice: Heat the butter and fry the spring onions for 1 minute. Add the saffron and the rice and toss over a moderate heat for 2 minutes. Combine the stock, orange juice and rind. Cook by the absorption method (*page 307*), until the rice is tender, about 20 to 25 minutes. Remove the lid and allow to stand for 5 minutes, then season and toss with a fork.

Pasta and Rice

Capricorn Chicken and Rice

Serves 3

3 whole chicken breasts or chicken pieces
seasoned flour
3 tablespoons peanut oil
¼ cup chopped spring onions (scallions)
1 garlic clove, crushed
2 teaspoons soy sauce
3 cups cooked rice

Sauce
1 x 450 g (11 ½ oz) can pineapple pieces, with liquid
½ cup canned sliced cucumber, chopped
1 tablespoon cucumber liquid
½ cup chopped spring onions (scallions)
½ cup (4 fl oz) chicken stock, made with stock cubes
2 tomatoes, chopped
2 tablespoons (¾ oz) sugar
1 tablespoon lemon juice or vinegar
½ teaspoon ground ginger
3 teaspoons soy sauce, or to taste
3 teaspoons cornflour (cornstarch), dissolved in a little water

Halve the chicken breasts, toss in the flour and sauté in hot oil until golden brown. Remove. Add more oil if needed and fry the spring onions and garlic until just tender. Add the soy sauce and the rice and toss until well blended. Spoon the rice into a greased ovenproof dish. Arrange the chicken on top.

Sauce: Combine all the ingredients and stir over moderate heat until the mixture boils and thickens. Spoon half the sauce over the chicken and rice. Cover and bake in a 180°C (350°F/Gas 4) oven for about 35 minutes or until chicken is tender. Spoon over remaining sauce and serve.

Chicken Croquettes

Serves 4 - 6

3 cups cooked diced chicken
1 onion, finely chopped
2 cups cooked rice
3 stalks celery, finely chopped
1 teaspoon salt
freshly ground pepper
1 tablespoon lemon juice
3 eggs
2 tablespoons water
1 cup (4 oz) fine breadcrumbs
oil

Put the chicken through a mincing machine or chop very finely. Combine chicken, onion and celery. Add rice, salt, pepper and lemon juice. Lightly beat 2 eggs, add to the mixture and blend well. Chill in refrigerator for 1 hour. Shape into 16 croquettes or patties. Lightly beat the water and the remaining egg together. Dip the croquettes in the egg and roll in breadcrumbs. Cook in hot oil until golden.

Sultana Orange Chicken

Serves 4

½ cup (4 fl oz) lemon juice
1 small onion, finely chopped
1 tablespoon grated orange rind
1 teaspoon salt
freshly ground black pepper, to taste
½ teaspoon ground cinnamon
8 chicken drumsticks
90 g (3 oz) ghee or butter

Glaze
2-3 tablespoons (2-3 oz) sieved orange marmalade or apricot conserve
crushed peppercorns
2 tablespoons crumbled dried mint or thyme leaves

Orange Sultana Rice
1 cup (6 oz) rice
1 ½ cups chicken stock, made with stock cubes
½ cup (4 fl oz) orange juice
grated rind of 1 orange
2-3 cups (12 oz-1 lb) sultanas sultanas
¼ cup (1 oz) flaked or slivered toasted almonds
thin strips of orange rind

Curried Sultanas
¼ cup (2 fl oz) oil
1 teaspoon curry powder
¼ cup (1 oz) whole blanched almonds
1 cup (6 oz) sultanas

Combine the lemon juice, onion, orange rind, salt, pepper and cinnamon and pour over chicken. Marinate in the refrigerator for 1 to 2 hours, turning several times. Remove from the marinade and pat dry.

Heat 60 g (2 oz) of ghee in a pan and brown chicken lightly. Brush an ovenproof dish with the remaining ghee and add the drumsticks. Brush with marmalade and sprinkle with crushed peppercorns and mint. Bake at 180°C (350°F/Gas 4) for 45 minutes or until cooked, basting occasionally with ghee. Serve with Orange Sultana Rice and Curried Sultanas.

Orange Sultana Rice: Cook rice by absorption method (*page 307*) using the chicken stock, orange juice and rind in place of water. Stir the sultanas and almonds through the rice and sprinkle with strips of orange rind.

Curried Sultanas: Heat the oil, add the curry powder and cook for 1 minute. Add the almonds and toss over moderate heat for 2 minutes. Add the sultanas and stir until plump.

Chicken Pineapple Curry

Serves 4

1 kg (2 lb) chicken pieces
15 g (½ oz) butter
1 tablespoon oil
1 onion, finely chopped
1 garlic clove, crushed
1 red and 1 green pepper (capsicum), cut into thin strips
1-2 tablespoons curry powder
1 tablespoon (⅓ oz) flour
1 tablespoon (½ oz) brown sugar
1 x 850 g (1 lb 11 ½ oz) can pineapple pieces
1 cup (8 fl oz) chicken stock, made with stock cubes
salt to taste
1 tablespoon (1 oz) fruit chutney
1 tablespoon lemon juice
1 tablespoon coconut cream or desiccated coconut

Pat the chicken pieces quite dry. Heat the butter and oil, fry the chicken until golden. Remove, and fry the onion, garlic and peppers until tender. Add the curry powder, flour and brown sugar. Cook, stirring, for 1 minute to develop the flavour. Drain the pineapple and reserve the syrup. Add 1 cup (8 fl oz) each of syrup and the stock gradually to the curry mixture and stir until the mixture boils. Replace the chicken, season with salt, cover and simmer on low heat for about 35 to 50 minutes, or until the chicken is tender. Add the pineapple pieces, chutney, lemon juice and coconut cream and heat for another 5 to 10 minutes. Serve with Citrus Curried Rice (*page 313*).

Stir-Fried Chicken and Rice

Serves 4

1 whole chicken breast
2 tablespoons peanut oil
1 small red and 1 green pepper (capsicum), cut into thin strips
4 spring onions (scallions), cut into thin strips
1 garlic clove, crushed
½ teaspoon chopped fresh ginger or ¼ teaspoon ground ginger
2 chicken stock cubes dissolved in ¾ cup (6 fl oz) hot water
1 tablespoon soy sauce, or to taste
1 tablespoon tomato sauce
2 teaspoons cornflour (cornstarch)
1 tablespoon dry sherry or water
6 cups hot cooked rice

Remove the skin and bone from the chicken. Cut the breast in half lengthwise and slice crosswise into thin strips. Heat oil in a frypan and fry peppers, spring onions, garlic and ginger, stir frying with a fork for about 2 minutes. The vegetables should be slightly crisp. Remove vegetables and reserve. Add extra oil if required and stir fry the chicken until it just starts to colour. Replace the vegetables. Combine the chicken stock, soy sauce, tomato sauce, cornflour blended in sherry and pour over the chicken. Stir over heat until the mixture boils and thickens.

Serve the chicken spooned over hot rice.

Ham and Rice New Orleans

Serves 6

2 tablespoons oil
2 onions, thinly sliced
1 cup chopped celery
1 green pepper (capsicum), chopped
1 garlic clove, crushed
2 cups (12 oz) rice
3 ½ cups (28 fl oz) chicken stock, made with stock cubes
¼ teaspoon dried thyme
1 bay leaf
dash of Tabasco sauce or pinch of chilli powder
2 tomatoes, peeled and diced
1 cup sliced mushrooms cooked in a little butter
salt and pepper
6 thick slices ham
1 tablespoon chopped fresh parsley

Heat the oil, add the onions, celery, pepper and garlic and cook over moderate heat for about 2 minutes. Add the rice to the pan and continue cooking and stirring for about 3 to 4 minutes. Add the stock, thyme, bay leaf, Tabasco, tomatoes, mushrooms, and salt and pepper to taste. Bring to the boil, cover, lower the heat to simmer and cook for 15 minutes. Cut the ham into fingers and arrange over the rice. Cover and continue cooking until the rice is tender, about 10 minutes. Serve sprinkled with parsley.

Fried Chicken Raisin Rice

Serves 4

60 g (2 oz) butter
¼ cup (1 oz) almonds
2 onions, chopped
1 garlic clove, crushed
½ teaspoon chopped fresh or ground ginger
3 crushed cardamom pods, optional
1 piece cinnamon stick
½ teaspoon ground turmeric
½ cup (3 oz) raisins or sultanas
3 cups cooked chicken, cut into serving sized pieces (reserve some for garnish)
4 cups cooked rice, refrigerated overnight

Heat the butter and sauté the almonds until golden. Remove and reserve. Add the onions to the pan, cook until tender. Add the garlic, ginger, cardamom, cinnamon and turmeric. Cook over moderate heat for 1 minute, add the raisins and chicken pieces and toss in the spice mixture. Add the rice to the pan and continue tossing until heated. Serve rice garnished with the reserved chicken and fried almonds.

Pasta and Rice

Sweet and Sour Chicken

Serves 4

2 whole chicken breasts
cornflour (cornstarch)
oil for frying
2 onions
1 red pepper (capsicum)
½ cup sliced canned cucumber, drained
1 x 450 g (14½ oz) can pineapple pieces
1 x 375 g (12 oz) can sweet and sour sauce
3 teaspoons soy sauce
1 tablespoon tomato sauce
2 cups hot cooked rice
shredded spring onions (scallions), to garnish

Cut the chicken breasts in half, remove the bones and cut each half into cubes. Toss in cornflour and shake off excess. Deep fry the chicken until golden brown then drain on absorbent paper. Pour off all but 1 tablespoon of oil. Cut the onions into quarters then each quarter into segments. Cut the pepper into large dice. Fry the onions and diced pepper in oil for just 2 minutes then add the sliced cucumber, pineapple pieces, sweet and sour sauce, soy sauce and tomato sauce. Stir over moderate heat, then add chicken. When hot, spoon over a bed of rice. Garnish with finely shredded spring onions.

Chicken and Almonds

Serves 2

500 g (1 lb) chicken breasts
2 teaspoons cornflour (cornstarch)
salt
1 egg white
1 tablespoon dry sherry
oil for frying

Seasoning
½ cup (4 fl oz) chicken stock, made with stock cubes
3 teaspoons cornflour (cornstarch)

2 slices fresh ginger
1 cup diced red and green pepper
1 onion or 6 spring onions (scallions)
1 cup (5 oz) almonds, fried in oil until golden
1 cup hot cooked rice

2 teaspoons soy sauce
½ teaspoon sesame oil, optional

Bone chicken breasts and cut into 1.25 cm (½ inch) cubes. Mix the cornflour, salt, egg white and sherry. Add to the chicken and mix well. Heat oil in a hot pan or wok, add the ginger slices, then add the chicken and stir fry until the chicken turns white. Remove and drain. In 2 tablespoons of oil fry the peppers and onion until just coloured but still crisp. Add the well mixed seasoning ingredients and allow to boil then replace chicken. Add almonds and serve immediately, spooned over steaming hot rice.

Chinese Spiced Chicken Wings

Serves 4 – 6

1 kilo (2 lb) chicken wings   1 tablespoon sesame seeds

Marinade
2 tablespoons soy sauce
1 tablespoon peanut oil
1 tablespoon sherry, optional
2 tablespoons (2 oz) honey

1 tablespoon lemon juice
½ teaspoon Chinese five spice powder
½ teaspoon minced garlic
1 teaspoon ground ginger

Lemon Pepper Rice
2 cups (12 oz) rice
1 teaspoon pre-soaked diced dried red pepper (capsicum)

1 teaspoon pre-soaked parsley flakes
1 teaspoon lemon pepper

Remove the tips from the chicken wings, pat dry. Blend the marinade ingredients. Place the chicken wings in a glass or ceramic dish, pour over marinade, cover and refrigerate for at least 2 hours, turning occasionally.

Remove the chicken from the marinade and place in a single layer in a greased ovenproof dish. Spoon over half the marinade and bake uncovered in a 180°C (350°F/Gas 4) oven for about 30 to 35 minutes (alternatively grill (broil) or barbecue, basting with remaining marinade). Place the sesame seeds in a small heavy saucepan, toss over moderate heat until golden brown and sprinkle over the chicken during the last 5 minutes of baking. Serve with Lemon Pepper Rice.

Lemon Pepper Rice: Cook rice and toss with diced capsicum and parsley flakes. Sprinkle with lemon pepper.

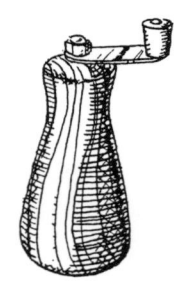

Spiced Chicken Pilaf

Serves 4

60 g (2 oz) butter
¼ cup (1 oz) almonds
2 onions, thinly sliced
1 garlic clove, crushed
½ teaspoon chopped fresh ginger or ¼ teaspoon ground ginger
1 small cinnamon stick
6 cardamom pods or cloves
¼ cup (2 fl oz) yoghurt
½ teaspoon ground turmeric
½ cup (3 oz) sultanas
4 cups cooked rice, refrigerated overnight
375 g (12 oz) cooked chicken, cut into serving sized pieces

Heat the butter and sauté the almonds until pale golden, remove and reserve. Add the onions and garlic and cook until golden brown, removing a few onion slices for use as a garnish. Add the ginger, cinnamon and cardamom and cook over moderate heat for a few minutes. Mix the yoghurt and turmeric together and add to the pan with the sultanas, rice and 2 cups of chicken pieces. Toss the mixture frequently over moderate heat. Place the remaining chicken, almonds and reserved onions on the top of the rice, cover and heat. Serve with the following accompaniments: toasted coconut, chopped tomatoes, cucumber and chutney.

Russian Chicken Fillets, Lemon Butter Rice

Serves 4

60 g (2 oz) butter
½ cup chopped spring onions (scallions)
½ cup chopped red pepper (capsicum)
1 garlic clove, crushed
250 g (8 oz) mushrooms, sliced
3 teaspoons flour
1¼ cups (10 fl oz) sour cream
¼ cup chopped dill pickle or canned sliced cucumber
salt and pepper
750 g (1½ lb) chicken fillets or boned chicken breasts
1 recipe Lemon Butter Rice (page 308)
2 firm red tomatoes, sliced and fried
black olives, to garnish

Heat half of the butter in a pan and sauté the spring onions, red pepper, garlic and mushrooms until just tender. Sprinkle the flour in the pan, toss to blend and cook for 1 minute. Gradually add the sour cream and stir well. Then add the dill pickle and season to taste. Remove and keep warm.

Heat the remaining butter in a pan. Pat the chicken fillets dry and sauté until golden brown and cooked. Remove and keep warm.

Spoon the Lemon Butter Rice onto a serving platter. Overlap the chicken on the rice, spoon over the mushroom sauce and top with fried tomato slices and black olives.

Chinese Stir Fried Chicken

Serves 2

2 whole chicken breasts
1 tablespoon peanut oil
1 stalk celery, cut into thin strips
1 small green or red pepper (capsicum), cut into thin strips
4 spring onions (scallions), chopped
1 garlic clove, crushed
½ teaspoon chopped fresh ginger or ¼ teaspoon ground ginger
1 cup cooked peas or beans
1 chicken stock cube, dissolved in ½ cup (4 fl oz) water
salt
1 tablespoon soy sauce
1 teaspoon cornflour (cornstarch)

Remove bone and skin from the chicken and cut each breast in half. Slice crosswise into thin strips, 5 cm (2 inch) long and 2 cm (¾ inch) wide. Heat the oil in a frypan or wok and stir fry the celery, green pepper, spring onions, garlic and ginger for about 2 to 3 minutes. Remove the vegetables and reserve. Add extra oil if required and stir fry the chicken until chicken meat turns white. Replace the vegetables, add the cooked peas or beans, and pour in chicken stock. Season to taste. Blend the soy sauce and cornflour until smooth, add to the chicken mixture and stir constantly until the mixture has boiled and thickened. Ideal to serve with Fried Rice (page 307).

Malaysian Chicken Curry

Serves 4 – 6

1.5 kg (3 lb) chicken breasts and wings
15 g (½ oz) butter
1 tablespoon oil
1 tablespoon curry powder
3 onions, sliced
1 garlic clove, crushed
2 tomatoes, peeled and chopped
1 x 450 g (14 ½ oz) can pineapple pieces, drained, liquid retained
1 cup chicken stock, made with cubes
salt and pepper
½ cup (4 fl oz) coconut milk
1 cup diced cucumber

Cut the chicken into bite-sized pieces. Heat the butter and oil, brown the chicken and remove. Add the curry powder, onions and garlic. Cook, stirring, for 2 minutes. Then add the tomatoes, pineapple liquid and the chicken stock. Season with salt and pepper. Add the coconut milk, replace the chicken and simmer until tender, for about 25 minutes. Add the pineapple pieces and cucumber and simmer until heated. Serve spooned over rice.

Pasta and Rice

Spicy Arroz con Pollo

Serves 6

1 x 1.5 kg (3 lb) chicken
¼ teaspoon saffron
4 cups (1 litre) chicken stock
2 tablespoons oil
2 onions, chopped
1 garlic clove, crushed
1 mild green chilli pepper, finely chopped, optional
2 cups (12 oz) rice
salt and pepper
1 cup frozen peas
2 tomatoes, peeled and cut into wedges
½ cup (2 ½ oz) stuffed olives, sliced

Wipe the chicken with damp paper towels. Cut into 8 serving sized pieces. Place the saffron in a saucepan large enough to hold the stock. Add the stock and bring to the boil so that it takes on a saffron colour.

Set an electric frypan at 175°C (340°F) and heat the oil. Add the chicken pieces and sauté until golden brown. Remove from the pan. Add the onion, garlic and chilli to the pan and cook until softened. Add the rice, mix well and fry for about 3 to 5 minutes. Add the stock and season to taste.

Spread the mixture evenly to the edge of the pan. Add the chicken, peas, tomatoes and olives, pressing into the rice to form a decorative pattern. Do not stir. Cover and cook at 130°C (260°F) until the rice and other ingredients are cooked. If necessary add more stock if the rice appears too dry or does not appear to be cooking sufficiently.

Speedy Chicken and Rice Ring

Serves 4

2 tablespoons oil
1 kg (2 lb) chicken wings or chicken pieces
1 ¾ cups (14 fl oz) canned tomato juice
1 x 40 g (1 ¼ oz) packet French onion soup mix
3 teaspoons brown sugar
¼ teaspoon dried oregano or basil
1 red pepper (capsicum), chopped
1 green pepper (capsicum), chopped

Rice Ring

1 ½ cups (10 oz) rice
fresh parsley to garnish

Fry the chicken wings in the hot oil until golden. Drain away the excess oil then add the tomato juice, soup mix, brown sugar and oregano. Cover and cook over moderate heat until the wings are tender, about 20 to 25 minutes. During the last 5 minutes of cooking add the peppers. Serve with the Rice Ring.

Rice Ring: Cook the rice (*page 307*). Grease a mould or cake tin and spoon the hot rice into the mould, press firmly, then turn out onto a serving plate. Garnish with the parsley.

Chicken Rice Casserole

Serves 4

1.5 kg (3 lb) chicken pieces
2 tablespoons oil
2 onions, chopped
1 green and 1 red pepper (capsicum), chopped
1 garlic clove, crushed
½ cup chopped fresh parsley
1 cup (6 oz) rice
1 ½ cups (12 fl oz) chicken stock
1 x 440 g (14 oz) can tomatoes
salt and pepper
pinch of dried rosemary
pinch of dried basil
1 cup (4 oz) grated cheese

Pat the chicken dry and place skin side up in a shallow greased ovenproof dish. Brush with oil. Place in a 200°C (400°F/Gas 6) oven and bake, covered, for about 35 minutes or until golden.

Add the onions and peppers, garlic, parsley and rice. Bring the stock and tomatoes to the boil and pour over the chicken and the rice mixture. Add the seasoning and herbs and stir to blend. Cover the dish with a lid or foil, lower heat to 190°C (375°F/Gas 5) and bake until the chicken and rice are tender, about 30 minutes. Serve sprinkled with cheese.

Coq au Vin with Rice

Serves 6 – 8

1.5 kg (3 lb) roasting chicken or chicken pieces
2-3 rashers bacon
12 small onions
125 g (4 oz) button mushrooms
2 tablespoons oil
2 tablespoons brandy
2 cups (16 fl oz) red wine
chopped fresh parsley
2 cups (12 oz) rice
4 cups (1 litre) chicken stock

If using a whole chicken cut into 6-8 serving sized pieces. Remove the rind from the bacon and cut into small pieces. Peel the onions, wipe and trim the mushrooms. Heat the oil in a heavy based flameproof casserole dish and fry the bacon with the onions and mushrooms. Drain on absorbent paper. Fry the chicken pieces until well browned. Return the bacon, mushrooms and onions to the pan. Pour over the brandy and light with a long match. When the flames die down, add the red wine. Cover and cook over low heat for 40 minutes or until chicken is tender. Thicken with cornflour (cornstarch) if necessary. Sprinkle with the chopped parsley. Serve with rice cooked with chicken stock, by the absorption method (*page 307*).

Rice and Chicken California

Serves 4

½ cup (2 oz) slivered almonds
45 g (1 ½ oz) butter
1 small onion, chopped
2 tablespoons (¾ oz) flour
2 cups (16 fl oz) chicken stock
1 cup (8 fl oz) cream or milk
salt and freshly ground pepper
3 cups cooked rice
2 cups diced, cooked chicken
½ cup (3 oz) sultanas
½ cup diced red or green pepper (capsicum)
1 tablespoon chopped fresh parsley
½ cup (2 oz) grated cheese

Fry the almonds in butter until golden, remove and reserve. Add the onion to the pan, cook until tender then add the flour and blend thoroughly. Gradually add the stock, stirring until smooth. Add the cream gradually. Simmer for 1 minute, do not boil. Season to taste with salt and pepper. Add the rice, chicken, sultanas, red pepper and parsley. Spoon into an ovenproof dish and sprinkle with the cheese. Bake in a 180°C (350°F/Gas 4) oven for about 20 to 25 minutes, until the cheese is golden. Serve with a tossed salad.

California Chicken Casserole

Serves 4

45 g (1 ½ oz) butter
1 onion, finely chopped
½ green pepper (capsicum), chopped
1 cup thinly sliced button mushrooms
2 tablespoons (¾ oz) flour
2 cups (16 fl oz) chicken stock
salt and pepper
3 cups cubed cooked chicken
1 tablespoon dry sherry
2 teaspoons lemon juice
½ cup (4 fl oz) sour cream or evaporated milk
3 cups hot cooked rice
15 g (½ oz) butter
1 tablespoon chopped fresh parsley
2 tablespoons chopped canned pimiento or sliced stuffed olives

Heat the butter and cook the onion, green pepper and mushrooms until just tender. Add the flour, blend thoroughly then gradually add the chicken stock, stirring until the sauce boils. Add salt and pepper to taste. Add the chicken, sherry and lemon juice and stir until boiling, then add the sour cream and heat without boiling. Combine the hot rice with the butter and parsley. Serve the chicken over rice and garnish with the pimiento or sliced olives.

Creamy Curried Chicken

Serves 4

60 g (2 oz) butter
1 tablespoon mild curry powder
2 medium-sized onions, thinly sliced
1.2 kg (2 ½ lb) roasting chicken cut into 8 portions, or chicken pieces
2 cups (16 fl oz) water
2 chicken stock cubes, crumbled
1 tablespoon lemon juice
1 tablespoon fruit chutney
2 green apples, peeled, cored and diced
½ cup (2 oz) full cream milk powder
1 tablespoon cornflour (cornstarch) dissolved in a little water

Butternut Rice
4 cups hot cooked rice
15 g (½ oz) butter
2 tablespoons (1 oz) sultanas
¼ cup (1 ½ oz) peanuts

Melt the butter in a large heavy based saucepan. Add the curry powder, onions and chicken and sauté over gentle heat for 15 minutes, turning regularly. Add the water and stock cubes, bring to the boil, then simmer for a further 15 minutes. Add the remaining ingredients and stir until boiling. Serve on Butternut Rice.

Butternut Rice: Toss the rice with the butter, sultanas and peanuts.

Golden Apricot Chicken

Serves 4

2 tablespoons peanut oil
1 kg (2 lb) chicken pieces
1 x 40 g (1 ¼ oz) packet French onion soup
1 x 470 g (15 oz) can apricot nectar

Lemon Pilaf
15 g (½ oz) butter
3 cups cooked rice
grated rind of 1 lemon
1 tablespoon chopped fresh chives or parsley
salt and pepper
¼ cup (1 oz) chopped walnuts

Heat the oil and brown the chicken pieces. Add the soup mix and apricot nectar and stir to blend thoroughly. Cover and simmer over moderate heat for 35 to 40 minutes or until the chicken is tender.

Lemon Pilaf: Melt the butter in a pan. Combine the rice and the remaining ingredients and toss in the pan until the rice is heated. Spoon the Golden Apricot Chicken around the Lemon Pilaf.

Pasta and Rice

Chicken and Peppers

Serves 3

500 g (1 lb) chicken breasts
1 tablespoon cornflour (cornstarch)
1 egg white
½ teaspoon sesame oil, optional
1 tablespoon dry sherry

4 tablespoons peanut oil
1 onion, diced
1 cup red or green peppers (capsicum), diced
1 cup celery, diced
½ cup (3 oz) almonds, fried in oil until golden

Sauce
½ cup (4 fl oz) chicken stock, made with stock cubes
3 teaspoons soy sauce
2 teaspoons cornflour (cornstarch)

Remove bones from the chicken and cut into small 2.5 cm (1 inch) dice. Mix cornflour, egg white, sesame oil and sherry. Pour over the chicken and allow to stand for 5 minutes. Heat the peanut oil and deep fry the chicken until just golden. Remove and drain. In 2 tablespoons of hot oil sauté the onion, peppers and celery until just tender. Add the sauce ingredients (mixed together) and bring to the boil.

Replace the chicken and vegetables and mix well. Add the almonds and serve with rice.

Cheddar Chicken Rice

Serves 4–6

30 g (1 oz) butter
4 spring onions (scallions), sliced diagonally
1 cup sliced mushrooms
⅓ cup chopped green pepper (capsicum)
1 tablespoon flour
1 cup (8 fl oz) milk
250 g (8 oz) processed cheddar cheese, grated

salt and pepper
2 cups diced cooked chicken
⅓ cup (2 oz) sliced stuffed olives, optional
½ cup (2 oz) slivered almonds, toasted
2 cups (12 oz) rice
¼ cup chopped fresh parsley

Melt the butter and gently sauté the onions, mushrooms and green pepper. Remove from the pan. Add the flour and cook for 1 minute then gradually stir in the milk and bring to the boil, adding three quarters of the cheese and the salt and pepper. Stir until the cheese has melted. Add the chicken, cooked vegetables, olives and almonds, and simmer until heated through.

Cook the rice then gently stir in the chopped parsley. Place the rice on a heated serving plate and mound the chicken in the centre. Sprinkle the remaining cheese over the chicken.

Casablanca Chicken and Yellow Rice

Serves 6

1.5 kg (3 lb) chicken pieces
45 g (1 ½ oz) butter
2 tablespoons oil
2 large onions, thinly sliced
1 garlic clove, crushed
½ teaspoon chopped fresh ginger
¼ teaspoon saffron threads or ground turmeric
1 cinnamon stick, broken in half
1 cup (8 fl oz) apricot nectar

½ cup (4 fl oz) dry white wine
salt and pepper
½ cup (3 oz) prunes, stoned and soaked
1 cup (4 oz) dried apricots, soaked
1 tablespoon (1 oz) honey
3 teaspoons lemon juice
extra soaked apricots and prunes, to garnish
1 tablespoon toasted sesame seeds

Yellow Rice
2 cups (12 oz) rice
3½ cups (28 fl oz) chicken stock
½ teaspoon ground turmeric

Fry the chicken pieces in the butter and oil until golden. Remove and set aside. Fry the onions, garlic and spices, then replace the chicken and toss in the spice-onion mixture. Add the apricot nectar, wine, salt and pepper. Cover and cook over moderate heat until tender, about 30 to 40 minutes. During the last 10 minutes of cooking add the prunes, apricots, honey and lemon juice. Check the seasoning. Serve on a bed of Yellow Rice. Garnish with extra fruit and sprinkle with the sesame seeds.

Yellow Rice: Cook the rice by the absorption method (*page 307*), with the chicken stock and turmeric.

Opposite: *Casablanca Chicken and Yellow Rice*

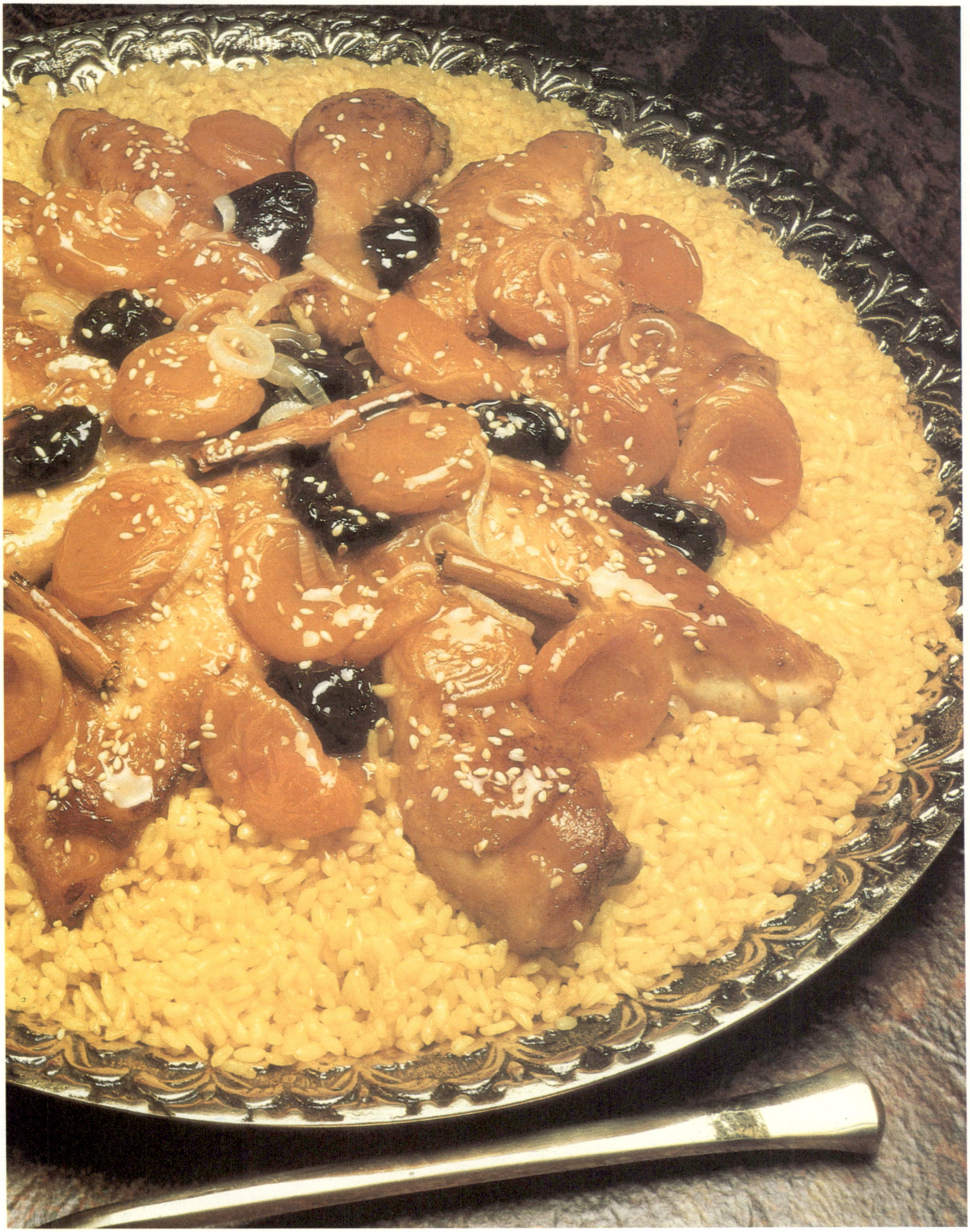

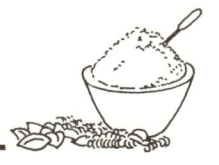

Pasta and Rice

Rice Ring with Salmon in Lemon Sauce

Serves 4

- 3 tablespoons oil
- 1 onion, chopped or 4 chopped spring onions (scallions)
- 1 garlic clove, crushed
- 1 red pepper, chopped or 1 cup cooked peas
- 3 cups cooked rice
- 1 teaspoon soy sauce
- 1 teaspoon ground paprika
- salt
- 2 hard-boiled eggs
- 1 tablespoon lemon juice
- 1 teaspoon chopped fresh parsley
- 1 cup (8 fl oz) chicken stock, made with stock cube
- 3 teaspoons arrowroot or cornflour (cornstarch), dissolved in a little water
- 1 x 220 g (7 oz) can pink salmon, drained

Heat the oil in a frypan and fry the onion, garlic and red pepper until just tender. Add the rice and toss well with a fork until heated through. Add the soy sauce, paprika, salt to taste and 1 chopped hard-boiled egg. When the rice is thoroughly heated, spoon into a well-greased ring tin and put aside to keep warm. Add lemon juice and parsley to the hot chicken stock. Mix in the arrowroot and boil until the sauce thickens. Add the flaked salmon to the sauce.

Turn the rice ring out onto a plate, garnish with the remaining egg cut in slices and a few red pepper pieces. Fill the centre of the ring with the salmon mixture.

Rice Tuna Pie

Serves 4

- 1 tablespoon melted butter
- 2 cups cooked rice
- 1 egg, beaten with salt and pepper to taste
- 1 cup (4 oz) grated cheese
- 2 rashers bacon, chopped
- 1 onion or 4 spring onions (scallions), thinly sliced
- ½ cup chopped celery
- oil for frying
- 1 x 500 g (1 lb) can tuna
- 1 extra egg, beaten
- 1 tablespoon mayonnaise
- ¾ cup (6 fl oz) milk
- 1 tablespoon flour
- salt and pepper

Combine the butter, rice, egg and blend well. Place in a well greased 30 cm (12 inch) pie plate or similarly shaped ovenproof dish, pressing well against the bottom and sides of the plate. Sprinkle three quarters of the cheese over the rice crust. Fry the bacon, onion and celery in a little oil for a few minutes, then spoon into the pie crust. Drain and flake the tuna before adding to the pie crust.

Combine the extra egg, mayonnaise, milk, flour, salt and pepper and beat together until well blended. Pour the egg mixture over the tuna. Place in a 180°C (350°F/Gas 4) oven and cook for 35 to 40 minutes, or until the filling has set. Garnish with the remaining cheese, tomato wedges and bacon rolls. Return to oven to melt the cheese. Serve hot or cold, cut into wedges, with salad.

Salmon and Rice Casserole

Serves 6

- 15 g (½ oz) butter
- 1 onion, chopped
- 3 cups cooked rice
- 1 x 450 g (14 ½ oz) can salmon, drained and flaked
- juice and rind of ½ a lemon
- 1 tablespoon chopped fresh parsley
- salt and freshly ground pepper
- 2 cups frozen broccoli, cooked, or 2 zucchini (courgettes), parboiled, or canned asparagus cuts, drained
- 1 cup (4 oz) grated cheese
- 2 cups (16 fl oz) hot thick white sauce, or canned chicken or celery soup
- sliced tomatoes, to garnish
- capers, to garnish

Heat the butter and sauté the onion until golden. Set aside.

Mix together the rice, salmon, lemon juice and rind, onion and parsley and place in a well-greased ovenproof dish. Season with salt and pepper. Cut the cooked broccoli into small florets and trim the stalks to match. Spoon the broccoli in a border around the dish. Add half of the cheese to the hot white sauce and stir until melted. Spoon the sauce over the salmon mixture. Sprinkle the top with the reserved cheese. Place the oven dish on a baking tray and bake at 180°C (350°F/Gas 4) until the top is golden. During the last 10 minutes of cooking, garnish with the tomato slices and capers.

Seafood Risotto

Serves 4

- 2 tablespoons oil
- 1 onion, chopped
- 1 garlic clove, crushed
- 1 cup (6 oz) rice
- 2 tomatoes, peeled and chopped
- 250 g (8 oz) fresh fish, diced
- 1 tablespoon tomato paste
- 2 cups (16 fl oz) chicken stock
- 1 bay leaf
- ¼ teaspoon dried oregano or basil
- salt and pepper
- 250 g (8 oz) fresh, frozen or cooked prawns (shrimp), tuna or salmon
- 1 cup sliced mushrooms, cooked in 1 tablespoon butter for 2 minutes
- chopped fresh parsley, to garnish

Heat the oil and sauté the onion, garlic and rice for a few minutes, tossing well. Add the tomatoes, fish, tomato paste, chicken stock, bay leaf, oregano and salt and pepper. Stir once to distribute the rice evenly, then cook over low heat, covered, for about 20 minutes. Reserve a few prawns, add the remainder to the rice with the mushrooms, and continue cooking until the rice is tender. Add a little extra hot stock if needed. Garnish with the reserved prawns and parsley.

Seafood Gumbo

Serves 6

45 g (1 ½ oz) butter
3 rashers bacon, chopped
1 onion, chopped
1 garlic clove, crushed
250 g (8 oz) okra, thinly sliced
1 x 410 g (13 oz) can peeled tomatoes
1 bay leaf
2 lemon slices
8 cups (2 litres) chicken stock, made with stock cubes
1 x 500 g (1 lb) can crab meat or equal amount fresh or canned prawns (shrimp)
salt and pepper
3 cups hot cooked rice
2 tablespoons chopped fresh parsley

Heat the butter and fry the bacon for a few minutes. Add the onion, garlic and okra to the pan and fry over moderate heat until the okra is golden. Add the tomatoes, bay leaf, lemon slices and chicken stock. Simmer for about 15 minutes, or until the okra is tender then add the crab meat and heat. Adjust the seasoning with salt and pepper to taste. Spoon about ½ cup of the hot rice into each soup bowl and pour the soup over the rice. Sprinkle with parsley.

Fish Rice Rollups

Serves 4 – 6

45 g (1 ½ oz) margarine
1 medium-sized onion, finely chopped
4 cups cooked rice
salt and pepper
750 g (1 ½ lb) fresh or frozen fish fillets
1 hard-boiled egg, finely chopped
1 tablespoon chopped fresh parsley
a little grated lemon rind
2 tablespoons mayonnaise
1 x 440 g (14 oz) can cream of tomato, celery or mushroom soup
½ cup (4 fl oz) milk
1 cup cooked broccoli, or spinach or peas
½ cup (2 oz) buttered breadcrumbs or grated cheese

Heat the margarine and sauté the onion until tender. Add the rice and toss to blend. Season to taste. Pat the fish dry with paper towels and season. Cut wide fillets in half lengthwise. Remove 6 tablespoons rice from the pan and combine with the egg, parsley, lemon rind and mayonnaise. Place 2 teaspoons rice mixture at the end of each fillet, roll up and secure with a toothpick or tie with thread. Spoon the remaining rice into a greased ovenproof dish. Blend the soup and milk. Add ½ cup (4 fl oz) soup to the rice and blend. Place the broccoli in the centre of the rice. Lay fish rolls around the broccoli and pour over the remaining soup. Sprinkle with breadcrumbs or cheese. Cover and cook in a 180°C (350°F/Gas 4) oven until the fish flakes with a fork, about 25 to 30 minutes.

Prawn Risotto

Serves 6

1.25 kg (2 ½ lb) green prawns (shrimp)

Stock
2 tablespoons olive oil
1 medium-sized onion, finely chopped
1 small carrot, finely chopped
1 stalk celery, finely chopped
1 garlic clove, crushed
reserved prawn (shrimp) heads and shells
1 cup (8 fl oz) dry white wine
5 cups (1.25 litres) water
1 teaspoon salt

Risotto
60 g (2 oz) butter
1 medium-sized onion, chopped
1 small red pepper (capsicum), diced
1 small green pepper (capsicum), diced
2 stalks celery, thinly sliced
2 cups (12 oz) rice
spring onions (scallions), to garnish
extra cooked prawns (shrimp), to garnish

Peel and devein the prawns. Set aside and reserve the heads and shells for use in the stock.

Stock: Heat the olive oil in a large saucepan and add the chopped vegetables and garlic. Cook gently until the onion becomes transparent. Add the reserved prawn heads and shells, white wine, water and salt. Bring the liquid to the boil and simmer for 40 minutes.

Risotto: Melt half the butter in another large saucepan and lightly sauté the onion, peppers and celery until soft. Lift out wih a slotted spoon and reserve.

Add the remaining butter, heat until foaming and add the prawns. Cook for about 3 to 4 minutes, until the prawns turn pink and are lightly cooked. Remove from pan. Add the rice to the pan and stir well to coat each grain with butter. Strain the stock and add 1 cup (8 fl oz) to the rice. Cook over medium heat until the stock is absorbed. Add a further 3 cups (24 fl oz) of stock, a cupful at a time, cooking until each cupful is absorbed. Stir the reserved vegetables and prawns through the rice with a fork, taking care not to crush the rice grains. Cover and cook for 5 minutes more or until the rice is tender, adding a little more stock if necessary. Garnish the risotto with spring onion curls, and extra cooked prawns with heads left on.

Pasta and Rice

Rice with Mussels

Serves 6

- 2 bay leaves
- 1 stalk celery, chopped
- 3 peppercorns
- 24 mussels, scrubbed clean and bearded, or canned mussels or other shellfish
- ¼ cup (2 fl oz) olive oil
- 2 onions, chopped
- 1 cup (6 oz) rice
- 1 cup (8 fl oz) tomato juice or 1 tablespoon tomato paste
- chopped fresh parsley

Fill a large saucepan with about 2.5 cm (1 inch) of cold water. Add the bay leaves, celery and peppercorns and bring to the boil. When boiling rapidly, add enough mussels to fit in the bottom of the saucepan. Replace the lid and reboil rapidly until the mussels open. Remove the cooked mussels from the pan and cook more mussels while allowing the opened ones to cool. When all the mussels have opened, strain the liquid through a cloth and reserve. Take the mussels out of their shells and set aside.

Heat the oil in a frying pan and sauté the onions until transparent. Add the rice, stirring until each grain is covered with oil, then remove from the heat. Measure the strained cooking liquid and add the tomato juice (or paste) and enough water to make up 2 cups. Add to the rice, replace the pan over heat and bring the liquid to the boil, stirring occasionally. Cover and cook over a low heat until the rice has absorbed all the liquid and is tender. If necessary add more boiling water.

Stir the mussels and parsley into the cooked rice with a wooden fork, cover the pan with a thick cloth and then the lid, folding the cloth over it, and stand for 10 minutes away from the heat.

Rice with Mussels

Pacific Prawn Curry

Serves 4

3 tablespoons peanut oil
1 teaspoon finely chopped root ginger
1 garlic clove, crushed
500 g (1 lb) green or cooked prawns (shrimp), peeled and deveined
2 onions, sliced
1 tablespoon curry powder, or to taste
1½ cups (12 fl oz) coconut milk or use chicken stock
1 green cucumber, halved lengthwise, seeded, then cut in thick slices
2 teaspoons lemon juice
1 teaspoon sugar
salt
3 teaspoons cornflour (cornstarch), dissolved in a little water
shredded spring onions (scallions)

Pacific Prawn Curry

Heat the oil in a wok or frying pan. Add the ginger and garlic – when they change colour discard. Add the prawns to the flavoured oil, and fry until they turn pink, remove and reserve. Add more oil if needed and cook the onions for 2 minutes. Then add the curry powder and stir fry for 1 minute. Blend in the coconut milk and heat until boiling. Add cucumber and simmer for a few minutes then add lemon juice, sugar and salt to taste. Return the prawns to the wok, and stir until the mixture boils and thickens. Serve with Lemon Rice, garnish with spring onions.

Lemon Rice: Cook 2 cups (12 oz) of rice. When drained add 15 g (½ oz) butter and the grated rind of 1 lemon, toss to blend.

Prawns in Black Bean Sauce

Serves 4

6 dried Chinese mushrooms
500 g (1 lb) green prawns (shrimp)
1 tablespoon canned black beans
2 tablespoons Chinese wine or dry sherry
2 garlic cloves, crushed
1 teaspoon finely grated fresh ginger
oil for frying
1 onion, thinly sliced
1 cup (8 fl oz) chicken stock, made with stock cubes
½ teaspoon sugar
1 teaspoon soy sauce
2 teaspoons cornflour (cornstarch)

Soak the mushrooms in hot water for 20 minutes. Discard stems and cut in thin strips. Peel and devein the prawns. Wash the black beans in a sieve under running cold water. Drain well, mash with a fork and mix with the wine, garlic and ginger. Heat oil in a wok or frypan, add the prawns, mushrooms and onion and stir for 1 minute. Add the bean mixture, lower heat and cook for 1 minute. Blend the chicken stock with the sugar, soy sauce and cornflour. Add to the prawns and stir until the sauce thickens and boils.

Serve spooned over hot rice.

Pasta and Rice

Prawn Asopao

Serves 4

¼ cup (2 fl oz) olive oil
1 large onion, chopped
1 green pepper (capsicum), chopped
4 rashers bacon, chopped
1 cup (6 oz) rice
2 ½ cups (20 fl oz) chicken stock
1 cup frozen peas, thawed
¼ cup capers, drained
¼ cup stuffed olives, sliced
750 g (1 ½ lb) king prawns (shrimps), cooked
1 whole canned pimiento
salt and pepper

Heat the oil in a large saucepan and cook the onion, green pepper and bacon, covered, over low heat for 10 minutes. Stir in the rice and the stock and bring to the boil. Reduce the heat, cover tightly and simmer for 20 minutes until the rice is tender.

Add the peas, capers and olives to the casserole and lightly toss through. Arrange the peeled and deveined prawns on top and decorate with the pimiento cut into 1 cm (½ inch) strips. Cover and simmer for 4 to 5 minutes to cook the peas and heat the prawns through. Adjust the seasoning and serve from the casserole.

Speedy Rice Supper

Serves 6

500 g (1 lb) rice
3 tablespoons oil
4 rashers bacon, chopped
2 onions or 6 spring onions (scallions), chopped
1 cup chopped green or red pepper (capsicum), celery or drained corn kernels
1 garlic clove, crushed
3 cups chopped cooked chicken
salt and pepper
soy sauce
2 tomatoes, chopped
1 x 425 g (13 ½ oz) can whole champignons, drained and fried in a little butter until golden
¼ cup (1 ½ oz) peanuts or chopped almonds
chopped fresh parsley

Cook the rice by the rapid boil method (*page 307*). Allow to drain well in colander and keep warm. Heat 2 tablespoons of the oil in a pan. Add the bacon, onions, green pepper and garlic and fry until the bacon is golden. Add 2 cups of the chicken to the vegetable mixture and toss until heated through.

Add the remaining oil to the pan with the rice. Lightly toss, but do not stir, with a large fork until rice and chicken mixture are blended. Season to taste with salt, pepper and soy sauce. If serving direct from the pan, spoon a ring of the reserved cup of chicken onto the rice mixture, then add a ring of chopped tomato. Spoon the champignons into the centre of the pan, replace the lid and allow to heat for a few minutes. Uncover, garnish with nuts and parsley, and serve with coleslaw or a tossed salad.

Seafood Supper Pie

Serves 4

Crust
2 cups cooked rice
2 teaspoons curry powder
1 onion, finely chopped
60 g (2 oz) melted butter

Filling
1 x 185 g (6 oz) can salmon, drained and flaked
2 eggs
1 ½ cups (12 fl oz) milk
½ cup (2 oz) grated cheese
salt and pepper
a squeeze of lemon juice
1 tablespoon chopped fresh parsley
lemon and olive slices, to garnish

Crust: Combine all ingredients and press into a greased 20 cm (8 inch) tart plate.

Filling: Thoroughly combine all the ingredients except the garnish and carefully spoon into the prepared crust. Bake in a 180°C (350°F/Gas 4) oven for 35 to 40 minutes or until set. Serve garnished with lemon and olives.

Rice Seafood Supper

Serves 4

500 g (1 lb) cooked fish, haddock is ideal or canned salmon or tuna
3 cups hot cooked brown rice cooked by absorption method (*page 307*)
45 g (1 ½ oz) butter
1 onion, finely chopped
1 cup finely chopped celery
1 teaspoon grated lemon rind
salt and pepper
½ cup (4 fl oz) milk
2 eggs, beaten
½ cup (2 oz) grated cheese
lemon slices and parsley to garnish

Flake the fish into small pieces with a fork and combine with the rice. Heat the butter and sauté onion and celery until just tender then spoon into the rice along with the lemon rind. Season to taste with salt and pepper.

Grease 4 small ramekins or a medium-sized oven dish. Combine the milk and beaten eggs, pour over the rice mixture and blend with a fork. Spoon the rice mixture into the ramekins, sprinkle with the cheese and bake in a 180°C (350°F/Gas 4) oven for about 15 to 20 minutes. Serve with lemon slices and parsley sprigs.

Quick Spanish Risotto

Serves 6

butter, for frying
1 garlic clove, chopped
2 onions, chopped
2 green peppers (capsicum), sliced
6 cups cooked rice
2 tomatoes, sliced
500 g (1 lb) prawns (shrimp), cooked, peeled and deveined
1 x 450 g (14 ½ oz) can corn kernels, drained
salt and pepper

Heat the butter in a frypan and sauté the garlic, onions and peppers. Add the rice and heat through. Add the rest of the ingredients and toss until heated through.

Salmon Cakes with Caper Sauce

Serves 4

1 x 500 g (1 lb) can pink salmon
3 cups cooked rice
1 onion, grated or finely chopped
1 egg, beaten
salt and pepper
pinch of nutmeg, optional
butter for frying

Caper Sauce
15 g (½ oz) butter
1 tablespoon flour
1 ¼ cups (10 fl oz) milk
2 tablespoons capers, drained
2 tablespoons chopped fresh parsley
1 tablespoon lemon juice
1 teaspoon salt
pepper

Flake the salmon, add 1 cup of the rice and combine with the remaining ingredients, except the butter. Form into 8 even-sized cakes on a well floured board. Fry in hot butter until well browned. Drain, keep hot. Add a little extra butter to the pan and toss the remaining 2 cups rice until heated through. Serve with Caper Sauce.

Caper Sauce: Melt the butter, blend in the flour and cook for 1 minute, then remove from heat. Gradually blend in the milk until smooth. Replace over heat, stirring constantly until the mixture boils and thickens. Add the capers, parsley, lemon juice and seasoning. Spoon sauce over the Salmon Cakes. Serve with lemon wedges.

Salmon Rice Sorrento

Serves 4

1 x 220 g (7 oz) can pink salmon
2 tablespoons margarine
3 onions, thinly sliced
1 garlic clove, crushed
1 x 425 g (13 ½ oz) can tomatoes
1 tablespoon chopped fresh parsley
2 teaspoons brown sugar
1 bay leaf or a little chopped fresh basil
½ cup (4 fl oz) dry white wine or chicken stock
salt and freshly ground pepper
4 cups cooked rice
juice and rind of ½ lemon
2 tomatoes, sliced
extra chopped fresh parsley or black olives, to garnish

Drain and flake the salmon. Heat the margarine and cook 2 of the onions and the garlic until just tender. Add the tomatoes, parsley, brown sugar, bay leaf, wine, salt and pepper and allow to simmer for a few minutes. Place the rice, lemon juice and rind in a well-greased ovenproof dish and top with the flaked salmon. Pour over the tomato/wine sauce and top with the tomato slices and reserved sliced onions. Bake in a 180°C (350°F/Gas 4) oven for about 20 minutes. Serve dusted with parsley and garnished with a few black olives.

Easy Paella Pronto

Serves 4

½ cup (4 fl oz) olive or peanut oil
3 cups chopped cooked chicken
3 rashers bacon, chopped
2 onions, chopped
1 green pepper (capsicum),
2 garlic cloves, crushed
1 x 450 g (14 oz) can peeled tomatoes
¼ teaspoon saffron threads, soaked in boiling water or ½ teaspoon turmeric
6 cups cooked rice, refrigerated overnight
2 cups (16 fl oz) chicken stock
1 cup cooked peas or beans
250 g (8 oz) fresh or canned prawns (shrimp)
1 x 220 g (7 oz) can tuna or salmon, drained
1 x 105 g (3 ½ oz) can smoked oysters or mussels
lemon wedges

Heat the oil in a paella pan or frypan and add the chicken, bacon, onions, green pepper and garlic. Toss over moderate heat until the bacon is golden. Add the tomatoes and saffron, then the rice and toss (don't stir) with a large fork. Add the chicken stock, peas and two thirds of the prawns. Flake the tuna and add to the rice with the smoked oysters. Toss over moderate heat until the rice is hot. Garnish the centre with the reserved prawns and serve with lemon wedges.

Note: Any cooked meat, sausage or ham may replace the chicken, and cooked fresh fish may replace the prawns.

Pasta and Rice

Seafood Rice Kedgeree

Serves 2

60 g (2 oz) butter
1 cup sliced mushrooms
1 onion, sliced
1 x 125 g (4 oz) can smoked oysters, drained or small can tuna
3 cups cooked rice
2 hard-boiled eggs
1 tablespoon cream
parsley, to garnish

Heat the butter in a pan and cook the mushrooms and onion for 2 minutes. Then add smoked oysters, rice and 1 chopped hard-boiled egg. Toss lightly with a fork and season to taste. Fold the cream through the rice. Garnish with hard-boiled egg wedges and parsley.

Seafood Rice Kedgeree

Prawn Kebabs on Summer Rice

Serves 2

2 cups cooked rice
2 tablespoons French dressing
1 tablespoon chopped chives
1 red pepper (capsicum), cut into cubes
1 green pepper, (capsicum) cut into cubes
125 g (4 oz) cheese, cut into cubes
6 king prawns (shrimp), peeled and cleaned
6 canned peach slices

Carefully combine the rice, French dressing and chives, place on a serving plate and chill while preparing kebabs. Thread the peppers, cheese, prawns and peaches alternately on thin metal skewers. Serve on a bed of Summer Rice Pilaf (*page 313*), and accompany with a salad.

Spanish-Style Fish and Rice

Serves 4

- 3 tablespoons oil
- 4 fish fillets
- 1 garlic clove, crushed
- 1 green pepper, thinly sliced
- 2 onions, thinly sliced
- 4 tomatoes, sliced
- 1 tablespoon fresh parsley, chopped
- ½ cup (4 fl oz) dry white wine or chicken stock
- salt and pepper

Spanish Rice
- 2 cups (12 oz) rice
- 3½ cups (28 fl oz) chicken stock, made with a stock cube
- ½ teaspoon ground turmeric
- 1 tablespoon tomato paste
- ½ cup (2 ½ oz) sliced stuffed olives
- salt and pepper

Heat the oil and sauté the fish until golden on both sides. Remove from pan and keep warm. Place the garlic, green pepper, onions, tomatoes and parsley in the pan and cook for about 5 minutes. Replace the fish and add the wine, salt and pepper to taste. Simmer for about 5 to 10 minutes.

Serve the fish on a bed of Spanish Rice, topped with the sauce.

Spanish Rice: Cook the rice in the chicken stock with the turmeric and tomato paste. Follow directions for absorption method of cooking the rice (*page 307*). When cooked, allow to stand for 5 minutes, uncovered, then mix the stuffed olives through the rice. Season to taste with salt and pepper.

South Pacific Prawn Pilaf

Serves 4

- 15 g (½ oz) butter
- 4 spring onions (scallions), chopped
- 1 garlic clove, crushed
- 1 teaspoon chopped fresh ginger
- ½ teaspoon turmeric
- 1 cup (6 oz) rice
- 2 cups (16 fl oz) chicken stock
- 250 g (8 oz) peeled prawns (shrimp)
- 1 cup chopped cooked chicken
- salt and pepper
- toasted almonds

Heat the butter, add the spring onions, garlic, ginger and turmeric and cook for 1 minute. Add the rice and cook for 2 minutes, tossing. Add the chicken stock and cook by the absorption method (*page 307*). When cooked add the prawns and chicken, toss through the rice until heated through and season. Sprinkle with toasted almonds.

Rice Tuna Rissoles

Serves 4

- 1 x 500 g (1 lb) can tuna, drained
- 1 onion, finely chopped
- 2 stalks celery, finely chopped
- 2 cups cooked brown rice
- salt and pepper
- 1 tablespoon lemon juice
- 2 eggs, beaten
- flour
- 1 egg, blended with 2 tablespoons water
- breadcrumbs
- oil for frying
- chopped fresh parsley
- ¼ cup (2 fl oz) mayonnaise

Flake the tuna finely with a fork. Combine the onion, celery, rice, salt, pepper and lemon juice. Add 2 eggs and blend well. Form into patty or rissole shapes. Dip the rissoles into the flour then into the remaining egg blended with water and roll in breadcrumbs. If possible, refrigerate for 30 minutes. Fry in hot oil until golden. Add a little chopped parsley to the mayonnaise and spoon over the rissoles.

South Pacific Prawn Pilaf

Pasta and Rice

Quick 'n' Easy Rice and Cheese Salad

Serves 6

- 2 cups cooked rice
- ¼ cup chopped fresh parsley
- ¼ cup chopped mint or 2 teaspoons dried mint
- ½ cup chopped tomatoes
- salad dressing
- salt and pepper
- lettuce leaves
- 60 g (2 oz) cheese, cubed
- tomato wedges, to garnish
- sprigs of parsley, to garnish

Combine the rice, chopped parsley, mint and tomatoes. Pour on sufficient salad dressing to thoroughly moisten all ingredients and toss lightly. Season with salt and pepper. Chill until ready to serve.

Spoon the rice salad into a lettuce-lined bowl. Top with cubes of cheese, and garnish with the tomato wedges and parsley sprigs.

Creole Rice Salad

Serves 4

- 3 cups cooked rice
- ½ cup chopped green pepper (capsicum)
- ½ cup chopped red pepper (capsicum)
- 1 cup finely chopped mushrooms
- ½ cup chopped spring onions (scallions)
- 1 cup corn kernels, drained
- 1 cup diced ham or salami sausage
- salt and pepper
- ⅔ cup (5 fl oz) Italian or French dressing
- ¼ teaspoon instant garlic
- ¼ teaspoon paprika
- a little Tabasco sauce or chilli powder
- 1 tomato, chopped, to garnish
- a little chopped fresh parsley, to garnish

Combine the rice, peppers, mushrooms, spring onions, corn and ham. Season with salt and pepper. Blend the Italian dressing with the garlic, paprika and Tabasco. Pour over the rice mixture and toss well. Season to taste with salt and pepper and garnish with chopped tomato and parsley.

Tuna Rice Salad

Serves 4

- lettuce leaves
- 3 cups cooked rice
- 4 spring onions (scallions), chopped
- 1 cup corn kernels
- ½ red or green pepper (capsicum)
- 1 cup cooked peas
- 1 x 220 g (7 oz) can tuna or salmon
- ¼ cup (1 oz) peanuts, to garnish
- a little chopped fresh parsley, to garnish

Curry Dressing

- 3 tablespoons peanut oil
- 1 tablespoon vinegar
- 1 small garlic clove, crushed
- ½ teaspoon salt
- freshly ground pepper
- 1 teaspoon curry powder or paprika

Line a salad bowl with the lettuce leaves. Combine the rice, spring onions, corn, red pepper, peas and tuna in a basin. Place the dressing ingredients in a screw-topped jar and shake until well blended. Pour the dressing over the rice and toss to blend well. Spoon into a salad bowl and sprinkle with the peanuts and parsley. You may substitute ¼ cup (2 fl oz) of bottled French dressing for the Curry Dressing if you wish.

Note: This salad will keep in a plastic container in the refrigerator for several days. It can even be served hot. Simply make up the salad as the recipe suggests, including the dressing. Place in a greased frypan and toss over moderate heat until heated thoroughly. It will make a quick meal and is ideal served with a green salad.

Minted Rice and Ham Salad

Serves 4

- 1 cup rice cooked by the absorption method (*page 307*), in 2 cups (16 fl oz) blended orange juice and pineapple liquid
- 1 x 450g (14 ½ oz) can crushed pineapple, drained
- 1 tablespoon finely chopped fresh mint
- grated rind of 1 orange
- ¼ cup (2 fl oz) sour cream
- 1 x 1 kg (2 lb) can ham, chilled
- mint sprigs, to garnish
- fresh orange slices, to garnish

Combine the rice, crushed pineapple, mint, orange rind and sour cream. Press into a ring mould or tin and chill thoroughly. Slice the ham and arrange on a platter

Unmould the rice ring and decorate with mint sprigs and fresh orange slices. Serve with a tossed green salad.

Ham and Peach Salad

Serves 4

1 x 825 g (1 lb 10 ½ oz) can peach halves
¼ cup (2 oz) sugar
1 tablespoon vinegar
1 cinnamon stick
½ teaspoon whole cloves
¼ cup (2 fl oz) brandy
1 cup rice cooked by absorption method (*page 307*)
¼ cup chopped chives
⅓ cup (2 ½ fl oz) mayonnaise
500 g (1 lb) ham
¼ cup (1 oz) toasted slivered almonds

Drain the syrup from the peaches and combine it with the sugar, vinegar, cinnamon and cloves. Simmer, uncovered, for 5 minutes. Add the peach halves, cool, then stir in the brandy. Allow to chill for 6 hours or overnight.

Combine the rice, chopped chives and mayonnaise. Spoon into peach halves. Slice the ham and arrange with the filled peaches. Strain the peach marinade and serve separately. Top with slivered almonds and serve with the peach halves and a green salad.

Parma Rice Salad

Serves 6

½ lettuce, coarsely shredded
6 cups cooked rice
1 cup diced cheese
8 tomatoes, thinly sliced
1 cucumber, peeled and sliced
2 white onions, thinly sliced
3 hard-boiled eggs, cut in quarters
a few black olives, to garnish
chopped fresh parsley

Italian Style Dressing
1 cup (8 fl oz) French dressing
½ teaspoon sugar
½ teaspoon mixed mustard
1 garlic clove, crushed
1 tablespoon chopped fresh parsley
1 teaspoon chopped fresh chives or basil

Line a salad platter with lettuce. Toss the rice in half the dressing, add the cheese and spoon onto the lettuce. Top with the tomato and cucumber slices and the onion rings. Garnish the salad with the hard-boiled eggs and olives. Pour the remaining dressing over the salad and sprinkle with parsley.

Italian Style Dressing: Combine all the dressing ingredients and blend thoroughly.

Pagoda Rice Salad

Serves 6

Rice
2 ½ cups (1 lb) rice
5 ½ cups (1.3 litres) boiling chicken stock, made with cubes
pinch of saffron or ¼ teaspoon turmeric
¼ teaspoon grated lemon rind

Malaysian Dressing
1 garlic clove, crushed
½ teaspoon finely chopped fresh ginger
1 cup (8 fl oz) peanut oil
⅓ cup (2 ½ fl oz) vinegar
¼ cup (2 fl oz) pineapple liquid
1 teaspoon soy sauce
1 tablespoon toasted sesame seeds
½ teaspoon salt
freshly ground pepper

To Serve
1 cup thinly sliced canned water chestnuts or radishes
1 green or red pepper (capsicum), chopped
1 x 450 g (14 ½ oz) can pineapple slices or pieces, drained
1 cup chopped spring onions (scallions), optional
250 g (8 oz) cooked chicken, cut in thin strips
125 g (4 oz) peeled prawns, (shrimp), optional
toasted almonds or peanuts, to garnish

Rice: Cook the rice by the absorption method (*page 307*), using the above ingredients. Drain well and blend the rice with half the Malaysian Dressing while still warm.

Malaysian Dressing: Combine all the ingredients in a screw-top jar and shake well.

To Serve: Toss the rice with a little bit more of the Malaysian Dressing, a few water chestnuts, green pepper, pineapple and spring onions. Place the rice on a large platter, surround with the remaining ingredients and serve with extra dressing.

Pasta and Rice

Barbecue Rice Salad

Serves 8

6 cups cooked brown rice
1 onion, finely chopped
1 x 450 g (14 ½ oz) can 3-bean mix, drained or
1 x 440 g (14 oz) can corn kernels
1 cup diced cheese
3 rashers bacon, cooked and diced

1 red or green pepper (capsicum), chopped
1 cup chopped celery
tomato wedges
onion rings
olives

Dressing
½ cup (4 fl oz) oil
2 tablespoons vinegar or lemon juice
1 teaspoon brown sugar
1 teaspoon salt
a little freshly ground pepper
½ teaspoon dry mustard
pinch of chilli powder
1 garlic clove, crushed
1 tablespoon chopped olives or fresh parsley

Combine the rice, onion, beans, cheese, bacon, red pepper and celery. Combine all the dressing ingredients and blend well. Add to the rice mixture and blend thoroughly. Refrigerate to develop the flavour. Toss again before serving and garnish with tomato wedges, onion rings and olives.

Barbecue Rice Salad

Seafood Rice Salad

Serves 4

500 g (1 lb) small prawns (shrimp)
12 stuffed olives
2 cups cooked rice, chilled
1 x 105 g (3 ½ oz) can smoked mussels, drained
1 cup cauliflower florets, blanched in boiling water for 7 to 9 minutes and drained

1 green pepper (capsicum), finely sliced
3 tablespoons lemon juice
4 tablespoons French dressing
1 tablespoon finely chopped onion
freshly ground black pepper

Put aside 6 of the larger prawns and 6 olives for garnishing. Finely chop the remaining olives and add to the rice with the remaining prawns and the mussels, cauliflower and green pepper. Add all other ingredients, mix well and spoon into a salad bowl lined with lettuce leaves. Garnish with the reserved prawns and olives.

Sunshine Rice Salad

Serves 6

½ cup (4 fl oz) French dressing
2 tablespoons orange juice
a little grated orange rind
½ teaspoon paprika
salt and pepper
1 teaspoon chopped chives or parsley
4 cups cooked rice
1 cup thinly sliced celery
4 spring onions (scallions), thinly sliced

1 x 312 g (10 oz) can mandarin orange segments
shredded lettuce
1 x 220 g (7 oz) can salmon, drained and flaked with a fork
onion rings, celery curls or mint sprigs

Combine the French dressing, orange juice and rind, paprika, salt and pepper, and chives, and mix until well blended. Combine the rice, celery, spring onions and half the mandarin orange segments. Add two thirds of the dressing, toss until rice mixture is coated and check the seasoning. Surround a salad platter with shredded lettuce. Spoon the rice mixture into the centre, top with the salmon, surround with the remaining mandarin orange segments and pour over the remaining dressing. Garnish with onion rings, celery curls or mint sprigs.

Note: For special occasions, the rice mixture may be pressed into a well oiled ring mould or cake tin and refrigerated. Invert the mould onto a salad platter and surround with the remaining ingredients.

St Clements Rice Salad

Serves 6

1 cup (8 fl oz) orange juice
grated rind of 1 orange
2 ½ cups (20 fl oz) chicken stock
2 cups (12 oz) rice
4 spring onions (scallions), chopped
2 oranges, cut into segments
3 cups cooked chicken, cut into bite-sized pieces
mint sprigs

Citrus Dressing
½ cup (4 fl oz) oil
2 tablespoons lemon juice
grated rind and juice of 1 orange
½ teaspoon paprika
salt and pepper
2 teaspoons sherry, optional

Bring the orange juice, rind and chicken stock to the boil. Add the rice, stir well, cover and simmer for about 20 to 25 minutes until the rice is tender. Remove from heat, uncover and allow to stand 10 minutes. Toss with a fork and refrigerate until cold.

Add the spring onions to the rice mixture. Blend all the dressing ingredients thoroughly, then pour two thirds of the dressing over the rice. Place the rice on a salad platter and garnish the centre with the orange segments and chicken. Pour over the remaining dressing and decorate with mint sprigs.

St Clements Rice Salad

Pasta and Rice

Summer's Day Salad

Serves 6

- 250 g (½ lb) corned beef
- 4 cups cold, cooked rice
- ½ cup chopped spring onions (scallions)
- ½ cup chopped mixed pickles (onion, gherkins, cauliflower)
- ½ cup chopped celery
- ½ cup chopped fresh parsley
- ½ teaspoon mustard
- ½ cup (4 fl oz) French dressing
- salt
- freshly ground black pepper
- lettuce
- 3 tomatoes, quartered

Use home-cooked, canned or ready-cooked corned beef and cut in cubes or strips according to the type of meat used.

Mix together the rice, spring onions, pickles, celery and parsley. Blend the mustard into the French dressing and pour over the rice mixture. Toss well, add the corned beef, salt and pepper to taste and toss to mix evenly. Pile in the centre of a lettuce-lined platter. Pour a little French dressing over the tomato wedges and arrange around the edge of the platter.

Italian Rice Salad

Serves 4

- 3 cups cooked brown rice
- 125 g (4 oz) ham or salami, cut into small cubes
- 125 g (4 oz) cheese, cubed
- 2 tomatoes, chopped
- 1 small cucumber, peeled and cubed
- 3 tablespoons oil
- 1 tablespoon lemon juice
- ½ teaspoon mixed mustard
- ½ teaspoon salt
- ⅛ teaspoon lemon pepper
- ⅛ teaspoon minced garlic
- ⅛ teaspoon dried oregano leaves
- ¼ teaspoon dried basil leaves
- black olives, to garnish

Combine the brown rice, salami, cheese, tomatoes and cucumber. Blend the remaining ingredients together, reserving the olives for a garnish. Toss the dressing through the rice and refrigerate to allow the flavour to develop. Before serving toss thoroughly and garnish with olives.

Seafood Salad Indienne

Serves 6

- 3 cups cooked rice
- 4 spring onions (scallions), chopped
- 1 x 440 g (14 oz) can corn kernels drained
- 1 red pepper (capsicum), finely chopped
- 1 cup cooked peas
- ¾ cup (3 oz) blanched almonds, chopped
- 2 teaspoons curry powder
- 1 teaspoon salt
- pepper to taste
- ⅓ cup (2 ½ fl oz) white vinegar
- ¼ cup (2 fl oz) oil
- 1 garlic clove, crushed
- lettuce
- 500 g (1 lb) prawns (shrimp), peeled
- lemon slices and parsley, to garnish

Curry Mayonnaise

- 30 g (1 oz) butter
- 2 teaspoons curry powder
- 2 teaspoons flour
- 2 tablespoons sugar
- ½ cup (4 fl oz) milk
- 1 egg, beaten
- ¼ cup (2 fl oz) white vinegar
- salt and pepper

Combine the first 6 ingredients in a basin. Place the curry powder, salt, pepper, vinegar, oil and garlic in a screw-top jar and shake. Pour into the rice mixture and toss. Press into a lightly oiled ring tin or mould and chill. Turn onto a serving platter and surround with crisp lettuce cups and prawns. Spoon over Curry Mayonnaise. Chill well before serving, garnished with lemon and parsley.

Curry Mayonnaise: Melt the butter and fry the curry powder very gently for 2 minutes. Remove from heat and stir in the flour and sugar. Cook for 3 minutes. Carefully blend in the combined milk and egg. Heat, stirring until mixture thickens. Add the vinegar very gradually, stirring constantly. Season to taste.

Capricornia Rice Salad

Serves 8

- 6 cups cooked rice
- ½ cup chopped spring onions (scallions)
- ½ cup grated carrot
- ½ cup each red and green pepper (capsicum), diced
- ½ cup chopped celery
- 1 cup diced cheese
- 1 x 450 g (14 ½ oz) can pineapple pieces, drained and juice reserved
- 1 cup (8 fl oz) French dressing
- salt and pepper
- 1 tablespoon chopped fresh parsley

Combine the rice, spring onions, carrot, red and green pepper and celery with the cheese and pineapple pieces. Add 2 tablespoons of the reserved pineapple liquid to the French dressing and pour over the rice. Toss well and season to taste with salt and pepper. Sprinkle with pastry.

Golden Ham with Golden Nut Rice Salad

Serves 8

1 x 905 g (1 lb 13 oz) can ham
½ cup (4 fl oz) apricot nectar
¼ cup (3 oz) apricot jam
¼ cup (1 ½ oz) brown sugar
1 tablespoon sherry
1 tablespoon lemon juice
1 teaspoon dry mustard
¼ teaspoon ground ginger

Golden Nut Rice Salad
6 cups cooked rice
1 cup finely chopped celery
½ cup finely chopped spring onions (scallions)
½ cup (2 oz) chopped toasted almonds
½ cup (4 fl oz) French dressing
½ cup (4 fl oz) apricot nectar
salt and pepper

Cut the ham into slices, removing any jelly. Re-form and tie with string to retain the shape. Combine the apricot nectar with the remaining ingredients, heat, stirring, until boiling, then sieve. Spoon half the glaze over the ham. Bake at 180°C (350°F/Gas 4) for about 10 minutes, basting frequently with the pan juices. Raise temperature to 190°C (375°F/Gas 5). Spoon over the remaining glaze and bake until the ham is well glazed, about 10 to 15 minutes. Remove and cool slightly, then refrigerate. Remove the string and serve the ham with Golden Nut Rice Salad. Garnish with apricot halves filled with cranberry sauce.

Golden Nut Rice Salad: Combine the rice with the celery, spring onions and almonds. Blend the French dressing, nectar and seasoning. Pour over the rice mixture and toss well.

Oriental Rice Salad

Serves 4

250 g (8 oz) button mushrooms, sliced
1 onion, or 4 spring onions scallions), thinly sliced
½ cup (4 fl oz) peanut oil
2 tablespoons vinegar
1 garlic clove, crushed
½ teaspoon salt
½ teaspoon ground ginger
2 teaspoons soy sauce
3 cups cooked brown rice
1 cup thinly sliced celery
1 cup grated carrot
¼ cup (1 oz) toasted sesame seeds or slivered toasted almonds

Combine the mushrooms and onion. Blend together the next 6 ingredients, pour over the mushrooms and allow to marinate for 30 minutes. Mix the mushrooms with the rice, celery and carrot, tossing to combine thoroughly. Chill before serving, sprinkled with sesame seeds.

Greek Rice Salad

Serves 4

1 small cucumber
2 tomatoes
3 tablespoons oil
1 tablespoon lemon juice
½ teaspoon grated lemon rind
½ teaspoon mixed mustard
1 teaspoon chopped fresh herbs (parsley, mint, basil)
salt and pepper
3 cups cooked rice
1 lettuce heart, coarsely shredded
125 g (4 oz) cream cheese or feta cheese, cubed
a few olives, to garnish

Peel the cucumber, halve lengthwise, and scoop out the seeds with a spoon. Cut into thin slices. Cut the tomatoes into thin wedges. Blend together the oil, lemon juice, lemon rind, mustard, herbs, salt and pepper. Place the rice in the centre of a salad platter, surround with the lettuce, cucumber slices, tomato wedges and cheese cubes. Garnish the centre with cucumber slices and black olives. Pour the lemon herb dressing over the salad and toss before serving.

Cool Island Salad

Serves 6

3 cups (24 fl oz) chicken stock
grated rind of 1 lemon
1 ½ cups (9 oz) rice
2 cups cooked chicken cut into bite-sized pieces
1 cup diced honeydew melon
2 cups seedless green grapes

Lemon Dressing
6 tablespoons oil
1 tablespoon orange juice
2 tablespoons lemon juice
salt and pepper
2 teaspoons dry sherry
1 tablespoon chopped fresh parsley or mint

Bring the chicken stock and lemon rind to the boil, add the rice and cover. Lower heat and simmer for about 20 to 25 minutes until the rice is tender. Remove from the heat, uncover and allow to stand 5 minutes. Toss with a fork, then refrigerate. When chilled, add the chicken, melon and grapes. Blend all the Lemon Dressing ingredients thoroughly. Pour over the rice salad and toss until well mixed. Garnish with a small bunch of grapes.

Pasta and Rice

Citrus Rice Salad

Serves 4

2 oranges, peeled and sliced
1 grapefruit, peeled and sectioned
3 cups chilled cooked rice
1 onion, thinly sliced
1 tablespoon chopped fresh parsley
¾ cup (6 fl oz) mayonnaise
juice from oranges and grapefruit
extra orange slices, to garnish

Collect the juice while peeling and slicing the citrus fruit. Combine the orange, grapefruit, rice, onion and parsley in a large bowl. Blend with the mayonnaise and moisten with the juice from the fruit if necessary. Chill. Garnish with extra orange slices.

Summer Rice Salad

Serves 6

3 cups cooked rice
1 cup chopped corned beef, ham or prawns (shrimp)
1 onion or 4 spring onions (scallions), finely chopped
½ cup (4 fl oz) French dressing or mayonnaise
½ teaspoon paprika
salt and pepper
2 oranges, thinly sliced
½ cucumber, sliced
1 tablespoon chopped chives

Combine the rice, corned beef and onion. Blend the French dressing and paprika and add to the rice with salt and pepper, tossing to blend well. Pile the rice in the centre of a salad platter, surround with orange and cucumber slices, and sprinkle with chives.

Rice Coleslaw Salad

Serves 6

3 cups cooked rice
1 cup grated carrot
2 cups shredded cabbage
1 cup pineapple pieces, drained
½ cup chopped spring onions (scallions)
⅓ cup (2 ½ fl oz) French dressing
⅓ cup (2 ½ fl oz) mayonnaise or sour cream
½ teaspoon sugar
pinch of ground ginger
salt and pepper
extra pineapple pieces, to garnish
toasted almonds, to garnish

Combine the rice, carrot, cabbage, pineapple pieces and spring onions.
Blend the French dressing with the mayonnaise, then add the sugar and a pinch of ginger. Season the salad with salt and pepper, add the dressing and blend well.
Garnish with extra pineapple and toasted almonds.

Rice Waldorf Salad

Serves 4

3 cups cooked brown rice
1 cup (4 oz) diced cheese
½ cup chopped celery
2 apples, unpeeled, diced and soaked in a little lemon juice
1 cup grated carrot
½ cup (3 oz) sultanas
1 cup finely shredded cabbage or lettuce
½ cup (2 oz) chopped pecan nuts or walnuts
⅔ cup (5 fl oz) French dressing or mayonnaise
salt and pepper

Combine the rice with the cheese, celery, apples, carrot, sultanas, cabbage and pecan nuts. Pour over the dressing and toss to blend well. Season with salt and pepper to taste.

Note: Pineapple pieces may be substituted for apples.

Rice Garden Salad

Serves 6

2 cups (16 fl oz) chicken stock (can be made with stock cubes)
1 tablespoon lemon juice
½ teaspoon grated lemon rind
1 cup (6 oz) brown rice
1 cup peeled diced cucumber
½ cup diced green or red pepper (capsicum)
½ cup diced celery
4 spring onions (scallions), chopped
salt and freshly ground pepper
lettuce
2 tomatoes, diced
a few black olives
chopped fresh parsley

Tomato Juice Dressing
½ cup (4 fl oz) unsweetened tomato juice
2 teaspoons vinegar or lemon juice
1 small garlic clove, crushed
pinch of dried oregano or dry mustard
dash of Worcestershire sauce
salt and freshly ground pepper
¼ teaspoon grated lemon rind

Combine the chicken stock with the lemon juice and rind. Bring to the boil, add the rice, stir once and cover. Place over moderate heat and cook until rice is tender, 55 to 60 minutes. Add a little extra hot stock or water if required. Allow the rice to cool, then add the cucumber, green pepper, celery, spring onions and seasoning, tossing well to combine. Place the rice salad in a lettuce-lined salad platter or bowl. Spoon over sufficient Tomato Juice Dressing to moisten and toss to combine. Spoon the tomatoes into the centre of the rice salad and garnish with olives and parsley.

Tomato Juice Dressing: Combine all ingredients and blend well. Refrigerate for 30 minutes if possible. Shake well before using.

VEGETABLES

Vegetables are one of the most important elements of any diet. Australia is blessed with an abundant supply of the very freshest vegetables and fruits available anywhere in the world and with the introduction of the new style fruit markets, we have the opportunity to purchase vegetables and fruits previously unknown in Australia. Most of these new varieties are accompanied by leaflets showing their uses and approximate flavour. This new international look to our fruit and vegetable shopping will enable us to try the best of the new cultures introduced to our country.

Do not cook vegetables until soft. Leave them a little crisp and give the family something to taste and chew. In fact, it is not necessary to cook many vegetables at all.

The majority of the recipes in this chapter have been supplied by the Primary Products Promotion Unit of the **Department of Agriculture**, while others have been provided by contributors whose credits appear elsewhere in the book.

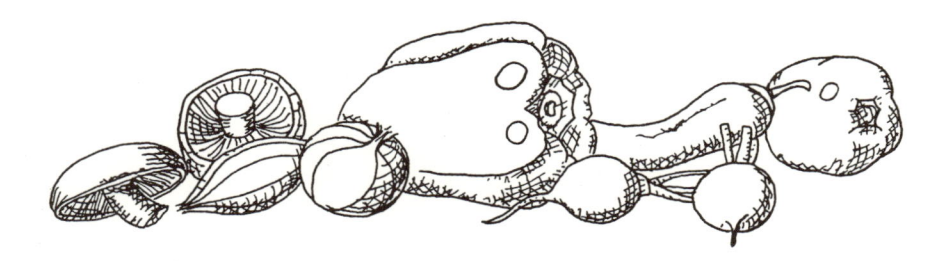

The **Primary Products Promotions Unit** was created in 1981 by the New South Wales Department of Agriculture out of a need to service and educate the community, from producer to consumer. It was established to develop and promote the 'Fresh is Best' campaign.

The functions of the PPP Unit are considerable, covering media publicity and promotion, point-of-sale promotion, education, product testing, recipe development and grower/wholesaler/retailer/consumer communications.

Product tests are conducted to assess quality and cooking performance in relation to geographical area and variety. Recipe development follows the Dietary Guidelines for Australians in increasing the consumption of complex carbohydrates and dietary fibre while decreasing the intake of fat, refined sugar, salt and alcohol.

As a result of the 'Fresh is Best' campaign, a bigger and better variety of fresh fruit and vegetables now take their rightful place in the home with Australians realising the immeasurable importance of fresh fruit and vegetables in the diet.

The recipes here were supplied by Anne Marshall.

Vegetables

Artichokes with Lemon Butter

Serves 4

4 large artichokes
2 garlic cloves, finely chopped
75 g (2½ oz) butter
juice of ½ lemon

Cook the trimmed artichokes in lightly salted water with a squeeze of lemon juice for about 20 minutes. Drain and keep warm in a cloth.

Simmer the garlic in the butter until soft. Add the lemon juice and simmer for 1 minute. Serve the artichokes on individual plates with small separate bowls of lemon butter.

To eat, pull the artichoke leaves off the base. Dip in the lemon butter, then draw the fleshy end of the leaf through your teeth.

Scalloped Asparagus Parcels

Serves 8 as a first course or 4 as a main course

½ cup (4 fl oz) water
½ cup (4 fl oz) white wine
500 g (1 lb) Tasmanian scallops, debearded
8 sheets filo pastry, halved
250 g (8 oz) butter, melted

1 bunch thin asparagus, trimmed and blanched
1 cup chopped spring onions (scallions)
1 cup (4 oz) grated Swiss cheese

Wine Mustard Sauce
30 g (1 oz) butter
2 tablespoons flour
reserved stock from poaching scallops
1 teaspoon grain seed mustard

freshly ground black pepper
¼ cup (2 fl oz) cream

Bring the water and wine to the boil. Add the scallops and return to the boil. Drain and reserve the stock. Lay one sheet of filo pastry on a board, keeping the remaining sheets covered to prevent drying out. Brush with melted butter, top with a second sheet and brush again. Lay 3-4 spears of asparagus on the filo, top with 2 tablespoons scallops and a sprinkling of spring onions and cheese. Fold in the sides of the pastry and roll to form a neat parcel.

Place the parcel on a baking tray. Repeat with the remaining pastry and filling to make 8 parcels. Bake at 190°C (375°F/Gas 5) for 15 to 20 minutes or until golden brown.

Wine Mustard Sauce: Melt the butter in a saucepan. Add the flour and stir over a medium heat for 1 minute. Add the reserved stock and stir until boiling and thickened. Season with the mustard and pepper. Stir in the cream.

Asparagus Chinese Style

Serves 4 – 6

2 tablespoons peanut oil
2 garlic cloves, crushed
1 teaspoon grated fresh ginger
3 bunches asparagus, trimmed and sliced diagonally
250 g (8 oz) oyster mushrooms, sliced
250 g (8 oz) snow peas (mange-tout), strung

1 cup (8 fl oz) chicken stock
1 tablespoon soy sauce
1 tablespoon dry sherry
½ teaspoon sesame oil
2 teaspoons cornflour (cornstarch)
1 tablespoon cold water
¼ cup sesame seeds, toasted

Heat a wok and add the oil. Stir fry the garlic and ginger for 1 minute. Add the asparagus and stir fry for 3 to 4 minutes. Add the mushrooms and snow peas and stir fry for 1 minute.

Stir in the chicken stock, soy sauce, sherry and sesame oil. Cover and cook for 1 minute. Blend the cornflour with water. Add to the vegetables and stir for 1 minute until thick and glossy. Serve hot, sprinkled with toasted sesame seeds.

Filo Silverbeet Triangles

Makes 24

1 kg (2 lb) silverbeet
1 cup chopped spring onions (scallions)
⅓ cup (2 ½ fl oz) olive oil
125 g (4 oz) feta cheese
1 cup (8 oz) cottage cheese
2 tablespoons grated Parmesan cheese

2 tablespoons chopped fresh parsley
1 tablespoon chopped fresh dill
4 eggs, beaten
freshly ground nutmeg
freshly ground pepper
500 g (1 lb) filo pastry
250 g (8 oz) butter, melted

Remove and reserve the stalks of the silverbeet for another dish. Shred and steam the leaves. Sauté the spring onions in heated oil.

Mix the silverbeet leaves with the spring onions, feta, cottage and Parmesan cheeses, parsley, dill, eggs, nutmeg and pepper in a food processor. Process until smooth.

Cut each filo pastry sheet into 3 strips. Stack and keep covered. Lay a strip on the work bench. Brush with the melted butter. Place a teaspoonful of filling onto the edge of the pastry. Fold a corner over the filling to form a triangle. Continue to fold in triangles to the end of the strip, then place seam side down on a baking tray. Continue in this way until all the filling is used.

Bake at 190°C (375°F/Gas 5) for 15 to 20 minutes, until puffed and golden. Serve hot.

Creamy Filled Mushrooms

Makes 24

24 medium-sized mushrooms
½ cup (4 oz) cream cheese, softened
¾ cup finely chopped ham or salami
¼ cup finely chopped spring onions (scallions)
¼ cup (1 oz) pecans, finely chopped
2 tablespoons chopped fresh parsley
1 teaspoon lemon rind
1 teaspoon lemon juice
freshly ground black pepper
paprika or parsley for garnish

Remove the stalks from the mushrooms. Finely chop the stalks and mix with the remaining ingredients.

Mound the mixture into the mushrooms caps and chill well. Sprinkle with paprika or top each with a tiny sprig of parsley before serving.

Fennel with Mushrooms

Serves 4

2 bulbs fennel
1 large tomato
15 g (½ oz) butter
1 garlic clove, crushed
500 g (1 lb) mushrooms, thinly sliced
1 chicken stock cube
¼ cup (2 fl oz) water
salt and freshly ground black pepper
1 tablespoon chopped fresh basil
extra chopped fresh basil for garnish

Wash the fennel and discard any tough or withered outer pieces. Slice thinly. Peel and chop the tomato.

Melt the butter in a frying pan and sauté the garlic for 1 minute. Add the fennel and tomato and cook for 5 minutes. Add the remaining ingredients and stir to combine. Cover and simmer for 6 to 8 minutes or until the fennel is tender. Serve hot, sprinkled with the extra basil. Delicious with beef or grilled (broiled) fish.

Italian Fried Peppers

Serves 4

3 tablespoons olive oil
2 garlic cloves, crushed
2 green peppers (capsicums), cut into strips
2 red peppers (capsicums), cut into strips
½ teaspoon chopped fresh oregano
½ teaspoon salt
1-2 tablespoons water

Heat the oil in a large frying pan and fry the garlic. Add the peppers, oregano, salt and water. Cover and cook over a low heat until tender-crisp, stirring occasionally.

Serve hot as a vegetable. Delicious with chicken, veal, lamb and beef.

Prawn and Cauliflower Stir Fry

Serves 4 – 6

3 tablespoons peanut oil
500 g (1 lb) green prawns (shrimps), peeled and deveined
2 garlic cloves, crushed
2 teaspoons grated fresh ginger
2 onions, each cut into 8 segments
2 carrots, diagonally sliced
2 cups cauliflower florets
2 cups shredded Chinese cabbage
¾ cup (6 fl oz) chicken or fish stock
1 tablespoon light soy sauce
2 teaspoons cornflour (cornstarch), blended with water
½-1 cup (2-4 oz) pecan nuts, coarsely chopped

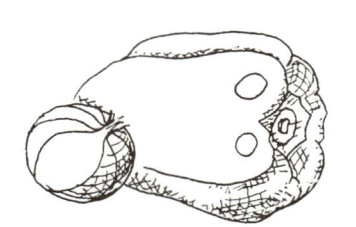

Heat 1 tablespoon of the oil in a wok. Add the prawns and stir fry until just cooked, about 2 minutes. Remove. Add the remaining oil to the wok, add the garlic, ginger and onions and stir fry until the onions are transparent. Add the carrots and cauliflower, stir fry a further 1 to 2 minutes. Add the Chinese cabbage, stock and soy sauce. Toss the vegetables well to coat. Cover and simmer for 2 to 3 minutes or until the vegetables are tender.

Return the prawns to the wok with the blended cornflour and stir fry until slightly thickened and glossy. Serve immediately with rice.

Vegetables

Nutty Eggplant Bake

Serves 4

- 2 eggplants (aubergines)
- 2 eggs
- ½ cup (4 fl oz) natural yoghurt
- 4 tablespoons finely chopped almonds
- 2 tablespoons wholemeal flour
- ¼ teaspoon paprika
- ¼ teaspoon freshly ground black pepper
- 1 cup (4 oz) grated cheese
- 2 tablespoons oil
- 2 small onions, thinly sliced

Slice the eggplants, and sprinkle with salt. Allow to stand for 30 minutes. Rinse and dry with paper towels. Mix together the eggs, yoghurt, almonds, flour, paprika, pepper and half the cheese.

Heat the oil and fry the onions until tender. Fry the eggplant slices until golden and drain well.

Place the eggplants and onions in a medium-sized ovenproof dish and pour the yoghurt mixture over the top. Sprinkle with the remaining cheese and bake at 180°C (350°F/Gas 4) for 20 minutes.

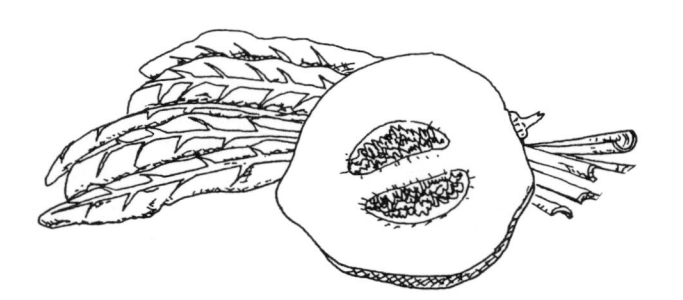

Indonesian Fried Sweet Corn

Serves 4

- 1 cup freshly cooked sweet corn kernels
- 1 small onion, finely chopped
- 1 stalk celery, finely chopped
- 2 tablespoons fresh coriander leaves, chopped
- 1 egg, lightly beaten
- 1 teaspoon flour
- 2 finely chopped red chillies, optional
- 3 tablespoons oil

Place all the ingredients except the oil in a large bowl and mix thoroughly. Heat the oil in a wok or large frying pan. Add the vegetable mixture and stir fry over a high heat for about 5 minutes or until the vegetables are golden. Serve hot as an accompaniment to a curry meal.

Savoury Sprouts with Bacon

Serves 4

- 500 g (1 lb) Brussels sprouts
- 30 g (1 oz) butter
- 2 rashers bacon, diced
- ½ red pepper (capsicum), diced
- 1 tablespoon lemon juice
- salt and pepper

Trim and wash the sprouts, and cut a cross in the stalks. Steam until just tender. Melt the butter in a small frying pan and sauté the bacon until crisp. Add the red pepper and sauté for 1 minute.

Place bacon and red pepper in a serving dish with the Brussels sprouts and lemon juice, and toss well to combine. Season to taste before serving.

Opposite: *Savoury Sprouts with Bacon*

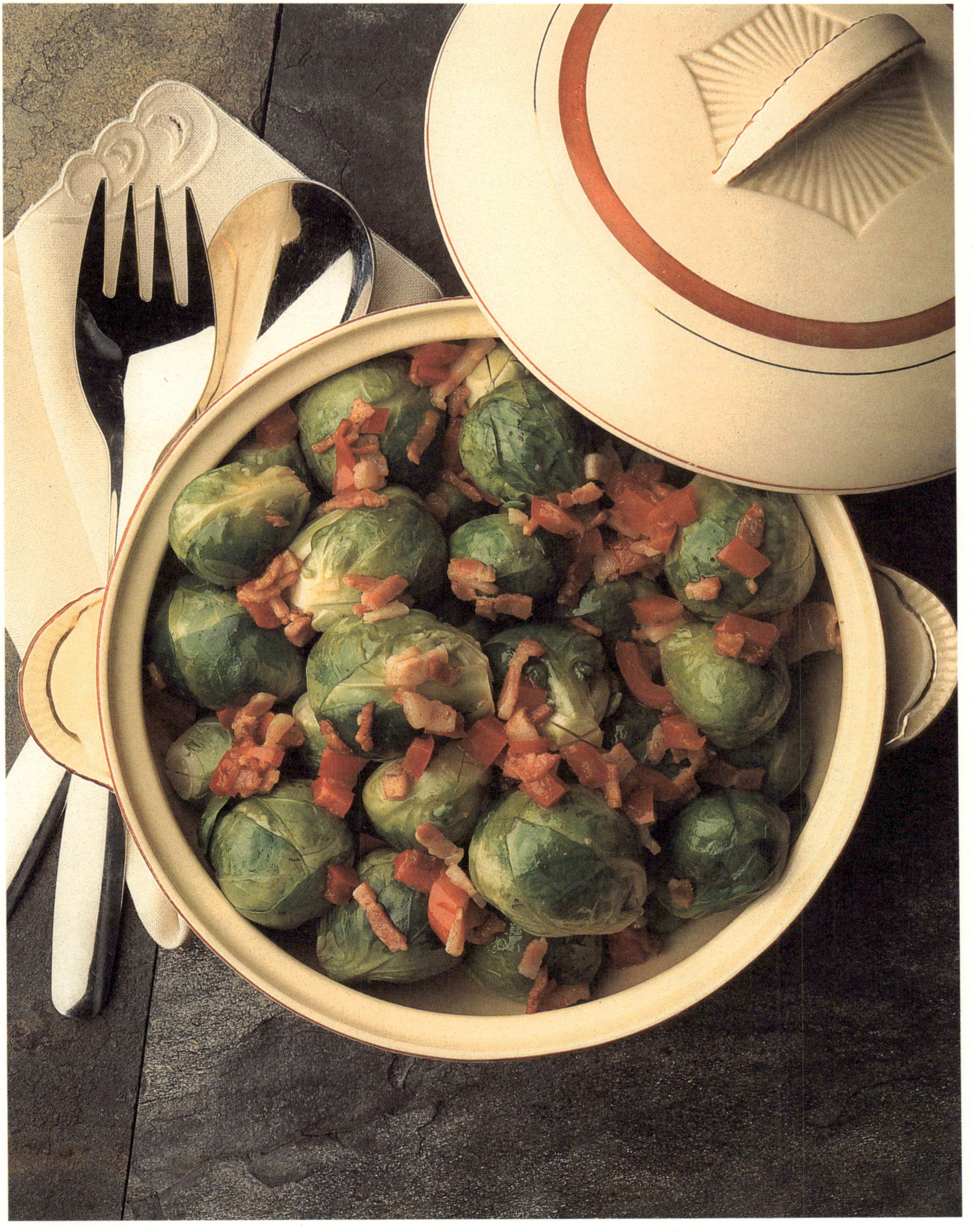

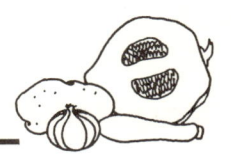

Vegetables

Mexican Chokos

Serves 4

4 chokos (summer squash)
15 g (½ oz) margarine
1 onion, finely chopped
1 red pepper (capsicum), diced
1 x 250 g (8 oz) can red kidney beans, drained
1 teaspoon chilli sauce
1 cup (8 oz) grated cheese

Peel, halve and remove the seeds from the chokos. Cook the chokos in boiling water until tender, about 10 minutes. Drain.

Heat the margarine in a pan. Gently fry the onion until soft. Add the red pepper and cook until tender. Add the kidney beans and chilli sauce. Simmer for 5 to 8 minutes.

Spoon the mixture onto the choko halves and top with grated cheese. Grill (broil) for 5 minutes or until the cheese has browned and melted. Serve hot as a vegetarian dish or a snack.

Chinese Vegetable Stir Fry

Serves 4 – 8

1 teaspoon grated fresh ginger
2 garlic cloves, crushed
2 tablespoons oil
½ small Chinese cabbage, stems sliced, leaves torn into pieces
1 bunch bok choy, stems sliced, leaves torn into pieces
1 medium-sized white radish, peeled and cut into thin strips
½ cup (4 fl oz) chicken stock
1 ½ tablespoons cornflour (cornstarch), blended with 3 tablespoons water
2 teaspoons soy sauce
1 teaspoon sesame oil
pinch of five spice powder

Stir fry the ginger and garlic in the heated oil. Add the stems of the Chinese cabbage and bok choy and stir fry for 2 minutes. Add the white radish and stir fry a further 2 minutes. Add the leaves of the Chinese cabbage and bok choy and toss well.

Drizzle the chicken stock over the vegetables. Cover and steam for 3 minutes or until tender crisp. Add the remaining ingredients, stirring until a glossy sauce is formed. Serve immediately.

Note: This dish has a delicate flavour and is the ideal accompaniment to rich meat dishes. Any combination of Chinese vegetables may be substituted for those used in the recipe.

Stuffed Peppers with Beef

Serves 6

12 red or green peppers (capsicums)
2 onions, chopped
3 garlic cloves, crushed
2 tablespoons oil
6 fresh tomatoes, peeled and chopped
¾ cup (6 fl oz) beef stock
½ cup corn kernels
1 teaspoon sugar
pepper
750 g (1 ½ lb) minced topside (ground beef)
3 tablespoons tomato paste
3 tablespoons chopped fresh parsley
¾ cup cooked rice

Remove the tops and seeds from the peppers. Gently fry the onions and garlic in 1 tablespoon of the oil for 3 minutes. Add the tomatoes, stock, corn, sugar and pepper to taste. Cover and simmer for 10 minutes.

Heat the remaining oil in a heavy pan and add the meat. Brown, then add the onion-tomato mixture, tomato paste, parsley and rice. Stir well and cook for 10 minutes.

Loosely fill the peppers with the meat mixture. Place in a baking dish. Pour in water to cover the bottom of the dish. Bake at 180°C (350°F/Gas 4) for 35 to 45 minutes until cooked. Serve hot with boiled brown rice.

Oriental Stuffed Avocados

Serves 4

2 avocados, halved and stoned
4 lettuce leaves
1 cup alfalfa sprouts or mung bean sprouts
2 stalks celery, finely sliced

Dressing

2 tablespoons cider vinegar
1 tablespoon tamari or soy sauce
6 spring onions (scallions), finely chopped
½ cup (2 oz) chopped toasted almonds

2 cm (¾ inch) piece fresh ginger, finely chopped
½ cup (4 fl oz) salad oil
1 tablespoon honey

Place each avocado half on a lettuce leaf on four small plates. Toss the remaining ingredients in a bowl and pile into the avocados. Top with dressing and serve as a first course.

Dressing: Blend all the ingredients in a jar and shake well. Allow to stand in the refrigerator for at least 1 hour to develop the flavours. Shake again just before serving.

Hot Cabbage and Prosciutto Toss

Serves 8

1 very small cabbage, sliced
15 g (½ oz) butter
2 stalks celery, chopped
250 g (8 oz) prosciutto, thinly sliced
¾ cup (3 oz) cashews
freshly ground black pepper
freshly ground nutmeg
1 teaspoon caraway seeds

Boil the cabbage in a little water for 5 minutes until tender-crisp. Drain well. Melt the butter in a large frying pan and stir fry the cooked cabbage, celery, prosciutto, cashews, pepper and nutmeg until heated through. Serve hot sprinkled with caraway seeds. Delicious with pork chops or sausages.

Green Grapefruit Salad

Serves 4–6

2 knobs whitloof (chicory), leaves separated
1 bunch asparagus, trimmed and steamed
1 ripe avocado, sliced
3 grapefruit, segmented
1 Spanish onion, thinly sliced
½ cup (2½ oz) black olives, pitted
3 tablespoons olive oil
1 tablespoon orange juice
1 teaspoon grain seed mustard
freshly ground black pepper

Arrange the whitloof leaves and asparagus like spears on a round platter. Layer the avocado and grapefruit segments, onion and olives attractively over the whitloof.

Combine the remaining ingredients in a screw-top jar and shake well. Drizzle over the salad. Serve well chilled as an accompaniment to cold meats.

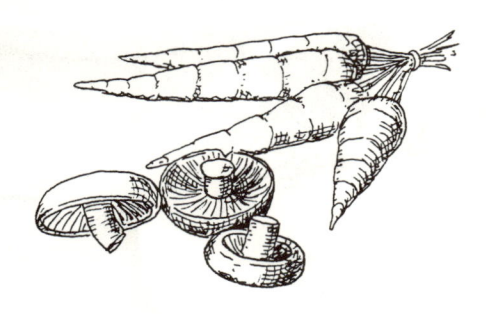

Stir Fried Baby Vegetables

Serves 8

3 rashers bacon, rind and bones removed
1 onion, finely chopped
1 garlic clove, crushed
500 g (1 lb) prepared baby vegetables, any variety or mixture
500 g (1 lb) English spinach, washed and torn into small pieces
1 punnet cherry tomatoes, halved
juice of 1 lemon
1 tablespoon light soy sauce
1 tablespoon toasted sesame seeds

Chop the bacon and stir fry until crisp in a wok or large, heavy frying pan. Remove and drain on kitchen paper. Add the onion and garlic to the wok and stir fry in the bacon fat for 1 minute. Add the prepared baby vegetables and stir fry for 2 minutes. Add the spinach and tomatoes and stir fry for a further 1 minute until the spinach is limp. Stir in the lemon juice and soy sauce and heat through.

Serve the vegetables immediately, sprinkled with the fried bacon and toasted sesame seeds. Delicious with grilled (broiled) lamb chops or fish.

Devilled Carrots

Serves 4

500 g (1 lb) carrots, julienned or sliced thinly into rounds
30 g (1 oz) butter or margarine
1 teaspoon soft brown sugar
2 teaspoons dry mustard
1 tablespoon Worcestershire sauce
2 tablespoons brandy
freshly ground black pepper
2 tablespoons toasted sesame seeds

Toss the carrots lightly in melted butter in a heavy based pan. Mix the brown sugar with the mustard and sprinkle over the carrots. Add the Worcestershire sauce and brandy. Season to taste with pepper. Add the sesame seeds.

Cover the pan and shake gently over low heat for 5 minutes or until the carrots are just tender. Serve as a vegetable accompaniment. Delicious with chicken or game.

Vegetables

Ricotta Spinach Bake

Serves 4 – 6

Batter

1 cup (8 fl oz) pancake mix
2 eggs, separated, whites reserved
¾ cup (6 fl oz) milk
seasonings to taste

Spinach Ricotta Filling

1 x 280 g (9 oz) packet frozen spinach, thawed
1 cup (4 oz) grated Australian ricotta cheese
1 medium-sized onion, grated
¼ cup (1 oz) chopped blanched almonds
½ teaspoon nutmeg
black pepper to taste
reserved egg whites from batter (above)

Pour half the batter into the base of a 5 cup (1.25 litre) glass ovenproof dish. Bake at 200°C (400°F/Gas 6) for 10 minutes. Remove from the oven. Spread the Spinach Ricotta Filling over the cooked base. Pour over the remaining batter. Reduce the oven to 190°C (375°F/Gas 5) and bake a further 25 minutes. Serve warm with oven-baked seasoned tomatoes.

Batter: Beat all the ingredients together until smooth.

Spinach Ricotta Filling: Combine all the ingredients except the egg whites. Beat the egg whites to soft peaks. Fold into the spinach mixture.

Vegetable Spaghetti with Tasty Tomato Sauce

Serves 6 – 8

1.5 kg (3 lb) vegetable spaghetti (spaghetti squash)

Tasty Tomato Sauce

1 tablespoon olive oil
15 g (½ oz) butter
½ onion, finely chopped
1 garlic clove, crushed
½ cup chopped celery
½ green pepper (capsicum), finely chopped
2 tomatoes, coarsely chopped
2 tablespoons chopped fresh parsley
pinch of salt
freshly ground black pepper

Cook the vegetable spaghetti according to the directions on *page 380* and keep hot.

Spoon the sauce over the vegetable spaghetti and serve.

Tasty Tomato Sauce: Heat the oil and butter in a pan. Add the onion, garlic, celery and green pepper and gently fry until tender. Add the tomatoes and parsley and simmer until the mixture is hot. Season to taste with salt and pepper.

Ricotta Spinach Bake

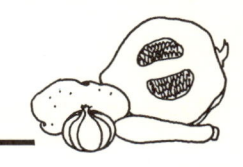

Stir Fry Vegetables
Serves 6

60 g (2 oz) butter
1 onion, cut into wedges
2 stalks celery, sliced
1 carrot, cut into sticks
½ red pepper (capsicum), sliced
125 g (4 oz) green beans
250 g (8 oz) broccoli florets
100 g (3 ½ oz) mushrooms, sliced
1 x 425 g (13 ½ oz) can baby corn, drained
⅓ cup water chestnuts
1 tablespoon soy sauce
100 g (3 ½ oz) Australian cheese, diced

Melt the butter in a large frying pan. Fry the onion, celery, carrot and red pepper for 3 minutes. Add the beans, broccoli, mushrooms, corn and water chestnuts. Cook for a further 2 minutes. Sprinkle the soy sauce over. Remove from the heat and stir through the cheese.

Nectarine and Silverbeet Salad
Serves 6

½ bunch silverbeet, washed, trimmed and torn into pieces
4 spring onions (scallions), chopped
4 nectarines, washed and sliced
30 g (1 oz) pine nuts
1 cup (8 fl oz) plain yoghurt
2 tablespoons finely chopped fresh mint

Place the silverbeet and spring onions in a colander and pour boiling water over the pieces. Refresh immediately with cold water and dry. Mix with the nectarine segments and pine nuts. Combine the yoghurt and mint and add to the salad.

Fruity Pilaf
Serves 4

30 g (1 oz) butter
2 garlic cloves, crushed
1 onion, chopped
1-2 tablespoons curry powder
1 ½ cups (10 oz) brown rice
¼ cup (1½ oz) sultanas
1 x 425 g (13½ oz) can whole tomatoes
2 cups (16 fl oz) orange juice
2 cups fresh or frozen peas
1 cup (4 oz) grated Australian cheese

Melt the butter in a large frying pan and fry the garlic, onion and curry powder for 3 to 4 minutes. Add the rice and cook for 5 minutes. Stir in the remaining ingredients except for the cheese. Cover well and simmer for 45 minutes or until the rice is cooked and the liquid evaporated. Stir through the cheese. Serve with stir-fried vegetables.

Country Garden Quiche
Serves 6

Wholemeal Pastry

1 cup (4 oz) wholemeal flour
½ cup (2 oz) self-raising flour
100 g (3 ½ oz) margarine, cut into pieces
1 egg yolk
3 tablespoons cold water

Filling

250 g (8 oz) broccoli florets, blanched and drained well
1 teaspoon oil
1 onion, chopped
½ green pepper (capsicum), chopped
250 g (8 oz) mushrooms, sliced
¼ cup (1 oz) grated cheese
½ teaspoon chopped fresh basil
1 cup (8 fl oz) milk
2 eggs, beaten
1 tablespoon grated Parmesan cheese

Wholemeal Pastry: Sieve the flours together into a bowl. Return the husks to the bowl. Lightly rub in the margarine until the mixture resembles fine breadcrumbs. Mix together the egg yolk and water. Add to the flour mixture to make a stiff dough.

Knead the dough lightly and form into a round cake shape. Wrap in foil or greaseproof paper and chill in the refrigerator for at least 15 minutes. Roll the pastry out to fit a 23 cm (9 inch) flan tin. Bake blind, at 200°C (400°F/Gas 6), for 15 minutes or until straw coloured. Remove the paper and baking beans and cool the pastry shell.

Filling: Arrange the broccoli in the pastry shell. Heat the oil in a pan and gently sauté the onion and green pepper until tender. Sprinkle the mushrooms over the broccoli. Combine the cheese, basil, milk and eggs and pour into the pastry shell, coating the broccoli in a little of the liquid. Sprinkle with the Parmesan.

Bake at 200°C (400°F/Gas 6) for 10 minutes. Reduce the heat to 190°C (375°F/Gas 5) and bake a further 30 minutes until golden brown and set. Serve hot while puffy, accompanied by a salad.

Vegetables

Cheese Crumble
Serves 6

30 g (1 oz) butter
6 spring onions (scallions), cut into 2 cm (¾ inch) slices
2 stalks celery, sliced
2 medium-sized carrots, cut into straws
2 zucchini (courgettes), sliced
2 tablespoons flour

Topping
30 g (1 oz) butter
1 clove garlic, crushed
6 slices bread, crusts removed and cut into 1 cm (½ inch) cubes

1 ½ cups (12 fl oz) skim milk
¼ cup (1 oz) grated Australian Parmesan cheese
freshly ground black pepper to taste
1 cup macaroni, cooked until tender

¼ cup (1 oz) grated Australian Parmesan cheese

Melt butter in a large saucepan. Sauté spring onions, celery, carrots and zucchini until tender. Gently stir in flour, gradually adding milk and bring to the boil, stirring constantly. Add cheese, pepper and macaroni and pour into an 18 cm (7 inch) round casserole dish. Sprinkle with topping. Bake at 180°C (350°F/Gas 4) for 20 minutes or until golden brown.

Topping: Melt butter with garlic, add bread cubes and toss in butter for 5 to 6 minutes. Stir in cheese.

Vegetable Layer Pot
Serves 6 – 8

1 kg (2 lb) potatoes, peeled and cooked
60 g (2 oz) butter
2 tablespoons milk
nutmeg
seasonings
1 large onion, sliced

2 medium-sized carrots, grated
1 tablespoon pine nuts
2 zucchini (courgettes), grated
2 tablespoons grated Australian Parmesan cheese

Mash the potatoes with a little butter, milk, a shake of nutmeg and seasonings to taste. Fry the onion rings in the remaining butter for 4 to 5 minutes or until transparent. Grease a 23 x 7 cm (9 x 3 inch) glass casserole dish. Spoon one third of the potato across the base, then layer with half the carrot, the pine nuts, half the zucchini, one third of the potato, the remaining carrot and zucchini, the onion rings, and finish with potato. Season where necessary. Sprinkle the Parmesan cheese on top then bake at 180°C (350°F/Gas 4) for 15 to 20 minutes until golden brown on top. Serve accompanied with meat, poultry or fish.

Savoury-Filled Tomatoes
Serves 6

6 whole firm tomatoes
salt and pepper
1 small red apple
3 eggs, hard-boiled and chopped
¼ cup (1 oz) chopped walnuts

2 tablespoons diced green pepper (capsicum)
¼ cup (2 fl oz) mayonnaise
lettuce leaves
chopped fresh parsley

Cut the tops off the tomatoes and scoop the pulp out carefully. Drain the pulp. Sprinkle with salt and invert to drain. Dice the apple, leaving the skin on. Mix all the ingredients lightly together. Add the well drained tomato pulp and season to taste. Pile into the tomato cases and arrange on a bed of lettuce leaves. Garnish with parsley and chill for 1 hour before serving.

Stuffed Cheese Mushrooms
Serves 6

12 large mushrooms
60 g (2 oz) butter
1 onion, finely chopped
1 rasher bacon, finely chopped
½ cup cooked rice

1 tablespoon chopped fresh parsley
salt and pepper
½ cup cheese, cut into small cubes
extra chopped fresh parsley

Remove the mushroom stalks and chop finely. Heat half the butter and fry the stalks, onion and bacon for about 2 minutes. Add the rice and parsley, toss to mix well. Brush the mushroom caps on both sides with the remaining melted butter. Arrange, hollow side up, in a greased shallow ovenproof dish. Season the rice mixture with salt and pepper and place equal portions of mixture on the mushroom caps, topping each with cheese cubes. Spoon a little extra melted butter over the mushrooms. Bake in a 180°C (350°F/Gas 4) oven for about 15 minutes or until golden and the cheese is melted. Add extra butter if mushrooms appear to become dry. Sprinkle with extra chopped parsley.

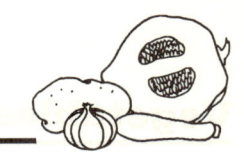

Savoury Stuffed Peppers

Serves 6

3 medium-sized green peppers (capsicums)
1 x 440 g (14 oz) can savoury mince
4 ½ cups cooked rice
1 cup (4 oz) grated cheese
1 tablespoon (½ oz) brown sugar
¼ teaspoon ground oregano
¼ teaspoon ground basil
1 x 440 g (14 oz) can tomato soup

Cut the peppers in halves lengthwise and remove the stems and seeds. Drop the peppers into boiling salted water and cook for 5 minutes. Drain and run under cold water. Blend the mince with 1 ½ cups of rice and ½ cup (2 oz) of the cheese. Spoon the rice/mince mixture into the pepper halves. Place the peppers in a shallow ovenproof dish, just large enough to fit firmly. Add the brown sugar and herbs to the tomato soup. Spoon the soup over the stuffed peppers. Sprinkle with the remaining cheese. Bake in a 180°C (350°F/Gas 4) oven for about 35 minutes. Serve on a bed of the remaining hot rice. Spoon over the sauce or serve separately.

Potato Chips

Serves 6

6 large old potatoes
4 cups (1 litre) cooking oil
salt

Peel the potatoes and wash if dirty. Dry them well. Cut the potatoes into finger length pieces, about 6 mm (¼ inch) square. Dry the chips well with absorbent paper.

Heat the oil in a deep pan, until smoking. Immerse the chips, using a wire basket if preferred. Leave to cook until golden brown. Remove from the oil with a slotted spoon if no basket is used. Drain on absorbent paper. Sprinkle with salt and serve immediately.

Note: Chips may be partially cooked and then re-immersed in hot oil just before serving.

Potato Casserole

Serves 6

6 large old potatoes
½ cup (4 fl oz) milk
1 cup (4 oz) grated cheese
salt and pepper

Grease a medium-sized shallow casserole. Slice the potatoes thinly and place in layers in the casserole. Pour over the milk and sprinkle with grated cheese. Season well.

Bake at 180°C (350°F/Gas 4) for 1 hour or until the potato is cooked and the cheese is golden brown.

Cut in slices and serve hot.

Green Beans and Bacon

Serves 4 – 6

500 g (1 lb) green beans
2 rashers bacon, rind removed

Top and tail the beans and remove any strings. Slice diagonally into pieces about 2.5 cm (1 inch) long. Cut the bacon into tiny strips and fry until crisp. Drain well on absorbent paper.

Steam the beans for a few minutes only and serve hot, sprinkled with the bacon.

Cinnamon Carrots

Serves 4 – 6

4-6 medium-sized carrots
30 g (1 oz) butter or margarine
1 teaspoon ground cinnamon
1 teaspoon sugar

Peel the carrots and cut into julienne strips. Steam for a few minutes to retain the crisp texture. Add the butter and gently stir through the carrots until melted.

Place in a serving dish and sprinkle with the cinnamon and sugar. Serve hot.

Purée of Peas

Serves 4

2 cups frozen peas
2 lettuce leaves, shredded
pinch of salt
pinch of sugar
15 g (½ oz) butter
1 tablespoon cream
freshly ground black pepper

Place the peas, lettuce leaves, salt and sugar in a pan. Cover with cold water and cook until tender. Drain and reserve the liquid. Purée the peas and lettuce in a food processor. Boil the reserved cooking liquid until reduced to ½ cup (4 fl oz).

Put the pea purée in a pan with the butter and boil until the butter melts. Add the cream and concentrated pea liquid and season to taste with pepper. Serve hot as a vegetable accompaniment.

Vegetables

Vegetable Curry

Serves 4

2 tablespoons oil
1 garlic clove, crushed
2.5 cm (1 inch) piece fresh ginger, finely chopped
2 tablespoons curry powder
4 large potatoes, peeled and cubed
4 carrots, peeled and sliced
2 onions, peeled and sliced
½ small head cauliflower, broken into florets
250 g (8 oz) green beans, strings removed and sliced
1 x 250 g (8 oz) can peeled tomatoes

Heat the oil in a large saucepan. Sauté the garlic and ginger in the oil. Add the curry powder and stir to bring out the flavour. Add the vegetables and stir to coat in the curry mixture. Add the undrained tomatoes and mix through. Cover and bake at 180°C (350°F/Gas 4) for 1 hour or until the vegetables are tender. Serve hot with rice.

Vegetable Spaghetti with Pesto Sauce

Serves 6 – 8

1.5 kg (3 lb) vegetable spaghetti (spaghetti squash)

Pesto Sauce
1 cup fresh basil leaves, stripped from the stems
2-3 garlic cloves, crushed
¼ cup (1 oz) pecan nuts, roughly chopped
1 cup (8 fl oz) olive oil, chilled
2-3 tablespoons grated Parmesan cheese

Boil the whole vegetable spaghetti in lightly salted boiling water for 20 to 30 minutes. Cut in half, remove the seeds and tease the flesh away from the skin with a fork.

To cook the vegetable spaghetti in the microwave, cut the vegetable into four slices, remove the seeds, and place in plastic bags in the microwave oven. Cook on high for 10 to 12 minutes, then tease the flesh out with a fork. Keep hot.

Pour the pesto sauce over the vegetable spaghetti and mix through gently before serving.

Pesto Sauce: Combine the basil, garlic and nuts and process in a blender or food processor until fairly fine. Slowly add the olive oil in a thin stream with the motor turned on. Add the Parmesan cheese and blend until smooth.

Cauliflower in Black Bean Sauce

Serves 4 – 6

½ head cauliflower
2 tablespoons water
1 tablespoon sherry
2 tablespoons black bean sauce

Break the cauliflower into small florets. Heat the water in a wok and add the cauliflower. Cook over high heat, stirring occasionally until the cauliflower is tender. Stir in the sherry and sauce. Stir gently to distribute the sauce. Serve hot.

French Fries

Serves 6

6 large old potatoes
4 cups (1 litre) cooking oil
salt

Peel the potatoes and wash if dirty. Dry them well. Slice the potatoes very finely to produce thin flat pieces. Dry the fries well with absorbent paper.

Heat the oil in a deep pan until smoking. Immerse the fries, using a wire basket if preferred. Leave to cook until golden brown. The fries will curl during cooking. Remove from the oil with a slotted spoon if no basket is used. Drain on absorbent paper. Sprinkle with salt and serve immediately.

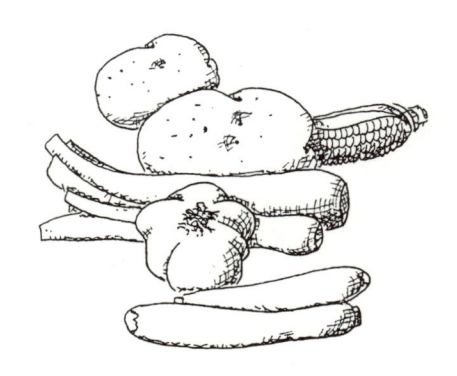

SALADS

Australians are known as great salad eaters. Our climate is temperate so it is ideal for the quick preparation of meals that can be eaten outside.

Salads have come a long way from a wedge of tomato and a limp lettuce leaf lurking on the side of the plate. They are now complete meals with such a wide variety of goodies that almost anything goes. Some can even be served warm. Try combining fruit with your favourite salad, serving crusty bread and a good wine, and you have a complete meal which requires no cooking.

The recipes in this chapter have been provided by a number of the contributors whose credits appear elsewhere in the book.

Salads

Cool Potato Salad

Serves 6 - 8

500 g (1 lb) small potatoes
1 small onion, finely chopped
1 bunch chives, snipped
1 Granny Smith apple, peeled, cored and chopped
1 fresh gherkin or small cucumber, chopped
1 bunch radishes, thinly sliced
2 tablespoons chopped fresh parsley
1 ¼ cups (10 fl oz) sour cream
juice of ½ lemon
salt and pepper
parsley sprigs, sunflower and sesame seeds, for garnish

Boil the potatoes in their skins until just tender. Drain and cool. Peel the potatoes if old, leave the skin on new potatoes, and cut into 1-2 cm (½-¾ inch) cubes.

Place the potatoes in a bowl. Add the onion, chives, apple, gherkin, radishes, parsley, sour cream and lemon juice and mix gently until all the potatoes are coated. Season to taste with salt and pepper. Chill well.

Serve in a salad bowl garnished with sprigs of parsley and sprinkle with sunflower and sesame seeds.

Onion Salad

Serves 8

4 tablespoons olive oil
2 carrots, chopped
750 g (1 ½ lb) small pickling onions
1 ½ cups (12 fl oz) water
¾ cup (6 fl oz) dry white wine
4 tablespoons lemon juice
2 tablespoons tomato paste
⅓ cup (2 oz) sultanas
2 bay leaves
1 teaspoon salt
freshly ground black pepper
pinch of cayenne pepper
1 tablespoon chopped fresh parsley

Heat the oil in a large heavy pan. Add the carrots, cover and sauté until the carrots are soft, about 5 to 10 minutes, shaking the pan frequently. Peel the onions and add to the pan with the water, wine, lemon juice, tomato paste, sultanas, bay leaves, salt, pepper and cayenne. Bring slowly to the boil, then simmer, partly covered, for 1 hour or until the onions are tender and the sauce has reduced a little and thickened.

Cool the onion mixture and place in a serving bowl. Cover and chill well in the refrigerator. Before serving, adjust the seasoning to taste and sprinkle with chopped parsley. Serve chilled.

German Potato Salad with Horseradish

Serves 6 - 8

1 kg (2 lb) medium-sized potatoes cooked in their jackets
½ cup (4 fl oz) olive oil
½ teaspoon salt
1 small onion, finely chopped
3 tablespoons lemon juice
½ cup (4 fl oz) sour cream or mayonnaise
½ teaspoon honey, optional
1 tablespoon chopped fresh parsley or dill
1 tablespoon horseradish

Peel the potatoes and cut into 2.5 cm (1 inch) cubes. Place in a bowl, add the other ingredients and mix gently. Serve lightly chilled.

Note: The flavour of the salad will improve if prepared 2 hours before serving.

Lebanese Salad

Serves 6 - 8

1 cup burghul
2 cups finely chopped fresh parsley
4 medium-sized tomatoes, chopped
4 spring onions (scallions), finely chopped
½ cup finely chopped fresh mint
½ cup (4 fl oz) olive oil
½ cup (4 fl oz) lemon juice
2 garlic cloves, crushed
freshly ground black pepper

Soak the burghul in cold water for 30 minutes. Rinse and drain, then squeeze dry in the fingertips. Mix the burghul with the parsley, tomatoes, spring onions and mint.

Shake the remaining ingredients together in a screw-top jar. Pour over the salad. Serve well chilled.

Mushroom Salad

Serves 6

500 g (1 lb) button mushrooms, sliced
125 g (4 oz) ham, cut into thin strips
3 spring onions (scallions), chopped
½ cucumber, sliced
½ cup (4 fl oz) olive oil
¼ cup (2 fl oz) lemon juice
1 garlic clove, crushed
salt and pepper
½ cup (2 oz) chopped pecans

Place the first four ingredients in a salad bowl. Combine the oil, lemon juice, garlic and seasonings. Pour over the mushrooms, ham, spring onions and cucumber. Marinate for 30 minutes.

Sprinkle with pecans just before serving.

Bean and Prawn Salad

Serves 4

500 g (1 lb) cooked king prawns (shrimp), shelled, deveined and cut into bite-sized pieces
½ red pepper (capsicum), finely diced
½ green pepper (capsicum), finely diced
2 cups French beans, strung, blanched and sliced
1 bunch chives, snipped into 2.5 cm (1 inch) lengths

Lime Mayonnaise
¼ cup (2 fl oz) sour cream
¼ cup (2 fl oz) mayonnaise
finely grated rind and juice of 2 limes

Combine all salad ingredients thoroughly in a salad bowl. Fold the mayonnaise in gently. Serve chilled with wholemeal bread rolls.

Lime Mayonnaise: Mix all ingredients well.

Coleslaw with Grapes

Serves 4 - 6

250 g (8 oz) cabbage, finely shredded
2 green apples, cored and diced
2 large carrots, peeled and grated
1 cup seedless grapes
½ cup (2 oz) coarsely chopped pecans
2 tablespoons snipped chives
¾ cup (6 fl oz) yoghurt
juice of ½ lemon
salt and pepper to taste

Place the cabbage, apples, carrots, grapes, pecans and chives in a salad bowl. Mix the yoghurt with the lemon juice and salt and pepper to taste.
Pour the yoghurt dressing over the salad and toss well. Chill before serving.

Hot Beetroot Salad

Serves 4 [M]

2 large beetroot
juice of 1 orange
1 apple, peeled, cored and diced
2 tablespoons sour cream
1 tablespoon white wine vinegar

Peel the beetroot and grate or chop finely in a food processor. Place the beetroot in a microwave dish, add the orange juice, cover with a lid or clear plastic wrap. Cook in a microwave oven on high for **5** minutes.
Remove from the microwave, add the diced apple, sour cream and vinegar and stir gently until evenly mixed. Serve hot with roast or grilled (broiled) beef or lamb, or cold with a mixed salad.

Red Cabbage and Silverbeet Salad

Serves 6 - 8

¼ red cabbage, finely shredded
½ bunch silverbeet, finely shredded
1 green apple, cored and sliced
60 g (2 oz) pecan nuts
3 tablespoons lemon juice
3 tablespoons oil
½ teaspoon prepared whole-grain mustard
1 teaspoon sugar

Toss the cabbage, silverbeet, apple and pecan nuts together.
Make a dressing by placing the lemon juice, oil, mustard and sugar in a screw-top jar and shake well. Pour the dressing over the salad. Toss well and serve chilled.

Oriental Broccoli Salad

Serves 6

250 g (8 oz) broccoli, broken into florets
2 carrots, peeled and thinly sliced
250 g (8 oz) cauliflower, broken into florets
1 cup bean sprouts
½ cup (4 fl oz) peanut oil
2 tablespoons white wine vinegar
freshly ground black pepper
1 teaspoon mustard
¼ cup toasted sesame seeds

Blanch the broccoli, carrots and cauliflower. Drain and refresh with cold water. Toss the vegetables with the bean sprouts in a salad bowl.
Combine the remaining ingredients in a screw-top jar, shake well, then drizzle over the vegetables and chill.

Note: The salad may be served in a bowl lined with Chinese cabbage.

Cauliflower Salad

Serves 4 - 6

½ cauliflower, cut into small florets
1 cup (8 fl oz) mayonnaise
2 tablespoons mango chutney
½ teaspoon ground cumin or coriander
freshly ground black pepper
1 tablespoon chopped fresh mint
1 tablespoon chopped fresh chives

Blanch the cauliflower by dropping into boiling water for 1 minute, then remove and refresh with cold water immediately and drain. Combine the mayonnaise with the chutney, cumin, pepper, mint and chives. Add the cauliflower and toss gently. Serve chilled.

Note: Delicious with cold rare roast beef fillet.

Salads

Beetroot and Buckwheat Salad

Serves 6

- 2 whole beetroot, stalks removed
- 1 cup buckwheat
- 6 spring onions (scallions), chopped
- 1 cup alfalfa sprouts
- 1 cup bean sprouts
- 1 red pepper (capsicum), blanched and thinly sliced
- 2 tablespoons olive oil
- 1 tablespoon soy sauce
- 1 tablespoon vinegar
- freshly ground black pepper
- 1 bunch chives, finely chopped
- 2 garlic cloves, crushed
- 2 teaspoons chopped fresh ginger
- 1 cup (4 oz) coarsely chopped pecans
- ½ extra red pepper (capsicum), thinly sliced, for garnish

Cook the beetroot in boiling water for 20 to 30 minutes or until tender. Peel the beetroot, then thinly slice half the beetroot and reserve for garnish. Julienne the remaining beetroot. Cook the buckwheat in boiling water for 10 minutes. Drain and cool.

Combine the beetroot, buckwheat, spring onions, sprouts and red pepper in a salad bowl. Combine the oil, soy sauce, vinegar, pepper, chives, garlic and ginger in a screw-top jar and shake. Drizzle over the salad and chill well.

Serve sprinkled with pecans, and garnished with beetroot and capsicum slices.

Spring Salad with Strawberry Sauce

Brussels Salad

Serves 6

- 500 g (1 lb) Brussels sprouts, cooked and halved
- 250 g (8 oz) cap mushrooms, sliced
- 1 cup finely sliced spring onions (scallions)

Dressing:
- ¾ cup (6 fl oz) yoghurt
- ⅓ cup (2 ½ fl oz) tomato juice
- 1 teaspoon grain seed mustard
- 125 g (4 oz) bacon, finely chopped
- ½ cup (2 oz) chopped pecans
- ½ teaspoon chopped fresh basil
- 2 tablespoons chopped fresh parsley

Combine the Brussels sprouts, mushrooms and spring onions in a salad bowl.

Pour the dressing over the salad and chill well. Cook the bacon until very crisp, add the pecans and sprinkle over the salad. Serve immediately.

Dressing: Combine yoghurt, tomato juice, mustard, basil and parsley and mix well.

Spring Salad with Strawberry Sauce

Serves 4

- 1 bunch asparagus, trimmed
- 1 punnet strawberries
- freshly ground black pepper
- ½ teaspoon horseradish cream
- ½ teaspoon grated orange rind
- 2 teaspoons orange juice
- 1 cup (8 fl oz) olive oil
- ⅓ cup (2 ½ fl oz) tarragon vinegar
- 1 teaspoon dry mustard
- ½ teaspoon sugar
- salt
- pepper
- 1 garlic clove, crushed
- 2 oranges
- 1 grapefruit
- 1 large ripe avocado

Drop the asparagus into boiling water. Simmer for 3 to 4 minutes, or until just tender. Drain and cool. Reserve 4 strawberries. Hull the remaining strawberries and purée them in a blender or food processor. Add the pepper, horseradish, orange rind and juice. Combine thoroughly.

Combine the olive oil, vinegar, mustard, sugar, salt, pepper and garlic in a screw-top jar. Shake until a thick dressing is formed. Peel and segment the oranges and grapefruit. Peel and thinly slice the avocado.

Arrange the asparagus spears, fruit segments and avocado slices attractively on plates. Mask the asparagus with the strawberry sauce and drizzle French dressing over the other salad ingredients. Prepare 4 strawberry fans as a garnish for salad.

Opposite: *Beetroot and Buckwheat Salad*

385

Salads

Caesar Salad

Serves 6

2 rashers bacon, rind removed
¼ loaf unsliced bread, crusts removed
1 lettuce
freshly ground black pepper
¼ cup (2 fl oz) French dressing

Cut the bacon into tiny pieces and fry until crisp. Remove the bacon and set aside. Cut the bread into 1.25 cm (½ inch) cubes. Fry the cubes in the bacon fat until golden brown and crisp. Drain well on absorbent paper.

Tear the lettuce into bite-sized pieces and place in a bowl. Sprinkle over the bacon and bread cubes and season with black pepper. Just before serving pour over the dressing.

Cucumber Salad

Serves 4

2 large cucumbers
salt
2 tablespoons toasted sesame seeds
½ cup (4 fl oz) thick sour cream

Peel the cucumber and cut into quarters lengthwise. Remove the row of seeds from each strip. Slice the cucumbers and place in a colander. Sprinkle liberally with salt and leave to stand for at least 2 hours. Stir occasionally during this time. Dry the cucumber well on absorbent paper and place in a bowl. Stir the sesame seeds through the sour cream and then spoon over the cucumber. Stir gently to mix. Serve at a barbecue or as an accompaniment to a curry.

Tomato and Orange Salad

Serves 4

500 g (1 lb) tomatoes, cut into wedges
2 oranges, segmented
2 stalks celery, chopped
1 tablespoon chopped fresh parsley
freshly ground black pepper
1 tablespoon olive oil
¼ cup (2 fl oz) orange juice
2 spring onions (scallions), chopped
1 teaspoon dry mustard
1 tablespoon chopped fresh parsley

Place tomatoes, orange segments, celery and parsley in a salad bowl. Season with pepper. Chill. Combine the remaining ingredients in a screw-top jar and shake well.

Toss the salad with the dressing to serve.

Waldorf Salad

Serves 6

6 stalks celery
2 Granny Smith apples
1 lettuce
½ cup (2 oz) chopped walnuts
½ cup (4 fl oz) mayonnaise

Wash the celery and slice diagonally. Chop the unpeeled apples into small pieces, removing the core. Place the celery and apple in a large salad bowl. Tear the lettuce into bite-sized pieces and add to the bowl. Sprinkle in the walnuts. Spoon over the mayonnaise and serve immediately.

Avocado and Tomato Salad

Serves 4

2 large avocados
2 large tomatoes
¼ cup (2 fl oz) French dressing

Peel the avocados and cut into bite-sized pieces. Place in a bowl. Cut the tomatoes into bite-sized pieces and add to the avocado. Stir gently to mix then add the dressing and stir again. Stand for at least 30 minutes before serving.

Note: The acid in the dressing and tomatoes will prevent the avocado from discolouring.

Beetroot Yoghurt Salad

Serves 4

2 large cooked beetroot
½ cup (4 fl oz) yoghurt

Peel the beetroot and cut into julienne strips. Place in a bowl and spoon over the yoghurt. Serve as an accompaniment to curry or other spicy dishes.

Mandarin and Coconut Salad

Serves 4

1 x 250 g (8 oz) can mandarin segments
½ cup (4 fl oz) yoghurt
¼ cup desiccated coconut

Drain the mandarin segments and blend with the yoghurt. Sprinkle on the coconut.

Hot Broad Bean Salad

Serves 6 - 8 [M]

30 g (1 oz) butter
1 cup spring onions (scallions), diagonally sliced
500 g (1 lb) broad beans, shelled
1 small bunch asparagus, trimmed and sliced
1 small lettuce, finely shredded
½ cup (4 fl oz) chicken stock
freshly ground black pepper
2 tablespoons light soy sauce

Melt the butter in a microwave dish in a microwave oven for 30 seconds on high. Add the spring onions and toss well to coat in butter. Cook for 2 minutes on high.

Add the broad beans, asparagus, lettuce, stock and pepper. Cover and cook for 8 minutes on high. Drain, toss with soy sauce and serve.

Broad Bean and Tuna Salad

Serves 3 - 4

1 x 200 g (6 ½ oz) can tuna, drained and flaked
250 g (8 oz) broad beans, lightly steamed
2 hard-boiled eggs, quartered
1 small cucumber, thinly sliced
4 tablespoons French dressing
1 garlic clove, crushed
anchovy fillets
black olives
12 cherry tomatoes

Place the tuna, broad beans, eggs and cucumber in a salad bowl. Toss lightly with the dressing and garlic. Garnish with latticed anchovy fillets, olives and tomatoes. Serve chilled with French bread.

Grapes, Cheese and Nut Salad

Serves 4 - 6

2 cups ricotta or cottage cheese
½ cup (4 fl oz) natural yoghurt
2 teaspoons lemon juice
pinch of cayenne pepper
1 cup mixed white and black grapes
½ cup corn kernels
1 stalk celery, diced
¼ cup (1 oz) chopped pecans
¼ cup (1 oz) chopped toasted almonds

Combine the cheese with the yoghurt, lemon juice and cayenne pepper. Fold in the remaining ingredients. Chill well.

Serve in crisp lettuce cups accompanied by rye crispbread.

Fruity Orange Salad

Serves 8 - 12

1 cup (8 fl oz) orange juice
1 tablespoon honey
1 cinnamon stick
4 oranges, peeled and segmented
1 medium-sized pineapple, peeled and cubed
1 small honeydew melon, halved, seeded and cut into balls
1 small rockmelon, halved, seeded and cut into balls
1 punnet strawberries, hulled and halved
½ cup chopped fresh mint
½ cup (2 oz) pecan nuts

Place the orange juice, honey and cinnamon stick in a small pan. Heat gently to dissolve the honey. Cool, pour into a bowl and remove the cinnamon stick.

Add the prepared fruit to the syrup and mix thoroughly. Chill well. Serve the fruit salad sprinkled with mint and pecan nuts.

Chinese Bean Sprout Salad

Serves 4

1 cup Chinese broccoli stems, sliced and blanched
1 cup carrot straws, blanched
1 cup bean sprouts
½ cup (2 oz) slivered almonds
2 tablespoons sesame seeds
2 tablespoons soy sauce
2 tablespoons vinegar
1 tablespoon oil
2 teaspoons sesame oil
1 teaspoon dry mustard
1 teaspoon honey

Place the vegetables and nuts in a salad bowl. Shake the remaining ingredients together in a screw-top jar, then drizzle over the salad. Toss and chill well before serving.

Note: Broccoli leaves may be reserved for a stir fry dish.

Fruity Pork Salad

Serves 4

250 g (8 oz) cold roast pork, cut into thin strips
1 persimmon, peeled and sliced
1 grapefruit, segmented
1 cup fresh pineapple pieces
¼ teaspoon ground cardamom
lettuce cups

Combine the meat with the fruits. Drizzle with lime juice and sprinkle with cardamom.

Pile into lettuce cups and chill well before serving.

Salads

Seafood Salad

Serves 4

- 150 g (5 oz) cuttlefish or squid
- milk
- 100 g (3½ oz) green prawns peeled and cut in half lengthwise
- 150 g (5 oz) scallops
- 100 g (3½ oz) smoked salmon, cut in strips
- 2 cups (16 fl oz) water
- peppercorns, salt, lemon juice and parsley
- 150 g snow peas (mange-tout)
- 1 tablespoon chopped parsley
- 60 g (2 oz) oyster mushrooms cut into bite-sized pieces if large
- 1 large onion, sliced
- ½ punnet strawberries, hulled
- 1 green pepper (capsicum), cut in strips

Dressing

- ⅔ cup (5 fl oz) olive oil
- ⅓ cup (2 ½ fl oz) lemon juice
- ⅓ teaspoon green peppercorns
- ½ garlic clove, crushed
- 1 teaspoon grated fresh ginger

Slice the cuttlefish in a criss-cross pattern and marinate in milk for 1 hour to tenderise. Rinse the cuttlefish under cold running water. Cook the seafood in a saucepan with simmering water seasoned with peppercorns, salt, lemon juice and parsley. Drain the seafood and chill.

Blanch the snow peas in salted, boiling water for 2 minutes and refresh. Frozen snow peas may be used straight from the packet. Combine all the ingredients and toss gently in the salad dressing.

Dressing: Combine all the ingredients in a blender for 30 seconds.

Seafood Salad

Prawn and Macaroni Salad

Prawn and Macaroni Salad

Serves 4

- 2 cups cooked macaroni
- 500 g (1 lb) cooked prawns (shrimp), (peeled bay prawns are ideal for this salad)
- 2 tablespoons chopped spring onions (scallions)
- 1 tablespoon chopped fresh parsley
- 2 tablespoons finely chopped celery

Sauce
- ½ cup (4 fl oz) mayonnaise
- 2 tablespoons tomato sauce
- dash of Worcestershire sauce
- dash of Tabasco sauce
- squeeze of lemon juice

Combine the liquid ingredients for the sauce and check seasoning. Combine with salad ingredients and mix well. Refrigerate for 1 hour. Serve on a bed of lettuce or in 4 lettuce cups garnished with a sprig of parsley.

Sesame Crab Salad

Serves 4

- 250 g (8 oz) crab meat (flesh from 2 crabs)
- 2 tablespoons sesame seeds, lightly toasted
- 100 g (3½ oz) celery, sliced diagonally
- 1 tablespoon chopped fresh parsley
- ½ head lettuce, torn into bite-sized pieces
- 1 bunch fresh asparagus, blanched and cut into 2.5 cm (1 inch) pieces

Dressing
- ⅓ cup (2½ fl oz) sesame oil
- ⅓ cup (2½ fl oz) lemon juice
- ½ teaspoon Worcestershire sauce
- freshly ground pepper
- dash of Tabasco sauce

Combine all the ingredients for the dressing in a blender and mix for 30 seconds. Combine the salad ingredients and gently toss in the dressing.

Salads

Nutty Pineapple Salad

Serves 6

- 1 pineapple
- ¾ cup cooked brown rice
- 2 tablespoons sultanas
- 2 tablespoons peanuts (unsalted)
- ½ green pepper (capsicum), seeded and chopped
- 30 g (1 oz) butter
- 1 onion, diced
- 1 teaspoon curry powder
- 1 tablespoon mayonnaise, optional

Cut the pineapple in half lengthwise. Remove the flesh and cut into cubes. Reserve the shell for serving. Combine the rice, sultanas, pineapple cubes, peanuts and green pepper. Melt the butter in a pan. Sauté the onion until tender, add the curry powder and cook for 1 minute, stirring continually. Add to rice mixture. Spoon back into the shells. Garnish with dill or mint. Add mayonnaise if desired.

Harlequin Health Salad

Serves 6

- 4 cups cooked brown rice
- ½ cup thinly sliced celery
- ½ cup shredded cabbage
- ½ cup thinly sliced spring onions (scallions)
- 1 small carrot, grated
- 1 tomato, seeded and diced
- 2 tablespoons chopped capers, optional
- French dressing to moisten

Combine all the ingredients except the dressing in a large bowl and moisten with the French dressing. Transfer to a serving platter and garnish with thinly sliced cucumber.

Note: A little curry powder and raisins can be added for an interesting variation.

Southern Cross Salad

Serves 6

- 1 avocado, sliced
- 1 Granny Smith apple, halved and sliced
- juice of 2 lemons
- 3 spring onions (scallions), sliced
- 1 stalk celery, sliced
- 1 lettuce, washed and broken into bite-sized pieces
- 4 eggs, hard-boiled and sliced
- French dressing

Dip the avocado and apple in the lemon juice. Gently combine the salad vegetables and the eggs and sprinkle with French dressing.

Pineapple Chicken Salad

Serves 6

- 3 cups cooked rice
- 2 cups cooked diced chicken
- 1 x 450 g (14 ½ oz) can pineapple pieces, drained
- ½ cup each red and green pepper (capsicum), chopped
- ½ cup chopped spring onions (scallions)
- ½ cup (2 oz) slivered almonds
- 1 cup (8 fl oz) French dressing
- ½ teaspoon chopped fresh ginger, or ½ teaspoon ground
- 1 teaspoon soy sauce
- salt and pepper

Combine the rice, chicken, pineapple pieces, red and green pepper, spring onions and almonds. Blend the French dressing with the ginger and soy sauce. Season with salt and pepper, add the dressing to the rice-chicken mixture and toss to mix well. Garnish with extra pineapple pieces and spring onions.

Health Salad

Serves 6

- 3 red-skinned eating apples
- 2 tablespoons lemon juice
- 1 cup celery, chopped
- 1 cup (4 oz) grated cheese
- ½ cup (3 oz) sultanas
- 4 cups cooked brown rice
- ¼ cup (1 oz) chopped walnuts
- salt and pepper
- ½ cup (4 fl oz) mayonnaise or salad dressing
- 1 teaspoon grated orange rind
- 1 tablespoon orange juice

Chop the apples, toss in the lemon juice and drain. Combine the apples with the celery, cheese, sultanas, rice and walnuts. Season to taste. Blend the mayonnaise, orange rind and juice. Pour over the rice mixture and toss until well blended. Garnish with extra apple slices and a few chopped walnuts.

Bean and Watercress Salad

Serves 6 – 8

- 1 bunch watercress, washed and broken into sprigs
- 2 stems dill, broken into sprigs
- 4 oranges, peeled and segmented
- 1 tablespoon small capers
- 2 cups green beans, blanched and sliced
- 1 punnet cherry tomatoes, washed
- 4 tablespoons French dressing

Combine all the ingredients in a salad bowl with the French dressing. Toss lightly until well coated with dressing. Serve chilled.

Egg Spinach Salad

Serves 4 – 6

½ bunch of uncooked spinach
½ cup (4 fl oz) salad oil
¼ cup (2 oz) sugar
2 tablespoons vinegar
2 teaspoons finely grated onion
½ teaspoon salt
¼ teaspoon dry mustard
1 cup peas
250 g (8 oz) bacon, crisply cooked and crumbled
6 eggs, hard-boiled

Wash the spinach and chill. Combine the oil, sugar, vinegar, onion, salt and mustard in a blender and blend until thick. Tear the spinach into bite-sized portions. Combine with the peas, bacon and eggs and toss lightly. Pour the dressing over the salad and let stand for about 30 minutes. Toss again lightly to mix, then serve.

Garden Egg Salad

Serves 4

½ cup (4 fl oz) mayonnaise or salad dressing
⅓ cup sweet pickle relish
½ teaspoon dried onion flakes
8 eggs, hard-boiled and chopped
1 x 310 g (10 oz) packet frozen peas
¼ cup chopped celery
lettuce leaves, optional

Stir together the mayonnaise, relish and onion until blended. Toss with the eggs, peas and celery until combined. Cover and chill to blend flavours. Serve on lettuce leaves, if desired.

Egg and Potato Salad

Serves 4

500 g (1 lb) small new potatoes, boiled and skinned
125 g (4 oz) piece salami, diced
2 celery stalks, finely chopped
1 tablespoon chopped chives
1 tablespoon chopped fresh parsley
6-8 tablespoons mayonnaise
4 eggs, hard-boiled
1 small lettuce
paprika

Thinly slice the potatoes and combine with diced salami, celery, chives, parsley and mayonnaise. Cut the eggs in half and remove the yolks. Chop the whites and sieve the yolks. Add the whites to the mixture along with half the sieved yolks. Turn the ingredients gently until mixed and serve on a bed of lettuce leaves. Garnish with the remaining sieved egg yolk and paprika.

Egg Salad

Serves 4

200 g (6 ½ oz) small button mushrooms
125 g (4 oz) cold cooked roast meat
½ cup (4 fl oz) mayonnaise
1 teaspoon prepared mustard
4 eggs, hard-boiled
chopped fresh parsley

Slice the mushrooms and the meat into thin strips and place in a large bowl. Combine the mayonnaise and mustard and pour over the mixture. Slice the eggs. Very carefully fold 3 of the sliced eggs into the meat. Place in a salad bowl lined with lettuce leaves and arrange the other sliced egg on top and sprinkle with chopped parsley.

Ham and Egg Salad

Serves 4

1 ½ cups diced cooked ham
6 eggs, hard-boiled and chopped
½ cup diced pickled onions
½ cup sliced gherkins
⅓ cup (2 ½ fl oz) mayonnaise
1 tablespoon prepared mustard
2 teaspoons lemon juice
salt and pepper
4 lettuce cups

Combine the ham, eggs, onions and gherkins. Blend the mayonnaise, mustard and lemon juice. Add to the ham mixture and toss lightly. Season to taste. Chill. Spoon into lettuce cups.

Crunchy Egg Salad

Serves 4

8 eggs, hard boiled
½ small white onion
4 tablespoons chopped crispy chicken skin (see note)
salt and freshly ground black pepper
lettuce, tomato and cucumber to garnish

Chop the eggs and onion finely. Mix with the crispy chicken skin, salt and pepper. Spoon into a bowl lined with lettuce leaves and decorate with tomato wedges and cucumber slices.

Note: To make crisp chicken skin, take uncooked chicken skin and cut into 1.5 cm (1 inch) squares. Place in a heavy frying pan with a little chopped onion and a little chicken fat or butter and two tablespoons of water. Leave the pan on the heat until the onion is brown and the skin is crisp. When done, drain on absorbent paper and store in a cool place. The skin goes crispy when cool.

Salads

Curried Egg Salad

Serves 4

8 eggs, hard-boiled and chopped
2 stalks celery, thinly sliced
4 spring onions (scallions), chopped

3 tablespoons chopped parsley
2 tablespoons grated Parmesan cheese
lettuce leaves

Curried Mayonnaise
60 g (2 oz) butter
1 medium-sized onion, chopped
1 tablespoon curry powder

½ cup (4 fl oz) mayonnaise
1 tablespoon lemon juice
salt and pepper
½ cup (4 fl oz) cream

Combine the chopped eggs, celery, spring onions and parsley in a bowl and mix well. Sprinkle with the cheese and refrigerate until ready to serve. Serve with Curry Mayonnaise.

Curry Mayonnaise: Heat the butter in a pan. Add the chopped onion and sauté lightly. Add the curry powder and cook for 1 minute and allow to cool completely. When cold combine with the mayonnaise, lemon juice, salt and pepper. Beat the cream until soft peaks form and fold through the mayonnaise mixture.

Good Health Salad

Serves 6

1 cup chopped fresh parsley
1 cup fresh or canned bean shoots
1 cup alfalfa shoots or finely chopped celery
4 cups cooked brown rice
1 onion, finely chopped

¼ cup chopped fresh mint
2 firm red tomatoes, diced
½ cup (4 fl oz) olive or peanut oil
3 tablespoons lemon juice
1 teaspoon salt
freshly ground pepper

Add the parsley, bean shoots and alfalfa shoots to the rice together with the onion, mint and tomatoes. Blend together the oil, lemon juice, salt and pepper. Spoon the dresssing over the rice mixture and toss well. Chill for at least 1 hour before serving.

Creamy Chicken Peach Salad

Serves 6 – 8

1 ½ cups smoked chicken or turkey breast
4 peaches, peeled, stoned and cubed
1 red pepper (capsicum), seeded and cut into strips
1 cup (8 fl oz) natural yoghurt
pulp of 3 passionfruit
freshly ground black pepper

1 teaspoon grain seed mustard
1 teaspoon coriander
½ teaspoon cumin
½ teaspoon grated lime rind
½ teaspoon lime juice
2 rashers bacon, rind removed and chopped
1 mignonette lettuce

Cut the meat into strips. Toss with the peaches and red pepper. Combine the yoghurt with the passionfruit, pepper, mustard, spices and lime rind and juice. Pour over the turkey mixture, toss and chill well.

Just prior to serving, sauté the bacon until crisp. Drain well. Serve the salad in a large bowl lined with lettuce leaves and sprinkled with the hot bacon. Serve immediately.

Prawn Salad Mould

Serves 4

3 cups cooked rice
4 spring onions (scallions), chopped
½ cup chopped red pepper (capsicum)
½ cup chopped green pepper (capsicum)
1 cup chopped celery

½ cup (3 oz) sultanas
¾ cup (6 fl oz) French dressing
1 teaspoon curry powder
1 garlic clove, crushed
500 g (1 lb) peeled prawns (shrimp)

Combine the rice, spring onions, red and green peppers, celery and sultanas in a bowl. Blend the French dressing with the curry powder and garlic. Pour over the rice mixture and toss well. Press rice into a lightly oiled mould or ring tin and refrigerate. When ready to serve, turn out onto a platter. Fill the centre of the mould with prawns and garnish with spring onion curls or lettuce leaves. Chopped chicken or canned salmon may be used instead of prawns.

DESSERTS

Dessert is the ultimate indulgence, usually eaten when satisfied. Whether it be a smooth chocolate mousse or a simple cheese and fruit platter, it always forms a mellow end to a fine meal.

Never serve a rich dessert after a heavy main course and if serving a saucy dessert then it is best to avoid sauces in the other courses. Three courses are very filling so sometimes it is best to serve what is, strictly speaking, a first course followed by a delectable dessert. This is becoming a new trend overseas. Whatever your choice, make the end of your meal memorable and leave your guests craving for another invitation.

The majority of the recipes in this chapter have been provided by the **Meadowbank Technical College** while others have been provided by contributors whose credits appear elsewhere in the book.

Within the **Department of Technical and Further Education** (TAFE) in New South Wales, the School of Home Science conducts a variety of courses in both city and country centres. These courses are for full and part-time students and provide a wide range of subjects which include Nutrition, Consumer Education, Community and Family Studies and Household and Financial Management.

Full-time students are trained for a career as Home Economists in industry, while part-time students learn a variety of living skills suitable for family use and the areas of management and small scale catering.

Practical cookery classes range from Modern Basic, Special Culinary Skills and Gourmet Cookery to Italian, Continental, Chinese and Asian, as well as practical nutrition and budget control.

The following recipes have been selected and prepared by the teachers at Meadowbank College of TAFE, particularly Margaret Bolderstone.

Desserts

Hazelnut Chocolate Dip

Serves 6

1 ¼ cups (10 fl oz) cream
6 butternut snap biscuits, finely crushed
100 g (3 ½ oz) cooking chocolate, roughly chopped
½ cup (2 oz) chopped hazelnuts
fresh seasonal fruits

Lightly whip the cream. Fold through the crushed biscuits, chocolate and hazelnuts. Spoon into a serving bowl. Serve as a dip for bite-sized pieces of fresh seasonal fruits arranged on 1 central or 6 individual platters, e.g. strawberries, pineapple wedges, grapes, melon, banana, apricot halves or pear pieces. Alternately, serve as a topping over a selection of the above fruit.

Liqueured Coffee Ice Cream

Serves 4 – 6

1 tablespoon instant coffee
¼ cup (2 fl oz) coffee liqueur
2 cups (16 fl oz) thickened cream
2 tablespoons sugar

Dissolve the coffee in the liqueur. Beat the cream with the sugar until firm peaks form. Blend in the coffee and liqueur thoroughly. Pour into an ice cream tray or plastic container. Freeze for several hours until softly frozen. Serve decorated with chocolate curls or nuts.

Brandied Chestnut Mousse

Serves 4

1 cup (8 fl oz) canned chestnut purée
2 tablespoons sugar, or to taste
2 tablespoons brandy
1 cup (8 fl oz) cream, semi-whipped
melted chocolate
fresh orange segments

Beat the chestnut purée until smooth. Beat in the sugar, then brandy and fold in the cream. Spoon into 4 individual glass dessert dishes. Chill well. Drizzle over a little melted chocolate. Decorate with orange segments.

Basic Cheesecake

Serves 6 – 8

Base
1 x 250 g (8 oz) packet plain sweet biscuits
125 g (4 oz) butter, melted
1 teaspoon cinnamon

Filling
375 g (12 oz) cream cheese
¾ cup (6 oz) caster (powdered) sugar plus 1 tablespoon
1 whole egg, plus 2 eggs, separated
1 cup (8 fl oz) sour cream
1 tablespoon lemon juice
whipped cream
cinnamon

Base: Crush the biscuits and mix well with the melted butter and cinnamon. Press firmly onto the base and sides of a 20 cm (8 inch) spring form tin. Refrigerate until set.

Filling: Beat the cream cheese until soft and fluffy. Add the ¾ cup (6 oz) sugar and beat well. Add the whole egg, 2 egg yolks, sour cream and lemon juice and beat well. Beat the egg whites until peaks form, then beat in the extra sugar. Fold the egg whites through the cream cheese mixture. Pour into the base and cook at 160°C (325°F/Gas 3) for 1 to 1¼ hours. Refrigerate until firm. Decorate with whipped cream and a sprinkle of cinnamon.

Coconut Cheesecake

Serves 8 – 10

60 g (2 oz) unsalted butter
1 cup (3 ½ oz) wholemeal biscuit crumbs
1 ½ cups (4 ½ oz) desiccated coconut
2 teaspoons hot water
500 g (1 lb) ricotta cheese
3 eggs, separated
½ cup (5 oz) honey
vanilla essence
¼ cup (1 oz) cornflour (cornstarch)
½ cup (4 fl oz) buttermilk
1 teaspoon cinnamon
yoghurt and chopped almonds for decoration

Melt the butter in a pan and combine with the biscuit crumbs, 1 cup (3 oz) of the coconut and 2 teaspoons of water until well mixed. Press into a buttered 23 cm (9 inch) spring form tin and chill.

Place the cheese, egg yolks, honey, vanilla and cornflour in a blender, then add the buttermilk and blend. Beat the egg whites until stiff and fold into the blended mixture. Pour into the crumb case and sprinkle with remaining coconut and cinnamon. Bake at 150°C (300°F/Gas 2) for 45 minutes to 1 hour or until set. Leave in the open oven until cool, remove and chill. Decorate with yoghurt and almonds.

Chocolate Rum Cheesecake

Serves 10 – 12

Crumb Crust
375 g (12 oz) plain sweet biscuits, crushed
125 g (4 oz) butter, melted

Filling
185 g (6 oz) dark cooking chocolate
750 g (1½ lb) Australian cream cheese, softened
1 cup (8 oz) sugar
1 tablespoon gelatine
2 tablespoons water
2 tablespoons rum
1½ cups (12 fl oz) milk
1 cup (8 fl oz) light sour cream
2 egg whites

Crumb Crust: Mix the biscuits and butter together. Press into the base and sides of a 23 cm (9 inch) spring form tin. Refrigerate.

Filling: Melt the chocolate in the top of a double boiler or in a basin over hot water. Beat the cheese and sugar together until smooth and creamy. Beat in the chocolate thoroughly. Dissolve the gelatine in water and rum over low heat. Mix into the chocolate mixture adding the milk and sour cream. Beat thoroughly. Whip the egg whites until stiff. Fold into the chocolate mixture. Pour into the chilled crumb crust and refrigerate until set. Remove the sides of the tin and decorate with whipped cream and chocolate curls or cherries.

Cherry Brandy Cheesecake

Serves 8

Crumb Crust
125 g (4 oz) shortbread biscuits, crushed
¼ cup (1 oz) walnuts, finely chopped
60 g (2 oz) butter, melted

Filling
500 g (1 lb) Australian cream cheese
½ cup (4 oz) caster (powdered) sugar
2-3 tablespoons cherry brandy
100 g (3 ½ oz) cooking chocolate, melted over hot water
1 ¼ cups (10 fl oz) sour cream
1 tablespoon gelatine, dissolved in 2 tablespoons boiling water

Crumb Crust: Combine the biscuits, walnuts and butter and press onto the base of a 20 cm (8 inch) spring form tin. Refrigerate until firm.

Filling: Beat the cream cheese and sugar together until smooth. Beat in the cherry brandy, then the melted chocolate. Fold in the sour cream and dissolved gelatine. Blend thoroughly. Pour over the biscuit base and refrigerate until firm. Serve decorated with whipped cream and cherries.

Strawberry Cheesecake

Serves 5 – 6   [M]

Crust
30 g (1 oz) butter
1 ½ cups (6 oz) crushed ginger nut, granita or coconut biscuits
½ teaspoon ground ginger

Filling
125 g (4 oz) cottage cheese
125 g (4 oz) cream cheese
¼ cup (2 oz) caster (powdered) sugar
1 egg yolk
1 teaspoon grated lemon rind
1 tablespoon lemon juice
1 egg white, very lightly beaten

Topping
1 cup (8 fl oz) light sour cream
1 tablespoon caster (powdered) sugar
½ teaspoon vanilla essence
1 punnet strawberries

Crust: Melt the butter in a microwave on high for 30 seconds. Mix the butter, biscuit crumbs and ginger. Press into a 20 cm (8 inch) pie plate. Cook for 1 minute on high. Cool.

Filling: Mix the cottage cheese, cream cheese, sugar, egg yolk, lemon rind and juice together in a food processor. Fold in the egg white. Pour into the pie crust. Cook on defrost for 20 minutes. Chill.

Topping: Mix the sour cream, sugar and vanilla together. Spread over the chilled cheesecake. Cut the strawberries in half. Place on top of the sour cream.

Rhubarb Fool

Serves 5 – 6

1 bunch rhubarb, washed and cut up into 2.5 cm (1 inch) lengths, or 500 g (1 lb) frozen rhubarb
½ cup (4 fl oz) concentrated orange juice
½ teaspoon ground ginger
2 tablespoons brandy
⅓-½ cup (3-4 oz) sugar
1 ¼ cups (10 fl oz) cream
2 passionfruit

Cook the rhubarb, orange concentrate and ginger together until soft. Stir in the brandy and sugar. Purée the mixture and chill.

Whip the cream. Fold half the cream through the chilled purée. Pour into 5-6 individual dessert dishes and pipe the remaining cream on top. Decorate with passionfruit pulp.

Desserts

Apple Banana Shortcake

Serves 6

125 g (4 oz) butter
½ cup (4 oz) sugar
1 egg
1 cup (4 oz) self-raising flour
1 cup (4 oz) flour
2 tablespoons lemon butter (*page 454*)
2 cooking apples, peeled and grated
1 sliced banana
grated rind and juice of ½ lemon
caster (powdered) sugar

Cream the butter and sugar lightly. Add the egg. Sift in the flours and mix well. Divide the mixture into two. Roll each into a circle to fit a 20 cm (8 inch) greased cake tin. Place one circle in the tin and spread with lemon butter, then top with the remaining ingredients except caster sugar. Place the second circle on top pressing down firmly around the sides. Brush with water and sprinkle evenly with caster sugar. Bake at 180°C (350°F/Gas 4) for 40 minutes. Serve hot or cold with whipped cream, custard or ice cream.

Apple Noodle Meringue

Serves 8

125 g (4 oz) twist ribbon egg noodles
5 large cooking apples
1 ½ cups (12 fl oz) water
3 tablespoons sugar
3 eggs, separated
3 teaspoons cornflour (cornstarch)
15 g (½ oz) butter
2 tablespoons apricot jam
½ teaspoon cinnamon
½ teaspoon mixed spice
½ cup (4 oz) caster (powdered) sugar

Cook the noodles and drain. Peel, core and quarter the apples, stew gently until soft in the water and sugar. Drain and reserve the juice and make up to 1 ½ cups (12 fl oz), with water if necessary. Blend the egg yolks with the cornflour, gradually stirring in the apple juice. Melt the butter and pour in the egg yolk mixture and stir over a low heat until thickened. Arrange half the noodles in a 30 cm (12 inch) square casserole dish. Dot with jam. Cover with half the apples, sprinkle with half the cinnamon and mixed spice. Repeat the layers. Pour the sauce over. Beat the egg whites until stiff and gradually add the caster sugar. Spread roughly over the top. Bake at 180°C (350°F/Gas 4) for 15 minutes.

Opposite: *Old Fashioned Pudding and Brandy Sauce*

Yoghurt Rice Cream

Serves 6

1 cup (6 oz) short grain rice
3 cups (24 fl oz) skim milk
¾ cup (6 fl oz) non-fat apricot yoghurt
1 x 425 g (13 ½ oz) can unsweetened apricots, drained
nutmeg

Place the rice and milk in a saucepan. Bring to the boil then simmer for 15 to 20 minutes until the rice is cooked and the liquid absorbed, stirring occasionally. Stir in the yoghurt and apricots. Heat gently. Serve with a little nutmeg sprinkled on top.

Note: Any flavoured yoghurt and fruit may be used.

Old-Fashioned Pudding and Brandy Sauce

Serves 8 - 10

1½ cups (8 oz) chopped raisins
1½ cups (8 oz) sultanas
1½ cups (7 oz) currants
⅓ cup (2 oz) chopped mixed peel
2 tablespoons rum
2 tablespoons brandy
250 g (8 oz) butter, softened
1 ¼ cups (6 oz) packed soft brown sugar
grated rind of 1 lemon and 1 orange
4 eggs
1 cup (4 oz) flour
½ teaspoon each bicarbonate of soda (baking soda); salt; ground ginger; nutmeg; cinnamon and mixed spice
2 cups (4 oz) soft breadcrumbs

Brandy Sauce

¼ cup (2 oz) sugar
2 tablespoons cornflour (cornstarch)
1 tablespoon flour
2 cups (16 fl oz) milk
4 egg yolks
30 g (1 oz) butter
½ teaspoon vanilla essence
3 tablespoons brandy

Combine the fruits and spirits in a large bowl. Cover and allow to stand overnight. Cream together the butter, sugar and rind until creamy. Add the eggs one at a time. Beat well. Gradually add the sifted dry ingredients, except the breadcrumbs, alternately with the fruit mixture and the breadcrumbs.

Turn into a greased 10 cup (2.5 litre) bowl, lined on the bottom only. Cover securely with greased foil or paper. Steam for 4 hours on a rack in a large covered saucepan, with water coming halfway up sides of basin. Serve with Brandy Sauce.

Brandy Sauce: Place all the ingredients together in a saucepan and whisk until smooth. Cook gradually over a low heat, stirring all the time, until the sauce thickens.

397

Desserts

Pineapple Meringue

Serves 4 – 6

1 ripe medium-sized pineapple
1 cup sultana grapes
2 bananas, sliced
½ cup (3 oz) maraschino cherries
¼ cup (2 fl oz) dry sherry
⅓ cup (3 oz) caster (powdered) sugar
3 egg whites
2 tablespoons flaked almonds

Leave the top on the pineapple and cut it through lengthwise. Carefully remove the flesh, taking care that the case is not cut. Chop the flesh and add the grapes, bananas and cherries. Add the sherry and 2 tablespoons of the sugar and mix well. Press into the pineapple shells.

Beat the egg whites until stiff then gradually add the remaining caster sugar to form a smooth, glossy meringue. Pile over the fruit and sprinkle with the almonds. Bake at 150°C (300°F/Gas 2) for 5 to 10 minutes until the meringue is lightly browned. Serve warm or cold.

Caramel Oranges

Serves 8

8 oranges
¼ cup (2 fl oz) brandy
2 tablespoons Cointreau or Grand Marnier
1 cup (8 fl oz) water
1 ½ cups (12 oz) sugar
ice cream

Thinly peel the rind from 1 orange, then cut this into fine strips approximately 2.5 cm (1 inch) in length. Place in a saucepan, cover with water, blanch, drain and reserve for garnish. Peel the oranges, removing all the white pith. Segment or cut into slices, reserving any juice.

Combine the brandy, Cointreau and juice and pour over the oranges. Refrigerate for a few hours. Place the water and sugar in a saucepan over low heat until the sugar dissolves. Bring to the boil and boil until the mixture becomes a very light caramel colour. Cool a little. Pour over the oranges. Serve with the ice cream and sprinkle the top with the orange strips.

Individual Apricot Strudels

Serves 12

24 sheets filo pastry

185 g (6 oz) butter, melted

Filling

1 x 500 g (1 lb) can pie apricots
finely grated rind of 1 lemon
squeeze lemon juice
½ cup (4 oz) sugar
1 teaspoon mixed spice
⅓ cup (2 oz) sultanas
½ cup (2 oz) toasted slivered almonds
icing (confectioners') sugar
cream or ice cream

Drain off any excess liquid from the apricots. Combine the fruit with the lemon rind and juice, sugar, spice, sultanas and almonds.

Take one sheet of pastry and brush with the butter. Fold in halves lengthwise. Place 1 tablespoon of mixture on the short end of the pastry 2.5 cm (1 inch) from the edges. Fold in all edges and brush the pastry with butter.

Roll up and place on a greased tray with the seam side underneath. Brush with melted butter and make two slits in the top of the pastry. Bake at 190°C (375°F/Gas 5) for approximately 25 minutes. Cool a little, sprinkle with icing sugar and serve with cream or ice cream.

Harlequin Cassata

Serves 12

8 cups (2 litres) ice cream, softened in the refrigerator

Divide the ice cream into three equal portions. To each portion add one of the following:

a.
1 x 35 g (1 oz) cherry ripe bar, chopped

b.
1 x 425 g (13 ½ oz) can wild loganberries, drained, juice reserved
½ cup (4 fl oz) cream
½ cup (4 fl oz) reserved berry juice

c.
2 tablespoons cocoa, blended with a little water
½ cup (4 fl oz) cream
1 tablespoon chocolate or coffee liqueur

Freeze, layer by layer, in a 6 cup (1.5 litre) fancy mould. Freeze for several hours until firm throughout. Dip up to the rim in very hot water. Invert the mould and drop abruptly onto a wooden board. Repeat until the ice cream loosens. Place on a serving dish. Serve sliced with cream.

Pavlova Roll

Serves 6 – 8

4 egg whites
¾ cup (6 oz) sugar
½ cup (2 oz) slivered almonds
1 tablespoon cinnamon sugar
1 cup (8 fl oz) cream, whipped

Preheat the oven to 190°C (375°F/Gas 5). Grease, line, grease and cornflour a Swiss roll tin. Beat the egg whites until stiff peaks form. Gradually beat in the sugar until completely dissolved.

Spread the meringue over the base of the prepared tin. Sprinkle with the nuts and cinnamon sugar. Bake for 8 to 10 minutes until firm and the nuts have coloured. Cool. Turn out carefully, fill with cream and roll carefully.

Note: Serve either with an assortment of fresh fruit in the centre e.g. strawberries, passionfruit, kiwifruit, or purée 1 punnet of strawberries, flavoured with sugar and Grand Marnier.

Tamarillo Sorbet

Serves 8 – 10

1 ½ cups (12 fl oz) water
¾ cup (6 oz) sugar
finely grated rind of 1 lemon
strained juice of 2 lemons
¾ cup (6 fl oz) cream
1 ½ cups tamarillo pulp

Place the water and sugar in a saucepan over low heat until the sugar has dissolved. Bring to the boil and boil for 5 minutes. Remove and add the lemon rind and juice and cool. Add the lightly whipped cream and tamarillo pulp.

Place in a tray and freeze, stirring every 15 minutes until the mixture thickens, or place in an ice cream maker and mix until it thickens. Serve in small quantities.

Chocolate Cherry and Ginger Squares

Serves 8 – 10

375 g (12 oz) dark chocolate, melted
1 egg
½ cup (4 oz) caster (powdered) sugar
¾ cup (4 oz) chopped glacé cherries
¾ cup (4 oz) chopped glacé ginger
1 ⅓ cups (4 oz) desiccated coconut

Line a Swiss roll tin with baking paper or greased greaseproof paper. Spread the chocolate over base of tin. Combine the egg, sugar, cherries, ginger and coconut and spread over the chocolate.

Bake at 190°C (375°F/Gas 5) for 15 minutes. Cool and cut into squares.

Zuppa Inglese

Serves 8 – 10

1 cup (8 fl oz) strong black coffee
¼ cup (2 fl oz) marsala

Filling
3 tablespoons flour
3 tablespoons sugar
2 cups (16 fl oz) milk
3 eggs
vanilla essence

Topping
1 ¾ cups (14 fl oz) cream
2 tablespoons caster (powdered) sugar
1 packet savoyard biscuits
grated chocolate
½ teaspoon grated lemon rind
pink colouring
3 tablespoons grated chocolate
2 tablespoons coffee liqueur

Combine the coffee and marsala. Divide the biscuits into three lots. Using the first lot, dip each biscuit very quickly into the coffee mixture. Place 5 or 6 biscuits in a line on the serving plate. Spread with the chocolate filling.

Dip the second 5 or 6 biscuits into the coffee mixture and place on top of the chocolate. Spread with the pink filling. Top with the third layer of biscuits, also dipped in the coffee liquid. Refrigerate for 30 minutes.

Spread the topping over the top and sides of the biscuits and filling. Sprinkle with the grated chocolate. Make several hours before using. Slice to serve.

Filling: Combine the flour and sugar and blend with a little of the milk. Beat the eggs and ½ cup (4 fl oz) of the milk. Heat the remaining milk and add to the blended flour mixture. Return to the saucepan and cook, stirring, until thickened, then simmer for 2 minutes. Add the blended egg mixture and stir until it comes to the boil. Remove and add the vanilla and lemon rind to taste. Cool.

Divide the mixture into two. Add colouring to one half and chocolate to the second half.

Topping: Whip the cream and add the sugar and liqueur.

Desserts

Fruit Salad Slice

Serves 8 – 10

1 x 650 g (1 ¼ lb) can fruit salad	1 tablespoon gelatine
1 tablespoon chopped glacé cherries	1 x 250 g (8 oz) packet macaroons
finely grated rind and juice of 1 lemon	1 cup (8 fl oz) thickened cream

Drain the syrup from the fruit salad. Add the cherries, lemon rind and juice to the fruit. Place 3 tablespoons of the fruit syrup in a basin and add the gelatine. Dissolve the gelatine over moderately hot water. Cool. Add to the fruit mixture and chill for a while.

Line a bar or loaf tin with foil. Crush the macaroons and place half on the foil to form a layer of 3 mm (⅛ inch). Beat the cream and add to the fruit mixture and pour carefully over the macaroon base. Place another layer of macaroon on top. Allow to set. Remove from the tin and cut into slices to serve.

Individual Chocolate Baskets

Serves 12

250 g (8 oz) good quality cooking chocolate	3 passionfruit
60 g (2 oz) copha	Cointreau or Grand Marnier
1 punnet strawberries	1 cup (8 fl oz) thickened cream
3 kiwifruit	
2 oranges, segmented	

Select 12 strong paper patty cases or use two cases together for each basket. Place chocolate and copha in a basin and soften over moderately hot water. Place 2 teaspoons of chocolate mixture in each patty case and rotate to completely cover the surface. Repeat until all the cases have been covered. Allow to set.

Rinse and dry the strawberries. Keep 12 aside for decoration and chop the remainder. Peel and slice the kiwifruit and keep twelve half slices for decoration. Segment oranges and keep 12 slices for decoration. Combine the remaining fruits and sprinkle with a little Cointreau.

Whip the cream, adding a little sugar if liked. Carefully peel away the paper from the chocolate shapes and place on a serving plate. Spoon the fruit into these cases. Top with the cream. Decorate with the strawberries, kiwifruit slices and orange segments.

Dôme à l'Orange

Serves 8 – 10

Outer Coating

4 medium-sized oranges	½ cup (4 fl oz) Grand Marnier
3 ½ cups (28 fl oz) water	1 x 3-egg sponge, cooked in a slab tin
2 ¾ cups (1 ⅓ lb) sugar	¼ cup (2 fl oz) milk

Filling

8 cups (2 litres) vanilla ice cream	¼ cup (2 fl oz) Grand Marnier
½ cup (2 oz) finely chopped macadamia nuts	

Outer Coating: Slice the unpeeled oranges thinly and remove any seeds. Place the water and sugar in a saucepan. Slowly dissolve the sugar and bring to the boil. Add half the Grand Marnier and the oranges and simmer gently for 2 hours. Stand overnight.

Filling: Soften the ice cream a little and add the nuts and Grand Marnier.

Assembly: Line a 10 cup (2.5 litre) mould with foil, making sure it is very smooth. Top this with the orange slices, overlapping them a little. Cut a round of sponge to fit the base of the mould, then cut the remaining sponge into fingers to cover the sides. Place the sponge base and slices over the orange slices. Combine the remaining Grand Marnier and the milk and brush over the sponge. Add the ice cream filling. Trim the top of the sponge fingers level with the top of the ice cream. Cover with foil and freeze. Carefully turn out and remove foil.

Individual Chocolate Baskets

Bombe Alaska

Serves 8 - 10

Sponge Base
2 eggs, separated
½ cup (4 oz) caster (powdered) sugar
⅔ cup (2 ½ oz) self-raising flour
2 tablespoons hot water
pinch of salt

Filling
4 cups (1 litre) ice cream
500 g (1 lb) fresh or canned fruit, e.g. pineapple, kiwifruit, peaches, strawberries

Topping
4 egg whites
1 cup (8 oz) caster (powdered) sugar

Sponge Base: Preheat the oven to 180°C (350°F/Gas 4). Beat the egg whites until stiff. Gradually add the sugar while continuing to beat. Beat until the sugar has dissolved. Mix in the egg yolks and then fold in the sifted flour. Add the hot water and salt and fold in quickly. Pour into a greased and lined Swiss roll tin. Bake for about 15 minutes or until lightly browned on top and springy to touch. Turn out onto a cooling rack and peel off the paper. Allow to cool.

Filling: Cut the sponge into 3 even pieces. Place one piece on an ovenproof dish and spread with slightly softened ice cream. Sandwich this with another piece of sponge and repeat. Freeze.

Drain the fruits if they are canned or cut the fresh fruits into bite-sized pieces. Remove the sponge sandwich from the freezer and cover with fruit. Return to the freezer.

Meringue: Beat the egg whites until stiff. Gradually add the sugar and continue to beat until the mixture is very stiff. Spread or pipe this mixture over the sponge sandwich until completely covered. Bake in a very hot oven, 240°C (475°F/Gas 9), for 3 to 5 minutes. Serve at once. Decorate with lighted sparklers for a stunning effect.

Caramel Fondue with Fruit

Serves 8 – 10

½ cup (4 oz) caster (powdered) sugar
2 tablespoons cornflour (cornstarch)
2 cups (16 fl oz) cream
selection of fresh fruits, cut into bite-sized pieces

Place the sugar in a fondue pot and cook gently until lightly caramelised. Blend the cornflour with a little of the cream, add the remaining cream and mix, then add to the sugar mixture.

Cook over moderate heat, stirring all the time until the caramel dissolves and the mixture thickens. Cool and use to dip the fruits.

Barbecue Fruit Kebabs

Serves 6 – 8

3 bananas, cut into thick slices
2 apples, unpeeled and cut into chunks
1 pineapple, cubed
2 grapefruit, segmented
1 punnet strawberries
any other fresh fruit in season e.g. peaches; apricots; nectarines

Marinade
¾ cup (6 fl oz) orange juice
¼ cup (2 fl oz) lemon juice
½ cup (5 oz) honey
2 tablespoons Cointreau
1 tablespoon finely chopped mint

Combine the ingredients for the marinade and mix well. Combine the fruit, add the marinade and stand for 30 minutes to 1 hour. Thread the fruit onto bamboo sticks which have been soaked in water.

Barbecue for 5 to 7 minutes, turning frequently to prevent burning. During cooking baste with the marinade.

Chocolate Orange Mousse

Serves 6

125 g (4 oz) good quality cooking chocolate
1 tablespoon Grand Marnier
4 eggs, separated
finely grated rind of 1 orange
2 tablespoons orange juice
1 cup (8 fl oz) cream
extra ½ cup (4 fl oz) cream, whipped
chocolate curls
very thin slices of orange

Melt the chocolate over moderately hot water or in a microwave. Beat together the Grand Marnier, egg yolks, orange rind and juice and add to the chocolate to form a smooth thick mixture. Whip the cream and fold into the chocolate mixture.

Beat the egg whites to soft peaks and fold lightly into the chocolate mixture. Place in individual serving dishes and refrigerate. Top with whipped cream, chocolate curls and orange slices.

Ice Cream

Serves 6 – 8

2 ½ cups (20 fl oz) cream
¾ cup (4 oz) sieved icing (confectioners') sugar
4 egg whites
flavouring
colouring

Whip the cream lightly and add the icing sugar. Whip the egg whites and fold into the cream mixture. Add the flavouring and colouring as desired. Place in refrigerator trays and freeze or place in an ice cream maker and churn until set.

Flavourings: Use a variety of essences such as vanilla, peppermint or coffee. Chopped chocolate, glacé fruits or fresh fruits may also be used.

Desserts

Walnut Torte

Serves 8 – 10

3 eggs
1 cup (7 oz) caster (powdered) sugar plus 2 tablespoons
125 g walnuts, very finely chopped
½ cup (2 oz) flour
salt
2 ½ cups (20 fl oz) thickened cream
vanilla essence
2 tablespoons rum
walnut halves

Grease and base line a 23 cm (8 inch) spring form tin. Beat the eggs well, then gradually add 1 cup (7 oz) sugar, beating well until the mixture is very thick and glossy. Gently fold in the walnuts and the sieved flour and salt. Pour into the tin and bake in a moderate oven at 180°C (350°F/Gas 4) for about 40 minutes or until set. Remove and stand for 15 minutes before removing from the tin. Allow to cool.

Beat the cream and the remaining caster sugar, vanilla and rum. Slice the cake into three rounds and sandwich together with the cream. Spread the remaining cream over the top and sides. Decorate with walnut halves.

Coffee Dessert Cake

Serves 8 – 10

185 g (6 oz) unsalted butter
¾ cup (6 oz) caster (powdered) sugar
3 eggs, separated
1 ½ cups (6 oz) flour
1 teaspoon baking powder
pinch of salt
½ teaspoon bicarbonate of soda (baking soda)
½ cup (4 fl oz) sour cream
½ cup (2 oz) chopped walnuts
sour cream for serving

Coffee Syrup
1 cup (8 fl oz) strong black coffee
2 tablespoons rum
⅓ cup (3 oz) sugar
⅓ cup (2 ½ fl oz) water

Thoroughly grease a 20 cm (8 inch) tube pan and sprinkle with flour. Tap out any excess flour. Cream the butter, gradually add the sugar and beat very well. Add the egg yolks and beat well.

Sieve the flour, baking powder, salt and bicarbonate of soda together. Fold in the cream and walnuts, then the sieved flour. Beat the egg whites to a soft peak and fold into the cake mixture. Pour into the prepared tin and bake at 180°C (350°F/Gas 4) for about 40 to 45 minutes. Test with a skewer. Remove and stand for 5 minutes. Turn onto a cake cooler, leave for 5 minutes then return to the cake tin.

Combine the coffee and rum. Heat the sugar and water and bring to the boil when the sugar is dissolved. Add the coffee mixture and warm but do not boil. Slowly pour the liquid over the cake mixture and stand until cool. Turn onto a serving plate. Serve with the sour cream.

Fruit Shortcake Dessert

Serves 6 – 8

2 cups (8 oz) self-raising flour
½ teaspoon mixed spice
pinch of salt
90 g (3 oz) butter
1 egg
¼ cup (2 oz) sugar
1 tablespoon honey
3 tablespoons milk
icing (confectioners') sugar
sour cream

Filling
fruits in season e.g. combinations of berry fruits; grated apple with chopped dates; banana, passionfruit and pineapple

Sieve the flour, spice and salt. Add the butter and rub in until the mixture resembles breadcrumbs. Beat the egg and add the sugar, honey and milk. Mix into the flour mixture to form a soft dough.

Grease a 20 cm (8 inch) cake tin. Divide the mixture in two. Knead one half lightly and press into the tin. Top with the filling. Place the remaining dough evenly over the filling.

Bake at 180°C (350°F/Gas 4) for about 40 minutes. Cool a little and remove. Cool and sprinkle with icing sugar. Serve with sour cream.

Fudge Pudding

Serves 6

1 cup (4 oz) flour
2 teaspoons baking powder
pinch of salt
¾ cup (6 oz) sugar
6 tablespoons cocoa
½ cup (4 fl oz) milk
15 g (½ oz) butter, melted
1 cup (4 oz) chopped nuts
1 cup (6 oz) soft brown sugar
1 ¾ cups (14 fl oz) hot water
whipped cream
icing (confectioners') sugar

Grease a 6-8 cup (1 ½-2 litre) casserole dish. Sieve the flour, baking powder, salt, sugar and 2 tablespoons cocoa into a bowl. Add the milk, melted butter and nuts and stir. Spread into the prepared dish and sprinkle with the brown sugar and remaining cocoa, mixed together. Pour over the hot water. Bake at 180°C (350°F/Gas 4) for 45 minutes.

The cake mixture will rise to the surface with the sauce mixture underneath. Serve warm with whipped cream, flavoured with icing sugar.

Opposite: Walnut Torte

403

Desserts

Quick Fruit Sponge Dessert

Serves 8 – 10

1 cup (4 oz) wholemeal or white self-raising flour
½ cup (4 oz) sugar
½ cup (4 fl oz) milk
1 beaten egg
⅓ cup (2½ fl oz) melted butter
hot stewed fruit
icing (confectioners') sugar

Mix all the ingredients except the butter, fruit and icing sugar. Stir in the butter. Beat well and pour over **hot** stewed fruit in a deep pie dish. Bake at 190°C (375°F/Gas 5) for 30 minutes. Sprinkle with icing sugar. Serve with custard, ice cream or cream.

Note: Any stewed or canned fruit is suitable.

Lemon Loaf Cake

Makes 1 loaf

125 g (4 oz) butter
2 teaspoons grated lemon rind
1 ¼ cups (12 oz) sugar
1 ½ cups (6 oz) self-raising flour
3 eggs
¾ cup (6 fl oz) milk
¼ cup (2 fl oz) lemon juice
whipped cream

Combine the butter, lemon rind and 1 cup (8 oz) of sugar in a saucepan. Heat until the butter is melted. Do not boil. Stir in half the sifted flour then the eggs, beaten with the remaining sifted flour and the milk. Beat with a wooden spoon until smooth.

Pour into a well greased 23 x 10 cm (9 x 4 inch) loaf tin. Bake at 190°C (375°F/Gas 5) for 50 minutes or until cooked. Leave in the tin to cool.

Combine the lemon juice and remaining sugar in a saucepan. Stir over low heat until the sugar dissolves. Bring to the boil. Pour the hot syrup over the hot cake, leave to cool. Serve warm with whipped cream.

Pawpaw in Passionfruit Sauce

Serves 4

1 large pawpaw (papaya), peeled, seeded and cubed
⅔ cup (5 fl oz) freshly squeezed orange juice
pulp of 6 large passionfruit
¼ cup (2 fl oz) lime juice

Combine all the ingredients. Chill and serve.

Chocolate Rum Soufflé

Makes 6

250 g (8 oz) dark chocolate
¼ cup (2 fl oz) milk
2 tablespoons rum
4 egg yolks
4 egg whites
pinch of salt
3 tablespoons caster (powdered) sugar
soft unsalted butter and caster (powdered) sugar for lining the moulds
icing (confectioners') sugar

Melt the chocolate over hot water. Add the milk and rum. Remove from the heat and beat in the egg yolks. Beat the egg whites with the salt until the mixture forms peaks. Gradually beat in the sugar.

Fold the chocolate mixture into the egg white mixture. Spoon carefully into six individual soufflé dishes which have been greased with unsalted butter and sprinkled with caster sugar. Cook on the centre shelf of a preheated oven at 220°C (425°F/Gas 7) for 15 minutes. Sprinkle with icing sugar.

Pears in Ginger Sauce

Serves 4 [M]

4 pears, halved, peeled and cored
½ cup (4 fl oz) white wine
1 teaspoon grated fresh ginger
2 teaspoons lemon juice
60 g (2 oz) butter
½ cup (3 oz) soft brown sugar
1 ¼ cups (10 fl oz) cream, whipped

Place the pears, wine, ginger and lemon juice in a large heatproof bowl. Cover and microwave on high for 10 minutes. Stand for 10 minutes. Melt the butter in a heatproof glass bowl on high for 1 minute. Add the sugar. Cook uncovered for 2 minutes and stir twice during cooking.

Remove the pears from the syrup. Place in a serving dish. Mix the caramel and syrup together and pour over the pears. Serve chilled, with whipped cream.

Self-Saucing Chocolate Pudding

Serves 4–6 [M]

- 1 cup (4 oz) flour
- ¾ cup (6 oz) caster (powdered) sugar
- ⅓ cup (1 ½ oz) cocoa
- 2 teaspoons baking powder
- ½ teaspoon salt
- ½ cup (4 fl oz) milk
- 30 g (1 oz) butter, melted
- 1 teaspoon vanilla essence
- ½ cup (2 oz) chopped pecans
- ¾ cup (4 oz) soft brown sugar
- 1 ¼ cups (10 fl oz) hot water

Sift the flour, sugar, ¼ cup (1 oz) of the cocoa, the baking powder and salt into a large casserole. Stir in the milk, butter, vanilla and nuts. Mix to a thick paste.

Blend the remaining cocoa and brown sugar with the water and pour over the mixture in the casserole. Microwave on high for 8 minutes. Serve warm with ice cream.

Rich Steamed Pudding

Serves 8–10 [M]

- 2¼ cups (12 oz) mixed fruit
- 1 cup (6 oz) sultanas
- 250 g (8 oz) butter
- 1 cup (6 oz) soft brown sugar
- 1 cup (8 fl oz) water
- 1 tablespoon syrup or treacle
- 1 teaspoon bicarbonate of soda (baking soda)
- 1 teaspoon cinnamon
- 1 teaspoon mixed spice
- ½ teaspoon ground ginger
- 1 cup (4 oz) flour
- 1 cup (4 oz) self-raising flour
- 1 teaspoon parisienne essence

Place the first six ingredients in a large heatproof bowl and microwave on high for 8 to 10 minutes. Stir twice during heating. Cool to a warm temperature.

Add the bicarbonate of soda and spices to the flours. Add to the fruit. Stir in the parisienne essence. Pour into a microwave ring mould.

Cook on medium-low for 18 to 20 minutes. Allow to stand for 5 minutes, loosely covered. Serve warm with custard.

Choc-Meringue Tart

Serves 8

- 1 cup (4 oz) self-raising flour
- 1 cup (4 oz) flour
- 1 cup (7 oz) caster (powdered) sugar
- 125 g (4 oz) butter, roughly chopped
- 2 egg yolks plus 2 whole eggs
- 2 tablespoons cold water
- 500 g (1 lb) Australian ricotta cheese
- ¼ cup (1 oz) cocoa or instant coffee
- ½ cup (4 fl oz) light sour cream

Meringue
- 2 egg whites
- ¼ cup (2 oz) caster (powdered) sugar
- ¼ teaspoon vanilla essence

Sift together the flours, add half the sugar, then rub in the butter until the mixture resembles fine breadcrumbs. Combine one egg yolk and the water, add and mix to a firm dough. Knead lightly on a floured surface, cover and leave for 30 minutes. Roll out the pastry and line a 23 cm (9 inch) tart plate. Prick the base with a fork and bake in a hot oven, 200°C (400°F/Gas 6), for 15 minutes (protect the edges with foil if becoming too browned). Remove from the oven and cool.

Beat the cheese until smooth then gradually beat in the remaining sugar and the cocoa. Beat in the remaining egg yolk and the eggs, then beat in the sour cream. Pour into the pastry case, place in a moderate oven, 180°C (350°F/Gas 4), and bake for 1 hour.

Meringue: Beat the egg whites until soft peaks form then gradually beat in the sugar and beat again until stiff peaks form. Mix in the vanilla essence. Spoon the meringue over the filling and swirl into peaks. Return to the oven and bake for another 10 minutes. Serve warm or cold with softly whipped cream.

Apricot Delights

Serves 4

- 125 g (4 oz) plain marshmallows
- 2 tablespoons lemon juice
- ¼ teaspoon grated lemon rind
- ½ cup (4 fl oz) apricot flavoured yoghurt
- ¼ cup (2 fl oz) apricot purée
- 125 g (4 oz) Australian cottage cheese
- ½ cup (4 fl oz) cream
- 2 tablespoons toasted chopped almonds

Reserve 4 whole marshmallows. Melt the remaining marshmallows with the lemon juice and rind in a small saucepan. Combine the next four ingredients in a bowl. Add the marshmallow mixture and mix well. Pour into 4 individual parfait dishes. Top with a whole marshmallow and almonds. Chill for at least 30 minutes.

Desserts

Chocolate Date Nut Torte

Serves 8 – 10

4 eggs
1 ¾ cups (13 oz) caster (powdered) sugar
4 tablespoons flour
2 teaspoons baking powder
½ teaspoon cinnamon
1 cup (4 oz) coarsely chopped walnuts
2 cups (10 oz) finely chopped dates
125 g (4 oz) chocolate, grated
1 ¼ cups (10 fl oz) thickened cream, whipped
extra grated chocolate

Beat the eggs until light then gradually add the sugar and beat until light and fluffy. Sieve the flour, baking powder and cinnamon and gently fold into the egg mixture. Fold in the walnuts, dates and chocolate.

Grease and line a 23 cm (9 inch) spring form tin. Pour in the mixture and bake at 150°C (300°F/Gas 2) for 45 to 50 minutes. Cool in the tin. Remove, spread with the cream and sprinkle with grated chocolate to serve.

Passionfruit Pears

Serves 4

½ cup (4 oz) sugar
1 cup (8 fl oz) water
strips of orange rind
½ cup (4 fl oz) orange juice
4 firm pears, peeled leaving stalk intact
¼ cup (2 fl oz) cream
2 passionfruit

Combine the sugar and water and stir over medium heat until the sugar is dissolved. Add the orange rind and juice and bring to the boil. Add the pears and simmer, covered, for 10 to 15 minutes or until cooked. Baste frequently with the syrup. Remove and drain the pears.

Add the cream to the syrup and simmer, uncovered, until reduced and thickened. Add the passionfruit pulp. Pour over the pears to glaze. Serve warm.

Passionfruit Pears

Pineapple Upside-down Pudding

Serves 6 [M]

Topping
60 g (2 oz) butter
⅓ cup (2 oz) soft brown sugar
3 slices pineapple, cut in half
6 glacé cherries

Cake Mixture
60 g (2 oz) butter
⅓ cup (3 oz) caster (powdered) sugar
3 eggs
1 cup (4 oz) self-raising flour
2 tablespoons water

Topping: Cream the butter and brown sugar together, then spread over the bottom of a microwave ring mould. Place the half pineapple rings and cherries on the creamed mixture.

Cake Mixture: Cream the butter and sugar together until light and fluffy. Beat in the eggs one at a time. Add the flour and fold in. Stir in the water.

Spoon mixture over the pineapple and cherries. Cook on medium for 5 to 6 minutes. Cover loosely with plastic wrap and stand for 5 minutes. Turn out and serve with cream or custard.

Pecan Pie

Serves 6 – 8

1 quantity biscuit pastry (*page 412*)
1 cup (4 oz) chopped pecan nuts
2 eggs
2 tablespoons flour
2 tablespoons soft brown sugar
2 tablespoons golden syrup
½ cup (4 fl oz) milk
¼ cup (2 fl oz) cream
vanilla essence
cream or ice cream to serve

Place a 20 cm (8 inch) flan ring on a baking slide. Roll out the pastry thinly and place in the flan ring, taking care not to stretch the pastry. Trim the top. Place the pecan nuts in the pastry shell. Lightly beat the eggs, then add the flour, brown sugar and golden syrup, and mix until well blended. Mix in the milk, cream and vanilla essence to taste. Pour into the pastry shell.

Bake at 200°C (400°F/Gas 6) for 15 minutes, then at 160°C (325°F/Gas 3) for 25 to 30 minutes, until the filling has set. Remove from the oven. Serve warm or cold with cream or ice cream.

Peach Crumble

Serves 4 – 5 [M]

Filling
1 x 220 g (7 oz) can pie peaches
1 teaspoon grated lemon rind
¼ cup (2 oz) sugar
¼ teaspoon ground ginger

Topping
½ cup (2 oz) self-raising flour
½ cup (1½ oz) coconut
½ cup (3 oz) soft brown sugar
60 g (2 oz) butter, melted

Filling: Mix the peaches, lemon rind, sugar and ginger together. Put into a microwaveproof casserole.

Topping: Mix the self-raising flour, coconut, brown sugar and melted butter together. Sprinkle over the peach filling. Microwave for 8 to 9 minutes on high. Serve warm with cream or ice cream.

Strawberry Puffs

Makes 18

1 quantity choux pastry (*page 408*)
1 ¼ cups (10 fl oz) thickened cream
2 tablespoons icing (confectioners') sugar
1 punnet strawberries, hulled
2 tablespoons strawberry jam

Preheat the oven to 200°C (400°F/Gas 6). Grease a baking slide. Place 18 heaped teaspoons of choux pastry on the tray, leaving 4 cm (1 ½ inch) between each one. Bake the puffs for 25 to 30 minutes until well browned. Remove from the oven and make a small slit in each to allow the steam to escape.

Whip the cream and sweeten with the icing sugar. Purée the strawberries with the strawberry jam. Fill the puffs with sweetened cream. Place on a serving plate and drizzle with strawberry sauce.

Strawberry Puffs

Desserts

Blitz Torte

Serves 8 – 10

125 g (4 oz) butter
1 ¼ cups (9 oz) caster (powdered) sugar
1 teaspoon vanilla essence
4 egg yolks
1 cup (4 oz) flour
1 teaspoon baking powder
pinch of salt
⅓ cup (2 ½ fl oz) milk
4 egg whites
¼ cup (1 oz) slivered almonds
½ teaspoon cinnamon

Filling

2 tablespoons custard powder
⅓ cup (3 oz) caster sugar
1 cup (8 fl oz) milk
1 egg
vanilla essence
60 g (2 oz) unsalted butter

Grease and line the bases of two 23 cm (9 inch) cake tins. Thoroughly cream the butter and ½ cup (4 oz) of the sugar, then add the vanilla and egg yolks. Beat well. Sieve the flour, baking powder and salt together. Fold this into the butter mixture alternately with the milk. Spread into the prepared tins.

Beat the egg whites until stiff and gradually beat in the remaining sugar until the meringue is stiff and glossy. Spread over the cake mixture, then sprinkle with the almonds and cinnamon. Bake at 180°C (350°F/Gas 4) for 25 to 30 minutes. Cool, carefully remove from the tins and sandwich together with the filling.

Filling: Combine the custard powder and sugar and blend with a little of the milk. Beat the egg and add 2 tablespoons of the milk to this.

Heat the remaining milk and pour onto the custard powder mixture. Return to the saucepan, bring to the boil, stirring, and simmer for 2 minutes. Pour a little of this onto the egg mixture. Return to the saucepan and stir until the mixture comes to the boil. Remove and add vanilla. Cool. Cream the butter and gradually beat in the cooled custard.

Choux Pastry

1 cup (8 fl oz) water
60 g (2 oz) butter
¾ cup (3 oz) flour
3 eggs

Place the water and butter in a saucepan and heat until boiling. Remove from the heat and add the flour all at once and beat until smooth. Return to a medium heat and cook for approximately 3 to 5 minutes, stirring continually until the mixture starts to come away from the sides of the saucepan. Allow to cool a little.

Beat the eggs and gradually add to the flour mixture, beating well. The mixture should be stiff and glossy. Use as desired.

Blueberry Bavarois

Serves 6

¾ cup (6 fl oz) milk
3 egg yolks
2 tablespoons sugar
1 teaspoon vanilla essence
3 teaspoons gelatine
2 tablespoons water
¾ cup (6 fl oz) cream
100 g (3 ½ oz) blueberries

Sauce

200 g (6 ½ oz) blueberries
¼ cup (2 oz) sugar
¼ cup (2 fl oz) water
2 tablespoons brandy

Bring the milk to the boil. Beat the yolks and sugar together until well mixed. Pour in the hot milk and vanilla essence and whisk over heat until the mixture coats the back of a metal spoon. Cool.

Soak the gelatine in cold water, dissolve over hot water and add to the custard. Whip the cream until stiff. When the custard is as thick as the whipped cream, fold in the cream and blueberries. Pour the mixture into 6 wetted moulds and set in the refrigerator overnight. Serve with the sauce.

Sauce: Place the blueberries and sugar in a saucepan, add the water and stir until the sugar is dissolved. Bring to the boil. Simmer until the mixture is thick. Add the brandy and strain the sauce.

Lemon Mousse with Raspberry Yoghurt Sauce

Serves 6

3 teaspoons gelatine
3 tablespoons water
3 eggs, separated
¾ cup (6 oz) caster (powdered) sugar
½ cup (4 fl oz) lemon juice
2 teaspoons finely grated lemon rind
1 ¼ cups (10 fl oz) cream

Sauce

125 g (4 oz) fresh or frozen raspberries
2 tablespoons icing (confectioners') sugar
¾ cup (6 fl oz) natural yoghurt
1 tablespoon Grand Marnier

Combine the gelatine and water and dissolve the gelatine over hot water. Beat the egg yolks and sugar until very thick and creamy. Add the gelatine and lemon juice and rind. Allow to thicken a little.

Beat the egg whites until soft peaks form. Beat the cream. Fold the egg whites and cream into the mixture. Pour into a wetted 4 cup (1 litre) mould or 6 individual moulds and allow to set. Turn onto a serving plate and serve with the sauce.

Sauce: Combine the raspberries and icing sugar and add to the yoghurt. Add the Grand Marnier.

Marsala Crème

Serves 6

- 1 x 250 g (8 oz) packet macaroons
- ½ cup (4 fl oz) marsala
- 185 g (6 oz) cooking chocolate
- 2 tablespoons sugar
- 1 teaspoon instant coffee
- ¼ teaspoon cinnamon
- 4 eggs, separated
- 1 tablespoon gelatine, soaked in 3 tablespoons water
- 1 ¼ cups (10 fl oz) thickened cream
- extra chocolate, made into curls

Crush the macaroons and sprinkle with half the marsala. Place the chocolate in a bowl and place over moderately hot water until softened. Add the sugar, coffee and cinnamon. Beat in the egg yolks and remaining marsala and cool.

Dissolve the gelatine over hot water, then add to the chocolate mixture. Chill until beginning to set. Beat the cream and fold half into the mixture. Beat the egg whites to soft peaks and fold in.

Divide half the chocolate into 6 individual serving dishes, sprinkle with the macaroon mixture then add the remaining chocolate mixture. Allow to set and pipe the remaining cream on top and sprinkle with chocolate curls.

Soufflé Carmen

Serves 6

- 1 cup (4 oz) dried apricots
- ¾ cup (6 fl oz) water
- finely grated rind of 1 lemon
- juice of 2 lemons
- 1½ tablespoons gelatine
- 4 eggs, separated
- 1 cup (7 oz) caster (powdered) sugar
- 1 cup (8 fl oz) cream

Garnish
- ½ cup (4 fl oz) cream
- vanilla essence
- 1 tablespoon sugar
- 1 tablespoon chopped pistachio nuts

Combine the apricots and water and cook gently until soft. Add the lemon rind and cool. Combine the lemon juice and gelatine and dissolve over hot water.

Beat the egg yolks and sugar until light and creamy, then add the apricot mixture and gelatine. Allow to cool and refrigerate until beginning to set. Beat the cream and fold into the mixture. Beat the egg whites until soft peaks form then fold in.

Place in 6 individual serving dishes and allow to set. Beat the cream for the garnish and add the vanilla and sugar. Pipe onto each serving and sprinkle with pistachio nuts.

Crêpe Batter

Makes about 20

- 1 cup (4 oz) flour
- pinch of salt
- 3 eggs
- ¾ cup (6 fl oz) milk
- ¾ cup (6 fl oz) water
- oil for frying

Sieve the flour and salt into a bowl and make a well in the centre. Add the eggs and half the milk. Gradually beat with a wooden spoon, drawing in the flour from the edges to the centre. Beat until smooth, adding a little more liquid if needed. Beat in more liquid, if necessary, to form a creamy consistency which will pour readily.

Heat a 13-15 cm (5-6 inch) crêpe pan and add a little oil. Lift the pan off the heat and pour in 2 tablespoons of batter, tilting the pan so that it covers the whole surface. Heat until lightly browned then toss or turn the crêpe and lightly brown the second side. Use as required.

Note: The crêpe batter may be mixed in a food processor. Crêpes freeze well.

Cherry Cream Crêpe Stack

Makes 20

- 1 quantity crêpe batter (*see above*)

Cream Filling
- ½ cup (4 oz) sugar
- 2 tablespoons flour
- 1 tablespoon cornflour (cornstarch)
- pinch of salt
- 2 cups (16 fl oz) milk
- 3 egg yolks
- ¼ teaspoon almond essence

Cherry Topping
- ¾ cup (6 oz) sugar
- 2 tablespoons cornflour (cornstarch)
- ½ cup (4 fl oz) cherry juice
- 2 cups drained sour cherries
- 1 tablespoon lemon juice
- 3 tablespoons port
- red food colouring

Make the crêpes. Spread the cream filling on each crêpe and place in two stacks. Spoon sauce over the top of the stacks.

Cream Filling: Combine the sugar, flour, cornflour and salt and blend with a little of the milk. Beat 3 tablespoons of the milk into the egg yolks. Heat the remaining milk and pour onto the blended flour mixture. Return to the saucepan and stir until the mixture thickens, then simmer for 2 minutes. Pour in the egg mixture, stirring continually, and heat until just boiling. Cool and add the almond essence.

Cherry Topping: Combine the sugar and cornflour and mix with the cherry juice. Add the cherries and cook, stirring until the mixture thickens and boils. Simmer for 2 minutes. Remove and cool and add the lemon juice, port and food colouring.

Desserts

Hazelnut Pancakes with Caramel Sauce

Makes 20

1 quantity crêpe batter (*page 409*)
90 g (3 oz) butter
1 cup (5 oz) soft brown sugar
1 ½ cups (12 fl oz) water
3 tablespoons flour
3 eggs
90 g (3 oz) toasted hazelnuts, chopped

Caramel Sauce

¾ cup (6 oz) sugar
1 ½ cups (12 fl oz) water
1 teaspoon finely grated lemon rind
5 cm (2 inch) stick cinnamon
pinch of ground cloves
vanilla essence
1 tablespoon sherry
juice of 1 lemon

Make the crêpes. Combine the butter, brown sugar and 1 cup (8 fl oz) of the water in a saucepan and place over a moderate heat until the sugar dissolves and the mixture comes to the boil. Blend the flour with the remaining liquid and add to the saucepan, stirring well. Bring to the boil and simmer for 2 minutes.

Beat the eggs and add 3 tablespoons of water to them. Pour in the caramel mixture and return to the saucepan and stir until it comes to the boil. Cool a little and add the hazelnuts. Spread on each crêpe and roll up.

Place in a greased ovenproof dish and cover with foil. Heat for approximately 15 to 20 minutes at 150°C (300°F/Gas 2). Pour a little sauce over for serving and serve the remaining sauce separately.

Caramel Sauce: Place the sugar and one third of the water in a saucepan. Cook gently until the sugar dissolves, then boil to form a caramel. Carefully add the remaining water, lemon rind, cinnamon and cloves and simmer for 3 minutes. Remove the cinnamon and add the vanilla, sherry and lemon juice.

Mango Liqueur Crêpes

Makes 20

1 quantity crêpe batter (*page 409*)
2-3 fresh mangoes, peeled and seeded
1 tablespoon chopped crystallised ginger
2 tablespoons ginger syrup
185 g (6 oz) ricotta cheese
finely grated rind and juice of 1 lemon
2 tablespoons Cointreau
slivered, lightly browned almonds

Sauce

2 small mangoes, peeled, seeded, and sliced
2 tablespoons Cointreau

Make the crêpes. Chop the mangoes and add the ginger and syrup. Beat the cheese and add the lemon rind and juice and Cointreau. Combine the mango and cheese mixtures. Place the mixture on the crêpes, arrange on a serving dish and sprinkle with the almonds. Serve with the sauce.

Sauce: Purée the mango slices and add the Cointreau. Warm slightly to serve.

Apple Crêpes

Makes 20

6 Granny Smith apples
½ cup (4 fl oz) water
30 g (1 oz) butter
3 cloves
½ teaspoon cinnamon
3 tablespoons soft brown sugar
finely grated rind of 1 orange
juice of ½ orange
1 quantity crêpe batter (*page 409*)
3 tablespoons melted butter
1 tablespoon sugar
extra ½ teaspoon cinnamon
cream or ice cream, to serve

Peel, core and slice the apples and place in a saucepan. Add the water, butter, cloves and cinnamon. Cook until the apples are soft. Add the brown sugar and cook a further 5 minutes. Add the orange rind and juice. Cool.

Make the crêpes. Place 1½-2 tablespoons of the apple mixture in each crêpe and roll up. Place in a greased ovenproof dish. Sprinkle with the melted butter, sugar and cinnamon. Place under a griller (broiler) for a few minutes before serving. Serve with cream or ice cream.

Opposite: *Hazelnut Pancakes with Caramel Sauce*

411

Desserts

Fruity Almond Pears
Serves 4 [M]

4 medium-sized pears, peeled and sliced, or 4 bananas, halved, or 4 slices fresh pineapple
½ cup (2 oz) chopped dried apricots
½ cup (3 oz) pitted, chopped prunes
½ cup (3 oz) chopped raisins
½ cup (2 oz) ground almonds
1 egg white
¼ cup (2 fl oz) water
4 tablespoons honey
1 cup (4 oz) flaked almonds, toasted

Lay the fresh fruit in a heated shallow casserole. Combine the dried fruit and ground almonds with the egg white. Sprinkle the fruit with this mixture and drizzle with water and honey. Cover.

Cook on high in a microwave oven for 6 to 8 minutes or until the fruit is tender, or bake at 180°C (350°F/Gas 4) for 15 to 20 minutes. Serve sprinkled with flaked almonds.

Basic Biscuit Pastry
Makes 24

⅔ cup (2 ½ oz) flour
⅔ cup (2 ½ oz) self-raising flour
pinch of salt
90 g (3 oz) butter
1 x 55 g egg
2 tablespoons sugar

Sieve together the flours and salt. Add the butter and rub into the flour mixture until well blended. Lightly beat the egg and sugar and add to the flour mixture. Mix in to form a ball. Knead gently on a lightly floured board. Cover and refrigerate for 1 hour before using. Roll out evenly on a lightly floured board to the shape required.

Grape Flan
Serves 6 – 8

1 quantity biscuit pastry (see above)
2 ½ cups seedless grapes
2 tablespoons flour
2 tablespoons sugar
1 tablespoon honey
¼ teaspoon mixed spice
1 cup (8 fl oz) light sour cream

Place a 20 cm (8 inch) flan ring on a baking slide. Roll out the pastry thinly and place in the flan ring taking care not to stretch it. Trim off the top. Rinse and dry the grapes and place in the pastry. Combine the flour, sugar, honey, spice and sour cream. Mix well and spread over the grapes.

Bake at 200°C (400°F/Gas 6) for 15 minutes, then lower the heat and continue cooking at 160°C (325°F/Gas 3) for approximately 25 minutes or until the mixture is set. Serve warm or cold with cream or ice cream.

Lemon Tart
Serves 6 – 8

1 quantity biscuit pastry (see above)
2 eggs, separated
3 tablespoons sugar
1 cup (8 fl oz) milk
finely grated rind of 1 lemon
⅓ cup (2 ½ fl oz) lemon juice
¾ cup (1½ oz) soft breadcrumbs
4 tablespoons caster (powdered) sugar

Roll out pastry and line a 20 cm (8 inch) pie plate. Make a frill around the edge of the plate. Beat the egg yolks. Add the sugar then the milk, lemon rind and juice and breadcrumbs.

Pour into the pastry case and bake at 200°C (400°F/Gas 6) for 10 to 15 minutes, then at 160°C (325°F/Gas 3) for a further 20 to 25 minutes or until the filling is set.

Beat the egg whites until stiff and gradually add the caster sugar.

Spread on top of the lemon filling and place in the oven for approximately 5 minutes until the meringue is set and lightly browned.

Apple Galette
Serves 6 – 8

2 quantities biscuit pastry (see above)
6 cooking apples
finely grated rind of 1 lemon
juice of 1 lemon
3 tablespoons sugar
4 passionfruit
300 g (9 ½ oz) ricotta or neufchâtel cheese
2 tablespoons caster (powdered) sugar
2 tablespoons brandy
⅔ cup (5 fl oz) light sour cream
½ cup (2 oz) chopped flaked almonds, lightly browned

Divide the pastry into three sections and roll out one piece to a 20 cm (8 inch) round. Lift onto a baking slide and bake at 200°C (400°F/Gas 6) for about 12 minutes or until golden brown. Do not overcook. Remove from the oven, cool a little then carefully remove from the slide. Allow to cool. Prepare and cook the other two sections in the same way.

Peel, core and slice the apples finely. Place in a saucepan and add the lemon rind and juice. Cook over a very low heat until the apples are soft. This can be done in a microwave. Add the sugar and stir, cool a little and add the pulp from the passionfruit. Cool completely.

Beat the cheese, add the caster sugar and brandy and beat until creamy. Beat in the sour cream.

To assemble, place one pastry round on a serving plate and spread with one third of the cream mixture. Spread half the apple mixture over this. Place the second pastry round on top of this and add cream and apple. Place the third pastry round on top, spread with cream and sprinkle with the almonds.

Moccha Liqueur Tart

Serves 6 – 8

- 1 quantity biscuit pastry (*page 412*)
- 3 tablespoons water
- 1 tablespoon gelatine
- 250 g (8 oz) ricotta or neufchâtel cheese
- 2 egg yolks
- ⅓ cup (3 oz) caster (powdered) sugar
- 1 tablespoon instant coffee
- ½ cup (4 fl oz) warm milk
- 1 tablespoon Tia Maria
- 2 egg whites
- 1 cup (8 fl oz) cream
- vanilla essence
- extra caster (powdered) sugar
- 60 g (2 oz) chocolate
- 1 teaspoon copha
- perfect ivy leaves, washed

Roll out the pastry to fit a 20 cm (8 inch) flan ring. Bake blind until lightly golden brown. Combine the water and gelatine and dissolve the gelatine over hot water. Cool.

Beat the cheese, egg yolks and sugar. Add the coffee to the milk and beat into the cheese mixture. Add the Tia Maria and gelatine mixture. When beginning to set, fold in the beaten egg whites. Beat the cream with the vanilla and a little caster sugar and fold in half the cheese mixture. Pour into the prepared pastry case and allow to set.

Melt the chocolate over warm water and add the copha. Spread over the ivy leaves and allow to set.

To serve, pipe rosettes from the remaining cream. Carefully peel off the ivy leaves and place the chocolate leaves on top of the tart.

Peach Berry Crêpes

Serves 8

- 8 crêpes (*page 409*)
- 1 x 425 g (13 ½ oz) can raspberries or 1 punnet fresh raspberries plus 2 tablespoons each water and sugar
- 2 teaspoons cornflour (cornstarch)
- 1 tablespoon cold water
- 4 ripe peaches, peeled and sliced or 1 x 425 g (13 ½ oz) can sliced peaches, drained
- 8 scoops vanilla ice cream

Prepare the crêpes and keep warm. Place canned raspberries, or fresh raspberries with water and sugar, in a clean pan. Slowly bring to the boil, stirring occasionally. Blend the cornflour with the water. Add to the raspberries and bring to the boil, stirring continuously until the sauce thickens. Add the peaches and heat thoroughly.

To serve, place a hot crêpe on each plate. Place a scoop of ice cream on top, fold over and spoon on the sauce. Serve immediately.

Blushing Mousse

Serves 8

- 4 eggs, separated
- ½ cup (4 fl oz) milk
- ½ cup (5 oz) honey
- 1 teaspoon vanilla essence
- 1 tablespoon gelatine
- ¼ cup (2 fl oz) cold water
- 3 green apples, peeled and sliced
- ½ cup (4 fl oz) water
- 6 tamarillos, peeled
- 1 ¼ cups (10 fl oz) cream, whipped
- extra 2 tamarillos for decoration

Combine the egg yolks, milk and honey in the top of a double boiler. Whisk over simmering water until the mixture coats the back of a spoon. Cool slightly and add the vanilla. Sprinkle the gelatine over cold water. Dissolve over hot water and stir into the hot custard. Stew the apples in water until just tender, about 8 to 10 minutes.

Purée the apples and tamarillos in a food processor or blender. Add the fruit purée to the custard mixture and allow to cool until partially set. Whisk the egg whites until soft peaks form. Fold into the setting fruit custard with the softly whipped cream. Pour into 8 glasses for serving. Chill well. Serve decorated with slices of tamarillo.

Mango Sublime

Serves 4 – 6

- 2 mangoes, peeled and sliced
- juice of 1 lime
- 1 punnet raspberries
- 2 tablespoons Cointreau
- 1 tablespoon icing (confectioners') sugar

Arrange the mango slices on a serving plate and brush with lime juice. Purée the raspberries, Cointreau and icing sugar together in a blender or food processor. Drizzle the raspberry purée over the mango slices.

Pears in Red Wine

Serves 4   [M]

- 3 cups (24 fl oz) red wine
- ½ cup (4 oz) sugar
- 1 cinnamon stick
- 4 cloves
- 4 pears

Place the wine, sugar, cinnamon stick and cloves in a heatproof mixing bowl. Cover with plastic wrap and microwave on high for 6 minutes. Stir to dissolve the sugar.

Peel the pears, leaving the stalks on. Place the pears neatly in the bowl, and ensure pears are totally covered with the wine. Cover and microwave on high for 8 to 10 minutes, turning after 4 minutes. Test with a fine skewer or vegetable knife. Allow the pears to cool before serving. Rotate the pears in the wine occasionally until ready to serve. This ensures a good colour.

Desserts

Custard Apple and Passionfruit Mousse

Serves 6 – 8

2 teaspoons gelatine
2 tablespoons cold water
1 large custard apple, peeled, seeded and chopped
1 cup (8 fl oz) cream, whipped
2 egg whites, stiffly beaten
2 passionfruit
extra 4 passionfruit

Sprinkle the gelatine over the cold water and dissolve in a hot water-bath. Stir into the chopped custard apple. Fold in the whipped cream and whisked egg whites and the pulp of the passionfruit. Spoon the mixture into 6-8 glasses. Chill and set for 2-3 hours.
Serve decorated with extra passionfruit pulp.

Creamy Grape Crunch

Serves 6 – 8

1 kg (2 lb) seedless grapes
3 tablespoons brandy
3 tablespoons honey
juice of ½ lemon
2 ½ cups (20 fl oz) sour cream
1 teaspoon cinnamon
¾ cup (4 oz) soft brown sugar, sieved

Wash and drain the grapes and dry in a clean tea towel. Remove the stems from the grapes and then mix with the brandy, honey and lemon juice. Chill in an ovenproof dish for 2 hours.
Preheat a grill (broiler). Smother the grapes with the sour cream and sprinkle with cinnamon. Top with the sieved brown sugar. Grill (broil) until the sugar caramelizes. Serve immediately.

Custard Apple and Passionfruit Mousse

Grapefruit Blush

Serves 4

2 grapefruit
¼ teaspoon cinnamon
4 bananas
squeeze of lemon juice
desiccated coconut
angelica

Cut the grapefruit into halves crosswise. Remove and discard the central pith and membranes. Reserve the shells. Lift out fruit. Pulp and place in a bowl and sprinkle with cinnamon.
Peel the bananas, mash into a pulp and add a squeeze of lemon juice.
Mix the mashed banana with the grapefruit. Put the mixture into the grapefruit shells, sprinkle with coconut and decorate with angelica.

Citron Touché

Serves 4

1 egg white
caster sugar
3 teaspoons gelatine
½ cup (4 fl oz) water
2 eggs, separated
¼ cup (2 oz) caster (powdered) sugar
¼ cup (2 fl oz) lemon juice
grated rind of 1 lemon
whipped cream
mint sprigs

Dip the rims of 4 dessert glasses into lightly beaten egg white, then caster sugar, forming a decoration on the glass.
Soak the gelatine in the water then dissolve over hot water. Combine the egg yolks, caster sugar and lemon juice in the top of a double boiler. Whisk continually until thick. Remove from the heat, cool to tepid and add the dissolved tepid gelatine mixture and grated lemon rind. Beat over ice until partially set.
Whisk the egg whites until stiff. Fold into the lemon mixture and pour into the prepared glasses. Chill until set. Decorate with cream and a sprig of mint.

Mandarin Blossoms

Serves 4

8 mandarins
1 cup (8 fl oz) Grand Marnier
¾ cup (6 fl oz) cream
2 teaspoons sugar
½ teaspoon cinnamon
nutmeg

Peel and segment the mandarins, removing as much pith as possible. Soak the mandarins in Grand Marnier for 1 hour then heat very gently for 5 minutes. Whip the cream and sugar in a small bowl until soft peaks form. Spoon the mandarin segments and juices into a serving dish and decorate with cream and a sprinkle of nutmeg.

Apricot Ambrosia

Serves 6

3 cups cooked rice
1 x 820 g (1 lb 10 oz) can apricots, liquid reserved
grated rind and juice of 1 orange
2 tablespoons honey or sugar
3 passionfruit
1 cup (8 fl oz) cream
4 tablespoons (2 oz) sugar
1 teaspoon vanilla

Combine the rice, apricot liquid, rind and juice of the orange with the honey. Cook over moderate heat, stirring frequently until the liquid is absorbed. Leave to cool. Reserve 6 apricots, cut the remainder in halves and add to the rice along with the pulp of 2 passionfruit. Whip the cream and sugar until soft peaks form, then add the vanilla. Fold lightly through apricot rice. Decorate with extra whipped cream and apricot halves. Spoon over a little passionfruit pulp.

Sour Cream Raisin Flan

Serves 6

1 x 20 cm (8 inch) precooked shortcrust pastry case

Filling
2/3 cup (5 oz) sugar
4 tablespoons flour
4 tablespoons cornflour (cornstarch)
1 teaspoon cinnamon
pinch of salt
1/4 teaspoon nutmeg
pinch of ground cloves
1/2 cup (3 oz) chopped raisins
1 cup (8 fl oz) sour cream
1/2 cup (4 fl oz) milk
3 egg yolks

Meringue
3 egg whites
1/4 teaspoon cream of tartar
4 teaspoons cornflour (cornstarch)
1/3 cup (3 oz) caster (powdered) sugar

Filling: Combine the sugar, flours, cinnamon, salt, nutmeg, cloves and raisins in a medium saucepan. Gradually mix in the sour cream, then stir in the milk and the egg yolks. Mix well until smooth. Cook gradually until the mixture thickens, stirring continuously. Do not boil. Allow to cool slightly. Spoon the filling into the precooked pastry case and allow to set.

Meringue: Whisk together the egg whites and the cream of tartar to form soft peaks. Blend the cornflour evenly through the sugar. Add the sugar to the egg whites, beating until stiff peaks form. Place mixture in a piping bag and decorate the top of the flan or spoon the mixture onto the flan and spread over the filling. Place in the oven at 180°C (350°F/Gas 4) for 5 to 10 minutes or until the meringue is lightly browned. Serve warm or hot.

Plum Delight

Serves 4

1/4 cup (2 fl oz) rosé wine
1 tablespoon orange juice
2 teaspoons lemon juice
2 1/2 teaspoons gelatine
1 1/2 cups plum purée
2 egg whites
1/4 cup (2 oz) caster (powdered) sugar
1/2 cup (2 fl oz) natural yoghurt
cinnamon or nutmeg
toasted flaked almonds

Combine the wine and fruit juices and sprinkle in the gelatine. Stand over hot water until the gelatine is dissolved. Stir into the plum purée and cool. Beat egg whites until soft peaks form. Gradually add the caster sugar and beat until smooth. Fold through the plum mixture with the yoghurt.

Place in 4 individual serving dishes and chill for at least 4 hours. Sprinkle with cinnamon or nutmeg and toasted flaked almonds.

Apple Berry Pancakes

Serves 8

1 cup (4 oz) self-raising flour
1 tablespoon caster (powdered) sugar
1 egg
3/4-1 cup (6-8 fl oz) cultured buttermilk
1 apple, grated
1 punnet blackberries, raspberries or any berry in season

Custard Sauce
3 tablespoons custard powder
2 cups (16 fl oz) skim milk
liquid sweetener

Sift the flour and sugar into a bowl. Lightly beat the egg and make up to 1 cup (8 fl oz) with the buttermilk. Stir into the flour until smooth. Stir through the grated apple. Drop large spoonfuls of batter into a hot non-stick frypan. Flatten out slightly. When golden brown on the bottom and bubbles appear on the surface, turn over and cook until browned. Serve hot with berries on top and hot custard sauce poured over.

Custard Sauce: Mix the custard powder with a little milk to form a smooth paste. Heat the remaining milk in a saucepan. Add the custard powder and stir until thickened. Add the liquid sweetener to taste, or the equivalent in sugar.

Desserts

Pavlova

Serves 6

6 egg whites
1¼ cups (8 oz) caster (powdered) sugar
1 teaspoon vinegar

Preheat the oven to 150°C (300°F/Gas 2). Cover a scone tray or suitable flat metal dish with aluminium foil or baking paper. Whisk the egg whites until thick. Gradually add half the sugar to the whites while continuing to beat. Whip until soft peaks form. Fold in the remainder of the sugar and the vinegar until just mixed. Spread on the tray in a circle keeping the sides slightly higher than the middle. Bake for 1 hour. Remove from the oven and allow to cool.

Decorate with whipped cream (no sugar added), passionfruit, kiwifruit and strawberries.

Pavlova au Rhum

Serves 6

2 tablespoons currants
2 tablespoons raisins
1 tablespoon black rum
1 cup (8 fl oz) unthickened cream
1-2 teaspoons coffee liqueur or liquid coffee
1 cooked pavlova shell (*see above*)
60 g (2 oz) dark chocolate, grated

Soak the currants and raisins in a small amount of boiling water for about 30 minutes. Drain well and cover with the black rum. The longer the fruit is soaked in rum, the stronger the flavour. Whip the cream until thick. Fold in the coffee liqueur and spread over the pavlova. Drain the fruit and place on top of the cream. Sprinkle on the grated chocolate.

Hints for Successful Pavlovas

- Use either crockery, glass or stainless steel bowls, not plastic. Though clean they can harbour grease.

- Make sure the beaters and bowl are spotlessly clean and use a warm dry bowl. It will give a greater volume of egg white.

- Do not attempt to beat egg whites that contain the slightest spot of egg yolk.

- Do not allow the egg whites and sugar to stand after preparation – bake straight away.

Sunshine Pineapple Pie

Serves 6 – 8

1 x 20 cm (8 inch) precooked shortcrust pastry case

Filling

1 x 440 g (14 oz) can crushed pineapple, drained
½ cup (3 oz) fruit mince or mixed dried fruit
1 teaspoon dark rum, optional
2 egg yolks

Meringue

2 egg whites
4 tablespoons caster (powdered) sugar

Filling: Combine the pineapple, fruit mince and rum in a saucepan and heat. When starting to bubble, remove from heat, stir in the egg yolks and pour into the pastry case. Cool.

Meringue: Beat the egg whites and sugar until peaks form. Spoon over the filling. Place in 220°C (440°F/Gas 6) oven for a few minutes to set and lightly brown.

Meringue Roll

Serves 6 – 8

1½ teaspoons vinegar
10 egg whites
2½ cups (1 lb) caster (powdered) sugar
1 tablespoon cornflour (cornstarch)
extra caster sugar
cinnamon
1 cup (8 fl oz) cream, whipped
2 passionfruit

Preheat the oven to 150°C (300°F/Gas 2). Grease a Swiss roll tin and line with greaseproof paper on base and sides. Grease the lining paper. Add the vinegar to the egg whites and whip until thick. Gradually add half the sugar while continuing to beat. Whip until soft peaks form. Lightly fold in the remaining sugar which has been mixed with the cornflour. Spread the mixture into the Swiss roll tin. Bake immediately for 10 to 15 minutes or until the top is golden brown.

Remove from oven and invert onto greaseproof sheet which has been sprinkled with caster sugar mixed with cinnamon. Gently remove the lining paper and allow to cool thoroughly. Spread the surface of the roll with the cream and splash with passionfruit pulp. Roll up as for a Swiss roll and serve by cutting slices off the roll with fresh fruits such as kiwifruit and strawberries.

Lemon Meringue Pie

Serves 6 – 8

1 x 375 g (12 oz) packet sweet shortcrust pastry

Filling

4 tablespoons flour
4 tablespoons cornflour (cornstarch)
2 teaspoons grated lemon rind
¾ cup (6 fl oz) lemon juice
1 cup (8 oz) sugar
1¼ cups (10 fl oz) water
90 g (3 oz) butter, melted
4 egg yolks

Meringue

4 egg whites
pinch of salt
¾ cup (6 oz) caster (powdered) sugar

Pastry: Roll out pastry and line a 23 cm (9 inch) pie dish. Trim and decorate the edges. Prick the base and sides of the pastry with a fork. Bake blind at 190°C (375°F/Gas 5) for 10 to 15 minutes or until lightly browned. Allow to cool.

Filling: Combine the sifted flours, lemon rind, juice and sugar in a saucepan. Add the water and blend until smooth. Stir over low heat until the mixture boils and thickens. Reduce the heat and stir a further 2 minutes. Remove from the heat and stir in the butter and lightly beaten egg yolks. Stir until the butter has melted. Cool. Spread the cold lemon filling evenly into the pastry case.

Meringue: Combine the egg whites and salt in a small bowl and beat until soft peaks form. Gradually add the sugar and beat well until the sugar has dissolved. Spoon on top of the lemon filling, spreading the meringue to the edges of the pie to seal. Peak the meringue decoratively with a knife. Bake at 180°C (350°F/Gas 4) for 5 to 10 minutes or until lightly browned. Cool and refrigerate.

Meringues

Makes 12 – 15

6 egg whites
1 teaspoon vinegar
1½ cups (10 oz) caster (powdered) sugar

Preheat the oven to 110°C (225°F/Gas ¼). Whip the egg whites and vinegar until stiff peaks form. Add half the sugar on fast speed and continue whipping for 30 seconds. Add remaining sugar on slow speed and continue whipping for approximately 30 seconds. Place the mixture in a piping bag. Pipe onto a foil-lined baking tray. Bake for approximately 4 hours or until dried out. Cool and store in an airtight container.

Strawberry Mousse

Serves 4

375 g (12 oz) strawberries
1 tablespoon Cointreau or sherry
2 tablespoons sifted icing (confectioners') sugar
1 tablespoon chopped crystallised ginger
1¾ cups (14 fl oz) cream
2 egg whites
12 extra strawberries for garnish

Purée the strawberries in a blender or rub through a sieve. Add the Cointreau, sugar and ginger to the purée. Whip the cream until just stiff and whisk the egg whites until stiff. Fold the cream and egg whites alternately into the strawberry purée mixture. Pile into 4 tall glasses and chill. Just before serving, decorate with whole strawberries.

Chocolate Mousse

Serves 4

90 g (3 oz) dark cooking chocolate
2 eggs, separated
1 cup (8 fl oz) cream
¼ cup (2 oz) caster (powdered) sugar
rum, brandy or liqueur, optional
whipped cream
almonds or cherries

Melt the chocolate in a bowl over hot water. Stir in the egg yolks until smooth, then gradually blend in the cream. Whip the egg whites with the caster sugar to form a stiff meringue. Fold this into the chocolate mixture. Add a dash of rum if desired and pour into 4 individual dishes. Chill for a few hours. Decorate with whipped cream and almonds.

Zabaglione

Serves 4

4 egg yolks
½ cup (4 fl oz) marsala or Madeira
3 tablespoons caster (powdered) sugar
whipped cream
grapes or strawberries
nutmeg

Put the egg yolks, marsala and caster sugar into the top of a double boiler. Stir gently. When thoroughly blended place over simmering water. Do not boil. Keep stirring in the same direction with a rotary whisk. When the eggs are thick and fluffy, remove from the heat, but keep beating. Add a tablespoon of whipped cream for each serve and pour into glasses. Refrigerate. Decorate with grapes or strawberries and a sprinkle of nutmeg. For hot zabaglione serve immediately.

Desserts

Cream Puffs

Makes 12 – 15

1 cup (8 fl oz) water
75 g (2½ oz) butter
1 cup (4 oz) flour
pinch of salt
4 eggs
whipped cream
icing (confectioners') sugar

Put water and butter in a pan over low heat until the butter is melted. Bring to the boil. Remove from the heat and add the sifted flour and salt all at once.

Stir over low heat until the mixture forms a ball and leaves the sides of the pan. Remove from the heat immediately.

Put mixture into a small bowl. Using a wooden spoon, spread the mixture up the sides of the bowl to allow the mixture to cool slightly, approximately 5 minutes.

Beat the eggs until just combined. Beat the choux pastry on low speed. Add the eggs gradually, beating well after each addition. The mixture should be very thick, smooth and glossy. Drop rounded spoonfuls of mixture onto lightly greased baking trays, allowing room for spreading. Bake at 220°C (425°F/Gas 7) for 10 minutes. Reduce the heat to moderate, 180°C (350°F/Gas 4), and cook for a further 20 minutes or until the puffs are golden brown and firm to the touch. The cooking time will depend on the size of the puffs. When cooked, remove from the oven, make a small slit in the side to allow steam to escape. Return to the oven for a few minutes to dry out. When cold, carefully cut the puffs in half and remove any soft filling. Fill with whipped cream, sprinkle the top with icing sugar or pour over Chocolate Sauce *(see below)*.

Chocolate Sauce

Makes 1 cup (8 fl oz)

185 g (6 oz) dark cooking
   chocolate
15 g (½ oz) butter
2 tablespoons caster
   (powdered) sugar
⅓ cup (2 ½ fl oz) cream
   or evaporated milk
1 teaspoon vanilla essence

Place the chocolate, butter, caster sugar and cream in the top of a double boiler. Melt over simmering water. Beat in the vanilla essence and leave to cool for 3 to 5 minutes.

Old English Rice Pudding

Serves 4

4 cups (1 litre) milk
2 tablespoons rice
2 tablespoons sugar, or to
   taste
30 g (1 oz) butter
a little nutmeg

Butter a deep ovenproof dish and add the milk, rice, sugar and butter. Stir and cook at 180°C (350°F/Gas 4) for 2 to 3 hours. When cooled sprinkle with the nutmeg.

While baking, stir occasionally and add a little more milk if needed. The ideal pudding should not be too firm or dry – but thick, soft and still creamy. Serve warm with cream or stewed, canned or fresh fruits. If eaten cold, you may remove the skin, top with a layer of brown or white sugar and place under a hot griller (broiler) for a few minutes. Serve with ice cream.

Amaretti Crêpes

Makes 20

1 quantity crêpe batter
   (*page 409*)
125 g (4 oz) unsalted butter
100 g (3 ½ oz) icing
   (confectioners') sugar
4 tablespoons Amaretti
   liqueur
8 Amaretti biscuits or
   almond macaroons
extra icing (confectioners')
   sugar

Make the crêpes. Beat the butter and sugar together until creamy. Gradually add the liqueur and stir in the crushed biscuits. Spread the filling onto the crêpes and fold into four. Sprinkle with extra icing sugar and serve immediately.

Opposite: *Cream Puffs with Chocolate Sauce*

419

Desserts

Custard

Makes 3 cups (24 fl oz)

2 eggs
¼ cup (2 oz) sugar
2½ cups (20 fl oz) milk

Whisk the eggs and sugar together in a bowl. Warm the milk in the top of a double boiler. Pour into the egg and sugar mixture, stirring all the time. Return to the double boiler and cook gently, stirring until the custard thickens.

Baked Custard

Serves 6

4 eggs
¼ cup (2 oz) sugar
2½ cups (20 fl oz) milk

Whisk the eggs and sugar together. Pour in the slightly warmed milk and blend until smooth. Pour into a dish and stand in a baking tray of warm water. Place in the oven and bake at 160°C (325°F/Gas 3) for 1 hour. Remove the custard immediately or it will overcook.

Custard Tart

Serves 6

1 x 20 cm (8 inch) precooked shortcrust pastry case

Filling
3 eggs
1 teaspoon vanilla essence
2 tablespoons sugar
2 cups (16 fl oz) milk
1 egg white, beaten
nutmeg

Filling: Beat eggs, vanilla and sugar together. Heat the milk until lukewarm then gradually stir into the egg mixture. Lightly brush the pastry with beaten egg white. Put the pie plate onto a baking tray and carefully pour half the custard mixture into the pastry case. Place the oven tray with pie dish into the oven and carefully pour the remaining mixture into the case (this prevents spilling the custard as the pie is put into the oven).

Bake at 180°C (350°F/Gas 4) for 50 to 55 minutes. After 15 minutes cooking time, sprinkle with nutmeg. Do not overcook. The custard becomes firm on cooling.

Baked Egg Custard

Serves 6

2 cups (16 fl oz) milk
¼ cup (2 oz) sugar
pinch of salt
½ teaspoon vanilla essence
3 eggs, beaten

Beat the milk, sugar, salt and vanilla together, add the eggs and mix again. Pour the mixture into an ovenproof dish or individual ramekins and place in a baking dish half filled with water. Bake at 120°C (250°F/Gas ½) for 1 hour for a large custard and about 20 minutes for small ramekins. To check if cooked, insert a sharp knife into the centre. If clean, custard is cooked. May be served hot or cold.

Golden Pecan Pie

Serves 6–8

Pastry
1 cup (4 oz) flour
60 g (2 oz) butter or margarine
2 tablespoons water, approximately

Filling
3 large eggs
½ cup (3 oz) soft brown sugar
3 tablespoons melted butter
1 cup (12 oz) golden syrup
1 cup (4 oz) chopped pecans
2 tablespoons cornflour (cornstarch)
whipped cream and extra pecan halves to decorate

Pastry: Sift the flour and rub in the butter until the mixture resembles fine breadcrumbs. Add sufficient water to make a firm dough. Wrap and refrigerate for about 20 minutes. Roll out to fit a 23 cm (9 inch) pie plate.

Filling: Beat the eggs lightly with the sugar. Add the remaining ingredients and stir well to combine. Pour carefully into the pie case and bake at 180°C (350°F/Gas 4) for about 1 hour or until the filling is well browned and just set. The filling will set firmly on cooling. Decorate with whipped cream and pecan halves.

Tangy Banana Bavarois

Serves 8

- 3 eggs, separated
- ½ cup (4 oz) caster (powdered) sugar
- 2 tablespoons lemon juice
- 2 teaspoons gelatine
- ½ cup (4 fl oz) cold water
- pulp of 6 passionfruit
- 3 bananas, mashed
- 1 cup (8 fl oz) cream, whipped

Whisk the egg yolks, sugar and lemon juice in the top of a double boiler over simmering water until thickened. Remove from the heat. Sprinkle the gelatine over cold water then place over simmering water to dissolve. Pour the gelatine into the custard. Stir two thirds of the passionfruit and the bananas into the custard mixture. Allow to cool until partially set.

Whisk the egg whites until soft peaks form. Fold into the fruity custard with the whipped cream. Pour into eight ½ cup (4 fl oz) wetted moulds. Chill until set. Unmould to serve and drizzle with the remaining passionfruit.

Apple and Cinnamon Droplets

Makes 36

- 125 g (4 oz) butter
- ½ cup (4 oz) caster (powdered) sugar
- 1 egg
- ¼ cup (2 fl oz) milk
- ½ teaspoon vanilla essence
- 1 teaspoon cinnamon
- ½ cup (2 oz) chopped almonds
- 2 cups (8 oz) wholemeal self-raising flour
- ½ cup bran
- 2 apples, peeled, cored and grated
- ½ cup (3 oz) sultanas

Cream the butter and sugar until light and fluffy. Gradually add the egg, milk and vanilla and beat well. Combine the mixture with the remaining ingredients. Mix thoroughly.

Place small spoonfuls of mixture on a greased baking tray. Bake at 200°C (400°F/Gas 6) for 15 minutes. Cool on a wire cooling tray. Store in an airtight tin.

Tropical Melon Salad

Serves 6 – 8

- 1 cup rockmelon balls
- 1 cup honeydew melon balls
- 1 cup watermelon balls
- 1 cup pineapple pieces
- 1 punnet strawberries, halved
- 2 kiwifruit, peeled and sliced
- 1 cup (8 fl oz) sour cream
- 2 tablespoons honey
- 2 tablespoons orange juice
- ¼ cup (¾ oz) coconut

Combine the fruit in a bowl and chill. Mix the remaining ingredients and fold through the fruit or serve drizzled on top of the fruit as a dessert.

Blackberry and Yoghurt Cream

Serves 2 – 4

- 1 cup (8 fl oz) natural yoghurt
- 2 tablespoons maple syrup
- ½ teaspoon cinnamon
- 1 cup blackberries
- toasted flaked almonds, optional

Blend together the yoghurt, maple syrup and cinnamon. Chill well. Place the blackberries in a dessert dish and top with the yoghurt cream. Garnish with almonds if desired. Serve with petits fours.

Boysenberry and Pear Crumble

Serves 6 – 8

- 2 punnets boysenberries
- 4 firm, ripe pears, peeled, cored, and sliced
- ⅓ cup (3 oz) sugar
- ¾ cup (4 oz) soft brown sugar
- ¾ cup (2½ oz) rolled oats
- ½ cup (2 oz) flour
- 125 g (4 oz) butter, cut into small pieces

Grease a 25 cm (10 inch) round pie dish. Combine the boysenberries, pears and sugar and place in the pie dish. Place the brown sugar, oats and flour in a mixing bowl and rub in the butter. Sprinkle over the fruit in the pie dish.

Bake in a moderately hot oven at 190°C (375°F/Gas 5) for 25 minutes or until the topping is golden brown.

Serve warm with custard, cream, yoghurt or ice cream.

Citrus Sorbet

Serves 8 – 10

- 1 lemon
- 1 lime
- 1 orange
- ⅓ cup (3 oz) sugar
- 1 teaspoon gelatine, soaked in 1 tablespoon water
- 2 egg whites

Finely grate the rind of the lemon, lime and orange. Juice the fruit and add water to make up 1 cup (8 fl oz) liquid. Place 3 cups (24 fl oz) water and the sugar in a saucepan and bring to the boil. Boil gently for 5 minutes. Remove and add the gelatine, fruit juice mixture and grated rind. Cool.

Place in freezer trays until beginning to set. Beat the egg whites to soft peaks and whisk into the fruit mixture. Return to the freezer and when setting, whisk again. Freeze to serve.

Note: If using an ice cream maker, place the fruit mixture and beaten egg whites in the bowl and churn until the mixture thickens.

Desserts

Granny's Apple Soufflé
Serves 4

60 g (2 oz) butter
½ cup (2 oz) flour
¾ cup (6 fl oz) milk, boiling
4 eggs, separated
¼ cup (2 oz) sugar
1 ½ cups cooked, puréed apple
½ teaspoon mixed spice
1 tablespoon sultanas
knob of butter and 1 teaspoon sugar for greasing the soufflé dish

Melt the butter in a saucepan. Add the flour and stir until blended. Add the scalded milk and stir continuously over low heat until thick. Allow the sauce to cool. Beat the egg yolks and sugar until light and stir into the cooked sauce. Stir in the apple purée, mixed spice, and sultanas.

Whisk the egg whites until stiff and fold into the sauce mixture. Pour the mixture into the soufflé dish which has been lightly greased with the butter and sprinkled with sugar. Bake in the centre of the oven at 190°C (375°F/Gas 5) for 45 minutes or until the soufflé is puffed and golden. Serve immediately.

Boysenberry Sorbet
Serves 8

500 g (1 lb) boysenberries
1 cup (8 fl oz) water
½ cup (4 oz) sugar
juice of 1 ½ lemons

Wash the boysenberries and drain well. Purée the berries in a blender. Place in a bowl and set aside. Place the water and sugar in a saucepan over medium heat and stir until the sugar dissolves. Increase the heat and boil gently until mixture starts to become syrupy, about 5 minutes. Remove from the heat and allow to cool.

When the syrup is cold, stir in the boysenberry purée and lemon juice and chill for 30 minutes. Mix to a sorbet texture in a commercial ice cream churn. Alternatively, beat with an electric mixer until thick. Pour into a lamington tin and freeze until crystals begin to form. Transfer to a mixing bowl and beat again. Return the mixture to the lamington tin and freeze until firm.

Serve scoops of sorbet in champagne glasses and decorate with fresh boysenberries and a mint leaf.

Boysenberry Sorbet

Lemon Chiffon Pie

Lemon Chiffon Pie

Serves 6

Base

1 x 250 g (8 oz) packet sweet biscuits, crumbed

125 g (4 oz) butter, melted

Filling

3 eggs, separated
½ cup (4 oz) caster (powdered) sugar
juice and rind of 2 lemons
3 teaspoons gelatine
½ cup (4 fl oz) cream

Base: Pour the melted butter over the biscuit crumbs. Combine well and press onto the bottom and sides of a well-greased spring form tin.

Bake blind at 190°C (375°F/Gas 5) for 10 minutes. Remove from oven and chill thoroughly.

Filling: Combine the egg yolks, half the caster sugar, lemon juice and rind, and gelatine in a saucepan. Stir over low heat until the mixture thickens slightly. Remove from heat and leave to cool. Whisk the egg whites until stiff, then beat in the remaining caster sugar, a little at a time, until thick and glossy. Beat the cream until thick. Fold the lemon mixture and the cream into the meringue, blending well. Pile the mixture into the crumb base and chill until set.

Desserts

Raspberry Rice Parfait

Serves 6

3 cups cooked rice
3 cups (24 fl oz) milk
15 g (½ oz) butter
⅓ cup (3 oz) sugar
1 teaspoon vanilla essence
½ cup (4 fl oz) well-chilled evaporated milk and 2 teaspoons lemon juice, or use fresh cream
1 x 450 g (14 ½ oz) can raspberries, drained
3 teaspoons sherry
whipped cream, to decorate

Place the rice, milk and butter in a saucepan, and cook for about 15 minutes over moderate heat, stirring all the time, until the rice is thick and creamy. Remove from heat, add the sugar and vanilla and allow to cool. Whip the evaporated milk and lemon juice until thick. Fold through the rice with the raspberries and sherry. Spoon into parfait glasses, decorate with whipped cream.

Rice and Raisin Cream

Serves 4

¼ cup (2 oz) rice
2 ½ cups (20 fl oz) milk
½ cup (3 oz) raisins
grated rind of 1 lemon
2 eggs, separated
½ cup (3 oz) brown sugar
¼ cup (2 fl oz) evaporated milk
¼ cup (2 oz) sugar, for meringue
chopped walnuts, to decorate

Place the rice, milk, raisins and lemon rind in a well-greased saucepan. Cook over low heat, stirring occasionally, until the rice is tender, about 45 minutes. Remove from heat. Beat the egg yolks slightly, add to the rice and beat well. Replace over heat for a few minutes but do not boil. Cool slightly, then add the brown sugar and evaporated milk. Spoon into a well-greased ovenproof dish.

Beat the egg whites to stiff peaks, add the sugar very gradually and beat to meringue consistency. Spoon meringue over the rice, spreading right to the edge of the dish. Sprinkle with the walnuts and bake at 160°C (325°F/Gas 3), until meringue is golden.

Pineapple Parfait

Serves 4

2 cups cooked rice
1 x 425 g (13 ½ oz) can pineapple pieces, liquid reserved
grates rind and juice of 2 oranges
1 tablespoon sugar or honey
15 g (½ oz) butter
1 cup (8 fl oz) cream or chilled evaporated milk, whipped
2 passionfruit or sliced bananas

Combine the rice with pineapple liquid, rind and juice of the oranges, the sugar and butter. Place over moderate heat and just simmer until the liquid is absorbed. When quite cool add pineapple pieces, half the cream and half the passionfruit pulp. Spoon into parfait glasses or a serving bowl. Top with remaining whipped cream and passionfruit pulp.

Cottage Rice Pudding

Serves 4

2 ½ cups (20 fl oz) milk
¼ cup (2 oz) rice
1 tablespoon margarine
salt
½ cup (4 oz) sugar
2 tablespoons honey
½ cup (3 oz) sultanas
1 teaspoon vanilla
1 teaspoon grated lemon rind
1 cup (8 oz) cottage cheese
whipped cream
½ teaspoon cinnamon or nutmeg

Heat the milk, add the rice, margarine and salt. Stir until the mixture boils, then simmer, covered, over moderate heat. Stir occasionally and cook until tender, about 45 minutes. Remove from heat, add the sugar, honey, sultanas, vanilla, lemon rind and cottage cheese. May be served warm or cold. Serve with whipped cream sprinkled with cinnamon.

Honey Rice Buns

Makes 12

125 g (4 oz) butter
½ cup (5 oz) honey
½ teaspoon grated lemon rind
2 eggs
½ cup cooked brown rice
1 ¼ cups (6 oz) dates, roughly chopped
1 ¼ cups (5 oz) wholemeal self-raising flour
pinch of ground cloves

Cream the butter, honey and lemon rind together. Beat the eggs in thoroughly, one at a time. Mix in the rice and dates then fold in the flour and cloves. Spoon the mixture into paper patty cases or a buttered gem iron. Place on a flat tray. Bake at 190°C (375°F/Gas 5) for 20 minutes.

Pineapple Rice Crêpes

Makes 8 crêpes

Crêpes
1 egg
½ cup (4 fl oz) buttermilk
1 tablespoon oil or melted butter
2 tablespoons water
½ cup (2 oz) flour
¼ teaspoon salt
butter for frying

Filling
½ cup cooked rice
¼ cup (2 oz) caster (powdered) sugar
¾ cup drained crushed pineapple
¼ teaspoon vanilla essence
5 marshmallows, chopped finely
½ cup (4 fl oz) cream, whipped
icing (confectioners') sugar

Crêpes: Place all the ingredients for the crêpes in a blender or food processor. Cover and blend for about 20 to 30 seconds, or combine all the ingredients and beat well with a rotary whisk until smooth. Heat a little butter in a crêpe pan and when it starts to foam, pour in sufficient batter to cover the surface of the pan with a thin layer. Rotate the pan quickly to spread the batter as thinly and evenly as possible. Pour off any excess. Cook the crêpe for 1 minute on one side until bubbles appear on the surface and then flip it over with a metal spatula and cook for another minute. Stack the crêpes flat, one on top of the other, with greaseproof paper between each one.

Filling: Combine rice, sugar, pineapple, vanilla and marshmallows. Fold in the whipped cream. Spoon some filling onto each crêpe and roll up. Sprinkle with icing sugar and serve at once. The crêpes may be garnished with mandarin or fresh orange segments.

Brown Rice Brûlée

Serves 6

3 cups cooked apple or pie apples
½ cup (3 oz) sultanas
3 cups cooked brown rice
45 g (1 ½ oz) butter, melted
grated rind and juice of 1 orange
½ cup (3 oz) brown sugar
¼ cup (1 oz) chopped walnuts or almonds

Combine the apple and sultanas and place half this mixture in a well-greased ovenproof dish or pie plate. Mix the brown rice, butter, rind and orange juice. Spoon this over the apple and finish with the remaining apple mixture. Top with the brown sugar and walnuts. Place in a 180°C (350°F/Gas 4) oven to heat and melt the sugar. Serve warm or cold with ice cream or cream.

Note: Any stewed or canned fruit may be used instead of the apples.

Brown Rice Apple Betty

Serves 6

3 cups cooked brown rice
2 cups cooked or canned apple slices
½ cup (3 oz) sultanas
¼ teaspoon ground nutmeg or ginger
½ cup (3 oz) brown sugar
½ cup (4 fl oz) orange juice
2 tablespoons melted butter

Place half the rice in the base of a well-greased ovenproof dish. Mix together the apples, sultanas, nutmeg and half the brown sugar and spoon this mixture over the rice. Place the remaining rice over the apple, leaving a border of apple around the edge of the dish. Sprinkle the surface with the remaining brown sugar. Spoon over the orange juice and melted butter. Cover the dish with a lid or foil and bake at 180°C (350°F/Gas 4) for 25 minutes.

Note: You may substitute canned pineapple or apricots in this recipe. Use ½ cup (4 fl oz) syrup to replace the orange juice.

Sunshine-Spiced Rice

Serves 6

3 cups cooked rice
1 x 450 g (14 ½ oz) can pineapple pieces
½ cup (2 ½ oz) chopped dates or sultanas
¼ cup (1 ½ oz) chopped glacé ginger
¼ cup (1 oz) chopped pecans or walnuts
½ cup (3 oz) brown sugar
½ teaspoon each cinnamon and ground ginger
15 g (½ oz) butter

Place half the rice in a greased ovenproof dish. Drain the pineapple and reserve the syrup. Combine pineapple pieces, dates, ginger and pecans. Spoon half the pineapple mixture over the rice. Sprinkle with half the brown sugar and spices. Repeat layers. Top with dabs of butter then spoon over the reserved pineapple syrup. Cover with a lid or foil and bake at 180°C (350°F/Gas 4) for about 25 minutes. Serve warm with cream or ice cream.

Desserts

Golden Rice Dessert

Serves 4

½ cup (3 oz) rice
1 ¾ cups (14 fl oz) cold water
pinch of salt
½ cup (3 oz) chopped dried figs or apricots
1 cup (5 oz) sultanas
3 tablespoons golden syrup
¼ cup (1 ½ oz) preserved glacé ginger, chopped
½ cup (2 oz) chopped pecans or walnuts
1 teaspoon vanilla essence
1 cup (8 fl oz) cream, whipped
extra whipped cream and nuts to decorate

Place the rice and water in a saucepan with the salt and simmer, covered, for 10 minutes. Add the figs, sultanas and golden syrup and continue cooking until the liquid is absorbed and the rice tender. Remove from heat, add the ginger, nuts and vanilla. Allow to cool. Fold in the whipped cream and blend well. Serve in individual dishes and decorate with the extra whipped cream and nuts.

Tropical Touch Parfait

Serves 4

2 cups cooked rice
1 x 450 g (14½ oz) can pineapple pieces or fruit salad, liquid reserved
grated rind and juice of 2 oranges
1 tablespoon honey or sugar to taste
30 g (1 oz) butter
1 cup (8 fl oz) cream, whipped
3 passionfruit
1 banana, sliced and soaked in lemon juice

Combine the rice with the pineapple liquid, orange rind and juice, honey and butter. Place over moderate heat and stir occasionally until the liquid is almost absorbed. Allow to cool. Fold half the cream and half the passionfruit pulp into the rice mixture. Add the pineapple pieces, and blend thoroughly. Spoon into parfait glasses. Decorate with remaining cream and top with the banana slices and remaining passionfruit.

Fruit Salad Rice

Serves 4

2 ½ cups (20 fl oz) orange juice
3 cups cooked rice
2 tablespoons honey, or sugar to taste
1 cup (8 fl oz) cream, whipped
2 kiwifruit, sliced
1 cup diced honeydew melon
1 cup diced pawpaw (papaya)
1 punnet strawberries, sliced
3 passionfruit

Heat the orange juice, add rice, bring to the boil, then lower heat to simmer, stirring occasionally until almost all the juice is absorbed. Remove from the heat, add the honey and cool. Fold the whipped cream through the rice then spoon the rice into a serving bowl. Combine kiwifruit, honeydew, pawpaw and strawberries, and spoon this fruit mixture into a circle over the rice. Top with passionfruit pulp and serve with extra whipped cream.

Orange Rice Pudding

Serves 4

1 cup (6 oz) rice
2 cups (16 fl oz) boiling water
½ cup (4 fl oz) orange juice
1 ½ cups (12 fl oz) water
15 g (½ oz) butter
½ cup (5 oz) honey or sugar to taste
extra 2 tablespoons orange juice
grated rind of 1 orange
2 peeled oranges, thinly sliced
½ cup (5 oz) orange marmalade or apricot jam
2 teaspoons sherry, optional

Boil the rice in the water until the water has been absorbed, about 15 minutes. Add the orange juice, water and butter, bring to the boil then simmer until the rice is quite tender, about 25 minutes. Add the honey, extra orange juice and rind. Spoon into a serving dish and top with a ring of sliced oranges. Heat the marmalade with the sherry then spoon over the orange slices. Serve with cream or ice cream.

Note: Canned mandarin segments may be used instead of fresh oranges.

Rice Apple Flan

Serves 6

⅓ cup (2 oz) rice
3 cups (24 fl oz) milk
⅓ cup (3 oz) sugar
¼ cup (2 fl oz) evaporated milk
1 teaspoon vanilla essence
1 egg, beaten
2 cups stewed or canned fruit (apples, apricots, peaches or cherries)
1 egg white, beaten
cinnamon
sugar
coconut
chopped nuts

Simmer the rice in the milk over low heat, stirring occasionally, until just tender, about 40 minutes. Remove from heat and add the sugar, evaporated milk, then the vanilla and beaten egg. Spread the fruit over the base of a pie plate or ovenproof dish, leaving a little for decoration. Add the beaten egg white to the rice mixure and spread over the fruit. Spoon the reserved fruit into the centre. Blend together a little cinnamon, sugar, coconut and nuts. Sprinkle this mixture over the rice and bake at 180°C (350°F/Gas 4) for about 25 minutes. Serve with whipped cream or ice cream.

Spicy Apple Pancakes

Serves 6

1 cup cooked rice
1 cup (8 fl oz) milk
1 egg, separated
⅔ cup (2 ½ oz) self-raising flour, sifted
3 teaspoons honey or sugar to taste
15 g (½ oz) melted butter
grated rind of ½ lemon
pinch of salt
1 apple, peeled and grated
¼ teaspoon nutmeg
butter, for frying
1 tablespoon sugar
½ teaspoon cinnamon
honey, apple jelly or maple syrup
whipped cream

Heat the rice gently in ¼ cup (2 fl oz) of milk until the milk is absorbed. Remove from the heat and add the beaten egg yolk and remaining milk. Add the next 7 ingredients and blend well. Beat the egg white until stiff and fold through the mixture. Melt some butter and fry spoonfuls of mixture in the pan, when brown turn and cook the other side. Serve warm sprinkled with sugar, cinnamon and honey. Top with whipped cream.

Spicy Apple Pancakes

Desserts

Pineapple Marshmallow Rice

Serves 6

3 cups cooked rice
3 cups (24 fl oz) milk
15 g (½ oz) butter
⅓ cup (3 oz) sugar
1 teaspoon vanilla essence
1 cup (8 fl oz) cream, whipped
1 x 450 g (14 ½ oz) can crushed pineapple, liquid reserved
1 cup chopped marshmallows
a few extra chopped marshmallows and glacé cherries, to decorate

Combine the rice, milk and butter in a heavy saucepan and cook over moderate heat, stirring occasionally until the rice is thick and creamy. Remove from heat and add the sugar. Allow to cool, then add the vanilla, cream, pineapple and marshmallows. Spoon into a serving dish, decorate with cherries and chopped marshmallows. Reserved liquid from the pineapple may be served over the rice.

Pineapple Rice Whip

Serves 4

1 x 85 g packet orange or lemon jelly
1 x 425 g (13 ½ oz) can crushed pineapple, liquid reserved
rind and juice of 1 orange
1 tablespoon honey
1 cup (8 fl oz) evaporated milk, chilled
1 ½ cups cooked rice
whipped cream and passionfruit or banana, to decorate

Place the jelly crystals in a bowl. Drain the pineapple and combine the pineapple liquid with the orange rind and juice, adding water if required to make 1 cup (8 fl oz). Bring the pineapple liquid to the boil, pour over the jelly, add the honey and stir until quite dissolved. Refrigerate until just thickening, then stir in the crushed pineapple. Beat the evaporated milk until peaks form, fold into the pineapple mixture, whip again, then add the rice. Refrigerate until set. The dessert may be decorated with whipped cream and passionfruit pulp or sliced bananas.

Creamy Rice with Pineapple

Serves 4

¼ cup (2 fl oz) rice
2 ½ cups (20 fl oz) milk
1 egg, beaten
2 tablespoons sugar or honey
1 x 425 g (13 ½ oz) can crushed pineapple, drained

Place the rice and milk in a well-greased saucepan and cook over low heat, stirring occasionally, for about 45 minutes, until the rice is soft and creamy. Use an asbestos mat if required to keep the heat low. Remove the rice from the heat and gradually add the egg, beating well. Return to heat, add the sugar and the drained pineapple and reheat. Serve warm with cream or ice cream.

Note: You may use any canned, stewed or fresh fruit such as peaches, apricots, raspberries, apples, bananas or passionfruit.

Pineapple Rice Ambrosia

Serves 4

1 ½ cups cooked rice
1 x 450 g (14 ½ oz) can crushed pineapple, liquid reserved
grated rind of 1 orange
1 tablespoon honey
2 bananas, finely chopped or mashed with the juice of ½ lemon
2 egg whites
¼ cup (2 oz) sugar
whipped cream, toasted coconut or passionfruit pulp, to decorate

Combine the rice, pineapple liquid and orange rind and cook over moderate heat until almost all the liquid is absorbed. Add the honey and allow to cool. When cool, add the crushed pineapple and bananas. Whip the egg whites, add the sugar gradually and beat to a meringue consistency. Fold into the pineapple rice and serve in a glass bowl or individual serving dishes. Top with the whipped cream and toasted coconut or passionfruit pulp.

Pineapple Rice Torte

Serves 4 - 6

3 cups (24 fl oz) milk
pinch of salt
¾ cup (5 oz) rice
½ cup (4 oz) sugar
1 tablespoon fine dry breadcrumbs or biscuit crumbs
2 eggs, separated
¼ cup (1 oz) toasted almonds
½ cup (3 oz) diced glacé or dried fruits such as apricots, mixed peel, cherries
1 x 450 g (14 ½ oz) can pineapple slices, drained; finely chop 2 slices; reserve the remainder for decoration
grated rind of 1 orange
grated rind of 1 lemon
1 teaspoon vanilla essence
2 tablespoons fruit liqueur or sherry or 1 tablespoon orange juice and 1 tablespoon pineapple liquid
1 cup (8 fl oz) cream, whipped, to decorate
pineapple slices and cherries to decorate

Bring the milk to the boil in a well-greased saucepan, add the salt, rice and half the sugar. Bring to the boil, stirring all the time, then cover, reduce heat and simmer for 25 minutes. Stir occasionally to avoid lumps. Remove from heat and allow rice to cool. Thoroughly grease a 20 cm (8 inch) spring form tin. Sprinkle with breadcrumbs until base and sides are evenly coated, then shake to remove excess crumbs.

Beat the egg yolks, add the remaining sugar and continue to beat until thick. Fold into the rice mixture with almonds, glacé fruits and well drained, chopped pineapple, the orange and lemon rind, and vanilla. Beat egg whites to stiff peaks and lightly fold into the rice mixture.

Spoon into the prepared cake tin and cook at 180°C (350°F/Gas 4) until the cake is golden brown and quite set (about 1 ¼ hours). Allow to cool in tin, then prick surface with a fine skewer and sprinkle the liqueur, sherry or fruit juice over cake. Allow to stand overnight. Decorate with whipped cream and fruits.

Date Spiced Creamy Rice

Serves 4

1 quantity Speedy Creamy Rice (page 436)
½ cup (2 ½ oz) chopped dates or raisins or sultanas
2 tablespoons brown sugar
pinch of cinnamon
pinch of nutmeg
1½ tablespoons chopped nuts

Prepare the basic Speedy Creamy Rice. Add the dates to this mixture and spoon into a greased ovenproof dish. Sprinkle with the brown sugar, cinnamon, nutmeg and nuts. Place under a hot grill (broiler) for a few minutes. Serve with ice cream.

Maple Peach Rice

Serves 4

3 cups cooked brown rice
1 x 450 g (14 ½ oz) can sliced peaches, liquid reserved
½ cup (3 oz) sultanas
3 tablespoons maple syrup or honey
½ cup (2 oz) chopped walnuts or pecans
½ teaspoon cinnamon
½ teaspoon nutmeg
15 g (½ oz) butter, melted
extra chopped walnuts

Combine the rice with the peach syrup, sultanas, 2 tablespoons of the maple syrup, walnuts, cinnamon and nutmeg. Spoon the rice into a well-greased ovenproof dish and top with peach slices. Spoon over the remaining maple syrup, combined with the melted butter, and sprinkle with extra walnuts. Bake at 180°C (350°F/Gas 4) for about 15 to 20 minutes until heated through. Serve with cream or ice cream.

Rhubarb Rice Crisp

Serves 6

2 cups cooked rice
2 cups cooked rhubarb or plums
2 teaspoons lemon juice
1 cup (6 oz) brown sugar
½ teaspoon cinnamon
½ teaspoon ground ginger
salt
¾ cup (3 oz) flour
75 g (2 ½ oz) butter
½ cup (2 oz) chopped nuts

Combine the rice, rhubarb, lemon juice, ½ cup (3 oz) of the sugar, and cinnamon in a buttered shallow ovenproof dish or pie plate. Mix the ginger, a pinch of salt and the flour with the remaining sugar. Cut in the butter until the mixture is crumbly then stir in the nuts and sprinkle over the rice mixture. Bake at 180°C (350°F/Gas 4) for about 30 minutes. Serve warm with whipped cream or ice cream.

Spiced Rice Custard

Serves 4

¼ cup (2 oz) rice
4 cups (1 litre) milk
2 cardamom pods
3 eggs, beaten
45 g (1 ½ oz) butter
3 tablespoons sugar
1 teaspoon vanilla essence
½ teaspoon nutmeg

Combine the rice, 2 cups (16 fl oz) of milk and the cardamom pods in a well-greased saucepan and cook over moderate heat, stirring occasionally for about 15 minutes, until the rice is just tender. Combine the remaining milk, eggs, butter, sugar and vanilla. Add to the hot rice and blend well. Pour into a well-buttered ovenproof dish and sprinkle with the nutmeg. Bake at 150°C (300°F/Gas 2) until set, about 45 minutes.

Desserts

Greek Rice Pudding (Rizogalo)

Serves 4

1 cup (8 fl oz) water
pinch of salt
½ cup (3 oz) rice, washed
4 cups (1 litre) milk
¾ cup (6 oz) sugar
½ teaspoon grated lemon rind or more to taste
1 ½ teaspoons cornflour (cornstarch), mixed with 4 tablespoons cold water
cinnamon

Bring the water and salt to the boil, add the rice and boil for 5 minutes. Drain. Rinse a large saucepan with boiling water, pour in the milk to scald, add the sugar, stirring to dissolve, and when simmering add the parboiled rice and lemon rind. Reduce the heat and just simmer until the rice is very soft, thick and creamy, about 35 minutes.

Add the blended cornflour slowly to the rice mixture and stir. Return to the heat and simmer for 15 minutes. Remove from heat, pour into dishes and sprinkle each serving with a little cinnamon. Serve hot or cold.

Apple Cottage Rice

Serves 4

2 cups cooked apple, sweetened with sugar
2 cups cooked brown rice
4 tablespoons cottage cheese
grated rind and juice of 1 orange
4 tablespoons yoghurt
sugar
cinnamon

Combine the apple, rice, cottage cheese and orange rind and juice. Spoon into individual serving dishes and chill. Serve topped with yoghurt sweetened with a little sugar and sprinkled with cinnamon or extra grated orange rind.

Sunshine Rice Cream

Serves 6

3 cups cooked rice
3 cups (24 fl oz) milk
15 g (½ oz) butter
2 tablespoons sugar
1 teaspoon vanilla essence
1 cup (8 fl oz) cream, whipped
1 x 450 g (14 ½ oz) can pineapple pieces
3 passionfruit
extra cream, to decorate

Place the rice, milk and butter in a saucepan and cook over medium heat, stirring occasionally, until the rice is thick and creamy and the milk is absorbed, about 15 minutes. Remove from the heat and add the sugar and vanilla. Allow to cool. Fold in the whipped cream. Drain the pineapple pieces, and add two thirds to the rice along with the pulp of 2 passionfruit. Serve in a bowl or individual dishes, and decorate with the extra cream and the remaining pineapple and passionfruit.

Date and Apple Rice

Serves 4

3 cups cooked brown rice
grated rind of 1 orange
1 cup (8 fl oz) orange juice
60 g (2 oz) butter
½ cup (2 ½ oz) chopped dates or prunes
¼ cup (1 ½ oz) chopped glacé ginger, optional
2 tablespoons honey
2 cups stewed apples

Topping
3 tablespoons brown sugar
¼ cup (1 oz) chopped walnuts
¼ teaspoon nutmeg
¼ teaspoon cinnamon

Place the rice, orange rind and juice and two thirds of the butter in a saucepan, simmer and stir occasionally for about 5 minutes, then add the dates, ginger and honey and cook for another few minutes. Place half the rice in an ovenproof dish and top with half the apple, repeat the layers. Combine the topping ingredients and sprinkle over the rice. Dot with the reserved butter. Place in a 180°C (350°F/Gas 4) oven or under the grill (broiler) until the topping melts.

Cherry Rice Flan

Serves 4

¾ cup cooked rice
½ cup (3 oz) chopped glacé cherries
2 tablespoons brandy
2 eggs
¾ cup (6 fl oz) cream
½ cup (4 oz) caster (powdered) sugar
a few drops of vanilla essence
icing (confectioners') sugar

Yoghurt Pastry
1 cup (4 oz) flour
pinch of salt
45 g (1 ½ oz) butter
3 tablespoons plain yoghurt

Place the rice and the cherries in a small bowl with the brandy and stand for 1 to 2 hours at room temperature. Prepare the yoghurt pastry (*see below*). Roll the pastry out thinly and line a 20 cm (8 inch) flan ring. Chill. Bake the pastry case blind at 220°C (425°/Gas 7) for 10 minutes. Set aside.

Drain off any excess brandy from the cherry and rice mixture and spread over the base of the flan. Beat the eggs lightly and combine with the cream, caster sugar and vanilla. Spoon the custard mixture into the flan case. Bake at 190°C (375°F/Gas 5) for 30 minutes or until the custard is set. Cool for 10 minutes. Dust the top with the icing sugar and serve at once. The flan may also be served cold.

Yoghurt Pastry: Sift the flour and salt into a bowl. Rub in the butter with your fingertips until the mixture resembles coarse breadcrumbs. Add the yoghurt and mix to a firm dough. Chill for 30 minutes.

Creamy Rice with Cherry Sauce

Serves 4

½ cup (3 oz) rice
1 cup (8 fl oz) water
15g (½ oz) butter
2 ½ cups (20 fl oz) milk
½ cup (4 oz) sugar or
 ½ cup (5 oz) honey
juice of ½ a small lemon
1 teaspoon grated lemon rind

Cherry Sauce
1 x 440 g (15 ½ oz) can cherries, liquid reserved
1 tablespoon brandy or sherry
½ teaspoon cinnamon
strip of orange rind
2 teaspoons arrowroot, dissolved in a little water

Creamy Rice: Cook the rice in the water until all the water is absorbed. Add the butter and milk, cover and cook over low heat until the rice is tender. Add extra milk if required. Remove from the heat and stir in the sugar, lemon juice and rind. Serve warm or cold, topped with Cherry Sauce.

Cherry Sauce: Drain the cherries and blend the liquid with the brandy, cinnamon and orange rind. Bring to the boil and thicken with the arrowroot. Add the cherries and a little extra brandy if desired. Heat and pour over the rice.

Peach Ginger Rice Cream

Serves 4

½ cup (3 oz) rice
1 cup (8 fl oz) boiling water
2 cups (16 fl oz) milk
3 tablespoons caster (powdered) sugar
1 cup (8 fl oz) cream, whipped
1 x 220 g (7 ½ oz) can peach halves
¼ cup (1 ½ oz) sliced glacé ginger
2 teaspoons lemon juice
2 tablespoons redcurrant jelly or apricot jam
3 teaspoons arrowroot or cornflour (cornstarch), dissolved in a little water
extra whipped cream
toasted almond slivers, to decorate

Boil the rice in the water until the water has been absorbed, about 5 minutes. Add the milk to the pan and cook over low heat until the rice is quite tender, about 25 to 30 minutes. Add the sugar and allow to cool. Fold in the whipped cream.

Drain the peaches and reserve the syrup. Chop half the peaches and fold through the rice with the glacé ginger. Place the remaining peaches on the rice in a serving dish. Blend the peach liquid, lemon juice, redcurrant jelly and arrowroot, and stir until the mixture boils and thickens. Allow to cool then spoon over the peaches. Serve with whipped cream and top with almond slivers.

Peach Ginger Rice Cream

Desserts

Austrian Rice Cream

Serves 4

¼ cup (2 oz) rice
3 cups (24 fl oz) milk
2 tablespoons sugar
2 tablespoons caster (powdered) sugar
2 teaspoons gelatine
juice and rind of 1 orange
1 cup sliced strawberries
½ cup seedless grapes
1 apple, diced and tossed in lemon juice
3 teaspoons brandy, sherry or Cointreau
½ cup (4 fl oz) cream, whipped
sliced kiwifruit, to garnish

Simmer the rice and milk, stirring occasionally, until the rice is tender, about 40 to 45 minutes. Add extra milk if required. Add the sugar and allow the rice to cool. Dissolve the gelatine in the orange juice and add to the rice with the rind, the strawberries, grapes, apple and brandy. Fold in the whipped cream. Spoon into an oiled mould or serving dish and chill until firm. Garnish with sliced kiwifruit. Ideal served with a fruit purée or sauce.

Swedish Rice Pudding

Serves 6

1 cup (6 oz) rice
5 cups (1.25 litres) milk
3 Granny Smith (or similar type) apples, peeled and thinly sliced
1 teaspoon grated lemon rind
2 eggs, beaten with ½ cup (4 oz) sugar
45 g (1 ½ oz) butter
½ cup (2 oz) slivered toasted almonds
¾ cup (4 oz) raisins
2 tablespoons sherry
½ teaspoon nutmeg
½ teaspoon cinnamon

Cook the rice by the rapid boil method (*page 307*) for 12 minutes. Drain, then add the milk and apple slices, and cook over moderate heat until the rice is quite tender, about 20 minutes.

Remove from the heat and add the remaining ingredients, except for the spices. Spoon into a buttered pie plate or an ovenproof dish. Sprinkle with the spices, then set the dish in a pan of hot water and bake at 180°C (350°F/Gas 4) for about 40 minutes.

Grand Marnier Rice Imperial

Serves 8

Praline
½ cup (3 oz) blanched almonds
⅓ cup (3 oz) granulated sugar

2 tablespoons cold water

Mousse
250 g (8 oz) cottage cheese, sieved
⅓ cup (3 oz) caster (powdered) sugar
2 eggs, separated
½ cup (4 fl oz) milk
2 tablespoons gelatine dissolved in ¼ cup (2 fl oz) water

4 tablespoons Grand Marnier
½ cup (3 oz) rice, cooked and drained well
1 ¼ cups (10 fl oz) cream, semi-whipped
extra whipped cream
finely chopped mixed peel

Praline: Brown the almonds in a 180°C (350°F/Gas 4) oven. Set aside. In a small saucepan, dissolve the sugar with the water. Do not allow to boil until the sugar is dissolved, then boil steadily until caramel in colour. Remove and quickly stir in the almonds. Pour onto a buttered tin plate and cool thoroughly. Crush roughly with the end of a rolling pin or with a pestle and mortar. Set aside.

Mouse: Beat the cottage cheese, caster sugar, egg yolks and milk together and pour into the top of a double boiler. Stir over gentle heat until it reaches the consistency of a custard. Fold the dissolved gelatine into the custard then add the liqueur. Pour into a large bowl and chill until the mixture begins to thicken and set. Beat the egg whites until stiff. Quickly fold in the rice, praline, cream and egg whites. Pour into an 8 cup (2 litre) mould and chill until set. Unmould onto a serving platter and decorate with extra whipped cream and mixed peel.

Baked Rice Custard

Serves 6

3 eggs, beaten
½ cup (4 oz) sugar
1 teaspoon vanilla essence
3 cups (24 fl oz) milk
1 cup cooked rice
½ cup (3 oz) sultanas
15 g (½ oz) butter
a little nutmeg

Beat the eggs, sugar and vanilla until creamy, then add the milk and blend well. Add the rice and sultanas. Pour into a well-greased ovenproof dish, top with knobs of butter and sprinkle with nutmeg. Place the dish in a pan of hot water and bake at 150°C (300°F/Gas 2) for 45 minutes or until set. Stir occasionally during the first 20 minutes. Serve with cream or ice cream.

Rice Imperatrice Mould

Serves 4

- 15 g (½ oz) butter
- 1 ½ cups cooked rice
- 1 ½ cups (12 fl oz) milk
- ⅓ cup (3 oz) sugar
- 3 teaspoons gelatine
- 2 tablespoons hot orange juice
- ½ cup (3 oz) chopped glacé fruit (apricots, cherries, pineapple)
- ¼ cup (2 fl oz) Grand Marnier or your favourite liqueur or orange juice
- ½ cup (4 fl oz) cream, whipped
- extra whipped cream
- glacé cherries, to decorate
- angelica strips, to decorate

In a heavy based saucepan, simmer the butter, rice and milk over low heat until the rice is soft and creamy, about 15 to 20 minutes. Remove from the heat and add the sugar, and gelatine dissolved in hot orange juice. Place the rice mixture in the refrigerator until almost set.

Soak the glacé fruits in the Grand Marnier and add them, and the whipped cream, to the almost-set rice. Place the rice in an oiled mould or serving dish and refrigerate until firm. Unmould on a serving plate. Decorate with the extra whipped cream, cherries and angelica strips.

Prunicot Rice Dessert

Serves 4

- 3 cups cooked rice
- ½ cup (5 oz) honey, melted
- 1 x 425 g (13 ½ oz) can prunes
- 1 x 425 g (13 ½ oz) can apricot halves
- 1 tablespoon gelatine, dissolved in ½ cup (4 fl oz) hot water
- 1 tablespoon sherry
- juice and rind of 1 orange
- 1 cup chopped marshmallows
- 1 cup (8 fl oz) cream, whipped
- toasted almonds, to decorate

Combine the rice and honey. Drain the fruits and combine both syrups, adding the dissolved gelatine. Blend the sherry with the orange juice and rind. Reserve some of the fruit for decoration and fold the remainder through the rice with the syrup. Blend thoroughly. Fold in the marshmallows and half the whipped cream. Spoon into a serving dish and chill. Decorate with the remaining whipped cream and reserved fruits. Sprinkle with almonds.

Honey Rice

Serves 4

- 15 g (½ oz) butter
- 3 cups cooked rice
- ½ cup (3 oz) sultanas or raisins
- 2 ½ cups (20 fl oz) milk
- ½ cup (5 oz) honey
- 1 teaspoon grated orange rind
- 1 tablespoon orange juice

Melt the butter in a saucepan and add the rice, sultanas, milk and honey. Bring to the boil, then reduce the heat and simmer for about 15 minutes, stirring occasionally. Remove from the heat and stir in the orange rind and juice.

Note: This dessert is delicious served warm with ice cream or cold with stewed or canned fruits. It keeps well in the refrigerator.

Apricot Rice Parfait

Serves 6

- 15 g (½ oz) butter
- 3 cups cooked rice
- 3 cups (24 fl oz) milk
- 1 teaspoon vanilla essence
- 2 tablespoons sugar or to taste
- ½ cup (4 fl oz) cream, whipped
- 1 x 825 g (1 lb 10 ½ oz) can apricot halves
- extra whipped cream, to decorate
- ¼ cup (1 oz) slivered toasted almonds, to decorate

Place the butter, rice and milk in a heavy based saucepan. Bring to the boil, then reduce the heat and simmer, stirring occasionally, until the rice is thick and creamy, about 15 to 20 minutes. Remove from the heat, and add the vanilla and sugar. Refrigerate until cool and then add the whipped cream.

Drain the apricots and place the rice and apricots in alternate layers in parfait glasses or a serving dish. Decorate with the extra whipped cream and slivered almonds.

Yoghurt Raisin Rice Pudding

Serves 6

- 2 cups cooked rice
- ¾ cup (6 fl oz) cream
- ¾ cup (6 fl oz) milk
- 1 ½ cups (12 fl oz) natural yoghurt
- ½ cup (5 oz) honey
- 3 eggs, lightly beaten
- 1 cup (5 oz) chopped raisins

Combine the rice, cream, milk, yoghurt and honey. Mix in the eggs and raisins. Spoon the mixture into a lightly buttered 6 cup (1.5 litre) casserole. Bake at 180°C (350°F/Gas 4) for about 45 to 55 minutes.

Serve warm with extra natural yoghurt if desired.

Desserts

Caramel Crunch Rice

Serves 4

3 cups cooked rice
3 cups (24 fl oz) milk
15 g (½ oz) butter
⅓ cup (3 oz) sugar, or to taste
2 teaspoons instant coffee
3 tablespoons caramel syrup
1 cup (8 fl oz) cream, whipped
1 teaspoon vanilla
½ cup finely chopped butterscotch or peanut brittle toffee
extra whipped cream
¼ cup (1 oz) chopped pecans or walnuts

Place the rice, milk and butter in a saucepan and cook over medium heat, stirring occasionally, until the rice is thick and creamy, about 15 to 20 minutes. Remove from heat, add the sugar, coffee and caramel syrup. Allow to cool. Fold in the whipped cream, vanilla and half the crushed butterscotch. Place in a serving dish, decorate with extra whipped cream and sprinkle with remaining butterscotch and pecan nuts.

Apricot Honey Rice

Serves 6

3 cups cooked brown rice
1 x 425 g (13 ½ oz) can apricot halves
⅓ cup (4 oz) honey, or to taste
1 teaspoon grated orange rind
juice of 1 orange
½ teaspoon ground nutmeg
½ cup (3 oz) brown sugar
¼ cup (1 oz) chopped nuts
15 g (½ oz) butter
glacé cherries, to decorate

Place the rice in a well-buttered ovenproof dish. Drain the apricots and combine the apricot syrup, honey, and orange rind and juice. Spoon the syrup over the rice and toss with a fork. Place the apricot halves around the border of the rice. Combine the nutmeg, brown sugar and nuts and sprinkle over the rice. Place small dots of butter on the rice and place in a 180°C (350°F/Gas 4) oven for about 15 minutes or until the rice is heated. Decorate with glacé cherries in the apricot halves. Serve with cream or ice cream.

Spiced Rice Balls

Serves 4

½ cup (3 oz) rice
2 ½ cups (20 fl oz) milk
⅓ cup (3 oz) sugar, or to taste
small cinnamon stick
desiccated coconut
cream
brown sugar

Place the rice, milk, sugar and cinnamon stick in the top of a double boiler. Set over boiling water and cook for about 1 hour, stirring occasionally until the rice is tender and milk absorbed. Remove the cinnamon stick and cool the rice. When cold, roll the rice into small balls and toss in the coconut. Serve with cream and brown sugar.

Rice Ginger Snaps

Makes 12 - 18

30 g (1 oz) butter
½ cup (3 oz) lightly packed brown sugar
¼ cup (3 oz) golden syrup

Ginger Cream
125 g (4 oz) cream cheese
1 tablespoon caster (powdered) sugar
1 teaspoon ground ginger
2 tablespoons maraschino liqueur or orange juice

1 tablespoon finely chopped mixed peel
¼ cup cooked rice
½ cup (2 oz) flour

1 ¼ cups (10 fl oz) cream
strawberries, to decorate
icing (confectioners') sugar, to decorate

Rice Ginger Snaps: Melt the butter, brown sugar and golden syrup. Cool slightly. Thoroughly stir in mixed peel, rice and flour. Place small tablespoonfuls of the mixture onto flat buttered trays, approximately four on each. Bake at 180°C (350°F/Gas 4) for about 8 to 10 minutes or until outer edges of the biscuits are golden brown. Leave on the tray for 1 minute then carefully lift off with a spatula. Either roll around the handle of a wooden spoon or leave flat.

Ginger Cream: Beat the cream cheese, sugar, ginger and liqueur together. Add the cream and beat until mixture has the consistency of whipped cream. Pipe into rolled snaps and decorate tops or, alternatively, stack 3 or 4 snaps together, filling between each layer with the cream. Decorate tops with small, hulled strawberries and dust with sifted icing sugar.

Creamy Rice Camden

Serves 4

2 ½ cups (20 fl oz) milk
¼ cup (2 oz) rice
salt
2 tablespoons sugar
2 egg yolks, beaten
1 teaspoon vanilla essence
cinnamon or nutmeg

Grease a heavy based saucepan with butter. Pour in the milk and bring to the boil. Add the rice and a pinch of salt. Stir, bring back to the boil, then lower the heat and simmer, stirring occasionally. Cook for about 45 to 50 minutes or until the rice is soft.

Combine the rice and sugar and add the beaten egg yolks. Remove from heat and stir until blended. Add the vanilla and pour into a serving dish. Sprinkle with cinnamon. This is a quick version of the old style rice pudding. It may be served with cream, ice cream, stewed or fresh fruit.

Variation: Top with raspberry or apricot jam. Whip remaining egg whites with ¼ cup (2 oz) of sugar to meringue consistency. Spread over the rice, bake at 180°C (350°F/Gas 4) for 15 minutes until golden.

Apricot Honey Rice

435

Desserts

Peachy Rice Parfaits

Serves 6

- 1 x 470 g (15 oz) can sliced peaches
- 3 cups cooked rice
- 1 teaspoon vanilla essence
- 6 glacé cherries, chopped
- 2 tablespoons sugar
- 1 cup chopped marshmallows
- ½ cup (4 fl oz) chilled evaporated milk, whipped or ⅔ cup (5 ½ fl oz) cream, whipped
- extra cream, to decorate
- extra glacé cherries, to decorate

Drain the peaches, then add the rice to the peach syrup and cook over low heat in a greased saucepan until the syrup is absorbed. Cool the rice. Fold the rice, vanilla, cherries, sugar and marshmallows into the whipped evaporated milk. Spoon into parfait glasses alternately with the peaches. Top with whipped cream and glacé cherries.

Peach Rice Treat

Serves 4

- 1 egg
- ¼ cup (2 oz) sugar
- 1 tablespoon cornflour (cornstarch)
- a few drops of vanilla essence
- 2 cups (16 fl oz) milk
- 1 cup cooked rice
- 1 x 425 g (13 ½ oz) can sliced peaches

Beat together the egg, sugar, cornflour and vanilla. Bring the milk to the boil and gradually add the egg mixture, stirring until thick and smooth. Add the cooked rice and blend well. Drain the peaches, chop half and add them to the rice. Spoon into individual serving dishes and decorate with the remaining peach slices.

Mocha Cream Parfait

Serves 6

- 3 cups cooked rice
- 3 cups (24 fl oz) milk
- 2-3 teaspoons instant coffee
- 15 g (½ oz) butter
- ½ cup (4 oz) brown or white sugar
- 1 teaspoon vanilla essence
- 1 cup (8 fl oz) cream, whipped
- ½ cup grated chocolate or crushed peanut toffee
- extra whipped cream, to decorate
- 8 chocolate bits or grated chocolate

Place the rice in a heavy based saucepan, blend the milk and coffee together and add to the rice with the butter. Stir frequently over low heat until the rice is thick and creamy, about 15 to 20 minutes. Remove from the heat. Add the sugar and vanilla and allow to cool. When cool fold in the whipped cream and chocolate. Spoon into parfait glasses or a serving dish. Top with the extra whipped cream and chocolate bits or grated chocolate.

Speedy Creamy Rice

Serves 4

- 3 cups cooked rice
- 3 cups (24 fl oz) milk
- 15 g (½ oz) butter or margarine
- ½ cup (4 oz) sugar or ½ cup (5 oz) honey
- 1 tablespoon vanilla essence

Place the rice, milk and butter in a greased saucepan and cook over moderate heat for about 15 minutes, stirring frequently. Add the sugar and vanilla.

Serve hot or cold with cream, ice cream or fruit.

Note: For a flavour change, add grated chocolate, coffee essence, orange rind and juice, or marmalade. Any one may replace vanilla in the basic recipe. Try combining coffee and chocolate to produce a mocha flavoured rice.

Peach Meringue Creamy Rice

Serves 4

- 1 quantity Speedy Creamy Rice (*above*)
- 2 eggs, separated
- canned sliced peaches, drained
- 4 tablespoons caster (powdered) sugar

Add the beaten egg yolks to the basic Speedy Creamy Rice and place in a greased ovenproof dish. Top with the peaches. Beat the egg whites with the caster sugar to a meringue consistency and spread over the rice-peach mixture. Bake at 160°C (325°F/Gas 3) for 15 minutes or until the meringue is golden.

Rice Custard Imperial

Serves 4

- 1 x 85 g (2 ½ oz) packet instant vanilla custard
- 2 ¼ cups (18 fl oz) milk
- 1 cup cooked rice
- ½ cup (3 oz) finely chopped glacé fruits (cherries, ginger, apricots or mixed fruits)
- 1 tablespoon rum, brandy or orange juice
- 2 tablespoons apricot jam, heated and sieved
- whipped cream
- toasted slivered almonds

Make up the custard, using the milk, and add the rice. Soak the fruit in rum and when the custard starts to cool a little, add the fruit. Pour into a glass serving bowl or individual serving dishes. When set spread with the apricot jam and top with whipped cream and almonds. This is an ideal dessert to serve when you have guests. It can be made well in advance.

Variation: Make up chocolate instant custard, replace fruits with choc bits, flavour with coffee. Top with whipped cream and grated chocolate.

Jamaican Rum Rice Pudding

Serves 6

2 cups freshly cooked rice
½ cup (4 oz) caster (powdered) sugar
¼ teaspoon vanilla essence
½ cup (3 oz) raisins
1 tablespoon rum
4 eggs, lightly beaten
2 ½ cups (20 fl oz) milk
¼ cup (¾ oz) toasted coconut

In a large bowl, mix together the rice, sugar, vanilla, raisins and rum. In another bowl combine the eggs and milk. Add the eggs and milk to the rice and combine well. Turn into a well-buttered baking dish. Bake at 180°C (350°F/Gas 4) for 30 minutes. Sprinkle the top with coconut during the last 5 minutes of baking. Serve warm with thin crisp biscuits. The dessert can also be chilled and served with whipped cream.

Note: This pudding is rather sweet so reduce the sugar to ⅓ cup (3 oz) if preferred.

Honey Rice Muffins

Makes 12

90 g (3 oz) butter
½ cup (5 oz) honey
½ teaspoon grated lemon rind
2 eggs
½ cup cooked rice
1 ¼ cups (6 oz) roughly chopped dates
1 ¼ cups (5 oz) wholemeal self-raising flour
½ teaspoon ground cloves

Cream the butter, honey and lemon rind together. Beat in the eggs thoroughly, one at a time. Mix in the rice and the dates and fold in the flour and cloves. Spoon the mixture into paper patty cases or a buttered gem iron. Place on a flat tray and bake at 190°C (375°F/Gas 5) for 20 minutes.

Brown Rice Pudding

Serves 4

2 cups cooked brown rice
3 cups (24 fl oz) milk
⅓ cup (1 ½ oz) chopped walnuts
¼ teaspoon nutmeg
2 tablespoons mixed peel
3 eggs, beaten
3 tablespoons honey

Combine all the ingredients and spoon into a greased ovenproof dish. Bake at 180°C (350°F/Gas 4) for about 35 minutes or until set. The pudding may be glazed with a little extra honey while still hot. Serve hot or cold with cream, ice cream or sour cream.

Jamaican Scrambled Rice

Serves 4 - 6

¼ cup (2 fl oz) white rum
¼ cup (1 oz) raisins
1 cup (6 oz) rice
¼ teaspoon salt
1 cup (8 oz) sugar
3 cups (24 fl oz) milk
2 tablespoons chopped nuts
grated rind of 1 lemon
1 egg, beaten
60 g (2 oz) butter
¼ cup (2 oz) caster (powdered) sugar
½ teaspoon cinnamon
whipped cream

Place the rum and raisins in a small bowl and set aside for several hours. Place the rice, salt, sugar and milk in the top half of a double boiler. Cook over simmering water, stirring occasionally, until the rice is tender and the milk is absorbed. Allow to cool slightly. Stir in the raisins, nuts, lemon rind and beaten egg and combine gently but thoroughly.

Melt the butter in a medium to large frying pan, add the rice mixture and cook until a golden crust forms on the bottom. Place the pan under a griller (broiler) and grill (broil) until the top is golden. Combine the caster sugar and cinnamon and sprinkle over. Serve in wedges with whipped cream.

Brown Rice Dessert

Serves 4

4 cups cooked brown rice
grated rind and juice of 1 orange
15 g (½ oz) butter
½ cup (4 fl oz) milk
½ cup (2 ½ oz) chopped dates or prunes or sultanas
¼ cup (3 oz) golden syrup or honey

Topping
3 tablespoons brown sugar
¼ teaspoon each nutmeg and ground ginger or cinnamon
15 g (½ oz) butter

Combine the rice, orange rind and juice, butter and milk in a well-greased saucepan. Stir over moderate heat for about 5 minutes, then add the dates and golden syrup. Blend and transfer to a greased ovenproof dish.

Topping: Combine the brown sugar, nutmeg and ginger and sprinkle over the rice. Dot with the butter and place in a 220°C (425°F/Gas 7) oven or under the grill (broiler) for a few minutes to heat the topping.

Desserts

Golden Apricot Rice Pudding

Serves 4

- 1 ½ cups cooked brown rice
- ¼ cup (¾ oz) desiccated coconut
- 3 eggs, separated
- ⅓ cup (4 oz) honey
- ½ cup (4 fl oz) water
- 1 ½ cups (12 fl oz) apricot nectar
- a little grated lemon rind
- 1 teaspoon vanilla essence
- ⅓ cup (3 oz) sugar
- ½ cup (5 oz) apricot jam
- a few toasted slivered almonds

Combine the rice, coconut and beaten egg yolks and place in a well-greased ovenproof dish. Combine the honey and water and bring to the boil. Stir in the apricot nectar, lemon rind and vanilla and pour over the rice. Place the dish in a pan of hot water and bake at 180°C (350°F/Gas 4) for about 45 minutes or until set.

Beat the egg whites until stiff peaks form, gradually add the sugar and beat to meringue consistency. Allow the pudding to cool slightly, then spread the surface with the apricot jam and top with meringue. Sprinkle with the almond slivers and bake for 10 to 15 minutes or until golden.

Strawberry Rice Cheesecake

Serves 4 - 6

- 2 cups cooked rice
- 1 ½ cups (12 fl oz) milk
- 125 g (4 oz) cream cheese
- 250 g (8 oz) cottage cheese
- ⅔ cup (5 oz) caster (powdered) sugar
- 3 medium-sized eggs
- 1 teaspoon vanilla essence
- grated rind of 1 lemon
- 1 tablespoon fine dry breadcrumbs
- 1 cup (8 fl oz) cream, whipped
- 1 punnet strawberries

Slowly simmer the rice in the milk, stirring occasionally, for about 15 to 20 minutes or until the rice is creamy and the milk absorbed. Cool. Cream together the cream cheese, cottage cheese and caster sugar. Continue beating, adding the eggs one at a time, the vanilla and lemon rind. Add the cooled rice and blend well. Thoroughly grease a 20 cm (8 inch) spring form pan and sprinkle with breadcrumbs to evenly coat the base and sides. Spoon the mixture into the pan. Bake at 180°C (350°F/Gas 4) for about 1 to 1 ¼ hours or until the cake is firm. Cool in the tin then remove, top with whipped cream and strawberries.

Note: Bananas, passionfruit, cherries or peaches can be substituted.

Rice Muffins

Makes 12

- 1 cup cooked rice
- 1 cup (8 fl oz) milk
- 2 tablespoons sugar
- 45 g (1 ½ oz) butter, melted
- 2 eggs, well beaten
- 1 teaspoon vanilla essence
- 1 ½ cups (6 oz) flour
- pinch of salt
- ¼ teaspoon nutmeg
- ¼ teaspoon cinnamon
- 2 teaspoons baking powder

Place the rice in a bowl and stir in the milk, sugar, butter, eggs and vanilla. Sift together the flour, salt and spices. Gradually add the flour to the rice mixture, beating well until batter consistency. Sift the baking powder over the batter and very lightly fold into the mixture. Pour the batter into well-greased patty tins until about two thirds full and bake at 200°C 400°F/Gas 6) for about 20 to 25 minutes or until golden. Split open while warm and serve buttered with honey or golden syrup.

Rice Apricot Cream Delight

Serves 6

- ⅔ cup (4 oz) rice
- 2¾ cups (22 fl oz) milk
- ½ teaspoon vanilla essence
- ⅓ cup (3 oz) sugar
- 1 x 822 g (1 lb 10 ½ oz) can apricots, drained and with liquid reserved
- 1 cup (8 fl oz) cream, whipped
- 1 egg white, stiffly beaten
- whipped cream and slivered toasted almonds to decorate

Apricot Sauce

- 2 cups (16 fl oz) apricot nectar
- 1-2 tablespoons brandy
- 2 teaspoons arrowroot or cornflour (cornstarch), mixed with a little water
- pinch of cinnamon

Rice Apricot Cream Delight: Pour 1 cup (8 fl oz) of boiling water over the rice and let it stand, covered, for 10 minutes. Drain and place the rice in a greased saucepan with the milk. Simmer over low heat until the rice is tender, stirring occasionally. Add the vanilla and sugar and stir until dissolved. Put aside to cool.

Chop one third of the apricots and fold into the rice with the cream and egg white. Place in a serving dish, chill, then decorate with the whipped cream, remaining apricot halves and sprinkle with slivered almonds. Serve with Apricot Sauce.

Apricot Sauce: Heat the apricot nectar and brandy, thicken with the blended arrowroot and add the cinnamon. Cool before serving.

BAKING

The aroma of freshly baked bread or scones straight from the oven will bring family from everywhere and it is unwise to leave a cake cooling with children in the house.

Save your baking for the cooler days and store it up in the freezer to produce delectable snacks. Let the children make muffins for breakfast and help you knead the bread. Everything tastes better if you participate in its making.

The majority of the recipes in this chapter have been supplied by the **Bread Research Institute of Australia Ltd**, while others have been provided by contributors whose credits appear elsewhere in the book.

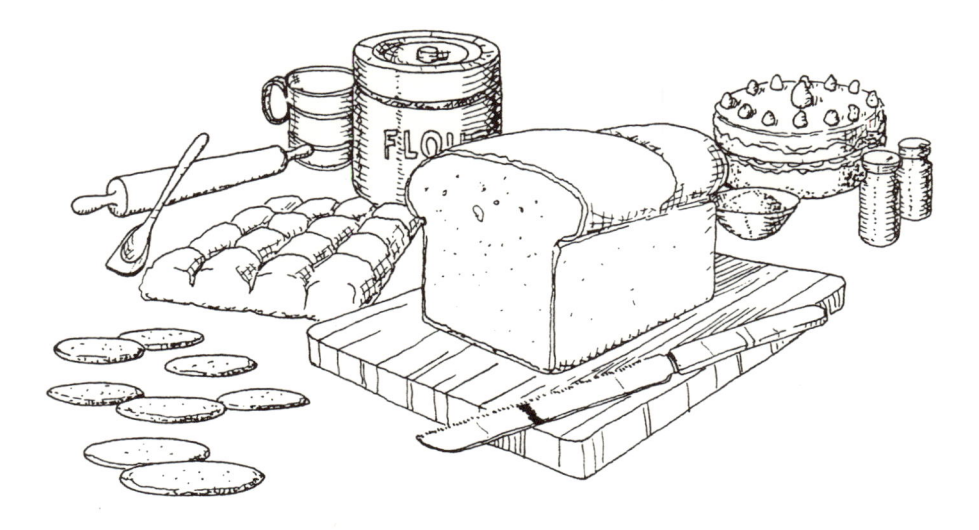

The **Bread Research Institute** (BRI), formed in 1947, is a scientific research organisation supported by the Australian bread and flour milling industries, the Australian Wheat Board and the Commonwealth Department of Industry, Technology and Commerce. Located at North Ryde, New South Wales, its work covers a wide range of activities, from the evaluation of wheat varieties through to flour milling and the use of flour in a variety of products such as bread, noodles, pasta and other baked products.

Information on the nutritional value of flour and bread is available from the Consumer Information Division together with recipes, posters, educational leaflets and pamphlets. The recipes here have been supplied by Penny Stone and Doreen Badger from the Consumer Information Division of the Institute.

Baking

Whole-Wheat Nut Bread

Makes 1 loaf

1 cup (4 oz) flour
2 teaspoons baking powder
¼ teaspoon salt
½ teaspoon cinnamon
¼ teaspoon nutmeg
¼ teaspoon allspice
½ cup (2 oz) wholemeal flour
60 g (2 oz) butter or margarine
¾ cup (6 oz) sugar
2 eggs
½ cup (4 fl oz) milk
½ teaspoon vanilla essence
½ cup (2 oz) chopped walnuts

Sift together the flour, baking powder, salt and spices. Stir in the wholemeal. Cream the butter and sugar together, add the eggs one at a time, beating well after each addition. Add the dry ingredients alternately with the milk and vanilla. Beat until smooth after each addition. Stir in the nuts. Turn into a greased loaf pan and bake at 180°C (350°F/Gas 4) for 55 minutes or until a skewer inserted in the centre comes out clean. Cool for 10 minutes then remove from the pan.

Peanut Butter Coffee Cake

Makes 1 cake

1½ cups (6 oz) self-raising flour
½ cup (4 oz) sugar
1 egg
⅔ cup (5 fl oz) milk
30 g (1 oz) butter
¼ cup (2 oz) peanut butter

Sift the dry ingredients together. Beat the egg and add to the milk. Melt the butter and peanut butter together and add to the egg and milk. Stir the liquids into the dry ingredients, mixing only enough to dampen all the flour. Pour into a greased and lined 18 cm (7 inch) sandwich tin. Bake at 190°C (375°F/Gas 5) for 35 minutes.

Quick Fruit Bread

Makes 1 loaf

2 cups (10 oz) mixed dried fruit
1½ cups (6 oz) self-raising flour
½ teaspoon salt
½ cup (4 oz) sugar
185 g (6 oz) butter
2 eggs, beaten
1 tablespoon milk
¼ teaspoon almond essence

Soak the dried fruit in boiling water to cover for 10 minutes. Drain well. Sift the dry ingredients into a mixing bowl. Cut in the butter and stir in the dried fruit. Add remaining ingredients and beat thoroughly.

Spread in a well greased loaf pan and bake at 180°C (350°F/Gas 4) for 1 hour. This cake freezes well.

Crunchy Orange Coffee Cake

Makes 1 cake

1½ cups (6 oz) self-raising flour
½ cup (4 oz) sugar
1 egg
½ cup (4 fl oz) milk
60 g (2 oz) butter, melted

Topping
60 g (2 oz) softened butter
¼ cup (1½ oz) soft brown sugar
2 tablespoons grated orange rind
2 tablespoons flour
½ cup (1½ oz) coconut

Preheat the oven to 190°C (375°F/Gas 5). Grease an 18 cm (7 inch) sandwich tin and line the bottom with paper. Sift the dry ingredients together. Beat the egg and add to the milk and melted butter. Stir the liquids into the dry ingredients, mixing only enough to dampen all the flour. Pour into the pan and sprinkle with the topping. Bake for 40 minutes or until golden.

Topping: Mix all the ingredients together thoroughly with a fork.

Cinnamon Streusel Coffee Cake

Makes 1 cake

1½ cups (6 oz) self-raising flour
½ cup (4 oz) sugar
1 egg
½ cup (4 fl oz) milk
60 g (2 oz) butter, melted

Streusel Topping
¼ cup (2 oz) sugar
½ teaspoon cinnamon
1 tablespoon flour
1 tablespoon softened butter
½ teaspoon vanilla essence
2 tablespoons chopped nuts

Preheat the oven to 190°C (375°F/Gas 5). Grease a deep 20 cm (8 inch) cake tin and line the bottom with paper. Sift the dry ingredients together. Beat the egg and add to the milk and melted butter. Stir the liquids into the dry ingredients, mixing only enough to dampen all the flour. Pour into the prepared tin. Sprinkle with Streusel Topping and bake for 45 minutes.

Streusel Topping: Mix the sugar, cinnamon and flour together. Cut in the butter until the mixture resembles breadcrumbs. Add the vanilla and nuts. Sprinkle over the cake before baking.

Coffee Cake

Makes 1 cake

1½ cups (6 oz) self-raising flour
½ cup (4 oz) sugar
1 egg
½ cup (4 fl oz) milk
3 tablespoons melted butter

Sift the dry ingredients together. Beat the egg and add to the milk and melted butter. Stir the liquids into the dry ingredients, mixing only enough to dampen all the flour. Pour into a greased 18 cm (7 inch) sponge tin. Bake for 25 minutes at 190°C (375°F/Gas 5). Cool slightly in the tin before turning onto a cake rack.

Toppings for Coffee Cake

Each covers 1 cake

Streusel

¼ cup (2 oz) sugar
½ teaspoon cinnamon
1 tablespoon flour
15 g (½ oz) butter, softened
2 tablespoons chopped nuts
½ teaspoon vanilla essence

Mix the sugar, cinnamon and flour together. Cut in the butter until the mixture resembles breadcrumbs. Add the nuts and vanilla. Sprinkle over the cake before baking.

Crunchy Citrus Topping

30 g (1 oz) butter, softened
2 tablespoons flour
½ cup (1½ oz) coconut
¼ cup (1½ oz) soft brown sugar, firmly packed
2 tablespoons grated orange or lemon rind

Mix all ingredients together thoroughly with a fork. Sprinkle on top of cake before baking.

Sugared Almond Topping

1 tablespoon sugar
2 tablespoons almond meal

Mix the sugar and almond meal together and sprinkle on top of cake. Smooth over with a knife. Bake as directed.

Pineapple Walnut Cookies

Makes 72

250 g (8 oz) butter
1 cup (8 oz) sugar
1 egg
1 cup drained crushed pineapple
1 teaspoon bicarbonate of soda (baking soda)
¼ teaspoon nutmeg
3 cups (12 oz) flour
½ cup (2 oz) chopped walnuts

Cream the butter and sugar together until fluffy. Beat in the egg, add the pineapple, the sifted dry ingredients and mix thoroughly. Stir in the nuts and chill the mixture in the refrigerator for at least 1 hour. Place rounded teaspoonfuls about 5 cm (2 inch) apart on greased oven trays. Bake at 180°C (350°F/Gas 4) for 8 to 10 minutes.

Cheese Biscuits

Makes 36

2 cups (8 oz) self-raising flour
250 g (8 oz) butter
2 cups (8 oz) grated cheese
toasted sesame seeds or coconut

Sift the flour. Rub in the butter and cheese. Lightly knead the mixture together. (During hot weather it may be necessary to chill the dough.) Roll into small balls and toss in sesame seeds or coconut.
 Press on cold greased trays with a fork, allowing room to spread. Bake at 180°C (350°F/Gas 4) for 20 to 25 minutes.

Apricot Cream Biscuits

250 g (8 oz) butter or margarine
4 level tablespoons icing (confectioners') sugar
½ cup (2 oz) finely chopped dried apricots
1 cup (4 oz) self-raising flour
1½ cups (6 oz) cornflour (cornstarch)

Filling

30 g (1 oz) butter
¾ cup (6 oz) icing (confectioners') sugar
1 tablespoon apricot conserve
½ teaspoon sherry

Cream the butter with the icing sugar. Add the apricots. Sift the flour and cornflour together and fold into the creamed ingredients to make a dry mixture. Roll into small balls and place on a greased tray. Flatten slightly with the back of a fork. Bake at 180°C (350°F/Gas 4) for 10 to 15 minutes. Cool and join together with the filling.

Filling: Cream the butter and sugar. Add the conserve and sherry and mix to a spreading consistency.

Baking

Lemon Coconut Buttons

Makes 40 - 45

125 g (4 oz) butter
½ cup (4 oz) caster (powdered) sugar
1 egg
1 cup (4 oz) self-raising flour
1 cup (3 oz) coconut
1 teaspoon vanilla essence
a few drops of lemon essence
sliced glacé cherries or crystallised ginger, optional

Cream the butter and sugar until light. Beat in the egg. Add the flour, coconut, vanilla and lemon essences. Mix well. Roll into balls and place on greased trays leaving plenty of room to spread. They will flatten out so do not make them too big. Place a small slice of cherry or ginger in the centre of each one if liked. Bake at 180°C (350°F/Gas 4) for 15 to 20 minutes.

Sesame Biscuits

Makes 72

185 g (6 oz) butter
1 cup (6 oz) soft brown sugar, firmly packed
1 egg
1 teaspoon vanilla essence
1 cup toasted sesame seeds
½ cup (¾ oz) toasted shredded coconut
1¾ cups (7 oz) flour
1 teaspoon baking powder
½ teaspoon bicarbonate of soda (baking soda)
pinch of salt

Cream the butter and sugar together. Add the egg, vanilla, sesame seeds and coconut. Sift the dry ingredients, add to the mixture and mix well. Roll into small balls, or pipe in 5 cm (2 inch) strips on ungreased oven trays. Bake for 10 to 12 minutes at 180°C (350°F/Gas 4).

Crunchies

Cherry Raisin Nut Bread

Makes 1 loaf

3 cups (12 oz) flour, sifted
3 teaspoons baking powder
½ teaspoon salt
1 egg, beaten
1 teaspoon vanilla essence
½ teaspoon almond essence
¾ cup (6 oz) sugar
60 g (2 oz) butter, melted
1¼ cups (10 fl oz) milk
½ cup (2 oz) walnuts
¼ cup (1½ oz) finely chopped maraschino cherries
½ cup (3 oz) seedless raisins

Preheat the oven to 180°C (350°F/Gas 4). Grease and line a loaf tin. Sift the flour with the baking powder and salt. Combine the egg, vanilla and almond essences, sugar and butter and beat until blended. Add the milk, blending well. Add the flour mixture, beating until smooth then stir in the nuts, cherries and raisins.

Pour the batter into the prepared pan and bake for 60 to 65 minutes. Let cool in the pan for 10 minutes, then remove from the pan. Serve cut into thin slices.

Shortbread Creams

Makes 24

185 g (6 oz) butter
⅓ cup (2 oz) icing (confectioners') sugar
½ teaspoon vanilla essence
1½ cups (6 oz) flour
½ cup (2 oz) custard powder

Cream the butter and sugar together. Add the vanilla, then the sifted dry ingredients. Mix well. Roll into small balls and place on a greased tray.

Flatten slightly and bake for 20 minutes at 150°C (300°F/Gas 2). When cold sandwich together with Vanilla Butter Icing (*page 459*). The biscuits may be piped.

Crunchies

Makes 36

1¼ cups (5 oz) self-raising flour
1 cup (8 oz) sugar
1 cup (3 oz) coconut
1 cup (3 oz) rolled oats
pinch of salt
125 g (4 oz) butter or margarine
1 tablespoon golden syrup
1 level teaspoon bicarbonate of soda (baking soda)
2 tablespoons boiling water

Combine the flour, sugar, coconut, rolled oats and salt. Melt the butter and add the golden syrup, and the soda dissolved in the boiling water. Add the liquids to the dry ingredients and mix. The mixture will be dry. Roll teaspoonfuls into small balls and press flat with a fork. Bake at 180°C (350°F/Gas 4) for 15 to 20 minutes.

Sponge Roll or Sandwich

Makes 1 two-layer cake or 1 roll

3 eggs
½ cup (4 oz) sugar
¾ cup (3 oz) flour
1 teaspoon baking powder
30 g (1 oz) butter, melted

Beat the eggs, add the sugar and beat until thick. Sift the flour and baking powder and fold in lightly. Do not beat. Lastly add the melted butter.

Sponge Sandwich: Bake in greased and floured 18 cm (7 inch) sandwich tins at 190°C (375°F/Gas 5) for 15 to 20 minutes.

Sponge Roll: Bake in a greased Swiss roll tin at 200°C (400°F/Gas 6) for 8 to 10 minutes. Turn out on a cloth or greaseproof paper sprinkled with icing (confectioners') sugar. Spread with jam and roll quickly.

Sour Cream Sugar Cookies

Makes 36

2½ cups (10 oz) flour
pinch of salt
½ teaspoon bicarbonate of soda (baking soda)
1½ teaspoons baking powder
½ teaspoon nutmeg
¼ teaspoon allspice
125 g (4 oz) butter
1 egg, well beaten
1 cup (8 fl oz) thick sour cream
⅔ cup (3½ oz) soft brown sugar
1 cup (4 oz) chopped nuts
1 cup (6 oz) raisins

Mix and sift the dry ingredients together. Cut in the butter as for pastry. Add the egg to the sour cream with the sugar. Combine with the dry ingredients and add the nuts and fruit. Roll into small balls and place onto greased oven trays. Press lightly with a fork. Bake at 180°C (350°F/Gas 4) for 16 minutes.

Sour Cream Sugar Cookies

Baking

Fruit Flan with Streusel
Makes 2 flans

Base
250 g (8 oz) butter or margarine
¾ cup (4 oz) icing (confectioners') sugar
1 egg yolk
3 cups (12 oz) flour

Vanilla Custard
1 tablespoon cornflour (cornstarch)
2 teaspoons sugar
1¼ cups (10 fl oz) milk
knob of butter
½ teaspoon vanilla essence
1 egg, beaten
4 large apples, peeled, cored and thinly sliced

Streusel
60 g (2 oz) butter
¼ cup (2 oz) sugar
1 cup (4 oz) flour
½ teaspoon cinnamon

Base: Cream the butter and sugar together. Add the egg yolk, then the sifted flour. Refrigerate overnight. Roll out into two 20 cm (8 inch) flan rings. Rest pastry for 15 minutes. Bake at 160°C (325°F/Gas 3) for 20 to 25 minutes. Cool.

Vanilla Custard: Combine the cornflour and sugar and mix with the milk. Bring to the boil, stirring constantly. Cool. Add the butter, vanilla and beaten egg. Spread a thin layer of custard on the base of each flan. Blanch the apple slices for 5 minutes. Layer the apple slices on top and sprinkle with the streusel. Bake at 180°C (350°F/Gas 4) until the apples are tender.

Streusel: Cream the butter and sugar together. Blend in the flour and cinnamon.

Spiced Pumpkin Cake
Makes 1 cake

1 x packet golden buttercake cake mix
2 eggs
60 g (2 oz) soft butter
¾ cup cooked mashed pumpkin
1 teaspoon cinnamon
½ teaspoon bicarbonate of soda (baking soda)
½ teaspoon nutmeg
½ teaspoon ground ginger
½ teaspoon ground cloves
1 cup (5 oz) mixed dried fruit

Preheat the oven to 180°C (350°F/Gas 4). Place all ingredients in a mixer bowl and beat according to the directions on the packet. Pour into a deep 20 cm (8 inch) cake tin. Bake for 40 to 50 minutes and ice with Lemon Icing (*page 459*).

Chocolate Rum Biscuits
Makes 12

185 g (6 oz) butter
1 cup (8 oz) icing (confectioners') sugar
1 egg, beaten
1¼ cups (6 oz) self-raising flour
1 cup (4 oz) cornflour (cornstarch)
3 tablespoons cocoa
pinch of mixed spice
½ teaspoon vanilla essence

Filling
1 cup (8 oz) icing (confectioners') sugar, sifted
½ teaspoon vanilla essence
1 tablespoon cocoa
90 g (3 oz) butter
2 teaspoons rum, optional

Cream the butter and icing sugar. Add the egg and sifted dry ingredients, then the vanilla. Mix well and chill for 15 minutes in the refrigerator. Pipe onto greased oven trays and bake at 180°C (350°F/Gas 4) for 10 to 12 minutes.
Cool on a rack, then sandwich together with the filling.

Filling: Beat all ingredients together.

Cheesecake
Makes 1 cake

Base
¾ packet plain sweet biscuits
90 g (3 oz) butter, melted

Filling
1 x 250 g (8 oz) packet cream cheese
½ cup (4 oz) sugar
2 eggs, beaten
1 teaspoon vanilla essence

Topping
2 tablespoons sugar
1¼ cups (10 fl oz) sour cream
1 teaspoon vanilla essence

Base: Crush the biscuits into fine crumbs, add the butter and combine well. Press into a spring form tin and bake for 5 minutes at 180°C (350°F/Gas 4). Cool.

Filling: Beat the cheese with the sugar. Add the eggs and vanilla and beat until smooth. Pour into the crust. Bake for 20 to 25 minutes or until skewer comes out clean. Remove and cool.

Topping: Mix the sugar with the sour cream and vanilla. Spread over the cake. Bake for 10 minutes. Cool and chill. Store overnight before cutting.

Chocolate Rough

Makes 1 slab

125 g (4 oz) butter
½ cup (4 oz) sugar
1 teaspoon vanilla essence
1 cup (4 oz) self-raising flour
¾ cup (2½ oz) coconut
2 tablespoons cocoa

Icing
¼ cup (2 fl oz) condensed milk
1½ tablespoons melted butter
1 cup (6 oz) icing (confectioners') sugar
1 cup (3 oz) coconut
1 tablespoon cocoa

Preheat the oven to 190°C (375°F/Gas 5). Cream the butter and sugar, add the vanilla, then the sifted dry ingredients. Press into a greased and lined Swiss roll tin and bake for 20 to 25 minutes. Ice while hot.

Icing: Mix all the ingredients together and spread quickly over the cake while hot.

Chocaroon Cake

Makes 1 cake

90 g (3 oz) butter
½ cup (4 oz) sugar
grated rind of ½ lemon
½ teaspoon vanilla essence
2 egg yolks
1½ cups (6 oz) self-raising flour
¼ cup (2 fl oz) milk
apricot or raspberry jam

Chocaroon Layers
2 tablespoons sugar
1 tablespoon cocoa
½ cup (1½ oz) coconut
2 egg whites

Preheat the oven to 180°C (350°F/Gas 4). Grease and line a deep loaf tin. Cream the butter, sugar, lemon rind and vanilla. Add the egg yolks and beat well. Fold in the sifted flour alternately with the milk. Spoon half the mixture into the tin, then half of the chocaroon mixture. Cover with the remaining cake mixture and brush lightly with a little jam. Top with the remaining chocaroon mixture. Bake for 50 to 60 minutes.

Chocaroon Layers: Combine the sugar, cocoa and coconut. Beat the egg whites until stiff but not dry. Fold in the dry ingredients.

Fudge Bars

Makes 1 slab

60 g (2 oz) plain dark chocolate
60 g (2 oz) butter
3 eggs, beaten
1 cup (8 oz) sugar
1½ cups (6 oz) flour
½ teaspoon salt
1 teaspoon baking powder
½ cup (4 fl oz) milk
1 cup (4 oz) chopped walnuts

Melt the chocolate and pour over the butter. Mix well. Beat the eggs until thick and lemon coloured then add the sugar gradually, beating well after each addition. Combine the mixtures and add a little of the flour. Sift the remaining flour with the other dry ingredients and add alternately with the milk. Stir in the nuts. Pour into a greased Swiss roll tin and bake at 180°C (350°F/Gas 4) for 35 to 40 minutes. Ice with Chocolate Icing (*page 459*) while still warm.

Banana Caramel Cake

Makes 1 square cake

1 cup (8 oz) sugar
¼ cup (2 fl oz) water
125 g (4 oz) butter
2 eggs, separated
1 cup mashed banana
2½ cups (10 oz) self-raising flour
1 teaspoon bicarbonate of soda (baking soda)
pinch of salt

Preheat the oven to 180°C (350°F/Gas 4). Grease a 20 cm (8 inch) square cake tin and line with paper. Place half the sugar in a heavy pan and caramelise over a medium heat. Add the water and stir until the mixture has dissolved. Cool. Cream the butter and ¼ cup (2 oz) of the remaining sugar. Beat in the egg yolks and caramel. Add the mashed banana, then the sifted dry ingredients. Beat the egg whites until stiff. Beat in the remaining sugar to make a stiff meringue and fold into the cake mixture. Spoon into the prepared tin and bake for 40 to 45 minutes. Ice with Lemon Icing when cold (*page 459*).

Baking

Cheese Scones

Makes 12

2 cups (8 oz) self-raising flour
pinch of salt
1 tablespoon sugar
60 g (2 oz) butter, melted
2/3 cup (6 fl oz) milk

Cheese Topping
30 g (1 oz) softened butter
1/2 cup (2 oz) grated cheese
pinch of cayenne pepper
1/2 level teaspoon dry mustard

Sift the dry ingredients together. Add the melted butter and the milk and mix thoroughly. Cut with a small circular cutter and place on a greased oven slide. Place 3/4 teaspoon of the topping on each scone. Bake at 230°C (450°F/Gas 8) for 10 minutes.

Cheese Topping: Mix all the ingredients.

Banana Nut Bread

Makes 1 loaf

125 g (4 oz) butter
3/4 cup (6 oz) sugar
2 eggs, beaten
1 cup mashed ripe bananas
1 teaspoon lemon juice
2 cups (8 oz) self-raising flour
1/2 teaspoon bicarbonate of soda (baking soda)
1 cup (4 oz) chopped walnuts

Cream the butter and sugar together. Add the well beaten eggs. Press the bananas through a sieve and add the lemon juice. Blend with the creamed mixture. Sift the dry ingredients together and mix with the banana mixture. Add the nuts. Bake in a greased loaf pan at 160°C (325°F/Gas 3) for 1 to 1 1/4 hours.

Wheatgerm Biscuits

Makes 24

125 g (4 oz) butter
1/2 cup (4 oz) sugar
1 egg
2 cups (8 oz) flour
1/2 cup (1 3/4 oz) wheatgerm
2 teaspoons baking powder
1/2 teaspoon salt
1/4 cup (2 fl oz) milk
vanilla essence

Cream the butter and sugar. Add the egg. Sift the flour, wheatgerm, baking powder and salt together. Add the creamed mixture alternately with the milk and vanilla. Mix together to form a dough. Chill. Roll out 6 mm (1/4 inch) thick and cut into 5 cm (2 inch) squares. Prick with a fork, place on a greased tray and bake at 180°C (350°F/Gas 4) for 10 to 12 minutes.

Coffee Sponge

Makes 1 two-layer cake

90 g (3 oz) butter
3/4 cup (6 oz) sugar
3 tablespoons coffee essence
1/2 teaspoon vanilla essence
3 eggs, separated
1 cup (4 oz) self-raising flour
1/2 cup (2 oz) cornflour (cornstarch)
3 tablespoons milk

Preheat the oven to 200°C (400°F/Gas 6). Grease 2 sponge sandwich tins and line with waxed paper. Cream the butter, sugar, coffee essence and vanilla together. Beat in the egg yolks one at a time, then add the sifted flour and cornflour alternately with the stiffly beaten egg white. Mix well and add the milk. Spoon into the sandwich tins. Bake for 20 to 25 minutes. Ice and fill with coffee icing. Decorate with walnuts and cherries.

Cinnamon Apple Slice

Makes 1 slab

2 medium-sized Granny Smith apples, peeled
2 cups (8 oz) self-raising flour
2 teaspoons cinnamon
3/4 cup (6 oz) sugar
1 cup (3 oz) coconut
1 cup (6 oz) sultanas
1 cup (5 oz) currants
250 g (8 oz) margarine
2 tablespoons golden syrup
2 eggs

Preheat the oven to 180°C (350°F/Gas 4). Peel and coarsely grate the apples into a large bowl. Add the sifted flour and cinnamon, sugar, coconut and fruit.

Melt the margarine and golden syrup. Add to the bowl with the lightly beaten eggs. Mix well. Spread in a greased 30 x 25 cm (12 x 10 inch) Swiss roll tin. Bake for 45 minutes, or until cooked. Cool in the pan.

Opposite: *Coffee Sponge*

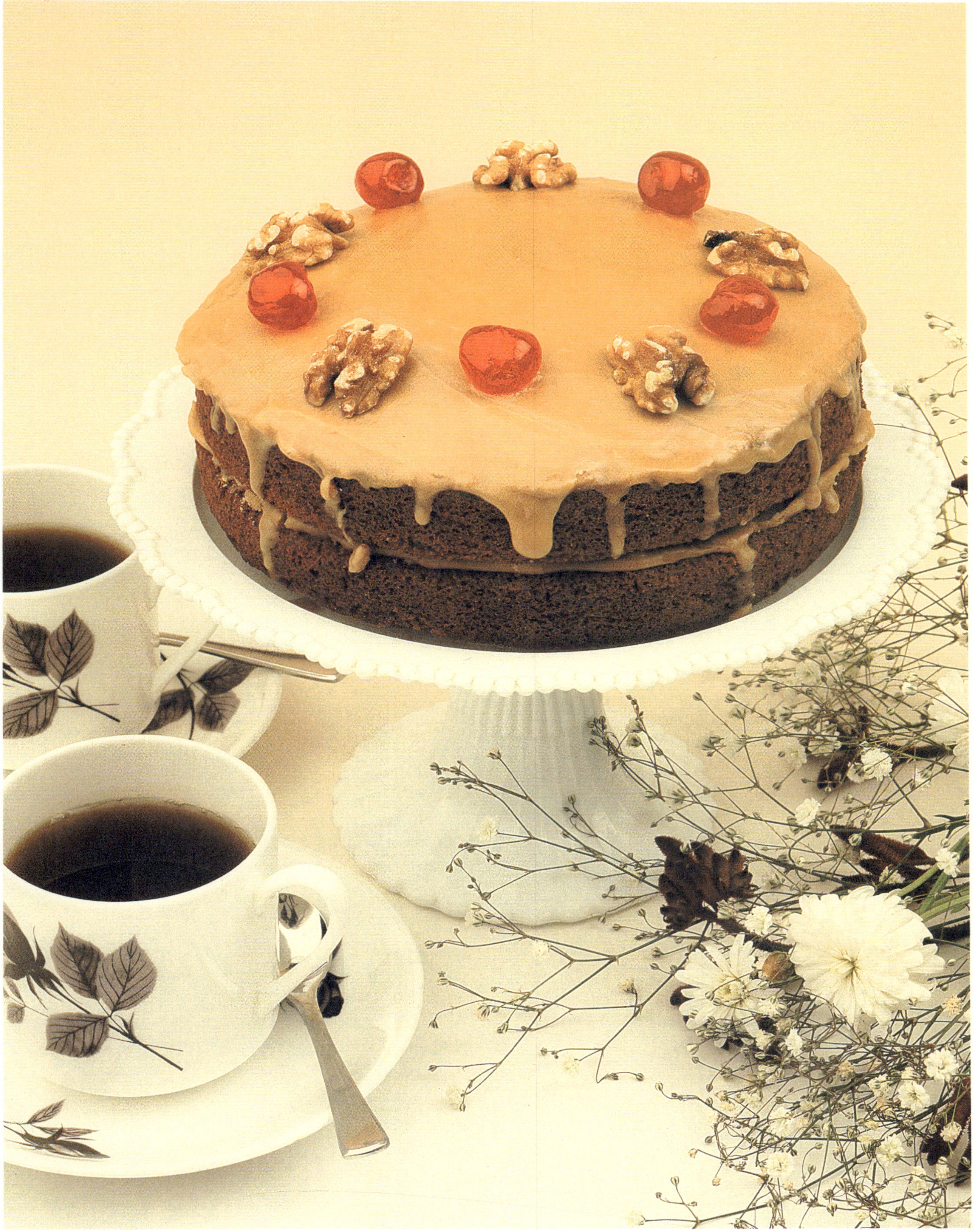

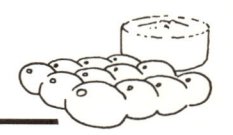

Baking

Danish Apple Coconut Coffee Cake

Makes 1 cake

185 g (6 oz) butter
1 cup (8 oz) plus 2 tablespoons sugar
3 eggs
2½ cups (10 oz) self-raising flour
¼ cup (2 fl oz) milk
1¼ cups (3¾ oz) coconut
2 large cooking apples, peeled, cored and diced
¼ cup (1 oz) sliced almonds

Preheat the oven to 180°C (350°F/Gas 4). Grease a 23 x 30 cm (9 x 12 inch) slab tin and line the bottom with paper. Cream the butter and 1 cup (8 oz) of the sugar until smooth. Stir in the eggs, blending very well. Sift the flour and add to the creamed mixture alternately with the milk. Blend until smooth. Stir in the coconut then fold in the apples. Pour into the prepared tin. Sprinkle with the almonds then the remaining sugar. Serve warm.

Boiled Fruit Cake

Makes 1 cake

1 teaspoon cinnamon
1¼ cups (6 oz) chopped dates
¼ cup (1½ oz) chopped crystallised ginger
315 g (10 oz) dried mixed fruit
1 x 470 g (15 oz) can crushed pineapple
1 cup (8 oz) sugar
125 g (4 oz) butter or margarine
1 teaspoon bicarbonate of soda (baking soda)
1 cup (4 oz) flour
1¼ cups (5 oz) self-raising flour
1 egg
1 tablespoon rum

Preheat the oven to 180°C (350°F/Gas 4). Grease and line a deep 20 cm (8 inch) square tin. Boil the cinnamon, dates, ginger, mixed fruit, pineapple, sugar and butter together for 10 minutes. Allow to cool. Sift the bicarbonate of soda and flours together. Add the egg and the rum to the boiled mixture, then add the dry ingredients and mix thoroughly. Bake for 1 to 1½ hours or until done.

Cinnamon-Sugar Muffins

Makes 12

1 quantity plain muffin batter *(next)*
1½ teaspoons cinnamon
3 tablespoons sugar

Make the plain muffins. Mix the cinnamon and sugar together and sprinkle on top of each muffin. Bake as directed above.

Plain Muffins

Makes 12

250 g (8 oz) self-raising flour
½ teaspoon salt
¼ cup (2 oz) sugar
90 g (3 oz) butter, melted
1 cup (8 fl oz) milk
1 egg

Preheat the oven to 200°C (400°F/Gas 6). Grease two trays of deep muffin tins. Sift the flour and salt. Add the sugar and mix well. Add the melted butter to the milk and beat in the egg.
Make a well in the centre of the dry ingredients and pour in the liquid ingredients all at once. Stir quickly with a fork, just until the dry ingredients are moistened. The batter should be lumpy. Three quarters fill each muffin tin and bake for 20 to 25 minutes. Serve hot.

Bran Muffins

Makes 18

1 cup (2 oz) bran
1 cup (4 oz) self-raising flour
½ teaspoon salt
2 tablespoons golden syrup
30 g (1 oz) butter
¾ cup (6 fl oz) milk
1 egg
¼ cup (1 oz) raisins, optional

Mix the dry ingredients together. Put the golden syrup, butter and milk in a saucepan and heat until the butter has melted. Beat the egg until thick and foamy, then add to the milk mixture. Add the liquid to the dry ingredients. Stir quickly but do not beat. Stir in the raisins, if desired. Bake in greased muffin tins at 200°C (400°F/Gas 6) for 15 to 20 minutes.

Apricot Muffins

Makes 12

2 teaspoons grated orange rind
½ teaspoon bicarbonate of soda (baking soda)
½ cup (2 oz) finely chopped dried apricots
1 quantity plain muffin batter *(above)*

Add the orange rind, soda and apricots to the muffin batter. Mix and bake as directed above.

Lemon Coconut Pie

Serves 6

Pastry
1¼ cups (5 oz) flour
pinch of salt
½ level teaspoon baking powder
90 g (3 oz) margarine
cold water
1 teaspoon lemon juice
⅓ cup (1 oz) desiccated coconut

Filling
1 level tablespoon flour
2 level tablespoons cornflour (cornstarch)
⅞ cup (7 oz) sugar
1 cup (8 fl oz) hot water
grated rind of 1 lemon
2 egg yolks
15 g (½ oz) butter
½ cup (4 fl oz) lemon juice

Meringue
2 egg whites
4 level tablespoons sugar
½ cup (1½ oz) desiccated coconut
1 teaspoon lemon juice

Pastry: Sift the flour, salt and baking powder. Rub in the margarine lightly until the mixture resembles coarse breadcrumbs. Mix to a dry dough with water and lemon juice. Knead until smooth on a floured board. Put between two sheets of greaseproof paper and roll out until half the size required for a 23 cm (9 inch) pie plate. Peel off the paper. Sprinkle the dough with half the coconut. Replace the paper, reverse the pastry and repeat with the remaining coconut on the other side. Roll to the size of the dish. Line the dish with the pastry and pinch the edges. Prick the pastry with a fork. Bake at 190°C (375°F/Gas 5) for 15 minutes. Cool.

Filling: Blend both flours with the sugar, hot water and lemon rind. Stir over heat until thickened. Remove from the heat, add the beaten egg yolks and butter. Stir over heat then add the lemon juice and cool. Pour into the pastry case.

Meringue: Beat the egg whites stiffly, gradually add the sugar and beat well. Fold in the coconut and lemon juice. Pile on top of the filling. Bake at 110°C (225°F/Gas 2) until meringue turns pale golden brown.

Apricot Nut Loaf

Makes 1 cake

¾ cup (3 oz) chopped dried apricots
1¼ cups (10 fl oz) milk
90 g (3 oz) butter
2¾ cups (11 oz) self-raising flour
¼ teaspoon salt
½ cup (4 oz) sugar
1 egg
½ cup (2 oz) chopped walnuts

Preheat the oven to 180°C (350°F/Gas 4). Grease and line a deep loaf tin.

Soak the apricots in the milk for 30 minutes. Rub the butter into the flour and salt. Add the sugar and the egg, then the soaked apricots. Stir through the walnuts. Pour into the prepared tin and bake for 50 to 60 minutes or until a skewer comes out clean. Do not cut until the following day.

Orange Macaroon Tartlets

Makes 30

Pastry
1¾ cups (7 oz) flour
½ cup (3 oz) icing (confectioners') sugar
1½ teaspoons baking powder
125 g (4 oz) butter or margarine
2 egg yolks

Filling
3 oranges
soft brown sugar

Topping
2 egg whites
½ cup (4 oz) sugar
¾ cup (2½ oz) coconut

Pastry: Sift the flour, icing sugar and baking powder together. Rub the butter through lightly. Make a well in the centre, add the egg yolks and mix thoroughly to a soft dough. Chill for 30 minutes. Roll out 3 mm (⅛ inch) thick on a lightly floured board. Cut into rounds and fit into greased patty tins.

Filling: Peel the oranges, discard the pith and cut into slices 6 mm (¼ inch) thick. Cut each slice into small pieces. Place several small pieces of orange in each patty case to cover the bottom. Sprinkle with a little brown sugar.

Topping: Beat the egg whites until stiff. Beat in the sugar until the mixture forms peaks. Fold in the coconut. Spoon 1 level tablespoon onto the top of each orange tartlet. Bake at 180°C (350°F/Gas 4) for 20 to 25 minutes.

Baking

Kringle

Makes 1

- 30 g (1 oz) compressed yeast
- ¼ cup (2 fl oz) warm water
- ¾ cup (6 fl oz) evaporated milk
- 1 teaspoon salt
- 3 tablespoons sugar
- 1 egg, beaten
- 500 g (1 lb) flour, sifted
- 185 g (6 oz) butter or margarine, melted
- milk
- caster (powdered) sugar
- flaked almonds, optional

Filling
- 2 tablespoons cornflour (cornstarch)
- 2 tablespoons sugar
- 1 teaspoon vanilla essence
- ⅓ cup (2½ fl oz) evaporated milk
- ¼ cup (2 fl oz) water
- 2 tablespoons sultanas, soaked in 2 tablespoons sweet sherry

Mix the yeast with the water. Add the milk, salt, sugar, egg and ½ cup (2 oz) of the flour. Beat until smooth. Melt one third of the butter and stir into the milk mixture. Cut the remaining butter into the remaining flour, until butter particles are the size of a pea. Pour the yeast batter over the top and carefully turn the mixture over with a spatula until all the flour is moistened. Place in a covered bowl and refrigerate for 30 minutes. Roll and fold 3 times.

Roll the dough into a long strip 10 x 60 cm (4 x 24 inch) and spread with the filling mixture. Sprinkle with the sultanas. Roll up as for a Swiss roll, starting with the long side. Moisten the edges and seal. Place seam side down on a greased oven tray, bending into a pretzel shape. Cover with a clean cloth and leave in a warm place for 30 minutes. Glaze with milk, sprinkle with caster sugar, and flaked almonds if desired. Bake at 190° (375°F/Gas 5) for 20 minutes.

Filling: Mix all ingredients together except the sultanas. Bring to the boil, stirring constantly. Add the sherry, drained from the sultanas, and mix well.

Coconut Apricot Pie

Serves 6 – 8

- ⅓ Kringle dough mixture (see above)
- 3 tablespoons coconut
- 1 x 500 g (1 lb) can pie apricots
- 2 tablespoons soft brown sugar

Roll the dough to fit a 23 cm (9 inch) sponge tin and save the trimmings. Sprinkle the base of the dough with coconut, then spread with the apricots. Sprinkle the top with the brown sugar. Roll the trimmings into long strips to make a lattice top. Cover and leave in a warm place for 20 minutes. Bake at 190°C (375°F/Gas 5) for 25 to 30 minutes.

French Apple Pie

Serves 6 – 8

- ⅓ Kringle dough mixture (see above)
- 1 x 500 g (1 lb) can pie apples
- ½ teaspoon ground cloves
- 1 cup (8 fl oz) sour cream
- 1 teaspoon vanilla essence
- 1 tablespoon sugar
- 1 egg, beaten

Roll the dough out to fit a 23 cm (9 inch) sponge tin. Spread the apples on the dough in the tin and sprinkle with the cloves. Cover and leave in a warm place for 30 minutes. Bake at 190°C (375°F/Gas 5) for 20 minutes. Remove from the oven and pour over the sour cream, mixed with the vanilla, sugar and beaten egg. Bake for a further 10 minutes. Cool.

Apricot Cream Pie

Serves 6 – 8

- ⅓ Kringle dough mixture (see above)
- 1 x 500 g (1 lb) can apricot halves, drained

Topping
- 1 egg white
- 2 tablespoons sugar
- 1 cup (8 fl oz) sour cream
- 1 teaspoon vanilla essence

Roll the dough to fit a greased flan ring. Spread the apricots on the base of the flan. Cover and leave in a warm place for 20 minutes. Bake at 190°C (375°F/Gas 5) for 20 minutes. Remove from the oven. Beat the egg white until stiff. Beat in the sugar, then fold the meringue mixture into the sour cream and vanilla. Pour onto the apricots. Bake for a further 10 minutes. Cool.

Quick Sweet Pastries

Make these crisp, sweet pastries with the dough trimmings from the Kringle and store in an airtight tin. Serve with fruit and cream or ice cream, or other light desserts.

Roll the trimmings into a square 3 mm (⅛ inch) thick. Sprinkle the surface of the dough with sugar and press down lightly with a rolling pin. Roll the dough to the centre from opposite sides and pinch the edges of the rolls together in the centre. Cut into 6 mm (¼ inch) slices. Dip one cut side in vanilla sugar and place on a greased oven slide, sugar side up. Leave in a warm place for 30 minutes. Bake for 10 to 15 minutes at 180°C (350°F/Gas 4) until golden.

Note: Dough may be kept for up to 4 days covered in the refrigerator.

Blueberry Muffins

Makes 12

- 2 x 250 g (8 oz) punnets blueberries
- 1¾ cups (7 oz) flour
- 2½ teaspoons baking powder
- ½ cup (4 oz) sugar
- 1 egg
- ¾ cup (6 fl oz) vegetable oil
- 60 g (2 oz) pecans, finely chopped, optional

Reserve 12 whole berries and cut the remainder in half. Sift the flour and baking powder into a mixing bowl. Stir in the sugar and make a well in the centre. Beat the egg, mix with the milk and vegetable oil. Pour into the centre of the bowl, add the halved blueberries and pecans and stir with a fork until the mixture forms a soft consistency. Spoon the mixture into 12 well-greased deep muffin pans. Place a whole blueberry on top of each muffin.

Bake in a moderate oven at 180°C (350°F/Gas 4) for 20 to 25 minutes or until done. Remove the muffins from the pans and cool slightly. Serve warm, split and filled with home-made blueberry jam if liked.

Banana and Sultana Cake

Makes 1 cake

- 90 g (3 oz) butter
- ½ cup (4 oz) raw sugar
- 1 egg
- 2 ripe bananas, mashed
- ½ cup (3 oz) sultanas
- 1½ cups (6 oz) wholemeal self-raising flour
- ½ cup (4 fl oz) milk
- ½ teaspoon ground nutmeg
- 90 g (3 oz) pecan nuts, chopped
- 1 teaspoon ground cinnamon mixed with 1 tablespoon sugar

Cream the butter and sugar. Add the egg and mix thoroughly. Fold in the bananas and sultanas. Add the flour, milk, nutmeg and pecan nuts. Mix by hand until combined.

Spoon the mixture evenly into a greased loaf tin. Sprinkle with the cinnamon sugar.

Bake in a moderate oven at 180°C (350°F/Gas 4) for 45 to 60 minutes or until cooked. Serve with butter curls for afternoon tea.

Banana and Sultana Cake

Baking

Orange Raisin Plait

Makes 1 cake

- ¼ cup (2 fl oz) boiling water
- 1 cup (5 oz) raisins
- ⅓ cup (2 oz) chopped mixed peel
- 125 g (4 oz) butter or margarine
- ⅓ cup (2 oz) plus 1 tablespoon soft brown sugar
- 1 egg
- ½ cup (4 fl oz) concentrated orange juice (undiluted) or ½ cup (4 fl oz) fresh orange juice and grated rind of 1 orange
- 3½ cups (14 oz) self-raising flour
- milk
- 1 tablespoon chopped candied orange peel, optional

Pour the boiling water over the raisins and mixed peel and let stand for 10 minutes. Cream the butter and the ⅓ cup (2 oz) sugar. Add the egg and beat well. Add the concentrated or fresh orange juice and rind. Add the raisin mixture, then the flour, to make a dough. Knead very lightly and divide the mixture into 3 equal pieces. Form each portion into a roll 2.5 cm (1 inch) in diameter. Plait the three strands together and place on a greased oven tray. Brush the surface of the plait with a little milk and sprinkle with the tablespoon of brown sugar and, if desired, 1 tablespoon of chopped candied orange peel. Bake at 230°C (450°F/Gas 8) for 15 minutes. Reduce the heat to 180°C (350°F/Gas 4) and bake for a further 15 minutes.

Sicillia Cake

Serves 8

- 1 x 345 g (11 oz) packet chocolate cake mix
- 1 cup (6 oz) chopped glacé fruit
- 2 tablespoons rum
- 1 ¼ cups (10 fl oz) cream
- ¼ cup (2 oz) caster (powdered) sugar
- chopped almonds

Chocolate Cream
- 1¼ cups (10 fl oz) cream
- 2 tablespoons dark cocoa, sifted
- 1 tablespoon caster (powdered) sugar

Make the cake as directed on packet and cook in an oblong cake pan. Cool thoroughly. Soak the fruit in rum for 30 minutes. Whip the cream and sugar until firm. Stir in the fruit and rum. Slice the cake horizontally into 4. Sandwich together with fruit cream. Wrap the cake in foil and chill several hours or overnight. Remove the foil. Spread the Chocolate Cream over the sides and top of cake. If desired, press the chopped almonds into the sides with a spatula and decorate with chocolate curls or extra glacé fruit.

Chocolate Cream: Beat all the ingredients together to a spreading consistency.

Orange Gâteau

Makes 4 thin layers

- 3 large eggs, at room temperature
- ½ cup (4 oz) caster (powdered) sugar
- ¾ cup (3 oz) flour
- 2 tablespoons cornflour (cornstarch)
- ⅓ cup (2 ½ fl oz) melted butter or margarine
- 4 teaspoons rum
- ⅔ cup (5 fl oz) cream, whipped
- extra grated orange rind or grated chocolate

Filling
- ½ cup (4 oz) sugar
- 2 tablespoons cornflour (cornstarch)
- ½ cup (4 fl oz) water
- 1 egg, beaten
- 2 tablespoons orange juice
- 2 teaspoons grated orange rind
- knob of butter

Line the bottoms of two 20 cm (8 inch) cake tins and grease the sides of the tins. Beat the eggs and sugar together on fast speed in an electric mixer until very thick. Spoon the sifted dry ingredients onto the eggs and fold in by hand. Add the melted butter and fold in very gently with a figure-of-eight movement. Pour into the prepared tins and bake at 190°C (375°F/Gas 5) for 20 minutes or until the centre feels springy. Remove from the oven and let stand in the tins for 10 to 15 minutes, then turn out onto a rack to cool. When completely cool, split the cakes through the centre and lightly sprinkle the cut surfaces with the rum.

Filling: Mix the sugar and cornflour together in a saucepan. Add the water gradually. Cook, stirring, until boiling. Boil for 1 minute. Remove from the heat and stir in the beaten egg. Return to the saucepan and cook a further 1 minute. Remove from the heat and stir in the juice, rind and butter. Cool completely.

Spread the mixture between the layers of cake. Spread the top of the cake with whipped cream and sprinkle with orange rind or grated chocolate. Chill before serving.

Sour Cream Scones

Makes 14 - 16

- ½ cup (2 oz) self-raising flour
- ½ cup (2 oz) wholemeal self-raising flour
- 1 cup (4 oz) grated Australian cheese
- ½ cup (4 fl oz) sour cream
- 2 tablespoons milk

Combine the flours. Add the cheese and sour cream. Mix in the milk to form a soft dough. Knead lightly and quickly on a floured board. Pat out into a rectangle about 1 cm (½ inch) thick. Cut the scone dough into 5 cm (2 inch) squares. Bake at 230°C (450°F/Gas 8) for about 8 to 10 minutes.

Orange Date Shortcake

Makes 1 slab

Make the filling first for these well-flavoured bars. Serve with tea or coffee, or pack with school lunches.

Filling
- 3 cups (15 oz) finely chopped dates
- ¼ cup (2 oz) sugar
- ¾ cup (6 fl oz) water
- juice of 2 oranges
- grated rind of 1 orange

Shortcake
- 185 g (6 oz) butter or margarine
- 1 cup (6 oz) soft brown sugar, lightly packed
- 2 cups (8 oz) flour
- 1½ cups (4½ oz) quick cooking rolled oats
- ½ teaspoon bicarbonate of soda (baking soda)
- grated rind of 1 orange

Filling: Mix the dates, sugar and water together in a saucepan. Bring to the boil, reduce the heat and simmer for 10 minutes, stirring occasionally. Add the orange juice and rind. Cool.

Shortcake: Cream the butter and sugar together. Combine the dry ingredients and orange rind, then add to the creamed mixture. Press half into a greased lamington tin and spread with the cooled date filling. Crumble the remaining shortcake over the dates. Press lightly. Bake at 200°C (400°F/Gas 6) for 25 to 30 minutes or until golden. Cut into bars while warm.

Quick Cheese Loaf

Makes 1 loaf

This quick, tasty bread makes a welcome change from rich foods. It will keep well for some days in an airtight tin. Good for picnics, barbecues, or to serve at morning tea.

- 90 g (3 oz) butter or margarine
- 2½ cups (10 oz) self-raising flour
- 1 teaspoon baking powder
- ½ teaspoon salt
- ½ teaspoon dry mustard pepper
- 1½ cups (6 oz) finely grated cheese
- 1¼ cups (10 fl oz) milk
- 1 egg

Melt the butter and cool slightly. Line the bottom of a greased loaf tin with greased paper. Sift the dry ingredients into a bowl and stir in the cheese. Add the melted butter to the milk and egg. Make a well in the centre of the dry ingredients, pour in the milk mixture and mix to a very soft dough adding a little more milk if necessary. Turn into the prepared loaf tin, spread evenly and bake at 190°C (375°F/Gas 5) for 1¼ hours.

Herb Onion Bread

Makes 2 loaves

- 45 g (1½ oz) compressed yeast
- ½ cup (4 fl oz) lukewarm water
- 3 cups (12 oz) flour
- 3 cups (12 oz) wholemeal flour
- 1 tablespoon sugar
- 2 teaspoons salt
- ½ teaspoon freshly ground black pepper
- 2 tablespoons mixed herbs
- 2 tablespoons onion flakes
- 1 egg
- ½ cup (4 fl oz) evaporated milk
- 125 g (4 oz) butter or margarine, melted and cooled
- semolina

Crumble the yeast into ¼ cup (2 fl oz) of the lukewarm water and set aside. Combine the dry ingredients in a large mixing bowl. Beat the egg with the evaporated milk and remaining warm water, then add the butter. Make a well in the centre of the dry ingredients, add the egg mixture and yeast and mix well to make a soft dough. Add extra lukewarm water if necessary. Turn onto a lightly floured board and knead thoroughly until the dough is smooth and satiny.

Divide the dough in half. Roll out each piece to a rectangle approximately 15 x 30 cm (6 x 12 inch), then roll up each rectangle to make long, thin loaves. Make four or five slashes with a sharp knife across the top of each loaf. Cover a cake rack with a clean cloth and dust lightly with semolina. Place the loaves on the rack, cover with a piece of plastic wrap and a cloth and stand in a warm place until the loaves have doubled in bulk, about 30 minutes. Lift the loaves carefully onto hot oven trays which have been lightly dusted with semolina. Bake at 230°C (450°F/Gas 8) for 25 to 30 minutes. The loaves should sound hollow when tapped on the bottom.

Apricot Tea Cake

Serves 8 - 10

- 100 g (3 ½ oz) butter
- ¾ cup (6 oz) caster (powdered) sugar
- 1 egg
- ½ teaspoon vanilla essence
- 2 cups (8 oz) self-raising flour
- ¾ cup (6 fl oz) buttermilk
- 1 x 425 g (13 ½ oz) can apricots, drained

Preheat the oven to 180°C (350°F/Gas 4). Grease a 20 cm (8 inch) sandwich tin and line the base with paper. Cream butter and sugar and beat in the egg and vanilla essence. Mix in the sifted flour and the buttermilk alternately. Mix well and spoon the mixture into the tin. Arrange the apricots on top in a pattern radiating from the centre. Bake for 35 to 40 minutes. Serve warm with butter.

Baking

Cherry Ripe Bars

Makes 24

Biscuit Base
30 g (1 oz) butter
¼ cup (2 oz) sugar
2 egg yolks
a few drops of vanilla essence
½ cup (2 oz) flour
½ cup (2 oz) self-raising flour

Topping
2 egg whites
½ cup (2 oz) sugar
125 g (4 oz) chopped glacé cherries
1 ½ cups (4½ oz) desiccated coconut
60 g (2 oz) grated chocolate

Biscuit Base: Cream butter and sugar, add egg yolks and vanilla essence. Fold through the sifted flours. Turn onto a board, roll light or press out with your fingers to line the base of an 18 cm x 28 cm (7 x 11 inch) shallow tin.

Topping: Whip the egg whites until stiff, beating in the sugar gradually. Fold through the cherries and coconut and spoon over the base. Mark in squares with a sharp knife. Bake in moderately hot oven, 190°C (375°F/Gas 5), for 10 minutes then reduce the temperature to 160°C (325°F/Gas 3) for a further 10 to 15 minutes. Remove and sprinkle with chocolate. Cool and cut into squares.

Carrot and Zucchini Cake

Serves 8 - 10

2½ cups (10 oz) wholemeal self-raising flour
½ teaspoon cinnamon
125 g (4 oz) butter
¾ cup (6 oz) sugar
2 eggs
½ cup (4 fl oz) natural yoghurt
1 cup firmly packed grated carrot
1 cup firmly packed grated zucchini (courgette)
¼ cup (1 oz) roughly chopped walnuts
¼ cup sunflower seeds
extra sunflower seeds

Sift the flour and cinnamon together adding the coarser particles left in the sieve. Cream the butter and sugar until light and fluffy. Add the eggs, one at a time, beating between each addition. Fold in the yoghurt, carrot, zucchini, walnuts, ¼ cup sunflower seeds and then the flour. Spoon into a greased 20 cm (8 inch) square cake pan. Sprinkle with extra sunflower seeds. Bake at 190°C (375°F/Gas 5) for 1 hour 10 minutes. Serve hot or cold spread generously with butter.

Lemon Tarts

Makes 12

Pastry
100 g (3 ½ oz) butter
1½ cups (6 oz) flour
¼ cup (2 oz) caster (powdered) sugar
1 egg yolk
1-2 tablespoons water

Lemon Butter
125 g (4 oz) butter
1 cup (8 oz) sugar
grated rind of 3 lemons
½ cup (4 fl oz) lemon juice
4 eggs, lightly beaten

Pastry: Rub the butter into the flour until resembling fine breadcrumbs. Stir in the sugar. Mix the egg yolk with the water, add to the flour. Mix together and knead lightly to form a smooth ball. Cover with plastic wrap and refrigerate for 30 minutes. Roll out on a floured board. Cut into circles to line twelve 8 cm (3 inch) fluted tartlet tins. Fill with baking beans or rice and bake blind at 180°C (350°F/Gas 4) for 20 to 25 minutes. Remove the baking beans and paper and cook for 5 minutes until light brown. Remove from the tins, cool. Fill with Lemon Butter and serve with whipped cream.

Lemon Butter: Melt the butter over a double boiler. Add the sugar and stir until dissolved. Mix in the lemon rind and juice. Stir in the eggs and continue stirring until thick enough to coat a wooden spoon, about 5 minutes. Remove from the heat. Use when cold.

Cheddar Wheat Round

Serves 8

2 cups (8 oz) wholemeal self-raising flour
2 teaspoons dry mustard
¼ teaspoon black pepper
½ teaspoon mixed herbs
30 g (1 oz) butter
1 tablespoon finely chopped onion
¾ cup (6 fl oz) milk, approximately
½ cup (2 oz) grated Australian cheese
sesame or poppy seeds

Combine the flour and seasonings. Rub in the butter with your fingertips. Add the onion. Add the milk and mix to a soft dough. Knead lightly on a floured board, shaping into a ball. Place on a greased baking tray. Press out with the palm of the hand to an 18 cm (7 inch) circle. Mark into 8 wedges by pressing the back of a knife halfway through the dough. Sprinkle with cheese and sesame seeds. Bake at 230°C (450°F/Gas 8) for 25 minutes. Lift onto a rack and break into wedges. Split and spread with butter. Serve hot or cold.

Opposite: *Lemon Tarts*

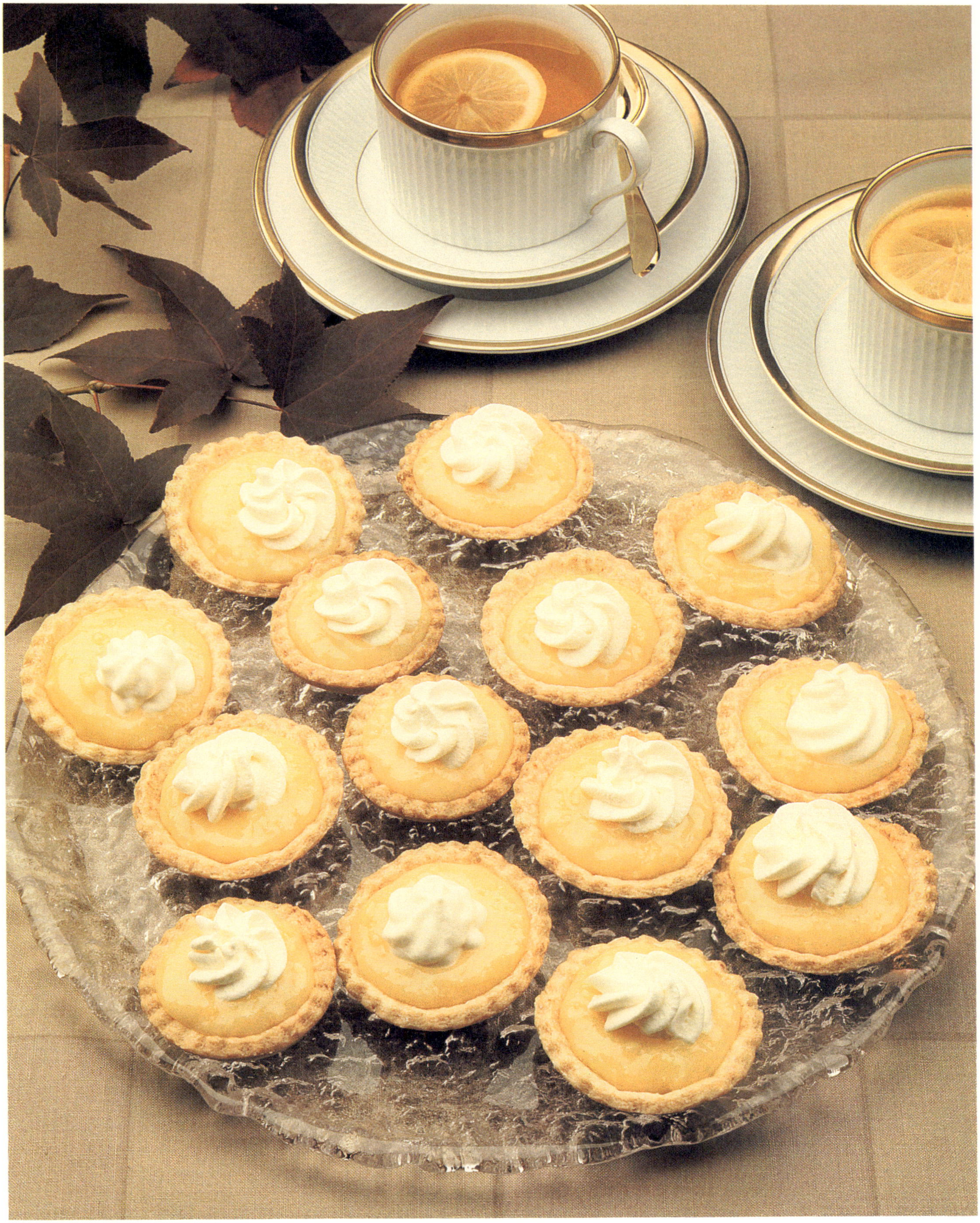

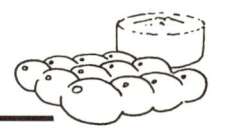

Baking

Chelsea Butter Bun

Serves 6 - 8

60 g (2 oz) butter
3 cups (12 oz) self-
    raising flour, sifted

1 cup (8 fl oz) milk

Filling
60 g (2 oz) butter
¼ cup (1 ½ oz) soft brown
    sugar
½ cup (3 oz) sultanas
¼ cup (1 oz) currants
cinnamon

Rub the butter into the flour with fingertips. Add the milk and mix to a soft dough with a knife. Turn onto a lightly floured board and knead lightly. Roll the dough into an oblong shape 6 mm (¼ inch) thick. Spread with the creamed butter and brown sugar and sprinkle with fruit and cinnamon. Moisten the dough edge and roll lengthwise. Cut the roll into 2 cm (¾ inch) slices and pack into a greased 20 cm (8 inch) cake tin. Brush lightly with milk. Bake in a hot oven, 220°C (425°F/Gas 7), for 15 to 20 minutes or until golden.

Angel Cake

Serves 6 - 8

10 egg whites
1 ½ cups (11 oz) caster
    (powdered) sugar
⅓ cup (1 ½ oz) flour
2 ½ tablespoons cornflour
    (cornstarch)

pinch of bicarbonate of
    soda (baking soda)
¼ teaspoon citric acid

Preheat the oven to 180°C (350°F/Gas 4). Coat the inside of a round or ring tin with water. Do NOT grease or line. Whip the egg whites until thick. While continuing to beat add the caster sugar slowly to form stiff peaks.

Sift together the remaining ingredients and blend into the egg whites until just mixed. Spoon into the wetted tin and bake for 45 minutes, or until a fork inserted in the centre comes out clean. When cooked invert onto a cooling rack and allow to cool. Do NOT attempt to remove tin. Once cool remove the tin and invert the cake onto its right side.

Serve plain or a a dessert with ice cream, cream and fresh fruits or fruit toppings.

Carrot and Walnut Cake

Serves 6 - 8

1 ¾ cups (7 oz) wholemeal
    self-raising flour
1 teaspoon baking powder
1 cup (4 oz) crushed walnuts
300 g (9 ½ oz) carrots,
    grated

1 apple, grated
1 ⅓ cups (7 oz) soft brown
    sugar
4 eggs
¾ cup (6 fl oz) vegetable oil

Frosting
225 g (7 oz) cream cheese
2 teaspoons honey
2 teaspoons icing
    (confectioner's) sugar
1 teaspoon lemon juice

Preheat the oven to 180°C (350°F/Gas 4). Grease and line a 23 cm (9 inch) round deep cake tin. Place all the ingredients in a mixing bowl and beat until well blended. Pour into the tin and bake for approximately 1 hour. When cold, top with frosting.

Frosting: Beat all the ingredients together until smooth.

American Fruit Cake

Serves 14 - 16

⅔ cup (4 oz) pitted prunes,
    halved
1 ⅔ cups (8 oz) currants
1 ½ cups (8 oz) sultanas
¼ cup (2 fl oz) sherry
¼ cup (2 fl oz) brandy
¾ cup (4 oz) glacé cherries
¾ cup (4 oz) pitted dates,
    halved
¾ cup (4 oz) chopped
    mixed peel
1 cup (4 oz) walnut pieces
1 ¾ cups (7 oz) self-raising
    flour
1 tablespoon cocoa

1 teaspoon cinnamon
½ teaspoon each mixed
    spice and nutmeg
⅛ teaspoon each
    bicarbonate of soda
    (baking soda) and salt
1 tablespoon instant coffee
    powder
¼ cup (2 fl oz) hot water
125 g (4 oz) butter or
    margarine, softened
1 cup (4 oz) lightly packed
    soft brown sugar
3 eggs
¼ cup (3 oz) plum jam

Preheat the oven to 150°C (300°F/Gas 2). Combine the first five ingredients in a bowl and allow to stand overnight, covered. Stir in the next four ingredients and 1 cup (4 oz) of the flour. Mix well. Sift the remaining flour with the cocoa, spices, soda and salt. Dissolve the coffee in the hot water.

Cream the butter and sugar until fluffy. Then add the eggs one at a time and beat well. Mix in the flour alternately with the coffee. Add the marinated fruit mixture and all remaining ingredients. Mix well. Turn the cake into a greased deep 25 cm (10 inch) round or 23 cm (9 inch) square cake tin. Bake until firm, approximately 2 ½ hours. Cool completely and store in an airtight container.

Almond Honey Cake

Serves 6 - 8

185 g (6 oz) butter
¾ cup (6 oz) caster (powdered) sugar
4 tablespoons honey
3 eggs
1 ½ cups (6 oz) self-raising flour
1 teaspoon cinnamon
1 teaspoon mixed spice
1 tablespoon finely grated lemon peel
2 tablespoons slivered almonds

Glaze
60 g (2 oz) butter
2 ½ tablespoons honey
extra almonds

Preheat the oven to 180°C (350°F/Gas 4). Cream the butter, sugar and honey until light and fluffy. Beat in the eggs one at a time. Sift together the flour, spices and lemon peel and fold into the creamed mixture. Spoon the mixture into a greased and lined 25 x 12 cm (10 x 5 inch) loaf tin and sprinkle the top with slivered almonds. Bake for 50 to 60 minutes and turn onto a cooling rack when done.

Glaze: Melt the butter and honey and brush over the top of the cooled cake. Decorate with extra almonds.

Golden Fruit Cake

Serves 14 - 16

1 ⅓ cups (7 oz) halved glacé cherries
⅓ cup (2 oz) mixed peel
⅔ cup (3 ½ oz) sultanas
½ cup (3 oz) chopped glacé pineapple
½ cup (2 oz) chopped glacé apricots
½ cup (2 oz) coarsely chopped, blanched almonds
1 cup (4 oz) flour
1 teaspoon baking powder
¼ teaspoon salt
250 g (8 oz) butter
1 tablespoon grated orange peel
1 tablespoon grated lemon peel
1 cup (7 oz) caster (powdered) sugar
5 eggs
¼ cup (2 fl oz) sweet sherry

Preheat the oven to 180°C (350°F/Gas 4). Toss the fruits and almonds in ¼ cup (1 oz) of the flour. Sift the remaining flour, baking powder and salt. Beat the butter and grated peel, gradually adding the sugar until creamy and light. Beat in the eggs, one at a time. Stir in the flour alternately with the sherry. Fold in the fruit-nut mixture.

Turn into a lined, deep 20 cm (8 inch) square tin. Bake until firm, 1 ½ to 1 ¾ hours. Cool slightly, turn out of tin and cool completely. Store in an airtight container.

Plain Sponge

Serves 8 - 10

4 medium-sized eggs
¾ cup (6 oz) caster (powdered) sugar
⅔ cup (2 ½ oz) flour
⅓ cup (1 ½ oz) cornflour (cornstarch)
1 teaspoon baking powder
whipped cream

Preheat the oven to 200°C (400°F/Gas 6). Beat the eggs until foamy, about 5 to 8 minutes on medium-high speed. Gradually beat in the sugar until thick and creamy. Sift all the dry ingredients together to thoroughly blend. Fold the dry ingredients into the egg mixture with a metal spoon or spatula. This must be done lightly and quickly but make sure the flour is totally mixed.

Pour the mixture into two well-greased and lined 20 cm (8 inch) round sponge tins. Bake for 15 to 20 minutes. To test if the sponge is done, check that it has shrunk away from the sides of the tin, or that the top springs back after pressing lightly. When cooked, immediately invert the sponges onto a rack covered with a tea towel. This stops wire marks on top of the sponge. When completely cold, spread one cake with whipped cream or your favourite filling, and place the second sponge on top. Ice, or decorate with whipped cream or icing (confectioners') sugar sprinkled through a sieve.

Swiss Roll

Serves 6 - 8

2 medium-sized eggs
½ cup (4 oz) caster (powdered) sugar
½ cup (2 oz) self-raising flour
1 teaspoon milk
1 tablespoon water

Preheat the oven to 220°C (425°F/Gas 6). Grease and line a Swiss roll tin with greaseproof paper. Beat the eggs until foamy, add the sugar and beat until thick and creamy. Fold in the sifted flour with a spatula or metal spoon, then lightly stir in the combined milk and water. Pour into the prepared Swiss roll tin and bake in the preheated oven for about 15 minutes. Sprinkle a greaseproof paper sheet with caster sugar, turn the cooked Swiss roll onto this and remove paper from the base.

Trim off the crusty ends if necessary and quickly roll up, starting from the wide side. Roll up the greaseproof paper with the sponge. Leave until cool, then unroll. Discard the paper. Fill the roll with jam and whipped cream, fruit and cream. Reroll, sprinkle with additional caster or icing (confectioners') sugar to serve.

Baking

Scones

Makes 12

2 cups (8 oz) self-raising flour
pinch of salt
30 g (1 oz) butter or margarine
2/3 cup (5 fl oz) milk, approximately

Sift the flour and salt together and mix in the butter to resemble breadcrumbs. Stir in the milk to form a soft dough. Turn onto a floured surface and knead lightly.

Press out to 1.25 cm (½ inch) thickness and cut out rounds using a scone cutter. Place on a greased baking tray and glaze, if desired, with milk. Bake in a preheated oven at 230°C (450°F/Gas 8) for 7 to 10 minutes. Serve hot with jam and cream.

Pumpkin Scones

Makes 24

30 g (1 oz) butter, softened
¼ cup (3 oz) honey
1 egg, beaten
1 cup cooked, mashed pumpkin
2 cups (8 oz) wholemeal self-raising flour
2 cups (8 oz) self-raising flour
½ teaspoon nutmeg
½ teaspoon cinnamon
¾ cup (6 fl oz) milk
½ cup (3 oz) chopped glacé ginger
½ cup (3 oz) chopped raisins

Cream the butter and honey until fluffy. Add the egg and pumpkin and beat well. Fold in the sifted dry ingredients alternately with the milk. Add the fruit and mix lightly. Turn the mixture onto a floured board and knead lightly. Roll out to 2.5 cm (1 inch) thick. Cut into small rounds with a scone cutter and place close together on a lightly greased baking tray.

Bake at 220°C (425°F/Gas 7) for 15 minutes. Serve warm, buttered and topped with honey.

Shortcrust Pastry

Makes 250 g (8 oz)

2 cups (8 oz) self-raising flour
pinch of salt
125 g (4 oz) butter or margarine
1 egg yolk
2-3 tablespoons iced water

Sift the flour and salt together and place in a food processor. Add the butter and process for a few seconds until the mixture resembles fine breadcrumbs. Add the egg yolk and process for a few seconds.

With the processor running, add the water, a little at a time, until the mixture forms a ball. Place on a lightly floured surface and knead gently. Use as directed.

Damper

Serves 6 - 8

4 cups (1 lb) self-raising flour
1 x 375 ml (12 fl oz) can beer

Place the flour in a large bowl. Add the beer and mix to a soft dough. Place in a large greased pan with a lid in the coals of an open fire and cook for 20 to 30 minutes depending on the heat of the fire. Check if done and replace the lid if a skewer does come out clean. Break apart and serve with lashings of butter and jam or honey.

Note: The dough may be formed into strips and wound around the ends of thick sticks. Make sure that the dough seals over the end of the stick. Hold over the fire. When cooked the damper and will pull off the end of the stick and may be filled with butter and jam and honey. Children love cooking their own damper.

Zucchini Cake

Makes 1 ring cake

125 g (4 oz) soft butter or margarine
¾ cup (4 oz) soft brown sugar
2 eggs, beaten
grated rind of 1 lemon
1 cup (4 oz) wholemeal self-raising flour, sifted with 1 teaspoon bicarbonate of soda (baking powder) and 1 teaspoon cinnamon
1 cup grated zucchini (courgettes)
½ cup (2 oz) chopped pecans

Place all the ingredients in the order given in a large mixing bowl and beat with a wooden spoon until well combined.

Place the mixture in a 20 cm (8 inch) ring tin brushed with melted butter, and bake on the middle shelf of the oven at 180°C (350°F/Gas 4) for 40 to 45 minutes or until a warm skewer inserted in the cake comes out clean. Turn out and cool on a rack.

Vanilla Butter Icing

Covers 1 cake

1 ½ cups (8 oz) icing (confectioners') sugar
30 g (1 oz) butter, softened
2-4 tablespoons water
a few drops of vanilla essence

Sift the icing sugar. Stir in the butter, then add sufficient water to make a smooth paste. Stir in vanilla essence to taste.

Chocolate Icing

Covers 1 cake

1 ½ cups (8 oz) icing (confectioners') sugar
2 tablespoons cocoa
15 g (½ oz) butter, softened
2-4 tablespoons water

Sift the icing sugar and cocoa. Blend in the butter and then add sufficient water to make a smooth icing.

Royal Icing

3 cups (1 lb 2 oz) pure icing (confectioners') sugar
3 egg whites

Gradually add the sugar to the egg whites on slow speed until desired peak is obtained. Do NOT use a plastic bowl. Keep covered with a damp cloth until ready to use.

Coffee Icing

Covers 1 cake

1 ½ cups (8 oz) icing (confectioner's) sugar
2 teaspoons instant coffee
2-4 tablespoons water

Sift the icing sugar. Mix the coffee into the water and add slowly to the icing sugar until smooth.

Orange or Lemon Icing

Covers 1 cake

1 ½ cups (8 oz) icing (confectioners') sugar
2-4 tablespoons orange juice or lemon juice

Sift the icing sugar. Blend in the juice a little at a time to a smooth consistency.

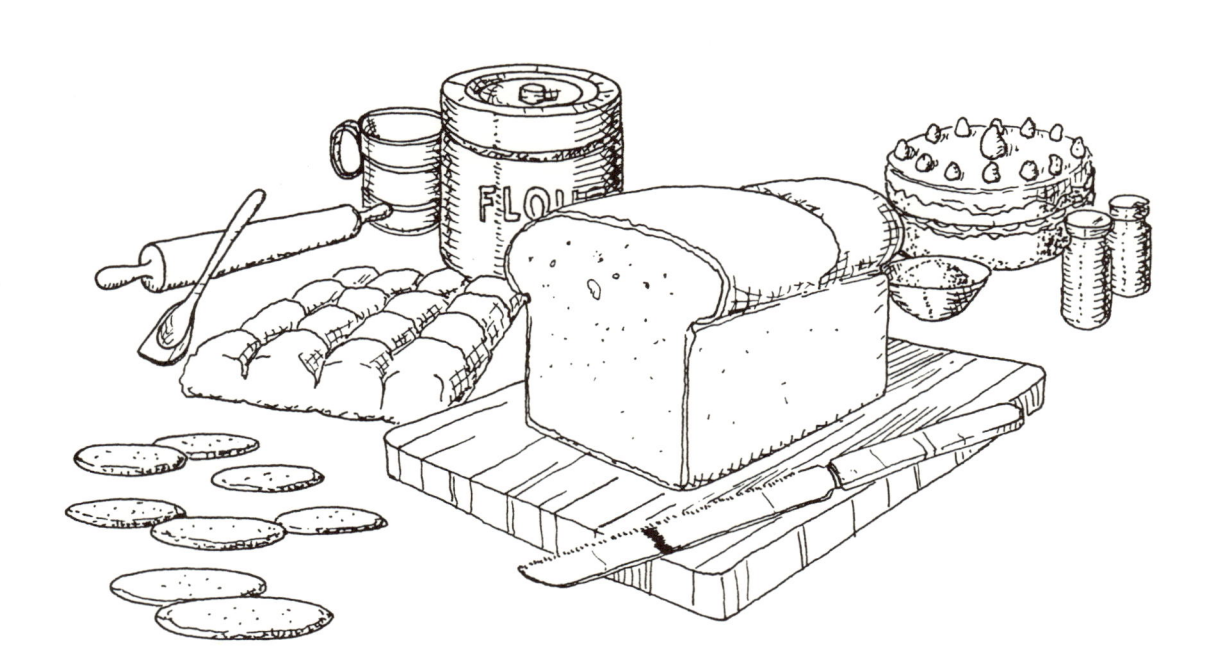

Glossary of Cooking Terms and Ingredients

Au gratin: Food sprinkled with breadcrumbs, often covered with cheese sauce and browned until a crisp coating forms.

Bain-marie: A saucepan standing in a large pan which is filled with boiling water to keep liquids at simmering point. A double boiler will do the same job.

Bake blind: To bake a pastry case without filling. To avoid the pastry cooking unevenly it is usually necessary to fill the shell with rice or special baking beans available at most kitchen shops.

Beurre manié: Equal quantities of butter and flour kneaded together and added a little at a time to thicken a stew or casserole.

Blanch: To heat in boiling water or steam to to preserve colour.

Bouquet garni: A bunch of herbs, usually consisting of sprigs of parsley, thyme, marjoram, rosemary, a bay leaf, peppercorns and cloves, tied in muslin and used to flavour stews and casseroles.

Consommé: A clear soup usually made from beef.

Court bouillon: The liquid in which fish, poultry or meat is cooked. It usually consists of water with bay leaf, onion, carrots and salt and freshly ground black pepper to taste. Other additives can include wine, vinegar, stock, garlic or spring onions (scallions).

Cream: To cream butter and sugar by beating with a wooden spoon or an electric mixer until light, white and fluffy like whipped cream.

Croûtes: Pieces of fried or toasted sliced bread, usually used under beef fillet, etc. Small pieces are sometimes used in soup.

Croûton: Fried or toasted cubes of bread usually used as a garnish or topping, or an accompaniment to soup.

Dutch oven: A heavy casserole with a lid usually made from cast iron or pottery.

Flake: To break into small pieces with a fork.

Flame: To ignite warmed alcohol over food.

Fold in: To cut in ingredients to a mixture which has been beaten until light and fluffy, using a plastic spatula.

Garnish: To decorate food for presentation.

Glaze: To brush pastry, etc. with beaten egg to enhance the golden appearance.

Julienne: To cut into fine strips resembling matchsticks.

Knead: To work dough usually with hands until it is of the desired consistency.

Marinade: A mixture of an oil and seasonings in which food is soaked to give more flavour or to soften tough food.

Mascarpone cheese: A cream or non-fat cheese from Italy. Usually used as a dessert cheese.

Reduce: To cook over a very high heat, uncovered, until the liquid is reduced by evaporation.

Sauté: To fry quickly in a small amounts of hot butter or oil.

Seasoned flour: Plain (all-purpose) flour seasoned with plenty of salt and pepper.

Skim: To remove any substance from the surface of a mixture.

Stock: A liquid containing the flavours, extracts and nutrients of bones, meat, fish or vegetables in which they are cooked.

Sweat: To cook vegetables over heat only until the juices run.

Vegetable spaghetti: A large fruit which shreds and tastes exactly like cooked spaghetti. Available at large fruit markets.

INDEX

A

Abalone Amandine 288
Aberdeen Sausage 93
Advocaat 54
Almond Honey Cake 457
Amaretti Crêpes 418
American Fruit Cake 456
Angel Cake 456
Appetisers
    Baby Quiche 30
    Calypso Eggs 34
    Camembert Hot Bread 28
    Camembert Puffs 36
    Cheese Pillows 29
    Crab and Asparagus Pâté 28
    Crabmeat Ramekins 27
    Creamy Blue Cheese Celery Sticks 27
    Curry Nibblers 35
    Dip à la Ritz 32
    Drunken Prawns 28
    Egg and Anchovy Pâté 35
    Egg and Apple Croquettes 33
    Egg 'n' Apple Dip 31
    Egg 'n' Celery Dip 31
    Egg 'n' Cheese Dip 31
    Egg 'n' Chicken and Almond Spread 31
    Egg 'n' Corn Relish Dip 31
    Egg 'n' Crunchy Peanut Butter Dip 31
    Egg Mousse 30
    Egg Nibblers 33
    Egg 'n' Onion Dip 31
    Egg 'n' Pine Dip 32
    Egg and Salmon Dip 31
    Egg and Tuna Aspic 34
    Ham and Melon Wraps 34
    Herb and Blue Cheese Pinwheels 36
    Hot Mozzarella Avocados 30
    Irish Eggs 35
    Mediterranean Dip 27
    Melba Toast 32
    Mini Edam Quiches 29
    Mozzarella Stacks 28
    Mushroom Roulade with Cheesy Sauce 30
    Mustardy Yoghurt Dip 29
    Peppered Eggs 33
    Pickled Eggs 30
    Prawn Pâté 28
    Salmon Salad Dip 32
    Savoury Bites 33
    Savoury Egg Rolls 32
    Scotch Egg Roll 34
    Scots Eggs 32
    Shrimp Pâté 36
    Souffléed Beer Pots 27
    Stuffed Cottage Eggs 32
    Tarragon Chicken Mousse 35
    Vegetable Terrine 34
    Vol au Vent Provençale 36
Apple Baked Ling 276
Apple Banana Shortcake 396
Apple Berry Pancakes 415
Apple Butter Chicken 248
Apple Chicken Soup 20
Apple and Cinnamon Droplets 421
Apple-Cinnamon Rice 222
Apple Cottage Rice 430
Apple and Cream Combo Filling 44
Apple Crêpes 410
Apple Galette 412
Apple-Glazed Chicken Thighs 259
Apple Isle Lamb 139
Apple Lamb Loin 135
Apple Nog 52
Apple Noodle Meringue 396
Apple Rice 307
Apricot Ambrosia 415
Apricot Chicken 221
Apricot Cider Lamb 141
Apricot Cream Biscuits 441
Apricot Cream Pie 450
Apricot Delights 405
Apricot Egg Flip 54
Apricot Honey Rice 434
Apricot Lamb 114
Apricot Muffins 448
Apricot Nut Loaf 449
Apricot-Nut Rack of Lamb 113
Apricot and Pork Kebabs 188
Apricot Pork Roast 178
Apricot Rice Parfait 433
Apricot Sauce 438
Apricot Squid 286
Apricot Tea Cake 453
Arroz con Pollo 260
Artichokes with Lemon Butter 370
Asparagus Chinese Style 370
Aspic 98
Austrian Rice Cream 432
Avocado and Prawn Soup 20
Avocado Sauce 38
Avocado and Tomato Salad 386
Avocado Veal in Filo 149

B

Baby Quiche 30
Bacon Brown Rice 308
Bacon Rice Bake 313
Baked Chicken Remoulade 199
Baked Chicken Reuben 211
Baked Chilli Chicken 214
Baked Crayfish with Mustard Butter 290
Baked Custard 420
Baked Dinner for Two 80
Baked Egg Custard 420
Baked Fish Loaf 283
Baked Fish with Zucchini 272
Baked Flathead Fillets 273
Baked Ham, Spiced Apple Ring 344
Baked Lamb Dinner 107
Baked Lasagna with Eggplant 306
Baked Lasagna with Tomato and Meat Sauce 305
Baked Luncheon Rice 309
Baked Mustard Chicken 199
Baked Rice Custard 432
Baked Savoury Mushrooms 320
Baked Tomatoes 320
Baked Whole Fish with Macadamia Stuffing 281
Baked Whole Trevally 281
Banana Bender 54
Banana Caramel Cake 445
Banana Nut Bread 446
Banana Rice 332
Banana and Sultana Cake 451
Barbecue Beef Spare Ribs 70
Barbecue Fruit Kebabs 401
Barbecue Rice Salad 364
Barbecue Spare Ribs 334
Barbecued Chicken Supreme 251
Barbecued Herbed Steaks 72
Barbecued Lemon Chops 145
Barbecued Pork Spareribs 187
Barbecued Prawns 266
Barbecued Rib Eye 58
Barbecued Roast Pork 179
Barbecued Sausages 76
Basic Biscuit Pastry 412
Basic Cheesecake 394
Basic Hot Soufflé 43
Basic Roulade 46
Basil-Garlic Chicken Pastries 204
Basil-Garlic Cream Sauce 204
Basil Sauce (Pesto) 38
Bean and Prawn Salad 383
Bean and Watercress Salad 390
Béarnaise Sauce 39
Béchamel Sauce 306
Beef
    Apricot Rolls 332
    Baked Dinner for Two 80
    Baked Lasagna with Tomato and Meat Sauce 305

INDEX

Barbecue Beef Spare Ribs 70
Barbecue Spare Ribs 334
Barbecued Herbed 72
Barbecued Rib Eye 58
Barbecued Sausages 76
Beefy Fried Rice 75
Beer Casserole 83
Beer-Sauced Garlic Steak 99
with BlackBerries 64
Blue Cheese Steaks 70
Blue Vein Cheese Roast 69
Bolognese Sauce 79
Bourguigonne 94
with Broccoli 333
Brochettes Tropicana 75
and Tomato Flan 67
Buderim Beef Salad 64
Burgundian Beef and Beans 88
Cabbage Rolls 321
Cabbage Rolls in Tomato Cream Sauce 324
Capricornia Beef and Rice Salad 66
Carbonnade for a Crowd 86
Carpetbag Steaks 67
Carving 56
Chilli Beef and Beans 85
Chilli con Carne 86
Chinese Beef 74
Chinese Strips 333
Chinese Sizzling Steak 77
Coconut Beef Curry 92
Cornucopias 92
Corned Beef Dinner 63
Corned Beef Hash 93
Corned Beef Orana 84
Corned Beef Richmond 89
Corned Silverside 88
Country Beef Casserole 62
Creole Beef Soup 21
Crockpot Apricot Beef 78
Cranberry Corned Beef 79
Curried Sausages 89
Curry (Mild) 333
Custard-Topped Noodle Casserole 298
Demi Glace 40
Dinner Loaf 95
Dipaway Meatballs 29
Dolmades 320
Drover's Dream 88
Easy-as-Pie 66
Economical Beef Stroganoff 85
Family Favourite Meatballs 337
Family-Size Meat Pie 90
Fillet with Avocado Béarnaise 68
Fillet with Béarnaise Sauce 61
Fillet Steak with Four Peppers 77

Florentine Beef Cakes 95
Freezer Beef Stew 97
French Onion Steak 100
Fruity Barbecued Blade
Frypan Moussaka 79
Ginger Beef Skewers 75
Goulash 92, 98
Goulash variation 97
Green Lasagne 96
Hamburgers 70
High Fibre Rissoles 71
Honey Beef Kebabs 102
Irish Pot Roast 95
Italian Sauce 334
Keema Curry 89
Kofta Curry 94
Meat Ring 57
Meatballs 318
Meatballs in Beer Sauce 90
Meatballs with Curry Fruit Sauce 332
Mexican Chilli Soup 20
Mexican Sausages with Chilli Bean 102
Mexicani Mince 335
Microgrill and Vegetables 71
Mini Meat Loaves 80
Mini Meat Loaves with Rice 335
Minute, 'n' Walnuts 332
Mustard Glazed Steaks 100
Olives 85
Open Steak Sandwiches 72
Ox Tongue with Cumberland Sauce 84
Party Chilli con Carne 98
Pasta with Summer Sauce 76
Pastrami 99
Pepper Steak 72
Peppered Beef in Filo 68
Peppered Rump Steak 58
Peppered Steak and Peaches 82
Pineapple Meat Loaf 57
Pizza 80
Pizza Burgers 71
Poached Fillet with Tapenade 96
Pronto Beef Parmigiana 102
Regal Roast Beef 67
Reuben Sandwich 84
Rib Eye Roast 57
Rice Lasagne 334
Rice and Pepper Pinwheel 336
'n' Rice Potage 25
Rice Shepherd's Pie 334
Riverina Beef Casserole 93
Riverina Rice Meat Loaf 336
Roast Beef with Vegetables Provençale 60

Rolls with Spinach and Pine Nuts 61
Roast Beef with Yorkshire Pudding 59
Roast Stuffed Topside 66
and Salad Pillows 103
Salisbury Steaks 71
Samosa with Meat Filling 78
Sang Cho Bau 104
Satays 100
Satays with Peanut Sauce 82
Sausage Breakfast for One 70
Sausage Roll 58
Scotch Eggs 75
Sherried Beef Stew 76
Skewered Beef Waldorf 104
Smoked Beef 82
Spiced Beef Loaf 99
Spiced Beef Pâté 98
Spicy, and Rice Casserole 337
Steak Canton 67
Steak Diane 78
Steak and Kidney Pie 86
Steak Rolls in Curry Sauce 83
Steak Rolls Teriyaki 81
Steaks Rosemary 74
Steak Satay 90
Steak with Tangy Apricots 101
Steak Teriyaki 74
Stock 40
Stroganoff 97
Stuffed Cannelloni with Mushrooms 300
Stuffed Rib Eye Steak with Hot Potato Salad 103
Summer Loafers 72
Swiss Steak 94
Teriyaki Meatballs 103
Toad-in-the-Hole 69
and Tomato Flan 67
Town and Country Hot Pot 102
Tripe and Onions 62
and Vegetable Casserole 97
Wellington 81
with Blackberries 64
Beer Casserole 83
Beer-Sauced Garlic Steak 99
Beetroot and Buckwheat Salad 384
Beetroot Yoghurt Salad 386
Benalla Lamb and Apricot Terrine 107
Biriyani Rice 315
Biscuits
　Apricot Cream 441
　Cheese 441
　Cherry Ripe Bars 454
　Chocolate Rum 444

INDEX

Crunchies 442
Lemon Coconut Buttons 442
Pineapple Walnut Cookies 441
Sesame 442
Shortbread Creams 442
Sour Cream Sugar Cookies 443
Wheat Germ 446
Blackberry and Yoghurt Cream 421
Blanquette of Veal 152
Blitz Torte 408
Blue Cheese Steaks 70
Blue Grenadier Chowder 266
Blue Vein Cheese Roast 69
Blueberry Bavarois 408
Blueberry Muffins 451
Blushing Mousse 413
Boiled Fruit Cake 448
Bolognese Sauce 79
Bombe Alaska 401
Bonjour Croissants 190
Borsch 26
Bouillabaisse 270
Boysenberry and Pear Crumble 421
Boysenberry Sorbet 422
Braised Chinese Spareribs 185
Braised Ling in Vegetables 275
Bran Muffins 448
Brandied Chestnut Mousse 394
Brandy, Chicken in 206
Brandy Egg Nog 52
Brandy Sauce 396
Bravo Chicken 231
Bread
   Herb Onion 453
Broad Bean and Tuna Salad 387
Broccoli Rice Bake 310
Broccoli and Scallop Soup 24
Brochettes Tropicana 75
Brown Baked Chicken 216
Brown Rice Apple Betty 425
Brown Rice Broth 18
Brown Rice Brûlée 425
Brown Rice and Cheese Casserole 309
Brown Rice Country Casserole 326
Brown Rice Dessert 437
Brown Rice Medley 312
Brown Rice Mushroom Medley 310
Brown Rice O'Reilly 328
Brown Rice Pie 310
Brown Rice Pudding 437
Brown Rice Scramble 312
Brunch Combo Filling 44
Brussels Salad 384
Buderim Beef Salad 64
Burgundian Beef and Beans 88
Butter Sauce 270
Buttered Honey Chicken Bites 243

Buttered Rice 341
Butterfly Flip 53
Butterfly Pork Steaks Supreme 177
Butterfly Steak Royale 177
Butternut Rice 351

C

Cabbage Rolls 321
Cabbage Rolls in Tomato Cream Sauce 324
Caesar Salad 386
Cake
   Almond Honey 457
   American Fruit 456
   Angel 456
   Apricot Nut Loaf 449
   Apricot Tea 453
   Banana Caramel 445
   Banana Nut Bread 446
   Banana and Sultana 451
   Boiled Fruit 448
   Carrot and Walnut 456
   Carrot and Zucchini 454
   Cheese 444
   Cherry Raisin Nut Bread 442
   Chocaroon 445
   Chocolate Rough 445
   Cinnamon Apple Slice 446
   Cinnamon Streusel Coffee 440
   Coffee 441
   Coffee Sponge 446
   Crunchy Orange Coffee 440
   Danish Apple Coconut Coffee 448
   Fudge Bars 445
   Golden Fruit 457
   Orange Date Shortcake 453
   Orange Gâteau 452
   Orange Raisin Plait 452
   Peanut Butter Coffee 440
   Plain Sponge 457
   Quick Cheese Loaf 453
   Quick Fruit Bread 440
   Sicillia 452
   Spiced Pumpkin 444
   Sponge Roll or Sandwich 443
   Swiss Roll 457
   Toppings, Coffee Cake 441
   Whole-Wheat Nut Bread 440
   Zucchini 458
California Chicken Casserole 351
Calypso Eggs 34
Camembert Hot Bread 28
Camembert Puffs 36
Canadian Pork Pie 181
Cannelloni Chicken 230
   'à la King' 301

   alla Napolitana 300
   Stuffed with Lamb 300
Caper Sauce 359
Capital Chicken Casserole 223
Capricorn Chicken and Rice 346
Capricornia Beef and Rice Salad 66
Capricornia Rice Salad 366
Caramel Crunch Rice 434
Caramel Fondue 401
Caramel Oranges 398
Caramel Sauce 410
Carbonnade for a Crowd 86
Carolina Chicken 222
Carpetbag Steaks 67
Carrot Scones 202
Carrot Topped Chicken 206
Carrot and Walnut Cake 456
Carrot and Zucchini Cake 454
Carving
   Beef 56
   Chicken 194
   Lamb 106
   Pork 160
Casablanca Chicken and Yellow Rice 352
Casanova Pork Rolls 172
Casserole Veal Chops 157
Cauliflower in Black Bean Sauce 380
Cauliflower Salad 383
Celery and Chicken Soup 23
Celery Rice 341
Chateaubriand 60
Cheddar Chicken Rice 352
Cheddar Wheat Round 454
Cheese Biscuits 441
Cheese Cake 444
Cheese and Corn Soup 20
Cheese Crumble 378
Cheese Fried Rice 310
Cheese Pillows 29
Cheese and Rice Puffs 326
Cheese Sauce 99
Cheese Scones 446
Cheese and Tomato Soufflé 43
Cheesecake
   Basic 394
   Cherry Brandy 395
   Chocolate Rum 395
   Coconut 394
   Strawberry 395
   Strawberry Rice 438
Cheesy Chicken and Cabbage Bake 220
Cheesy Rice Franks 336
Cheesy Sauce 30
Chelsea Butter Bun 456
Cherry Brandy Cheesecake 395

INDEX

Cherry Chicken 236
Cherry Chicken Salad 246
Cherry Cream Crêpe Stack 409
Cherry Raisin Nut Bread 442
Cherry Rice Flan 430
Cherry Ripe Bars 454
Cherry Sauce 262, 431
Chicken
    à la King 258
    and Almonds 348
    Andaluza 224
    Andouille 199
    Apple Butter 248
    Apple Chicken Soup 20
    Apple-Glazed Thighs
    Apricot 221
    Arroz con Pollo 350
    with Artichokes 231
    Asparagus Casserole 218
    with Avocado 237
    Baked Chilli 214
    Baked Mustard 199
    Baked Remoulade 199
    Baked South-of-the-Border 218
    Barbecued Supreme 251
    Basil 198
    Basil-Garlic Pastries 204
    in Brandy 206
    à la Brandy Wine 231
    Bravo 231
    Breast in Tarragon Cream 213
    Breasts, Cucumber Stuffed 247
    Breasts Provençale 209
    Breasts Rockefeller 254
    with Broccoli 251
    Broccoli Dinner 254
    Brown Baked 216
    and Brussel Sprouts Casserole 219
    Burgoo 230
    Buttered Honey Bites 243
    Cacciatore 240
    California Casserole 351
    Calypso 255
    Cannelloni 230
    Capricorn Chicken and Rice 346
    Carrot Topped 206
    Carving 194
    Capital Casserole 223
    Carolina 222
    Casablanca, and Yellow Rice 352
    Casserole Vegeroni 302
    Celery and Chicken Soup 23
    Chablis 209
    Cheddar Rice 352
    Cheesy Chicken and Cabbage Bake 220
    Cherry 236

Chow Mein 210
Chilli 250
Chilli Sandwich 229
Chinese Spiced Wings 348
Chinese Stir-Fried 349
Chinese Watercress Soup 22
Chinoise 258
Chutney 222
Cobbler 260
Cold Lemon 210
Colonial 244
Coq au Vin with Rice 350
Cordon Bleu 212
Coriander 224
Corn Pudding 196
and Corn Stew 250
Country Captain 226
Country Club 213
Country-Style 226
Cream Soup 16
Creamy Curried 351
Creamy Lemon 234
Creole 243
Crispy Lemon 228
Croquettes 346
Curried 227
Curried Amandine 260
Curried Pancakes 258
Curried Salad 247
in Curry Cream Sauce 232
Curry Soup 16
Deluxe 215
Divan 202
and Dumplings 226
Endive au Gratin 238
Escalope 216
Extraordinaire 212
-au-Feu 240
Fiesta with Chilli Sauce 220
Fillets on Orange Rice 345
Florentine 196
with Fresh Vegetables 250
Fried 195
Fried, Raisin Rice 347
Ginger Lemon 198
Ginger Wine 236
Gingered Lychees 246
Gingered Pear 242
Golden 224
Golden Apricot 351
Green Pepper 238
on the Grill 195
and Ham with Spaghetti 192
Hawaiian Salad 200
Hazelnut 220
Hot Tomato 251
Hungarian Paprika 246

Indian Savouries 216
Indienne Soup 25
Italian 247
Italian Liver Pâté 242
Jambalaya 230
Jointing 194
Kashmiri Curry 345
Kiev 206
à la King 258
Latin American 223
Lazy Day Chinese 234
Legs, Stuffed 238
Lemon-Coconut 199
Lemon Fillet 206
Lemon Honey 227
Licken Rice 217
Limacado 244
Lime 197
with Lime Butter 211
Little Legs Tempura 204
and Macaroni 243
Macaroni 305
Macedoine 214
Malaysian Curry 349
Marengo 217
Maryland 261
and Melon Salad with Ginger Mayonnaise 245
Merry Berry 202
Mini-Drumsticks 239
Mountains 259
Mushroom Dinner 243
Mushroom-Stuffed 248
Mustard 210
Mustard Vegetable 253
90 Second 209
Noodle Soup 227
and Noodles 226
North Carolina Grilled 221
Nugget 212
Nutty Oven-Fried 207
Old Style Broth 17
Olive-Rosemary Honey 232
with Olive Scones 207
Orange-Avocado 203
Orange-Ginger 197
Oven-Barbecued 195
Oven-Fried 195
Oyster-Stuffed 222
Pan Whiskied 255
Paprika 198
Peanut Butter 248
and Pears 223
Pecan with Dijon Sauce 210
and Peppers 352
Pepino Salad 245
Picante 207

INDEX

Pie 257
Pie, Herby 234
and Pineapple 230
Pineapple Curry 347
Pizza 217
Poached 195
au Poivre 234
Pollo Verde 203
Portuguese 213
in a Pot 232
Provençale 255
Puffed Chilli 257
Puffed Ricotta 215
Quick Cassoulet 255
Quick Pepper 228
Ratatouille 211
in Red Wine 261
Reuben Baked 211
Rice Athena 323
and Rice, California 351
Rice Casserole 350
Rice and Noodles 344
Riverboat Wheel 235
Roast 195
Roasted 255
Roasted Plum 200
Rolls 205
Rolls, Curried 211
Rosemary's 242
Rosemary Supreme 203
Russian Fillets, Lemon Butter Rice 349
St Basil 203
Salad, Cherry 246
Salad Drumsticks 219
Salad, Hot Chinese 223
Sautéed Breasts with Blueberry Sauce 246
Savoury, and Squash 216
Scallopini 213
Scampi 221
Sesame 242
Skillet Supreme 198
Slimmers Choko Salad 245
Soup Indienne 25
Southern Style 196
Spaghetti 254
Spanish 221
Spanish Paella 311
Speedy, and Rice Ring 350
Spiced Chicken Wings 348
Spiced Custard Apple 244
Spiced Microwave 217
Spiced Pilaf 349
Spicy Arroz con Pollo 350
Spicy Grilled 220
Spicy, and Peaches 239
Spicy, with Rice 235
Stew 250
Stir-Fried, and Broccoli 227
Stir-Fried, and Rice 347
Stock 40
Stuffed Thighs 252
Sultana Orange 346
Sunshine Pie 202
Sweet and Sour 348
Sweet 'n' Sour 200
Sweet and Spicy 200
Sweet Surprise 228
Taco Grill 251
Tahitian 214
Tamale 215
Tandori 261
Tangy Sweet 253
Tarragon Chicken Mousse 35
Tasty Thighs 218
Teen's Easy Cheesy 204
Tetrazzini 232
Texas 239
Thighs, Apple-Glazed 219
Tomato Chicken Soup 18
Tomato-Chilli 222
Topped Eggplant Boats 218
Touch o' Mint 247
Trussing 194
with Turnips 219
Vegetable 209
Vermouth 235
Veronique 260
Vino 239
Wellington 261
Yoghurt-Lemon 242
Yummy Balls 219
Zucchini Parmesan 214
Chilled Cherry Soup 23
Chilli Beef and Beans 85
Chilli Bitter Melon Beef 99
Chilli Chicken 250
Chilli con Carne 86
Chilli-Plum Glazed Cutlets 126
Chilli Sauce 220
Chinese Bean Sprout Salad 387
Chinese Beef 74
Chinese Beef Strips 333
Chinese Fried Rice 316
Chinese Fried Rice with Mixed Meats 342
Chinese Mixed Pickles 37
Chinese Sauce 317
Chinese Sizzling Steak 77
Chinese Spiced Chicken Wings 348
Chinese Spiced Pork 343
Chinese Stir-Fried Chicken 349
Chinese-Style Squid and Peppers 272
Chinese-Style Steamed Rice 308
Chinese Vegetable Stir Fry 374
Chinese Watercress Soup 22
Chocaroon Cake 445
Choc-Meringue Tart 405
Chocolate Cherry and Ginger Squares 399
Chocolate Date Nut Torte 406
Chocolate Icing 459
Chocolate Mousse 417
Chocolate Orange Mousse 401
Chocolate Rough 445
Chocolate Rum Biscuits 444
Chocolate Rum Cheesecake 395
Chocolate Rum Soufflé 404
Chocolate Sauce 418
Chocolate Soufflé 43
Choux Pastry 408
Chutney Chicken 222
Chutneyed Chops Banana 110
Cinnamon Apple Slice 446
Cinnamon Carrots 379
Cinnamon Streusel Coffee Cake 440
Cinnamon Sugar Muffins 448
Citron Touché 414
Citrus Curried Rice 316
Citrus Curried Rice with Orange Steaks 313
Citrus Dressing 365
Citrus Rack of Veal 148
Citrus Rice Salad 368
Citrus Sorbet 421
Coconut Apricot Pie 450
Coconut Beef Curry 92
Coconut Cheesecake 394
Coffee Cake 441
Coffee Sponge 446
Coffee Dessert Cake 402
Coffee Icing 459
Cold Lemon Chicken 210
Cold Veal Pie 154
Coleslaw with Grapes 383
Colonial Chicken 244
Condiments
    Chinese Mixed Pickles 37
    Plum and Ginger Chutney 37
Confetti Chicken Quiche 231
Cool Island Salad 367
Cool Potato Salad 382
Coq au Vin 224
Coq au Vin with Rice 350
Coral Trout Oskar 265
Coriander Chicken 224
Corn Bread 98
Corn and Rice Chowder with Prawns 19
Corned Beef Dinner 63

INDEX

Corned Beef Hash 93
Corned Beef Orana 84
Corned Beef Richmond 89
Corned Lamb with Cranberry Glaze 118
Corned Lamb with Mustard Sauce 120
Corned Silverside 88
Cornucopias 92
Cottage Rice Pudding 424
Country Beef Casserole 62
Country Club Chicken 213
Country Garden Quiche 377
Country Style Chicken 226
Cowra Lamb Casserole 338
Crab and Asparagus Pâté 28
Crabmeat Ramekins 27
Cranberry Corned Beef 79
Cranberry Pork Steaks 166
Cream of Carrot Soup 19
Cream of Chicken Soup 16
Cream Puffs 418
Cream of Vegetable Soup 16
Creamy Blue Cheese Celery Sticks 27
Creamy Chicken Peach Salad 392
Creamy Curried Chicken 351
Creamy Filled Mushrooms 371
Creamy Grape Crunch 414
Creamy Lemon Chicken 234
Creamy Rice with Cherry Sauce 431
Creamy Rice with Pineapple 428
Creole Beef Soup 21
Creole Chicken 243
Creole Jambalaya 337
Creole Rice Salad 362
Creole Stuffed Tomatoes 326
Crêpe Batter 409
Crêpes 45
Cressy Soup 23
Crispy Baked Orange Roughy 278
Crispy Fish Slices with Sweet and Sour Sauce 281
Crispy Lemon Chicken 228
Crispy Oysters 290
Crispy Trout 276
Crockpot Apricot Beef 78
Crown Roast with Cherries 108
Crown Roast with Fruit Stuffing 134
Crunchies 442
Crunchy Egg Salad 391
Crunchy Orange Coffee Cake 440
Crunchy Citrus Topping 441
Crunchy Pork Butterflies with Mushroom Sauces 172
Crunchy Pork Grill 185
Crusty Ham Grill 190
Cuban Beans and Rice 328

Cucumber Salad 386
Cucumber-Stuffed Chicken Breasts 247
Curried Chicken 227
Curried Chicken Amandine 260
Curried Chicken Pancakes 258
Curried Chicken Rolls 211
Curried Chicken Salad 247
Curried Egg Salad 392
Curried Eggs 309
Curried Eggs and Noodles 299
Curried Lamb Fingers 140
Curried Noodle Bake 299
Curried Puffs 313
Curried Sausages 89
Curried Sultanas 346
Curry
  Beef (Mild) 333
  Chicken Pineapple 347
  Chicken Soup 16
  Crumbed Cutlets 126
  Dressing 362
  Egg 48
  Fish 281
  Hurry Curry Soup 19
  Kashmiri Chicken Curry 345
  Kofta (Meatballs) 333
  Lamb and Coconut 124
  Lamb and Pawpaw 140
  Lamb Shank Casserole 122
  Malaysian Chicken Curry 349
  Mayonnaise 265
  Mayonnaise 366
  Mulligatawny Soup with Rice 16
  Nibblers 35
  Pacific Prawn 357
  Sauce 332
  Sweet Lamb 121
  Tropical Rice 312
Custard 420
Custard Apple and Passionfruit Mousse 414
Custard Sauce 415
Custard Tart 420
Custard-Topped Noodle Casserole 298

D

Damper 458
Danish Apple Coconut Coffee Cake 448
Date and Apple Rice 430
Date Spiced Creamy Rice 429
Deep-Fried Scallops 285
Deep-Fried Squid 286
Deep Pork Pie 174

Delicate Ham Puffs 192
Demi Glace 40
Desserts
  Amaretti Crêpes 418
  Apple Banana Shortcake 396
  Apple Berry Pancakes 415
  Apple and Cinnamon Droplets 421
  Apple Cottage Rice 430
  Apple Crêpes 410
  Apple Galette 412
  Apple Noodle Meringue 396
  Apricot Ambrosia 415
  Apricot Delights 405
  Apricot Honey Rice 434
  Apricot Rice Parfait 433
  Austrian Rice Cream 432
  Baked Custard 420
  Baked Egg Custard 420
  Baked Rice Custard 432
  Barbecue Fruit Kebabs 401
  Basic Cheesecake 394
  Blackberry and Yoghurt Cream 421
  Blitz Torte 408
  Blueberry Bavarois 408
  Blushing Mousse 413
  Bombe Alaska 401
  Boysenberry and Pear Crumble 421
  Boysenberry Sorbet 422
  Brandied Chestnut Mousse 394
  Brown Rice 437
  Brown Rice Apple Betty 425
  Brown Rice Brûlée 425
  Brown Rice Pudding 437
  Caramel Crunch Rice 434
  Caramel Fondue 401
  Caramel Oranges 398
  Cheese Cake 444
  Cherry Cream Crêpe Stack 409
  Cherry Rice Flan 430
  Choc-Meringue Tart 405
  Chocolate Cherry and Ginger Squares 399
  Chocolate Date Nut Torte 406
  Chocolate Mousse 417
  Chocolate Orange Mousse 401
  Chocolate Rum Cheesecake 395
  Chocolate Rum Soufflé 404
  Citron Touché 414
  Citrus Sorbet 421
  Coconut Cheesecake 394
  Coffee Dessert Cake 402
  Cream Puffs 418
  Creamy Grape Crunch 414
  Creamy Rice with Cherry Sauce 431

INDEX

Creamy Rice with Pineapple 428
Custard 420
Custard Apple and Passionfruit Mousse 414
Custard Tart 420
Date and Apple Rice 430
Date Spiced Creamy Rice 429
Dôme à l'Orange 400
Fruit Salad Rice 426
Fruit Salad Slice 400
Fruit Shortcake Dessert 402
Fruity Almond Pears 412
Fudge Pudding 402
Golden Apricot Rice Pudding 438
Golden Pecan Pie 420
Golden Rice 426
Grand Marnier Imperial 432
Granny's Apple Soufflé 422
Grape Flan 412
Grapefruit Blush 414
Greek Rice Pudding (Rizogalo) 430
Harlequin Cassata 398
Hazelnut Chocolate Dip 394
Hazelnut Pancakes with Caramel Sauce 410
Honey Rice 433
Honey Rice Buns 424
Honey Rice Muffins 437
Ice Cream 401
Individual Apricot Strudels 398
Individual Chocolate Baskets 400
Jamaican Rum Rice Pudding 437
Jamaican Scrambled Rice 437
Lemon Chiffon Pie 423
Lemon Loaf Cake 404
Lemon Meringue Pie 417
Lemon Mousse with Raspberry Yoghurt Sauce 408
Lemon Tart 412
Liqueured Coffee Ice Cream 394
Mandarin Blossoms 414
Mango Liqueur Crêpes 410
Mango Sublime 413
Maple Peach Rice 429
Marsala Crème 409
Meringue 417
Meringue Roll 416
Mocha Cream Parfait 436
Mocha Liqueur Tart 413
Old Fashioned Pudding and Brandy Sauce 396
Orange Rice Pudding 426
Old English Rice Pudding 418
Passionfruit Pears 406
Pavlova 416
Pavlova au Rhum 416

Pavlova Roll 399
Paw Paw in Passionfruit Sauce 404
Peach Berry Crêpes 413
Peach Crumble 407
Peach Ginger Rice Cream 431
Peach Meringue Creamy Rice 436
Peach Rice Treat 436
Peachy Rice Parfaits 436
Pears in Ginger Sauce 404
Pears in Red Wine 413
Pecan Pie 406
Pineapple Marshmallow Rice 428
Pineapple Meringue 398
Pineapple Parfait 424
Pineapple Rice Ambrosia 428
Pineapple Rice Crêpes 425
Pineapple Rice Torte 429
Pineapple Rice Whip 428
Pineapple Upside-down Pudding 406
Plum Delight 415
Prunicot Rice 433
Quick Fruit Sponge Dessert 404
Raspberry Rice Parfait 424
Rhubarb Fool 395
Rhubarb Rice Crisp 429
Rice Apple Flan 427
Rice Apricot Cream Delight 438
Rice Custard Imperial 436
Rice Imperatrice Mould 433
Rice Muffins 438
Rice and Raisin Cream 424
Rice Steamed Pudding 405
Self-Saucing Chocolate Puding 405
Soufflé Carmen 409
Sour Cream Raisin Flan 415
Speedy Creamy Rice 436
Spiced Rice Balls 434
Spiced Rice Custard 429
Spicy Apple Pancakes 427
Strawberry Cheesecake 395
Strawberry Mousse 417
Strawberry Puffs 407
Strawberry Rice Cheesecake 438
Sunshine Pineapple Pie 416
Sunshine Rice Cream 430
Sunshine-Spiced Rice 425
Swedish Rice Pudding 432
Tamarillo Sorbet 399
Tangy Banana Bavarois 421
Tropical Melon Salad 421
Tropical Touch Parfait 426
Walnut Torte 402
Yoghurt Raisin Rice Pudding 433
Yoghurt Rice Cream 396
Zabaglione 417
Zuppa Inglese 399

Devilled Carrots 375
Devilled Chops and Kidneys 126
Dill Sauce 212
Dinner Loaf 95
Dip à la Ritz 32
Dipaway Meatballs 29
Diver Whiting and Fennel 264
Dolmades 320
Dôme à l'Orange 400
Dory Fillets in Anchovy Sauce 273
Dory Fillets with Avocado Hazelnut Cream 278
Dressing
   Citrus 365
   Curry 362
   Italian Style 363
   Lemon 367
   Malaysian 363
   Tomato Juice 368
   Tomato-Onion 92
Drover's Dream 88
Drumsticks Italian Style 252
Drunken Prawns 28
Dry-Spiced Spareribs 285
Dutch Fish 274

E

East Coast Sauce 205
Eastern Spareribs 186
Easy-as-Pie 66
Easy Lamb Biriani 343
Easy Paella Pronto 359
Economical Beef Stroganoff 85
Edinburgh Egg Nog 52
Egg and Anchovy Pâté 35
Egg and Apple Croquettes 33
Egg 'n' Apple Dip 31
Egg and Bacon Rice 328
Egg 'n' Celery Dip 31
Egg 'n' Cheese Dip 31
Egg 'n' Chicken and Almond Spread 31
Egg Combos 44
   Apple and Cream Filling 44
   Brunch Filling 44
   Fruit Treat Filling 44
   Mushroom Filling 44
   Savoury Basic Mixture 44
   Savoury Fillings 44
   Seafood Filling 44
   Special Occasion Filling 45
   Sweet Basic Mixture 44
   Sweet Fillings 44
   Tomato Filling 44
Egg 'n' Corn Relish Dip 31

INDEX

Egg 'n' Crunchy Peanut Butter Dip 31
Egg Curry 48
Egg Curry with Raisin Brown Rice 329
Egg Flip 54
Egg Fondue 49
Egg Lasagne 48
Egg and Lemon Soup 26
Egg 'n' Malt Flip 54
Egg Mousse 30
Egg Nibblers 33
Egg Nog 52
Egg 'n' Onion Dip 31
Egg 'n' Pine Dip 32
Egg and Potato Salad 391
Egg Salad 391
Egg and Salmon Dip 31
Egg Spinach Salad 391
Egg Stroganoff 48
Egg and Tuna Aspic 34
Egg Whisk 54
Eggs
   Boiling 42
   Frying 42
   Poaching 42
   Scrambled 42
Eggs in Noodle Nests 298

F

Family Favourite Meatballs 337
Family-Size Meat Pie 90
Farmhouse Casserole 121
Farmland Treat 50
Fast Pork Burgers 179
Fennel with Mushrooms 371
Fiesta Chicken with Chilli Sauce 220
Fillet with Béarnaise Sauce 61
Fillet Steak with Four Peppers 77
Filo Silverbeet Triangles 370
Fish Curry 281
Fish Fillets in Ginger Sauce 274
Fish au Gratin 272
Fish Kiev 277
Fish with Mango and Kiwifruit 278
Fish Patties 284
Fish Rice Rollups 355
Fish Soufflé 43
Fish Soup 24
Fish Soup with Potatoes and Saffron 265
Fish Stock 40
Fish with Zucchini and Tomatoes 277
Flat Omelette 42
Florentine Beef Cakes 95
Flounder Parmesan 273

Fluffy Omelette 43
Formosa Fried Rice 316
Freezer Beef Stew 97
French Apple Pie 450
French Fries 380
French Ham Bake 191
French Onion Soup 22
French Onion Steak 100
Fresh Corn Chowder 23
Fried Brown Rice 312
Fried Chicken 195
Fried Chicken Raisin Rice 347
Fried Fillets with Lemon Caper Sauce 266
Fried Mushroom Rice 330
Fried Rice 307
Fruit Combo Treat Filling 44
Fruit Flan with Streusel 444
Fruit Kebabs, Barbecue 401
Fruit Salad Rice 426
Fruit Salad Slice 400
Fruit Sauce 157
Fruit Shortcake Dessert 402
Fruit Soup 23
Fruit Stuffing 116
Fruity Almond Pears 412
Fruity Barbecued Blade 103
Fruity Fried Rice 330
Fruity Lamb Pot Roast 113
Fruity Orange Salad 387
Fruity Pilaf 377
Fruity Pork Braise 162
Fruity Pork Parcels 173
Fruity Pork Salad 387
Fruity Rice Stuffing for Duck 328
Fruity Stuffing 110
Fruity Veal 'n' Pork Rolls 157
Frypan Moussaka 79
Fudge Bars 445
Fudge Pudding 402

G

Garden Egg Salad 391
Garlic Butter 277
Garlic Mussels 289
German Potato Salad with Horseradish 382
Ginger Beef Skewers 75
Ginger Bream 278
Ginger Honey Scallops 285
Ginger Lemon Chicken 198
Ginger Wine Chicken 236
Gingered Lychees with Chicken 246
Gingered Pear Chicken 242
Glazed Lamb Cutlets 142
Golden Apricot Chicken 351

Golden Apricot Rice Pudding 438
Golden Chicken 224
Golden Fruit Cake 457
Golden Ham with Golden Nut Rice Salad 367
Golden Pecan Pie 420
Golden Rice Dessert 426
Golden Risotto 322
Good Health Salad 392
Gourmet Rice and Mushrooms 324
Grand Marnier Rice 432
Grand Pork Chops 173
Granny's Apple Soufflé 422
Grape Flan 412
Grapefruit Blush 414
Grapefruit Bubbly 54
Grapes, Cheese and Nut Salad 387
Gravlax 282
Greek Kebabs and Salad 145
Greek Lemon Soup 18
Greek Rice Pudding (Rizogalo) 430
Greek Rice Salad 367
Green Beans and Bacon 379
Green Grapefruit Salad 375
Green Lasagne 96
Green Lasagna with Meat Sauce 306
Green Pepper Chicken 238
Green Peppers with Seafood Filling 268
Grilled Abalone Steaks 289
Guard of Honour 116

H

Ham
   Baked, Spiced Apple Ring 344
   Bonjour Croissants 190
   Crusty Grill 190
   Delicate Puffs 192
   French Bake 191
   Juicy Steaks with Curried Fruits 189
   Pantry Steak 190
   Pasta Salad 191
   Stand-by au Gratin 192
   Yummy Loaf 191
Ham and Chicken with Spaghetti 192
Ham and Egg Salad 391
Ham and Melon Wraps 34
Ham Milano Bake 191
Ham and Noodles in a Pot 191
Ham Paella 190
Ham and Parsley Flap Jacks 189
Ham Pasta 190
Ham and Peach Salad 363
Ham in Peppercorn Sauce 189
Ham Pizza Steak 190

INDEX

Ham Potato Boats 191
Ham Puff Pie 189
Ham and Rice Bake 308
Ham and Rice New Orleans 347
Ham Steaks with Pineapple Sauce 192
Hamburgers 70
Harlequin Cassata 398
Harlequin Health Salad 390
Hasty Tasty Lamb Casserole 117
Hawaiian Chicken Salad 200
Hazelnut Chicken 220
Hazelnut Chocolate Dip 394
Hazelnut Pancakes with Caramel Sauce 410
Health Salad 390
Hearty Cabbage Soup 17
Herb and Blue Cheese Pinwheels 36
Herb Onion Bread 453
Herb and Pine Nut Crust 111
Herb Pork Casserole 184
Herb Stuffing 85, 262
Herbed Lamb Chops 132
Herbed Lamb Skewers 137
Herbed Mussels 289
Herbed Roast Lamb 111
Herby Chicken Pie 234
Herby Tomato Quiche 47
High Fibre Rissoles 71
Highland Fish Soup 19
Hollandaise Sauce 39
Honey Beef Kebabs 102
Honey-Glazed Lamb Racks 114
Honey Lamb Chops 145
Honey Pork with Pineapple 186
Honey Rice 433
Honey Rice Buns 424
Honey Rice Muffins 437
Honey-Soy Lamb Chops 142
Honey Taro Root Pork 188
Honeyed Barbecue Lamb 109
Hot Beetroot Salad 383
Hot Broad Bean Salad 387
Hot Cabbage and Prosciutto Toss 375
Hot Chinese Chicken Salad 223
Hot Coffee Brandy Cream 53
Hot Mozzarella Avocado 30
Hot and Spicy Pork Strips 172
Hot Tomato Chicken 251
Hungarian Casserole 187
Hungarian Chicken Paprika 246
Hurry Curry Soup 19

I

Ice Cream 401
Iced Tomato Soup 22

Icing
    Chocolate 459
    Coffee 459
    Lemon 459
    Orange 459
    Royal 459
    Vanilla Butter 459
Indian Chicken Savouries 216
Individual Apricot Strudels 398
Individual Chocolate Baskets 400
Indonesian Fried Sweet Corn 372
Irish Eggs 35
Irish Fried Rice 324
Irish Pot Roast 95
Italian Chicken 247
Italian Chicken Liver Pâté 242
Italian Fried Peppers 371
Italian Mushroom Risotto 326
Italian Rice Salad 366
Italian Style Dressing 363
Italian Style Schnitzels 170
Italian Veal Roll 157

J

Jamaican Rum Rice Pudding 437
Jamaican Scrambled Rice 437
Jointing
    Chicken 194
Juicy Ham Steaks with Curried Fruits 189
Jumbuck Stew 122

K

Kashmiri Chicken Curry 345
Keema Curry 89
Kiwi Fish Fillets 265
Kofta Curry 94
Kofta Curry (Meatballs) 333
Kringle 450

L

Ladies' Fingers 116
Lamb
    Apple Isle 139
    Apple Loin 135
    Apricot 114
    Apricot Cider 141
    Apricot-Nut Rack 113
    Baked Dinner 107
    Balls with Egg and Lemon Sauce 113
    Barbecued Lemon Chops 145
    Benalla Lamb and Apricot Terrine 107
    Biriani 340
    Boulangére 107
    Cannelloni Stuffed with Lamb 300
    Carving 106
    Cassoulet 124
    Chilli-Plum Glazed Cutlets 126
    Chops with Mandarin Sauce 141
    Chops with Marmalade Sauce 131
    Chops with Plum Sauce 144
    Chutneyed Chops Banana 110
    and Coconut Curry 124
    Corned with Cranberry Glaze 118
    Corned with Mustard Sauce 120
    Crown Roast with Cherries 108
    Crown Roast with Fruit Stuffing 134
    Cowra Casserole 338
    Curried Fingers 140
    Curry Crumbed Cutlets 126
    Cutlets Parmigiana 132
    Cutlets in Pastry 108
    Cutlets and Vegetables in Pastry 144
    Devilled Chops and Kidneys 126
    Diane 129
    Easy Biriani 343
    Farmhouse Casserole 121
    Fruity Pot Roast 113
    Glazed Cutlets 142
    Greek Kebabs and Salad 145
    Guard of Honour 116
    Hasty Tasty Casserole 117
    Herbed Chops 132
    Herbed Roast 111
    Herbed Skewers 137
    Honey Chops 145
    Honey-Glazed Racks 114
    Honey-Soy Chops 142
    Honeyed Barbecue Lamb 109
    Hot Pot 121
    Jumbuck Stew 122
    Kebabs with Fruity Rice 338
    Ladies' Fingers 116
    Lamburgers Pizza-Style 133
    Lebanese Lamburgers 132
    Lebanese Pockets 146
    Lemon Casserole 338
    Lemon Mint Chops 128
    Lima 117
    Little Sausages 145
    Loin with Mustard 108
    Mango 121
    Mango Sauté 129
    Mediterranean Stew 119
    Middle Eastern Kebabs 117
    Middle Eastern Keftes 124
    Mildura 137

INDEX

Minced Kebabs 136
Minted Chops 142
and Mint Sausages 138
Mongolian 136
Montmorency 114
Navarin 112
Noisettes with Citrus Sauce 136
Noisettes with Mushroom Sauce 126
Noodles with Lamb 297
Orange Chops 125
Orange Ginger Chops 128
Orange Kebabs 122
Orange Steaks 313
Oregano with Quick Ratatouille 140
Oven Chops and Vegetables 122
and Pawpaw Curry 140
Peachy 135
and Pea Stroganoff 146
Peppercorn 141
Persian with Sour Cherries 120
Pineapple Riblets 130
in the Pink 141
Plum Casserole 119
Plum Chops for Two 117
Pommery with Parsnip Purée 137
Pot Roast 125
with Prunes 118
Quick Microroast Dinner 144
Rack of Lamb with Herb and Pine Nut Crust 111
Ragôut with Celery Rice 341
Rice with Lamb and Chick Peas 339
Rice Salad 339
Rich Scotch Broth 120
and Ricotta Casserole 340
Roast with Fruity Stuffing 110
Roast with Pears 114
Roast with Peppercorn Soufflé Crust 134
Roast Sesame 109
Roast Seville 142
Roman-Style 146
Rosemary 139
Satay 146
Satsuma 137
Shank Curry Casserole 122
Sherried Kidneys 133
Shogayaki 140
with Skewered Fruits 132
Skewered Lamb and Mushrooms 130
Smithon 110
Smoked with Blueberry Sauce 129
Smoked Leg with Marmalade Glaze 125
Spicy Barbecue Chops 129
Spicy Kebabs 341
Spicy Pilaf 338
and Spring Rice 339
Steaks with Port Sauce 138
Steaks Wangaratta 128
Sweet Curry 121
Sweet and Sour 128
Teppanyaki 133
Venetian Style 131
Lamb's Fry and Bacon Sauté 130
Lamburgers Pizza-Style 133
Lasagna
  Baked with Eggplant 306
  Baked, with Tomato and Meat Sauce 305
  with Butter and Grated Cheese 305
  Egg 48
  Green with Meat Sauce 306
  Rice 334
Latin American Chicken 223
Lazy Day Chinese Chicken 234
Lebanese Lamb Pockets 146
Lebanese Lamburgers 132
Lebanese Salad 382
Lemon Butter Rice 308, 343
Lemon Chiffon Pie 423
Lemon Coconut Buttons 442
Lemon-Coconut Chicken 199
Lemon Coconut Pie 449
Lemon Dressing 367
Lemon Fillet Chicken 206
Lemon Honey Chicken 227
Lemon Icing 459
Lemon Lamb Casserole 338
Lemon Loaf Cake 404
Lemon Meringue Pie 417
Lemon Mint Chops 128
Lemon Mousse with Raspberry Yoghurt Sauce 408
Lemon and Orange Sauce 38
Lemon Pepper Rice 348
Lemon Pilaf 351
Lemon Rice 307, 334
Lemon Sauce 228
Lemon-Spiced Spareribs 186
Lemon Tart 412
Lemon Tarts 454
Lettuce Roll-ups 273
Limacado Chicken 244
Lime Chicken 197
Lime Mayonnaise 383
Little Lamb Sausages 145
Little Legs Tempura 204
Liqueured Coffee Ice Cream 394

M

Malaysian Chicken Curry 349
Malaysian Dressing 363
Malted Mallow 53
Mandarin Blossoms 414
Mandarin and Coconut Salad 36
Mandarin Style Spareribs 187
Mango Chicken 257
Mango Lamb 121
Mango Lamb Sauté 129
Mango Liqueur Crêpes 410
Mango Sublime 413
Maple Peach Rice 429
Marinade
  Herb Wine 72
Marinated Octopus Greek Style 288
Marinated Pork Chops 183
Marsala Crème 4-09
Mayonnaise 39, 265
  Curry 366
  Lime 383
Meatballs in Beer Sauce 90
Meatballs with Curry Fruit Sauce 332
Meat Ring 57
Mediterranean Dip 27
Mediterranean Lamb Stew 199
Melba Toast 32
Meringue 405
Meringue Roll 416
Meringues 417
Merry Berry Chicken 202
Mexican Chilli Soup 10
Mexican Chokos 374
Mexican Fried Rice 328
Mexicani Mince 335
Mexican Noodles 298
Mexican Sausages with Chilli Beans 102
Mexicano Spareribs 187
Microgrill and Vegetables 71
Microwave Mackerel Bake 283
Middle Eastern Kebabs 117
Middle Eastern Keftes 124
Mild Pork Curry 161
Minced Lamb Kebabs 136
Minestrone Soup 18
Mini Edam Quiches 29
Mini Meat Loaves 80
Mini Meat Loaves with Rice 335
Minted Cucumber Soup 22
Minted Lamb Chops 142
Minted Rice and Ham Salad 362
Minute Beef 'n' Walnuts 332
Mocha Cream Parfait 436
Mocha Liqueur Tart 413

INDEX

Mock Rice Bouillabaisse 21
Mongolian Lamb 136
Mornay Mussels 289
Moroccan Lamb and Chick Pea Stew 119
Morwong Ambrosia 276
Mozzarella Stacks 28
Mud Crab in Black Bean Sauce 269
Muffins
    Apricot 448
    Blueberry 451
    Bran 448
    Cinnamon Sugar 448
    Plain 448
Mullet and Mushroom in Filo 267
Mullet Rollmops 264
Mulligatawny (Curried) Soup with Rice 16
Muscle Tucker 54
Mushroom Combo Filling 44
Mushroom Rice 308
Mushroom-Rice Piroshki 321
Mushroom Roulade with Cheesy Sauce 30
Mushroom Salad 382
Mushroom Stuffing 248
Mushrooms
    Stuffed 35
    Stuffed Cheese 378
    Stuffed Chicken 248
Mussels, The Italian Way 289
Mustard
    Chicken 210
    Cream Rack of Veal 148
    Glazed Steaks 100
    Sauce 120
    Vegetable Chicken 253
Mustardy Yoghurt Dip 29

N

Nasi Goreng 318
Navarin of Lamb 112
Nectarine and Silverbeet Salad 377
Nidi al Mascarpone 296
Nidi con Pesto di Formaggio 296
Nidi alla Romagnola 297
Nidi Smalzade 297
Nidi with Spinach 297
Nidi Verdi con Aglio 296
Nidi with Whiting 247
90-second Chicken 209
Nippy Pineapple Sauce 212
Noisettes with Citrus Sauce 136
Noisettes with Mushroom Sauce 126
Noodle Rice 332
Noodles 294

Noodles
    Baked Lasagna with Eggplant 306
    Cannelloni 'à la King' 301
    Cannelloni alla Napolitana 300
    Cannelloni Stuffed with Lamb 300
    alla Carbonara 298
    Curried Bake 299
    and Curried Eggs 299
    Chicken 226
    Custard-Topped Casserole 298
    Eggs in Noodle Nests 298
    Green Lasagne with Meat Sauce 306
    with Lamb 297
    Lasagne with Butter and Grated Cheese 305
    Macaroni, Chicken 305
    Mexican 298
    Nidi al Mascarpone 296
    Nidi con Pesto di Formaggio 296
    Nidi alla Romagnola 297
    Nidi Smalzade 297
    Nidi with Spinach 297
    Nidi Verdi con Aglio 296
    Nidi with Whiting 247
    Pasta alla Bolognese 304
    Pasta, Wholemeal with Capers and Anchovies 304
    Red, White and Green Pasta 304
    Short Pasta Salad 304
    Soyaroni alla Beppina 294
    Soyaroni and Butter 296
    Soyaroni alla Marinara 294
    Soyaroni with Mushrooms 296
    Soyaroni with Peas 296
    Soyaroni with Tuna and Béchamel Sauce 294
    Soyaroni with Tonno 296
    Stuffed Cannelloni with Mushroom 300
    Vegeroni con la Balsamella 303
    Vegeroni al Burro 301
    Vegeroni with Cheese and Onions 301
    Vegeroni, Chicken Casserole 302
    Vegeroni with Cottage Cheese 301
    Vegeroni with Ham and Mushroom Sauce 301
    Vegeroni al Mascarpone 302
    Vegeroni Niçoise 303
    Vegeroni con Tonno 302
    Vegeroni and Tuna Italian Style 302
    Vegeroni Tuna Salad 302
    Vegeroni Tuna Tomato 301
No-Name Eggs 50
North Carolina Grilled Chicken 221

Norwegian Egg Cream 53
Nugget Chicken 212
Nut Rice 316
Nutty Eggplant Bake 372
Nutty Oven-fried Chicken 207
Nutty Pineapple Salad 390

O

Octopus 288
Octopus Casserole 288
Old English Casserole 176
Old English Rice Pudding 418
Old Fashioned Pudding and Brandy Sauce 396
Old Style Chicken Broth 17
Old Style Egg Nog 52
Olive-Rosemary Honey Chicken 232
Olive Scones 207
Omelette
    Flat 42
    Fluffy 43
    Pizza 49
Onion, Cheddar, Poppy Seed Crumbs 216
Onion Rice 307
Onion Salad 382
Open Steak Sandwiches 72
Orange-Avocado Chicken 203
Orange Date Shortcake 453
Orange Gâteau 452
Orange-Ginger Chicken 197
Orange Ginger Lamb Chops 128
Orange Icing 459
Orange Lamb Chops 125
Orange Lamb Kebabs 122
Orange Macaroon Tartlets 449
Orange and Onion Pickled Scallops 282
Orange Raisin Plait 452
Orange Rice 307, 345
Orange Rice Pudding 426
Orange Roughy with Mushrooms 277
Orange Sauce 262
Orange Sultana Rice 346
Orange Steaks 313
Oregano Lamb with Quick Ratatouille 140
Oriental Broccoli Salad 383
Oriental Fried Rice 317
Oriental Rice Salad 367
Oriental Stuffed Avocados 374
Osso Buco 153
Oven-Baked Morwong with Yoghurt Sauce 275
Oven-Barbecued Chicken 195
Oven Chops and Vegetables 122

INDEX

Oven Fried Chicken 195
Oven Fried Pork Schnitzel 171
Oven Fried Steaks 176
Oyster Cocktail 290
Oyster and Dill Soup 20
Oyster Mushroom Prawns 280
Oyster-Stuffed Chicken 222
Oyster Stuffing 269
Oysters Casino 290
Ox Tongue with Cumberland Sauce 84

P

Pacific Prawn Curry 357
Pagoda Rice Salad 363
Pancake Pork Schnitzels 168
Pan Whiskied Chicken 255
Paprika Veal Chops 158
Parma Pork Schnitzels 168
Parma Rice Salad 363
Party Ham Steak 190
Parsley Fillets 276
Parsnip and Orange Soup 22
Party Chilli con Carne 98
Party Punch 53
Passionfruit Pears 406
Passionfruit Perch 280
Pasta alla Bolognese 304
Pasta Ham Salad 191
Pasta with Summer Sauce 76
Pastrami 99
Pastrami and Spinach Salad 92
Pastries
  Biscuit, Basic 412
  Choux 408
  Quick Sweet 450
  Shortcrust 458
  Sour Cream 321
  Wholemeal 377
  Yoghurt 430
Paupiettes of Veal 153
Pavlova 416
Pavlova au Rhum 416
Pavlova Roll 399
Paw Paw in Passionfruit Sauce 404
Peach Berry Crêpes 413
Peach Crumble 407
Peach Ginger Rice Cram 431
Peach Meringue Creamy Rice 436
Peach Rice Treat 436
Peachy Keen Nog 52
Peachy Lamb 135
Peachy Rice Parfaits 436
Peanut Butter Chicken 248
Peanut Butter Coffee Cake 440
Pears in Ginger Sauce 404
Pears in Red Wine 413
Peasant Style Pork 168
Pecan Chicken with Dijon Sauce, 210
Pecan Pie 406
Pepino Chicken Saled 245
Peppercorn Lamb 141
Peppercorn Sauce 38
Pepper Steaks 72
Peppered Beef in Filo 68
Peppered Eggs 33
Peppered Rump Steak 58
Persian Lamb with Sour Cherries 120
Pickled Eggs 30
Pie
  Apricot Cream 450
  Coconut Apricot 450
  French Apple 450
  Lemon Coconut 449
Pilau Rice 318
Pineapple Chicken Salad 390
Pineapple Lamb Riblets 130
Pineapple Marshmallow Rice 428
Pineapple Meat Loaf 57
Pineapple Meringue 398
Pineapple Parfait 424
Pineapple Pork Packets 343
Pineapple Rice Ambrosia 428
Pineapple Rice Crêpes 425
Pineapple Rice Torte 429
Pineapple Rice Whip 428
Pineapple Upside-down Pudding 406
Pineapple Walnut Cookies 441
Pizza Burgers 71
Pizza
  Chicken 217
  Omelette 49
Plain Muffins 448
Plain Sponge 457
Plum Delight 415
Plum and Ginger Chutney 37
Plum Lamb Casserole 119
Plum Lamb Chops for Two 117
Plum Pork Medallions 166
Poached Chicken 195
Poached Oranges 224
Poached Fillet with Tapenade 96
Polish Pork Roast 179
Pollo Verde Chicken 203
Pork
  Apricot Kebabs 188
  Apricot Roast 178
  and Bacon Loaf 180
  Balls and Bean Soup 181
  Barbecued Roast 179
  Barbecued Spareribs 187
  with Blackbean Sauce 169
  au Blanc 176
  Braised Chinese Spareribs 185
  Butterflies, Crunchy with Mushroom 172
  Butterfly Steak Royale 177
  Butterfly Steaks Supreme 177
  Cabbage Rolls 182
  Canadian Pie 181
  Carving 160
  Casanova Rolls 172
  with Chickpeas Creole 163
  Chinese Spiced 343
  Chops with Cheese 185
  Chops on Cider Rice 344
  Chops with Pernod 184
  Chops, Grand 173
  Chop Suey 161
  Cranberry Steaks 166
  Crunchy Grill 185
  Curry 162
  Deep Pie 174
  Dry-Spiced Spareribs 185
  Eastern Spareribs 186
  Fast Burgers 179
  Fruity Braise 162
  Fruity Parcels 173
  in Ginger Wine 165
  Ham and Melon Wraps 34
  and Ham in Pineapple Sauce 162
  and Ham Rolls 173
  Herb Casserole 184
  Honey with Pineapple 186
  Honey Taro Root 188
  Hot and Spicy Strips 172
  Hungarian Casserole 187
  in Lemon Sauce 161
  Lemon-Spiced Spareribs 186
  Mandarin Style Spareribs 187
  Marinated Chops 183
  Medallions in Tomato Sauce
  Mexicano Spareribs 187
  Mild Curry 161
  Minute Steak 164
  and Mushrooms in a Rice Ring 163
  and Mushroom Rolls 171
  Niçoise 173
  and Noodle Toss 164
  Old English Casserole 176
  Oven Fried Steaks 176
  Pantry Casserole 184
  Parmigiana 169
  Pâté Loaf 181
  in Peanut Sauce 174
  Peasant Style 168
  in Pepper Sauce 165
  and Pineapple Boats 188
  Pineapple Packets 343

INDEX

Plum Medallions 166
Polish Roast 179
Portuguese 183
Pot Luck Casserole 168
Pot Roast 179
and Quince Casserole 161
Ragout 172
Rarebit 165
Redcurrant-Glazed Spareribs 186
Roast Calvados 180
Roast with Mango 178
Rockets 183
Rosey Roast 178
Satay 164
Saucy Tomato 165
Sauté Médaillon Suzette 166
Schnitzel Kiev 169
Schnitzel, Oven Fried 171
Schnitzel, Pancake 168
Schnitzels, Italian Style 170
Schnitzels, Parma 168
Schnitzels, Swiss Style 165
Smoked, and Cucumber Sauce 184
with Snake Beans 188
Spareribs with Sauerkraut 185
Speedy Pies 181
Spinach-Stuffed 176
Steaks with Dates 174
'Stir-Fried' 172
Stuffed Chops 183
Stuffed Chops with
   Mushrooms 182
Stuffed with Herbs 178
Sukiyaki 182
Supreme Casserole 177
Tacos 180
in Taco Sauce 168
Tarragon Medallions 165
and Tomato Sauce (for pasta) 182
and Vegetable Creole 164
Wellington 179
Yankee Noodle Roast 180
Zippy, in Sauce 168
Portuguese Pork 183
Potato Cakes 74
Potato Casserole 379
Potato Chips 379
Pot Luck Pork Casserole 168
Prairie Oyster 53
Praline 432
Prawn Asopao 358
Prawn Bisque 24
Prawn and Cauliflower Stir Fry 371
Prawn Kebabs on Summer Rice 360
Prawn and Macaroni Salad 389
Prawn Pâté 28
Prawn and Pumpkin Soup 24

Prawn Risotto 355
Prawn Salad Mould 392
Prawns in Black Bean Sauce 357
Prawns with Snow Peas 280
Pronto Beef Parmigiana 102
Pronto Rice 355
Prune and Nut Stuffing 148
Prune and Nut Veal 148
Prunicot Rice Dessert 433
Puffed Chilli Chicken 357
Puffed Ricotta Chicken 215
Pumpkin and Apple Soup 22
Pumpkin Flan 50
Pumpkin Scones 458
Pumpkin Soup 26
Pumpkin Zucchini Soup 20
Purée of Peas 379

Q

Queensland Threadfin Salmon
   Parcel 284
Quiche
   Confetti Chicken 231
   Lorraine 49
Quick Cheese Loaf 453
Quick Chicken Cassolette 255
Quick and Easy Fish Casserole 276
Quick 'n' Easy Rice and Cheese
   Salad 362
Quick Fruit Bread 440
Quick Fruit Sponge Dessert 404
Quick Microroast Lamb Dinner 144
Quick Pepper Chicken 228
Quick Ratatouille 140
Quick Spanish Risotto 359
Quick Sweet Pastries 450
Quizza 47

R

Rack of Lamb with Herb and Pine
   Nut Crust 111
Raspberry Rice Parfait 424
Red Mexican Rice 314
Red Cabbage and Silverbeet
   Salad 383
Red, White and Green Pasta 304
Redcurrant-Glazed Pork
   Spareribs 186
Reef Seafood Terrine with Yoghurt
   and Dill Sauce 266
Regal Roast Beef 67
Reuben Sandwich 84
Rhubarb Fool 395
Rhubarb Rice Crisp 429
Rib Eye Roast 57

Rice
   Apple 307
   Apple-cinnamon 222
   Apple Cottage 430
   Apple Flan 427
   Apricot Cream Delight 438
   Apricot Honey 434
   Apricot Parfait 433
   Arroz Con Pollo 350
   Athena 323
   Austrian Cream 432
   Bacon Bake 313
   Bacon Brown 308
   Baked Custard 432
   Baked Ham, Spiced Apple
      Ring 344
   Baked Luncheon 309
   Baked Savoury Mushrooms 320
   Baked Tomatoes 320
   Banana 332
   Barbecue Salad 364
   Barbecue Spare Ribs 334
   Beef Apricot Rolls 332
   Beef with Broccoli 333
   Beef Curry (Mild) 333
   Bolognese 318
   Biriyani 315
   Broccoli Bake 310
   Brown, Absorption Method 307
   Brown, Apple Betty 425
   Brown Brûlée 425
   Brown, Cooking 307
   Brown, Country Casserole 326
   Brown, Dessert 437
   Brown, Fried 312
   Brown, Medley 312
   Brown, Mushroom Medley 310
   Brown, O'Reilly 328
   Brown, Pie 310
   Brown, Pudding 437
   Brown, Rapid Boil Method 307
   Brown Rice and Cheese
      Casserole 309
   Brown, Scramble 312
   Brown, Variations 307
   Buttered 341
   Butternut 351
   Cabbage Rolls 321
   Cabbage Rolls in Tomato
      Sauce 324
   California Chicken Casserole 351
   Capricorn Chicken and Rice 346
   Capricornia Salad 366
   Caramel Crunch 434
   Casablanca Chicken and Yellow
      Rice 352
   Celery 341

INDEX

Cheddar Chicken 352
Cheese Fried 310
Cheese Puffs 326
Cheesy Franks 336
Cherry Flan 430
Chicken and Almonds 348
and Chicken California 351
Chicken Casserole 350
Chicken Fillets on Orange Rice 345
Chicken Licken 217
Chicken and Noodles 344
Chicken and Peppers 352
Chicken Pineapple 347
Chinese Beef Strips 333
Chinese Fried 316
Chinese Fried with Mixed Meats 342
Chinese Spiced Chicken Wings 348
Chinese Spiced Pork 343
Chinese Stir-Fried Chicken 349
Citrus Curried 316
Citrus Curried, with Orange Steaks 313
Citrus Salad 368
Coleslaw Salad 368
Cool Island Salad 367
Coq au Vin 350
Cottage Pudding 424
Cowra Lamb Casserole 338
Creamy with Cherry Sauce 431
Creamy Curried Chicken 351
Creamy with Pineapple 428
Creole Casserole and Rice Puffs 329
Creole Jambalaya 337
Creole Salad 362
Creole Stuffed Tomatoes 326
Cuban Beans 328
Curried Eggs 309
Custard Imperial 436
Date and Apple 430
Date Spiced Creamy 429
Dolmades 320
Easy Lamb Biriani 343
Easy Paella Pronto 359
Egg and Bacon 328
Egg Curry with Raisin Brown Rice 329
Family Favourite Meatballs 337
Fish Rollups 355
Florentine Soup 18
Fried 307
Fried Formosa 316
Fried Mushroom 330
Fruit Salad 426
Fruity Fried 330
Fruity Stuffing for Duck 328
Garden Salad 368
Golden Apricot Pudding 438
Golden Chicken 351
Golden Dessert 426
Golden Ham with Golden Nut Salad 367
Golden Risotto 322
Gourmet, and Mushrooms 324
Grand Marnier Imperial 432
Greek Pudding (Rizogalo) 430
Greek Salad 367
Ham, Bake 308
Ham and Peach Salad 363
Ham and Rice New Orleans 347
Honey 433
Honey Buns 424
Honey Muffins 437
Imperatrice Mould 433
Irish Fried 324
Italian Salad 366
Italian Mushroom Risotto 326
Jamaican Rum Pudding 437
Jamaican Scrambled 4
Kashmiri Chicken Curry 345
Kofta Curry 333
Lamb Biriani 340
with Lamb and Chickpeas 339
Lamb Kebabs with Fruity Rice 338
Lamb Ragôut with Celery Rice 341
Lamb and Ricotta Casserole 340
Lamb Salad 339
Lasagne 334
Lemon 307
Lemon Butter 308, 343
Lemon Lamb Casserole 338
Lemon Pepper 348
Lemon Pilaf 351
Malaysian Chicken Curry 349
Maple Peach 429
Meatballs with Curry Fruit Sauce 332
Mexican Fried 328
Mexicani Mince 335
Mini Meat Loaves 335
Minted, and Ham Salad 362
Mocha Cream Parfait 436
Muffins 438
Mushroom 308, 342
Mushroom Piroshki 321
with Mussels (Pilafi Me Mithia) 356
Nasi Goreng 318
Noodle 332
Nut 316
Old English Pudding 418
Onion 307
Orange 307, 345
Orange Pudding 426
Orange Sultana 346
Oriental Fried 317
Oriental Salad 367
Pacific Prawn Curry 357
Pagoda Salad 363
Parma Salad 363
Peach Ginger Cream 431
Peach Meringue Creamy 436
Peach Treat 436
Peachy Parfaits 436
and Pepper Pinwheel 336
Pilaf with Spinach 325
Pilau 318
Pineapple Ambrosia 428
Pineapple Crêpes 425
Pineapple Marshmallow 428
Pineapple Parfait 424
Pineapple Pork Packets 343
Pineapple Torte 429
Pineapple Whip 428
Pork Chops on Cider Rice 344
Prawn Asopaos 358
Prawn Kebabs on Summer Rice 360
Prawn Risotto 355
Prawns in Black Bean Sauce 357
Pronto 335
Prunicot Dessert 433
Puffs 329
Quick 'n' Easy Rice and Cheese Salad 362
Quick Spanish Risotto 359
and Raisin Cream 424
Raspberry Parfait 424
Ravenna 308
with Red Beans 337
Red Mexican 314
Reheating 307
Rhubarb Crisp 429
Rich Scotch Broth 120
Rich Steamed Pudding 405
Ring with Salmon in Lemon Sauce 354
Rio Grande Fried 329
Rissoles, Chinese Style 317
Riverina Meat Loaf 336
Royale 324
Russian Chicken Fillets, Lemon Butter Rice 349
Saffron 314
St Clements Salad 365
Salmon Cakes with Caper Sauce 359
Salmon and Rice Casserole 354
Salmon Rice Sorrento 359
Sardine Pizza 322

INDEX

and Sardine Ramekins 321
Saturday Supper Pie 336
Savoury Fingers 321
Savoury Supper 309
Seafood Gumbo 355
Seafood Kedgeree 360
Seafood Risotto 354
Seafood Salad 364
Seafood Supper 358
Seafood Supper Pie 358
Shepherd's Pie 334
Siamese Fried 330
South Pacific Prawn Pilaf 361
South Pacific Salad 315
Spanish 361
Spanish Paella 311
Spanish-Style Fish and Rice 361
Speedy Creamy 436
Speedy Supper 358
Spiced 344
Spiced Balls 434
Spiced Chicken Pilaf 349
Spiced Custard 429
Spiced Indian 316
Spiced, and Lentils 325
Spicy Apple Pancakes 427
Spicy Beef and Rice Casserole 337
Spicy Lamb Kebabs 341
Spicy Lamb Pilaf 338
Spring Rice and Lamb 339
Steamed Chinese-Style 308
Stir-Fried Chicken and Rice 347
Storing 307
Strawberry Cheesecake 438
Stuffed Eggplant 320
Stuffed Tomatoes 323
Sultana Orange Chicken 346
Summer Pilaf 313
Summer Salad 367
Summer's Day Salad 366
Sunbrown Risotto 322
Sunshine Cream 430
Sunshine Salad 364
Sunshine-Spiced 425
Swedish Pudding 432
Sweet Yellow 317
Swiss Veal with Rice Ring 342
Tangy 315
Tomato 308
Tomato Salad 315
Tropical Curry 312
Tropical Touch Fried 330
Tropical Touch Parfait 426
Tuna Pie 354
Tuna Rissoles 361
Veal Bacon Rolls with Fried Rice 342

Vegetable Loaf 330
Vegetable Pilau 317
Venetian Ring 325
Waldorf Salad 368
White, Absorption Method 307
White, Cooking 307
White, Rapid Boil Method 307
Yellow 308, 345
Yoghurt Cream 396
Yoghurt Raisin Pudding 433
Ricotta Spinach Bake 376
Rio Grande Fried Rice 329
Riverboat Chicken Wheel 235
Riverina Beef Casserole 93
Riverina Rice Meat Loaf 336
Roast Beef with Vegetables Provençale 60
Roast Beef with Yorkshire Pudding 59
Roast Chicken 195
Roast Duck with Cherry Sauce 262
Roast Duck with Orange Sauce 262
Roast Lamb with Fruity Stuffing 110
Roast Lamb with Pears 114
Roast Lamb with Peppercorn Soufflé Crust 134
Roast Lamb Sesame 109
Roast Pork Calvados 180
Roast Pork with Mango 178
Roast Stuffed Topside 66
Roast Turkey 262
Roasted Chicken 255
Roasted Plum Chicken 200
Roman-Style Lamb 146
Rosemary Chicken Supreme 203
Rosemary's Chicken 242
Rosy Pork Roast 178
Roulade
  Basic 46
  Mushroom Filling 46
  Salmon Filling 46
  Spinach 46
  Tomato and Zucchini Filling 46
Royal Icing 459
Royal Soup 26
Royalty Sauce 212
Russian Chicken Fillets, Lemon Butter Rice 349

S

Saffron Rice 314
St Clements Rice Salad 365
Salad
  Avocado and Tomato 386
  Barbecue Rice 364
  Bean and Prawn 383

Bean and Watercress 390
Beetroot and Buckwheat 384
Beetroot Yoghurt 386
Broad Bean and Tuna 387
Brussels 384
Caesar 386
Capricornia Rice 366
Cauliflower 383
Chicken Drumsticks 219
Chinese Bean Sprout 387
Citrus Rice 368
Coleslaw with Grapes 383
Cool Island 367
Cool Potato 382
Creamy Chicken Peach 392
Creole Rice 362
Crunchy Egg 391
Cucumber 386
Curried Chicken 247
Curried Egg 392
Egg 391
Egg and Potato 391
Egg Spinach 391
Fruity Orange 387
Fruity Pork 387
German Potato Salad with Horseradish 382
Golden Ham with Golden Nut Rice 367
Good Health 392
Grapes, Cheese and Nut 387
Greek Rice 367
Green Grapefruit 375
Ham and Egg 391
Ham and Peach 363
Harlequin Health 390
Hawaiian Chicken 200
Health 390
Hot Beetroot 383
Hot Broad Bean 387
Hot Chinese Chicken 223
Italian Rice 366
Lamb Rice 339
Lebanese 382
Mandarin and Coconut 386
Minted Rice and Ham 362
Mushroom 382
Nectarine and Silverbeet Salad 377
Nutty Pineapple 390
Onion 382
Oriental Broccoli 383
Oriental Rice 367
Pagoda Rice 363
Parma Rice 363
Pasta Ham 191
Pepino Chicken 245
Pineapple Chicken 390

INDEX

Prawn and Macaroni 389
Prawn Mould 392
Quick 'n' Easy Rice and Cheese 362
Red Cabbage and Silverbeet 383
Rice Coleslaw 368
Rice Garden 368
Rice Waldorf 368
Seafood 388
Seafood Indienne 366
Seafood Rice 364
Sesame Crab 389
Short Pasta 304
Southern Cross 390
South Pacific Rice 315
Spring, with Strawberry Sauce 384
Tomato Rice 315
St Clements Rice 365
Summer Rice 368
Summer's Day 366
Sunshine Rice 364
Vegeroni Tuna 302
Salisbury Steaks 71
Salmon Cakes with Caper Sauce 359
Salmon and Rice Casserole 354
Salmon Rice Sorrento 359
Salmon Salad Dip 32
Salmon Tomato Chowder 19
Sambals 244
Sandwich
   Chicken-Chilli 229
Samosa with Meat Filling 78
Sang Cho Bau 104
Satay Lamb 146
Satays with Peanut Sauce 82
Saturday Supper Rice Pie 336
Sauce
   Apricot 438
   Avocado 38
   Avocado Béarnaise 68
   Barbecue Sauce 70
   Basil (Pesto) 38
   Basil-Garlic Cream 204
   Béarnaise 39
   Béchamel 306
   Beer 90
   Brandy 396
   Butter 270
   Caper 359
   Caramel 410
   Cheese 99
   Cheesy 30
   Cherry 431
   Chilli 220
   Chinese 317
   Chocolate 418
   Cumberland 84
   Curry 332

   Custard 415
   Dill 212
   East Coast 205
   Fruit 157
   Hollandaise 39
   Italian 334
   Lemon 228
   Lemon and Orange 38
   Mustard 120
   Nippy Pineapple 212
   Peanut 82, 174
   Peppercorn 38, 68
   Pork and Tomato (for pasta) 182
   Royalty 212
   Sherry Cream 149
   Sweet and Sour 38
   Tapenade 96
   Tartare 38
   Tomato 38
   Tomato 238
   Tomato and Orange 386
   Tuna 156
   Tuna Rice 362
   Velouté 38, 257
   Waldorf 386
   White 33, 96
   Wine Mustard 370
   Yoghurt 136
   Yoghurt and Dill 266
Saucy Tomato Pork 165
Sausage
   Aberdeen 93
   Breakfast for One 70
   Carpetbag 76
   Crunchy Sausage Sticks 76
   and Pineapple Skewers 76
   Mexican with Chilli Beans 102
   Mushroom 65
   Roll 58
   Rolls 76
Saucy Chicken 237
Sauté Médallon Suzette 166
Sautéed Chicken Breasts with
   Blueberry Sauce 246
Savoury Basic Combo Mixture 44
Savoury Bites 33
Savoury Chicken and Squash 216
Savoury Egg Pillow 47
Savoury Egg Rolls 32
Savoury Filled Tomatoes 378
Savoury Sprouts with Bacon 372
Savoury Stuffed Pepers 379
Scalloped Asparagus Parcels 370
Scallops Kebabs with Curry Mayonnaise 265
Scallops with Snow Peas 280

Scones 458
   Carrot 202
   Cheese 446
   Pumpkin 458
   Sour Cream 452
   Topping 88
Scotch Egg Roll 34
Scotch Eggs 75
Scots Eggs 32
Scrambled Eggs 42
Seafood
   Abalone Amandine 288
   Abalone, Grilled Steaks 289
   Apple Baked Ling 276
   Avocado and Prawn Soup 20
   Baked Fish Loaf 283
   Baked Fish with Zucchini 272
   Baked Flathead Fillets 273
   Baked Whole Fish with
     Macadamia Stuffing 281
   Baked Whole Trevally 281
   Barbecued Prawns 266
   Blue Grenadier Chowder 266
   Bouillabaisse 270
   Braised Ling in Vegetables 275
   Broccoli and Scallop Soup 24
   Calypso Eggs 34
   Chinese Style Squid and
     Peppers 272
   Collation 264
   Combo Filling 44
   Coral Trout Oskar 265
   Corn and Rice Chowder with
     Prawns 19
   Crab and Asparagus Pâté 28
   Crabmeat Ramekins 27
   Crayfish, Baked with Mustard
     Butter 290
   Crispy Baked Orange Roughy 278
   Crispy Fish Slices with Sweet and
     Sour Sauce 281
   Crispy Trout 276
   Curried Puffs 313
   Diver Whiting and Fennel 264
   Dory Fillets in Anchovy Sauce 273
   Dory Fillets with Avocado Hazelnut Cream 278
   Drunken Prawns 218
   Dutch Fish 274
   Easy Paella Pronto 359
   Egg and Salmon Dip 31
   Egg and Tuna Aspic 34
   Fish Curry 281
   Fish au Gratin 272
   Fish Kiev 277
   Fish Fillets in Ginger Sauce 274
   Fish with Mango and Kiwifruit 278

INDEX

Fish Patties 284
Fish Rice Rollups 355
Fish Soufflé 43
Fish Soup 24
Fish Soup with Potatoes and Saffron 265
Fish Stock 40
Fish with Zucchini and Tomatoes 277
Flounder Parmesan 273
Fried Fillets with Lemon Caper Sauce 266
Ginger Bream 278
Gravlax 282
Green Peppers with Seafood Filing 268
Gumbo 355
Highland Fish Soup 19
Kiwi Fish Fillets 265
Marinated Fish 284
Marinated Fish Salad 284
Microwave Mackeral Bake 283
Mock Rice Bouillabaisse 21
Morwong Ambrosia 276
Mud Crab in Black Bean Sauce 269
Mullet and Mushroom in Filo 267
Mullet Rollmops 264
Mussels, Garlic 289
Mussels, Herbed 289
Mussels, The Italian Way 289
Mussels, Mornay 289
Nidi with Whiting 297
Octopus 288
Octopus Casserole 288
Octopus, Marinated Greek Style 288
Orange and Onion Pickled Scallops 282
Orange Roughy with Mushrooms 277
Oven-Baked Morwong with Yoghurt Sauce 275
Oyster Cocktail 290
Oyster and Dill Soup 20
Oyster Mushroom Prawns 280
Oysters Casino 290
Oysters, Crispy 290
Pacific Prawn Curry 357
Parsley Fillets 276
Passionfruit Perch 280
Pie 270
Prawn Asopao 358
Prawn Bisque 24
Prawn and Cauliflower Stir Fry 371
Prawn Kebabs on Summer Rice 360
Prawn Pâté 28

Prawn and Pumpkin Soup 24
Prawn Risotto 355
Prawns in Black Bean Sauce 357
Prawns with Snow Peas 280
Queensland Treadfin Salmon Parcels 284
Quick Spanish Risotto 359
Reef Terrine with Yoghurt and Dill Sauce 266
Rice Kedgeree 360
Rice with Mussels (Pilafi Me Mithia) 356
Rice Ring with Salmon in Lemon Sauce 354
Rice Salad 364
Rice Supper 358
Rice Tuna Pie 354
Rice Tuna Rissoles 361
Risotto 354
Salad 388
Salad Indienne 366
Salmon Cakes with Caper Sauce 359
Salmon and Rice Casserole 354
Salmon Rice Sorrento 359
Salmon Salad Dip 32
Salmon Tomato Chowder 19
Scallops, Deep Fried 285
Scallops, Ginger Honey 285
Scallops Kebabs with Curry Mayonnaise 265
Sesame Sorcery 269
Soufflé 267
South Pacific Prawn Pilaf 361
Soyaroni alla Marinara 294
Soyaroni con Tonno 296
Soyaroni with Tuna and Béchamel Sauce 294
Spanish-Style Fish and Rice 361
Special Fish Pie 282
Spiced Trumpeter 277
Squid 285
Squid, Apricot 286
Squid, Deep-Fried 286
Squid, Stuffed or Calamarie Farcie 285
Squid, Stuffed, and Mushrooms 286
Supper Pie 358
Tahitian Fish Kiwi 278
Tangy Baked Fish 284
Scallops with Snow Peas 280
Shrimp Pâté 36
Stir Fry 272
Tomato Fish Casserole 266
Troppo Fish Fillets 268
Tuna Rice Salad 362

Vegeroni con Tonno 302
Vegeroni and Tuna Italian Style 302
Vegeroni Tuna Salad 302
Vegeroni Tuna Tomato 301
Whole Baked Fish 269
Whole Baked Mullet 270
Warehou in Parsley Wine Sauce 264
Seasoned Egg Ramekins 47
Self-Saucing Chocolate Pudding 405
Sesame Biscuits 442
Sesame Chicken 242
Sesame Crab Salad 389
Sesame Sorcery 269
Sherried Beef Stew 76
Sherried Lamb Kidneys 133
Sherry Cream Sauce 149
Shortbread Creams 442
Shortcrust Pastry 458
Short Pasta Salad 304
Shrimp Pâté 36
Siamese Fried Rice 330
Sicillia Cake 452
Skewered Beef Waldorf 104
Skewered Lamb and Mushrooms 130
Skillet Chicken 236
Slimmers Chicken and Choko Salad 245
Smoked Beef Carbonara 82
Smoked Lamb with Blueberry Sauce 129
Smoked Lamb Leg with Marmalade Glaze 125
Smoked Pork and Cucumber Sauce 184
Soufflé
  Basic Hot 43
  Carmen 409
  Cheese and Tomato 43
  Chocolate 43
  Fish 43
  Strawberry 43
Souffléd Beer Pots 27
Soup
  Apple Chicken 20
  Avocado and Prawn 20
  Beef 'n' Rice Potage 25
  Blue Grenadier Chowder 266
  Borsch 26
  Bouillabaisse 270
  Broccoli and Scallop 24
  Brown Rice Broth 18
  Celery and Chicken 23
  Cheese and Corn 20
  Chicken Curry 16

INDEX

Chicken Indienne 25
Chicken Noodle 227
Chilled Cherry 23
Chinese Watercress 22
Corn and Rice Chowder with Prawns 19
Cream of Carrot 19
Cream of Chicken 16
Cream of Vegetable 16
Creole Beef 21
Cressy 23
Egg and Lemon 26
Fish 24
Fish with Potatoes and Saffron 265
French Onion 22
Fresh Corn Chowder 23
Fruit 23
Greek Lemon 18
Hearty Cabbage 17
Highland Fish 19
Hurry Curry 19
Iced Tomato 22
Mexican Chilli 20
Minestrone 18
Minted Cucumber 22
Mock Rice Bouillabaisse 21
Mulligatawny (Curried) with Rice 16
Old Style Chicken Broth 17
Oyster and Dill 20
Parsnip and Orange 22
Prawn Bisque 24
Prawn and Pumpkin 24
Pumpkin 26
Pumpkin and Apple 22
Pumpkin Zucchini 20
Rice Florentine 18
Rich Scotch Broth 120
Royal 26
Salmon Tomato Chowder 19
Summer Day 16
Tomato Chicken Bouillon 18
Tomato and Egg 26
Sour Cream Pastry 321
Sour Cream Raisin Flan 415
Sour Cream Scones 452
Sour Cream Sugar Cookies 443
South-of-the-Border Baked Chicken 218
Southern Cross Salad 390
South Pacific Prawn Pilaf 361
South Pacific Rice Salad 315
Soyaroni alla Beppina 294
Soyaroni and Butter 296
Soyaroni alla Marinara 294
Soyaroni with Mushrooms 296
Soyaroni with Peas 296
Soyaroni con Tonno 296
Soyaroni with Tuna and Béchamel Sauce 294
Spaghetti 292
  Aglio e Olio 293
  alla Carbonara 293
  Chicken 254
  con Salsa di Pomodoro 293
  al Sugo 293
  Wholemeal with Butter and Vegetables 293
  Wholemeal and Chicken 292
  Wholemeal with Eggplant and Tomatoes 292
Spaghettini alla Marinara 292
Spanish Chicken 221
Spanish Paella 311
Spanish Rice 361
Spanish-Style Fish and Rice 361
Spareribs with Sauerkraut 185
Special Fish Pie 282
Special Occasion Combo Filling 45
Speedy Chicken and Rice Ring 350
Speedy Creamy Rice 436
Speedy Pork Pies 181
Speedy Rice Supper 358
Spiced Beef Loaf 99
Spiced Beef Pâté 98
Spiced Chicken Microwave 217
Spiced Chicken Pilaf 349
Spiced Custard Apple Chicken 244
Spiced Indian Pilau 316
Spiced Pumpkin Cake 444
Spiced Rice 344
Spiced Rice Balls 434
Spiced Rice Custard 429
Spiced Rice and Lentils 325
Spiced Trumpeter 277
Spicy Apple Pancakes 427
Spicy Arroz Con Pollo 350
Spicy Barbecue Chops 129
Spicy Beef and Rice Casserole 337
Spicy Chicken Peaches 239
Spicy Chicken with Rice 235
Spicy Grilled Chicken 220
Spicy Lamb Kebabs 341
Spicy Lamb Pilaf 338
Spicy Plum Pork 169
Spinach Pie (Spanakopita) 49
Spinach Roulade 46
Spinach-Stuffed Pork 176
Sponge Roll or Sandwich 443
Spring Rice and Lamb 339
Spring Salad with Strawberry Sauce 384
Squid 285
  Sweet and Sour 286
Stand-by Ham au Gratin 192
Steak Canton 67
Steak Diane 78
Steak and Kidney Pie 90, 97
Steak Rolls in Curry Sauce 83
Steak Rolls Teriyaki 81
Steak Satay 103
Steak with Tangy Apricots 101
Steak Teriyaki 74
Steaks Rosemary 74
Stir Fried Baby Vegetables 375
Stir Fried Chicken and Broccoli 227
Stir-Fried Chicken and Rice 347
'Stir-Fried' Pork 172
Stir Fry Seafood 272
Stir Fry Vegetables 377
Stock
  Beef 40
  Chicken 40
  Demi Glace 40
  Fish 40
Strawberry Cheesecake 395
Strawberry Mousse 417
Strawberry Puffs 407
Strawberry Rice Cheesecake 438
Strawberry Soufflé 43
Strawberry Wine Vinegar 39
Streusel Topping 441
Stuffed Cannelloni with Mushrooms 300
Stuffed Cheese Mushrooms 378
Stuffed Chicken Legs 238
Stuffed Chicken Thighs 252
Stuffed Cottage Eggs 32
Stuffed Eggplant 320
Stuffed Mushrooms 35
Stuffed Peppers 51
Stuffed Peppers with Beef 374
Stuffed Pork Chops 183
Stuffed Pork Chops with Mushrooms 182
Stuffed Pork with Herbs 178
Stuffed Rib Eye Steak with Hot Potato Salad 103
Stuffed Squid or Calamarie Farcie 285
Stuffed Squid and Mushrooms 286
Stuffed Tomatoes 323
Stuffing
  Fruit
  Fruity 110
  Fruity Rice for Duck 328
  Herb 85
  Oyster 269
  Prune and Nut 148
  Wild Rice 269
Sugared Almond Topping 441
Sultana Orange Chicken 346

INDEX

Summer Day Soup 16
Summer Loafers 72
Summer Rice Pilaf 313
Summer Rice Salad 368
Summer's Day Salad 366
Sunbrown Risotto 322
Sunrise Cocktail 53
Sunshine Chicken Pie 202
Sunshine Pineapple Pie 416
Sunshine Rice Cream 430
Sunshine Rice Salad 364
Sunshine-Spiced Rice 425
Suprêmes de Volaille Amandine 260
Swedish Rice Pudding 432
Sweet Basic Combo Mixture 44
Sweet Combo Fillings 44
Sweet Lamb Curry 121
Sweet and Sour Chicken 348
Sweet and Sour Sauce 38
Sweet and Sour Squid 286
Sweet and Spicy Chicken 200
Sweet Suprise Chicken 228
Sweet Yellow Rice 317
Swiss Roll 457
Swiss Steak 94
Swiss Style Schnitzels 165
Swiss Veal with Rice Ring 342

T

Taco Chicken Grill 251
Tahitian Chicken 214
Tahitian Fish Kiwi 278
Tamarillo Sorbet 399
Tangy Baked Fish 284
Tangy Banana Bavarois 421
Tangy Rice 315
Tangy Sweet Chicken 253
Tarragon Chicken Mousse 35
Tarragon Pork Medallions
Tarragon Veal Cutlets 150
Tarragon Vinegar 39
Tartare Sauce 38
Tasty Chicken Thighs 218
Teen's Easy Cheesy Chicken 204
Teriyaki Meatballs 103
Texas Chicken 239
The Snowie 52
Toad-in-the-Hole 69
Tomato Chicken Bouillon 18
Tomato-Chilli Chicken 222
Tomato Cocktail 53
Tomato Combo Filling 44
Tomato and Egg Soup 26
Tomato Fish Casserole 266
Tomato Juice Dressing 368
Tomato Nests 50

Tomato and Orange Salad 386
Tomato Rice 308
Tomato Rice Salad 315
Tomato Sauce 38, 238
Tomato Sugo 306
Tomato Toppa 28
Toppings
    Coffee Cake 441
    Crunchy Orange 441
    Streusel 441
    Sugared Almond 441
Touch O'Mint Chicken 247
Town and Country Hot Pot 102
Tripe and Onions 62
Tropical Curry 312
Tropical Melon Salad 421
Tropical Touch Fried Rice 330
Tropical Touch Parfait 426
Tropics 54
Troppo Fish Fillets 268
Trussing
    Chicken 194
Tuna Rice Salad 362
Tuna Sauce 156

V

Vanilla Butter Icing 459
Veal
    Avocado in Filo 149
    Bacon Rolls with Mushroom Rice 342
    Blanquette 152
    Casserole Chops 157
    Citrus Rack 148
    Cold Pie 154
    Fruity Veal 'n' Pork Rolls 157
    Goulash for Two 152
    Italian Roll 157
    Louisa 158
    with Mango 150
    Marengo 156
    Marsala 149
    with Mushrooms and Paprika 157
    Mustard Cream Rack 148
    Nidi Smalzade 297
    Osso Buco 153
    Pasta Allo Bolognese 304
    Paupiettes 153
    Paprika Chops 158
    and Pepper Casserole 156
    with Peppercorn Sauce 152
    Prune and Nut 148
    and Spinach Pie 155
    Steaks with Blueberry Sauce 150
    Swiss with Rice Ring 342
    Tarragon Cutlets 150

Vienna Schnitzels 149
Vitello Tonnato 156
Zarina and Lemon Rice 158
Vegeroni con la Balsamello 303
Vegeroni al Burro 301
Vegeroni with Cheese and Onions 301
Vegeroni with Cottage Cheese 301
Vegeroni with Ham and Mushroom Sauce 301
Vegeroni al Mascarpone 302
Vegeroni Niçoise 303
Vegeroni con Tonno 302
Vegeroni and Tuna Italian Style 302
Vegeroni Tuna Salad 302
Vegeroni Tuna Tomato 301
Vegetable Spaghetti with Pesto Sauce 380
Vegetable Spaghetti with Tasty Tomato Sauce 376
Vegetables
    Artichokes with Lemon Butter 370
    Asparagus Chinese Style 370
    Asparagus, Scalloped Parcels 370
    Avocado, Oriental Stuffed 374
    Baked Savoury Mushrooms 320
    Baked Tomatoes 320
    Borsch 26
    Cabbage, Hot and Prosciutto Toss 375
    Carrots, Cinnamon 379
    Carrots, Devilled 375
    Cauliflower in Black Bean Sauce 380
    Cauliflower and Prawn Stir Fry 371
    Cheese Crumble 378
    Chicken 209
    Chinese Stir Fry 374
    Chokos, Mexican 374
    Cream of Carrot Soup 19
    Cream Soup 16
    Creamy Blue Cheese Celery Sticks 27
    Creole Stuffed Tomatoes 326
    Curry
    Eggplant, Nutty Bake 372
    Fennel with Mushrooms 371
    French Fries 380
    French Onion Soup 22
    Fresh Corn Chowder 23
    Fruity Pilaf 377
    Green Beans and Bacon 379
    Hearty Cabbage Soup 17
    Herby Tomato Quiche 47
    Hot Mozzarella Avocados 30
    Iced Tomato Soup 22
    Italian Mushroom Risotto 326

INDEX

Layer Pot 378
Mediterranean Dip 27
Minted Cucumber Soup 22
Mushroom Roulade with Cheesy Sauce 30
Mushrooms, Creamy Filled 371
Parsnip and Orange Soup 22
Peas, Purée 379
Pepper, Savoury Stuffed 379
Peppers, Italian Fried 371
Peppers, Stuffed with Beef 374
Pilau 317
Potato Cakes 74
Potato Casserole 379
Potato Chips 379
Pumpkin and Apple Soup 22
Pumpkin Flan 50
Pumpkin Soup 26
Pumpkin Zucchini 20
Quiche, Wholemeal 377
Quick Ratatouille 140
Silverbeet, Filo Triangles 370
Spinach Pie 49
Spinach, Ricotta Bake 376
Sprouts, Savoury with Bacon 372
Stir Fried Baby 375
Stir Fry 377
Stuffed Eggplant 320
Stuffed Mushrooms 35
Stuffed Peppers 51
Stuffed Peppers with Beef 374
Summer Day Soup 16
Sweet Corn, Indonesian Fried 372
Terrine 34
Tomato and Egg Soup 26
Tomato Nests 50
Tomato Toppa 28
Tomatoes, Savoury Filled 378
Tomatoes, Stuffed 323
Zucchini Slice 46
Velouté Sauce 38, 257
Venetian Rice Ring 325
Vienna Schnitzels 149
Vinegar
  Strawberry Wine 39
  Tarragon 39
Vitello Tonnato 156
Vol au Vent Provençale 36

Whole Baked Fish 269
Whole Baked Mullet 270
Wholemeal Pasta with Capers and Anchovies 304
Wholemeal Pastry 377
Wholemeal Spaghetti with Butter and Vegetables 293
Wholemeal Spaghetti and Chicken 292
Wholemeal Spaghetti with Eggplant and Tomatoes 292
Wholemeal Spaghetti with Tomato and Basil 292
Whole Wheat Croûtons 227
Whole-Wheat Nut Bread 440
Wild Rice Stuffing 269
Wine Mustard Sauce 370

Y

Yankee Noodle Pork Roast 180
Yellow Rice 308, 345
Yoghurt 39
Yoghurt and Dill Sauce 266
Yoghurt-Lemon Chicken 242
Yoghurt Pastry 430
Yoghurt Raisin Rice Pudding 433
Yoghurt Rice Cream 396
Yoghurt Sauce 136
Yorkshire Pudding 69
Yummy Chicken Balls 219
Yummy Ham Loaf 191

Z

Zabaglione 417
Zippy Fruit Chicken 235
Zippy Pork in Sauce 168
Zucchini Cake 458
Zucchini Parmesan, Chicken 214
Zucchini Slice 46
Zuppa Inglese 399

W

Waldorf Salad 386
Walnut Torte 402
Warehou in Parsley Wine Sauce 264
Wheat Germ Biscuits 446
White Sauce 33, 96